# Microsoft®
# Visual Basic® 2005:
# RELOADED
# Second Edition

D1406704

## Diane Zak

**THOMSON**

**COURSE TECHNOLOGY** ™

Australia • Canada • Mexico • Singapore • Spain • United Kingdom • United States

THOMSON

COURSE TECHNOLOGY

**Microsoft® Visual Basic® 2005: RELOADED, Second Edition**
by Diane Zak

**Managing Editor:**
William Pitkin III

**Senior Product Manager:**
Tricia Coia

**Marketing Manager:**
Brian Berkeley

**Associate Product Manager:**
Sarah Santoro

**Editorial Assistant:**
Allison Murphy

**Production Editor:**
Melissa Panagos

**Cover Designer:**
Steve Deschene

**Compositor:**
Gex Publishing Services

**Manufacturing Coordinator:**
Justin Palmeiro

Disclaimer
Course Technology reserves the right to revise this publication and make changes from time to time in its content without notice.

ISBN 1-4188-3623-0

# Contents

Preface . . . . . . . . . . . . . . . . . . . . . . . . . . . . . . . . . . . . . . . . . . . . . . . . . . xiii

Read This Before You Begin . . . . . . . . . . . . . . . . . . . . . . . . . . . . . . . . . . . . xviii

**CHAPTER 1**
An Introduction to Visual Basic 2005 . . . . . . . . . . . . . . . . 1

Programmers . . . . . . . . . . . . . . . . . . . . . . . . . . . . . . . . . . . . . . . . . . . . . . . . 2
A Brief History of Programming Languages . . . . . . . . . . . . . . . . . . . . . . 2
    Machine Languages . . . . . . . . . . . . . . . . . . . . . . . . . . . . . . . . . . . . . . 3
    Assembly Languages . . . . . . . . . . . . . . . . . . . . . . . . . . . . . . . . . . . . . 3
    High-Level Languages . . . . . . . . . . . . . . . . . . . . . . . . . . . . . . . . . . . . 3
OOP Terminology . . . . . . . . . . . . . . . . . . . . . . . . . . . . . . . . . . . . . . . . . . . 4
Visual Studio 2005 . . . . . . . . . . . . . . . . . . . . . . . . . . . . . . . . . . . . . . . . . . 6
    The Common Language Runtime . . . . . . . . . . . . . . . . . . . . . . . . . . . . . 7
    Solutions, Projects, and Files . . . . . . . . . . . . . . . . . . . . . . . . . . . . . . 7
    Starting Microsoft Visual Studio 2005 . . . . . . . . . . . . . . . . . . . . . . . . 8
Creating a Visual Basic 2005 Windows-Based Application . . . . . . . . . . 10
    Managing the Windows in the IDE . . . . . . . . . . . . . . . . . . . . . . . . . . 11
The Windows Form Designer Window . . . . . . . . . . . . . . . . . . . . . . . . . . 12
The Solution Explorer Window . . . . . . . . . . . . . . . . . . . . . . . . . . . . . . . 13
The Properties Window . . . . . . . . . . . . . . . . . . . . . . . . . . . . . . . . . . . . . 15
    Properties of a Windows Form Object . . . . . . . . . . . . . . . . . . . . . . . . 16
The Toolbox Window . . . . . . . . . . . . . . . . . . . . . . . . . . . . . . . . . . . . . . . 19
    The Label Tool . . . . . . . . . . . . . . . . . . . . . . . . . . . . . . . . . . . . . . . . 21
    The Button Tool . . . . . . . . . . . . . . . . . . . . . . . . . . . . . . . . . . . . . . . . 22
The Code Editor Window . . . . . . . . . . . . . . . . . . . . . . . . . . . . . . . . . . . 24
    The Me.Close Method . . . . . . . . . . . . . . . . . . . . . . . . . . . . . . . . . . . 26
Saving a Solution . . . . . . . . . . . . . . . . . . . . . . . . . . . . . . . . . . . . . . . . . 27
Starting and Ending an Application . . . . . . . . . . . . . . . . . . . . . . . . . . . 27
Using an Assignment Statement . . . . . . . . . . . . . . . . . . . . . . . . . . . . . . 30
Printing Your Code . . . . . . . . . . . . . . . . . . . . . . . . . . . . . . . . . . . . . . . . 31
Closing the Current Solution . . . . . . . . . . . . . . . . . . . . . . . . . . . . . . . . . 32
Opening an Existing Solution . . . . . . . . . . . . . . . . . . . . . . . . . . . . . . . . 32
Programming Tutorial: Creating a Visual Basic 2005 Application . . . . . 33
    Starting Visual Studio .NET . . . . . . . . . . . . . . . . . . . . . . . . . . . . . . . 33
    Creating a Visual Basic 2005 Windows-based Application . . . . . . . . . . . . 34
    Managing the Windows in the IDE . . . . . . . . . . . . . . . . . . . . . . . . . . 35
    Using the Toolbox Window to Add Objects to a Form . . . . . . . . . . . . . . 36
    Using the Properties Window to Change an Object's Properties . . . . . . . . 40
    Using the Format Menu . . . . . . . . . . . . . . . . . . . . . . . . . . . . . . . . . . 43
    Displaying an Image in a Picture Box Control . . . . . . . . . . . . . . . . . . . 44
    Starting and Ending an Application . . . . . . . . . . . . . . . . . . . . . . . . . . 46
    Writing Visual Basic 2005 Code . . . . . . . . . . . . . . . . . . . . . . . . . . . . 49
    Closing the Current Solution . . . . . . . . . . . . . . . . . . . . . . . . . . . . . . . 53
    Opening an Existing Solution . . . . . . . . . . . . . . . . . . . . . . . . . . . . . . 53
    Printing Your Code . . . . . . . . . . . . . . . . . . . . . . . . . . . . . . . . . . . . . 53

Syntax Errors in Code .......................................... 54
Exiting Visual Studio .NET ..................................... 56
**Programming Example: State Capitals** ...................... 56
User Interface ................................................. 56
Code ......................................................... 58

**Quick Review** ............................................... 58
**Key Terms** ................................................. 60
**Self-Check Questions and Answers** ......................... 63
**Review Questions** .......................................... 64
**Review Exercises - Short Answer** .......................... 67
**Computer Exercises** ........................................ 67
**Case Projects** ............................................. 69
Castle's Ice Cream Parlor ...................................... 69
Allen School District .......................................... 69
Elvira Learning Center ......................................... 69
Mary Golds Flower Shop ....................................... 70

**CHATPER 2**

# Creating a User Interface ........................ 71

**Planning an Application** .................................... 72
**Skate-Away Sales** .......................................... 72
Identifying the Application's Tasks ............................. 72
Identifying the Objects ........................................ 74
Identifying the Events ......................................... 77
**Designing the User Interface** .............................. 78
Arranging the Controls ........................................ 81
Including Graphics in the User Interface ....................... 84
Including Different Fonts in the User Interface ................. 85
Including Color in the User Interface .......................... 85
**Assigning Access Keys** ..................................... 86
**Setting the TabIndex Property** ............................. 87
**Designating Default and Cancel Buttons** ................... 90
**Including Splash Screens and Dialog Boxes in an Application** ....... 91
**The Timer Tool** ............................................ 93
**Programming Tutorial: Creating the Color Game Application** ...... 95
Completing the MainForm's Interface .......................... 96
Coding the MainForm ......................................... 100
Coding the Color Buttons' Click Event Procedures .............. 101
Coding the Clear Colors Button's Click Event Procedure ......... 102
Adding the DialogForm to the Color Game Project .............. 102
Coding the DialogForm and the Options Button ................ 104
Adding the SplashScreenForm to the Color Game Project ........ 106
Completing the Color Game Application ........................ 107
**Programming Example: Moonbucks Coffee** .................. 111
TOE Chart ................................................... 112
User Interface ................................................ 112
Objects, Properties, and Settings ............................. 113
Tab Order .................................................... 114
Code ......................................................... 115

**Quick Review** .............................................. 115
**Key Terms** ................................................ 117
**Self-Check Questions and Answers** ........................ 118

Review Questions . . . . . . . . . . . . . . . . . . . . . . . . . . . . . . . . . . . . . . . . . . 119
Review Exercises – Short Answer . . . . . . . . . . . . . . . . . . . . . . . . . . . . . . 121
Computer Exercises . . . . . . . . . . . . . . . . . . . . . . . . . . . . . . . . . . . . . . . . 122
Case Projects . . . . . . . . . . . . . . . . . . . . . . . . . . . . . . . . . . . . . . . . . . . . . 124
    Crispies Bagels and Bites . . . . . . . . . . . . . . . . . . . . . . . . . . . . . . . . 124
    Perry Primary School . . . . . . . . . . . . . . . . . . . . . . . . . . . . . . . . . . . . 124
    Jasper Health Foods . . . . . . . . . . . . . . . . . . . . . . . . . . . . . . . . . . . . 125
    Sophia's Italian Deli . . . . . . . . . . . . . . . . . . . . . . . . . . . . . . . . . . . . 125

## CHAPTER 3
## Variables, Constants, Methods, and Calculations     127

Variables . . . . . . . . . . . . . . . . . . . . . . . . . . . . . . . . . . . . . . . . . . . . . . . . 128
    Selecting a Data Type for a Variable . . . . . . . . . . . . . . . . . . . . . . . . 128
    Selecting a Name for a Variable . . . . . . . . . . . . . . . . . . . . . . . . . . . . 130
Declaring A Variable . . . . . . . . . . . . . . . . . . . . . . . . . . . . . . . . . . . . . . 131
Assigning Data to an Existing Variable . . . . . . . . . . . . . . . . . . . . . . . . 132
    Using the TryParse Method . . . . . . . . . . . . . . . . . . . . . . . . . . . . . . 134
    Using the Convert Class . . . . . . . . . . . . . . . . . . . . . . . . . . . . . . . . . 140
Writing Arithmetic Expressions . . . . . . . . . . . . . . . . . . . . . . . . . . . . . . 141
The Scope and Lifetime of a Variable . . . . . . . . . . . . . . . . . . . . . . . . . 144
Static Variables . . . . . . . . . . . . . . . . . . . . . . . . . . . . . . . . . . . . . . . . . . 148
Named Constants . . . . . . . . . . . . . . . . . . . . . . . . . . . . . . . . . . . . . . . . 150
Option Explicit and Option Strict . . . . . . . . . . . . . . . . . . . . . . . . . . . . 152
Coding the Skate-Away Sales Application . . . . . . . . . . . . . . . . . . . . . . 154
    Using Pseudocode to Plan a Procedure . . . . . . . . . . . . . . . . . . . . . 155
    Using a Flowchart to Plan a Procedure . . . . . . . . . . . . . . . . . . . . . . 156
Coding the Clearbutton's Click Event Procedure . . . . . . . . . . . . . . . . . 158
    Clearing the Contents of a Control's Text Property . . . . . . . . . . . . . . 159
    Setting the Focus . . . . . . . . . . . . . . . . . . . . . . . . . . . . . . . . . . . . . . 160
Coding The Calcbutton's Click Event Procedure . . . . . . . . . . . . . . . . . 161
Testing and Debugging the Application . . . . . . . . . . . . . . . . . . . . . . . . 164
Formatting Numeric Output . . . . . . . . . . . . . . . . . . . . . . . . . . . . . . . . 166
Programming Tutorial: Creating the Change Game Application . . . . . 170
    Completing the Change Game Application . . . . . . . . . . . . . . . . . . . 171
    Coding the clearButton's Click Event Procedure . . . . . . . . . . . . . . . 172
    Coding the calcButton's Click Event Procedure . . . . . . . . . . . . . . . . 173
Programming Example: Currency Calculator . . . . . . . . . . . . . . . . . . . . 177
    TOE Chart . . . . . . . . . . . . . . . . . . . . . . . . . . . . . . . . . . . . . . . . . . . 178
    User Interface . . . . . . . . . . . . . . . . . . . . . . . . . . . . . . . . . . . . . . . . . 178
    Objects, Properties, and Settings . . . . . . . . . . . . . . . . . . . . . . . . . . 179
    Tab Order . . . . . . . . . . . . . . . . . . . . . . . . . . . . . . . . . . . . . . . . . . . 180
    Pseudocode . . . . . . . . . . . . . . . . . . . . . . . . . . . . . . . . . . . . . . . . . 180
    Code . . . . . . . . . . . . . . . . . . . . . . . . . . . . . . . . . . . . . . . . . . . . . . . 180

Quick Review . . . . . . . . . . . . . . . . . . . . . . . . . . . . . . . . . . . . . . . . . . . 181
Key Terms . . . . . . . . . . . . . . . . . . . . . . . . . . . . . . . . . . . . . . . . . . . . . . 183
Self-Check Questions and Answers . . . . . . . . . . . . . . . . . . . . . . . . . . . 184
Review Questions . . . . . . . . . . . . . . . . . . . . . . . . . . . . . . . . . . . . . . . . 186
Review Exercises – Short Answer . . . . . . . . . . . . . . . . . . . . . . . . . . . . 188
Computer Exercises . . . . . . . . . . . . . . . . . . . . . . . . . . . . . . . . . . . . . . 189
Case Projects . . . . . . . . . . . . . . . . . . . . . . . . . . . . . . . . . . . . . . . . . . . 193
    Willow Pools . . . . . . . . . . . . . . . . . . . . . . . . . . . . . . . . . . . . . . . . . 193

Builder's Inc. .................................................. 193
Tile Limited ................................................... 193
Quick Loans .................................................... 193

## CHAPTER 4
# Making Decisions in a Program .................... 195

The Selection Structure .......................................... 196
Writing Pseudocode for the If and If/Else Selection Structures ....... 197
Flowcharting the If and If/Else Selection Structures .............. 198
Coding the If and If/Else Selection Structures ................... 199
Comparison Operators ............................................ 200
    Using Comparison Operators – Swapping Numeric Values ............ 202
    Using Comparison Operators – Example 2 .......................... 206
Using the ToUpper and ToLower Methods .......................... 209
Logical Operators ............................................... 211
    Using the Truth Tables ......................................... 214
    Using Logical Operators in an If...Then...Else Statement .............. 216
The String.IsNullOrempty Method ................................ 217
Modifying the Skate-Away Sales Application ..................... 218
The MessageBox.Show Method .................................... 221
Nested Selection Structures ..................................... 226
The If/ElseIf/Else Selection Structure ........................... 231
The Case Selection Structure .................................... 233
    Using To and Is in an ExpressionList ............................. 235
Generating Random Integers ..................................... 237
Programming Tutorial: Creating the Rock, Paper,
Scissors Game Application ...................................... 239
    Creating the Rock, Paper, Scissors Game Interface ................... 240
    Coding the Rock, Paper, Scissors Game Application ................. 242
Programming Example: Fat Calculator Application ............... 248
    TOE Chart ..................................................... 249
    User Interface ................................................. 249
    Objects, Properties, and Settings ................................ 249
    Tab Order ..................................................... 250
    Pseudocode .................................................... 250
    Code .......................................................... 251

Quick Review ................................................... 252
Key Terms ...................................................... 253
Self-Check Questions and Answers .............................. 255
Review Questions ............................................... 256
Review Exercises – Short Answer ............................... 259
Computer Exercises ............................................. 263
Case Projects ................................................... 268
    Allenton Water Department ..................................... 268
    Professor Juarez ............................................... 268
    Barren Community Center ....................................... 268
    Willow Health Club ............................................ 268

## CHAPTER 5
# Repeating Program Instructions .................... 269

The Repetition Structure ........................................ 270
The For...Next Statement ........................................ 270

**The Financial.Pmt Method** . . . . . . . . . . . . . . . . . . . . . . . . . . . . . 274
    The Monthly Payment Calculator Application . . . . . . . . . . . . . . . . . . 277
    Selecting the Existing Text in a Text Box . . . . . . . . . . . . . . . . . . . . . . 278
    Coding a Control's TextChanged Event Procedure . . . . . . . . . . . . . . . 280
**Using a List Box in an Interface** . . . . . . . . . . . . . . . . . . . . . . . . . 281
    Adding Items to a List Box . . . . . . . . . . . . . . . . . . . . . . . . . . . . . . 282
    The SelectedItem and SelectedIndex Properties . . . . . . . . . . . . . . . . 284
    The SelectedValueChanged and SelectedIndexChanged Events . . . . . . . . 286
**Modifying the Monthly Payment Calculator Application** . . . . . . . . . . 287
**Using a Combo Box in an Interface** . . . . . . . . . . . . . . . . . . . . . . . 290
**The Do...Loop Statement** . . . . . . . . . . . . . . . . . . . . . . . . . . . . . 294
**Using Counters and Accumulators** . . . . . . . . . . . . . . . . . . . . . . . 300
    The InputBox Function . . . . . . . . . . . . . . . . . . . . . . . . . . . . . . . . 300
**The Sales Express Application** . . . . . . . . . . . . . . . . . . . . . . . . . . 302
**Programming Tutorial: Creating the Car Race Game Application** . . . . 307
    Completing the Car Race Game Interface . . . . . . . . . . . . . . . . . . . . . 308
    Coding the Car Race Game Application . . . . . . . . . . . . . . . . . . . . . . 312
    Moving a Control While an Application Is Running . . . . . . . . . . . . . . . 313
    Coding the raceTimer's Tick Event Procedure . . . . . . . . . . . . . . . . . . 315
**Programming Example: Grade Calculator** . . . . . . . . . . . . . . . . . . . 326
    TOE Chart . . . . . . . . . . . . . . . . . . . . . . . . . . . . . . . . . . . . . . . 326
    User Interface . . . . . . . . . . . . . . . . . . . . . . . . . . . . . . . . . . . . . 327
    Objects, Properties, and Settings . . . . . . . . . . . . . . . . . . . . . . . . . 327
    Tab Order . . . . . . . . . . . . . . . . . . . . . . . . . . . . . . . . . . . . . . . 328
    Pseudocode . . . . . . . . . . . . . . . . . . . . . . . . . . . . . . . . . . . . . . 328
    Code . . . . . . . . . . . . . . . . . . . . . . . . . . . . . . . . . . . . . . . . . . 329

**Quick Review** . . . . . . . . . . . . . . . . . . . . . . . . . . . . . . . . . . . . 330
**Key Terms** . . . . . . . . . . . . . . . . . . . . . . . . . . . . . . . . . . . . . . 332
**Self-Check Questions and Answers** . . . . . . . . . . . . . . . . . . . . . . . 333
**Review Questions** . . . . . . . . . . . . . . . . . . . . . . . . . . . . . . . . . 335
**Review Exercises – Short Answer** . . . . . . . . . . . . . . . . . . . . . . . . 338
**Computer Exercises** . . . . . . . . . . . . . . . . . . . . . . . . . . . . . . . . 340
**Case Projects** . . . . . . . . . . . . . . . . . . . . . . . . . . . . . . . . . . . . 347
    Sonheim Manufacturing Company . . . . . . . . . . . . . . . . . . . . . . . . 347
    Random Numbers Game . . . . . . . . . . . . . . . . . . . . . . . . . . . . . . 348
    Edmonton Bank . . . . . . . . . . . . . . . . . . . . . . . . . . . . . . . . . . . 348
    Powder Skating Rink . . . . . . . . . . . . . . . . . . . . . . . . . . . . . . . . 348

**CHAPTER 6**
**String Manipulation and More Controls** . . . . . . . . . . . . . . 349
**Manipulating Strings in Visual Basic** . . . . . . . . . . . . . . . . . . . . . . 350
**Determining the Number of Characters Contained in a String** . . . . . . 350
**Removing Characters from a String** . . . . . . . . . . . . . . . . . . . . . . . 352
    The Remove Method . . . . . . . . . . . . . . . . . . . . . . . . . . . . . . . . 356
**Replacing Characters in a String** . . . . . . . . . . . . . . . . . . . . . . . . 358
    The Mid Statement . . . . . . . . . . . . . . . . . . . . . . . . . . . . . . . . . 361
**Inserting Characters In a String** . . . . . . . . . . . . . . . . . . . . . . . . . 364
    The Insert Method . . . . . . . . . . . . . . . . . . . . . . . . . . . . . . . . . 368
**Search a String for One or More Characters** . . . . . . . . . . . . . . . . . 370
    The Contains Method . . . . . . . . . . . . . . . . . . . . . . . . . . . . . . . 375
    The IndexOf Method . . . . . . . . . . . . . . . . . . . . . . . . . . . . . . . . 378
**Accessing Characters Contained in a String** . . . . . . . . . . . . . . . . . 382

**Comparing Strings** . . . . . . . . . . . . . . . . . . . . . . . . . . . . . . . . . . . . . . . . . . . . **385**
    The Like Operator . . . . . . . . . . . . . . . . . . . . . . . . . . . . . . . . . . . . . . . . 388
**More Controls** . . . . . . . . . . . . . . . . . . . . . . . . . . . . . . . . . . . . . . . . . . . . . . . . . **393**
    Using Radio Buttons . . . . . . . . . . . . . . . . . . . . . . . . . . . . . . . . . . . . . . 393
    Using Check Boxes . . . . . . . . . . . . . . . . . . . . . . . . . . . . . . . . . . . . . . . 396
**Programming Tutorial: Hangman Game** . . . . . . . . . . . . . . . . . . . . . . . . . **399**
    TOE Chart . . . . . . . . . . . . . . . . . . . . . . . . . . . . . . . . . . . . . . . . . . . . . 400
    Coding the Hangman Game . . . . . . . . . . . . . . . . . . . . . . . . . . . . . . . . 400
**Programming Example: Glasgow Health Club Dues**
**Calculator Application** . . . . . . . . . . . . . . . . . . . . . . . . . . . . . . . . . . . . . . . **410**
    TOE Chart . . . . . . . . . . . . . . . . . . . . . . . . . . . . . . . . . . . . . . . . . . . . . 411
    User Interface . . . . . . . . . . . . . . . . . . . . . . . . . . . . . . . . . . . . . . . . . . 411
    Objects, Properties, and Settings . . . . . . . . . . . . . . . . . . . . . . . . . . . . 412
    Tab Order . . . . . . . . . . . . . . . . . . . . . . . . . . . . . . . . . . . . . . . . . . . . . 413
    Pseudocode . . . . . . . . . . . . . . . . . . . . . . . . . . . . . . . . . . . . . . . . . . . 414
    Code . . . . . . . . . . . . . . . . . . . . . . . . . . . . . . . . . . . . . . . . . . . . . . . . 414

**Quick Review** . . . . . . . . . . . . . . . . . . . . . . . . . . . . . . . . . . . . . . . . . . . . . . . . **417**
**Key Terms** . . . . . . . . . . . . . . . . . . . . . . . . . . . . . . . . . . . . . . . . . . . . . . . . . . . **418**
**Self-Check Questions and Answers** . . . . . . . . . . . . . . . . . . . . . . . . . . . . . **419**
**Review Questions** . . . . . . . . . . . . . . . . . . . . . . . . . . . . . . . . . . . . . . . . . . . . **420**
**Review Exercises – Short Answer** . . . . . . . . . . . . . . . . . . . . . . . . . . . . . . . **423**
**Computer Exercises** . . . . . . . . . . . . . . . . . . . . . . . . . . . . . . . . . . . . . . . . . . **424**
**Case Projects** . . . . . . . . . . . . . . . . . . . . . . . . . . . . . . . . . . . . . . . . . . . . . . . **429**
    Georgetown Credit . . . . . . . . . . . . . . . . . . . . . . . . . . . . . . . . . . . . . . 429
    Jacobson Finance . . . . . . . . . . . . . . . . . . . . . . . . . . . . . . . . . . . . . . . 430
    BobCat Motors . . . . . . . . . . . . . . . . . . . . . . . . . . . . . . . . . . . . . . . . . 430
    Delta Primary School . . . . . . . . . . . . . . . . . . . . . . . . . . . . . . . . . . . . 430


**CHAPTER 7**
**Sub and Function Procedures** . . . . . . . . . . . . . . . . . . . . . . . .**431**
**Procedures** . . . . . . . . . . . . . . . . . . . . . . . . . . . . . . . . . . . . . . . . . . . . . . . . . . **432**
**Sub Procedures** . . . . . . . . . . . . . . . . . . . . . . . . . . . . . . . . . . . . . . . . . . . . . . **432**
    The Gadis Antiques Application . . . . . . . . . . . . . . . . . . . . . . . . . . . . . 434
**Including Parameters in an Independent Sub Procedure** . . . . . . . . . . . **438**
**Passing Variables** . . . . . . . . . . . . . . . . . . . . . . . . . . . . . . . . . . . . . . . . . . . . **438**
    Passing Variables by Value . . . . . . . . . . . . . . . . . . . . . . . . . . . . . . . . 439
    Passing Variables by Reference . . . . . . . . . . . . . . . . . . . . . . . . . . . . . 444
**Associating a Procedure with Different Objects and Events** . . . . . . . . **448**
**Function Procedures** . . . . . . . . . . . . . . . . . . . . . . . . . . . . . . . . . . . . . . . . . **451**
    The Pine Lodge Application . . . . . . . . . . . . . . . . . . . . . . . . . . . . . . . . 452
**Programming Tutorial: Concentration Game Application** . . . . . . . . . . . **455**
    TOE Chart . . . . . . . . . . . . . . . . . . . . . . . . . . . . . . . . . . . . . . . . . . . . . 456
    Coding the Concentration Game Application . . . . . . . . . . . . . . . . . . . 457
    Converting Object Variables . . . . . . . . . . . . . . . . . . . . . . . . . . . . . . . 464
    Completing the Concentration Game Application . . . . . . . . . . . . . . . . 467
**Programming Example: Rainfall Application** . . . . . . . . . . . . . . . . . . . . . **476**
    TOE Chart . . . . . . . . . . . . . . . . . . . . . . . . . . . . . . . . . . . . . . . . . . . . . 476
    User Interface . . . . . . . . . . . . . . . . . . . . . . . . . . . . . . . . . . . . . . . . . . 476
    Objects, Properties, and Settings . . . . . . . . . . . . . . . . . . . . . . . . . . . . 477
    Tab Order . . . . . . . . . . . . . . . . . . . . . . . . . . . . . . . . . . . . . . . . . . . . . 478
    Pseudocode . . . . . . . . . . . . . . . . . . . . . . . . . . . . . . . . . . . . . . . . . . . 478
    Code . . . . . . . . . . . . . . . . . . . . . . . . . . . . . . . . . . . . . . . . . . . . . . . . 479

Quick Review ........................................................ 480
Key Terms .......................................................... 481
Self-Check Questions and Answers ................................. 482
Review Questions .................................................. 483
Review Exercises – Short Answer .................................. 486
Computer Exercises ................................................ 488
Case Projects ...................................................... 492
    Car Shoppers Inc. .............................................. 492
    Wallpaper Warehouse ........................................... 492
    Cable Direct .................................................. 493
    Harvey Industries ............................................. 493

**CHAPTER 8**

**Arrays** ................................................ **495**

Using Arrays ....................................................... 496
One-Dimensional Arrays ............................................ 496
Storing Data in a One-Dimensional Array ......................... 498
Manipulating One-Dimensional Arrays ............................. 499
    Displaying the Contents of a One-Dimensional Array ............. 500
    The For Each...Next Statement ................................. 502
    Using the Subscript to Access an Element in a One-Dimensional Array ... 503
    Searching a One-Dimensional Array ............................. 505
    Calculating the Average Amount Stored in a One-Dimensional
    Numeric Array ................................................. 507
    Determining the Highest Value Stored in a One-Dimensional Array ...... 509
    Updating the Values Stored in a One-Dimensional Array ......... 511
    Sorting the Data Stored in a One-Dimensional Array ............ 513
Parallel One-Dimensional Arrays ................................... 516
Two-Dimensional Arrays ............................................ 519
    Storing Data in a Two-Dimensional Array ....................... 521
    Searching a Two-Dimensional Array ............................. 522
Programming Tutorial: Lottery Game Application ................... 525
    TOE Chart ..................................................... 525
    Coding the Lottery Game Application ........................... 525
Programming Example: Perrytown Gift Shop Application ............ 530
    TOE Chart ..................................................... 531
    User Interface ................................................ 531
    Objects, Properties, and Settings ............................. 532
    Tab Order ..................................................... 533
    Pseudocode .................................................... 533
    Code .......................................................... 534

Quick Review ...................................................... 536
Key Terms ......................................................... 536
Self-Check Questions and Answers ................................. 537
Review Questions .................................................. 538
Review Exercises – Short Answer .................................. 542
Computer Exercises ................................................ 543
Case Projects ...................................................... 549
    JM Sales ...................................................... 549
    Waterglen Horse Farms ......................................... 549
    Conway Enterprises ............................................ 550
    Tic-Tac-Toe ................................................... 550

**CHAPTER 9**
## Structures and Sequential Access Files . . . . . . . . . . . . . . .551

**Structures** . . . . . . . . . . . . . . . . . . . . . . . . . . . . . . . . . . . . . . . . 552
    Using a Structure to Declare a Variable . . . . . . . . . . . . . . . . . . . . . . . . . 553
    Passing a Structure Variable to a Procedure . . . . . . . . . . . . . . . . . . . . . 554
    Creating an Array of Structure Variables . . . . . . . . . . . . . . . . . . . . . . 559
**File Types** . . . . . . . . . . . . . . . . . . . . . . . . . . . . . . . . . . . . . . . . . . . 562
**Sequential Access Files** . . . . . . . . . . . . . . . . . . . . . . . . . . . . . . . . . . 562
**Writing Information to a Sequential Access File** . . . . . . . . . . . . . . . . . 563
    Aligning Columns of Information in a Sequential Access File . . . . . . . . . . 566
**Reading Information from a Sequential Access File** . . . . . . . . . . . . . . 567
    Determining Whether a File Exists . . . . . . . . . . . . . . . . . . . . . . . . . . 568
**The FormClosing Event** . . . . . . . . . . . . . . . . . . . . . . . . . . . . . . . . . 570
**The Friends Application** . . . . . . . . . . . . . . . . . . . . . . . . . . . . . . . . . 571
**Programming Tutorial: Modified Car Race Game Application** . . . . . . . 575
    Modifying the Car Race Game Application . . . . . . . . . . . . . . . . . . . . . 576
**Programming Example: Glovers Application** . . . . . . . . . . . . . . . . . . 581
    TOE Chart . . . . . . . . . . . . . . . . . . . . . . . . . . . . . . . . . . . . . . . . . . 582
    User Interface . . . . . . . . . . . . . . . . . . . . . . . . . . . . . . . . . . . . . . . . 582
    Objects, Properties, and Settings . . . . . . . . . . . . . . . . . . . . . . . . . . 582
    Tab Order . . . . . . . . . . . . . . . . . . . . . . . . . . . . . . . . . . . . . . . . . . . 583
    Pseudocode . . . . . . . . . . . . . . . . . . . . . . . . . . . . . . . . . . . . . . . . . 583
    Code . . . . . . . . . . . . . . . . . . . . . . . . . . . . . . . . . . . . . . . . . . . . . . 584

**Quick Review** . . . . . . . . . . . . . . . . . . . . . . . . . . . . . . . . . . . . . . . . 586
**Key Terms** . . . . . . . . . . . . . . . . . . . . . . . . . . . . . . . . . . . . . . . . . . 586
**Self-Check Questions and Answers** . . . . . . . . . . . . . . . . . . . . . . . . 587
**Review Questions** . . . . . . . . . . . . . . . . . . . . . . . . . . . . . . . . . . . . 588
**Review Exercises – Short Answer** . . . . . . . . . . . . . . . . . . . . . . . . . 590
**Computer Exercises** . . . . . . . . . . . . . . . . . . . . . . . . . . . . . . . . . . 592
**Case Projects** . . . . . . . . . . . . . . . . . . . . . . . . . . . . . . . . . . . . . . . 595
    Warren High School . . . . . . . . . . . . . . . . . . . . . . . . . . . . . . . . . . . . 595
    WKRK-Radio . . . . . . . . . . . . . . . . . . . . . . . . . . . . . . . . . . . . . . . . . 595
    Shoe Circus . . . . . . . . . . . . . . . . . . . . . . . . . . . . . . . . . . . . . . . . . 595
    Revellos . . . . . . . . . . . . . . . . . . . . . . . . . . . . . . . . . . . . . . . . . . . 595

**CHAPTER 10**
## Creating Classes and Objects . . . . . . . . . . . . . . . . . . . . . . . .597

**Classes and Objects** . . . . . . . . . . . . . . . . . . . . . . . . . . . . . . . . . . . 598
**Defining a Class** . . . . . . . . . . . . . . . . . . . . . . . . . . . . . . . . . . . . . 598
**Example 1—Using a Class That Contains Public Variables Only** . . . . . . 601
**Example 2—Using a Class That Contains a Private Variable, a**
**Property Procedure, and Two Methods** . . . . . . . . . . . . . . . . . . . . . . . 604
    Constructors . . . . . . . . . . . . . . . . . . . . . . . . . . . . . . . . . . . . . . . . . 608
    Methods Other Than Constructors . . . . . . . . . . . . . . . . . . . . . . . . . . 609
**Example 3—Using a Class That Contains Two Constructors** . . . . . . . . 612
**Example 4—Using a Class That Contains Overloaded Methods** . . . . . . 617
**Example 5—Using a Base Class and a Derived Class** . . . . . . . . . . . . . 622
**Programming Tutorial: Card Game** . . . . . . . . . . . . . . . . . . . . . . . . . 626
    TOE Chart . . . . . . . . . . . . . . . . . . . . . . . . . . . . . . . . . . . . . . . . . . 627
    Coding the Card Game Application . . . . . . . . . . . . . . . . . . . . . . . . . . 627

**Programming Example: Kessler Landscaping Application** . . . . . . . . . . **638**
    TOE Chart . . . . . . . . . . . . . . . . . . . . . . . . . . . . . . . . . . . . . . . . 639
    User Interface . . . . . . . . . . . . . . . . . . . . . . . . . . . . . . . . . . . . . . 639
    Pseudocode . . . . . . . . . . . . . . . . . . . . . . . . . . . . . . . . . . . . . . . 639
    Code (MyRectangle.vb file) . . . . . . . . . . . . . . . . . . . . . . . . . . . . . 640
    Code (Main Form.vb file) . . . . . . . . . . . . . . . . . . . . . . . . . . . . . . 641

**Quick Review** . . . . . . . . . . . . . . . . . . . . . . . . . . . . . . . . . . . . . . . **642**
**Key Terms** . . . . . . . . . . . . . . . . . . . . . . . . . . . . . . . . . . . . . . . . . **643**
**Self-Check Questions and Answers** . . . . . . . . . . . . . . . . . . . . . . . **644**
**Review Questions** . . . . . . . . . . . . . . . . . . . . . . . . . . . . . . . . . . . **645**
**Review Exercises – Short Answer** . . . . . . . . . . . . . . . . . . . . . . . . **647**
**Computer Exercises** . . . . . . . . . . . . . . . . . . . . . . . . . . . . . . . . . . **649**
**Case Projects** . . . . . . . . . . . . . . . . . . . . . . . . . . . . . . . . . . . . . . **654**
    Glasgow Health Club . . . . . . . . . . . . . . . . . . . . . . . . . . . . . . . . 654
    Franklin Calendars . . . . . . . . . . . . . . . . . . . . . . . . . . . . . . . . . 655
    Bingo Game . . . . . . . . . . . . . . . . . . . . . . . . . . . . . . . . . . . . . . 655
    Pennington Book Store . . . . . . . . . . . . . . . . . . . . . . . . . . . . . . . 655

**CHAPTER 11**
# Using ADO.NET 2.0 . . . . . . . . . . . . . . . . . . . . . . . . . 657
**Database Terminology** . . . . . . . . . . . . . . . . . . . . . . . . . . . . . . . . **658**
**ADO.NET 2.0** . . . . . . . . . . . . . . . . . . . . . . . . . . . . . . . . . . . . . . **660**
**Connecting a Database to an Application** . . . . . . . . . . . . . . . . . . . **661**
    Previewing the Data Contained in a Dataset . . . . . . . . . . . . . . . . . 662
**Binding the Objects in a Dataset** . . . . . . . . . . . . . . . . . . . . . . . . **664**
    Having the Computer Create a Bound Control . . . . . . . . . . . . . . . . 664
    Binding to an Existing Control . . . . . . . . . . . . . . . . . . . . . . . . . . 670
**Accessing the Records in a Dataset** . . . . . . . . . . . . . . . . . . . . . . . **672**
**Dataset Designer** . . . . . . . . . . . . . . . . . . . . . . . . . . . . . . . . . . . **674**
    Creating a New Query . . . . . . . . . . . . . . . . . . . . . . . . . . . . . . . 678
    Using the Query Builder Dialog Box . . . . . . . . . . . . . . . . . . . . . . 680
    Allowing the User to Run a Query . . . . . . . . . . . . . . . . . . . . . . . 681
**Programming Tutorial: Trivia Game Application** . . . . . . . . . . . . . . . **684**
    TOE Chart . . . . . . . . . . . . . . . . . . . . . . . . . . . . . . . . . . . . . . . 685
    Coding the Trivia Game Application . . . . . . . . . . . . . . . . . . . . . . 685
**Programming Example: Cartwright Industries Application** . . . . . . . . . **694**
    TOE Chart . . . . . . . . . . . . . . . . . . . . . . . . . . . . . . . . . . . . . . . 695
    User Interface (drag the table to the form) . . . . . . . . . . . . . . . . . . 695
    Objects, Properties, and Settings . . . . . . . . . . . . . . . . . . . . . . . . 696
    Code . . . . . . . . . . . . . . . . . . . . . . . . . . . . . . . . . . . . . . . . . . 696

**Quick Review** . . . . . . . . . . . . . . . . . . . . . . . . . . . . . . . . . . . . . . . **697**
**Key Terms** . . . . . . . . . . . . . . . . . . . . . . . . . . . . . . . . . . . . . . . . . **698**
**Self-Check Questions and Answers** . . . . . . . . . . . . . . . . . . . . . . . **699**
**Review Questions** . . . . . . . . . . . . . . . . . . . . . . . . . . . . . . . . . . . **700**
**Review Exercises – Short Answer** . . . . . . . . . . . . . . . . . . . . . . . . **702**
**Computer Exercises** . . . . . . . . . . . . . . . . . . . . . . . . . . . . . . . . . . **703**
**Case Projects** . . . . . . . . . . . . . . . . . . . . . . . . . . . . . . . . . . . . . . **705**
    Addison Playhouse . . . . . . . . . . . . . . . . . . . . . . . . . . . . . . . . . 705
    College Courses . . . . . . . . . . . . . . . . . . . . . . . . . . . . . . . . . . . 705
    Sports Action . . . . . . . . . . . . . . . . . . . . . . . . . . . . . . . . . . . . . 705
    The Fiction Bookstore . . . . . . . . . . . . . . . . . . . . . . . . . . . . . . . 706

**APPENDIX A**
How To Boxes ................................707

**APPENDIX B**
GUI Design Rules .............................711

**APPENDIX C**
Visual Basic Type Conversion Functions ...............715

**APPENDIX D**
Creating a SQL Server Database .....................717

Glossary ................................................. 723
Index .................................................... 733

# Preface

*Microsoft Visual Basic 2005: RELOADED, Second Edition* uses Visual Basic 2005, an object-oriented language, to teach programming concepts. This book is designed for a beginning programming course; however, it assumes students have learned basic Windows skills and file management from one of Course Technology's other books that cover the Microsoft Windows operating system.

## ORGANIZATION AND COVERAGE

*Microsoft Visual Basic 2005: RELOADED, Second Edition* contains 11 chapters and 4 appendices. A twelfth chapter, which covers ASP.NET 2.0, can be obtained electronically from the Course Technology Web site (**www.course.com**), and then navigating to the page for this book. Also available electronically are additional appendices covering menus, printing, collections, and using ADO.NET 2.0 with Microsoft Access databases.

In the chapters, students with no previous programming experience learn how to plan and create their own interactive Windows applications. By the end of the book, students will have learned how to use TOE charts, pseudocode, and flowcharts to plan an application. They also will learn how to work with controls and write Visual Basic statements such as If...Then...Else, Select Case, Do...Loop, For...Next, and For Each...Next. Students also will learn how to create and manipulate variables, constants, strings, sequential access files, structures, classes, and arrays. Additionally, they will learn how to use ADO.NET 2.0 to connect an application to a SQL Server database. The text also introduces students to OOP concepts and terminology.

Appendix A lists the names and locations of the How To boxes included in the chapters. The How To boxes summarize important concepts and provide a quick reference for students. Appendix B lists the GUI design rules mentioned in the chapters, and Appendix C lists the Visual Basic type conversion functions. Finally, Appendix D teaches students how to use Visual Studio 2005 to create a SQL Server database.

## APPROACH

Like the first edition, *Microsoft Visual Basic 2005: RELOADED, Second Edition* focuses on programming concepts. However, the second edition includes several new features that were added in response to instructor feedback. One new feature is a Programming Tutorial, which appears after the concepts section in each chapter. The Programming Tutorial guides students through the process of creating an application. With the exception of Chapter 1, the applications in the Programming Tutorials are games. Game applications are used because research shows that the fun and exciting nature of games helps motivate students to learn.

Also added to each chapter are Self-Check Questions and Answers, which allow students to test their comprehension of the material. The Exercises section in the first edition is split into two sections in the second edition: Review Exercises – Short Answer and Computer Exercises. Additionally, completed applications (rather than partial applications) are used to illustrate the concepts in each chapter. The files for the completed applications are provided to the instructor.

## FEATURES

*Microsoft Visual Basic 2005: RELOADED, Second Edition* is an exceptional textbook because it also includes the following features:

- **Read This Before You Begin** This section is consistent with Course Technology's unequaled commitment to helping instructors introduce technology into the classroom. Technical considerations and assumptions about hardware, software, and default settings are listed in one place to help instructors save time and eliminate unnecessary aggravation.

- **Full-color interior** Interior design displays features of text in vibrant color for better illustration of important topics.

- **How To boxes** The How To boxes in each chapter summarize important concepts and provide a quick reference for students. For example, How To boxes show the steps for performing a task, such as starting Microsoft Visual Studio 2005. Additionally, each time a new control is introduced, its most commonly used properties are listed in a How To box. Similarly, when a new statement or method is covered, its syntax is shown in a How To box along with examples of using the syntax.

---

**HOW TO...**

### Add Items to a List Box

**Syntax**
*object*.**Items.Add**(*item*)

**Examples**
```
animalListBox.Items.Add("Dog")
animalListBox.Items.Add("Cat")
animalListBox.Items.Add("Horse")
```
displays Dog, Cat, and Horse in the animalListBox

```
For code As Integer = 100 To 105
    codeListBox.Items.Add(code.ToString)
Next code
```
displays 100, 101, 102, 103, 104, and 105 in the codeListBox

**FIGURE 5.16**    How to add items to a list box

---

- **Tip** Tips provide additional information about a procedure—for example, an alternate method of performing the procedure. They also relate the OOP terminology learned in Chapter 1 to applications created in Visual Basic 2005.

- **Programming Tutorials** A Programming Tutorial follows the concepts section in each chapter. The Programming Tutorial gives students step-by-step instructions on how to use the chapter's concepts to create and program a game application.

# PROGRAMMING TUTORIAL

## Creating the Rock, Paper, Scissors Game Application

In this tutorial, you create an application that simulates a game called Rock, Paper, Scissors. Typically, two people play the game. However, you will program the game so that one person can play against the computer.

"Rock, Paper, Scissors" refers to the three choices each player can indicate using hand gestures. To play the game, the players face each other, call out "Rock, paper, scissors, shoot," and then make the hand gesture corresponding to their choice: a fist (rock), a flat hand (paper), or two fingers forming a V shape (scissors). The rules for determining a win are shown in the following chart.

- Rock breaks scissors, so rock wins
- Paper covers rock, so paper wins
- Scissors cut paper, so scissors wins

- **Complete Programming Examples** After the Programming Tutorial in each chapter is an example of a completed program. The Programming Example shows the TOE chart and pseudocode used to plan the program, as well as the user interface, Objects/Properties/Settings chart, and Visual Basic 2005 code. The Programming Example demonstrates the concepts covered in the chapter.

# PROGRAMMING EXAMPLE

## Fat Calculator Application

Create a Visual Basic application that allows the user to enter the total number of calories and grams of fat contained in a specific food. The application should calculate and display two values: the food's fat calories (the number of calories attributed to fat) and its fat percentage (the ratio of the food's fat calories to its total calories). Additionally, the application should display the message "This food is high in fat." when the fat percentage is over 30%; otherwise, it should display the message "This food is not high in fat." Name the solution Fat Calculator Solution. Name the project Fat Calculator Project. Name the form file Main Form.vb. Save the application in the VbReloaded\Chap04 folder. Test the application using 150 and 6 as the number of calories and grams of fat, respectively. The fat calories should be 54 and the fat percentage should be 36.00%.

- **Quick Review** Following the Programming Example in each chapter is a Quick Review, which recaps the concepts covered in the chapter.

- **Key Terms** Following the Quick Review in each chapter is a collection of all the key terms found throughout the chapter. Definitions are also included in sentence format.

## Key Terms

The **selection structure**, also called the **decision structure**, allows a program to make a decision or comparison and then select the appropriate path, depending on the result of that decision or comparison.

The **condition** in a selection structure specifies the decision you are making and must be phrased so that it results in either a true or false answer only.

An **If selection structure** contains only one set of instructions, which are processed when the condition is true.

- **Self-check Questions and Answers** Following the Key Terms in each chapter are 10 Self-check Questions and Answers, which allow the student to determine whether they understand the chapter's concepts.

- **Review Questions, Review Exercises – Short Answer, and Computer Exercises** Following the Self-check Questions and Answers are the Review Questions and Review Exercises – Short Answer sections. These sections provide meaningful, conceptual questions and exercises that test students' understanding of what they learned in the chapter. The sections are followed by Computer Exercises, which provide students with additional practice of the skills and concepts they learned in the chapter.

- **Discovery Exercises** The Windows environment allows students to learn by exploring and discovering what they can do. The Discovery Exercises are designated by a "discovery" icon in the margin. They encourage students to challenge and independently develop their own programming skills while exploring the capabilities of Visual Basic 2005.

- **Debugging Exercises** One of the most important programming skills a student can learn is the ability to find and fix problems in an existing application. The Debugging Exercises are designated by the "debugging" icon in the margin and provide an opportunity for students to detect and correct errors in an existing application.

- **Case Projects** At the end of each chapter are four Case Projects. The Case Projects give the student the opportunity to independently synthesize and evaluate information, examine potential solutions, and make recommendations.

- **Think Tank Case Projects** The last Case Project in each chapter is designated by the "Think Tank" icon. The Think Tank Case Projects are more challenging than the other Case Projects.

- **Glossary** A glossary is included at the end of the book listing all the key terms in alphabetical order, along with definitions.

## TEACHING TOOLS

The following supplemental materials are available when this book is used in a classroom setting. All of the teaching tools available with this book are provided to the instructor on a single CD-ROM. Many can also be found at the Course Technology Web site (**www.course.com**).

- **Electronic Instructor's Manual** The Instructor's Manual that accompanies this textbook includes additional instructional material to assist in class preparation, including Sample Syllabi, Chapter Outlines, Technical Notes, Lecture Notes, Quick Quizzes, Teaching Tips, Discussion Topics, and Additional Case Projects.

- **ExamView®** This textbook is accompanied by ExamView, a powerful testing software package that allows instructors to create and administer printed, computer (LAN-based), and Internet exams. ExamView includes hundreds of questions that correspond to the topics covered in this text, enabling students to generate detailed study guides that include page references for further review. The computer-based and Internet testing components allow students to take exams at their computers, and also save time for the instructor by grading each exam automatically.

- **PowerPoint Presentations** This book comes with Microsoft PowerPoint slides for each chapter. These are included as a teaching aid for classroom presentation, to make available to students on the network for chapter review, or to be printed for classroom distribution. Instructors can add their own slides for additional topics they introduce to the class.

- **Data Files** Data Files, which are necessary for completing many of the Programming Tutorials and Computer Exercises, are provided on the Teaching Tools CD-ROM and may also be found on the Course Technology Web site at **www.course.com**.

- **Solution Files** Solutions to end-of-chapter Review Questions, Review Exercises – Short Answer, Computer Exercises, and Case Projects are provided on the Teaching Tools CD-ROM and may also be found on the Course Technology Web site at **www.course.com**. The Solution Files also include the applications that appear in the concepts section in each chapter; these applications are used to illustrate the concepts being taught. The solutions are password protected.

- **Distance Learning** Course Technology offers online WebCT and Blackboard (versions 5.0 and 6.0) courses for this text to provide the most complete and dynamic learning experience possible. When you add online content to one of your courses, you're adding a lot: automated tests, topic reviews, quick quizzes, and additional case projects with solutions. For more information on how to bring distance learning to your course, contact your local Course Technology sales representative.

## ACKNOWLEDGMENTS

Writing a book is a team effort rather than an individual one. I would like to take this opportunity to thank my team, especially Tricia Coia (Senior Product Manager), Melissa Panagos (Production Editor), and the Quality Assurance testers who carefully test each chapter. Thank you for your support, enthusiasm, patience, and hard work. I could not have completed this project without you. Last, but certainly not least, I want to thank the following reviewers for their invaluable ideas and comments:

Lorraine Bergkvist, University of Baltimore; Henry Bojack, Farmingdale State University; Deborah Green, Virginia College at Birmingham; Paula Ruby, Arkansas State University; Lawrence Eric Meyer, Miami Dade College – Kendall campus

*Diane Zak*

# Read This Before You Begin

## TO THE USER

### Data Files

To complete some of the tutorials and exercises, you will need the data files created for this book. Your instructor will provide the data files to you. You also can obtain the files electronically from the Course Technology Web site (**www.course.com**), and then navigating to the page for this book.

Each chapter in this book has its own set of data files, which are stored in a separate folder within the VbReloaded folder. For example, the files for Chapter 1 are stored in the VbReloaded\Chap01 folder. Similarly, the files for Chapter 2 are stored in the VbReloaded\Chap02 folder. Throughout this book, you will be instructed to open files from or save files to these folders.

You can use a computer in your school lab or your own computer to complete the Programming Tutorials, Programming Examples, Computer Exercises, and Case Projects in this book.

### Using Your Own Computer

To use your own computer to complete the material in this book, you will need the following:

- A PentiumII-class processor, 600 MHz or higher, personal computer running Microsoft Windows. This book was written and Quality Assurance tested using Microsoft Windows XP.

- Microsoft Visual Studio 2005 Standard Edition or Professional Edition or Team System Edition, or Microsoft Visual Basic 2005 Express Edition installed on your computer. This book was written using Microsoft Visual Studio 2005 Professional Edition and Quality Assurance tested using Microsoft Visual Studio 2005 Professional Edition and Microsoft Visual Basic Express Edition.

  If your book came with a copy of Microsoft Visual Basic 2005 Express Edition, then you may install that on your computer and use it to complete the material.

- **Data files** You will not be able to complete some of the Programming Tutorials and Computer Exercises in this book using your own computer unless you have them. You can get the data files from your instructor, or you can obtain them electronically from the Course Technology Web site (**www.course.com**), and then navigating to the page for this book.

## Figures

The figures in this book reflect how your screen will look if you are using Microsoft Visual Studio 2005 Professional Edition and a Microsoft Windows XP system. Your screen may appear slightly different in some instances if you are using another version of Microsoft Visual Studio, Microsoft Visual Basic, or Microsoft Windows.

## Visit Our World Wide Web Site

Additional materials designed especially for you might be available for your course on the World Wide Web. Go to **www.course.com**. Periodically search this site for more details.

## TO THE INSTRUCTOR

To complete some of the Programming Tutorials and Computer Exercises in this book, your users must use a set of data files. These files are included in the Instructor's Resource Kit. They also may be obtained electronically through the Course Technology Web site at **www.course.com**. Follow the instructions in the Help file to copy the data files to your server or standalone computer. You can view the Help file using a text editor such as WordPad or Notepad. Once the files are copied, you should instruct your users how to copy the files to their own computers or workstations.

The Programming Tutorials, Programming Examples, Computer Exercises, and Case Projects in this book were Quality Assurance tested using Microsoft Visual Studio 2005 Professional Edition and Microsoft Visual Basic Express Edition on a Microsoft Windows XP operating system.

## Course Technology Data Files

You are granted a license to copy the data files to any computer or computer network used by individuals who have purchased this book.

# An Introduction to Visual Basic 2005

**After studying Chapter 1, you should be able to:**

- Explain the history of programming languages
- Define the terminology used in object-oriented programming
- Explain the role of the .NET Framework class library and Common Language Runtime (CLR)
- Create a Visual Basic 2005 Windows-based application
- Manage the windows in the Integrated Development Environment (IDE)
- Set the properties of an object
- Add a control to a form
- Use the Label, Button, and PictureBox tools
- Enter code in the Code Editor window
- Save a solution
- Start and end an application
- Print a project's code
- Write an assignment statement
- Close and open an existing solution

## PROGRAMMERS

Although computers appear to be amazingly intelligent machines, they cannot yet think on their own. Computers still rely on human beings to give them directions. The directions are called **programs**, and the people who write the programs are called **programmers**. Programmers make it possible for us to communicate with our personal computers; without them, we wouldn't be able to use the computer to write a letter or play a game.

Typical tasks performed by a computer programmer include analyzing a problem statement or project specification, planning an appropriate solution, and converting the solution to a series of instructions that the computer can follow. Generally speaking, programmers are either applications programmers or systems programmers. **Applications programmers** write and maintain programs that handle a specific task, such as calculating a company's payroll. They also may customize off-the-shelf programs to match a company's unique requirements. **Systems programmers**, on the other hand, write and maintain programs that help the computer carry out its basic operating functions. Examples of such programs include operating systems, device drivers, and utilities.

According to the 2004–05 Edition of the *Occupational Outlook Handbook* (OOH), published by the U.S. Department of Labor's Bureau of Labor Statistics, "When hiring programmers, employers look for people with the necessary programming skills who can think logically and pay close attention to detail. The job calls for patience, persistence, and the ability to work on exacting analytical work, especially under pressure. Ingenuity, creativity, and imagination also are particularly important when programmers design solutions and test their work for potential failures. The ability to work with abstract concepts and to do technical analysis is especially important for systems programmers, because they work with the software that controls the computer's operation. Because programmers are expected to work in teams and interact directly with users, employers want programmers who are able to communicate with nontechnical personnel."

The Bureau of Labor Statistics predicts that employment of programmers will grow 10–20% between 2002 and 2012. "Jobs for both systems and applications programmers should be most plentiful in data processing service firms, software houses, and computer consulting businesses." The OOH also reports that "according to Robert Half International, a firm providing specialized staffing services, average annual starting salaries in 2003 ranged from $51,500 to $80,500 for applications development programmers/analysts, and from $55,000 to $87,750 for software developers. Average starting salaries for mainframe systems programmers ranged from $53,250 to $68,750 in 2003."

## A BRIEF HISTORY OF PROGRAMMING LANGUAGES

Just as human beings communicate with each other through the use of languages such as English, Spanish, Hindi, and Chinese, programmers use a variety of special languages, called **programming languages**, to communicate with the computer. Some popular programming languages are Visual Basic, Visual C#, C++, Visual C++, Java, Perl (Practical Extraction and Report Language), C, and COBOL (Common Business Oriented Language). In the next sections, you follow the progression of programming languages from machine languages to assembly languages, and then to high-level languages.

## Machine Languages

Within a computer, all data is represented by microscopic electronic switches that can be either off or on. The off switch is designated by a 0, and the on switch is designated by a 1. Because computers can understand only these on and off switches, the first programmers had to write the program instructions using nothing but combinations of 0s and 1s; for example, a program might contain the instruction 00101 10001 10000. Instructions written in 0s and 1s are called **machine language** or **machine code**. The machine languages (each type of machine has its own language) represent the only way to communicate directly with the computer. As you can imagine, programming in machine language is very tedious and error-prone and requires highly trained programmers.

## Assembly Languages

Slightly more advanced programming languages are called **assembly languages**. The assembly languages simplify the programmer's job by allowing the programmer to use mnemonics in place of the 0s and 1s in the program. **Mnemonics** are memory aids—in this case, alphabetical abbreviations for instructions. For example, most assembly languages use the mnemonic ADD to represent an add operation and the mnemonic MUL to represent a multiply operation. An example of an instruction written in an assembly language is MUL bl, ax.

Programs written in an assembly language require an **assembler**, which also is a program, to convert the assembly instructions into machine code—the 0s and 1s the computer can understand. Although it is much easier to write programs in assembly language than in machine language, programming in assembly language still is tedious and requires highly trained programmers.

## High-Level Languages

**High-level languages** represent the next major development in programming languages. High-level languages are a vast improvement over machine and assembly languages, because they allow the programmer to use instructions that more closely resemble the English language. An example of an instruction written in a high-level language is grossPay = hours * rate.

Programs written in a high-level language require either an interpreter or a compiler to convert the English-like instructions into the 0s and 1s the computer can understand. Like assemblers, both interpreters and compilers are separate programs. An **interpreter** translates the high-level instructions into machine code, line by line, as the program is running, whereas (in most cases) a **compiler** translates the entire program into machine code before running the program.

Like their predecessors, the first high-level languages were used to create procedure-oriented programs. When writing a **procedure-oriented program**, the programmer concentrates on the major tasks that the program needs to perform. A payroll program, for example, typically performs several major tasks, such as inputting the employee data, calculating the gross pay, calculating the taxes, calculating the net pay, and outputting a paycheck. The programmer must instruct the computer every step of the way, from the start of the task to its completion. In a procedure-oriented program, the programmer determines and controls the order in which the computer processes the instructions. In other words, the programmer must determine not only the proper instructions to give the computer, but the correct sequence of those instructions as well. Examples of high-level languages used to create procedure-oriented programs include COBOL, BASIC (Beginner's All-Purpose Symbolic Instruction Code), and C.

**TIP**

High-level languages are more machine-independent than are machine and assembly languages. Therefore, programs written in a high-level language can be used on many different types of computers.

TIP

Most objects in an object-oriented program have one or more tasks to perform. The tasks are programmed using the same techniques used in procedure-oriented programming.

Recently, more advanced high-level languages have emerged; these languages are used to create object-oriented programs. Different from a procedure-oriented program, which focuses on the individual tasks the program must perform, an **object-oriented program** requires the programmer to focus on the objects that the program can use to accomplish its goal. The objects can take on many different forms. For example, programs written for the Windows environment typically use objects such as check boxes, list boxes, and buttons. A payroll program, on the other hand, might utilize objects found in the real world, such as a time card object, an employee object, and a check object. Because each object is viewed as an independent unit, an object can be used in more than one program, usually with little or no modification. A check object used in a payroll program, for example, also can be used in a sales revenue program (which receives checks from customers) and an accounts payable program (which issues checks to creditors). The ability to use an object for more than one purpose saves programming time and money—an advantage that contributes to the popularity of object-oriented programming. Examples of high-level languages used to create object-oriented programs include Visual Basic, Java, C++, Visual C++, Visual J#, and Visual C#.

In this book, you learn how to create object-oriented programs using the Visual Basic 2005 language. Although you may have either heard or read that object-oriented programs are difficult to write, do not be intimidated. Admittedly, creating object-oriented programs does take some practice. However, you already are familiar with many of the concepts upon which object-oriented programming is based. Much of the anxiety of object-oriented programming stems from the terminology used when discussing it. Many of the terms are unfamiliar, because they typically are not used in everyday conversations. The next section will help to familiarize you with the terms used in discussions about object-oriented programming. Do not be concerned if you do not understand everything right away; you will see further explanations and examples of these terms throughout this book.

## OOP TERMINOLOGY

When discussing object-oriented programs, you will hear programmers use the terms OOP (pronounced like *loop*) and OOD (pronounced like *mood*). **OOP** is an acronym for object-oriented programming and simply means that you are using an object-oriented language to create a program that contains one or more objects. OOD, on the other hand, is an acronym for object-oriented design. Like top-down design, which is used to plan procedure-oriented programs, **OOD** also is a design methodology, but it is used to plan object-oriented programs. Unlike top-down design, which breaks up a problem into one or more tasks, OOD divides a problem into one or more objects.

An **object** is anything that can be seen, touched, or used; in other words, an object is nearly any *thing*. As mentioned earlier, the objects used in an object-oriented program can take on many different forms. The menus, check boxes, and buttons included in most Windows programs are objects. An object also can represent something encountered in real life—such as a wristwatch, a car, a credit card receipt, and an employee.

**TIP**

The class itself is not an object. Only an instance of the class is an object.

**TIP**

The term "encapsulate" means "to enclose in a capsule." In the context of OOP, the "capsule" is a class.

Every object has attributes and behaviors. The **attributes**, also called **properties**, are the characteristics that describe the object. When you tell someone that your wristwatch is a Farentino Model 35A, you are describing the watch (an object) in terms of some of its attributes—in this case, its maker and model number. A watch also has many other attributes, such as a crown, dial, hour hand, minute hand, and movement.

An object's **behaviors** include **methods**, which are the operations (actions) that the object is capable of performing. A watch, for example, can keep track of the time. Some watches also can keep track of the date. Still others can illuminate their dials when a button on the watch is pushed. (As you will learn later in this chapter, an object's behaviors also include events.)

You also will hear the term "class" in OOP discussions. A **class** is a pattern or blueprint used to create an object. Every object used in an object-oriented program comes from a class. A class contains—or, in OOP terms, it **encapsulates**—all of the attributes and behaviors that describe the object the class creates. The blueprint for the Farentino Model 35A watch, for example, encapsulates all of the watch's attributes and behaviors. Objects created from a class are referred to as **instances** of the class, and are said to be "instantiated" from the class. All Farentino Model 35A watches are instances of the Farentino Model 35A class.

"Abstraction" is another term used in OOP discussions. **Abstraction** refers to the hiding of the internal details of an object from the user. Hiding the internal details helps prevent the user from making inadvertent changes to the object. The internal mechanism of a watch, for example, is enclosed (hidden) in a case to protect the mechanism from damage. Attributes and behaviors that are not **hidden** are said to be **exposed** to the user. Exposed on a Farentino Model 35A watch are the crown used to set the hour and minute hands, and the button used to illuminate the dial. The idea behind abstraction is to expose to the user only those attributes and behaviors that are necessary to use the object, and to hide everything else.

Another OOP term, **inheritance**, refers to the fact that you can create one class from another class. The new class, called the **derived class**, inherits the attributes and behaviors of the original class, called the **base class**. For example, the Farentino company might create a blueprint of the Model 35B watch from the blueprint of the Model 35A watch. The Model 35B blueprint (the derived class) will inherit all of the attributes and behaviors of the Model 35A blueprint (the base class), but it then can be modified to include an additional feature, such as an alarm.

Finally, you also will hear the term "polymorphism" in OOP discussions. **Polymorphism** is the object-oriented feature that allows the same instruction to be carried out differently depending on the object. For example, you open a door, but you also open an envelope, a jar, and your eyes. Similarly, you can set the time, date, and alarm on a Farentino watch. Although the meaning of the verbs "open" and "set" are different in each case, you can understand each instruction because the combination of the verb and the object makes the instruction clear. Figure 1.1 uses the wristwatch example to illustrate most of the OOP terms discussed in this section.

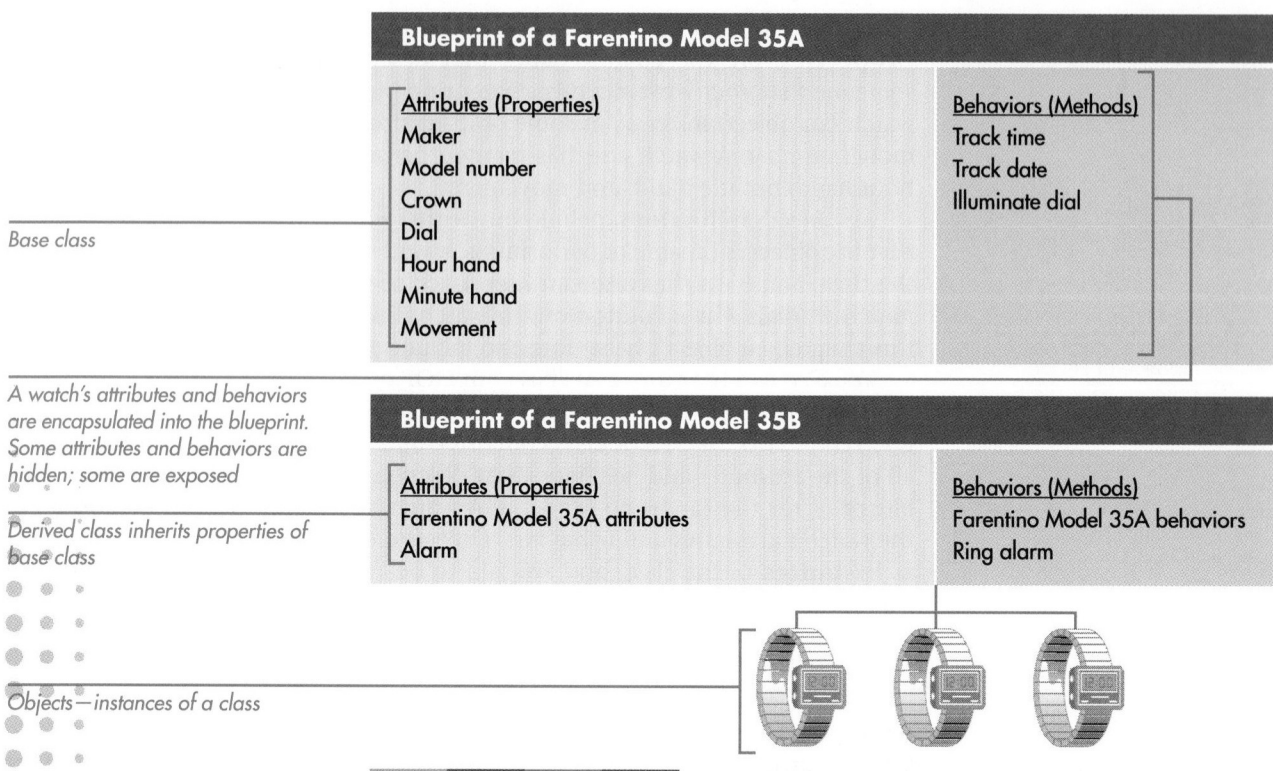

Base class

A watch's attributes and behaviors are encapsulated into the blueprint. Some attributes and behaviors are hidden; some are exposed

Derived class inherits properties of base class

Objects—instances of a class

**FIGURE 1.1**     Illustration of OOP terms

Visual Basic 2005, which is the programming language you will use in this book, is available as a stand-alone product or as part of Visual Studio 2005.

## VISUAL STUDIO 2005

Visual Studio 2005 is Microsoft's newest integrated development environment. An **integrated development environment** (**IDE**) is an environment that contains all of the tools and features you need to create, run, and test your programs. For example, an IDE contains an editor for entering your program instructions, and a compiler for running and testing the program.

Included in Visual Studio 2005 are the Visual Basic 2005, Visual C++ 2005, Visual C# 2005, and Visual J# 2005 programming languages. You can use the languages available in Visual Studio 2005 to create Windows-based or Web-based programs, referred to as **applications**. A **Windows-based application** has a Windows user interface and runs on a desktop computer. A **user interface** is what you see and interact with when using an application. Examples of Windows-based applications include graphics programs, data-entry systems, and games.

A **Web-based application**, on the other hand, has a Web user interface and runs on a server. You access a Web-based application using your computer's browser. Examples of Web-based applications include e-commerce applications available on the Internet and employee handbook applications accessible on a company's intranet.

The programming languages in Visual Studio 2005, as well as many other programming languages, run in the **Microsoft .NET Framework 2.0**, which is a platform on which you create applications. As a result, the programming

TIP

You also can create console applications in Visual Studio 2005. A console application runs in a Command Prompt window, which has a text user interface rather than a graphical one.

TIP

.NET is pronounced "dot net". A list of .NET languages can be found at *www.dotnetpowered. com/languages.aspx.*

languages are often referred to as **.NET languages**, and applications created using the .NET languages are commonly called **.NET applications**.

The driving force behind the .NET Framework is Microsoft's goal of connecting information, people, systems, and devices. To accomplish that goal, the Framework provides support for standard networking protocols and specifications (such as TCP/IP, SOAP, XML, and HTTP), as well as support for different platforms (such as Windows XP, Windows CE, and Unix).

The .NET Framework also provides for easier development of applications. One way it does so is by supporting a variety of programming languages. This support allows programmers to use their preferred .NET language when developing applications. An application can even be written in more than one .NET language.

Ease of development can also be attributed to a component of the .NET Framework, called the **.NET Framework class library**. Every .NET language has access to the class library, which contains an extensive set of classes that can be used in .NET applications. Using a class from the class library in an application is beneficial for two reasons: First, it saves you from having to create the class on your own. Second, it provides consistency among applications, making code easier to understand and reuse.

In addition to the class library, the .NET Framework also contains a component called the Common Language Runtime.

## The Common Language Runtime

Each .NET language has its own compiler, and each language-specific compiler performs the same task, which is to translate .NET program instructions into a language that the **Common Language Runtime** (**CLR**) can understand. The language is called **Microsoft Intermediate Language** (**MSIL**) or, more simply, **Intermediate Language** (**IL**). The CLR is responsible for managing the execution of the IL instructions. It does this by providing a **just-in-time** (**JIT**) compiler that converts the IL into native machine code that can be executed by the computer. Figure 1.2 illustrates the role of the CLR.

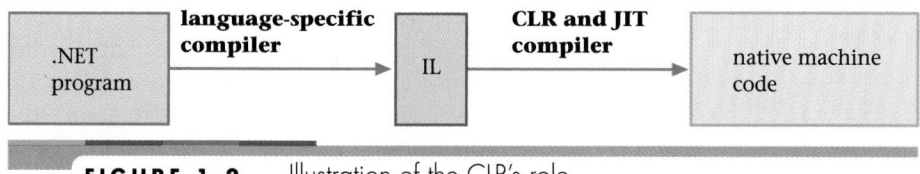

**FIGURE 1.2**    Illustration of the CLR's role

The CLR allows compiled IL to be reused in any application written in any .NET language. This is because the CLR does not make a distinction between the IL created by one language-specific compiler and the IL created by a different language-specific compiler. To the CLR, all IL is the same, regardless of the original language used to create it.

Applications created in Visual Studio 2005 are composed of solutions, projects, and files.

## Solutions, Projects, and Files

A **solution** is a container that stores the projects and files for an entire application. A **project** also is a container, but it stores files associated with only a specific piece of the solution. Although the idea of solutions, projects, and files may sound confusing, the concept of placing things in containers is nothing new to you. Think of a solution as being similar to a drawer in a filing cabinet. A project then is similar to a file folder that you store in the drawer, and a file is similar to a document that you store in the file folder. You can place many file folders in a filing cabinet drawer, just as you can place many projects in a solution. You also can store many documents in a file folder, similar to the way you can store many files in a project. Figure 1.3 illustrates this analogy.

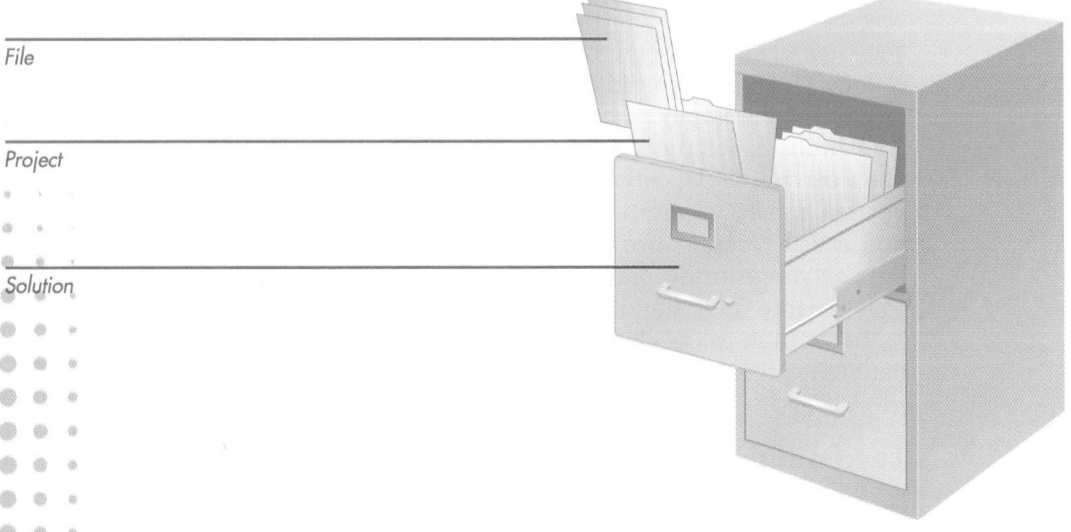

*File*

*Project*

*Solution*

**FIGURE 1.3**       Illustration of a solution, project, and file

### Starting Microsoft Visual Studio 2005

Figure 1.4 shows the steps you follow to start Microsoft Visual Studio 2005, which is the version of Visual Studio used in this book. If you are using a previous version of Microsoft Visual Studio, your steps will be slightly different than the ones shown in Figure 1.4.

*Note:* As mentioned in the Read This Before You Begin section of this book, you are not expected to follow the steps listed in the How To boxes right now. The How To boxes provide a quick reference that you can use when completing the Programming Example, Programming Tutorial, Exercises, and Case Projects found at the end of the chapter.

**TIP**

Projects stored in the same solution can be written in different .NET languages.

## HOW TO...

### Start Microsoft Visual Studio 2005

1. Click the Start button on the taskbar.
2. Point to All Programs, then point to Microsoft Visual Studio 2005.
3. Click Microsoft Visual Studio 2005.

**FIGURE 1.4**       How to start Microsoft Visual Studio 2005

When you start the Professional Edition of Microsoft Visual Studio 2005, your screen will appear similar to Figure 1.5; however, your Recent Projects list might include the names of projects or solutions with which you have recently worked. If you are using a different edition or a previous version of Visual Studio, your startup screen will look different than the one shown in Figure 1.5. For example, you might see the Database Explorer window instead of the Server Explorer window. Or, you may not see the Class View window.

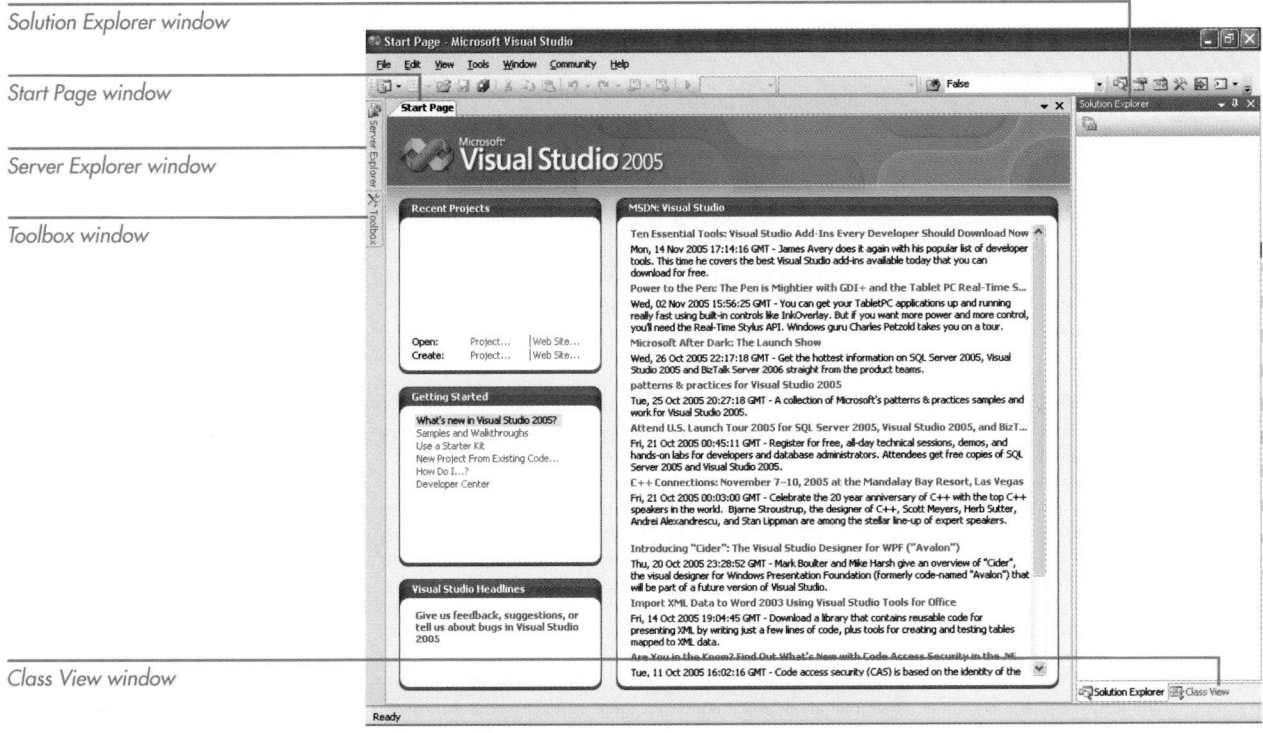

**FIGURE 1.5**    Microsoft Visual Studio 2005 startup screen

As Figure 1.5 indicates, the IDE contains five windows: Start Page, Server (or Database) Explorer, Toolbox, Solution Explorer, and Class View. Figure 1.6 briefly describes the purpose of each window.

| Window | Purpose |
| --- | --- |
| Class View | display the classes, methods, and properties included in a solution |
| Server (Database) Explorer | display data connections and servers |
| Solution Explorer | display the names of projects and files included in a solution |
| Start Page | create and open projects, access information on how to get started using Visual Studio 2005, access news and technical articles regarding .NET |
| Toolbox | display items that you can use when creating a project |

**FIGURE 1.6**    Purpose of the windows included in the IDE

## CREATING A VISUAL BASIC 2005 WINDOWS-BASED APPLICATION

Figure 1.7 shows the steps you follow to create a Visual Basic 2005 Windows-based application, and Figure 1.8 shows an example of a completed New Project dialog box. (You learn how to create a Web-based application in a subsequent chapter.)

### HOW TO...

**Create a Visual Basic 2005 Windows-based Application**

1. Start Microsoft Visual Studio 2005, then click File on the menu bar.
2. Point to New, then click Project to open the New Project dialog box.
3. If necessary, expand the Visual Basic node in the Project types list, then click Windows.
4. If necessary, click Windows Application in the Visual Studio installed templates section of the Templates list.
5. Enter an appropriate name and location in the Name and Location boxes, respectively.
6. If necessary, select the Create directory for solution check box.
7. Enter an appropriate name in the Solution Name box.
8. Click the OK button.

**FIGURE 1.7**      How to create a Visual Basic 2005 Windows-based application

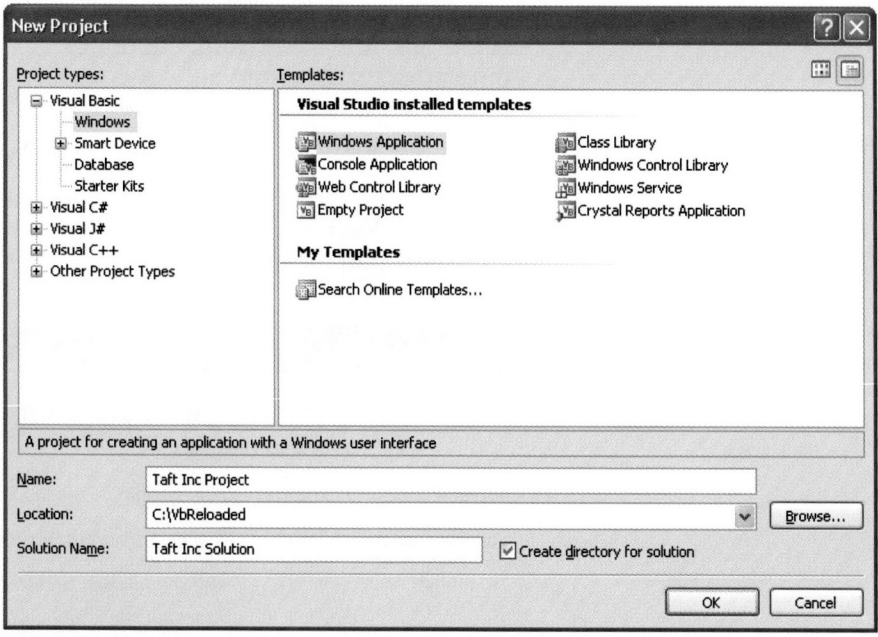

**FIGURE 1.8**      Completed New Project dialog box

When you click the OK button in the New Project dialog box, Visual Studio 2005 creates a solution and adds a Visual Basic project to the solution, as shown in Figure 1.9.

Auto Hide button

Solution name

Project name and information

Properties window

Windows Form Designer window

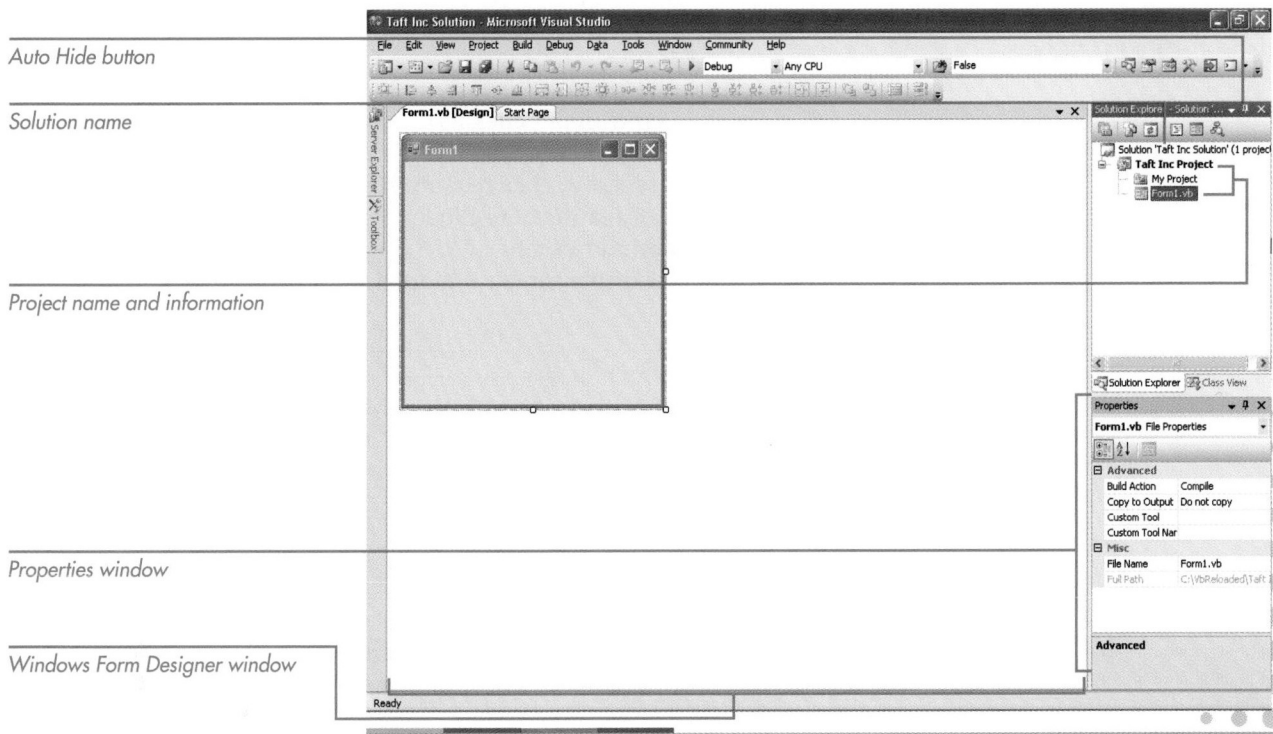

**FIGURE 1.9**    Solution and Visual Basic project created by Visual Studio 2005

Notice that, in addition to the five windows discussed earlier, two new windows appear in the development environment: the Windows Form Designer window and the Properties window. Having so many windows open at the same time can be confusing, especially when you are first learning the IDE. In most cases, you will find it easier to work in the IDE if you either close or auto-hide the windows you are not currently using. You learn how to auto-hide a window in the next section.

## Managing the Windows in the IDE

The easiest way to close an open window in the IDE is to click the Close button on the window's title bar. In most cases, the View menu provides an appropriate option for opening a closed window. To open the Toolbox window, for instance, you click View on the menu bar, and then click Toolbox on the menu. Similarly, you click View, point to Other Windows, and then click Start Page to open the Start Page window.

You can use the Auto Hide button (see Figure 1.9) on a window's title bar to auto-hide a window. When you auto-hide a window and then move the mouse pointer away from the window, the window is minimized and appears as a tab on the edge of the IDE. Additionally, the vertical pushpin on the Auto Hide button is replaced by a horizontal pushpin, which indicates that the window is auto-hidden. The Server Explorer and Toolbox windows shown in Figure 1.9 are examples of auto-hidden windows.

To temporarily display a window that has been auto-hidden, you simply place your mouse pointer on the window's tab; doing so slides the window into view. You can permanently display an auto-hidden window by clicking the Auto Hide button on the window's title bar. When you do this, the horizontal pushpin on the button is replaced by a vertical pushpin, which indicates that the window is not auto-hidden. Figure 1.10 summarizes what you learned in this section.

HOW TO...

**Manage the Windows in the IDE**

- To close an open window, click its Close button.
- To open a window, in most cases you use the View menu.
- To auto-hide a window, click its Auto Hide button.
- To temporarily display an auto-hidden window, place your mouse pointer on the window's tab.
- To permanently display an auto-hidden window, click its Auto Hide button.

**FIGURE 1.10**    How to manage the windows in the IDE

In the next several sections, you take a closer look at the Windows Form Designer, Solution Explorer, Properties, and Toolbox windows. You also look at two new windows: the Project Designer window and Code Editor window. (The Server Explorer window is covered in a subsequent chapter in this book.)

## THE WINDOWS FORM DESIGNER WINDOW

Figure 1.11 shows the **Windows Form Designer window**, where you create (or design) the graphical user interface, referred to as a **GUI**, for your project. Recall that a user interface is what you see and interact with when using an application.

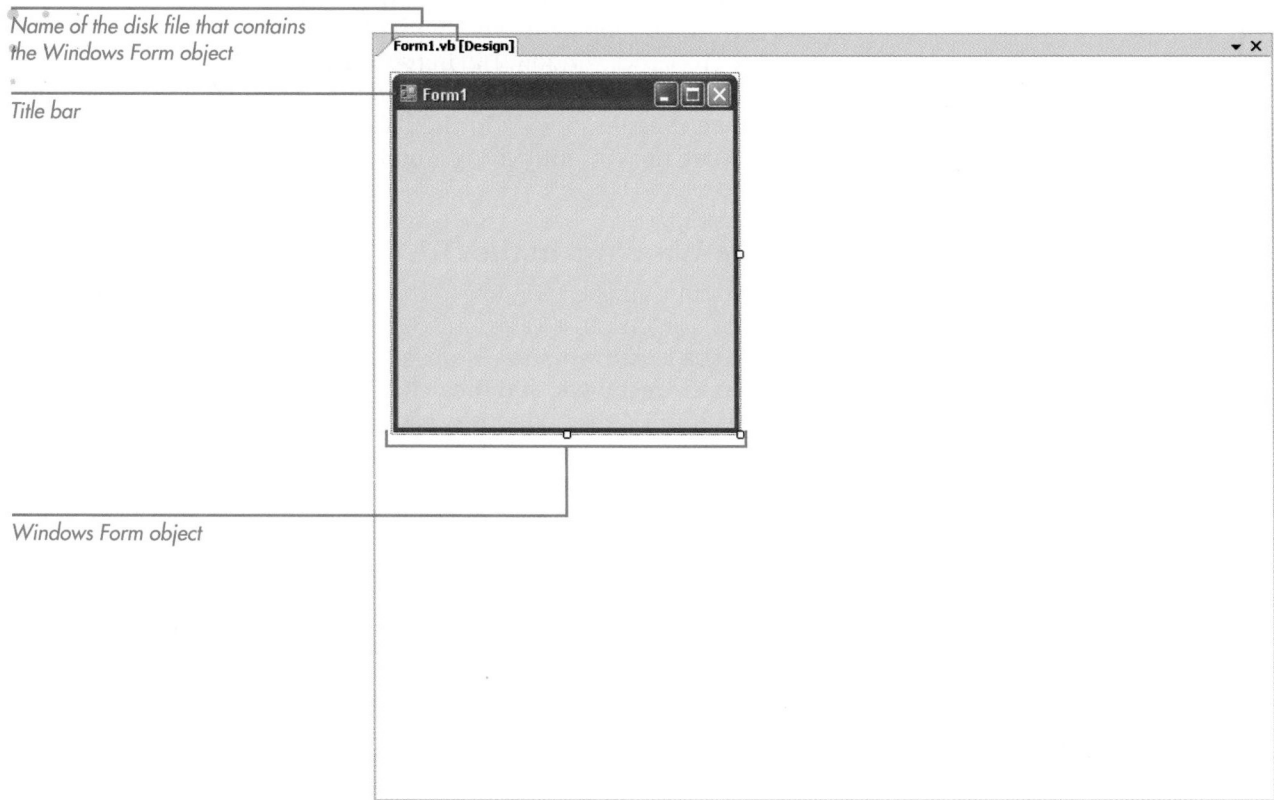

*Name of the disk file that contains the Windows Form object*

*Title bar*

*Windows Form object*

**FIGURE 1.11**    Windows Form Designer window

Only a Windows Form object appears in the designer window shown in Figure 1.11. A **Windows Form object**, or **form**, is the foundation for the user interface in a Windows-based application. You create the user interface by adding other objects, such as buttons and text boxes, to the form.

Notice that a title bar appears at the top of the Windows Form object. The title bar contains a default caption—in this case, Form1—as well as Minimize, Maximize, and Close buttons.

At the top of the designer window is a tab labeled Form1.vb [Design]. [Design] identifies the window as the designer window. Form1.vb is the name of the file (on your computer's hard disk) that contains Visual Basic instructions associated with the Windows Form object.

Recall that all objects in an object-oriented program come from—or, in OOP terms, are instances of—a class. The Windows Form object, for example, is an instance of the Windows Form class. The form object is automatically instantiated for you when you create a Windows-based application.

## THE SOLUTION EXPLORER WINDOW

The **Solution Explorer window** displays a list of the projects contained in the current solution, and the items contained in each project. Figure 1.12 shows the Solution Explorer window for the Taft Inc Solution. Notice that the solution contains one project named Taft Inc Project. Within the Taft Inc Project is a My Project folder and a file named Form1.vb.

*Show All Files button*

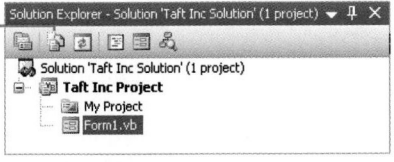

**FIGURE 1.12**   Solution Explorer window

You can use the My Project folder to open the Project Designer window; to do this, you right-click the folder and then click Open on the context menu. Figure 1.13 shows the Project Designer window opened in the IDE.

**TIP**

The Taft Inc Project contains items in addition to the ones shown in Figure 1.12. To display the additional items, which typically are kept hidden, click the Show All Files button located below the title bar in the Solution Explorer window.

*Right-click, then click Open to open the Project Designer window*

*Project Designer window*

*Tabs*

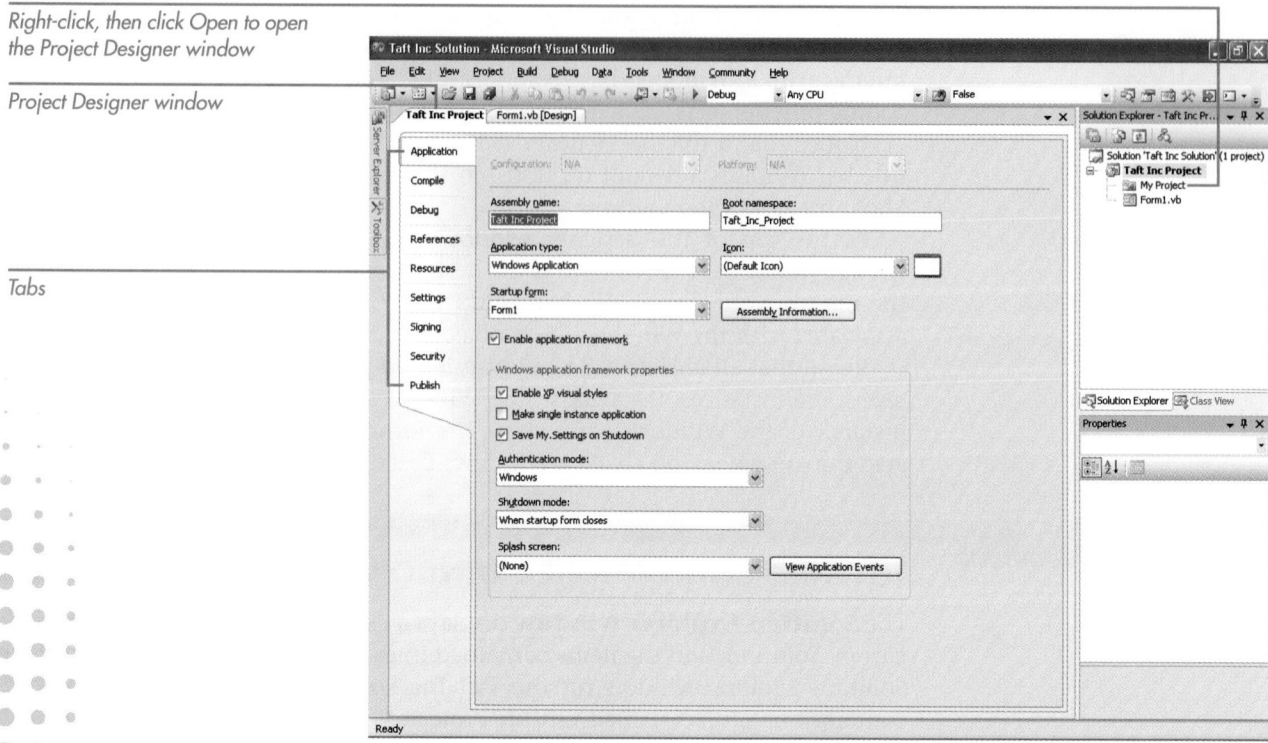

**FIGURE 1.13**     Project Designer window opened in the IDE

The **Project Designer window** contains nine tabs, with each tab displaying a different pane in the window. The Application pane appears in the Project Designer window shown in Figure 1.13. Figure 1.14 describes the purpose of each pane in the Project Designer window.

| Pane | Purpose |
|------|---------|
| Application | describe the application and its behavior, such as the application type and startup form |
| Compile | control compiler behavior, such as compiler warnings and optimizations |
| Debug | define debugging behavior, such as start action and start options |
| References | list the components referenced by the project |
| Settings | dynamically store and retrieve property settings and other information for the application |
| Resources | manage resources for the project, such as strings and images |
| Signing | sign an application with a public/private key pair |
| Security | set security permissions for a ClickOnce application |
| Publish | configure an application for ClickOnce publishing |

**FIGURE 1.14**     Purpose of the panes in the Project Designer window

Recall that the Taft Inc Project also contains a file named Form1.vb. The .vb on the filename indicates that the file is a "Visual Basic" source file. A **source file** is a file that contains program instructions, called **code**. The Form1.vb file contains the code associated with the Windows Form object, or form, displayed in the Windows Form Designer window. You can use the Code Editor window, which you learn about later in this chapter, to view the contents of the Form1.vb file.

The Form1.vb source file is also referred to as a **form file**, because it contains the code associated with a Windows Form object. The code associated with the first Windows Form object included in a project is automatically stored in a form file named Form1.vb. The code associated with the second Windows Form object in the same project is stored in a form file named Form2.vb, and so on. Because a project can contain many Windows Form objects and, therefore, many form files, it is a good practice to give each form file a more meaningful name; this will help you keep track of the various form files in the project. You can use the Properties window to change the filename.

## THE PROPERTIES WINDOW

As is everything in an object-oriented language, a file is an object. Each object has a set of attributes that determine its appearance and behavior. The attributes, called properties, are listed in the **Properties window**. In the context of OOP, the Properties window exposes the object's properties to the programmer.

When an object is created, a default value is assigned to each of its properties. The Properties window shown in Figure 1.15, for example, lists the default values assigned to the properties of the Form1.vb file contained in the Taft Inc Project.

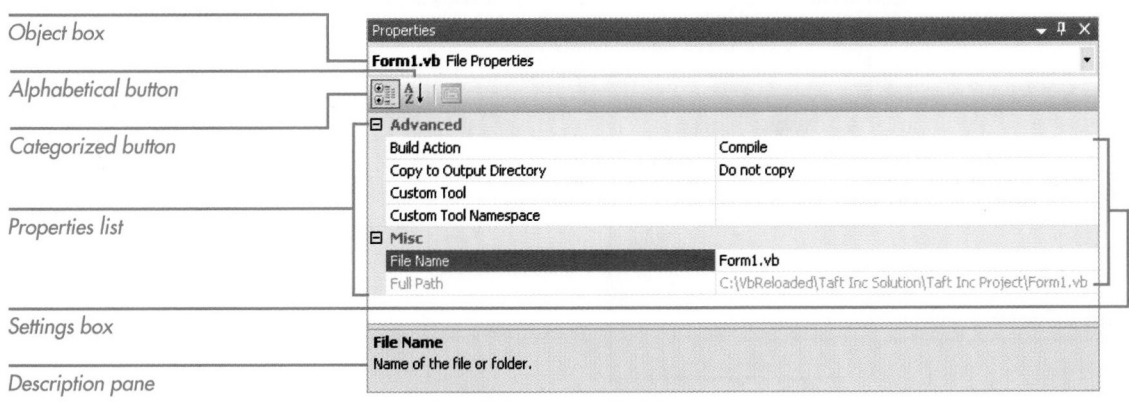

Object box

Alphabetical button

Categorized button

Properties list

Settings box

Description pane

**FIGURE 1.15**   Properties window showing the properties of the Form1.vb file object

**TIP**

To display the properties of the Form1.vb form file object, you first must click Form1.vb in the Solution Explorer window.

As indicated in Figure 1.15, the Properties window includes an Object box and a Properties list. The Object box is located immediately below the Properties window's title bar. The **Object box** contains the name of the selected object; in this case, it contains Form1.vb, which is the name of the form file object. When an object is selected, its properties appear in the Properties window.

The **Properties list** has two columns. The left column displays the names of the properties associated with the selected object. You can use the Alphabetical or

**TIP**

You also can change the File Name property by right-clicking Form1.vb in the Solution Explorer window, and then clicking Rename on the context menu.

**TIP**

It is easy to confuse the Windows Form object with the form file object. The Windows Form object is the form itself. A Windows Form object, or form, can be viewed in the designer window and appears on the screen when the application is running. The form file object, on the other hand, is the disk file that contains the code associated with the form.

Categorized buttons, which are located below the Object box, to display the property names either alphabetically or by category. The right column in the Properties list is called the **Settings box** and displays the current value, or setting, of each of the properties. For example, the current value of the File Name property shown in Figure 1.15 is Form1.vb. Notice that a brief description of the selected property appears in the Description pane located at the bottom of the Properties window.

Depending on the property, you can change the default value by selecting the property in the Properties list, and then either typing a new value in the Settings box or selecting a predefined value from a list or dialog box. For example, to change the value of the File Name property, you click File Name in the Properties list and then type the new filename in the Settings box. However, to change the value of the Build Action property, you click Build Action in the Properties list, then click the list arrow button in the Settings box, and then click one of the predefined settings from a drop-down list.

Like a file object, a Windows Form object also has a set of properties.

## Properties of a Windows Form Object

To display the properties of a Windows Form object in the Properties window, you first must select the object. You select the Windows Form object by clicking it in the designer window.

The Properties window in Figure 1.16 shows a partial listing of the properties of a Windows Form object. The vertical scroll bar on the Properties window indicates that there are more properties to view.

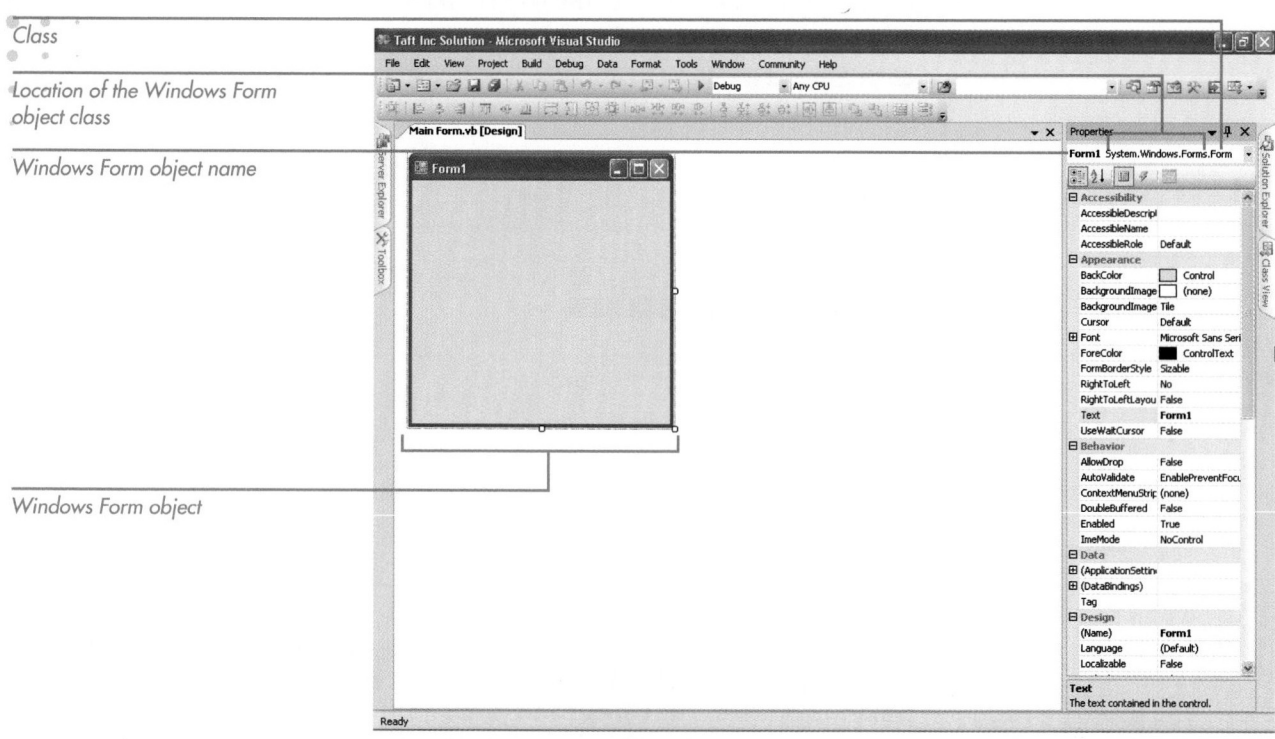

*Class*

*Location of the Windows Form object class*

*Windows Form object name*

*Windows Form object*

**FIGURE 1.16**　　Windows Form object properties listed in the Properties window

Notice that Form1 System.Windows.Forms.Form appears in the Object box in Figure 1.16. Form1 is the name of the Windows Form object. The name is automatically assigned to the form when the form is created—or, in OOP terms, instantiated. In System.Windows.Forms.Form, Form is the name of the class used to instantiate the Windows Form object. The forms in a project inherit the attributes and behaviors of the Form class. System.Windows.Forms, on the other hand, is the namespace that contains the Form class definition. A **class definition** is a block of code that specifies (or defines) the attributes and behaviors of an object. All class definitions in Visual Studio 2005 are contained in namespaces, which you can picture as blocks of internal memory cells. Each **namespace** contains the code that defines a group of related classes. The System.Windows.Forms namespace, for instance, contains the definition of the Windows Form class. It also contains the class definitions for objects you add to a form, such as buttons and text boxes.

The period that separates each word in System.Windows.Forms.Form is called the **dot member access operator**. Similar to the backslash (\) in a folder path, the dot member access operator indicates a hierarchy, but of namespaces rather than folders. In other words, the backslash in the path C:\VbReloaded\Taft Inc Solution\Taft Inc Project\Form1.vb indicates that the Form1.vb file is contained in (or is a member of) the Taft Inc Project folder, which is a member of the Taft Inc Solution folder, which is a member of the VbReloaded folder, which is a member of the C: drive. Likewise, the name System.Windows.Forms.Form indicates that the Form class is a member of the Forms namespace, which is a member of the Windows namespace, which is a member of the System namespace. The dot member access operator allows the computer to locate the Form class in the computer's internal memory, similarly to the way the backslash (\) allows the computer to locate the Form1.vb file on your computer's hard disk.

As you did with the file object, you should assign a more meaningful name to the Windows Form object; this will help you keep track of the various forms in a project. Keep in mind that the names of the forms within the same project must be unique.

Unlike a file object, a Windows Form object has a Name property rather than a File Name property. You use the name entered in an object's **Name property** to refer to the object in code. The name must begin with a letter and contain only letters, numbers, and the underscore character. You cannot use punctuation characters or spaces in the name.

For many years, most Visual Basic programmers used Hungarian notation when naming objects, and many programmers still follow this practice. **Hungarian notation** is a naming convention that uses the first three (or more) characters in the name to represent the object's type (form, button, and so on), and the remaining characters to represent the object's purpose. For example, using Hungarian notation, you might assign the name frmMain to the main (or primary) form in an application. The "frm" identifies the object as a form, and "Main" reminds you of the form's purpose. Similarly, a secondary form used to access an employee database might be named frmEmployeeData or frmPersonnel. Hungarian notation names are entered using **camel case**, which means that you lowercase the characters that represent the object's type and then uppercase the first letter of each word in the name.

Recently, a new naming convention for forms has emerged, and this is the naming convention used in this book. In the new naming convention, the name begins with the form's purpose, followed by the form's class (Form). Additionally, form names are entered using **Pascal case**, which means that the first letter in

TIP

Recall that every object used in an object-oriented program is instantiated from a class.

TIP

Camel case refers to the fact that the uppercase letters, which are taller than the lowercase letters, appear as "humps" in the name.

TIP

Pascal is a programming language created by Niklaus Wirth in the late 1960s. It was named in honor of the seventeenth-century French mathematician Blaise Pascal, and is used to develop scientific applications.

TIP

Visit *www.irritatedvowel.com/ Programming/Standards.aspx* for an interesting article on why Hungarian notation has fallen out of favor with many programmers.

TIP

Although this book uses the new naming convention for forms, your company (or instructor) may have a different naming convention you are expected to use. Your company's (or instructor's) naming convention supersedes the one used in this book.

TIP

The Name property is used by the programmer, whereas the Text property is read by the user.

the name, as well as the first letter of each subsequent word in the name, is capitalized. Using this new naming convention, you would assign the name MainForm to the main form in an application. "Main" reminds you of the form's purpose, and "Form" indicates the class used to instantiate the form. Similarly, a secondary form used to access an employee database might be named EmployeeDataForm or PersonnelForm.

In addition to changing the Form object's Name property, you also should change its **Text property**, which controls the caption displayed in the form's title bar. The caption also is displayed on the application's button on the taskbar while the application is running. The default caption, Form1, is automatically assigned to the first form in a project. Better, more descriptive captions include "Commission Calculator" and "Employee Information".

The Name and Text properties of a Form object always should be changed to more meaningful values. At times, you also may want to change the Form object's StartPosition property. You use the **StartPosition property** to determine where the form is positioned when the application is started and the form first appears on the screen. A form that represents a splash screen, for example, always should appear in the middle of the screen. As you may know, a **splash screen** is the first image that appears when an application is started. It is used to introduce the application and to hold the user's attention while the application is being read into the computer's memory. To display a Form object in the middle of the screen, you change its StartPosition property from WindowsDefaultLocation to CenterScreen.

Figure 1.17 lists the names and uses of several properties of a Windows Form object.

## HOW TO...

### Use a Windows Form Object

| Property | Use to |
| --- | --- |
| AcceptButton | specify a default button that will be "clicked" when the user presses the Enter key |
| CancelButton | specify a cancel button that will be "clicked" when the user presses the Esc key |
| Font | specify the font to use for text (usually set to Tahoma) |
| FormBorderStyle | control the border of the form |
| Name | give the form a meaningful name |
| StartPosition | specify the starting position of the form |
| Text | specify the caption that appears in the form's title bar and on the taskbar |

**FIGURE 1.17**    How to use a Windows Form object

You can use the Toolbox window to add other objects, such as text boxes and buttons, to a form.

## THE TOOLBOX WINDOW

The **Toolbox window**, or **toolbox**, contains the tools you use when creating your application. The contents of the toolbox vary depending on the designer in use. The toolbox shown in Figure 1.18 appears when you are using the Windows Form designer.

*This tab displays the tool names in alphabetical order*

*These tabs display the tool names by category*

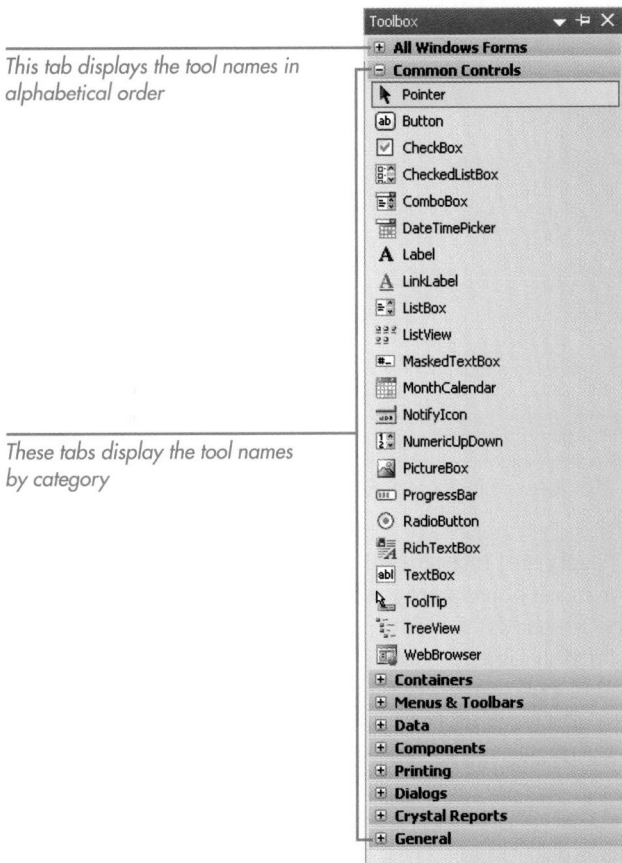

**FIGURE 1.18**   Toolbox window

Both an icon and a name identify each tool in the toolbox. The toolbox tabs allow you to view the tools by category or in alphabetical order by name. When you rest your mouse pointer on either the tool's name or its icon, the tool's purpose appears in a box, as shown in Figure 1.19.

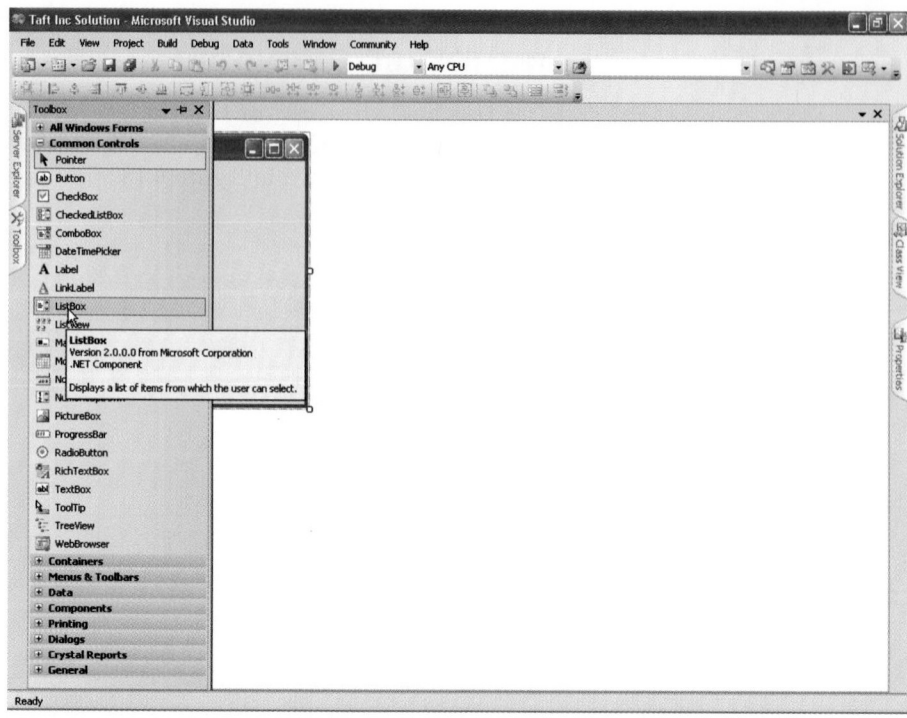

**FIGURE 1.19**        Box describing the purpose of the ListBox tool

In the context of OOP, each tool in the toolbox represents a class, which is a pattern from which one or more objects are instantiated. The object's attributes (properties) and behaviors (methods) are encapsulated (combined) in the tool. The tools allow you to instantiate objects such as text boxes, list boxes, and radio buttons. These objects, called **controls**, are displayed on the form. Figure 1.20 lists the steps you follow to add a control to a form.

**HOW TO...**

### Add a Control to a Form

1. Click a tool in the toolbox, but do not release the mouse button.
2. Hold down the mouse button as you drag the mouse pointer to the form. You will see a solid box, as well as an outline of a rectangle and a plus box, following the mouse pointer, as shown in Figure 1.21.
3. Release the mouse button.

Additional ways:
- Click a tool in the toolbox and then click the form.
- Click a tool in the toolbox, then place the mouse pointer on the form, and then press the left mouse button and drag the mouse pointer until the control is the desired size.

**FIGURE 1.20**        How to add a control to a form

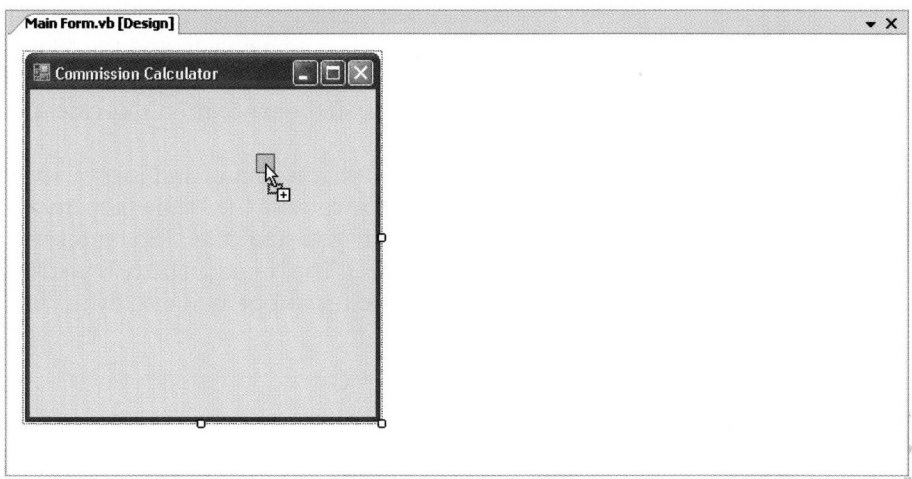

**FIGURE 1.21**     Tool being dragged to the form

Controls on a form can be selected, sized, moved, deleted, or locked and unlocked. The easiest way to select a control is to click it in the designer window; however, you also can use the list arrow button in the Properties window's Object box to select a control. You size a control using the sizing handles that appear around it when it is selected. You move a control by dragging it to the desired location, and you delete it by clicking it and then pressing the Delete key on your keyboard. To lock the controls in place, which prevents them from being inadvertently moved, you click the form (or any control on the form), then click Format on the menu bar, and then click Lock Controls; you follow the same procedure to unlock the controls. You also can lock and unlock the controls by right-clicking the form (or any control on the form), and then clicking Lock Controls on the context menu. When a control is locked, a small lock appears in the upper-left corner of the control.

In the next two sections, you learn about the Label tool and the Button tool. (You learn about the PictureBox tool in the Programming Tutorial section of this chapter.)

### The Label Tool

You use the **Label tool** to instantiate a label control. The purpose of a **label control** is to display text that the user is not allowed to edit while the application is running. Label controls are used in an interface to identify other controls and also display program output. The form shown in Figure 1.22, for example, includes three identifying labels and one display label.

**TIP**

The label controls shown in Figure 1.22 are instances of the Label class.

Identifies a list box

Identifies a text box

Identifies another label control

Displays program output

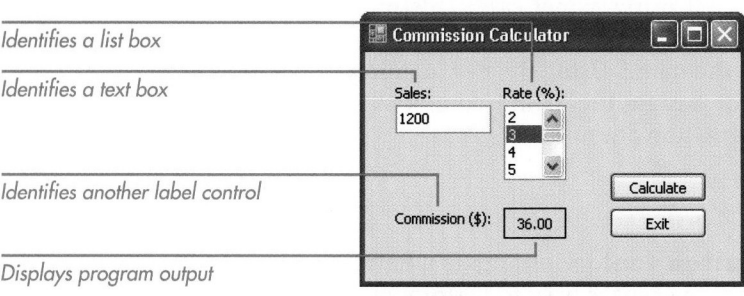

**FIGURE 1.22**     Label controls on a form

The "Sales:" label in Figure 1.22 tells the user the type of information to enter in the text box located below it, and the "Rate (%):" label describes the numbers listed in the list box. The "Commission ($):" label identifies the contents of the label control located next to it; in this case, the label control displays a commission amount.

Figure 1.23 lists the names and uses of several properties of a label control. As with all controls, you use the Name property to give the control a more meaningful name, and you use the Text property to specify the text to display inside the control. The Name property is used by the programmer when coding the application. The Text property is read by the user while the application is running.

**HOW TO...**

### Use a Label Control

| Property | Use to |
|---|---|
| AutoSize | automatically size the control to fit its current contents |
| BorderStyle | specify whether the control has a visible border (identifying labels should not have a visible border) |
| Font | specify the font to use for text (usually set to Tahoma) |
| Margin | specify the space between the control and another control |
| Name | give the control a meaningful name |
| TabIndex | indicate the control's position in the Tab order |
| Text | specify the text that appears inside the control |
| TextAlign | specify the position of the text within the control |

**FIGURE 1.23**     How to use a label control

Some programmers assign meaningful names to all of the label controls in an interface, while others do so only for label controls that display program output; in this book, you follow the latter convention.

As you learned earlier, for many years most Visual Basic programmers used Hungarian notation when naming objects. Using Hungarian notation, a programmer might assign the name lblCommission to a label control that displays a commission amount. The "lbl" identifies the object as a label control, and "Commission" indicates the control's purpose. In the new naming convention for controls, control names are made up of the control's purpose followed by the control's class. Unlike form names, which are entered using Pascal case, control names are entered using camel case. This means that you lowercase the first word in the control's name and then uppercase the first letter of each subsequent word in the name. Using the new naming convention for controls, a programmer might assign the name commissionLabel to a label control that displays a commission amount.

### The Button Tool

You use the **Button tool** to instantiate a button control. In Windows applications, a **button control** is used to perform an immediate action when clicked. The OK and Cancel buttons are examples of button controls found in most Windows applications.

**TIP**
The button controls shown in Figure 1.24 are instances of the Button class.

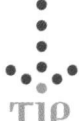

The form shown in Figure 1.24 contains two button controls labeled Calculate and Exit. The text that appears on each button's face is entered in the button's Text property.

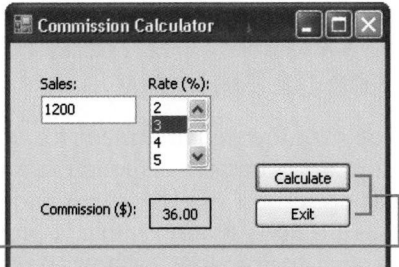

*Button controls*

**FIGURE 1.24** Button controls on a form

Figure 1.25 lists the names and uses of several properties of a button control.

**HOW TO...**

### Use a Button Control

| **Property** | **Use to** |
|---|---|
| BackgroundImage | specify the background image displayed in the control |
| BackgroundImageLayout | specify the layout for the background image |
| Enabled | indicate whether the control can respond to an action (such as clicking) |
| Font | specify the font to use for text (usually set to Tahoma) |
| Image | indicate the image to display on the face of the control |
| ImageAlign | specify the alignment of the image displayed on the face of the control |
| Margin | specify the space between the control and another control |
| Name | give the control a meaningful name |
| TabIndex | indicate the control's position in the Tab order |
| Text | specify the text that appears inside the control |
| TextAlign | specify the position of the text within the control |

**FIGURE 1.25** How to use a button control

You should assign meaningful names to the button controls in an interface. The names should end with the word Button, which is the name of the class used to instantiate a button control. Good names for the Calculate and Exit buttons shown in Figure 1.24 are calculateButton and exitButton.

After creating your application's user interface, you then write the Visual Basic instructions to tell the objects how to respond when they are clicked, double-clicked, and so on. You enter the instructions in the Code Editor window, which you view next.

## THE CODE EDITOR WINDOW

Think about the Windows environment for a moment. Did you ever wonder why the OK and Cancel buttons respond the way they do when you click them, or how the Exit option on the File menu knows to close the application? The answer to these questions is very simple: a programmer gave the menu option and buttons explicit instructions on how to respond to the actions of the user. Those actions—such as clicking, double-clicking, and scrolling—are called **events**. The set of Visual Basic instructions, or code, that tells an object how to respond to an event is called an **event procedure**. You enter an event procedure's code in the Code Editor window. Figure 1.26 shows various ways of opening the Code Editor window, and Figure 1.27 shows the Code Editor window opened in the IDE.

**HOW TO...**

**Open the Code Editor Window**

- Right-click the form, and then click View Code on the context menu.
- Verify that the designer window is the active window, then click View on the menu bar, and then click Code.
- Verify that the designer window is the active window, then press the F7 key on your keyboard.
- Click the form or a control on the form, then click the Events button in the Properties window, and then double-click the desired event.

**FIGURE 1.26**    How to open the Code Editor window

Designer window's tab

Code Editor window's tab

Click the minus box to collapse the code

Class statement

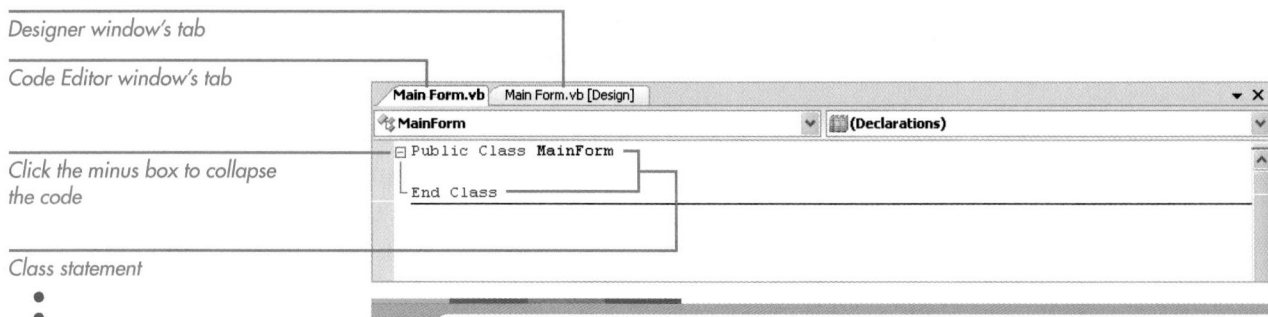

**FIGURE 1.27**    Code Editor window opened in the IDE

**TIP**

The **Public** keyword in the Class statement indicates that the class can be used by code defined outside of the class.

The Code Editor window shown in Figure 1.27 contains the Visual Basic Class statement, which is used to create a class. In this case, the Class statement begins with the `Public Class MainForm` instruction and ends with the `End Class` instruction. Within the Class statement you enter the code to tell the form and its objects how to react to the user's actions.

If the Code Editor contains many lines of code, you might want to hide the sections of code with which you are not presently working or that you do not want to print. You hide, or collapse, a section of code by clicking the minus box that appears next to it. Figure 1.28 shows the code collapsed in the Code Editor window. To expand the code, you click the plus box that appears next to the code.

*Method Name list box*

*Class Name list box*

*Click the plus box to expand the code*

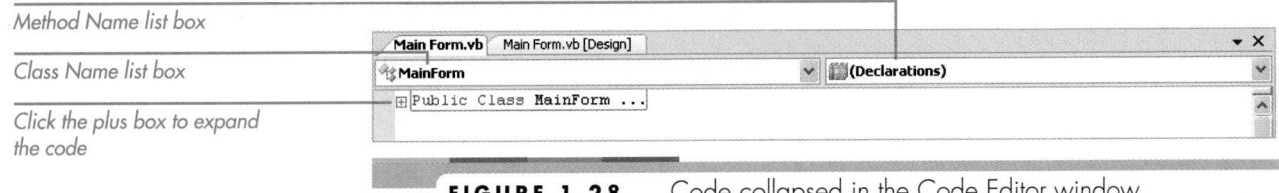

**FIGURE 1.28**    Code collapsed in the Code Editor window

As indicated in Figure 1.28, the Code Editor window contains a Class Name list box and a Method Name list box. The **Class Name list box** lists the names of the objects included in the user interface. The **Method Name list box** lists the events to which the selected object is capable of responding. In OOP, the events are considered behaviors, because they represent actions that the object can have performed on it. (Recall that methods, which are actions that an object can perform, are considered behaviors also.) The Code Editor window exposes an object's behaviors to the programmer.

You use the Class Name and Method Name list boxes to select the object and event, respectively, that you want to code. For example, to code the exitButton's Click event, you select exitButton in the Class Name list box and select Click in the Method Name list box. When you do this, a code template for the exitButton's Click event procedure appears in the Code Editor window, as shown in Figure 1.29. The first line in the code template is called the **procedure header**, and the last line is called the **procedure footer**.

*Procedure header*

*Procedure footer*

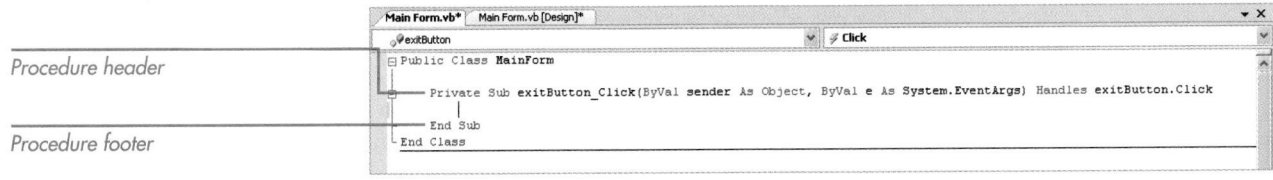

**FIGURE 1.29**    Code template for the exitButton's Click event procedure

The procedure header begins with the two keywords `Private Sub`. A **keyword** is a word that has a special meaning in a programming language. The `Private` keyword indicates that the procedure can be used only within the class in which it is defined—in this case, only within the MainForm class. The `Sub` keyword is an abbreviation of the term **sub procedure**, which, in programming terminology, refers to a block of code that performs a specific task. Following the `Sub` keyword is the name of the object (`exitButton`), an underscore ( `_` ), the name of the event (`Click`), and parentheses containing `ByVal sender as Object, ByVal e As System.EventArgs`. The items within the parentheses are called parameters and represent information that is passed to the procedure when it is invoked. For now, you do not need to worry about the parameters; you learn more about parameters later in this book.

**TIP**

To display line numbers in the Code Editor window, click Tools, then click Options. Expand the Text Editor node, then click Basic. Select the Line numbers check box, then click the OK button.

Following the items in parentheses in the procedure header is `Handles exitButton.Click`. This part of the procedure header indicates that the procedure handles (or is associated with) the exitButton's Click event. In other words, the procedure will be processed when the exitButton is clicked. As you learn later in this book, you can associate the same procedure with more than one event. To do so, you list each event, separated by commas, in the `Handles` section of the procedure header.

The code template ends with the procedure footer, which contains the keywords `End Sub`. You enter your Visual Basic instructions at the location of the insertion point, which appears between the `Private Sub` and `End Sub` lines in Figure 1.29. The Code Editor automatically indents the line between the procedure header and footer. Indenting the lines within a procedure makes the instructions easier to read and is a common programming practice.

Notice that the keywords in the code appear in a different color from the rest of the code. The Code Editor window displays keywords in a different color to help you quickly identify these elements. In this case, the color-coding helps you easily locate the procedure header and footer.

When the user clicks the Exit button shown earlier in Figure 1.24, it indicates that he or she wants to end the application. If an application contains only one form, you stop the application by entering the `Me.Close` method in a procedure within the form. In this case, the `Me.Close` method should be entered in the Exit button's Click event procedure, because you want the method processed when the user clicks the button.

### The Me.Close Method

You use the **Me.Close method** to instruct the computer to close the current form, which you refer to using the keyword `Me`. If the current form is the main form, closing it terminates the application. A **method** is a predefined Visual Basic procedure that you can call (or invoke) when needed. You call the `Me.Close` method by entering the instruction `Me.Close()` in a procedure in the Code Editor window. Notice the empty set of parentheses after the method's name in the instruction. The parentheses are required when calling any of the Visual Basic methods; however, depending on the method, the parentheses may or may not be empty. Figure 1.30 shows the `Me.Close` method entered in the Exit button's Click event procedure. In this application, the Exit button's name is exitButton.

*The asterisk indicates that the solution has been changed since the last time it was saved*

**TIP**

If you forget to enter the parentheses after a method's name, the Code Editor will enter them for you when you move the insertion point to another line in the Code Editor window.

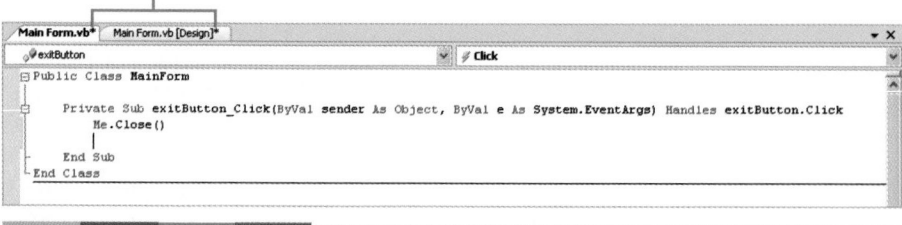

**FIGURE 1.30**    Me.Close method entered in the exitButton's Click event procedure

When the user clicks the Exit button, the computer processes the instructions shown in the exitButton_Click procedure one after another in the order in which they appear in the procedure. In programming, this is referred to as **sequential processing** or as the **sequence structure**. (You learn about two other programming structures [selection and repetition] in future chapters.)

Notice the asterisk (*) that appears on the designer and Code Editor tabs in Figure 1.30. The asterisk indicates that a change was made to the solution since the last time it was saved. It is a good practice to save the current solution every 10 or 15 minutes so that you will not lose a lot of your work if the computer loses power.

## SAVING A SOLUTION

Figure 1.31 shows two ways to save a solution. When you save a solution, the computer saves any changes made to the files included in the solution. Saving the solution also removes the asterisk that appears on the designer and Code Editor tabs.

**HOW TO...**

### Save a Solution

- Click File on the menu bar, and then click Save All.
- Click the Save All button 🖫 on the Standard toolbar.

**FIGURE 1.31**    How to save a solution

When you are finished coding the application, you need to start it to verify that it is working correctly.

## STARTING AND ENDING AN APPLICATION

Before you start an application for the first time, you need to specify the name of the **startup form**, which is the form that the computer automatically displays each time the application is started. You select the name from the Startup form list box in the Project Designer window. Figure 1.32 shows the steps you follow to specify the startup form's name, and Figure 1.33 shows the name of the startup form (in this case, MainForm) selected in the Project Designer window. The asterisk that appears on the Application tab in Figure 1.33 indicates that a change was made to one or more settings in the Application pane.

**HOW TO...**

### Specify the Startup Form

1. Open the Project Designer window. You can open the window by right-clicking My Project in the Solution Explorer window, and then clicking Open on the context menu.  You also can click Project on the menu bar, and then click <project name> Properties on the menu.
2. Click the Startup form list arrow in the Application pane, and then click the appropriate form name in the list.
3. Click the Close button on the Project Designer window.

**FIGURE 1.32**    How to specify the startup form

Close button

The asterisk indicates that a change was made in the pane

Startup form name

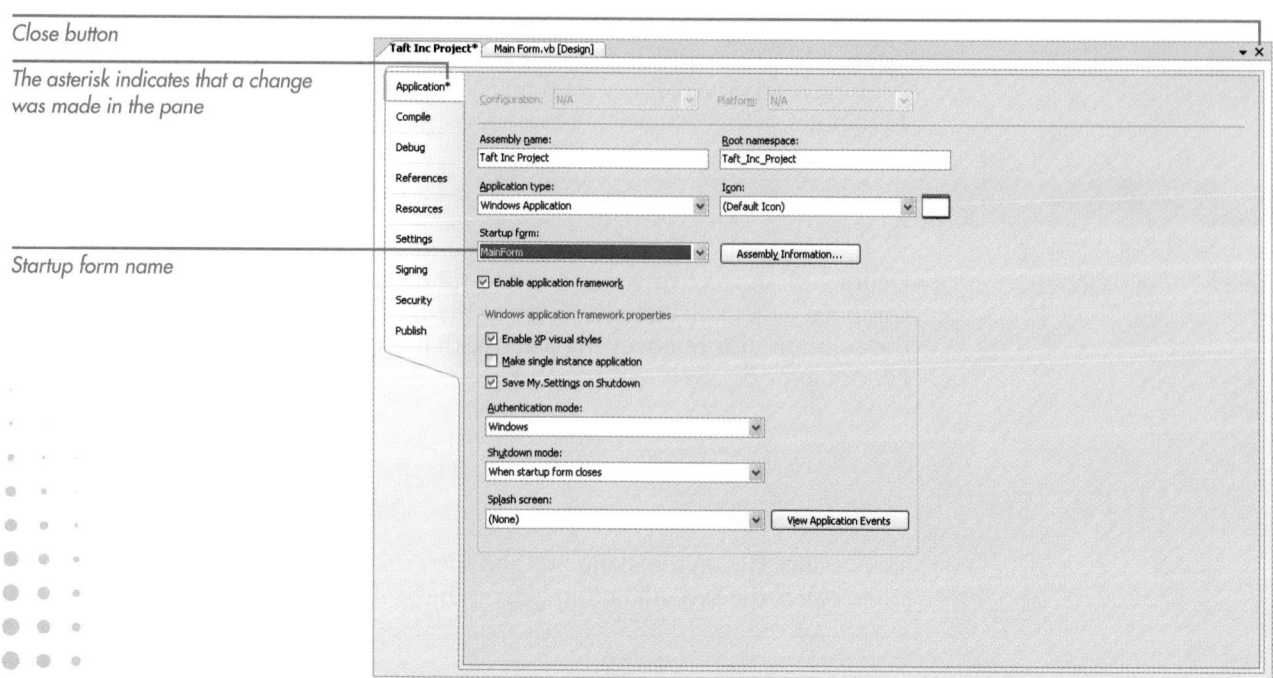

**FIGURE 1.33**    Name of the startup form selected in the Project Designer window

Figure 1.34 shows two ways to start an application, and Figure 1.35 shows the result of starting the Taft Inc Commission Calculator application. Notice that the computer automatically displays the startup form, which in this case is the form named MainForm. (At this point, you do not need to be concerned about the windows that appear at the bottom of the screen in Figure 1.35.)

## HOW TO...

**Start an Application**

- Save the solution. Click Debug on the menu bar, then click Start Debugging.
- Save the solution, then press the F5 key on your keyboard.

**FIGURE 1.34**    How to start an application

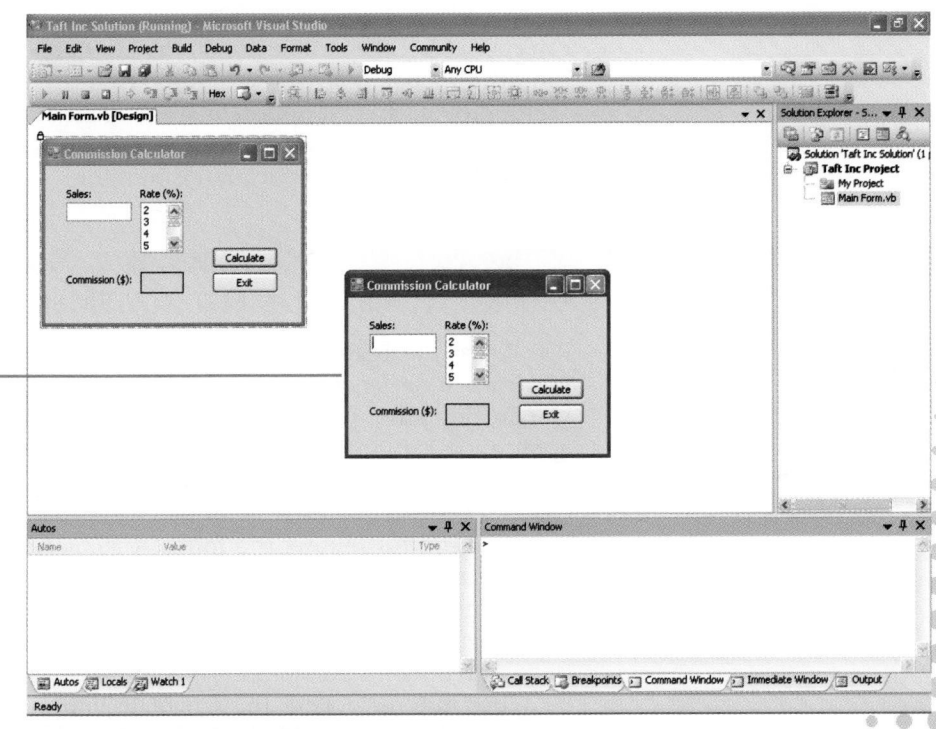

Startup form

**FIGURE 1.35**    Result of starting the Commission Calculator application

When you start a Visual Basic application, the computer automatically creates a file that can be run outside of the Visual Studio 2005 IDE; for example, it can be run from the Run dialog box in Windows. The file, referred to as an **executable file**, has the same name as the project, but with an .exe filename extension. The name of the executable file for the Taft Inc Project is Taft Inc Project.exe. The computer stores the executable file in the project's bin\Debug folder. In this case, for example, the Taft Inc Project.exe file is stored in the VbReloaded\Taft Inc Solution\Taft Inc Project\bin\Debug folder.

The way you end (or close) an application depends on the application's interface. Figure 1.36 lists various ways of ending an application.

**HOW TO...**    **End an Application**

- Click an Exit button in the interface.
- Click File on the menu bar, then click Exit.
- Click the Close button on the application's title bar.

**FIGURE 1.36**    How to end an application

To end the Commission Calculator application shown in Figure 1.35, you can click either the Exit button in the interface or the Close button on the application's title bar. Many applications, such as Visual Studio 2005 and Microsoft Word, provide an Exit option on a File menu for this purpose.

Next, you learn how to use an assignment statement to change the contents of a control while an application is running.

## USING AN ASSIGNMENT STATEMENT

Recall that the Text property determines the text displayed inside a control. As you learned earlier, you can set the Text property in the Properties window while you are designing your application. You also can set the Text property while an application is running; you do so using an assignment statement.

An **assignment statement** assigns a value to something, such as the property of a control. An assignment statement that assigns a value to the Text property of a control follows the format *control*.**Text** = *string*, where *control* is the control's name and *string* is zero or more characters enclosed in quotation marks. For example, to assign the word "Hello" to the greetingLabel control, you use the assignment statement `greetingLabel.Text = "Hello"`. The equal sign (=) in an assignment statement is called the **assignment operator**.

When the user clicks the Calculate button in the Commission Calculator interface, the button's Click event procedure should calculate the appropriate commission amount, and then display the calculated amount in the commissionLabel control. You can accomplish this by using an assignment statement to assign the calculated amount to the commissionLabel control's Text property. For now, however, you will simply assign the word "OK" to the Text property. (You learn how to perform calculations in Chapter 3.) Figure 1.37 shows the assignment statement entered in the calculateButton's Click event procedure in the Code Editor window. Figure 1.38 shows the result of the user starting the application and clicking the Calculate button.

*Assignment statement*

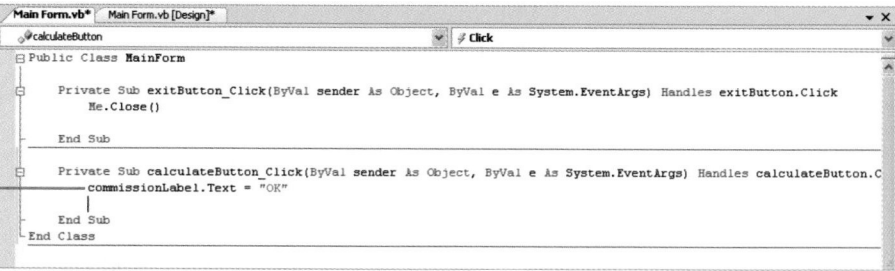

**FIGURE 1.37**    Assignment statement entered in the calculateButton's Click event procedure

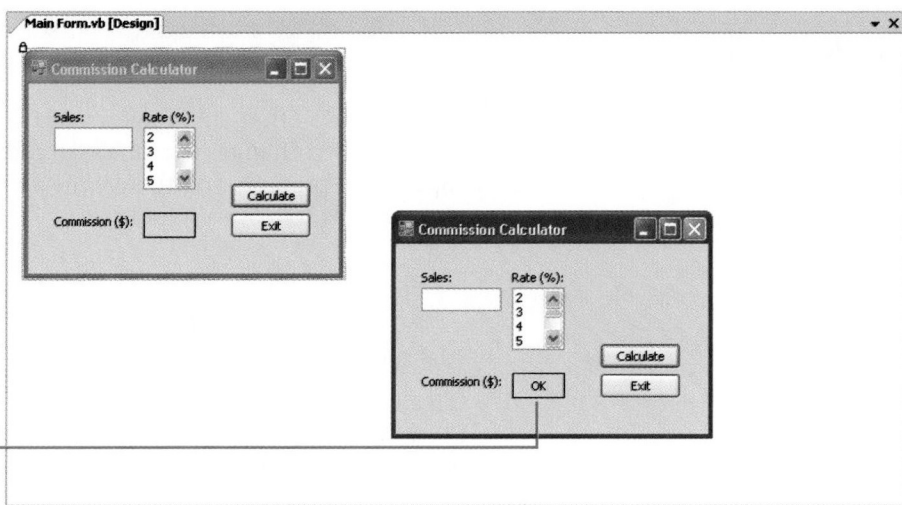

*Displayed by the Calculate button's
assignment statement*

**FIGURE 1.38**    Result of clicking the Calculate button

You will learn more about assignment statements in subsequent chapters in this book. Next, you learn how to print the code entered in the Code Editor window.

## PRINTING YOUR CODE

You always should print a copy of your application's code, because the printout will help you understand and maintain the application in the future. Figure 1.39 shows the steps you follow to print the code.

**HOW TO...**

### Print an Application's Code

1. Verify that the Code Editor window is the active window.
2. Collapse any code that you do not want to print. You do this by clicking the minus box that appears next to the code.
3. Click File on the menu bar, and then click Print.
4. If you don't want to print the collapsed code, select the Hide collapsed regions check box.
5. To print line numbers, select the Include line numbers check box.
6. Click the OK button to begin printing.

**FIGURE 1.39**    How to print an application's code

In the remainder of this chapter, you learn how to close the current solution and how to open an existing solution.

## CLOSING THE CURRENT SOLUTION

When you close a solution, all projects and files contained in the solution also are closed. If unsaved changes were made to the solution, project, or form, a dialog box opens and prompts you to save the appropriate files. Figure 1.40 shows the steps you follow to close a solution.

**HOW TO...**

### Close a Solution

1. Click File on the menu bar.
2. Click Close Solution.

**FIGURE 1.40**     How to close a solution

Notice that you use the Close Solution option, rather than the Close option, on the File menu. The Close option does not close the solution; it only closes the open windows, such as the designer and Code Editor windows, in the IDE.

## OPENING AN EXISTING SOLUTION

Figure 1.41 shows the steps you follow to open an existing solution. If a solution is already open in the IDE, it is closed before another solution is opened. In other words, only one solution can be open in the IDE at any one time.

**HOW TO...**

### Open an Existing Solution

1. Click File on the menu bar, point to Open, and then click Project/Solution to open the Open Project dialog box.
2. Locate and then click the solution filename, which is contained in the application's solution folder. The solution filename has an .sln filename extension, which stands for "solution."
3. Click the Open button in the Open Project dialog box.
4. If the Windows Form Designer window is not displayed, click View on the menu bar, and then click Designer.

**FIGURE 1.41**     How to open an existing solution

You have completed the concepts section of Chapter 1. The next section is the Programming Tutorial section, which gives you step-by-step instructions on how to apply the chapter's concepts to an application. A Programming Example follows the Programming Tutorial. The Programming Example is a completed program that demonstrates the concepts taught in the chapter. Following the Programming Example are the Quick Review, Key Terms, Self-Check Questions and Answers, Review Questions, Review Exercises – Short Answer, Computer Exercises, and Case Projects sections.

# PROGRAMMING TUTORIAL

## Creating a Visual Basic 2005 Application

In this tutorial, you create a Visual Basic 2005 application that contains a label, a picture box, and three buttons. The first button displays the picture box on the form, and the second button hides the picture box. The third button ends the application.

### Starting Visual Studio 2005

Before you can create a Visual Basic 2005 application, you first must start Visual Studio 2005.

**To start Visual Studio 2005:**

1. Click the **Start** button on the Windows taskbar to open the Start menu.
2. Point to **All Programs**, then point to **Microsoft Visual Studio 2005**, and then click **Microsoft Visual Studio 2005**. The Microsoft Visual Studio copyright screen appears momentarily, and then the Microsoft Visual Studio window opens. See Figure 1.42. (Your screen might not look identical to Figure 1.42.)

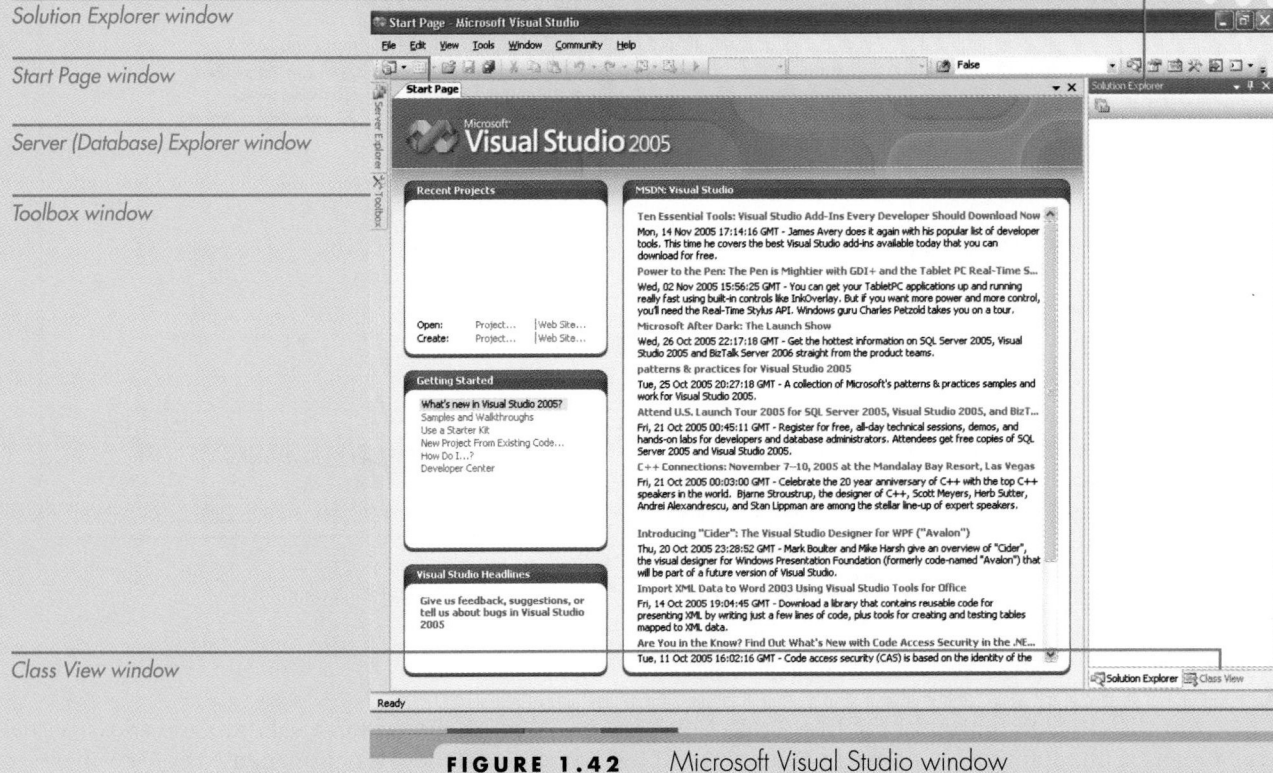

*Solution Explorer window*

*Start Page window*

*Server (Database) Explorer window*

*Toolbox window*

*Class View window*

**FIGURE 1.42**   Microsoft Visual Studio window

3. If the Server (Database) Explorer, Toolbox, Start Page, Solution Explorer, and Class View windows are not open, click **View** on the menu bar, and then click the appropriate option.

Next, you create a Visual Basic 2005 Windows-based application. Recall that a Windows-based application has a Windows user interface and runs on a desktop computer.

## Creating a Visual Basic 2005 Windows-based Application

As you learned in the concepts section of this chapter, Visual Basic 2005 applications are composed of solutions, projects, and files. A solution is a container that stores the projects and files for an entire application. A project also is a container, but it stores files associated with only a specific piece of the solution.

**To create a Visual Basic 2005 Windows-based application:**

1. Click **Tools** on the menu bar, then click **Options**. Click **Projects and Solutions**. If necessary, select the **Save new projects when created** and **Always show solution** check boxes, then click the **OK** button.
2. Click **File** on the Visual Studio menu bar, point to **New**, and then click **Project**. The New Project dialog box opens.
3. If necessary, expand the Visual Basic node in the Project types list, then click **Windows**.
4. If necessary, click **Windows Application** in the Visual Studio installed templates section of the Templates list.
5. Type **First Project** in the Name box.
6. Use the **Browse** button, which appears next to the Location box, to open the Project Location dialog box. Locate the **VbReloaded\Chap01** folder, then click the **Open** button to open the folder.
7. If necessary, select the **Create directory for solution** check box in the New Project dialog box.
8. Type **First Solution** in the Solution Name box. The completed New Project dialog box is shown in Figure 1.43.

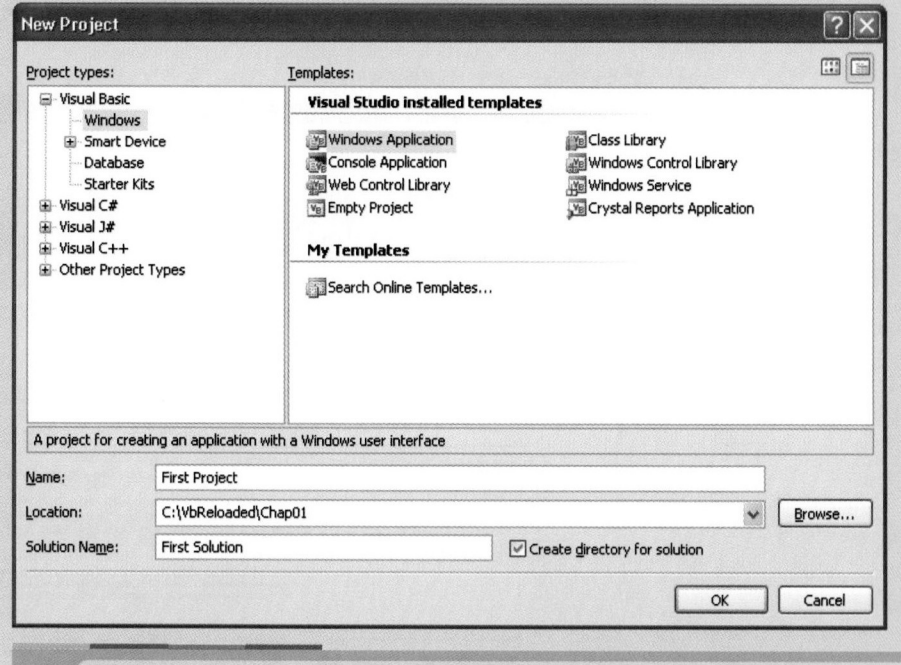

**FIGURE 1.43**     Completed New Project dialog box

9. Click the **OK** button to close the New Project dialog box.

When you click the OK button in the New Project dialog box, Visual Studio creates a solution and adds a Visual Basic project to the solution, as shown in Figure 1.44. If the Properties window is not open, use the View menu to open it.

Auto Hide button

Solution name

Project name and information

Properties window

Windows Form Designer window

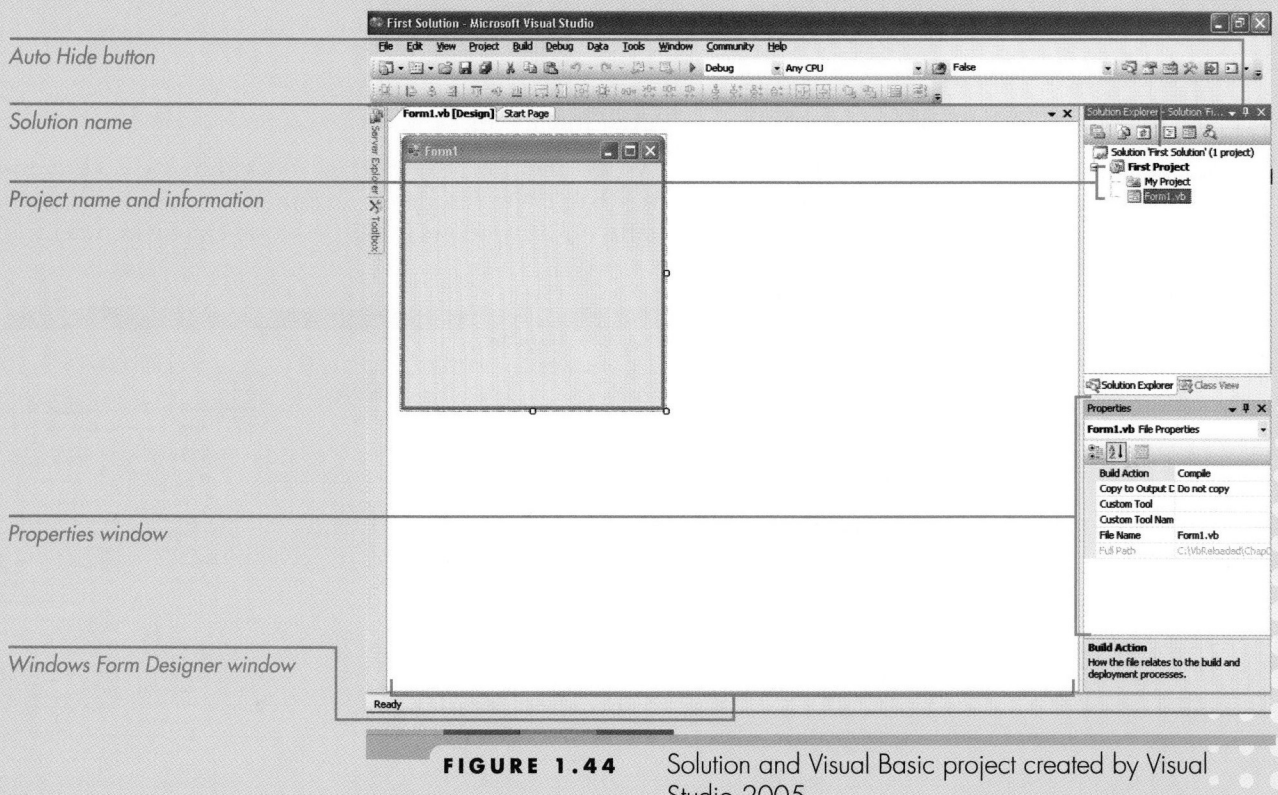

**FIGURE 1.44**    Solution and Visual Basic project created by Visual Studio 2005

10. If necessary, click the Alphabetical button in the Properties window to display the property names in alphabetical order. (Most times, it's easier to work with the Properties window when the property names are listed in alphabetical order.)

In the next section, you learn how to manage the windows in the IDE.

### Managing the Windows in the IDE

In the next set of steps, you learn how to close, auto-hide, and display the windows in the IDE.

**To close, auto-hide, and display the windows in the IDE:**

1. Place your mouse pointer on the **Server Explorer** (or Database Explorer) tab. When the Server (Database) Explorer window slides into view, which may take several moments, click the **Close** button on its title bar.

Now close the Start Page and Class View windows.

2. Click the **Start Page** tab to make the Start Page window the active window, and then click the **Close** button on its title bar.
3. Click the **Class View** tab to make the Class View window the active window, and then click the **Close** button on its title bar.

Next, auto-hide the Solution Explorer window.

4. Click the **Auto Hide** button (the vertical pushpin) on the Solution Explorer window's title bar, then move the mouse pointer away from the window. The Solution Explorer window is minimized and appears as a tab on the right edge of the IDE.

Now temporarily display the Solution Explorer window.

5. Place your mouse pointer on the **Solution Explorer** tab. The Solution Explorer window slides into view.

6. Move your mouse pointer away from the Solution Explorer window. The window is minimized and appears as a tab again.

Next, use the Auto Hide button to permanently display the Toolbox window.

7. Place your mouse pointer on the **Toolbox** tab. When the Toolbox window slides into view, click the **Auto Hide** button (the horizontal pushpin) on its title bar. The vertical pushpin button replaces the horizontal pushpin button. Figure 1.45 shows the current status of the windows in the development environment.

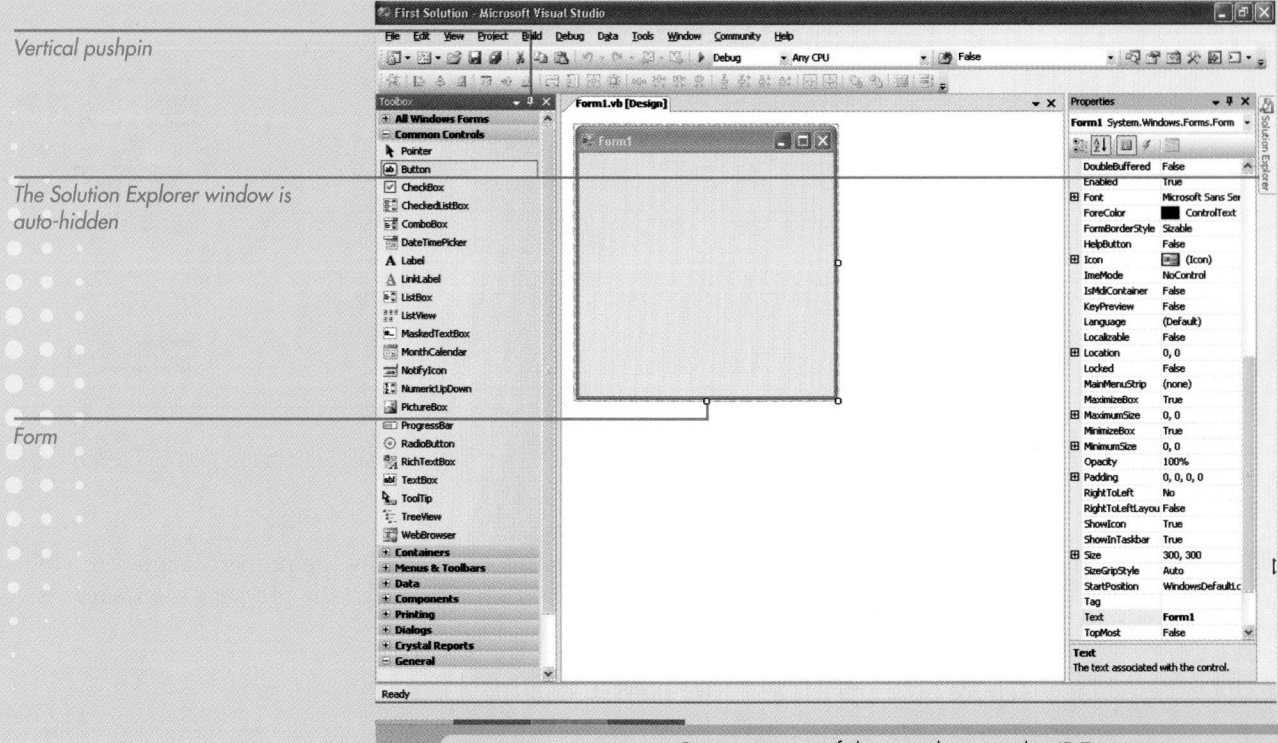

**FIGURE 1.45**     Current status of the windows in the IDE

Only a form appears in the Windows Form designer window shown in Figure 1.45. A form is the foundation for the user interface in a Windows-based application. You create the user interface by adding other objects, such as buttons and labels, to the form. You add the objects using the Toolbox window.

## Using the Toolbox Window to Add Objects to a Form

The Toolbox window, or toolbox, contains the tools you use when creating your application. You use the tools to add objects, called controls, to a form. In the next set of steps, you add button controls, a label control, and a picture box control to the current form. You also learn how to size, move, delete, and undelete a control.

**To add and manipulate a control:**

1. Click the **Button** tool in the toolbox, but do not release the mouse button. Hold down the mouse button as you drag the mouse pointer to the lower-left corner of the form. As you drag the mouse pointer, you will see a solid box, as well as an outline of a rectangle and a plus box, following the mouse pointer, as shown in Figure 1.46.

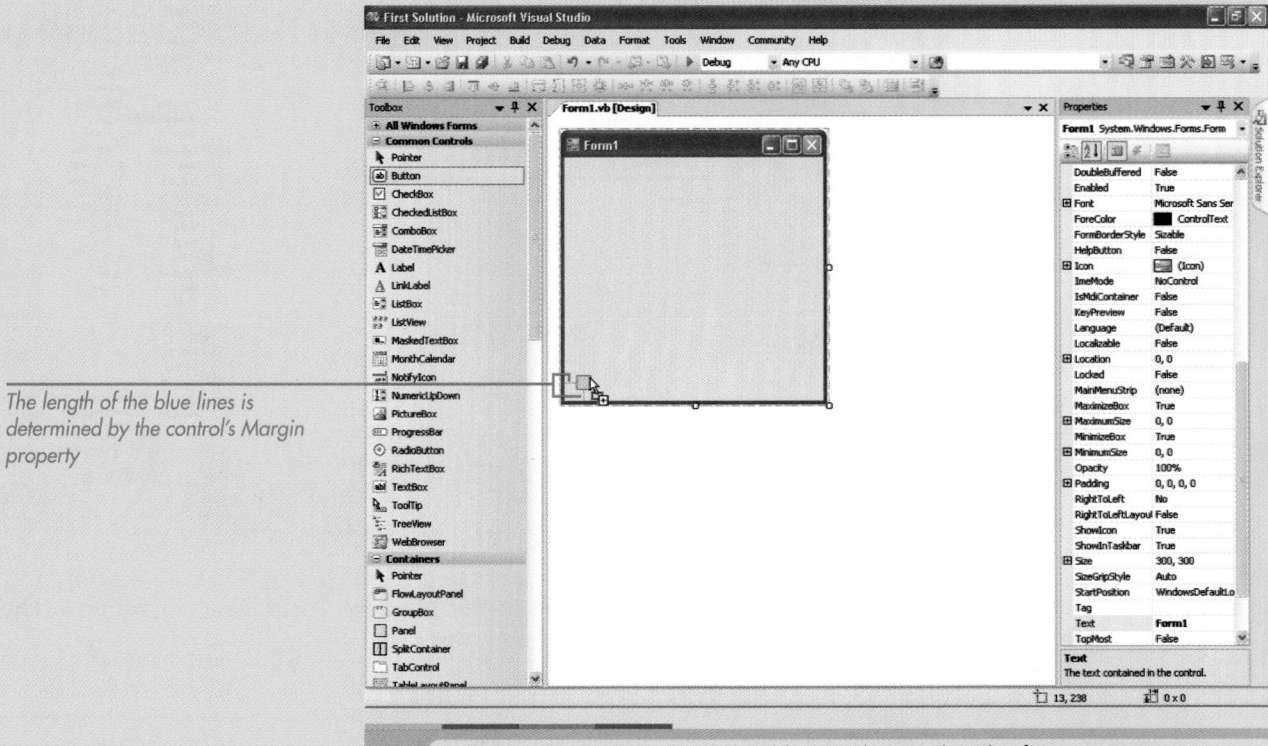

*The length of the blue lines is determined by the control's Margin property*

**FIGURE 1.46**   Button tool being dragged to the form

Notice that a blue line appears between the form's left border and the control's left border, and between the form's bottom border and the control's bottom border. The blue lines are called margin lines, because their size is determined by the contents of the control's Margin property. The purpose of the margin lines is to assist you in spacing the controls properly on a form.

2. Release the mouse button. A button control appears on the form, as shown in Figure 1.47. The sizing handles on the control indicate that the control is selected. You can use the sizing handles to make a control bigger or smaller.

*The asterisk indicates that the form has been changed since the last time it was saved*

*Sizing handle*

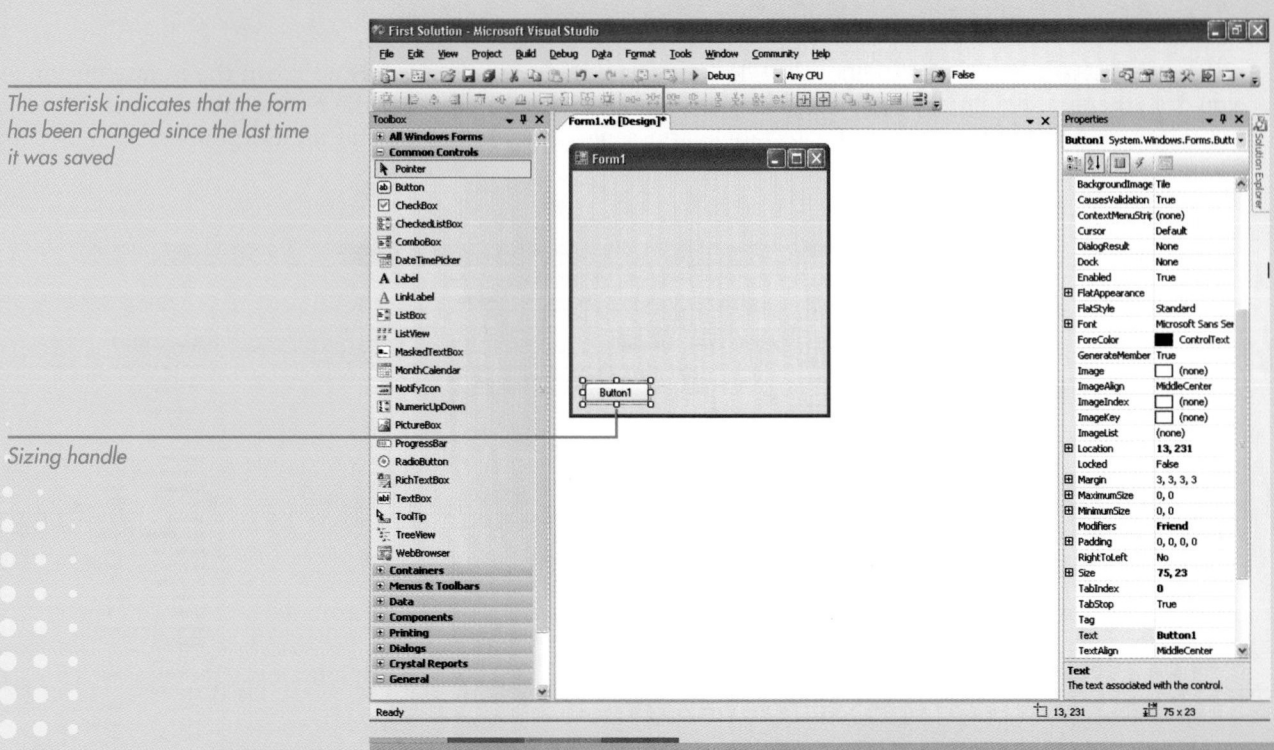

**FIGURE 1.47**      Button control added to the form

Notice that an asterisk (*) appears on the Form1.vb [Design] tab in the Windows Form Designer window. The asterisk indicates that the form has been changed since the last time it was saved.

3. Practice using the sizing handles to make the button control bigger.

Now reposition the button control on the form.

4. Place your mouse pointer on the center of the button control, then press the left mouse button and drag the control to another area of the form. Release the mouse button.

Next, delete and then undelete the button control.

5. Press the **Delete** key on your keyboard to delete the control.
6. Click **Edit** on the menu bar, and then click **Undo** to reinstate the button control.
7. Drag the button control back to its original location in the lower left-hand corner of the form.

You also can add a control to a form by clicking the appropriate tool and then clicking the form.

8. Click the **Button** tool in the toolbox, then click the **form**. (You do not need to worry about the exact location.)
9. Drag the second button control until the top of the control is aligned with the top of the first button control. When the tops of both controls are aligned, the designer displays a blue snap line, as shown in Figure 1.48.

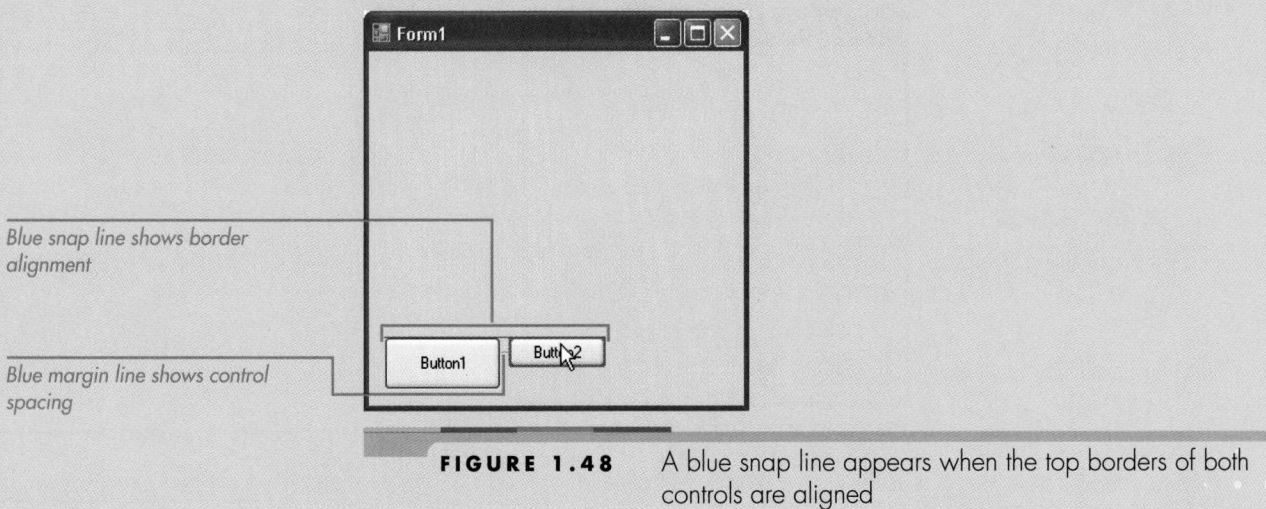

Blue snap line shows border
alignment

Blue margin line shows control
spacing

**FIGURE 1.48**    A blue snap line appears when the top borders of both
controls are aligned

**10.** Now drag the second button control down slightly, until the Button2 text is aligned with the Button1 text. When the text in both controls is aligned, the designer displays a pink snap line, as shown in Figure 1.49.

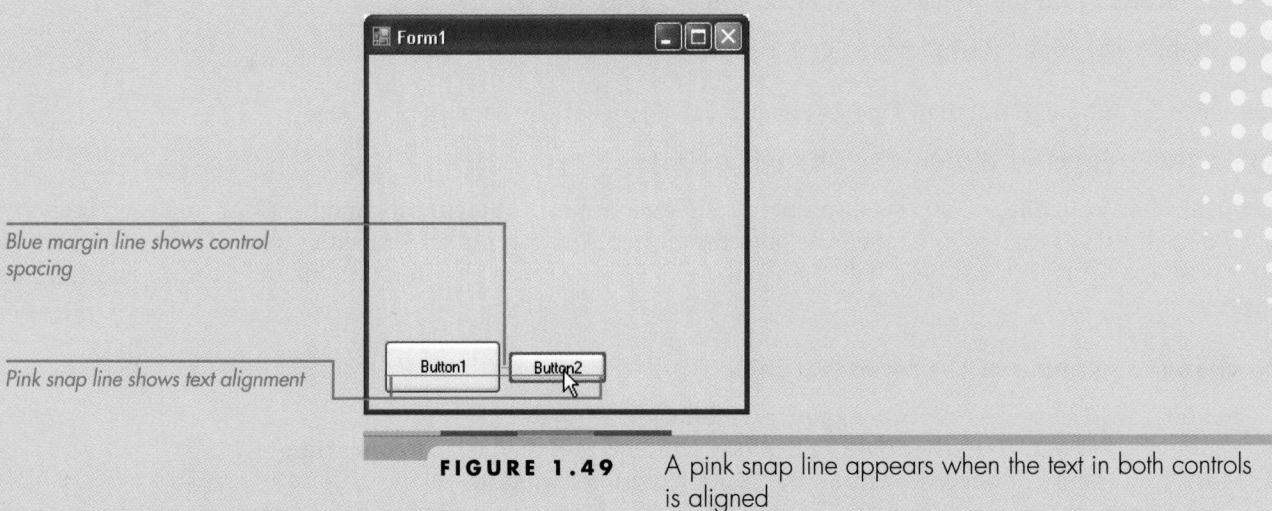

Blue margin line shows control
spacing

Pink snap line shows text alignment

**FIGURE 1.49**    A pink snap line appears when the text in both controls
is aligned

**11.** Release the mouse button.

Additionally, you can add a control to a form by clicking the appropriate tool, then placing the mouse pointer on the form, and then pressing the left mouse button and dragging the mouse pointer until the control is the desired size.

**12.** Click the **Button** tool in the toolbox, and then place the mouse pointer on the form. Press the left mouse button and drag the mouse pointer until the control is the desired size, then release the mouse button. (You do not need to worry about the exact location and size.)

**13.** Drag the third button control until the Button3 text is aligned with the Button2 text, then release the mouse button.

**14.** Add a label control and a picture box control to the form. Position the controls as shown in Figure 1.50. (You do not need to worry about the exact location and size of the controls in the interface.)

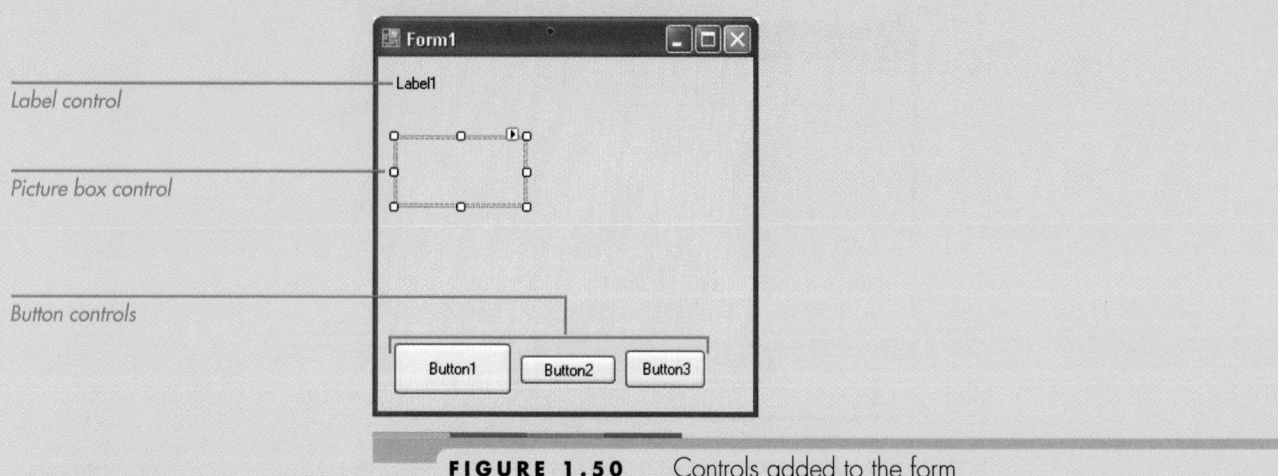

Label control

Picture box control

Button controls

**FIGURE 1.50**    Controls added to the form

15. Save the solution by clicking **File** on the menu bar, and then clicking **Save All**. Notice that an asterisk (*) no longer appears on the Form1.vb [Design] tab. This indicates that no changes were made to the form since the last time it was saved.

You are finished with the Toolbox window, so you can auto-hide it.

16. Auto-hide the Toolbox window.

Next, you learn how to use the Properties window to change the properties of an object.

### Using the Properties Window to Change an Object's Properties

Each object in Visual Basic has a set of properties that determine its appearance and behavior, and each property has a default value assigned to it when the object is created. You can use the Properties window to assign a different value to a property. First, you will change the File Name property of the form file object from Form1.vb to MainForm.vb.

### To change the name of the form file object:

1. Temporarily display the Solution Explorer window.
2. Right-click **Form1.vb** in the Solution Explorer window, and then click **Properties**.
3. Move your mouse pointer away from the Solution Explorer window.
4. Click **File Name** in the Properties window, then type **MainForm.vb** and press **Enter**. Notice that you do not have to erase the old value in the Settings box before entering the new value; as you type the new value, it replaces the old value.

In the next set of steps, you assign values to some of the properties of the form object.

### To assign values to some of the properties of the form:

1. Click the **form** (but not a control on the form). Sizing handles appear on the form to indicate that the form is selected, and the form's properties appear in the Properties window, as shown in Figure 1.51. If the property names do not appear in alphabetical order, click the **Alphabetical** button in the Properties window.

Programming Tutorial                                                                                        **41**

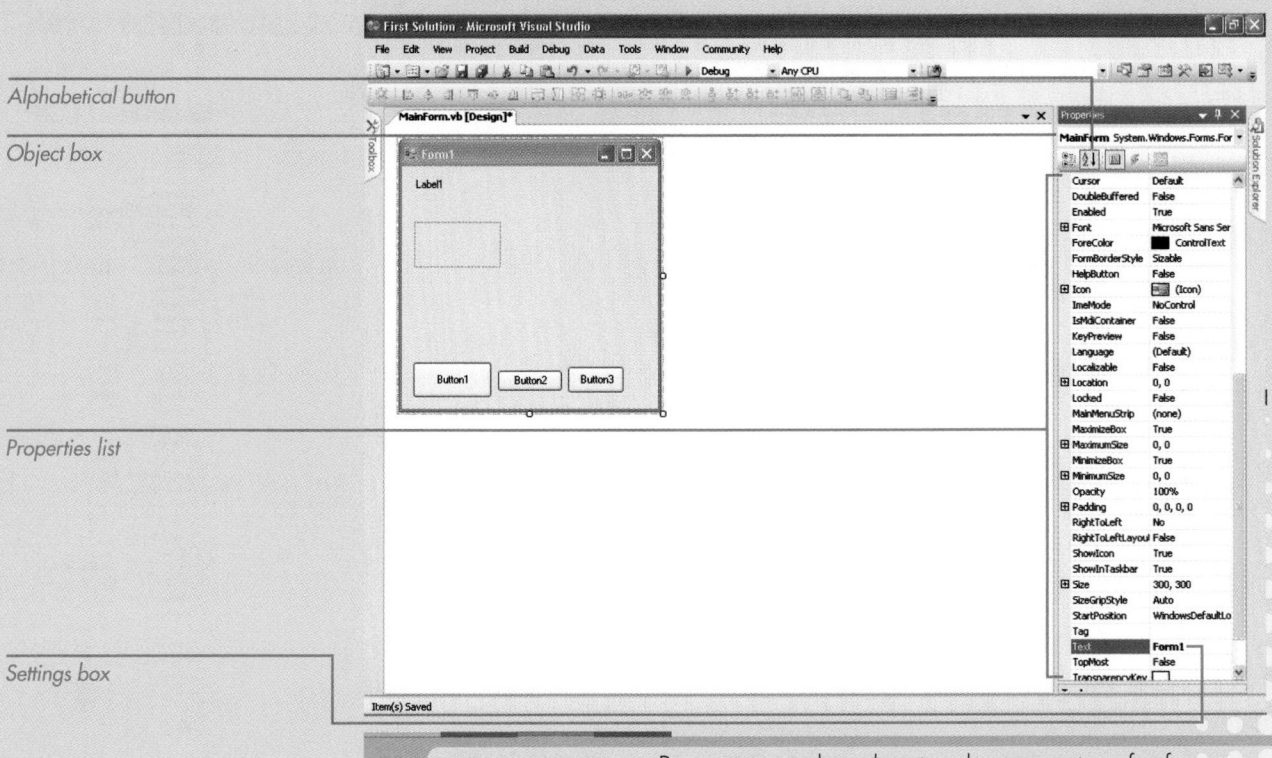

FIGURE 1.51     Properties window showing the properties of a form

As indicated in Figure 1.51, the Properties window includes an Object box and a Properties list. The Object box contains the name of the selected object. The Properties list has two columns. The left column displays the names of the properties associated with the selected object, and the right column (called the Settings box) displays the current value, or setting, of each of the properties.

**First, change the type and size of the font used to display text on the form.**

2. Click **Font** in the Properties list, then click the **...** (ellipsis) button in the Settings box. When the Font dialog box opens, click **Tahoma** in the Font box and **10** in the Size box, and then click the **OK** button. (Notice that this change affects the text displayed in the controls on the form.)

Recall that a form's StartPosition property, which specifies where the form is positioned when the application is started and the form first appears on the screen.

3. Click **StartPosition** in the Properties list. Click the **list arrow** in the Settings box, and then click **CenterScreen**.

Recall that a form's Text property specifies the text to display in the form's title bar.

4. Click **Text** in the Properties list. Type **First Application** and press **Enter**.

Recall that a form's name is stored in the form's Name property.

5. Use the scroll bar in the Properties window to scroll to the top of the Properties list, then click **(Name)** in the Properties list.
6. If necessary, type **MainForm** and press **Enter**. Figure 1.52 shows the current status of the form.

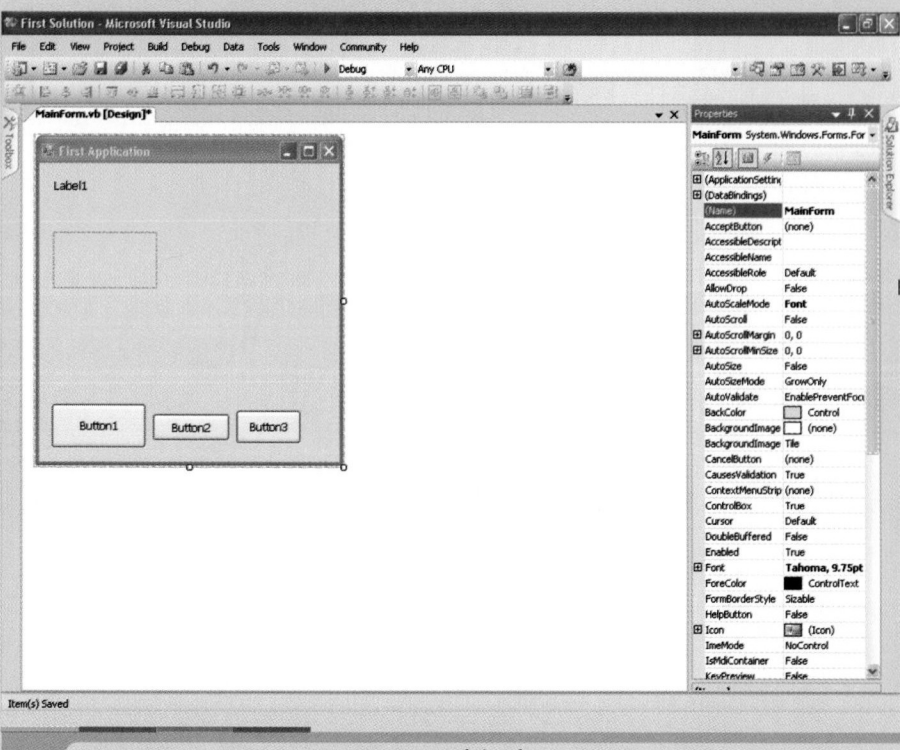

**FIGURE 1.52**    Current status of the form

Next, you will assign values to some of the properties of the Label1 control.

**To assign values to some of the properties of the Label1 control:**

1. Click the **Label1** control in the form. The control's properties appear in the Properties window.

First, display the text "My First Application" in the control.

2. Click **Text** in the Properties list, then type **My First Application** and press **Enter**. Notice that the label control automatically sizes to fit its current contents. This occurs because the control's AutoSize property is set to True.

Now set the label control's Location property, which determines the position of the control's upper-left corner on the form.

3. Click the **plus box** that appears next to the Location property in the Properties list. The X below the Location property refers to the control's horizontal location; the Y refers to its vertical location.
4. Type **115** in the X settings box, then type **15** in the Y settings box. Notice that 115, 15 appears in the Location settings box. Click the **minus box** that appears next to the Location property.

**TIP** You also could have set the Location property by typing 115, 15 in the property's settings box.

In the next set of steps, you assign values to some of the properties of the button controls.

**To assign values to some of the properties of the button controls:**

1. Click the **Button1** control in the form. The control's properties appear in the Properties window. Set the Name property to **onButton**, and set the Text property to **On**.
2. Click the **Button2** control in the form. Set the Name property to **offButton**, and set the Text property to **Off**.
3. Click the **Button3** control in the form. Set the Name property to **exitButton**, and set the Text property to **Exit**.

Now assume that you want to make the On and Exit buttons the same size as the Off button. You can do so by individually setting the On and Exit buttons' Size properties to the same value as the Off button's Size property; or, you can use the Format menu.

### Using the Format Menu

The Format menu provides options that allow you to manipulate the controls in the user interface. The Align option, for example, allows you to align two or more controls by their left, right, top, or bottom borders. You can use the Make Same Size option to make two or more controls the same width and/or height. The Format menu also has a Center in Form option that centers one or more controls either horizontally or vertically on the form.

Before you can use the Format menu to make the three button controls the same size, you first must select the controls. The first control you select should always be the one whose size and/or location you want to match. In this case, for example, you want the size of the On and Exit buttons to match the size of the Off button. Therefore, the Off button should be the first control you select. The first control selected is referred to as the reference control.

**To make the On and Exit buttons the same size as the Off button:**

1. Click the **Off** button in the form. Press and hold down the **Control** (**Ctrl**) key as you click the **On** button and then the **Exit** button, then release the Control key. The three buttons are now selected. Notice that the sizing handles on the reference control (the Off button) are white, whereas the sizing handles on the On and Exit buttons are black.
2. Click **Format** on the menu bar. Point to **Make Same Size**, and then click **Both**. The On and Exit buttons are now the same size as the Off button.

Next, you will use the Format menu to align the top borders of the On and Exit buttons with the top border of the Off button.

**To align the top borders of the selected buttons:**

1. Click **Format** on the menu bar.
2. Point to **Align**, and then click **Tops**. The top borders of the On and Exit buttons are now aligned with the top border of the Off button.
3. Click the **form** to deselect the buttons.
4. If necessary, position the buttons to match those shown in Figure 1.53.

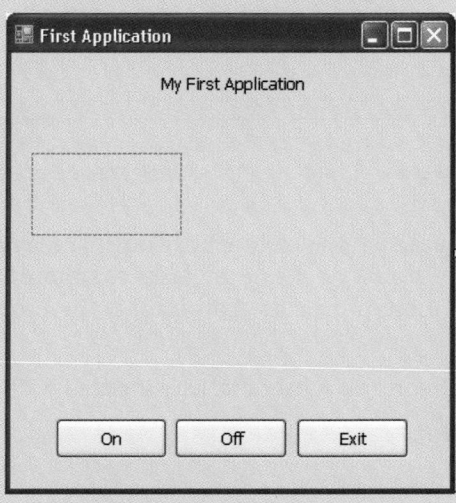

**FIGURE 1.53**   Location of the buttons on the form

**TIP** You also can select a group of controls on the form by placing the mouse pointer slightly above and to the left of the first control you want to select, then pressing the left mouse button and dragging. A dotted rectangle appears as you drag. When all of the controls you want to select are within (or at least touched by) the dotted rectangle, release the mouse button. All of the controls surrounded or touched by the dotted rectangle will be selected.

Next, you learn how to display an image in a picture box control.

### Displaying an Image in a Picture Box Control

You can use a picture box control to display an image. The image you will display in the current interface is stored in the Square (Square.JPG) file contained in the VbReloaded\Chap01 folder.

**To display an image in a picture box control:**

1. Click the **PictureBox1** control on the form. The control's properties appear in the Properties window, as shown in Figure 1.54.

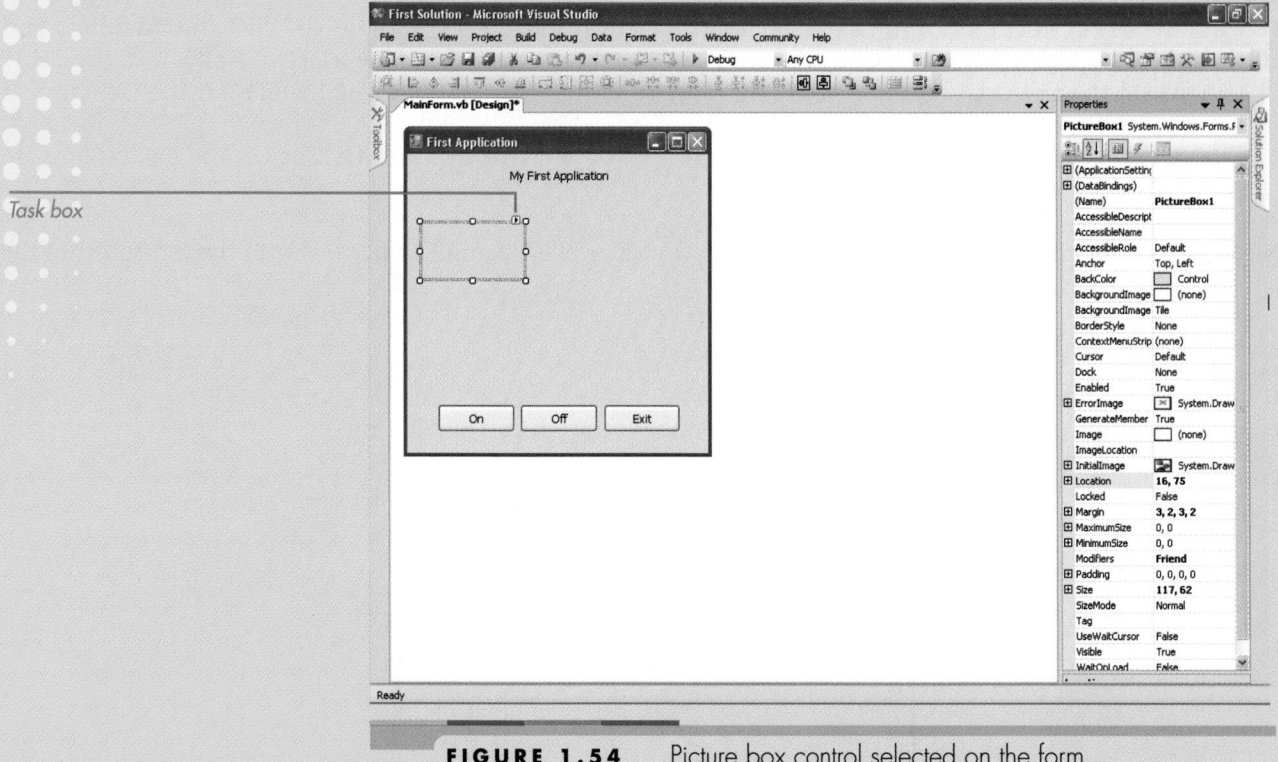

**FIGURE 1.54**     Picture box control selected on the form

Notice that a box containing a triangle appears on the picture box control in Figure 1.54. The box is referred to as the task box because, when you click it, it displays a list of the tasks commonly performed by the control. Each task in the list is associated with one or more properties. You can set the properties using the task list or the Properties window.

2. Click the **task box** on the PictureBox1 control. A list of tasks associated with a picture box appears, as shown in Figure 1.55.

**FIGURE 1.55**   Task list for a picture box control

3. Click **Choose Image**. The Select Resource dialog box opens.
4. Verify that the Project resource file radio button is selected in the dialog box.
5. Click the **Import** button. The Open dialog box opens.
6. Open the VbReloaded\Chap01 folder, then click **Square** (**Square.JPG**) in the list of filenames. Click the **Open** button. The completed Select Resource dialog box is shown in Figure 1.56.

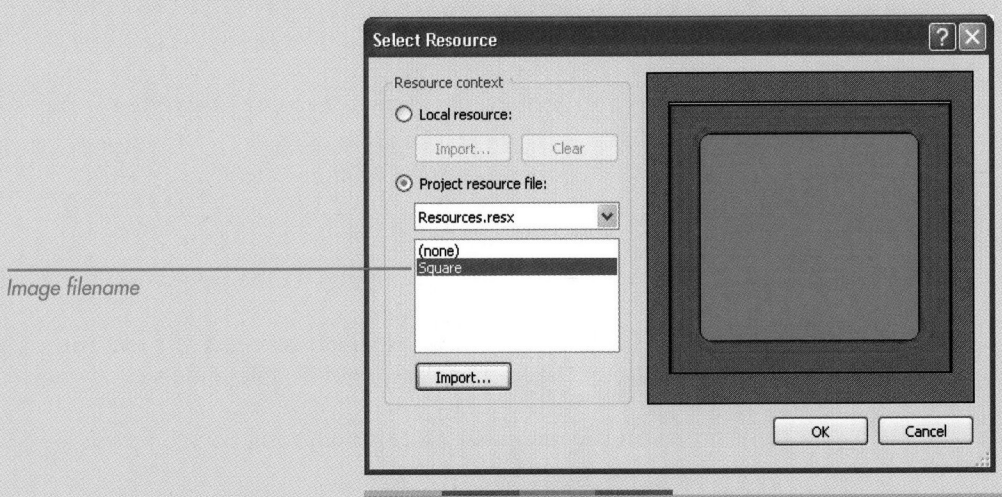

*Image filename*

**FIGURE 1.56**   Completed Select Resource dialog box

7. Click the **OK** button. The image appears in the picture box control on the form.
8. Click the **Size Mode** list arrow, and then click **AutoSize** in the list. The picture box control automatically sizes to fit its contents.
9. Click the picture box control to close the task list.
10. Use the Properties window to set the picture box's Name property to **squarePictureBox** and its Location property to **62, 54**. The completed user interface is shown in Figure 1.57.

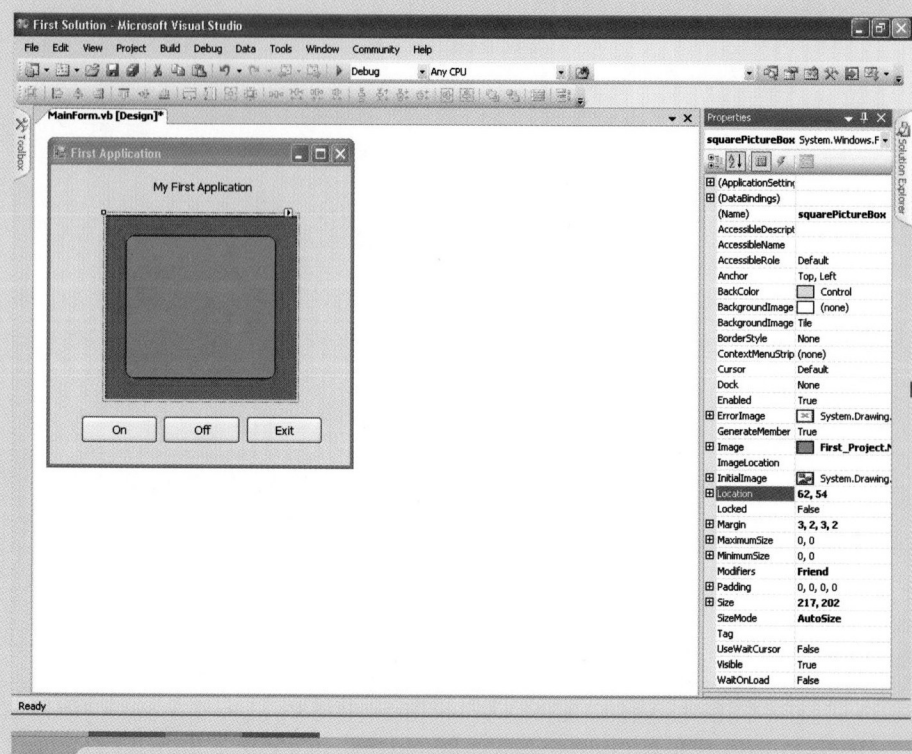

**FIGURE 1.57**    Completed user interface

11. Auto-hide the Properties window.

Now lock the controls in place on the form. Locking the controls prevents them from being inadvertently moved as you work in the IDE.

**To lock the controls:**

1. Right-click the **form**.
2. Click **Lock Controls** on the context menu. Notice that a small lock appears in the upper-left corner of the form.
3. Click the **On** button. Here again, notice that a small lock appears in the upper-left corner of the control.
4. Try dragging one of the controls to a different location on the form. You will not be able to do so.

**TIP**  You also can lock the controls by clicking Format on the menu bar, and then clicking Lock Controls.

If you need to move a control after you have locked the controls in place, you can change the control's Location property setting in the Properties list. You also can unlock the control by changing its Locked property to False. Or, you can unlock all of the controls by clicking Format on the menu bar, and then clicking Lock Controls. The Lock Controls option is a toggle option: selecting it once activates it, and selecting it again deactivates it.

Now that the user interface is complete, you can start the application to see how it will look to the user.

### Starting and Ending an Application

You can start an application by clicking Debug on the menu bar, and then clicking Start Debugging; or you can simply press the F5 key on your keyboard.

**To start and stop the current application:**

1. Temporarily display the Solution Explorer window. Right-click the **My Project** folder in the Solution Explorer window, and then click **Open** on the context menu. The Project Designer window opens.
2. If necessary, click the **Startup form** list arrow in the Application pane, and then click **MainForm** in the list. See Figure 1.58.

Project Designer window's Close button

Startup form name

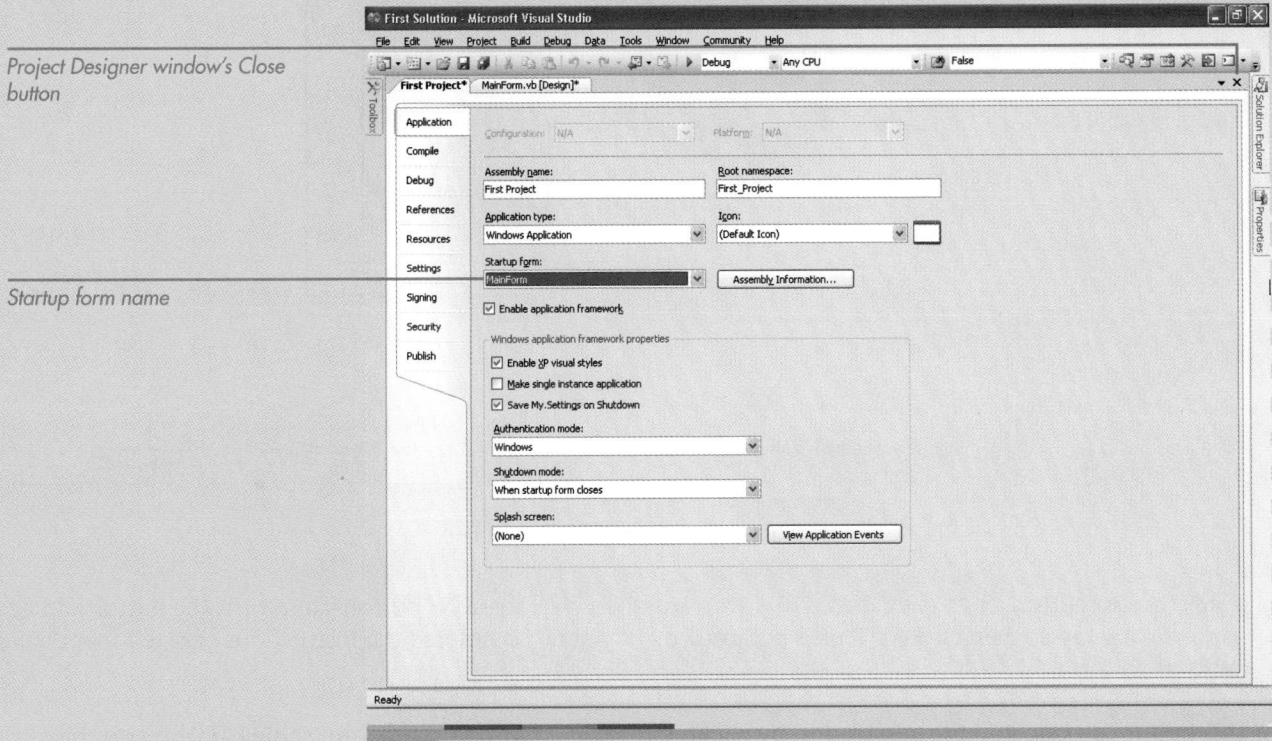

**FIGURE 1.58**    Name of the startup form selected in the Application pane

3. Close the Project Designer window.

Now save the solution and then start the application. (You should always save the solution before starting the application.)

4. Save the solution by clicking the **Save All** button on the Standard toolbar.
5. To start the application, click **Debug** on the menu bar, and then click **Start Debugging**. See Figure 1.59. (Do not be concerned about any windows that appear at the bottom of the screen.)

Form's Close button

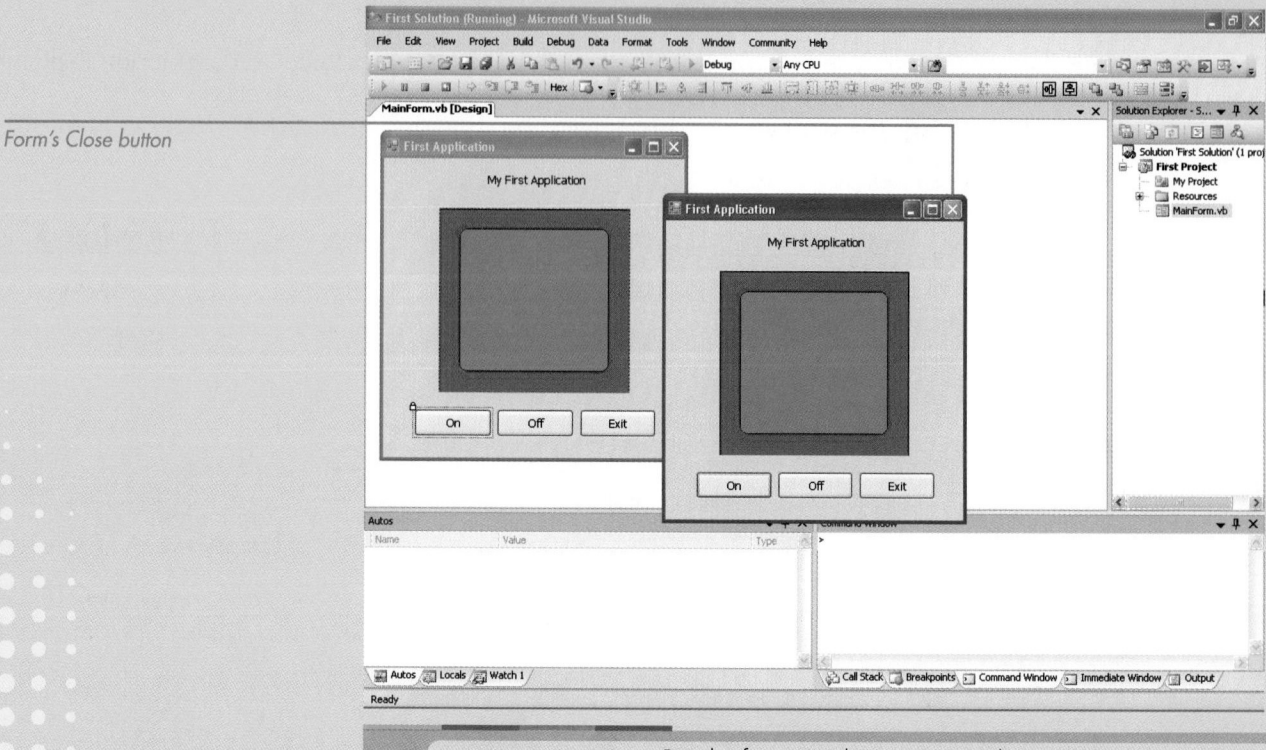

**FIGURE 1.59**   Result of starting the current application

6. Click the **On** button, then click the **Off** button, and then click the **Exit** button. Currently, the buttons do not perform any tasks when clicked. This is because you have not yet entered the instructions that tell them what tasks to perform.

At this point, you can stop the application by clicking the Close button on the form's title bar. You also can click the designer window to make it the active window, then click Debug on the menu bar, and then click Stop Debugging.

7. Click the **Close** button on the form's title bar. When the application ends, you are returned to the IDE. An Output window may appear at the bottom of the screen, as shown in Figure 1.60.

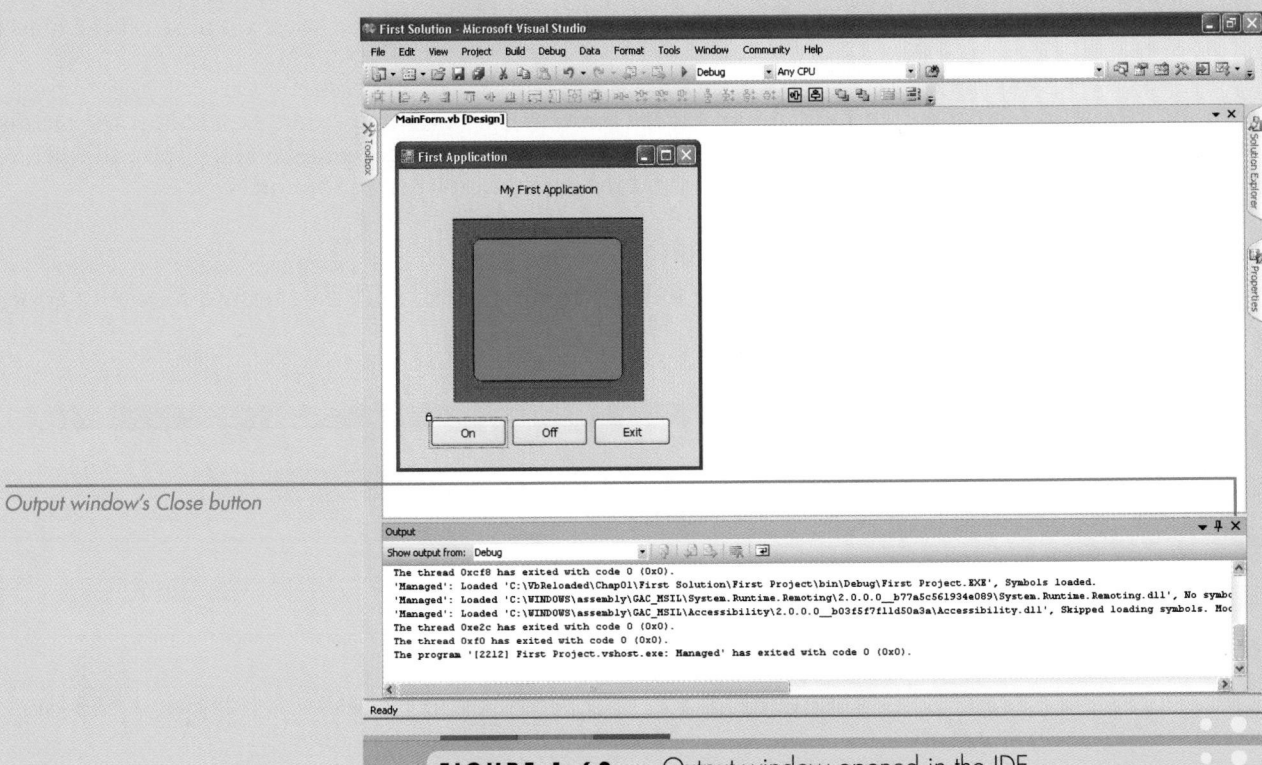

*Output window's Close button*

**FIGURE 1.60**     Output window opened in the IDE

**8.** If necessary, close the Output window by clicking the **Close** button on its title bar.

You use Visual Basic code to tell a button how to respond when the user clicks it.

### Writing Visual Basic 2005 Code

At this point, the On, Off, and Exit buttons on the form do not know what tasks they should perform when they are clicked by the user. You tell a button what to do by writing an event procedure for it. You write the event procedure in the Code Editor window.

**To open the Code Editor window:**

1. Right-click the **form**.
2. Click **View Code**. The Code Editor window opens in the IDE, as shown in Figure 1.61. Notice that the Code Editor window already contains some Visual Basic code (instructions).

*Method Name list box*

*Class Name list box*

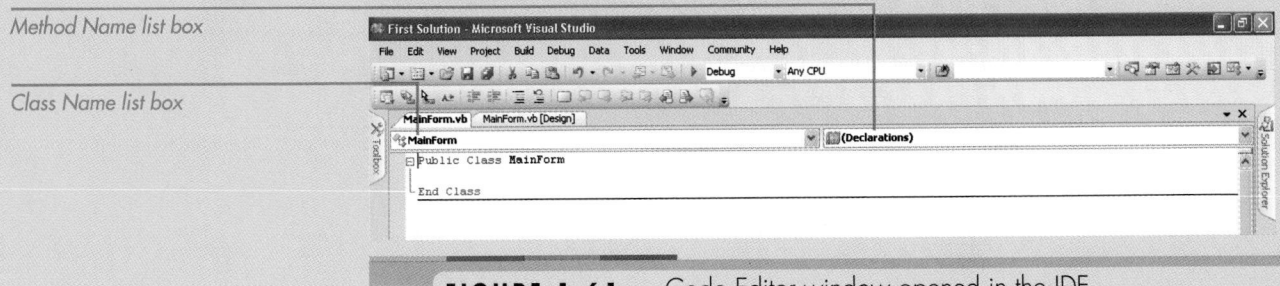

**FIGURE 1.61**     Code Editor window opened in the IDE

As Figure 1.61 indicates, the Code Editor window contains a Class Name list box and a Method Name list box. The Class Name list box lists the names of the objects included in the user interface. The Method Name list box lists the events to which the selected object is capable of responding. You use the list boxes to select the object and event that you want to code.

When the user clicks the Off button in the interface, the button's Click event procedure should hide the picture box. Similarly, when the user clicks the On button, the button's Click event procedure should display the picture box. The Exit button's Click event procedure should end the application when the button is clicked.

**To code the Exit button's Click event procedure:**

1. Click the **Class Name** list arrow, and then click **exitButton** in the list. Click the **Method Name** list arrow, and then click **Click** in the list. See Figure 1.62.

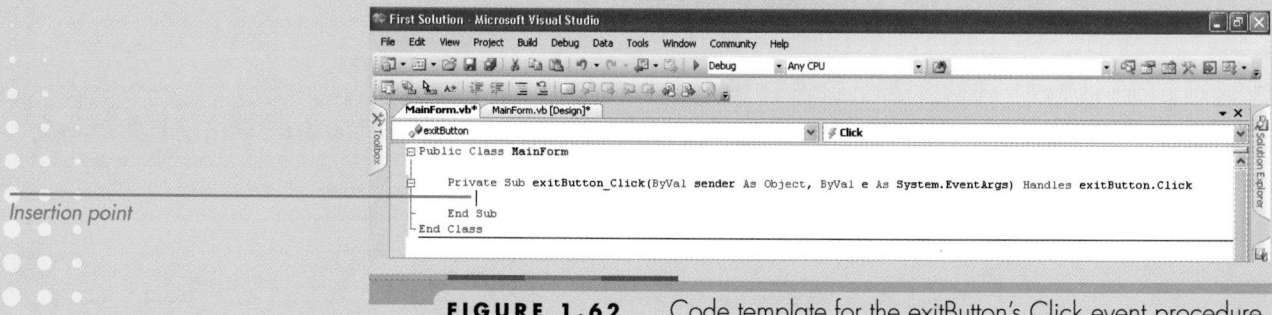

Insertion point

**FIGURE 1.62**     Code template for the exitButton's Click event procedure shown in the Code Editor window

Notice that, when you select an object and event, additional code automatically appears in the Code Editor window. To help you follow the rules of the Visual Basic 2005 programming language, called **syntax**, the Code Editor provides you with a code template for every event procedure.

The insertion point located in the event procedure indicates where you enter your code for the object. In this case, you want to instruct the button to end the application. Recall that you use the `Me.Close()` instruction to accomplish the task. You can type the instruction on your own; or you can use the IntelliSense feature that is built into the Code Editor. In this set of steps, you use the IntelliSense feature.

2. Type **me.** (but don't press Enter). When you type the period, the IntelliSense feature displays a list of properties, methods, and so on from which you can select. If necessary, click the **All** tab. See Figure 1.63. The All tab on the list displays all of the items, whereas the Common tab displays only the most commonly used items.

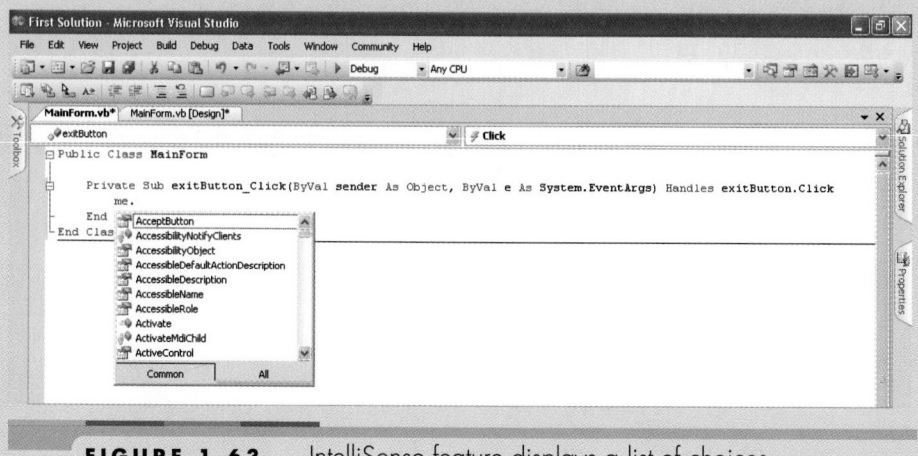

**FIGURE 1.63**     IntelliSense feature displays a list of choices

**HELP?** If the list of choices does not appear, the IntelliSense feature may have been turned off on your computer. To turn it on, click Tools on the menu bar, and then click Options. Expand the Text Editor node in the Options dialog box, and then click Basic. Select the Auto list members check box. Click the OK button to close the Options dialog box.

3. Click the **Common** tab.
4. Type **cl** (but don't press Enter). The IntelliSense feature highlights the Close method in the list, as shown in Figure 1.64.

*Description of the Close method*

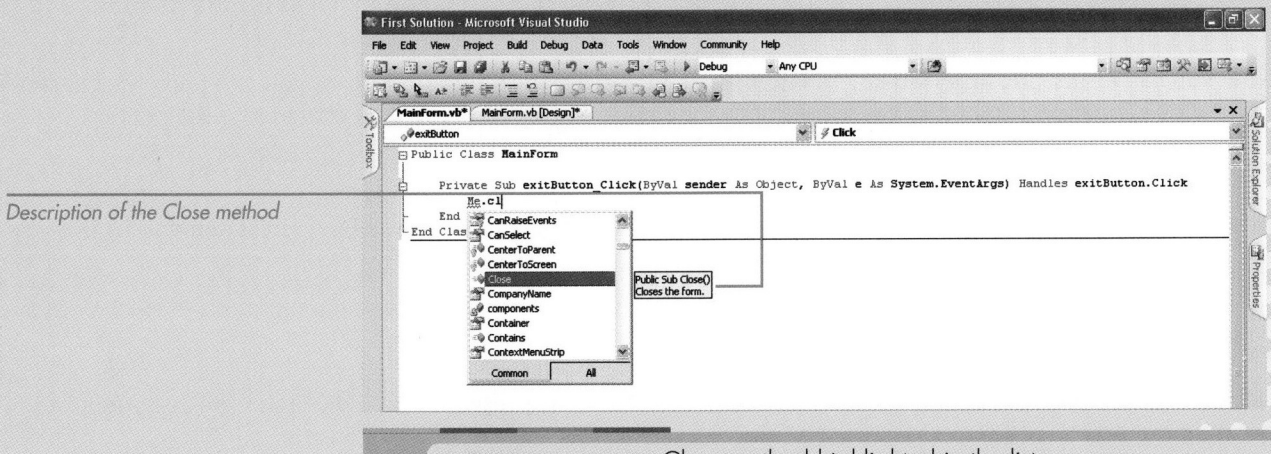

**FIGURE 1.64**     Close method highlighted in the list

5. Press the **Enter** key on your keyboard to select the Close method. The Code Editor enters the `Me.Close()` instruction in the procedure, as shown in Figure 1.65.

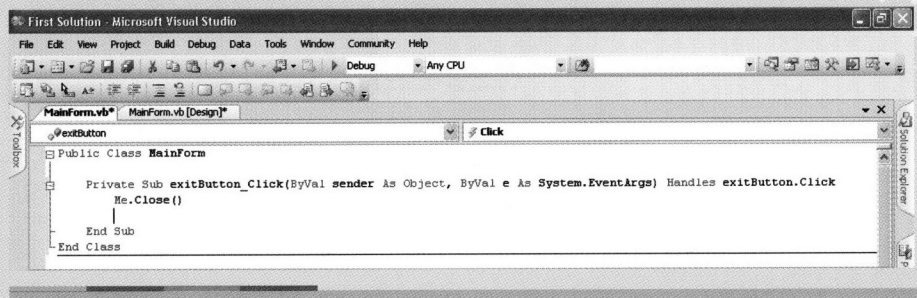

**FIGURE 1.65**     Me.Close() instruction entered in the procedure

Recall that when the user clicks the On and Off buttons, the buttons' Click event procedures should display and hide, respectively, the picture box control. You can use assignment statements to accomplish both tasks.

**To code the On and Off buttons' Click event procedures:**

1. Use the Class Name and Method Name list boxes to open the code template for the onButton's Click event procedure.

In the previous set of steps, you learned that the IntelliSense feature displays a list of choices when you type the word me followed by a period in the Code Editor window. It also displays the list of choices when you press and hold down the Control (Ctrl) key as you press the Spacebar on your keyboard.

2. Press and hold down the **Ctrl** key as you press the **Spacebar**, then release the **Ctrl** key. The IntelliSense feature displays a list of properties, methods, and so on. If necessary, click the **Common** tab.

To display the picture box, which is named squarePictureBox, you need to set the control's Visible property to True. You do this using the assignment statement `squarePictureBox.Visible = True`.

3. Type **squ** to highlight squarePictureBox in the list.

Now you can either press the Tab key to enter squarePictureBox in the procedure, or you can press the character that follows squarePictureBox in the assignment statement. In this case, the next character is the period.

4. Type **.** (a period), then type the letter **v**. The IntelliSense feature highlights Visible in the list.

Here again, you can either press the Tab key or type the next character in the assignment statement. In this case, the next character is the equal sign.

5. Type **=**, then type **t** and press **Enter**. The Code Editor enters the `squarePictureBox.Visible = True` statement in the procedure.

Finally, you will code the Off button's Click event procedure. The procedure should contain the assignment statement `squarePictureBox.Visible = False`.

6. Open the code template for the offButton's Click event procedure.
7. Enter the following assignment statement into the procedure: **squarePictureBox.Visible = False**. Figure 1.66 shows the code you entered in the Code Editor window.

*Me.Close method*

*Assignment statements*

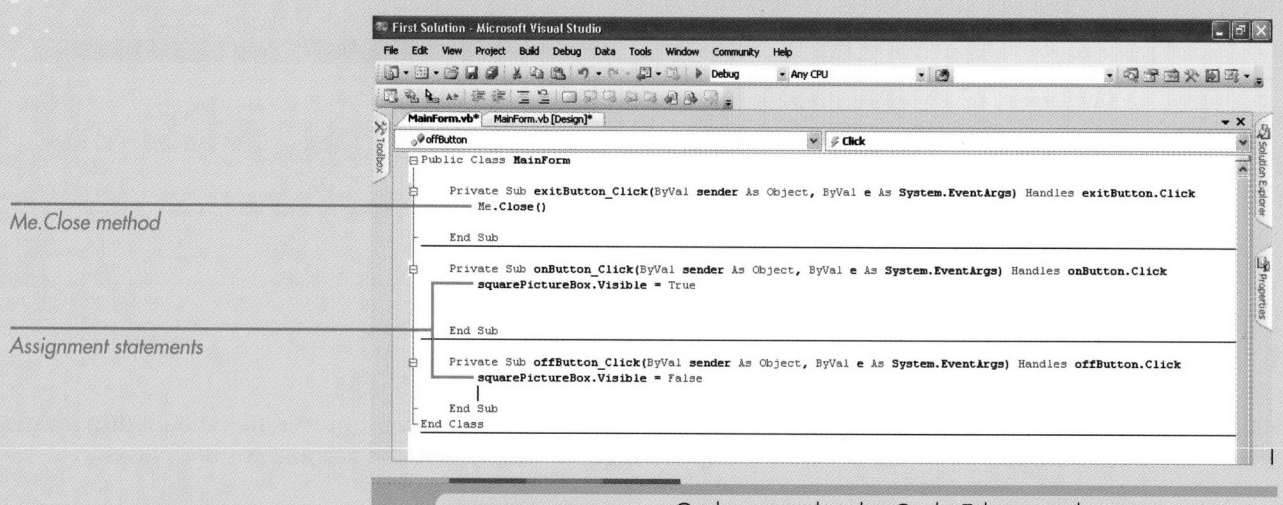

**FIGURE 1.66**    Code entered in the Code Editor window

Now close the Code Editor window, then save the solution and start the application.

**To close the Code Editor window, then save the solution, and start the application:**

1. Click the **Close** button on the Code Editor window's title bar.
2. Click **File** on the menu bar, and then click **Save All**.
3. Click **Debug** on the menu bar, and then click **Start Debugging**.

First verify that the Off and On buttons are working correctly.

4. Click the **Off** button. The picture box disappears.
5. Click the **On** button. The picture box reappears.

Now verify that the Exit button ends the application.

6. Click the **Exit** button. The application ends and you are returned to the designer window.
7. If necessary, close the Output window.

When you are finished working on a solution, you should close the solution.

### Closing the Current Solution

You close a solution using the Close Solution option on the File menu. When you close a solution, all projects and files contained in the solution also are closed. If unsaved changes were made to the solution, project, or form, a dialog box opens and prompts you to save the appropriate files. The dialog box contains Yes, No, and Cancel buttons. You click the Yes button to save the files before the solution is closed. You click the No button to close the solution without saving the files, and you click the Cancel button to leave the solution open.

**To close the current solution:**

1. Click **File** on the menu bar.
2. Click **Close Solution**.

You can use the Solution Explorer window to verify that the solution is closed.

3. Temporarily display the Solution Explorer window to verify that no solutions are open in the IDE.

Next, you learn how to open a solution that was saved previously.

### Opening an Existing Solution

You can use the File menu or the Start Page to open an existing solution. If a solution is already open in the IDE, it is closed before another solution is opened. In other words, only one solution can be open in the IDE at any one time.

**To open the First Solution:**

1. Click **File** on the menu bar, point to **Open**, and then click **Project/Solution**. The Open Project dialog box opens.
2. Locate and then open the **VbReloaded\Chap01\First Solution** folder.
3. If necessary, click **First Solution** (First Solution.sln) in the list of filenames, and then click the **Open** button.
4. If the Windows Form Designer window is not displayed, click **View** on the menu bar, and then click **Designer**.
5. Temporarily display the Solution Explorer window to verify that the solution is open.

### Printing Your Code

You always should print a copy of the code entered in the Code Editor window, because the printout will help you understand and maintain the application in the future. To print the code, the Code Editor window must be the active, or current, window.

**To print the current application's code:**

1. Right-click the **form**, then click **View Code** to open the Code Editor window.
2. Click **File** on the menu bar, then click **Print**. The Print dialog box opens. Notice that you can include line numbers in the printout.
3. If your computer is connected to a printer, click the **OK** button to begin printing; otherwise, click the **Cancel** button. If you clicked the OK button, your printer prints the code.

In the next section, you will intentionally introduce a syntax error in the code. This will allow you to observe how the Code Editor and compiler treat syntax errors.

### Syntax Errors in Code

You create a syntax error when you enter an instruction that does not follow the rules of the programming language. Most syntax errors are typing errors—for example, typing `Flse` rather than `False`.

**To introduce a syntax error in the current application:**

1. In the offButton's Click event procedure, change the word `False` in the assignment statement to **Flse**, then click in **the line below the assignment statement**. Notice that a squiggly blue line appears below the mistyped word, `Flse`. The squiggly blue line indicates that the code contains a syntax error.
2. Position your mouse pointer on the word `Flse`. The Code Editor displays a box that contains an appropriate error message, as shown in Figure 1.67. In this case, the message indicates that the Code Editor does not recognize the word `Flse`.

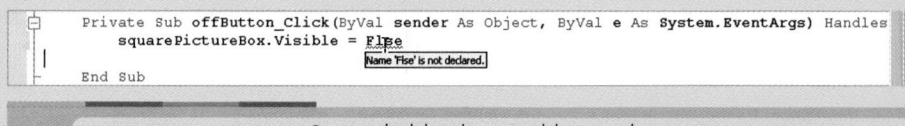

**FIGURE 1.67**      Squiggly blue line and box indicate a syntax error

At this point, you should correct the error before starting the application. However, observe what happens when you start an application without correcting a syntax error.

3. Save the solution, then start the application. The computer displays the message box shown in Figure 1.68.

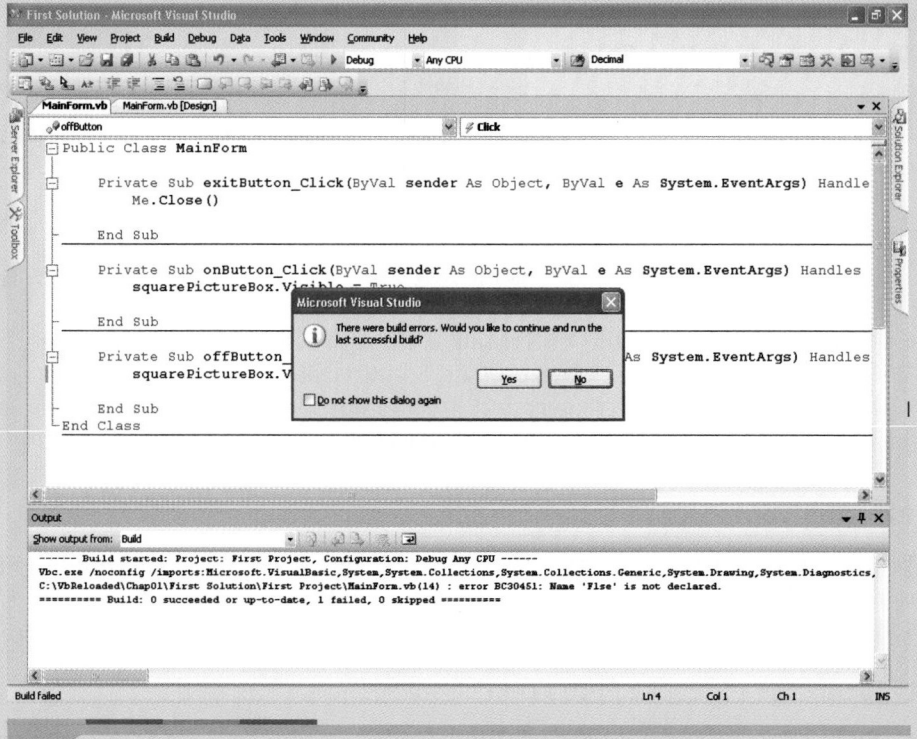

**FIGURE 1.68**      Message box indicates that the code contains errors

4. Click the **No** button. The Error List window shown in Figure 1.69 opens. Notice that the Error List window indicates that the code has one error: Name 'Flse' is not declared.

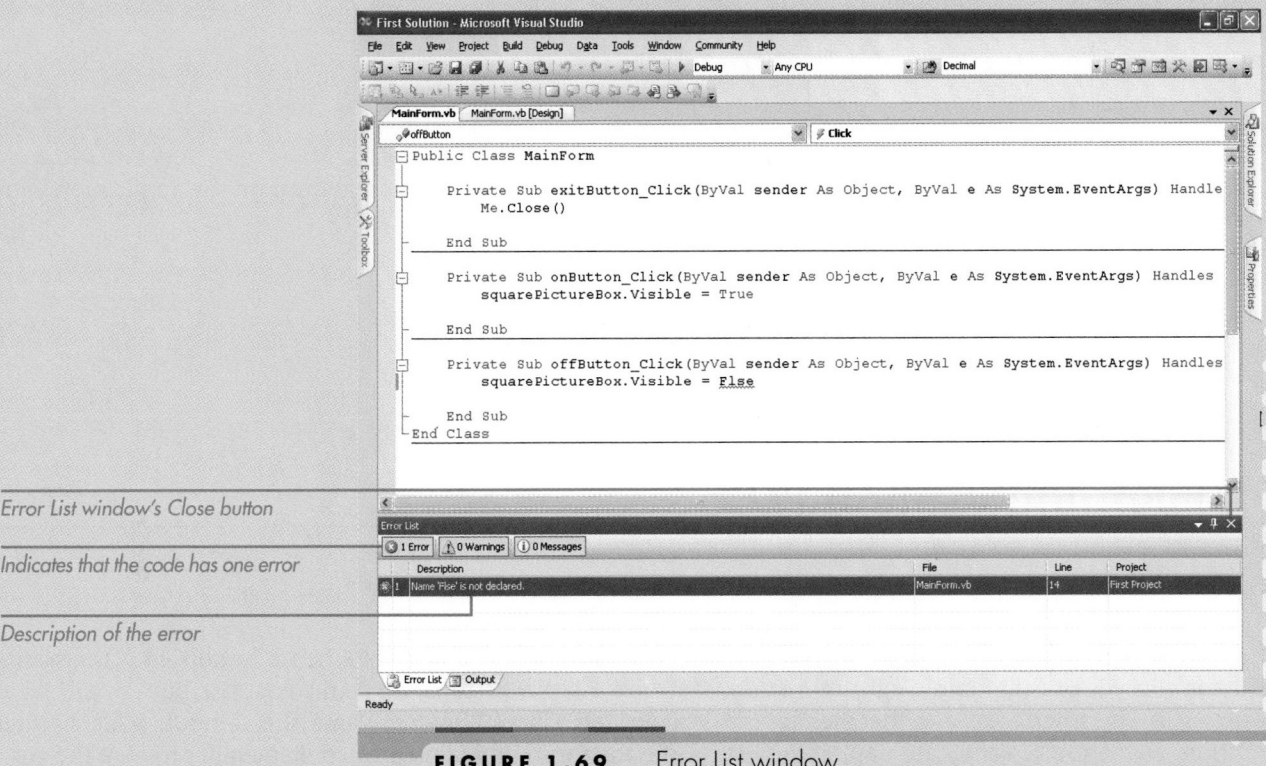

**FIGURE 1.69**    Error List window

5. Double-click the **description of the error** in the Error List window. The Code Editor highlights the error—in this case, the mistyped word F1se—in the code, as shown in Figure 1.70.

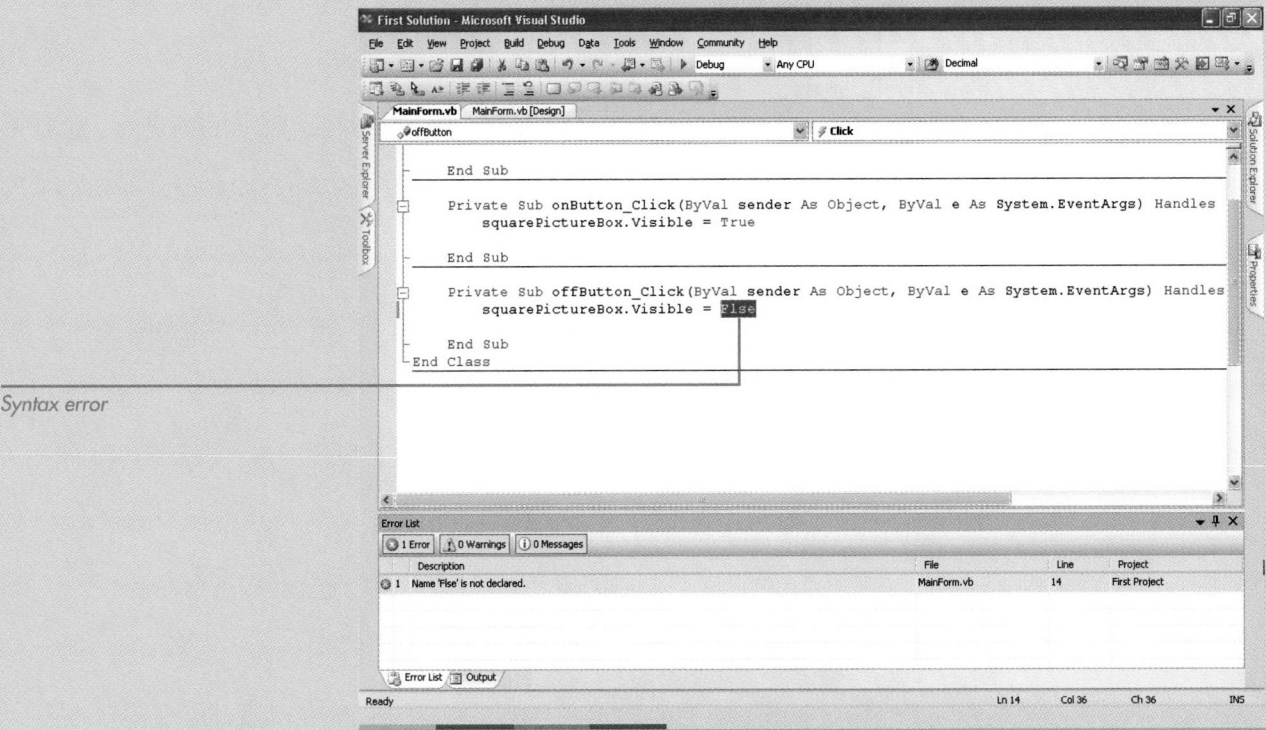

**FIGURE 1.70**    Syntax error highlighted in the code

6. Type **False** to correct the syntax error.
7. Save the solution, then start the application. Test the Off button to verify that it is working correctly.
8. Click the **Exit** button to end the application. If necessary, close the Output and Error List windows.
9. Close the Code Editor window.

Lastly, you learn how to exit Visual Studio 2005.

### Exiting Visual Studio 2005

As in most Windows applications, you exit an application using either the Close button on the application window's title bar, or the Exit option on the File menu.

**To exit Visual Studio 2005:**

1. Click **File** on the menu bar.
2. Click **Exit** on the menu.

# PROGRAMMING EXAMPLE

## State Capitals

Create a Visual Basic 2005 application that displays the state capital in a label when a button with the state's name is clicked. Use the following state names: Alabama, Alaska, Arizona, and Arkansas. Use button and label controls in the interface. Save the files in the VbReloaded\Chap01 folder. Name the solution State Capital Solution. Name the project State Capital Project. Name the form file Main Form.vb. Remember to lock the controls in the interface.

### User Interface:

Labels

Buttons

**FIGURE 1.71**

| Object | Property | Setting |
|---|---|---|
| Form1 | Name | MainForm (be sure to change the startup form to this name) |
| | Font | Tahoma |
| | Size | |
| |    Width | 300 |
| |    Height | 215 |
| | StartPosition | CenterScreen |
| | Text | State Capitals |
| Button1 | Name | alabamaButton |
| | Text | Alabama |
| Button2 | Name | alaskaButton |
| | Text | Alaska |
| Button3 | Name | arizonaButton |
| | Text | Arizona |
| Button4 | Name | arkansasButton |
| | Text | Arkansas |
| Button5 | Name | exitButton |
| | Text | Exit |
| Label1 | AutoSize | True |
| | Text | Capital: |
| Label2 | Name | capitalLabel |
| | AutoSize | False |
| | BorderStyle | FixedSingle |
| | Size | |
| |    Width | 100 |
| |    Height | 23 |
| | Text | (empty) (*Hint*: delete the text that appears in the Settings box in the Properties window.) |
| | TextAlign | MiddleCenter |

**FIGURE 1.72**

**Code:**

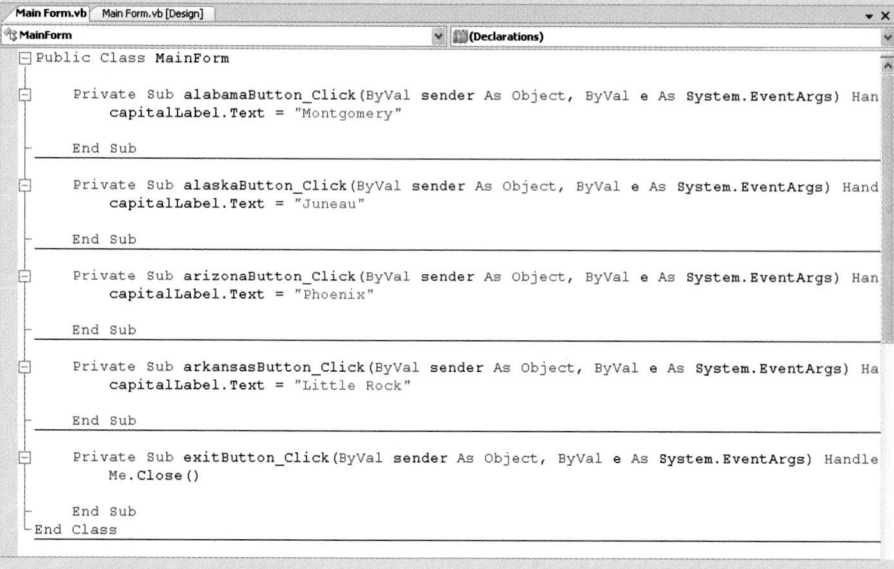

```vb
Public Class MainForm

    Private Sub alabamaButton_Click(ByVal sender As Object, ByVal e As System.EventArgs) Han
        capitalLabel.Text = "Montgomery"

    End Sub

    Private Sub alaskaButton_Click(ByVal sender As Object, ByVal e As System.EventArgs) Hand
        capitalLabel.Text = "Juneau"

    End Sub

    Private Sub arizonaButton_Click(ByVal sender As Object, ByVal e As System.EventArgs) Han
        capitalLabel.Text = "Phoenix"

    End Sub

    Private Sub arkansasButton_Click(ByVal sender As Object, ByVal e As System.EventArgs) Ha
        capitalLabel.Text = "Little Rock"

    End Sub

    Private Sub exitButton_Click(ByVal sender As Object, ByVal e As System.EventArgs) Handle
        Me.Close()

    End Sub
End Class
```

**FIGURE 1.73**

## Quick Review

- The directions given to a computer are called programs and are written by programmers using a variety of programming languages.
- Generally speaking, programmers are either applications programmers or systems programmers.
- Programming languages have progressed from machine languages to assembly languages, and then to high-level languages.
- An assembler translates assembly language programs into machine language.
- Programs written in a high-level language require either an interpreter or a compiler to convert the program instructions into machine language.
- Procedure-oriented programs focus on tasks, whereas object-oriented programs focus on objects.
- An object is anything that can be seen, touched, or used. All objects have attributes (properties) and behaviors (methods and events).
- A class is a pattern from which an object can be instantiated (created). A class encapsulates the object's attributes and behaviors. Some attributes and behaviors are hidden, while others are exposed.
- You can create one class (the derived class) from another class (the base class). The derived class inherits the attributes and behaviors of the base class.
- You create, run, and test your programs in the Visual Studio IDE.
- You can use Visual Studio 2005 to create Windows-based and Web-based applications.
- The Microsoft .NET Framework 2.0 is a platform on which .NET applications are created.

- The .NET Framework contains a class library and the CLR, which manages execution of an intermediate language called IL (or MSIL).
- Applications created in Visual Studio are composed of solutions, projects, and files.
- You create your application's GUI in the Windows Form Designer window.
- A form is the foundation for the user interface in a Windows-based application.
- A Windows Form object is an instance of the Windows Form class.
- The Solution Explorer window displays the names of projects and files contained in the current solution.
- The Project Designer window contains panes that contain project settings.
- The Properties window exposes an object's properties to the programmer.
- All class definitions are contained in namespaces.
- The System.Windows.Forms namespace contains the definition of the Windows Form class, as well as the class definitions for objects you add to a form.
- The forms you create inherit the attributes and behaviors of the Form class.
- The dot member access operator indicates a hierarchy of namespaces.
- You use the value stored in an object's Name property to refer to the object in code.
- The value stored in the form's Text property displays in the form's title bar and on the taskbar when the application is running.
- The form's StartPosition property determines the position of the form when it first appears on the screen when the application is started.
- The Toolbox window contains the tools you use when creating your application's GUI.
- The value stored in a control's Text property displays inside the control.
- Controls on a form can be selected, sized, moved, deleted, or locked and unlocked.
- A label control displays text that the user is not allowed to edit while the application is running.
- You use a button control to perform an immediate action when clicked.
- You tell an object how to respond to an event by coding an event procedure. You enter the code in the Code Editor window.
- You use the Class Name and Method Name list boxes in the Code Editor window to select the object and event, respectively, that you want to code.
- The Code Editor provides a code template for each of an object's event procedures. The code template begins with the `Private Sub` line and ends with the `End Sub` line. You enter your Visual Basic instructions between those lines.
- You can use the `Me.Close` method to terminate an application.
- You should save the solution every 10 or 15 minutes.
- Before you start an application for the first time, you need to specify the name of the startup form.
- When you start a Visual Basic application, the computer automatically creates an executable file. This is the file given to the user.
- You can use an assignment statement to assign a value to a property while an application is running.
- You should print an application's code, because the printout will help you understand and maintain the application in the future.
- Closing a solution closes all projects and files contained in the solution.
- Only one solution can be open in the IDE at any one time.

## Key Terms

The directions given to computers are called **programs**.

The people who write programs are called **programmers**.

**Applications programmers** write and maintain programs that handle a specific task.

**Systems programmers** write and maintain programs that help the computer carry out its basic operating functions.

Programmers use **programming languages** to communicate with the computer.

Computer instructions written in 0s and 1s are called **machine language** or **machine code**.

**Assembly languages** were developed after machine languages and allow the programmer to use mnemonics in place of the 0s and 1s in a program.

The alphabetic abbreviations used to represent instructions in assembly languages are called **mnemonics**.

An **assembler** is a program that converts assembly instructions into machine code.

**High-level languages** were developed after assembly languages and allow the programmer to use computer instructions that more closely resemble the English language.

An **interpreter** is a program that translates high-level instructions into machine code, line by line, as the program is running.

A **compiler** is a program that, in most cases, translates all of a program's high-level instructions into machine code before running the program. The .NET language-specific compilers, however, translate the program instructions into IL (or MSIL). The JIT compiler then translates the IL into machine code.

When writing a **procedure-oriented program**, the programmer concentrates on the major tasks that the program needs to perform.

When writing an **object-oriented program**, the programmer concentrates on the objects that the program can use to accomplish its goal. However, the programmer uses procedure-oriented programming when coding an object's tasks.

**OOP** is an acronym for object-oriented programming and means that you are using an object-oriented language to create a program that contains one or more objects.

**OOD** is an acronym for object-oriented design—a design methodology used to plan object-oriented programs.

An **object** is anything that can be seen, touched, or used.

**Attributes**, also called **properties**, are the characteristics that describe an object.

**Behaviors** include **methods**, which are the operations (actions) that an object is capable of performing. Behaviors also include **events**, which are actions to which an object can respond.

A **class** is a pattern or blueprint used to create an object.

A class **encapsulates** (contains) all of the attributes and behaviors that describe the object created by the class.

Objects created from a class are referred to as **instances** of the class.

**Abstraction** refers to the hiding of the internal details of an object from the user.

Some attributes and behaviors of an object are **hidden** from the user, while others are **exposed** to the user.

**Inheritance** refers to the fact that you can create one class from another class. The new class is called the **derived class**, and the original class is called the **base class**.

**Polymorphism** is the object-oriented feature that allows the same instruction to be carried out differently depending on the object.

An **integrated development environment** (**IDE**) is an environment that contains all of the tools and features you need to create, run, and test your programs.

**Application** is another name for program.

A **Windows-based application** has a Windows user interface and runs on a desktop computer, whereas a **Web-based application** has a Web user interface and runs on a server.

A **user interface** is what you see and interact with when using an application.

The **Microsoft .NET Framework 2.0** is a platform on which you create .NET applications.

A **.NET language** is a language that runs in the .NET Framework.

A **.NET application** is an application created using a .NET language.

The **.NET Framework class library** contains an extensive set of classes that can be used in any .NET application.

The **Common Language Runtime** (**CLR**) is responsible for managing the execution of the IL (MSIL) instructions.

Each language-specific compiler in .NET translates program instructions into **Microsoft Intermediate Language** (**MSIL**), also called **Intermediate Language** (**IL**).

The CLR provides a **just-in-time** (**JIT**) compiler that converts IL (MSIL) into native machine code.

A **solution** is a container that stores the projects and files for an entire application.

A **project** is a container that stores files associated with only a specific piece of a solution.

You use the **Windows Form Designer window** to create your application's GUI.

**GUI** stands for graphical user interface.

A **Windows Form object**, or **form**, is the foundation for the user interface in a Windows-based application.

The **Solution Explorer window** displays a list of the projects contained in the current solution, and the items contained in each project.

The **Project Designer window** allows you to access various settings for the project.

A **source file** is a file that contains code.

**Code** is another name for program instructions.

A **form file** contains the code associated with a Windows Form object.

An object's attributes (properties) are listed in the **Properties window**.

The **Object box** in the Properties window contains the name of the selected object.

The left column of the **Properties list** displays the names of the properties associated with the selected object. The right column is called the **Settings box** and displays the current value (setting) of each of the properties.

A **namespace** contains the code that defines a group of related classes.

A **class definition** is a block of code that specifies (or defines) the attributes and behaviors of an object.

The **dot member access operator**, which is a period, indicates a hierarchy of namespaces.

You use the name entered in an object's **Name property** to refer to the object in code.

**Hungarian notation** is a naming convention that uses the first three (or more) characters in the name to represent the object's type, and the remaining characters to represent the object's purpose.

When entering an object's name using **camel case**, you lowercase the first word (or, in the case of Hungarian notation, the characters that represent the object's type), and then uppercase the first letter of each subsequent word in the name.

When entering an object's name using **Pascal case**, you uppercase the first letter in the name, as well as the first letter of each subsequent word in the name.

The **Text property** of a form displays in the form's title bar and on the taskbar while the application is running.

The **Text property** of a control appears inside the control.

You use the **StartPosition property** to determine where the form is positioned when the application is started and the form first appears on the screen.

A **splash screen** is the first image that appears when an application is started. It is used to introduce the application and hold the user's attention while the application is being read into the computer's internal memory.

The **Toolbox window**, or **toolbox**, contains the tools you use when creating your application. Each tool represents a class.

A **control** is another name for an object displayed on a form.

You use the **Label tool** to instantiate a **label control**, which displays text that the user is not allowed to edit while the application is running.

You use the **Button tool** to instantiate a button control. In a Windows application, a **button control** is used to perform an immediate action when clicked.

**Events** are actions to which an object can respond. Examples include clicking, double-clicking, and scrolling.

An **event procedure** is a set of Visual Basic instructions that tells an object how to respond to an event.

The **Class Name list box** in the Code Editor window lists the names of the objects included in the user interface.

The **Method Name list box** in the Code Editor window lists the events to which the selected object is capable of responding.

The first line in the code template is called the **procedure header**, and the last line is called the **procedure footer**.

A **keyword** is a word that has a special meaning in a programming language.

The term **sub procedure** refers to a block of code that performs a specific task.

The **Me.Close method** instructs the computer to terminate the current application.

A **method** is a predefined Visual Basic procedure that you can call (or invoke) when needed.

The computer processes a procedure's instructions, one after another, in the order in which they appear in the procedure. This is referred to as **sequential processing** or as the **sequence structure**.

The **startup form** is the form that is automatically displayed when an application is started.

An **executable file** is a file that can be run outside of the Visual Studio 2005 IDE.

An **assignment statement** is an instruction that assigns a value to something, such as a property of a control.

The equal sign in an assignment statement is called the **assignment operator**.

The rules of a programming language are called its **syntax**.

## Self-Check Questions and Answers

1. Each .NET language compiler translates program instructions into _____.
   a. assembly code
   b. IL
   c. machine language
   d. systems code

2. The .NET Framework 2.0 contains _____.
   a. a class library
   b. the CLR
   c. support for different programming languages and different platforms
   d. All of the above

3. The _____ translates intermediate language into machine code.
   a. CLR
   b. JIT compiler
   c. MSIL
   d. None of the above.

4. Assume that a form contains a button control named exitButton. When the button is selected in the interface, _____ will appear in the Object box in the Properties window.
   a. Button System.Windows.Forms.exitButton
   b. Button System.Windows.Button.exitButton
   c. exitButton System.Windows.Button
   d. exitButton System.Windows.Forms.Button

5. You use _____ case for control names, which means you lowercase the first word in the name, and then uppercase the first letter of each subsequent word in the name.
   a. camel
   b. control
   c. Hungarian
   d. Pascal

6. Assume an application needs to calculate and display a sales tax amount. The application should display the calculated amount in a _____ control.
   a. button
   b. form
   c. label
   d. text

7. To end an application when a button is clicked, you enter the _____ instruction in the button's Click event procedure.
   a. `Close.Me()`
   b. `CloseMe()`
   c. `Me.Close()`
   d. None of the above.

8. When a form has been modified since the last time it was saved, _____ appears on its tab in the designer window.
   a. an ampersand (&)
   b. a percent sign (%)
   c. a plus sign (+)
   d. None of the above.

9. Which of the following assigns the string "Las Vegas" to the cityLabel control?
   a. `cityLabel.Label = "Las Vegas"`
   b. `cityLabel.String = "Las Vegas"`
   c. `cityLabel.Text = "Las Vegas"`
   d. None of the above.

10. Which of the following assigns the string "785.23" to the amountTextBox control?
    a. `amountTextBox = "785.23"`
    b. `amountTextBox.Label = "785.23"`
    c. `amountTextBox.String = "785.23"`
    d. `amountTextBox.Text = "785.23"`

Answers: 1) b, 2) d, 3) b, 4) d, 5) a, 6) c, 7) c, 8) d, 9) c, 10) d

## Review Questions

1. The set of directions given to a computer is called _____.
   a. computerese
   b. commands
   c. instructions
   d. a program

2. Instructions written in 0s and 1s are called _____.
   a. assembly language
   b. booleans
   c. machine code
   d. mnemonics

3. Assuming the program is not created using a .NET language, _____ translates the entire high-level program into machine code before running the program.
   a. an assembler
   b. a compiler
   c. an interpreter
   d. a translator

4. In procedure-oriented programs, the emphasis is on the major tasks needed to accomplish the program's goal.
   a. True
   b. False

5. In object-oriented programs, the emphasis is on objects needed to accomplish the program's goal.
   a. True
   b. False

6. A(n) _____ is a pattern or blueprint for creating an object.
   a. attribute
   b. behavior
   c. class
   d. instance

7. The object that you create from a class is called _____ of the class.
   a. an abstraction
   b. an attribute
   c. an instance
   d. a subclass

8. In the context of OOP, the combining of an object's attributes and behaviors into one package is called _____.
   a. abstraction
   b. combining
   c. encapsulation
   d. inheritance

9. In the context of OOP, the hiding of the internal details of an object from the user is called _____.
   a. abstraction
   b. combining
   c. encapsulation
   d. inheritance

10. Alcon Toys manufactures several versions of a basic doll. Assume that the basic doll is called Model A and the versions are called Models B, C, and D. In the context of OOP, the Model A doll is called the _____ class; the other dolls are called the _____ class.
    a. base, derived
    b. base, inherited
    c. derived, base
    d. inherited, derived

11. In the context of OOP, _____ refers to the fact that you can create one class from another class.
    a. abstraction
    b. combining
    c. encapsulation
    d. inheritance

12. A _____ is a container that stores the projects and files for an entire application.
    a. form file
    b. profile
    c. solution
    d. template

13. The _____ window lists the projects and files included in a solution.
  a. Object
  b. Project
  c. Properties
  d. Solution Explorer

14. You use the _____ window to set the characteristics that control an object's appearance and behavior.
  a. Characteristics
  b. Object
  c. Properties
  d. Toolbox

15. CLR stands for _____.
  a. Common Language Runtime
  b. Compiler Language Runtime
  c. Computer Language Runtime
  d. None of the above.

16. Which of the following instructions displays the text "Sales:" in a label control named Label1?
  a. `Label1.Caption = "Sales:"`
  b. `Label1.Text = "Sales:"`
  c. `Label1.Name = "Sales:"`
  d. `Label1.Label = "Sales:"`

17. You can use the _____ method to terminate the current application.
  a. Me.Close
  b. Me.Done
  c. Me.Finish
  d. Me.Stop

18. The text that appears on the face of a button control is stored in the control's _____ property.
  a. Caption
  b. Command
  c. Label
  d. Text

19. Actions such as clicking and double-clicking are called _____.
  a. actionEvents
  b. events
  c. happenings
  d. procedures

20. The _____ list box in the Code Editor window lists the events to which the selected object is capable of responding.
  a. Event Name
  b. Method Name
  c. Object Name
  d. Procedure Name

## Review Exercises - Short Answer

1. Define the following terms:
   a. OOP
   b. OOD
   c. attribute
   d. behavior

2. Explain the difference between assembly languages and high-level languages.

3. Explain the difference between a Windows-based application and a Web-based application.

4. Explain the difference between a Windows Form object's Text property and its Name property.

5. Explain the difference between a form file object and a Windows Form object.

6. Define the term "namespace".

7. What does the dot member access operator indicate in the text System.Windows.Forms.Label?

8. Explain the purpose of the following: the .NET language-specific compilers, the .NET Framework class library, the CLR, and the JIT compiler.

9. What property determines whether the value stored in the form's Text property appears on the Windows taskbar when the application is running? (*Hint*: Use the Description pane in the Properties window.)

10. What property determines whether an icon is displayed in the form's title bar?

## Computer Exercises

1. In this exercise, you modify this chapter's Programming Example.
   a. Create the State Capitals application shown in this chapter's Programming Example. Save the application in the VbReloaded\Chap01 folder.
   b. Add another label control to the form. Give it an appropriate name. Modify the application so that it displays a message that indicates the state's U.S. Constitution signing order. For example, when the user clicks the Alabama button, the button's Click event procedure should display the message "Alabama was the 22nd state to sign the U.S. Constitution." (Alaska was the 49th state to sign the Constitution, Arizona was the 48th state, and Arkansas was the 25th state.)
   c. Save the solution, then start and test the application. Close the solution.
   d. Locate the application's .exe file. Run the file from the Run dialog box in Windows.

2. In this exercise, you add label and button controls to a form. You also change the properties of the form and its controls.
   a. Open the Mechanics Solution (Mechanics Solution.sln) file, which is contained in the VbReloaded\Chap01\Mechanics Solution folder.
   b. Assign the filename Main Form.vb to the form file object.

    c. Assign the name MainForm to the Windows Form object.

    d. The Windows Form object's title bar should say IMA. Set the appropriate property.

    e. The Windows Form object should be centered on the screen when it first appears. Set the appropriate property.

    f. Add a label control to the form. Change the label control's name to companyLabel.

    g. The label control should display the caption "International Mechanics Association" (without the quotation marks). Set the appropriate property.

    h. Display the label control's text in italics using the Tahoma font. Change the size of the text to 12 points.

    i. Center the label control horizontally and vertically on the form.

    j. Add a button control to the form. Change the button control's name to exitButton.

    k. The button control should display the caption "Exit" (without the quotation marks). Set the appropriate property.

    l. Display the button control's caption using the Tahoma font. Change the size of the text to 12 points. Size the button appropriately.

    m. The Exit button should terminate the application when it is clicked. Enter the appropriate code in the Code Editor window.

    n. Change the project's startup form to MainForm.

    o. Save the solution, then start and test the application. Close the solution.

3. In this exercise, you add label and button controls to a form. You also change the properties of the form and its controls.

    a. Create the user interface shown in Figure 1.74. Name the solution Costello Solution. Name the project Costello Project. Name the form file object Main Form.vb. Save the application in the VbReloaded\Chap01 folder.

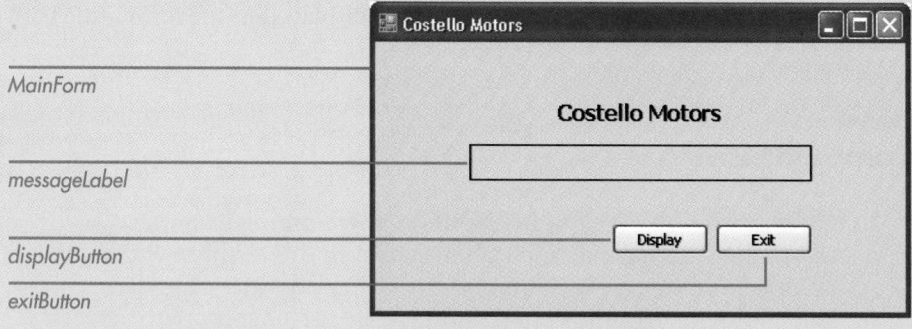

**FIGURE 1.74**

    b. The Exit button should terminate the application when it is clicked. Enter the appropriate code in the Code Editor window.

    c. When the Display button is clicked, it should display the message "We have the best deals in town!" in the messageLabel control. Enter the appropriate code in the Code Editor window.

    d. Save the solution. Start and then test the application. Close the solution.

4. In this exercise, you find and correct an error in an application. The process of finding and correcting errors is called debugging.

    a. Open the Debug Solution (Debug Solution.sln) file, which is contained in the VbReloaded\Chap01\Debug Solution folder.

    b. Start the application. Click the Exit button. Notice that the Exit button does not end the application.

c.  Click the Close button on the form's title bar to end the application.

d.  Open the Code Editor window. Locate and then correct the error.

e.  Save the solution, then start and test the application. Close the solution.

## Case Projects

### Castle's Ice Cream Parlor

Create an application that displays the price of an item in a label when a button with the item's name is clicked.

| Item | Price |
|------|-------|
| Banana Split | 1.79 |
| Sundae | .99 |
| Milkshake | 2.25 |

Use button and label controls in the interface. Include a button control that allows the user to terminate the application. Be sure to assign meaningful names to the form, the button controls, and the label control that displays the price. Save the application in the VbReloaded\Chap01 folder.

### Allen School District

Create an application that displays the name of the principal and the school's phone number in labels when a button with the school's name is clicked.

| School | Principal | Phone number |
|--------|-----------|--------------|
| Primary Center | June Davis | 111-9999 |
| Lewis Middle School | Matt Hayes | 111-8888 |
| Kaufman Junior High | Sandy Jenkins | 111-8978 |
| Allen High School | Perry Thomas | 111-2222 |

Use button and label controls in the interface. Include a button control that allows the user to terminate the application. Be sure to assign meaningful names to the form, the button controls, and the label controls that display the name and phone number. Save the application in the VbReloaded\Chap01 folder.

### Elvira Learning Center

Create an application that displays the equivalent Spanish word in a label when a button with an English word is clicked.

| English | Spanish |
|---------|---------|
| Hello | Hola |
| Good-bye | Adios |
| Love | Amor |
| Cat | Gato |
| Dog | Perro |

Use button and label controls in the interface. Include a button control that allows the user to terminate the application. Be sure to assign meaningful names to the form, the button controls, and the label control that displays the Spanish word. Save the application in the VbReloaded\Chap01 folder.

## Mary Golds Flower Shop

Create an eye-catching splash screen for the flower shop. You can use the tools you learned about in this chapter, or you can experiment with other tools from the toolbox. (For example, the Timer tool creates a timer control, which you can use to close the splash screen after a specified period of time. You can look ahead to Chapter 2 to learn how to use a timer control.) Save the application in the VbReloaded\Chap01 folder.

# Creating a User Interface

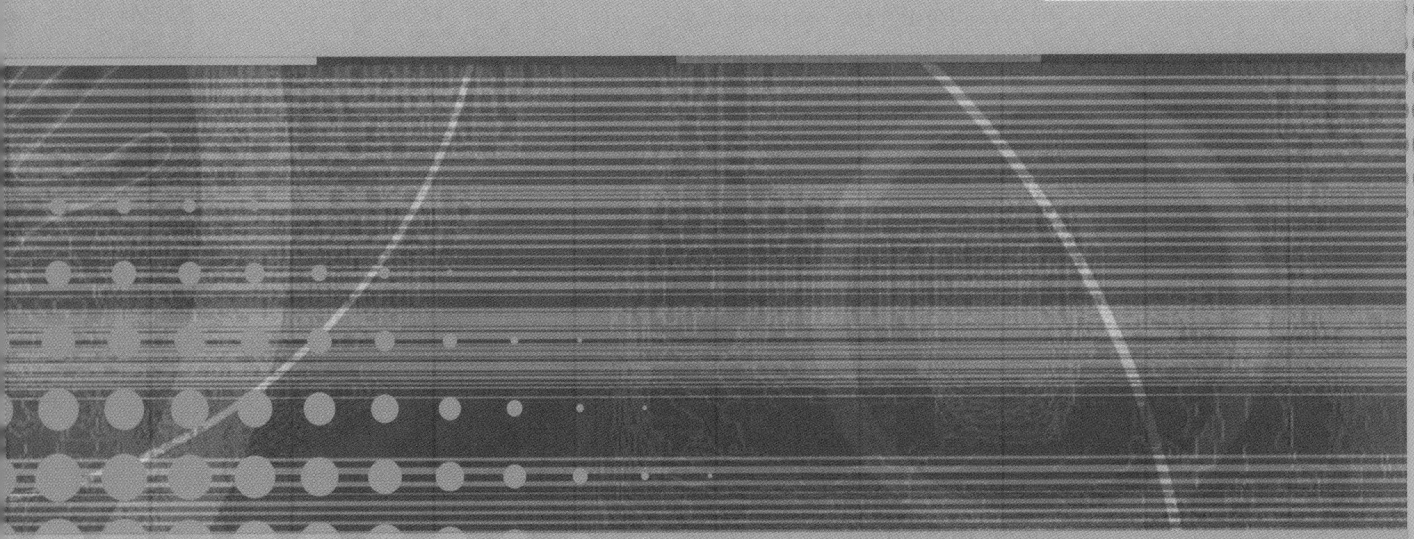

**After studying Chapter 2, you should be able to:**

- Plan an application
- Complete a TOE chart
- Use a text box, table layout panel, and timer
- Explain the difference between a primary window and a dialog box
- Follow the Windows standards regarding the layout and labeling of controls
- Follow the Windows standards regarding the use of graphics, fonts, and color
- Assign access keys to controls
- Set the tab order
- Designate a default button and a cancel button
- Explain the difference between a modal form and a modeless form
- Add a splash screen and a dialog box to an application

## PLANNING AN APPLICATION

Before you can create the user interface for your application, you need to plan the application. The plan should be developed jointly with the user to ensure that the application meets the user's needs. It cannot be stressed enough that the only way to guarantee the success of an application is to actively involve the user in the planning phase. Figure 2.1 lists the steps you follow when planning an application.

HOW TO...

### Plan an Application

1. Identify the tasks the application needs to perform.
2. Identify the objects to which you will assign those tasks.
3. Identify the events required to trigger an object into performing its assigned tasks.
4. Design the user interface.

**FIGURE 2.1**        How to plan an application

You can use a TOE (Task, Object, Event) chart to record the application's tasks, objects, and events, which are identified in the first three steps of the planning phase. In the next several sections, you complete a TOE chart for the Skate-Away Sales Company.

## SKATE-AWAY SALES

Skate-Away Sales sells skateboards by phone. The skateboards are priced at $100 each and are available in two colors—yellow and blue. The company employs 20 salespeople to answer the phones. The salespeople record each order on a form that contains the customer's name, address, and the number of blue and yellow skateboards ordered. The salespeople then calculate the total number of skateboards ordered and the total price of the skateboards, including a 5% sales tax. The company's sales manager, Jacques Cousard, feels that having the salespeople manually perform the necessary calculations is much too time-consuming and prone to errors. He wants you to create a computerized application that will solve the problems of the current order-taking system. The first step in planning this application is to identify the application's tasks.

### Identifying the Application's Tasks

Realizing that it is essential to involve the user when planning the application, you meet with the sales manager of Skate-Away Sales, Mr. Cousard, to determine his requirements. You ask Mr. Cousard to bring the form the salespeople currently use to record the orders. Viewing the current forms and procedures will help you gain a better understanding of the application. You also can use the current form as a guide when designing the user interface. Figure 2.2 shows the current order form used by Skate-Away Sales.

**Skate-Away Sales Order Form:**

Customer name: _____

Address: _____

City: _____ State: _____ ZIP: _____

| Number of blue skateboards ordered: | Number of yellow skateboards ordered: | Total number of skateboards ordered: | Total price: |
|---|---|---|---|
|  |  |  |  |
|  |  |  |  |
|  |  |  |  |
|  |  |  |  |
|  |  |  |  |
|  |  |  |  |
|  |  |  |  |
|  |  |  |  |
|  |  | Grand total: |  |

**FIGURE 2.2**      Current order form used by Skate-Away sales

When identifying the tasks an application needs to perform, it is helpful to ask the following questions:

- What information, if any, will the application need to display on the screen and/or print on the printer?
- What information, if any, will the user need to enter into the user interface to display and/or print the desired information?
- What information, if any, will the application need to calculate to display and/or print the desired information?
- How will the user end the application?
- Will previous information need to be cleared from the screen before new information is entered?

The answers to these questions will help you identify the application's major tasks. The answers for each question for the Skate-Away Sales application are as follows.

*What information, if any, will the application need to display on the screen and/or print on the printer?* (Notice that "display" refers to the screen, and "print" refers to the printer.) The Skate-Away Sales application should display the customer's name, street address, city, state, ZIP code, the number of blue skateboards ordered, the number of yellow skateboards ordered, the total number of skateboards ordered, and the total price of the order. In this case, the application does not need to print anything on the printer.

*What information, if any, will the user need to enter into the user interface to display and/or print the desired information?* In the Skate-Away Sales application, the salesperson (the user) must enter the customer's name, street address, city, state, ZIP code, and the number of blue and yellow skateboards ordered.

*What information, if any, will the application need to calculate to display and/or print the desired information?* The Skate-Away Sales application needs to calculate the total number of skateboards ordered and the total price of the order.

*How will the user end the application?* All applications should give the user a way to exit the program. The Skate-Away Sales application will use an Exit button for this task.

*Will previous information need to be cleared from the screen before new information is entered?* After Skate-Away's salesperson enters and calculates an order, he or she will need to clear the order's information from the screen before entering the next order.

Figure 2.3 shows the Skate-Away Sales application's tasks listed in a TOE chart. The tasks in a TOE chart do not need to be listed in any particular order. In this case, the data entry tasks are listed first, followed by the calculation tasks, display tasks, application ending task, and screen clearing task.

| Task | Object | Event |
| --- | --- | --- |
| Get the following order information from the user:<br>    Customer's name<br>    Street address<br>    City<br>    State<br>    ZIP code<br>    Number of blue skateboards ordered<br>    Number of yellow skateboards ordered | | |
| Calculate the total skateboards ordered and the total price | | |
| Display the following information:<br>    Customer's name<br>    Street address<br>    City<br>    State<br>    ZIP code<br>    Number of blue skateboards ordered<br>    Number of yellow skateboards ordered<br>    Total skateboards ordered<br>    Total price | | |
| End the application | | |
| Clear the screen for the next order | | |

**FIGURE 2.3**     Tasks entered in a TOE chart

Next, you identify the objects that will perform the tasks listed in the TOE chart.

### Identifying the Objects

After completing the Task column of the TOE chart, you then assign each task to an object in the user interface. For this application, the only objects you will use, besides the Windows form itself, are the button, label, and text box controls. As you learned in Chapter 1, you use a label control to display information that you do not want the user to change while your application is running, and you use a button control to perform an action immediately after the user clicks it. You use a

**TIP**

You can draw a TOE chart by hand, or you can use the table feature in a word processor (such as Microsoft Word) to draw one.

**text box** to give the user an area in which to enter data. You instantiate (create) a text box using the **TextBox tool** in the toolbox. Figure 2.4 lists the names and uses of several properties of a text box. Notice that you can control the case of the characters entered into a text box, as well as the maximum number of characters that the text box will accept. You also can specify whether the text in the text box can appear on one line, and whether scroll bars appear on the text box.

## HOW TO...

### Use a Text Box

| Property | Use to |
|---|---|
| BackColor | specify the background color of the text box |
| CharacterCasing | indicate whether the text should be left alone or converted to uppercase or lowercase |
| Font | specify the font to use for text (usually set to Tahoma) |
| ForeColor | specify the color of the text displayed in the text box |
| Margin | specify the space between the text box and another control on the form |
| MaxLength | specify the maximum number of characters that can be entered into the text box |
| Multiline | indicate whether the text in the text box can appear on more than one line |
| Name | give the text box a meaningful name |
| PasswordChar | specify the character to display when entering a password |
| ScrollBars | indicate whether scroll bars appear on the text box (used with a multiline text box) |
| TabIndex | indicate the control's position in the Tab order |
| TabStop | indicate whether the user can use the Tab key to give focus to the text box |
| Text | specify the text that appears inside the text box |
| TextAlign | specify the position of the text within the text box |

**FIGURE 2.4**   How to use a text box

Now you assign each of the tasks in the TOE chart shown in Figure 2.3 to an object. The first task listed in the figure is to get the order information from the user. For each order, the salesperson will need to enter the customer's name, address, city, state, and ZIP code, as well as the number of blue skateboards ordered and the number of yellow skateboards ordered. Because you need to provide the salesperson with areas in which to enter the information, you assign the first task to seven text boxes—one for each item of information. The names of the text boxes will be nameTextBox, addressTextBox, cityTextBox, stateTextBox, zipTextBox, blueTextBox, and yellowTextBox.

The second task listed in the TOE chart is to calculate both the total number of skateboards ordered and the total price. So that the salesperson can calculate these amounts at any time, you assign the task to a button named calcButton.

The third task listed in the TOE chart is to display the order information, the total number of skateboards ordered, and the total price. The order information will be displayed automatically when the user enters that information in the seven text boxes. The total skateboards ordered and the total price, however, are not entered by the user; rather, those amounts are calculated by the calcButton. Because the user should not be allowed to change the calculated results, you will have the calcButton display the total skateboards ordered and the total price in two label controls named totalBoardsLabel and totalPriceLabel. Recall from Chapter 1 that a user cannot access the contents of a label control while the application is running. Notice that the task of displaying the total skateboards ordered involves two objects (calcButton and totalBoardsLabel). The task of displaying the total price also involves two objects (calcButton and totalPriceLabel).

The last two tasks listed in the TOE chart are "End the application" and "Clear the screen for the next order." You assign these tasks to buttons so that the user has control over when the tasks are performed. You name the buttons exitButton and clearButton. Figure 2.5 shows the TOE chart with the Task and Object columns completed.

| Task | Object | Event |
|---|---|---|
| Get the following order information from the user: | | |
|    Customer's name | nameTextBox | |
|    Street address | addressTextBox | |
|    City | cityTextBox | |
|    State | stateTextBox | |
|    ZIP code | zipTextBox | |
|    Number of blue skateboards ordered | blueTextBox | |
|    Number of yellow skateboards ordered | yellowTextBox | |
| Calculate the total skateboards ordered and the total price | calcButton | |
| Display the following information: | | |
|    Customer's name | nameTextBox | |
|    Street address | addressTextBox | |
|    City | cityTextBox | |
|    State | stateTextBox | |
|    ZIP code | zipTextBox | |
|    Number of blue skateboards ordered | blueTextBox | |
|    Number of yellow skateboards ordered | yellowTextBox | |
|    Total skateboards ordered | calcButton, totalBoardsLabel | |
|    Total price | calcButton, totalPriceLabel | |
| End the application | exitButton | |
| Clear the screen for the next order | clearButton | |

**FIGURE 2.5**     Tasks and objects entered in a TOE chart

After defining the application's tasks and assigning those tasks to objects in the user interface, you then determine which objects need an event (such as clicking or double-clicking) to occur for the object to do its assigned task. In the next section, you identify the events required by the objects listed in the TOE chart in Figure 2.5.

## Identifying the Events

The seven text boxes listed in the TOE chart in Figure 2.5 are assigned the task of getting and displaying the order information. Text boxes accept and display information automatically, so no special event is necessary for them to do their assigned task.

The two label controls listed in the TOE chart are assigned the task of displaying the total number of skateboards ordered and the total price of the order. Label controls automatically display their contents; so, here again, no special event needs to occur. (Recall that the two label controls will get their values from the calcButton.)

The remaining objects listed in the TOE chart are the three buttons: calcButton, clearButton, and exitButton. You will have the buttons perform their assigned tasks when the user clicks them. Figure 2.6 shows the TOE chart with the tasks, objects, and events necessary for the Skate-Away Sales application.

**TIP**

Not all objects in a user interface will need an event to occur in order for the object to perform its assigned tasks.

| Task | Object | Event |
|------|--------|-------|
| Get the following order information from the user: | | |
|     Customer's name | nameTextBox | None |
|     Street address | addressTextBox | None |
|     City | cityTextBox | None |
|     State | stateTextBox | None |
|     ZIP code | zipTextBox | None |
|     Number of blue skateboards ordered | blueTextBox | None |
|     Number of yellow skateboards ordered | yellowTextBox | None |
| Calculate the total skateboards ordered and the total price | calcButton | Click |
| Display the following information: | | |
|     Customer's name | nameTextBox | None |
|     Street address | addressTextBox | None |
|     City | cityTextBox | None |
|     State | stateTextBox | None |
|     ZIP code | zipTextBox | None |
|     Number of blue skateboards ordered | blueTextBox | None |
|     Number of yellow skateboards ordered | yellowTextBox | None |
|     Total skateboards ordered | calcButton, totalBoardsLabel | Click, None |
|     Total price | calcButton, totalPriceLabel | Click, None |
| End the application | exitButton | Click |
| Clear the screen for the next order | clearButton | Click |

**FIGURE 2.6**   Completed TOE chart ordered by task

If the application you are creating is small, as is the Skate-Away Sales application, you can use the TOE chart in its current form to help you write the Visual Basic code. When the application you are creating is large, however, it is helpful to rearrange the TOE chart so that it is ordered by object instead of by task. To do so, you simply list all of the objects in the Object column, being sure to list each object only once. Then list the tasks you have assigned to each object in the Task column, and list the events in the Event column. Figure 2.7 shows the rearranged TOE chart, ordered by object rather than by task.

| Task | Object | Event |
|---|---|---|
| 1. Calculate the total skateboards ordered and the total price<br>2. Display the total skateboards ordered and the total price in totalBoardsLabel and totalPriceLabel | calcButton | Click |
| Clear the screen for the next order | clearButton | Click |
| End the application | exitButton | Click |
| Display the total skateboards ordered (from calcButton) | totalBoardsLabel | None |
| Display the total price (from calcButton) | totalPriceLabel | None |
| Get and display the order information | nameTextBox,<br>addressTextBox,<br>cityTextBox, stateTextBox,<br>zipTextBox, blueTextBox,<br>yellowTextBox | None |

**FIGURE 2.7**     Completed TOE chart ordered by object

After completing the TOE chart, the next step is to design the user interface.

## DESIGNING THE USER INTERFACE

Although the TOE chart lists the objects you need to include in the application's user interface, it does not tell you *where* to place those objects in the interface. While the design of an interface is open to creativity, there are some guidelines to which you should adhere so that your application is consistent with the Windows standards. This consistency will make your application easier to both learn and use, because the user interface will have a familiar look to it. The guidelines are referred to as GUI guidelines, because they pertain to Graphical User Interfaces. The first GUI guideline you learn in this chapter relates to the form itself.

Most Windows applications consist of a main window, possibly some other primary windows, and one or more secondary windows, called dialog boxes. The primary viewing and editing of your application's data take place in a **primary window**. The primary window shown in Figure 2.8, for example, allows you to view and edit documents created using the Notepad application. **Dialog boxes** are used to support and supplement a user's activities in the primary windows. The Font dialog box shown in Figure 2.8, for instance, allows you to specify the font of the text selected in the primary window.

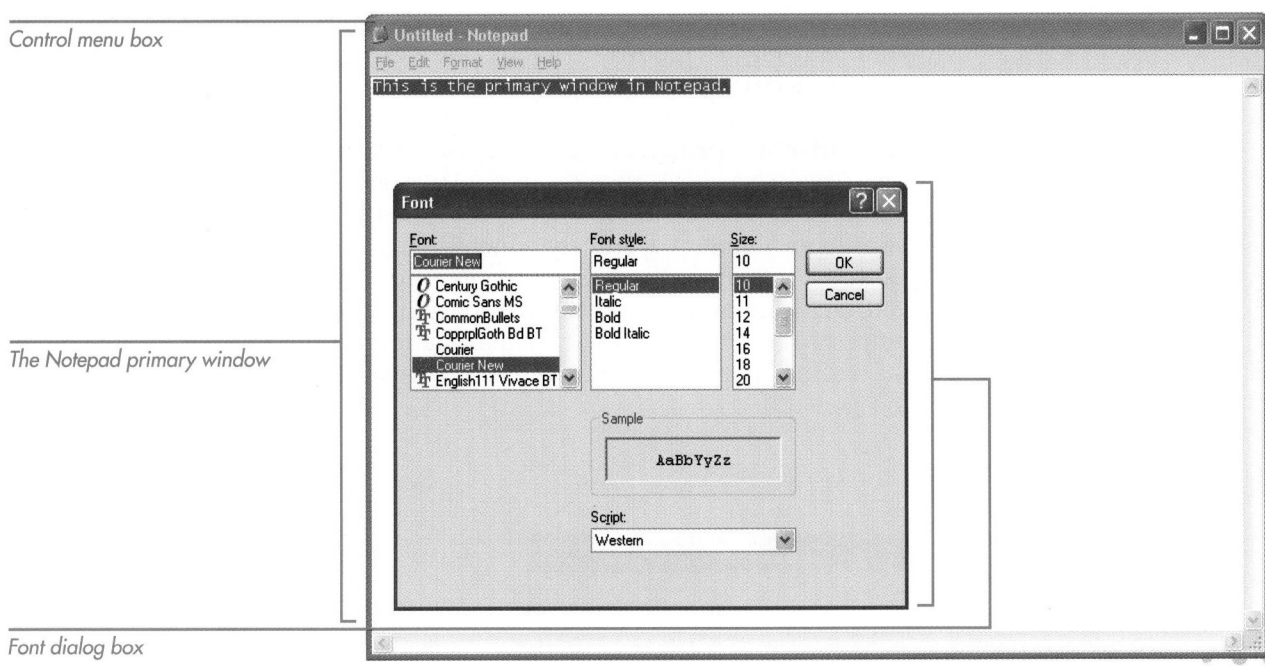

Control menu box

The Notepad primary window

Font dialog box

**FIGURE 2.8**    Primary window and Font dialog box in Notepad

Primary windows can be resized, minimized, maximized, and closed by the user. To resize a primary window, the user simply drags the window's border. To minimize, maximize, or close a primary window, the user clicks the Minimize, Maximize, or Close buttons that appear on the window's title bar. The user also can click the Control menu box to display the Control menu, which contains Minimize, Maximize, and Close options.

Unlike primary windows, dialog boxes can be closed only. They cannot be resized, minimized, or maximized by the user. The only buttons that appear in a dialog box's title bar are the Close button and, in some cases, the Help button. Additionally, a dialog box does not contain a Control menu box.

In Visual Basic, you use a Windows Form object, or form, to create both primary windows and dialog boxes. You specify the border style of the window or dialog box using the form's **FormBorderStyle property**. Figure 2.9 lists the valid settings for the FormBorderStyle property and provides a brief description of the border provided by each setting.

| FormBorderStyle setting | Description of the border |
|---|---|
| Fixed3D | fixed, three-dimensional |
| FixedDialog | fixed, thick dialog-style |
| FixedSingle | fixed, thin line |
| FixedToolWindow | fixed, tool window style |
| None | no border |
| Sizable | sizable, normal style (default setting) |
| SizableToolWindow | sizable, tool window style |

**FIGURE 2.9**    FormBorderStyle settings

If the form represents a primary window, you typically leave the form's FormBorderStyle property at its default setting, Sizable. When the FormBorderStyle property is set to Sizable, the user can drag the form's borders to change the form's size while the application is running. You also leave the form's **MinimizeBox property** and **MaximizeBox property** set at the default setting, True. This allows the user to minimize and maximize the form using the Minimize and Maximize buttons on the form's title bar. The user always should be able to minimize a primary window and, in most cases, also maximize it. However, if you want to prevent the user from maximizing a primary window, you can do so by setting the form's MaximizeBox property to False. When the property is set to False, the Maximize button on the title bar, as well as the Maximize option on the Control menu, appears dimmed (grayed-out), as shown in Figure 2.10.

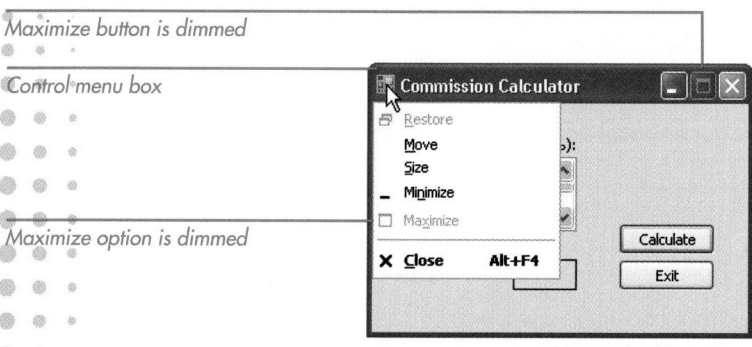

**FIGURE 2.10**      Result of setting the form's MaximizeBox property to False

If the form represents a dialog box, you usually set the form's FormBorderStyle property to FixedDialog. The FixedDialog setting draws a fixed, thick dialog-style border around the form. It also removes the Control menu box from the form's title bar.

Recall that a dialog box should not have the Minimize and Maximize buttons on its title bar. You remove the Minimize and Maximize buttons from the title bar by setting both the MinimizeBox and MaximizeBox properties of the form to False.

In addition to using a form to create primary windows and dialog boxes, you also can use a form to create splash screens. As you learned in Chapter 1, a splash screen is the first image that appears when an application is started. It is used to introduce the application and to hold the user's attention as the application is being read into the computer's internal memory. Figure 2.11 shows the Visual Studio 2005 splash screen.

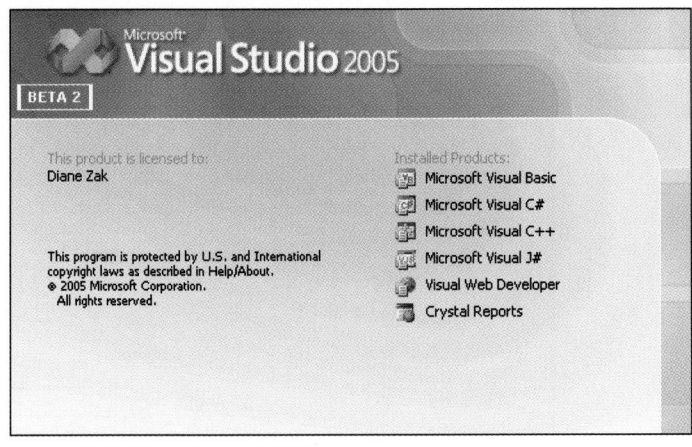

**FIGURE 2.11**   Visual Studio 2005 splash screen

If a form represents a splash screen, you typically set the form's FormBorderStyle property to FixedSingle. You also set the form's **ControlBox property** to False; doing this removes the Control menu box, as well as the Minimize, Maximize, and Close buttons, from the title bar. You can remove the entire title bar from the form by setting the ControlBox property to False, and then deleting the text that appears in the form's Text property.

Next, you learn how to arrange the controls in an interface.

## Arranging the Controls

In Western countries, you should organize the user interface so that the information flows either vertically or horizontally, with the most important information always located in the upper-left corner of the screen. In a vertical arrangement the information flows from top to bottom; the essential information is located in the first column of the screen, while secondary information is placed in subsequent columns. In a horizontal arrangement, on the other hand, the information flows from left to right; the essential information is placed in the first row of the screen, with secondary information placed in subsequent rows. You can group together related controls using either white (empty) space or one of the tools located in the Containers section of the toolbox.

Figures 2.12 and 2.13 show two different interfaces for the Skate-Away Sales application. In Figure 2.12, the information is arranged vertically, and white space is used to group related controls together. In Figure 2.13, the information is arranged horizontally. Related controls in Figure 2.13 are grouped together using a **group box control**, a **panel control**, and a **table layout panel control**. You instantiate group box, panel, and table layout panel controls using the GroupBox, Panel, and TableLayoutPanel tools, respectively; these tools are located in the Containers section of the toolbox.

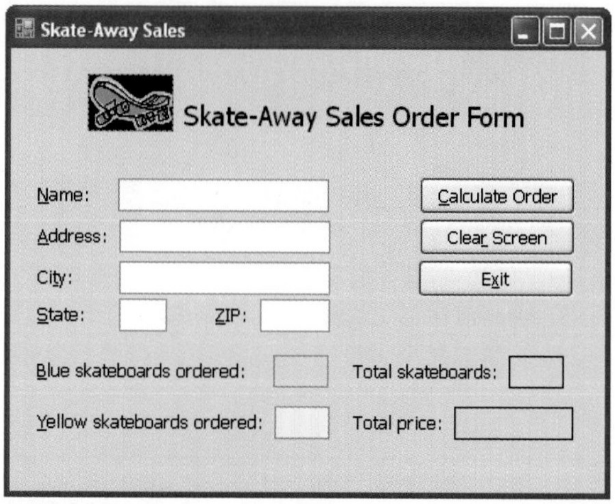

**FIGURE 2.12**    Vertical arrangement of the Skate-Away Sales interface

Group box control

Panel control

TableLayoutPanel control

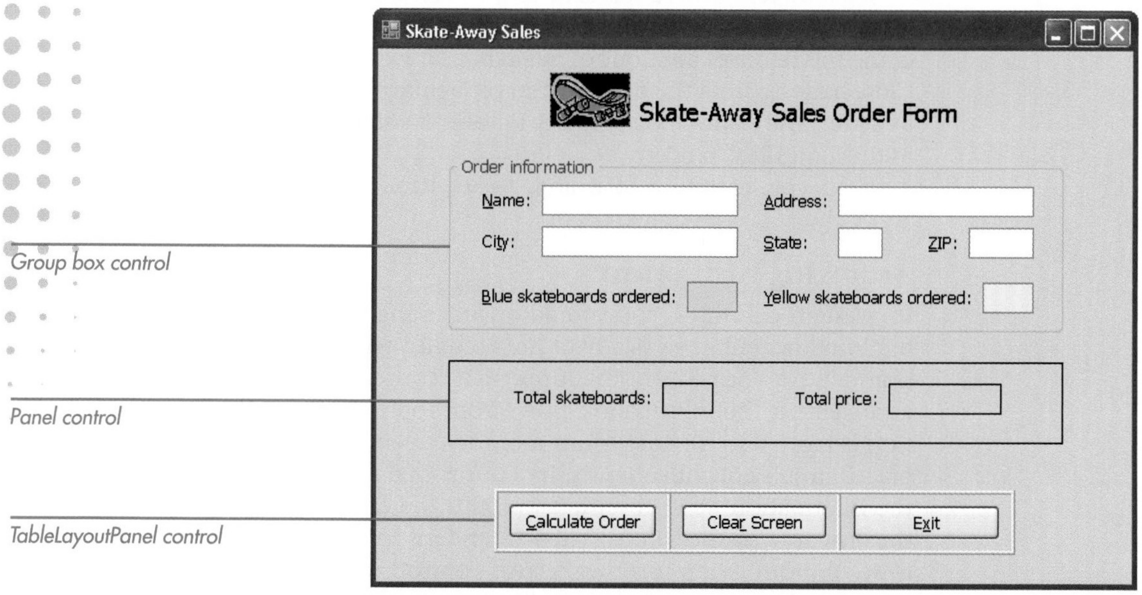

**FIGURE 2.13**    Horizontal arrangement of the Skate-Away Sales interface

Figures 2.14, 2.15, and 2.16 list the names and uses of several properties of the group box, panel, and table layout panel controls. The difference between a panel and a group box is that, unlike a group box, a panel can have scroll bars. Additionally, unlike a panel, a group box has a Text property that you can use to indicate the contents of the control. Unlike the panel and group box controls, the table layout panel control provides a table structure in which you place other controls.

HOW TO...

**Use a Group Box**

| Property | Use to |
|---|---|
| Name | give the group box a meaningful name |
| Padding | specify the internal space between the edges of the group box and the edges of the controls contained within the group box |
| Text | specify the text that appears in the upper-left corner of the control |

**FIGURE 2.14**   How to use a group box

HOW TO...

**Use a Panel**

| Property | Use to |
|---|---|
| Name | give the panel a meaningful name |
| BorderStyle | specify whether the panel has a visible border |
| Padding | specify the internal space between the edges of the panel and the edges of the controls contained within the panel |

**FIGURE 2.15**   How to use a panel

HOW TO...

**Use a TableLayoutPanel**

| Property | Use to |
|---|---|
| Name | give the panel a meaningful name |
| CellBorderStyle | specify whether the table cells have a visible border |
| ColumnCount | indicate the number of columns in the table |
| Columns | specify the style of each column in the table |
| Padding | specify the internal space between the edges of the panel and the edges of the controls contained within the panel |
| RowCount | indicate the number of rows in the table |
| Rows | specify the style of each row in the table |

**FIGURE 2.16**   How to use a table layout panel

Notice that each text box and button control in the interfaces shown in Figures 2.12 and 2.13 is labeled so the user knows the control's purpose. The text contained in label controls that identify text boxes should be left-aligned within the label control. Additionally, the identifying label should be positioned either above or to the left of the text box it identifies. As you learned in Chapter 1, buttons are identified by a caption that appears on the button itself. Identifying labels and captions should be from one to three words only, and each should appear on one line. Labels and captions should be meaningful. The label identifying a text box, for example, should tell the user the type of information to enter. A button's caption, on the other hand, should indicate the action the button will perform when it is clicked.

A text box's identifying label should end with a colon (:), as shown in Figures 2.12 and 2.13. The colon distinguishes an identifying label from other text in the user interface, such as the heading text "Skate-Away Sales Order Form". The Windows standard is to use sentence capitalization for identifying labels. **Sentence capitalization** means you capitalize only the first letter in the first word and in any words that are customarily capitalized. The Windows standard for button captions is to use book title capitalization. When using **book title capitalization**, you capitalize the first letter in each word, except for articles, conjunctions, and prepositions that do not occur at either the beginning or the end of the caption.

When positioning the controls, be sure to maintain a consistent margin from the edge of the form. Related controls should be placed close to each other on the form. Controls that are not part of any logical grouping are typically positioned farther away from other controls.

Always size the buttons in the interface relative to each other. When the buttons are positioned horizontally, as they are in Figure 2.13, all the buttons should be the same height; their widths, however, may vary if necessary. If the buttons are stacked vertically, as they are in Figure 2.12, all the buttons should be the same height and the same width.

When laying out the controls in the interface, try to minimize the number of different margins so that the user can more easily scan the information. You can do so by aligning the borders of the controls wherever possible, as shown in Figures 2.12 and 2.13. You can align the borders using the snap lines that appear as you are building the interface. Or, you can use the Format menu to align (and also size) the controls.

When designing the user interface, keep in mind that you want to create a screen that no one notices. Snazzy interfaces may get "oohs" and "aahs" during their initial use, but they become tiresome after a while. The most important point to remember is that the interface should not distract the user from doing his or her work. Unfortunately, it is difficult for some application developers to refrain from using the many different colors, fonts, and graphics available in Visual Basic. Actually, using these elements is not the problem—overusing them is. So that you do not overload your user interfaces with too much color, too many fonts, and too many graphics, the next three sections provide some guidelines to follow regarding these elements. Consider the graphics first.

## Including Graphics in the User Interface

The human eye is attracted to pictures before text, so include a graphic only if it is necessary to do so. Graphics typically are used to either emphasize or clarify a portion of the screen. You also can use a graphic for aesthetic purposes, as long as the graphic is small and placed in a location that does not distract the user. For example, the small graphic in the Skate-Away Sales interfaces (shown earlier in Figures 2.12 and 2.13) is included for aesthetics only. The graphic is purposely located in the upper-left corner of the interface, which is where you want the user's eye to be drawn first anyway. The graphic adds a personal touch to the Skate-Away Sales order form without being distracting to the user.

Next, you learn some guidelines pertaining to the use of different fonts in the interface.

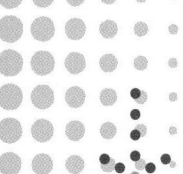

**TIP**

You learned how to use the Format menu in the Programming Tutorial section of Chapter 1.

**TIP**

The graphics, font, and color guidelines do not pertain to game applications.

## Including Different Fonts in the User Interface

You can use an object's **Font property** to change the type, style, and size of the font used to display the text in the object. A **font** is the general shape of the characters in the text. Tahoma, Courier, and Microsoft Sans Serif are examples of font types. Font styles include regular, bold, and italic. The numbers 8.25, 10, and 18 are examples of font sizes, which typically are measured in points, with one **point** equaling $1/72$ of an inch.

Some fonts are serif, and some are sans serif. A **serif** is a light cross stroke that appears at the top or bottom of a character. The characters in a serif font have the light strokes, whereas the characters in a sans serif font do not. ("Sans" is a French word meaning "without.") Books use serif fonts, because those fonts are easier to read on the printed page. Sans serif fonts, on the other hand, are easier to read on the screen, so you should use a sans serif font for the text in a user interface. For applications that will run on systems running Windows 2000 or Windows XP, it is recommended that you use the Tahoma font, because it offers improved readability and globalization support. You should use only one font type for all of the text in the interface. The Skate-Away Sales interfaces, for example, use only the Tahoma font.

You can use 8-, 9-, 10-, 11-, or 12-point fonts for the elements in the user interface; however, text displayed using a 12-point font is easier to read at high screen resolutions. Be sure to limit the number of font sizes used to either one or two. The Skate-Away Sales interfaces (shown earlier in Figures 2.12 and 2.13) use two font sizes: 14 point for the heading at the top of the interface, and 10 point for everything else.

Visual Basic automatically assigns the value Microsoft Sans Serif, 8.25 point to a form's Font property when the form is created. When you add a control to the form, the form's Font property value is automatically assigned to the control's Font property. Therefore, if you want to change the font used in an interface—perhaps to Tahoma, 10 point—you should change the form's Font property before adding any controls to the form. This will ensure that all of the controls on the form use the same font, and you will not need to set each control's Font property separately.

Avoid using italics and underlining in an interface, because both make text difficult to read. Additionally, limit the use of bold text to titles, headings, and key items that you want to emphasize.

In addition to overusing graphics and fonts, many application developers make the mistake of using either too much color or too many different colors in the user interface. In the next section, you learn some guidelines pertaining to the use of color.

## Including Color in the User Interface

Just as the human eye is attracted to graphics before text, it also is attracted to color before black and white, so use color sparingly. It is a good practice to build the interface using black, white, and gray first, then add color only if you have a good reason to do so. Keep the following three points in mind when deciding whether to include color in an interface:

1. Many people have some form of either color-blindness or color confusion, so they will have trouble distinguishing colors.
2. Color is very subjective; a pretty color to you may be hideous to someone else.
3. A color may have a different meaning in a different culture.

Usually, it is best to use black text on a white, off-white, or light gray background. This is because dark text on a light background is the easiest to read.

TIP

If the Tahoma font is not available, use either Microsoft Sans Serif or Arial.

TIP

You also can change the form's Font property after adding the controls. Any control whose Font property has not been set individually will assume the form's setting.

Never use a dark color for the background or a light color for the text, because a dark background is hard on the eyes, and light-colored text can appear blurry.

If you are going to include color in the interface, limit the number of colors to three, not including white, black, and gray. Be sure that the colors you choose complement each other.

Although color can be used to identify an important element in the interface, you should never use it as the only means of identification. For example, in the Skate-Away Sales interfaces, the blue and yellow text boxes help the salesperson quickly identify where to enter the order for blue and yellow skateboards, respectively. However, color is not the only means of identifying those areas in the interfaces; the labels to the left of the text boxes also tell the user where to enter the orders for blue and yellow skateboards.

## ASSIGNING ACCESS KEYS

Looking closely at the Skate-Away Sales interface shown in Figure 2.17, you will notice that the captions for many of the controls contain an underlined letter, called an access key. An **access key** allows the user to select an object using the Alt key in combination with a letter or number. For example, you can select the File menu in Visual Studio by pressing Alt+F, because the letter "F" is the File menu's access key. Access keys are not case sensitive; in other words, you can select the File menu by pressing either Alt+F or Alt+f. Similarly, you can select the Calculate Order button in the interface shown in Figure 2.17 by pressing either Alt+C or Alt+c.

*Access key for the Calculate Order button*

*nameTextBox*

*Access key for the nameTextBox*

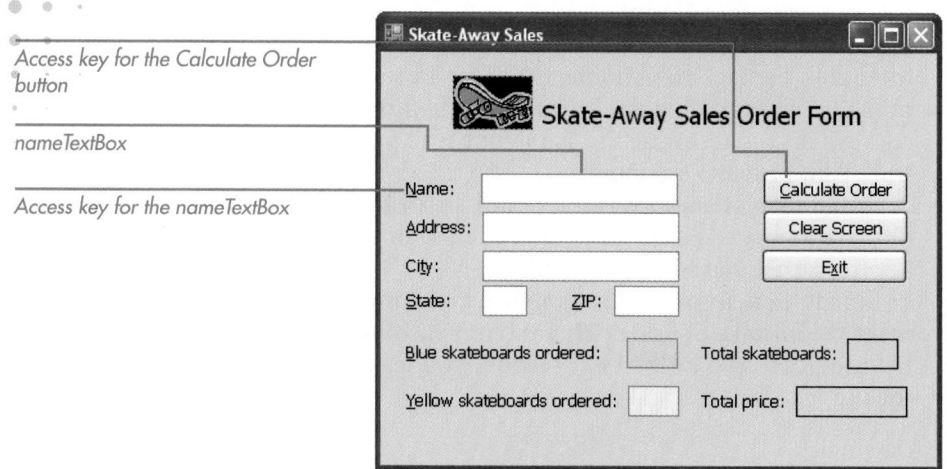

**FIGURE 2.17**    Skate-Away Sales interface

You should assign access keys to each of the controls (in the interface) that can accept user input. Examples of such controls include text boxes and buttons, because the user can enter information in a text box and he or she can click a button. The only exception to this rule is the OK and Cancel buttons typically found in dialog boxes. In Windows applications, the OK and Cancel buttons do not have access keys.

It is important to assign access keys to controls for the following three reasons:

1. Access keys allow a user to work with the application even if the mouse becomes inoperative.

2. Access keys allow users who are fast typists to keep their hands on the keyboard.

3. Access keys allow people with disabilities, which may prevent them from working with a mouse, to use the application.

You assign an access key by including an ampersand (&) in the control's caption or identifying label. For example, to assign an access key to a button, you include the ampersand in the button's Text property, which is where a button's caption is stored. To assign an access key to a text box, on the other hand, you include the ampersand in the Text property of the label control that identifies the text box. (As you learn later in this chapter, you also must set the identifying label's TabIndex property to a value that is one number less than the value stored in the text box's TabIndex property.) You enter the ampersand to the immediate left of the character you want to designate as the access key. For example, to assign the letter C as the access key for the Calculate Order button, you enter &Calculate Order in the button's Text property. To assign the letter N as the access key for the nameTextBox control, you enter &Name: in the Text property of its identifying label control.

Each access key appearing in the interface should be unique. The first choice for an access key is the first letter of the caption or identifying label, unless another letter provides a more meaningful association. For example, the letter X typically is the access key for an Exit button, because the letter X provides a more meaningful association than does the letter E. If you can't use the first letter (perhaps because it already is used as the access key for another control) and no other letter provides a more meaningful association, then use a distinctive consonant in the caption or label. The last choices for an access key are a vowel or a number.

Most times, the order in which controls are added to a form does not represent the desired tab order, which is the order that each control should receive the focus when the user presses the Tab key. You specify the desired order using the TabIndex property, which you learn about next.

## SETTING THE TABINDEX PROPERTY

The **TabIndex property** determines the order in which a control receives the focus when the user presses either the Tab key or an access key while the application is running. A control having a TabIndex of 2, for instance, will receive the focus immediately after the control whose TabIndex is 1. Likewise, a control with a TabIndex of 18 will receive the focus immediately after the control whose TabIndex is 17. When a control has the **focus**, it can accept user input.

When you add to a form a control that has a TabIndex property, Visual Basic sets the control's TabIndex property to a number that represents the order in which the control was added to the form. The TabIndex property for the first control added to a form is 0 (zero), the TabIndex property for the second control is 1, and so on. In most cases, you will need to change the TabIndex values of the controls, because the order in which controls are added to a form rarely represents the desired tab order.

To determine the appropriate TabIndex settings for an interface, you first make a list of the controls (in the interface) that can accept user input. The list should reflect the order in which the user will want to access the controls. For example, in the Skate-Away Sales interface shown in Figure 2.17, the user typically will want to access the nameTextBox first, then the addressTextBox, the cityTextBox, and so on. If a control that accepts user input is identified by a label control, you also include the label control in the list. (A text box is an example

TIP

If a control does not have a
TabIndex property, you do not
assign it a TabIndex value. You
can tell if a control has a
TabIndex property by viewing
its Properties list.

of a control that accepts user input and is identified by a label control.) You place the name of the label control immediately above the name of the control it identifies in the list. For example, in the Skate-Away Sales interface, the Label2 control (which displays Name:) identifies the nameTextBox; therefore, Label2 should appear immediately above nameTextBox in the list. The names of controls that do not accept user input, and those that do not identify controls that accept user input, should be listed at the bottom of the list; these names do not need to appear in any specific order.

After listing the controls, you then assign each control in the list a TabIndex value, beginning with the number 0. Figure 2.18 shows the list of controls for the Skate-Away Sales interface (shown in Figure 2.17) along with the appropriate TabIndex values.

| Controls that accept user input, along with their identifying label controls | TabIndex setting |
| --- | --- |
| Label1 (Name:) | 0 |
| nameTextBox | 1 |
| Label2 (Address:) | 2 |
| addressTextBox | 3 |
| Label3 (City:) | 4 |
| cityTextBox | 5 |
| Label4 (State:) | 6 |
| stateTextBox | 7 |
| Label5 (ZIP:) | 8 |
| zipTextBox | 9 |
| Label6 (Blue skateboards ordered:) | 10 |
| blueTextBox | 11 |
| Label7 (Yellow skateboards ordered:) | 12 |
| yellowTextBox | 13 |
| calcButton | 14 |
| clearButton | 15 |
| exitButton | 16 |

| Other controls | TabIndex setting |
| --- | --- |
| Label10 (Skate-Away Sales Order Form) | 17 |
| Label8 (Total skateboards:) | 18 |
| Label9 (Total price:) | 19 |
| totalBoardsLabel | 20 |
| totalPriceLabel | 21 |
| PictureBox1 | This control does not have a TabIndex property. |

**FIGURE 2.18**    List of controls and TabIndex settings

Notice that the first column in the list contains two sections. The first section is titled "Controls that accept user input, along with their identifying label controls." This section contains the names of the seven text boxes and three buttons in the Skate-Away Sales interface, because those controls can accept user input. Notice that each text box in the list is associated with an identifying label control, whose name appears immediately above the text box name in the list. Also notice that the TabIndex value assigned to each text box's identifying label control is one number less than the value assigned to the text box itself. For example, the Label1 control has a TabIndex value of 0, and its corresponding text box (nameTextBox) has a TabIndex value of 1. Likewise, the Label2 control and its corresponding text box have TabIndex values of 2 and 3, respectively. For a text box's access key (which is defined in the identifying label) to work appropriately, you must be sure to set the identifying label control's TabIndex property to a value that is one number less than the value stored in the text box's TabIndex property.

The second section in the list shown in Figure 2.18 is titled "Other controls." In this section you list the names of controls that neither accept user input nor identify controls that accept user input.

You can use the Properties list to set the TabIndex property of each control; or, you can use the Tab Order option on the View menu. When you use the Tab Order option, the current TabIndex value for each control (except controls that do not have a TabIndex property) appears in blue boxes on the form. You begin specifying the desired tab order by placing the mouse pointer on the first control you want in the tab order. In this case, you place the mouse pointer on the Label1 control, which contains the text &Name:. A rectangle surrounds the control and the mouse pointer becomes a crosshair, as shown in Figure 2.19.

*Crosshair*

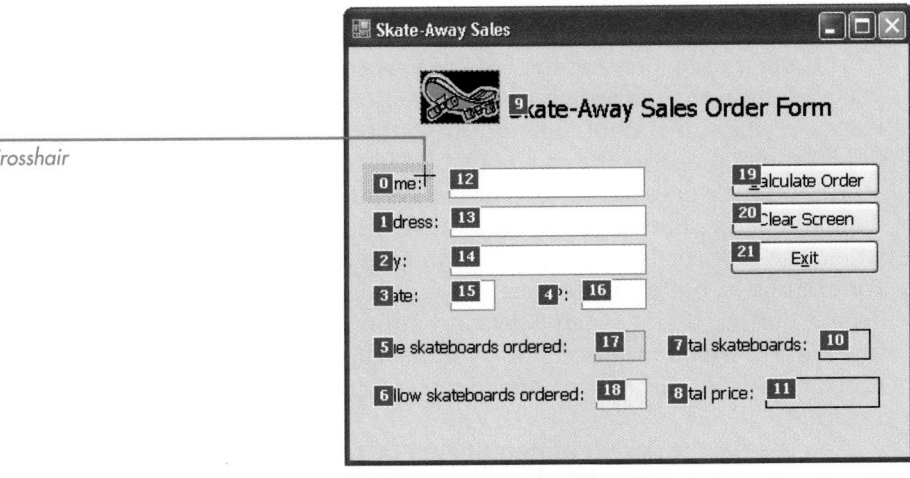

**FIGURE 2.19**    Crosshair positioned on the Name: label

**TIP**

The Tab Order option on the View menu is available only when the designer window is the active window.

You then click the control; when you do, the number 0 appears in the blue box, and the color of the box changes from blue to white to indicate that you have set the TabIndex value for that control. You then click the next control you want in the tab order, and so on. When you have finished setting all of the TabIndex values, the color of the boxes will automatically change from white to blue, as shown in Figure 2.20.

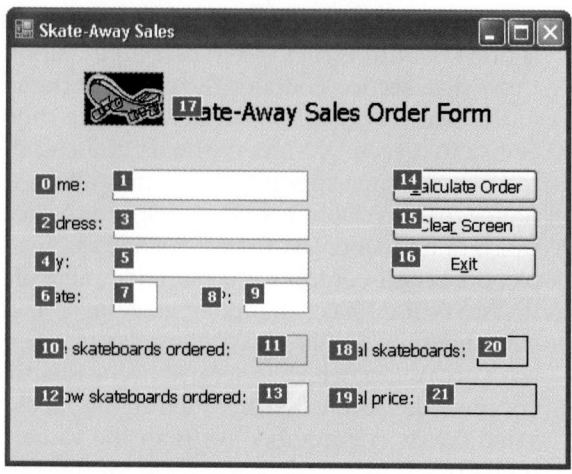

**FIGURE 2.20**          Correct TabIndex values shown in the form

You remove the TabIndex boxes from the form by pressing the Esc key on your keyboard. Alternatively, you can click View on the menu bar, and then click Tab Order.

In many interfaces, one of the buttons is designated as the default button, and another is designated as the cancel button. You learn about default and cancel buttons next.

**TIP**

If you make a mistake when specifying the tab order, you can press the Esc key and then start over again.

## DESIGNATING DEFAULT AND CANCEL BUTTONS

As you already know from using Windows applications, you can select a button by clicking it or by pressing the Enter key when the button has the focus. If you make a button the **default button**, you also can select it by pressing the Enter key even when the button does not have the focus. When a button is selected, the computer processes the code contained in the button's Click event procedure.

An interface does not have to have a default button. However, if one is used, it should be the button that is most often selected by the user, except in cases where the tasks performed by the button are both destructive and irreversible. For example, a button that deletes information should not be designated as the default button. If you assign a default button in an interface, it typically is the first button, which means that it is on the left when the buttons are positioned horizontally on the screen, and on the top when the buttons are stacked vertically.

You specify the default button (if any) by setting the form's **AcceptButton property** to the name of the button. For example, to make the Calculate Order button the default button in the Skate-Away Sales interface, you set the form's AcceptButton property to calcButton. The default button in an interface has a darkened border, as shown in Figure 2.21.

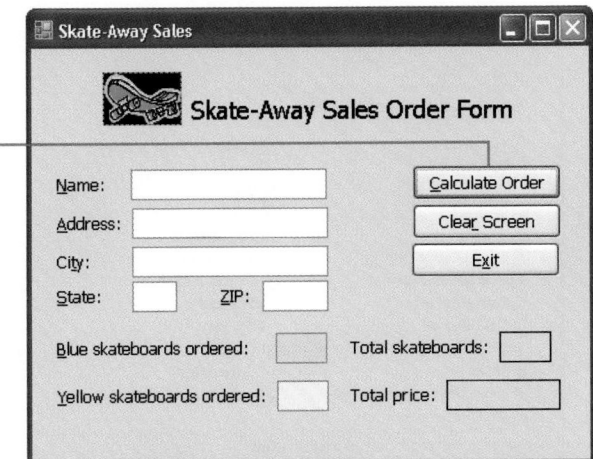

The default button has a darkened border

**FIGURE 2.21**    Default button shown in the interface

TIP

A form can have only one default button and one cancel button.

You also can designate a cancel button in an interface. Unlike the default button, the **cancel button** is automatically selected when the user presses the Esc key. You specify the cancel button (if any) by setting the form's **CancelButton property** to the name of the button. For example, to make the Exit button the cancel button in the Skate-Away Sales interface, you set the form's CancelButton property to exitButton.

Next, you learn how to include splash screens and dialog boxes in an application.

## INCLUDING SPLASH SCREENS AND DIALOG BOXES IN AN APPLICATION

Figure 2.22 shows the steps you follow to add either a splash screen or a dialog box to an application, and Figure 2.23 shows an example of a completed Add New Item - <projectname> dialog box.

HOW TO...

### Add a Splash Screen or a Dialog Box to an Application

1. Click Project on the menu bar, then click Add Windows Form to open the Add New Item – *<projectname>* dialog box.
2. Click the desired template in the list of Visual Studio installed templates.
3. Enter an appropriate name in the Name box.
4. Click the Add button.

**FIGURE 2.22**    How to add a splash screen or a dialog box to an application

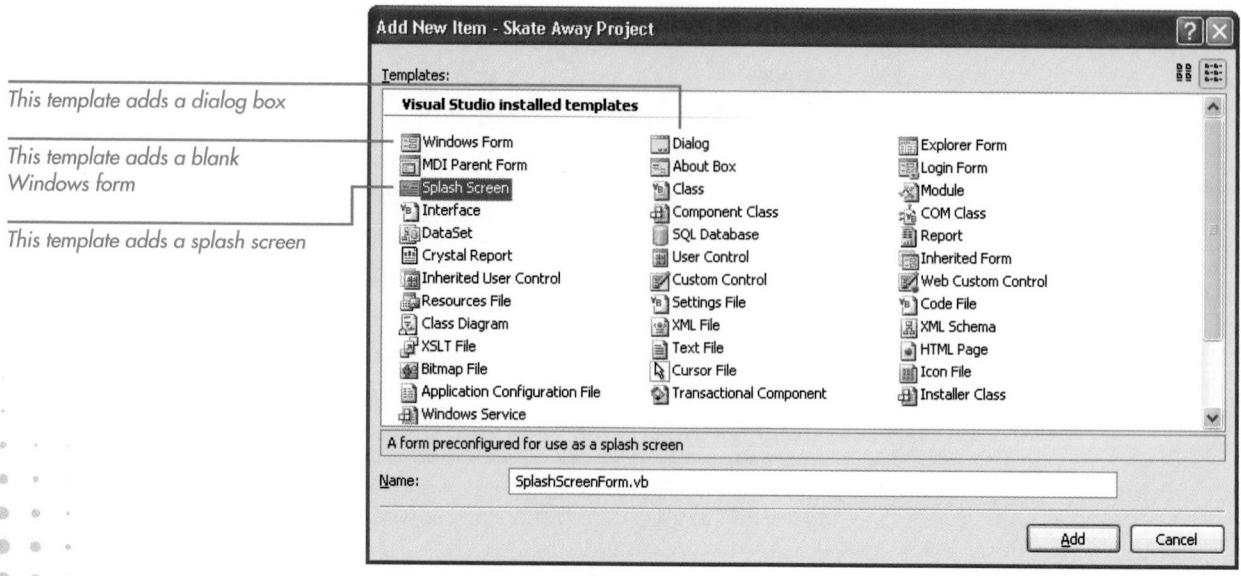

This template adds a dialog box

This template adds a blank
Windows form

This template adds a splash screen

**FIGURE 2.23**    Completed Add New Item - *<projectname>* dialog box

You can use the templates listed in the Add New Item - *<projectname>* dialog box to add many different items to an application. For example, the Splash Screen template adds a form that is already configured for use as a splash screen. The Dialog template, on the other hand, adds a form that resembles a standard dialog box. If you prefer to create your splash screen or dialog box from scratch, you can use the Windows Form template to add a blank Windows form to the application.

As you learned in Chapter 1, the computer automatically displays an application's startup form each time the application is started. In contrast, you must give the computer an explicit instruction to display a form that is not the startup form—for example, a form that represents a splash screen or dialog box. To display a form that is not the startup form, you use either the Show method or the ShowDialog method.

If you use the **Show method** in a form's code to open another form, then the newly opened form is modeless. A **modeless form** can remain displayed on the screen while the user completes other actions in the application, such as accessing the controls located on the original form. The user closes a modeless form by clicking the Close button on its title bar, or by clicking a button designated for this purpose on the form. Several modeless forms can be displayed at the same time in an application, and the user can switch the focus from one form to another. The Windows Form Designer, Solution Explorer, and Properties windows in Visual Basic are examples of modeless forms. The Find and Replace dialog box in Visual Studio is another example of a modeless form.

If you use the **ShowDialog method** in a form's code to open another form, then the newly opened form is modal. A **modal form** requires the user to take some action in the form before he or she can continue working in the application. The Font dialog box shown earlier in Figure 2.8 is an example of a modal form. When a modal form is displayed, no input from the keyboard or mouse can occur in the application until the form is closed.

Figure 2.24 shows the syntax of the Show and ShowDialog methods and includes an example of using each method. Most times, you will use the ShowDialog method to display the splash screens and dialog boxes in your applications.

TIP

To open the Find and Replace dialog box in Visual Studio, click Edit on the menu bar, point to Find and Replace, and then click an option on the menu.

TIP

Although you cannot access other forms in your application when a modal form is displayed, you can access other applications. You do so by clicking the application's button on the Windows taskbar.

## HOW TO...

**Use the Show and ShowDialog Methods**

**Syntax**
*formname*.**Show**()
*formname*.**ShowDialog**()

**Examples**
```
FindReplaceForm.Show()
```
displays the FindReplaceForm as a modeless form

```
FontForm.ShowDialog()
```
displays the FontForm as a modal form

**FIGURE 2.24**    How to use the Show and ShowDialog methods

When the Show method is used in code, the next line of code executes immediately after the modeless form is opened. In other words, if a procedure contains the `FindReplaceForm.Show()` instruction followed by the `stateTextBox.Text = "TN"` instruction, the "TN" will be assigned to the stateTextBox immediately after the FindReplaceForm is opened. In contrast, when the ShowDialog method is used in code, the next line of code does not execute until the modal form is closed. In this case, if a procedure contains the `FontForm.ShowDialog()` instruction followed by the `stateTextBox.Text = "TN"` instruction, the "TN" will not be assigned to the stateTextBox until after the FontForm is closed.

In most applications, a form that represents a splash screen closes after a specified period of time, without any intervention from the user. This typically is accomplished by including a timer control on the form. You create a timer control using the Timer tool in the toolbox.

## THE TIMER TOOL

The **Timer tool** is located in the Components section of the toolbox, and it is used to instantiate timer controls. The purpose of a **Timer control** is to process code at one or more regular intervals. The length of each interval is specified in milliseconds and entered in the timer's **Interval property**. A millisecond is $\frac{1}{1000}$ of a second. In other words, there are 1000 milliseconds in a second.

A timer's **Enabled property** indicates the timer's state, which can be either running (Enabled = True) or stopped (Enabled = False). If the timer is running, its Tick event occurs each time an interval has elapsed. Therefore, you enter the code you want processed in the timer's Tick event procedure. If the timer is stopped, on the other hand, the Tick event does not occur and the code entered in the Tick event procedure is not processed. Figure 2.25 lists the names and uses of several properties of a timer control.

# HOW TO...

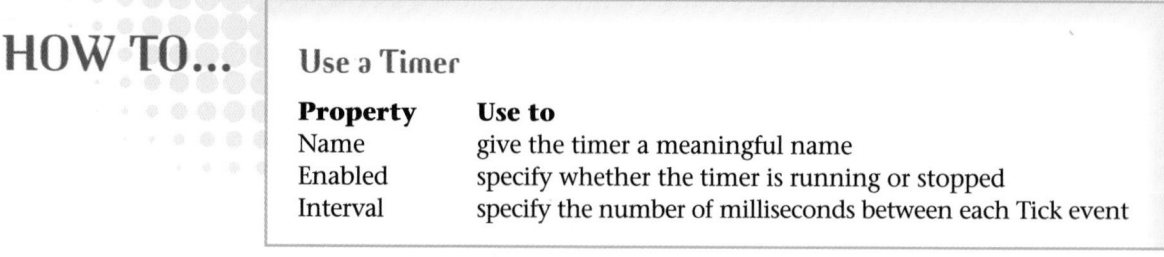

### Use a Timer

| Property | Use to |
|----------|--------|
| Name | give the timer a meaningful name |
| Enabled | specify whether the timer is running or stopped |
| Interval | specify the number of milliseconds between each Tick event |

**FIGURE 2.25**     How to use a timer

When you instantiate a timer control, the control does not appear on the form in the designer window. Instead, it is placed in a special area in the IDE, as shown in Figure 2.26. The special area is called the component tray.

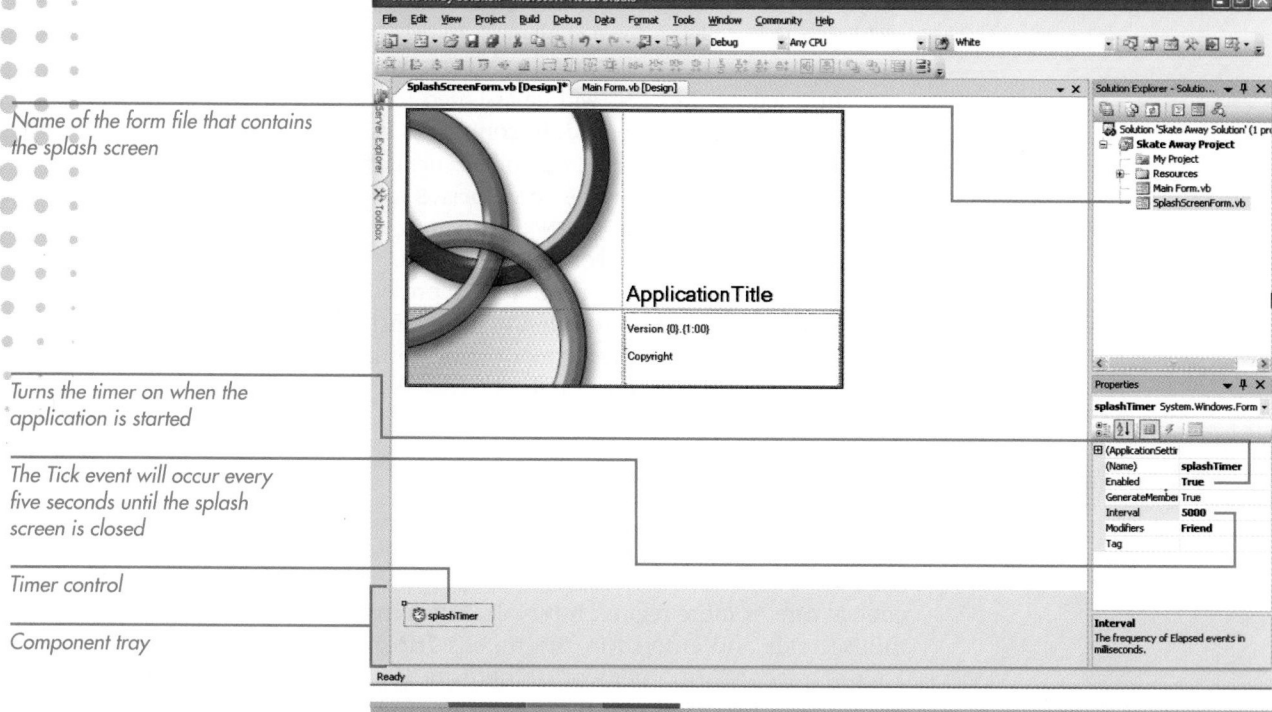

*Name of the form file that contains the splash screen*

*Turns the timer on when the application is started*

*The Tick event will occur every five seconds until the splash screen is closed*

*Timer control*

*Component tray*

**FIGURE 2.26**     Timer shown in the component tray

The **component tray** stores all controls that do not appear in the user interface when an application is running. In other words, the user will not see the timer when the splash screen appears on the screen.

Notice that the name of the form file that contains the splash screen is listed in the Solution Explorer window. Also notice that the timer's Enabled property is set to True, and its Interval property is set to 5000. Setting the timer's Enabled property to True tells the computer to start the timer as soon as the splash screen is opened. The number 5000 in the Interval property tells the computer to fire the timer's Tick event after five seconds, and continue to do so until the timer is disabled. You learn how to code a timer's Tick event procedure in the Programming Tutorial section of the chapter.

You have completed the concepts section of Chapter 2. The next section is the Programming Tutorial section, which gives you step-by-step instructions on how to apply the chapter's concepts to an application. A Programming Example follows the Programming Tutorial. The Programming Example is a completed program that demonstrates the concepts taught in the chapter. Following the Programming Example are the Quick Review, Key Terms, Self-Check Questions and Answers, Review Questions, Review Exercises – Short Answer, Computer Exercises, and Case Projects sections.

# PROGRAMMING TUTORIAL

## Creating the Color Game Application

In this tutorial, you create an application that can be used to teach a child the names of nine different colors. The application contains a primary window, a splash screen, and a dialog box, which are shown in Figures 2.27, 2.28, and 2.29, respectively.

*Table layout panel control*

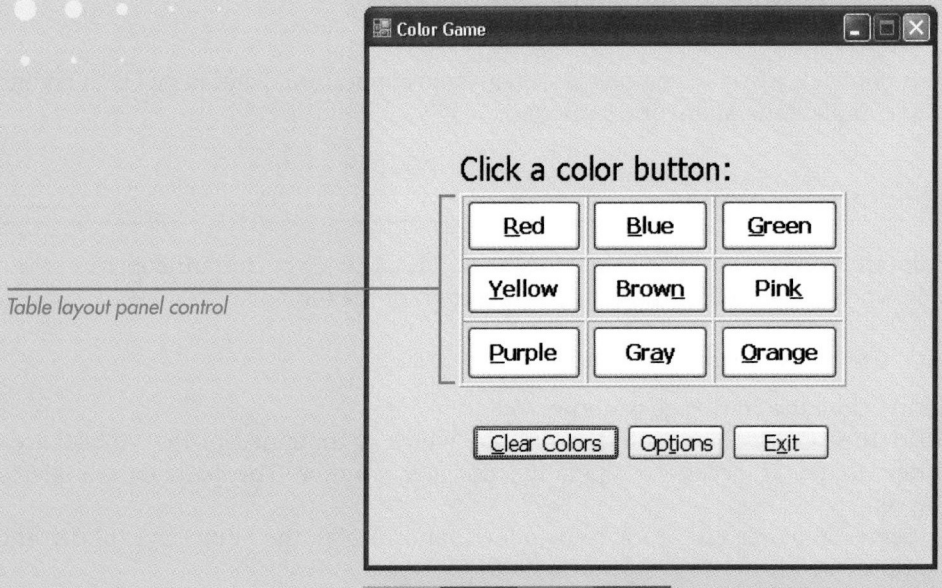

**FIGURE 2.27**   Primary window - MainForm

**FIGURE 2.28**    Splash screen - SplashScreenForm

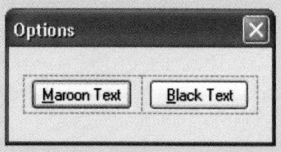

**FIGURE 2.29**    Dialog box - DialogForm

Included in the data files for this book is a partially completed Color Game application. Before you begin coding the application, you will need to complete the MainForm's interface.

## Completing the MainForm's Interface

Missing from the MainForm's interface is a table layout panel control. Recall that you instantiate the control using the TableLayoutPanel tool, which is located in the Containers section of the toolbox.

**To complete the MainForm's user interface:**

1. Start Visual Studio. If necessary, close the Start Page window.
2. Open the **Color Game Solution** (Color Game Solution.sln) file, which is contained in the VbReloaded\ Chap02\Color Game Solution folder. If necessary, open the designer window. The partially completed MainForm appears on the screen.
3. If necessary, auto-hide the Server Explorer and Toolbox windows, and display the Solution Explorer and Properties windows.
4. Set the MainForm's StartPosition property to **CenterScreen**.
5. In this application, you will not allow the user to maximize the MainForm. Set the MainForm's MaximizeBox property to **False**.
6. Use the TableLayoutPanel tool to add a table layout panel control to the form, as shown in Figure 2.30. If the task list is not open, click the **task box**.

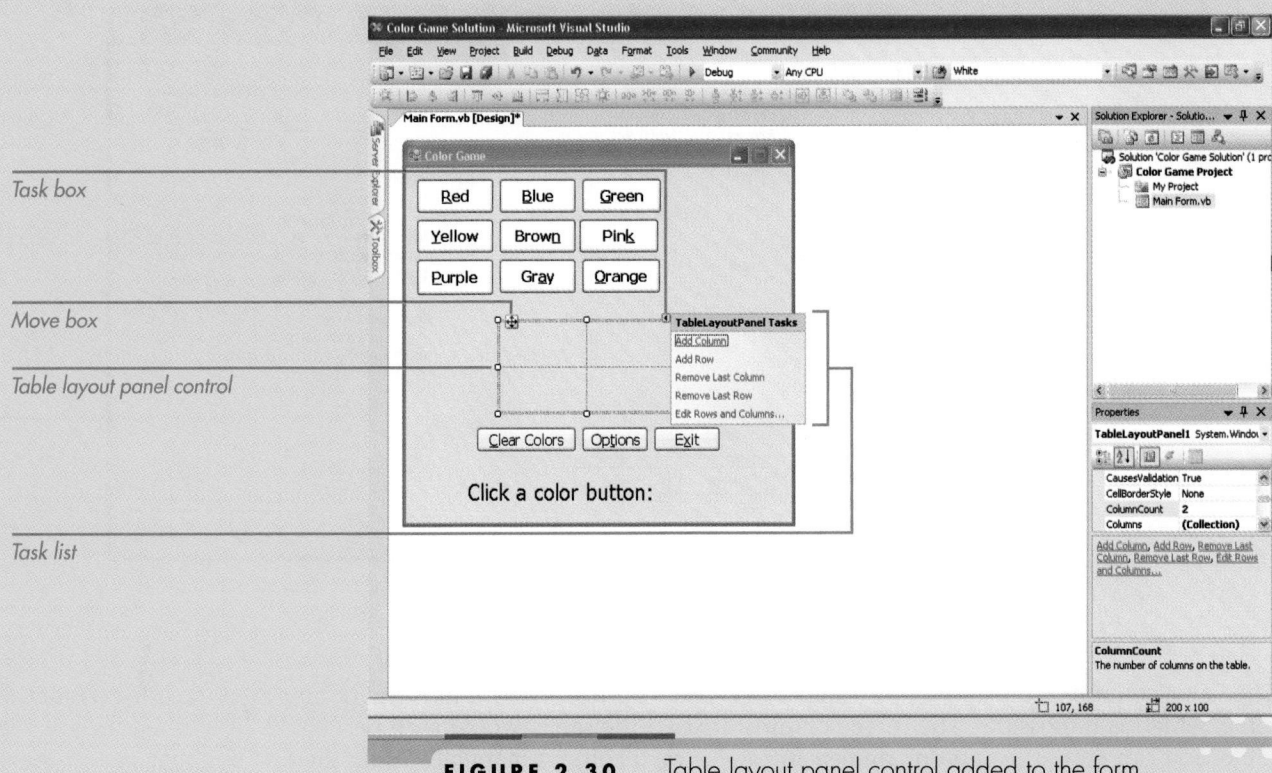

Task box

Move box

Table layout panel control

Task list

**FIGURE 2.30**   Table layout panel control added to the form

Notice that the table layout panel control contains a move box, which you can use to move the control to another area of the form. You move the control by placing your mouse pointer on the move box, and then dragging the control to the desired location.

Currently, the table layout panel control contains two rows and two columns. You will use the Add Column and Add Row options on the task list to add another column and row to the control.

7. Click **Add Column**, then click **Add Row**. The table layout panel control now contains three rows and three columns.

Next, you will use the Edit Rows and Columns option on the task list to make each column the same size, and also to make each row the same size.

8. Click **Edit Rows and Columns**. The Column and Row Styles dialog box opens. Click **Column3** in the Member list, then click the **Percent** radio button in the Size Type section of the dialog box, as shown in Figure 2.31.

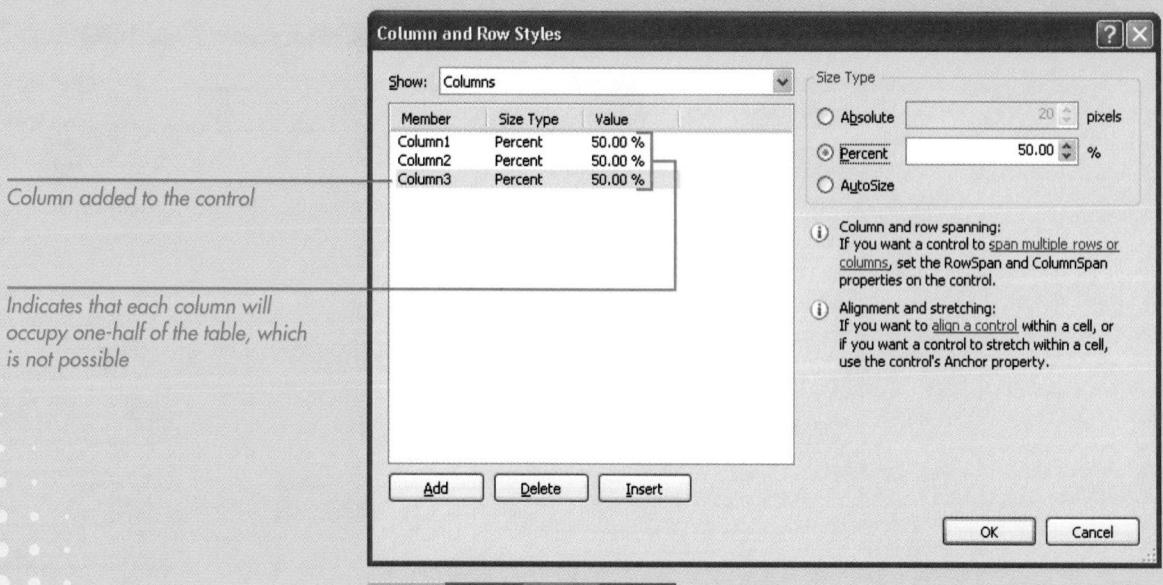

Column added to the control

Indicates that each column will
occupy one-half of the table, which
is not possible

**FIGURE 2.31**     Column and Row Styles dialog box

The Value column in the dialog box indicates that each of the three columns will occupy 50.00% (one-half) of the table, which is impossible. The three columns, if sized the same, would each occupy 33.33% (one-third) of the table. You can enter the appropriate percentage for each column manually, using the text box that appears next to the Percent radio button. Or, you can let the computer change the percentages for you; to do so, you simply click the OK button.

9. Click the **OK** button. The Column and Row Styles dialog box closes. Now verify that the computer changed the percentages to 33.33%. Click **Edit Rows and Columns** on the task list to open the Column and Row Styles dialog box. The dialog box now contains the correct percentages, as shown in Figure 2.32.

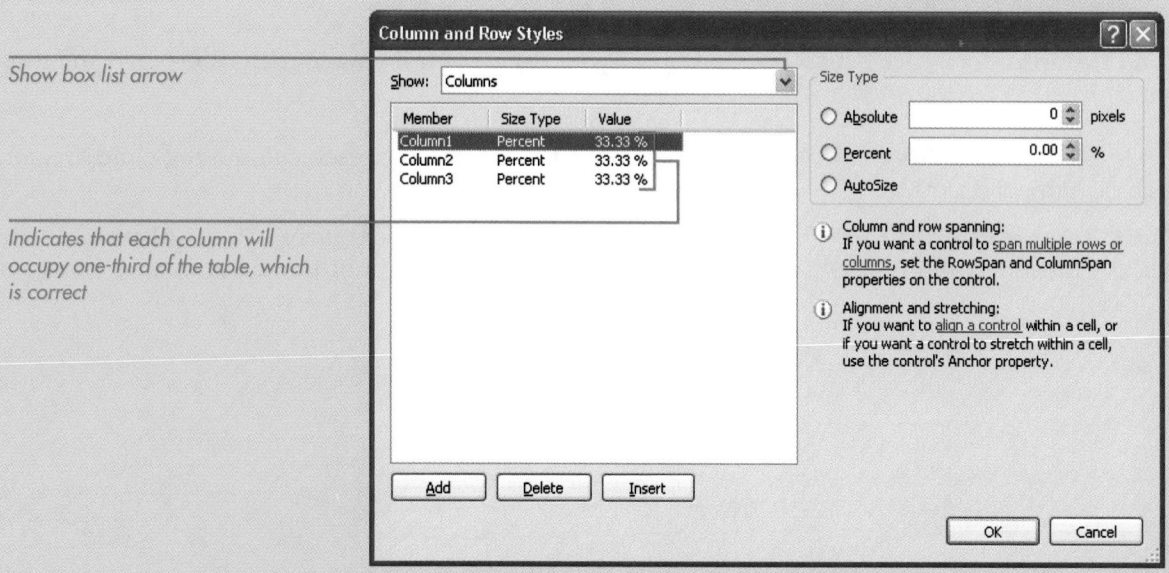

Show box list arrow

Indicates that each column will
occupy one-third of the table, which
is correct

**FIGURE 2.32**     Correct percentages shown in the Column and Row
Styles dialog box

Next, you will make the rows the same size.

10. Click the **list arrow** in the Show box, then click **Rows**. Click **Row3** in the Member list, then click the **Percent** radio button in the Size Type section of the dialog box. Click the **OK** button.

11. On your own, verify that the computer changed each row's percentage to 33.33% in the Column and Row Styles dialog box, then close the dialog box.

12. Now you will put a border around each cell in the table layout panel control. A cell is an intersection of a row and a column. The table layout panel control contains nine cells. Click **CellBorderStyle** in the Properties window, then click **OutsetDouble**.

13. Now make the table layout panel control larger. Click **Size** in the Properties window, then type **300, 146** and press **Enter**.

14. Now drag each of the nine color buttons into its own cell in the table layout panel. As you are dragging the buttons, try placing more than one button in the same cell. You will find that each cell in the table layout panel accepts only one control. Figure 2.33 shows the correct placement of the buttons in the table layout panel.

**TIP** If you need to put several controls in a cell, you can do so by first putting the controls in a panel control, and then placing the panel control in the cell.

You can put only one control in each cell

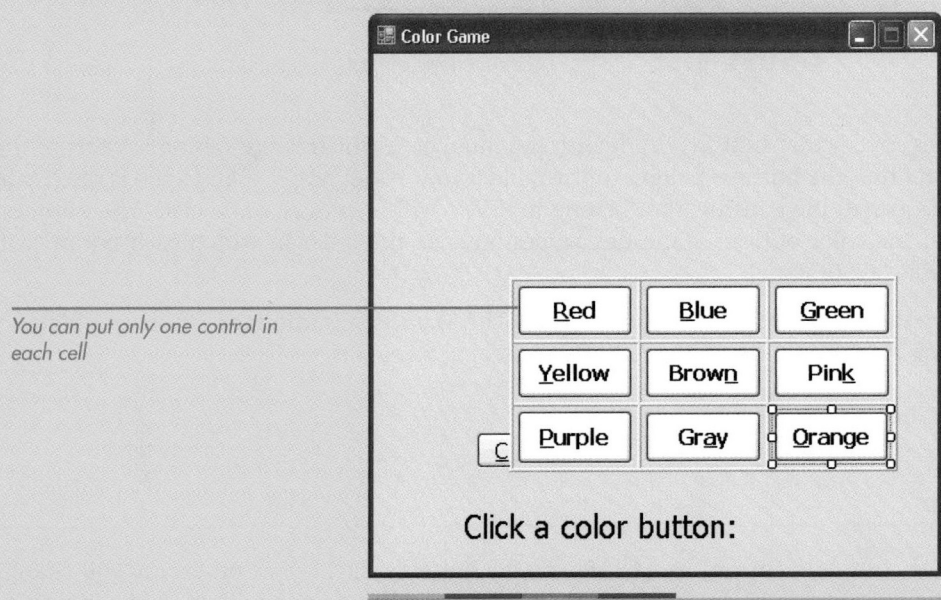

**FIGURE 2.33**    Buttons positioned in the table layout panel

15. Now you will position the table layout panel and the "Click a color button:" label appropriately. Click the **TableLayoutPanel1** control, then set its Location property to **71, 110**. Click the **Label1** control, then set its Location property to **68, 77**.

16. Now lock the controls in place on the form. Right-click the **MainForm**, then click **Lock Controls**.

17. Now set the TabIndex property for the controls. Click **View** on the menu bar, then click **Tab Order**. Use the information shown in Figure 2.34 to set the tab order.

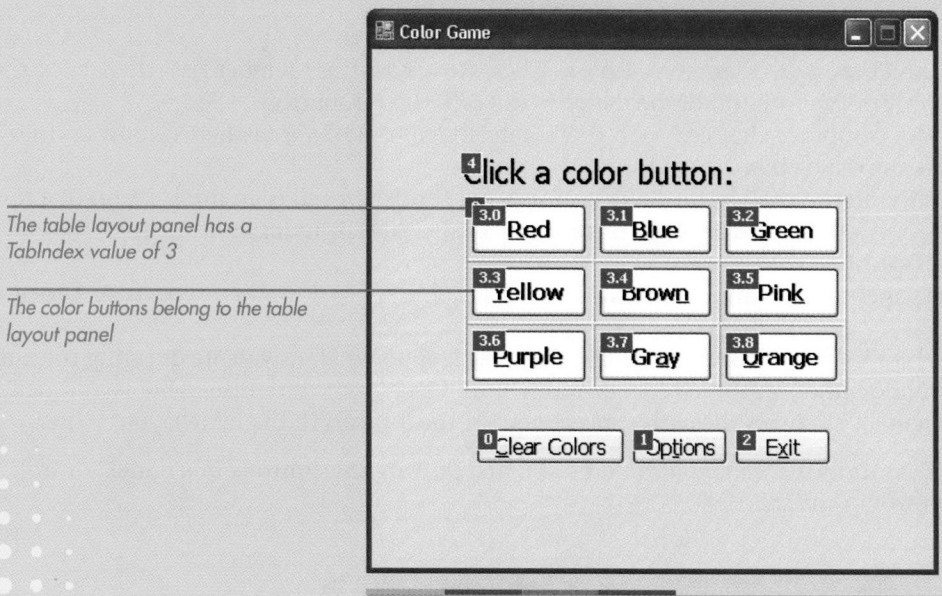

*The table layout panel has a TabIndex value of 3*

*The color buttons belong to the table layout panel*

**FIGURE 2.34**    Tab order for the controls in the interface

Notice that the TabIndex values of the color buttons begin with the number 3, which is the TabIndex value of the table layout panel; this indicates that the buttons belong to the table layout panel rather than to the form. If you move or delete the table layout panel, the controls that belong to it also will be moved or deleted. The numbers that appear after the period in the color buttons' TabIndex values indicate the order in which each button will receive the focus within the table layout panel.

18. Press the **Esc** key to remove the tab order boxes from the form. The MainForm's interface is now complete.
19. Save the solution by clicking **File** on the menu bar, and then clicking **Save All**.

Next, you begin coding the MainForm.

## Coding the MainForm

When the user clicks one of the color buttons on the MainForm, the button's Click event procedure will change the button's background to the appropriate color. For example, clicking the Red button will cause the button to be colored red. Similarly, when the user clicks the Clear Colors button, the button's Click event procedure will change each color button's background to white. The user can click the Exit button to end the application, and he or she can click the Options button to open the dialog box shown earlier in Figure 2.29.

Figure 2.35 shows the TOE chart for the MainForm. For now, do not worry about the last task, which is to "Display the SplashScreenForm" (shown earlier in Figure 2.28). You learn how to display the splash screen later in this tutorial.

| Task | Object | Event |
|---|---|---|
| Change the button's background to the appropriate color | blueButton, brownButton, grayButton, greenButton, orangeButton, pinkButton, purpleButton, redButton, yellowButton | Click |
| Change the background of the nine color buttons to white | clearButton | Click |
| End the application | exitButton | Click |
| Display the DialogForm | optionsButton | Click |
| Display the SplashScreenForm | MainForm | Load |

**FIGURE 2.35**    TOE chart for the MainForm

First you will code the color buttons' Click event procedures.

### Coding the Color Buttons' Click Event Procedures

According to the TOE chart, each color button's Click event procedure is responsible for changing the button's background to the appropriate color. The background color of a control is specified in the control's **BackColor property**. To change the value stored in the BackColor property while an application is running, you use an assignment statement in the following format: *controlname*.**BackColor** = *color*. In the assignment statement, *controlname* is the name of the control whose BackColor property you want to change, and *color* is the name of a color.

**To code the color buttons' Click event procedures:**

1. Open the Code Editor window by right-clicking the **form** and then clicking **View Code**. Notice that the exitButton's Click event procedure already contains the `Me.Close()` instruction.
2. Click the **Class Name** list arrow, and then click **blueButton** in the list. Click the **Method Name** list arrow, and then click **Click** in the list. The code template for the blueButton's Click event procedure appears in the Code Editor window.
3. Type **bluebutton.backcolor = color.blue** and press **Enter**.
4. On your own, code the Click event procedures for the remaining eight color buttons. You should assign the following colors to the buttons' BackColor properties: Color.Brown, Color.Gray, Color.Green, Color.Orange, Color.Pink, Color.Purple, Color.Red, and Color.Yellow. (If you need help, you can refer to the MainForm's code shown in Figure 2.45.)
5. Save the solution.
6. Start the application by clicking **Debug** on the menu bar, and then clicking **Start Debugging**.
7. Click **each of the color buttons** to verify that the code you entered is working correctly. Figure 2.36 shows the MainForm after all of the color buttons were clicked.

**FIGURE 2.36**     Result of clicking the color buttons

8. Click the **Exit** button to end the application. If necessary, close the Output window.

Next, you code the Click event procedure for the Clear Colors button.

### Coding the Clear Colors Button's Click Event Procedure

According to the TOE chart, the Clear Colors button, which is named clearButton, should change the background of each color button to white.

**To code the clearButton's Click event procedure:**

1. Open the code template for the clearButton's Click event procedure.
2. Type **bluebutton.backcolor = color.white** and press **Enter**.
3. On your own, assign Color.White to the BackColor property of the remaining eight color buttons. (If you need help, you can refer to the MainForm's code shown in Figure 2.45.)
4. Save the solution, then start the application by pressing the **F5** key on your keyboard.
5. Click **each of the color buttons**, then click the **Clear Colors** button. The background of each color button should be white.
6. Click the **Exit** button to end the application. If necessary, close the Output window.

According to the TOE chart for the MainForm, the optionButton's Click event procedure should display the DialogForm (shown earlier in Figure 2.29). As you may remember, the form represents a dialog box. Before you can code the event procedure, you need to add the DialogForm to the Color Game project.

## Adding the DialogForm to the Color Game Project

Recall that you use the Add New Item - *<projectname>* dialog box to add a form to a project.

**To add a dialog box form to the Color Game project:**

1. Click **Project** on the menu bar, then click **Add Windows Form**. The Add New Item – Color Game Project dialog box opens.
2. Click **Dialog** in the list of templates.
3. Type **Dialog Form.vb** in the Name box. See Figure 2.37.

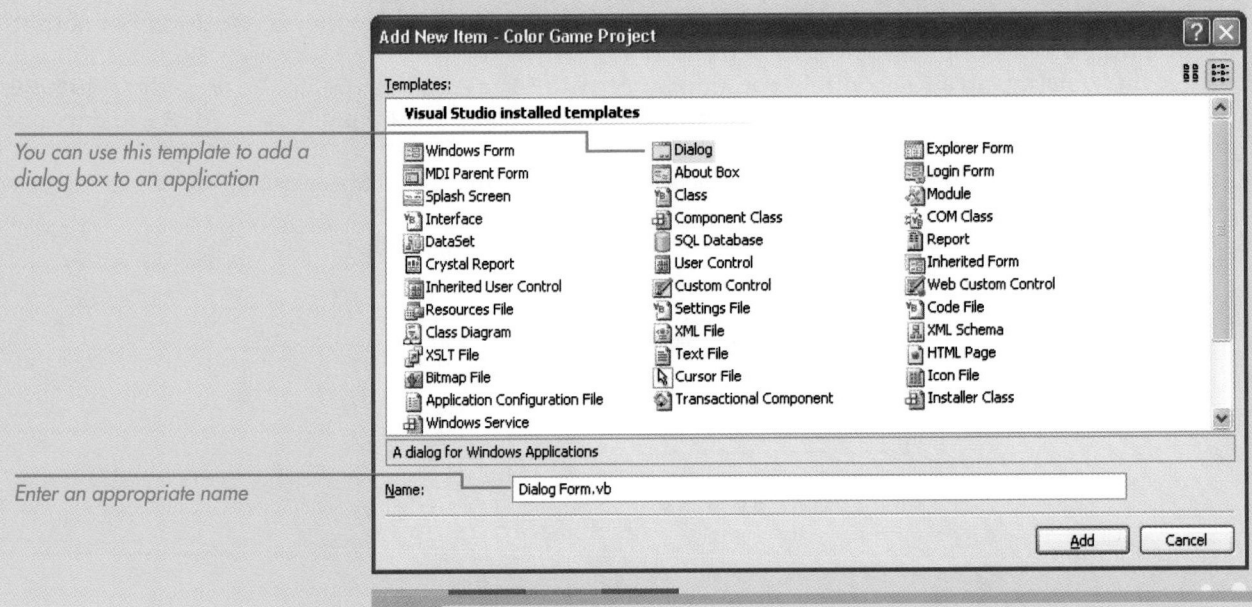

You can use this template to add a dialog box to an application

Enter an appropriate name

**FIGURE 2.37**     Completed Add New Item - Color Game Project dialog box

4. Click the **Add** button. A form representing a dialog box is added to the project, as shown in Figure 2.38. Automatically included on the form is a table layout panel control, which contains the OK and Cancel buttons found in most dialog boxes.

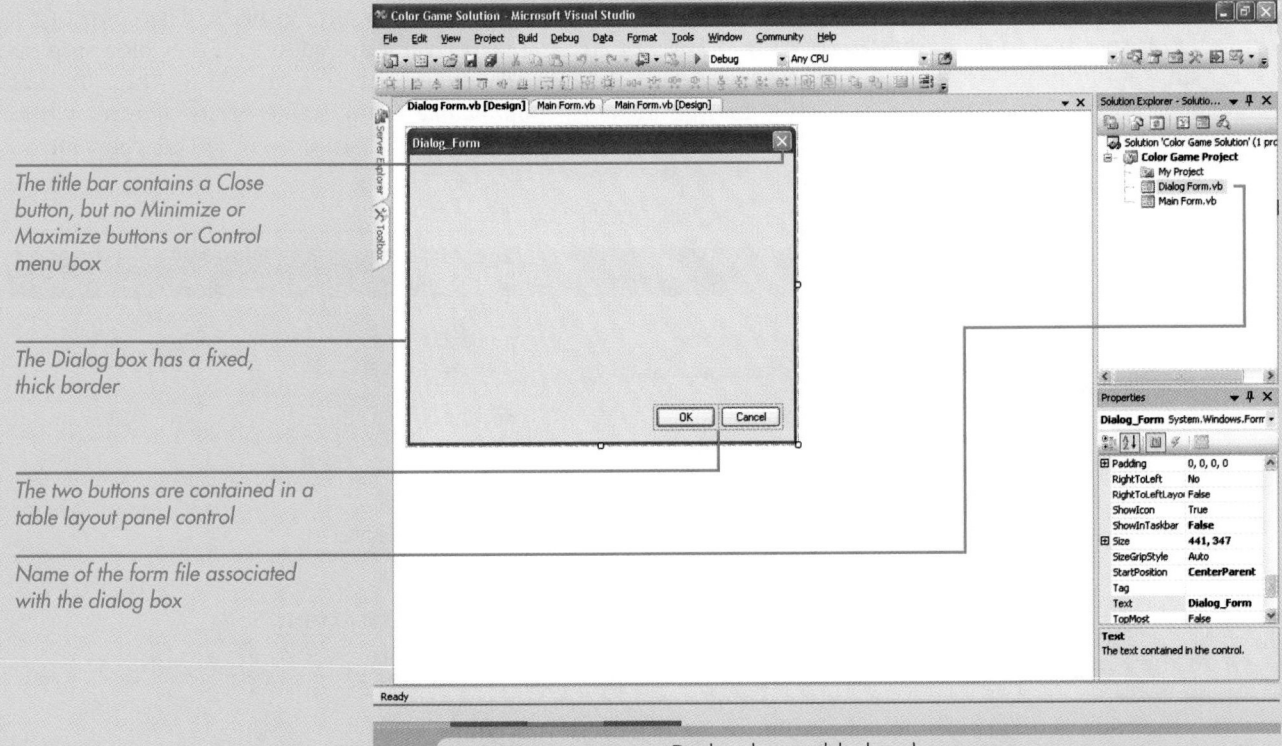

The title bar contains a Close button, but no Minimize or Maximize buttons or Control menu box

The Dialog box has a fixed, thick border

The two buttons are contained in a table layout panel control

Name of the form file associated with the dialog box

**FIGURE 2.38**     Dialog box added to the project

5. Change the form's name from Dialog_Form to **DialogForm**.
6. Scan the DialogForm's Properties list. Notice that the FormBorderStyle property is already set to FixedDialog, and the MaximizeBox and MinimizeBox properties are set to False.

7. Change the DialogForm's Size property to **210, 103**, and change its Text property to **Options**. Set both its AcceptButton and CancelButton properties to **(none)**.
8. Change the TableLayoutPanel1 control's Location property to **11, 21**, and change its Size property to **182, 29**.
9. Change the OK button's Name property to **maroonButton**. Change its Size property to **78, 23**, and its Text property to **&Maroon Text**.
10. Change the Cancel button's Name property to **blackButton**. Change its Size property to **78, 23**, and its Text property to **&Black Text**. Change its DialogResult property to **None**.
11. Lock the controls on the form. Figure 2.39 shows the completed DialogForm.

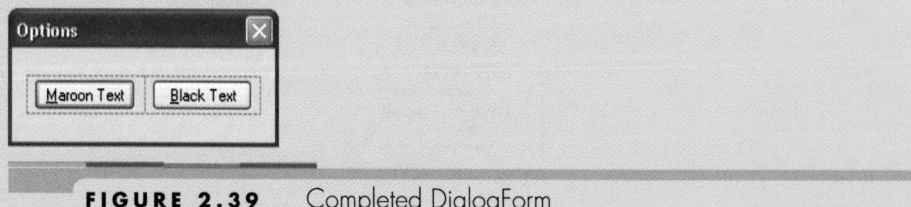

**FIGURE 2.39**   Completed DialogForm

12. Save the solution.

Now you can code the appropriate events in the DialogForm, and also code the Options button on the MainForm.

## Coding the DialogForm and the Options Button

When the user clicks the Maroon Text button in the DialogForm, the button's Click event procedure should change the color of the MainForm's text to maroon. Similarly, when the user clicks the Black Text button in the DialogForm, the button's Click event procedure should change the MainForm's text to black. The color of the form's text is specified in the form's **ForeColor property**. To change the value stored in the ForeColor property while an application is running, you use an assignment statement in the following format: *controlname*.**ForeColor** = *color*. In the assignment statement, *controlname* is the name of the control whose ForeColor property you want to change, and *color* is the name of a color. Figure 2.40 shows the TOE chart for the DialogForm.

| Task | Object | Event |
|------|--------|-------|
| Change the color of the MainForm's text to maroon | maroonButton | Click |
| Change the color of the MainForm's text to black | blackButton | Click |

**FIGURE 2.40**   TOE chart for the DialogForm

**To code the Click event procedures for the maroonButton and blackButton:**

1. Open the Code Editor window. Delete the code that appears between the `Public Class` and `End Class` statements.
2. Open the code template for the maroonButton's Click event procedure.
3. Type **mainform.forecolor = color.maroon** and press **Enter**.
4. Open the code template for the blackButton's Click event procedure.
5. Enter the appropriate assignment statement to change the MainForm's text to black.
6. Close the Dialog Form.vb window, then save the solution.

Next, you will code the Click event procedure for the optionsButton, which is on the MainForm. The procedure is assigned the task of displaying the DialogForm. Recall that you can display a form using either the Show method or the ShowDialog method. The method you choose depends on whether you want the form to be modal (ShowDialog) or modeless (Show). To give you an opportunity to use both methods, you will display the DialogForm as a modeless form, and, later in this tutorial, you will display the SplashScreenForm as a modal form.

**To code the Click event procedure for the optionsButton:**

1. Click the **Main Form.vb** tab in the IDE to display the Code Editor window for the MainForm.
2. Open the code template for the optionsButton's Click event procedure.
3. Type **dialogform.show()** and press **Enter**.
4. Save the solution, then start the application.
5. Click the **Options** button to open the DialogForm.
6. Click the **Maroon Text** button. The color of the text on the MainForm changes from black to maroon.
7. Click the **Pink** button on the MainForm. Notice that you can access the MainForm without having to close the DialogForm; this is because the DialogForm is modeless. See Figure 2.41. (Do not be concerned if the DialogForm on your screen appears in a different location.)

*The DialogForm is modeless*

*You can work in the MainForm while the DialogForm is open*

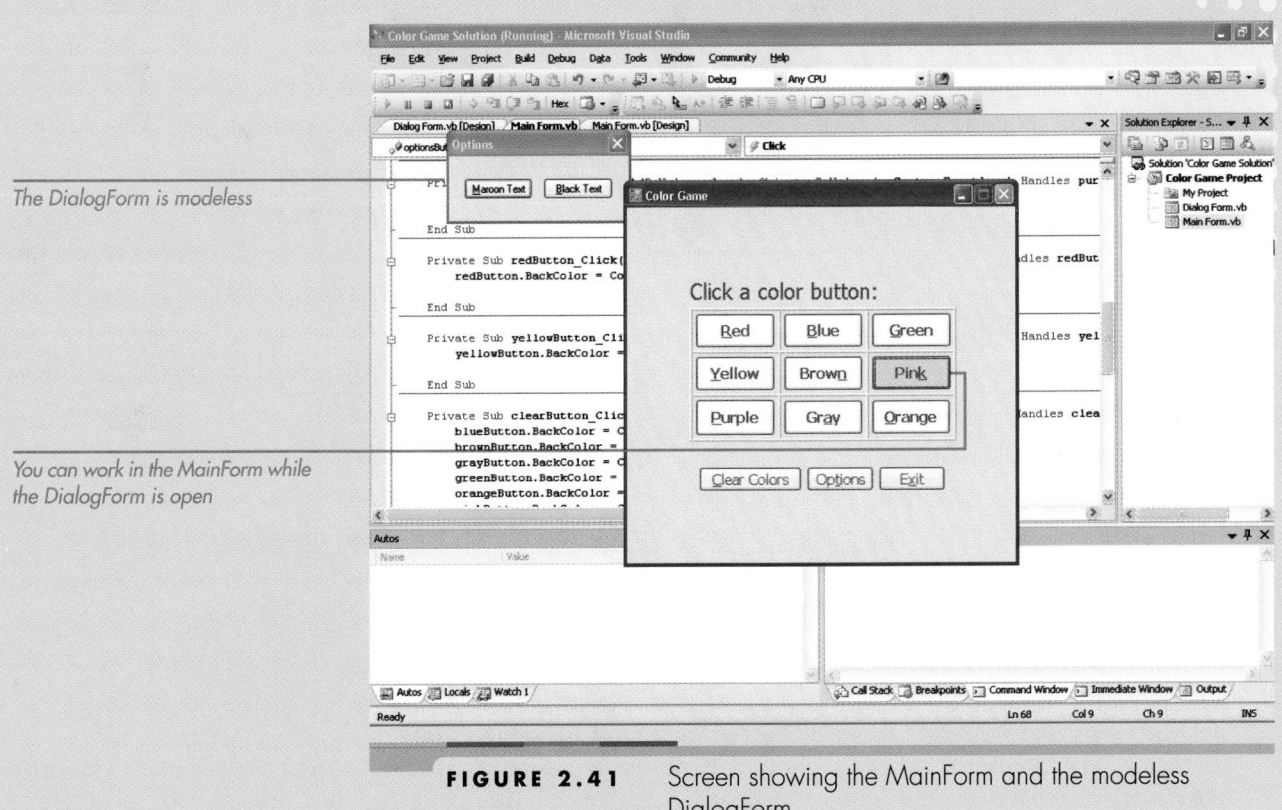

**FIGURE 2.41**   Screen showing the MainForm and the modeless DialogForm

8. Click the **Black Text** button on the DialogForm. The color of the text on the MainForm changes from maroon to black.
9. Close the DialogForm by clicking the **Close** button on its title bar.
10. Click the **Exit** button to end the application. If necessary, close the Output window.

According to the MainForm's TOE chart (shown earlier in Figure 2.35), you still need to code the MainForm's Load event procedure. The procedure is assigned the task of displaying the SplashScreenForm. Before you can code the event procedure, you need to add the SplashScreenForm to the Color Game project.

## Adding the SplashScreenForm to the Color Game Project

Just as you did earlier, you will use the Add New Item - *<projectname>* dialog box to add another form to the project. In this case, however, the form will represent a splash screen rather than a dialog box.

**To add a splash screen form to the Color Game project, and then add a timer control to the form:**

1. Click **Project** on the menu bar, then click **Add Windows Form**. The Add New Item – Color Game Project dialog box opens.
2. Click **Splash Screen** in the list of templates. Type **SplashScreenForm.vb** in the Name box, and then click the **Add** button. A form representing a splash screen is added to the project, as shown in Figure 2.42. Automatically included on the form are three labels and two table layout panel controls.

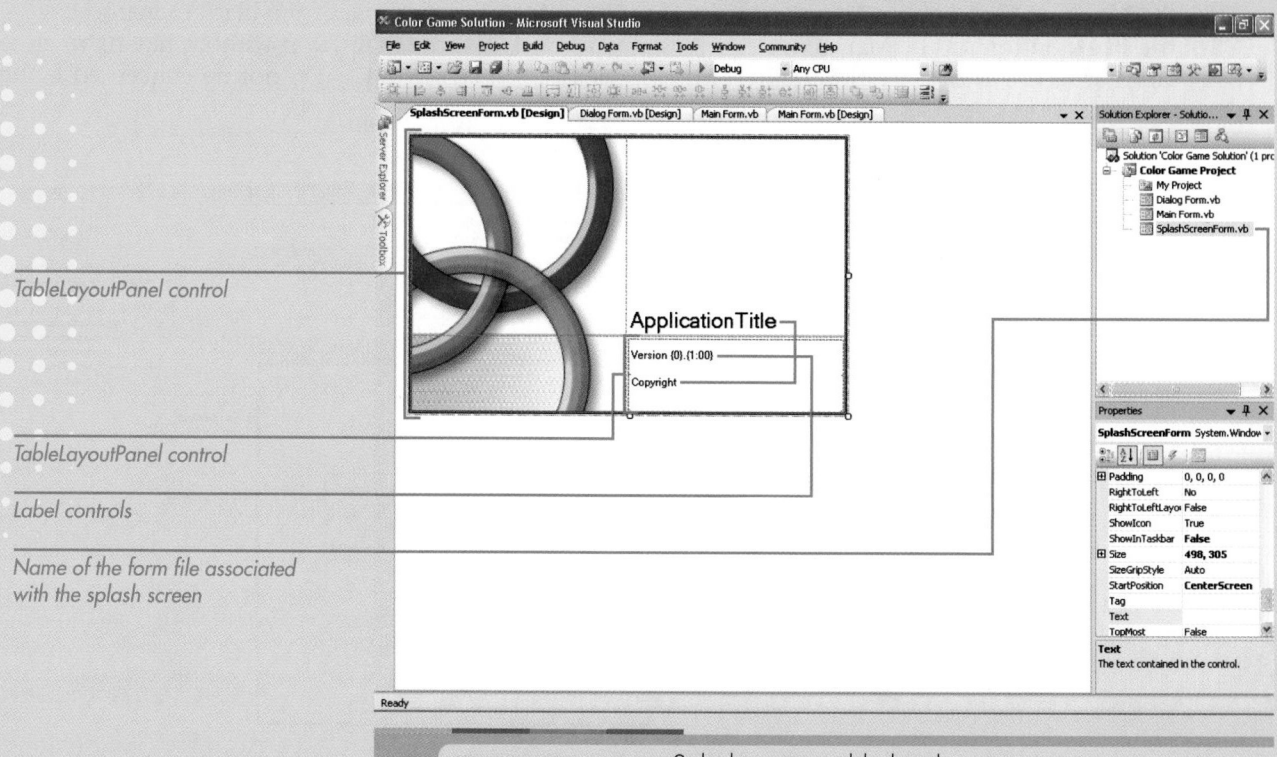

**FIGURE 2.42**     Splash screen added to the project

3. Click the **ApplicationTitle** label, then set its Text property to **Color Game**.
4. Click the **Version** label, then set its Text property to **Version 1**.
5. Click the **Copyright** label, then set its Text property to **Copyright 2007**.
6. Right-click **My Project** in the Solution Explorer window, then click **Open**. Click the **Assembly Information** button on the Application pane. Change the Title box's text to **Color Game**. If necessary, change the year number in the Copyright box to **2007**. Click the **OK** button, then close the Color Game Project window.

As you learned in the concepts section of the chapter, most splash screens use a timer control to close the splash screen after a specified period of time has elapsed. You will add a timer control to the SplashScreenForm, and you will specify the period of time as five seconds, which is 5000 milliseconds.

7. Double-click the **Timer tool**, which is located in the Components section of the toolbox. A timer control appears in the component tray. Change the timer control's Name property to **splashTimer**. Change its Enabled property to **True**, and its Interval property to **5000**. See Figure 2.43.

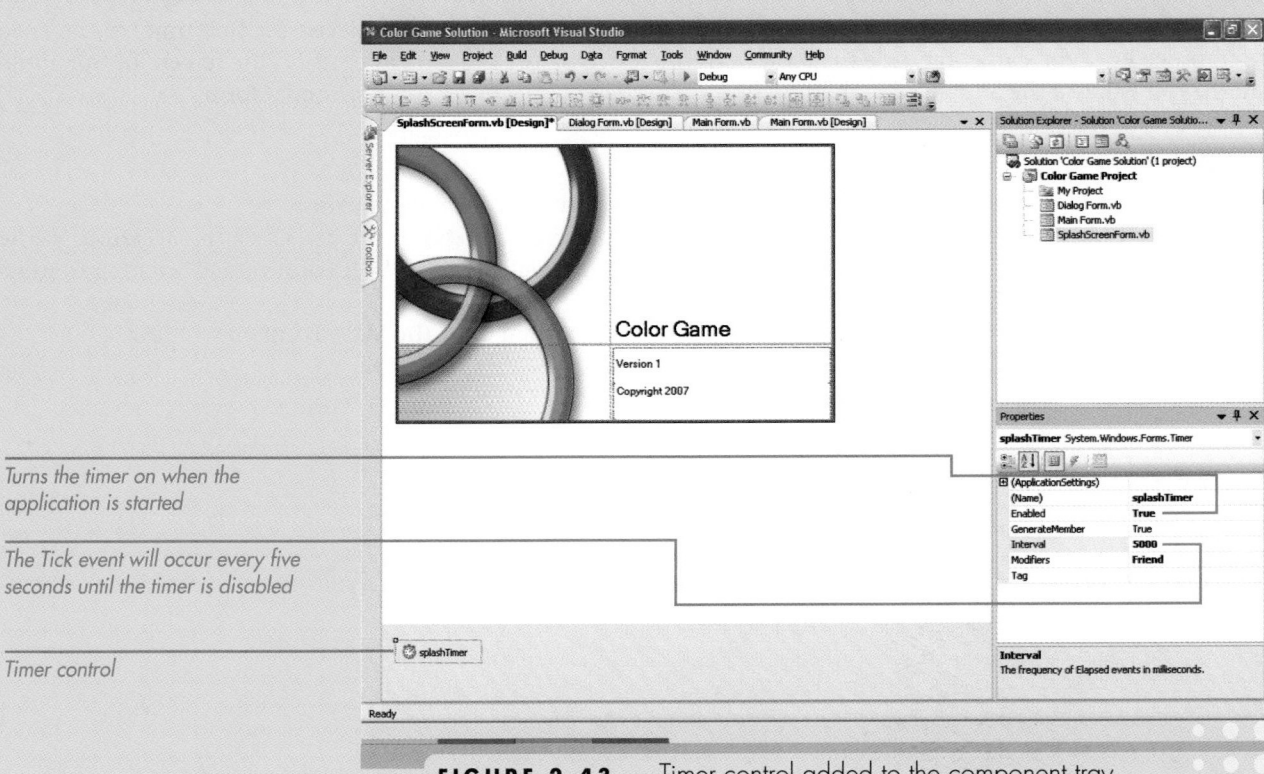

*Turns the timer on when the application is started*

*The Tick event will occur every five seconds until the timer is disabled*

*Timer control*

**FIGURE 2.43**    Timer control added to the component tray

Now you can finish coding the Color Game application. All you have left to code is the Tick event procedure for the splashTimer, and the MainForm's Load event procedure.

## Completing the Color Game Application

Figure 2.44 shows the TOE chart for the SplashScreenForm. Notice that you have only one event procedure to code in this form: the splashTimer's Tick event procedure. The procedure is assigned the tasks of disabling the timer and closing the SplashScreenForm.

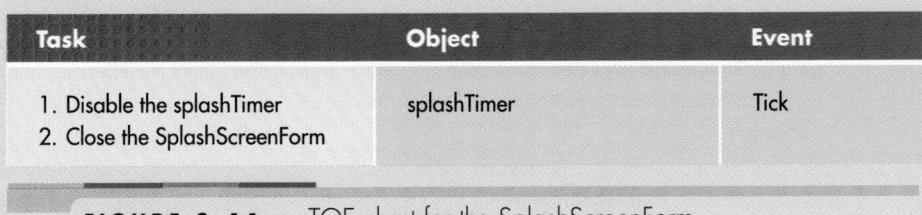

| Task | Object | Event |
|------|--------|-------|
| 1. Disable the splashTimer<br>2. Close the SplashScreenForm | splashTimer | Tick |

**FIGURE 2.44**    TOE chart for the SplashScreenForm

**To code the splashTimer's Tick event procedure:**

1. Open the Code Editor window by right-clicking the **form**, and then clicking **View Code**. For now, do not be concerned about the code that appears in the Code Editor window.
2. Open the code template for the splashTimer's Tick event procedure.
3. Type **splashtimer.enabled = false** and press **Enter**, then type **me.close()** and press **Enter**.
4. Close the SplashScreenForm.vb window, then save the solution.

The last procedure you need to code is the MainForm's Load event procedure. As you may remember from the TOE chart shown earlier in Figure 2.35, the MainForm's Load event procedure is assigned the task of displaying the SplashScreenForm.

A form's **Load event** occurs when an application is started and the form is displayed the first time. In the Load event procedure, you can enter code that you want processed before the form appears on the screen. In this application, you will use the ShowDialog method to display the SplashScreenForm as a modal form.

**To code the MainForm's Load event procedure:**

1. Click the **Main Form.vb** tab to display the Code Editor window for the MainForm.
2. Click the **Class Name** list arrow, and then click **(MainForm Events)** in the list. Click the **Method Name** list arrow, and then click **Load** in the list. The code template for the MainForm's Load event procedure appears in the Code Editor window.
3. Type **splashscreenform.showdialog()** and press **Enter**, then close the Main Form.vb window.
4. Save the solution. Figure 2.45 shows the code for the Color Game application.

---

**MainForm's code**

```vb
Public Class MainForm
    Private Sub exitButton_Click(ByVal sender As Object, _
        ByVal e As System.EventArgs) Handles exitButton.Click
        Me.Close()
    End Sub


    Private Sub blueButton_Click(ByVal sender As Object, _
        ByVal e As System.EventArgs) Handles blueButton.Click
        blueButton.BackColor = Color.Blue
    End Sub


    Private Sub brownButton_Click(ByVal sender As Object, _
        ByVal e As System.EventArgs) Handles brownButton.Click
        brownButton.BackColor = Color.Brown
    End Sub


    Private Sub grayButton_Click(ByVal sender As Object, _
        ByVal e As System.EventArgs) Handles grayButton.Click
        grayButton.BackColor = Color.Gray
    End Sub


    Private Sub greenButton_Click(ByVal sender As Object, _
        ByVal e As System.EventArgs) Handles greenButton.Click
        greenButton.BackColor = Color.Green
    End Sub


    Private Sub orangeButton_Click(ByVal sender As Object, _
        ByVal e As System.EventArgs) Handles orangeButton.Click
        orangeButton.BackColor = Color.Orange
    End Sub


    Private Sub pinkButton_Click(ByVal sender As Object, _
        ByVal e As System.EventArgs) Handles pinkButton.Click
        pinkButton.BackColor = Color.Pink
    End Sub
```

*(Figure is continued on next page)*

```
        Private Sub purpleButton_Click(ByVal sender As Object, _
            ByVal e As System.EventArgs) Handles purpleButton.Click
            purpleButton.BackColor = Color.Purple
        End Sub

        Private Sub redButton_Click(ByVal sender As Object, _
            ByVal e As System.EventArgs) Handles redButton.Click
            redButton.BackColor = Color.Red
        End Sub

        Private Sub yellowButton_Click(ByVal sender As Object, _
            ByVal e As System.EventArgs) Handles yellowButton.Click
            yellowButton.BackColor = Color.Yellow
        End Sub

        Private Sub clearButton_Click(ByVal sender As Object, _
            ByVal e As System.EventArgs) Handles clearButton.Click
            blueButton.BackColor = Color.White
            brownButton.BackColor = Color.White
            grayButton.BackColor = Color.White
            greenButton.BackColor = Color.White
            orangeButton.BackColor = Color.White
            pinkButton.BackColor = Color.White
            purpleButton.BackColor = Color.White
            redButton.BackColor = Color.White
            yellowButton.BackColor = Color.White
        End Sub

        Private Sub optionsButton_Click(ByVal sender As Object, _
            ByVal e As System.EventArgs) Handles optionsButton.Click
            DialogForm.Show()
        End Sub

        Private Sub MainForm_Load(ByVal sender As Object, _
            ByVal e As System.EventArgs) Handles Me.Load
            SplashScreenForm.ShowDialog()
        End Sub
    End Class
```

**DialogForm's code**

```
Public Class DialogForm

    Private Sub maroonButton_Click(ByVal sender As Object, _
        ByVal e As System.EventArgs) Handles maroonButton.Click
        MainForm.ForeColor = Color.Maroon
    End Sub

    Private Sub blackButton_Click(ByVal sender As Object, _
        ByVal e As System.EventArgs) Handles blackButton.Click
```

*(Figure is continued on next page)*

```
            MainForm.ForeColor = Color.Black
        End Sub
    End Class
```

**SplashScreenForm's code (only the code you entered is shown)**

```
    Private Sub splashTimer_Tick(ByVal sender As Object, _
        ByVal e As System.EventArgs) Handles splashTimer.Tick
        splashTimer.Enabled = False
        Me.Close()
    End Sub
```

**FIGURE 2.45**    Color Game application's code

Now test the application to verify that it is working correctly.

**To test the application:**

1. Start the application. Because the MainForm is the startup form, the computer will automatically display it. Before doing so, however, the computer processes the `SplashScreenForm.ShowDialog()` instruction contained in the MainForm's Load event procedure. The instruction tells the computer to display the SplashScreenForm first, and display it as a modal form. See Figure 2.46.

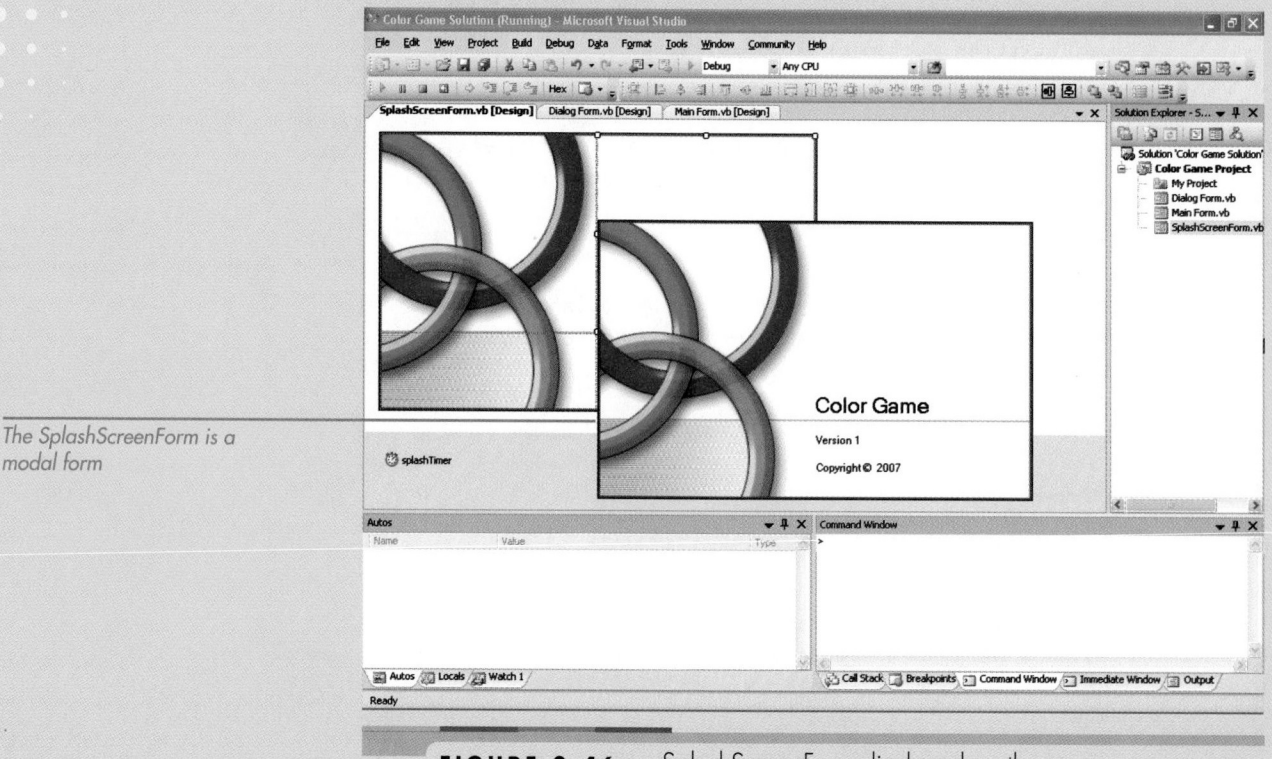

*The SplashScreenForm is a modal form*

**FIGURE 2.46**    SplashScreenForm displayed on the screen

Because the SplashScreenForm is a modal form, no further activity can occur in the application until the SplashScreenForm is closed. Recall that you assigned the task of closing the form to the splashTimer, which begins counting as soon as the SplashScreenForm is displayed. When five seconds have elapsed, the splashTimer's Tick event occurs and the instructions contained in the Tick event procedure are processed. The instructions tell the computer to disable the timer and then close the current form, which is the SplashScreenForm. After the computer closes the modal SplashScreenForm, it then displays the startup form, MainForm.

2. Click the **Options** button on the MainForm. The computer processes the `DialogForm.Show()` instruction contained in the optionsButton's Click event procedure. The instruction tells the computer to display the DialogForm as a modeless form. See Figure 2.47.

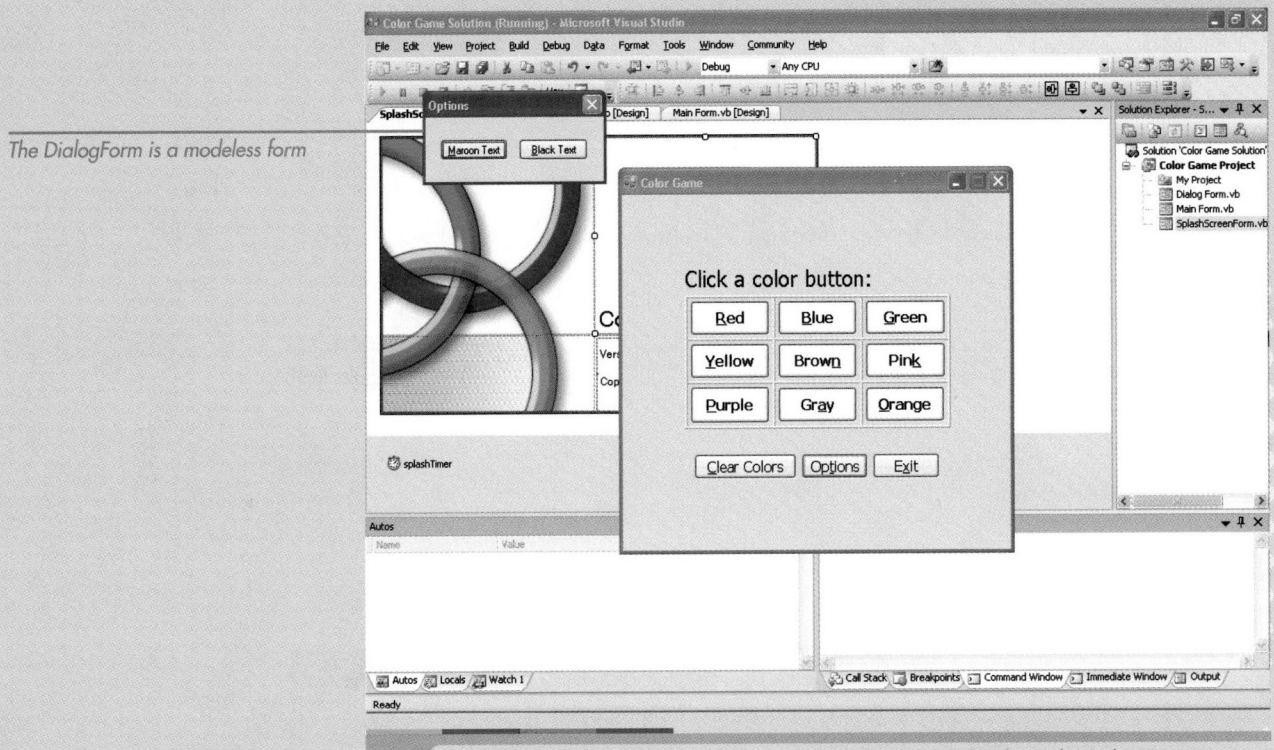

*The DialogForm is a modeless form*

**FIGURE 2.47**    MainForm and DialogForm displayed on the screen

Because the DialogForm is modeless, you can leave it displayed while you are working in the MainForm.

3. Close the DialogForm by clicking its **Close** button.
4. Click the **Exit** button to end the application. If necessary, close the Output window.
5. Click **File** on the menu bar, and then click **Close Solution**.

# PROGRAMMING EXAMPLE

## Moonbucks Coffee

Create a user interface that allows the user to enter the following customer information: name, address, city, state, ZIP code, the number of pounds of regular coffee ordered, and the number of pounds of decaffeinated coffee ordered. The interface will need to display the total number of pounds of coffee ordered and the total price of the order. Name the solution Moonbucks Solution. Name the project Moonbucks Project. Name the form file Main Form.vb. Save the files in the VbReloaded\Chap02 folder.

**TOE Chart:**

| Task | Object | Event |
|---|---|---|
| 1. Calculate the total pounds of coffee ordered and the total price of the order<br>2. Display the total pounds of coffee ordered and the total price of the order in totalPoundsLabel and totalPriceLabel | calcButton | Click |
| Clear the screen for the next order | clearButton | Click |
| End the application | exitButton | Click |
| Display the total pounds of coffee ordered (from calcButton) | totalPoundsLabel | None |
| Display the total price of the order (from calcButton) | totalPriceLabel | None |
| Get and display the order information | nameTextBox, addressTextBox, cityTextBox, stateTextBox, zipTextBox, regularTextBox, decafTextBox | None |

**FIGURE 2.48**

**User Interface:**

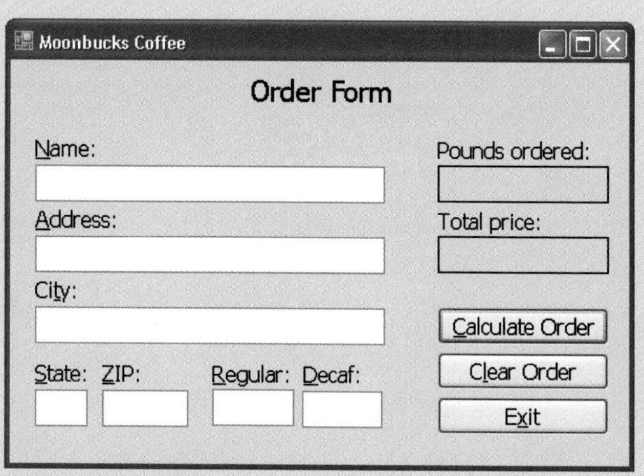

**FIGURE 2.49**

## Objects, Properties, and Settings:

| Object | Property | Setting |
|--------|----------|---------|
| Form1 | Name | MainForm (be sure to change the startup form to this name) |
| | AcceptButton | calcButton |
| | CancelButton | exitButton |
| | Font | Tahoma, 12 point (change this before adding any controls) |
| | Size | 480, 330 |
| | StartPosition | CenterScreen |
| | Text | Moonbucks Coffee |
| Label1 | AutoSize | True |
| | Font | Tahoma, 16 point |
| | Text | Order Form |
| | | Use the Format menu to center this label horizontally |
| Label2 | AutoSize | True |
| | Text | &Name: |
| Label3 | AutoSize | True |
| | Text | &Address: |
| Label4 | AutoSize | True |
| | Text | Ci&ty: |
| Label5 | AutoSize | True |
| | Text | &State: |
| Label6 | AutoSize | True |
| | Text | &ZIP: |
| Label7 | AutoSize | True |
| | Text | &Regular: |
| Label8 | AutoSize | True |
| | Text | &Decaf: |
| Label9 | AutoSize | True |
| | Text | Pounds ordered: |
| Label10 | AutoSize | True |
| | Text | Total price: |
| Label11 | Name | totalPoundsLabel |
| | AutoSize | False |
| | BorderStyle | FixedSingle |
| | Text | (empty) |
| | TextAlign | MiddleCenter |
| Label12 | Name | totalPriceLabel |
| | AutoSize | False |
| | BorderStyle | FixedSingle |
| | Text | (empty) |
| | TextAlign | MiddleCenter |
| *(Figure is continued on next page)* | | |

| Object | Property | Setting |
|--------|----------|---------|
| TextBox1 | Name | nameTextBox |
| TextBox2 | Name | addressTextBox |
| TextBox3 | Name | cityTextBox |
| TextBox4 | Name<br>CharacterCasing<br>MaxLength | stateTextBox<br>Upper<br>2 |
| TextBox5 | Name | zipTextBox |
| TextBox6 | Name | regularTextBox |
| TextBox7 | Name | decafTextBox |
| Button1 | Name<br>Text | calcButton<br>&Calculate Order |
| Button2 | Name<br>Text | clearButton<br>C&lear Order |
| Button3 | Name<br>Text | exitButton<br>E&xit |

**FIGURE 2.50**

**Tab Order:**

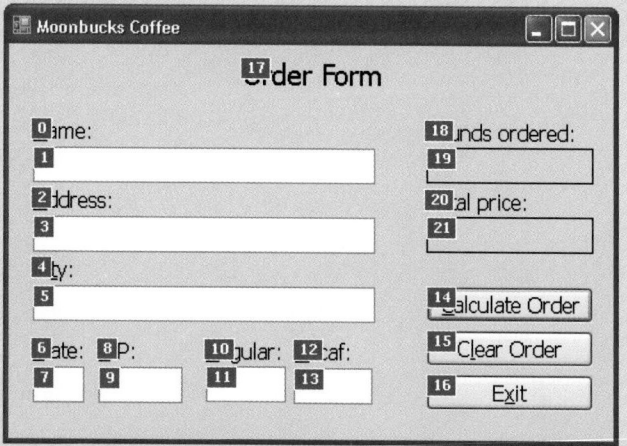

**FIGURE 2.51**

**Code:**

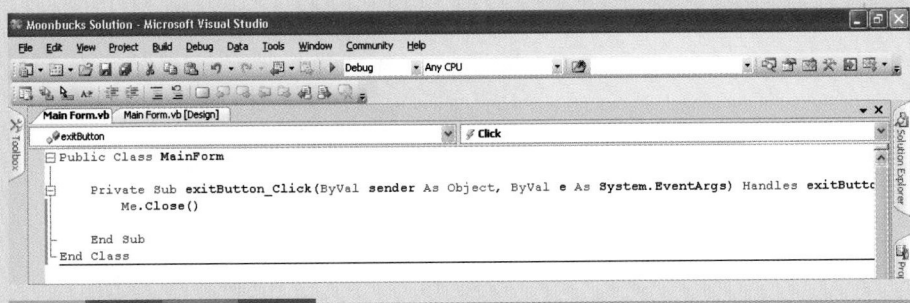

**FIGURE 2.52**

## Quick Review

- You should plan an application jointly with the user to ensure that the application meets the user's needs.
- Planning an application requires that you identify the tasks, objects, and events. You then build the interface.
- You can use a TOE chart to record an application's tasks, objects, and events.
- You use a text box control to give the user an area in which to enter data.
- The primary viewing and editing of your application's data takes place in a primary window.
- Dialog boxes are used to support and supplement a user's activities in a primary window.
- Primary windows can be resized, minimized, maximized, and closed by the user. Dialog boxes can be closed only.
- You use the form's FormBorderStyle property to specify the border style of a primary window or dialog box.
- You use the form's MinimizeBox and MaximizeBox properties to control whether minimize and maximize buttons appear darkened or dimmed on the title bar.
- If a form represents a splash screen, you typically set the form's ControlBox property to False.
- In Western countries, you should organize the user interface so that the information flows either vertically or horizontally, with the most important information always located in the upper-left corner of the screen.
- You can group related controls together using either white space or one of the tools located in the Containers section of the toolbox.
- Labels that identify text boxes should be left-aligned and positioned either above or to the left of the text box. They also should end with a colon and be entered using sentence capitalization.
- Identifying labels and button captions should be from one to three words only, and each should appear on one line.

- Identifying labels and button captions should be meaningful. Button captions should be entered using book title capitalization.
- When positioning the controls, you should maintain a consistent margin from the edge of the form.
- Related controls typically are placed close together in the interface. Controls that are not part of any logical grouping may be positioned farther away from other controls.
- When buttons are positioned horizontally on the screen, all the buttons should be the same height; their widths, however, may vary if necessary. When buttons are stacked vertically on the screen, all the buttons should be the same height and the same width.
- Align the borders of the controls wherever possible to minimize the number of different margins used in the interface.
- You can use the Format menu to align, size, and center the controls in an interface.
- Graphics and color should be used sparingly in an interface.
- You can use an object's Font property to change the type, style, and size of the font used to display the text in the object. It is recommended that you use the Tahoma font for applications that will run on systems running Windows 2000 or Windows XP.
- You can use 8-, 9-, 10-, 11-, or 12-point fonts for the text in an interface. Avoid using italics and underlining in an interface, and limit the use of bold text to titles, headings, and key items that you want to emphasize.
- You should assign access keys to each of the controls (in the interface) that can accept user input—such as text boxes and buttons. You assign an access key by including an ampersand (&) in the control's caption or identifying label.
- The TabIndex property determines the order in which a control receives the focus when the user presses either the Tab key or an access key. The TabIndex property of a text box should be set to a value that is one number more than the value stored in the TabIndex property of its identifying label.
- You use the form's AcceptButton property to designate a default button, and its CancelButton property to designate a cancel button.
- You use the Show method to display a modeless form. You use the ShowDialog method to display a modal form.
- You can use the Timer tool to instantiate a timer control. You use a timer control when you want to process code at one or more specified intervals. The timer is stored in the component tray.
- When using a timer, you set its Enabled property to True. You set its Interval property to the number of milliseconds that must elapse before the timer's Tick event occurs. You place the code you want processed in the timer's Tick event procedure.
- You disable a timer by setting its Enabled property to False.
- If you want code processed before a form is displayed, you place the code in the form's Load event procedure.

## Key Terms

You use a **text box** to give the user an area in which to enter data. A text box is instantiated using the **TextBox tool**.

A **primary window** is a window in which the primary viewing and editing of your application's data takes place.

A **dialog box** is a window that supports and supplements a user's activities in a primary window.

A form's **FormBorderStyle property** allows you to specify the border style of the form.

The **MinimizeBox property** and **MaximizeBox property** control the display of the Minimize and Maximize buttons, respectively, on a form's title bar.

The **ControlBox property** allows you to remove the Control menu box, as well as the Minimize, Maximize, and Close buttons, from a form's title bar.

You can use the **group box control**, the **panel control**, and the **table layout panel control** to group related controls together.

**Sentence capitalization** means you capitalize only the first letter in the first word and in any words that are customarily capitalized.

**Book title capitalization** means you capitalize the first letter in each word, except for articles, conjunctions, and prepositions that do not occur at either the beginning or the end of the caption.

An object's **Font property** allows you to change the type, style, and size of the font used to display the text in the object.

A **font** is the general shape of the characters in the text.

A **point** is a font measurement and is equal to $\frac{1}{72}$ of an inch.

A **serif** is a light cross stroke that appears at the top or bottom of a character.

An **access key** is the underlined character in an object's identifying label or caption. An access key allows the user to select the object using the Alt key in combination with the character.

The **TabIndex property** determines the order in which a control receives the focus when the user presses either the Tab key or an access key while the application is running.

When a control has the **focus**, it can accept user input.

A **default button** can be selected by pressing the Enter key even when the button does not have the focus. You specify the default button (if any) by setting the form's **AcceptButton property**.

A **cancel button** can be selected by pressing the Esc key. You specify the cancel button (if any) by setting the form's **CancelButton property**.

You use the **Show method** to display a **modeless form**, which is a form that can remain on the screen while the user completes other actions in the application.

You use the **ShowDialog method** to display a **modal form**, which is a form that requires the user to take some action in the form before he or she can continue working in the application.

You use the **Timer tool** to create a **timer control**, whose purpose is to process code at one or more regular intervals. The interval is specified in the timer control's **Interval property**.

A timer's **Enabled property** indicates the timer's state, which is either running or stopped.

The **component tray** is a special area in the IDE. It stores controls that do not appear in the interface when the application is running.

The background color of a control is specified in the control's **BackColor property**.

The color of a control's text is specified in the control's **ForeColor property**.

A form's **Load event** occurs when an application is started and the form is displayed the first time.

## Self-Check Questions and Answers

1. You can use a text box's _____ property to ensure that the text entered into the text box is in uppercase.
   a. Case
   b. CharacterCasing
   c. Upper
   d. UpperCase

2. Assume you want to allow the user to enter a maximum of five characters into a text box. You can do so by setting the text box's _____ property.
   a. CharacterMaximum
   b. MaxCharacters
   c. MaxLength
   d. MaxNumber

3. The text "January sales:" is an example of _____ capitalization.
   a. book title
   b. sentence

4. Tahoma is a _____ font.
   a. sans serif
   b. serif

5. The default button on a form can be selected by _____.
   a. clicking it
   b. pressing the Enter key when the button has the focus
   c. pressing the Enter key when the button does not have the focus
   d. All of the above.

6. TabIndex values begin with the number _____.
   a. 0
   b. 1

7. You use the _____ method to display a modal form.
   a. Show
   b. ShowDialog
   c. ShowFormModal
   d. ShowModal

8. The _____ property indicates the number of milliseconds that must elapse before a timer's Tick event occurs.
   a. TickTime
   b. Time
   c. TimeElapsed
   d. None of the above.

9. The _____ occurs when a form is displayed the first time while an application is running.
   a. Display
   b. DisplayForm
   c. Load
   d. None of the above.

10. A timer control appears _____ in the IDE.
    a. in the component tray
    b. in the control tray
    c. on the form
    d. None of the above.

Answers: 1) b, 2) c, 3) b, 4) a, 5) d, 6) a, 7) b, 8) d, 9) c, 10) a

## Review Questions

1. You use _____ control to accept or display information that can be changed while the application is running.
   a. an entry
   b. a label
   c. a text box
   d. a word-processing

2. When designing a user interface, you should organize the information _____.
   a. either horizontally or vertically
   b. horizontally only
   c. vertically only

3. When designing a user interface, the most important information should be placed in the _____ of the screen.
   a. center
   b. lower-left corner
   c. upper-left corner
   d. upper-right corner

4. You can use _____ to group together related controls in an interface.
   a. a group box control
   b. a panel control
   c. white space
   d. All of the above.

5. Which of the following statements is false?
   a. A button's caption should appear on one line.
   b. A button's caption should be from one to three words only.
   c. A button's caption should be entered using book title capitalization.
   d. A button's caption should end with a colon (:).

6. The labels that identify text boxes should be entered using _____.
   a. book title capitalization
   b. sentence capitalization
   c. either a or b

7. Which of the following statements is false?
   a. The text that identifies a text box should be aligned on the left in a label control.
   b. An identifying label should be positioned either above or to the left of the text box it identifies.
   c. Labels that identify text boxes should be entered using book title capitalization.
   d. Labels that identify text boxes should end with a colon (:).

8. The _____ property determines the order in which a control receives the focus when the user presses the Tab key or an access key.
   a. OrderTab
   b. SetOrder
   c. TabIndex
   d. TabOrder

9. All controls have a TabIndex property.
   a. True
   b. False

10. If the buttons are positioned horizontally on the screen, then each button should be _____.
    a. the same height
    b. the same width
    c. the same height and the same width

11. If the buttons are stacked vertically on the screen, then each button should be _____.
    a. the same height
    b. the same width
    c. the same height and the same width

12. When building an interface, always use _____.
    a. dark text on a dark background
    b. dark text on a light background
    c. light text on a dark background
    d. light text on a light background

13. You use the _____ character to assign an access key to a control.
    a. &
    b. *
    c. @
    d. ^

14. You assign an access key using a control's _____ property.
    a. Access
    b. Caption
    c. KeyAccess
    d. Text

15. Use a _____ font for the text in the user interface.
    a. sans serif
    b. serif

16. The human eye is attracted to _____.
    a. color before black and white
    b. graphics before text
    c. text before graphics
    d. both a and b

17. You use the _____ property to designate a default button in the interface.
    a. button's AcceptButton
    b. button's DefaultButton
    c. form's AcceptButton
    d. form's DefaultButton

18. If a text box has a TabIndex value of 7, its identifying label should have a TabIndex value of _____.
    a. 6
    b. 7
    c. 8
    d. 9

19. When a _____ form is displayed, the user cannot perform any actions in the application until the form is closed.
    a. modal
    b. modeless

20. In most cases, you would use the _____ instruction to open a splash screen named SplashForm.
    a. `SplashForm.Show()`
    b. `SplashForm.ShowDialog()`
    c. `SplashForm.ShowForm()`
    d. None of the above.

## Review Exercises – Short Answer

1. Define the following terms:
   a. book title capitalization
   b. sentence capitalization

2. List the four steps you should follow when planning a Visual Basic application.

3. Explain the procedure for choosing a control's access key.

4. Explain how you give users keyboard access to a text box.

5. Explain the difference between a primary window and a dialog box.

6. Explain the difference between a modal form and a modeless form.

7. Write the instruction to display the TypeDialogForm as a modeless form.

8. How do you specify that a modeless form should remain on top of other windows in the interface?

9. How do you specify that you do not want the form's name to appear in the taskbar when the application is running?

## Computer Exercises

1. In this exercise, you modify the chapter's Programming Example.
   a. Create the Moonbucks Coffee application shown in this chapter's Programming Example. Save the application in the VbReloaded\Chap02 folder.
   b. Close the Moonbucks Coffee application. Then use Windows to make a copy of the Moonbucks Solution folder. Rename the folder Moonbucks Solution—Modified.
   c. Open the Moonbucks Solution (Moonbucks Solution.sln) file contained in the VbReloaded\Chap02\Moonbucks Solution—Modified folder.
   d. Modify the user interface so that it displays the total number of pounds of coffee ordered, the price of the order without any sales tax, the sales tax amount, and the total price of the order. Place the calculated amounts, along with their identifying labels, in a table layout panel control. Be sure to reset the tab order.
   e. Also modify the TOE chart shown in Figure 2.48 and the OPS (Object, Property, Setting) chart shown in Figure 2.50.
   f. Save the solution, then start the application. Click the Exit button, then close the solution.

2. In this exercise, you modify an existing application's user interface so that the interface follows the design guidelines you learned in this chapter.
   a. Open the Time Solution (Time Solution.sln) file contained in the VbReloaded\Chap02\Time Solution folder.
   b. Lay out and organize the interface so that it follows all of the design guidelines specified in this chapter.
   c. Save the solution, then start the application. Click the Exit button, then close the solution.

3. In this exercise, you modify the application created in this chapter's Programming Tutorial.
   a. Use Windows to make a copy of the Color Game Solution folder, which is contained in the VbReloaded\Chap02 folder. Rename the folder Color Game Solution—Modified.
   b. Open the Color Game Solution (Color Game Solution.sln) file contained in the VbReloaded\Chap02\Color Game Solution—Modified folder.
   c. Include a Cancel button on the DialogForm. The button's Click event procedure should simply close the DialogForm.
   d. In the MainForm, modify the optionsButton's Click event procedure. The procedure should now display the DialogForm as a modal form.
   e. Save the solution, then start and test the application. When you are finished testing the application, click the Exit button, then close the solution.

4. In this exercise, you prepare a TOE chart and build an interface.
   Scenario: Sarah Brimley is the accountant at Paper Products. The salespeople at Paper Products are paid a commission, which is a percentage of the sales they make. (In other words, if you have sales totaling $2,000 and your commission rate is 10%, then your commission is $200.) Sarah wants you to create an application that will compute the commission after she enters the salesperson's name, sales, and commission rate.
   a. Prepare a TOE chart ordered by object.
   b. Build an appropriate interface. Name the solution, project, and form file Paper Solution, Paper Project, and Main Form.vb, respectively. Save the solution in the VbReloaded\Chap02 folder.

c. Add a splash screen to the application. The splash screen should remain on the screen for eight seconds. Code the MainForm's Load event, as well as the Exit button and timer control.

d. Save the solution, then start and test the application. When you are finished testing the application, close it and then close the solution.

5. In this exercise, you prepare a TOE chart and build an interface.

Scenario: RM Sales divides its sales territory into four regions: North, South, East, and West. Robert Gonzales, the sales manager, wants an application in which he can enter the current year's sales for each region and the projected increase (expressed as a percentage) in sales for each region. He then wants the application to compute the following year's projected sales for each region. (For example, if Robert enters 10000 as the current sales for the South region, and then enters a 10% projected increase, the application should display 11000 as next year's projected sales.)

a. Prepare a TOE chart ordered by object.

b. Build an appropriate interface. Name the solution, project, and form file RMSales Solution, RMSales Project, and Main Form.vb, respectively. Save the solution in the VbReloaded\Chap02 folder. Code the Exit button.

c. Save the solution, then start and test the application. When you are finished testing the application, close it and then close the solution.

6. In this exercise, you learn how to bypass a control in the tab order when the user is tabbing.

a. Open the Johnson Solution (Johnson Solution.sln) file, which is contained in the VbReloaded\Chap02\Johnson Solution folder.

b. Start the application. Press the Tab key several times and notice where the focus is placed each time. Click the Exit button.

c. Assume that most of Johnson's customers are located in California. Enter CA in the stateTextBox control's Text property.

d. Find a way to bypass (skip over) the stateTextBox control when the user is tabbing. If the user needs to place the focus in the stateTextBox control—perhaps to change the control's contents—he or she will need to click or double-click the control, or use its access key.

e. Save the solution, then start and test the application. Click the Exit button, then close the solution.

7. In this exercise, you learn about the group box and panel controls.

a. Open the GroupPanel Solution (GroupPanel Solution.sln) file, which is contained in the VbReloaded\Chap02\GroupPanel Solution folder.

b. Use the GroupBox tool to add a group box control to the form. Change the group box control's Text property to Shirts. Change its Size property to 200, 136, and its Location property to 40, 24.

c. Drag four label controls and two text boxes into the group box. Give three of the label controls the following captions: Red:, Green:, and Total:. The remaining label control should have a fixed border and be empty. Name the empty label control totalLabel, and set its AutoSize property to False. Name the text boxes redTextBox and greenTextBox. Align and size the label and text box controls appropriately within the group box control.

d. Use the Panel tool to add a panel control to the form. Change the panel control's BorderStyle property to FixedSingle. Change its Size property to 200, 64, and its Location property to 40, 168.

e. Drag two button controls into the panel control. Name the buttons calcButton and exitButton. Give the buttons the following captions: Calculate and Exit. Align and size the buttons appropriately within the panel control. Lock the controls.

f. Click View on the menu bar, and then click Tab Order. Click the group box control, and then click the Red: label, the redTextBox control, the Green: label, the greenTextBox control, the Total: label, and the totalLabel control. What values appear in the tab order boxes for these controls?

g. Click the panel control, the calcButton control, and the exitButton control. What values appear in the tab order boxes for these controls?

h. Press the Esc key on your keyboard.

i. Code the Exit button so that it ends the application.

j. Save the solution, then start the application. Verify that the tab order and access keys work correctly.

k. Click the Exit button, then close the solution.

8. In this exercise, you modify the application created in this chapter's Programming Tutorial.

a. Use Windows to make a copy of the Color Game Solution folder, which is contained in the VbReloaded\Chap02 folder. Rename the folder Color Game Solution—Discovery.

b. Open the Color Game Solution (Color Game Solution.sln) file contained in the VbReloaded\Chap02\Color Game Solution—Discovery folder.

c. Assume you want the DialogForm to always be the top-most window. Set the appropriate property.

d. Assume you want the DialogForm's name to appear on the taskbar when the application is running. Set the appropriate property.

e. Save the solution, then start and test the application. When you are finished testing the application, click the Exit button, then close the solution.

9. In this exercise, you find and correct an error in an application. The process of finding and correcting errors is called debugging.

a. Open the Debug Solution (Debug Solution.sln) file, which is contained in the VbReloaded\Chap02\Debug Solution folder.

b. Start the application. Test all of the access keys in the interface. Notice that not all of them are working. Stop the application.

c. Locate and then correct any errors.

d. Save the solution, then start the application and test the access keys again. Click the Exit button, then close the solution.

## Case Projects

### Crispies Bagels and Bites

Create a TOE chart and a user interface for an application that allows the user to enter the number of bagels, donuts, and cups of coffee a customer orders. The application should display the total price of the order. Include a button control that allows the user to terminate the application. Be sure to assign meaningful names to the form, the button controls, the text boxes, and the label control that displays the total price. Name the solution, project, and form file Crispies Solution, Crispies Project, and Main Form.vb, respectively. Save the solution in the VbReloaded\Chap02 folder.

### Perry Primary School

Create TOE charts and a user interface for an application that allows the user to enter two numbers. The application should display the sum of and difference between both numbers. Include a button control that allows the user to terminate the application. Be sure to assign meaningful names to the form, the button controls, the text boxes, and the label controls that display the sum and difference. Name the solution, project, and form file Perry Solution, Perry Project, and Main Form.vb, respectively. Save the solution in the VbReloaded\Chap02 folder. Include a splash screen in the application. Also include a dialog box that allows the user to change the color of the text used in the MainForm to either red or black. (If you use the Dialog template, be sure to set the form's AcceptButton and CancelButton properties to (none), and set the Cancel button's DialogResult property to None.)

## Jasper Health Foods

Create a TOE chart and a user interface for an application that allows the user to enter the sales amounts for four states: Illinois, Indiana, Kentucky, and Ohio. The application should display the total sales and the sales commission earned. Include a button control that allows the user to terminate the application. Be sure to assign meaningful names to the form, the button controls, the text boxes, and the label controls that display the total sales and commission. Name the solution, project, and form file Jasper Solution, Jasper Project, and Main Form.vb, respectively. Save the solution in the VbReloaded\Chap02 folder. Include a splash screen in the application.

## Sophia's Italian Deli

Sophia's offers the following items on its lunch menu: Italian sub, meatball sandwich, slice of pizza, sausage sandwich, meatball/sausage combo, chicken fingers, ravioli plate, lasagna plate, bowl of soup, Caesar salad, calamari, spumoni, and cheesecake. Create a TOE chart and a user interface for an application that allows the user to enter a customer's lunch order. The application should display the price of the order without sales tax, the sales tax amount, and the total price of the order. Name the solution, project, and form file Sophia Solution, Sophia Project, and Main Form.vb, respectively. Save the solution in the VbReloaded\Chap02 folder. Include an About box in the application. The About box should display when the user clicks an About button on the MainForm.

# 3

# Variables, Constants, Methods, and Calculations

**After studying Chapter 3, you should be able to:**

- Declare variables and named constants
- Assign data to an existing variable
- Convert data to the appropriate type using the TryParse method and the Convert class methods
- Write arithmetic expressions
- Understand the scope and lifetime of variables and named constants
- Understand the purpose of the Option Explicit, Option Strict, and Imports statements
- Use a TOE chart, pseudocode, and a flowchart to code an application
- Clear the contents of a control's Text property while an application is running
- Send the focus to a control while the application is running
- Explain the difference between syntax errors and logic errors
- Format an application's numeric output

## VARIABLES

**Variables** are computer memory locations where programmers can temporarily store data while an application is running. The user at the keyboard may enter the data, or it may be read from a file, or it may be the result of a calculation made by the computer. The memory locations are called variables because the contents of the locations can change as the application is running.

Every variable has a name, data type, scope, and lifetime. First, you learn how to select an appropriate data type.

### Selecting a Data Type for a Variable

Each variable used in an application must be assigned a data type by the programmer. The **data type** determines the type of data the variable can store. Figure 3.1 describes most of the basic data types available in Visual Basic 2005. Each data type is a class, which means that each data type is a pattern from which one or more objects—in this case, variables—are created (instantiated).

| Type | Stores | Memory required | Values |
|------|--------|-----------------|--------|
| Boolean | logical value | 2 bytes | True, False |
| Byte | binary number | 1 byte | 0 to 255 (unsigned) |
| Char | one Unicode character | 2 bytes | one Unicode character |
| Date | date and time information | 8 bytes | dates from January 1, 0001 to December 31, 9999, and times from 0:00:00 to 23:59:59 |
| Decimal | fixed-point number | 16 bytes | +/-79,228,162,514,264,337,593,543, 950,335 number with no decimal point; +/-7.92281625142643375935 43950335 with a decimal point; smallest non-zero number is +/- 0.0000000000000000000000000001 |
| Double | floating-point number | 8 bytes | +/- 4.94065645841247E-324 to 1.79769313486231E308 |
| Integer | integer | 4 bytes | -2,147,483,648 to 2,147,483,647 |
| Long | integer | 8 bytes | -9,223,372,036,854,775,808 to 9,223,372,036,854,775,807 |
| Object | object reference | 4 bytes | N/A |
| Short | integer | 2 bytes | -32,768 to 32,767 |
| Single | floating-point number | 4 bytes | +/- 1.401298E-45 to 3.402823E38 |
| String | text | varies | 0 to approximately 2 billion characters |

**TIP**

Also available in Visual Basic 2005 are the SByte, UInteger, ULong, and UShort data types. The "S" in SByte stands for "signed." The "U" in the other data types stands for "Unsigned."

**FIGURE 3.1**     Basic data types in Visual Basic 2005

As Figure 3.1 indicates, variables assigned the Integer, Long, or Short data type can store **integers**, which are whole numbers—numbers without any decimal places. The differences among these three data types are in the range of integers each type can store and the amount of memory each type needs to store the integer.

Figure 3.1 indicates that Single and Double variables can store a **floating-point number**, which is a number that is expressed as a multiple of some power of 10. Floating-point numbers are written in E (exponential) notation, which is similar to scientific notation. For example, the number 3,200,000 written in E (exponential) notation is 3.2E6; written in scientific notation it is $3.2 \times 10^6$. Notice that exponential notation simply replaces "X $10^6$" with the letter E followed by the power number—in this case, 6. Floating-point numbers also can have a negative number after the E. For example, 3.2E-6 means 3.2 divided by 10 to the sixth power, or .0000032.

Floating-point numbers are used to represent both extremely small and extremely large numbers. The differences between the Single and Double types are in the range of numbers each type can store and the amount of memory each type needs to store the numbers. Although a Double variable can store numbers in a Single variable's range, a Double variable takes twice as much memory to do so.

Variables declared using the Decimal data type store numbers with a fixed decimal point. Unlike floating-point numbers, fixed-point numbers are not expressed as a multiple of some power of 10. To illustrate this point, the number 32000 expressed as a floating-point number is 3.2E4, but that same number expressed as a fixed-point number is simply 32000. Calculations involving fixed-point numbers are not subject to the small rounding errors that may occur when floating-point numbers are used. In most cases, the small rounding errors do not create any problems in an application. One exception, however, is when the application contains complex equations dealing with money, where you need accuracy to the penny. In those cases, the Decimal data type is the best type to use.

Also listed in Figure 3.1 are the Char data type, which can store one Unicode character, and the String data type, which can store from zero to approximately two billion Unicode characters. **Unicode** is the universal coding scheme for characters. It assigns a unique numeric value to each character used in the written languages of the world. For more information, see The Unicode Standard at *www.unicode.org*.

You use a Boolean variable to store the Boolean values True and False, and a Date variable to store date and time information. The Byte data type is used to store binary numbers.

If you do not assign a specific data type to a variable, Visual Basic assigns the Object type to it. Unlike other variables, an Object variable can store many different types of data, and it also can freely change the type of stored data while the application is running. For example, you can store the number 40 in an Object variable at the beginning of the application and then, later on in the application, store the text "John Smith" in that same variable. Although the Object data type is the most flexible data type, it is less efficient than the other data types. At times it uses more memory than necessary to store a value and, because the computer has to determine which type of data is currently stored in the variable, your application will run more slowly.

In this book, you will use the Integer data type to store integers. You will use either the Decimal data type or the Double data type for numbers that contain decimal places and are used in calculations. You will use the String data type for text and numbers not used in calculations.

In addition to assigning a data type to the variables used in an application, the programmer also must assign a name to each variable.

## Selecting a Name for a Variable

You should assign a descriptive name to each variable used in an application. The name, also called the **identifier**, should help you remember the variable's purpose. In other words, it should help you remember the meaning of the value stored inside the variable. For example, the names `length` and `width` are much more meaningful than are the names `x` and `y`, because `length` and `width` remind you that the numbers stored in the variables represent a length and width measurement, respectively.

For many years, most Visual Basic programmers used Hungarian notation when naming variables, and many programmers still follow this practice. As you learned in Chapter 1, Hungarian notation is a naming convention that uses the first three (or more) characters in the name to represent the object's type, and the remaining characters in the name to represent the object's purpose. Using Hungarian notation, a Decimal variable that stores a sales amount might be named `decSales`. The "dec" identifies the variable as a Decimal variable, and "Sales" reminds the programmer of the variable's purpose—in this case, to store a sales amount.

More recently, a new naming convention for variables has emerged. In the new naming convention, you no longer state the data type in a variable's name. Rather, you name the variable by its intended purpose only. Variable names are entered using camel case, which means you lowercase the first word in the variable's name and then uppercase the first letter of each subsequent word in the name. Using the new naming convention, a programmer might assign the name `sales`, or the name `salesAmount`, to a variable that stores a sales amount. In this book, you will use the new naming convention for variables.

In addition to being descriptive, a variable name must follow the rules listed in Figure 3.2. The figure also includes examples of valid and invalid variable names.

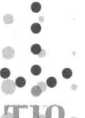

**TIP**

Although Microsoft recommends the new naming convention for variables, your company (or instructor) may have a different naming convention you are expected to use. Your company's (or instructor's) naming conventions supersede the ones recommended by Microsoft.

## HOW TO...        Name a Variable

### Rules

1. The name must begin with a letter or an underscore.
2. The name must contain only letters, numbers, and the underscore character. No punctuation characters or spaces are allowed in the name.
3. Although the name can contain a maximum of 16383 characters, 32 characters is the recommended maximum number of characters to use.
4. The name cannot be a reserved word, such as `Print`.

### Examples

| Valid variable names | Invalid variable names |
|---|---|
| `printReport` | `print` (the name cannot be a reserved word) |
| `sales2007` | `2007Sales` (the name must begin with a letter) |
| `westRegion` | `west Region` (the name cannot contain a space) |
| `firstName` | `first.Name` (the name cannot contain punctuation) |

**FIGURE 3.2**    How to name a variable

Now that you know how to select an appropriate data type and name for a variable, you can learn how to declare a variable in code. Declaring a variable tells the computer to set aside a small section of its internal memory, and it allows you to refer to the location by the variable's name. The size of the section is determined by the variable's data type.

## DECLARING A VARIABLE

You use a declaration statement to declare, or create, a variable. Figure 3.3 shows the syntax of a declaration statement and includes several examples of declaring variables.

**HOW TO...**

### Declare a Variable

**Syntax**
{Dim | Private | Static} *variablename* As *datatype* [= *initialvalue*]

**Examples**
```
Dim carPayment As Double
```
declares a Double variable named `carPayment`; the variable is automatically initialized to 0

```
Dim itemPrice As Decimal
Dim discount As Decimal
```
declares two Decimal variables named `itemPrice` and `discount`; the variables are automatically initialized to 0

```
Dim isDataOk As Boolean = True
```
declares a Boolean variable named `isDataOk` and initializes it using the keyword `True`

```
Dim studentName As String
Dim age As Integer
```
declares a String variable named `studentName` and an Integer variable named `age`; the String variable is automatically initialized to `Nothing`, and the Integer variable is automatically initialized to 0

**FIGURE 3.3**    How to declare a variable

**TIP**

A declaration statement also can begin with a keyword other than the ones shown in Figure 3.3. You will learn about the other keywords later in this book.

**TIP**

Dim comes from the word "dimension," which is how programmers in the 1960s referred to the process of allocating the computer's memory. "Dimension" refers to the "size" of something.

The {**Dim** | **Private** | **Static**} portion of the syntax shown in Figure 3.3 indicates that you can select only one of the keywords appearing within the braces. In this case, you can select `Dim`, `Private`, or `Static`. In most instances, you declare a variable using the keyword `Dim`. (You learn about the `Private` and `Static` keywords later in this chapter.)

*Variablename* in the syntax is the variable's name, and *datatype* is the variable's data type. As mentioned earlier, a variable is considered an object in Visual Basic and is an instance of the class specified in the *datatype* information. The `Dim carPayment As Double` statement, for example, creates an object named `carPayment`. The `carPayment` object is an instance of the Double class.

*Initialvalue* in the syntax is the value you want stored in the variable when it is created in the computer's internal memory. The square brackets in the syntax indicate that the "*= initialvalue*" part of a declaration statement is optional. If you do not assign an initial value to a variable when it is declared, Visual Basic stores a default value in the variable; the default value depends on the variable's data type. A variable declared using one of the numeric data types is automatically initialized to—in other words, given a beginning value of—the number zero. Visual Basic automatically initializes a Boolean variable using the keyword `False`, and a Date variable to 1/1/0001 12:00:00 AM. Object and String variables are automatically initialized using the keyword `Nothing`. Variables initialized to `Nothing` do not actually contain the word "Nothing"; rather, they contain no data at all.

After a variable is created, you can use an assignment statement to store other data in the variable.

## ASSIGNING DATA TO AN EXISTING VARIABLE

In the previous chapters, you used assignment statements to assign values to the properties of controls while an application is running. You also use assignment statements to assign values to variables while an application is running. Figure 3.4 shows the syntax of an assignment statement that assigns a value to a variable. The figure also includes several examples of such assignment statements. As you learned in Chapter 1, the equal sign (=) that appears in an assignment statement is referred to as the assignment operator.

**HOW TO...**

### Assign a Value to a Variable

**Syntax**
*variablename = value*

**Examples**
```
Dim quantityOrdered As Integer
quantityOrdered = 500
```
assigns the integer 500 to an Integer variable named `quantityOrdered`

```
Dim firstName As String
firstName = "Mary"
```
assigns the string "Mary" to a String variable named `firstName`

```
Dim zipCode As String
zipCode = zipTextBox.Text
```
assigns the string contained in the zipTextBox's Text property to a String variable named `zipCode`

```
Dim discountRate As Double
discountRate = .03
```
assigns the Double number .03 to a Double variable named `discountRate`

```
Dim taxRate As Decimal
taxRate = .05D
```
converts the number .05 from Double to Decimal, and then assigns the result to a Decimal variable named `taxRate`

**FIGURE 3.4**    How to assign a value to a variable

When the computer processes an assignment statement, it assigns the value that appears on the right side of the assignment operator to the variable whose name appears on the left side of the assignment operator. In other words, the computer stores the value in the variable (memory location). The data type of the value should be the same data type as the variable. For example, the `quantityOrdered = 500` assignment statement shown in Figure 3.4 stores the number 500, which is an integer, in an Integer variable named `quantityOrdered`. Similarly, the `firstName = "Mary"` assignment statement stores the string "Mary" in a String variable named `firstName`. A **string** is a group of characters enclosed in quotation marks. When the computer processes an assignment statement that assigns a string to a String variable, it assigns only the characters that appear between the quotation marks; it does not assign the quotation marks themselves.

The number 500 and the string "Mary" are called literal constants. A **literal constant** is an item of data whose value does not change while the application is running. The number 500 is a numeric literal constant, and the string "Mary" is a string literal constant. Notice that you can store literal constants in variables. Also notice that string literal constants are enclosed in quotation marks, but numeric literal constants and variable names are not. The quotation marks differentiate a string from both a number and a variable name. In other words, "500" is a string, but 500 is a number. Similarly, "Mary" is a string, but Mary (without the quotation marks) would be interpreted by Visual Basic as the name of a variable.

Keep in mind that the value stored in the Text property of an object is always treated as a string rather than as a number. Therefore, the `zipCode = zipTextBox.Text` assignment statement shown in Figure 3.4 assigns the string contained in the zipTextBox's Text property to a String variable named `zipCode`.

In Visual Basic, a numeric literal constant that has a decimal place is automatically treated as a Double number. As a result, the `discountRate = .03` assignment statement in Figure 3.4 assigns the Double number .03 to a Double variable named `discountRate`. The last assignment statement in the figure, `taxRate = .05D`, shows how you convert a numeric literal constant of the Double data type to the Decimal data type, and then assign the result to a Decimal variable. The D that follows the number .05 in the statement is one of the literal type characters in Visual Basic. A **literal type character** forces a literal constant to assume a data type other than the one its form indicates. In this case, the D forces the Double number .05 to assume the Decimal data type, which causes the computer to store the number with a fixed-point rather than with a floating-point.

Figure 3.5 lists the literal type characters in Visual Basic and includes an example of using each character. Notice that you append a literal type character to the end of the literal constant.

## HOW TO...

### Use the Literal Type Characters

| Literal type character | Data type | Example |
|---|---|---|
| S | Short | age = 35S |
| I | Integer | hours = 40I |
| L | Long | population = 20500L |
| D | Decimal | rate = .03D |
| F | Single | payRate = .03F |
| R | Double | sales = 2356R |
| C | Char | initial = "A"C |

**FIGURE 3.5**  How to use the literal type characters

Technically, the I in the hours = 40I example in Figure 3.5 is not necessary, because Visual Basic treats a numeric literal constant that does not have a decimal place as an Integer number. The only exception to this treatment is when the number is too large to fit into an Integer variable; in that case, Visual Basic treats the number as a Long.

Many times, the data type of the value you need to assign to a variable is different from the data type of the variable itself. As you just learned, if the value is a literal constant, you can use a literal type character to change the literal constant's data type to match the variable's data type. If the value is not a literal constant, however, you can use the TryParse method or one of the methods contained in the Convert class. You learn about the TryParse method first.

## Using the TryParse Method

Recall that each data type in Visual Basic is a class, which is a group of instructions used to create an object; in this case, the object is a variable. Most classes have methods. A **method** is a specific portion of the class instructions, and its purpose is to perform a task for the class. For example, every numeric data type in Visual Basic has a **TryParse method** that can be used to convert a string to that numeric data type. Figure 3.6 shows the syntax of the TryParse method and includes examples of using the method.

---

**HOW TO...**      **Use the TryParse Method**

**Syntax**
*datatype*.**TryParse**(*string*, [*numberStyles, IFormatProvider,*] *variable*)

**Examples**
```
Dim sales As Decimal
Dim isConverted As Boolean
isConverted = Decimal.TryParse(salesTextBox.Text, sales)
```

- If the string stored in the salesTextBox can be converted to Decimal, the TryParse method converts the string and stores the result in the sales variable. It also returns the Boolean value True, which is assigned to the isConverted variable. Examples of strings that the method can convert to Decimal include "34", "12.55", "-4.23", "7.88-", "1,457.99", and " 33 ". The strings will be converted to the numbers 34, 12.55, -4.23, -7.88, 1457.99, and 33, respectively.

- If the string stored in the salesTextBox cannot be converted to Decimal, the TryParse method stores the number zero in the sales variable. It also returns the Boolean False, which is assigned to the isConverted variable. Examples of strings that the method cannot convert to Decimal include "$5.67", "(4.23)", "7%", "122o", and "1 345".

*(Figure is continued on next page)*

Line continuation character

```
Dim sales As Decimal
Dim isConverted As Boolean
isConverted = Decimal.TryParse(salesTextBox.Text, _
    NumberStyles.Currency, NumberFormatInfo.CurrentInfo, _
    sales)
```

- The TryParse method works exactly the same as in the previous example, except it now will also convert (to Decimal) the strings "$5.67" and "(4.23)". The strings will be converted to the numbers 5.67 and -4.23, respectively.

```
Dim num As Integer
Dim isConverted As Boolean
isConverted = Integer.TryParse(numTextBox.Text, num)
```

- If the string stored in the numTextBox can be converted to an Integer, the TryParse method converts the string and stores the result in the num variable. It also returns the Boolean value True, which is assigned to the isConverted variable. Examples of strings that the method can convert to Integer include "6", " 7 ", and "-896". The strings will be converted to 6, 7, and -896, respectively.
- If the string stored in the numTextBox cannot be converted to an Integer, the TryParse method assigns the number zero to the num variable. It also returns the Boolean value False, which is assigned to the isConverted variable. Examples of strings that the method cannot convert to Integer include "5,889", "$78", "(11)", and "4-".

```
Dim num As Integer
Dim isConverted As Boolean
isConverted = Integer.TryParse(numTextBox.Text, _
    NumberStyles.Integer _
    Or NumberStyles.AllowCurrencySymbol, _
    Or NumberStyles.AllowThousands, _
    NumberFormatInfo.CurrentInfo, num)
```

- The TryParse method works exactly the same as in the previous example, except it now will also convert (to Integer) the strings "5,889" and "$78". The strings will be converted to the numbers 5889 and 78, respectively.

Important Note: To use the *numberStyles* and `NumberFormatInfo.CurrentInfo` values shown in the second and last examples, you first need to enter the Imports `System.Globalization` statement in the General Declarations section in the Code Editor window.

**FIGURE 3.6**    How to use the TryParse method

In the TryParse method's syntax, *datatype* is one of the numeric data types available in Visual Basic, such as Decimal, Double, and Integer. Notice that the TryParse method has four arguments. You learn about the required arguments, *string* and *variable*, first.

The *string* argument represents the string you want converted to a number of the *datatype* type and typically is the Text property of a control. The *variable* argument is the name of a numeric variable where the TryParse method can store the number. The numeric variable must be the same data type as specified in the *datatype* portion of the syntax. In other words, if you want to convert a string to a Decimal number, then you will need to give the TryParse method the name of a Decimal variable in which to store the number.

The TryParse method parses the string, which means it looks at each character in the string, to determine whether the string can be converted to a number of the specified data type. If the string can be converted, the TryParse method converts the string to a number and stores the number in the variable specified in the *variable* argument. In addition, the TryParse method returns the Boolean value True to indicate that the conversion was successful.

However, if the TryParse method determines that the string cannot be converted to a number of the specified data type, the method assigns the number zero to the variable specified in the *variable* argument. In this case, the method returns the Boolean value False to indicate that it was not able to convert the string.

You typically assign the TryParse method's return value to a Boolean variable, as shown in the examples in Figure 3.6. This is done because in most cases you will want the computer to process different instructions depending on whether the conversion was successful or unsuccessful. For example, assume you are using the TryParse method to convert (to a number) a string that represents a sales amount. If the Boolean variable contains the value True, it indicates that the conversion was successful. Therefore, you can have the computer process instructions to calculate and display a bonus amount, which is a percentage of the sales amount. However, if the Boolean variable contains the value False, it indicates that the TryParse method could not convert the string—perhaps because the user entered 122o rather than 1220. In that case, you will probably have the computer process instructions that prompt the user to re-enter the sales amount.

In this chapter, you will always assign the TryParse method's return value to a Boolean variable. Although the Boolean variable will be named `isConverted` in most of the examples you view, you can use any name for the variable. However, the new naming convention for variables recommends that you begin Boolean variable names with the word "is" to denote a True/False value. In Chapter 4, which covers the selection structure, you will learn how to use the Boolean variable's value to determine the appropriate instructions to process.

Study closely the code shown in the first example in Figure 3.6. The code begins by declaring a Decimal variable named `sales` and a Boolean variable named `isConverted`. The `isConverted = Decimal.TryParse` `(salesTextBox.Text, sales)` statement uses the TryParse method to convert the string stored in the salesTextBox to a Decimal number. You will need to do this before you can use the sales amount in a calculation. If the conversion is successful, the TryParse method stores the number in the `sales` variable. It also returns the Boolean value True, which the statement assigns to the `isConverted` variable. However, if the string cannot be converted to a Decimal number, the TryParse method stores the number zero in the `sales` variable. It also returns the Boolean value False, which the statement assigns to the `isConverted` variable.

As indicated in Figure 3.6, the `Decimal.TryParse(salesTextBox.Text,` `sales)` method can convert (to Decimal) a string that contains only numbers, as well as one that also contains a decimal point, a leading or trailing sign, a

**TIP**

The Customize Regional Options dialog box resides outside of Visual Studio .NET and is part of the Windows operating system.

**TIP**

To open the Customize Regional Options dialog box using the Classic style of Windows, click Start, and then click Control Panel. Double-click Regional and Language Options, and then click the Customize button.

comma, or leading and/or trailing spaces. It cannot, however, convert a string that contains a dollar sign, parentheses, a percent sign, a letter, or a space within the string.

In some applications, you might want to allow the user to enter a number that contains a dollar sign (to denote currency) or parentheses (to denote a negative number). You can do so using the TryParse method's optional arguments: *IFormatProvider* and *numberStyles*. The *IFormatProvider* argument specifies the characters used by your computer system to format numbers, dates, and times. Examples of such characters include the currency symbol, thousands separator, decimal point indicator, date separator, and time separator. Although the *IFormatProvider* argument can take on many different values, in this book you will use the value `NumberFormatInfo.CurrentInfo`. The `NumberFormatInfo.CurrentInfo` value tells the TryParse method to use the formatting characters specified in the Customize Regional Options dialog box. To open the dialog box, click Start on the taskbar, and then click Control Panel. When the Control Panel dialog box opens, click Date, Time, Language, and Regional Options. When the Date, Time, Language, and Regional Options dialog box opens, click Regional and Language Options. Finally, click the Customize button in the Regional and Language Options dialog box. Figure 3.7 shows an open Customize Regional Options dialog box. You can use the dialog box to change the characters used to format numbers, currency, dates, and times.

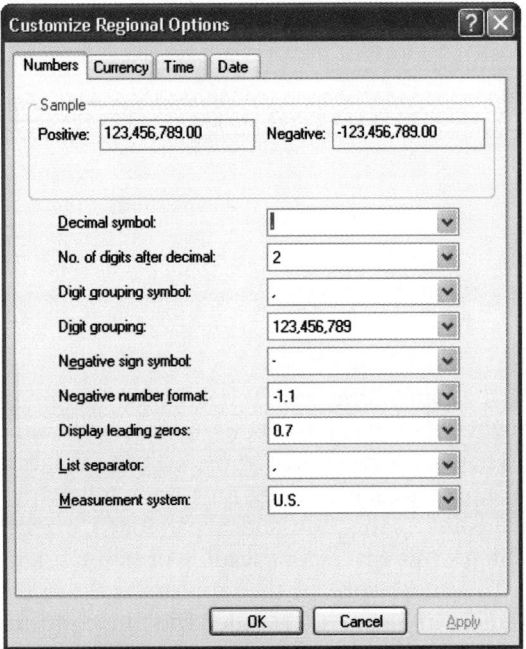

**FIGURE 3.7**    The Customize Regional Options dialog box

The *numberStyles* argument indicates the formatting characters that can appear in a string and still allow the string to be converted to a number. Figure 3.8 describes the styles commonly used for the *numberStyles* argument in the TryParse method.

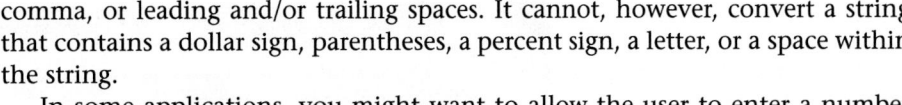

| Style | Description |
|---|---|
| AllowCurrencySymbol | allows the string to contain a currency symbol |
| AllowDecimalPoint | allows the string to contain a decimal point |
| AllowExponent | allows the string to be in exponential notation |
| AllowLeadingSign | allows the string to begin with a sign |
| AllowLeadingWhite | allows the string to begin with one or more spaces |
| AllowParentheses | allows the string to be enclosed in parentheses |
| AllowThousands | allows the string to have group separators |
| AllowTrailingSign | allows the string to end with a sign |
| AllowTrailingWhite | allows the string to end with one or more spaces |
| Currency | composite style that contains the AllowCurrencySymbol, AllowDecimalPoint, AllowLeadingSign, AllowLeadingWhite, AllowParentheses, AllowThousands, AllowTrailingSign, and AllowTrailingWhite styles |
| Float | composite style that contains the AllowDecimalPoint, AllowLeadingSign, AllowLeadingWhite, AllowTrailingWhite, and AllowExponent styles |
| Integer | composite style that contains the AllowLeadingSign, AllowLeadingWhite, and AllowTrailingWhite styles |
| Number | composite style that contains the AllowDecimalPoint, AllowLeadingSign, AllowLeadingWhite, AllowThousands, AllowTrailingSign, and AllowTrailingWhite styles |

**FIGURE 3.8**     Styles for the TryParse method's *numberStyles* argument

The *numberStyles* and *IFormatProvider* arguments are used in the second example shown earlier in Figure 3.6. In the second example, the NumberStyles.Currency and NumberFormatInfo.CurrentInfo values allow the TryParse method to convert the string if it contains any of the following: the currency symbol ($), the decimal point (.), the thousands separator (,), parentheses, one or more leading and/or trailing white spaces, or a leading or trailing sign.

The underscore (_) that appears at the end of two of the lines in the second example in Figure 3.6 is called the line continuation character. You use the **line continuation character** to break up a long instruction into two or more physical lines in the Code Editor window. Breaking up an instruction in this manner makes the instruction easier to read and understand. The line continuation character must be immediately preceded by a space, and it must appear at the end of a physical line of code.

In the third example shown in Figure 3.6, the isConverted = Integer.TryParse(numTextBox.Text, num) statement uses the TryParse method to convert the string stored in the numTextBox to an Integer. If the string can be converted, the method stores the result in an Integer variable named num. It then returns the Boolean value True, which the statement assigns to a Boolean variable named isConverted. If, on the other hand, the string cannot be converted to an Integer, the method stores the number zero in the num variable. It then returns the Boolean value False, which the statement assigns to the `isConverted` variable. Notice that, in this example, the TryParse method can convert strings containing numbers, as well as one that also contains a leading sign, leading spaces, or trailing spaces. It cannot, however, convert a string that contains a comma, a dollar sign, parentheses, or a trailing sign.

The code shown in the last example in Figure 3.6 is identical to the code shown in the third example, except the TryParse method in the last example contains values for the *numberStyles* and *IFormatProvider* arguments. In this example, the `NumberStyles.Integer Or NumberStyles.AllowCurrencySymbol Or NumberStyles.AllowThousands` and `NumberFormatInfo.CurrentInfo` values allow the TryParse method to convert the string if it contains any of the following: the currency symbol ($), the thousands separator (,), one or more leading and/or trailing white spaces, or a leading sign. Notice that you can include more than one style in the *numberStyles* argument; to do this, you separate each style with the keyword `Or`.

As you just learned, you can use the TryParse method to convert a string to a numeric data type. The method's *IFormatProvider* argument indicates the characters used to format numeric and date/time information on your computer system. The method's *numberStyles* argument specifies the formatting characters allowed in a string. As indicated in the "Important Note" shown earlier in Figure 3.6, before you can use the *numberStyles* and `NumberFormatInfo.CurrentInfo` values shown in the second and last examples, you first need to enter the `Imports System.Globalization` statement in the General Declarations section of the Code Editor window. The General Declarations section appears above the Public Class statement in the Code Editor window, as shown in Figure 3.9.

*General Declarations section*

*Statement*

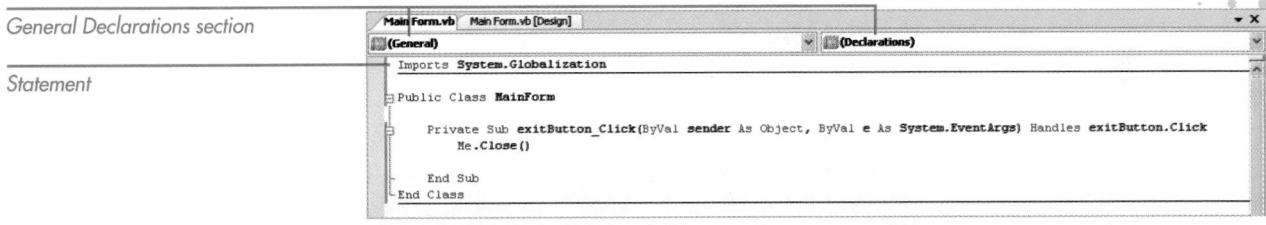

**FIGURE 3.9**    Statement entered in the General Declarations section

The `Imports System.Globalization` statement imports the System.Globalization namespace, which contains the definitions for the *numberStyles* and `NumberFormatInfo.CurrentInfo` values. If you do not import the System.Globalization namespace, then you will need to precede each *numberStyle* in the TryParse method with System.Globalization followed by a period. For example, you will need to enter `System.Globalization. NumberStyles.Currency` rather than `NumberStyles.Currency`. You also will need to enter `System.Globalization.NumberFormatInfo. CurrentInfo` rather than `NumberFormatInfo.CurrentInfo`. The advantage of importing a namespace is that it allows you to access its members without having to specify the namespace itself.

At times, you may need to convert a number (rather than a string) from one data type to another. Visual Basic provides several ways of accomplishing this task. For example, you can use the Visual Basic conversion functions, which are listed in Appendix C in this book. You also can use one of the methods defined in the Convert class. In this book, you will use the Convert class methods, because they have an advantage over the conversion functions: the methods can be used in any .NET language, whereas the conversion functions can be used only in Visual Basic.

## Using the Convert Class

The **Convert class** contains methods that you can use to convert a numeric value to a specified data type. Figure 3.10 lists the most commonly used methods contained in the Convert class, and it includes examples of using the methods. Notice that you use a period to separate the class name (`Convert`) from the method name (`ToDecimal`, `ToDouble`, `ToInt32`, and `ToString`). As you learned in Chapter 1, the period is called the dot member access operator, and it indicates that what appears to the right of the operator is a member of what appears to the left of the operator. In this case, the dot member access operator indicates that the `ToDecimal`, `ToDouble`, `ToInt32`, and `ToString` methods are members of the Convert class.

**HOW TO...**

### Use the Methods in the Convert Class

| Syntax | Purpose |
|---|---|
| Convert.ToDecimal(*value*) | convert *value* to the Decimal data type |
| Convert.ToDouble(*value*) | convert *value* to the Double data type |
| Convert.ToInt32(*value*) | convert *value* to the Integer data type |
| Convert.ToString(*value*) | convert *value* to the String data type |

**Examples**
```
Dim sales As Integer = 4500
Dim newSales As Double
newSales = Convert.ToDouble(sales)
```
converts the contents of an Integer variable named `sales` to Double, and assigns the result to a Double variable named `newSales`

```
Dim rate As Decimal = Convert.ToDecimal(.05)
```
converts the Double number .05 to Decimal before storing it in a Decimal variable named `rate`

```
Dim testScore As Integer = 98
totalLabel.Text = Convert.ToString(testScore)
```
converts the contents of an Integer variable named `testScore` to String, and then assigns the result to the totalLabel's Text property

**FIGURE 3.10**   How to use the methods contained in the Convert class

**TIP**

You also can use the Convert methods to convert a String value to a numeric data type. However, the TryParse method is the recommended method to use for that task because, unlike the TryParse method, the Convert methods result in an error if the string cannot be converted to a number.

In the syntax for each method, *value* is the numeric value you want to convert to a different data type. In the first example shown in Figure 3.10, the `newSales = Convert.ToDouble(sales)` statement converts the contents of the `sales` variable to Double, and then assigns the result to the `newSales` variable. In the second example, the `Dim rate As Decimal = Convert.ToDecimal(.05)` statement converts the Double number .05 to

**TIP**

Later in the chapter, you will learn how to format strings using the ToString method contained in each numeric data type.

Decimal, and stores the result in the `rate` variable. The statement is equivalent to the `Dim rate As Decimal = .05D` statement. However, many programmers would argue that using the Convert.ToDecimal method, rather than the literal type character (D), makes the code clearer. The last assignment statement shown in Figure 3.10, `totalLabel.Text = Convert.ToString(testScore)`, converts the contents of the `testScore` variable to String before assigning it to the totalLabel's Text property.

Keep in mind that a variable can store only one item of data at any one time. When you use an assignment statement to assign another item to the variable, the new data replaces the existing data. To illustrate this point, assume that a button's Click event procedure contains the following three lines of code:

```
Dim number As Integer
number = 500
number = number * 2
```

When you run the application and click the button, the three lines of code are processed as follows:

- The Dim statement creates the `number` variable in memory and automatically initializes it to the number zero.
- The `number = 500` assignment statement removes the zero from the `number` variable and stores the number 500 there instead. The `number` variable now contains the number 500 only.
- The `number = number * 2` assignment statement first multiplies the contents of the `number` variable (500) by the number two, giving 1000. The assignment statement then replaces the current contents of the `number` variable (500) with 1000. Notice that the calculation appearing on the right side of the assignment operator (=) is performed first, and then the result is assigned to the variable whose name appears on the left side of the assignment operator.

As you can see, after data is stored in a variable, you can use the variable in calculations. When a statement contains the name of a variable, the computer uses the value stored inside the variable to process the statement. You learn more about statements containing calculations in the next section.

## WRITING ARITHMETIC EXPRESSIONS

Most applications require the computer to perform one or more calculations. You instruct the computer to perform a calculation by writing an arithmetic expression that contains one or more arithmetic operators. Figure 3.11 lists the most commonly used arithmetic operators available in Visual Basic, along with their precedence numbers. The **precedence numbers** indicate the order in which the computer performs the operation in an expression. Operations with a precedence number of 1 are performed before operations with a precedence number of 2, which are performed before operations with a precedence number of 3, and so on. However, you can use parentheses to override the order of precedence, because operations within parentheses always are performed before operations outside parentheses.

| Operator | Operation | Precedence number |
|----------|-----------|-------------------|
| ^ | exponentiation (raises a number to a power) | 1 |
| – | negation | 2 |
| *, / | multiplication and division | 3 |
| \ | integer division | 4 |
| Mod | modulus arithmetic | 5 |
| +, – | addition and subtraction | 6 |

Important Note: You can use parentheses to override the order of precedence. Operations within parentheses are always performed before operations outside parentheses.

**FIGURE 3.11**    Most commonly used arithmetic operators and their order of precedence

**TIP**

The difference between the negation and subtraction operators shown in Figure 3.11 is that the negation operator is unary, whereas the subtraction operator is binary. Unary and binary refer to the number of operands required by the operator. Unary operators require one operand, whereas binary operators require two operands. The expression –7 uses the negation operator to turn the positive number 7 into a negative number. The expression 9 – 4 uses the subtraction operator to subtract the number 4 from the number 9.

Notice that some operators shown in Figure 3.11 have the same precedence number. For example, both the addition and subtraction operators have a precedence number of 6. If an expression contains more than one operator having the same priority, those operators are evaluated from left to right. In the expression 3 + 12 / 3 – 1, for instance, the division (/) is performed first, then the addition (+), and then the subtraction (–). In other words, the computer first divides 12 by 3, then adds the result of the division (4) to 3, and then subtracts 1 from the result of the addition (7). The expression evaluates to 6.

You can use parentheses to change the order in which the operators in an expression are evaluated. For example, the expression 3 + 12 / (3 – 1) evaluates to 9, not 6. This is because the parentheses tell the computer to subtract 1 from 3 first, then divide the result of the subtraction (2) into 12, and then add the result of the division (6) to 3, giving 9.

Two of the arithmetic operators listed in Figure 3.11 might be less familiar to you; these are the integer division operator (\) and the modulus arithmetic operator (Mod). You use the **integer division operator** (\) to divide two integers, and then return the result as an integer. For example, the expression 211\4 results in 52, which is the integer result of dividing 211 by 4. (If you use the standard division operator [/] to divide 211 by 4, the result is 52.75 rather than 52.)

The modulus arithmetic operator also is used to divide two numbers, but the numbers do not have to be integers. After dividing the numbers, the **modulus arithmetic operator** returns the remainder of the division. For example, 211 Mod 4 equals 3, which is the remainder of 211 divided by 4. One use for the modulus arithmetic operator is to determine whether a year is a leap year—one that has 366 days rather than 365 days. As you may know, if a year is a leap year, then its year number is evenly divisible by the number four. In other words, if you divide the year number by four and the remainder is zero, then the year is a leap year. You can determine whether the year 2008 is a leap year by using the expression 2008 Mod 4. This expression evaluates to zero (the remainder of 2008 divided by four), so the year 2008 is a leap year. Similarly, you can determine whether the year 2009 is a leap year by using the expression 2009 Mod 4. This expression evaluates to one (the remainder of 2009 divided by four), so the year 2009 is not a leap year.

When entering an arithmetic expression in code, you do not enter the dollar sign ($) or the percent sign (%). If you want to enter a percentage in an arithmetic expression, you first must change the percentage to its decimal equivalent; for example, you would change 5% to .05. Figure 3.12 shows examples of arithmetic expressions in assignment statements.

## HOW TO... Include Arithmetic Expressions in Assignment Statements

```
Dim age As Integer
age = age + 1
```
adds the integer 1 to the contents of an Integer variable named `age`, then assigns the result to the `age` variable

```
Dim sales As Decimal
Dim bonus As Decimal
Dim isConverted As Boolean
isConverted = Decimal.TryParse(salesTextBox.Text, sales)
bonus = sales * Convert.ToDecimal(.05)
```
converts the Double number .05 to Decimal before multiplying it by the contents of a Decimal variable named `sales`, then assigns the result to a Decimal variable named `bonus`

```
Dim total As Decimal = 250.55D
Dim number As Integer = 5
averageLabel.Text = Convert.ToString(total /
Convert.ToDecimal(number))
```
converts the contents of an Integer variable named `number` to Decimal, then divides the result into the contents of a Decimal variable named `total`, and then converts the result of the division to a String before assigning it to the averageLabel's Text property

```
Dim currentPay As Double = 1500.65
Dim newPay As Double
newPay = currentPay + (currentPay * .02)
```
multiplies the contents of a Double variable named `currentPay` by the Double number .02, then adds the result to the contents of the `currentPay` variable, and then assigns the sum to a Double variable named `newPay`

**FIGURE 3.12** How to include arithmetic expressions in assignment statements

The assignment statement shown in the first example in Figure 3.12 adds the number one (an Integer) to an Integer variable named `age`, and then assigns the result to the `age` variable. Notice that the variable and the literal constant have the same data type, Integer. As you learned earlier, the value assigned to a variable should have the same data type as the variable itself.

The `bonus = sales * Convert.ToDecimal(.05)` assignment statement in the second example converts the Double number .05 to Decimal before multiplying it by the contents of a Decimal variable named `sales`. The statement assigns the result to a Decimal variable named bonus. In this case, the variables and literal constant in the assignment statement have the Decimal data type.

The third example in the figure contains the `averageLabel.Text = Convert.ToString(total / Convert.ToDecimal(number))` assignment

**TIP**
In the second example, you could have used `.05D` rather than `Convert.ToDecimal(.05)`.

statement. Notice that the calculation in this statement involves two variables: `total` and `number`. Also notice that the `number` variable is converted to Decimal to match the data type of the `total` variable; this is done because all variables included in a calculation should have the same data type. If a calculation contains variables of different data types, you should convert the variables to match the one having the widest data type. A data type is considered wider than another data type if it can store larger values. In this case, the Decimal data type is wider than the Integer data type, so the Integer variable (`number`) is converted to Decimal before the calculation is performed. When the calculation is completed, the assignment statement converts the result to a String before assigning it to the averageLabel's Text property.

In the last example shown in Figure 3.12, the `newPay = currentPay + (currentPay * .02)` assignment statement multiplies the contents of a Double variable named `currentPay` by the Double number .02. The statement adds the result to the contents of the `currentPay` variable, assigning the sum to a Double variable named `newPay`. Here again, notice that the variables and literal constant in the statement have the same data type, Double.

Technically, the parentheses in the `newPay = currentPay + (currentPay * .02)` assignment statement are not necessary, because the computer always performs multiplication before addition. In other words, you could write the statement as `newPay = currentPay + currentPay * .02`. However, many programmers feel that the parentheses make the arithmetic expression easier to understand.

You now know how to use a variable declaration statement to declare a variable. Recall that the statement allows you to assign a name, data type, and initial value to the variable you are declaring. You also know how to use an assignment statement to store literal constants and the result of arithmetic expressions in an existing variable. There are just two more things about variables that you need to learn: in addition to a name and a data type, every variable also has both a scope and a lifetime.

## THE SCOPE AND LIFETIME OF A VARIABLE

A variable's **scope** indicates where in the application's code the variable can be used, and its **lifetime** indicates how long the variable remains in the computer's internal memory. Most of the variables used in an application should have procedure scope because fewer unintentional errors occur in applications when the variables are declared using the minimum scope needed. However, some variables used in applications may have module scope or block scope. The scope is determined by where you declare the variable—in other words, where you enter the variable's declaration statement. Typically, you enter the declaration statement either in a procedure, such as an event procedure, or in the Declarations section of a form. (The Declarations section of a form is not the same as the General Declarations section.)

When you declare a variable in a procedure, the variable is called a **procedure-level variable** and is said to have **procedure scope** because only that procedure can use the variable. For example, if you enter the `Dim number As Integer` statement in the calcButton's Click event procedure, only the calcButton's Click event procedure can use the `number` variable. No other procedures in the application are allowed to use the variable. As a matter of fact, no other procedures in the application will even be aware of the `number` variable's existence. Procedure-level variables remain in the computer's internal memory

only while the procedure in which they are declared is running; they are removed from memory when the procedure ends. In other words, a procedure-level variable has the same lifetime as the procedure that declares it. As mentioned earlier, most of the variables in your applications will be procedure-level variables.

The Sales Tax application that you view next illustrates the use of procedure-level variables. Figure 3.13 shows the MainForm in the application, and Figure 3.14 shows the Click event procedures for the Calculate 2% Tax and Calculate 5% Tax buttons.

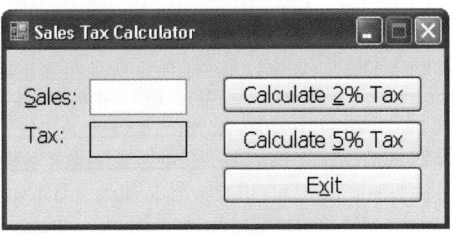

**FIGURE 3.13**    The MainForm in the Sales Tax application

Comment

Procedure-level variables declared in the calcTax2Button's Click event procedure

Procedure-level variables declared in the calcTax5Button's Click event procedure

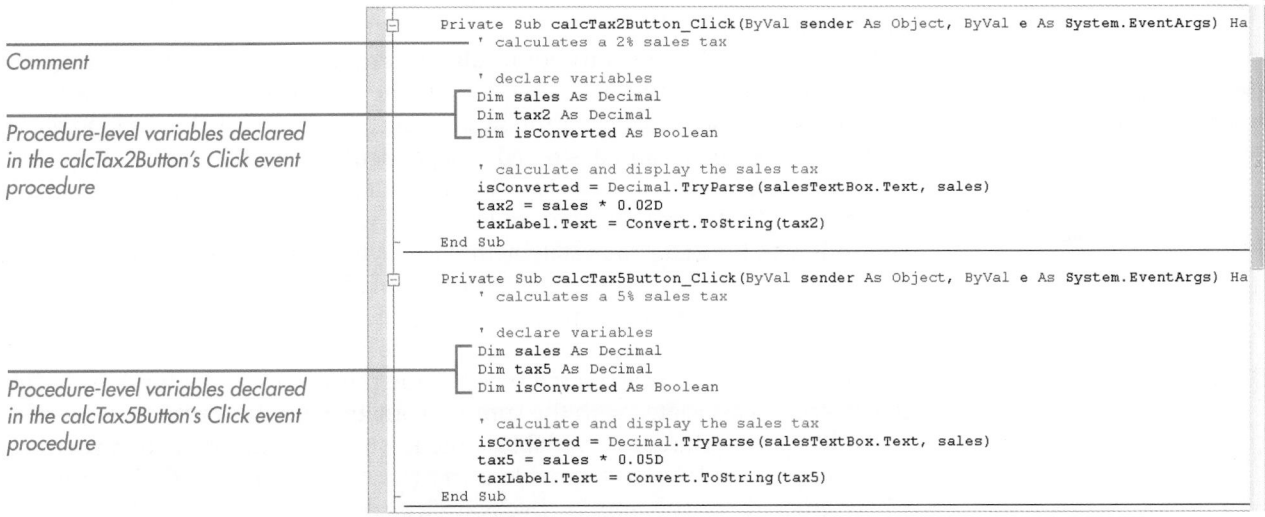

```
Private Sub calcTax2Button_Click(ByVal sender As Object, ByVal e As System.EventArgs) Ha
    ' calculates a 2% sales tax

    ' declare variables
    Dim sales As Decimal
    Dim tax2 As Decimal
    Dim isConverted As Boolean

    ' calculate and display the sales tax
    isConverted = Decimal.TryParse(salesTextBox.Text, sales)
    tax2 = sales * 0.02D
    taxLabel.Text = Convert.ToString(tax2)
End Sub

Private Sub calcTax5Button_Click(ByVal sender As Object, ByVal e As System.EventArgs) Ha
    ' calculates a 5% sales tax

    ' declare variables
    Dim sales As Decimal
    Dim tax5 As Decimal
    Dim isConverted As Boolean

    ' calculate and display the sales tax
    isConverted = Decimal.TryParse(salesTextBox.Text, sales)
    tax5 = sales * 0.05D
    taxLabel.Text = Convert.ToString(tax5)
End Sub
```

**FIGURE 3.14**    Click event procedures

As the MainForm shown in Figure 3.13 indicates, the application allows the user to enter a sales amount. It then calculates and displays either a 2% sales tax or a 5% sales tax, depending on the button selected by the user.

Notice that both procedures shown in Figure 3.14 declare procedure-level variables. It is customary to enter the variable declaration statements at the beginning of the procedure, as shown in the figure. Also notice that each procedure contains three lines of green text; the lines, called **comments**, are used to internally document the procedure. You create a comment in Visual Basic by placing an apostrophe (') before the text that represents the comment. Visual Basic ignores everything that appears after the apostrophe on that line. Although it is not required, many programmers use a space to separate the apostrophe from the comment, as shown in the figure. It is a good programming practice to use a comment to document each procedure's purpose. You enter the comment below the `Private Sub` line in the procedure. Here again, although it is not required, many programmers follow the comment with a blank line. You also should include comments that explain various sections of the procedure's code, because comments make the code more readable and easier to understand by anyone viewing it.

When the user enters a sales amount and then clicks the Calculate 2% Tax button, the calcTax2Button's Click event procedure creates and initializes the `sales`, `tax2`, and `isConverted` variables; only the calcTax2Button's Click event procedure can use the variables. The procedure then converts the sales amount to Decimal and stores the result in the `sales` variable. Then the procedure multiplies the contents of the `sales` variable by .02 and stores the result in the `tax2` variable. Finally, the procedure assigns the contents of the `tax2` variable, converted to String, to the taxLabel's Text property. When the procedure ends, the computer removes the `sales`, `tax2`, and `isConverted` procedure-level variables from memory. The variables will be created again the next time the user clicks the Calculate 2% Tax button. A similar process is followed when the user clicks the Calculate 5% Tax button, except the variable that stores the tax amount is named `tax5`, and the tax is calculated using a rate of .05 rather than .02.

Notice that both procedures shown in Figure 3.14 declare variables named `sales` and `isConverted`. When you use the same name to declare a variable in more than one procedure, each procedure creates its own variable when the procedure is invoked. Each procedure also destroys its own variable when the procedure ends. In other words, although the `sales` and `isConverted` variables in both procedures have the same name, they are not the same variable; rather, each is created and destroyed independently from the other.

In addition to declaring a variable in a procedure, you also can declare a variable in the form's Declarations section, which begins with the `Public Class` statement and ends with the `End Class` statement. When you declare a variable in the form's Declarations section, the variable is called a **module-level variable** and is said to have **module scope**. You typically use a module-level variable when you need more than one procedure in the *same* form to use the *same* variable, because a module-level variable can be used by all of the procedures in the form, including the procedures associated with the controls contained on the form.

Unlike a procedure-level variable, which you declare using the `Dim` keyword, you declare a module-level variable using the `Private` keyword. For example, when entered in the form's Declarations section, the statement `Private number As Integer` creates a module-level variable named `number`. Because the variable has module scope, it can be used by every procedure in the form. Module-level variables retain their values and remain in the computer's internal memory until the application ends. In other words, a module-level variable has the same lifetime as the application itself.

The Total Sales application that you view next illustrates the use of a module-level variable. Figure 3.15 shows the MainForm in the application, and Figure 3.16 shows the MainForm's code.

**TIP**

The form's Declarations section is not the same as the General Declarations section, which you learned about earlier. The General Declarations section is located above the `Public Class` statement, whereas the form's Declarations section is located within the `Public Class` statement. Figure 3.16 shows the location of both sections.

**TIP**

You also can use the `Dim` keyword to declare a module-level variable. However, most Visual Basic programmers use the `Private` keyword, because it makes the scope more obvious to anyone reading the code.

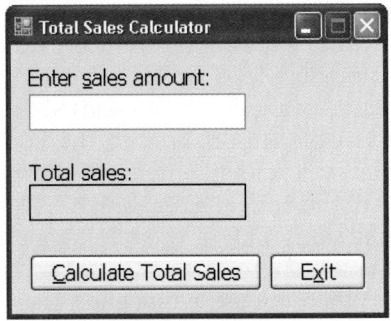

**FIGURE 3.15**    The MainForm in the Total Sales application

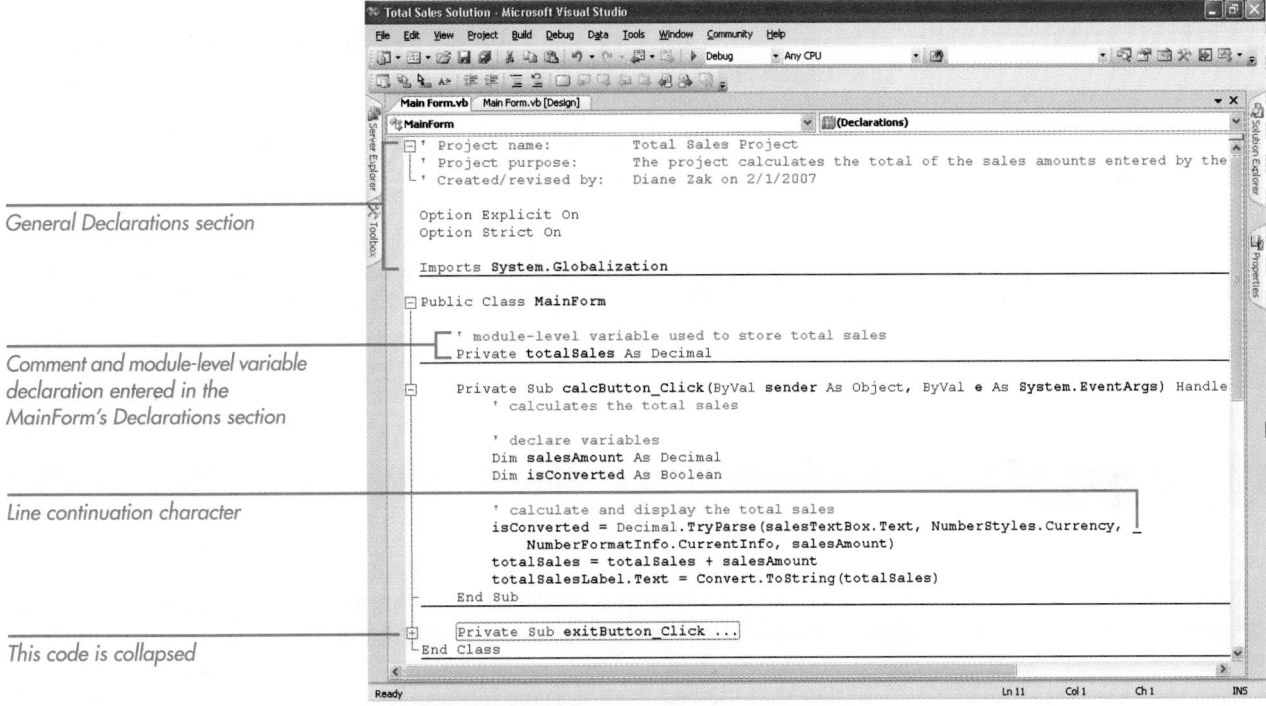

General Declarations section

Comment and module-level variable declaration entered in the MainForm's Declarations section

Line continuation character

This code is collapsed

**FIGURE 3.16**    MainForm's code using a module-level variable

The Total Sales application uses the module-level variable, which is named `totalSales`, to accumulate (add together) the sales amounts entered by the user. Notice that you place the declaration statement for a module-level variable after the `Public Class` statement, but before the first `Private Sub` statement, in the form's Declarations section. (For now, don't worry about the two Option statements that appear in the code shown in Figure 3.16. You learn about Option statements later in this chapter.)

When the Total Sales application is started, the `Private` statement contained in the MainForm's declarations section is processed first. The statement creates and initializes (to the number zero) a Decimal variable named `totalSales`. The variable is created and initialized only once, when the application is first started. It remains in the computer's internal memory until the application ends.

Each time the user enters a sales amount in the interface and then clicks the Calculate Total Sales button, the button's Click event procedure creates and initializes two procedure-level variables named `salesAmount` and `isConverted`. The `salesAmount` variable is initialized to the number zero, and the `isConverted` variable is initialized to the Boolean value, False. The procedure then converts the sales amount entered by the user to Decimal, and adds the result to the contents of the `totalSales` variable. At this point, the `totalSales` variable contains the sum of all of the sales amounts entered so far. The procedure then displays the contents of the `totalSales` variable, converted to String, in the totalSalesLabel. When the procedure ends, the computer removes the procedure-level variables (`salesAmount` and `isConverted`) from its memory; however, it does not remove the module-level variable (`totalSales`). The `totalSales` variable is removed from the computer's memory only when the application ends. (In the next section, you will code the Total Sales application using a static variable rather than a module-level variable.)

As mentioned earlier, variables also can have **block scope**; such variables are called **block-level variables**. Block-level variables are declared within specific blocks of code, such as within `If...Then...Else` statements or `For...Next` statements. Only the block of code in which it is declared can use a block-level variable. You learn more about block-level variables in Chapter 4.

As the syntax shown earlier in Figure 3.3 indicates, you can declare a variable using the `Dim`, `Private`, or `Static` keywords. You have already learned how to use the `Dim` keyword to declare a procedure-level variable, and how to use the `Private` keyword to declare a module-level variable. Next, you learn how to use the `Static` keyword to declare a special type of procedure-level variable, called a static variable.

## STATIC VARIABLES

A **static variable** is a procedure-level variable that retains its value even when the procedure in which it is declared ends. Similar to a module-level variable, a static variable is not removed from the computer's internal memory until the application ends. You declare a static variable using the `Static` keyword.

Earlier you viewed the interface (Figure 3.15) and code (Figure 3.16) for the Total Sales application. Recall that the application used a module-level variable to accumulate the total sales. Rather than using a module-level variable for that purpose, you also can use a static variable.

As mentioned earlier, you can prevent many unintentional errors from occurring in an application by declaring the variables using the minimum scope needed. Because a static variable, which is simply a special type of procedure-level variable, has a narrower scope than does a module-level variable, it is better to use a static variable instead of a module-level variable. Figure 3.17 shows the Total Sales application's code using a static variable.

**TIP**

The **Static** keyword can be used in a procedure only.

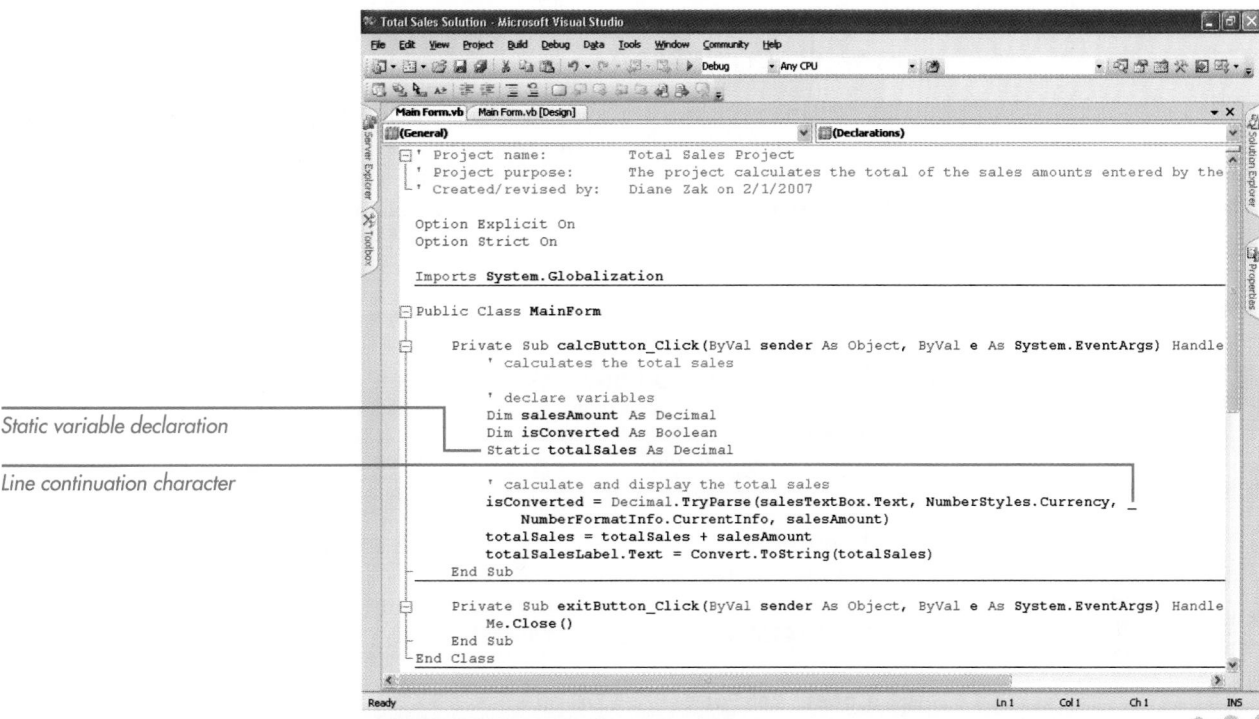

Static variable declaration

Line continuation character

**FIGURE 3.17**    MainForm's code using a static variable

The first time the user clicks the Calculate Total Sales button in the interface, the button's Click event procedure creates and initializes two procedure-level variables named salesAmount and isConverted, and one static variable named totalSales. The procedure then converts the sales amount entered by the user to Decimal, and adds the result to the contents of the totalSales variable. It then displays the contents of the totalSales variable, converted to String, in the totalSalesLabel. When the procedure ends, the computer removes from its internal memory the variables declared using the Dim keyword (salesAmount and isConverted). But it does not remove the variable declared using the Static keyword (totalSales).

Each subsequent time the user clicks the Calculate Total Sales button, the computer re-creates and re-initializes the salesAmount and isConverted variables declared in the button's Click event procedure. However, it does not re-create or re-initialize the totalSales variable, because that variable is still in the computer's memory. After re-creating and re-initializing the appropriate variables, the computer processes the remaining instructions contained in the button's Click event procedure. Here again, each time the procedure ends, the salesAmount and isConverted variables are removed from the computer's internal memory. The totalSales variable is removed only when the application ends.

In addition to literal constants and variables, you also can use named constants in your code.

## NAMED CONSTANTS

Like a variable, a **named constant** is a memory location inside the computer. However, unlike a variable, the contents of a named constant cannot be changed while the application is running. You create a named constant using the **Const statement**. Figure 3.18 shows the syntax of the Const statement and includes several examples of declaring named constants.

HOW TO...

### Declare a Named Constant

**Syntax**
Const *constantname* [As *datatype*] = *expression*

**Examples**
```
Const Pi As Decimal = 3.141593D
```
declares Pi as a Decimal named constant, and initializes it to the number 3.141593 (converted to Decimal)

```
Const MaxHours As Integer = 40
```
declares MaxHours as an Integer named constant, and initializes it to the integer 40

```
Private Const CoTitle As String = "ABC Company"
```
declares CoTitle as a String named constant, and initializes it to the string "ABC Company"

**FIGURE 3.18**       How to declare a named constant

**TIP**

Recall that Pascal case is also used for the names of forms.

In the syntax shown in Figure 3.18, *constantname* is the name of the named constant. Many programmers capitalize the names of constants to help distinguish the constants from the variables used in a program. However, the new naming convention uses Pascal case for the names of named constants. Recall that Pascal case means that you capitalize the first letter in the name, as well as the first letter of each subsequent word in the name. (Recall that variable names are entered using camel case rather than Pascal case.)

*Datatype* in the syntax is the named constant's data type, and *expression* is the value you want stored in the named constant. The *expression* must have the same data type as the named constant. The *expression* can contain a literal constant, another named constant, or an arithmetic operator. However, it cannot contain a variable.

The square brackets in the Const statement's syntax indicate that the "**As** *datatype*" portion is optional. If you do not assign a data type to a constant, Visual Basic assigns a data type based on the *expression*. For example, if you create a named constant for the number 45.6 and do not assign a data type to the constant, Visual Basic assigns the Double data type to it, because a numeric literal constant having a decimal place is assumed to be a Double number. It is a good programming practice to include the "**As** *datatype*" portion in a constant declaration statement, because doing so gives you control over the constant's data type.

**TIP**

Using a named constant to represent a value has another advantage: if the value changes in the future, you need to modify only the Const statement, rather than all of the statements that use the value.

The `Const` statements shown in the first two examples in Figure 3.18 can be used to create procedure-level named constants. To do so, you need simply to enter the statements in the appropriate procedure. However, you would use the `Const` statement shown in the last example in the figure to create a module-level named constant. Notice that you precede the `Const` keyword with the `Private` keyword when creating a module-level constant. Additionally, you would need to enter the `Private Const CoTitle As String = "ABC Company"` statement in the form's Declarations section.

Named constants make code more self-documenting and, therefore, easier to modify, because they allow you to use meaningful words in place of values that are less clear. The named constant Pi, for example, is much more meaningful than is the number 3.141593, which is the value of pi rounded to six decimal places. Once you create a named constant, you then can use the constant's name rather than its value in the application's code. Unlike variables, named constants cannot be inadvertently changed while the application is running.

The Area Calculator application that you view next illustrates the use of a named constant. Figure 3.19 shows the MainForm in the application, and Figure 3.20 shows the MainForm's code.

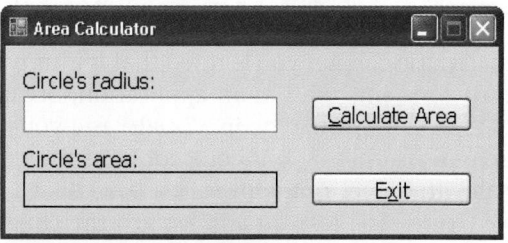

**FIGURE 3.19**     The MainForm in the Area Calculator application

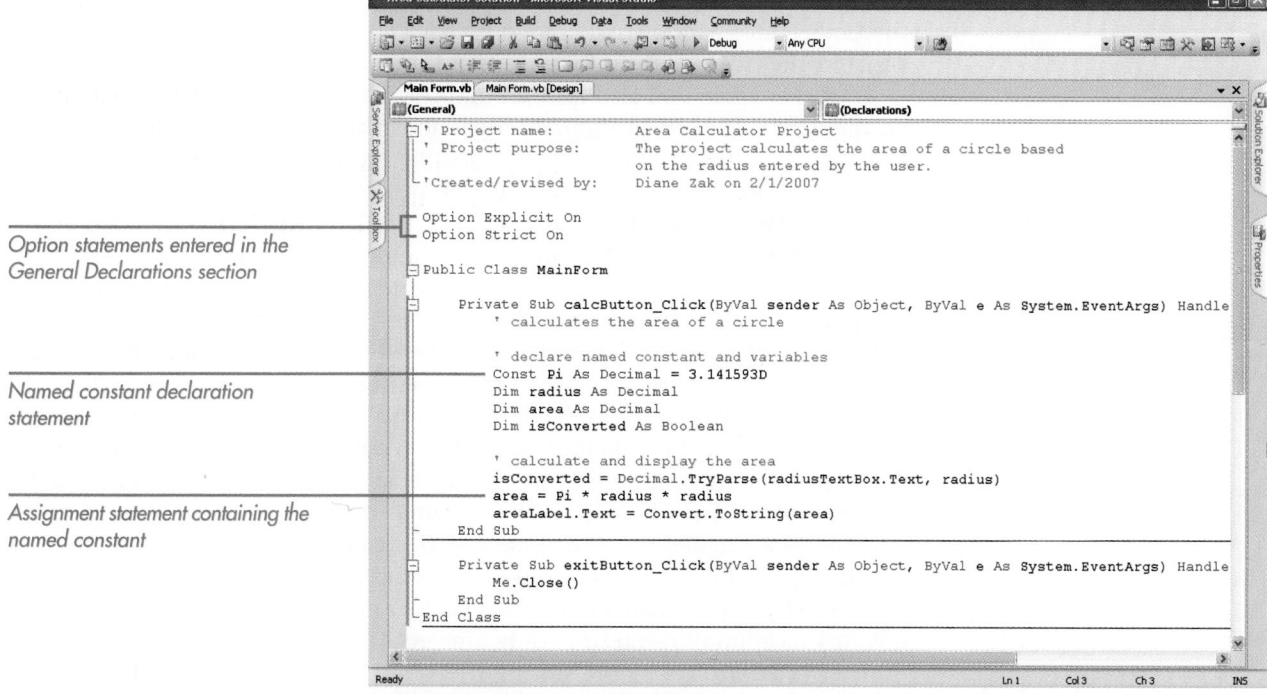

*Option statements entered in the General Declarations section*

*Named constant declaration statement*

*Assignment statement containing the named constant*

**FIGURE 3.20**     MainForm's code using a named constant

As the MainForm shown in Figure 3.19 indicates, the application allows the user to enter the radius of a circle. It then calculates and displays the area of the circle. Recall that the formula for calculating the area of a circle is πr2, where π stands for pi (3.141593).

The calcButton's Click event procedure, which is shown in Figure 3.20, declares and initializes a named constant (`Pi`) and three variables (`radius`, `area`, and `isConverted`). It then converts (to Decimal) the radius value entered by the user and stores the result in the `radius` variable. The `area = Pi * radius * radius` statement calculates the circle's area using the values stored in the `Pi` named constant and `radius` variable, and then assigns the result to the `area` variable. Lastly, the procedure displays the contents of the `area` variable in the areaLabel. When the procedure ends, the computer removes the named constant and the three variables from its internal memory.

Notice that two Option statements appear in the General Declarations section of the code shown in Figure 3.20. Both statements also appear in the Total Sales application's code, shown earlier in Figures 3.16 and 3.17. The purpose of each Option statement is explained in the next section.

## OPTION EXPLICIT AND OPTION STRICT

Earlier in the chapter you learned that it is important to declare the variables and named constants used in an application, because it allows you to control their data type. Unfortunately, in Visual Basic you can create variables "on the fly," which means that if your code contains the name of an undeclared variable—a variable that does not appear in a `Dim`, `Static`, or `Private` statement—Visual Basic creates one for you and assigns the Object data type to it. Recall that the Object type is not a very efficient data type. Because it is so easy to forget to declare a variable—and so easy to misspell a variable's name while coding, thereby inadvertently creating an undeclared variable—Visual Basic provides a way that prevents you from using undeclared variables in your code. You simply enter the statement `Option Explicit On` in the General Declarations section of the Code Editor window. Then if your code contains the name of an undeclared variable, the Code Editor informs you of the error.

In this chapter, you also learned that the data type of the value that appears on the right side of the assignment operator in an assignment statement should be the same as the data type of the variable that appears on the left side of the assignment operator. If the value's data type does not match the memory location's data type, the computer uses a process called **implicit type conversion** to convert the value to fit the memory location. For example, if you assign the integer 9 to a Decimal memory location, which stores fixed-point numbers, the computer converts the integer to a fixed-point number before storing the value in the memory location. It does this by appending a decimal point and the number 0 to the end of the integer. In this case, for example, the integer 9 is converted to the fixed-point number 9.0, and it is the fixed-point number 9.0 that is assigned to the Decimal memory location. When a value is converted from one data type to another data type that can store larger numbers, the value is said to be **promoted**. In this case, if the Decimal memory location is used subsequently in a calculation, the results of the calculation will not be adversely affected by the implicit promotion of the number 9 to the number 9.0.

However, if you inadvertently assign a Double number—such as 3.2—to a memory location that can store only integers, the computer converts the Double number to an integer before storing the value in the memory location. It does this by rounding the number to the nearest whole number and then truncating (dropping off) the decimal portion of the number. In this case, the computer converts the Double number 3.2 to the integer 3. As a result, the number 3, rather than the number 3.2, is assigned to the memory location. When a value is converted from one data type to another data type that can store only smaller numbers, the value is said to be **demoted**. If the memory location is used subsequently in a calculation, the results of the calculation probably will be adversely affected by the implicit demotion of the number 3.2 to the number 3; more than likely, the demotion will cause the calculated results to be incorrect.

With implicit type conversions, data loss can occur when the value of one data type (for example, Double) is converted to a narrower data type, which is a data type with less precision or smaller capacity (for example, Integer). You can eliminate the problems that occur as a result of implicit type conversions by entering the `Option Strict On` statement in the General Declarations section of the Code Editor window. When the `Option Strict On` statement appears in an application's code, Visual Basic uses the following type conversion rules:

- Strings will not be implicitly converted to numbers, and vice versa.
- Narrower data types will be implicitly promoted to wider data types. A data type is wider than another data type if it can store larger numbers. For example, a Short will be implicitly promoted to an Integer or Long, and a Single will be implicitly promoted to a Double.
- Wider data types will not be implicitly demoted to narrower data types. For example, a Double will not be implicitly demoted to a Single. Similarly, a Long will not be implicitly demoted to an Integer or Short.

You can turn on the settings for Option Explicit and Option Strict from code, as shown earlier in Figure 3.20, or you can use either the Project Designer window or the Options dialog box. Figure 3.21 lists the various ways you can turn on Option Explicit and Option Strict.

## HOW TO...

### Turn On Option Explicit and Option Strict

- Enter the `Option Explicit On` and `Option Strict On` statements in the General Declarations section of the Code Editor window. If a project contains more than one form, the statements must be entered in each form's Code Editor window.
- To turn the settings on for an entire project, open the solution that contains the project, then right-click My Project in the Solution Explorer window. Click Open to open the Project Designer window, then click the Compile tab. Use the Option explicit and Option strict boxes to turn on the settings.
- To turn the settings on for all of the projects you create, click Tools on the menu bar, and then click Options. When the Options dialog box opens, expand the Projects and Solutions node, then click VB Defaults. Use the Option Explicit and Option Strict boxes to turn on the settings.

**FIGURE 3.21**    How to turn on Option Explicit and Option Strict

Although you can use either the Project Designer window or the Options dialog box to turn on the Option Explicit and Option Strict settings, it is strongly recommended that you enter the Option Explicit On and Option Strict On statements in your code. Entering the statements in your code ensures that the options are set to On, and it makes the code more self-documenting.

Next, you will use what you learned in this chapter to code the Skate-Away Sales application. You also will learn how programmers plan a procedure's code.

## CODING THE SKATE-AWAY SALES APPLICATION

In Chapter 2, you learned how to plan an application. Recall that planning an application requires you to:

1. Identify the tasks the application needs to perform.
2. Identify the objects to which you will assign those tasks.
3. Identify the events required to trigger an object into performing its assigned tasks.
4. Design the user interface.

After planning an application, you then can begin coding the application so that the objects in the interface perform their assigned tasks when the appropriate event occurs. The objects and events that need to be coded are listed in the application's TOE chart, along with the tasks assigned to each object and event.

In Chapter 2, you created a TOE chart and a user interface for the Skate-Away Sales application. As you may remember, Skate-Away Sales sells skateboards by phone. The skateboards are priced at $100 each and are available in two colors—yellow and blue. Recall that the salespeople enter the order information using the interface shown in Figure 3.22.

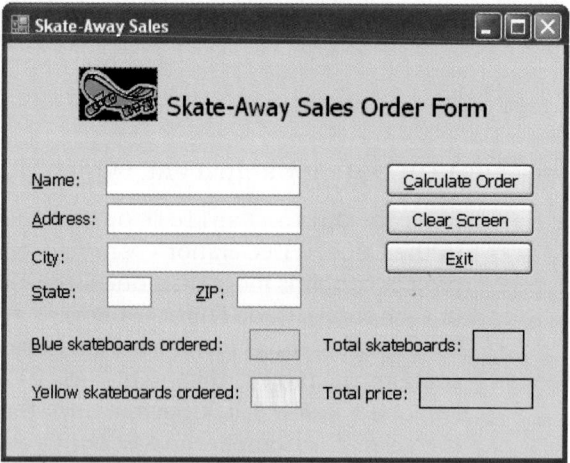

**FIGURE 3.22**     Interface for the Skate-Away Sales application

The Skate-Away Sales application should calculate and display the total number of skateboards ordered and the total price of the skateboards, including a 5% sales tax. Figure 3.23 shows the TOE chart created in Chapter 2.

| Task | Object | Event |
|---|---|---|
| 1. Calculate the total skateboards ordered and the total price<br>2. Display the total skateboards ordered and the total price in totalBoardsLabel and totalPriceLabel | calcButton | Click |
| Clear the screen for the next order | clearButton | Click |
| End the application | exitButton | Click |
| Display the total skateboards ordered (from calcButton) | totalBoardsLabel | None |
| Display the total price (from calcButton) | totalPriceLabel | None |
| Get and display the order information | nameTextBox, addressTextBox, cityTextBox, stateTextBox, zipTextBox, blueTextBox, yellowTextBox | None |

**FIGURE 3.23**    TOE chart for the Skate-Away Sales application

According to the TOE chart shown in Figure 3.23, only the three buttons require coding, as they are the only objects with an event—in this case, the Click event—listed in the third column of the chart. Before you begin coding an object's event procedure, you should plan the procedure. Programmers commonly use either pseudocode or a flowchart when planning a procedure's code.

## Using Pseudocode to Plan a Procedure

**Pseudocode** uses short phrases to describe the steps a procedure needs to take to accomplish its goal. Even though the word *pseudocode* might be unfamiliar to you, you already have written pseudocode without even realizing it. Think about the last time you gave directions to someone. You wrote each direction down on paper, in your own words; your directions were a form of pseudocode. Figure 3.24 shows the pseudocode for the procedures that need to be coded in the Skate-Away Sales application.

### calcButton Click Event Procedure (pseudocode)

1. calculate total skateboards ordered = blue skateboards ordered + yellow skateboards ordered
2. calculate total price = total skateboards ordered * skateboard price * (1 + sales tax rate)
3. display total skateboards ordered and total price in totalBoardsLabel and totalPriceLabel

### clearButton Click Event Procedure (pseudocode)

1. clear the Text property of the nameTextBox, addressTextBox, cityTextBox, stateTextBox, zipTextBox, blueTextBox, and yellowTextBox
2. clear the Text property of the totalBoardsLabel and totalPriceLabel
3. send the focus to the nameTextBox so the user can begin entering the next order

### exitButton Click Event Procedure (pseudocode)

1. end the application

**FIGURE 3.24**     Pseudocode for the Skate-Away Sales application

As the pseudocode indicates, the calcButton's Click event procedure is responsible for calculating the total skateboards ordered and the total price, and then displaying the calculated results in the appropriate label controls in the interface. The clearButton's Click event procedure will prepare the screen for the next order by removing the contents of the text boxes and two label controls, and then sending the focus to the nameTextBox. The exitButton's Click event procedure will simply end the application.

## Using a Flowchart to Plan a Procedure

Unlike pseudocode, which consists of short phrases, a **flowchart** uses standardized symbols to show the steps a procedure must follow to reach its goal. Figure 3.25 shows the flowcharts for the procedures that need to be coded in the Skate-Away Sales application. Notice that the logic pictured in the flowcharts is the same as the logic shown in the pseudocode.

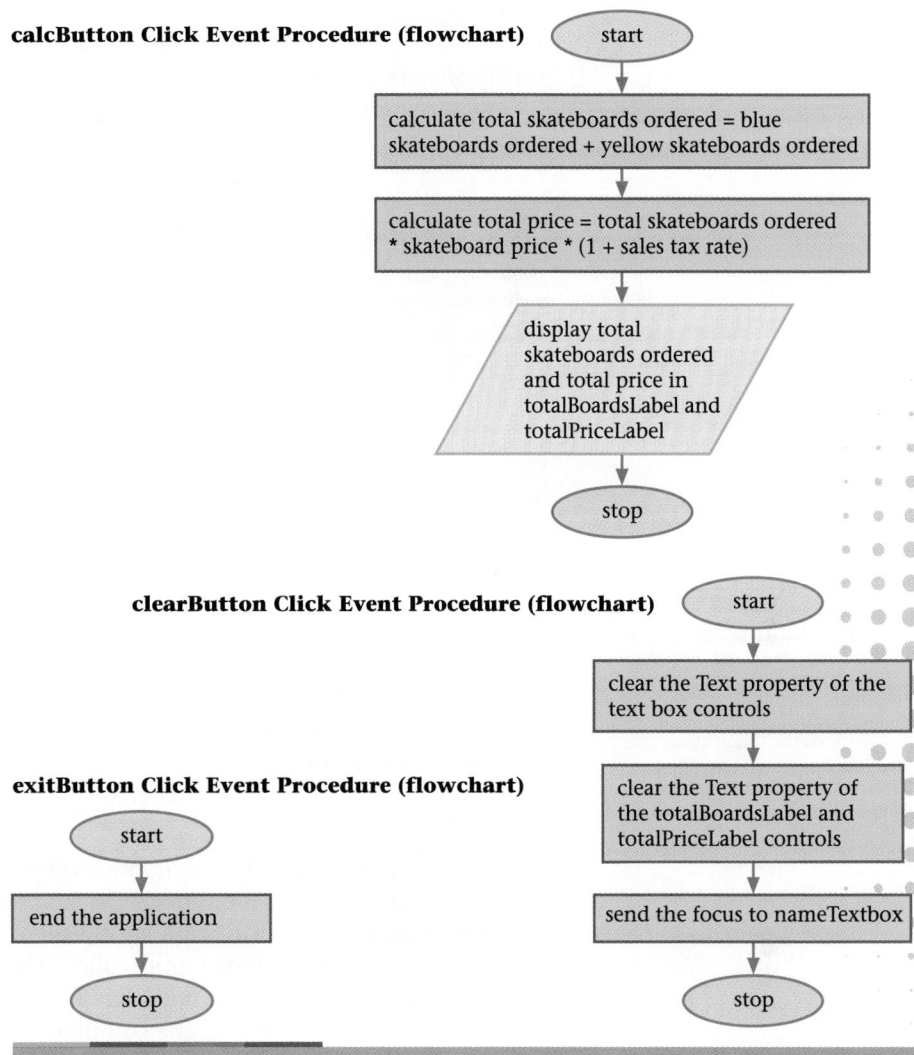

**FIGURE 3.25** Flowcharts for the Skate-Away Sales application

The flowcharts shown in Figure 3.25 contain three different symbols: an oval, a rectangle, and a parallelogram. The symbols are connected with lines, called **flowlines**. The oval symbol is called the **start/stop symbol**. The start oval indicates the beginning of the flowchart, and the stop oval indicates the end of the flowchart. The rectangles that appear between the start and the stop ovals are called **process symbols**. You use the process symbol to represent tasks such as making calculations.

The parallelogram in a flowchart is called the **input/output symbol** and is used to represent input tasks, such as getting information from the user, and output tasks, such as displaying information. The parallelogram shown in Figure 3.25 represents an output task.

When planning a procedure, you do not need to create both a flowchart and pseudocode; you need to use only one of these planning tools. The tool you use is really a matter of personal preference. For simple procedures, pseudocode works just fine. When a procedure becomes more complex, however, the procedure's steps may be easier to understand in a flowchart. In this book, you usually will use pseudocode when planning procedures.

**TIP**

In Chapters 4 and 5, you learn the purpose of another flowchart symbol: the diamond.

The programmer uses either the procedure's pseudocode or its flowchart as a guide when coding the procedure. For example, according to the pseudocode and flowchart shown in Figures 3.24 and 3.25, the exitButton control's Click event procedure has one task, and that is to end the application. The task is accomplished by the `Me.Close()` statement shown in Figure 3.26.

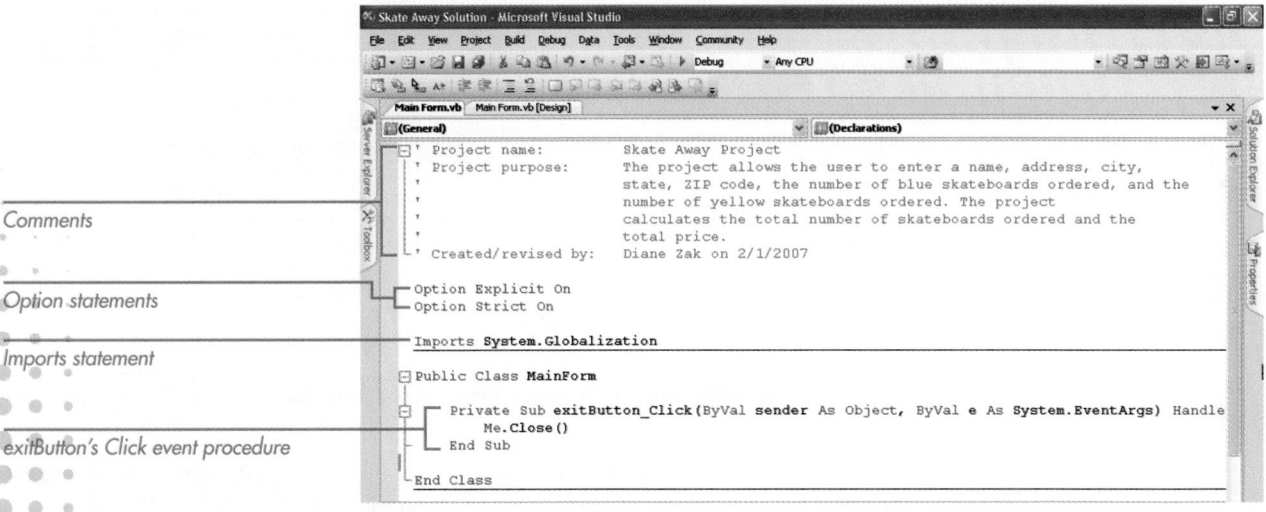

Comments

Option statements

Imports statement

exitButton's Click event procedure

**FIGURE 3.26**    Comments and statements entered in the Code Editor window

Notice that the Code Editor window shown in Figure 3.26 contains some comments and statements in its General Declarations section. The comments document the project's name and purpose, as well as the programmer's name and the date the code was either created or modified. The `Option Explicit On` statement prevents you from using an undeclared variable in your code. The `Option Strict On` statement prevents the computer from performing any implicit type conversions that may lead to a loss of data. Recall that the `Imports System.Globalization` statement imports the System.Globalization namespace, which contains the definitions for the *numberStyles* and `NumberFormatInfo.CurrrentInfo` values used in the TryParse method.

Next, you learn how to code the clearButton's Click event procedure.

## CODING THE CLEARBUTTON'S CLICK EVENT PROCEDURE

According to the TOE chart shown earlier in Figure 3.23, the clearButton's Click event procedure is assigned the task of clearing the screen for the next order. The procedure's pseudocode, shown in Figure 3.27, indicates that the task involves clearing the Text property of seven text boxes and two labels in the interface, and then sending the focus to the nameTextBox.

---

**clearButton Click Event Procedure (pseudocode)**

1. clear the Text property of the nameTextBox, addressTextBox, cityTextBox, stateTextBox, zipTextBox, blueTextBox, and yellowTextBox
2. clear the Text property of the totalBoardsLabel and totalPriceLabel
3. send the focus to the nameTextBox so the user can begin entering the next order

**FIGURE 3.27**    Pseudocode for the clearButton's Click event procedure

Before viewing the code for the procedure, you first learn how to clear the contents of a control's Text property while an application is running. You then learn how to set the focus while an application is running.

## Clearing the Contents of a Control's Text Property

Figure 3.28 lists several techniques for clearing a control's Text property while an application is running. The figure also includes examples of using these techniques.

**HOW TO...**

**Clear a Control's Text Property While An Application Is Running**

- Assign a zero-length string ("") to the Text property.
- Assign the value `String.Empty` to the Text property.
- If the control is a text box, use the Clear method.

**Examples**

```
nameTextBox.Text = ""
totalLabel.Text = String.Empty
stateTextBox.Clear()
```

**FIGURE 3.28**    How to clear a control's Text property while an application is running

As Figure 3.28 indicates, you can clear the Text property of a control by assigning a zero-length string to it. Recall that a string is a group of characters enclosed in quotation marks. The word "Jones", for example, is a string. Likewise, "45" is a string, but 45 is not; 45 is a number. "Jones" is a string with a length of five, because there are five characters between the quotation marks. "45" is a string with a length of two, because there are two characters between the quotation marks. Following this logic, a **zero-length string**, also called an **empty string**, is a set of quotation marks with nothing between them, like this: "". Assigning a zero-length string to the Text property of a control while an application is running removes the contents of the control.

Notice that you also can assign the value **String.Empty** to the Text property of a control. When you do this, the computer assigns the empty string ("") to the Text property, thereby removing its contents. In other words, the statement `totalLabel.Text = String.Empty` is equivalent to the statement `totalLabel.Text = ""`.

**TIP**

You cannot use the Clear method to remove the contents of a label control's Text property.

## HOW TO...

**TIP**

If you can anticipate the control the user will employ next, you can use the Focus method to send the focus to the control. Doing this gives the user immediate access to the control, and it saves the user the time and effort needed to either click the control or tab to it.

If the control is a text box, you also can use the **Clear method** to remove the contents of the Text property. In other words, the statement `stateTextBox.Clear()` is equivalent to the statement `stateTextBox.Text = ""` and to the statement `stateTextBox.Text = String.Empty`.

Next, you learn how to set the focus while an application is running.

### Setting the Focus

You can use the **Focus method** to move the focus to a specified control while the application is running. As you learned in Chapter 2, when a control has the focus, it can accept user input. Figure 3.29 shows the syntax of the Focus method and includes two examples of using the method.

---

**Use the Focus method**

**Syntax**
*object*.**Focus()**

**Examples**
`nameTextBox.Focus()`
sends the focus to the nameTextBox

`clearButton.Focus()`
sends the focus to the clearButton

---

**FIGURE 3.29**     How to use the Focus method

In the syntax shown in Figure 3.29, *object* is the name of the object to which you want the focus sent. For example, to send the focus to the nameTextBox, you use the statement `nameTextBox.Focus()`. Similarly, to send the focus to the clearButton, you use the statement `clearButton.Focus()`. Figure 3.30 shows the code for the clearButton's Click event procedure in the Skate-Away Sales application. The procedure sends the focus to the nameTextBox so that the user can begin entering the next order.

```
Public Class MainForm

    Private Sub exitButton_Click(ByVal sender As Object, ByVal e As System.EventArgs) Handle
        Me.Close()
    End Sub

    Private Sub clearButton_Click(ByVal sender As Object, ByVal e As System.EventArgs) Handl
        ' prepare the screen for the next order

        ' clear the text boxes and labels, then set the focus
        nameTextBox.Clear()
        addressTextBox.Clear()
        cityTextBox.Clear()
        stateTextBox.Clear()
        zipTextBox.Clear()
        blueTextBox.Clear()
        yellowTextBox.Clear()
        totalBoardsLabel.Text = ""
        totalPriceLabel.Text = ""
        nameTextBox.Focus()
    End Sub

End Class
```

*clearButton's Click event procedure*

**FIGURE 3.30**     The clearButton's Click event procedure

The calcButton's Click event procedure is the only procedure that still needs to be coded.

## CODING THE CALCBUTTON'S CLICK EVENT PROCEDURE

According to the TOE chart shown earlier in Figure 3.23, the calcButton's Click event procedure is responsible for calculating both the total number of skateboards ordered and the total price of the order, and then displaying the calculated amounts in the totalBoardsLabel and totalPriceLabel. The procedure's pseudocode is shown in Figure 3.31.

---

**calcButton Click Event Procedure (pseudocode)**

1. calculate total skateboards ordered = blue skateboards ordered + yellow skateboards ordered

2. calculate total price = total skateboards ordered * skateboard price * (1 + sales tax rate)

3. display total skateboards ordered and total price in totalBoardsLabel and totalPriceLabel

---

**FIGURE 3.31** Pseudocode for the calcButton's Click event procedure

The first step listed in the pseudocode shown in Figure 3.31 is to calculate the total number of skateboards ordered. This is accomplished by adding the number of blue skateboards ordered to the number of yellow skateboards ordered. Recall that the number of blue skateboards ordered is recorded in the blueTextBox's Text property as the user enters that information in the interface. Likewise, the number of yellow skateboards ordered is recorded in the yellowTextBox's Text property.

The next step listed in the pseudocode is to calculate the total price of the order. You do this by multiplying the total number of skateboards ordered by the skateboard price ($100), and then adding a 5% sales tax to the result. Step 3 in the pseudocode indicates that the total skateboards ordered and the total price should be displayed in the totalBoardsLabel and totalPriceLabel, respectively, in the interface. Figure 3.32 shows two of the many ways of writing the code for the calcButton's Click event procedure.

---

**Version 1**

```
Private Sub calcButton_Click(ByVal sender As Object, ByVal e As System.EventArgs) _
    Handles calcButton.Click
    ' calculates the total number of skateboards ordered and the total price

    ' declare variables
    Dim blueBoards As Integer
    Dim yellowBoards As Integer
    Dim isConverted As Boolean
```

*(Figure is continued on next page)*

```
    ' convert input
    isConverted = Integer.TryParse(blueTextBox.Text, _
        NumberStyles.AllowThousands, NumberFormatInfo.CurrentInfo, blueBoards)
    isConverted = Integer.TryParse(yellowTextBox.Text, _
        NumberStyles.AllowThousands, NumberFormatInfo.CurrentInfo, yellowBoards)

    ' calculate and display total skateboards and total price
    totalBoardsLabel.Text = Convert.ToString(blueBoards + yellowBoards)
    totalPriceLabel.Text = _
        Convert.ToString(Convert.ToDecimal(totalBoardsLabel.Text) * 100D * (1D + 0.05D))
End Sub
```

**Version 2**

```
Private Sub calcButton_Click(ByVal sender As Object, ByVal e As System.EventArgs) _
    Handles calcButton.Click
    ' calculates the total number of skateboards ordered and the total price

    ' declare constants and variables
    Const TaxRate As Decimal = 0.05D
    Const SkateboardPrice As Decimal = 100D
    Dim blueBoards As Integer
    Dim yellowBoards As Integer
    Dim totalSkateboards As Integer
    Dim totalPrice As Decimal
    Dim isConverted As Boolean

    ' convert input
    isConverted = Integer.TryParse(blueTextBox.Text, _
        NumberStyles.AllowThousands, NumberFormatInfo.CurrentInfo, blueBoards)
    isConverted = Integer.TryParse(yellowTextBox.Text, _
        NumberStyles.AllowThousands, NumberFormatInfo.CurrentInfo, yellowBoards)

    ' calculate total skateboards and total price
    totalSkateboards = blueBoards + yellowBoards
    totalPrice = (totalSkateboards * SkateboardPrice) * (1 + TaxRate)

    ' display calculated results
    totalBoardsLabel.Text = Convert.ToString(totalSkateboards)
    totalPriceLabel.Text = Convert.ToString(totalPrice)
End Sub
```

**FIGURE 3.32** Two versions of the code for the calcButton's Click event procedure

Notice that Version 1's code uses three variables, while Version 2's code uses five variables and two named constants. Although Version 2's code is longer than Version 1's code, the variables and named constants in Version 2's code make the calculation statements easier to understand.

Figure 3.33 shows the completed code for the Skate-Away Sales application.

```
' Project name:          Skate Away Project
' Project purpose:       The project allows the user to enter a name, address, city,
'                        state, ZIP code, the number of blue skateboards ordered, and the
'                        number of yellow skateboards ordered. The project
'                        calculates the total number of skateboards ordered and the
'                        total price.
' Created/revised by:    Diane Zak on 2/1/2007

Option Explicit On
Option Strict On

Imports System.Globalization

Public Class MainForm

    Private Sub exitButton_Click(ByVal sender As Object, ByVal e As System.EventArgs) _
        Handles exitButton.Click
        Me.Close()
    End Sub

    Private Sub clearButton_Click(ByVal sender As Object, ByVal e As System.EventArgs) _
        Handles clearButton.Click
        ' prepare the screen for the next order

        ' clear the text boxes and labels, then set the focus
        nameTextBox.Clear()
        addressTextBox.Clear()
        cityTextBox.Clear()
        stateTextBox.Clear()
        zipTextBox.Clear()
        blueTextBox.Clear()
        yellowTextBox.Clear()
        totalBoardsLabel.Text = ""
        totalPriceLabel.Text = ""
        nameTextBox.Focus()
    End Sub

    Private Sub calcButton_Click(ByVal sender As Object, ByVal e As System.EventArgs) _
        Handles calcButton.Click
        ' calculates the total number of skateboards ordered and the total price

        ' declare constants and variables
        Const TaxRate As Decimal = 0.05D
        Const SkateboardPrice As Decimal = 100D
        Dim blueBoards As Integer
        Dim yellowBoards As Integer
        Dim totalSkateboards As Integer
        Dim totalPrice As Decimal
        Dim isConverted As Boolean
```

*(Figure is continued on next page)*

```
            ' convert input
            isConverted = Integer.TryParse(blueTextBox.Text, _
                NumberStyles.AllowThousands, NumberFormatInfo.CurrentInfo, blueBoards)
            isConverted = Integer.TryParse(yellowTextBox.Text, _
                NumberStyles.AllowThousands, NumberFormatInfo.CurrentInfo, yellowBoards)

            ' calculate total skateboards and total price
            totalSkateboards = blueBoards + yellowBoards
            totalPrice = (totalSkateboards * SkateboardPrice) * (1 + TaxRate)

            ' display calculated results
            totalBoardsLabel.Text = Convert.ToString(totalSkateboards)
            totalPriceLabel.Text = Convert.ToString(totalPrice)
        End Sub
    End Class
```

**FIGURE 3.33**   Completed code for the Skate-Away Sales application

After coding an application, you then need to test the application to verify that the code works correctly. If the code contains an error, called a **bug**, you need to correct the error before giving the application to the user.

## TESTING AND DEBUGGING THE APPLICATION

You test an application by starting it and entering some sample data. You should use both valid and invalid test data. **Valid data** is data that the application is expecting. For example, the Skate-Away Sales application is expecting the user to enter a numeric value as the number of blue skateboards ordered. **Invalid data**, on the other hand, is data that the application is not expecting. The Skate-Away Sales application, for example, is not expecting the user to enter a letter for the number of either blue or yellow skateboards ordered. You should test the application as thoroughly as possible, because you don't want to give the user an application that ends abruptly when invalid data is entered.

**Debugging** refers to the process of locating errors in the program. Program errors can be either syntax errors or logic errors. Most **syntax errors** are simply typing errors that occur when entering instructions. For example, typing `Me.Clse()` instead of `Me.Close()` results in a syntax error. The Code Editor detects most syntax errors as you enter the instructions. An example of a much more difficult type of error to find, and one that the Code Editor cannot detect, is a logic error. You create a **logic error** when you enter an instruction that does not give you the expected results. An example of a logic error is the instruction `average = num1 + num2 / 2`, which is supposed to calculate the average of two numbers. Although the instruction is syntactically correct, it is logically incorrect. The instruction to calculate the average of two numbers, written correctly, is `average = (num1 + num2) / 2`. Because division has a higher precedence number than does addition, you must place parentheses around the `num1 + num2` part of the expression.

First, you will test the Skate-Away Sales application using valid data. Assume that you start the application and then enter your name, address, city, state, and ZIP code. You also enter 5 as the number of blue skateboards ordered and 10 as the number of yellow skateboards ordered. After clicking the Calculate Order button, the interface will appear similar to the one shown in Figure 3.34.

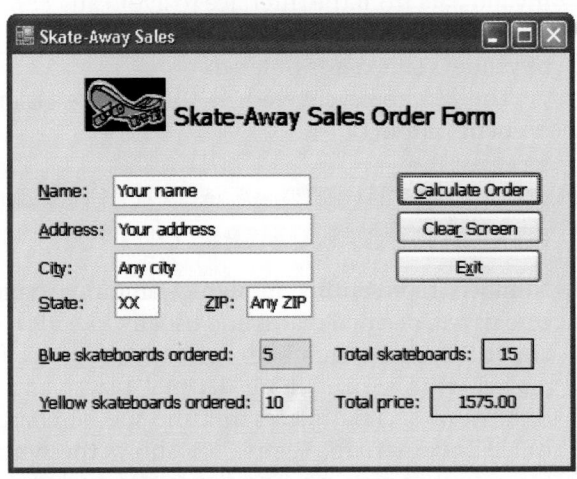

**FIGURE 3.34**     Result of testing the application using valid data

The interface shown in Figure 3.34 indicates that a total of 15 skateboards were ordered at a cost of 1575.00; both amounts are correct.

Now you will test the Skate-Away Sales application using invalid data. More specifically, you will enter a letter as the number of yellow skateboards ordered. In this test, assume that you start the application and then enter your name, address, city, state, and ZIP code. You also enter 5 as the number of blue skateboards ordered, but you inadvertently enter the letter "t" as the number of yellow skateboards ordered. After clicking the Calculate Order button, the interface will appear similar to the one shown in Figure 3.35.

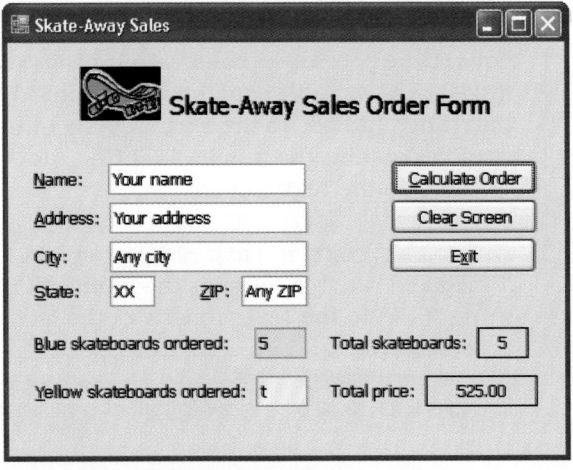

**FIGURE 3.35**     Result of testing the application using invalid data

In this case, the interface indicates that a total of 5 skateboards were ordered at a cost of 525.00. Notice that the application ignores the letter "t" entered as the number of yellow skateboards ordered. Although the invalid data did not cause the application to end abruptly, you should check with the person for whom you wrote the application to verify that this is how he or she wants the application to work. The person might want the application to remove the invalid data from the interface to avoid any confusion. Or, he or she might want the application to display a message prompting the user to re-enter the number of yellow skateboards ordered.

The last topic covered in this chapter is how to format an application's numeric output.

## FORMATTING NUMERIC OUTPUT

Numbers representing monetary amounts typically are displayed with either zero or two decimal places and usually include a dollar sign and a thousands separator. Similarly, numbers representing percentage amounts usually are displayed with zero or more decimal places and a percent sign. Specifying the number of decimal places and the special characters to display in a number is called **formatting**. Figure 3.36 shows the syntax you use to format a number for output as a string. The figure also includes several examples of formatting numbers.

### HOW TO...

**Format a Number for Output as a String**

**Syntax**

*variablename*.**ToString**(*formatString*)

**Examples**
```
commissionLabel.Text = commission.ToString("C")
```
if the `commission` variable contains the number 1250, the statement assigns the string "$1,250.00" to the Text property of the commissionLabel

```
totalLabel.Text = total.ToString("N2")
```
if the `total` variable contains the number 123.675, the statement assigns the string "123.68" to the Text property of the totalLabel; however, if the variable contains the number 123.674, the statement assigns the string "123.67" to the Text property

```
rateLabel.Text = rate.ToString("P0")
```
if the `rate` variable contains the number .06, the statement assigns the string "6 %" to the Text property of the rateLabel

**FIGURE 3.36**    How to format a number for output as a string

In the syntax shown in Figure 3.36, *variablename* is the name of a numeric variable, and ToString is a method that can be used with any of the numeric data types. The *formatString* argument in the syntax is a string that specifies the format you want to use. The *formatString* argument, which must be enclosed in double quotation marks, takes the form *Axx*, where *A* is an alphabetic character called the **format specifier**, and *xx* is a sequence of digits called the **precision specifier**. The format specifier must be one of the built-in format characters; the most commonly used format characters are listed in Figure 3.37. The precision specifier controls the number of significant digits or zeros to the right of the decimal point in the formatted number. As the second example shown in Figure 3.36 indicates, the ToString method rounds the number up if the number to its right is 5 or greater; otherwise, it truncates the excess digits.

| Format specifier | Name | Description |
|---|---|---|
| C or c | Currency | displays a number with a dollar sign; the precision specifier indicates the desired number of decimal places; if appropriate, displays a number with a thousands separator; negative numbers are enclosed in parentheses |
| D or d | Decimal | formats only integers; the precision specifier indicates the minimum number of digits desired; if required, the number is padded with zeros to its left to produce the number of digits specified by the precision specifier; negative numbers are preceded by a minus sign |
| F or f | Fixed-point | the precision specifier indicates the desired number of decimal places; negative numbers are preceded by a minus sign |
| N or n | Number | the precision specifier indicates the desired number of decimal places; if appropriate, displays a number with a thousands separator; negative numbers are preceded by a minus sign |
| P or p | Percent | the precision specifier indicates the desired number of decimal places; multiplies the number by 100 and displays the number with a percent sign; negative numbers are preceded by a minus sign |

**FIGURE 3.37** Most commonly used format specifiers

Notice that you can use either an uppercase letter or a lowercase letter as the format specifier. Figure 3.38 shows examples of how various *formatString*s format numeric values.

| formatString | Value | Result |
|---|---|---|
| C | 3764 | $3,764.00 |
| C0 | 3764 | $3,764 |
| C2 | 3764 | $3,764.00 |
| C2 | 456.783 | $456.78 |
| C2 | 456.785 | $456.79 |
| C2 | -75.31 | ($75.31) |
| D | 3764 | 3764 |
| D | -53 | -53 |
| D3 | 8 | 008 |
| D3 | 15 | 015 |
| F | 3764 | 3764.00 |
| F0 | 3764 | 3764 |
| F2 | 3764 | 3764.00 |
| F2 | 456.783 | 456.78 |
| F2 | 456.785 | 456.79 |
| F2 | -75.31 | -75.31 |
| N | 3764 | 3,764.00 |
| N0 | 3764 | 3,764 |
| N2 | 3764 | 3,764.00 |
| N2 | 456.783 | 456.78 |
| N2 | 456.785 | 456.79 |
| N2 | -75.31 | -75.31 |
| P | .364 | 36.40% |
| P | -.05 | -5.00% |
| P1 | .3645 | 36.5% |
| P2 | 1.1 | 110.00% |

**FIGURE 3.38**    *Examples of how various formatStrings format numeric values*

**TIP**

To learn how to create custom *formatStrings*, click Help on the menu bar, and then click Index. Click Visual Basic in the Filtered by list box, then type *custom numeric format strings* in the Look for text box, and then press Enter.

Recall that the Skate-Away Sales application displays the total price of the order in the totalPriceLabel. To include a dollar sign, thousands separator, and two decimal places when displaying the total price, you need simply to change the `totalPriceLabel.Text = Convert.ToString(totalPrice)` statement in the calcButton's Click event procedure to `totalPriceLabel.Text = totalPrice.ToString("C2")`. You also could use the statement `totalPriceLabel.Text = totalPrice.ToString("C")`, because the default precision specifier for the Currency format is two decimal places. However, including the precision specifier in the *formatString* makes the statement more self-documenting. Figure 3.39 shows the calcButton's modified Click event procedure, and Figure 3.40 shows the formatted output in the interface.

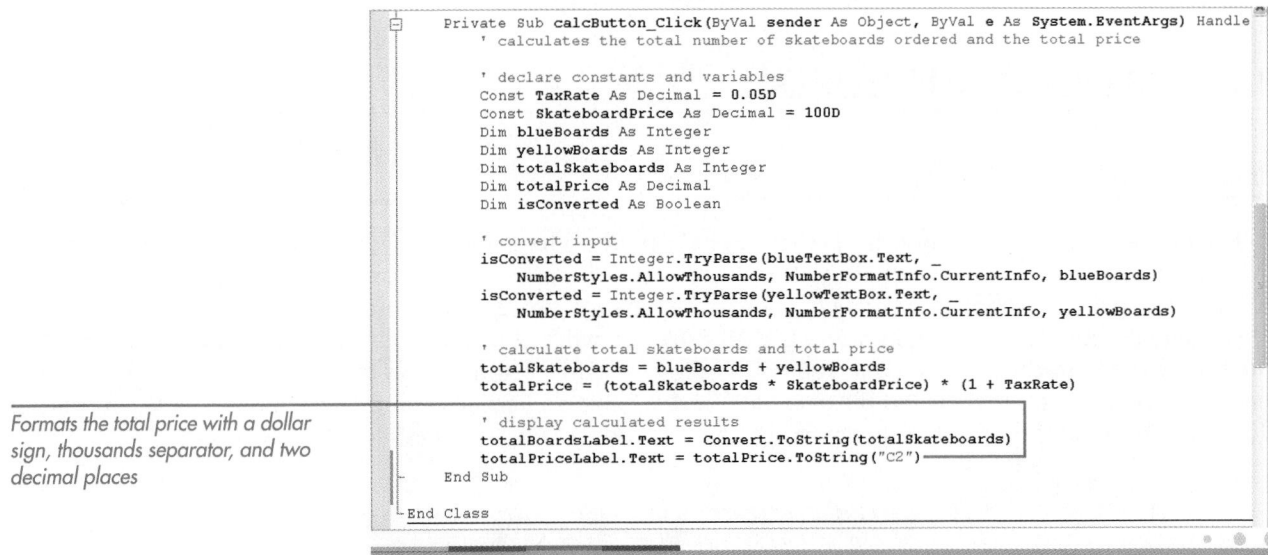

```
Private Sub calcButton_Click(ByVal sender As Object, ByVal e As System.EventArgs) Handle
    ' calculates the total number of skateboards ordered and the total price

    ' declare constants and variables
    Const TaxRate As Decimal = 0.05D
    Const SkateboardPrice As Decimal = 100D
    Dim blueBoards As Integer
    Dim yellowBoards As Integer
    Dim totalSkateboards As Integer
    Dim totalPrice As Decimal
    Dim isConverted As Boolean

    ' convert input
    isConverted = Integer.TryParse(blueTextBox.Text, _
        NumberStyles.AllowThousands, NumberFormatInfo.CurrentInfo, blueBoards)
    isConverted = Integer.TryParse(yellowTextBox.Text, _
        NumberStyles.AllowThousands, NumberFormatInfo.CurrentInfo, yellowBoards)

    ' calculate total skateboards and total price
    totalSkateboards = blueBoards + yellowBoards
    totalPrice = (totalSkateboards * SkateboardPrice) * (1 + TaxRate)

    ' display calculated results
    totalBoardsLabel.Text = Convert.ToString(totalSkateboards)
    totalPriceLabel.Text = totalPrice.ToString("C2")
End Sub

End Class
```

*Formats the total price with a dollar sign, thousands separator, and two decimal places*

**FIGURE 3.39**    calcButton's modified Click event procedure

*Total price formatted with a dollar sign, thousands separator, and two decimal places*

**FIGURE 3.40**    Formatted output shown in the interface

You have completed the concepts section of Chapter 3. The next section is the Programming Tutorial section, which gives you step-by-step instructions on how to apply the chapter's concepts to an application. A Programming Example follows the Programming Tutorial. The Programming Example is a completed program that demonstrates the concepts taught in the chapter. Following the Programming Example are the Quick Review, Key Terms, Self-Check Questions and Answers, Review Questions, Review Exercises – Short Answer, Computer Exercises, and Case Projects sections.

# PROGRAMMING TUTORIAL

## Creating the Change Game Application

In this tutorial, you create an application that can help students in grades 1 through 6 learn how to make change. The application will allow the student to enter the amount of money a customer owes and the amount of money the customer paid. It then will calculate the amount of change, as well as the number of dollars, quarters, dimes, nickels, and pennies to return to the customer. For now, you will not worry about the situation where the amount owed is greater than the amount paid. You will assume that the customer pays either the exact amount or more than the exact amount. Included in the data files for this book is a partially completed Change Game application. The application's user interface is shown in Figure 3.41, and its TOE chart is shown in Figure 3.42.

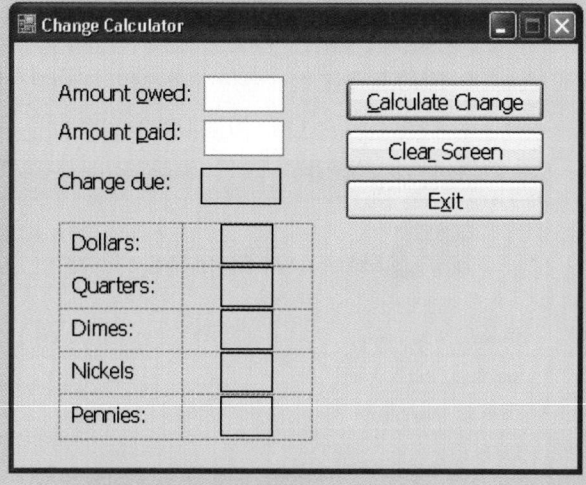

**FIGURE 3.41**    MainForm

| Task | Object | Event |
|---|---|---|
| 1. Calculate the change<br>2. Calculate the number of dollars, quarters, dimes, nickels, and pennies<br>3. Display the change and number of dollars, quarters, dimes, nickels, and pennies in the appropriate label controls | calcButton | Click |
| 1. Clear the screen for the next calculation<br>2. Send the focus to the owedTextBox | clearButton | Click |
| End the application | exitButton | Click |
| Get and display the amount owed | owedTextBox | None |
| Get and display the amount paid | paidTextBox | None |
| Display the change (from calcButton) | changeLabel | None |
| Display the number of dollars (from calcButton) | dollarLabel | None |
| Display the number of quarters (from calcButton) | quarterLabel | None |
| Display the number of dimes (from calcButton) | dimeLabel | None |
| Display the number of nickels (from calcButton) | nickelLabel | None |
| Display the number of pennies (from calcButton) | pennyLabel | None |

**FIGURE 3.42**   TOE Chart

## Completing the Change Game Application

As the TOE chart shown in Figure 3.42 indicates, only three Click event procedures need to be coded.

**To begin coding the application:**

1. Start Visual Studio. If necessary, close the Start Page window.
2. Open the **Change Solution** (Change Solution.sln) file, which is contained in the VbReloaded\ Chap03\Change Solution folder. If necessary, open the designer window. The MainForm shown earlier in Figure 3.41 appears on the screen.
3. Open the Code Editor window. Notice that the exitButton's Click event procedure has already been coded for you.
4. In the comments that appear in the General Declarations section, replace the <your name> and <current date> text with your name and the current date.

The application will use variables and the optional arguments in the TryParse method, so you will need to enter the appropriate Option and Imports statements in the General Declarations section.

5. Enter the Option and Imports statements shown in Figure 3.43.

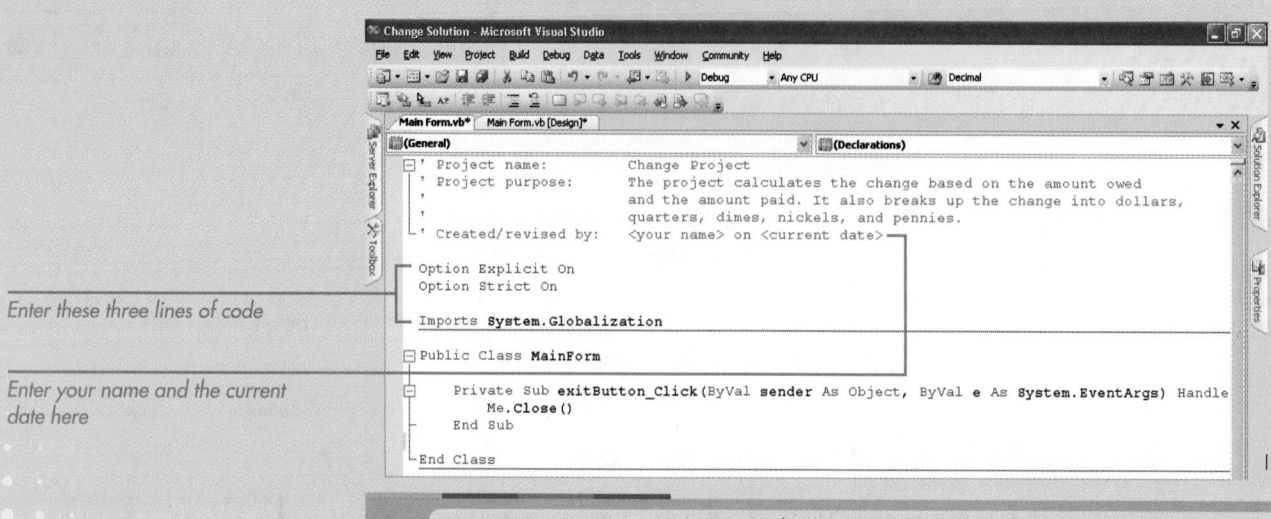

Enter these three lines of code

Enter your name and the current date here

**FIGURE 3.43**    Option and Imports statements entered in the General Declarations section

The first procedure you will code is the clearButton's Click event procedure.

## Coding the clearButton's Click Event Procedure

According to the TOE chart shown earlier in Figure 3.42, the clearButton's Click event procedure is responsible for clearing the screen for the next calculation, and then sending the focus to the owedTextBox. Clearing the screen involves removing the contents of the two text boxes and six of the labels in the interface. Figure 3.44 shows the procedure's pseudocode.

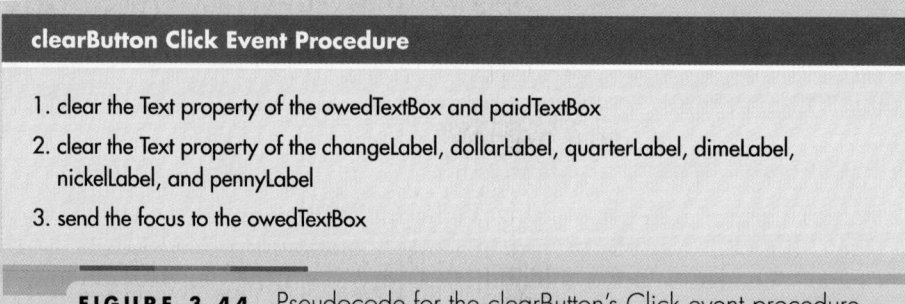

**clearButton Click Event Procedure**

1. clear the Text property of the owedTextBox and paidTextBox
2. clear the Text property of the changeLabel, dollarLabel, quarterLabel, dimeLabel, nickelLabel, and pennyLabel
3. send the focus to the owedTextBox

**FIGURE 3.44**    Pseudocode for the clearButton's Click event procedure

**To code the clearButton's Click event procedure:**

1. Open the code template for the clearButton's Click event procedure.

You will use the Clear method to remove the contents of the two text boxes. You will remove the contents of the labels by assigning a zero-length string to their Text properties. You will use the Focus method to send the focus to the owedTextBox.

2. Enter the code indicated in Figure 3.45, which shows the completed procedure.

```
Private Sub clearButton_Click(ByVal sender As Object, ByVal e As System.EventArgs) Handl
    ' clears the screen for the next calculation

    'clear the text boxes and labels, then set the focus
    owedTextBox.Clear()
    paidTextBox.Clear()
    changeLabel.Text = ""
    dollarLabel.Text = ""
    quarterLabel.Text = ""
    dimeLabel.Text = ""
    nickelLabel.Text = ""
    pennyLabel.Text = ""
    owedTextBox.Focus()
End Sub
```

*Enter these comments and lines of code*

**FIGURE 3.45**    clearButton's Click event procedure

3. Save the solution.

Next, you will code the calcButton's Click event procedure.

### Coding the calcButton's Click Event Procedure

According to the TOE chart shown earlier in Figure 3.42, the calcButton's Click event procedure is responsible for calculating and displaying the amount of change to give the customer. It also must calculate and display the number of dollars, quarters, dimes, nickels, and pennies to return. Figure 3.46 shows the procedure's pseudocode.

---

**calcButton Click Event Procedure**

1. calculate the change by subtracting the amount owed from the amount paid

2. assign the change to a temporary variable named temp

3. calculate the number of dollars by multiplying the contents of the temp variable by 100.0, and then dividing the result by 100

4. calculate the remaining change by subtracting the number of dollars from the contents of the temp variable

5. calculate the number of quarters by multiplying the contents of the temp variable by 100.0, and then dividing the result by 25

6. calculate the remaining change by multiplying the number of quarters by .25, and then subtracting the result from the contents of the temp variable

7. calculate the number of dimes by multiplying the contents of the temp variable by 100.0, and then dividing the result by 10

8. calculate the remaining change by multiplying the number of dimes by .1, and then subtracting the result from the contents of the temp variable

9. calculate the number of nickels by multiplying the contents of the temp variable by 100.0, and then dividing the result by 5

10. calculate the remaining change by multiplying the number of nickels by .05, and then subtracting the result from the contents of the temp variable

11. calculate the number of pennies by multiplying the contents of the temp variable by 100.0

12. display the change in the changeLabel

13. display the number of dollars, quarters, dimes, nickels, and pennies in the dollarLabel, quarterLabel, dimeLabel, nickelLabel, and pennyLabel

---

**FIGURE 3.46**    Pseudocode for the calcButton's Click event procedure

**To code the calcButton's Click event procedure:**

1. Open the code template for the calcButton's Click event procedure.
2. Enter the comments, variable declaration statements, and assignment statements shown in Figure 3.47. Then position the insertion point as shown in the figure. Do not worry about the green squiggly lines that appear below some of the variable names. The lines indicate that the variable has been declared, but it does not appear in any other statement in the code. The squiggly lines do not appear below the owed, paid, or isConverted variable names, because those names are included in the two assignment statements entered in the code.

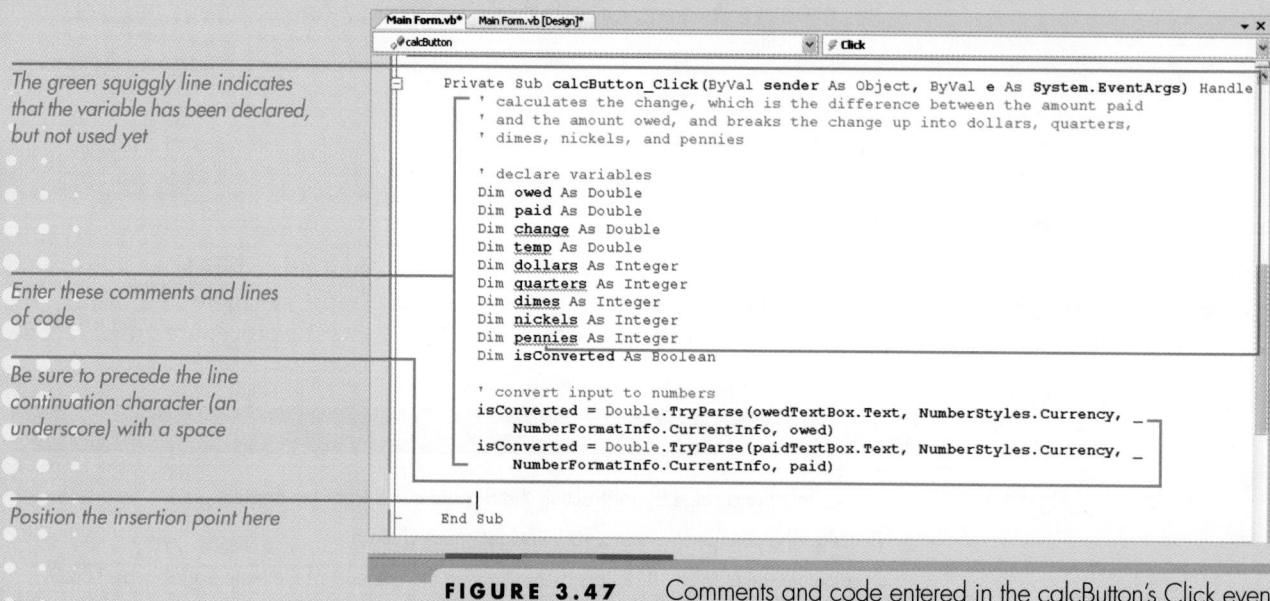

*The green squiggly line indicates that the variable has been declared, but not used yet*

*Enter these comments and lines of code*

*Be sure to precede the line continuation character (an underscore) with a space*

*Position the insertion point here*

**FIGURE 3.47** Comments and code entered in the calcButton's Click event procedure

The first 11 steps in the pseudocode pertain to calculating the change, as well as calculating the number of dollars, quarters, dimes, nickels, and pennies.

3. Enter the following comment and code. Press **Enter** twice after typing the last line.

```
' calculate the change
change = paid - owed
temp = change
dollars = Convert.ToInt32(temp * 100.0) \ 100
temp = temp - Convert.ToDouble(dollars)
quarters = Convert.ToInt32(temp * 100.0) \ 25
temp = temp - Convert.ToDouble(quarters) * 0.25
dimes = Convert.ToInt32(temp * 100.0) \ 10
temp = temp - Convert.ToDouble(dimes) * 0.1
nickels = Convert.ToInt32(temp * 100.0) \ 5
temp = temp - Convert.ToDouble(nickels) * 0.05
pennies = Convert.ToInt32(temp * 100.0)
```

The last two steps in the pseudocode pertain to displaying the calculated amounts.

4. Enter the following comment and code.

```
' display change, dollars, quarters, dimes, nickels, and pennies
changeLabel.Text = Convert.ToString(change)
dollarLabel.Text = Convert.ToString(dollars)
quarterLabel.Text = Convert.ToString(quarters)
dimeLabel.Text = Convert.ToString(dimes)
nickelLabel.Text = Convert.ToString(nickels)
pennyLabel.Text = Convert.ToString(pennies)
```

5. Save the solution. Figure 3.48 shows the Change Game application's code.

```
' Project name:          Change Project
' Project purpose:       The project calculates the change based on the amount owed
'                        and the amount paid. It also breaks up the change into dollars,
'                        quarters, dimes, nickels, and pennies.
' Created/revised by:    <your name> on <current date>


Option Explicit On
Option Strict On


Imports System.Globalization


Public Class MainForm

    Private Sub exitButton_Click(ByVal sender As Object, ByVal e As System.EventArgs) _
        Handles exitButton.Click
        Me.Close()
    End Sub


    Private Sub clearButton_Click(ByVal sender As Object, ByVal e As System.EventArgs) _
        Handles clearButton.Click
        ' clears the screen for the next calculation

        'clear the text boxes and labels, then set the focus
        owedTextBox.Clear()
        paidTextBox.Clear()
        changeLabel.Text = ""
        dollarLabel.Text = ""
        quarterLabel.Text = ""
        dimeLabel.Text = ""
        nickelLabel.Text = ""
        pennyLabel.Text = ""
        owedTextBox.Focus()
    End Sub


    Private Sub calcButton_Click(ByVal sender As Object, ByVal e As System.EventArgs) _
        Handles calcButton.Click
        ' calculates the change, which is the difference between the amount paid
        ' and the amount owed, and breaks the change up into dollars, quarters,
        ' dimes, nickels, and pennies
```

*(Figure is continued on next page)*

```
            ' declare variables
            Dim owed As Double
            Dim paid As Double
            Dim change As Double
            Dim temp As Double
            Dim dollars As Integer
            Dim quarters As Integer
            Dim dimes As Integer
            Dim nickels As Integer
            Dim pennies As Integer
            Dim isConverted As Boolean

            ' convert input to numbers
            isConverted = Double.TryParse(owedTextBox.Text, NumberStyles.Currency, _
                NumberFormatInfo.CurrentInfo, owed)
            isConverted = Double.TryParse(paidTextBox.Text, NumberStyles.Currency, _
                NumberFormatInfo.CurrentInfo, paid)

            ' calculate the change
            change = paid - owed
            temp = change
            dollars = Convert.ToInt32(temp * 100.0) \ 100
            temp = temp - Convert.ToDouble(dollars)
            quarters = Convert.ToInt32(temp * 100.0) \ 25
            temp = temp - Convert.ToDouble(quarters) * 0.25
            dimes = Convert.ToInt32(temp * 100.0) \ 10
            temp = temp - Convert.ToDouble(dimes) * 0.1
            nickels = Convert.ToInt32(temp * 100.0) \ 5
            temp = temp - Convert.ToDouble(nickels) * 0.05
            pennies = Convert.ToInt32(temp * 100.0)

            ' display change, dollars, quarters, dimes, nickels, and pennies
            changeLabel.Text = Convert.ToString(change)
            dollarLabel.Text = Convert.ToString(dollars)
            quarterLabel.Text = Convert.ToString(quarters)
            dimeLabel.Text = Convert.ToString(dimes)
            nickelLabel.Text = Convert.ToString(nickels)
            pennyLabel.Text = Convert.ToString(pennies)
        End Sub

End Class
```

**FIGURE 3.48** The Change Game application's code

Now test the application to verify that it is working correctly.

**To test the application:**

1. Start the application. Type **39.67** as the amount owed, and **50.00** as the amount paid. Click the **Calculate Change** button. The button's Click event procedure calculates the change, as well as the number of dollars, quarter, dimes, nickels, and pennies. It then displays the calculated results in the interface, as shown in Figure 3.49.

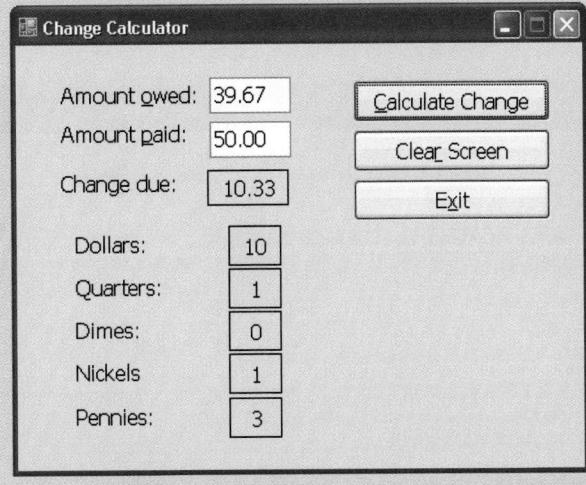

**FIGURE 3.49**    Calculated results shown in the interface

2. Click the **Clear Screen** button.
3. Test the application several more times using your own values for the amount owed and amount paid.
4. Click the **Exit** button to end the application. If necessary, close the Output window.
5. Close the solution.

# PROGRAMMING EXAMPLE

## Currency Calculator

Create an application that allows the user to enter the number of American dollars that he or she wants to convert to both British pounds and Mexican pesos. The application should make the appropriate calculations and then display the results on the screen. Name the solution Currency Calculator Solution. Name the project Currency Calculator Project. Name the form file Main Form.vb. Save the files in the VbReloaded\Chap03 folder.

**TOE Chart:**

| Task | Object | Event |
|------|--------|-------|
| 1. Convert the American dollars to British pounds<br>2. Convert the American dollars to Mexican pesos<br>3. Display the number of British pounds and the number of Mexican pesos in the britishLabel and mexicanLabel<br>4. Send the focus to the americanTextBox | calcButton | Click |
| End the application | exitButton | Click |
| Display the number of British pounds (from calcButton) | britishLabel | None |
| Display the number of Mexican pesos (from calcButton) | mexicanLabel | None |
| Get and display the number of American dollars | americanTextBox | None |

**FIGURE 3.50**

**User Interface:**

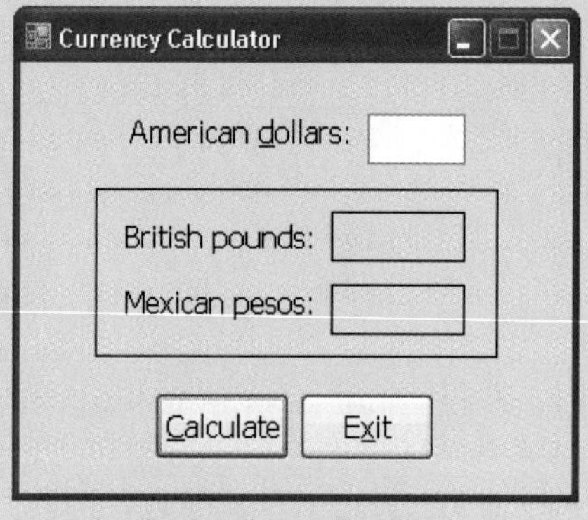

**FIGURE 3.51**

## Objects, Properties, and Settings:

| Object | Property | Setting |
|---|---|---|
| Form1 | Name | MainForm |
| | AcceptButton | calcButton |
| | Font | Tahoma, 12 point |
| | MaximizeBox | False |
| | Size | 316, 264 |
| | StartPosition | CenterScreen |
| | Text | Currency Calculator |
| Label1 | AutoSize | True |
| | Text | American &dollars: |
| Label2 | AutoSize | True |
| | Text | British pounds: |
| Label3 | AutoSize | True |
| | Text | Mexican pesos: |
| Label4 | Name | britishLabel |
| | AutoSize | False |
| | BorderStyle | FixedSingle |
| | Size | 75, 27 |
| | Text | (empty) |
| | TextAlign | MiddleCenter |
| Label5 | Name | mexicanLabel |
| | AutoSize | False |
| | BorderStyle | FixedSingle |
| | Size | 75, 27 |
| | Text | (empty) |
| | TextAlign | MiddleCenter |
| TextBox1 | Name | americanTextBox |
| Button1 | Name | calcButton |
| | Text | &Calculate |
| Button2 | Name | exitButton |
| | Text | E&xit |
| Panel1 | BorderStyle | FixedSingle |
| | Size | 225, 90 |

**FIGURE 3.52**

**Tab Order:**

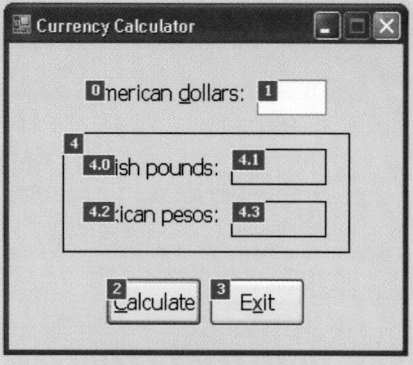

**FIGURE 3.53**

**Pseudocode:**

**exitButton Click event procedure**

1. end the application

**calcButton Click event procedure**

1. calculate number of British pounds by multiplying American dollars by .571505
2. calculate number of Mexican pesos by multiplying American dollars by 10.7956
3. display number of British pounds and number of Mexican pesos in britishLabel and mexicanLabel
4. send the focus to the americanTextBox

**FIGURE 3.54**

**Code:**

```
' Project name:        Currency Calculator Project
' Project purpose:     The project converts the number of American dollars entered by the
'                      user to the number of British pounds and Mexican pesos.
' Created/revised by:  <your name> on <current date>

Option Explicit On
Option Strict On

Imports System.Globalization

Public Class MainForm
```

*(Figure is continued on next page)*

```
    Private Sub exitButton_Click(ByVal sender As Object, ByVal e As System.EventArgs) _
        Handles exitButton.Click
        Me.Close()
    End Sub

    Private Sub calcButton_Click(ByVal sender As Object, ByVal e As System.EventArgs) _
        Handles calcButton.Click
        ' converts American dollars to British pounds and Mexican pesos

        ' declare constants and variables
        Const BritishRate As Decimal = 0.571505D
        Const MexicanRate As Decimal = 10.7956D
        Dim americanDollars As Decimal
        Dim britishPounds As Decimal
        Dim mexicanPesos As Decimal
        Dim isConverted As Boolean

        ' calculate number of British pounds and Mexican pesos
        isConverted = Decimal.TryParse(americanTextBox.Text, _
            NumberStyles.Currency, NumberFormatInfo.CurrentInfo, americanDollars)
        britishPounds = americanDollars * BritishRate
        mexicanPesos = americanDollars * MexicanRate

        ' display number of British pounds and Mexican pesos, then set focus
        britishLabel.Text = britishPounds.ToString("N2")
        mexicanLabel.Text = mexicanPesos.ToString("N2")
        americanTextBox.Focus()
    End Sub
End Class
```

**FIGURE 3.55**

## Quick Review

- Variables and named constants are computer memory locations that store data. The contents of a variable can change while the application is running. However, the contents of a named constant cannot change while the application is running.
- All variables and named constants have a name, data type, scope, and lifetime.
- The name assigned to a variable or named constant should help you remember the memory location's purpose.
- You use a declaration statement to declare a variable. If the variable has either block or procedure scope, you begin the declaration statement with the keyword Dim. If the variable has module scope, you begin the declaration statement with the keyword Private.

- You can use an assignment statement to assign a value to an existing variable while the application is running. The data type of the value should be the same as the data type of the variable.
- Unlike variables and named constants, which are computer memory locations, a literal constant is an item of data. The value of a literal constant does not change while the application is running.
- String literal constants are enclosed in quotation marks (""), whereas numeric literal constants are not enclosed in quotation marks.
- A literal type character is a letter that is appended to the end of a literal constant. You use a literal type character to specify the data type of a literal constant.
- You can use the TryParse method to convert a string to a number. If the string can be converted, the method converts the string to a number and stores the number in a numeric variable; it also returns the Boolean value True. If the string cannot be converted, the method stores the number zero in the numeric variable and returns the Boolean value False.
- You use the Imports statement to import a namespace. Importing a namespace allows you to access its members without having to specify the namespace itself.
- The Convert class contains methods that convert values to a specified data type.
- A variable can store only one item of data at any one time.
- The integer division operator divides two integers, and then returns the result.
- The modulus arithmetic operator divides two numbers, and then returns the remainder.
- A procedure-level memory location can be used only by the procedure in which it is declared. A module-level memory location can be used by all of the procedures in the form. A block-level memory location can be used only within the block of code in which it is declared.
- It is a good programming practice to use comments to internally document your application's code. Comments begin with the apostrophe.
- A static variable is a procedure-level variable that retains its value even when the procedure ends.
- You use the Const statement to declare a named constant.
- The `Option Explicit On` statement tells the computer to warn you if your code contains the name of an undeclared variable.
- The `Option Strict On` statement tells the computer not to perform any implicit type conversions that may lead to a loss of data. The computer also should not implicitly convert strings to numbers, and vice versa.
- Programmers commonly use either pseudocode (short phrases) or a flow-chart (standardized symbols) when planning a procedure's code.
- While an application is running, you can remove the contents of text box and label controls by assigning either the empty string ("") or the `String.Empty` value to the control's Text property. You also can use the Clear method to remove the contents of a text box while an application is running.
- You can use the Focus method to move the focus to a control while the application is running.
- After coding an application, you should test the application (with both valid and invalid data) to verify that the code works correctly.
- You can format an application's numeric output so that it displays special characters (such as dollar signs and percent signs) and the desired number of decimal places.

## Key Terms

**Variables** are computer memory locations where programmers can temporarily store data while an application is running.

A variable's **data type** determines the type of data the variable can store.

An **integer** is a whole number, a number without any decimal places.

A **floating-point number** is a number that is expressed as a multiple of some power of 10.

**Unicode** is the universal coding scheme that assigns a unique number to each character in the written languages of the world.

The name of an object is also called an **identifier**.

The equal sign (=) in an assignment statement is called the **assignment operator**.

A **string** is a group of characters enclosed in quotation marks.

A **literal constant** is an item of data whose value does not change while an application is running.

You can use a **literal type character** to convert a literal constant to a different data type.

A **method** performs a task for the class in which it is defined.

The **TryParse method** converts a string to a number.

You can use the **line continuation character**, which is the underscore, to break up a long instruction into two or more physical lines in the Code Editor window.

The **Convert class** contains methods that return the result of converting a value to a specified data type.

The **precedence numbers** for the arithmetic operators indicate the order in which the computer performs the arithmetic operation in an expression.

The **integer division operator** (\) divides two integers, and then returns the result as an integer.

The **modulus arithmetic operator** (Mod) returns the remainder of a division.

A variable's **scope** indicates where in the application's code the variable can be used.

A variable's **lifetime** indicates how long the variable remains in the computer's internal memory.

A **procedure-level variable** is declared in a procedure and has **procedure scope**.

**Comments** are used to document a program internally and are created using the apostrophe.

A **module-level variable** is declared in the form's Declarations section and has **module scope**.

**Block-level variables** are declared within a specific block of code and have **block scope**.

A **static variable** is a special type of procedure-level variable that retains its value even when the procedure ends.

A **named constant** is a computer memory location whose contents cannot be changed while the application is running. You create a named constant using the **Const statement**.

**Implicit type conversion** is the process by which a value is automatically converted to fit the memory location to which it is assigned.

A value is **promoted** when it is converted from one data type to another that can store larger numbers.

A value is **demoted** when it is converted from one data type to another that can store only smaller numbers.

**Pseudocode** uses phrases to describe the steps a procedure needs to take to accomplish its goal.

A **flowchart** uses standardized symbols to show the steps a procedure needs to take to accomplish its goal.

The lines connecting the symbols in a flowchart are called **flowlines**.

The oval symbol in a flowchart is called the **start/stop symbol**.

The rectangle symbol in a flowchart is called the **process symbol**.

The parallelogram in a flowchart is called the **input/output symbol**.

A **zero-length string**, also called an **empty string**, is a set of quotation marks with nothing between them.

You can remove the contents of a control by assigning the value **String.Empty** to the control's Text property.

You can use the **Clear method** to remove the contents of a text box.

You use the **Focus method** to move the focus to a control while the application is running.

An error in a program is called a **bug**.

**Valid data** is data that the application is expecting.

**Invalid data** is data that the application is not expecting.

**Debugging** refers to the process of locating errors in the program.

Most **syntax errors** are typing errors that occur when entering instructions.

A **logic error** occurs when you enter an instruction that is syntactically correct, but does not give you the expected results.

Specifying the number of decimal places and the special characters to display in a number is called **formatting**.

When formatting a number, the **format specifier** determines the special characters that will appear in the formatted number. The **precision specifier** controls the number of significant digits or zeros to the right of the decimal point in the formatted number.

## Self-Check Questions and Answers

1. Every variable and named constant has _____.
   a. a data type
   b. a lifetime
   c. a scope
   d. All of the above.

2. Which of the following statements converts the number 1.5 to Decimal, and assigns the result to a Decimal variable named `number`?
   a. `number = Convert.Decimal(1.5)`
   b. `number = Convert.ToDecimal(1.5)`
   c. `number = D(1.5)`
   d. Both b and c.

3. Which of the following statements converts the string stored in the `inputValue` variable to the Double data type, and then stores the result in a Double variable named `number`?
   a. `isConverted = Double.TryParse(inputValue, number)`
   b. `isConverted = Double.TryParse(inputValue,`
      `NumberStyles.Currency, NumberFormatInfo.CurrentInfo,`
      `number)`
   c. `isConverted = Double.TryParse(number, inputValue)`
   d. Both a and b.

4. The NumberStyles.AllowThousands value is defined in the _____ namespace.
   a. System.Global
   b. System.Globalization
   c. System.Info
   d. System.NumberStyles

5. Which of the following is the line continuation character?
   a. _ (underscore)
   b. - (hyphen)
   c. & (ampersand)
   d. None of the above.

6. What will be assigned to an Integer variable named `answer` when the following statement is processed? `answer = 45 Mod 2`
   a. 1
   b. 22
   c. 22.5
   d. None of the above.

7. Static variables can be declared in _____.
   a. the form's Declarations section
   b. the General Declarations section
   c. a procedure
   d. All of the above.

8. The _____ statement prevents variables from being created "on the fly."
   a. `Option Declare On`
   b. `Option Explicit On`
   c. `Option Strict On`
   d. None of the above.

9. Which of the following can be used to delete the contents of the cityTextBox?
   a. `cityTextBox.Text = ""`
   b. `cityTextBox.Text = String.Empty`
   c. `cityTextBox.Clear()`
   d. All of the above.

10. Which of the following can be used to place an insertion point in the cityTextBox while an application is running?
    a. `cityTextBox.Focus()`
    b. `cityTextBox.PlacePoint()`
    c. `cityTextBox.SendFocus()`
    d. None of the above.

Answers: 1) d, 2) b, 3) d, 4) b, 5) a, 6) a, 7) c, 8) b, 9) d, 10) a

## Review Questions

1. _____ are memory locations in which you store information, temporarily.
   a. Literal constants
   b. Named constants
   c. Variables
   d. both b and c

2. Which of the following are valid variable names?
   a. income94
   b. inc_94
   c. incomeTax
   d. All of the above.

3. A(n) _____ variable is known only to the procedure in which it is declared.
   a. block-level
   b. module-level
   c. procedure-level
   d. open-level

4. A _____ is a data item whose value does not change while the program is running.
   a. literal constant
   b. literal variable
   c. named constant
   d. variable

5. A _____ is a memory location whose value can change while the program is running.
   a. literal constant
   b. literal variable
   c. named constant
   d. variable

6. If you do not provide a data type in a variable declaration statement, Visual Basic assigns the _____ data type to the variable.
   a. Decimal
   b. Integer
   c. Object
   d. String

7. Which of the following assigns the number 2.89 to a Decimal variable named `price`? (Assume that the application contains the `Option Strict On` statement.)
   a. `price = 2.89`
   b. `price = 2.89D`
   c. `price = D2.89`
   d. None of the above.

8. Which of the following assigns the string contained in the `inputRate` variable to a Decimal variable named `rate`?
   a. `isConverted = Decimal.TryParse(inputRate, rate)`
   b. `isConverted = Decimal.TryParse(rate, inputRate)`
   c. `isConverted = TryParse.Decimal(inputRate, rate)`
   d. `isConverted = TryParse.Decimal(rate, inputRate)`

9. Which of the following assigns the sum of two Integer variables, named `score1` and `score2`, to the Text property of the answerTextBox? (Assume that the application contains the `Option Strict On` statement.)
   a. `answerTextBox.Text = Convert.ToString(score1 + score2)`
   b. `answerTextBox.Text = Convert.ToString(score1) + Convert.ToString(score2)`
   c. `answerTextBox.Text = score1 + score2`
   d. All of the above.

10. Which of the following assigns, to a Single variable named `commission`, a number that is 5% of the amount stored in an Integer variable named `sales`? (Assume that the application contains the `Option Strict On` statement.)
    a. `commission = sales * .05S`
    b. `commission = Convert.ToSingle(sales) * 5%`
    c. `commission = Convert.ToSingle(sales) * .05F`
    d. `commission = Convert.ToSingle(sales) * .05S`

11. Which of the following declares a Double named constant?
    a. `Const Rate As Double = .09`
    b. `Const Rate As Double = .09D`
    c. `Constant Rate = .09D`
    d. both a and b

12. Which of the following assigns the sum of two Integer variables to the Text property of the totalLabel? (Assume that the application contains the `Option Strict On` statement.)
    a. `totalLabel.Text = Convert.ToInteger(num1 + num2)`
    b. `totalLabel.Text = Convert.ToInt32(num1 + num2)`
    c. `totalLabel.Text = Convert.ToString(num1 + num2)`
    d. None of the above.

13. Comments in an application's code begin with the _____ character.
    a. apostrophe (')
    b. asterisk (*)
    c. caret (^)
    d. None of the above.

14. Most of the variables used in an application are _____.
    a. block-level
    b. module-level
    c. procedure-level
    d. variable-level

15. The _____ statement prevents data loss due to implicit type conversions.
    a. `Option Explicit On`
    b. `Option Strict On`
    c. `Option Implicit Off`
    d. `Option Convert Off`

16. Which of the following sends the focus to the numberTextBox?
    a. `numberTextBox.Focus()`
    b. `numberTextBox.SendFocus()`
    c. `numberTextBox.SetFocus()`
    d. `SetFocus(numberTextBox)`

17. Which of the following is a valid assignment statement?
    a. `nameTextBox = 'Jones'`
    b. `nameTextBox.Caption = 'Jones'`
    c. `nameTextBox.Text = "Jones"`
    d. `nameTextBox.Text = 'Jones'`

18. The statement `total = num1 + num2 * 3D`, which should multiply by 3 the sum of two Decimal variables and then assign the result to a Decimal variable, is an example of a _____.
    a. logic error
    b. syntax error
    c. correct instruction

19. The statement `janSales + febSales = totalSales`, which should add together the January and February sales amounts and then assign the result to the `totalSales` variable, is an example of a _____.
    a. logic error
    b. syntax error
    c. correct instruction

20. Assume that the `sales` variable contains the number 12345.89. Which of the following displays the number as 12,345.89?
    a. `salesLabel.Text = sales.ToString("C2")`
    b. `salesLabel.Text = sales.ToString("N2")`
    c. `salesLabel.Text = sales.ToString("D2")`
    d. `salesLabel.Text = sales.ToString("F2")`

## Review Exercises – Short Answer

1. Assume a procedure needs to store an item's name and its price. The price may have a decimal place. Write the appropriate Dim statements to create the necessary procedure-level variables.

2. Assume a procedure needs to store the name of an item in inventory and its height and weight. The height may have decimal places; the weight will be whole numbers only. Write the appropriate Dim statements to create the necessary procedure-level variables.

3. Write an assignment statement that assigns Miami to an existing String variable named `city`.

4. Write an assignment statement that adds the contents of the `sales1` variable to the contents of the `sales2` variable, and then assigns the sum to an existing variable named `totalSales`. All of the variables have the Decimal data type.

5. Write an assignment statement that multiplies the contents of the `salary` variable by the number 1.5, and then assigns the result to the `salary` variable. The `salary` variable has the Decimal data type.

6. Assume a form contains two buttons named salaryButton and bonusButton. Both buttons' Click event procedures need to use the same variable, which is a String variable named `employeeName`. Write the appropriate statement to declare the `employeeName` variable. Also specify where you will need to enter the statement and whether the variable is a procedure-level or module-level variable.

7. Write the statement to declare a procedure-level named constant named `Tax_Rate` whose value is .05. The named constant should have the Double data type.

8. Write the statement to declare a module-level named constant named `Tax_Rate` whose value is .05. The named constant should have the Decimal data type.

9. Write the statement to convert the contents of the unitsTextBox to an integer. Store the integer in an Integer variable named `numberOfUnits`. Use `isConverted` as the name of the Boolean variable.

10. Write the statement to assign, to the unitsLabel, the contents of an Integer variable named `numberOfUnits`.

11. Write the statement to assign, to a String variable named `totalSales`, the sum of the values stored in two Decimal variables named `westSales` and `eastSales`.

12. Write the statement to assign, to the payLabel, the value stored in a Decimal variable named `grossPay`. The value should be displayed with a dollar sign and two decimal places.

13. Write the statement that prevents the computer from implicitly converting a number to a string.

14. Write two statements that you can use to delete the contents of the totalLabel.

15. What is a static variable?

## Computer Exercises

1. In this exercise, you modify the chapter's Programming Example.
   a. Create the Currency Calculator application shown in the chapter's Programming Example. Save the application in the VbReloaded\ Chap03 folder.
   b. Modify the application so that it also displays the number of Canadian dollars and the number of Japanese yen. Use the following conversion rates:
      1 American dollar = 1.23679 Canadian dollar
      1 American dollar = 112.212 Japanese yen
   c. Modify the application so that it displays the number of pounds, pesos, Canadian dollars, and yen using three decimal places only. Be sure to modify the TOE chart and pseudocode before modifying the code. Also be sure to modify the comments contained in the Code Editor window.
   d. Save the solution, then start and test the application. Close the application, then close the solution.

2. In this exercise, you complete the application from Chapter 2's Computer Exercise 2.
   a. Copy the Time Solution folder from the VbReloaded\Chap02 folder to the VbReloaded\Chap03 folder.
   b. Open the Time Solution (Time Solution.sln) file contained in the VbReloaded\Chap03\Time Solution folder.
   c. Open the Code Editor window and enter the appropriate comments at the beginning of the code. Also enter the Option Explicit On and Option Strict On statements.
   d. The application should calculate and display the total number of weekday hours and the total number of weekend hours. Write the appropriate pseudocode, then code the application. Use variables to temporarily store the input and calculated values.
   e. Save the solution, then start and test the application. Close the application, then close the solution.

3. In this exercise, you complete the application from Chapter 2's Computer Exercise 4.
   a. Copy the Paper Solution folder from the VbReloaded\Chap02 folder to the VbReloaded\Chap03 folder.
   b. Open the Paper Solution (Paper Solution.sln) file contained in the VbReloaded\Chap03\Paper Solution folder.
   c. Open the Code Editor window and enter the appropriate comments at the beginning of the code. Also enter the Option Explicit On and Option Strict On statements.
   d. Use the TOE chart you created in Chapter 2 to write the appropriate pseudocode, then code the application. Use variables to temporarily store the sales amount, commission rate, and commission amount. Display the commission amount with a dollar sign and two decimal places.
   e. Save the solution, then start the application. Test the application using your name, 2000 as the sales amount, and 10 as the commission rate. The commission should be $200.00.
   f. Close the application, then close the solution.

4. In this exercise, you complete the application from Chapter 2's Computer Exercise 5.
   a. Copy the RMSales Solution folder from the VbReloaded\Chap02 folder to the VbReloaded\Chap03 folder.
   b. Open the RMSales Solution (RMSales Solution.sln) file contained in the VbReloaded\Chap03\RMSales Solution folder.
   c. Open the Code Editor window and enter the appropriate comments at the beginning of the code. Also enter the Option Explicit On and Option Strict On statements.
   d. Use the TOE chart you created in Chapter 2 to write the appropriate pseudocode, then code the application. Use variables to temporarily store the sales amounts, projected increase rates, and projected sales amounts. Allow the user to include a dollar sign and comma when entering the sales amounts. Display the projected sales amounts with a dollar sign and zero decimal places.

e. Save the solution, then start the application. Test the application by entering the following sales amounts and rates:

| Region | Sales | Projected Increase (%) |
|--------|-------|------------------------|
| North  | 25000 | 5 |
| South  | 30000 | 7 |
| East   | 10,000 | 4 |
| West   | $15000 | 11 |

f. Close the application, then close the solution.

5. Scenario: John Lee wants an application in which he can enter the following three pieces of information: his cash balance at the beginning of the month, the amount of money he earned during the month, and the amount of money he spent during the month. He wants the application to compute his ending balance.
   a. Prepare a TOE chart ordered by object.
   b. Build an appropriate interface. Name the solution JohnLee Solution. Name the project JohnLee Project. Save the application in the VbReloaded\Chap03 folder.
   c. Write the pseudocode, then code the application. Allow the user to include a dollar sign and comma when entering the information.
   d. Save the solution, then start the application. Test the application using the following data:
   Beginning cash balance: 5000    Earnings: 2500    Expenses: 3000
   e. Close the application, then close the solution.

6. Scenario: Jackets Unlimited is having a 25% off sale on all its merchandise. The store manager asks you to create an application that requires the clerk simply to enter the original price of a jacket. The application should then compute the discount and new price.
   a. Prepare a TOE chart ordered by object.
   b. Build an appropriate interface. Name the solution Jackets Solution. Name the project Jackets Project. Save the application in the VbReloaded\Chap03 folder.
   c. Write the pseudocode, then code the application. Display a dollar sign and two decimal places in the discount and new price amounts.
   d. Test the application using the following data:
   Jacket's original price: 50
   e. Close the application, then close the solution.

7. Scenario: Colfax Industries needs an application that allows the shipping clerk to enter the quantity of an item in inventory and the number of items that can be packed in a box for shipping. When the shipping clerk clicks a button, the application should compute and display the number of full boxes that can be packed and how many items are left over.
   a. Prepare a TOE chart ordered by object.
   b. Build an appropriate interface. Name the solution Colfax Solution. Name the project Colfax Project. Save the application in the VbReloaded\Chap03 folder.
   c. Write the pseudocode, then code the application.
   d. Test the application using the following information. Colfax has 45 skateboards in inventory. If six skateboards can fit into a box for shipping, how many full boxes could the company ship, and how many skateboards will remain in inventory?
   e. Close the application, then close the solution.

8. Scenario: Management USA, a small training center, plans to run two full-day seminars on December 1. The seminars are called "How to Be an Effective Manager" and "How to Run a Small Business." Each seminar costs $200. Registration for the seminars will be done by phone. When a company calls to register its employees, the phone representative will ask for the following information: the company's name, address (including city, state, and ZIP code), the number of employees registering for the "How to Be an Effective Manager" seminar, and the number of employees registering for the "How to Run a Small Business" seminar. Claire Jenkowski, the owner of Management USA, wants the application to calculate the total number of employees the company is registering and the total cost.
   a. Prepare a TOE chart ordered by object.
   b. Build an appropriate interface. Name the solution Management Solution. Name the project Management Project. Save the application in the VbReloaded\Chap03 folder. The state entry should contain a maximum of two characters and should always appear in uppercase.
   c. Write the pseudocode, then code the application.
   d. Test the application using the following data:
      Company Name: ABC Company
      Address: 345 Main St.
      City, State, ZIP: Glen, tx 70122
      Registrants for "How to Be an Effective Manager": 10
      Registrants for "How to Run a Small Business": 5
   e. Close the application, then close the solution.

9. In this exercise, you experiment with a static variable.
   a. Open the Static Solution (Static Solution.sln) file contained in the VbReloaded\Chap03\Static Solution folder.
   b. Start the application. Click the Count button. The message indicates that you have clicked the Count button once, which is correct.
   c. Click the Count button several more times. Each time you click the Count button, the message changes to indicate the number of times the button was clicked.
   d. Click the Exit button to end the application.
   e. Open the Code Editor window and study the code. Notice that the code uses a module-level variable to keep track of the number of times the Count button is clicked. Modify the code so that it uses a static variable rather than a module-level variable.
   f. Save the solution, then start the application. Click the Count button several times. Each time you click the Count button, the message should change to indicate the number of times the button was clicked.
   g. Click the Exit button to end the application, then close the solution.

10. In this exercise, you experiment with the Visual Basic conversion functions listed in Appendix C.
   a. Open the Conversion Functions Solution (Conversion Functions Solution.sln) file contained in the VbReloaded\Chap03\Conversion Functions Solution folder.
   b. Test the application by entering a letter as the item price and number purchased. Record the results on a piece of paper.
   c. Modify the code so that it uses the Visual Basic conversion functions listed in Appendix C rather than the TryParse and Convert methods.
   d. Save the solution, then start and test the application by entering a letter as the item price and number purchased. What is the difference between the methods and conversion functions?
   e. Click the Exit button to end the application, then close the solution.

11. In this exercise, you find and correct an error in an application. The process of finding and correcting errors is called debugging.
   a. Open the Debug Solution (Debug Solution.sln) file contained in the VbReloaded\Chap03\Debug Solution folder.
   b. Start the application, then test the application.
   c. Locate and then correct any errors.
   d. Save the solution, then start and test the application. When the application is working correctly, close the solution.

## Case Projects

### Willow Pools

Create an application that allows the user to enter the length, width, and height of a rectangle. The application should calculate and display the volume of the rectangle. Test the application using the following data. The swimming pool at a health club is 100 feet long, 30 feet wide, and 4 feet deep. How many cubic feet of water will the pool contain?

### Builder's Inc.

Create an application that allows the user to enter both the diameter of a circle and the price of railing material per foot. The application should calculate and display the circumference of the circle and the total price of the railing material. Test the application using the following information. Jack Jones, one of Builders Inc.'s customers, is building a railing around a circular deck having a diameter of 36 feet. The railing material costs $2 per foot. What is the circumference of the deck and the total price of the railing material?

### Tile Limited

Create an application that allows the user to enter the length and width (in feet) of a rectangle, and the price of a square foot of tile. The application should calculate and display the area of the rectangle and the total price of the tile. Test the application using the following data. Susan Caper, one of Tile Limited's customers, is tiling a floor in her home. The floor is 12 feet long and 14 feet wide. The price of a square foot of tile is $1.59. What is the area of the floor and how much will the tile cost?

### Quick Loans

Create an application that allows the user to enter the amount of a loan, the interest rate, and the term of the loan (in years). The application should calculate and display the total amount of interest and the total amount to be repaid. (*Hint*: Visual Basic provides the Financial.Pmt method that you can use to calculate a loan payment. You can use the Help menu to research the method.) Test the application using the following data. You visit Quick Loans because you want to borrow $9000 to buy a new car. The loan is for three years at an annual interest rate of 12%. How much will you pay in interest over the three years, and what is the total amount you will repay?

# Making Decisions in a Program

- Include the selection structure in pseudocode and in a flowchart
- Write an If...Then...Else statement
- Write code that uses comparison operators and logical operators
- Create a variable having block-scope
- Concatenate strings
- Use the `ControlChars.NewLine` constant
- Change the case of a string
- Determine whether a string contains data
- Display a message in a message box
- Include a nested selection structure in pseudocode, a flowchart, and code
- Code an If/ElseIf/Else selection structure
- Include a Case selection structure in pseudocode, a flowchart, and code
- Generate random numbers

TIP

As you may remember from Chapter 1, the selection structure is one of the three programming structures. The other two programming structures are sequence (which you used in the previous chapters) and repetition (which is covered in Chapter 5).

## THE SELECTION STRUCTURE

The applications you created in the previous three chapters used the sequence programming structure only, where a procedure's instructions are processed, one after another, in the order in which each appears in the procedure. In many applications, however, the next instruction processed depends on the result of a decision or comparison that the program must make. For example, a payroll program typically compares the number of hours the employee worked with the number 40 to determine whether the employee should receive overtime pay in addition to regular pay. Based on the result of that comparison, the program then selects either an instruction that computes regular pay only or an instruction that computes regular pay plus overtime pay.

You use the **selection structure**, also called the **decision structure**, when you want a program to make a decision or comparison and then select one of two paths, depending on the result of that decision or comparison. Although the idea of using the selection structure in a program is new, the concept of the selection structure is already familiar to you, because you use it each day to make hundreds of decisions. For example, every morning you have to decide whether you are hungry and, if you are, what you are going to eat. Figure 4.1 shows other examples of selection structures you might use today.

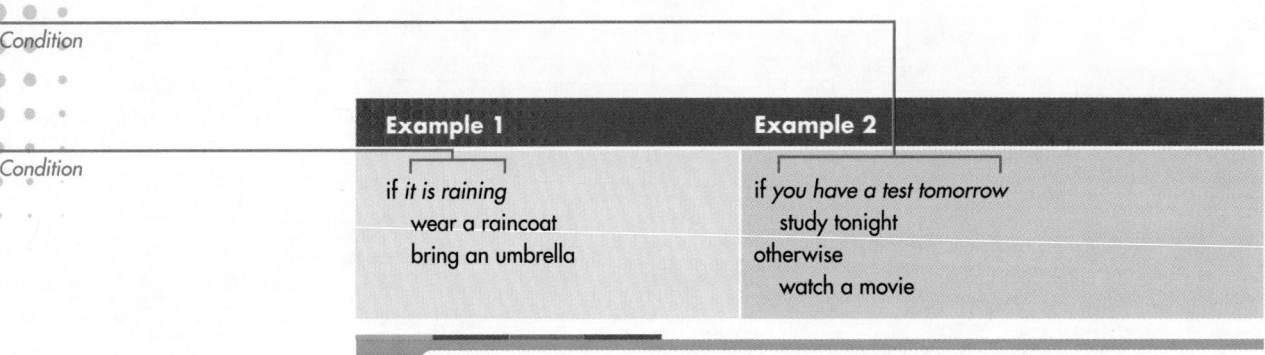

**FIGURE 4.1**     Selection structures you might use today

In the examples shown in Figure 4.1, the portion in *italics*, called the **condition**, specifies the decision you are making and is phrased so that it results in either a true or false answer only. For example, it is either raining (true) or not raining (false); either you have a test tomorrow (true) or you do not have a test tomorrow (false).

If the condition is true, you perform a specific set of tasks. If the condition is false, on the other hand, you might or might not need to perform a different set of tasks. For instance, look at the first example shown in Figure 4.1. If it is raining (a true condition), then you will wear a raincoat and bring an umbrella. Notice that you do not have anything in particular to do if it is not raining (a false condition). Compare this with the second example shown in Figure 4.1. If you have a test tomorrow (a true condition), then you will study tonight. However, if you do not have a test tomorrow (a false condition), then you will watch a movie.

Like you, the computer also can evaluate a condition and then select the appropriate tasks to perform based on that evaluation. When using the selection structure in a program, the programmer must be sure to phrase the condition so that it results in either a true or a false answer only. The programmer also must specify the tasks to be performed when the condition is true and, if necessary, the tasks to be performed when the condition is false.

Visual Basic provides four forms of the selection structure: If, If/Else, If/ElseIf/Else, and Case. First you learn about the If and If/Else selection structures.

## WRITING PSEUDOCODE FOR THE IF AND IF/ELSE SELECTION STRUCTURES

An **If selection structure** contains only one set of instructions, which are processed when the condition is true. An **If/Else selection structure**, on the other hand, contains two sets of instructions: one set is processed when the condition is true and the other set is processed when the condition is false. Figure 4.2 shows examples of both the If and the If/Else selection structures written in pseudocode.

**If selection structure**

Condition

True path

```
1.  get the part number and price
2.  if the part number is "AB203"
        calculate the price by multiplying the price by 1.1
        display "Price increase" message
    end if
3.  display the part number and price
```

**If/Else selection structure**

Condition

True path

False path

```
1.  get the sales amount
2.  if the sales amount is greater than 1500
        calculate the commission by multiplying the sales amount by .02
    else
        calculate the commission by multiplying the sales amount by .01
    end if
3.  display the commission
```

**FIGURE 4.2**    Examples of the If and If/Else selection structures written in pseudocode

Although pseudocode is not standardized—every programmer has his or her own version—you will find some similarities among the various versions. For example, many programmers begin the selection structure with the word "if" and end the structure with the two words "end if". They also use the word "else" to designate the instructions to be performed when the condition is false.

In the examples shown in Figure 4.2, the italicized portion of the instruction indicates the condition to be evaluated. Notice that each condition results in either a true or a false answer only. In Example 1, either the part number is "AB203" or it isn't. In Example 2, either the sales amount is greater than the number 1500 or it isn't.

When the condition is true, the set of instructions following the condition is selected for processing. The instructions following the condition are referred to as the **true path**—the path you follow when the condition is true. The true path ends when you come to the "else" or, if there is no "else", when you come to the end of the selection structure (the "end if"). After the true path instructions are processed, the instruction following the "end if" is processed. In the examples shown in Figure 4.2, the display instructions are processed after the instructions in the true path.

The instructions processed when the condition is false depend on whether the selection structure contains an "else". When there is no "else", as in the first example shown in Figure 4.2, the selection structure ends when its condition is false, and processing continues with the instruction following the "end if". In the first example, for instance, the "display the part number and price" instruction is processed when the part number is not "AB203." In cases where the selection structure contains an "else", as in the second example shown in Figure 4.2, the instructions between the "else" and the "end if"—referred to as the **false path**—are processed before the instruction after the "end if" is processed. In the second example, the "calculate the commission by multiplying the sales amount by .01" instruction is processed first, followed by the "display the commission" instruction.

Recall from Chapter 3 that, in addition to using pseudocode to plan the code for a procedure, programmers also use flowcharts. In the next section, you learn how to show the If and If/Else selection structures in a flowchart.

## FLOWCHARTING THE IF AND IF/ELSE SELECTION STRUCTURES

Unlike pseudocode, which consists of short phrases, a flowchart uses standardized symbols to show the steps the computer must take to accomplish a task. Figure 4.3 shows Figure 4.2's examples in flowchart form.

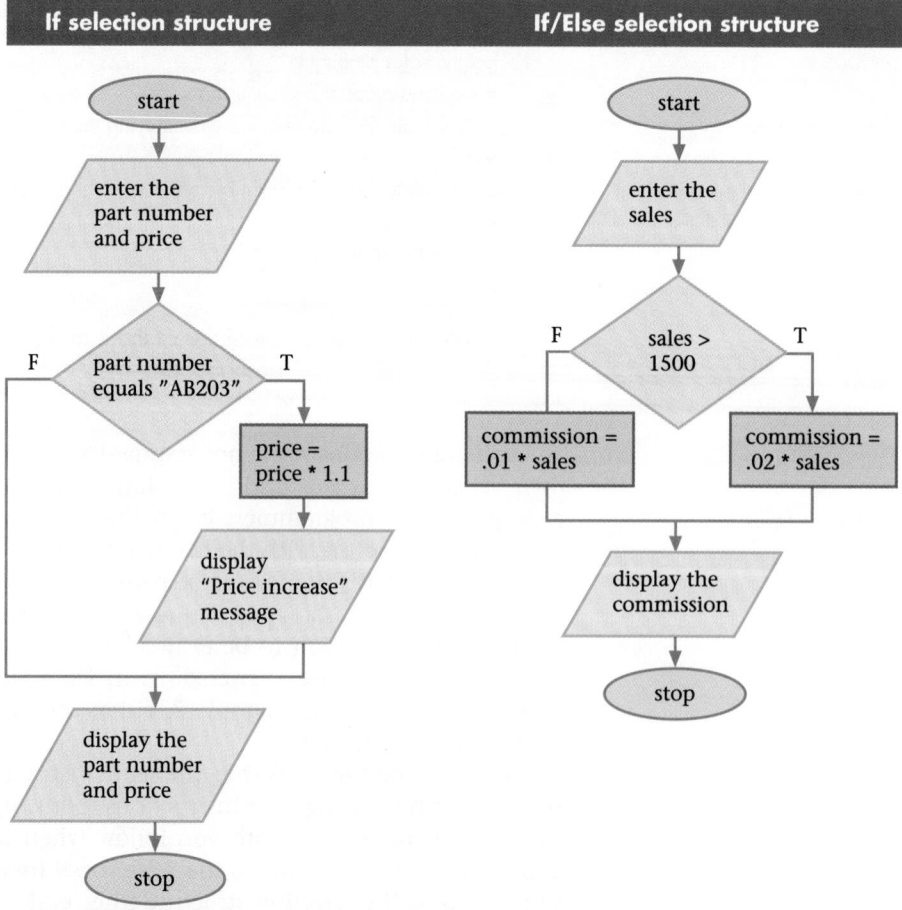

**FIGURE 4.3**    Examples of the If and If/Else selection structures drawn in flowchart form

As you learned in Chapter 3, the oval in the figure is the start/stop symbol, the rectangle is the process symbol, and the parallelogram is the input/output symbol. The new symbol in the flowcharts, the diamond, is called the **selection/repetition symbol**, because it is used to represent both the selection and repetition structures. In Figure 4.3's flowcharts, the diamonds represent the selection structure. (You learn how to use the diamond to represent the repetition structure in Chapter 5.) Notice that inside each diamond is a comparison that evaluates to either true or false only. Each diamond also has one flowline entering the symbol and two flowlines leaving the symbol. The two flowlines leading out of the diamond should be marked so that anyone reading the flowchart can distinguish the true path from the false path. You mark the flowline leading to the true path with a "T" (for true), and you mark the flowline leading to the false path with an "F" (for false).

Next, you learn how to code the If and If/Else selection structures in Visual Basic.

## CODING THE IF AND IF/ELSE SELECTION STRUCTURES

You use the **If...Then...Else statement** to code the If and If/Else selection structures in Visual Basic. Figure 4.4 shows the syntax of the If...Then...Else statement and includes two examples of using the statement.

**HOW TO...**

### Use the If...Then...Else Statement to Code the If and If/Else Selection Structures

**Syntax**
**If** *condition* **Then**
    *statement block containing one or more statements to be processed when the condition is true*
**[Else**
    *statement block containing one or more statements to be processed when the condition is false]*
**End If**

**Examples**
```
If partNumber = "AB203" Then
     price = price * 1.1
     messageLabel.Text = "Price increase"
End If
```

If the `partNumber` variable contains the string "AB203", the first instruction in the true path multiplies the contents of a Double variable named `price` by 1.1 and assigns the result to the `price` variable. The second instruction in the true path displays the message "Price increase" in the messageLabel.

*(Figure is continued on next page)*

```
If sales > 1500D Then
     commission = .02D * sales
Else
     commission = .01D * sales
End If
```

If a Decimal variable named `sales` contains a number that is greater than 1500, the instruction in the true path multiplies the contents of the `sales` variable by .02 and assigns the result to a Decimal variable named `commission`; otherwise, the instruction in the false path multiplies the contents of the `sales` variable by .01 and assigns the result to the `commission` variable.

**FIGURE 4.4**    How to use the If…Then…Else statement to code the If and If/Else selection structures

The items in square brackets in the syntax are optional. For example, you do not always need to include the Else portion of the syntax, referred to as the **Else clause**, in an If…Then…Else statement. Words in **bold**, however, are essential components of the statement. The words If, Then, and End If, for instance, must be included in the If…Then…Else statement. The word Else must be included only when the programmer needs to use the false path of the selection structure.

Items in *italics* in the syntax indicate where the programmer must supply information pertaining to the current application. For instance, the programmer must supply the *condition* to be evaluated. The *condition* must be a Boolean expression, which is an expression that results in a Boolean value (True or False). In addition to supplying the *condition*, the programmer must supply the statements to be processed in the true path and, if used, the false path. The set of statements contained in the true path, as well as the set of statements contained in the false path, is referred to as a **statement block**.

The If…Then…Else statement's *condition* can contain variables, literal constants, named constants, properties, methods, arithmetic operators, comparison operators, and logical operators. You already know about variables, literal constants, named constants, properties, methods, and arithmetic operators from previous chapters. You will learn about comparison operators and logical operators in this chapter.

**TIP**

In Visual Basic, a statement block is a set of statements terminated by an Else, End If, Loop, or Next clause.

## COMPARISON OPERATORS

Visual Basic provides nine **comparison operators**, also referred to as **relational operators**. Figure 4.5 lists the six most commonly used comparison operators and includes examples of using the operators in the If…Then…Else statement's *condition*. (The remaining comparison operators are covered in subsequent chapters.)

# HOW TO...

## Use the Most Commonly Used Comparison Operators

| Operator | Operation |
|---|---|
| = | equal to |
| > | greater than |
| >= | greater than or equal to |
| < | less than |
| <= | less than or equal to |
| <> | not equal to |

### Examples

`If number1 = number2 Then`
Compares the contents of the `number1` variable with the contents of the `number2` variable. The *condition* evaluates to True when the contents of both variables are equal; otherwise, it evaluates to False.

`If weight > 190 Then`
Compares the contents of the `weight` variable with the number 190. The *condition* evaluates to True when the `weight` variable contains a number that is greater than 190; otherwise, it evaluates to False.

`If age >= 21 Then`
Compares the contents of the `age` variable with the number 21. The *condition* evaluates to True when the `age` variable contains a number that is greater than or equal to 21; otherwise, it evaluates to False.

`If price < 45.75D Then`
Compares the contents of the `price` variable with the number 45.75. The *condition* evaluates to True when the `price` variable contains a number that is less than 45.75; otherwise, it evaluates to False.

`If primeRate <= rate Then`
Compares the contents of the `primeRate` variable with the contents of the `rate` variable. The *condition* evaluates to True when the `primeRate` variable contains a number that is less than or equal to the number stored in the `rate` variable; otherwise, it evaluates to False.

`If state <> "MA" Then`
Compares the contents of the `state` variable with the string "MA". The *condition* evaluates to True when the `state` variable does not contain the string "MA"; otherwise, it evaluates to False.

**FIGURE 4.5**  How to use the most commonly used comparison operators

Notice that the expression contained in each *condition* shown in Figure 4.5 evaluates to one of two Boolean values—either True or False. All expressions containing a comparison operator will result in an answer of either True or False only.

Unlike arithmetic operators, comparison operators do not have an order of precedence. If an expression contains more than one comparison operator, the computer evaluates the comparison operators from left to right in the expression. Keep in mind, however, that comparison operators are evaluated after any arithmetic operators in the expression. In other words, in the expression 12 / 2 * 3 < 7 + 4, the three arithmetic operators (/, *, +) are evaluated before the comparison operator (<) is evaluated. The result of the expression is the Boolean value False, as shown in Figure 4.6.

| Evaluation steps | Result |
| --- | --- |
| Original expression | 12 / 2 * 3 < 7 + 4 |
| 12 / 2 is evaluated first | 6 * 3 < 7 + 4 |
| 6 * 3 is evaluated second | 18 < 7 + 4 |
| 7 + 4 is evaluated third | 18 < 11 |
| 18 < 11 is evaluated last | False |

**FIGURE 4.6**    Evaluation steps for an expression containing arithmetic and comparison operators

Next, you view two examples of procedures that contain a comparison operator in an If...Then...Else statement. The first procedure uses the If selection structure, and the second procedure uses the If/Else selection structure.

## Using Comparison Operators – Swapping Numeric Values

Assume you want to create a procedure that displays both the lowest and highest of two numbers entered by the user. Figures 4.7 and 4.8 show the pseudocode and flowchart, respectively, for a procedure that will accomplish this task. Figure 4.9 shows the corresponding Visual Basic code for the displayButton's Click event procedure, and Figure 4.10 shows a sample run of the application that contains the procedure.

**Pseudocode**

1. store the text box values in the number1 and number2 variables
2. if the number contained in the number1 variable is greater than the number contained in the number2 variable
    swap the numbers so that the number1 variable contains the smaller number
  end if
3. display (in messageLabel) a message stating the lowest number and the highest number

**FIGURE 4.7**    Pseudocode showing the If selection structure

**Flowchart**

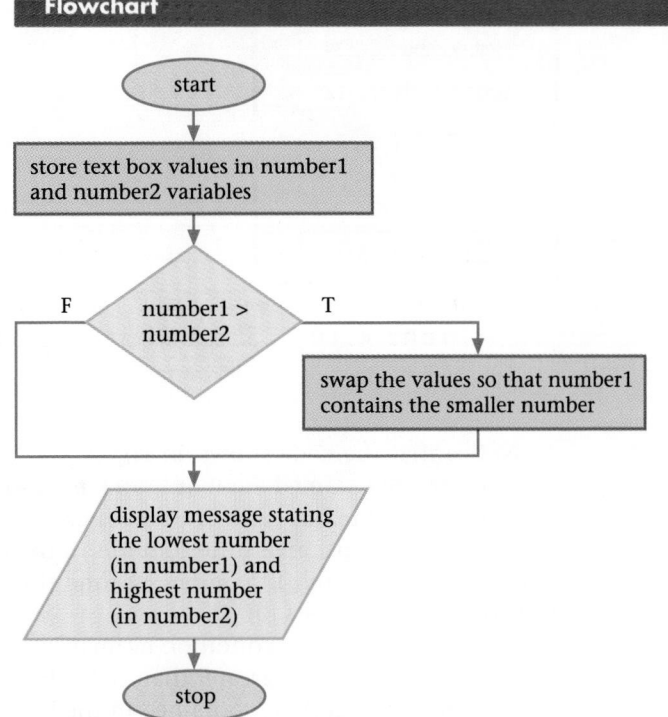

**FIGURE 4.8**    Flowchart showing the If selection structure

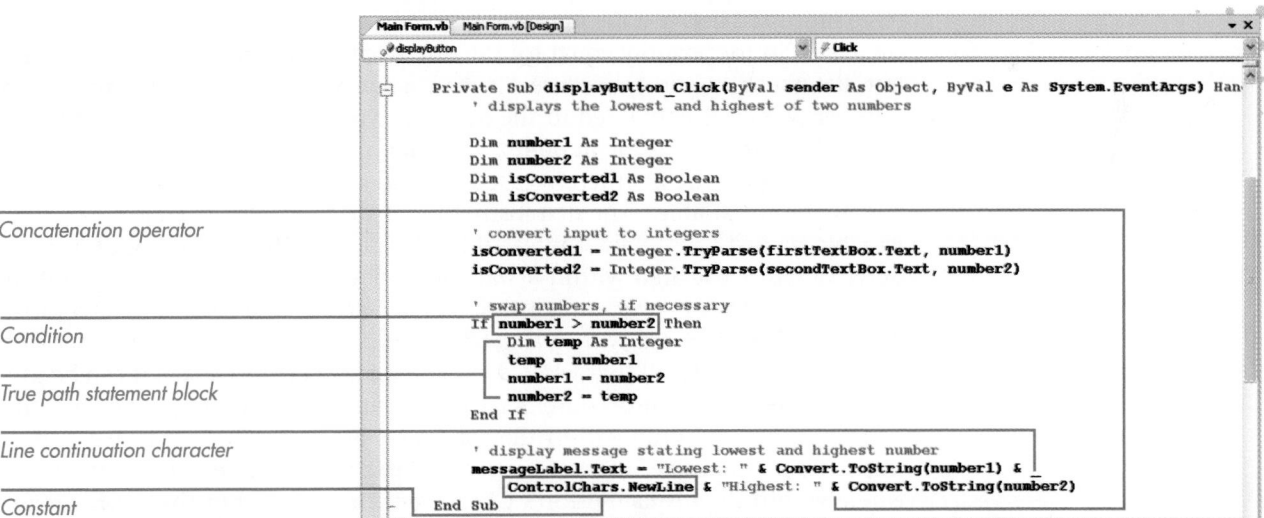

**FIGURE 4.9**    The If selection structure shown in the displayButton's Click event procedure

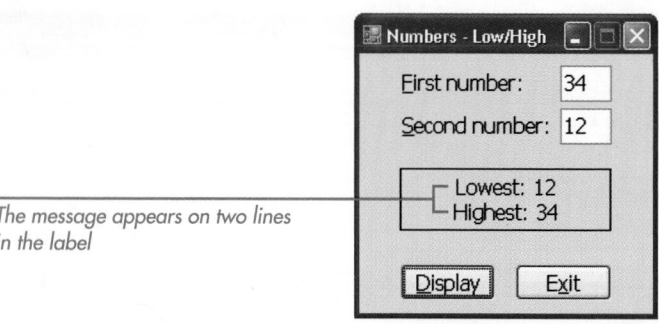

*The message appears on two lines in the label*

**FIGURE 4.10**    Sample run of the application that contains the displayButton's Click event procedure

Notice that the code shown in Figure 4.9 first declares two procedure-level Integer variables named `number1` and `number2`, and two Boolean variables named `isConverted1` and `isConverted2`. The procedure then uses the TryParse method to convert the contents of the firstTextBox and secondTextBox to integers. The `number1 > number2` condition in the If...Then...Else statement compares the contents of the `number1` variable with the contents of the `number2` variable. If the condition evaluates to True, it means that the value in the `number1` variable is greater than the value in the `number2` variable. In that case, the four instructions contained in the If...Then...Else statement's true path swap the values contained in those variables. Swapping the values places the smaller number in the `number1` variable, and the larger number in the `number2` variable. If the `number1 > number2` condition evaluates to False, on the other hand, the true path instructions are skipped over. The instructions do not need to be processed because the `number1` variable already contains a number that is smaller than (or possibly equal to) the one stored in the `number2` variable. The last statement in the procedure displays a message that indicates the lowest number (which is contained in the `number1` variable) and the highest number (which is contained in the `number2` variable).

Study closely the instructions used to swap the values stored in the `number1` and `number2` variables. The first instruction, `Dim temp As Integer`, declares a variable named `temp`. Like the variables declared at the beginning of a procedure, variables declared within a statement block remain in memory until the procedure ends. However, unlike variables declared at the beginning of a procedure, variables declared within a statement block have block scope rather than procedure scope. Recall that when a variable has procedure scope, it can be used anywhere within the procedure. A variable that has **block scope**, on the other hand, can be used only within the statement block in which it is declared. In this case, for example, the `number1` and `number2` variables can be used anywhere within the displayButton's Click event procedure, but the `temp` variable can be used only within the If...Then...Else statement's true path. You may be wondering why the `temp` variable was not declared at the beginning of the procedure, along with the `number1` and `number2` variables. Although there is nothing wrong with declaring all variables at the beginning of a procedure, in this case the `temp` variable is not needed unless a swap is necessary, so there is no reason to create the variable until it is needed.

The second instruction in the If...Then...Else statement's true path, `temp = number1`, assigns the value in the `number1` variable to the `temp` variable. The `temp` variable is necessary to store the contents of the `number1` variable temporarily so that the swap can be made. If you did not store the `number1` variable's value in the `temp` variable, the `number1` variable's value would be lost when the computer processes the next statement, `number1 = number2`, which replaces the contents of the `number1` variable with the contents of the `number2` variable. Finally, the `number2 = temp` instruction assigns the value in the `temp` variable to the `number2` variable. Figure 4.11 illustrates the concept of swapping, assuming the user enters the numbers eight and four in the firstTextBox and secondTextBox, respectively.

|  | temp | number1 | number2 |
|---|---|---|---|
| values stored in the variables immediately before the `temp = number1` instruction is processed | 0 | 8 | 4 |
| result of the `temp = number1` instruction | 8 | 8 | 4 |
| result of the `number1 = number2` instruction | 8 | 4 | 4 |
| result of the `number2 = temp` instruction, which completes the swapping process | 8 | 4 | 8 |

*Values were swapped*

**FIGURE 4.11**     Illustration of the swapping concept

The code shown in Figure 4.9 contains two items that were not covered in the previous three chapters: the concatenation operator and the `ControlChars.NewLine` constant. You use the **concatenation operator**, which is the ampersand (&), to concatenate (connect or link) strings together. When concatenating strings, you must be sure to include a space before and after the ampersand; otherwise, the Visual Basic compiler will not recognize the ampersand as the concatenation operator. Figure 4.12 shows some examples of string concatenation. As the last example shows, you do not need to use the Convert.ToString method when concatenating a numeric value to a string. This is because the Visual Basic compiler automatically converts, to a string, a numeric value preceded by the concatenation operator.

## HOW TO...

### Concatenate Strings

Assume you have the following variables:

| Variables | Data type | Contents |
|---|---|---|
| firstName | String | Sue |
| lastName | String | Chen |
| age | Integer | 21 |

| Using the above variables, this concatenated string: | Would result in: |
|---|---|
| firstName & lastName | SueChen |
| firstName & " " & lastName | Sue Chen |
| lastName & ", " & firstName | Chen, Sue |
| "She is " & Convert.ToString(age) & "!" | She is 21! |
| "She is " & age & "!" | She is 21! |

**FIGURE 4.12**     How to concatenate strings

**TIP**

You also can use the plus sign (+) to concatenate strings. To avoid confusion, however, you should use the plus sign for addition and the ampersand for concatenation.

The concatenation operator appears four times in the `messageLabel.Text = "Lowest: " & Convert.ToString(number1) & ControlChars.NewLine & "Highest: " & Convert.ToString(number2)` statement, which is included in the code shown in Figure 4.9. The statement concatenates five strings: the string "Lowest: ", the contents of the `number1` variable converted to a string, the `ControlChars.NewLine` constant, the string "Highest: ", and the contents of the `number2` variable converted to a string. The **ControlChars.NewLine constant** in the statement advances the insertion point to the next line in the messageLabel and is the reason that the "Highest: 34" text appears on the second line in the label, as shown in Figure 4.10.

## Using Comparison Operators – Example 2

Now assume you want to give the user the option of displaying either the sum of two numbers that he or she enters, or the difference between the two numbers. Figures 4.13 and 4.14 show the pseudocode and flowchart, respectively, for a procedure that will accomplish this task. Figure 4.15 shows the corresponding Visual Basic code for the calcButton's Click event procedure, and Figure 4.16 shows a sample run of the application that contains the procedure.

---

**Pseudocode**

1. store text box values in operation, number1, and number2 variables
2. if the operation variable contains "A"
    calculate the sum by adding together the numbers contained in the number1 and number2 variables
    display (in answerLabel) the message "Sum:" and the sum
   else
    calculate the difference by subtracting the number contained in the number2 variable from the number contained in the number1 variable
    display (in answerLabel) the message "Difference:" and the difference
   end if

**FIGURE 4.13**    Pseudocode showing the If/Else selection structure

**Flowchart**

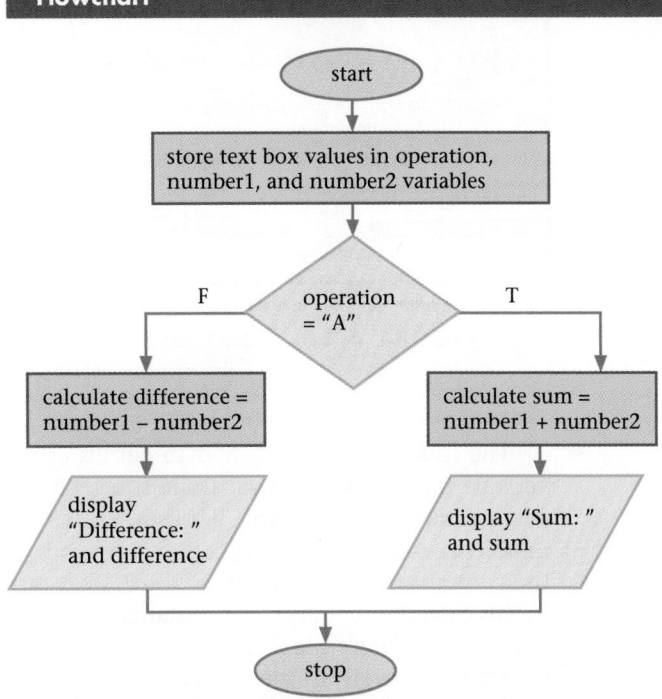

**FIGURE 4.14**    Flowchart showing the If/Else selection structure

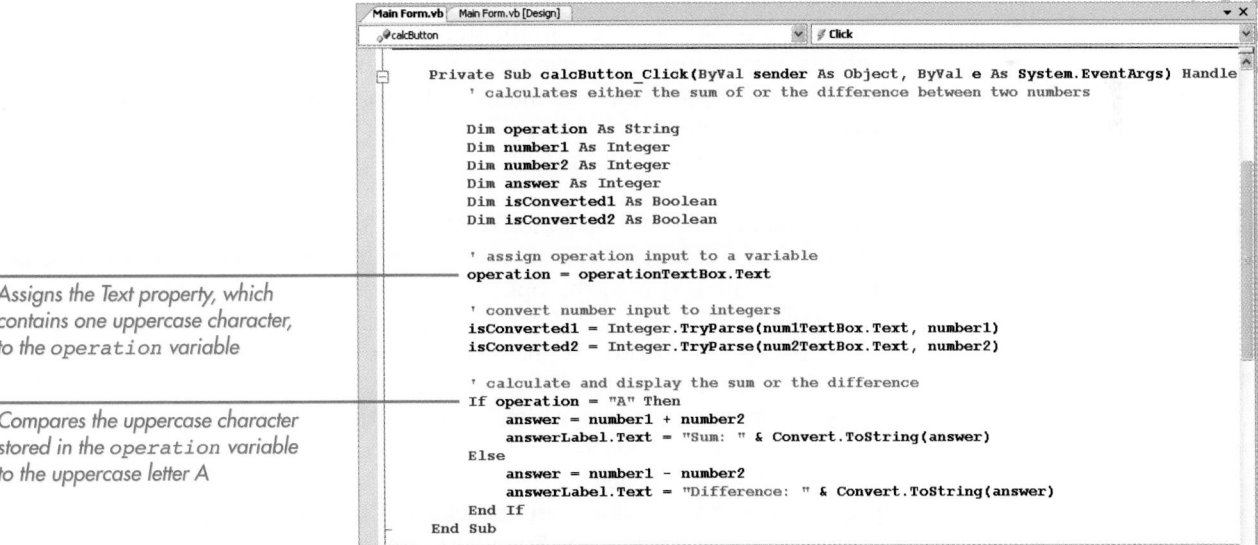

Assigns the Text property, which contains one uppercase character, to the operation variable

Compares the uppercase character stored in the operation variable to the uppercase letter A

```vb
Private Sub calcButton_Click(ByVal sender As Object, ByVal e As System.EventArgs) Handle
    ' calculates either the sum of or the difference between two numbers

    Dim operation As String
    Dim number1 As Integer
    Dim number2 As Integer
    Dim answer As Integer
    Dim isConverted1 As Boolean
    Dim isConverted2 As Boolean

    ' assign operation input to a variable
    operation = operationTextBox.Text

    ' convert number input to integers
    isConverted1 = Integer.TryParse(num1TextBox.Text, number1)
    isConverted2 = Integer.TryParse(num2TextBox.Text, number2)

    ' calculate and display the sum or the difference
    If operation = "A" Then
        answer = number1 + number2
        answerLabel.Text = "Sum: " & Convert.ToString(answer)
    Else
        answer = number1 - number2
        answerLabel.Text = "Difference: " & Convert.ToString(answer)
    End If
End Sub
```

**FIGURE 4.15**    The If/Else selection structure shown in the calcButton's Click event procedure

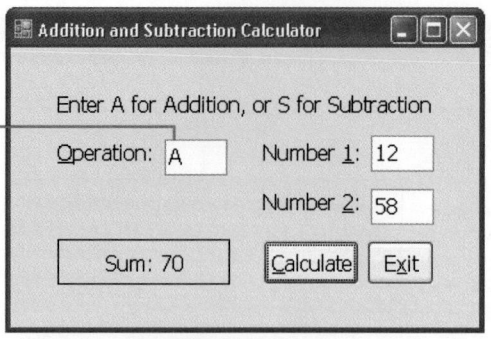

**FIGURE 4.16**     Sample run of the application that contains the calcButton's Click event procedure

The code shown in Figure 4.15 declares six procedure-level variables: a String variable named operation, three Integer variables named number1, number2, and answer, and two Boolean variables named isConverted1 and isConverted2. The operation = operationTextBox.Text statement assigns the contents of the operationTextBox's Text property to the operation variable. In this case, the Text property contains one uppercase character; this is because the operationTextBox's MaxLength and CharacterCasing properties are set to 1 and Upper, respectively, in the Properties window. As you learned in Chapter 2, a text box's MaxLength property specifies the maximum number of characters that can be entered in the text box, and its CharacterCasing property indicates whether the text should be left alone or converted to uppercase or lowercase.

The calcButton's Click event procedure uses the TryParse method to convert the contents of both the num1TextBox and num2TextBox to integers. The operation = "A" condition in the If...Then...Else statement then compares the contents of the operation variable with the uppercase letter "A". If the condition is true, the procedure calculates and displays the sum of the two numbers entered by the user, as shown in Figure 4.16. If the condition is false, on the other hand, the procedure calculates and displays the difference between the two numbers.

Now assume that the operationTextBox's CharacterCasing property is not set to Upper, but is left at its default value, Normal. If the user enters an uppercase letter "A" in the text box, the operation = operationTextBox.Text statement assigns an uppercase letter "A" to the operation variable, and the operation = "A" condition in the selection structure evaluates to True. As a result, the selection structure's true path calculates and displays the sum of the numbers entered by the user, which is correct. However, if the user enters a lowercase letter "a" in the text box, the operation = operationTextBox.Text statement assigns a lowercase letter "a" to the operation variable, and the operation = "A" condition in the selection structure evaluates to False; this is because string comparisons in Visual Basic are case-sensitive. As a result, the selection structure's false path calculates and displays the difference between the numbers entered by the user, which is incorrect.

Visual Basic provides two methods that you can use to solve the case problems that occur when comparing strings: ToUpper and ToLower.

**TIP**

The uppercase letter A has a Unicode value of 41, whereas the lowercase letter a has a Unicode value of 61. As you learned in Chapter 3, Unicode is the universal coding scheme for characters.

## USING THE TOUPPER AND TOLOWER METHODS

As is true in most programming languages, string comparisons in Visual Basic are case-sensitive, which means that the string "Yes" is not the same as the string "YES" or the string "yes". A problem occurs when you need to include, in a comparison, a string that is either entered by the user or read from a file, because you cannot always control the case of the string. Although you can set a text box's CharacterCasing property to Upper or Lower, you may not want to change the case of the user's entry as he or she is typing it. And it's entirely possible that you may not be aware of the case of strings that are read from a file. Before using a string in a comparison, you can convert it to either uppercase or lowercase, and then use the converted string in the comparison.

You use the **ToUpper method** to convert a string to uppercase, and the **ToLower method** to convert a string to lowercase. Figure 4.17 shows the syntax of both methods and includes several examples of using the methods.

**HOW TO...**

### Use the ToUpper and ToLower Methods

**Syntax**
*string*.**ToUpper()**
*string*.**ToLower()**

**Examples**
```
If letter.ToUpper() = "P" Then
```
compares the uppercase version of the string stored in the `letter` variable to the uppercase letter "P"

```
If state.ToLower() = "ca" Then
```
compares the lowercase version of the string stored in the `state` variable to the lowercase letters "ca"

```
If item1.ToUpper() <> item2.ToUpper() Then
```
compares the uppercase version of the string stored in the `item1` variable to the uppercase version of the string stored in the `item2` variable

```
If "reno" = cityTextBox.Text.ToLower() Then
```
compares the lowercase letters "reno" to the lowercase version of the string stored in the cityTextBox

```
nameLabel.Text = name.ToUpper()
```
assigns the uppercase version of the string stored in the `name` variable to the Text property of the nameLabel

```
newName = newName.ToUpper()
```
changes the contents of the `newName` variable to uppercase

```
nameTextBox.Text = nameTextBox.Text.ToLower()
```
changes the contents of the nameTextBox to lowercase

**FIGURE 4.17**    How to use the ToUpper and ToLower methods

**TIP**

The ToUpper and ToLower methods affect only characters that represent letters of the alphabet, as these are the only characters that have uppercase and lowercase forms.

In each syntax shown in Figure 4.17, *string* typically is the name of a String variable that contains the string you want to convert. However, as the fourth example shows, *string* also can be the property of an object. Both methods temporarily convert the string to the appropriate case. For example, `letter.ToUpper()` temporarily converts the contents of the `letter` variable to uppercase, and `state.ToLower()` temporarily converts the contents of the `state` variable to lowercase.

You also can use the ToUpper and ToLower methods to permanently convert the contents of a String variable or property to uppercase or lowercase, respectively. To do so, you simply include the variable or property, along with the appropriate method, in an assignment statement. For example, to permanently change the contents of the `newName` variable to uppercase, you use the assignment statement `newName = newName.ToUpper()`. You use the assignment statement `nameTextBox.Text = nameTextBox.Text.ToLower()` to convert the contents of the nameTextBox's Text property to lowercase.

When using the ToUpper method in a comparison, be sure that everything you are comparing is uppercase. In other words, the clause `If letter.ToUpper() = "p" Then` will not work correctly: the *condition* will always evaluate to False, because the uppercase version of a letter will never be equal to its lowercase counterpart. Likewise, when using the ToLower method in a comparison, be sure that everything you are comparing is lowercase.

As mentioned earlier, if the CharacterCasing property of the operationTextBox (shown earlier in Figure 4.16) was left at its default value, Normal, the code shown in Figure 4.15 will not work correctly when the user enters a lowercase letter "a" in the text box. Recall that the code will calculate and display the difference between, rather than the sum of, the two numbers entered by the user. Figures 4.18 and 4.19 show two different ways of using the ToUpper method to fix this problem. In Figure 4.18, the ToUpper method is included in the statement that assigns the text box value to the `operation` variable. In Figure 4.19, the ToUpper method is included in the If...Then...Else statement's condition. The assignment statement in Figure 4.18 will permanently change the value in the `operation` variable to uppercase, while the condition in Figure 4.19 will change the value to uppercase only temporarily. In this instance, neither way is better than the other; both simply represent two different ways of performing the same task.

ToUpper method

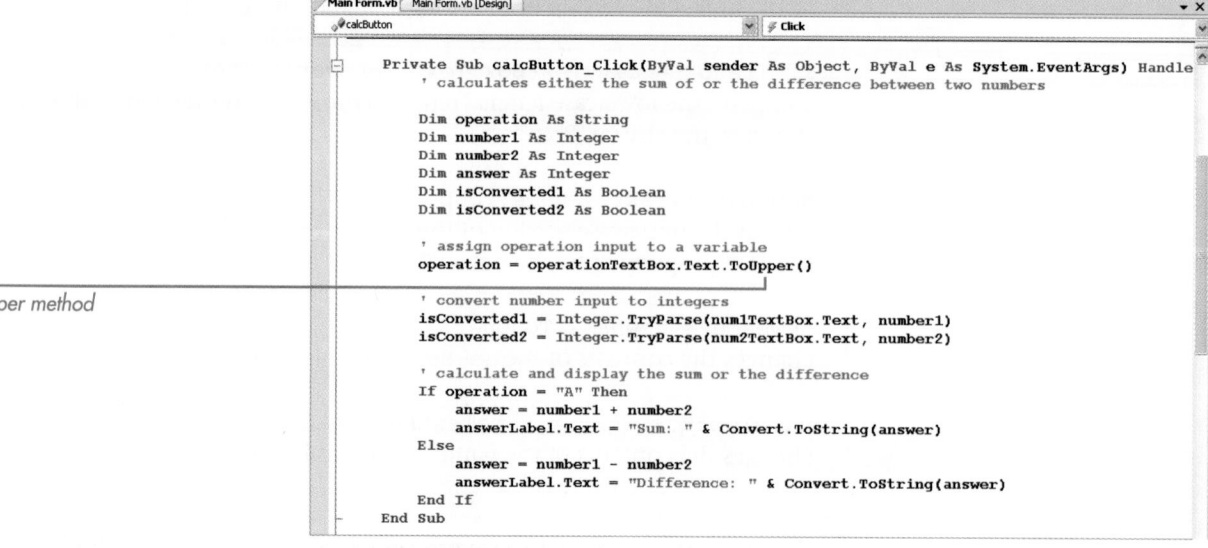

**FIGURE 4.18** Code showing the ToUpper method in the assignment statement

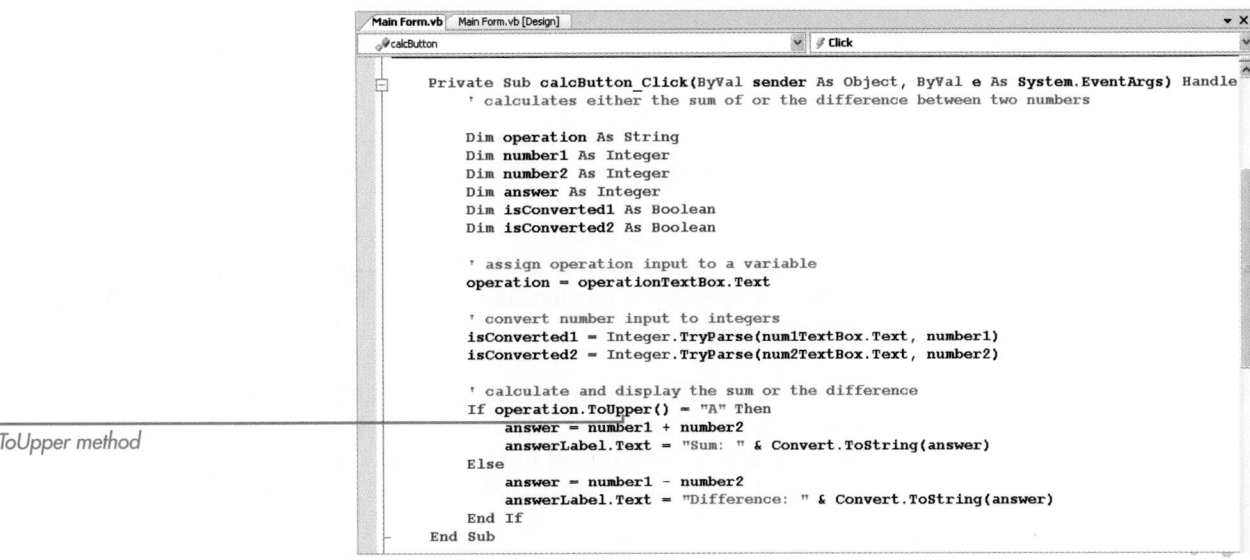

*ToUpper method*

**FIGURE 4.19** Code showing the ToUpper method in the If...Then...Else statement's condition

Recall that you also can use logical operators in the If...Then...Else statement's *condition*.

## LOGICAL OPERATORS

**Logical operators**, sometimes referred to as **Boolean operators**, allow you to combine two or more *conditions* into one compound *condition*. Visual Basic provides six logical operators, which are listed along with their order of precedence in Figure 4.20. The figure also contains examples of using logical operators in the If...Then...Else statement's *condition*.

**HOW TO...**

### Use the Logical Operators

| Operator | Operation | Precedence number |
|---|---|---|
| Not | reverses the value of the condition; True becomes False, and False becomes True | 1 |
| And | all conditions must be true for the compound condition to be true | 2 |
| AndAlso | same as the And operator, except performs short-circuit evaluation | 2 |
| Or | only one of the conditions must be true for the compound condition to be true | 3 |
| OrElse | same as the Or operator, except performs short-circuit evaluation | 3 |
| Xor | one and only one condition can be true for the compound condition to be true | 4 |

*(Figure is continued on next page)*

**Examples**
```
If Not isInsured Then
```
The condition evaluates to True when the `isInsured` variable contains the Boolean value False; otherwise, it evaluates to False.

```
If hours > 0 And hours <= 40 Then
```
The compound condition evaluates to True when the `hours` variable contains a number that is greater than zero, but less than or equal to 40; otherwise, it evaluates to False.

```
If state = "TN" AndAlso sales > 50000D Then
```
The compound condition evaluates to True when the `state` variable contains the letters "TN" and, at the same time, the `sales` variable contains a number that is greater than 50000; otherwise, it evaluates to False.

```
If rating = "A" Or rating = "B" Then
```
The compound condition evaluates to True when the `rating` variable contains either the letter "A" or the letter "B"; otherwise, it evaluates to False.

```
If state = "TN" OrElse sales > 50000D Then
```
The compound condition evaluates to True when the `state` variable contains the letters "TN" or when the `sales` variable contains a number that is greater than 50000; otherwise, it evaluates to False.

```
If coupon1 = "USED" Xor coupon2 = "USED" Then
```
The compound condition evaluates to False when neither or both variables contain the string "USED"; otherwise, it evaluates to True.

**FIGURE 4.20**   How to use the logical operators

The tables shown in Figure 4.21, called **truth tables**, summarize how Visual Basic evaluates the logical operators in an expression. Like expressions containing comparison operators, expressions containing logical operators always evaluate to a Boolean value.

**Truth table for the Not operator**

| value of *condition* | value of Not *condition* |
|---|---|
| True | False |
| False | True |

**Truth table for the And operator**

| value of *condition1* | value of *condition2* | value of *condition1* And *condition2* |
|---|---|---|
| True | True | True |
| True | False | False |
| False | True | False |
| False | False | False |

*(Figure is continued on next page)*

| Truth table for the AndAlso operator | | |
|---|---|---|
| value of *condition1* | value of *condition2* | value of *condition1* **AndAlso** *condition2* |
| True | True | True |
| True | False | False |
| False | (not evaluated) | False |

| Truth table for the Or operator | | |
|---|---|---|
| value of *condition1* | value of *condition2* | value of *condition1* **Or** *condition2* |
| True | True | True |
| True | False | True |
| False | True | True |
| False | False | False |

| Truth table for the OrElse operator | | |
|---|---|---|
| value of *condition1* | value of *condition2* | value of *condition1* **OrElse** *condition2* |
| True | (not evaluated) | True |
| False | True | True |
| False | False | False |

| Truth table for the Xor operator | | |
|---|---|---|
| value of *condition1* | value of *condition2* | value of *condition1* **Xor** *condition2* |
| True | True | False |
| True | False | True |
| False | True | True |
| False | False | False |

**FIGURE 4.21** Truth tables for the logical operators

As Figure 4.21 indicates, the Not operator reverses the truth-value of the *condition*. If the value of the *condition* is True, then the value of Not *condition* is False. Likewise, if the value of the *condition* is False, then the value of Not *condition* is True.

Now look at the truth tables for the And and AndAlso logical operators. When you use the And or AndAlso operators to combine two conditions, the resulting compound condition is True only when both conditions are True. If either condition is False or if both conditions are False, then the compound condition is False. The difference between the And and AndAlso operators is that the And operator always evaluates both conditions, while the AndAlso operator performs a **short-circuit evaluation**, which means that it does not always evaluate *condition2*. Because both conditions combined with the AndAlso operator need to be True for the compound condition to be True, the AndAlso operator does not evaluate *condition2* when *condition1* is False. Although the And and AndAlso operators produce the same results, the AndAlso operator is more efficient.

Now look at the truth tables for the Or and OrElse logical operators. When you combine conditions using the Or or OrElse operators, the compound condition is False only when both conditions are False. If either condition is True or if both conditions are True, then the compound condition is True. The difference between the Or and OrElse operators is that the Or operator always evaluates both conditions, while the OrElse operator performs a short-circuit evaluation. Because only one of the conditions combined with the OrElse operator needs to be True for the compound condition to be True, the OrElse operator does not evaluate *condition2* when *condition1* is True. Although the Or and OrElse operators produce the same results, the OrElse operator is more efficient.

Finally, look at the truth table for the Xor operator. When you combine conditions using the Xor operator, the compound condition is True only when one and only one condition is True. If both conditions are True or both conditions are False, then the compound condition is False. In the next section, you use the truth tables to determine the appropriate logical operator to use in the If...Then...Else statement's compound condition.

## Using the Truth Tables

Assume that you want to pay a bonus to every A-rated salesperson whose monthly sales total more than $10,000. To receive a bonus, the salesperson must be rated A and he or she must sell more than $10,000 in product. Assuming a String variable named `rating` and a Decimal variable named `sales` contain the salesperson's rating and sales amount, respectively, you can phrase *condition1* as `rating = "A"` and *condition2* as `sales > 10000D`. Now the question is, which logical operator should you use to combine both conditions into one compound condition? You can use the truth tables shown in Figure 4.21 to answer this question.

For a salesperson to receive a bonus, remember that both *condition1* (`rating = "A"`) and *condition2* (`sales > 10000D`) must be True at the same time. If either condition is False, or if both conditions are False, then the compound condition should be False and the salesperson should not receive a bonus. According to the truth tables, the And, AndAlso, Or, and OrElse operators evaluate the compound condition as True when both conditions are True. However, only the And and AndAlso operators evaluate the compound condition as False when either one or both of the conditions is False. The Or and OrElse operators, you will notice, evaluate the compound condition as False only when *both* conditions are False. Therefore, the correct compound condition to use here is either `rating = "A" And sales > 10000D` or `rating = "A" AndAlso sales > 10000D`. Recall, however, that the AndAlso operator is more efficient than the And operator.

Now assume that you want to send a letter to all A-rated salespeople and all B-rated salespeople. Assuming the rating is stored in the `rating` variable, you can phrase *condition1* as `rating = "A"` and *condition2* as `rating = "B"`. Now which operator do you use?

At first it might appear that either the And or AndAlso operator is the correct one to use, because the example says to send the letter to "all A-rated salespeople and all B-rated salespeople." In everyday conversations, you will find that people sometimes use the word *and* when what they really mean is *or*. Although both words do not mean the same thing, using *and* instead of *or* generally does not cause a problem, because we are able to infer what another person means. Computers, however, cannot infer anything; they simply process the directions you give them, word for word. In this case, you actually want to send a letter to all salespeople with either an A or a B rating (a salesperson cannot have both an A rating and a B rating), so you will need to use either the Or or OrElse operator. As the truth tables indicate, the Or and OrElse operators are the only operators that evaluate the compound condition as True when one or more of the conditions is True. Therefore, the correct compound condition to use here is either `rating = "A" Or rating = "B"` or `rating = "A" OrElse rating = "B"`. However, recall that the OrElse operator is more efficient than the Or operator.

Finally, assume that when placing an order, a customer is allowed to use only one of two coupons. Assuming the program uses the variables `coupon1` and `coupon2` to keep track of the coupons, you can phrase *condition1* as `coupon1 = "USED"` and *condition2* as `coupon2 = "USED"`. Now which operator should you use to combine both conditions? According to the truth tables, the Xor operator is the only operator that evaluates the compound condition as True when one and only one condition is True. Therefore, the correct compound condition to use here is `coupon1 = "USED" Xor coupon2 = "USED"`.

Figure 4.22 shows the order of precedence for the arithmetic, comparison, and logical operators you have learned so far.

| Operator | Operation | Precedence number |
|----------|-----------|-------------------|
| ^ | exponentiation | 1 |
| – | negation | 2 |
| *, / | multiplication and division | 3 |
| \ | integer division | 4 |
| Mod | modulus arithmetic | 5 |
| +, – | addition and subtraction | 6 |
| & | concatenation | 7 |
| =, >, >=, <, <=, <> | equal to, greater than, greater than or equal to, less than, less than or equal to, not equal to | 8 |
| Not | reverses truth value of condition | 9 |
| And, AndAlso | all conditions must be true for the compound condition to be true | 10 |
| Or, OrElse | only one condition needs to be true for the compound condition to be true | 11 |
| Xor | one and only one condition can be true for the compound condition to be true | 12 |

**FIGURE 4.22**    Order of precedence for arithmetic, comparison, and logical operators

Notice that logical operators are evaluated after any arithmetic operators or comparison operators in an expression. In other words, in the expression 12 > 0 AndAlso 12 < 10 * 2, the arithmetic operator (*) is evaluated first, followed by the two comparison operators (> and <), followed by the logical operator (AndAlso). The expression evaluates to True, as shown in Figure 4.23.

| Evaluation steps | Result |
|------------------|--------|
| Original expression | 12 > 0 AndAlso 12 < 10 * 2 |
| 10 * 2 is evaluated first | 12 > 0 AndAlso 12 < 20 |
| 12 > 0 is evaluated second | True AndAlso 12 < 20 |
| 12 < 20 is evaluated third | True AndAlso True |
| True AndAlso True is evaluated last | True |

**FIGURE 4.23**    Evaluation steps for an expression containing arithmetic, comparison, and logical operators

In the next section, you view the Visual Basic code for a procedure that contains a logical operator in an If...Then...Else statement.

## Using Logical Operators in an If...Then...Else Statement

Assume you want to create a procedure that calculates and displays an employee's gross pay. To keep this example simple, assume that no one at the company works more than 40 hours per week, and everyone earns the same hourly rate, $10.65. Before making the gross pay calculation, the procedure should verify that the number of hours entered by the user is greater than or equal to zero, but less than or equal to 40. Programmers refer to the process of verifying that the input data is within the expected range as **data validation**. In this case, if the number of hours is valid, the procedure should calculate and display the gross pay; otherwise, it should display an error message alerting the user that the input data is incorrect. Figure 4.24 shows two ways of writing the Visual Basic code for the procedure. Notice that the If...Then...Else statement in the first example uses the AndAlso logical operator, whereas the If...Then...Else statement in the second example uses the OrElse logical operator.

### Example 1: using the AndAlso operator

```
Private Sub calcButton_Click(ByVal sender As Object, _
        ByVal e As System.EventArgs) Handles calcButton.Click
        ' calculates and displays a gross pay amount

        Dim hoursWorked As Decimal
        Dim grossPay As Decimal
        Dim isConverted As Boolean

        ' calculate and display gross pay, or display an error message
        isConverted = Decimal.TryParse(hoursTextBox.Text, hoursWorked)
        If hoursWorked >= 0D AndAlso hoursWorked <= 40D Then
            grossPay = hoursWorked * 10.65D
            grossLabel.Text = grossPay.ToString("C2")
        Else
            grossLabel.Text = "Error"
        End If
    End Sub
```

### Example 2: using the OrElse operator

```
Private Sub calcButton_Click(ByVal sender As Object, _
        ByVal e As System.EventArgs) Handles calcButton.Click
        ' calculates and displays a gross pay amount

        Dim hoursWorked As Decimal
        Dim grossPay As Decimal
        Dim isConverted As Boolean
```

*(Figure is continued on next page)*

```
        ' calculate and display gross pay, or display an error message
        isConverted = Decimal.TryParse(hoursTextBox.Text, hoursWorked)
        If hoursWorked < 0D OrElse hoursWorked > 40D Then
            grossLabel.Text = "Error"
        Else
            grossPay = hoursWorked * 10.65D
            grossLabel.Text = grossPay.ToString("C2")
        End If
End Sub
```

**FIGURE 4.24**    AndAlso and OrElse logical operators in the
If...Then...Else statement

The compound condition in the first example shown in Figure 4.24 determines whether the value stored in the hoursWorked variable is greater than or equal to the number 0 and, at the same time, less than or equal to the number 40. If the compound condition evaluates to True, the selection structure calculates and displays the gross pay; otherwise, it displays the "Error" message.

The compound condition in the second example shown in Figure 4.24 determines whether the value stored in the hoursWorked variable is less than the number 0 or greater than the number 40. If the compound condition evaluates to True, the selection structure displays the "Error" message; otherwise, it calculates and displays the gross pay. Both If...Then...Else statements shown in Figure 4.24 produce the same results and simply represent two different ways of performing the same task. Figure 4.25 shows a sample run of the application that contains either of the calcButton Click event procedures shown in Figure 4.24.

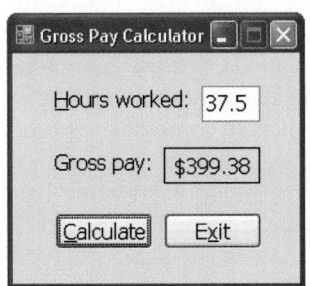

**FIGURE 4.25**    Sample run of the application that contains the calcButton's
Click event procedure

Next, you learn about the String.IsNullOrEmpty method, which you will often find in an If...Then...Else statement's condition.

## THE STRING.ISNULLOREMPTY METHOD

You can use the **String.IsNullOrEmpty method** to determine whether a control's Text property contains data before attempting to parse it. You also can use the method to determine whether a String variable contains data. Figure 4.26 shows the syntax of the String.IsNullOrEmpty method and includes examples of using the method.

# HOW TO...

## Use the String.IsNullOrEmpty Method

**Syntax**
**String.IsNullOrEmpty(***string***)**

**Examples**
```
If String.IsNullOrEmpty(quantityTextBox.Text) Then
```
the condition evaluates to True when the quantityTextBox is empty; otherwise, it evaluates to False

```
If String.IsNullOrEmpty(quantityTextBox.Text) = True Then
```
same as the previous example

```
If Not String.IsNullOrEmpty(inputHours) Then
```
the condition evaluates to True when the inputHours variable contains data; otherwise, it evaluates to False

```
If String.IsNullOrEmpty(inputHours) = False Then
```
same as the previous example

**FIGURE 4.26**    How to use the String.IsNullOrEmpty method

In the syntax, *string* is the item whose contents you want to verify. The String.IsNullOrEmpty method returns the Boolean value True when the *string* does not contain any data; otherwise, it returns the Boolean value False.

As the first two examples shown in Figure 4.26 indicate, you can use either the `String.IsNullOrEmpty(quantityTextBox.Text)` condition or the `String.IsNullOrEmpty(quantityTextBox.Text) = True` condition to determine whether the quantityTextBox is empty. The last two examples show that you can use either the `Not String.IsNullOrEmpty(inputHours)` condition or the `String.IsNullOrEmpty(inputHours) = False` condition to determine whether the inputHours variable contains a value.

In Chapter 3, as well as in some of the procedures you viewed in this chapter, you assigned the TryParse method's return value to a Boolean variable. Recall that the method returns the Boolean value True when the conversion is successful, but returns the Boolean value False when the conversion is not successful. In the next section, you modify the Skate-Away Sales application so that it uses the value returned by the TryParse method to determine the instructions to process when the method succeeds and when it fails.

## MODIFYING THE SKATE-AWAY SALES APPLICATION

In Chapter 3, you created an application for Skate-Away Sales, a company that sells skateboards by phone. Figure 4.27 shows the application's user interface, and Figure 4.28 shows the calcButton's modified Click event procedure. Changes made to the original code are shaded in Figure 4.28.

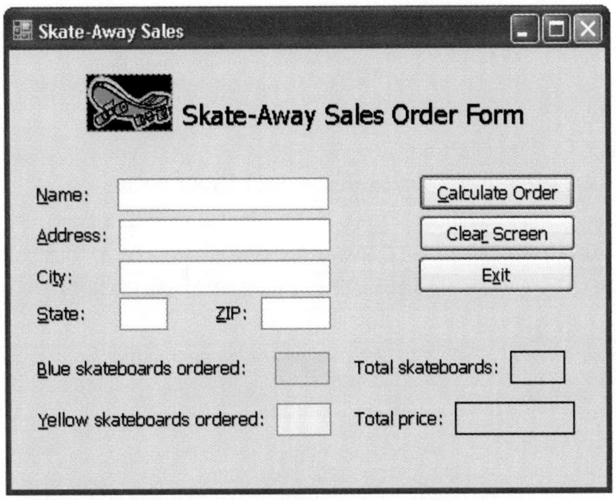

**FIGURE 4.27** User interface for the Skate-Away Sales application

**Visual Basic code**

```vb
Private Sub calcButton_Click(ByVal sender As Object, ByVal e As System.EventArgs) _
    Handles calcButton.Click
    ' calculates the total number of skateboards ordered and the total price

    ' declare constants and variables
    Const TaxRate As Decimal = 0.05D
    Const SkateboardPrice As Decimal = 100D
    Dim blueBoards As Integer
    Dim yellowBoards As Integer
    Dim totalSkateboards As Integer
    Dim totalPrice As Decimal
    Dim isConverted1 As Boolean
    Dim isConverted2 As Boolean

    ' if a skateboards ordered text box is empty, then
    ' display 0 in it
    If String.IsNullOrEmpty(blueTextBox.Text) Then
        blueTextBox.Text = "0"
    End If
    If String.IsNullOrEmpty(yellowTextBox.Text) Then
        yellowTextBox.Text = "0"
    End If

    ' convert input
    isConverted1 = Integer.TryParse(blueTextBox.Text, _
        NumberStyles.AllowThousands, NumberFormatInfo.CurrentInfo, blueBoards)
    isConverted2 = Integer.TryParse(yellowTextBox.Text, _
        NumberStyles.AllowThousands, NumberFormatInfo.CurrentInfo, yellowBoards)
```

*(Figure is continued on next page)*

```
' if the input is converted to Integer, then
' calculate and display total skateboards and total price
' otherwise, display an error message
If isConverted1 = True AndAlso isConverted2 = True Then
    totalSkateboards = blueBoards + yellowBoards
    totalPrice = (totalSkateboards * SkateboardPrice) * (1 + TaxRate)
    totalBoardsLabel.Text = Convert.ToString(totalSkateboards)
    totalPriceLabel.Text = totalPrice.ToString("C2")
Else
    MessageBox.Show("The skateboards ordered entries must be numbers.", _
        "Skate-Away Sales", MessageBoxButtons.OK, MessageBoxIcon.Information)
End If
End Sub
```

**FIGURE 4.28**      The calcButton's modified Click event procedure

The modified procedure declares two Boolean variables named `isConverted1` and `isConverted2`. The procedure then uses the String.IsNullOrEmpty method in two If...Then...Else statements to determine whether the blueTextBox and yellowTextBox contain data. If either text box is empty, the procedure assigns the string "0" to its Text property to indicate that no skateboards of that color were ordered.

The two TryParse methods in the procedure attempt to convert the values entered in the blueTextBox and yellowTextBox to Integer, assigning the return values (either True or False) to the Boolean variables, `isConverted1` and `isConverted2`. The compound condition in the If...Then...Else statement determines whether the TryParse methods were successful. It does this by comparing the contents of the `isConverted1` variable with the value True, and also comparing the contents of the `isConverted2` variable with the value True. Because the compound condition contains the AndAlso logical operator, both conditions must be true for the compound condition to be true. In this case, if the compound condition evaluates to True, it means that both TryParse methods were successful in converting the contents of their respective text boxes to Integer. Therefore, the instructions in the If...Then...Else statement's true path calculate and display the total number of skateboards ordered and the total price.

However, if one or both of the Boolean variables does not contain the value True, it means that at least one of the TryParse methods failed to convert its text box value to Integer. In that case, the instruction in the If...Then...Else statement's false path uses the MessageBox.Show method to display an appropriate message to the user, as shown in Figure 4.29.

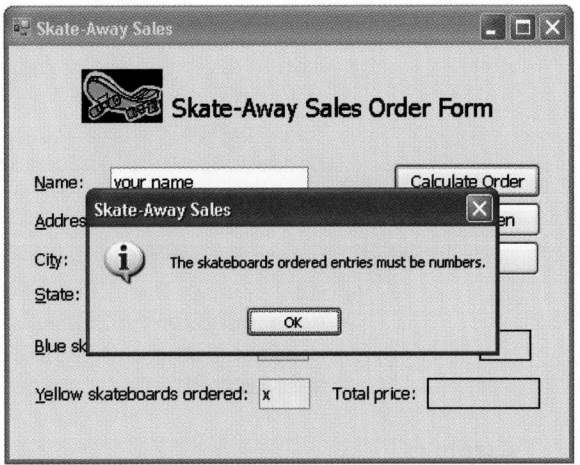

**FIGURE 4.29**  Message box displayed when the compound condition evaluates to False

You learn how to use the MessageBox.Show method next.

## THE MESSAGEBOX.SHOW METHOD

You can use the **MessageBox.Show method** to display a message box that contains text, one or more buttons, and an icon. Figure 4.30 shows the syntax of the MessageBox.Show method. It also lists the meaning of each argument used by the method, and includes two examples of using the method to create a message box.

### HOW TO...

**Use the MessageBox.Show Method**

**Syntax**
**MessageBox.Show**(*text, caption, buttons, icon*[, *defaultButton*])

| Argument | Meaning |
|---|---|
| *text* | text to display in the message box |
| *caption* | text to display in the title bar of the message box |
| *buttons* | buttons to display in the message box; can be one of the following constants: |

```
MessageBoxButtons.AbortRetryIgnore
MessageBoxButtons.OK
MessageBoxButtons.OKCancel
MessageBoxButtons.RetryCancel
MessageBoxButtons.YesNo
MessageBoxButtons.YesNoCancel
```

*(Figure is continued on next page)*

| icon | icon to display in the message box; typically, one of the following constants:<br>`MessageBoxIcon.Exclamation`<br>`MessageBoxIcon.Information`<br>`MessageBoxIcon.Stop` |
| defaultButton | button automatically selected when the user presses Enter; can be one of the following constants:<br>`MessageBoxDefaultButton.Button1`  (default setting)<br>`MessageBoxDefaultButton.Button2`<br>`MessageBoxDefaultButton.Button3` |

**Examples**
```
MessageBox.Show("Record deleted.", "Payroll", _
    MessageBoxButtons.OK, MessageBoxIcon.Information)
```
displays an informational message box that contains the message "Record deleted."

```
MessageBox.Show("Delete this record?", "Payroll", _
    MessageBoxButtons.YesNo, MessageBoxIcon.Exclamation, _
    MessageBoxDefaultButton.Button2)
```
displays a warning message box that contains the message "Delete this record?"

**FIGURE 4.30**     How to use the MessageBox.Show method

As Figure 4.30 indicates, the *text* argument specifies the text to display in the message box. The *text* argument can be a String literal constant, String named constant, or String variable. The message in the *text* argument should be concise but clear, and should be entered using sentence capitalization. You should avoid using the words "error," "warning," or "mistake" in the message, as these words imply that the user has done something wrong.

The *caption* argument specifies the text to display in the title bar of the message box, and typically is the application's name. Like the *text* argument, the *caption* argument can be a String literal constant, String named constant, or String variable. Unlike the *text* argument, however, the *caption* argument is entered using book title capitalization.

The *buttons* argument indicates the buttons to display in the message box and can be one of six different constants. For example, a *buttons* argument of `MessageBoxButtons.AbortRetryIgnore` displays the Abort, Retry, and Ignore buttons in the message box. A *buttons* argument of `MessageBoxButtons.OK`, on the other hand, displays only the OK button in the message box.

The *icon* argument specifies the icon to display in the message box and typically is one of the following constants: `MessageBoxIcon.Exclamation`, `MessageBoxIcon.Information`, or `MessageBoxIcon.Stop`. A message box's icon indicates the type of message being sent to the user. The `MessageBoxIcon.Exclamation` constant, for example, displays the Warning Message icon, which alerts the user to a condition or situation that requires him or her to make a decision before the application can proceed. The message to the user can be phrased as a question, such as "Save changes to the document?"

The `MessageBoxIcon.Information` constant displays the Information Message icon. The Information Message icon indicates that the message in the message box is for information only and does not require the user to make a decision. An example of an informational message is "The changes were saved." A message box with an Information Message icon should contain only an OK button; in other words, you always use `MessageBoxButtons.OK` for the *buttons* argument when using `MessageBoxIcon.Information` for the *icon* argument. The user acknowledges the informational message by clicking the OK button.

The `MessageBoxIcon.Stop` constant displays the Stop Message icon, which alerts the user to a serious problem that requires intervention or correction before the application can continue. You would use the Stop Message icon in a message box that alerts the user that the disk in the disk drive is write-protected.

The *defaultButton* argument in the MessageBox.Show method identifies the default button, which is the button that is selected automatically when the user presses the Enter key on the computer keyboard. To designate the first button in the message box as the default button, you either set the *defaultButton* argument to `MessageBoxDefaultButton.Button1`, or you simply omit the argument. To have the second or third button be the default button, you set the *defaultButton* argument to `MessageBoxDefaultButton.Button2` or `MessageBoxDefaultButton.Button3`, respectively. The default button should be the button that represents the user's most likely action, as long as that action is not destructive.

Study the two examples shown in Figure 4.30. In the first example, the `MessageBox.Show("Record deleted.", "Payroll", MessageBoxButtons.OK, MessageBoxIcon.Information)` instruction displays the informational message box shown in Figure 4.31. The user can close the message box by clicking either the OK button or the Close button. The `MessageBox.Show("Delete this record?", "Payroll", MessageBoxButtons.YesNo, MessageBoxIcon.Exclamation, MessageBoxDefaultButton.Button2)` instruction in the second example displays the warning message box shown in Figure 4.32. Notice that the Close button in a warning message box is automatically disabled. In this case, the user must select either the Yes button or the No button (which is the default button) to close the message box.

*The user can close an information message box using either the OK button or the Close button*

**FIGURE 4.31**   Message box displayed by the first example shown in Figure 4.30

*The Close button is automatically disabled*

*The user must select one of these buttons to close the warning message box*

*Default button*

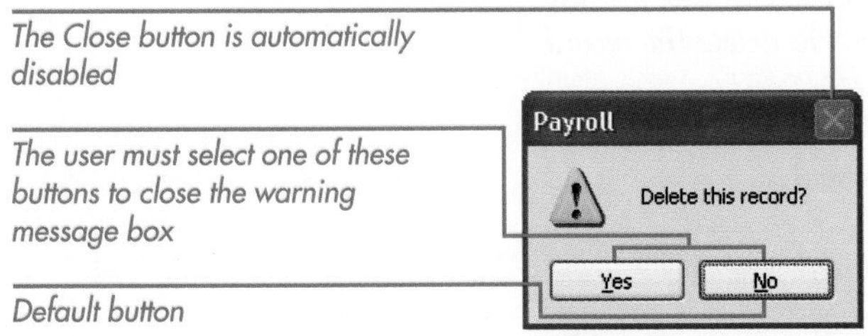

**FIGURE 4.32**   Message box displayed by the second example shown in Figure 4.30

After displaying the message box, the MessageBox.Show method waits for the user to choose one of the buttons displayed in the message box. It then closes the message box and returns an integer that indicates which button the user chose.

Sometimes you are not interested in the value returned by the MessageBox.Show method. This is the case when the message box is for informational purposes only, like the message boxes shown in Figures 4.29 and 4.31. Recall that the only button in an informational message box is the OK button. Many times, however, the button selected by the user determines the next task performed by an application. For example, selecting the Yes button in the message box shown in Figure 4.32 tells the application to delete the record; selecting the No button tells the application not to delete the record.

Figure 4.33 lists the integer values returned by the MessageBox.Show method; each value is associated with a button that can appear in a message box. The figure also lists the DialogResult values assigned to each integer, and the meaning of the integers and DialogResult values. Additionally, the figure contains three examples of using the value returned by the MessageBox.Show method.

## HOW TO... Use the Value Returned by the MessageBox.Show Method

| Number | DialogResult Value | Meaning |
|---|---|---|
| 1 | DialogResult.OK | user chose the OK button |
| 2 | DialogResult.Cancel | user chose the Cancel button |
| 3 | DialogResult.Abort | user chose the Abort button |
| 4 | DialogResult.Retry | user chose the Retry button |
| 5 | DialogResult.Ignore | user chose the Ignore button |
| 6 | DialogResult.Yes | user chose the Yes button |
| 7 | DialogResult.No | user chose the No button |

**Examples**

```
Dim button As DialogResult
button = MessageBox.Show("Delete this record?", _
        "Payroll", MessageBoxButtons.YesNo, _
        MessageBoxIcon.Exclamation, _
        MessageBoxDefaultButton.Button2)
If button = DialogResult.Yes Then
    instructions to delete the record
End If


If MessageBox.Show("Delete this record?", _
        "Payroll", MessageBoxButtons.YesNo, _
        MessageBoxIcon.Exclamation, _
        MessageBoxDefaultButton.Button2) _
        = DialogResult.Yes Then
            instructions to delete the record
End If
```

**(Figure is continued on next page)**

```
Dim button As DialogResult
button = MessageBox.Show("Play another game?", _
        "Math Monster", MessageBoxButtons.YesNo, _
        MessageBoxIcon.Exclamation)
If button = DialogResult.Yes Then
    instructions to start another game
Else  'DialogResult.No
    instructions to close the game application
End If
```

**FIGURE 4.33**    How to use the value returned by the
MessageBox.Show method

As Figure 4.33 indicates, the MessageBox.Show method returns the integer 6 when the user selects the Yes button. The integer 6 is represented by the DialogResult value, `DialogResult.Yes`. When referring to the MessageBox.Show method's return value in code, you should use the DialogResult values listed in Figure 4.33 rather than the integers, because the values make the code easier to understand.

Look closely at the three examples shown in Figure 4.33. In the first example, the value returned by the MessageBox.Show method is assigned to a DialogResult variable named `button`. If the user selects the Yes button in the message box, the integer 6 is stored in the `button` variable; otherwise, the integer 7 is stored in the variable to indicate that the user selected the No button. The selection structure in the example compares the contents of the `button` variable to the DialogResult value, `DialogResult.Yes`. If the `button` variable contains the integer 6, which is the value of `DialogResult.Yes`, then the instructions to delete the record are processed; otherwise, the deletion instructions are skipped.

You do not have to store the value returned by the MessageBox.Show method in a variable, although doing so can make your code more readable. For instance, in the second example shown in Figure 4.33, the method's return value is not stored in a variable. Instead, the method appears in the selection structure's condition, where its return value is compared to `DialogResult.Yes`.

The selection structure shown in the third example in Figure 4.33 performs one set of tasks when the user selects the Yes button in the message box, and another set of tasks when the user selects the No button. It is a good programming practice to document the Else portion of the selection structure as shown in the figure, because it makes it clear that the Else portion is processed only when the user selects the No button.

As you learned earlier, you use the selection structure when you want a procedure to make a decision and then select one of two paths—either the true path or the false path—based on the result of that decision. Both paths in a selection structure can include instructions that declare variables, perform calculations, and so on. Both paths also can include other selection structures, called nested selection structures.

## NESTED SELECTION STRUCTURES

When either a selection structure's true path or its false path contains another selection structure, the inner selection structure is referred to as a **nested selection structure**, because it is contained (nested) within the outer selection structure. You use a nested selection structure when more than one decision must be made before the appropriate action can be taken. For example, assume you want to create a procedure that determines voter eligibility and displays one of three messages. The messages and the criteria for displaying each message are shown in the following chart:

| Message | Criteria |
|---------|----------|
| "You are too young to vote." | person is younger than 18 years old |
| "You can vote." | person is at least 18 years old and is registered to vote |
| "You need to register before you can vote." | person is at least 18 years old but is not registered to vote |

As the chart indicates, the person's age and voter registration status determine the appropriate message to display. If the person is younger than 18 years old, the procedure should display the message "You are too young to vote." However, if the person is at least 18 years old, the procedure should display one of two different messages. The correct message to display is determined by the person's voter registration status. If the person is registered, then the appropriate message is "You can vote."; otherwise, it is "You need to register before you can vote." Notice that determining the person's voter registration status is important only *after* his or her age is determined. You can think of the decision regarding the age as being the **primary decision**, and the decision regarding the registration status as being the **secondary decision**, because whether the registration decision needs to be made depends on the result of the age decision. The primary decision is always made by the outer selection structure, while the secondary decision is always made by the inner (nested) selection structure.

Figures 4.34 and 4.35 show the pseudocode and Visual Basic code, respectively, for the displayButton's Click event procedure, which displays the appropriate message based on a person's voter eligibility. Figure 4.36 shows the corresponding flowchart. In the figures, the outer selection structure determines the age (the primary decision), and the nested selection structure determines the voter registration status (the secondary decision). Notice that the nested selection structure appears in the outer selection structure's true path in the figures. (The lines connecting the selection structures in the pseudocode and code are included to help you see the clauses that are related to each other.)

**Pseudocode**

if the age is greater than or equal to 18
    if the registration status is Y
        display "You can vote."
    else
        display "You need to register before you can vote."
    end if
else
    display "You are too young to vote."
end if

**FIGURE 4.34**    Pseudocode showing the nested selection structure in the true path

**Visual Basic code**

```vb
Private Sub displayButton_Click(ByVal sender As Object, _
    ByVal e As System.EventArgs) Handles displayButton.Click
    ' displays a message based on a person's age and voter status

    Dim age As Integer
    Dim status As String
    Dim isConverted As Boolean

    ' convert age input to Integer
    isConverted = Integer.TryParse(ageTextBox.Text, age)

    ' display appropriate message
    If age >= 18 Then
        status = statusTextBox.Text
        If status = "Y" Then
            messageLabel.Text = "You can vote."
        Else
            messageLabel.Text = _
                "You need to register before you can vote."
        End If
    Else
        messageLabel.Text = "You are too young to vote."
    End If
End Sub
```

**FIGURE 4.35**    The displayButton's Click event procedure showing the nested selection structure in the true path

**Flowchart**

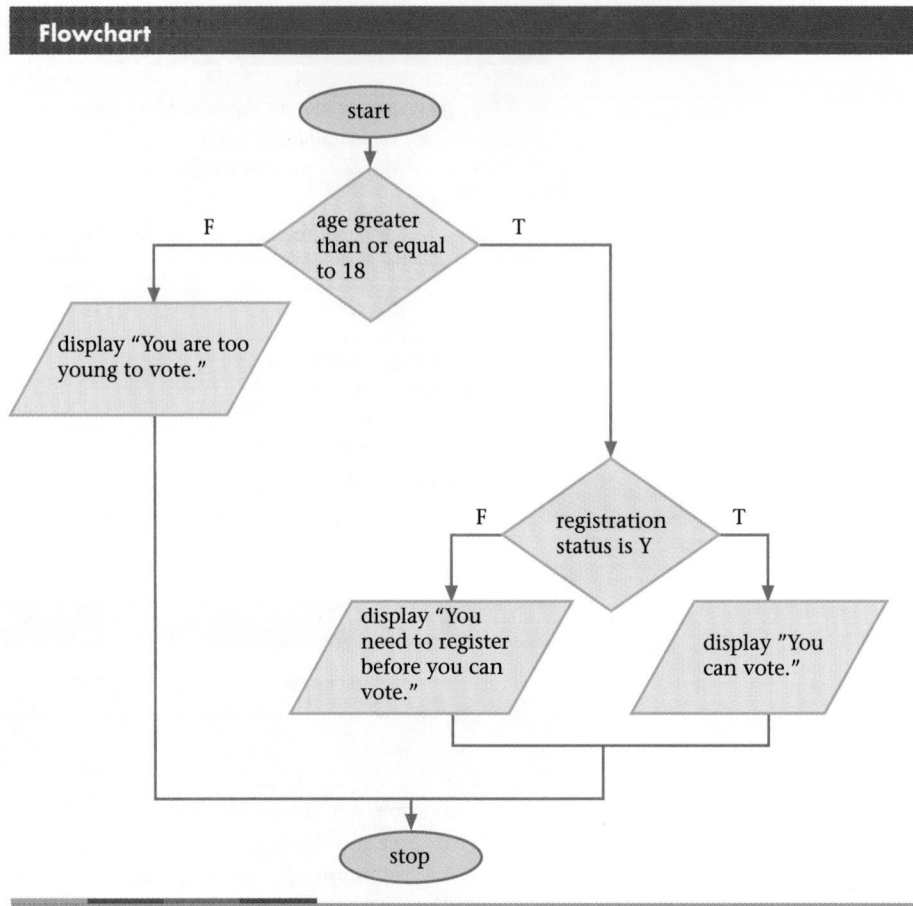

Look closely at the displayButton's Click event procedure shown in Figure 4.35. The procedure declares three variables named age, status, and isConverted. It then uses the TryParse method to convert the contents of the ageTextBox to an integer. The condition in the outer selection structure checks whether the integer stored in the age variable is greater than or equal to 18. If the condition is false, it means that the person is not old enough to vote. In that case, only one message— the "You are too young to vote." message—is appropriate. After the message is displayed, both the outer selection structure and the procedure end.

If the outer selection structure's condition is true, on the other hand, it means that the person *is* old enough to vote. Before displaying the appropriate message, the instructions in the outer selection structure's true path assign the contents of the statusTextBox to the status variable. A nested selection structure then is used to determine whether the person is registered. If he or she is registered, the instruction in the nested selection structure's true path displays the "You can vote." message; otherwise, the instruction in the nested selection structure's false path displays the "You need to register before you can vote." message. After the appropriate message is displayed, both selection structures and the procedure end. Notice that the nested selection structure in this procedure is processed only when the outer selection structure's condition is true.

Figures 4.37, 4.38, and 4.39 show the pseudocode, Visual Basic code, and flowchart, respectively, for a different version of the displayButton's Click event procedure. As in the previous version, the outer selection structure in this version determines the age (the primary decision), and the nested selection structure determines the voter registration status (the secondary decision). In this version of the procedure, however, the nested selection structure appears in the false path of the outer selection structure.

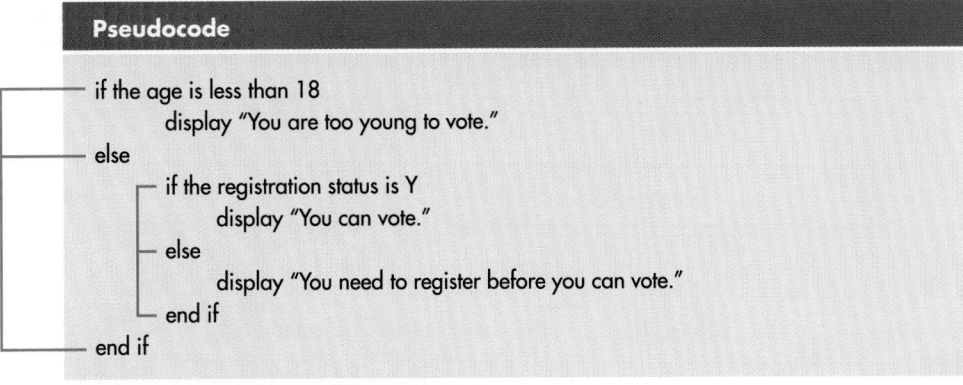

**Pseudocode**

```
if the age is less than 18
        display "You are too young to vote."
else
        if the registration status is Y
                display "You can vote."
        else
                display "You need to register before you can vote."
        end if
end if
```

**FIGURE 4.37**   Pseudocode showing the nested selection structure in the false path

**Visual Basic code**

```
Private Sub displayButton_Click(ByVal sender As Object, _
    ByVal e As System.EventArgs) Handles displayButton.Click
    ' displays a message based on a person's age and voter status

    Dim age As Integer
    Dim status As String
    Dim isConverted As Boolean

    ' convert age input to Integer
    isConverted = Integer.TryParse(ageTextBox.Text, age)

    ' display appropriate message
    If age < 18 Then
        messageLabel.Text = "You are too young to vote."
    Else
        status = statusTextBox.Text
        If status = "Y" Then
            messageLabel.Text = "You can vote."
        Else
            messageLabel.Text = "You need to register before
            you can vote."
        End If
    End If
End Sub
```

**FIGURE 4.38**   The displayButton's Click event procedure showing the nested selection structure in the false path

**Flowchart**

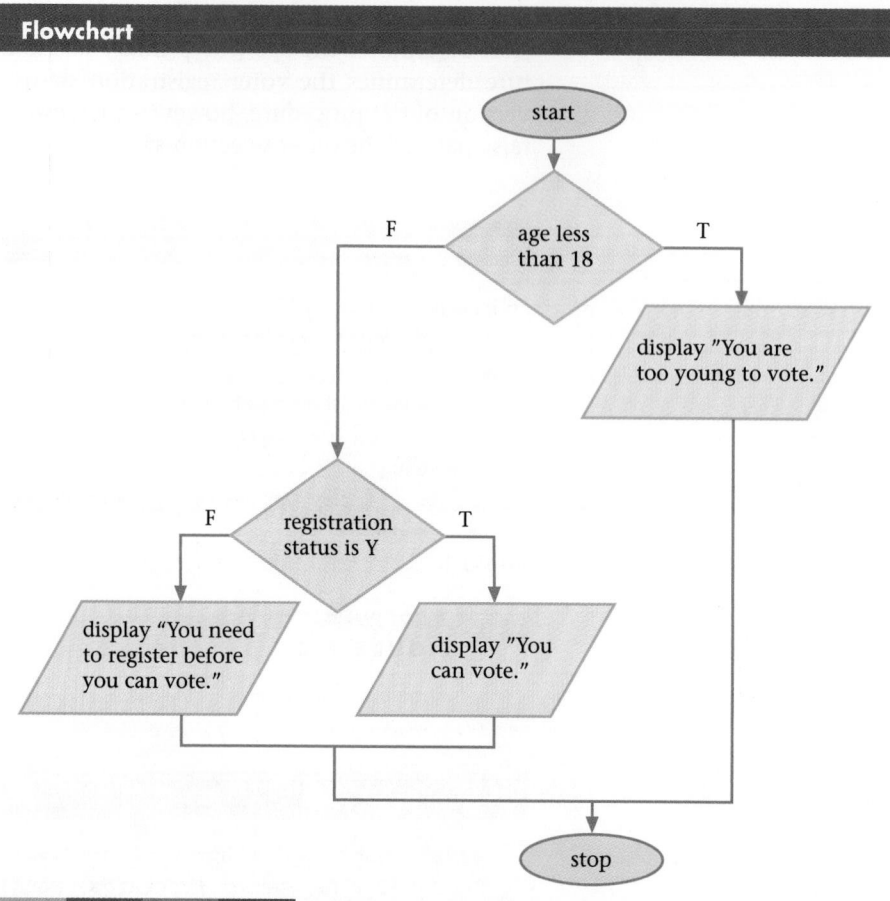

**FIGURE 4.39**     Flowchart showing the nested selection structure in the false path

Like the version shown earlier, this version of the displayButton's Click event procedure first declares the necessary variables, and then converts the contents of the ageTextBox to Integer. However, rather than checking whether the integer stored in the age variable is greater than or equal to 18, the outer selection structure in this version checks whether the integer is less than 18. If the condition is true, the instruction in the outer selection structure's true path displays the message "You are too young to vote." If the condition is false, the instructions in the outer selection structure's false path assign the contents of the statusTextBox to the status variable, and then use a nested selection structure to determine whether the person is registered. If the person is registered, the instruction in the nested selection structure's true path displays the "You can vote." message; otherwise, the instruction in the nested selection structure's false path displays the "You need to register before you can vote." message. Unlike in the previous version, the nested selection structure in this version of the procedure is processed only when the outer selection structure's condition is false.

Both versions of the displayButton's Click event procedure produce the same results. Neither version is better than the other; each simply represents a different way of solving the same problem. Figure 4.40 shows a sample run of the application that contains either version of the procedure.

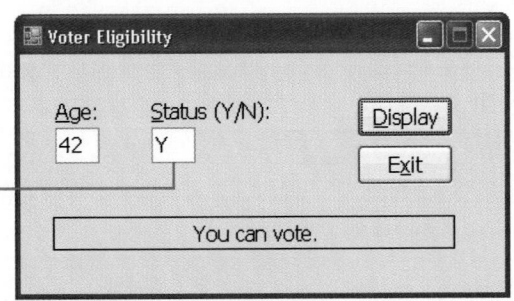

*The statusTextBox's CharacterCasing and MaxLength properties are set to Upper and 1, respectively*

**FIGURE 4.40**    Sample run of the application that contains the displayButton's Click event procedure

In addition to the If and If/Else forms of the selection structure, Visual Basic also provides the If/Elself/Else and Case forms. The If/Elself/Else and Case forms of the selection structure are commonly referred to as **extended selection structures** or **multiple-path selection structures**.

## THE IF/ELSEIF/ELSE SELECTION STRUCTURE

At times, you may need to create a selection structure that can choose from several alternatives. For example, assume you are asked to create a procedure that displays a message based on a letter grade that the user enters. The valid letter grades and their corresponding messages are shown in the following chart:

| Letter grade | Message |
|---|---|
| A | Excellent |
| B | Above Average |
| C | Average |
| D | Below Average |
| F | Below Average |

As the chart indicates, when the letter grade is an A, the procedure should display the message "Excellent." When the letter grade is a B, the procedure should display the message "Above Average," and so on. Figure 4.41 shows two versions of the Visual Basic code for the displayMsgButton's Click event procedure. The first version uses nested If/Else structures to display the appropriate message, while the second version uses the If/Elself/Else structure. As you do with the If/Else selection structure, you use the If...Then...Else statement to code the If/Elself/Else selection structure.

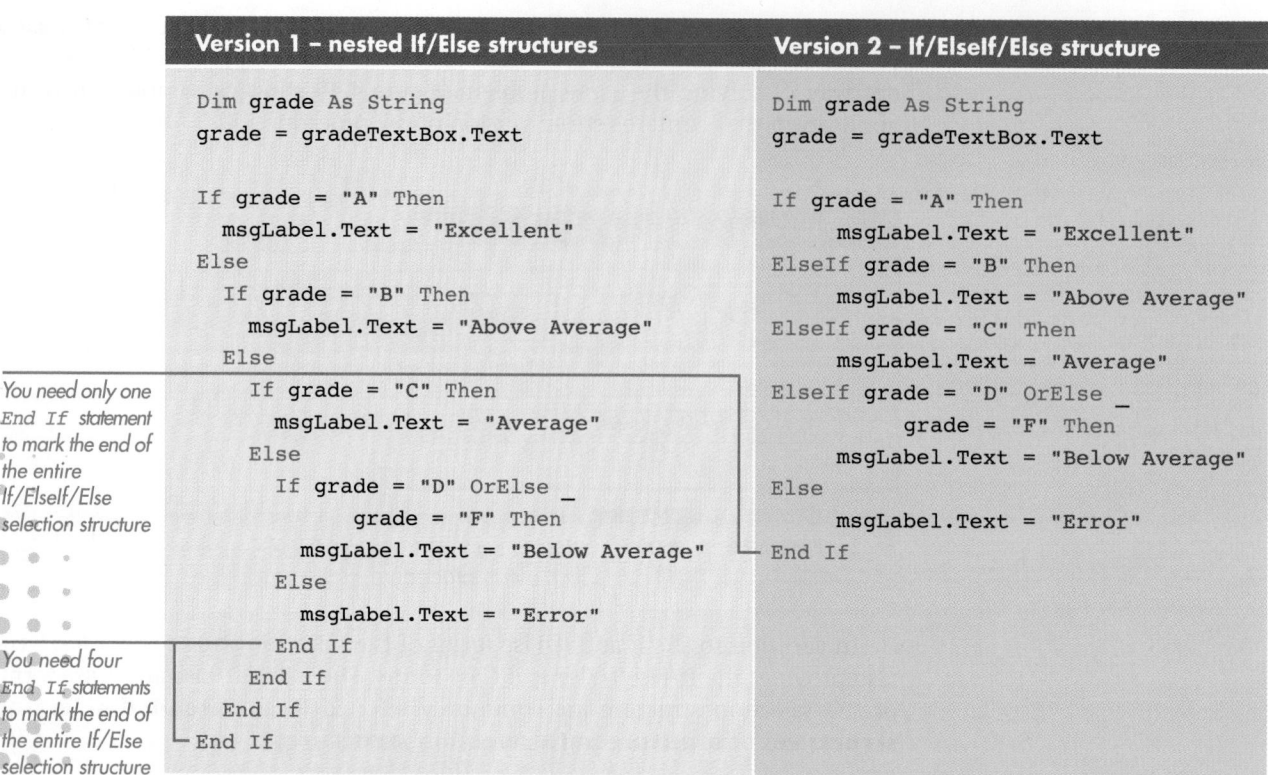

| Version 1 – nested If/Else structures | Version 2 – If/ElseIf/Else structure |
|---|---|

```
Dim grade As String
grade = gradeTextBox.Text

If grade = "A" Then
  msgLabel.Text = "Excellent"
Else
  If grade = "B" Then
    msgLabel.Text = "Above Average"
  Else
    If grade = "C" Then
      msgLabel.Text = "Average"
    Else
      If grade = "D" OrElse _
          grade = "F" Then
        msgLabel.Text = "Below Average"
      Else
        msgLabel.Text = "Error"
      End If
    End If
  End If
End If
```

```
Dim grade As String
grade = gradeTextBox.Text

If grade = "A" Then
    msgLabel.Text = "Excellent"
ElseIf grade = "B" Then
    msgLabel.Text = "Above Average"
ElseIf grade = "C" Then
    msgLabel.Text = "Average"
ElseIf grade = "D" OrElse _
        grade = "F" Then
    msgLabel.Text = "Below Average"
Else
    msgLabel.Text = "Error"
End If
```

*You need only one End If statement to mark the end of the entire If/ElseIf/Else selection structure*

*You need four End If statements to mark the end of the entire If/Else selection structure*

**FIGURE 4.41**     Two versions of the displayMsgButton's Click event procedure

Although you can write the displayMsgButton's Click event procedure using either nested If/Else selection structures (as shown in Version 1) or the If/ElseIf/Else selection structure (as shown in Version 2), the **If/ElseIf/Else structure** provides a much more convenient way of writing a multiple-path selection structure. Figure 4.42 shows a sample run of the application that contains either version of the displayMsgButton's Click event procedure.

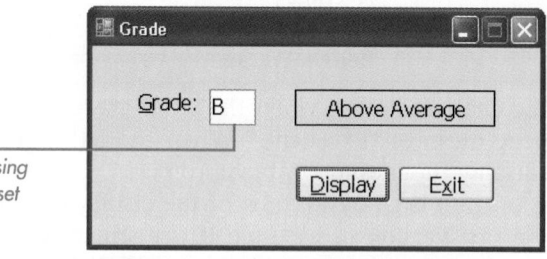

*The gradeTextBox's CharacterCasing and MaxLength properties are set to Upper and 1, respectively*

**FIGURE 4.42**     Sample run of the application that contains the displayMsgButton's Click event procedure

Next, you learn about the Case form of the selection structure.

## THE CASE SELECTION STRUCTURE

In situations where the selection structure has many paths from which to choose, it is often simpler and clearer to use the Case form of the selection structure, rather than the If/ElseIf/Else form. Figures 4.43 and 4.44 show the pseudocode and flowchart, respectively, for the displayMsgButton's Click event procedure, using the Case selection structure.

**Pseudocode**

1. grade value
   - A       display "Excellent"
   - B       display "Above Average"
   - C       display "Average"
   - D, F    display "Below Average"
   - Other    display "Error"

**FIGURE 4.43**    Pseudocode showing the Case selection structure

**Flowchart**

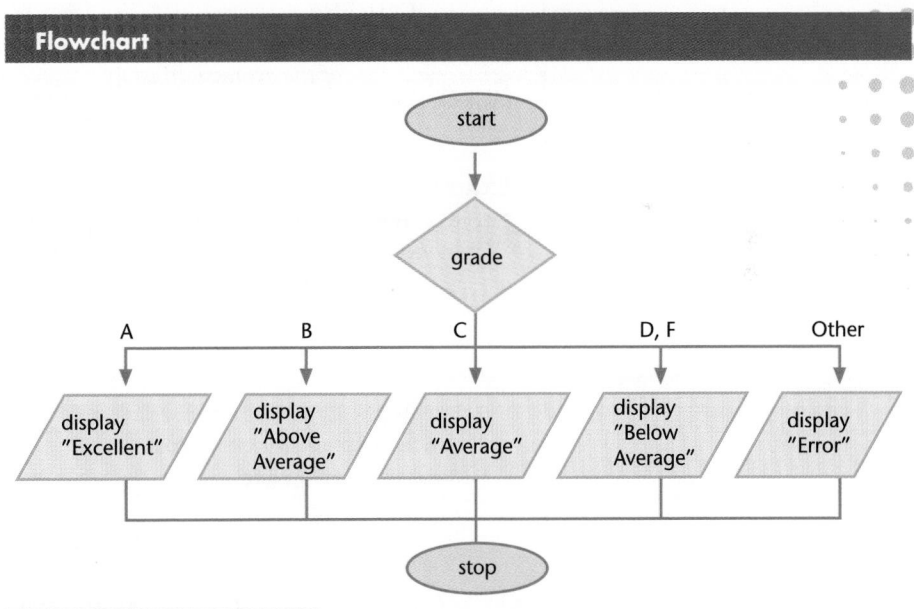

**FIGURE 4.44**    Flowchart showing the Case selection structure

The flowchart symbol for the Case form of the selection structure is the same as the flowchart symbol for the If, If/Else, and If/ElseIf/Else forms—a diamond. However, unlike the diamonds used in the other selection structures, the Case diamond does not contain a condition requiring a true or false answer. Instead, the Case diamond contains an expression whose value determines which path is chosen. In Figure 4.44, the expression is *grade*.

Like the If, If/Else, and If/ElseIf/Else diamond, the Case diamond has one flowline leading into the symbol. Unlike the other diamonds, however, the Case diamond has many flowlines leading out of the symbol. Each flowline represents a possible path for the selection structure. The flowlines must be marked appropriately, indicating which value(s) are necessary for each path to be chosen.

Figure 4.45 shows the syntax of the **Select Case statement**, which is used to code the Case selection structure in Visual Basic. It also shows how to use the Select Case statement to code the displayMsgButton's Click event procedure. It is customary to indent each Case clause, as well as the instructions within each Case clause, as shown in the figure.

HOW TO...

**Use the Select Case Statement**

**Syntax**
Select Case *selectorExpression*
        **Case** *expressionList1*
                [*instructions for the first Case*]
        [**Case** *expressionList2*
                [*instructions for the second Case*]]
        [**Case** *expressionListn*
                [*instructions for the nth case*]]
        [**Case Else**
                [*instructions for when the selectorExpression does not match any of the expressionLists*]]
**End Select**

**Example**
```
Private Sub displayMsgButton_Click(ByVal sender As Object, _
    ByVal e As System.EventArgs) Handles displayMsgButton.Click
    ' displays a message corresponding to a grade

    Dim grade As String

    'display appropriate message
    grade = gradeTextBox.Text
    Select Case grade
        Case "A"
            msgLabel.Text = "Excellent"
        Case "B"
            msgLabel.Text = "Above Average"
        Case "C"
            msgLabel.Text = "Average"
        Case "D", "F"
            msgLabel.Text = "Below Average"
        Case Else
            msgLabel.Text = "Error"
    End Select
End Sub
```

**FIGURE 4.45**    How to use the Select Case statement

The Select Case statement begins with the Select Case clause and ends with the End Select clause. Between the Select Case and End Select clauses are the individual Case clauses. Each Case clause represents a different path that the selection structure can follow. You can have as many Case clauses as necessary in a Select Case statement. If the Select Case statement includes a Case Else clause, the Case Else clause must be the last clause in the statement.

Notice that the Select Case clause must include a *selectorExpression*. The *selectorExpression* can contain any combination of variables, constants, methods, operators, and properties. In the procedure shown in Figure 4.45, the *selectorExpression* is a String variable named `grade`.

Each of the individual Case clauses, except the Case Else clause, must contain an *expressionList*, which can include one or more expressions. To include more than one expression in an *expressionList*, you simply separate each expression with a comma, as in the *expressionList* `Case "D", "F"`. The *selectorExpression* needs to match only one of the expressions listed in an *expressionList*.

The data type of the expressions must be compatible with the data type of the *selectorExpression*. In other words, if the *selectorExpression* is numeric, the expressions in the Case clauses should be numeric. Likewise, if the *selectorExpression* is a string, the expressions should be strings. In the procedure shown in Figure 4.45, the *selectorExpression* (`grade`) is a string, and so are the expressions—"A", "B", "C", "D", and "F"—as the quotation marks indicate.

When processing the Select Case statement, the computer first compares the value of the *selectorExpression* with the values listed in *expressionList1*. If a match is found, the computer processes the instructions for the first Case, stopping when it reaches either another Case clause (including the Case Else clause) or the End Select clause (which marks the end of the selection structure). It then skips to the instruction following the End Select clause. If a match is not found in *expressionList1*, the computer skips to the second Case clause, where it compares the *selectorExpression* with the values listed in *expressionList2*. If a match is found, the computer processes the instructions for the second Case clause and then skips to the instruction following the End Select clause. If a match is not found, the computer skips to the third Case clause, and so on. If the *selectorExpression* does not match any of the values listed in any of the *expressionLists*, the computer processes the instructions listed in the Case Else clause or, if there is no Case Else clause, it processes the instruction following the End Select clause. Keep in mind that if the *selectorExpression* matches a value in more than one Case clause, only the instructions in the first match are processed.

You also can specify a range of values in an *expressionList*—such as the values 1 through 4, and values greater than 10. You do so using the keywords `To` and `Is`.

## Using To and Is in an ExpressionList

You can use either the keyword `To` or the keyword `Is` to specify a range of values in a Case clause's *expressionList*. You use the `To` keyword when you know both the upper and lower bounds of the range, and you use the `Is` keyword when you know only one end of the range—either the upper or lower end. For example, assume that the price of an item sold by ABC Corporation depends on the number of items ordered, as shown in the following chart:

| Number of items ordered | Price per item |
|---|---|
| 1 – 5 | $ 25 |
| 6 – 10 | $ 23 |
| More than 10 | $ 20 |

Figure 4.46 shows the Visual Basic code for the displayPriceButton's Click event procedure, which displays the appropriate price per item.

**Visual Basic code**

```
Private Sub displayPriceButton_Click(ByVal sender As Object, _
    ByVal e As System.EventArgs) Handles _
    displayPriceButton.Click
    ' displays the price per item

    Dim numberOrdered As Integer
    Dim itemPrice As Integer
    Dim isConverted As Boolean

    ' assign the appropriate price per item to the
    ' itemPrice variable
    isConverted = _
        Integer.TryParse(numberTextBox.Text, numberOrdered)
    Select Case numberOrdered
        Case 1 To 5
            itemPrice = 25
        Case 6 To 10
            itemPrice = 23
        Case Is > 10
            itemPrice = 20
        Case Else
            itemPrice = 0
    End Select

    'display the price per item
    priceLabel.Text = itemPrice.ToString("C2")
End Sub
```

**FIGURE 4.46**    Example of using the **To** and **Is** keywords in a Select Case statement

TIP

Because **numberOrdered** is an Integer variable, you also can write the third Case clause shown in Figure 4.46 as
Case Is >= 11.

TIP

If you neglect to type the keyword **Is** in an expression, the Code Editor types it in for you. In other words, if you enter
Case > 10, the Code Editor changes the clause to
Case Is > 10.

According to the ABC Corporation's price chart, the price for one to five items is $25 each. Therefore, you could have written the first Case clause in Figure 4.46 as Case 1, 2, 3, 4, 5. However, a more convenient way of writing that range of numbers is to use the keyword To in the Case clause, but you must follow this syntax to do so: **Case** *smallest value in the range* **To** *largest value in the range*. The expression 1 To 5 in the first Case clause, for example, specifies the range of numbers from one to five, inclusive. The expression 6 To 10 in the second Case clause specifies the range of numbers from six to 10, inclusive. Notice that both Case clauses state both the lower (1 and 6) and upper (5 and 10) ends of each range.

The third Case clause in Figure 4.46, Case Is > 10, contains the Is keyword rather than the To keyword. Recall that you use the Is keyword when you know only one end of the range of values—either the upper or lower end. In this case, for example, you know only the lower end of the range, 10. You always use the Is keyword in combination with one of the following comparison

(relational) operators: =, <, <=, >, >=, <>. The `Case Is > 10` clause, for example, specifies all numbers that are greater than the number 10.

The `Case Else` clause shown in Figure 4.46 is processed only when the `numberOrdered` variable contains a value that is not included in any of the previous Case clauses—namely, a zero or a negative number. Figure 4.47 shows a sample run of the application that contains the displayPriceButton's Click event procedure.

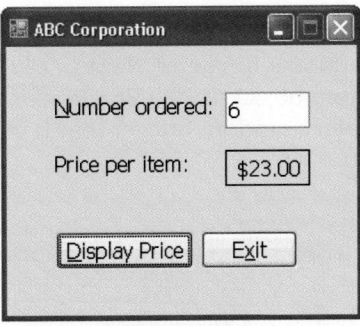

**FIGURE 4.47**   Sample run of the application that contains the displayPriceButton's Click event procedure

The last concept you learn in this chapter is how to generate random integers. You will use random integers in the Rock, Paper, Scissors game that you code in the Programming Tutorial section of the chapter.

## GENERATING RANDOM INTEGERS

Visual Basic provides a **pseudo-random number generator**, which is a device that produces a sequence of numbers that meet certain statistical requirements for randomness. Figure 4.48 shows how you use the pseudo-random number generator to generate random integers. The figure also includes several examples of generating random integers.

TIP

Pseudo-random numbers are chosen with equal probability from a finite set of numbers. The chosen numbers are not completely random because a definite mathematical algorithm is used to select them, but they are sufficiently random for practical purposes.

**HOW TO...**    Generate Random Numbers

**Syntax**
Dim *randomObjectName* **As New Random**
*randomObjectName*.**Next**(*minValue*, *maxValue*)

**Examples**
```
Dim number As Integer
Dim randomGenerator As New Random
number = randomGenerator.Next(0, 51)
```
creates a Random object named `randomGenerator`, then assigns (to the `number` variable) a random integer that is greater than or equal to 0, but less than 51

*(Figure is continued on next page)*

```
Dim number As Integer
Dim randomGenerator As New Random
number = randomGenerator.Next(50, 100)
```
creates a Random object named `randomGenerator`, then assigns (to the number variable) a random integer that is greater than or equal to 50, but less than 100

```
Dim number As Integer
Dim randomGenerator As New Random
number = randomGenerator.Next(-10, 0)
```
creates a Random object named `randomGenerator`, then assigns (to the number variable) a random integer that is greater than or equal to -10, but less than 0

**FIGURE 4.48**     How to generate random numbers

In Computer Exercise 12, you will learn how to use the Random.NextDouble method to generate a random floating-point number.

To use the pseudo-random number generator in a procedure, you first create a Random object using a Dim statement, as shown in Figure 4.48. The Random object represents the pseudo-random number generator in the procedure.

After creating a Random object, you can generate random integers using the **Random.Next method**. In the method's syntax (shown in Figure 4.48), *randomObjectName* is the name of the Random object. The *minValue* and *maxValue* arguments in the syntax must be integers, and *minValue* must be less than *maxValue*. The Random.Next method returns an integer that is greater than or equal to *minValue*, but less than *maxValue*.

In the first example shown in Figure 4.48, the `number = randomGenerator.Next(0, 51)` statement assigns (to the number variable) a random integer that is greater than or equal to 0, but less than 51. The `number = randomGenerator.Next(50, 100)` statement in the second example assigns (to the number variable) a random integer that is greater than or equal to 50, but less than 100. In the last example, the `number = randomGenerator.Next(-10, 0)` statement assigns (to the number variable) a random integer that is greater than or equal to -10, but less than 0.

Figure 4.49 shows the code for the generateButton's Click event procedure, which generates and displays random numbers between one and 10. Figure 4.50 shows a sample run of the application that contains the procedure.

**Visual Basic code**

```
Private Sub generateButton_Click(ByVal sender As Object, _
    ByVal e As System.EventArgs) Handles generateButton.Click
    ' displays random numbers between 1 and 10, inclusive

    Dim number As Integer
    Dim randomGenerator As New Random

    ' generate and display random number
    number = randomGenerator.Next(1, 11)
    randomLabel.Text = Convert.ToString(number)
End Sub
```

**FIGURE 4.49**     The generateButton's Click event procedure

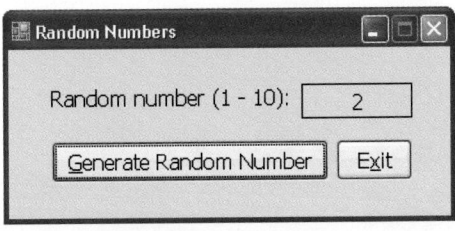

**FIGURE 4.50**    Sample run of the application that contains the generateButton's Click event procedure

You have completed the concepts section of Chapter 4. The next section is the Programming Tutorial section, which gives you step-by-step instructions on how to apply the chapter's concepts to an application. A Programming Example follows the Programming Tutorial. The Programming Example is a completed program that demonstrates the concepts taught in the chapter. Following the Programming Example are the Quick Review, Key Terms, Self-check Questions and Answers, Review Questions, Review Exercises – Short Answer, Computer Exercises, and Case Projects sections.

# PROGRAMMING TUTORIAL

## Creating the Rock, Paper, Scissors Game Application

In this tutorial, you create an application that simulates a game called Rock, Paper, Scissors. Typically, two people play the game. However, you will program the game so that one person can play against the computer.

"Rock, Paper, Scissors" refers to the three choices each player can indicate using hand gestures. To play the game, the players face each other, call out "Rock, paper, scissors, shoot," and then make the hand gesture corresponding to their choice: a fist (rock), a flat hand (paper), or two fingers forming a V shape (scissors). The rules for determining a win are shown in the following chart:

- Rock breaks scissors, so rock wins
- Paper covers rock, so paper wins
- Scissors cut paper, so scissors wins

The application's user interface is shown in Figure 4.51, and its TOE chart is shown in Figure 4.52.

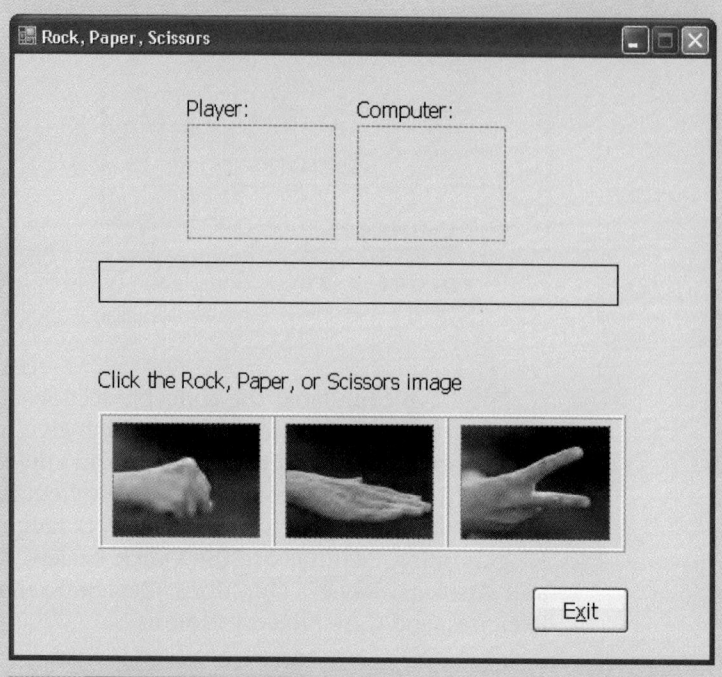

**FIGURE 4.51**     MainForm

| Task | Object | Event |
|---|---|---|
| 1. Display the appropriate image in the playerPictureBox<br>2. Generate a random number from 1 to 3, inclusive<br>3. Use the random number to display the rock, paper, or scissors image in the computerPictureBox<br>4. Determine whether there is a winner and display an appropriate message in winnerLabel | rockPictureBox,<br>paperPictureBox,<br>scissorsPictureBox | Click |
| End the application | exitButton | Click |
| Display a message that indicates either the winner or a tie game | winnerLabel | None |
| Display the image corresponding to the player's choice | playerPictureBox | None |
| Display the image corresponding to the computer's choice | computerPictureBox | None |

**FIGURE 4.52**     TOE Chart

## Creating the Rock, Paper, Scissors Game Interface

Before you can code the Rock, Paper, Scissors game application, you need to create the user interface.

**To create the user interface:**

1. Start Visual Studio. If necessary, close the Start Page window.
2. Create a Visual Basic Windows-based application. Name the solution RockPaperScissorsGame Solution, and name the project RockPaperScissorsGame Project. Name the form file Main Form.vb. Save the application in the VbReloaded\Chap04 folder.
3. Use the chart shown in Figure 4.53 to create the user interface shown in Figure 4.51. The Rock.jpg, Paper.jpg, and Scissors.jpg image files are contained in the VbReloaded\Chap04 folder. (The three image files were downloaded from the stock.XCHNG site and were contributed by the photographer, Laura Kennedy. You can browse and optionally download other free images at *www.sxc.hu*.) Use the Edit Rows and Columns option in the TableLayoutPanel Tasks box to change the size of each column in the TableLayoutPanel1 control to 33.33%.

| Object | Property | Setting |
|---|---|---|
| Form1 | Name | MainForm |
| | MaximizeBox | False |
| | Size | 549, 485 |
| | StartPosition | CenterScreen |
| | Text | Rock, Paper, Scissors |
| TableLayoutPanel1 | CellBorderStyle | OutsetDouble |
| | ColumnCount | 3 |
| | Location | 67, 268 |
| | RowCount | 1 |
| | Size | 409, 103 |
| Label1 | Text | Player: |
| Label2 | Text | Computer: |
| Label3 | Text | Click the Rock, Paper, or Scissors image |
| Label4 | Name | winnerLabel |
| | AutoSize | False |
| | BorderStyle | FixedSingle |
| | Location | 67, 155 |
| | Size | 403, 31 |
| | Text | (empty) |
| | TextAlign | MiddleCenter |
| PictureBox1 | Name | playerPictureBox |
| | Location | 136, 52 |
| | Size | 115, 86 |
| | SizeMode | AutoSize |
| PictureBox2 | Name | computerPictureBox |
| | Location | 268, 52 |
| | Size | 115, 86 |
| | SizeMode | AutoSize |
| PictureBox3 | Name | rockPictureBox |
| | Image | Rock.jpg |
| | Size | 115, 86 |
| | SizeMode | AutoSize |
| *(Figure is continued on next page)* | | |

| PictureBox4 | Name | paperPictureBox |
| | Image | Paper.jpg |
| | Size | 115, 86 |
| | SizeMode | AutoSize |
| PictureBox5 | Name | scissorsPictureBox |
| | Image | Scissors.jpg |
| | Size | 115, 86 |
| | SizeMode | AutoSize |
| Button1 | Name | exitButton |
| | Location | 404, 397 |
| | Size | 75, 35 |
| | Text | E&xit |

**FIGURE 4.53**   Object, Property, Setting chart

4. Verify that MainForm appears as the name of the startup form.
5. Save the solution.

Now that the interface is created, you can begin coding the application.

### Coding the Rock, Paper, Scissors Game Application

First you will enter comments to document the project's name and purpose, as well as the programmer's name and the date the code was created or last revised. You also will enter the appropriate Option statements.

**To enter the comments and Option statements:**

1. Open the Code Editor window.
2. Enter the comments and Option statements shown in Figure 4.54. Replace the <your name> and <current date> text with your name and the current date.

Enter these comments and Option statements

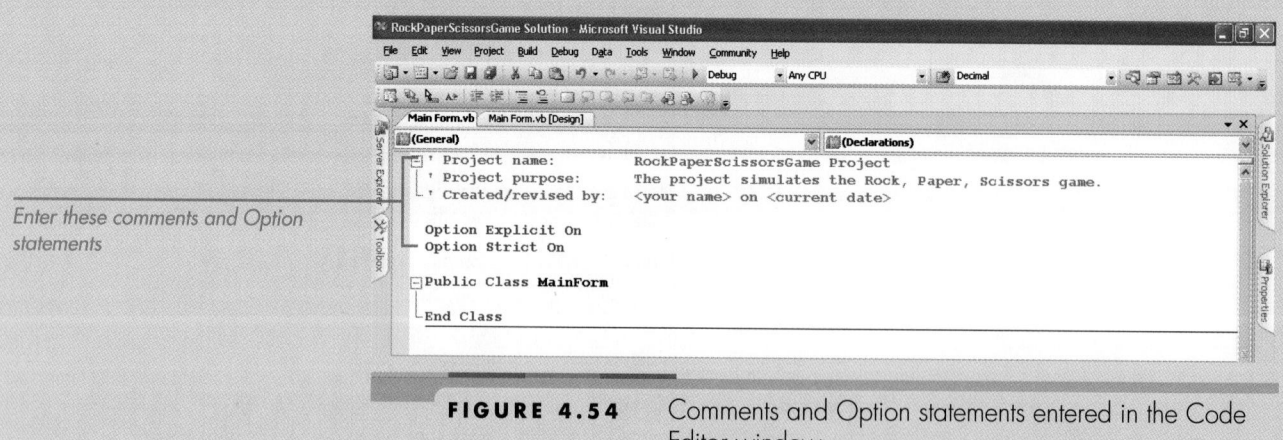

**FIGURE 4.54**   Comments and Option statements entered in the Code Editor window

According to the TOE chart, shown earlier in Figure 4.52, you will need to code the Click event procedures for the exitButton, rockPictureBox, paperPictureBox, and scissorsPictureBox. The first procedure you will code is the exitButton's Click event procedure, which should end the application.

**To code the exitButton's Click event procedure, then test the procedure's code:**

1. Open the code template for the exitButton's Click event procedure.
2. Type **me.close()** and press **Enter**.
3. Save the solution, then start the application. Click the **Exit** button to end the application. If necessary, close the Output window.

Before coding the Click event procedures for the picture boxes, study closely the chart shown in Figure 4.55. The chart indicates the combinations that can occur when playing the game, and the corresponding outcomes.

| Player's choice | Computer's choice | Outcome |
|---|---|---|
| Rock | Rock | Tie |
| | Paper | Computer wins because paper covers rock |
| | Scissors | Player wins because rock breaks scissors |
| Paper | Rock | Player wins because paper covers rock |
| | Paper | Tie |
| | Scissors | Computer wins because scissors cut paper |
| Scissors | Rock | Computer wins because rock breaks scissors |
| | Paper | Player wins because scissors cut paper |
| | Scissors | Tie |

**FIGURE 4.55**  Chart showing combinations and outcomes

Figure 4.56 shows the pseudocode for the rockPictureBox's Click event procedure.

**Pseudocode**

1. display the player's choice, which is represented by the rockPictureBox image, in the playerPictureBox
2. generate a random number from 1 to 3, inclusive
3. use the random number to display (in the computerPictureBox) the image that represents the computer's choice, and to display the appropriate message in the winnerLabel

   random number
   1  display the rockPictureBox image in the computerPictureBox
      display the string "Tie" in the winnerLabel
   2  display the paperPictureBox image in the computerPictureBox
      display the string "Computer wins because paper covers rock." in the winnerLabel
   3  display the scissorsPictureBox image in the computerPictureBox
      display the string "Player wins because rock breaks scissors." in the winnerLabel

**FIGURE 4.56**  Pseudocode for the rockPictureBox's Click event procedure

**To code the rockPictureBox's Click event procedure, then test the procedure's code:**

1. Open the code template for the rockPictureBox's Click event procedure.
2. Type ' **displays the appropriate message when the player selects this choice** and press **Enter** twice.

The procedure will use a Random object to represent the pseudo-random number generator, and an Integer variable to store the random number.

3. Type **dim randomGenerator as new random** and press **Enter**, then type **dim computerChoice as integer** and press **Enter** twice.

The first step in the pseudocode is to display the rockPictureBox image, which represents the player's choice, in the playerPictureBox.

4. Type ' **display the image corresponding to the player's choice** and press **Enter**, then type **playerpicturebox.image = rockpicturebox.image** and press **Enter** twice.

The next step is to generate a random number from 1 to 3, inclusive. You will assign the random number to the `computerChoice` variable.

5. Type ' **generate a random number from 1 to 3, inclusive** and press **Enter**. Type ' **then use the random number to display the image** and press **Enter**, then type ' **corresponding to the computer's choice** and press **Enter**.
6. Type **computerchoice = randomgenerator.next(1, 4)** and press **Enter**.

The last step is to use the random number to display the appropriate image and message in the computerPictureBox and winnerLabel, respectively.

7. Enter the additional code shown in Figure 4.57, which shows the completed rockPictureBox's Click event procedure.

Enter the Select Case statement

```
Main Form.vb   Main Form.vb [Design]
rockPictureBox                                        Click

    Private Sub rockPictureBox_Click(ByVal sender As Object, ByVal e As System.EventArgs) Ha
        ' displays the appropriate message when the player selects this choice

        Dim randomGenerator As New Random
        Dim computerChoice As Integer

        ' display the image corresponding to the player's choice
        playerPictureBox.Image = rockPictureBox.Image

        ' generate a random number from 1 to 3, inclusive
        ' then use the random number to display the image
        ' corresponding to the computer's choice
        computerChoice = randomGenerator.Next(1, 4)
        Select Case computerChoice
            Case 1
                computerPictureBox.Image = rockPictureBox.Image
                winnerLabel.Text = "Tie"
            Case 2
                computerPictureBox.Image = paperPictureBox.Image
                winnerLabel.Text = "Computer wins because paper covers rock."
            Case 3
                computerPictureBox.Image = scissorsPictureBox.Image
                winnerLabel.Text = "Player wins because rock breaks scissors."
        End Select

    End Sub
```

**FIGURE 4.57** Completed Click event procedure for the rockPictureBox

8. Save the solution, then start the application. Click the **rockPictureBox** several times to verify that its Click event procedure is working properly. Figure 4.58 shows a sample run of the application. Because the procedure generates a random number for the computer's choice, the image and message displayed in your computerPictureBox and winnerLabel, respectively, might be different from the ones shown in the figure.

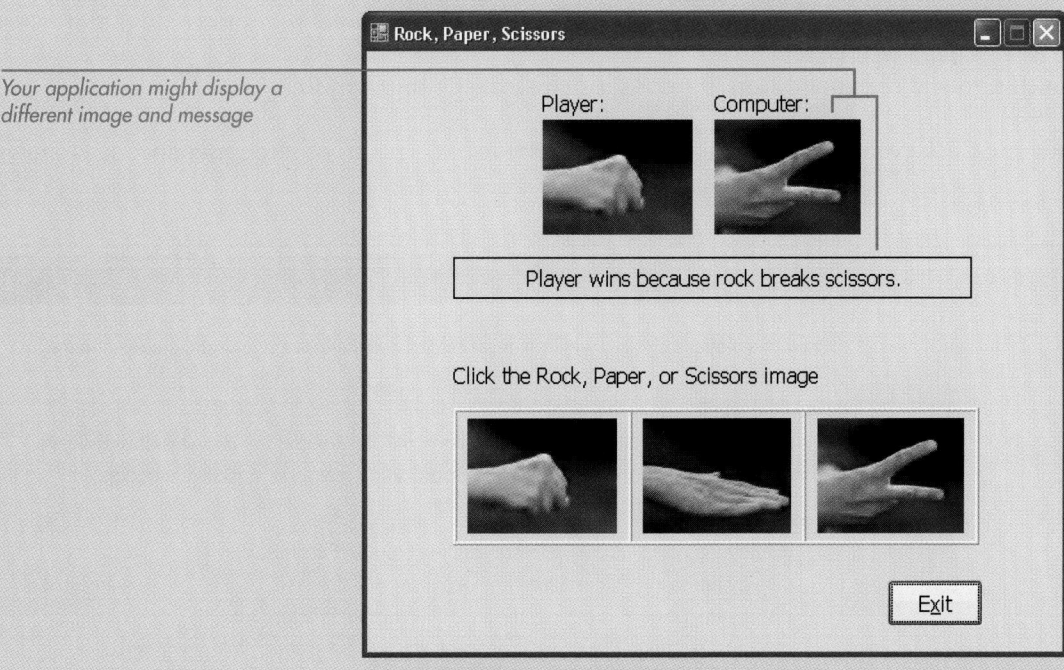

*Your application might display a different image and message*

**FIGURE 4.58**   Sample run of the Rock, Paper, Scissors application

**9.** Click the **Exit** button to end the application. If necessary, close the Output window.

Next, you will code the Click event procedure for the paperPictureBox. The procedure's pseudocode is shown in Figure 4.59.

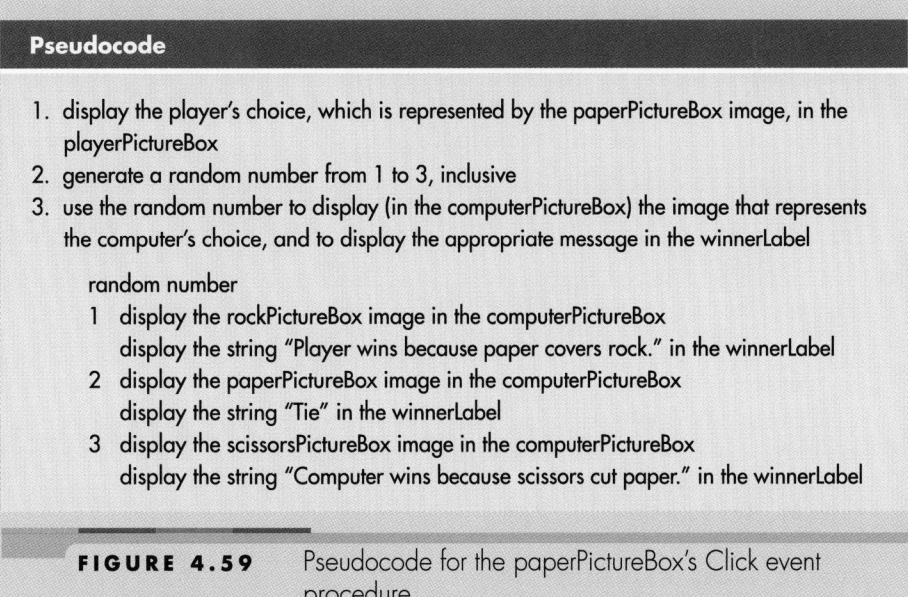

**Pseudocode**

1. display the player's choice, which is represented by the paperPictureBox image, in the playerPictureBox
2. generate a random number from 1 to 3, inclusive
3. use the random number to display (in the computerPictureBox) the image that represents the computer's choice, and to display the appropriate message in the winnerLabel

   random number
   1  display the rockPictureBox image in the computerPictureBox
      display the string "Player wins because paper covers rock." in the winnerLabel
   2  display the paperPictureBox image in the computerPictureBox
      display the string "Tie" in the winnerLabel
   3  display the scissorsPictureBox image in the computerPictureBox
      display the string "Computer wins because scissors cut paper." in the winnerLabel

**FIGURE 4.59**   Pseudocode for the paperPictureBox's Click event procedure

**To code the paperPictureBox's Click event procedure, then test the procedure's code:**

1. Open the code template for the paperPictureBox's Click event procedure.
2. Copy the code from the rockPictureBox's Click event procedure to the paperPictureBox's Click event procedure.
3. Modify the paperPictureBox's Click event procedure appropriately.

4. Save the solution, then start the application. Click the **paperPictureBox** several times to verify that its Click event procedure is working properly.
5. Click the **Exit** button to end the application. If necessary, close the Output window.

Finally, you will code the Click event procedure for the scissorsPictureBox. The procedure's pseudocode is shown in Figure 4.60.

**Pseudocode**

1. display the player's choice, which is represented by the scissorsPictureBox image, in the playerPictureBox
2. generate a random number from 1 to 3, inclusive
3. use the random number to display (in the computerPictureBox) the image that represents the computer's choice, and to display the appropriate message in the winnerLabel

    random number
    1  display the rockPictureBox image in the computerPictureBox
       display the string "Computer wins because rock breaks scissors." in the winnerLabel
    2  display the paperPictureBox image in the computerPictureBox
       display the string "Player wins because scissors cut paper." in the winnerLabel
    3  display the scissorsPictureBox image in the computerPictureBox
       display the string "Tie" in the winnerLabel

**FIGURE 4.60**    Pseudocode for the scissorsPictureBox's Click event procedure

**To code the scissorsPictureBox's Click event procedure, then test the procedure's code:**

1. Open the code template for the scissorsPictureBox's Click event procedure.
2. Copy the code from the rockPictureBox's Click event procedure to the scissorsPictureBox's Click event procedure.
3. Modify the scissorsPictureBox's Click event procedure appropriately.
4. Save the solution, then start the application. Click the **scissorsPictureBox** several times to verify that its Click event procedure is working properly.
5. Click the **Exit** button to end the application. If necessary, close the Output window.
6. Close the solution. Figure 4.61 shows the code for the Rock, Paper, Scissors Game application.

```
' Project name:        RockPaperScissorsGame Project
' Project purpose:     The project simulates the Rock, Paper, Scissors game.
' Created/revised by:  <your name> on <current date>

Option Explicit On
Option Strict On

Public Class MainForm

    Private Sub exitButton_Click(ByVal sender As Object, _
        ByVal e As System.EventArgs) Handles exitButton.Click
        Me.Close()
    End Sub
```

*(Figure is continued on next page)*

```
Private Sub rockPictureBox_Click(ByVal sender As Object, _
    ByVal e As System.EventArgs) Handles rockPictureBox.Click
    ' displays the appropriate message when the player selects this choice

    Dim randomGenerator As New Random
    Dim computerChoice As Integer

    ' display the image corresponding to the player's choice
    playerPictureBox.Image = rockPictureBox.Image

    ' generate a random number from 1 to 3, inclusive
    ' then use the random number to display the image
    ' corresponding to the computer's choice
    computerChoice = randomGenerator.Next(1, 4)
    Select Case computerChoice
        Case 1
            computerPictureBox.Image = rockPictureBox.Image
            winnerLabel.Text = "Tie"
        Case 2
            computerPictureBox.Image = paperPictureBox.Image
            winnerLabel.Text = "Computer wins because paper covers rock."
        Case 3
            computerPictureBox.Image = scissorsPictureBox.Image
            winnerLabel.Text = "Player wins because rock breaks scissors."
    End Select
End Sub

Private Sub paperPictureBox_Click(ByVal sender As Object, _
    ByVal e As System.EventArgs) Handles paperPictureBox.Click
    ' displays the appropriate message when the player selects this choice

    Dim randomGenerator As New Random
    Dim computerChoice As Integer

    ' display the image corresponding to the player's choice
    playerPictureBox.Image = paperPictureBox.Image

    ' generate a random number from 1 to 3, inclusive
    ' then use the random number to display the image
    ' corresponding to the computer's choice
    computerChoice = randomGenerator.Next(1, 4)
    Select Case computerChoice
        Case 1
            computerPictureBox.Image = rockPictureBox.Image
            winnerLabel.Text = "Player wins because paper covers rock."
        Case 2
            computerPictureBox.Image = paperPictureBox.Image
            winnerLabel.Text = "Tie"
        Case 3
            computerPictureBox.Image = scissorsPictureBox.Image
            winnerLabel.Text = "Computer wins because scissors cut paper."
    End Select
```

*(Figure is continued on next page)*

```
End Sub

    Private Sub scissorsPictureBox_Click(ByVal sender As Object, _
        ByVal e As System.EventArgs) Handles scissorsPictureBox.Click
        ' displays the appropriate message when the player selects this choice

        Dim randomGenerator As New Random
        Dim computerChoice As Integer

        ' display the image corresponding to the player's choice
        playerPictureBox.Image = scissorsPictureBox.Image

        ' generate a random number from 1 to 3, inclusive
        ' then use the random number to display the image
        ' corresponding to the computer's choice
        computerChoice = randomGenerator.Next(1, 4)
        Select Case computerChoice
            Case 1
                computerPictureBox.Image = rockPictureBox.Image
                winnerLabel.Text = "Computer wins because rock breaks scissors."
            Case 2
                computerPictureBox.Image = paperPictureBox.Image
                winnerLabel.Text = "Player wins because scissors cut paper."
            Case 3
                computerPictureBox.Image = scissorsPictureBox.Image
                winnerLabel.Text = "Tie"
        End Select
    End Sub
End Class
```

**FIGURE 4.61**    Code for the Rock, Paper, Scissors Game application

# PROGRAMMING EXAMPLE

## Fat Calculator Application

Create a Visual Basic application that allows the user to enter the total number of calories and grams of fat contained in a specific food. The application should calculate and display two values: the food's fat calories (the number of calories attributed to fat) and its fat percentage (the ratio of the food's fat calories to its total calories). Additionally, the application should display the message "This food is high in fat." when the fat percentage is over 30%; otherwise, it should display the message "This food is not high in fat." Name the solution Fat Calculator Solution. Name the project Fat Calculator Project. Name the form file Main Form.vb. Save the application in the VbReloaded\Chap04 folder. Test the application using 150 and 6 as the number of calories and grams of fat, respectively. The fat calories should be 54 and the fat percentage should be 36.00%.

**TOE Chart:**

| Task | Object | Event |
|------|--------|-------|
| 1. Calculate the fat calories<br>2. Calculate the fat percentage<br>3. Display the fat calories and fat percentage in fatCalsLabel and fatPercentLabel<br>4. Display (in a message box) either the "This food is high in fat." message or the "This food is not high in fat." message | calcButton | Click |
| End the application | exitButton | Click |
| Display the fat calories (from calcButton) | fatCalsLabel | None |
| Display the fat percentage (from calcButton) | fatPercentLabel | None |
| Get and display the calories and fat grams | caloriesTextBox, fatGramsTextBox | None |

**FIGURE 4.62**

**User Interface:**

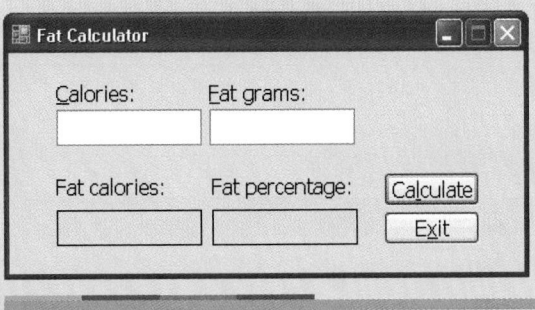

**FIGURE 4.63**

**Objects, Properties, and Settings:**

| Object | Property | Setting |
|--------|----------|---------|
| Form1 | Name<br>AcceptButton<br>Font<br>Size<br>StartPosition<br>Text | MainForm<br>calcButton<br>Tahoma, 12 point<br>408, 200<br>CenterScreen<br>Fat Calculator |
| Label1 | Text | &Calories: |
| Label2 | Text | &Fat grams: |
| Label3 | Text | Fat calories: |
| *(Figure is continued on next page)* | | |

| Label4 | Text | Fat percentage: |
|--------|------|-----------------|
| Label5 | Name | fatCalsLabel |
|        | AutoSize | False |
|        | BorderStyle | FixedSingle |
|        | Size | 112, 27 |
|        | Text | (empty) |
|        | TextAlign | MiddleCenter |
| Label6 | Name | fatPercentLabel |
|        | AutoSize | False |
|        | BorderStyle | FixedSingle |
|        | Size | 112, 27 |
|        | Text | (empty) |
|        | TextAlign | MiddleCenter |
| TextBox1 | Name | caloriesTextBox |
|          | Size | 112, 27 |
| TextBox2 | Name | fatGramsTextBox |
|          | Size | 112, 27 |
| Button1 | Name | calcButton |
|         | Text | Ca&lculate |
| Button2 | Name | exitButton |
|         | Text | E&xit |

**FIGURE 4.64**

**Tab Order:**

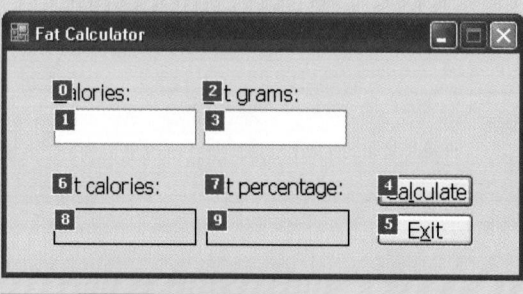

**FIGURE 4.65**

**Pseudocode:**

**exitButton Click event procedure**

1. close the application

## calcButton Click event procedure

1. if the contents of the caloriesTextBox and fatGramsTextBox can be converted to numbers
   calculate the fat calories by multiplying the total calories by 9
   calculate the fat percentage by dividing the fat calories by the total calories
   display the fat calories and fat percentage in fatCalsLabel and fatPercentLabel

   if the fat percentage is over 30%
   display the "This food is high in fat." message in a message box
   else
   display the "This food is not high in fat." message in a message box
   end if
   else
   display the "The calories and fat grams must be numbers." message in a message box
   end if

2. send the focus to the caloriesTextBox

**Code:**

```
' Project name:          Fat Calculator Project
' Project purpose:       The project allows the user to enter the number of
'                        calories and grams of fat contained in a specific food.
'                        It then calculates the food's fat calories and its
'                        fat percentage.
' Created/revised by:    <your name> on <current date>

Option Explicit On
Option Strict On

Public Class MainForm

    Private Sub exitButton_Click(ByVal sender As Object, _
        ByVal e As System.EventArgs) Handles exitButton.Click
        Me.Close()
    End Sub

    Private Sub calcButton_Click(ByVal sender As Object, _
        ByVal e As System.EventArgs) Handles calcButton.Click
        ' calculates a food's fat calories and its fat percentage

        Dim calories As Integer
        Dim fatGrams As Integer
        Dim fatCalories As Integer
        Dim fatPercent As Decimal
        Dim message As String
        Dim isConverted1 As Boolean
        Dim isConverted2 As Boolean

        ' convert input to Integer
        isConverted1 = Integer.TryParse(caloriesTextBox.Text, calories)
        isConverted2 = Integer.TryParse(fatGramsTextBox.Text, fatGrams)
```

*(Figure is continued on next page)*

```
' if the input is converted to Integer, then
' calculate and display fat calories and fat percentage, and
' then display message indicating whether or not the food is
' high in fat
' otherwise, display an appropriate message
If isConverted1 = True AndAlso isConverted2 = True Then
    fatCalories = fatGrams * 9
    fatPercent = Convert.ToDecimal(fatCalories) / _
        Convert.ToDecimal(calories)
    fatCalsLabel.Text = Convert.ToString(fatCalories)
    fatPercentLabel.Text = fatPercent.ToString("P2")
    If fatPercent > 0.3D Then
        message = "This food is high in fat."
    Else
        message = "This food is not high in fat."
    End If
    MessageBox.Show(message, "Fat Calculator", _
        MessageBoxButtons.OK, MessageBoxIcon.Information)
Else
    message = "The calories and fat grams must be numbers."
    MessageBox.Show(message, "Fat Calculator", _
            MessageBoxButtons.OK, MessageBoxIcon.Information)
End If

caloriesTextBox.Focus()
    End Sub
End Class
```

**FIGURE 4.66**

## Quick Review

- The selection structure allows a program to make a decision or comparison and then select one of two paths, depending on the result of that decision or comparison.
- Visual Basic provides four forms of the selection structure: If, If/Else, If/ElseIf/Else, and Case.
- In a flowchart, you use the diamond, called the selection/repetition symbol, to represent the selection structure's condition.
- In Visual Basic, you use the If...Then...Else statement to code the If, If/Else, and If/ElseIf/Else forms of the selection structure.
- All expressions containing a comparison operator will result in an answer of either True or False only.
- Comparison operators do not have an order of precedence in Visual Basic. Rather, they are evaluated from left to right in an expression, and are evaluated after any arithmetic operators in the expression.
- Variables declared in either the true or false path of a selection structure have block scope.
- You connect (or link) strings together using the concatenation operator.
- The ControlChars.NewLine constant advances the insertion point to the next line in a control.
- String comparisons in Visual Basic are case-sensitive. When comparing strings, you can use either the ToUpper method or the ToLower method to temporarily convert the strings to uppercase or lowercase, respectively.

- You use logical operators to create compound conditions. All expressions containing a logical operator will result in an answer of either True or False only.
- Like arithmetic operators, logical operators have an order of precedence and are evaluated after any arithmetic and comparison operators in an expression.
- Before using the TryParse method to parse a string, you can use the String.IsNullOrEmpty method to determine whether the string contains data.
- The MessageBox.Show method allows you to communicate with the user by displaying a message box.
- The MessageBox.Show method returns an integer that indicates the message box button chosen by the user. You should use the DialogResult value associated with the button when referring to the integer in code.
- Use sentence capitalization for the *text* argument in the MessageBox.Show method, but book title capitalization for the *caption* argument. The name of the application typically appears in the *caption* argument.
- Avoid using the words "error," "warning," or "mistake" in the MessageBox.Show method's message, as these words imply that the user has done something wrong.
- Display the Warning Message icon in a message box that alerts the user that he or she must make a decision before the application can continue. You can phrase the message as a question.
- Display the Information Message icon in a message box that displays an informational message along with an OK button only.
- Display the Stop Message icon when you want to alert the user of a serious problem that must be corrected before the application can continue.
- The default button in the message box should be the one that represents the user's most likely action, as long as that action is not destructive.
- You can nest selection structures, which means that you can place one selection structure in either the true or false path of another selection structure.
- The primary decision is always made by the outer selection structure. The secondary decision is always made by the inner (nested) selection structure.
- Typically, you use the If/ElseIf/Else and Case forms of the selection structure when the structure must choose from several alternatives.
- In Visual Basic, you use the Select Case statement to code the Case form of the selection structure.
- You use the keyword To in a Case clause's *expressionList* when you know both the upper and lower bounds of the range you want to specify. You use the keyword Is when you know only one end of the range.
- You use the pseudo-random number generator in Visual Basic to generate random numbers.

## Key Terms

The **selection structure**, also called the **decision structure**, allows a program to make a decision or comparison and then select the appropriate path, depending on the result of that decision or comparison.

The **condition** in a selection structure specifies the decision you are making and must be phrased so that it results in either a true or false answer only.

An **If selection structure** contains only one set of instructions, which are processed when the condition is true.

An **If/Else selection structure** contains two sets of instructions: one set is processed when the condition is true and the other set is processed when the condition is false.

The **true path** in a selection structure contains the instructions that are processed when the condition evaluates to True.

The **false path** in a selection structure contains the instructions that are processed when the condition evaluates to False.

The diamond in a flowchart is called the **selection/repetition** symbol.

You use the **If...Then...Else statement** to code the If, If/Else, and If/ElseIf/Else forms of the selection structure in Visual Basic.

The **Else clause** in an If...Then...Else statement contains the instructions that are processed when the condition evaluates to False.

A **statement block** is a set of statements terminated by an Else, End If, Loop, or Next statement.

**Comparison operators**, also called **relational operators**, allow you to compare values in a selection structure's condition.

A variable that has **block scope** can be used only within the statement block in which it is declared.

The **concatenation operator** is the ampersand (&). It is used to concatenate strings together and must be preceded and followed by a space character.

You can use the **ControlChars.NewLine constant** to advance the insertion point to the next line in a control.

The **ToUpper method** temporarily converts a string to uppercase.

The **ToLower method** temporarily converts a string to lowercase.

**Logical operators**, sometimes referred to as **Boolean operators**, allow you to combine two or more *conditions* into one compound *condition*.

**Truth tables** summarize how Visual Basic evaluates the logical operators in an expression.

The AndAlso and OrElse logical operators perform a **short-circuit evaluation**, which means that they do not always evaluate the second condition in a compound condition.

**Data validation** is the process of verifying that a program's input data is within the expected range.

You can use the **String.IsNullOrEmpty method** to determine whether a *string* contains data.

The **MessageBox.Show method** displays a message box that contains text, one or more buttons, and an icon.

In a nested selection structure, the **primary decision** is always made by the outer selection structure. The **secondary decision**, which depends on the result of the primary decision, is always made by the inner (nested) selection structure.

The **If/ElseIf/Else** and **Case** forms of the selection structure are commonly referred to as **extended selection structures** or **multiple-path selection structures**, because they have several alternatives from which to choose.

In Visual Basic, you use the **Select Case statement** to code the Case selection structure.

Visual Basic provides a **pseudo-random number generator** that you use to generate random numbers.

You use the **Random.Next method** to generate a random integer that is greater than or equal to a minimum value, but less than a maximum value.

## Self-Check Questions and Answers

1. What is the scope of variables declared in an If...Then...Else statement's false path?
   a. the entire application
   b. the procedure in which the If...Then...Else statement appears
   c. the entire If...Then...Else statement
   d. only the false path in the If...Then...Else statement

2. Which of the following concatenates the message "Do they live in ", the contents of a String variable named `state`, and a question mark?
   a. `"Do they live in " & state & "?"`
   b. `"Do they live in & state & ?"`
   c. `"Do they live in _ " state _ "?"`
   d. `"Do they live in " # state # "?"`

3. Which of the following methods converts the string stored in the `item` variable to lowercase?
   a. `item.Lower()`
   b. `Lower(item)`
   c. `LowerCase(item)`
   d. None of the above.

4. If the value of *condition1* is True and the value of *condition2* is False, then the value of *condition1* OrElse *condition2* is _____.
   a. True
   b. False

5. Which of the following logical operators performs a short-circuit evaluation?
   a. And
   b. AndAlso
   c. Or
   d. XOr

6. Assuming the priceTextBox is empty, the `String.IsNullOrEmpty(priceTextBox.Text)` method returns _____.
   a. "" (the empty string)
   b. 0
   c. True
   d. the contents of the priceTextBox

7. If the user clicks the Abort button in a message box, the MessageBox.Show method returns the integer 3, which is equivalent to the _____ value.
   a. Abort
   b. AbortButton
   c. ButtonAbort
   d. DialogResult.Abort

8. In a selection structure, the primary decision is always made by the _____ selection structure, while the secondary decision is always made by the _____ selection structure.
   a. inner, outer
   b. outer, inner

9. Assume that the *selectorExpression* in a Select Case statement is an Integer variable named `colorCode`? Which of the following Case clauses can be used to process the same instructions for color codes of 10 to 15, inclusive?
   a. `Case 10, 11, 12, 13, 14, 15`
   b. `Case 15 To 10`
   c. `Case >= 10 And <=15`
   d. All of the above.

10. Which of the following can be used in a procedure to declare an object that represents the pseudo-random number generator?
    a. `Dim randomGenerator As Generator`
    b. `Dim randomGenerator As Random`
    c. `Dim randomGenerator As RandomGenerator`
    d. None of the above.

Answers: 1) d, 2) a, 3) d, 4) a, 5) b, 6) c, 7) d, 8) b, 9) a, 10) d

## Review Questions

1. Which of the following is a valid condition for an If...Then...Else statement?
   a. `priceLabel.Text > 0 AndAlso priceLabel.Text <10`
   b. `sales > 500D OrElse <800D`
   c. `number > 100 AndAlso number <=1000`
   d. `state.ToUpper() = "Alaska" OrElse state.ToUpper() = "Hawaii"`

2. Assume you want to compare the string contained in the Text property of the firstNameTextBox with the name Bob. Which of the following conditions should you use in the If...Then...Else statement? (Be sure the condition will handle Bob, BOB, bob, and so on.)
   a. `firstNameTextBox.Text = ToUpper("BOB")`
   b. `firstNameTextBox.Text.ToUpper() = "Bob"`
   c. `firstNameTextBox.Text.ToUpper() = "BOB"`
   d. `ToUpper(firstName.Text) = "BOB"`

3. The expression 3 > 6 AndAlso 7 > 4 evaluates to _____.
   a. True
   b. False

4. The expression 4 > 6 OrElse 10 < 2 * 6 evaluates to _____.
   a. True
   b. False

5. The expression 7 >= 3 + 4 Or 6 < 4 And 2 < 5 evaluates to _____.
   a. True
   b. False

Use the following code to answer Questions 6 through 9.

```
If num = 1 Then
        nameLabel.Text = "Janet"
ElseIf num = 2 OrElse num = 3 Then
        nameLabel.Text = "Paul"
ElseIf num = 4 Then
        nameLabel.Text = "Jerry"
Else
        nameLabel.Text = "Sue"
End If
```

6. What will the preceding code display when the num variable contains the number 2?
   a. Janet
   b. Jerry
   c. Paul
   d. Sue

7. What will the preceding code display when the num variable contains the number 4?
   a. Janet
   b. Jerry
   c. Paul
   d. Sue

8. What will the preceding code display when the num variable contains the number 3?
   a. Janet
   b. Jerry
   c. Paul
   d. Sue

9. What will the preceding code display when the num variable contains the number 8?
   a. Janet
   b. Jerry
   c. Paul
   d. Sue

10. A nested selection structure can appear in _____ of another selection structure.
    a. only the true path
    b. only the false path
    c. either the true path or the false path

11. If the *selectorExpression* used in the Select Case statement is an Integer variable named `code`, which of the following Case clauses is valid?
    a. `Case Is > 7`
    b. `Case 3, 5`
    c. `Case 1 To 4`
    d. All of the above.

Use the following Select Case statement to answer Questions 12 through 14.

```
Select Case num
        Case 1
                nameLabel.Text = "Janet"
        Case 2 To 4
                nameLabel.Text = "Paul"
        Case 5, 7
                nameLabel.Text = "Jerry"
        Case Else
                nameLabel.Text = "Sue"
End Select
```

12. What will the preceding Select Case statement display when the num variable contains the number 2?
    a. Janet
    b. Jerry
    c. Paul
    d. Sue

13. What will the preceding Select Case statement display when the `num` variable contains the number 3?
    a. Janet
    b. Jerry
    c. Paul
    d. Sue

14. What will the preceding Select Case statement display when the `num` variable contains the number 6?
    a. Janet
    b. Jerry
    c. Paul
    d. Sue

15. Which of the following constants can be used to advance the insertion point to the next line in the answerLabel?
    a. `Advance.NewLine`
    b. `ControlChars.NewLine`
    c. `NewLine.Advance`
    d. None of the above.

16. Which of the following methods determines whether the `cityName` variable contains data?
    a. `String.IsData(cityName)`
    b. `String.IsEmptyData(cityName)`
    c. `String.IsEmptyOrNull(cityName)`
    d. `String.IsNullOrEmpty(cityName)`

17. If the user clicks the OK button in a message box displayed by the MessageBox.Show method, the message box returns the number 1, which is equivalent to which value?
    a. `DialogResult.OK`
    b. `DialogResult.OKButton`
    c. `MessageBox.OK`
    d. `MessageResult.OK`

18. Which of the following generates a random integer from 10 to 55, inclusive? (The Random object is named `randomGenerator`.)
    a. `randomGenerator.Next(10, 56)`
    b. `randomGenerator.Next(10, 55)`
    c. `randomGenerator.Next(9, 55)`
    d. None of the above.

19. Assume the `city` variable contains the string "Boston" and the `state` variable contains the string "MA". Which of the following will display the string "Boston, MA" (the city, a comma, a space, and the state) in the addressLabel control?
    a. `addressLabel.Text = "city" & ", " & "state"`
    b. `addressLabel.Text = city $ ", " $ state`
    c. `addressLabel.Text = city & ", " & state`
    d. `addressLabel.Text = "city," & "state"`

20. Assume that a Select Case statement's *selectorExpression* is an Integer variable. Which of the following Case clauses tells the computer to process the instructions when the Integer variable contains one of the following numbers: 1, 2, 3, 4, or 5?
    a. `Case 1, 2, 3, 4, And 5`
    b. `Case 1 To 5`
    c. `Case 5 To 1`
    d. Both a and b.

## Review Exercises – Short Answer

1. The six logical operators are listed below. Indicate their order of precedence by placing a number (1, 2, and so on) on the line to the left of the operator. (If two or more operators have the same precedence, assign the same number to each.)

   _____ Xor

   _____ And

   _____ Not

   _____ Or

   _____ AndAlso

   _____ OrElse

2. An expression can contain arithmetic, comparison, and logical operators. Indicate the order of precedence for the three types of operators by placing a number (1, 2, or 3) on the line to the left of the operator type.

   _____ Arithmetic

   _____ Logical

   _____ Comparison

Use the following selection structure to answer Questions 3 and 4:

```
If number <=100 Then
    number = number * 2
Else
    number = number * 3
End If
```

3. Assume the number variable contains the number 90. What value will be in the number variable after the above selection structure is processed?

4. Assume the number variable contains the number 1000. What value will be in the number variable after the above selection structure is processed?

5. Assume that you need to create a procedure that displays the appropriate fee to charge a golfer. The fee is based on the following fee schedule:

   | Fee | Criteria |
   | --- | --- |
   | 0 | Club members |
   | 15 | Non-members golfing on Monday through Thursday |
   | 25 | Non-members golfing on Friday through Sunday |

   In this procedure, which is the primary decision and which is the secondary decision? Why?

6. Draw the flowchart that corresponds to the following pseudocode:

   if hours are greater than 40
           display "Overtime pay"
   else
           display "Regular pay"
   end if

7. Write an If...Then...Else statement that displays the string "Pontiac" in the carMakeLabel when the carTextBox contains the string "Grand Am" (in any case).

8. Write an If...Then...Else statement that displays the string "Entry error" in the messageLabel when the `units` variable contains a number that is less than 0; otherwise, display the string "Valid Number".

9. Write an If...Then...Else statement that displays the string "Reorder" in the messageLabel when the `quantity` variable contains a number that is less than 10; otherwise, display the string "OK".

10. Write an If...Then...Else statement that assigns the number 10 to the `bonus` variable when the `sales` variable contains a number that is less than or equal to $250; otherwise, assign the number 15.

11. Write an If...Then...Else statement that displays the number 25 in the shippingLabel when the `state` variable contains the string "Hawaii" (in any case); otherwise, display the number 50.

12. Assume you want to calculate a 3% sales tax when the `state` variable contains the string "Colorado" (in any case); otherwise, you want to calculate a 4% sales tax. You can calculate the sales tax by multiplying the tax rate by the contents of the `sales` variable. Display the sales tax in the salesTaxLabel. Draw the flowchart, then write the Visual Basic code.

13. Assume you want to calculate an employee's gross pay. Employees working more than 40 hours should receive overtime pay (time and one-half) for the hours over 40. Use the variables `hours`, `hourRate`, and `gross`. Display the contents of the `gross` variable in the grossLabel. Write the pseudocode, then write the Visual Basic code.

14. Write the If...Then...Else statement that displays the string "Dog" in the animalLabel when the `animal` variable contains the letter "D" (in any case); otherwise, display the string "Cat". Draw the flowchart, then write the Visual Basic code.

15. Assume you want to calculate a 10% discount on desks sold to customers in Colorado. Use the variables `item`, `state`, `sales`, and `discount`. Format the discount using the "C2" format and display it in the discountLabel. Write the pseudocode, then write the Visual Basic code.

16. Assume you want to calculate a 2% price increase on all red shirts, but a 1% price increase on all other items. In addition to calculating the price increase, also calculate the new price. You can use the variables `itemColor`, `item`, `origPrice`, `increase`, and `newPrice`. Format the original price, price increase, and new price using the "N2" format. Display the original price, price increase, and new price in originalLabel, increaseLabel, and newLabel, respectively. Write the Visual Basic code.

17. Write the Visual Basic code that swaps the values stored in the `marySales` and `jeffSales` variables, but only if the value stored in the `marySales` variable is less than the value stored in the `jeffSales` variable.

18. Write the Visual Basic code that displays the message "Highest honors" when a student's test score is 90 or above. When the test score is 70 through 89, display the message "Good job". For all other test scores, display the message "Retake the test". Use the If/ElseIf/Else selection structure. The test score is stored in the `score` variable. Display the appropriate message in the msgLabel.

19. Write the Visual Basic code that compares the contents of the `quantity` variable with the number 10. When the `quantity` variable contains a number that is equal to 10, display the string "Equal" in the msgLabel. When the `quantity` variable contains a number that is greater than 10, display the string "Over 10". When the `quantity` variable contains a number that is less than 10, display the string "Not over 10". Use the If/ElseIf/Else selection structure.

20. Write the Visual Basic code that corresponds to the flowchart shown in Figure 4.67. Store the salesperson's code, which is entered in the codeTextBox, in an Integer variable named `code`. Store the sales amount, which is entered in the salesTextBox, in a Decimal variable named `sales`. Display the result of the calculation, or the error message, in the msgLabel.

**Flowchart**

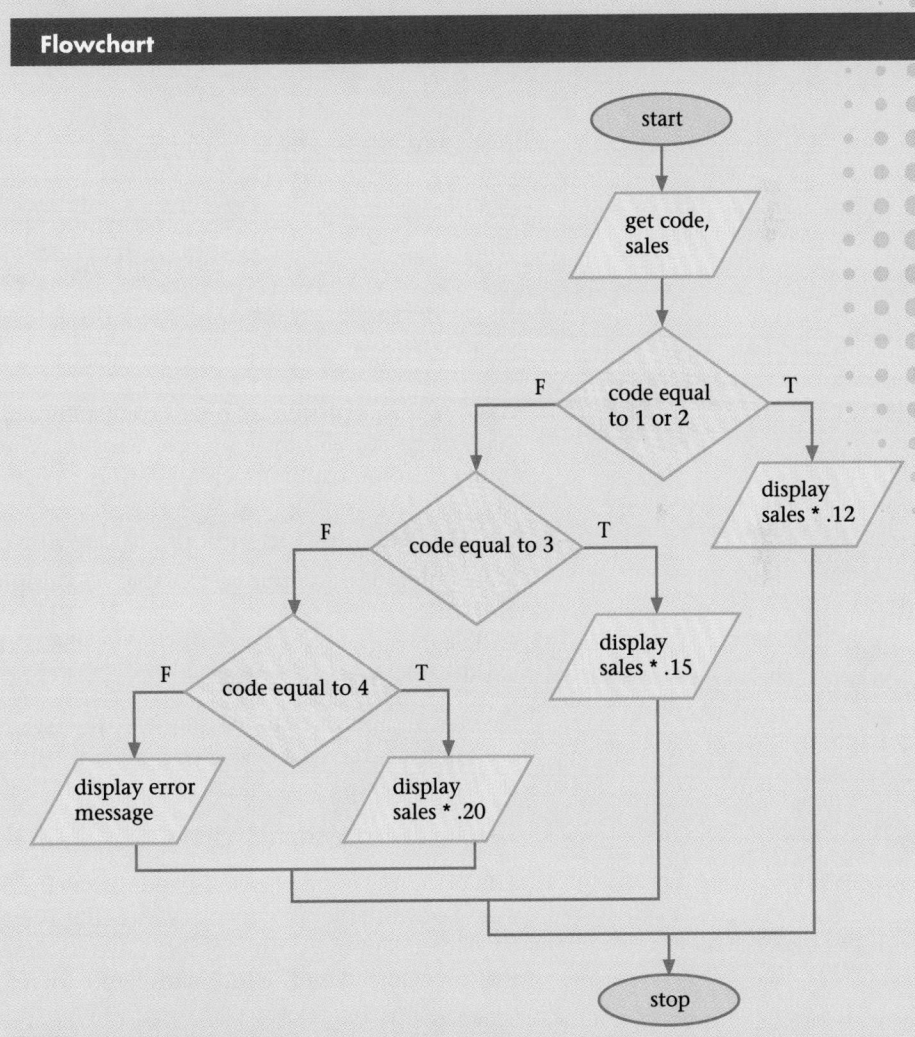

**FIGURE 4.67**

21. Write the Visual Basic code that corresponds to the flowchart shown in Figure 4.68. Store the salesperson's code, which is entered in the codeTextBox, in an Integer variable named `code`. Store the sales amount, which is entered in the salesTextBox, in a Decimal variable named `sales`. Display the result of the calculation, or the error message, in the msgLabel.

**Flowchart**

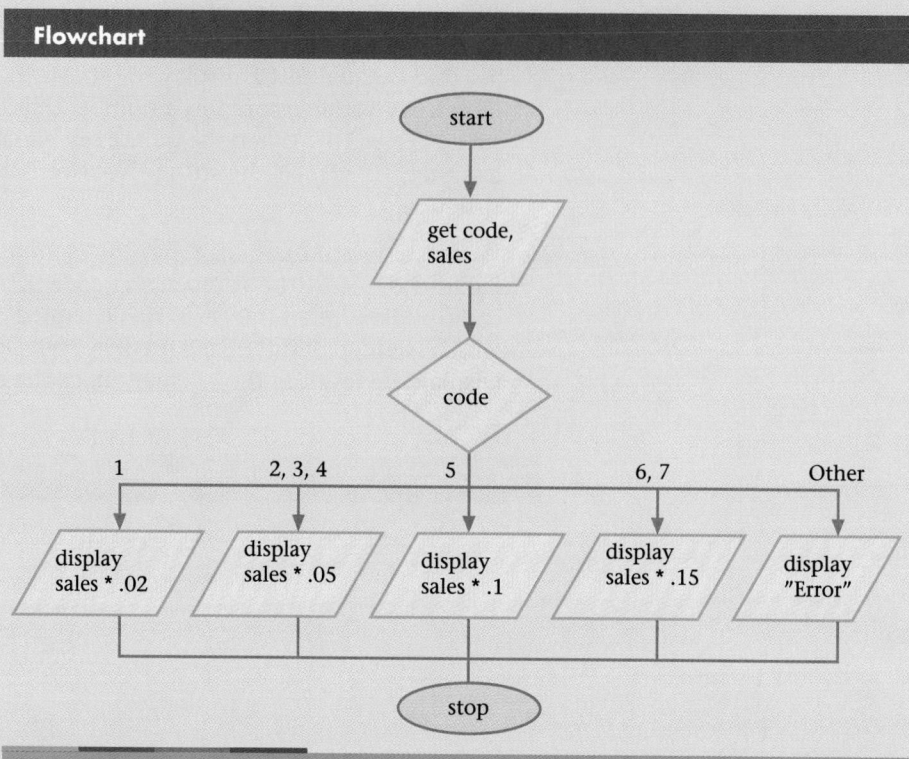

**FIGURE 4.68**

22. Assume that a procedure needs to display a shipping charge based on the state name stored in the `state` variable. (You can assume that the state name is stored using uppercase letters.) Write a Select Case statement that assigns the shipping charge to the `shipping` variable. Use the following table to determine the appropriate shipping charge.

| State entered in the `state` variable | Shipping charge |
| --- | --- |
| HAWAII | $25.00 |
| OREGON | $30.00 |
| CALIFORNIA | $32.50 |

Display an appropriate message in the msgLabel when the `state` variable contains a value that does not appear in the table. Also assign the number 0 to the `shipping` variable.

23. Rewrite the code from Exercise 22 using an If...Then...Else statement.

24. The price of a concert ticket depends on the seat location stored in the `seatLoc` variable. (You can assume that the seat location is stored using uppercase letters.) Write a Select Case statement that displays the price in the priceLabel. Use the following table to determine the appropriate price:

| Seat location | Concert ticket price |
| --- | --- |
| BOX | $75.00 |
| PAVILION | $30.00 |
| LAWN | $21.00 |

Display an appropriate message in the priceLabel if the `seatLoc` variable contains a value that does not appear in the table.

25. Rewrite the code from Exercise 24 using an If...Then...Else statement.

26. In the chapter, you learned about the `ControlChars.NewLine` constant. Technically, `NewLine` is the constant; `ControlChars` is the class that contains the definition for the constant. Use the Help screens to research the `ControlChars` class. What other constants (called fields) are contained in the class?

## Computer Exercises

1. In this exercise, you modify the Rock, Paper, Scissors Game application created in the chapter's Programming Tutorial.
   a. Use Windows to make a copy of the RockPaperScissorsGame Solution folder, which is contained in the VbReloaded\Chap04 folder. Rename the folder RockPaperScissorsGame Solution-Modified.
   b. Open the RockPaperScissorsGame Solution (RockPaperScissorsGame Solution.sln) file contained in the RockPaperScissorsGame Solution-Modifed folder.
   c. Modify the application so that it uses If...Then...Else statements rather than Select Case statements.
   d. Save the solution, then start and test the application. Click the Exit button to end the application, then close the solution.

2. In this exercise, you modify the chapter's Programming Example.
   a. Create the Fat Calculator application shown in the chapter's Programming Example. Save the application in the VbReloaded\Chap04 folder.
   b. Modify the application so that it displays the message "The calories entry must be numeric." in a message box when the Text property of the caloriesTextBox cannot be converted to a number. The application should display the message "The fat grams entry must be numeric." in a message box when the Text property of the fatGramsTextBox cannot be converted to a number. (You no longer need to display the message "The calories and fat grams must be numbers.") Be sure to modify the TOE chart and pseudocode before modifying the code.
   c. Save the solution, then start and test the application. Click the Exit button to end the application, then close the solution.

3. In this exercise, you code an application that swaps two values entered by the user.
   a. Open the Number Swap Solution (Number Swap Solution.sln) file, which is contained in the VbReloaded\Chap04\Number Swap Solution folder.
   b. Open the Code Editor window and enter the appropriate comments at the beginning of the code. Also enter the appropriate Option statements.
   c. Code the exitButton's Click event procedure so that it ends the application.
   d. Enter the code for the displayButton's Click event procedure, which is shown in Figure 4.9 in the chapter.
   e. Save the solution, then start the application. Test the application by entering the two values 34 and 12, and then clicking the Display button. The user interface should appear as shown earlier in Figure 4.10.
   f. Now test the application by entering the two values 5 and 9, and then clicking the Display button.
   g. Click the Exit button to end the application.
   h. Modify the displayButton's Click event procedure so that it displays an appropriate message (in a message box) if the contents of the text boxes cannot be converted to a number.

     i.  Save the solution, then start the application. Test the application.

     j.  Click the Exit button to end the application, then close the solution.

4.  In this exercise, you code an application that either adds or subtracts two numbers.

     a.  Open the AddSub Solution (AddSub Solution.sln) file, which is contained in the VbReloaded\Chap04\AddSub Solution folder.

     b.  Open the Code Editor window and enter the appropriate comments at the beginning of the code. Also enter the appropriate Option statements.

     c.  Code the exitButton's Click event procedure so that it ends the application.

     d.  Enter the code for the calcButton's Click event procedure, which is shown in Figure 4.15 in the chapter.

     e.  Save the solution, then start the application. Test the application by entering the letter a and the two numbers 12 and 58, and then clicking the Calculate button. The interface should appear as shown earlier in Figure 4.16.

     f.  Now test the application by entering the letter X and the two values 5 and 9, and then clicking the Calculate button. Although you entered the letter X rather than the letter S, notice that the application displays the difference between the two numbers. Click the Exit button to end the application.

     g.  Modify the calcButton's Click event procedure so that it displays (in a message box) an appropriate message if the user does not enter either the letter A (in any case) or the letter S (in any case). Also display an appropriate message if the Text properties of the text boxes cannot be converted to numbers.

     h.  Save the solution, then start the application. Test the application.

     i.  Click the Exit button to end the application, then close the solution.

5.  In this exercise, you modify the application from Exercise 4.

     a.  Use Windows to make a copy of the AddSub Solution folder, which is contained in the VbReloaded\Chap04 folder. Rename the folder AddSub Solution-Modified.

     b.  Open the AddSub Solution (AddSub Solution.sln) file contained in the AddSub Solution-Modified folder.

     c.  If the user enters a letter other than A, a, S, or s, use the MessageBox.Show method to display a message box that asks the user if he or she meant to enter the letter A. Include Yes and No buttons in the message box. If the user clicks the Yes button, the application should display the sum of the two numbers. If the user clicks the No button, the application should assume that the user wants to display the difference between the two numbers. (You will no longer need to display a message if the user does not enter either the letter A or the letter S.) As before, the application also should verify that the text box values were converted to integers. Also display the appropriate letter (A or S) in the Operation box.

     d.  Save the solution, then start the application. Test the application.

     e.  Click the Exit button to end the application, then close the solution.

6.  In this exercise, you complete two procedures that display a message based on a code entered by the user.

     a.  Open the Animal Solution (Animal Solution.sln) file, which is contained in the VbReloaded\Chap04\Animal Solution folder.

     b.  Open the Code Editor window. Complete the If...Then...Else button's Click event procedure by writing an If...Then...Else statement that displays the string "Dog" if the `animal` variable contains the number 1.

Display the string "Cat" if the `animal` variable contains the number 2. Display the string "Bird" if the `animal` variable contains anything other than the number 1 or the number 2. Display the appropriate string in the msgLabel.

c. Save the solution, then start the application. Test the If...Then...Else button three times, using the numbers 1, 2, and 5.

d. Click the Exit button to end the application.

e. Complete the Select Case button's Click event procedure by writing a Select Case statement that displays the string "Dog" if the `animal` variable contains either the letter "D" or the letter "d". Display the string "Cat" if the `animal` variable contains either the letter "C" or the letter "c". Display the string "Bird" if the `animal` variable contains anything other than the letters "D", "d", "C", or "c". Display the appropriate string in the msgLabel.

f. Save the solution, then start the application. Test the Select Case button three times, using the letters D, c, and x.

g. Click the Exit button to end the application, then close the solution.

7. In this exercise, you code an application that calculates a bonus.

a. Open the Bonus Solution (Bonus Solution.sln) file, which is contained in the VbReloaded\Chap04\Bonus Solution folder.

b. The user will enter the sales amount in the salesTextBox. The sales amount will always be an integer. Code the calcButton's Click event procedure so that it calculates the salesperson's bonus. Display the bonus, formatted with a dollar sign and two decimal places, in the bonusLabel. The following rates should be used when calculating the bonus:

| Sales amount ($) | Bonus |
|---|---|
| 0–5000 | 1% of the sales amount |
| 5001–10000 | 3% of the sales amount |
| Over 10000 | 7% of the sales amount |

Display an appropriate message when the sales amount is negative or cannot be converted to a number.

c. Save the solution, then start the application. Test the application with both valid and invalid data.

d. Click the Exit button to end the application, then close the solution.

8. In this exercise, you complete a procedure that calculates and displays the total amount owed by a company.

a. Open the Seminar Solution (Seminar Solution.sln) file, which is contained in the VbReloaded\Chap04\Seminar Solution folder.

b. Open the Code Editor window. Assume you offer programming seminars to companies. Your price per person depends on the number of people the company registers. (For example, if the company registers seven people, then the total amount owed is $560, which is calculated by multiplying the number 7 by the number 80.) Display the total amount owed in the totalLabel. Use the Select Case statement and the following table to complete the Calculate button's Click event procedure:

| Number of registrants | Criteria |
|---|---|
| 1 – 4 | $100 per person |
| 5 – 10 | $ 80 per person |
| 11 or more | $ 60 per person |
| Less than 1 | $  0 per person |

Display an appropriate message if the number registered is not numeric.

c. Save the solution, then start the application. Test the application four times, using the following data: 7, 4, 11, and −3.

d. Click the Exit button to end the application, then close the solution.

9. In this exercise, you create an application for Golf Pro, a U.S. company that sells golf equipment both domestically and abroad. Each of Golf Pro's salespeople receives a commission based on the total of his or her domestic and international sales. The application you create should allow the user to enter the amount of domestic sales and the amount of international sales. It then should calculate and display the commission. Use the following information to code the application:

| Sales | Commission |
|---|---|
| 1 – 100,000 | 2% * sales |
| 100,001 – 400,000 | 2,000 + 5% * sales over 100,000 |
| 400,001 and over | 17,000 + 10% * sales over 400,000 |

a. Build an appropriate interface. Name the solution Golf Pro Solution. Name the project Golf Pro Project. Save the application in the VbReloaded\Chap04 folder.

b. Code the application. Keep in mind that the sales amounts may contain decimal places.

c. Save the solution, then start the application. Test the application using both valid and invalid data.

d. End the application, then close the solution.

10. Jacques Cousard has been playing the lottery for four years and has yet to win any money. He wants an application that will select the six lottery numbers for him. Each lottery number can range from 1 to 54 only. (An example of six lottery numbers would be: 4, 8, 35, 15, 20, 3.)

a. Build an appropriate interface. Name the solution Lottery Solution. Name the project Lottery Project. Save the application in the VbReloaded\Chap04 folder.

b. Code the application. For now, do not worry if the lottery numbers are not unique. You learn how to display unique numbers in Chapter 8.

c. Save the solution, then start the application. Test the application.

d. End the application, then close the solution.

11. In this exercise, you learn about the SelectAll method and a text box control's Enter event.

a. Open the Name Solution (Name Solution.sln) file, which is contained in the VbReloaded\Chap04\Name Solution folder.

b. Start the application. Type your first name in the First text box, then press Tab. Type your last name in the Last text box, then click the Concatenate Name button. Your full name appears in the fullNameLabel.

c. Press Tab twice to move the focus to the First text box. Notice that the insertion point appears after your first name in the text box. It is customary in Windows applications to have a text box's existing text selected (highlighted) when the text box receives the focus. You can select a text box's existing text by entering the text box's SelectAll method in the text box's Enter event.

d. Click the Exit button to end the application.

e. Open the Code Editor window. Enter the SelectAll method in the Enter event procedures for the firstTextBox and lastTextBox controls.

f. Save the solution, then start the application. Type your first name in the First text box, then press Tab. Enter your last name in the Last text box, then click the Concatenate Name button. Your full name appears in the fullNameLabel.

g. Press Tab twice to move the focus to the First text box. Notice that your first name is selected in the text box. Press Tab to move the focus to the Last text box. Notice that your last name is selected in the text box.

h. Click the Exit button to end the application, then close the solution.

12. In this exercise, you generate and display random floating-point numbers.

a. Open the Random Float Solution (Random Float Solution.sln) file, which is contained in the VbReloaded\Chap04\Random Float Solution folder.

b. You can use the Random.NextDouble method to return a floating-point random number that is greater than or equal to 0.0, but less than 1.0. The syntax of the Random.NextDouble method is *randomObjectName*.**NextDouble**. Code the Display Random Number button's Click event procedure so that it displays a random floating-point number in the numberLabel.

c. Save the solution, then start the application. Click the Display Random Number button several times. Each time you click the button, a random number that is greater than or equal to 0.0, but less than 1.0, appears in the numberLabel.

d. Click the Exit button to end the application.

e. You can use the following formula to generate random floating-point numbers within a specified range: (*maxValue* – *minValue* + **1**) * *randomObjectName*.**NextDouble** + *minValue*. For example, the formula `(10 - 1 + 1) * randomGenerator.NextDouble + 1` generates floating-point numbers that are greater than or equal to 1.0, but less than 11.0. Modify the Display Random Number button's Click event procedure so that it displays a random floating-point number that is greater than or equal to 25.0, but less than 51.0. Display two decimal places in the floating-point number.

f. Save the solution, then start the application. Click the Display Random Number button several times to verify that the code you entered is working correctly.

g. Click the Exit button to end the application, then close the solution.

13. In this exercise, you find and correct an error in an application. The process of finding and correcting errors is called debugging.

a. Open the Debug Solution (Debug Solution.sln) file, which is contained in the VbReloaded\Chap04\Debug Solution folder.

b. Open the Code Editor window. Review the existing code. The calcButton's Click event procedure should calculate a 10% bonus when the code entered by the user is either 1 or 2 and, at the same time, the sales amount is greater than $10,000. Otherwise, the bonus rate is 5%.

c. Start the application. Type the number 1 in the Code text box. Type 200 in the Sales amount text box, then click the Calculate Bonus button. A message box appears and indicates that the bonus amount is $20.00 (10% of $200), which is incorrect; it should be $10.00 (5% of $200).

d. Click the OK button to close the message box. Click the Exit button to end the application.

e. Make the appropriate change to the calcButton's Click event procedure.

f. Save the solution, then start the application. Type the number 1 in the Code text box. Type 200 in the Sales amount text box, then click the Calculate Bonus button. The message box correctly indicates that the bonus amount is $10.00.

g. Click the Exit button to end the application, then close the solution.

## Case Projects

### Allenton Water Department

Create an application that calculates a customer's water bill. The user will enter the current meter reading and the previous meter reading. The application should calculate and display the gallons of water used and the total charge for the water. The charge for water is $1.75 per 1000 gallons, or .00175 per gallon. Before making the calculations, verify that the meter readings entered by the user are valid. To be valid, both meter readings must be numeric, and the current meter reading must be greater than or equal to the previous meter reading. Display appropriate messages if the meter readings are not valid.

### Professor Juarez

Create an application that displays a letter grade based on the average of three test scores entered by Professor Juarez. Each test is worth 100 points. Verify that the test scores entered by the professor are numeric. Use the following information to complete the application:

| Test average | Grade |
|---|---|
| 90–100 | A |
| 80–89 | B |
| 70–79 | C |
| 60–69 | D |
| below 60 | F |

### Barren Community Center

Create an application that displays a seminar fee, which is based on the membership status and age entered by the user. Verify that the data entered by the user is valid. Use the following information to code the application:

| Seminar fee | Criteria |
|---|---|
| 10 | Club member younger than 65 years old |
| 5 | Club member at least 65 years old |
| 20 | Non-member |

### Willow Health Club

Create an application that displays the number of daily calories needed to maintain your current weight. Use the following information to code the application:

Moderately active female: total calories per day = weight multiplied by 12 calories per pound

Relatively inactive female: total calories per day = weight multiplied by 10 calories per pound

Moderately active male: total calories per day = weight multiplied by 15 calories per pound

Relatively inactive male: total calories per day = weight multiplied by 13 calories per pound

# 5

# Repeating Program Instructions

**After studying Chapter 5, you should be able to:**

- Include the repetition structure in pseudocode and in a flowchart
- Write a For...Next statement
- Calculate a periodic payment using the Financial.Pmt method
- Include a list box and a combo box in an interface
- Write a Do...Loop statement
- Initialize and update counters and accumulators
- Display a dialog box using the InputBox function
- Create a multiline text box that cannot be edited
- Animate a control by moving it across a form
- Have the computer sound a beep

## THE REPETITION STRUCTURE

As you learned in Chapter 1, the three programming structures are sequence, selection, and repetition. Every program contains the sequence structure, where the program instructions are processed one after another in the order they appear in the program. Most programs also contain the selection structure, which you learned about in Chapter 4. Recall that programmers use the selection structure when they need the computer to make a decision and then take the appropriate action based on the result of the decision.

In addition to including the sequence and selection structures, many programs also include the repetition structure. Programmers use the **repetition structure**, referred to more simply as a **loop**, when they need the computer to repeatedly process one or more program instructions until some condition is met, at which time the repetition structure ends. For example, you may want to process a set of instructions—such as the instructions to calculate net pay—for each employee in a company. Or, you may want to process a set of instructions until the user enters a negative sales amount, which indicates that he or she has no more sales amounts to enter.

A repetition structure can be either a pretest loop or a posttest loop. In both types of loops, the condition is evaluated with each repetition, or iteration, of the loop. In a **pretest loop**, the evaluation occurs *before* the instructions within the loop are processed. In a **posttest loop**, the evaluation occurs *after* the instructions within the loop are processed. Depending on the result of the evaluation, the instructions in a pretest loop may never be processed. The instructions in a posttest loop, however, always will be processed at least once. Of the two types of loops, the pretest loop is the most commonly used.

You code a repetition structure (loop) in Visual Basic using one of the following statements: For...Next, Do...Loop, and For Each...Next. You learn about the For...Next and Do...Loop statements in this chapter. The For Each...Next statement is covered in Chapter 8.

**TIP**

As with the sequence and selection structures, you already are familiar with the repetition structure. For example, shampoo bottles typically include a direction that tells you to repeat the "apply shampoo to hair," "lather," and "rinse" steps until your hair is clean.

**TIP**

Pretest and posttest loops also are called top-driven and bottom-driven loops, respectively.

## THE FOR...NEXT STATEMENT

You can use the **For...Next statement** to code a loop whose instructions you want processed a precise number of times. The loop created by the For...Next statement is a pretest loop, because the loop's condition is evaluated *before* the instructions in the loop are processed. Figure 5.1 shows the syntax of the For...Next statement and includes two examples of using the statement. (Notice that you can use either the Convert.ToString method or a numeric data type's ToString method to convert the contents of a numeric variable to a String.)

**HOW TO...**

**Use the For...Next Statement**

**Syntax**
**For** *counter* [**As** *datatype*] = *startvalue* **To** *endvalue* [**Step** *stepvalue*]
      [*statements*]
**Next** *counter*

*(Figure is continued on next page)*

**Examples**

```
Dim numberSquared As Integer
For number As Integer = 1 To 3
     numberSquared = number * number
     MessageBox.Show(Convert.ToString(number) & " squared is " _
          & Convert.ToString(numberSquared), "Number Squared", _
          MessageBoxButtons.OK, MessageBoxIcon.Information)
Next number
```
displays the squares of the numbers 1, 2, and 3 in message boxes

```
Dim numberSquared As Integer
For number As Integer = 3 To 1 Step -1
     numberSquared = number * number
     MessageBox.Show(number.ToString & " squared is " _
          & numberSquared.ToString, "Number Squared", _
          MessageBoxButtons.OK, MessageBoxIcon.Information)
Next number
```
displays the squares of the numbers 3, 2, and 1 in message boxes

```
Dim x As Decimal
For x = .05D To .1D Step .01D
     rateLabel.Text = rateLabel.Text & x.ToString("P0") _
          & ControlChars.NewLine
Next x
```
displays the values 5%, 6%, 7%, 8%, 9%, and 10% in the rateLabel

**FIGURE 5.1**     How to use the For...Next statement

**TIP**

You can use the **Exit For** statement to exit the For...Next statement prematurely—in other words, exit it before it has finished processing. You may need to do so if the loop encounters an error when processing its instructions.

**TIP**

You can nest For...Next statements, which means that you can place one For...Next statement within another For...Next statement.

The For...Next statement begins with the For clause and ends with the Next clause. Between the two clauses, you enter the instructions you want the loop to repeat.

In the syntax for the For...Next statement, *counter* is the name of a numeric variable that the computer can use to keep track of the number of times it processes the loop instructions. Notice that *counter* appears in both the For clause and the Next clause. Although, technically, you do not need to specify the name of the *counter* variable in the Next clause, doing so is highly recommended because it makes your code more self-documenting.

You can use the **As** *datatype* portion of the For clause to declare the *counter* variable, as shown in the first two examples in Figure 5.1. When you declare a variable in the For clause, the variable has block scope and can be used only by the For...Next loop. Alternatively, you can declare the *counter* variable in a Dim statement, as shown in the last example in Figure 5.1. As you know, when a variable is declared in a Dim statement at the beginning of a procedure, it has procedure scope and can be used by the entire procedure.

When deciding where to declare the *counter* variable, keep in mind that if the variable is needed only by the For...Next loop, then it is a better programming practice to declare it in the For clause. As you learned in Chapter 3, this is because fewer unintentional errors occur in applications when the variables are declared using the minimum scope needed. You should declare the *counter* variable in a Dim statement only when other statements in the procedure need to use its value.

The *startvalue*, *endvalue*, and *stepvalue* items control the number of times the loop instructions are processed. The *startvalue* tells the computer where to begin counting, and the *endvalue* tells the computer when to stop counting. The *stepvalue* tells the computer how much to count by—in other words, how much to add to (or subtract from if the *stepvalue* is a negative number) the *counter* variable each time the loop is processed. If you omit the *stepvalue*, a *stepvalue* of positive 1 is used.

In the first example shown in Figure 5.1, the *startvalue* is 1, the *endvalue* is 3, and the *stepvalue* (which is omitted) is 1. Those values tell the computer to start counting at 1 and, counting by 1s, stop at 3—in other words, count 1, 2, and then 3. The computer will process the loop instructions shown in the first example three times.

The For clause's *startvalue*, *endvalue*, and *stepvalue* must be numeric and can be either positive or negative, integer or non-integer. If the *stepvalue* is positive, the *startvalue* must be less than or equal to the *endvalue* for the loop instructions to be processed. In other words, the instruction For number = 1 To 3 is correct, but the instruction For number = 3 To 1 is not correct because you cannot count from 3 (the *startvalue*) to 1 (the *endvalue*) by adding increments of 1 (the *stepvalue*). If, on the other hand, the *stepvalue* is negative, then the *startvalue* must be greater than or equal to the *endvalue* for the loop instructions to be processed. In other words, the instruction For number = 3 To 1 Step –1 is correct, but the instruction For number = 1 To 3 Step –1 is not correct because you cannot count from 1 to 3 by subtracting increments of 1.

When processing the For...Next statement, the computer performs the three tasks listed in Figure 5.2.

**Tasks performed when processing the For...Next statement**

1. If the *counter* variable is declared in the For clause, the computer creates the variable and initializes it to the *startvalue*; otherwise, it just performs the initialization task. This is done only once, at the beginning of the loop.

2. If the *stepvalue* is positive, the computer checks whether the value in the *counter* variable is greater than the *endvalue*. (Or, if the *stepvalue* is negative, the computer checks whether the value in the *counter* variable is less than the *endvalue*.) If it is, the computer stops processing the loop, and processing continues with the statement following the Next clause. If it is not, the computer processes the instructions within the loop, and then the next task, task 3, is performed. Notice that the computer evaluates the loop condition *before* processing the instructions within the loop.

3. The computer adds the *stepvalue* to the contents of the *counter* variable. It then repeats tasks 2 and 3 until the *counter* variable's value is greater than (or less than, if the *stepvalue* is negative) the *endvalue*.

**FIGURE 5.2**    Processing tasks for the For...Next statement

Figure 5.3 describes how the computer processes the code shown in the first example in Figure 5.1. Notice that when the For...Next statement in that example ends, the value stored in the number variable is 4.

## Processing steps for the first example in Figure 5.1

1. The computer creates the `numberSquared` variable and initializes it to the number zero.
2. The computer creates the `number` (*counter*) variable and initializes it to 1 (*startvalue*).
3. The computer checks whether the value in the `number` variable is greater than 3 (*endvalue*). It's not.
4. The assignment statement multiplies the value in the `number` variable by itself and assigns the result to the `numberSquared` variable.
5. The MessageBox.Show method displays the message "1 squared is 1".
6. The computer processes the Next clause, which adds 1 (*stepvalue*) to the contents of the `number` variable, giving 2.
7. The computer checks whether the value in the `number` variable is greater than 3 (*endvalue*). It's not.
8. The assignment statement multiplies the value in the `number` variable by itself and assigns the result to the `numberSquared` variable.
9. The MessageBox.Show method displays the message "2 squared is 4".
10. The computer processes the Next clause, which adds 1 (*stepvalue*) to the contents of the `number` variable, giving 3.
11. The computer checks whether the value in the `number` variable is greater than 3 (*endvalue*). It's not.
12. The assignment statement multiplies the value in the `number` variable by itself and assigns the result to the `numberSquared` variable.
13. The MessageBox.Show method displays the message "3 squared is 9".
14. The computer processes the Next clause, which adds 1 (*stepvalue*) to the contents of the `number` variable, giving 4.
15. The computer checks whether the value in the `number` variable is greater than 3 (*endvalue*). It is, so the computer stops processing the For...Next loop. Processing continues with the statement following the Next clause.

**FIGURE 5.3**    Processing steps for the code shown in the first example in Figure 5.1

Figures 5.4 and 5.5 show the pseudocode and flowchart, respectively, corresponding to the first example in Figure 5.1.

## Pseudocode

1. repeat for number = 1 to 3
        calculate numberSquared by multiplying number by number
        display message and numberSquared
   end repeat

**FIGURE 5.4**    Pseudocode for the first example in Figure 5.1

**Flowchart**

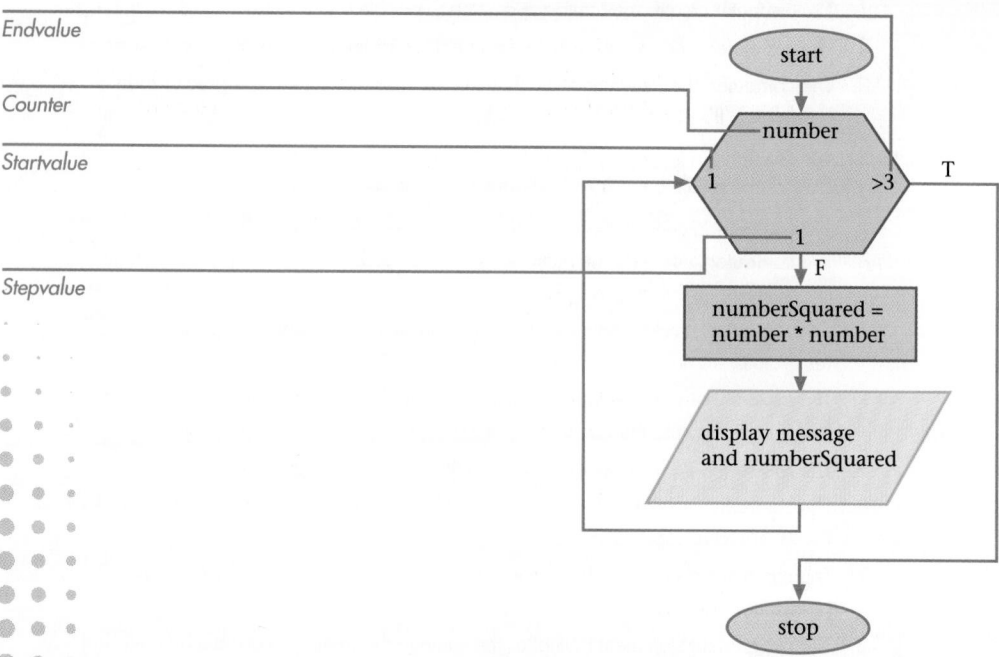

Endvalue

Counter

Startvalue

Stepvalue

**FIGURE 5.5**     Flowchart for the first example in Figure 5.1

The For...Next loop is represented in a flowchart by a hexagon, which is a six-sided figure. Four values are recorded inside the hexagon: the name of the *counter* variable, the *startvalue*, the *stepvalue*, and the *endvalue*. Notice that a greater-than sign (>) precedes the *endvalue* in the hexagon shown in Figure 5.5. The greater-than sign reminds you that the loop stops when the value in the *counter* variable is greater than the *endvalue*. When the *stepvalue* is a negative number, a less-than sign (<) should precede the *endvalue* in the hexagon, as a loop with a negative *stepvalue* stops when the value in the *counter* variable is less than the *endvalue*.

Before viewing the Payment Calculator application, which uses the For...Next statement to calculate and display the monthly payments on a loan amount, you learn about the Financial.Pmt method.

## THE FINANCIAL.PMT METHOD

You can use the **Financial.Pmt method** to calculate a periodic payment on either a loan or an investment. ("Pmt" stands for "Payment.") The method returns the periodic payment as a Double type number. Figure 5.6 shows the syntax of the Financial.Pmt method and lists the meaning of each argument included in the method. The figure also includes three examples of using the method.

HOW TO...          Use the Financial.Pmt Method

**Syntax**
**Financial.Pmt**(*Rate, NPer, PV*[, *FV, Due*])

*(Figure is continued on next page)*

| Argument | Meaning |
|----------|---------|
| *Rate* | interest rate per period |
| *NPer* | total number of payment periods (the term) |
| *PV* | present value of the loan or investment; the present value of a loan is the loan amount, whereas the present value of an investment is zero |
| *FV* | future value of the loan or investment; the future value of a loan is zero, whereas the future value of an investment is the amount you want to accumulate; if omitted, the number 0 is assumed |
| *Due* | due date of payments; can be either the constant `DueDate.EndOfPeriod` or the constant `DueDate.BegOfPeriod`; if omitted, `DueDate.EndOfPeriod` is assumed |

**Example 1** – Calculates the annual payment for a loan of $9,000 for 3 years at 5% interest. The payments are due at the end of each period (year).

*Rate*: .05
*NPer*: 3
*PV*: 9000
*FV*: 0
*Due*: `DueDate.EndOfPeriod`
Method: `Financial.Pmt(.05, 3, 9000, 0, DueDate.EndOfPeriod)`
    *or*
    `Financial.Pmt(.05, 3, 9000)`
Annual payment (rounded to the nearest cent): -3,304.88

**Example 2** – Calculates the monthly payment for a loan of $12,000 for 5 years at 6% interest. The payments are due at the beginning of each period (month).

*Rate*: .06/12
*NPer*: 5 * 12
*PV*: 12000
*FV*: 0
*Due*: `DueDate.BegOfPeriod`
Method: `Financial.Pmt(.06/12, 5 * 12, 12000, 0, DueDate.BegOfPeriod)`
Monthly payment (rounded to the nearest cent): -230.84

**Example 3** – Calculates the amount you need to save each month to accumulate $40,000 at the end of 20 years. The interest rate is 6%, and deposits are due at the beginning of each period (month).

*Rate*: .06/12
*NPer*: 20 * 12
*PV*: 0
*FV*: 40000
*Due*: `DueDate.BegOfPeriod`
Method: `Financial.Pmt(.06/12, 20 * 12, 0, 40000, DueDate.BegOfPeriod)`
Monthly payment (rounded to the nearest cent): -86.14

**FIGURE 5.6**   How to use the Financial.Pmt method

Notice that the Financial.Pmt method contains five arguments. Three of the arguments (*Rate*, *NPer*, and *PV*) are required, and two (*FV* and *Due*) are optional. If the *FV* (future value) argument is omitted, the Financial.Pmt method uses the default value, 0. If the *Due* argument is omitted, the Financial.Pmt method uses the constant `DueDate.EndOfPeriod` as the default value. The `DueDate.EndOfPeriod` constant indicates that payments are due at the end of each period.

The *Rate* and *NPer* (number of periods) arguments in the Financial.Pmt method must be expressed using the same units. For example, if *Rate* is a monthly interest rate, then *NPer* must specify the number of monthly payments. Likewise, if *Rate* is an annual interest rate, then *NPer* must specify the number of annual payments.

Study closely the three examples shown in Figure 5.6. Example 1 uses the Financial.Pmt method to calculate the annual payment for a loan of $9,000 for 3 years at 5% interest, where payments are due at the end of each period; in this case, a period is a year. As the example indicates, the annual payment returned by the Financial.Pmt method and rounded to the nearest cent is -3,304.88. In other words, if you borrow $9,000 for 3 years at 5% interest, you will need to make three annual payments of $3,304.88 to pay off the loan.

When calculating an annual payment, the *Rate* argument should specify the annual interest rate, and the *NPer* argument should specify the life of the loan or investment in years. In Example 1, the *Rate* argument is .05, which is the annual interest rate, and the *NPer* argument is the number 3, which is the number of years you have to pay off the loan. As the example indicates, you can use the `Financial.Pmt(.05, 3, 9000, 0, DueDate.EndOfPeriod)` method to calculate the annual payment. You also can use the `Financial.Pmt(.05, 3, 9000)` method, because the default values for the optional *FV* and *Due* arguments are 0 and `DueDate.EndOfPeriod`, respectively.

Notice that the Financial.Pmt method returns a negative number. To change the negative number to a positive number, you can precede the Financial.Pmt method with the negation operator, like this: `-Financial.Pmt(.05, 3, 9000, 0, DueDate.EndOfPeriod)`. As you learned in Chapter 3, the negation operator is one of the arithmetic operators. Its purpose is to reverse the sign of a number: A negative number preceded by the negation operator becomes a positive number. Likewise, a positive number preceded by the negation operator becomes a negative number.

The Financial.Pmt method shown in Example 2 in Figure 5.6 calculates the monthly payment for a loan of $12,000 for 5 years at 6% interest, where payments are due at the beginning of each period; in this case, a period is a month. Notice that the *Rate* and *NPer* arguments are expressed in monthly terms rather than in annual terms. The monthly payment for this loan, rounded to the nearest cent, is -230.84.

In addition to using the Financial.Pmt method to calculate the payments required to pay off a loan, you also can use the Financial.Pmt method to calculate the amount you need to save each period to accumulate a specific sum. The `Financial.Pmt(.06/12, 20 * 12, 0, 40000, DueDate.BegOfPeriod)` method shown in Example 3 in Figure 5.6, for instance, indicates that you need to save $86.14 (rounded to the nearest cent) each month to accumulate $40,000 at the end of 20 years, assuming a 6% interest rate and the appropriate amount deposited at the beginning of each period.

Next, you view the Monthly Payment Calculator application, which uses the For...Next statement and the Financial.Pmt method.

## The Monthly Payment Calculator Application

Herman Juarez has been shopping for a new car and has asked you to create an application that he can use to calculate and display his monthly car payment, using a term of five years and annual interest rates of 5%, 6%, 7%, 8%, 9%, and 10%. Figure 5.7 shows the Visual Basic code for a procedure that performs this task, and Figure 5.8 shows a sample run of the Monthly Payment Calculator application that contains the procedure.

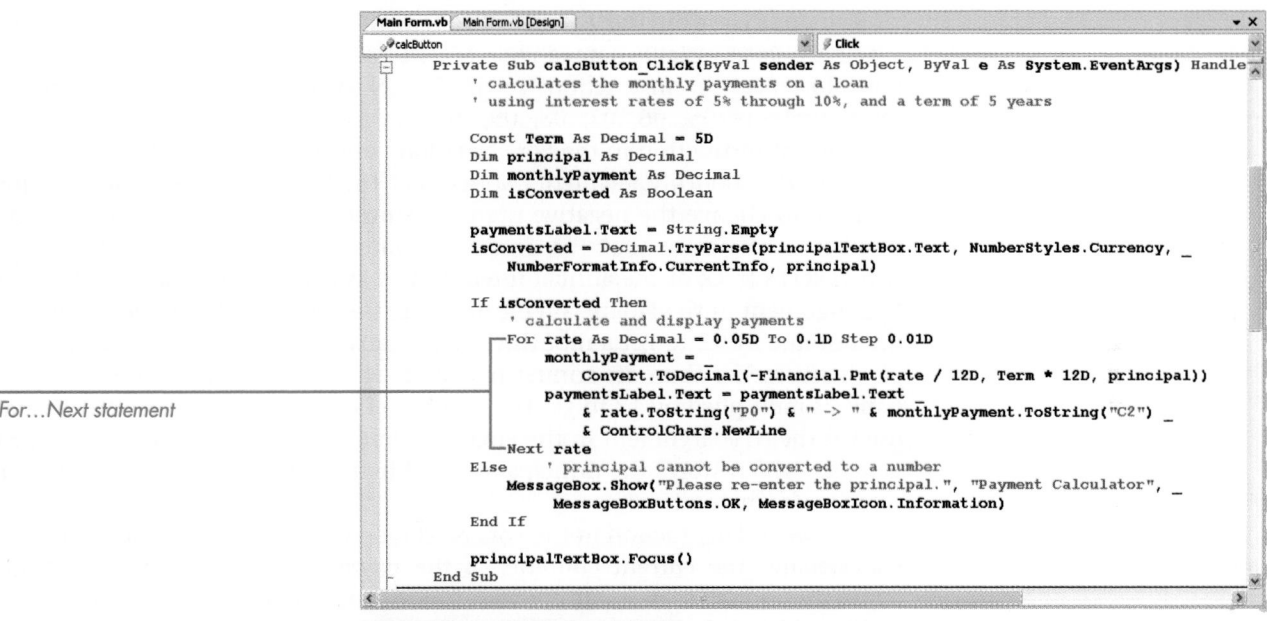

*For...Next statement*

**FIGURE 5.7**     Code for the calcButton's Click event procedure

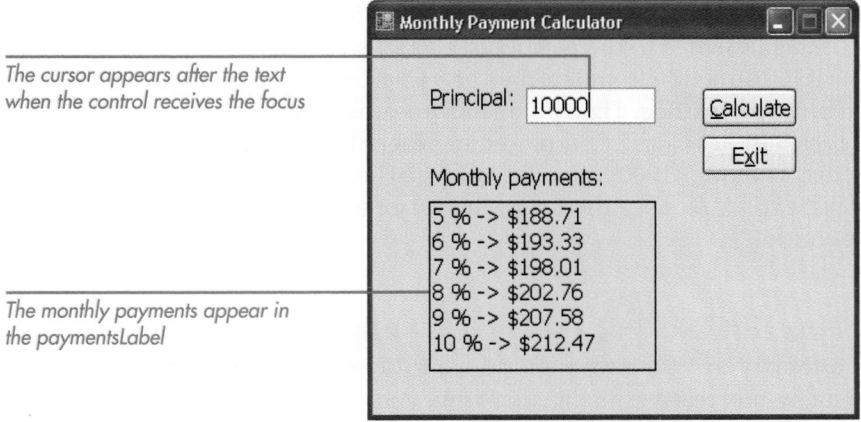

*The cursor appears after the text when the control receives the focus*

*The monthly payments appear in the paymentsLabel*

**FIGURE 5.8**     Sample run of the application that contains the calcButton's Click event procedure

The procedure shown in Figure 5.7 begins by declaring a named constant for the term and initializing it to the number five, which is the number of years Herman has to pay off the loan. The procedure also declares two variables to store the principal and payment amounts, and a variable to store the value returned by the TryParse method.

After declaring the constant and variables, the procedure clears the contents of the paymentsLabel, and then uses the TryParse method to convert the contents of the principalTextBox to a Decimal number. If the contents of the text box cannot be converted to a number, the statement in the selection structure's false path displays an appropriate message in a message box. If the conversion is successful, on the other hand, the computer processes the For...Next statement located in the selection structure's true path.

The For clause in the For...Next statement tells the computer to create a Decimal *counter* variable named `rate` and initialize it to .05. It also tells the computer to repeat the instructions in the For...Next loop six times, using annual interest rates of .05, .06, .07, .08, .09, and .1.

The first instruction in the For...Next loop uses the Financial.Pmt method to calculate the monthly payment. Notice that the instruction uses the negation operator to change the negative number returned by the method to a positive number. Also notice that the For...Next statement's *counter* variable (`rate`), which keeps track of the annual interest rates, is divided by 12 and used as the *Rate* argument in the Financial.Pmt method. It is necessary to divide the annual interest rate by 12 to get a monthly rate, because you want to display monthly payments rather than an annual payment. The `Term` constant, on the other hand, is multiplied by 12 to get the number of monthly payments; the result is used as the *NPer* argument in the Financial.Pmt method. Lastly, the `principal` variable, which stores the principal entered by the user, is used as the *PV* argument in the method.

The second instruction in the For...Next loop is an assignment statement that concatenates the current contents of the paymentsLabel with the following items: the annual interest rate converted to a string and formatted to a percentage with zero decimal places, the string " -> " (a space, a hyphen, a greater than sign, and a space), the monthly payment amount converted to a string and formatted with a dollar sign and two decimal places, and the `ControlChars.NewLine` constant. As you learned in Chapter 4, the `ControlChars.NewLine` constant advances the insertion point to the next line in a control. The concatenated string is then assigned to the paymentsLabel's Text property.

The last instruction in the calcButton's Click event procedure sends the focus to the principalTextBox. Figure 5.8 (shown earlier) shows the output displayed by the calcButton's Click event procedure when the user clicks the Calculate button after entering 10000 in the principalTextBox. Notice that when the principalTextBox receives the focus, the cursor appears after the text contained in the control.

## Selecting the Existing Text in a Text Box

It is customary in Windows applications to select (highlight) the existing text when a text box receives the focus. When you select the existing text, the user can remove the text simply by pressing a key—for example, the letter "n" on the keyboard. The key that is pressed—in this case, the letter "n"—replaces the selected text in the text box.

You use the **SelectAll method** to select all of the text contained in a text box. Figure 5.9 shows the syntax of the SelectAll method and includes an example of using the method.

# HOW TO...

### Select the Existing Text in a Text Box

**Syntax**
*textbox*.**SelectAll()**

**Example**
`nameTextBox.SelectAll()`
selects (highlights) the contents of the nameTextBox

---

**FIGURE 5.9**     How to select the existing text in a text box

In the syntax shown in Figure 5.9, *textbox* is the name of the text box whose contents you want to select. The `nameTextBox.SelectAll()` statement shown in the figure tells the computer to select, or highlight, the contents of the nameTextBox.

You can use the SelectAll method in the Monthly Payment Calculator application to select the contents of the principalTextBox when the text box receives the focus. You do this by entering the SelectAll method in the text box's Enter event procedure. A text box's **Enter event** occurs when the text box receives the focus. This can happen as a result of the user tabbing to the control or using the control's access key. It also occurs when the Focus method is used in code to send the focus to the control. Figure 5.10 shows the principalTextBox's Enter event procedure, and Figure 5.11 shows the result of the computer processing the procedure's code.

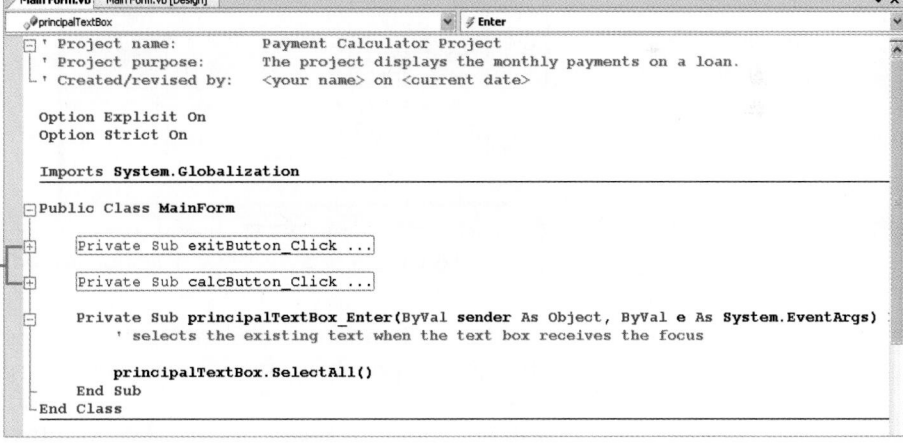

*The code in these two procedures is collapsed*

---

**FIGURE 5.10**     The principalTextBox's Enter event procedure

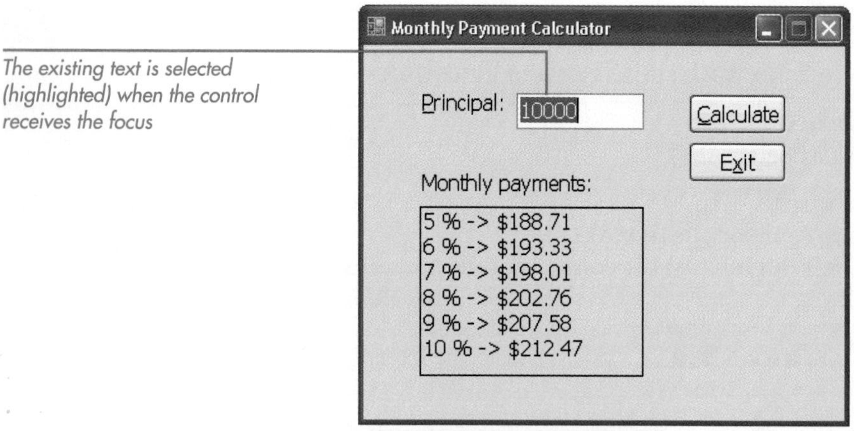

*The existing text is selected (highlighted) when the control receives the focus*

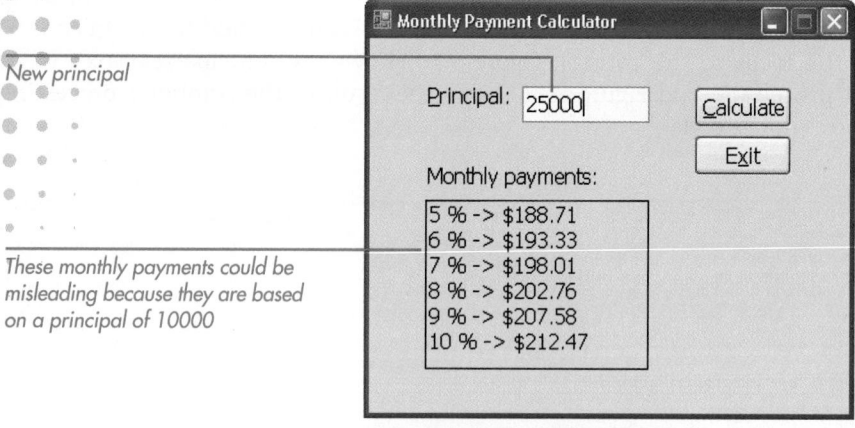

**FIGURE 5.11**    Result of processing the Enter event procedure

Now assume that, after calculating the monthly payments on a principal of $10,000, the user enters the number 25000 as the principal, as shown in Figure 5.12.

*New principal*

*These monthly payments could be misleading because they are based on a principal of 10000*

**FIGURE 5.12**    New principal entered in the Principal text box

The information shown in Figure 5.12 could be misleading, because even though the principal amount has changed, the paymentsLabel still lists the monthly payments for a $10,000 loan. The monthly payments for a $25,000 loan will not appear in the paymentsLabel until the user clicks the Calculate button. To prevent any confusion, it would be better to clear the contents of the paymentsLabel when the principal amount has changed. You can do so by coding the principalTextBox's TextChanged event procedure.

## Coding a Control's TextChanged Event Procedure

A control's **TextChanged event** occurs when a change is made to the contents of the control's Text property. This can happen as a result of either the user entering data into the control, or the application's code assigning data to the control's Text property.

In the Monthly Payment Calculator application, the principalTextBox's TextChanged event procedure should clear the contents of the paymentsLabel when the user changes the principal. Figure 5.13 shows the code for the principalTextBox's TextChanged event procedure, and Figure 5.14 shows a sample run of the application. In the sample run, the user enters the number 25000 in the principalTextBox after calculating the monthly payments for a $10,000 principal. Notice that the monthly payments no longer appear in the paymentsLabel.

The code in these three procedures is collapsed

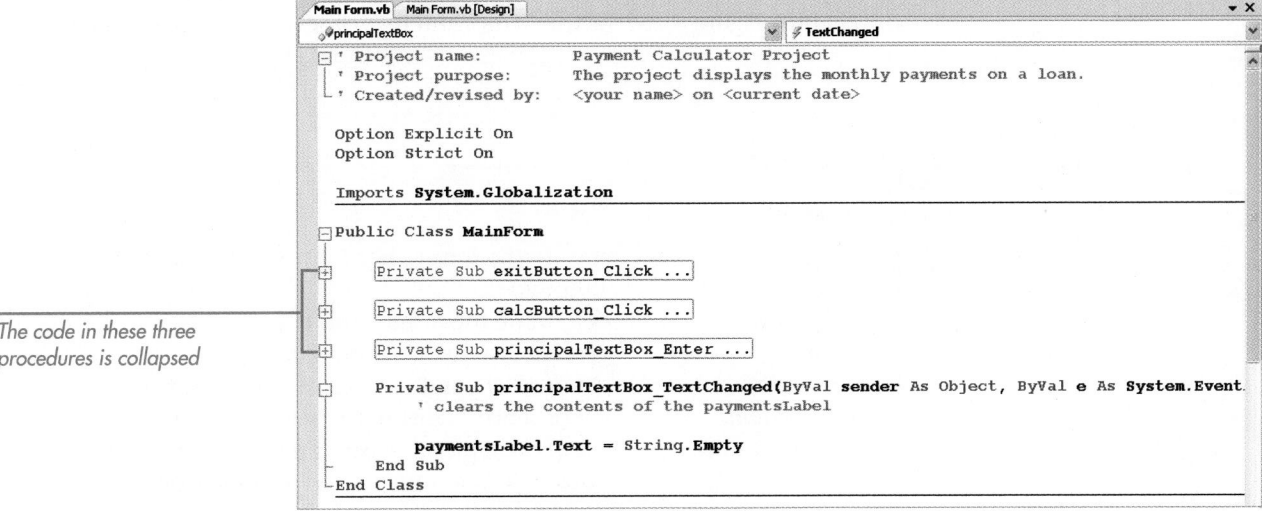

**FIGURE 5.13** The principalTextBox's TextChanged event procedure

New principal

The previous monthly payments are removed from the paymentsLabel

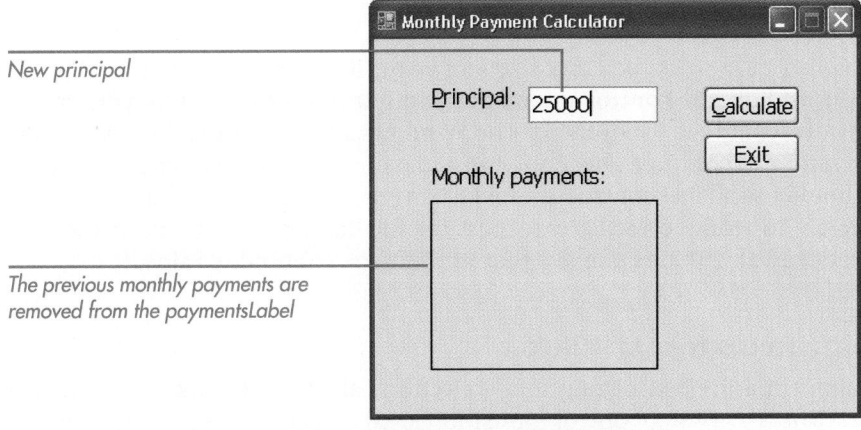

**FIGURE 5.14** Status of the paymentsLabel after entering the new principal

Next, you learn how to include list boxes in an interface. You often will use the For...Next statement to fill a list box with values.

## USING A LIST BOX IN AN INTERFACE

You use the **ListBox tool** in the toolbox to add a list box to an interface. You can use a **list box** to display a list of choices from which the user can select zero choices, one choice, or more than one choice. The number of choices the user is allowed to select is controlled by the list box's SelectionMode property. The default value for the property is One, which allows the user to select only one choice at a time in the list box. However, you also can set the property to None, MultiSimple, or MultiExtended. The None setting allows the user to scroll the list box, but not make any selection in it. The MultiSimple and MultiExtended settings allow the user to select more than one choice. In the concept section of this chapter, you learn how to use the One setting. You learn how to use the MultiSimple and MultiExtended settings in Computer Exercise 16 at the end of the chapter. Figure 5.15 lists the names and uses of several properties of a list box.

## HOW TO...

### Use a List Box

| Property | Use to |
| --- | --- |
| Font | specify the font to use for text (usually set to Tahoma) |
| Items.Count | determine the number of items in the list box |
| Name | give the list box a meaningful name |
| SelectedIndex | get or set the index of the selected item |
| SelectedItem | get or set the value of the selected item |
| SelectionMode | specify whether the user can select zero choices, one choice, or more than one choice; one choice is the default |
| Sorted | control whether the items in the list are sorted |

**FIGURE 5.15**     How to use a list box

You can make a list box any size you want. If you have more items than fit into the list box, the control automatically displays a scroll bar that you can use to view the complete list of items. The Windows standard for list boxes is to display a minimum of three selections and a maximum of eight selections at a time. You should use a label control to provide keyboard access to the list box. For the access key to work correctly, you must set the TabIndex property of the label control to a value that is one less than the list box's TabIndex value.

### Adding Items to a List Box

The items in a list box belong to a collection called the **Items collection**. A **collection** is a group of one or more individual objects treated as one unit. The first item in the Items collection appears as the first item in the list box, the second item appears as the second item in the list box, and so on.

A unique number called an **index** identifies each item in a collection. The first item in the Items collection—and, therefore, the first item in the list box—has an index of zero. The second item has an index of one, and so on.

You use the Items collection's **Add method** to specify each item you want displayed in a list box. You typically enter the Add methods in the form's Load event procedure. As you learned in Chapter 2, a form's Load event occurs before the form is displayed the first time.

Figure 5.16 shows the syntax of the Add method and includes two examples of using the method to add items to a list box. In the syntax, *object* is the name of the control to which you want the item added, and *item* is the text you want displayed in the control. Each item in a list box is considered an object.

# HOW TO...

## Add Items to a List Box

**Syntax**
*object*.**Items.Add**(*item*)

**Examples**
```
animalListBox.Items.Add("Dog")
animalListBox.Items.Add("Cat")
animalListBox.Items.Add("Horse")
```
displays Dog, Cat, and Horse in the animalListBox

```
For code As Integer = 100 To 105
    codeListBox.Items.Add(code.ToString)
Next code
```
displays 100, 101, 102, 103, 104, and 105 in the codeListBox

**FIGURE 5.16**    How to add items to a list box

**TIP**

You also can use the String Collection Editor dialog box to add items to a list box. You learn how to use the dialog box in Computer Exercise 18 at the end of the chapter.

The Add methods shown in the first example in Figure 5.16 add the strings "Dog", "Cat", and "Horse" to the animalListBox. In the second example, the `codeListBox.Items.Add(code.ToString)` instruction contained in the For...Next statement displays numbers from 100 through 105, in increments of 1, in the codeListBox. Notice that the ToString method is used to convert each number to a String before adding it to the list box. Figure 5.17 shows the Add methods entered in the form's Load event procedure, and Figure 5.18 shows the animalListBox and codeListBox after the computer processes the Add methods.

```
Main Form.vb   Main Form.vb [Design]                                                               ▼ × 
(General)                                          ▼    (Declarations)                             ▼
' Project name:          List Box Example Project
' Project purpose:       The project demonstrates the use of the Add method.
' Created/revised by:    <your name> on <current date>

Option Explicit On
Option Strict On

Public Class MainForm

    Private Sub MainForm_Load(ByVal sender As Object, ByVal e As System.EventArgs) Handles M

        ' add items to the animalListBox
        animalListBox.Items.Add("Dog")
        animalListBox.Items.Add("Cat")
        animalListBox.Items.Add("Horse")

        ' add items to the codeListBox
        For code As Integer = 100 To 105
            codeListBox.Items.Add(code.ToString)
        Next code
    End Sub

    Private Sub exitButton_Click(ByVal sender As Object, ByVal e As System.EventArgs) Handle
        Me.Close()
    End Sub
End Class
```

**FIGURE 5.17**    Add methods entered in the form's Load event procedure

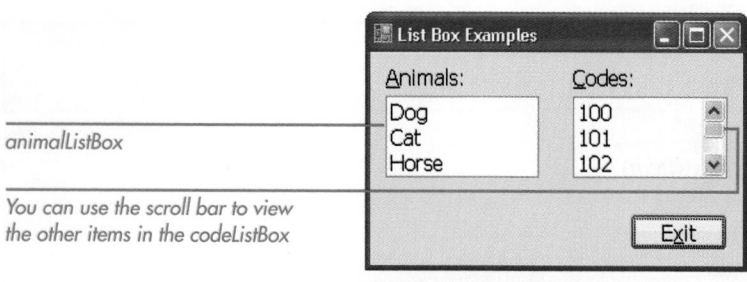

*animalListBox*

*You can use the scroll bar to view the other items in the codeListBox*

**FIGURE 5.18**    Items added to the animalListBox and codeListBox

When you use the Add method to add an item to a list box, the position of the item in the list depends on the value stored in the list box's Sorted property. If the Sorted property contains its default value, False, the item is added at the end of the list. If the Sorted property is set to True, on the other hand, the item is sorted along with the existing items, and then placed in its proper position in the list. For example, if the Sorted property of the animalListBox shown in Figure 5.18 were set to True, the list box items would appear in the following order: Cat, Dog, Horse.

Visual Basic sorts the list box items in dictionary order, which means that numbers are sorted before letters, and a lowercase letter is sorted before its uppercase equivalent. The items in a list box are sorted based on the leftmost characters in each item. Because of this, the items "Personnel", "Inventory", and "Payroll" will appear in the following order when the list box's Sorted property is set to True: Inventory, Payroll, Personnel. Similarly, the items 1, 2, 3, and 10 will appear in the following order when the list box's Sorted property is set to True: 1, 10, 2, 3.

The application determines whether you display the list box items in sorted order, or display them in the order in which they are added to the list box. If several list items are selected much more frequently than other items, you typically leave the list box's Sorted property set to False, and then add the frequently used items first so that the items appear at the beginning of the list. However, if the list box items are selected fairly equally, you typically set the list box's Sorted property to True, because it is easier to locate items when they appear in a sorted order.

## The SelectedItem and SelectedIndex Properties

When you select an item in a list box, the item appears highlighted in the list, as shown in Figure 5.19. Additionally, the computer stores the item's value in the list box's SelectedItem property, and stores the item's index in the list box's SelectedIndex property. In this case, for example, it stores the value "Dog" in the animalListBox's SelectedItem property, and stores the integer zero in its SelectedIndex property.

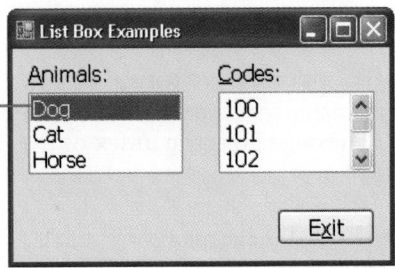

*The computer stores the string "Dog" in the list box's SelectedItem property, and stores the number zero in its SelectedIndex property*

**FIGURE 5.19**   Item selected in the animalListBox

You can use the SelectedItem and SelectedIndex properties to determine whether an item is selected in a list box. When no item is selected, the SelectedItem property contains the empty string, and the SelectedIndex property contains the number –1. Otherwise, the SelectedItem and SelectedIndex properties contain the value of the selected item and the item's index, respectively.

If a list box allows the user to make only one selection, it is customary in Windows applications to have one of the list box items already selected when the interface appears. The selected item, called the **default list box item**, should be either the item selected most frequently or, if all of the items are selected fairly equally, the first item in the list. You can use the SelectedItem and SelectedIndex properties to select the default list box item from code. Figure 5.20 shows examples of using the SelectedItem and SelectedIndex properties.

## HOW TO...   Use the SelectedItem and SelectedIndex Properties

**SelectedItem property examples**

```
animalLabel.Text = Convert.ToString(animalListBox.SelectedItem)
```
converts the item selected in the animaListBox to String, and then assigns the result to the animalLabel

```
If Convert.ToInt32(codeListBox.SelectedItem) = 103 Then
```
converts the item selected in the codeListBox to Integer, and then compares the result with the integer 103

```
If Convert.ToString(codeListBox.SelectedItem) <> "" Then
```
the condition evaluates to True when an item is selected in the codeListBox; otherwise, it evaluates to False

```
animalListBox.SelectedItem = "Cat"
```
selects the Cat item in the animalListBox

```
codeListBox.SelectedItem = "101"
```
selects the 101 item in the codeListBox

*(Figure is continued on next page)*

**SelectedIndex property examples**

```
MessageBox.Show(animalListBox.SelectedIndex.ToString)
```
displays (in a message box) the index of the item selected in the animalListBox

```
If codeListBox.SelectedIndex = 0 Then
```
determines whether the first item is selected in the codeListBox

```
codeListBox.SelectedIndex = 2
```
selects the third item in the codeListBox

**FIGURE 5.20** How to use the SelectedItem and SelectedIndex properties

**TIP**

In the first SelectedIndex property example shown in Figure 5.20, you also can use the Convert.ToString method to convert the SelectedIndex property to String.

The first five examples shown in Figure 5.20 use the SelectedItem property. The statement in the first example converts the item selected in the animalListBox to a String, and then assigns the string to the animalLabel. If "Horse" is selected in the animaListBox, the statement assigns "Horse" to the animalLabel. However, if no item is selected, the statement assigns the empty string to the animalLabel.

The If clause in the second example converts the item selected in the codeListBox to Integer, and then compares the result with the integer 103. You also could write the If clause as `If Convert.ToString(codeListBox.SelectedItem) = "103" Then` or as `If codeListBox.SelectedItem.ToString = "103"`.

You can use the If clause in the third example to determine whether an item is selected in the codeListBox. The statements in the fourth and fifth examples show how you can use the SelectedItem property to select a list box item.

The last three examples shown in Figure 5.20 use the SelectedIndex property. The `MessageBox.Show(animalListBox.SelectedIndex.ToString)` statement displays in a message box the index of the item selected in the animalListBox. If the second item is selected in the animalListBox, the statement displays the number 1. However, if no item is selected, the statement displays the number -1. In the next example, the `If codeListBox.SelectedIndex = 0 Then` clause compares the contents of the codeListBox's SelectedIndex property with the number zero to determine whether the first item is selected in the list box. You can use the `codeListBox.SelectedIndex = 2` statement shown in the last example to select the third item in the codeListBox.

## The SelectedValueChanged and SelectedIndexChanged Events

Each time either the user or a statement selects an item in a list box, the list box's **SelectedValueChanged** and **SelectedIndexChanged events** occur. You can use the procedures associated with these events to perform one or more tasks when the selected item has changed, as shown in Figure 5.21. The SelectedValueChanged procedure shown in the figure displays in a message box the value of the selected item. The SelectedIndexChanged event procedure displays a message box that contains the index of the selected item.

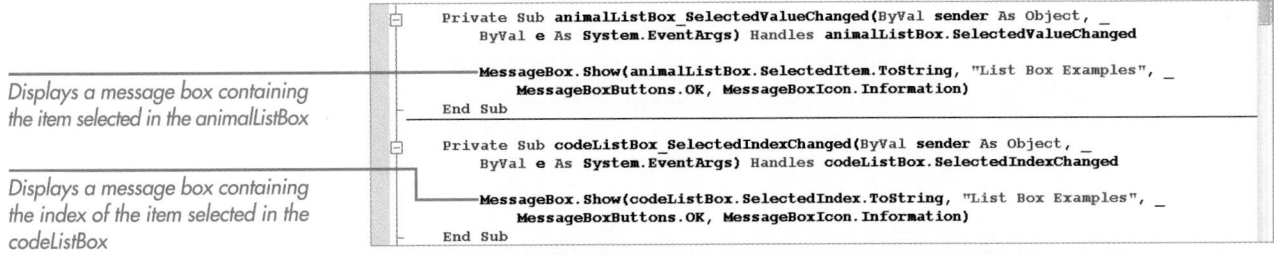

*Displays a message box containing the item selected in the animalListBox*

*Displays a message box containing the index of the item selected in the codeListBox*

**FIGURE 5.21** SelectedValueChanged and SelectedIndexChanged event procedures

Now use your knowledge about list boxes to modify the Monthly Payment Calculator application.

## MODIFYING THE MONTHLY PAYMENT CALCULATOR APPLICATION

The Monthly Payment Calculator application that you viewed earlier in the chapter calculates the monthly payments based on a five-year term only. In this section, you view a modified Monthly Payment Calculator application. The modified application calculates the monthly payments based on a term of 2, 3, 4, or 5 years; the appropriate term is chosen from a list box. Figure 5.22 shows a sample run of the modified application, and Figure 5.23 shows the application's code. Changes made to the original code are shaded in Figure 5.23.

*termListBox*

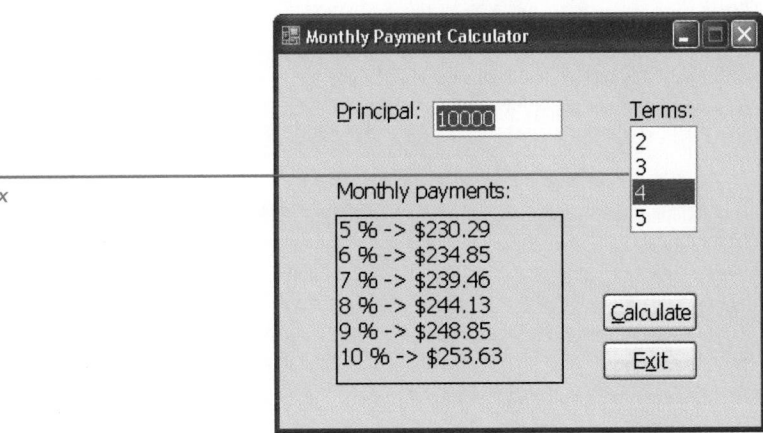

**FIGURE 5.22** Sample run of the Monthly Payment Calculator application using a list box

```vbnet
' Project name:          Payment Calculator Project
' Project purpose:       The project displays the monthly payments on a loan.
' Created/revised by:    <your name> on <current date>

Option Explicit On
Option Strict On

Imports System.Globalization

Public Class MainForm

    Private Sub exitButton_Click(ByVal sender As Object, _
        ByVal e As System.EventArgs) Handles exitButton.Click
        Me.Close()
    End Sub

    Private Sub MainForm_Load(ByVal sender As Object, _
        ByVal e As System.EventArgs) Handles Me.Load
        ' fills the termListBox with terms of 2, 3, 4, and 5 years

        For term As Integer = 2 To 5
            termListBox.Items.Add(term.ToString)
        Next term

        ' select the 4-year term
        termListBox.SelectedItem = "4"
    End Sub

    Private Sub calcButton_Click(ByVal sender As Object, _
        ByVal e As System.EventArgs) Handles calcButton.Click
        ' calculates the monthly payments on a loan
        ' using interest rates of 5% through 10%, and terms of 2, 3, 4, or 5 years

        Dim term As Decimal
        Dim principal As Decimal
        Dim monthlyPayment As Decimal
        Dim isConverted As Boolean

        paymentsLabel.Text = String.Empty
        isConverted = Decimal.TryParse(principalTextBox.Text, NumberStyles.Currency, _
            NumberFormatInfo.CurrentInfo, principal)

        If isConverted Then
            ' calculate and display payments
            term = Convert.ToDecimal(termListBox.SelectedItem)
            For rate As Decimal = 0.05D To 0.1D Step 0.01D
                monthlyPayment = _
                    Convert.ToDecimal(-Financial.Pmt(rate / 12D, term * 12D, principal))
```

*(Figure is continued on next page)*

```vb
                  paymentsLabel.Text = paymentsLabel.Text _
                      & rate.ToString("P0") & " -> " & monthlyPayment.ToString("C2") _
                      & ControlChars.NewLine
            Next rate
        Else    ' principal cannot be converted to a number
            MessageBox.Show("Please re-enter the principal.", "Payment Calculator", _
                MessageBoxButtons.OK, MessageBoxIcon.Information)
        End If

        principalTextBox.Focus()
    End Sub

    Private Sub principalTextBox_Enter(ByVal sender As Object, _
        ByVal e As System.EventArgs) Handles principalTextBox.Enter
        ' selects the existing text when the text box receives the focus

        principalTextBox.SelectAll()
    End Sub

    Private Sub principalTextBox_TextChanged(ByVal sender As Object, _
        ByVal e As System.EventArgs) Handles principalTextBox.TextChanged
        ' clears the contents of the paymentsLabel

        paymentsLabel.Text = String.Empty
    End Sub


    Private Sub termListBox_SelectedValueChanged(ByVal sender As Object, _
        ByVal e As System.EventArgs) Handles termListBox.SelectedValueChanged
        ' clears the contents of the paymentsLabel


        paymentsLabel.Text = String.Empty
    End Sub
End Class
```

**FIGURE 5.23** Modified application's code using a list box

The modified application uses the MainForm's Load event procedure to fill the termListBox with values and then select the four-year term in the list. The Term named constant defined in the calcButton's original Click event procedure (shown earlier in Figure 5.7) was changed to a variable named term in the modified procedure. The term = Convert.ToDecimal(termListBox.SelectedItem) statement in the modified procedure converts the item selected in the termListBox to Decimal, and then assigns the result to the term variable. Notice that the term variable, rather than the Term named constant, is used in the Financial.Pmt method. Additionally, the modified application uses the termListBox's SelectedValueChanged event procedure to remove the contents of the paymentsLabel when the term changes.

Next, you learn about combo boxes, which are many times used in place of list boxes in an interface.

## USING A COMBO BOX IN AN INTERFACE

You use the **ComboBox tool** in the toolbox to add a combo box to an interface. A **combo box** is similar to a list box in that it allows the user to select from a list of choices. However, unlike a list box, a combo box also can contain a text field that allows the user to type an entry that is not on the list. Additionally, a combo box can save space on a form because, unlike a list box, the full list of choices can be hidden.

Three styles of combo boxes are available in Visual Basic. The style is controlled by the combo box's DropDownStyle property, which can be set to Simple, DropDown (the default), or DropDownList. Each style of combo box contains a text portion and a list portion. When the DropDownStyle property is set to either Simple or DropDown, the text portion of the combo box is editable. However, in a Simple combo box the list portion is always displayed, while in a DropDown combo box the list portion appears only when the user clicks the combo box's list arrow. When the DropDownStyle property is set to the third style, DropDownList, the text portion of the combo box is not editable, and the user must click the combo box's list arrow to display the list of choices. Figure 5.24 shows an example of each combo box style, and Figure 5.25 shows the code used to fill the combo boxes with values. Notice that you use the Items collection's Add method to add an item to a combo box. Also notice that you can use a combo box's SelectedIndex, SelectedItem, or Text property to select the default item in the list portion of the control.

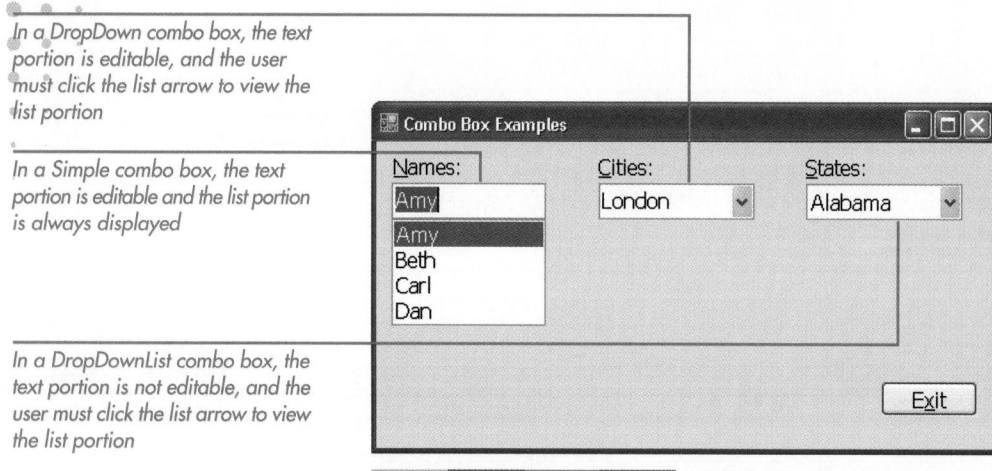

In a DropDown combo box, the text portion is editable, and the user must click the list arrow to view the list portion

In a Simple combo box, the text portion is editable and the list portion is always displayed

In a DropDownList combo box, the text portion is not editable, and the user must click the list arrow to view the list portion

**FIGURE 5.24**     Examples of the combo box styles

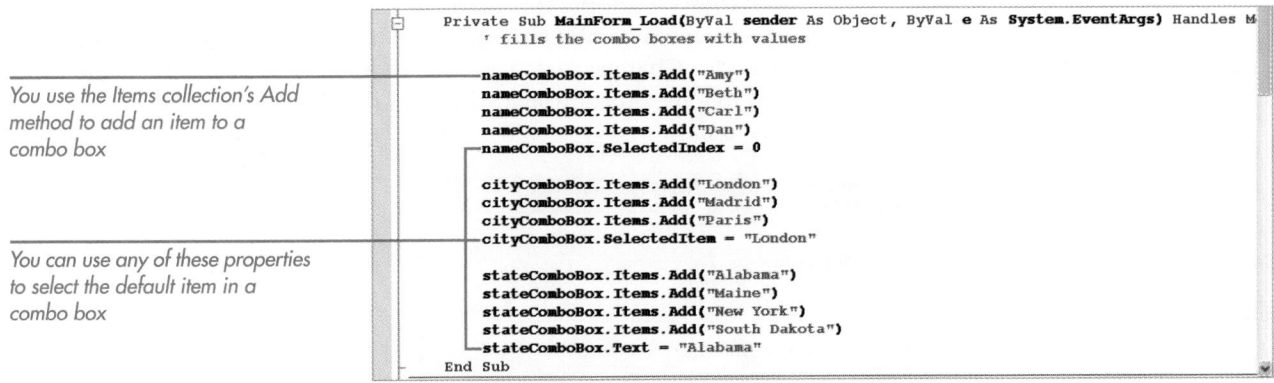

You use the Items collection's Add method to add an item to a combo box

You can use any of these properties to select the default item in a combo box

```
Private Sub MainForm_Load(ByVal sender As Object, ByVal e As System.EventArgs) Handles M
    ' fills the combo boxes with values

    nameComboBox.Items.Add("Amy")
    nameComboBox.Items.Add("Beth")
    nameComboBox.Items.Add("Carl")
    nameComboBox.Items.Add("Dan")
    nameComboBox.SelectedIndex = 0

    cityComboBox.Items.Add("London")
    cityComboBox.Items.Add("Madrid")
    cityComboBox.Items.Add("Paris")
    cityComboBox.SelectedItem = "London"

    stateComboBox.Items.Add("Alabama")
    stateComboBox.Items.Add("Maine")
    stateComboBox.Items.Add("New York")
    stateComboBox.Items.Add("South Dakota")
    stateComboBox.Text = "Alabama"
End Sub
```

**FIGURE 5.25**    Code used to fill the combo boxes in Figure 5.24 with values

You should use a label control to provide keyboard access to the combo box, as shown in Figure 5.24. For the access key to work correctly, you must set the TabIndex property of the label control to a value that is one less than the combo box's TabIndex value.

Figure 5.26 lists the names and uses of several properties of a combo box.

**HOW TO...**

### Use a Combo Box

| Property | Use to |
|---|---|
| DropDownStyle | specify the style of the combo box |
| Font | specify the font to use for text (usually set to Tahoma) |
| Items.Count | determine the number of items in the list portion of the combo box |
| Name | give the combo box a meaningful name |
| SelectedIndex | get or set the index of the selected item |
| SelectedItem | get or set the value of the selected item |
| Sorted | control whether the items in the list portion are sorted |
| Text | get or set the value that appears in the text portion of the combo box |

**FIGURE 5.26**    How to use a combo box

It is easy to confuse a combo box's SelectedItem property with its Text property. The SelectedItem property contains the value of the item selected in the list portion of the combo box, whereas the Text property contains the value that appears in the text portion. A value can appear in the text portion as a result of the user either selecting an item in the list portion of the control, or typing an entry in the text portion itself. If the combo box is a DropDownList style, where the text portion is not editable, you can use the SelectedItem and Text properties interchangeably. However, if the combo box is either a Simple or DropDown style, where the user can type an entry in the text portion, you should use the Text property because it contains the value either selected or entered by the user.

Figure 5.27 shows a sample run of the Monthly Payment Calculator application using a DropDown combo box rather than a list box. Figure 5.28 shows the application's code. Changes made to the code shown earlier in Figure 5.23, which referred to a list box, are shaded in Figure 5.28.

*termComboBox*

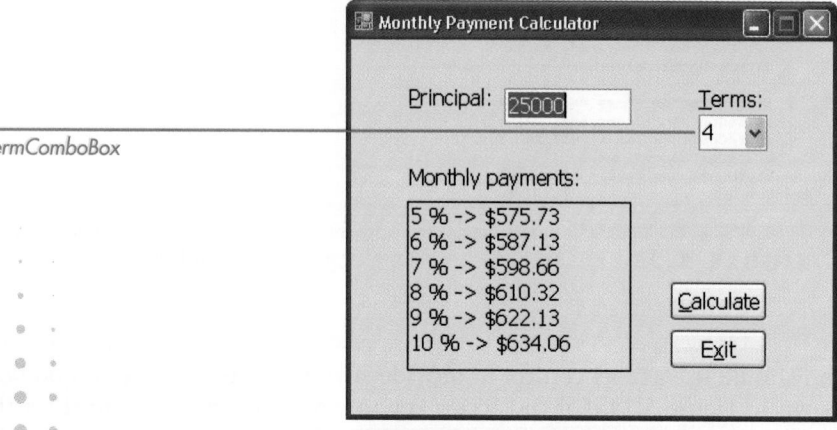

**FIGURE 5.27**  Sample run of the Monthly Payment Calculator application using a combo box

```
' Project name:        Payment Calculator Project
' Project purpose:     The project displays the monthly payments on a loan.
' Created/revised by:  <your name> on <current date>

Option Explicit On
Option Strict On

Imports System.Globalization

Public Class MainForm

    Private Sub exitButton_Click(ByVal sender As Object, _
        ByVal e As System.EventArgs) Handles exitButton.Click
        Me.Close()
    End Sub

    Private Sub MainForm_Load(ByVal sender As Object, _
        ByVal e As System.EventArgs) Handles Me.Load
        ' fills the termComboBox with terms of 2, 3, 4, and 5 years

        For term As Integer = 2 To 5
            termComboBox.Items.Add(term.ToString)
        Next term

        ' select the 4-year term
        termComboBox.Text = "4"
    End Sub
```

**(Figure is continued on next page)**

```
Private Sub calcButton_Click(ByVal sender As Object, _
    ByVal e As System.EventArgs) Handles calcButton.Click
    ' calculates the monthly payments on a loan
    ' using interest rates of 5% through 10%, and terms of 2, 3, 4, or 5 years

    Dim term As Decimal
    Dim principal As Decimal
    Dim monthlyPayment As Decimal
    Dim isConverted As Boolean

    paymentsLabel.Text = String.Empty
    isConverted = Decimal.TryParse(principalTextBox.Text, NumberStyles.Currency, _
        NumberFormatInfo.CurrentInfo, principal)
    If isConverted Then
        ' calculate and display payments
        Dim isTermConverted As Boolean
        isTermConverted = Decimal.TryParse(termComboBox.Text, term)
        If isTermConverted Then
            For rate As Decimal = 0.05D To 0.1D Step 0.01D
                monthlyPayment = _
                    Convert.ToDecimal(-Financial.Pmt(rate / 12D, term * 12D, principal))
                paymentsLabel.Text = paymentsLabel.Text _
                    & rate.ToString("P0") & " -> " & monthlyPayment.ToString("C2") _
                    & ControlChars.NewLine
            Next rate
        Else    ' term cannot be converted to a number
            MessageBox.Show("Please re-enter the term.", "Payment Calculator", _
                MessageBoxButtons.OK, MessageBoxIcon.Information)
        End If

    Else    ' principal cannot be converted to a number
        MessageBox.Show("Please re-enter the principal.", "Payment Calculator", _
            MessageBoxButtons.OK, MessageBoxIcon.Information)
    End If

    principalTextBox.Focus()
End Sub

Private Sub principalTextBox_Enter(ByVal sender As Object, _
    ByVal e As System.EventArgs) Handles principalTextBox.Enter
    ' selects the existing text when the text box receives the focus

    principalTextBox.SelectAll()
End Sub

Private Sub principalTextBox_TextChanged(ByVal sender As Object, _
    ByVal e As System.EventArgs) Handles principalTextBox.TextChanged
    ' clears the contents of the paymentsLabel

    paymentsLabel.Text = String.Empty
End Sub
```

**(Figure is continued on next page)**

```
Private Sub termComboBox_TextChanged(ByVal sender As Object, _
    ByVal e As System.EventArgs) Handles termComboBox.TextChanged
    ' clears the contents of the paymentsLabel

    paymentsLabel.Text = String.Empty
End Sub
End Class
```

**FIGURE 5.28**    Code for the Monthly Payment Calculator application using a combo box

Notice that the contents of the paymentsLabel are cleared in the combo box's TextChanged event procedure. The TextChanged event of a combo box occurs when the user either selects an item in the list portion or types a value in the text portion. (Recall that, in Figure 5.23, the list box's SelectedValueChanged procedure cleared the contents of the paymentsLabel.)

In all of the applications you have viewed so far in this chapter, the For...Next statement was used to code the repetition structure. Recall that you also can use the Do...Loop statement to code a repetition structure in Visual Basic.

## THE DO...LOOP STATEMENT

Unlike the For...Next statement, the **Do...Loop statement** can be used to code both a pretest loop and a posttest loop. Figure 5.29 shows two slightly different versions of the Do...Loop statement's syntax. You use the first version to code a pretest loop, and the second version to code a posttest loop. Figure 5.29 also includes an example of using each syntax to display the numbers 1, 2, and 3 in message boxes.

**HOW TO...**

**TIP**

You can use the Exit Do statement to exit the Do...Loop statement prematurely—in other words, exit it before the loop has finished processing. You may need to do this if the loop encounters an error when processing its instructions.

### Use the Do...Loop Statement

**Do...Loop syntax (pretest loop)**
Do {While | Until} *condition*
    [*instructions to be processed either while the condition is true or until the condition becomes true*]
Loop

**Do...Loop syntax (posttest loop)**
Do
    [*instructions to be processed either while the condition is true or until the condition becomes true*]
Loop {While | Until} *condition*

**Pretest loop example**
```
Dim number As Integer = 1
Do While number <= 3
```

**(Figure is continued on next page)**

```
        MessageBox.Show(number.ToString, "Numbers", _
            MessageBoxButtons.OK, MessageBoxIcon.Information)
        number = number + 1
Loop
```

**Posttest loop example**

```
Dim number As Integer = 1
Do
        MessageBox.Show(number.ToString, "Numbers", _
            MessageBoxButtons.OK, MessageBoxIcon.Information)
        number = number + 1
Loop Until number > 3
```

**FIGURE 5.29**     How to use the Do...Loop statement

**TIP**

You can nest Do...Loop statements, which means that you can place one Do...Loop statement within another Do...Loop statement.

The Do...Loop statement begins with the Do clause and ends with the Loop clause. Between both clauses, you enter the instructions you want the computer to repeat.

The {**While | Until**} portion of each syntax shown in Figure 5.29 indicates that you can select only one of the keywords appearing within the braces. In this case, you can choose either the keyword While or the keyword Until. As both examples shown in Figure 5.29 indicate, you do not type the braces ({}) or the pipe symbol (|) when entering the Do...Loop statement.

You follow the While or Until keyword with a *condition*, which can contain variables, constants, properties, methods, and operators. Like the condition used in the If...Then...Else statement, the condition used in the Do...Loop statement also must evaluate to a Boolean value—either True or False. The condition determines whether the computer processes the loop instructions. The keyword While indicates that the loop instructions should be processed *while* the condition is true. The keyword Until, on the other hand, indicates that the loop instructions should be processed *until* the condition becomes true. Notice that the keyword (either While or Until) and the condition appear in the Do clause in a pretest loop, but appear in the Loop clause in a posttest loop.

Figures 5.30 and 5.31 describe how the computer processes the code shown in the examples in Figure 5.29.

**Processing steps for the pretest loop example**

1. The computer creates the number variable and initializes it to 1.
2. The computer processes the Do clause, which checks whether the value in the number variable is less than or equal to 3. It is.
3. The MessageBox.Show method displays 1 (the contents of the number variable).
4. The number = number + 1 statement adds 1 to the contents of the number variable, giving 2.
5. The computer processes the Loop clause, which returns processing to the Do clause (the beginning of the loop).

*(Figure is continued on next page)*

6. The computer processes the Do clause, which checks whether the value in the `number` variable is less than or equal to 3. It is.

7. The MessageBox.Show method displays 2 (the contents of the `number` variable).

8. The `number = number + 1` statement adds 1 to the contents of the `number` variable, giving 3.

9. The computer processes the Loop clause, which returns processing to the Do clause (the beginning of the loop).

10. The computer processes the Do clause, which checks whether the value in the `number` variable is less than or equal to 3. It is.

11. The MessageBox.Show method displays 3 (the contents of the `number` variable).

12. The `number = number + 1` statement adds 1 to the contents of the `number` variable giving 4.

13. The computer processes the Loop clause, which returns processing to the Do clause (the beginning of the loop).

14. The computer processes the Do clause, which checks whether the value in the `number` variable is less than or equal to 3. It isn't, so the computer stops processing the Do…Loop statement. Processing continues with the statement following the Loop clause.

**FIGURE 5.30**   Processing steps for the pretest loop example shown in Figure 5.29

## Processing steps for the posttest loop example

1. The computer creates the `number` variable and initializes it to 1.

2. The computer processes the Do clause, which marks the beginning of the loop.

3. The MessageBox.Show method displays 1 (the contents of the `number` variable).

4. The `number = number + 1` statement adds 1 to the contents of the `number` variable, giving 2.

5. The computer processes the Loop clause, which checks whether the value in the `number` variable is greater than 3. It isn't, so processing returns to the Do clause (the beginning of the loop).

6. The MessageBox.Show method displays 2 (the contents of the `number` variable).

7. The `number = number + 1` statement adds 1 to the contents of the `number` variable, giving 3.

8. The computer processes the Loop clause, which checks whether the value in the `number` variable is greater than 3. It isn't, so processing returns to the Do clause (the beginning of the loop).

9. The MessageBox.Show method displays 3 (the contents of the `number` variable).

10. The `number = number + 1` statement adds 1 to the contents of the `number` variable, giving 4.

11. The computer processes the Loop clause, which checks whether the value in the `number` variable is greater than 3. It is, so the computer stops processing the Do…Loop statement. Processing continues with the statement following the Loop clause.

**FIGURE 5.31**   Processing steps for the posttest loop example shown in Figure 5.29

Figure 5.32 shows the flowchart and pseudocode associated with the pretest example in Figure 5.29. Figure 5.33 shows the flowchart and pseudocode for the posttest example.

**Pseudocode for the pretest loop example**

1. assign 1 to the number variable
2. repeat while the value in the number variable is less than or equal to 3
   display the contents of the number variable
   add 1 to the number variable
   end repeat

**Flowchart for the pretest loop example**

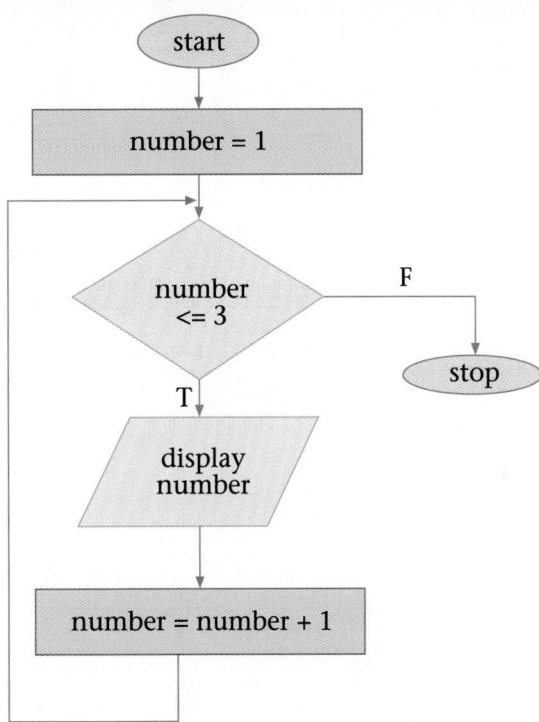

**FIGURE 5.32**    Pseudocode and flowchart for the pretest loop example shown in Figure 5.29

**Pseudocode for the posttest loop example**

1. assign 1 to the number variable
2. repeat
          display the contents of the number variable
          add 1 to the number variable
   end repeat until the value in the number variable is greater than 3

**Flowchart for the posttest loop example**

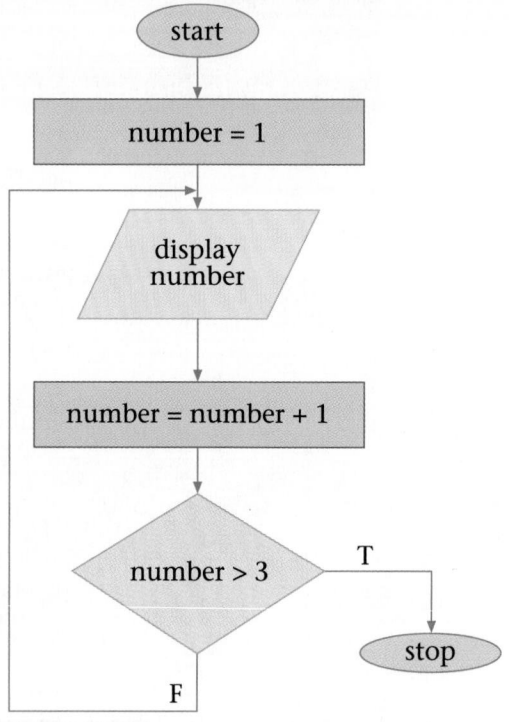

**FIGURE  5.33**    Pseudocode and flowchart for the posttest loop example shown in Figure 5.29

Notice that a diamond represents the loop condition in the flowcharts shown in Figures 5.32 and 5.33. As with the selection structure diamond, which you learned about in Chapter 4, the repetition structure diamond contains a comparison that evaluates to either True or False only. The result of the comparison determines whether the computer processes the instructions within the loop.

Like the selection diamond, the repetition diamond has one flowline entering the diamond and two flowlines leaving the diamond. The two flowlines leaving the diamond should be marked with a "T" (for True) and an "F" (for False).

In the flowchart of the pretest loop shown in Figure 5.32, the flowline entering the repetition diamond, as well as the symbols and flowlines within the True path, form a circle or loop. In the posttest loop's flowchart shown in Figure 5.33, the loop is formed by all of the symbols and flowlines in the False path. It is this loop, or circle, that distinguishes the repetition structure from the selection structure in a flowchart.

Although it appears that the pretest and posttest loops produce the same results—in this case, for instance, both examples shown in Figure 5.29 display the numbers 1 through 3—that will not always be the case. In other words, the two loops are not always interchangeable. The difference between both loops is demonstrated in the examples shown in Figure 5.34.

---

### Examples and processing steps

#### Pretest loop example

```
Dim number As Integer = 10
Do While number <= 3
    MessageBox.Show(number.ToString, "Numbers", _
        MessageBoxButtons.OK, MessageBoxIcon.Information)
    number = number + 1
Loop
```

#### Processing steps for the pretest loop

1. The computer creates the number variable and initializes it to 10.
2. The computer processes the Do clause, which checks whether the value in the number variable is less than or equal to 3. It isn't, so the computer stops processing the Do...Loop statement. Processing continues with the statement following the Loop clause.

#### Posttest loop example

```
Dim number As Integer = 10
Do
    MessageBox.Show(number.ToString, "Numbers", _
        MessageBoxButtons.OK, MessageBoxIcon.Information)
    number = number + 1
Loop Until number > 3
```

#### Processing steps for the posttest loop

1. The computer creates the number variable and initializes it to 10.
2. The computer processes the Do clause, which marks the beginning of the loop.
3. The MessageBox.Show method displays 10 (the contents of the number variable).
4. The number = number + 1 statement adds 1 to the contents of the number variable, giving 11.
5. The computer processes the Loop clause, which checks whether the value in the number variable is greater than 3. It is, so the computer stops processing the Do...Loop statement. Processing continues with the statement following the Loop clause.

---

**FIGURE 5.34**    Examples showing that the pretest and posttest loops do not always produce the same results

Comparing the processing steps shown in both examples in Figure 5.34, you will notice that the instructions in the pretest loop are not processed. This is because the number <= 3 condition, which is evaluated before the instructions are processed, evaluates to False. The instructions in the posttest loop, on the other hand, are processed one time, because the number > 3 condition is evaluated *after* (rather than *before*) the loop instructions are processed.

# USING COUNTERS AND ACCUMULATORS

**TIP**

Counters are used to answer the question, "How many?"—for example, "How many salespeople live in Virginia?" Accumulators are used to answer the question, "How much?"—for example, "How much did the salespeople sell this quarter?"

Many times an application will need to display a subtotal, a total, or an average. You calculate this information using a repetition structure that includes a counter, or an accumulator, or both. A **counter** is a numeric variable used for counting something—such as the number of employees paid in a week. An **accumulator** is a numeric variable used for accumulating (adding together) something—such as the total dollar amount of a week's payroll.

Two tasks are associated with counters and accumulators: initializing and updating. **Initializing** means to assign a beginning value to the counter or accumulator. Typically, counters and accumulators are initialized to zero; however, they can be initialized to any number, depending on the value required by the application. The initialization task is performed before the loop is processed, because it needs to be performed only once.

**Updating**, also called **incrementing**, means adding a number to the value stored in the counter or accumulator. The number can be either positive or negative, integer or non-integer. A counter is always incremented by a constant value—typically the number 1—whereas an accumulator is incremented by a value that varies. The assignment statement that updates a counter or an accumulator is placed within the loop in a procedure, because the update task must be performed each time the loop instructions are processed. You use both a counter and an accumulator, as well as a repetition structure, in the Sales Express application, which you view later in the chapter. You also use the InputBox function, which you learn about next.

## The InputBox Function

The **InputBox function** displays one of the Visual Basic predefined dialog boxes. The dialog box contains a message, along with an OK button, a Cancel button, and an input area in which the user can enter information. Figure 5.35 shows an example of a dialog box created by the InputBox function.

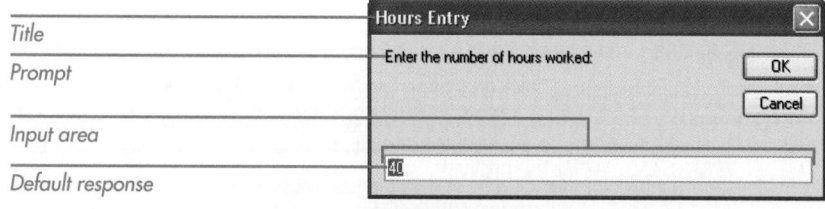

*Title*
*Prompt*
*Input area*
*Default response*

**FIGURE 5.35**     Example of a dialog box created by the InputBox function

The message that you display in the dialog box should prompt the user to enter the appropriate information in the input area of the dialog box. The user then needs to click either the OK button or the Cancel button to continue working in the application. Figure 5.36 shows the syntax of the InputBox function and includes several examples of using the function.

HOW TO...

## Use the InputBox Function

### Syntax
**InputBox**(*prompt*[, *title*][, *defaultResponse*])

### Examples
```
firstName = InputBox("Enter your first name:")
```
Displays a dialog box that shows "Enter your first name:" as the prompt, the project's name as the title, and an empty input area. Assigns the user's response to a String variable named `firstName`.

```
city = InputBox("City name:", "City")
```
Displays a dialog box that shows "City name:" as the prompt, "City" as the title, and an empty input area. Assigns the user's response to a String variable named `city`.

```
state = InputBox("State name:", "State", "Alaska")
```
Displays a dialog box that shows "State name:" as the prompt, "State" as the title, and "Alaska" in the input area. Assigns the user's response to a String variable named `state`.

```
state = InputBox("State name:",, "Alaska")
```
Displays a dialog box that shows "State name:" as the prompt, the project's name as the title, and "Alaska" in the input area. Assigns the user's response to a String variable named `state`.

```
Const InputPrompt As String = "Enter the rate:"
Const InputTitle As String = "Rate Entry"
rate = InputBox(InputPrompt, InputTitle, "0.0")
```
Displays a dialog box that shows the contents of the InputPrompt constant as the prompt, the contents of the InputTitle constant as the title, and "0.0" in the input area. Assigns the user's response to a String variable named `rate`.

**FIGURE 5.36**   How to use the InputBox function

In the syntax for the InputBox function, *prompt* is the message to display inside the dialog box, *title* is the text to display in the dialog box's title bar, and *defaultResponse* is the text you want displayed in the input area of the dialog box. In the dialog box shown in Figure 5.35, "Enter the number of hours worked:" is the *prompt*, "Hours Entry" is the *title*, and "40" is the *defaultResponse*.

When entering the InputBox function in the Code Editor window, the *prompt*, *title*, and *defaultResponse* arguments must be enclosed in quotation marks, unless that information is stored in a String named constant or String variable. The Windows standard is to use sentence capitalization for the *prompt*, but book title capitalization for the *title*. The capitalization (if any) you use for the *defaultResponse* depends on the text itself.

Notice that the *title* and *defaultResponse* arguments are optional, as indicated by the square brackets in the syntax. If you omit the *title*, the project name appears in the title bar. If you omit the *defaultResponse* argument, a blank input area appears when the dialog box opens.

TIP

The InputBox function's syntax also includes *XPos* and *YPos* arguments, which allow you to specify the horizontal and vertical position of the dialog box on the screen. Both arguments are optional; if omitted, the dialog box appears centered on the screen.

A **function** is a predefined procedure that performs a specific task and then returns a value after completing the task. The task performed by the InputBox function is to display a dialog box. The value returned by the InputBox function depends on whether the user clicks the dialog box's OK button, Cancel button, or Close button. If the user clicks the OK button, the InputBox function returns the value contained in the input area of the dialog box; this value is always treated as a string. However, if the user clicks either the Cancel button in the dialog box or the Close button on the dialog box's title bar, the InputBox function returns an empty (or zero-length) string.

As mentioned earlier, you use the InputBox function, as well as the repetition structure, a counter, and an accumulator, in the Sales Express application.

## THE SALES EXPRESS APPLICATION

Assume that Sales Express wants an application that the sales manager can use to display the average amount the company sold during the prior year. The sales manager will enter the amount of each salesperson's sales. The application will use a counter to keep track of the number of sales amounts entered by the sales manager, and an accumulator to total the sales amounts. After all of the sales amounts are entered, the application will calculate the average sales amount by dividing the value stored in the accumulator by the value stored in the counter; it then will display the average sales amount on the screen. Figure 5.37 shows the pseudocode for a possible solution to the Sales Express problem.

---

### Pseudocode for the Sales Express application

1.  get a sales amount from the user  *(Priming read)*
2.  repeat while the user entered a sales amount
        if the sales amount can be converted to a number
                add 1 to the counter variable
                add the sales amount to the accumulator variable
        else
                display an appropriate message in a message box
        end if
        get a sales amount from the user
    end repeat
3.  if the counter variable contains a value that is greater than zero
        calculate the average sales amount by dividing the accumulator variable by the counter variable
        display the average sales amount in the averageLabel
    else
        display the number 0 in the averageLabel
    end if

**FIGURE 5.37**    Pseudocode for the Sales Express application

---

Step 1 in the pseudocode is to get a sales amount from the user. Step 2 is a pretest loop whose instructions are processed as long as the user enters a sales amount. The first instruction in the loop is a selection structure that checks whether the sales amount can be converted to a number. If it can be converted to a number, the counter variable is incremented by one and the accumulator variable is incremented by the sales amount; otherwise, an appropriate message is displayed in a message box.

After the selection structure within the loop is processed, the application requests another sales amount from the user. It then checks whether a sales amount was entered to determine whether the loop instructions should be processed again. When the user has finished entering sales amounts, the loop ends and processing continues with Step 3 in the pseudocode.

Step 3 in the pseudocode is a selection structure that checks whether the counter variable contains a value that is greater than zero. Before using a variable as the divisor in an expression, you always should verify that the variable does not contain the number zero because, as in math, division by zero is not mathematically possible. Dividing by zero in a program will cause the program to end abruptly with an error.

As Step 3 indicates, if the counter variable contains a value that is greater than zero, the average sales amount is calculated and then displayed in the averageLabel. Otherwise, the number zero is displayed in the averageLabel.

Notice that "get a sales amount from the user" appears twice in the pseudocode shown in Figure 5.37: immediately above the loop and also within the loop. The "get a sales amount from the user" entry that appears above the loop is referred to as the **priming read**, because it is used to prime (prepare or set up) the loop. In this case, the priming read gets only the first salesperson's sales amount from the user. Because the loop in Figure 5.37 is a pretest loop, the first value determines whether the loop instructions are processed at all. The "get a sales amount from the user" entry that appears within the loop gets the sales amounts for the remaining salespeople (if any) from the user.

Figure 5.38 shows the Visual Basic code for the Sales Express application, and Figures 5.39 and 5.40 show sample runs of the application.

```
' Project name:        Sales Express Project
' Project purpose:     The project calculates the average sales
'                      amount entered by the user.
' Created/revised by:  <your name> on <current date>

Option Explicit On
Option Strict On

Imports System.Globalization

Public Class MainForm

    Private Sub exitButton_Click(ByVal sender As Object, _
        ByVal e As System.EventArgs) Handles exitButton.Click
        Me.Close()
    End Sub

    Private Sub calcButton_Click(ByVal sender As Object, _
        ByVal e As System.EventArgs) Handles calcButton.Click
        ' calculates and displays the average sales amount

        Const Prompt As String = "Enter a sales amount. Click Cancel to end."
        Const Title As String = "Sales Entry"
```

*(Figure is continued on next page)*

```
        Dim inputSales As String
        Dim sales As Decimal
        Dim salesCounter As Integer
        Dim salesAccumulator As Decimal
        Dim salesAverage As Decimal
        Dim isConverted As Boolean

        ' get first sales amount
        inputSales = InputBox(Prompt, Title, "0")

        ' repeat as long as the user enters a sales amount
        Do While inputSales <> String.Empty
            ' try to convert the sales amount to a number
            isConverted = Decimal.TryParse(inputSales, NumberStyles.Currency, _
                    NumberFormatInfo.CurrentInfo, sales)
            ' if the sales amount can be converted to a number, then
            ' update the counter and accumulator; otherwise, display a message
            If isConverted = True Then
                salesCounter = salesCounter + 1
                salesAccumulator = salesAccumulator + sales
            Else
                MessageBox.Show("Please re-enter the sales amount.", _
                    "Sales Express", MessageBoxButtons.OK, _
                    MessageBoxIcon.Information)
            End If

            ' get the next sales amount
            inputSales = InputBox(Prompt, Title, "0")
        Loop

        ' if salesCounter is greater than 0, then calculate and
        ' display the average sales amount; otherwise, display 0 as
        ' the average sales amount
        If salesCounter > 0 Then
            salesAverage = salesAccumulator / Convert.ToDecimal(salesCounter)
            averageLabel.Text = salesAverage.ToString("C2")
        Else
            averageLabel.Text = "0"
        End If
    End Sub
End Class
```

**FIGURE 5.38**    Code for the Sales Express application

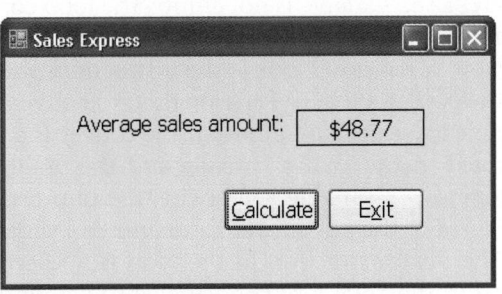

Dialog box created by the InputBox
function in the calcButton's Click
event procedure

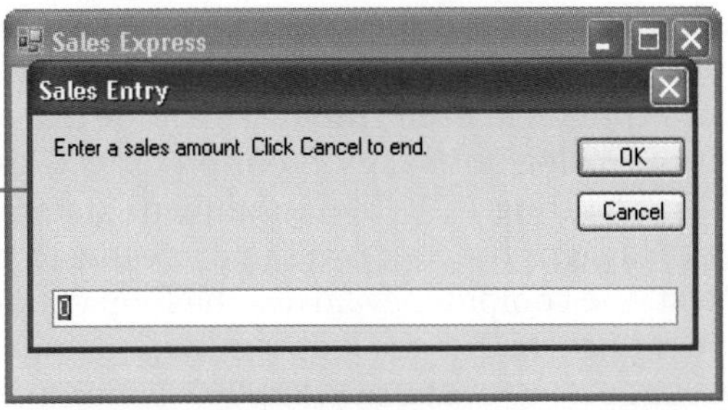

**FIGURE 5.39**     Sample run of the application showing the Sales Entry
dialog box

**FIGURE 5.40**     Sample run of the application showing the average
sales amount

The calcButton's Click event procedure declares two constants and six variables. The `Prompt` and `Title` constants are used as arguments in the InputBox function, and the `inputSales` variable is used to store the sales amount returned by the function as a String. The `sales` and `isConverted` variables are used by the TryParse method. The `sales` variable will store the sales amount after it has been converted to Decimal, and the `isConverted` variable will store a Boolean value that indicates whether the conversion was successful. The `salesCounter` variable is the counter variable that will keep track of the number of sales amounts entered. The `salesAccumulator` variable is the accumulator variable that the computer will use to total the sales amounts. The remaining variable, `salesAverage`, will store the average sales amount after it has been calculated.

Recall that counters and accumulators must be initialized, or given a beginning value; typically, the beginning value is the number zero. Because the Dim statement automatically assigns a zero to Integer and Decimal variables when the variables are created, you do not need to enter any additional code to initialize the `salesCounter` or `salesAccumulator` variables. In cases where you need to initialize a counter or an accumulator to a value other than zero, you can do so either in the Dim statement that declares the variable or in an assignment statement. For example, to initialize the `salesCounter` variable to the number one, you could use either the declaration statement `Dim  salesCounter  As Integer = 1` or the assignment statement `salesCounter = 1` in your code. (To use the assignment statement, the variable must already be declared.)

After the variables are declared, the InputBox function in the code displays a dialog box that prompts the user to either enter a sales amount or click the Cancel button, which indicates that the user has no more sales amounts to enter. As you learned earlier, the value returned by the InputBox function depends on whether the user clicks the dialog box's OK button, Cancel button, or Close

button. In this case, if the user enters a sales amount and then clicks the OK button in the dialog box, the InputBox function returns (as a string) the sales amount contained in the input area of the dialog box. However, if the user clicks either the dialog box's Cancel button or its Close button, the function returns a zero-length string (""). The assignment statement that contains the InputBox function assigns the function's return value to the `inputSales` variable.

Next, the computer evaluates the loop condition in the Do...Loop statement to determine whether the loop instructions should be processed. In this case, the `inputSales <> String.Empty` condition compares the contents of the `inputSales` variable to the `String.Empty` value. As you learned in Chapter 3, the `String.Empty` value represents a zero-length, or empty, string. If the `inputSales` variable is empty, the loop condition evaluates to True and the computer processes the loop instructions. If, on the other hand, the `inputSales` variable is not empty, the loop condition evaluates to False and the computer skips over the loop instructions.

Now take a closer look at the instructions within the loop. The first instruction in the loop uses the TryParse method to convert the contents of the `inputSales` variable to a Decimal number. If the conversion is successful, the Decimal number is stored in the `sales` variable and the Boolean value True is assigned to the `isConverted` variable. Otherwise, the number zero and the Boolean value False are stored in the `sales` and `isConverted` variables, respectively.

The next instruction in the loop is a selection structure that uses the value stored in the `isConverted` variable to determine whether the loop instructions should be processed. If the `isConverted` variable does not contain the Boolean value True, the MessageBox.Show method in the selection structure's false path displays an appropriate message. However, if the `isConverted` variable does contain the Boolean value True, the two instructions in the selection structure's true path are processed. The first instruction, `salesCounter = salesCounter + 1`, updates the counter variable by adding a constant value of one to it. Notice that the counter variable, `salesCounter`, appears on both sides of the assignment operator. The statement tells the computer to add one to the contents of the `salesCounter` variable, and then place the result back in the `salesCounter` variable. The `salesCounter` variable's value will be incremented by one each time the loop is processed. The second instruction in the true path, `salesAccumulator = salesAccumulator + sales`, updates the accumulator variable by adding a sales amount to it. Notice that the `salesAccumulator` variable also appears on both sides of the assignment operator. The statement tells the computer to add the contents of the `sales` variable to the contents of the `salesAccumulator` variable, and then place the result back in the `salesAccumulator` variable. The `salesAccumulator` variable's value will be incremented by a sales amount, which will vary, each time the loop is processed.

The last instruction in the loop, `inputSales = InputBox(Prompt, Title, "0")`, displays a dialog box that prompts the user for another sales amount. Notice that the instruction appears twice in the code—before the Do...Loop statement and within the Do...Loop statement. Recall that the input instruction located above the loop is referred to as the priming read, and its task is to get only the first sales amount from the user. The input instruction located within the loop gets each of the remaining sales amounts (if any) from the user. If you forget to enter the input instruction within the loop, you will create an endless or infinite loop. You can stop an endless loop by clicking Debug on the menu bar, and then clicking Stop Debugging.

After the user enters another sales amount, the computer returns to the Do clause, where the loop condition is tested again. If the condition evaluates to True, the loop instructions are processed again. If the condition evaluates to False, the loop stops and the instruction after the Loop clause is processed.

The instruction after the Loop clause is a selection structure that determines whether the `salesCounter` variable contains a value that is greater than zero. Recall that before using a variable as the divisor in an expression, you first should verify that the variable does not contain the number zero, because division by zero is mathematically impossible and will cause the program to end with an error. In this case, if the `salesCounter` variable contains a value that is greater than zero, the computer processes the instructions in the selection structure's true path. The first instruction in the true path calculates the average sales amount and assigns the result to the `salesAverage` variable. The second instruction in the true path displays the contents of the `salesAverage` variable in the averageLabel. However, if the value in the `salesCounter` variable is not greater than zero, the computer processes the instruction in the selection structure's false path. The instruction in the false path displays the number zero in the averageLabel.

You have completed the concepts section of Chapter 5. The next section is the Programming Tutorial section, which gives you step-by-step instructions on how to apply the chapter's concepts to an application. A Programming Example follows the Programming Tutorial. The Programming Example is a completed program that demonstrates the concepts taught in the chapter. Following the Programming Example are the Quick Review, Key Terms, Self-Check Questions and Answers, Review Questions, Review Exercises – Short Answer, Computer Exercises, and Case Projects sections.

# PROGRAMMING TUTORIAL

## Creating the Car Race Game Application

In this tutorial, you create an application that simulates a race between two cars. The application allows the user to guess the race results by selecting an item from a list box. The list box items are "Tie", "Red car wins", "White car wins", and "No guess". The "No guess" item is provided in case the user does not want to make a guess. The application keeps track of the number of times the user guesses the correct race results, as well as the number of times the user selects an incorrect race result. The Car Race Game application's user interface is shown in Figure 5.41, and its TOE chart is shown in Figure 5.42. (The car image files that appear in the interface are part of the Microsoft Clip Art collection. You can view other image files at *http://office.microsoft.com/clipart*.)

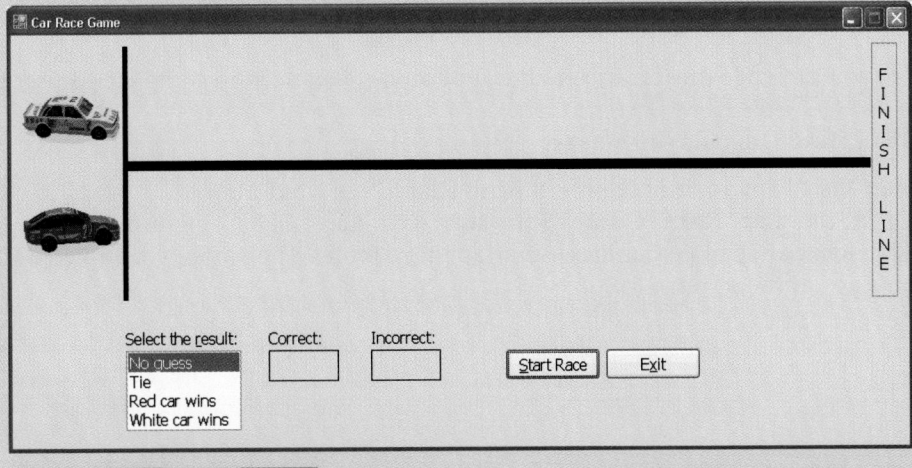

**FIGURE 5.41**   MainForm

| Task | Object | Event |
|------|--------|-------|
| 1. Fill the resultListBox with values<br>2. Select the first item in the list | MainForm | Load |
| End the application | exitButton | Click |
| Enable the raceTimer | startButton | Click |
| 1. Save the resultListBox selection<br>2. Disable the resultListBox to prevent the user from selecting during the race<br>3. Generate a random number for the white car and a random number for the red car<br>4. Use the random numbers to move the cars toward the finish line<br>5. When either or both cars have reached the finish line, disable the raceTimer and have the computer beep to indicate the end of the race<br>6. Display a message indicating that the race is over and the results of the race<br>7. Move the cars back to the starting line<br>8. Calculate and display the number of correct and incorrect guesses in the correctLabel and incorrectLabel<br>9. Enable the resultListBox | raceTimer | Tick |
| Display the white car image | whitePictureBox | None |
| Display the red car image | redPictureBox | None |
| Display the starting line | Label1 | None |
| Display the lane line | Label2 | None |
| Display the finish line | finishTextBox | None |
| Display the race result guesses | resultListBox | None |
| Display the number of correct guesses | correctLabel | None |
| Display the number of incorrect guesses | incorrectLabel | None |

**FIGURE 5.42**     TOE chart

## Completing the Car Race Game Interface

Before you can code the Car Race Game application, you need to complete its user interface.

**To complete the user interface:**

1. Start Visual Studio. If necessary, close the Start Page window.
2. Open the **Car Race Game Solution** (Car Race Game Solution.sln) file, which is contained in the VbReloaded\Chap05\Car Race Game Solution folder. The partially completed interface shown in Figure 5.43 appears on the screen.

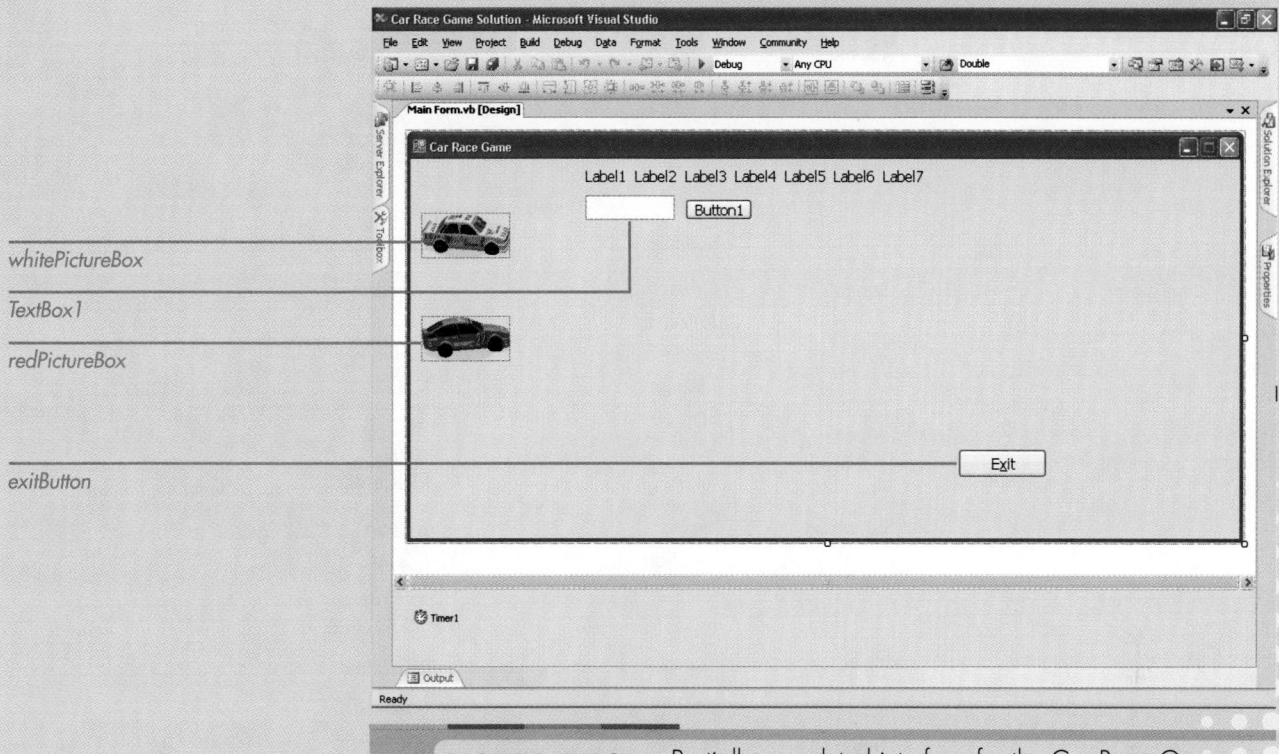

whitePictureBox

TextBox1

redPictureBox

exitButton

**FIGURE 5.43**    Partially completed interface for the Car Race Game application

3. Use the chart shown in Figure 5.44 to begin completing the user interface.

| Object | Property | Setting |
|---|---|---|
| Label1 | AutoSize<br>BackColor<br>Location<br>Size<br>Text | False<br>ControlText (on the System tab)<br>116, 12<br>5, 255<br>(empty) |
| Label2 | AutoSize<br>BackColor<br>Location<br>Size<br>Text | False<br>ControlText (on the System tab)<br>120, 127<br>779, 10<br>(empty) |
| Label3 | Location<br>Text | 116, 296<br>Select the &result: |
| Label4 | Location<br>Text | 265, 296<br>Correct: |
| Label5 | Location<br>Text | 371, 296<br>Incorrect: |
| *(Figure is continued on next page)* | | |

| Label6 | Name | correctLabel |
| --- | --- | --- |
| | AutoSize | False |
| | BorderStyle | FixedSingle |
| | Location | 267, 318 |
| | Size | 73, 31 |
| | Text | (empty) |
| | TextAlign | MiddleCenter |
| Label7 | Name | incorrectLabel |
| | AutoSize | False |
| | BorderStyle | FixedSingle |
| | Location | 373, 318 |
| | Size | 73, 31 |
| | Text | (empty) |
| | TextAlign | MiddleCenter |
| Button1 | Name | startButton |
| | Location | 514, 318 |
| | Size | 100, 31 |
| | Text | &Start Race |
| TextBox1 | Name | finishTextBox |
| | Location | 900, 12 |
| Timer | Name | raceTimer |
| | Enabled | False |
| | Interval | 100 |

**FIGURE 5.44**    Object, Property, Setting chart

4. The text "FINISH LINE" should appear in the finishTextBox, with each character in the text appearing on a separate line. Click the **finishTextBox** on the form, then set its Multiline property to **True**. Click **Text** in the Properties list, then click the Text property's **list arrow**. Press **Enter**, then do the following:

type **F** and press **Enter**
type **I** and press **Enter**
type **N** and press **Enter**
type **I** and press **Enter**
type **S** and press **Enter**
type **H** and press **Enter** twice
type **L** and press **Enter**
type **I** and press **Enter**
type **N** and press **Enter**
type **E** and press **Enter**

Figure 5.45 shows most of the text entered in the Text property.

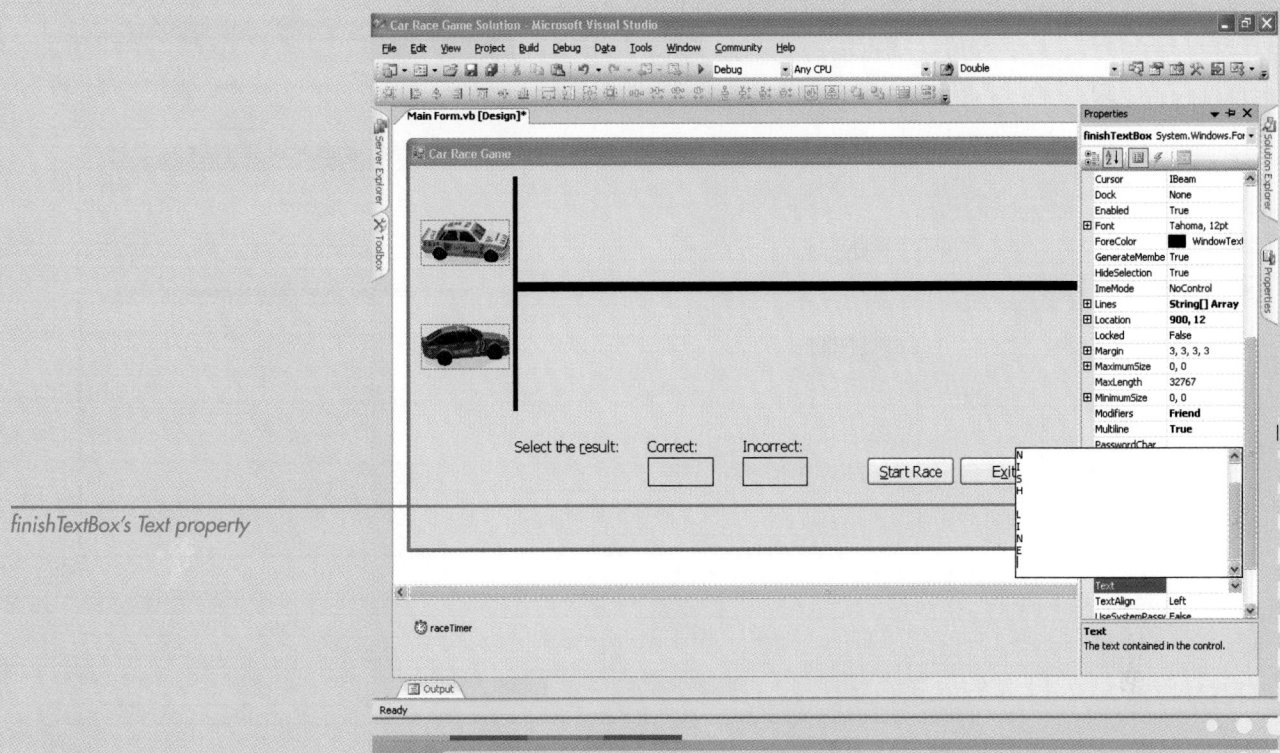

finishTextBox's Text property

**FIGURE 5.45**     Text entered in the finishTextBox's Text property

5. Click the **form** to close the Text property box.
6. Each character in the finishTextBox should be centered horizontally within the text box. Click the **finishTextBox**, then set its TextAlign property to **Center**.
7. The user should not be allowed to change the contents of the finishTextBox's Text property. Set the finishTextBox's ReadOnly property to **True**.
8. Set the finishTextBox's Size property to **27, 255**.
9. Click the **ListBox** tool in the toolbox, then drag a list box control to the form. Set the list box's properties as follows:

| | |
|---|---|
| Name | **resultListBox** |
| Location | **118, 318** |
| Size | **120, 80** |

10. Lock the controls on the form, then use Figure 5.46 to set the appropriate tab order.

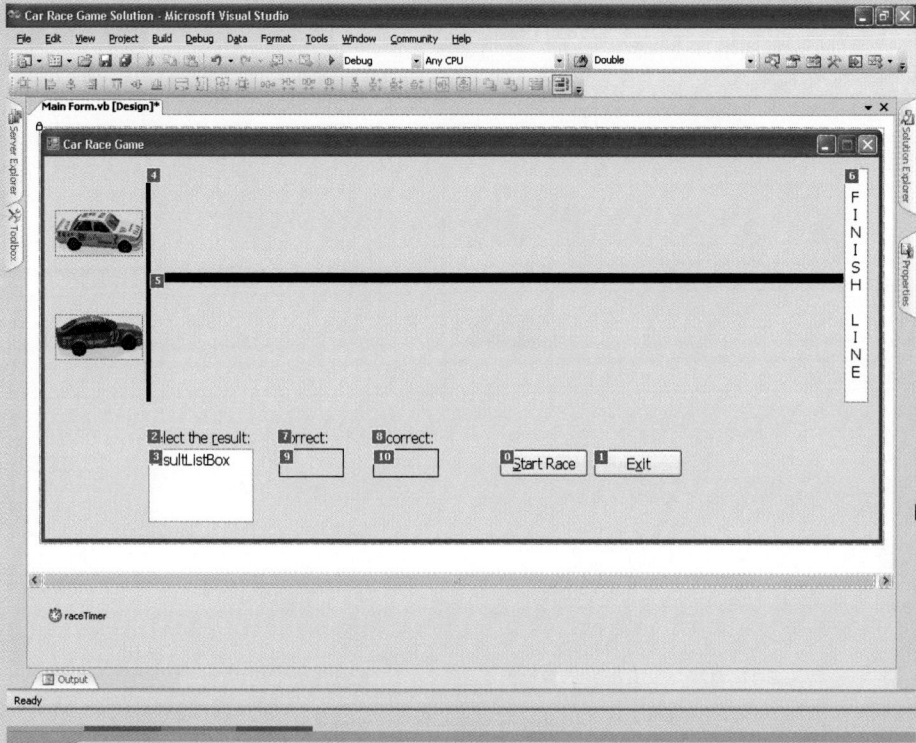

**FIGURE 5.46**    Tab order for the Car Race Game application

11. Press the **Esc** key to remove the tab order boxes, then save the solution.

Now that the interface is finished, you can begin coding the application.

### Coding the Car Race Game Application

According to the application's TOE chart (shown earlier in Figure 5.42), four event procedures need to be coded: the MainForm's Load event procedure, the Click event procedures for the exitButton and startButton, and the Tick event procedure for the raceTimer.

**To begin coding the application:**

1. Open the Code Editor window, which already contains the appropriate comments and Option statements. It also contains the code for the exitButton's Click event procedure.
2. Replace the <your name> and <current date> text in the comments with your name and the current date.

The first procedure you will code is the MainForm's Load event procedure. The procedure is responsible for displaying the items in the resultListBox and also selecting the first item.

3. Open the code template for the MainForm's Load event procedure, then enter the comment and code shown in Figure 5.47.

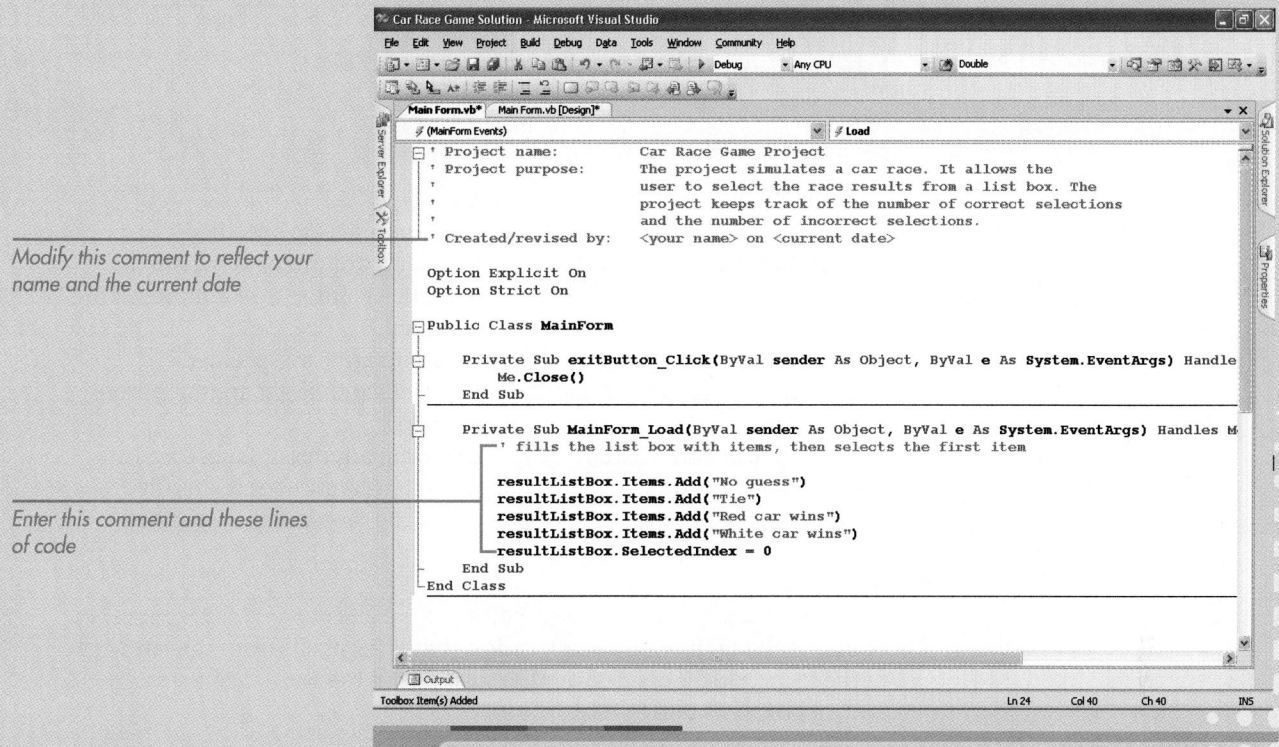

*Modify this comment to reflect your name and the current date*

*Enter this comment and these lines of code*

**FIGURE 5.47**   MainForm's Load event procedure

**HELP?**   To open the code template for the MainForm's Load event procedure, click (MainForm Events) in the Class Name box, then click Load in the Method Name box.

Next, you will code the startButton's Click event procedure. The procedure is responsible for enabling the raceTimer.

4.  Open the startButton's Click event procedure. Type **racetimer.enabled = true**.
5.  Save the solution.

Before you can code the raceTimer's Tick event procedure, you need to learn how to move a control while an application is running.

### Moving a Control While an Application Is Running

You can use the **SetBounds method** to change the location and/or size of a control while an application is running. Figure 5.48 shows the syntax of the SetBounds method. It also lists the values that you can enter in the method's *specified* argument. Additionally, the figure includes examples of using the method.

# HOW TO...

## Use the SetBounds Method

### Syntax
*control*.**SetBounds**(*x*, *y*, *width*, *height*, *specified*)

| *specified* values | Meaning |
|---|---|
| BoundsSpecified.All | all arguments are specified |
| BoundsSpecified.Height | the *height* argument is specified |
| BoundsSpecified.Location | the *x* (left) and *y* (top) arguments are specified |
| BoundsSpecified.None | no arguments are specified |
| BoundsSpecified.Size | the *width* and *height* arguments are specified |
| BoundsSpecified.Width | the *width* argument is specified |
| BoundsSpecified.X | the *x* (left) argument is specified |
| BoundsSpecified.Y | the *y* (top) argument is specified |

### Examples
```
carPictureBox.SetBounds(25, 50, 0, 0, BoundsSpecified.Location)
```
Positions the picture box at a location that is 25 pixels from the left edge of the form and 50 pixels from the top edge of the form. Leaves the picture box at its current size.

```
carPictureBox.SetBounds(25, 50, 0, 0, BoundsSpecified.All)
```
Positions the picture box at a location that is 25 pixels from the left edge of the form and 50 pixels from the top edge of the form. Changes the width and height of the picture box to zero pixels.

```
nameLabel.SetBounds(0, 0, 100, 0, BoundsSpecified.Width)
```
Leaves the label at its current location and current height. Changes the width of the label to 100 pixels.

```
cityTextBox.SetBounds(10, 0, 100, 0, BoundsSpecified.X Or
BoundsSpecified.Width)
```
Positions the text box at a location that is 10 pixels from the left edge of the form. Also changes the width of the picture box to 100 pixels. Leaves the text box at its current top location and current height.

**FIGURE 5.48**    How to use the SetBounds method

In the syntax, *control* is the name of the control whose location and/or size you want to change. You change the control's location by setting the SetBounds method's *x* and *y* arguments. The *x* argument specifies the location of the left edge of the control on the form, and the *y* argument specifies the location of the top edge of the control. In other words, the *x* argument indicates the control's horizontal location, while the *y* argument indicates its vertical location. You change the control's size by setting the SetBounds method's *width* and *height* arguments. The *x*, *y*, *width*, and *height* arguments are measured in pixels. A **pixel**, which is short for "picture element", is one spot in a grid of thousands of such spots that form an image produced on the screen by a computer or printed on a page by a printer.

When you do not want to change the location of either the left or top edge of a control, or when you do not want to change the control's height or width, you simply set the corresponding argument to the number zero. For example, to keep the control's left border at its current location, you set the *x* argument to 0. Similarly, to keep the control at its current size, you set both the *width* and *height* arguments to 0.

The *specified* argument in the SetBounds method indicates the arguments for which you are specifying a value. The *specified* argument can be one or more of the constants shown in Figure 5.48. For example, to indicate that you are specifying a value for the *height* argument only, you use the BoundsSpecified.Height constant as the *specified* argument. To indicate that only the *y* (top) argument is being specified in the SetBounds method, you use the BoundsSpecified.Y constant as the *specified* argument. Finally, to indicate that you are specifying both the *x* and *width* arguments, you use the Or operator to combine two constants in the *specified* argument, like this: BoundsSpecified.X Or BoundsSpecified.Width.

Study closely the four examples shown in Figure 5.48. In the first example, carPictureBox.SetBounds(25, 50, 0, 0, BoundsSpecified.Location), the *specified* argument indicates that only the arguments pertaining to the picture box's location are being specified. Therefore, the method uses only the values appearing in the *x* and *y* arguments. The values position the carPictureBox at a location that is 25 pixels from the left edge of the form, and 50 pixels from the top edge of the form.

The second example in the figure is almost identical to the first example, except it uses the BoundsSpecified.All constant as the *specified* argument. The BoundsSpecified.All constant indicates that all of the arguments are being specified in the SetBounds method. Like the SetBounds method in the first example, the SetBounds method in the second example positions the carPictureBox at a location that is 25 pixels from the left edge of the form, and 50 pixels from the top edge of the form. Unlike the SetBounds method in the first example, however, the SetBounds method in the second example changes both the width and height of the picture box to zero pixels. A control with a width and height of zero pixels is not visible on the form.

In the third example shown in Figure 5.48, the nameLabel.SetBounds(0, 0, 100, 0, BoundsSpecified.Width) method changes the width of the nameLabel to 100 pixels. The location and height of the nameLabel remain at their current values. In the fourth example, the cityTextBox.SetBounds(10, 0, 100, 0, BoundsSpecified.X Or BoundsSpecified.Width) method changes the location of the cityTextBox's left border, and also changes its width. The location of the cityTextBox's top border and its height remain at their current values.

You will use the SetBounds method in the raceTimer's Tick event procedure, which you code next.

### Coding the raceTimer's Tick Event Procedure

Figure 5.49 shows the pseudocode for the raceTimer's Tick event procedure.

**Pseudocode**

1. assign the resultListBox selection to a variable
2. disable the resultListBox to prevent the user from making a selection during the race
3. determine a new location for the white car, moving it toward the finish line:
   calculate the new location for the white car by adding a random number from 0 through 10 (inclusive) to the current value stored in the whitePictureBox's Right property, and assign the result to an Integer variable named whiteNewLocation

   if the new location will put the white car beyond the finish line, assign the value stored in the finishLine variable to the whiteNewLocation variable

*(Figure is continued on next page)*

**Pseudocode**

4. determine a new location for the red car, moving it toward the finish line:
   calculate the new location for the red car by adding a random number from 0 through 10 (inclusive) to the current value stored in the redPictureBox's Right property, and assign the result to an Integer variable named redNewLocation

   if the new location will put the red car beyond the finish line, assign the value stored in the finishLine variable to the redNewLocation variable

5. use the whiteNewLocation and redNewLocation variables to move the cars to their new locations

6. if one or both cars are at the finish line
   disable the raceTimer

   repeat five times
      have the computer sound a beep to indicate the end of the race
   end repeat

   if both cars are at the finish line
      assign "Tie" to the raceResult variable
   else if the white car is at the finish line
      assign "White car wins" to the raceResult variable
   else
      assign "Red car wins" to the raceResult variable
   end if

   display the message "Race Over!" and the race results in a message box

   return the cars to the starting line

   if the user did not select "No guess" in the resultListBox
      if the user selected the correct race result
         add 1 to the number of correct guesses counter
      else
         add 1 to the number of incorrect guesses counter
      end if

      display the number of correct and incorrect guesses in the correctLabel and incorrectLabel, respectively
   end if

   enable the resultListBox
   end if

**FIGURE 5.49**   Pseudocode for the raceTimer's Tick event procedure

**To begin coding the raceTimer's Tick event procedure:**

1. Open the code template for the raceTimer's Tick event procedure. Enter the comments shown in Figure 5.50, then position the insertion point as shown in the figure.

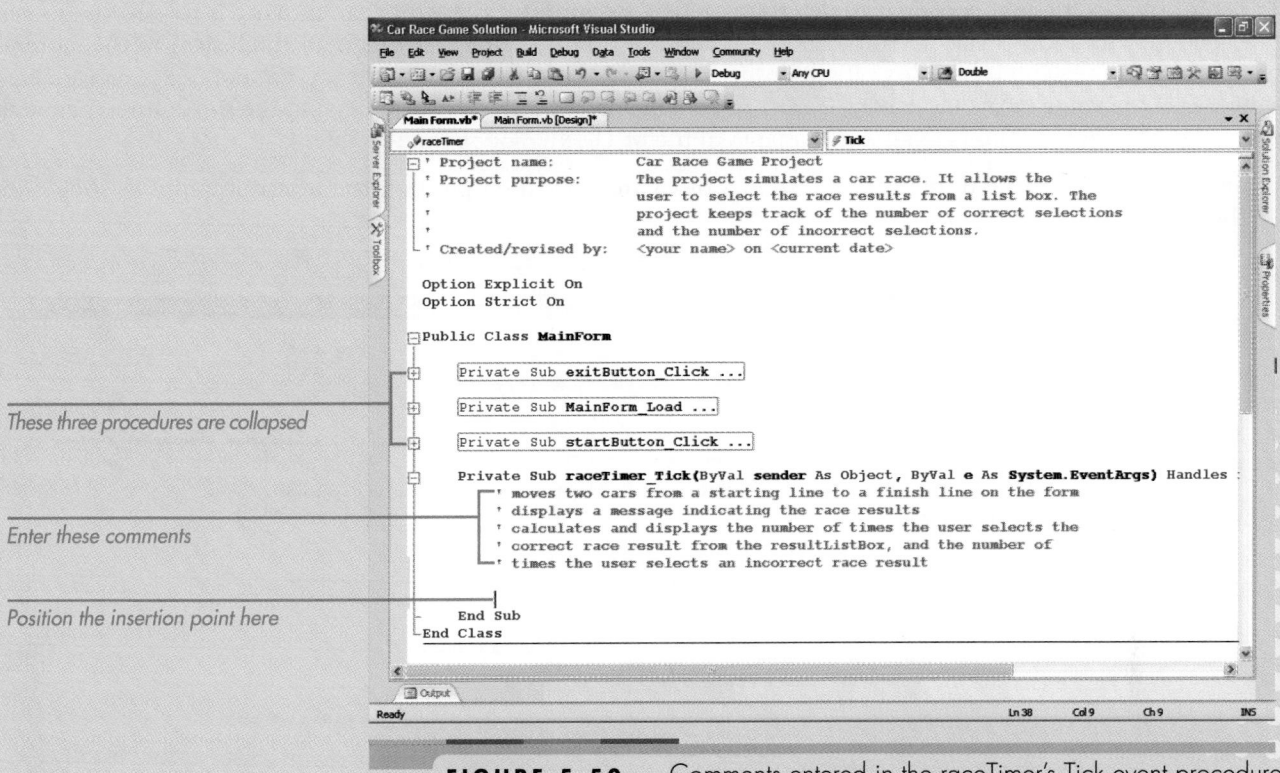

These three procedures are collapsed

Enter these comments

Position the insertion point here

**FIGURE 5.50**   Comments entered in the raceTimer's Tick event procedure

2. Enter the following Dim and Static statements. After typing the last Static statement, press **Enter** twice.
   **Dim randomGenerator As New Random**
   **Dim whiteNewLocation As Integer**
   **Dim redNewLocation As Integer**
   **Dim raceResult As String**
   **Dim userChoice As String**
   **Dim finishLine As Integer = finishTextBox.Left + 1**
   **Static numberCorrect As Integer**
   **Static numberIncorrect As Integer**

The randomGenerator variable will represent Visual Basic's pseudo-random number generator, which you learned about in Chapter 4. The whiteNewLocation and redNewLocation variables will store the new location for each car as it moves toward the finish line. The raceResult variable will store a string that indicates the result of the race. The string can be one of the following messages: "Tie", "White car wins", or "Red car wins". The userChoice variable will store the item that is selected in the resultListBox. The finishLine variable stores the location of the finish line, which is designated by the finishTextBox in the interface. In this case, because you want the winning car to cross over the finish line, the finishLine variable is assigned a value that is one number greater than the value stored in the finishTextBox's Left property. The numberCorrect and numberIncorrect variables are counter variables. The numberCorrect variable will keep track of the number of times the user guesses the race result correctly, and the numberIncorrect variable will keep track of the number of times the user makes an incorrect guess.

The first two steps in the pseudocode shown in Figure 5.49 are to assign to a variable the item selected in the resultListBox, and then disable the list box. You are disabling the list box to prevent the user from making a selection during the race.

3. Type **' save the user's list box selection, then disable the list box** and press **Enter**. Type **userchoice = resultlistbox.selecteditem.tostring** and press **Enter**. Type **resultlistbox.enabled = false** and press **Enter** twice.

The third step in the pseudocode is to determine a new location for the white car, moving it toward the finish line. The new location is calculated by adding a random number from 0 through 10 (inclusive) to the current value stored in the whitePictureBox's Right property. You will assign the sum to the whiteNewLocation variable. However, if the value in the whiteNewLocation variable will put the white car beyond the finish line, then you will assign the value in the finishLine variable to the whiteNewLocation variable.

4.  Enter the comments and lines of code shown in Figure 5.51, then position the insertion point as shown in the figure.

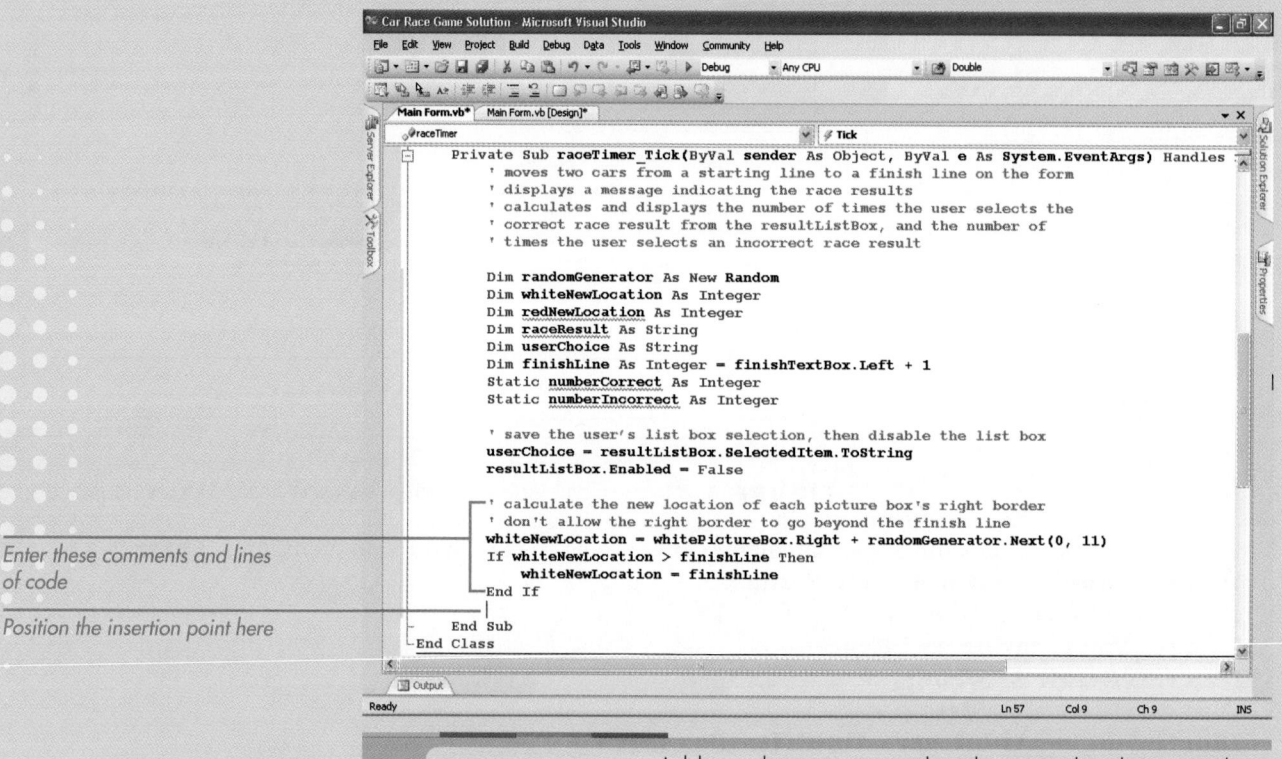

Enter these comments and lines of code

Position the insertion point here

**FIGURE 5.51**     Additional comments and code entered in the procedure

The fourth step in the pseudocode is to determine a new location for the red car, moving it toward the finish line. The new location is calculated by adding a random number from 0 through 10 (inclusive) to the current value stored in the redPictureBox's Right property. You will assign the sum to the redNewLocation variable. However, if the value in the redNewLocation variable will put the red car beyond the finish line, then you will assign the value in the finishLine variable to the redNewLocation variable.

5.  Type **rednewlocation = redpicturebox.right + randomgenerator.next(0, 11)** and press **Enter**.
6.  Enter the following selection structure, then position the insertion point two lines below the End If clause:

    **If redNewLocation > finishLine Then**
    **    redNewLocation = finishLine**
    **End If**

The fifth step in the pseudocode is to use the values stored in the whiteNewLocation and redNewLocation variables to move the two cars to their new locations. As you learned earlier, you can use the SetBounds method to move a control while an application is running. Recall that the method's *x* argument allows you to move a control horizontally by changing the location of the control's left border. The *y* argument allows you to move a control vertically by changing the location of the control's top border. In this case, you want to move each car horizontally, from the starting line to the finish line; therefore, you will use the *x* argument to set each picture box's left border.

The left border of each picture box control should be set to the difference between the new location for the control's right border and the width of the control. The new location for the whitePictureBox's right border is stored in the `whiteNewLocation` variable. The new location for the redPictureBox's right border is stored in the `redNewLocation` variable. You can use a control's Width property to determine its width.

7. Enter the comment and SetBounds methods shown in Figure 5.52, then position the insertion point as shown in the figure.

```
' calculate the new location of each picture box's right border
' don't allow the right border to go beyond the finish line
whiteNewLocation = whitePictureBox.Right + randomGenerator.Next(0, 11)
If whiteNewLocation > finishLine Then
    whiteNewLocation = finishLine
End If
redNewLocation = redPictureBox.Right + randomGenerator.Next(0, 11)
If redNewLocation > finishLine Then
    redNewLocation = finishLine
End If

' move each picture box toward the finish line
whitePictureBox.SetBounds(whiteNewLocation - whitePictureBox.Width, _
    0, 0, 0, BoundsSpecified.X)
redPictureBox.SetBounds(redNewLocation - redPictureBox.Width, _
    0, 0, 0, BoundsSpecified.X)

    End Sub
```

*Enter this comment and these lines of code*

*Position the insertion point here*

**FIGURE 5.52**    Comment and SetBounds methods entered in the procedure

Step 6 in the pseudocode is a selection structure that determines whether one or both cars are at the finish line.

8. Type ' **the following selection structure is processed only when at least** and press **Enter**. Type ' **one of the picture boxes is at the finish line** and press **Enter**.
9. Type **if whitepicturebox.right = finishline** _ and press **Enter**. Press **Tab**, then type **orelse redpicturebox.right = finishline then** and press **Enter**.
10. The first task in the selection structure's true path is to disable the raceTimer. Type ' **disable the timer** and press **Enter**, then type **racetimer.enabled = false** and press **Enter** twice.
11. Save the solution.

The second task in the true path is to have the computer sound a beep five times. You can use a repetition structure and the Console.Beep method to perform this task. The **Console.Beep method** plays the sound of a beep through the computer console speaker. Figure 5.53 shows the syntax of the Console.Beep method and includes examples of using the method.

## HOW TO...

### Use the Console.Beep Method

**Syntax**
**Console.Beep**([*frequency*, *duration*])

**Examples**
```
Console.Beep()
```
Sounds a beep through the computer console speaker.

```
Console.Beep(100, 25)
```
Sounds a beep through the computer console speaker. The beep has a frequency of 100 Hz and duration of 25 milliseconds.

**FIGURE 5.53**    How to use the Console.Beep method

The *frequency* and *duration* arguments are optional in the Console.Beep method's syntax. The *frequency* argument measures the frequency of the beep in Hertz (Hz) and must be an integer in the range of 37 through 32767. A Hertz is a unit of frequency of electrical vibrations and is named after Heinrich Hertz, who first detected electromagnetic waves. The *duration* argument is measured in milliseconds and must be an integer that is greater than zero.

**To finish coding the raceTimer's Tick event procedure:**

1. Type ' **sound a beep to indicate the end of the race** and press **Enter**, then enter the following repetition structure:
   **For x As Integer = 1 To 5**
   **    Console.Beep(100, 100)**
   **Next x**

The next task in the selection structure's true path is another selection structure. The nested selection structure should assign the appropriate message to the `raceResult` variable. Recall that the message indicates the outcome of the race.

2. Enter the comment and nested selection structure shown in Figure 5.54, then position the insertion point as shown in the figure.

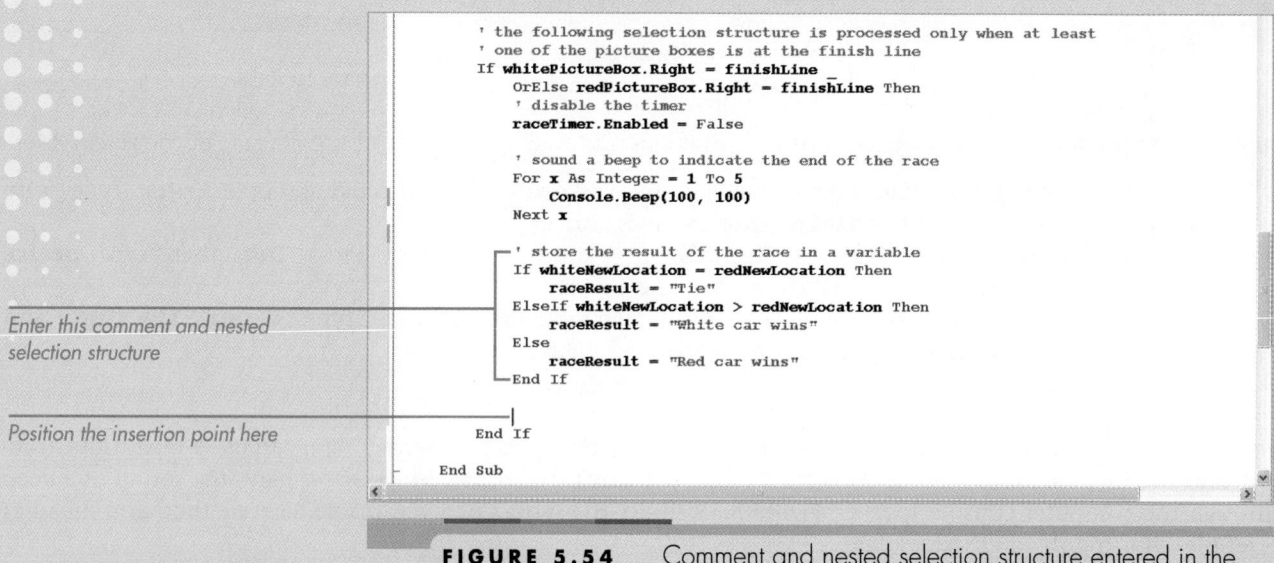

*Enter this comment and nested selection structure*

*Position the insertion point here*

**FIGURE 5.54**   Comment and nested selection structure entered in the procedure

3. The next task in the outer selection structure's true path is to display (in a message box) a message indicating the end of the race and also the race results. Type ' **display the race results** and press **Enter**. Type **messagebox.show("Race Over!" & controlchars.newline & raceresult, _** and press **Enter**. Press **Tab**, then type **"Car Race", messageboxbuttons.ok, messageboxicon.information)** and press **Enter** twice.
4. The next task is to return the cars to the starting line. Here again, you can use the SetBounds method to set the left border of each picture box. Type ' **move the picture boxes back to the starting line** and press **Enter**. Type **whitepicturebox.setbounds(12, 0, 0, 0, boundsspecified.x)** and press **Enter**. Type **redpicturebox.setbounds(12, 0, 0, 0, boundsspecified.x)** and press **Enter** twice.

The next task is a nested selection structure that determines whether the user chose the "No guess" option in the resultListBox. If the user did not select the "No guess" option, then the nested selection structure's true path updates the appropriate counter variable, and then displays the contents of each counter variable in the appropriate label control in the interface.

5. Enter the comments and selection structures shown in Figure 5.55, then position the insertion point as shown in the figure.

*Enter these comments and lines of code*

*Position the insertion point here*

```
                          ' display the race results
                          MessageBox.Show("Race Over!" & ControlChars.NewLine & raceResult, _
                              "Car Race", MessageBoxButtons.OK, MessageBoxIcon.Information)

                          ' move the picture boxes back to the starting line
                          whitePictureBox.SetBounds(12, 0, 0, 0, BoundsSpecified.X)
                          redPictureBox.SetBounds(12, 0, 0, 0, BoundsSpecified.X)

                          ' if the user did not want to guess the race results, then
                          ' don't update or display the counter values; otherwise,
                          ' compare the race results to the user's selection and update
                          ' the appropriate counter, then display both counter values
                          If userChoice <> "No guess" Then
                              If raceResult = userChoice Then
                                  numberCorrect = numberCorrect + 1
                              Else
                                  numberIncorrect = numberIncorrect + 1
                              End If
                              correctLabel.Text = Convert.ToString(numberCorrect)
                              incorrectLabel.Text = Convert.ToString(numberIncorrect)
                          End If

                      End If

                  End Sub
```

**FIGURE 5.55**    Comments and selection structures entered in the procedure

The last task in the outer selection structure's true path is to enable the resultListBox so that the user can make a selection before the next race.

6. Type **' enable the list box** and press **Enter**, then type **resultlistbox.enabled = true**.
7. Save the solution. Figure 5.56 shows the code for the Car Race Game application.

```
' Project name:        Car Race Game Project
' Project purpose:     The project simulates a car race. It allows the
'                      user to select the race results from a list box. The
'                      project keeps track of the number of correct selections
'                      and the number of incorrect selections.
' Created/revised by:  <your name> on <current date>

Option Explicit On
Option Strict On

Public Class MainForm

    Private Sub exitButton_Click(ByVal sender As Object, _
        ByVal e As System.EventArgs) Handles exitButton.Click
        Me.Close()
    End Sub

    Private Sub MainForm_Load(ByVal sender As Object, _
        ByVal e As System.EventArgs) Handles Me.Load
        ' fills the list box with items, then selects the first item
```

*(Figure is continued on next page)*

```
        resultListBox.Items.Add("No guess")
        resultListBox.Items.Add("Tie")
        resultListBox.Items.Add("Red car wins")
        resultListBox.Items.Add("White car wins")
        resultListBox.SelectedIndex = 0
End Sub

Private Sub startButton_Click(ByVal sender As Object, _
    ByVal e As System.EventArgs) Handles startButton.Click
    raceTimer.Enabled = True
End Sub

Private Sub raceTimer_Tick(ByVal sender As Object, _
    ByVal e As System.EventArgs) Handles raceTimer.Tick
    ' moves two cars from a starting line to a finish line on the form
    ' displays a message indicating the race results
    ' calculates and displays the number of times the user selects the
    ' correct race result from the resultListBox, and the number of
    ' times the user selects an incorrect race result

    Dim randomGenerator As New Random
    Dim whiteNewLocation As Integer
    Dim redNewLocation As Integer
    Dim raceResult As String
    Dim userChoice As String
    Dim finishLine As Integer = finishTextBox.Left + 1
    Static numberCorrect As Integer
    Static numberIncorrect As Integer

    ' save the user's list box selection, then disable the list box
    userChoice = resultListBox.SelectedItem.ToString
    resultListBox.Enabled = False

    ' calculate the new location of each picture box's right border
    ' don't allow the right border to go beyond the finish line
    whiteNewLocation = whitePictureBox.Right + randomGenerator.Next(0, 11)
    If whiteNewLocation > finishLine Then
        whiteNewLocation = finishLine
    End If
    redNewLocation = redPictureBox.Right + randomGenerator.Next(0, 11)
    If redNewLocation > finishLine Then
        redNewLocation = finishLine
    End If

    ' move each picture box toward the finish line
    whitePictureBox.SetBounds(whiteNewLocation - whitePictureBox.Width, _
        0, 0, 0, BoundsSpecified.X)
    redPictureBox.SetBounds(redNewLocation - redPictureBox.Width, _
        0, 0, 0, BoundsSpecified.X)
```

*(Figure is continued on next page)*

```vb
        ' the following selection structure is processed only when at least
        ' one of the picture boxes is at the finish line
    If whitePictureBox.Right = finishLine _
        OrElse redPictureBox.Right = finishLine Then
        ' disable the timer
        raceTimer.Enabled = False

        ' sound a beep to indicate the end of the race
        For x As Integer = 1 To 5
            Console.Beep(100, 100)
        Next x

        ' store the result of the race in a variable
        If whiteNewLocation = redNewLocation Then
            raceResult = "Tie"
        ElseIf whiteNewLocation > redNewLocation Then
            raceResult = "White car wins"
        Else
            raceResult = "Red car wins"
        End If

        ' display the race results
        MessageBox.Show("Race Over!" & ControlChars.NewLine & raceResult, _
            "Car Race", MessageBoxButtons.OK, MessageBoxIcon.Information)

        ' move the picture boxes back to the starting line
        whitePictureBox.SetBounds(12, 0, 0, 0, BoundsSpecified.X)
        redPictureBox.SetBounds(12, 0, 0, 0, BoundsSpecified.X)

        ' if the user did not want to guess the race results, then
        ' don't update or display the counter values; otherwise,
        ' compare the race results to the user's selection and update
        ' the appropriate counter, then display both counter values
        If userChoice <> "No guess" Then
            If raceResult = userChoice Then
                numberCorrect = numberCorrect + 1
            Else
                numberIncorrect = numberIncorrect + 1
            End If
            correctLabel.Text = Convert.ToString(numberCorrect)
            incorrectLabel.Text = Convert.ToString(numberIncorrect)
        End If

        ' enable the list box
        resultListBox.Enabled = True
    End If

    End Sub
End Class
```

**FIGURE 5.56**   Code for the Car Race Game application

Now that you have finished coding the application, you will test it to verify that it is working correctly.

**To test the Car Race Game application:**

1. Start the application. Click the **Start Race** button. Notice that when the picture boxes cross over the starting line, the line appears on top of the car images, as shown in Figure 5.57. You will fix that problem after the race ends.

**TIP** You can make the cars go faster by setting the raceTimer's Interval property, which is currently set at 100, to a smaller number.

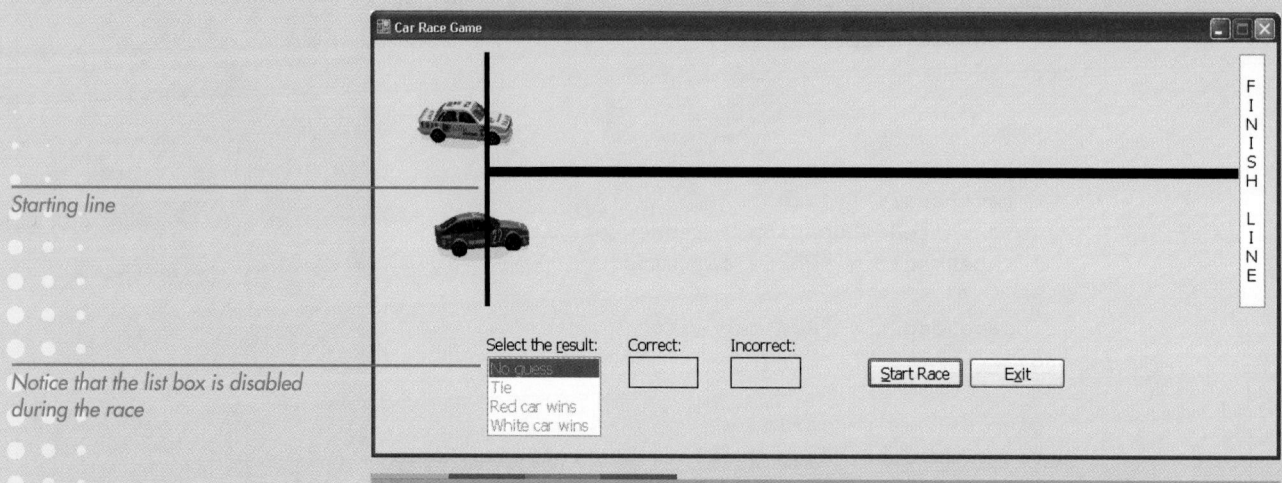

**FIGURE 5.57**      Starting line appears on top of the car images

When the race ends, you should hear several beeps. Additionally, a message box similar to the one shown in Figure 5.58 should appear. Because the application uses random numbers to control the race, your message box might say either "White car wins" or "Tie", rather than "Red car wins".

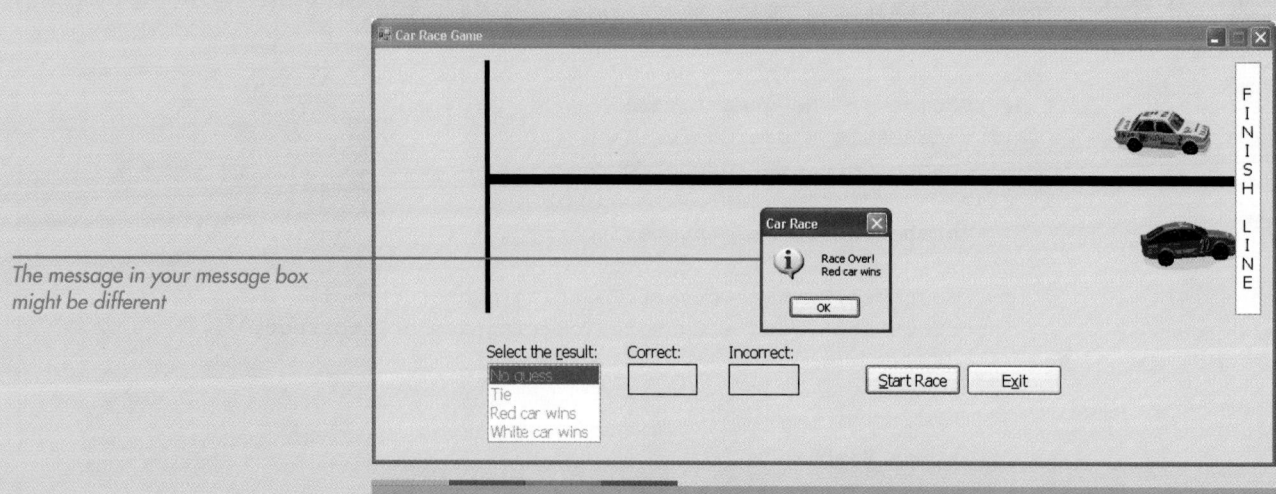

**FIGURE 5.58**      Message box that appears when the race is over

2. Click the **OK** button to close the message box. The raceTimer's Tick event procedure returns the cars to the starting line. It also enables the resultListBox.
3. Click the **Exit** button to end the application. If necessary, close the Output window.

Before testing the application again, you will fix the problem of the starting line appearing on top of the picture boxes.

**To have the picture boxes appear on top of the starting line, and then test the application again:**

1. Close the Code Editor window.
2. Right-click the **whitePictureBox** on the form, then click **Bring to Front**. Right-click the **redPictureBox** on the form, then click **Bring to Front**.
3. Save the solution, then start the application. Click the **Start Race** button. Notice that the car images now appear on top of the starting line, as shown in Figure 5.59.

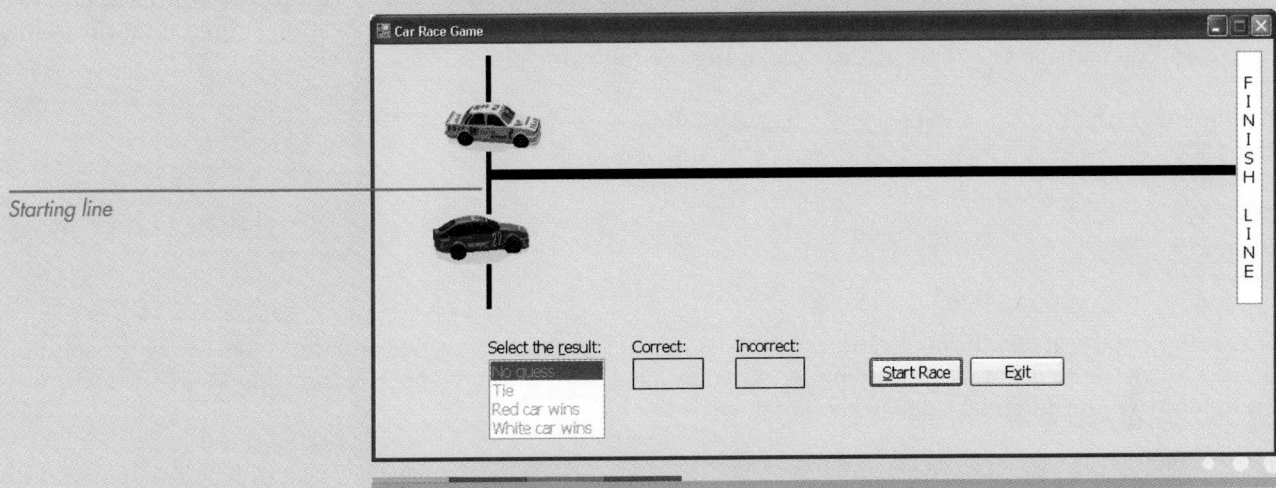

**FIGURE 5.59**     Car images now appear on top of the starting line

4. When the race ends, click the **OK** button to close the message box.
5. Click **Tie** in the list box, then click the **Start Race** button. When the race ends, click the **OK** button. The raceTimer's Tick event procedure updates the appropriate counter variable, and then displays the number of correct and incorrect guesses in the correctLabel and incorrectLabel, respectively. In Figure 5.60, the number 0 appears in the correctLabel and the number 1 appears in the incorrectLabel; this is because the race did not end in a tie. If your race did end in a tie, your correctLabel will show 1 and your incorrectLabel will show 0.

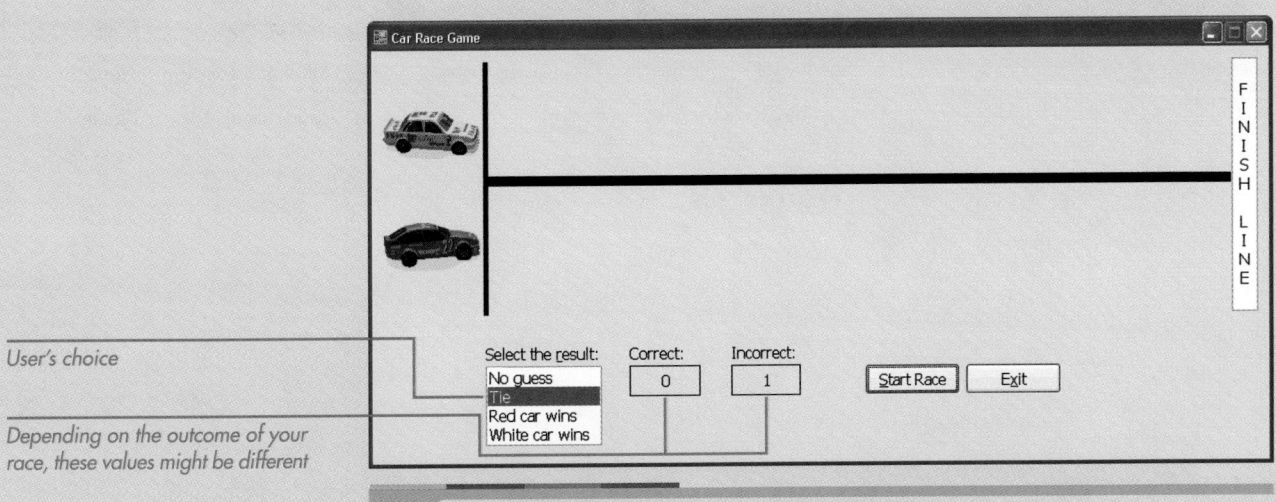

**FIGURE 5.60**     Number of correct and incorrect guesses shown in the interface

6. On your own, test the application several more times. When you are finished, click the **Exit** button to end the application. If necessary, close the Output window.
7. Close the solution.

# PROGRAMMING EXAMPLE

## Grade Calculator

Create a Visual Basic application that allows the user to enter the points a student earns on four projects and two tests. Each project is worth 50 points, and each test is worth 100 points. The application should total the points earned and then assign the appropriate grade, using the following chart:

| Total points earned | Grade |
|---|---|
| 360 – 400 | A |
| 320 – 359 | B |
| 280 – 319 | C |
| 240 – 279 | D |
| below 240 | F |

After assigning the grade, the application should display the total points earned and the grade. Name the solution Grade Calculator Solution. Name the project Grade Calculator Project. Name the form file Main Form.vb. Save the application in the VbReloaded\Chap05 folder.

**TOE Chart:**

| Task | Object | Event |
|---|---|---|
| 1. Get points earned on four projects and two tests<br>2. Display an appropriate message if the points earned cannot be converted to a number<br>3. Calculate the total points earned<br>4. Display the total points earned in the totalPointsLabel<br>5. Display the grade in the gradeLabel | assignButton | Click |
| End the application | exitButton | Click |
| Display the total points earned (from assignButton) | totalPointsLabel | None |
| Display the grade (from assignButton) | gradeLabel | None |

**FIGURE 5.61**

**User Interface:**

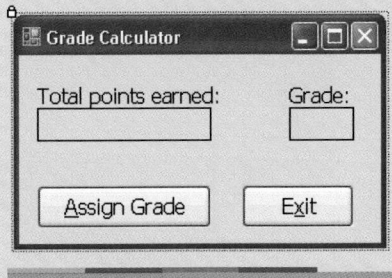

FIGURE 5.62

**Objects, Properties, and Settings:**

| Object | Property | Setting |
|---|---|---|
| Form1 | Name | MainForm |
| | Font | Tahoma, 12 point |
| | Size | 288, 176 |
| | StartPosition | CenterScreen |
| | Text | Grade Calculator |
| Label1 | Location | 12, 21 |
| | Text | Total points earned: |
| Label2 | Location | 207, 21 |
| | Text | Grade: |
| Label3 | Name | totalPointsLabel |
| | AutoSize | False |
| | BorderStyle | FixedSingle |
| | Location | 14, 40 |
| | Size | 135, 25 |
| | Text | (empty) |
| | TextAlign | MiddleCenter |
| Label4 | Name | gradeLabel |
| | AutoSize | False |
| | BorderStyle | FixedSingle |
| | Location | 209, 40 |
| | Size | 50, 25 |
| | Text | (empty) |
| | TextAlign | MiddleCenter |
| Button1 | Name | assignButton |
| | Location | 14, 98 |
| | Size | 135, 32 |
| | Text | &Assign Grade |
| Button2 | Name | exitButton |
| | Location | 173, 98 |
| | Size | 86, 32 |
| | Text | E&xit |

FIGURE 5.63

**Tab Order:**

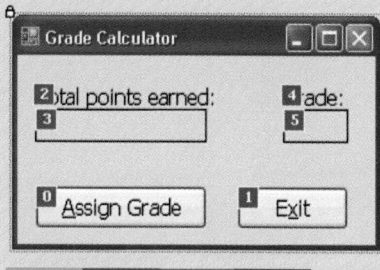

**FIGURE 5.64**

**Pseudocode:**

**exitButton Click event procedure**

1. close application

**assignButton Click event procedure**

1. repeat while the number of projects counter is less than 5
        get the points earned on the project
        if the points earned can be converted to a number
            add 1 to the number of projects counter
            add the project points to the total points accumulator
        else
            display an appropriate message in a message box
        end if
    end repeat
2. repeat while the number of tests counter is less than 3
        get the points earned on the test
        if the points earned can be converted to a number
            add 1 to the number of tests counter
            add the test points to the total points accumulator
        else
            display an appropriate message in a message box
        end if
    end repeat
3. assign the grade based on the total points earned value:
    >= 360        assign A as the grade
    >= 320        assign B as the grade
    >= 280        assign C as the grade
    >= 240        assign D as the grade
    < 240         assign F as the grade

4. display the total points earned in the totalPointsLabel
5. display the grade in the gradeLabel

## Code:

```
' Project name:        Grade Calculator Project
' Project purpose:     The project allows the user to enter the points a student
'                      earns on 4 projects and 2 tests. It then totals the
'                      points earned and displays the appropriate grade.
' Created/revised by:  <your name> on <current date>

Option Explicit On
Option Strict On

Public Class MainForm

    Private Sub exitButton_Click(ByVal sender As Object, _
        ByVal e As System.EventArgs) Handles exitButton.Click
        Me.Close()
    End Sub

    Private Sub assignButton_Click(ByVal sender As Object, _
        ByVal e As System.EventArgs) Handles assignButton.Click
        ' calculates the total points earned, then displays the total points
        ' earned and the appropriate grade

        Dim inputProjectPoints As String
        Dim inputTestPoints As String
        Dim grade As String
        Dim projectPoints As Integer
        Dim testPoints As Integer
        Dim totalPointsAccumulator As Integer
        Dim projectCounter As Integer = 1
        Dim testCounter As Integer = 1
        Dim isConverted As Boolean

        ' get and accumulate the project points
        Do While projectCounter < 5
            inputProjectPoints = InputBox("Enter the points earned on project " _
                & projectCounter, "Grade Calculator", "0")
            isConverted = Integer.TryParse(inputProjectPoints, projectPoints)
            If isConverted Then
                projectCounter = projectCounter + 1
                totalPointsAccumulator = totalPointsAccumulator + projectPoints
            Else
                MessageBox.Show("Please enter a number.", "Grade Calculator", _
                    MessageBoxButtons.OK, MessageBoxIcon.Information)
            End If
        Loop

        ' get and accumulate the test points
        Do While testCounter < 3
            inputTestPoints = InputBox("Enter the points earned on test " _
                & testCounter, "Grade Calculator", "0")
```

*(Figure is continued on next page)*

```
                isConverted = Integer.TryParse(inputTestPoints, testPoints)
            If isConverted Then
                testCounter = testCounter + 1
                totalPointsAccumulator = totalPointsAccumulator + testPoints
            Else
                MessageBox.Show("Please enter a number.", "Grade Calculator", _
                    MessageBoxButtons.OK, MessageBoxIcon.Information)
            End If
        Loop

        ' assign grade
        Select Case totalPointsAccumulator
            Case Is >= 360
                grade = "A"
            Case Is >= 320
                grade = "B"
            Case Is >= 280
                grade = "C"
            Case Is >= 240
                grade = "D"
            Case Else
                grade = "F"
        End Select

        'display the total points earned and the grade
        totalPointsLabel.Text = Convert.ToString(totalPointsAccumulator)
        gradeLabel.Text = grade
    End Sub
End Class
```

**FIGURE 5.65**

## Quick Review

- The three programming structures are sequence, selection, and repetition.
- The repetition structure, also called a loop, allows a program to repeatedly process one or more program instructions.
- A repetition structure can be either a pretest loop or a posttest loop.
- Depending on the loop condition, the instructions in a pretest loop may never be processed.
- The instructions in a posttest loop are always processed at least once.
- You can use the For...Next statement to code a pretest loop whose instructions you want processed a precise number of times.
- A variable declared in a For clause has block scope and can be used only by the For...Next loop.
- Typically, a hexagon is used in a flowchart to represent a repetition structure that is coded using the For...Next statement.
- The Financial.Pmt method calculates a periodic payment on either a loan or an investment.

- It is customary in Windows applications to highlight, or select, the existing text in a text box when the text box receives the focus. To do this, you enter the SelectAll method in the text box's Enter event procedure.
- When either the user or the application's code changes the text contained in a control, the control's TextChanged event occurs.
- A list box should contain a minimum of three selections.
- A list box should display a minimum of three selections and a maximum of eight selections at a time.
- Use a label control to provide keyboard access to a list box. Set the label control's TabIndex property to a value that is one number less than the list box's TabIndex value.
- You use the Items collection's Add method to add an item to a list box.
- List box items are either arranged by use, with the most used entries appearing first in the list, or sorted in ascending order.
- If a list box allows the user to make only one selection at a time, then a default item should be selected in the list box when the interface first appears. The default item should be either the item selected most frequently or the first item in the list.
- When an item is selected in a list box, the item appears highlighted in the list. The item's value is stored in the list box's SelectedItem property, and the item's index is stored in the list box's SelectedIndex property.
- When you select a different item in a list box, the list box's SelectedValueChanged and SelectedIndexChanged events occur.
- A list box's SelectedItem property and its SelectedIndex property can be used both to determine the item selected in the list box and to select a list box item from code.
- Combo boxes are similar to list boxes in that they allow the user to select from a list of choices. However, combo boxes also can have a text field.
- Three styles of combo boxes are available. The style is specified in a combo box's DropDownStyle property.
- You can use a combo box to save space in an interface.
- Use a label control to provide keyboard access to a combo box. Set the label control's TabIndex property to a value that is one number less than the combo box's TabIndex value.
- You use the Items collection's Add method to add an item to a combo box.
- Unlike a list box, a combo box has a Text property.
- A combo box's SelectedItem property contains the value of the item selected in the list portion of the combo box. A combo box's Text property contains the value that appears in the text portion of the combo box.
- You can use the Do...Loop statement to code either a pretest loop or a posttest loop.
- The *condition* used in the Do...Loop statement must evaluate to a Boolean value.
- When used in the Do...Loop statement, the keyword While indicates that the loop instructions should be processed *while* the condition is true. The keyword Until, on the other hand, indicates that the loop instructions should be processed *until* the condition becomes true.
- A diamond is used in a flowchart to represent the condition in a Do...Loop statement.
- You use a counter and/or an accumulator to calculate subtotals, totals, and averages.
- Counters and accumulators must be initialized and updated. The initialization is done outside of the loop that uses the counter, and the updating is done within the loop.

- The InputBox function displays a dialog box that contains a message, an OK button, a Cancel button, and an input area. The function returns a string.
- In the InputBox function, you should use sentence capitalization for the *prompt*, and book title capitalization for the *title*.
- Before using a variable as the divisor in an expression, you first should verify that the variable does not contain the number zero. Dividing by zero is mathematically impossible and will cause the program to end with an error.
- You can use a control's SetBounds method to move the control to a different location while an application is running. You also can use it to change the control's size while an application is running.
- The Console.Beep method allows you to play the sound of a beep through the computer console speaker.

## Key Terms

The **repetition structure** is also called a **loop**. You use a loop to repeatedly process one or more program instructions until some condition is met, at which time the loop ends.

In a **pretest loop**, the loop condition is evaluated before the instructions within the loop are processed.

In a **posttest loop**, the loop condition is evaluated after the instructions within the loop are processed.

The **For...Next statement** can be used to code a pretest loop whose instructions you want processed a precise number of times.

You can use the **Financial.Pmt method** to calculate a periodic payment on either a loan or an investment.

You can use the **SelectAll method** to select all of the text contained in a control.

A control's **Enter event** occurs when the user tabs to the control or uses the control's access key. It also occurs when the Focus method is used in code to send the focus to the control.

A control's **TextChanged event** occurs when a change is made to the text contained in the control's Text property.

You use the **ListBox tool** to add a list box to an interface.

A **list box** allows you to display a list of choices from which the user can select zero choices, one choice, or more than one choice.

The items in a list box belong to the **Items collection**.

A **collection** is a group of one or more individual objects treated as one unit. A unique number called an **index** identifies each item in a collection.

You use the Items collection's **Add method** to specify the items you want displayed in a list box.

The **default list box item** is the item that is automatically selected when the interface first appears.

A list box's **SelectedValueChanged** and **SelectedIndexChanged events** occur when a different value is selected in a list box.

You use the **ComboBox tool** to add a combo box to an interface.

Like a list box, a **combo box** allows the user to select from a list of choices. However, a combo box also can have a text field that allows the user to enter an item.

The **Do...Loop statement** can be used to code both a pretest loop and a posttest loop.

A **counter** is a numeric variable used for counting something and allows you to answer the question "How many?".

An **accumulator** is a numeric variable used for accumulating (adding together) something and allows you to answer the question "How much?".

**Initializing** means to assign a beginning value to a variable, such as a counter variable or an accumulator variable.

**Updating**, also called **incrementing**, means adding a number to the value stored in a counter or accumulator variable.

The **InputBox function** displays a dialog box that contains a message, OK and Cancel buttons, and an input area.

A **function** is a predefined procedure that performs a specific task and then returns a value after completing the task.

The **priming read** prepares the loop for processing.

The **SetBounds method** allows you to change the location and/or size of a control while an application is running.

A **pixel** is one spot in a grid of thousands of such spots that form an image produced on the screen by a computer or printed on a page by a printer. Pixel is short for "picture element."

You can use the **Console.Beep method** to play the sound of a beep through the computer console speaker.

## Self-Check Questions and Answers

1. A For...Next statement contains the following For clause: `For temp As Integer = 5 To 11 Step 2`. What value is stored in the `temp` variable when the For...Next statement ends?
   a. 11
   b. 12
   c. 13
   d. None of the above.

2. Which of the following calculates the monthly payment on a loan of $5,000 for two years at 4% interest? Payments are due at the end of the month and should be expressed as a positive number.
   a. `-Financial.Pmt(.04/12, 2 * 12, 5000)`
   b. `-Financial.Pmt(.04/12, 24, 5000)`
   c. `-Financial.Pmt(.04/12, 2 * 12, 5000, 0, DueDate.EndOfPeriod)`
   d. All of the above.

3. You use the _____ method to add items to a list box or combo box.
   a. Add
   b. AddList
   c. Item
   d. ItemAdd

4. The items in a list box or combo box belong to the _____ collection.
   a. Items
   b. List
   c. ListItems
   d. Values

5. Which of the following clauses stops the loop when the value in the `age` variable is less than the number zero?
   a. `Do While age >= 0`
   b. `Do Until age < 0`
   c. `Loop While age >= 0`
   d. All of the above.

6. Which of the following statements prompts the user for the name of a city, and then assigns the user's response to a String variable named `cityName`?
   a. `InputBox("Enter the city name:", "City", cityName)`
   b. `InputBox("Enter the city name:", cityName)`
   c. `cityName = InputBox("Enter the city name:", "City")`
   d. None of the above.

7. Which of the following statements can be used to change only the width and height of the nameLabel?
   a. `nameLabel.Bounds(0, 0, 50, 60, BoundsSpecified.Width And BoundSpecified.Height)`
   b. `nameLabel.Bounds(50, 60, 0, 0, BoundsSpecified.Width Or BoundSpecified.Height)`
   c. `nameLabel.SetBounds(0, 0, 50, 60, BoundsSpecified.Width And BoundSpecified.Height)`
   d. `nameLabel.SetBounds(0, 0, 50, 60, BoundsSpecified.Width Or BoundSpecified.Height)`

8. Which of the following plays a beep through the computer console's speaker?
   a. `Console.Beep()`
   b. `Console.DoBeep()`
   c. `Console.PlayBeep()`
   d. None of the above.

9. A text box's _____ property determines whether the user can enter data into the control.
   a. AccessOnly
   b. NoEdit
   c. OnlyRead
   d. ReadOnly

10. When a user tabs to a text box, the text box's _____ event occurs.
    a. Access
    b. Enter
    c. TabOrder
    d. None of the above.

Answers: 1) c, 2) d, 3) a, 4) a, 5) d, 6) c, 7) d, 8) a, 9) d, 10) b

## Review Questions

1. Which of the following flowchart symbols represents the condition in a Do...Loop statement?
   a. diamond
   b. hexagon
   c. parallelogram
   d. rectangle

2. How many times will the MessageBox.Show method in the following code be processed?
```
For counter As Integer = 4 To 11 Step 2
        MessageBox.Show("Hello")
Next counter
```
   a. 3
   b. 4
   c. 5
   d. 8

3. What is the value stored in the counter variable when the loop in Question 2 stops?
   a. 10
   b. 11
   c. 12
   d. 13

4. Assume you know the precise number of times the loop instructions should be processed. You can use the _____ statement to code this loop.
   a. Do...Loop
   b. For...Next
   c. either a or b

5. The _____ loop processes the loop instructions at least once, whereas the _____ loop instructions might not be processed at all.
   a. posttest, pretest
   b. pretest, posttest

6. How many times will the MessageBox.Show method in the following code be processed?
```
Dim counter As Integer
Do While counter > 3
        MessageBox.Show("Hello")
        counter = counter + 1
Loop
```
   a. 0
   b. 1
   c. 3
   d. 4

7. How many times will the MessageBox.Show method in the following code be processed?

```
Dim counter As Integer
Do
        MessageBox.Show("Hello")
        counter = counter + 1
Loop While counter > 3
```

   a. 0
   b. 1
   c. 3
   d. 4

Refer to Figure 5.66 to answer Questions 8 through 11.

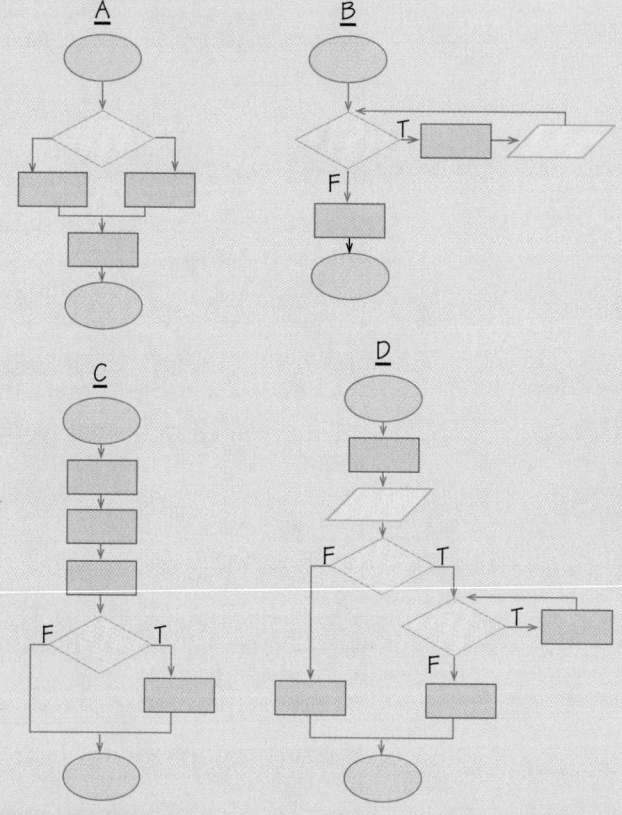

**FIGURE 5.66**

8. Which of the following programming structures are used in flowchart A in Figure 5.66? (Select all that apply.)
   a. sequence
   b. selection
   c. repetition

9. Which of the following programming structures are used in flowchart B in Figure 5.66? (Select all that apply.)
   a. sequence
   b. selection
   c. repetition

10. Which of the following programming structures are used in flowchart C in Figure 5.66? (Select all that apply.)
    a. sequence
    b. selection
    c. repetition

11. Which of the following programming structures are used in flowchart D in Figure 5.66? (Select all that apply.)
    a. sequence
    b. selection
    c. repetition

12. Assume a procedure allows the user to enter one or more values. The first input instruction will get the first value only and is referred to as the _____ read.
    a. entering
    b. initializer
    c. priming
    d. starter

13. Assume the InputBox function is used to display a dialog box. When the user clicks the Cancel button in the dialog box, the function returns _____.
    a. the number zero
    b. the empty string
    c. an error message
    d. None of the above.

14. Which of the following calculates the amount you need to save each month to accumulate $50,000 at the end of 10 years? The interest rate is 3% and deposits, which should be expressed as a positive number, are due at the beginning of the month.
    a. `-Pmt(.03/12, 10 * 12, 0, 50000, DueDate.BegOfPeriod)`
    b. `-Pmt(.03/12, 10 * 12, 50000, 0)`
    c. `Pmt(.03/12, 10 * 12, 50000, 0, DueDate.BegOfPeriod)`
    d. `-Pmt(.03/12, 120, 50000, 0, DueDate.BegOfPeriod)`

15. The _____ property stores the index of the item selected in a list box.
    a. Index
    b. SelectedIndex
    c. Selection
    d. SelectionIndex

16. Which of the following selects the "Cat" item, which appears third in the animalComboBox.
    a. `animalComboBox.SelectedIndex = 2`
    b. `animalComboBox.SelectedItem = "Cat"`
    c. `animalComboBox.Text = "Cat"`
    d. All of the above.

17. The _____ event occurs when the user selects a different item in a list box.
    a. SelectionChanged
    b. SelectedItemChanged
    c. SelectedValueChanged
    d. None of the above.

18. The _____ property stores the item that the user enters in the text portion of a combo box.
    a. SelectedItem
    b. SelectedValue
    c. Text
    d. TextItem

19. Which of the following updates an accumulator variable named `sumSales`?
    a. `sumSales = sumSales + sales`
    b. `sumSales = sales + sumSales`
    c. `sumSales = sumSales + 1`
    d. Both a and b.

20. Which of the following turns off a timer control named processTimer?
    a. `processTimer.Disabled = True`
    b. `processTimer.Enabled = False`
    c. `processTimer.Off = True`
    d. `processTimer.Status = False`

## Review Exercises – Short Answer

1. When processing the For...Next statement, the computer performs three tasks, as shown below. Put these tasks in their proper order by placing the numbers 1 through 3 on the line to the left of the task.
    _____ Adds the *stepvalue* to the *counter*.
    _____ Initializes the *counter* to the *startvalue*.
    _____ Checks whether the value in the *counter* is greater (less) than the *endvalue*.

2. Create a chart (similar to the one shown earlier in Figure 5.3) that lists the processing steps for the code shown in the second example in Figure 5.1.

3. Write a Visual Basic Do clause that processes the loop instructions as long as the value in the `quantity` variable is greater than the number 0. Use the `While` keyword.

4. Rewrite the Do clause from Exercise 3 using the `Until` keyword.

5. Write a Visual Basic Do clause that stops the loop when the value in the `inStock` variable is less than or equal to the value in the `reorder` variable. Use the `Until` keyword.

6. Rewrite the Do clause from Exercise 5 using the `While` keyword.

7. Write a Visual Basic Loop clause that processes the loop instructions as long as the value in the `letter` variable is either Y or y. Use the `While` keyword.

8. Rewrite the Loop clause from Exercise 7 using the `Until` keyword.

9. Write a Visual Basic Do clause that processes the loop instructions as long as the value in the `empName` variable is not "Done" (in any case). Use the `While` keyword.

10. Rewrite the Do clause from Exercise 9 using the `Until` keyword.

11. Write a Visual Basic assignment statement that updates the `quantity` counter variable by 2.

12. Write a Visual Basic assignment statement that updates the `total` counter variable by –3.

13. Write a Visual Basic assignment statement that updates the `totalPurchases` accumulator variable by the value stored in the `purchases` variable.

14. Write a Visual Basic assignment statement that subtracts the contents of the `salesReturns` variable from the `sales` accumulator variable.

15. What will the following code display in message boxes?
```
Dim x As Integer
Do While x < 5
    MessageBox.Show(Convert.ToString(x))
    x = x + 1
Loop
```

16. What will the following code display in message boxes?
```
Dim x As Integer
Do
    MessageBox.Show(Convert.ToString(x))
    x = x + 1
Loop Until x > 5
```

17. An instruction is missing from the following code. What is the missing instruction and where does it belong in the code?
```
Dim number As Integer = 1
Do While number < 5
    MessageBox.Show(number.ToString)
Loop
```

18. An instruction is missing from the following code. What is the missing instruction and where does it belong in the code?
```
Dim number As Integer = 10
Do
    MessageBox.Show(number.ToString)
Loop Until number = 0
```

19. What will the following code display in message boxes?
```
Dim totalEmp As Integer
Do While totalEmp <= 5
    MessageBox.Show(totalEmp.ToString)
    totalEmp = totalEmp + 2
Loop
```

20. What will the following code display in message boxes?
```
Dim totalEmp As Integer = 1
Do
    MessageBox.Show(totalEmp.ToString)
    totalEmp = totalEmp + 2
Loop Until totalEmp >= 3
```

21. Write the Visual Basic code that corresponds to the flowchart shown in Figure 5.67. (Display the calculated results on separate lines in the resultsLabel control.)

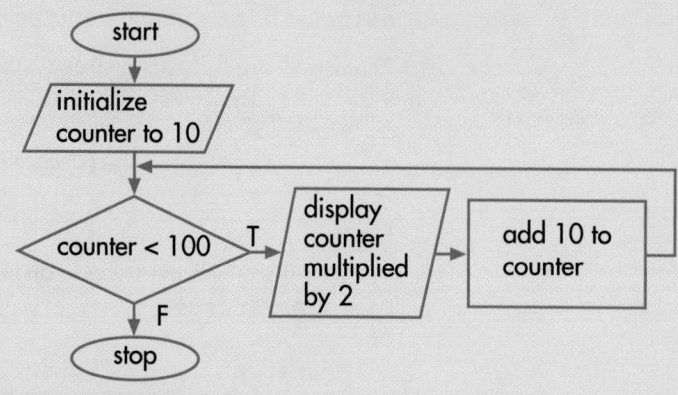

**FIGURE 5.67**

22. Write the Visual Basic statement that changes the size of the facePictureBox control to a width of 35 and a height of 50, and also changes the location of the control's left border to 10.

23. Write the Visual Basic statement that calculates the quarterly payment on a loan of $6,000 for three years at 9% interest. Payments are due at the beginning of the quarter and should be expressed as a negative number.

24. Write three different statements that you can use to select the first item in a combo box named deptComboBox. The first item is "Accounting."

25. Write the statement to select the existing text in the itemTextBox.

26. In the Monthly Payment Calculator application that you viewed in the concepts section of the chapter, why is it necessary to have the `paymentsLabel. Text = String.Empty` statement in both the calcButton's Click event procedure (shown in Figure 5.7) and the principalTextBox's TextChanged event procedure (shown in Figure 5.13)?

## Computer Exercises

1. In this exercise, you code three procedures that display the even integers between 1 and 9 in a label control.
   a. Open the Even Number Solution (Even Number Solution.sln) file, which is contained in the VbReloaded\Chap05\Even Number Solution folder.
   b. Code the For...Next button's Click event procedure so that it displays the even integers between 1 and 9 in the evenNumsLabel control; display each even integer on a separate line in the control. Use the For...Next statement.
   c. Code the Do...Loop Pretest button's Click event procedure so that it displays the even integers between 1 and 9 in the evenNumsLabel control; display each even integer on a separate line in the control. Use a pretest loop coded with the Do...Loop statement.

d. Code the Do...Loop Posttest button's Click event procedure so that it displays the even integers between 1 and 9 in the evenNumsLabel control; display each even integer on a separate line in the control. Use a posttest loop coded with the Do...Loop statement.

e. Save the solution, then start the application. Test each button in the interface.

f. Click the Exit button to end the application, then close the solution.

2. In this exercise, you code a procedure that displays the squares of the even integers from 2 through 12 in a label control.
   a. Open the Even Squares Solution (Even Squares Solution.sln) file, which is contained in the VbReloaded\Chap05\Even Squares Solution folder.
   b. Code the Display button's Click event procedure so that it displays the squares of the even integers from 2 through 12 in the squaresLabel control; display each square on a separate line in the control. Use the For...Next statement.
   c. Save the solution. Start and then test the application.
   d. Click the Exit button to end the application, then close the solution.

3. In this exercise, you code an application for Gwen Industries. The application calculates and displays the total sales and bonus amounts.
   a. Open the Gwen Solution (Gwen Solution.sln) file, which is contained in the VbReloaded\Chap05\Gwen Solution folder.
   b. Code the Calculate button's Click event procedure so that it allows the user to enter as many sales amounts as he or she wants to enter. Use the InputBox function to get the sales amounts. When the user has completed entering the sales amounts, the procedure should display the total sales in the totalSalesLabel control. It also should display a 10% bonus in the bonusLabel control.
   c. Save the solution, then start the application. Test the application using the following six sales amounts: 600.50, 4500.75, 3500, 2000, 1000, and 6500. Then test it again using the following four sales amounts: 75, 67, 88, and 30.
   d. Click the Exit button to end the application, then close the solution.

4. In this exercise, you code an application for Colfax Industries. The application calculates and displays the total company sales.
   a. Open the Colfax Solution (Colfax Solution.sln) file, which is contained in the VbReloaded\Chap05\Colfax Solution folder.
   b. Code the Add button's Click event procedure so that it adds the amount entered in the salesTextBox control to an accumulator variable, and then displays the contents of the accumulator variable in the totalSalesLabel control. Display the total sales with a dollar sign and two decimal places.
   c. Save the solution, then start the application. Test the application using the following sales amounts: 1000, 2000, 3000, and 4000.
   d. Click the Exit button to end the application, then close the solution.

5. In this exercise, you create an application for Premium Paper. The application allows the sales manager to enter the company's income and expense amounts. The number of income and expense amounts may vary each time the application is started. For example, the user may enter five income amounts and three expense amounts. Or, he or she may enter 20 income amounts and 30 expense amounts. The application should calculate and

display the company's total income, total expense, and profit (or loss). Use the InputBox function to get the individual income and expense amounts.

a. Name the solution Premium Solution. Name the project Premium Project. Save the application in the VbReloaded\Chap05 folder.

b. Design an appropriate interface. Use label controls to display the total income, total expenses, and profit (loss). Display the calculated amounts with a dollar sign and two decimal places. If the company experienced a loss, display the amount of the loss using a red font; otherwise, display the profit using a black font.

c. Code the application. Keep in mind that the income and expense amounts may contain decimal places.

d. Save the solution, then start the application. Test the application twice, using the following data:

First test:       Income amounts: 57.75, 83.23
                  Expense amounts: 200
Second test:   Income amounts: 5000, 6000, 35000, 78000
                  Expense amounts: 1000, 2000, 600

e. Stop the application, then close the solution.

6. In this exercise, you create an application that allows the user to enter a series of integers. The application then displays the sum of the odd integers and the sum of the even integers.

a. Build an appropriate interface. Name the solution SumOddEven Solution. Name the project SumOddEven Project. Save the application in the VbReloaded\Chap05 folder.

b. Code the application.

c. Save the solution, then start the application. Test the application using the following integers: 45, 2, 34, 7, 55, 90, and 32. The sum of the odd integers should be 107, and the sum of the even integers should be 158. Then test it again using the following integers: 5, 7, and 33.

d. Stop the application, then close the solution.

7. In this exercise, you create an application that allows the user to enter two integers. The application then displays all of the odd numbers between both integers and all of the even numbers between both integers.

a. Build an appropriate interface. Name the solution OddEven Solution. Name the project OddEven Project. Save the application in the VbReloaded\Chap05 folder.

b. Code the application.

c. Save the solution, then start the application. Test the application using the following integers: 6 and 25. The application should display the following odd numbers: 7, 9, 11, 13, 15, 17, 19, 21, and 23. It also should display the following even numbers: 8, 10, 12, 14, 16, 18, 20, 22, and 24. Then test it again using the following integers: 10 and 3.

d. Stop the application, then close the solution.

8. In this exercise, you modify this chapter's Programming Example.

a. Create the Grade Calculator application shown in this chapter's Programming Example. Save the application in the VbReloaded\Chap05 folder.

b. Modify the application so that it allows the user to display the grade for any number of students. Be sure to modify the TOE chart and pseudocode before modifying the code.

c. Save the solution, then start and test the application. Close the application, then close the solution.

9. In this exercise, you create an application that displays a shipping charge based on the state name selected in a list box.
   a. Create an appropriate interface, using a list box to display the following state names: Alabama, Georgia, Louisiana, and North Carolina. Name the solution Gentry Supplies Solution. Name the project Gentry Supplies Project. Save the application in the VbReloaded\Chap05 folder.
   b. Code the application using the following information:

   | State name | Shipping charge |
   | --- | --- |
   | Alabama | $20 |
   | Georgia | $35 |
   | Louisiana | $30 |
   | North Carolina | $28 |

   c. Save the solution, then start and test the application. Close the application, then close the solution.

10. In this exercise, you modify the application that you created in Computer Exercise 9. The modified application will use a combo box rather than a list box.
   a. Use Windows to make a copy of the Gentry Supplies Solution folder, which is contained in the VbReloaded\Chap05 folder. Rename the copy Modified Gentry Supplies Solution.
   b. Open the Gentry Supplies Solution (Gentry Supplies Solution.sln) file contained in the Modified Gentry Supplies Solution folder.
   c. Modify the application so that it uses a combo box rather than a list box to display the state names. Use the DropDown style.
   d. Also modify the application so that it displays the following message in a label control: "The shipping charge for *state* is *charge*.", where *state* is the name of the state selected or entered in the combo box, and *charge* is the shipping charge. If the user enters a state name that is not in the list portion of the combo box, the shipping charge should be $15.
   e. Save the solution, then start and test the application. Close the application, then close the solution.

11. In this exercise, you create an application that displays the telephone extension corresponding to the name selected in a list box. The names and extensions are shown here:

   | | |
   | --- | --- |
   | Smith, Joe | 3388 |
   | Jones, Mary | 3356 |
   | Adkari, Joel | 2487 |
   | Lin, Sue | 1111 |
   | Li, Vicky | 2222 |

   a. Open the Phone Solution (Phone Solution.sln) file, which is contained in the VbReloaded\Chap05\Phone Solution folder.
   b. The items in the list box should be sorted. Set the appropriate property.
   c. Code the form's Load event procedure so that it adds the five names shown above to the nameListBox. Select the first name in the list.
   d. Code the list box's SelectedValueChanged event procedure so that it assigns the item selected in the nameListBox to a variable. The procedure then should use the Select Case statement to display the telephone extension corresponding to the name stored in the variable.
   e. Save the solution, then start and test the application. Click the Exit button to end the application, then close the solution.

12. In this exercise, you modify the application that you created in Computer Exercise 11. The application will now assign the index of the selected item, rather than the selected item itself, to a variable.

    a. Use Windows to make a copy of the Phone Solution folder, which is contained in the VbReloaded\Chap05 folder. Rename the copy Modified Phone Solution.

    b. Open the Phone Solution (Phone Solution.sln) file contained in the Modified Phone Solution folder.

    c. Modify the list box's SelectedValueChanged event procedure so that it assigns the index of the item selected in the nameListBox to a variable. Modify the Select Case statement so that it displays the telephone extension corresponding to the index stored in the variable.

    d. Save the solution, then start and test the application. Click the Exit button to end the application, then close the solution.

13. In this exercise, you create an application that displays the first 10 Fibonacci numbers (1, 1, 2, 3, 5, 8, 13, 21, 34, and 55).

    a. Create an appropriate interface. Name the solution Fibonacci Solution. Name the project Fibonacci Project. Save the files in the VbReloaded\Chap05 folder.

    b. Code the application. Notice that, beginning with the third number in the series, each Fibonacci number is the sum of the prior two numbers. In other words, 2 is the sum of 1 plus 1, 3 is the sum of 1 plus 2, 5 is the sum of 2 plus 3, and so on. Display the numbers in a label control.

    c. Save the solution, then start and test the application. Close the application, then close the solution.

14. In this exercise, you create an application that displays a multiplication table similar to the one shown in Figure 5.68, where $x$ is a number entered by the user and $y$ is the result of multiplying $x$ by the numbers 1 through 9.

```
Multiplication Table
x * 1 = y
x * 2 = y
x * 3 = y
x * 4 = y
x * 5 = y
x * 6 = y
x * 7 = y
x * 8 = y
x * 9 = y
```

**FIGURE 5.68**

    a. Create an appropriate interface. Name the solution Multiplication Solution. Name the project Multiplication Project. Save the files in the VbReloaded\Chap05 folder.

    b. Code the application appropriately.

    c. Save the solution, then start and test the application. Close the application, then close the solution.

15. In this exercise, you create an application that allows the user to enter the gender (either F or M) and GPA for any number of students. The application should calculate the average GPA for all students, the average GPA for male students, and the average GPA for female students.

   a. Create an appropriate interface. Name the solution GPA Solution. Name the project GPA Project. Save the files in the VbReloaded\Chap05 folder.

   b. Code the application appropriately. Do not use the InputBox function in the application.

   c. Save the solution, then start and test the application. Close the application, then close the solution.

16. In this exercise, you learn how to create a list box that allows the user to select more than one item at a time.

   a. Open the Multi Solution (Multi Solution.sln) file, which is contained in the VbReloaded\Chap05\Multi Solution folder. The interface contains a list box named namesListBox. The list box's Sorted property is set to True, and its SelectionMode property is set to One.

   b. Open the Code Editor window. Notice that the form's Load event procedure adds five names to the namesListBox.

   c. Code the singleButton's Click event procedure so that it displays, in the resultLabel, the item selected in the namesListbox. For example, if the user clicks Debbie in the list box and then clicks the Single Selection button, the name Debbie should appear in the resultLabel.

   d. Save the solution, then start the application. Click Debbie in the list box, then click Ahmad, and then click Bill. Notice that, when the list box's SelectionMode property is set to One, you can select only one item at a time in the list.

   e. Click the Single Selection button. The name "Bill" appears in the resultLabel.

   f. Click the Exit button to end the application.

   g. Change the list box's SelectionMode property to MultiSimple. Save the solution, then start the application. Click Debbie in the list box, then click Ahmad, then click Bill, and then click Ahmad. Notice that, when the list box's SelectionMode property is set to MultiSimple, you can select more than one item at a time in the list. Also notice that you click to both select and deselect an item. (You also can use Ctrl+click and Shift+click, as well as press the Spacebar, to select and deselect items when the list box's SelectionMode property is set to MultiSimple.)

   h. Click the Exit button to end the application.

   i. Change the list box's SelectionMode property to MultiExtended. Save the solution, then start the application.

   j. Click Debbie in the list, then click Jim. Notice that, in this case, clicking Jim deselects Debbie. When a list box's SelectionMode property is set to MultiExtended, you use Ctrl+click to select multiple items in the list. You also use Ctrl+click to deselect items in the list. Click Debbie in the list, then Ctrl+click Ahmad, and then Ctrl+click Debbie.

   k. Next, click Bill in the list, then Shift+click Jim; this selects all of the names from Bill through Jim.

   l. Click the Exit button to end the application.
      As you know, when a list box's SelectionMode property is set to One, the item selected in the list box is stored in the SelectedItem property, and the item's index is stored in the SelectedIndex property. However, when a list box's SelectionMode property is set to either MultiSimple or MultiExtended, the items selected in the list box are stored (as strings) in

the SelectedItems property, and the indices of the items are stored (as integers) in the SelectedIndices property.

m. Code the multiButton's Click event procedure so that it first clears the contents of the resultLabel. The procedure should then display the selected names (which are stored in the SelectedItems property) on separate lines in the resultLabel.

n. Save the solution, then start the application.

o. Click Ahmad in the list box, then Shift+click Jim. Click the Multi-Selection button. The five names should appear on separate lines in the resultLabel.

p. Click the Exit button to end the application, then close the solution.

17. In this exercise, you learn how to use the Items collection's Insert, Remove, RemoveAt, and Clear methods. You also learn how to use the Items collection's Count property.

a. Open the Items Solution (Items Solution.sln) file, which is contained in the VbReloaded\Chap05\Items Solution folder.

b. The Items collection's Insert method allows you to add an item at a desired position in a list box or combo box while an application is running. The Insert method's syntax is *object*.**Items.Insert(***position*, *item***)**, where *position* is the index of the *item*. Code the Insert button's Click event procedure so it adds your name as the fourth item in the list box.

c. The Items collection's Remove method allows you to remove an item from a list box or combo box while an application is running. The Remove method's syntax is *object*.**Items.Remove(***item***)**, where *item* is the item's value. Code the Remove button's Click event procedure so it removes your name from the list box.

d. Like the Remove method, the Items collection's RemoveAt method also allows you to remove an item from a list box or combo box while an application is running. However, in the RemoveAt method you specify the item's index rather than its value. The RemoveAt method's syntax is *object*.**Items.RemoveAt(***index***)**, where *index* is the item's index. Code the Remove At button's Click event procedure so it removes the second name from the list box.

e. The Items collection's Clear method allows you to remove, or clear, all items from a list box or combo box while an application is running. The Clear method's syntax is *object*.**Items.Clear()**. Code the Clear button's Click event procedure so it clears the items from the list box.

f. The Items collections Count property stores the number of items in a list box or combo box. Code the Count button's Click event procedure so it displays the number of items in the list box.

g. Save the solution, then start and test the application. Click the Exit button to end the application, then close the solution.

18. In this exercise, you learn how to use the String Collection Editor dialog box to fill a list box with values.

a. Use Windows to make a copy of the Car Race Game Solution folder. Name the copy Modified Car Race Game Solution.

b. Open the Car Race Game Solution (Car Race Game Solution.sln) file contained in the Modified Car Race Game Solution folder.

c. Open the Code Editor window. Remove the four Add methods from the MainForm's Load event procedure. Also modify the comment. Close the Code Editor window.

d. Click the resultListBox on the form. Click the Items property in the Properties list, then click the ellipsis (...) button in the Settings box. The String Collection Editor dialog box opens.

e. Type the following four messages, pressing Enter after typing each one:
No guess
Tie
Red car wins
White car wins

f. Click the OK button to close the dialog box.

g. Save the solution, then start and test the application. Click the Exit button to end the application, then close the solution.

19. In this exercise, you find and correct an error in an application. The process of finding and correcting errors is called debugging.

a. Open the Debug Solution (Debug Solution.sln) file, which is contained in the VbReloaded\Chap05\Debug Solution folder.

b. Open the Code Editor window. Review the existing code.

c. Start and then test the application. Click the Exit button to end the application.

d. Correct any errors in the code.

e. Save the solution, then start and test the application again.

f. Click the Exit button to end the application, then close the solution.

## Case Projects

### Sonheim Manufacturing Company

Create an application that the company's accountant can use to calculate an asset's annual depreciation. The accountant will enter the asset's cost, useful life (in years), and salvage value (which is the value of the asset at the end of its useful life). Use a combo box to allow the user to select the useful life. Display the numbers from 3 through 20 in the list portion of the combo box, but allow the user to enter a number that is not on the list. The application should use the double-declining balance method to calculate the annual depreciation amounts, and then display the amounts in the interface. You can use the Financial.DDB method to calculate the depreciation. The method's syntax is **Financial.DDB**(*cost, salvage, life, period*). In the syntax, the *cost, salvage,* and *life* arguments are the asset's cost, salvage value, and useful life, respectively. The *period* argument is the period for which you want the depreciation amount calculated. The method returns the deprecation amount as a Double number. Figure 5.69 shows a sample depreciation schedule for an asset with a cost of $1,000, a useful life of 4 years, and a salvage value of $100.

| Year | Depreciation |
|---|---|
| 1 | 500.00 |
| 2 | 250.00 |
| 3 | 125.00 |
| 4 | 25.00 |

**FIGURE 5.69**

## Random Numbers Game

Create an application that allows the user to guess a random number generated by the computer. When the user makes an incorrect guess, the application should move an image either up or down, depending on how the guess compares to the random number. If the random number is greater than the user's guess, the application should move the image up to indicate that the user needs to guess a higher number. If the random number is less than the user's guess, the application should move the image down to indicate that the user needs to guess a lower number. The game ends when the user guesses the random number. However, the application should allow the user to stop the game prematurely. When that happens, the application should display the random number.

## Edmonton Bank

Create an application that allows the user to enter the amount a customer plans to deposit in a savings account at the end of each year. Assume that the bank is paying 10% interest, compounded annually and paid on the last day of each year. The application should calculate and display the value of the account at the end of 5 years, 10 years, 15 years, 20 years, 25 years, and 30 years. You can use the Financial.FV method to make the calculations. (The "FV" stands for "Future Value.") The syntax of the Financial.FV method is **Financial.FV(**Rate, NPer, Pmt[, PV, Due]**)**.

## Powder Skating Rink

Powder Skating Rink holds a weekly ice-skating competition. Competing skaters must perform a two-minute program in front of a panel of six judges. At the end of a skater's program, each judge assigns a score of zero through 10 to the skater. The manager of the ice rink wants an application that calculates and displays a skater's average score. Use list boxes to allow the user to select the names of the judges. (You will need to make up your own names to use.) Also use a list box to allow the user to select the score. After a judge's score has been recorded, remove his/her name from the list box. This will prevent the user from entering a judge's score more than once. (It might help to complete Computer Exercise 17 before coding this application.)

# String Manipulation and More Controls

- Determine the number of characters contained in a string
- Remove characters from a string
- Replace one or more characters in a string
- Insert characters within a string
- Search a string for one or more characters
- Access characters contained in a string
- Compare strings
- Include radio buttons in an interface
- Include check boxes in an interface

## MANIPULATING STRINGS IN VISUAL BASIC

Many times, an application will need to manipulate (process) string data. For example, an application may need to verify that an inventory part number begins with a specific letter to determine its location in the warehouse. Or, it may need to determine whether the last three characters in an employee number are valid. In this chapter, you learn several ways of manipulating strings in Visual Basic. You begin by learning how to determine the number of characters contained in a string.

## DETERMINING THE NUMBER OF CHARACTERS CONTAINED IN A STRING

If your application expects the user to enter a 10-digit phone number or a five-digit ZIP code, you should verify that the user entered the required number of characters. The number of characters contained in a string is stored in the string's **Length property**. Figure 6.1 shows the syntax of the Length property and includes several examples of using the property.

**HOW TO...**

### Use the Length Property of a String

**Syntax**
To determine the number of characters contained in a string:
   *string*.**Length**

**Examples**
```
Dim numChars As Integer
numChars = zipTextBox.Text.Length
```
assigns to the `numChars` variable the number of characters contained in the zipTextBox's Text property

```
Dim numChars As Integer
Dim fullName As String = "Paul Blackfeather"
numChars = fullName.Length
```
assigns the number 17 to the `numChars` variable

```
Dim phone As String
phone = InputBox("10-digit phone number:", "Phone")
Do Until phone.Length = 10
      phone = InputBox("10-digit phone number:", "Phone")
Loop
```
gets a phone number from the user until the number of characters contained in the phone number is equal to the number 10

```
Dim partNum As String
partNum = InputBox("Part number:", "Part Number")
If partNum.Length >= 4 Then
      instructions to process when the condition evaluates to True
```

*(Figure is continued on next page)*

```
Else
        instructions to process when the condition evaluates to False
End If
gets a part number from the user, and then determines whether the part
number contains at least four characters
```

**FIGURE 6.1**     How to use the Length property of a string

In the first example in Figure 6.1, the `numChars = zipTextBox.Text.Length` statement assigns to the `numChars` variable the number of characters contained in the zipTextBox's Text property. (Recall that the Text property of a control is treated as a string.) If the user enters the ZIP code 60111 in the zipTextBox, the statement assigns the number five to the `numChars` variable.

The `Dim fullName As String = "Paul Blackfeather"` statement in the second example assigns the string "Paul Blackfeather" to a String variable named `fullName`. The `numChars = fullName.Length` statement then uses the `fullName` variable's Length property to determine the number of characters contained in the variable, assigning the result to the `numChars` variable. In this case, the number 17 will be assigned, because the `fullName` variable contains 17 characters.

The pretest loop shown in the third example in Figure 6.1 processes the loop instruction, which prompts the user to enter a phone number, until the phone number entered contains 10 characters, at which time the loop ends. The code shown in the last example prompts the user to enter a part number, and stores the user's response in a String variable named `partNum`. The selection structure in the code then determines whether the `partNum` variable contains at least four characters.

Figure 6.2 shows the code for the ZIP Codes application, which uses the Length property to determine the number of characters contained in a ZIP code entered by the user. The If clause that contains the Length property is shaded in the code. If the ZIP code contains exactly five characters, it is added to the list box in the interface, as shown in the sample run in Figure 6.3; otherwise, an appropriate message is displayed.

**Visual Basic code**

```
' Project name:        Zip Codes Project
' Project purpose:     The project fills a list box with ZIP codes.
' Created/revised by:  <your name> on <current date>

Option Explicit On
Option Strict On

Public Class MainForm

    Private Sub addButton_Click(ByVal sender As Object, _
        ByVal e As System.EventArgs) Handles addButton.Click
        ' fills the list box with only 5-digit ZIP codes
```

*(Figure is continued on next page)*

```
        If zipTextBox.Text.Length = 5 Then
            zipListBox.Items.Add(zipTextBox.Text)
        Else
            MessageBox.Show("The ZIP code must contain 5 digits.", _
                "ZIP Codes", MessageBoxButtons.OK, _
                MessageBoxIcon.Information)
        End If

        zipTextBox.Focus()
    End Sub

    Private Sub zipTextBox_Enter(ByVal sender As Object, _
        ByVal e As System.EventArgs) Handles zipTextBox.Enter
        zipTextBox.SelectAll()
    End Sub

    Private Sub exitButton_Click(ByVal sender As Object, _
        ByVal e As System.EventArgs) Handles exitButton.Click
        Me.Close()
    End Sub
End Class
```

**FIGURE 6.2**     Code for the ZIP Codes application

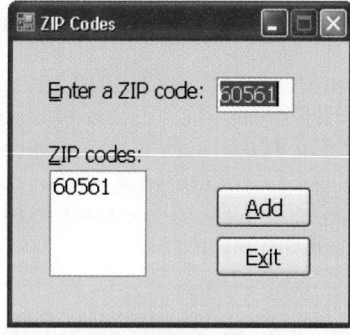

**FIGURE 6.3**     Sample run of the ZIP Codes application

## REMOVING CHARACTERS FROM A STRING

At times, you may need to remove one or more characters from an item of data entered by the user. For example, you may need to remove a percent sign from the end of a tax rate so that you can use the tax rate in a calculation. You can use the **TrimStart method** to remove one or more characters from the beginning of a string, and the **TrimEnd method** to remove one or more characters from the end of a string. To remove one or more characters from both the beginning and end of a string, you use the **Trim method**. Each method returns a string with the appropriate characters removed (trimmed). Figure 6.4 shows the syntax of the TrimStart, TrimEnd, and Trim methods and includes several examples of using each method.

# HOW TO...

## Use the TrimStart, TrimEnd, and Trim Methods

**Syntax**
To remove characters from the beginning of a string:
> *string*.**TrimStart**([*trimChars*])

To remove characters from the end of a string:
> *string*.**TrimEnd**([*trimChars*])

To remove characters from both the beginning and end of a string:
> *string*.**Trim**([*trimChars*])

**Examples**
```
Dim fullName As String
fullName = nameTextBox.Text.TrimStart()
```
assigns to the `fullName` variable the contents of the nameTextBox's Text property, excluding any leading spaces

```
nameTextBox.Text = nameTextBox.Text.TrimStart()
```
removes any leading spaces from the nameTextBox's Text property

```
Dim fullName As String
fullName = nameTextBox.Text.TrimEnd()
```
assigns to the `fullName` variable the contents of the nameTextBox's Text property, excluding any trailing spaces

```
Dim inputRate As String
Dim rate As String
inputRate = InputBox("Rate:", "Rate")
rate = inputRate.TrimEnd("%"c, " "c)
```
assigns to the `rate` variable the contents of the `inputRate` variable, excluding any trailing percent signs and spaces

```
nameTextBox.Text = nameTextBox.Text.Trim()
```
removes any leading and trailing spaces from the nameTextBox's Text property

```
Dim number As String
number = InputBox("Number:", "Number")
number = number.Trim("$"c, " "c, "%"c)
```
removes any leading and trailing dollar signs, spaces, and percent signs from the number variable

**FIGURE 6.4**    How to use the TrimStart, TrimEnd, and Trim methods

In each syntax, *trimChars* is a comma-separated list of characters that you want removed (trimmed) from the *string*. Notice that the *trimChars* argument is optional in each syntax. If you omit the *trimChars* argument, Visual Basic assumes that you want to remove one or more spaces from the beginning and/or end of the *string*. In other words, the default value for the *trimChars* argument is the space character (" ").

Study the examples shown in Figure 6.4. When processing the `fullName = nameTextBox.Text.TrimStart()` statement in the first example, the computer first makes a temporary copy of the string stored in the nameTextBox's Text property. It then removes any leading spaces from the temporary copy of the string, and assigns the resulting string to the `fullName` variable. If the user enters the string " Karen" (two spaces followed by the name Karen) in the nameTextBox, the statement assigns the name "Karen" to the `fullName` variable; however, the nameTextBox's Text property still contains " Karen" (two spaces followed by the name Karen). After the statement is processed, the computer removes the temporary copy of the string from its internal memory.

Notice that the `fullName = nameTextBox.Text.TrimStart()` statement does not remove the leading spaces from the nameTextBox's Text property. To remove the leading spaces from the Text property, you use the statement shown in the second example in Figure 6.4: `nameTextBox.Text = nameTextBox.Text.TrimStart()`.

When processing the `fullName = nameTextBox.Text.TrimEnd()` statement shown in the third example in Figure 6.4, the computer first makes a temporary copy of the string stored in the nameTextBox's Text property. It then removes any trailing spaces from the copied string, assigning the result to the `fullName` variable. After the statement is processed, the computer removes the copied string from its internal memory. If the user enters the string "Ned Yander    " (the name Ned Yander followed by four spaces) in the nameTextBox, the statement assigns the name "Ned Yander" to the `fullName` variable; however, the statement does not change the contents of the nameTextBox's Text property.

When processing the `rate = inputRate.TrimEnd("%"c, " "c)` statement shown in the fourth example in Figure 6.4, the computer first makes a copy of the string stored in the `inputRate` variable. It then removes any trailing percent signs and spaces from the copied string, and assigns the resulting string to the `rate` variable. For example, if the `inputRate` variable contains the string "3 %" (the number 3, a space, and a percent sign), the statement assigns the string "3" to the `rate` variable, but it does not change the value stored in the `inputRate` variable. Likewise, if the `inputRate` variable contains the string "15% " (the number 15, a percent sign, and two spaces), the statement assigns the string "15" to the `rate` variable, but leaves the contents of the `inputRate` variable unchanged. The letter c that appears after each string in the *trimChars* argument is one of the literal type characters you learned about in Chapter 3. Recall that a literal type character forces a literal constant to assume a different data type. In this case, the c forces each string in the *trimChars* argument to assume the Char (character) data type.

You can use the `nameTextBox.Text = nameTextBox.Text.Trim()` statement shown in the fifth example in Figure 6.4 to remove any leading and trailing spaces from the nameTextBox's Text property. Likewise, you can use the `number = number.Trim("$"c, " "c, "%"c)` statement shown in the last example to remove any leading and trailing dollar signs, spaces, and percent signs from the `number` variable.

Figure 6.5 shows the code for the City Names application, which uses the Trim method to remove any leading and trailing spaces from a city name entered by the user. The statement containing the Trim method is shaded in the figure. Figure 6.6 shows a sample run of the application.

**TIP**

The literal type characters are listed in Figure 3.5 in Chapter 3.

**Visual Basic code**

```vb
' Project name:        City Names Project
' Project purpose:     The project allows the user to add
'                      city names to a combo box.
' Created/revised by:  <your name> on <current date>

Option Explicit On
Option Strict On

Public Class MainForm

    Private Sub MainForm_Load(ByVal sender As Object, _
        ByVal e As System.EventArgs) Handles Me.Load
        ' fills the combo box with initial values

        cityComboBox.Items.Add("Chicago")
        cityComboBox.Items.Add("Nashville")
        cityComboBox.Items.Add("Atlanta")
        cityComboBox.SelectedIndex = 0

    End Sub

    Private Sub addButton_Click(ByVal sender As Object, _
        ByVal e As System.EventArgs) Handles addButton.Click
        ' trims any leading and trailing spaces from the
        ' city name before adding it to the combo box

        cityComboBox.Items.Add(cityComboBox.Text.Trim())
        cityComboBox.Focus()
    End Sub

    Private Sub exitButton_Click(ByVal sender As Object, _
        ByVal e As System.EventArgs) Handles exitButton.Click
        Me.Close()
    End Sub

End Class
```

**FIGURE 6.5**    Code for the City Names application

The city name entry contains leading and trailing spaces

The spaces are removed before the city name is added to the combo box

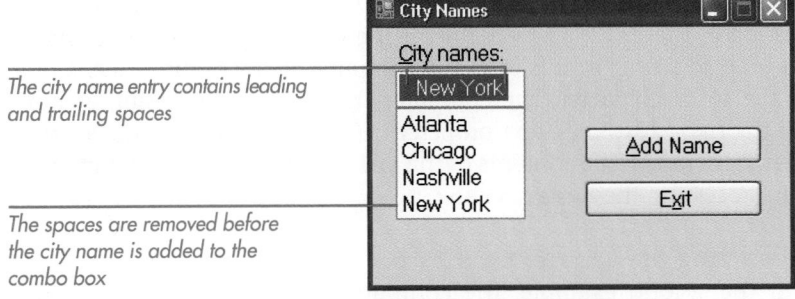

**FIGURE 6.6**    Sample run of the City Names application

## The Remove Method

Besides using the TrimStart, TrimEnd, and Trim methods, you also can use the Remove method to remove characters from a string. However, unlike the TrimStart, TrimEnd, and Trim methods, which remove characters from only the beginning and/or end of a string, the **Remove method** allows you to remove one or more characters located anywhere in a string. Figure 6.7 shows the syntax of the Remove method and includes several examples of using the method. Like the TrimStart, TrimEnd, and Trim methods, the Remove method returns a string with the appropriate characters removed.

**HOW TO...**

### Use the Remove Method

**Syntax**
To remove characters from anywhere in a string:
    *string*.**Remove**(*startIndex, count*)

**Examples**
```
Dim fullName As String = "John Cober"
nameTextBox.Text = fullName.Remove(0, 5)
```
assigns the string "Cober" to the nameTextBox's Text property

```
Dim fullName As String = "John"
nameTextBox.Text = fullName.Remove(2, 1)
```
assigns the string "Jon" to the nameTextBox's Text property

```
Dim fullName As String = "Janis"
fullName = fullName.Remove(3, 2)
```
assigns the string "Jan" to the fullName variable

**FIGURE 6.7**    How to use the Remove method

Each character in a string is assigned a unique number that indicates the character's position in the string; the number is called an **index**. The first character in a string has an index of zero; the second character has an index of one, and so on. In the Remove method's syntax, *startIndex* is the index of the first character you want removed from the *string*, and *count* is the number of characters you want removed. For example, to remove only the first character from a string, you use the number zero as the *startIndex*, and the number one as the *count*. To remove the fourth through eighth characters, you use the number three as the *startIndex*, and the number five as the *count*.

When processing the `nameTextBox.Text = fullName.Remove(0, 5)` statement shown in the first example in Figure 6.7, the computer makes a copy of the string stored in the `fullName` variable. It then removes the first five characters from the copied string; in this case, the computer removes the letters J, o, h, and n, and the space character. The computer then assigns the resulting string ("Cober") to the nameTextBox's Text property before removing the copied string from its internal memory. The contents of the `fullName` variable are not changed as a result of processing the `nameTextBox.Text = fullName.Remove(0, 5)` statement.

When processing the `nameTextBox.Text = fullName.Remove(2, 1)` statement in the second example, the computer makes a copy of the string stored in the `fullName` variable. It then removes one character, beginning with the character whose index is 2, from the copied string. The character with an index of 2 is the third character in the string—in this case, the letter h. The computer then assigns the resulting string ("Jon") to the nameTextBox's Text property. Here again, the statement does not change the string stored in the `fullName` variable.

You can use the `fullName = fullName.Remove(3, 2)` statement shown in the last example in Figure 6.7 to remove two characters, beginning with the character whose index is 3, from the string stored in the `fullName` variable. In this case, the letters i and s are removed, changing the contents of the `fullName` variable from "Janis" to "Jan".

Figure 6.8 shows the code for the Social Security application, which uses the Remove method to remove the dashes from a Social Security number. The statements containing the Remove method are shaded in the figure. Figure 6.9 shows a sample run of the application.

**Visual Basic code**

```
' Project name:        Social Security Project
' Project purpose:     The project removes the dashes
'                      from a social security number.
' Created/revised by:  <your name> on <current date>

Option Explicit On
Option Strict On

Public Class MainForm

    Private Sub exitButton_Click(ByVal sender As Object, _
        ByVal e As System.EventArgs) Handles exitButton.Click
        Me.Close()
    End Sub

    Private Sub removeButton_Click(ByVal sender As Object, _
        ByVal e As System.EventArgs) Handles removeButton.Click
        ' removes the dashes from a social security number

        Const message As String = _
            "The social security number must contain 11 characters."
        Dim socSecNumber As String

        socSecNumber = numberTextBox.Text

        If socSecNumber.Length = 11 Then
            socSecNumber = socSecNumber.Remove(3, 1)
            socSecNumber = socSecNumber.Remove(5, 1)
            numberLabel.Text = socSecNumber
        Else
            MessageBox.Show(message, "Social Security", _
                MessageBoxButtons.OK, MessageBoxIcon.Information)
        End If
```

*(Figure is continued on next page)*

```
            numberTextBox.Focus()
    End Sub
    Private Sub numberTextBox_Enter(ByVal sender As Object, _
        ByVal e As System.EventArgs) Handles numberTextBox.Enter
        numberTextBox.SelectAll()
    End Sub
End Class
```

**FIGURE 6.8**          Code for the Social Security application

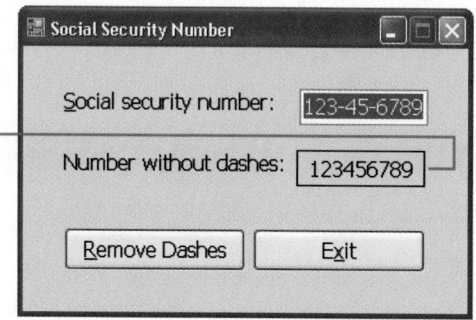

The dashes are removed from the Social Security number

**FIGURE 6.9**          Sample run of the Social Security application

At times, you may need to replace characters in a string, rather than just remove them.

## REPLACING CHARACTERS IN A STRING

You can use the **Replace method** to replace a sequence of characters in a string with another sequence of characters. For example, you can use the Replace method to replace area code "800" with area code "877" in a phone number. Or, you can use it to replace the dashes in a Social Security number with the empty string. Figure 6.10 shows the syntax of the Replace method and includes several examples of using the method.

**HOW TO...**          **Use the Replace Method**

**Syntax**
To replace all occurrences of a sequence of characters in a string with another sequence of characters:
        *string*.**Replace**(*oldValue*, *newValue*)

*(Figure is continued on next page)*

**Examples**
```
Dim name As String = "Mary James"
Dim newName As String
newName = name.Replace("James", "Smith")
```
assigns the string "Mary Smith" to the newName variable

```
Dim socialNum As String = "000-11-9999"
socialNum = socialNum.Replace("-", "")
```
assigns the string "000119999" to the socialNum variable

```
Dim word As String = "latter"
word = word.Replace("t", "d")
```
assigns the string "ladder" to the word variable

**FIGURE 6.10**    How to use the Replace method

In the syntax, *oldValue* is the sequence of characters that you want to replace in the *string*, and *newValue* is the replacement characters. The Replace method returns a string with all occurrences of *oldValue* replaced with *newValue*.

When processing the newName = name.Replace("James", "Smith") statement shown in the first example in Figure 6.10, the computer first makes a copy of the string stored in the name variable. It then replaces "James" with "Smith" in the copied string, and then assigns the result—in this case, "Mary Smith"—to the newName variable. If the name variable shown in the first example contained "James Jameston", the string "Smith Smithton" would be assigned to the newName variable, because the Replace method replaces all occurrences of *oldValue* with *newValue*.

In the second example, the socialNum = socialNum.Replace("-", "") statement replaces each dash (hyphen) in the string stored in the socialNum variable with a zero-length (empty) string. Replacing the dashes with the empty string is the same as removing the dashes, which was demonstrated earlier in Figure 6.8. The advantage of using the Replace method instead of the Remove method is that it takes one Replace method to remove both dashes, whereas it takes two Remove methods to accomplish the same task. After the statement in the second example is processed, the socialNum variable contains the string "000119999".

In the last example in Figure 6.10, the word = word.Replace ("t", "d") statement replaces each letter "t" in the string stored in the word variable with the letter "d". The statement changes the contents of the word variable from "latter" to "ladder".

Figure 6.11 shows the code for the modified Social Security application, which uses the Replace method to replace the dashes in a Social Security number with the empty string. The statement containing the Replace method is shaded in the figure. Figure 6.12 shows a sample run of the application.

**Visual Basic code**

```vb
' Project name:          Social Security Project
' Project purpose:       The project replaces, with the empty
'                        string, the dashes in a social
'                        security number.
' Created/revised by:    <your name> on <current date>

Option Explicit On
Option Strict On

Public Class MainForm

    Private Sub exitButton_Click(ByVal sender As Object, _
        ByVal e As System.EventArgs) Handles exitButton.Click
        Me.Close()
    End Sub

    Private Sub removeButton_Click(ByVal sender As Object, _
        ByVal e As System.EventArgs) Handles removeButton.Click
        ' replaces the dashes in a social security number
        ' with the empty string

        Const message As String = _
            "The social security number must contain 11 characters."
        Dim socSecNumber As String

        socSecNumber = numberTextBox.Text

        If socSecNumber.Length = 11 Then
            socSecNumber = socSecNumber.Replace("-", "")
            numberLabel.Text = socSecNumber
        Else
            MessageBox.Show(message, "Social Security", _
                MessageBoxButtons.OK, MessageBoxIcon.Information)
        End If

        numberTextBox.Focus()
    End Sub

    Private Sub numberTextBox_Enter(ByVal sender As Object, _
        ByVal e As System.EventArgs) Handles numberTextBox.Enter
        numberTextBox.SelectAll()
    End Sub
End Class
```

**FIGURE 6.11**    Code for the modified Social Security application

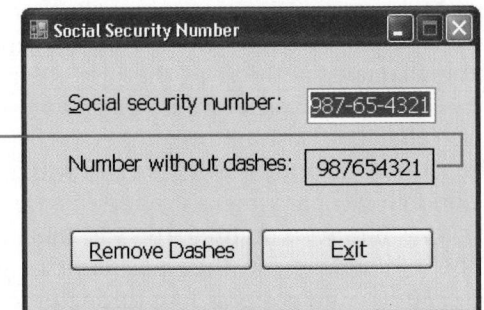

The dashes are replaced with the empty string

**FIGURE 6.12**    Sample run of the modified Social Security application

As mentioned earlier, the Replace method replaces all occurrences of *oldValue* with *newValue*. At times, however, you may need to replace only a specific occurrence of *oldValue* with *newValue*; for this, you use the Mid statement rather than the Replace method.

### The Mid Statement

You can use the **Mid statement** to replace a specified number of characters in a string with characters from another string. Figure 6.13 shows the syntax of the Mid statement and includes several examples of using the statement.

---

HOW TO...

**Use the Mid Statement**

**Syntax**

To replace a specific number of characters in a string with characters from another string:

   **Mid**(*targetString*, *start* [, *count*]) = *replacementString*

**Examples**

```
Dim fullName As String = "Rob Smith"
Mid(fullName, 7, 1) = "y"
```
changes the contents of the fullName variable to "Rob Smyth"

```
Dim fullName As String = "Rob Smith"
Mid(fullName, 7) = "y"
```
changes the contents of the fullName variable to "Rob Smyth"

```
Dim fullName As String = "Ann Johnson"
Mid(fullName, 5) = "Paul"
```
changes the contents of the fullName variable to "Ann Paulson"

```
Dim fullName As String = "Earl Cho"
Mid(fullName, 6) = "Liverpool"
```
changes the contents of the fullName variable to "Earl Liv"

---

**FIGURE 6.13**    How to use the Mid statement

In the Mid statement's syntax, *targetString* is the string in which you want characters replaced, and *replacementString* contains the replacement characters. *Start* is the character position of the first character you want replaced in the *targetString*. The first character in the *targetString* is in character position one, the second is in character position two, and so on. Notice that the character position is not the same as the index, which begins with zero.

The optional *count* argument specifies the number of characters to replace in the *targetString*. If *count* is omitted, the Mid statement replaces the lesser of either the number of characters in the *replacementString*, or the number of characters in the *targetString* from position *start* through the end of the *targetString*.

The `Mid(fullName, 7, 1) = "y"` statement shown in the first example in Figure 6.13 replaces the letter "i", which is located in character position seven in the `fullName` variable, with the letter "y". After the statement is processed, the `fullName` variable contains the string "Rob Smyth".

You also can omit the *count* argument and use the `Mid(fullName, 7) = "y"` statement, which is shown in the second example in Figure 6.13, to replace the letter "i" in the `fullName` variable with the letter "y". Recall that when the *count* argument is omitted from the Mid statement, the statement replaces the lesser of either the number of characters in the *replacementString* (in this case, one) or the number of characters in the *targetString* from position *start* through the end of the *targetString* (in this case, three).

The `Mid(fullName, 5) = "Paul"` statement in the third example in Figure 6.13 replaces four characters in the `fullName` variable, beginning with the character located in character position five in the variable (the letter J). Here again, because the *count* argument is omitted from the Mid statement, the statement replaces the lesser of either the number of characters in the *replacementString* (in this case, four) or the number of characters in the *targetString* from position *start* through the end of the *targetString* (in this case, seven). After the statement is processed, the `fullName` variable contains the string "Ann Paulson".

The `Mid(fullName, 6) = "Liverpool"` statement in the last example in Figure 6.13 replaces three characters in the `fullName` variable, beginning with the character located in character position six in the variable (the letter C). Here again, because the *count* argument is omitted from the Mid statement, the statement replaces the lesser of either the number of characters in the *replacementString* (in this case, nine) or the number of characters in the *targetString* from position *start* through the end of the *targetString* (in this case, three). After the statement is processed, the `fullName` variable contains the string "Earl Liv".

Figure 6.14 shows the code for the Phone application, which uses the Mid statement to change the area code in a phone number to "312". The Mid statement is shaded in the figure. Figure 6.15 shows a sample run of the Phone application.

**Visual Basic code**

```vb
' Project name:          Phone Project
' Project purpose:       The project changes the area code
'                        in a phone number to 877.
' Created/revised by:    <your name> on <current date>

Option Explicit On
Option Strict On

Public Class MainForm

    Private Sub exitButton_Click(ByVal sender As Object, _
        ByVal e As System.EventArgs) Handles exitButton.Click
        Me.Close()
    End Sub

    Private Sub reformatButton_Click(ByVal sender As Object, _
        ByVal e As System.EventArgs) Handles reformatButton.Click
        ' changes an area code to 877

        Dim newPhone As String

        newPhone = originalTextBox.Text

        ' reformat and display
        Mid(newPhone, 1, 3) = "877"
        newLabel.Text = newPhone

        originalTextBox.Focus()
    End Sub

    Private Sub originalTextBox_Enter(ByVal sender As Object, _
        ByVal e As System.EventArgs) Handles originalTextBox.Enter
        originalTextBox.SelectAll()
    End Sub
End Class
```

**FIGURE 6.14**    Code for the Phone application

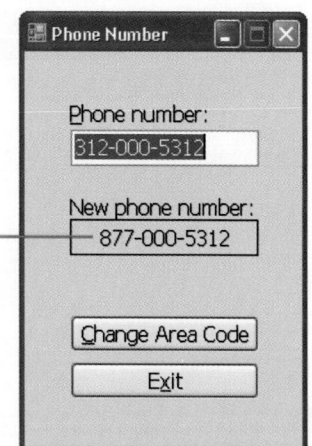

The 312 area code is replaced with area code 877

**FIGURE 6.15**   Sample run of the Phone application

## INSERTING CHARACTERS IN A STRING

In addition to removing and replacing characters in a string, you also can insert characters within a string. If you want to insert the characters at either the beginning or end of the string, you can use the PadLeft and PadRight methods, respectively. Both methods pad the string with a character until the string is a specified length, then they return the padded string. The **PadLeft method** pads the string on the left; in other words, it inserts the padded characters at the beginning of the string, which right-aligns the characters within the string. The **PadRight method**, on the other hand, pads the string on the right, which inserts the padded characters at the end of the string and left-aligns the characters within the string. Figure 6.16 shows the syntax of the PadLeft and PadRight methods and includes several examples of using the methods.

HOW TO...

### Use the PadLeft and PadRight Methods

**Syntax**
To insert characters at the beginning of a string:
     *string*.**PadLeft**(*length*[, *character*])
To insert characters at the end of a string:
     *string*.**PadRight**(*length*[, *character*])

**Examples**
```
Dim number as Integer = 42
Dim outputNumber As String
outputNumber = Convert.ToString(number)
outputNumber = outputNumber.PadLeft(5)
```
assigns "   42" (three spaces and the string "42") to the outputNumber variable

*(Figure is continued on next page)*

```
Dim number as Integer = 42
Dim outputNumber As String
outputNumber = number.ToString.PadLeft(5)
```
assigns " 42" (three spaces and the string "42") to the outputNumber variable

```
Dim netPay As Decimal = 767.89D
Dim formattedNetPay As String
formattedNetPay = netPay.ToString("C2").PadLeft(15, "*"c)
```
assigns "********$767.89" to the formattedNetPay variable

```
Dim firstName As String = "Sue"
Dim leftAlignedName As String
leftAlignedName = firstName.PadRight(10)
```
assigns "Sue    " (the string "Sue" and seven spaces) to the leftAlignedName variable

```
Dim firstName As String = "Sue"
firstName = firstName.PadRight(10)
```
assigns "Sue    " (the string "Sue" and seven spaces) to the firstName variable

**FIGURE 6.16**    How to use the PadLeft and PadRight methods

In each syntax shown in Figure 6.16, *length* is an integer that represents the desired length of the *string*. In other words, *length* represents the total number of characters you want the *string* to contain. The *character* argument is the character that each method uses to pad the *string* until it reaches the desired *length*. Notice that the *character* argument is optional in each syntax; if omitted, the default *character* is the space character.

The statements shown in the first two examples in Figure 6.16 produce the same results. In both examples, the code assigns five characters—three space characters, the character 4, and the character 2—to the outputNumber variable. However, the first example uses two assignment statements to accomplish the task, while the second example uses one assignment statement.

Study closely the two assignment statements shown in the first example. The first assignment statement, outputNumber = Convert.ToString(number), converts the contents of the number variable to String, and then assigns the result to the outputNumber variable. When processing the second assignment statement, outputNumber = outputNumber.PadLeft(5), the computer first makes a copy of the string stored in the outputNumber variable. It then pads the copied string with space characters until the string contains exactly five characters. In this case, the computer uses three space characters, which it inserts at the beginning of the string. The computer then assigns the resulting string—" 42"—to the outputNumber variable.

Now study the assignment statement shown in the second example. When processing the outputNumber = number.ToString.PadLeft(5) statement, the computer first makes a copy of the value stored in the number variable. It then converts the copied value to a string, inserts space characters at the beginning of the string until the string has exactly five characters, and then assigns the result to the `outputNumber` variable. Here again, notice that when two methods appear in an expression, the computer processes the methods from left to right. In this case, the computer processes the ToString method before processing the PadLeft method.

When processing the `formattedNetPay = netPay.ToString("C2").PadLeft(15, "*"c)` statement shown in the third example in Figure 6.16, the computer first makes a copy of the number stored in the `netPay` variable. It then converts the number to a string and formats it with a dollar sign and two decimal places. The computer then pads the string with asterisks until the string contains exactly 15 characters. In this case, the computer inserts eight asterisks at the beginning of the string. The computer assigns the resulting string ("********$767.89") to the `formattedNetPay` variable.

When processing the `leftAlignedName = firstName.PadRight(10)` statement shown in the fourth example, the computer first makes a copy of the string stored in the `firstName` variable. It then pads the copied string with space characters until the string contains exactly 10 characters. In this case, the computer uses seven space characters, which it inserts at the end of the string. The computer then assigns the resulting string—"Sue       "—to the `leftAlignedName` variable. Notice that the PadRight method left-aligns the name "Sue" within the `leftAlignedName` variable.

Keep in mind that the `leftAlignedName = firstName.PadRight(10)` statement does not change the contents of the `firstName` variable. To assign "Sue       " to the `firstName` variable, you would need to use the `firstName = firstName.PadRight(10)` statement shown in the last example in Figure 6.16.

Figure 6.17 shows the code for the Item Prices application, which uses the PadLeft method to right-align the numbers listed in a combo box. The statement containing the PadLeft method is shaded in the figure. Figure 6.18 shows a sample run of the Item Prices application.

---

**Visual Basic code**

```
' Project name:        Item Prices Project
' Project purpose:     The project increases the price
'                      selected or entered in each
'                      combo box.
' Created/revised by:  <your name> on <current date>

Option Explicit On
Option Strict On

Public Class MainForm

    Private Sub exitButton_Click(ByVal sender As Object, _
        ByVal e As System.EventArgs) Handles exitButton.Click
        Me.Close()
    End Sub
```

*(Figure is continued on next page)*

```
Private Sub MainForm_Load(ByVal sender As Object, _
    ByVal e As System.EventArgs) Handles Me.Load
    ' fills the combo boxes with values

    For price As Decimal = 9.45D To 11.45D Step 0.25D
        leftComboBox.Items.Add(price.ToString("N2"))
    Next price
    leftComboBox.SelectedIndex = 0

    For price As Decimal = 9.45D To 11.45D Step 0.25D
        rightComboBox.Items.Add(price.ToString("N2").PadLeft(5))
    Next price
    rightComboBox.SelectedIndex = 0

End Sub

Private Sub updateButton_Click(ByVal sender As Object, _
    ByVal e As System.EventArgs) Handles updateButton.Click
    ' increases the prices by 10% and 15%

    Const Percent1 As Decimal = 0.1D
    Const Percent2 As Decimal = 0.15D
    Dim leftPrice As Decimal
    Dim rightPrice As Decimal
    Dim leftNewPrice As Decimal
    Dim rightNewPrice As Decimal

    leftPrice = Convert.ToDecimal(leftComboBox.Text)
    rightPrice = Convert.ToDecimal(rightComboBox.Text)

    ' calculate and display new prices
    leftNewPrice = leftPrice + leftPrice * Percent1
    rightNewPrice = rightPrice + rightPrice * Percent2
    leftUpdatedLabel.Text = leftNewPrice.ToString("N2")
    rightUpdatedLabel.Text = rightNewPrice.ToString("N2")

End Sub

Private Sub leftComboBox_TextChanged(ByVal sender As Object, _
    ByVal e As System.EventArgs) Handles leftComboBox.TextChanged
    leftUpdatedLabel.Text = String.Empty
End Sub

Private Sub rightComboBox_TextChanged(ByVal sender As Object, _
    ByVal e As System.EventArgs) Handles rightComboBox.TextChanged
    rightUpdatedLabel.Text = String.Empty
End Sub
End Class
```

**FIGURE 6.17**    Code for the Item Prices application

*The prices are right-aligned using the PadLeft method*

*The prices are left-aligned automatically*

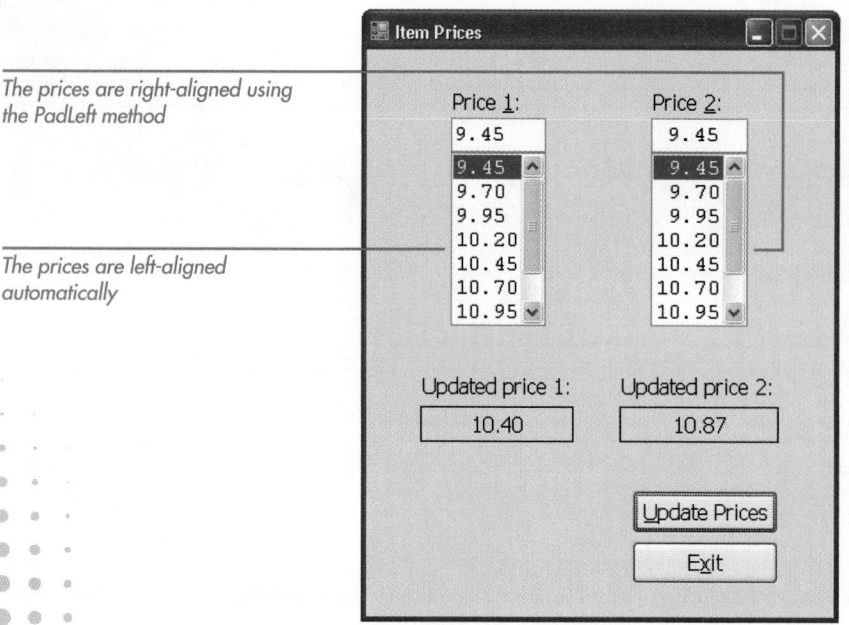

**FIGURE 6.18**    Sample run of the Item Prices application

Notice that the code shown in Figure 6.17 uses the Convert.ToDecimal method to convert to Decimal the string stored in each combo box's Text property. As you learned in Chapter 3, you typically use the TryParse method to convert a String value to a numeric data type because, unlike the TryParse method, the Convert methods result in an error when the string cannot be converted to a number. In this case, however, you do not have to worry about errors because you know that the values can be converted to a number.

The PadLeft and PadRight methods can be used to insert characters only at the beginning and end, respectively, of a string. To insert characters within a string, you use the Insert method.

### The Insert Method

Visual Basic provides the **Insert method** for inserting characters anywhere within a string. Possible uses for the method include inserting an employee's middle initial within his or her name, and inserting parentheses around the area code in a phone number. Figure 6.19 shows the syntax of the Insert method and includes two examples of using the method.

HOW TO...

**Use the Insert Method**

**Syntax**
To insert characters within a string:
      *string*.**Insert**(*startIndex*, *value*)

*(Figure is continued on next page)*

---

**Examples**
```
Dim name As String = "Rob Smith"
Dim fullName As String
fullName = name.Insert(4, "T. ")
```
assigns the string "Rob T. Smith" to the `fullName` variable

```
Dim phone As String = "3120501111"
phone = phone.Insert(0, "(")
phone = phone.Insert(4, ")")
phone = phone.Insert(8, "-")
```
changes the contents of the phone variable to "(312)050-1111"

---

**FIGURE 6.19**      How to use the Insert method

In the Insert method's syntax, *startIndex* specifies where in the *string* you want the *value* inserted. To insert the *value* at the beginning of the *string*, you use the number zero as the *startIndex*. To insert the *value* as the second character in the *string*, you use the number one as the *startIndex*, and so on. The Insert method returns a string with the appropriate characters inserted.

When processing the `fullName = name.Insert(4, "T. ")` statement shown in the first example in Figure 6.19, the computer first makes a copy of the string stored in the `name` variable, and then inserts the *value* "T. " (the letter T, a period, and a space) in the copied string. The letter T is inserted in *startIndex* position 4, which makes it the fifth character in the string. The period and space are inserted in *startIndex* positions 5 and 6, making them the sixth and seventh characters in the string. After the statement is processed, the `fullName` variable contains the string "Rob T. Smith"; however, the `name` variable still contains "Rob Smith".

In the second example shown in Figure 6.19, the `phone = phone.Insert(0, "(")` statement changes the contents of the phone variable from "3120501111" to "(3120501111". The `phone = phone.Insert(4, ")")` statement then changes the contents of the variable from "(3120501111" to "(312)0501111", and the `phone = phone.Insert(8, "-")` statement changes the contents of the variable from "(312)0501111" to "(312)050-1111".

Figure 6.20 shows the code for the Date application, which uses the Insert method to insert the string "20" in a date. The statement containing the Insert method is shaded in the figure. Figure 6.21 shows a sample run of the Date application.

---

**Visual Basic code**

```
' Project name:        Date Project
' Project purpose:     The project changes the year
'                      number in a date from "yy" to
'                      "20yy".
' Created/revised by:  <your name> on <current date>
```

**(Figure is continued on next page)**

```
Option Explicit On
Option Strict On

Public Class MainForm

    Private Sub exitButton_Click(ByVal sender As Object, _
        ByVal e As System.EventArgs) Handles exitButton.Click
        Me.Close()
    End Sub

    Private Sub changeButton_Click(ByVal sender As Object, _
        ByVal e As System.EventArgs) Handles changeButton.Click
        ' changes a year number from "yy" to "20yy"

        Dim newDate As String

        newDate = dateTextBox.Text
        dateLabel.Text = newDate.Insert(newDate.Length - 2, "20")

        dateTextBox.Focus()
    End Sub

    Private Sub dateTextBox_Enter(ByVal sender As Object, _
        ByVal e As System.EventArgs) Handles dateTextBox.Enter
        dateTextBox.SelectAll()
    End Sub
End Class
```

**FIGURE 6.20**     Code for the Date application

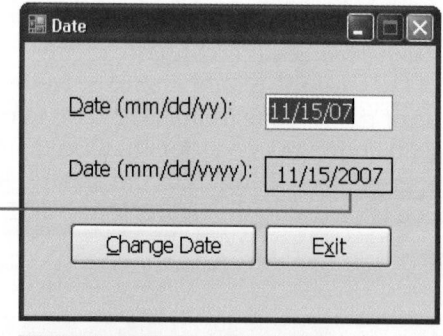

*The year number now begins with "20"*

**FIGURE 6.21**     Sample run of the Date application

## SEARCH A STRING FOR ONE OR MORE CHARACTERS

In some applications, you might need to determine whether a string begins or ends with a specific character or characters. For example, you may need to determine whether a phone number entered by the user begins with area code "312", which indicates that the customer lives in Chicago. Or, you may need to determine whether a tax rate entered by the user ends with a percent sign, because the percent sign will need to be removed before the tax rate can be used in a calculation.

In Visual Basic, you can use the **StartsWith method** to determine whether a specific sequence of characters occurs at the beginning of a string, and the **EndsWith method** to determine whether a specific sequence of characters occurs at the end of a string. Figure 6.22 shows the syntax of the StartsWith and EndsWith methods, along with examples of using each method.

## HOW TO...

### Use the StartsWith and EndsWith Methods

**Syntax**

To determine whether a specific sequence of characters occurs at the beginning of a string:

> *string*.**StartsWith**(*subString*)

To determine whether a specific sequence of characters occurs at the end of a string:

> *string*.**EndsWith**(*subString*)

**Examples**

```
Dim pay As String
pay = InputBox("Pay rate:", "Pay")
If pay.StartsWith("$") Then
        pay = pay.TrimStart("$"c)
End If
```
determines whether the string stored in the pay variable begins with the dollar sign; if it does, the dollar sign is removed from the string

```
Dim phone As String
phone = InputBox("10-digit phone number:", "Phone")
Do While phone.StartsWith("312")
        phoneListBox.Items.Add(phone)
        phone = InputBox("10-digit phone number", "Phone")
Loop
```
determines whether the string stored in the phone variable begins with "312"; if it does, the contents of the phone variable are added to the phoneListBox and the user is prompted to enter another phone number

```
Dim cityState As String = cityStateTextBox.Text.ToUpper()
If cityState.EndsWith("CA") Then
        stateLabel.Text = "California customer"
End If
```
determines whether the string stored in the cityState variable ends with "CA"; if it does, the string "California customer" is assigned to the stateLabel's Text property

```
Dim fullName As String
fullName = InputBox("Your name:", "Name")
fullName = fullName.ToUpper()
```

*(Figure is continued on next page)*

```
If Not fullName.EndsWith("SMITH") Then
      nameLabel.Text = fullName
End If
```
determines whether the string stored in the fullName variable ends with "SMITH"; if it does not, the variable's value is displayed in the nameLabel

```
Dim fullName As String
fullName = InputBox("Your name:", "Name")
If Not fullName.ToUpper.EndsWith("SMITH") Then
      nameLabel.Text = fullName
End If
```
determines whether the string stored in the fullName variable ends with "SMITH"; if it does not, the variable's value is displayed in the nameLabel

**FIGURE 6.22**    How to use the StartsWith and EndsWith methods

In the syntax for the StartsWith and EndsWith methods, *subString* is a string that represents the sequence of characters you want to search for either at the beginning or end of the *string*. The StartsWith method returns the Boolean value True when the *subString* is located at the beginning of the *string*; otherwise, it returns the Boolean value False. Similarly, the EndsWith method returns the Boolean value True when the *subString* is located at the end of the *string*; otherwise, it returns the Boolean value False. Both methods perform a case-sensitive search, which means that the case of the *subString* must match the case of the *string* for the methods to return the True value.

In the first example shown in Figure 6.22, the `If pay.StartsWith("$")` Then clause determines whether the string stored in the pay variable begins with the dollar sign. If it does, the `pay = pay.TrimStart("$"c)` statement removes the dollar sign from the variable's contents. You also can write the If clause in this example as `If pay.StartsWith("$") = True Then`.

Notice that, in the first example, the string `"$"` is used as the *subString* argument in the StartsWith method, but the character `"$"c` is used as the *trimChars* argument in the TrimStart method. This is because the *subString* argument in the StartsWith method must be a string, while the *trimChars* argument in the TrimStart method must be a listing of one or more characters.

In the second example shown in Figure 6.22, the `Do While phone.StartsWith("312")` clause determines whether the string stored in the phone variable begins with "312". If it does, the contents of the variable are added to the phoneListBox and the user is prompted to enter another phone number. You also can write the Do clause in this example as `Do While phone.StartsWith("312") = True`.

In the third example, the code assigns the string "California customer" to the stateLabel's Text property when the string stored in the cityState variable ends with the uppercase string "CA". Here again, you also can write the If clause in this example as `If cityState.EndsWith("CA") = True Then`.

The `fullName = fullName.ToUpper()` statement shown in the fourth example changes the contents of the fullName variable to uppercase. The `If Not fullName.EndsWith("SMITH")` Then clause then compares the contents of the fullName variable to the string "SMITH". If the fullName variable does not end with the string "SMITH", the `nameLabel.Text = fullName` statement displays the contents of the fullName variable in the nameLabel. You also can write the If clause in this example as `If fullName.EndsWith("SMITH") = False Then`.

The code shown in the last example in Figure 6.22 is similar to the code shown in the fourth example, except the ToUpper method is included in the If clause rather than in an assignment statement. When processing the `If Not fullName.ToUpper.EndsWith("SMITH")` Then clause, the computer first makes a copy of the string stored in the `fullName` variable; it then converts the copied string to uppercase. The computer then determines whether the copied string ends with the string "SMITH". Here again, notice that the computer processes the methods in the statement from left to right; in this case, it processes the ToUpper method before processing the EndsWith method. If the copied string does not end with the string "SMITH", the `nameLabel.Text = fullName` statement displays the contents of the `fullName` variable in the nameLabel. Unlike the code in the fourth example, the code in this example does not permanently change the contents of the `fullName` variable to uppercase. The If clause in this example also can be written as `If fullName.ToUpper.EndsWith("SMITH") = False Then`.

Figure 6.23 shows the code for the Sales Tax application, which uses the EndsWith method to determine whether a tax rate ends with a percent sign. The If clause that contains the EndsWith method is shaded in the figure. Figure 6.24 shows a sample run of the Sales Tax application.

**Visual Basic code**

```vb
' Project name:        Sales Tax Project
' Project purpose:     The project calculates a sales tax amount.
' Created/revised by:  <your name> on <current date>

Option Explicit On
Option Strict On

Public Class MainForm

    Private Sub exitButton_Click(ByVal sender As Object, _
        ByVal e As System.EventArgs) Handles exitButton.Click
        Me.Close()
    End Sub

    Private Sub calcButton_Click(ByVal sender As Object, _
        ByVal e As System.EventArgs) Handles calcButton.Click
        ' calculates a sales tax amount

        Const Message As String = _
            "The sales amount and tax rate must be numeric."
        Dim sales As Decimal
        Dim rate As Decimal
        Dim tax As Decimal
        Dim taxRate As String
        Dim isConvertedSales As Boolean
        Dim isConvertedRate As Boolean
```

*(Figure is continued on next page)*

```
    ' if necessary, remove the percent sign
    If rateTextBox.Text.EndsWith("%") Then
        taxRate = rateTextBox.Text.TrimEnd("%"c)
    Else
        taxRate = rateTextBox.Text
    End If

    isConvertedSales = Decimal.TryParse(salesTextBox.Text, sales)
    isConvertedRate = Decimal.TryParse(taxRate, rate)

    If isConvertedSales AndAlso isConvertedRate Then
        If rate > 1 Then
            rate = rate / 100
        End If
        tax = sales * rate
        taxLabel.Text = tax.ToString("C2")
    Else
        MessageBox.Show(Message, "Sales Tax Calculator", _
            MessageBoxButtons.OK, MessageBoxIcon.Information)
    End If

    salesTextBox.Focus()
End Sub

Private Sub salesTextBox_Enter(ByVal sender As Object, _
    ByVal e As System.EventArgs) Handles salesTextBox.Enter
    salesTextBox.SelectAll()
End Sub

Private Sub rateTextBox_Enter(ByVal sender As Object, _
    ByVal e As System.EventArgs) Handles rateTextBox.Enter
    rateTextBox.SelectAll()
End Sub

Private Sub salesTextBox_TextChanged(ByVal sender As Object, _
    ByVal e As System.EventArgs) Handles salesTextBox.TextChanged
    taxLabel.Text = String.Empty
End Sub

Private Sub rateTextBox_TextChanged(ByVal sender As Object, _
    ByVal e As System.EventArgs) Handles rateTextBox.TextChanged
    taxLabel.Text = String.Empty
End Sub
End Class
```

**FIGURE 6.23**    Code for the Sales Tax application

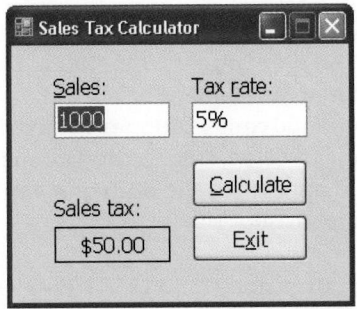

**FIGURE 6.24**   Sample run of the Sales Tax application

The StartsWith and EndsWith methods can be used only to determine whether a string begins or ends with a specific sequence of characters. To determine whether one or more characters appear anywhere in a string, you can use either the Contains method or the IndexOf method. You learn about the Contains method first.

### The Contains Method

You can use the **Contains method** to search a string to determine whether it contains a specific sequence of characters. For example, you can use the method to determine whether the area code "(312)" appears in a phone number, or whether the street name "Elm Street" appears in an address. Figure 6.25 shows the syntax of the Contains method and includes several examples of using the method.

**HOW TO...**

**Use the Contains Method**

**Syntax**
To search a string to determine whether it contains a specific sequence of characters, and then return a Boolean value that indicates whether the characters appear within the string:
> *string*.**Contains**(*subString*)

**Examples**
```
Dim address As String = "345 Main Street, Glendale, CA"
Dim isContained As Boolean
isContained = address.Contains("Main Street")
```
assigns the Boolean value True to the isContained variable, because "Main Street" appears in the address variable

```
Dim address As String = "345 Main Street, Glendale, CA"
Dim isContained As Boolean
isContained = address.Contains("Main street")
```
assigns the Boolean value False to the isContained variable, because "Main street" does not appear in the address variable

*(Figure is continued on next page)*

```
Dim address As String = "345 Main Street, Glendale, CA"
Dim isContained As Boolean
isContained = address.ToUpper.Contains("MAIN STREET")
```
assigns the Boolean value True to the isContained variable, because
"MAIN STREET" appears in the address variable when its contents are
converted to uppercase

```
Dim phone As String = "(312) 999-9999"
If phone.Contains("(312)") Then
```
the If...Then...Else statement's condition evaluates to True, because
"(312)" appears in the phone variable

**FIGURE 6.25**    How to use the Contains method

In the syntax shown in Figure 6.25, *subString* is a string that represents the
sequence of characters for which you want to search within the *string*. The
Contains method returns the Boolean value True when the *subString* is contained
anywhere within the string; otherwise, it returns the Boolean value False. Like
the StartsWith and EndsWith methods, the Contains method performs a case-
sensitive search.

In the first example shown in Figure 6.25, the isContained    =
address.Contains("Main Street") statement assigns the Boolean value True to
the isContained variable, because the *subString* "Main Street" is contained somewhere in the address variable. The isContained = address.Contains("Main
street") statement in the second example, however, assigns the Boolean value
False to the isContained variable. This is because the string stored in the address
variable ("Main Street") is not equivalent to the *subString* for which you are
searching ("Main street"). Remember that the Contains method performs a case-
sensitive search.

When processing the isContained = address.ToUpper.Contains("MAIN
STREET") statement shown in the third example, the computer first makes a copy
of the string stored in the address variable; it then converts the copied string to
uppercase. The computer then determines whether the copied string contains
the *subString* "MAIN STREET". In this case, the *subString* appears somewhere in
the copied string, so the computer assigns the Boolean value True to
the isContained variable.

In the first three examples shown in Figure 6.25, the Contains method
appears in an assignment statement, where its return value is assigned to a
Boolean variable. You also can use the Contains method in the condition of
either a selection or repetition structure. For instance, in the last example shown
in the figure, the Contains method appears in an If...Then...Else statement's condition. In the example, the Contains method returns the Boolean value True,
because the phone variable contains the *subString* "(312)"; therefore, the condition evaluates to True. The If clause in the example also can be written as
If phone.Contains("(312)") = True Then.

Figure 6.26 shows the code for the Part Number application, which uses the
Contains method to determine the appropriate delivery method. The If clauses
containing the Contains method are shaded in the figure. Figure 6.27 shows a
sample run of the Part Number application.

**Visual Basic code**

```vb
' Project name:        Part Number Project
' Project purpose:     The project selects the appropriate
'                      delivery method from a list box.
' Created/revised by:  <your name> on <current date>

Option Explicit On
Option Strict On

Public Class MainForm

    Private Sub exitButton_Click(ByVal sender As Object, _
        ByVal e As System.EventArgs) Handles exitButton.Click
        Me.Close()
    End Sub

    Private Sub MainForm_Load(ByVal sender As Object, _
        ByVal e As System.EventArgs) Handles Me.Load
        ' fills the list box with values

        deliveryListBox.Items.Add("Mail - Standard")
        deliveryListBox.Items.Add("Mail - Priority")
        deliveryListBox.Items.Add("FedEx - Standard")
        deliveryListBox.Items.Add("FedEx - Overnight")
        deliveryListBox.Items.Add("UPS")
    End Sub

    Private Sub partTextBox_Enter(ByVal sender As Object, _
        ByVal e As System.EventArgs) Handles partTextBox.Enter
        partTextBox.SelectAll()
    End Sub

    Private Sub partTextBox_TextChanged(ByVal sender As Object, _
        ByVal e As System.EventArgs) Handles partTextBox.TextChanged
        ' clears the list box selection

        deliveryListBox.SelectedIndex = -1
    End Sub

    Private Sub deliveryButton_Click(ByVal sender As Object, _
        ByVal e As System.EventArgs) Handles deliveryButton.Click
        ' selects the appropriate delivery method

        Dim partNum As String

        partNum = partTextBox.Text.ToUpper()
```

*(Figure is continued on next page)*

```
If partNum.Contains("MS") Then
    deliveryListBox.SelectedIndex = 0
ElseIf partNum.Contains("MP") Then
    deliveryListBox.SelectedIndex = 1
ElseIf partNum.Contains("FS") Then
    deliveryListBox.SelectedIndex = 2
ElseIf partNum.Contains("FO") Then
    deliveryListBox.SelectedIndex = 3
ElseIf partNum.Contains("U") Then
    deliveryListBox.SelectedIndex = 4
Else
    MessageBox.Show("Invalid part number", _
        "Part Numbers", MessageBoxButtons.OK, _
        MessageBoxIcon.Information)
End If

partTextBox.Focus()
End Sub

End Class
```

**FIGURE 6.26**      Code for the Part Number application

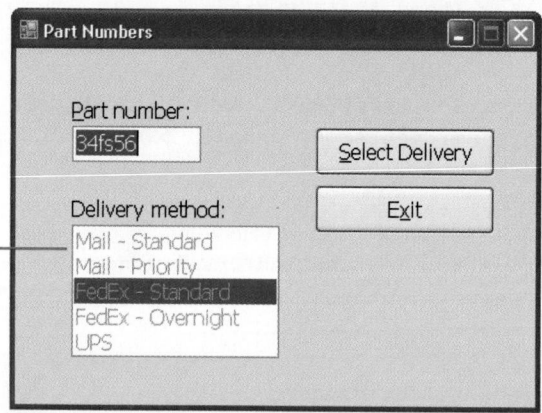

*The items appear dimmed because the list box's Enabled property is set to False*

**FIGURE 6.27**      Sample run of the Part Number application

### The IndexOf Method

In addition to using the Contains method to search for a *subString* anywhere within a string, you also can use the **IndexOf method**. Unlike the Contains method, which returns a Boolean value that indicates whether the *string* contains the *subString*, the IndexOf method returns an integer that represents the location of the *subString* within the *string*. Figure 6.28 shows the syntax of the IndexOf method and includes several examples of using the method.

# HOW TO...

## Use the IndexOf Method

### Syntax
To search a string to determine whether it contains a specific sequence of characters, and then return a number that indicates the location of the characters within the string:

      *string*.**IndexOf**(*subString*[, *startIndex*])

### Examples

```
Dim message As String = "Have a nice day"
Dim indexNum As Integer
indexNum = message.IndexOf("nice", 0)
```
assigns the number 7 to the indexNum variable

```
Dim message As String = "Have a nice day"
Dim indexNum As Integer
indexNum = message.IndexOf("nice")
```
assigns the number 7 to the indexNum variable

```
Dim message As String = "Have a nice day"
Dim indexNum As Integer
indexNum = message.IndexOf("Nice")
```
assigns the number -1 to the indexNum variable

```
Dim message As String = "Have a nice day"
Dim indexNum As Integer
indexNum = message.ToUpper.IndexOf("NICE")
```
assigns the number 7 to the indexNum variable

```
Dim message As String = "Have a nice day"
Dim indexNum As Integer
indexNum = message.IndexOf("nice", 5)
```
assigns the number 7 to the indexNum variable

```
Dim message As String = "Have a nice day"
Dim indexNum As Integer
indexNum = message.IndexOf("nice", 8)
```
assigns the number -1 to the indexNum variable

**FIGURE 6.28**    How to use the IndexOf method

In the syntax, *subString* is the sequence of characters for which you are searching in the *string*, and *startIndex* is the index of the character at which the search should begin; in other words, *startIndex* specifies the starting position for the search. Recall that the first character in a string has an index of zero, the second character has an index of one, and so on. Notice that the *startIndex* argument is optional in the IndexOf method's syntax. If you omit the *startIndex* argument, the IndexOf method begins the search with the first character in the *string*.

The IndexOf method searches for *subString* within *string*, beginning with the character whose index is *startIndex*. If the IndexOf method does not find the *subString*, it returns the number -1; otherwise, it returns the index of the starting position of *subString* within *string*.

You can use either the `indexNum = message.IndexOf("nice", 0)` statement shown in the first example in Figure 6.28, or the `indexNum = message.IndexOf("nice")` statement shown in the second example, to search for the word "nice" in the `message` variable, beginning with the first character in the variable. In each case, the word "nice" begins with the eighth character in the variable. The eighth character has an index of seven, so both statements assign the number seven to the `indexNum` variable.

Like the StartsWith, EndsWith, and Contains methods, the IndexOf method performs a case-sensitive search, as the third example in Figure 6.28 indicates. In the example, the `indexNum = message.IndexOf("Nice")` statement assigns the number -1 to the `indexNum` variable, because the word "Nice" is not contained in the `message` variable.

You can use the `indexNum = message.ToUpper.IndexOf("NICE")` statement shown in the fourth example to perform a case-insensitive search for the word "nice". When processing the statement, the computer first makes a copy of the string stored in the `message` variable. The ToUpper method then converts the copied string to uppercase, and the IndexOf method searches the uppercase string for the word "NICE". The statement assigns the number seven to the `indexNum` variable because, ignoring case, the word "nice" begins with the character whose index is seven.

The `indexNum = message.IndexOf("nice", 5)` statement shown in the fifth example searches for the word "nice" in the `message` variable, beginning with the character whose index is five; that character is the second letter "a". The statement assigns the number seven to the `indexNum` variable, because the word "nice" begins with the character whose index is seven.

The `indexNum = message.IndexOf("nice", 8)` statement shown in the last example in Figure 6.28 searches for the word "nice" in the `message` variable, beginning with the character whose index is eight; that character is the letter "i". Notice that the word "nice" does not appear anywhere in the "ice day" portion of the string stored in the `message` variable. Therefore, the statement assigns the number -1 to the `indexNum` variable.

Figure 6.29 shows the code for the Count application, which uses the IndexOf method to determine the number of times a sequence of characters appears in a string. The statements containing the IndexOf method are shaded in the figure. Figure 6.30 shows a sample run of the Count application.

**Visual Basic code**

```
' Project name:        Count Project
' Project purpose:     The project determines the number
'                      of times a sequence of characters
'                      appears in a string.
' Created/revised by:  <your name> on <current date>

Option Explicit On
Option Strict On
```

*(Figure is continued on next page)*

```
Public Class MainForm
    Private Sub exitButton_Click(ByVal sender As Object, _
        ByVal e As System.EventArgs) Handles exitButton.Click
        Me.Close()
    End Sub

    Private Sub stringTextBox_Enter(ByVal sender As Object, _
        ByVal e As System.EventArgs) Handles originalTextBox.Enter
        originalTextBox.SelectAll()
    End Sub

    Private Sub stringTextBox_TextChanged(ByVal sender As Object, _
        ByVal e As System.EventArgs) _
        Handles originalTextBox.TextChanged
        countLabel.Text = String.Empty
    End Sub


    Private Sub searchButton_Click(ByVal sender As Object, _
        ByVal e As System.EventArgs) Handles searchButton.Click
        ' displays a message that indicates the number
        ' of times a sequence of characters appears
        ' in the string entered in the stringTextBox

        Dim origString As String
        Dim searchFor As String
        Dim startIndex As Integer
        Dim searchIndex As Integer
        Dim counter As Integer

        origString = originalTextBox.Text

        ' get the subString
        searchFor = InputBox("Search for:", "Count")

        ' search for the subString
        ' continue the search until the subString
        ' can no longer be located
        searchIndex = origString.IndexOf(searchFor, startIndex)
        Do Until searchIndex = -1
            ' update the counter, then begin the next search
            ' with the character located immediately
            ' after where the subString was last located
            counter = counter + 1
            startIndex = searchIndex + 1
            searchIndex = origString.IndexOf(searchFor, startIndex)
        Loop
```

*(Figure is continued on next page)*

```
                ' display the results of the search
            countLabel.Text = "'" & searchFor _
                & "' appears in the string " _
                & counter.ToString & " time(s)."
        End Sub
End Class
```

**FIGURE 6.29**    Code for the Count application

**FIGURE 6.30**    Sample run of the Count application

## ACCESSING CHARACTERS CONTAINED IN A STRING

In some applications, it is necessary to access one or more characters contained in a string. For example, you may need to determine whether a specific letter appears as the third character in a string, because the letter identifies an employee's department. Or, you may need to display only the string's first five characters, which identify an item's location in the warehouse.

Visual Basic provides the **Substring method** for accessing any number of characters contained in a string. Figure 6.31 shows the syntax of the Substring method and includes several examples of using the method.

# HOW TO...

### Use the Substring Method

**Syntax**
To access one or more characters contained in a string:
      *string*.**Substring**(*startIndex*[, *count*])

**Examples**
```
Dim fullName As String = "Peggy Ryan"
firstName = fullName.Substring(0, 5)
lastName = fullName.Substring(6)
```
assigns "Peggy" to the firstName variable, and assigns "Ryan" to the lastName variable

*(Figure is continued on next page)*

```
Dim sales As String
sales = salesTextBox.Text
If sales.StartsWith("$") Then
        sales = sales.Substring(1)
End If
```
determines whether the string stored in the sales variable begins with the dollar sign; if it does, assigns the contents of the variable, excluding the dollar sign, to the sales variable

```
Dim inputRate As String
Dim rate As String
inputRate = InputBox("Enter rate:", "Tax Rate")
If inputRate.EndsWith("%") Then
        rate = inputRate.Substring(0, inputRate.Length - 1)
End If
```
determines whether the string stored in the inputRate variable ends with the percent sign; if it does, assigns the contents of the variable, excluding the percent sign, to the rate variable

**FIGURE 6.31**   How to use the Substring method

The Substring method contains two arguments: *startIndex* and *count*. *StartIndex* is the index of the first character you want to access in the *string*. As you learned earlier, the first character in a string has an index of zero; the second character has an index of one, and so on. The *count* argument, which is optional, specifies the number of characters you want to access. The Substring method returns a string that contains *count* number of characters, beginning with the character whose index is *startIndex*. If you omit the *count* argument, the Substring method returns all characters from the *startIndex* position through the end of the string.

The firstName = fullName.Substring(0, 5) statement shown in the first example in Figure 6.31 assigns the first five characters contained in the fullName variable ("Peggy") to the firstName variable. The lastName = fullName.Substring(6) statement assigns to the lastName variable all of the characters contained in the fullName variable, beginning with the character whose index is 6. In this case, the statement assigns "Ryan" to the lastName variable.

The code shown in the second example uses the StartsWith method to determine whether the string stored in the sales variable begins with the dollar sign. If it does, the sales = sales.Substring(1) statement assigns all of the characters from the sales variable, beginning with the character whose index is 1, to the sales variable. In other words, it assigns all but the first character to the sales variable. The sales = sales.Substring(1) statement is equivalent to the statement sales = sales.Remove(0, 1), as well as to the statement sales = sales.TrimStart("$"c).

The code shown in the last example in Figure 6.31 uses the EndsWith method to determine whether the string stored in the inputRate variable ends with the percent sign. If it does, the rate = inputRate.Substring(0, inputRate.Length - 1) statement assigns to the rate variable all of the characters contained in the inputRate variable, excluding the last character (which is the percent sign). The rate = inputRate.Substring(0, inputRate.Length - 1) statement is equivalent to the statement rate = inputRate.Remove(inputRate.Length - 1, 1), as well as to the statement rate = inputRate.TrimEnd("%"c).

Figure 6.32 shows the code for the Name application, which uses the Substring method to access only the first name from a person's full name. The statement containing the Substring method is shaded in the figure. Figure 6.33 shows a sample run of the Name application.

```vb
Visual Basic code

' Project name:        Name Project
' Project purpose:     The project displays a person's first name.
' Created/revised by:  <your name> on <current date>

Option Explicit On
Option Strict On

Public Class MainForm

    Private Sub exitButton_Click(ByVal sender As Object, _
        ByVal e As System.EventArgs) Handles exitButton.Click
        Me.Close()
    End Sub

    Private Sub fullTextBox_Enter(ByVal sender As Object, _
        ByVal e As System.EventArgs) Handles fullTextBox.Enter
        fullTextBox.SelectAll()
    End Sub

    Private Sub fullTextBox_TextChanged(ByVal sender As Object, _
        ByVal e As System.EventArgs) Handles fullTextBox.TextChanged
        firstLabel.Text = String.Empty
    End Sub

    Private Sub displayButton_Click(ByVal sender As Object, _
        ByVal e As System.EventArgs) Handles displayButton.Click
        ' displays the first name part of a full name

        Dim fullName As String
        Dim firstName As String
        Dim indexNum As Integer

        fullName = fullTextBox.Text

        ' search for the space character
        indexNum = fullName.IndexOf(" ")
        ' separate the first name
        firstName = fullName.Substring(0, indexNum)

        firstLabel.Text = firstName
        fullTextBox.Focus()
    End Sub
End Class
```

**FIGURE 6.32**    Code for the Name application

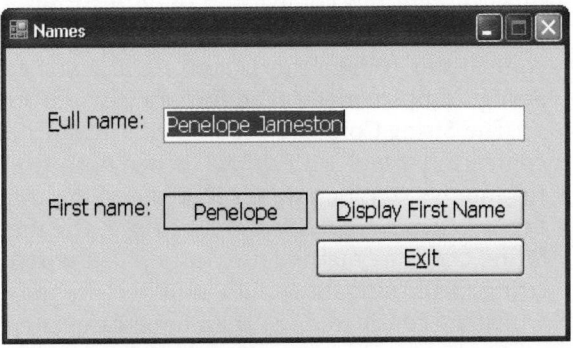

**FIGURE 6.33**    Sample run of the Name application

## COMPARING STRINGS

In addition to using the comparison operators to compare two strings, you also can use the **String.Compare method**. Figure 6.34 shows the syntax of the String.Compare method and includes several examples of using the method.

HOW TO...

### Use the String.Compare Method

**Syntax**
To compare two strings:
      **String.Compare**(*string1*, *string2*[, *ignoreCase*])

**Examples**
```
Dim result As Integer
result = String.Compare("Dallas", "Dallas")
```
assigns the number 0 to the result variable

```
Dim result As Integer
result = String.Compare("Dallas", "DALLAS")
```
assigns the number -1 to the result variable

```
Dim result As Integer
result = String.Compare("Dallas", "DALLAS", True)
```
assigns the number 0 to the result variable

```
Dim result As Integer
result = String.Compare("Dallas", "Boston")
```
assigns the number 1 to the result variable

**FIGURE 6.34**    How to use the String.Compare method

In the String.Compare method's syntax, the *string1* and *string2* arguments represent the two strings you want compared. The optional *ignoreCase* argument is a Boolean value that indicates whether you want to perform a case-insensitive or a case-sensitive comparison of both strings. When the *ignoreCase* argument is the Boolean value True, the String.Compare method performs a case-insensitive comparison. When the *ignoreCase* argument is the Boolean value False, the String.Compare method performs a case-sensitive comparison.

The String.Compare method returns an integer that indicates the result of comparing *string1* with *string2*. When both strings are equal, the method returns the number 0. When *string1* is greater than *string2*, the method returns the number 1. When *string1* is less than *string2*, the method returns the number -1. The String.Compare method uses rules called **word sort rules** when comparing the strings. Following these rules, numbers are considered less than lowercase letters, which are considered less than uppercase letters.

Study closely the examples shown in Figure 6.34. The `result = String.Compare("Dallas", "Dallas")` statement shown in the first example compares the string "Dallas" with the string "Dallas". Because both strings are equal, the String.Compare method returns the number 0, which the statement assigns to the `result` variable.

The second example shown in Figure 6.34 is identical to the first example, except the *string2* argument in the String.Compare method is capitalized. In this case, the String.Compare method returns the number –1 because the second character in *string1* (a) is less than the second character in *string2* (A).

The third example shown in the figure is almost identical to the second example, except the String.Compare method contains the Boolean value True in its *ignoreCase* argument. In this case, the String.Compare method returns the number 0 because, ignoring case, both strings are equal.

The `result = String.Compare("Dallas", "Boston")` statement shown in the last example in Figure 6.34 compares the string "Dallas" with the string "Boston". In this example, the String.Compare method returns the number 1 because the first character in *string1* (D) is greater than the first character in *string2* (B).

Figure 6.35 shows the code for the Alphabet application, which uses the String.Compare method to compare two letters entered by the user. The statement containing the String.Compare method is shaded in the figure. Figure 6.36 shows a sample run of the Alphabet application.

**Visual Basic code**

```
' Project name:        Alphabet Project
' Project purpose:     The project displays a message that
'                      indicates whether a letter is equal
'                      to another letter, or comes before
'                      or after the other letter.
' Created/revised by:  <your name> on <current date>

Option Explicit On
Option Strict On

Public Class MainForm
    Private Sub exitButton_Click(ByVal sender As Object, _
        ByVal e As System.EventArgs) Handles exitButton.Click
        Me.Close()
    End Sub
```

*(Figure is continued on next page)*

```vbnet
    Private Sub firstTextBox_Enter(ByVal sender As Object, _
        ByVal e As System.EventArgs) Handles firstTextBox.Enter
        firstTextBox.SelectAll()
    End Sub

    Private Sub firstTextBox_TextChanged(ByVal sender As Object, _
        ByVal e As System.EventArgs) Handles firstTextBox.TextChanged
        messageLabel.Text = String.Empty
    End Sub

    Private Sub secondTextBox_Enter(ByVal sender As Object, _
        ByVal e As System.EventArgs) Handles secondTextBox.Enter
        secondTextBox.SelectAll()
    End Sub

    Private Sub secondTextBox_TextChanged(ByVal sender As Object, _
        ByVal e As System.EventArgs) Handles secondTextBox.TextChanged
        messageLabel.Text = String.Empty
    End Sub

    Private Sub compareButton_Click(ByVal sender As Object, _
        ByVal e As System.EventArgs) Handles compareButton.Click
        ' displays the result of comparing two letters

        Dim letter1 As String
        Dim letter2 As String
        Dim result As Integer

        letter1 = firstTextBox.Text
        letter2 = secondTextBox.Text

        result = String.Compare(letter1, letter2, True)

        Select Case result
            Case 0
                messageLabel.Text = "Both letters are the same."
            Case 1
                messageLabel.Text = "The letter " & letter1 _
                    & " comes after the letter " _
                    & letter2 & " in the alphabet."
            Case -1
                messageLabel.Text = "The letter " & letter1 _
                    & " comes before the letter " _
                    & letter2 & " in the alphabet."
        End Select

        firstTextBox.Focus()
    End Sub
End Class
```

**FIGURE 6.35**    Code for the Alphabet application

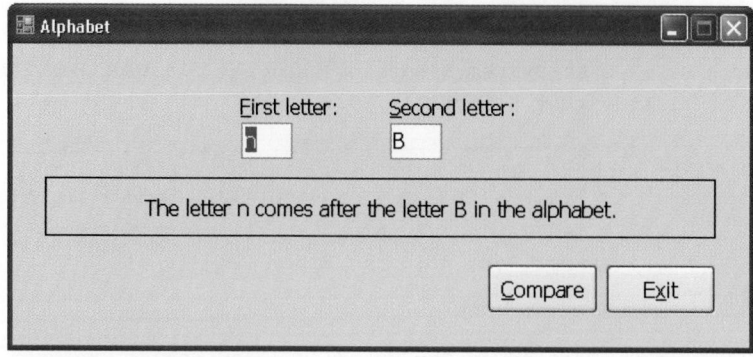

**FIGURE 6.36**      Sample run of the Alphabet application

In addition to using the String.Compare method to compare two strings, you also can use the Like operator.

## The Like Operator

Unlike the String.Compare method, the **Like operator** allows you to use pattern-matching characters to determine whether one string is equal to another string. Figure 6.37 shows the syntax of the Like operator and includes a listing of the operator's pattern-matching characters. The figure also shows several examples of using the Like operator.

### HOW TO...

**Use the Like operator**

**Syntax**

To use pattern-matching characters to determine whether one string is equal to another string:

      *string* **Like** *pattern*

| Pattern-matching characters | Matches in string |
|---|---|
| ? | any single character |
| * | zero or more characters |
| # | any single digit (0-9) |
| [*charlist*] | any single character in the *charlist* (for example, [a-z] matches any lowercase letter) |
| [!*charlist*] | any single character not in the *charlist* (for example, [!a-z] matches any character that is not a lowercase letter) |

**Examples**
```
isEqual = firstName.ToUpper() Like "B?LL"
```
assigns the Boolean value True to the `isEqual` variable when the string stored in the `firstName` variable begins with the letter B, followed by one character and then the two letters LL; otherwise, assigns the Boolean value False to the `isEqual` variable

*(Figure is continued on next page)*

```
If state Like "K*" Then
```
the If...Then...Else statement's condition evaluates to True when the string stored in the state variable begins with the letter K, followed by zero or more characters; otherwise, it evaluates to False

```
Do While idNum Like "###*"
```
the Do...Loop statement's condition evaluates to True when the string stored in the idNum variable begins with three digits, followed by zero or more characters; otherwise, it evaluates to False

```
If firstName.ToUpper() Like "T[OI]M" Then
```
the If...Then...Else statement's condition evaluates to True when the string stored in the firstName variable begins with the letter T, followed by either the letter O or the letter I, followed by the letter M; otherwise, it evaluates to False

```
isLowercase = letter Like "[a-z]"
```
assigns the Boolean value True to the isLowercase variable when the string stored in the letter variable is a lowercase letter; otherwise, it evaluates to False

```
For indexNum As Integer = 0 to name.Length - 1
        If name.Substring(indexNum, 1) Like "[!a-zA-Z]" Then
                nonLetter = nonLetter + 1
        End If
Next indexNum
```
compares each character contained in the name variable with the uppercase and lowercase letters of the alphabet, and counts the number of characters that are not letters

**FIGURE 6.37**    How to use the Like operator

In the Like operator's syntax, both *string* and *pattern* must be String expressions; however, *pattern* can contain one or more of the pattern-matching characters described in Figure 6.37. The Like operator evaluates to True if *string* matches *pattern*; otherwise it evaluates to False.

Study each example shown in Figure 6.37. The isEqual = firstName.ToUpper() Like "B?LL" statement shown in the first example contains the question mark (?) pattern-matching character, which is used to match one character in the *string*. Examples of *strings* that would make the firstName.ToUpper() Like "B?LL" expression evaluate to True include "Bill", "Ball", "bell", and "bull". Examples of *strings* for which the expression would evaluate to False include "BPL", "BLL", and "billy".

In the second example, the state Like "K*" condition in the If clause uses the asterisk (*) pattern-matching character to match zero or more characters. Examples of *strings* that would make the condition evaluate to True include "KANSAS", "Ky", and "Kentucky". Examples of *strings* for which the condition would evaluate to False include "kansas" and "ky".

In the third example, the idNum Like "###*" condition in the Do While clause contains two different pattern-matching characters: the number sign (#), which matches a digit, and the asterisk (*), which matches zero or more characters.

Examples of *strings* that would make the condition evaluate to True include "178" and "983Ab". Examples of *strings* for which the condition would evaluate to False include "X34" and "34Z".

In the fourth example, the `firstName.ToUpper() Like "T[OI]M"` condition in the If clause contains a *charlist* (character list)—in this case, the two letters O and I—enclosed in square brackets ([ ]). The condition evaluates to True when the string stored in the `firstName` variable is either "Tom" or "Tim" (entered in any case). When the `firstName` variable does not contain "Tom" or "Tim"—for example, when it contains "Tam" or "Tommy"—the expression evaluates to False.

The `isLowercase = letter Like "[a-z]"` statement shown in the fifth example in Figure 6.37 also contains a *charlist* enclosed in square brackets; however, the *charlist* represents a range of values—in this case, the lowercase letters "a" through "z". Notice that you use a hyphen (-) to specify a range of values. In this case, the statement assigns the Boolean value True to the `isLowercase` variable when the character stored in the `letter` variable is a lowercase letter; otherwise, it assigns the Boolean False.

The `name.Substring(indexNum, 1) Like "[!a-zA-Z]"` expression shown in the last example in Figure 6.37 also contains a *charlist* that specifies a range of values; however, the *charlist* is preceded by an exclamation point (!), which stands for "not". The expression evaluates to True when the current character in the `name` variable is *not* a letter; otherwise, it evaluates to False.

Earlier, in Figure 6.35, you viewed the code for the Alphabet application. Recall that the application used the String.Compare method to compare two characters entered by the user. Figure 6.38 shows the code for the modified Alphabet application, which uses the Like operator to ensure that the characters entered by the user are letters of the alphabet. The If clause that contains the Like operator is shaded in the figure. Figure 6.39 shows a sample run of the modified Alphabet application.

**Visual Basic code**

```
' Project name:        Alphabet Project
' Project purpose:     The project displays a message that
'                      indicates whether a letter is equal
'                      to another letter, or comes before
'                      or after the other letter.
' Created/revised by:  <your name> on <current date>

Option Explicit On
Option Strict On

Public Class MainForm

    Private Sub exitButton_Click(ByVal sender As Object, _
        ByVal e As System.EventArgs) Handles exitButton.Click
        Me.Close()
    End Sub

    Private Sub firstTextBox_Enter(ByVal sender As Object, _
        ByVal e As System.EventArgs) Handles firstTextBox.Enter
        firstTextBox.SelectAll()
    End Sub
```

*(Figure is continued on next page)*

```vb
    Private Sub firstTextBox_TextChanged(ByVal sender As Object, _
        ByVal e As System.EventArgs) Handles firstTextBox.TextChanged
        messageLabel.Text = String.Empty
    End Sub

    Private Sub secondTextBox_Enter(ByVal sender As Object, _
        ByVal e As System.EventArgs) Handles secondTextBox.Enter
        secondTextBox.SelectAll()
    End Sub

    Private Sub secondTextBox_TextChanged(ByVal sender As Object, _
        ByVal e As System.EventArgs) Handles secondTextBox.TextChanged
        messageLabel.Text = String.Empty
    End Sub

    Private Sub compareButton_Click(ByVal sender As Object, _
        ByVal e As System.EventArgs) Handles compareButton.Click
        ' displays the result of comparing two letters

        Dim letter1 As String
        Dim letter2 As String
        Dim result As Integer

        letter1 = firstTextBox.Text
        letter2 = secondTextBox.Text

        If letter1 Like "[a-zA-Z]" _
            AndAlso letter2 Like "[a-zA-Z]" Then
            result = String.Compare(letter1, letter2, True)

            Select Case result
                Case 0
                    messageLabel.Text = "Both letters are the same."
                Case 1
                    messageLabel.Text = "The letter " & letter1 _
                        & " comes after the letter " _
                        & letter2 & " in the alphabet."
                Case -1
                    messageLabel.Text = "The letter " & letter1 _
                        & " comes before the letter " _
                        & letter2 & " in the alphabet."
            End Select
        Else
            MessageBox.Show("Please enter two letters.", _
                "Alphabet", MessageBoxButtons.OK, _
                MessageBoxIcon.Information)
        End If

        firstTextBox.Focus()
    End Sub
End Class
```

**FIGURE 6.38**    Code for the modified Alphabet application

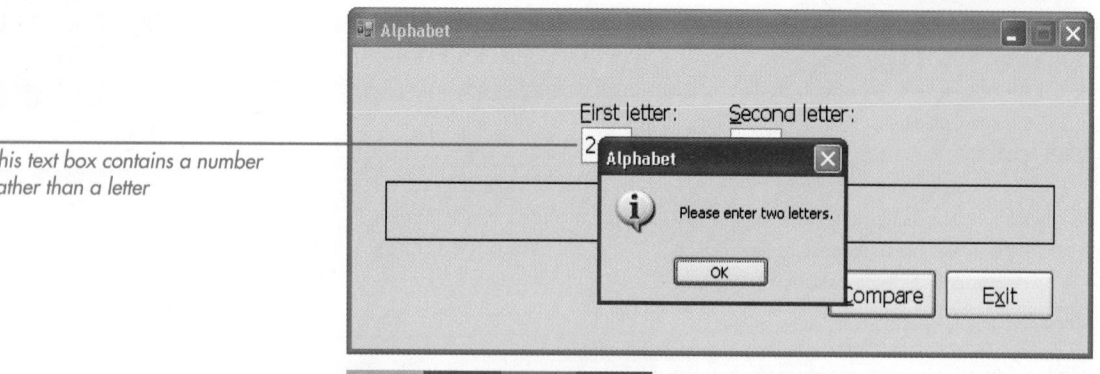

*This text box contains a number rather than a letter*

**FIGURE 6.39**   Sample run of the modified Alphabet application

Figure 6.40 summarizes the string manipulation techniques you learned in this chapter.

| Technique | Syntax | Purpose |
|---|---|---|
| Length property | *string*.**Length** | determine the number of characters in a string |
| Trim method | *string*.**Trim**([*trimChars*]) | remove characters from both the beginning and end of a string |
| TrimStart method | *string*.**TrimStart**([*trimChars*]) | remove characters from the beginning of a string |
| TrimEnd method | *string*.**TrimEnd**([*trimChars*]) | remove characters from the end of a string |
| Remove method | *string*.**Remove**(*startIndex, count*) | remove characters from anywhere in a string |
| Replace method | *string*.**Replace**(*oldValue, newValue*) | replace all occurrences of a sequence of characters in a string with another sequence of characters |
| Mid statement | **Mid**(*targetString, start* [, *count*]) = *replacementString* | replace a specific number of characters in a string with characters from another string |
| PadLeft method | *string*.**PadLeft**(*length*[, *character*]) | pads the beginning of a string with a character until the string is a specified length |
| PadRight method | *string*.**PadRight**(*length*[, *character*]) | pads the end of a string with a character until the string is a specified length |
| Insert method | *string*.**Insert**(*startIndex, value*) | insert characters within a string |
| StartsWith method | *string*.**StartsWith**(*subString*) | determine whether a string begins with a specific sequence of characters |
| EndsWith method | *string*.**EndsWith**(*subString*) | determine whether a string ends with a specific sequence of characters |
| Contains method | *string*.**Contains**(*subString*) | determine whether a string contains a specific sequence of characters; returns a Boolean value |
| IndexOf method | *string*.**IndexOf**(*subString*[, *startIndex*]) | determine whether a string contains a specific sequence of characters; returns an integer |
| Substring method | *string*.**Substring**(*startIndex*[, *count*]) | access one or more characters contained in a string |
| String.Compare method | **String.Compare**(*string1, string2*[, *ignoreCase*]) | compare two strings |
| Like operator | *string* **Like** *pattern* | use pattern-matching characters to determine whether one string is equal to another string |

**FIGURE 6.40**   String manipulation techniques

## MORE CONTROLS

So far, most of the applications you created in this book used text boxes to get user input. An advantage of using a text box for user input is that it can accept any data the user enters. A disadvantage is that it requires the application to perform data validation to ensure that the data was entered in the required format. In applications where the user is expected to enter one or more specific values, it is better to use other controls—such as list boxes, combo boxes, radio buttons, or check boxes—to display the values. Then, rather than typing the desired value in a text box, the user can select the appropriate value from one of these other controls. You learned how to use list boxes and combo boxes in Chapter 5. In this chapter, you learn how to use radio buttons and check boxes.

### Using Radio Buttons

You use the **RadioButton tool** in the toolbox to add a radio button to an interface. A **radio button** allows you to limit the user to only one choice in a group of two or more related and mutually exclusive choices. Figure 6.41 lists the names and uses of several properties of a radio button.

**TIP**

You also can use a list box, checked list box, or combo box to limit the user to only one choice in a group of related and mutually exclusive choices.

HOW TO...

**Use a Radio Button**

| Property | Use to |
|---|---|
| Checked | indicate whether the button is checked (selected) or unchecked (unselected) |
| Font | specify the font to use for text (usually set to Tahoma) |
| Name | give the radio button a meaningful name |
| Text | specify the text that appears inside the radio button |

**FIGURE 6.41**   How to use a radio button

Figure 6.42 shows the Gentry Supplies application's interface, which contains radio buttons.

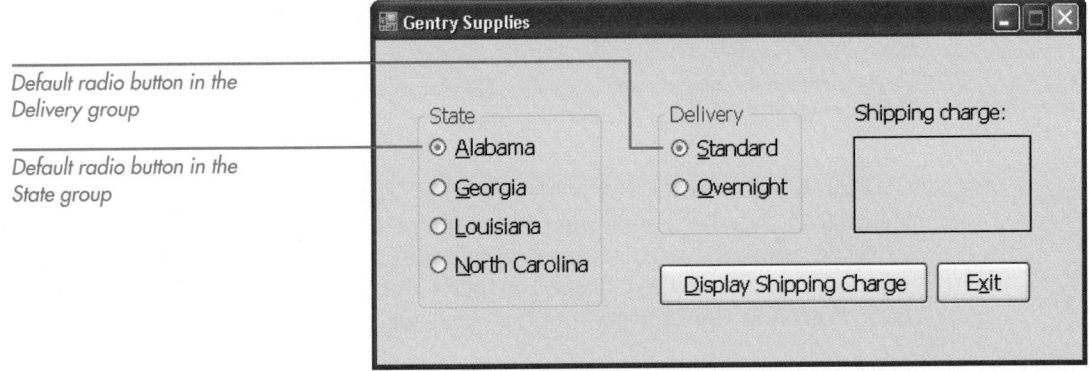

Default radio button in the Delivery group

Default radio button in the State group

**FIGURE 6.42**   Interface for the Gentry Supplies application

**TIP**

In the interface shown in Figure 6.42, it is not necessary to place both groups of radio buttons in a container. Only one of the groups needs to be placed in a container.

**TIP**

If you have more than seven choices from which the user can choose, you should consider using a list box, checked list box, or combo box rather than radio buttons.

Notice that each radio button in Figure 6.42 is labeled so that the user knows its purpose. You enter the label using sentence capitalization in the radio button's Text property. Each radio button also has a unique access key, which allows the user to select the button using the keyboard.

Radio buttons that are related should be grouped together. For example, two groups of radio buttons appear in the interface shown in Figure 6.42: one group contains the four state radio buttons, and the other contains the two delivery radio buttons. To include two groups of radio buttons in an interface, at least one of the groups must be placed within a container, such as a group box, panel, or table layout panel; otherwise, the radio buttons are considered to be in the same group and only one can be selected at any one time. In this case, the radio buttons pertaining to the state choice are contained in the GroupBox1 control, and the radio buttons pertaining to the delivery choice are contained in the GroupBox2 control. Placing each group of radio buttons in a separate group box allows the user to select one button from each group.

The minimum number of radio buttons in a group is two, because the only way to deselect a radio button is to select another radio button. The recommended maximum number of radio buttons in a group is seven.

It is customary in Windows applications to have one of the radio buttons in each group of radio buttons already selected when the user interface first appears. The selected button is called the **default radio button** and is either the radio button that represents the user's most likely choice or the first radio button in the group. You designate a radio button as the default radio button by setting the button's Checked property to the Boolean value True. When you set the Checked property to True in the Properties window, a black dot appears inside the circle in the button, as shown in Figure 6.42.

When the user clicks the Display Shipping Charge button in the Gentry Supplies application's user interface, the button's Click event procedure should calculate and display the appropriate shipping charge. The shipping charges are shown in Figure 6.43.

| State | Charge for standard delivery |
|---|---|
| Alabama | 20 |
| Georgia | 35 |
| Louisiana | 30 |
| North Carolina | 28 |
| Overnight delivery: add $10 to the charge for standard delivery | |

**FIGURE 6.43**    Shipping charges

Figure 6.44 shows the code for the Gentry Supplies application, and Figure 6.45 shows a sample run of the application. Notice that the code uses the Checked property to determine which radio button in the State group is selected. It also uses the Checked property to determine whether the Overnight radio button in the Delivery group is selected.

**Visual Basic code**

```
' Project name:          Gentry Supplies Project
' Project purpose:       The project displays a shipping charge
'                        based on the state and delivery method.
' Created/revised by:    <your name> on <current date>

Option Explicit On
Option Strict On

Public Class MainForm

    Private Sub exitButton_Click(ByVal sender As Object, _
        ByVal e As System.EventArgs) Handles exitButton.Click
        Me.Close()
    End Sub

    Private Sub displayButton_Click(ByVal sender As Object, _
        ByVal e As System.EventArgs) Handles displayButton.Click
        ' displays the appropriate shipping charge

        Dim shipCharge As Integer

        ' determine state shipping charge
        If alabamaRadioButton.Checked Then
            shipCharge = 20
        ElseIf georgiaRadioButton.Checked Then
            shipCharge = 35
        ElseIf louisianaRadioButton.Checked Then
            shipCharge = 30
        Else
            shipCharge = 28
        End If

        ' add $10 for overnight delivery
        If overnightRadioButton.Checked Then
            shipCharge = shipCharge + 10
        End If

        ' display shipping charge
        shipLabel.Text = shipCharge.ToString("C2")
    End Sub
End Class
```

Determines which State radio button is selected

Determines whether the Overnight radio button is selected

**FIGURE 6.44** Code for the Gentry Supplies application

**FIGURE 6.45**    Sample run of the Gentry Supplies application

## Using Check Boxes

You use the **CheckBox tool** in the toolbox to add a check box to an interface. Check boxes work like radio buttons in that they are either selected or deselected only; but that is where the similarity ends. You use radio buttons when you want to limit the user to only one choice from a group of related and mutually exclusive choices. You use **check boxes**, on the other hand, to allow the user to select any number of choices from a group of one or more independent and nonexclusive choices. Unlike radio buttons, where only one button in a group can be selected at any one time, any number of check boxes on a form can be selected at the same time. Figure 6.46 lists the names and uses of several properties of a check box.

**HOW TO...**

### Use a Check Box

| Property | Use to |
|---|---|
| Checked | indicate whether the check box is checked or unchecked |
| Font | specify the font to use for text (usually set to Tahoma) |
| Name | give the check box a meaningful name |
| Text | specify the text that appears inside the check box |

**FIGURE 6.46**    How to use a check box

Figure 6.47 shows a different version of the Gentry Supplies application's interface. This version uses a check box to indicate whether the user wants overnight delivery.

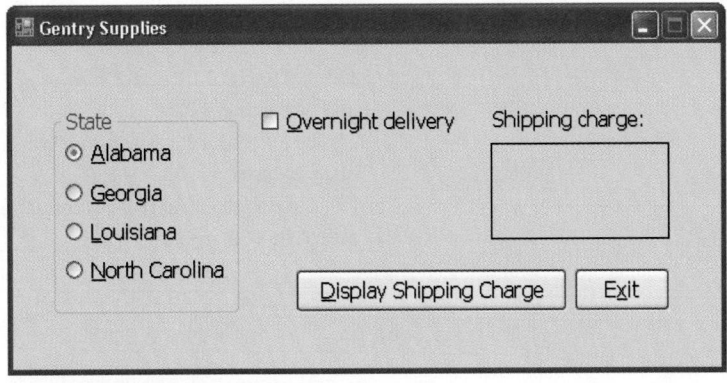

**FIGURE 6.47** A different version of the interface for the Gentry Supplies application

As with radio buttons, each check box in an interface should be labeled so that the user knows its purpose. You enter the label using sentence capitalization in the check box's Text property. Each check box also should have a unique access key.

Figure 6.48 shows the modified code for the Gentry Supplies application, and Figure 6.49 shows a sample run of the Gentry Supplies application using the new interface. The modification made to the original code is shaded in Figure 6.48. Notice that the modified code uses the Checked property to determine whether the Overnight delivery check box is selected.

**Visual Basic code**

```
' Project name:          Gentry Supplies Project
' Project purpose:       The project displays a shipping charge
'                        based on the state and delivery method.
' Created/revised by:    <your name> on <current date>

Option Explicit On
Option Strict On

Public Class MainForm

    Private Sub exitButton_Click(ByVal sender As Object, _
        ByVal e As System.EventArgs) Handles exitButton.Click
        Me.Close()
    End Sub

    Private Sub displayButton_Click(ByVal sender As Object, _
        ByVal e As System.EventArgs) Handles displayButton.Click
        ' displays the appropriate shipping charge

        Dim shipCharge As Integer
```

*(Figure is continued on next page)*

```
                       ' determine state shipping charge
                    ┌ If alabamaRadioButton.Checked Then
                    │      shipCharge = 20
                    │  ElseIf georgiaRadioButton.Checked Then
                    │      shipCharge = 35
                    │  ElseIf louisianaRadioButton.Checked Then
                    │      shipCharge = 30
                    │  Else
                    │      shipCharge = 28
                    └ End If

                       ' add $10 for overnight delivery
                    ┌ If overnightCheckBox.Checked Then
                    │      shipCharge = shipCharge + 10
                    └ End If

                       ' display shipping charge
                       shipLabel.Text = shipCharge.ToString("C2")
                   End Sub
               End Class
```

*Determines which State radio button is selected*

*Determines whether the Overnight check box is selected*

**FIGURE 6.48**　　Modified code for the Gentry Supplies application

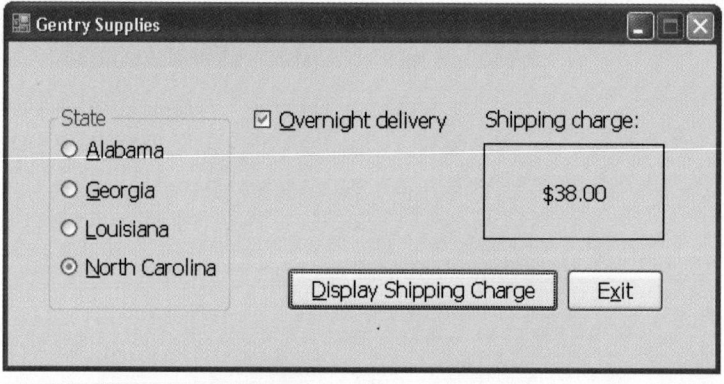

**FIGURE 6.49**　　Sample run of the modified Gentry Supplies application

You have completed the concepts section of Chapter 6. The next section is the Programming Tutorial section, which gives you step-by-step instructions on how to apply the chapter's concepts to an application. A Programming Example follows the Programming Tutorial. The Programming Example is a completed program that demonstrates the concepts taught in the chapter. Following the Programming Example are the Quick Review, Key Terms, Self-Check Questions and Answers, Review Questions, Review Exercises – Short Answer, Computer Exercises, and Case Projects sections.

# PROGRAMMING TUTORIAL

## Hangman Game

Mr. Mitchell teaches second grade at Hinsbrook School. On days when the weather is bad and the students cannot go outside to play, he spends recess time playing a simplified version of the Hangman game with his class. The game requires two people to play. Currently, Mr. Mitchell thinks of a word that has five letters. He then draws five dashes on the chalkboard—one for each letter in the word. One student then is chosen to guess the word, letter by letter. If the student guesses a correct letter, Mr. Mitchell replaces the appropriate dash or dashes with the letter. For example, if the original word is *moose* and the student guesses the letter *o*, Mr. Mitchell changes the fives dashes on the chalkboard to -oo--. If the student's letter does not appear in the word, Mr. Mitchell begins drawing the Hangman image, which contains nine lines and one circle. The game is over when the student guesses all of the letters in the word, or when he or she makes 10 incorrect guesses, whichever comes first. The Hangman game application's user interface is shown in Figure 6.50, and its TOE chart is shown in Figure 6.51.

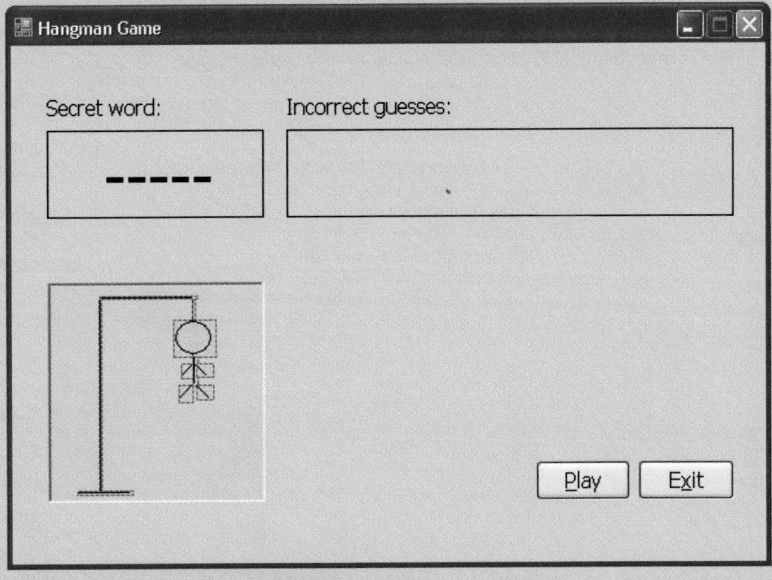

**FIGURE 6.50**   MainForm

**TOE Chart:**

| Task | Object | Event |
|---|---|---|
| 1. Hide the 10 picture boxes<br>2. Get a five-letter word from player 1<br>3. Display five dashes in the wordLabel<br>4. Clear the incorrectLabel<br>5. Get a letter from player 2<br>6. Search the word for the letter<br>7. If the letter is contained in the word, replace the appropriate dash(es)<br>8. If the letter is not contained in the word, display the letter in the incorrectLabel, then add 1 to the number of incorrect guesses, and then show the appropriate picture box<br>9. If all of the dashes have been replaced, the game is over, so display the message "Great guessing!" in a message box<br>10. If the user makes 10 incorrect guesses, the game is over, so display an appropriate message and the word in a message box | playButton | Click |
| End the application | exitButton | Click |
| Display the Hangman images | bottomPictureBox,<br>postPictureBox,<br>topPictureBox,<br>ropePictureBox,<br>headPictureBox,<br>bodyPictureBox,<br>rightArmPictureBox,<br>leftArmPictureBox,<br>rightLegPictureBox,<br>leftLegPictureBox | None |
| Display dashes and letters (from playButton) | wordLabel | None |
| Display the incorrect letters (from playButton) | incorrectLabel | None |

**FIGURE 6.51**    TOE chart

## Coding the Hangman Game

According to the application's TOE chart, the Click event procedures for the exitButton and the playButton need to be coded.

**To begin coding the Hangman Game application:**

1. Start Visual Studio. If necessary, close the Start Page window.
2. Open the **Hangman Game Solution** (Hangman Game Solution.sln) file, which is contained in the VbReloaded\Chap06\Hangman Game Solution folder. The interface shown earlier in Figure 6.50 appears on the screen.
3. Open the Code Editor window, which already contains the appropriate comments and Option statements. It also contains the code for the exitButton's Click event procedure.

4. Replace the <your name> and <current date> text in the comments with your name and the current date.

The only procedure you will need to code is the playButton's Click event procedure. The procedure's pseudocode is shown in Figure 6.52.

---

**Pseudocode**

1. hide the 10 picture boxes
2. get a 5-letter word from player 1
3. repeat until the word contains 5 letters
      get a 5-letter word from player 1
   end repeat
4. convert the word to uppercase
5. display 5 dashes in the wordLabel
6. clear the incorrectLabel

7. repeat until the game is over
      get a letter from player 2, then convert the letter to uppercase

      repeat for each letter in the word
        if the current letter is the same as the letter entered by player 2
          replace the appropriate dash in the wordLabel
          assign True to the isDashReplaced variable
        end if
      end repeat

      if a dash was replaced in the wordLabel
        if the wordLabel does not contain any more dashes
          assign True to the isGameOver variable
          display the "Great guessing!" message in a message box
        else
          assign False to the isDashReplaced variable
        end if
      else
        display the incorrect letter in the incorrectLabel
        add 1 to the number of incorrect guesses counter

        value of the number of incorrect guesses counter:
          1   show the bottomPictureBox
          2   show the postPictureBox
          3   show the topPictureBox
          4   show the ropePictureBox
          5   show the headPictureBox
          6   show the bodyPictureBox
          7   show the rightArmPictureBox
          8   show the leftArmPictureBox
          9   show the rightLegPictureBox
         10  show the leftLegPictureBox
              assign True to the isGameOver variable
              display the "Sorry, the word is" message and the word in a
              message box
      end if
   end repeat

---

**FIGURE 6.52**   Pseudocode for the playButton's Click event procedure

**To code the playButton's Click event procedure:**

1. Open the code template for the playButton's Click event procedure. Type ' **simulates the Hangman game** and press **Enter** twice.

The procedure will use five variables. The word variable will store the word entered by the first player. The letter variable will store the current letter entered by the second player. The isDashReplaced variable will keep track of whether a dash was replaced in the word, and the isGameOver variable will indicate whether the game is over. The incorrectCounter variable will keep track of the number of incorrect guesses made by the second player.

2. Enter the following Dim statements. Press **Enter** twice after typing the last Dim statement.
   **Dim word As String**
   **Dim letter As String**
   **Dim isDashReplaced As Boolean**
   **Dim isGameOver As Boolean**
   **Dim incorrectCounter As Integer**

3. The first step in the pseudocode is to hide the 10 picture boxes. Enter the following comment and assignment statements. After typing the last assignment statement, press **Enter** twice.
   **' hide the picture boxes**
   **bottomPictureBox.Visible = False**
   **postPictureBox.Visible = False**
   **topPictureBox.Visible = False**
   **ropePictureBox.Visible = False**
   **headPictureBox.Visible = False**
   **bodyPictureBox.Visible = False**
   **rightArmPictureBox.Visible = False**
   **leftArmPictureBox.Visible = False**
   **rightLegPictureBox.Visible = False**
   **leftLegPictureBox.Visible = False**

4. The second step in the pseudocode is to get a 5-letter word from the first player. Type ' **get a 5-letter word from the first player** and press **Enter**. Type **word = inputbox("Enter a 5-letter word:", "Hangman Game")** and press **Enter**.

5. The third step in the pseudocode is a repetition structure that repeats its one instruction until the user enters a word that contains five characters. Type the repetition structure shown in Figure 6.53, then position the insertion point as shown in the figure.

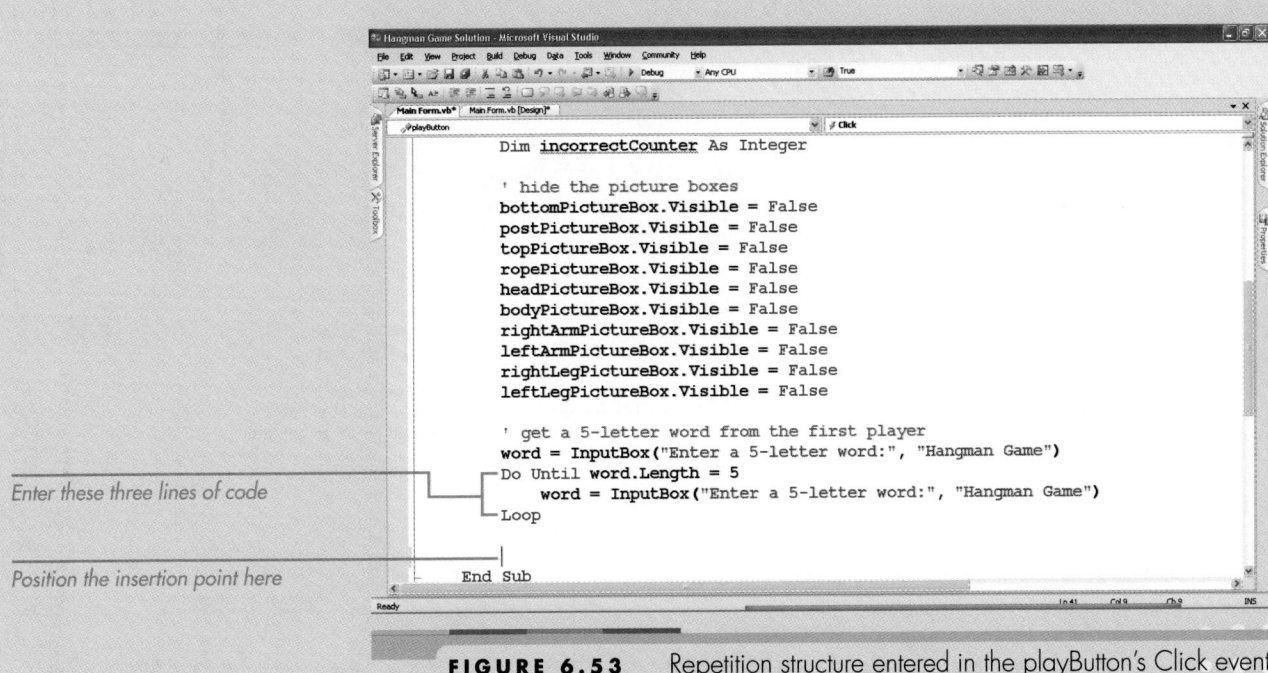

*Enter these three lines of code*

*Position the insertion point here*

**FIGURE 6.53**     Repetition structure entered in the playButton's Click event procedure

6.  The fourth step in the pseudocode is to convert to uppercase the word entered by the first player. Type **' convert the word to uppercase** and press **Enter**. Type **word = word.toupper()** and press **Enter** twice.

7.  Steps 5 and 6 in the pseudocode are to display five dashes in the wordLabel and then clear the incorrectLabel. Enter the following comments and assignment statements. After typing the last assignment statement, press **Enter** twice.

    **' display five dashes in the wordLabel**
    **' and clear the incorrectLabel**
    **wordLabel.Text = "-----"**
    **incorrectLabel.Text = String.Empty**

8.  Step 7 in the pseudocode is a repetition structure that repeats its instructions until the game is over. Enter the following comments and Do clause.

    **' allow the second player to guess a letter**
    **' the game is over when the second player**
    **' either guesses the word or makes 10**
    **' incorrect guesses**
    **Do Until isGameOver**

9.  The first task in the repetition structure is to get a letter from the second player, and then convert the letter to uppercase. Enter the following comments and assignment statements. After typing the last assignment statement, press **Enter** twice.

    **' get a letter from the second player, then**
    **' convert the letter to uppercase**
    **letter = InputBox("Enter a letter:", _**
        **"Letter", "", 550, 400)**
    **letter = letter.ToUpper()**

10. The next task in the repetition structure is a nested repetition structure that repeats its instructions for each letter in the word. Type **' search the word for the letter** and press **Enter**, then type **for indexNum as integer = 0 To 4** and press **Enter**. Change the Next clause to **Next indexNum**.

11. The nested repetition structure contains a selection structure that compares the current letter in the word with the letter entered by the second player. If both letters are the same, the selection structure's true path replaces the appropriate dash in the word. It also assigns the Boolean value True to the isDashReplaced variable to indicate that a dash was replaced in the word. Type the comments and selection structure shown in Figure 6.54, then position the insertion point as shown in the figure.

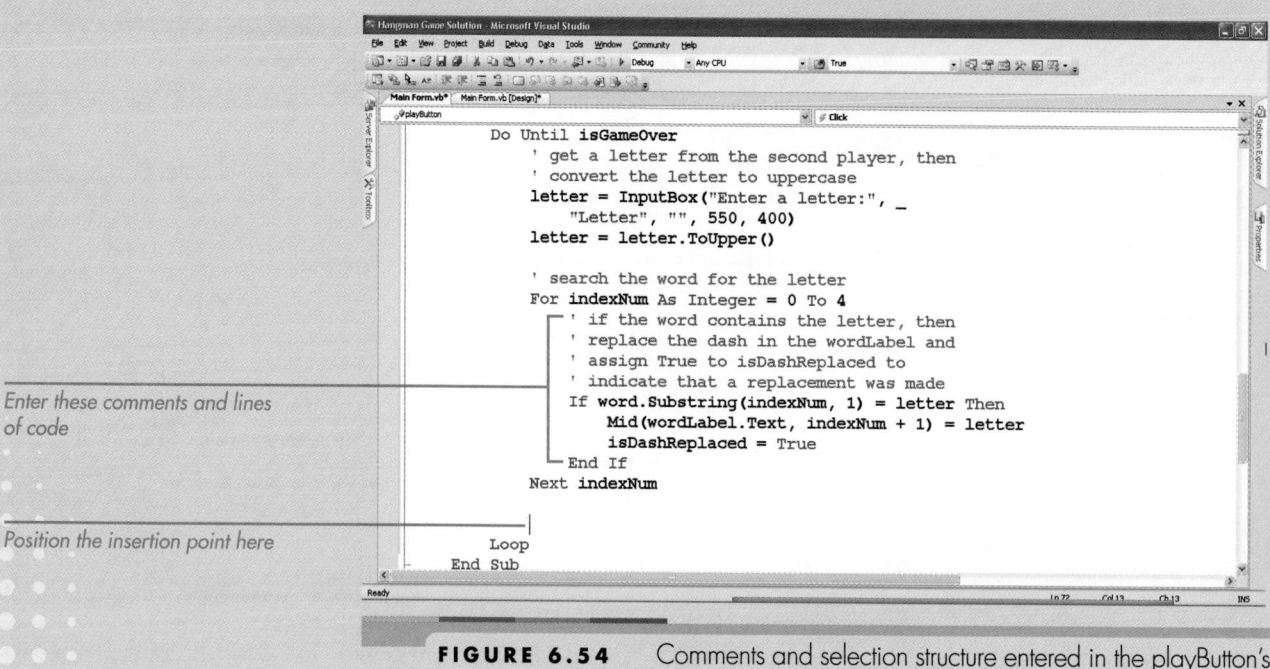

Enter these comments and lines of code

Position the insertion point here

**FIGURE 6.54**    Comments and selection structure entered in the playButton's Click event procedure

12. The next task in the outer repetition structure is a selection structure that determines whether a dash was replaced in the word. Type ' **determine whether a dash was replaced** and press **Enter**, then type **if isdashreplaced then** and press **Enter**.

13. If a dash was replaced in the word, the selection structure's true path uses a nested selection structure to determine whether the word contains any more dashes. If all of the dashes have been replaced in the word, then the game is over and the nested selection structure's true path assigns the Boolean value True to the isGameOver variable. It also displays the "Great guessing!" message in a message box. Otherwise, the nested selection structure's false path assigns the Boolean value False to the isDashReplaced variable; this resets the variable for the next search. Type the comments and selection structure shown in Figure 6.55, then position the insertion point as shown in the figure.

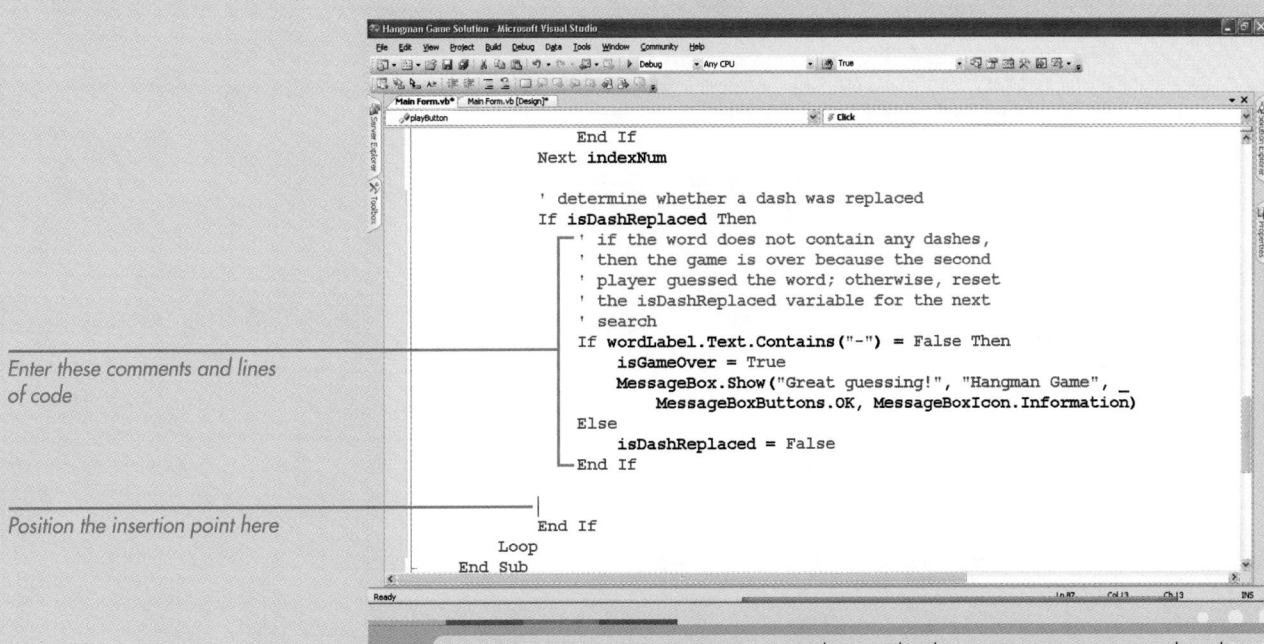

Enter these comments and lines of code

Position the insertion point here

**FIGURE 6.55**    Comments and nested selection structure entered in the playButton's Click event procedure

14. If a dash was not replaced in the word, it means that the letter entered by the second player does not appear in the word. In that case, the outer selection structure's false path displays the incorrect letter in the incorrectLabel, and also adds the number one to the contents of the incorrectCounter variable. Additionally, it uses a selection structure and the value stored in the incorrectCounter variable to determine which of the 10 picture boxes to display. If the incorrectCounter variable contains the number 10, the game is over because the second player reached the maximum number of incorrect guesses allowed. In that case, the selection structure assigns the Boolean value True to the isGameOver variable and also displays (in a message box) an appropriate message along with the word. Type the comments and additional lines of code shaded in Figure 6.56, which shows the code for the Hangman Game application.

```
' Project name:         Hangman Game Project
' Project purpose:      The project simulates the Hangman game.
' Created/revised by:   <your name> on <current date>

Option Explicit On
Option Strict On

Public Class MainForm

    Private Sub exitButton_Click(ByVal sender As Object, _
        ByVal e As System.EventArgs) Handles exitButton.Click
        Me.Close()
    End Sub

    Private Sub playButton_Click(ByVal sender As Object, _
        ByVal e As System.EventArgs) Handles playButton.Click
        ' simulates the Hangman game
```

**(Figure is continued on next page)**

```
Dim word As String
Dim letter As String
Dim isDashReplaced As Boolean
Dim isGameOver As Boolean
Dim incorrectCounter As Integer

' hide the picture boxes
bottomPictureBox.Visible = False
postPictureBox.Visible = False
topPictureBox.Visible = False
ropePictureBox.Visible = False
headPictureBox.Visible = False
bodyPictureBox.Visible = False
rightArmPictureBox.Visible = False
leftArmPictureBox.Visible = False
rightLegPictureBox.Visible = False
leftLegPictureBox.Visible = False

' get a 5-letter word from the first player
word = InputBox("Enter a 5-letter word:", "Hangman Game")
Do Until word.Length = 5
    word = InputBox("Enter a 5-letter word:", "Hangman Game")
Loop

' convert the word to uppercase
word = word.ToUpper()

' display five dashes in the wordLabel
' and clear the incorrectLabel
wordLabel.Text = "-----"
incorrectLabel.Text = String.Empty

' allow the second player to guess a letter
' the game is over when the second player
' either guesses the word or makes 10
' incorrect guesses
Do Until isGameOver
    ' get a letter from the second player, then
    ' convert the letter to uppercase
    letter = InputBox("Enter a letter:", _
        "Letter", "", 550, 400)
    letter = letter.ToUpper()

    ' search the word for the letter
    For indexNum As Integer = 0 To 4
        ' if the word contains the letter, then
        ' replace the dash in the wordLabel and
        ' assign True to isDashReplaced to
        ' indicate that a replacement was made
        If word.Substring(indexNum, 1) = letter Then
            Mid(wordLabel.Text, indexNum + 1) = letter
```

*(Figure is continued on next page)*

```
                        isDashReplaced = True
            End If
    Next indexNum


    ' determine whether a dash was replaced
    If isDashReplaced Then
        ' if the word does not contain any dashes,
        ' then the game is over because the second
        ' player guessed the word; otherwise, reset
        ' the isDashReplaced variable for the next
        ' search
        If wordLabel.Text.Contains("-") = False Then
            isGameOver = True
            MessageBox.Show("Great guessing!", "Hangman Game", _
                MessageBoxButtons.OK, MessageBoxIcon.Information)
        Else
            isDashReplaced = False
        End If


    Else     ' processed when no dash was replaced
        ' display the incorrect letter, then update
        ' the incorrect counter variable, then show
        ' the appropriate picture box
        incorrectLabel.Text = incorrectLabel.Text & " " & letter
        incorrectCounter = incorrectCounter + 1
        Select Case incorrectCounter
            Case 1
                bottomPictureBox.Visible = True
            Case 2
                postPictureBox.Visible = True
            Case 3
                topPictureBox.Visible = True
            Case 4
                ropePictureBox.Visible = True
            Case 5
                headPictureBox.Visible = True
            Case 6
                bodyPictureBox.Visible = True
            Case 7
                rightArmPictureBox.Visible = True
            Case 8
                leftArmPictureBox.Visible = True
            Case 9
                rightLegPictureBox.Visible = True
            Case 10
                leftLegPictureBox.Visible = True
                isGameOver = True
```

*(Figure is continued on next page)*

```
                    MessageBox.Show("Sorry, the word is " _
                        & word & ".", "Hangman Game", _
                        MessageBoxButtons.OK, _
                        MessageBoxIcon.Information)
                End Select
            End If
        Loop
    End Sub
End Class
```

**FIGURE 6.56**     Code for the Hangman Game application

Now that you have finished coding the application, you will test it to verify that it is working correctly.

**To test the Hangman Game application:**

1. Save the solution, then start the application. Click the **Play** button. The Hangman Game dialog box opens.
2. Type **cat** in the Hangman Game dialog box, then press **Enter** to select the OK button. Because the word does not contain five characters, the dialog box appears again and prompts you to enter a 5-letter word.
3. Type **puppy** in the Hangman Game dialog box, then press **Enter**. The Letter dialog box opens.
4. Type **p** in the Letter dialog box, then press **Enter** to select the OK button. The playButton's Click event procedure uses the letter P to replace three of the dashes in the wordLabel, as shown in Figure 6.57.

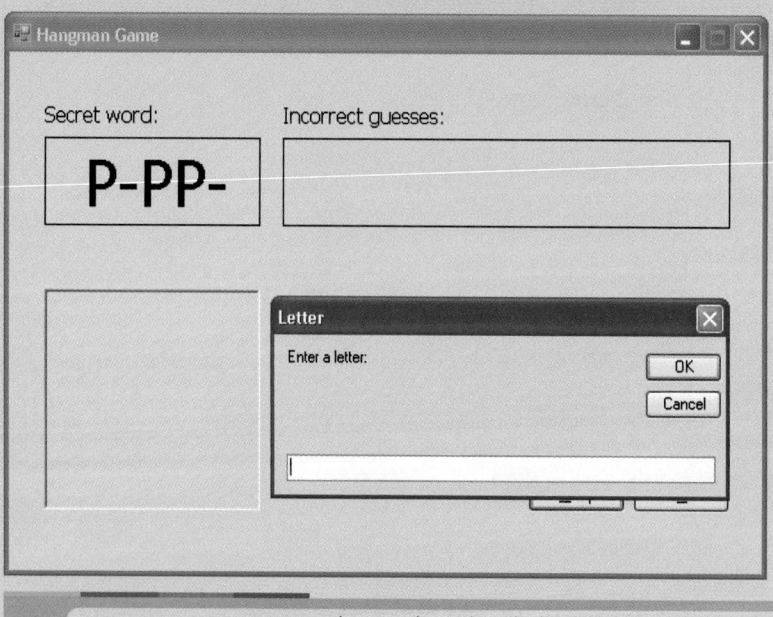

**FIGURE 6.57**     Dashes replaced with the letter P

5. Type **a** in the Letter dialog box, then press **Enter**. The playButton's Click event procedure displays the letter A in the incorrectLabel and also makes the bottomPictureBox visible, as shown in Figure 6.58.

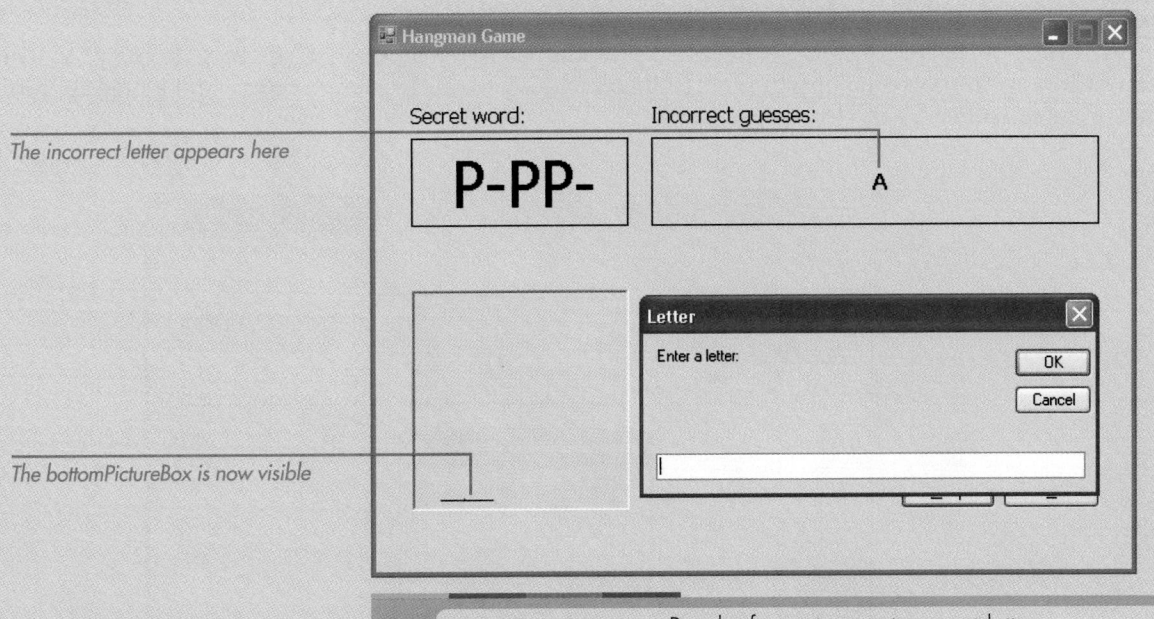

*The incorrect letter appears here*

*The bottomPictureBox is now visible*

**FIGURE 6.58**     Result of entering an incorrect letter

6. Type **b** in the Letter dialog box, then press **Enter**. The playButton's Click event procedure adds the letter B to the contents of the incorrectLabel and also makes the postPictureBox visible.

7. Type **u** in the Letter dialog box, then press **Enter**. Type **y** in the Letter dialog box, then press **Enter**. The playButton's Click event procedure displays the "Great guessing!" message in a message box, as shown in Figure 6.59.

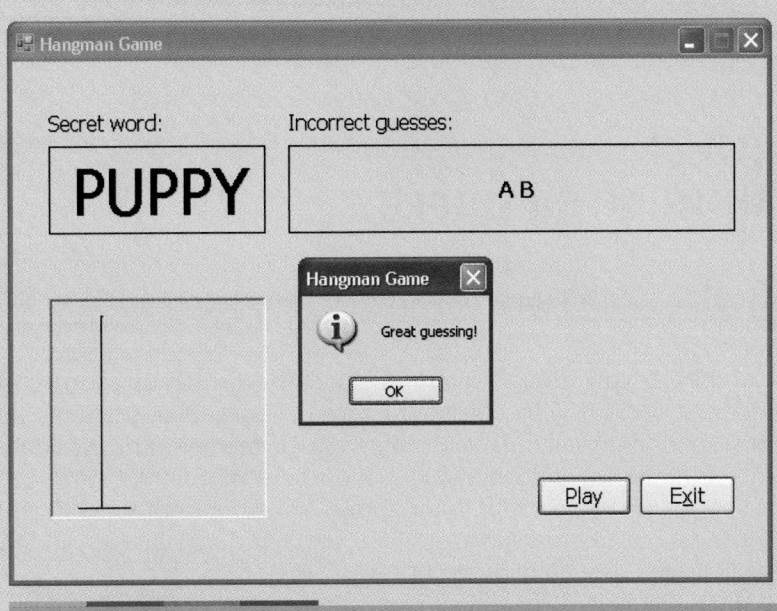

**FIGURE 6.59**     Result of guessing the word

8. Press **Enter** to close the message box.

Now you will enter a word followed by two correct guesses and 10 incorrect guesses.

9. Click the **Play** button. Type **basic** and press **Enter**.

10. Type **c** and press **Enter**, then type **a** and press **Enter**.

11. Type the following 10 letters, pressing **Enter** after typing each letter: **d, e, f, g, h, j, k, x, y, z**. The playButton's Click event procedure displays the 10 incorrect letters, the 10 picture boxes, and a message box, as shown in Figure 6.60.

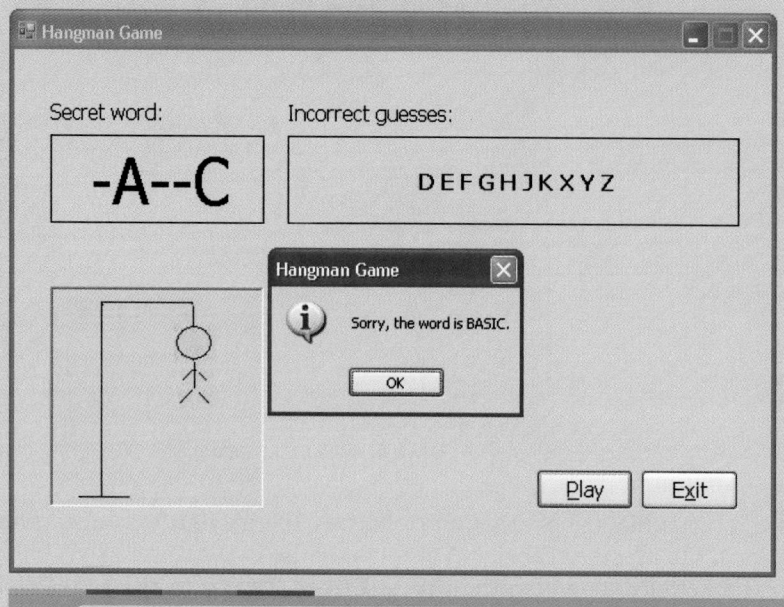

**FIGURE 6.60**    Result of making 10 incorrect guesses

12. Press **Enter** to close the message box, then click the **Exit** button to end the application. If necessary, close the Output window.

13. Close the Code Editor window, then close the solution.

# PROGRAMMING EXAMPLE

## Glasgow Health Club Dues Calculator Application

Each member of the Glasgow Health Club must pay monthly dues that consist of a basic fee and, optionally, one or more additional charges. The basic fee for a single membership is $50 per month. The basic fee for a family membership is $90 per month. If the member has a single membership, the additional charges are $30 per month for tennis, $25 per month for golf, and $20 per month for racquetball. If the member has a family membership, the additional charges are $50 per month for tennis, $35 per month for golf, and $30 per month for racquetball. The application should display the member's basic fee, additional charges, and monthly dues. Name the solution Glasgow Health Solution. Name the project Glasgow Health Project. Name the form file Main Form.vb. Save the application in the VbReloaded\Chap06 folder.

**TOE Chart:**

| Task | Object | Event |
|---|---|---|
| 1. Use the radio buttons to determine the basic fee<br>2. Use the check boxes to determine any additional fees<br>3. Calculate the monthly dues by adding together the basic fee and any additional fees<br>4. Display the basic fee in the basicLabel<br>5. Display any additional fees in the additionalLabel<br>6. Display the monthly dues in the duesLabel | calcButton | Click |
| End the application | exitButton | Click |
| Display the membership types | singleRadioButton, familyRadioButton | None |
| Display the additional options | golfCheckBox, TennisCheckBox, racquetCheckBox | None |
| Display the basic fee (from calcButton) | basicLabel | None |
| Display any additional fees (from calcButton) | additionalLabel | None |
| Display the monthly dues (from calcButton) | duesLabel | None |

**FIGURE 6.61**

**User Interface:**

**FIGURE 6.62**

**Objects, Properties, and Settings:**

| Object | Property | Setting |
| --- | --- | --- |
| Form1 | Name | MainForm |
| | Font | Tahoma, 12 point |
| | MaximizeBox | False |
| | Size | 340, 405 |
| | StartPosition | CenterScreen |
| | Text | Glasgow Health Club |
| Label1 | Location | 32, 174 |
| | Text | Basic fee: |
| Label2 | Location | 159, 174 |
| | Text | Additional: |
| Label3 | Location | 32, 257 |
| | Text | Monthly dues: |
| Label4 | Name | basicLabel |
| | AutoSize | False |
| | BorderStyle | FixedSingle |
| | Location | 34, 193 |
| | Size | 108, 26 |
| | Text | (empty) |
| | TextAlign | MiddleCenter |
| Label5 | Name | additionalLabel |
| | AutoSize | False |
| | BorderStyle | FixedSingle |
| | Location | 161, 193 |
| | Size | 132, 26 |
| | Text | (empty) |
| | TextAlign | MiddleCenter |
| Label6 | Name | duesLabel |
| | AutoSize | False |
| | BorderStyle | FixedSingle |
| | Location | 34, 282 |
| | Size | 104, 63 |
| | Text | (empty) |
| | TextAlign | MiddleCenter |
| RadioButton1 | Name | singleRadioButton |
| | Checked | True |
| | Location | 11, 31 |
| | Size | 65, 23 |
| | Text | &Single |
| RadioButton2 | Name | familyRadioButton |
| | Location | 11, 61 |
| | Size | 68, 23 |
| | Text | &Family |

*(Figure continued on next page)*

| CheckBox1 | Name | golfCheckBox |
|---|---|---|
|  | Location | 12, 26 |
|  | Size | 52, 23 |
|  | Text | &Golf |
| CheckBox2 | Name | tennisCheckBox |
|  | Location | 12, 55 |
|  | Size | 70, 23 |
|  | Text | &Tennis |
| CheckBox3 | Name | racquetCheckBox |
|  | Location | 12, 84 |
|  | Size | 104, 23 |
|  | Text | &Racquetball |
| GroupBox1 | Location | 34, 29 |
|  | Size | 108, 120 |
|  | Text | Membership |
| GroupBox2 | Location | 161, 29 |
|  | Size | 132, 120 |
|  | Text | Additional |
| Button1 | Name | calcButton |
|  | Location | 161, 312 |
|  | Size | 75, 33 |
|  | Text | &Calculate |
| Button2 | Name | exitButton |
|  | Location | 242, 312 |
|  | Size | 51, 33 |
|  | Text | E&xit |

**FIGURE 6.63**

**Tab Order:**

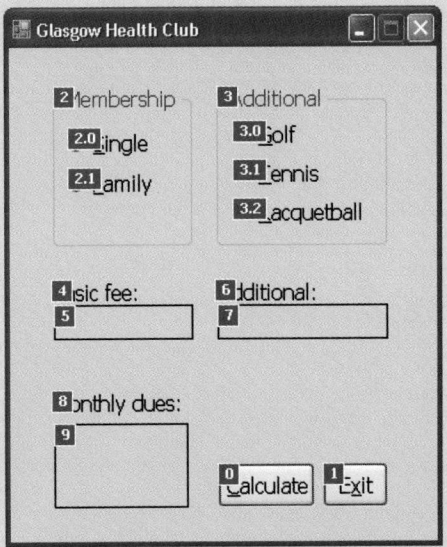

**FIGURE 6.64**

**Pseudocode:**

**exitButton Click event procedure**

1. close application

**calcButton Click event procedure**

1. if the Single radio button is selected
       assign 50 as the basic fee
       if the Golf check box is selected
           add 25 to the additional fee accumulator
       end if
       if the Tennis check box is selected
           add 30 to the additional fee accumulator
       end if
       if the Racquetball check box is selected
           add 20 to the additional fee accumulator
       end if
   else
       assign 90 as the basic fee
       if the Golf check box is selected
           add 35 to the additional fee accumulator
       end if
       if the Tennis check box is selected
           add 50 to the additional fee accumulator
       end if
       if the Racquetball check box is selected
           add 30 to the additional fee accumulator
       end if
   end if
2. calculate the total fee by adding together the basic fee and any additional fee
3. display the basic, additional, and total fees

**singleRadioButton, familyRadioButton, golfCheckBox, tennisCheckBox, and racquetCheckBox Click event procedures**

1. clear the Text property of the basicLabel, additionalLabel, and duesLabel

**Code:**

```
' Project name:        Glasgow Health Project
' Project purpose:     The project calculates a member's
'                      monthly dues.
' Created/revisd by:   <your name> on <current date>

Option Explicit On
Option Strict On

(Figure is continued on next page)
```

```
Public Class MainForm

    Private Sub exitButton_Click(ByVal sender As Object, _
        ByVal e As System.EventArgs) Handles exitButton.Click
        Me.Close()
    End Sub

    Private Sub calcButton_Click(ByVal sender As Object, _
        ByVal e As System.EventArgs) Handles calcButton.Click
        ' calculates the monthly dues, which include
        ' a basic fee and optional charges

        Const SingleBasicFee As Integer = 50
        Const FamilyBasicFee As Integer = 90
        Const SingleTennisFee As Integer = 30
        Const SingleGolfFee As Integer = 25
        Const SingleRacquetFee As Integer = 20
        Const FamilyTennisFee As Integer = 50
        Const FamilyGolfFee As Integer = 35
        Const FamilyRacquetFee As Integer = 30
        Dim basicFee As Integer
        Dim addFee As Integer
        Dim totalFee As Integer

        ' determine which radio button is checked
        ' and which check boxes (if any) are
        ' checked
        Select Case True
            Case singleRadioButton.Checked
                basicFee = SingleBasicFee
                If golfCheckBox.Checked Then
                    addFee = addFee + SingleGolfFee
                End If
                If tennisCheckBox.Checked Then
                    addFee = addFee + SingleTennisFee
                End If
                If racquetCheckBox.Checked Then
                    addFee = addFee + SingleRacquetFee
                End If
            Case familyRadioButton.Checked
                basicFee = FamilyBasicFee
                If golfCheckBox.Checked Then
                    addFee = addFee + FamilyGolfFee
                End If
                If tennisCheckBox.Checked Then
                    addFee = addFee + FamilyTennisFee
                End If
                If racquetCheckBox.Checked Then
                    addFee = addFee + FamilyRacquetFee
                End If
        End Select
```

*(Figure is continued on next page)*

```vb
      ' calculate the total fee
      totalFee = basicFee + addFee

      ' display the basic, additional, and total fees
      basicLabel.Text = basicFee.ToString("N2")
      additionalLabel.Text = addFee.ToString("N2")
      duesLabel.Text = totalFee.ToString("C2")
   End Sub

   Private Sub familyRadioButton_Click(ByVal sender As Object, _
      ByVal e As System.EventArgs) Handles familyRadioButton.Click
      basicLabel.Text = String.Empty
      additionalLabel.Text = String.Empty
      duesLabel.Text = String.Empty
   End Sub

   Private Sub singleRadioButton_Click(ByVal sender As Object, _
      ByVal e As System.EventArgs) Handles singleRadioButton.Click
      basicLabel.Text = String.Empty
      additionalLabel.Text = String.Empty
      duesLabel.Text = String.Empty
   End Sub

   Private Sub golfCheckBox_Click(ByVal sender As Object, _
      ByVal e As System.EventArgs) Handles golfCheckBox.Click
      basicLabel.Text = String.Empty
      additionalLabel.Text = String.Empty
      duesLabel.Text = String.Empty
   End Sub

   Private Sub racquetCheckBox_Click(ByVal sender As Object, _
      ByVal e As System.EventArgs) Handles racquetCheckBox.Click
      basicLabel.Text = String.Empty
      additionalLabel.Text = String.Empty
      duesLabel.Text = String.Empty
   End Sub

   Private Sub tennisCheckBox_Click(ByVal sender As Object, _
      ByVal e As System.EventArgs) Handles tennisCheckBox.Click
      basicLabel.Text = String.Empty
      additionalLabel.Text = String.Empty
      duesLabel.Text = String.Empty
   End Sub
End Class
```

**FIGURE 6.65**

## Quick Review

- You can use a string's Length property to determine the number of characters contained in the string.
- The TrimStart method removes one or more characters from the beginning of a string, and the TrimEnd method removes one or more characters from the end of a string. The Trim method removes one or more characters from both the beginning and end of a string. The TrimStart, TrimEnd, and Trim methods return a string with the appropriate characters removed (trimmed).
- You can use the Remove method to remove one or more characters from anywhere in a string. The Remove method returns a string with the appropriate characters removed.
- You can use the Replace method to replace all occurrences of a sequence of characters in a string with another sequence of characters. The method returns a string with all occurrences of the old value replaced with the new value.
- The Mid statement allows you to replace a specific number of characters in a string with characters from another string.
- The PadLeft method allows you to insert characters at the beginning of a string, until the string is a specified length. The PadRight method allows you to insert characters at the end of a string, until the string is a specified length. Both methods return a string with the appropriate characters inserted.
- You can use the Insert method to insert characters within a string. The method returns a string with the appropriate characters inserted.
- The StartsWith method determines whether a string begins with a specific sequence of characters. The method returns either the Boolean value True or the Boolean value False.
- The EndsWith method determines whether a string ends with a specific sequence of characters. The method returns either the Boolean value True or the Boolean value False.
- You can use the Contains method to search a string to determine whether it contains a specific sequence of characters. The method returns either the Boolean value True or the Boolean value False.
- The IndexOf method allows you to search a string to determine whether it contains a specific sequence of characters. The method returns the number -1 when the sequence of characters is not contained in the portion of the string being searched; otherwise, it returns the index of the starting position of the characters within the string.
- The Substring method allows you to access one or more characters contained in a string. The method returns a string that contains the specified number of characters.
- You can use the String.Compare method to determine whether one string is equal to another string. The method returns the number 0 when both strings are equal. It returns the number –1 when *string1* is less than *string2*, and returns the number 1 when *string1* is greater than *string2*.
- The Like comparison operator allows you to use pattern-matching characters to determine whether one string is equal to another string.
- Use radio buttons when you want to limit the user to one of two or more related and mutually exclusive choices.
- The minimum number of radio buttons in a group is two, and the recommended maximum is seven.
- The label in the radio button's Text property should be entered using sentence capitalization.
- Assign a unique access key to each radio button in an interface.

- Use a container (such as a group box, panel, or table layout panel) to create separate groups of radio buttons. Only one button in each group can be selected at any one time.
- Designate a default radio button in each group of radio buttons.
- Use check boxes when you want to allow the user to select any number of choices from a group of one or more independent and nonexclusive choices.
- The label in the check box's Text property should be entered using sentence capitalization.
- Assign a unique access key to each check box in an interface.

## Key Terms

A string's **Length property** stores an integer that represents the number of characters contained in the string.

The **TrimStart**, **TrimEnd**, **Trim**, and **Remove methods** remove one or more characters from a string, and then return a string with the appropriate characters removed.

The unique number assigned to each character in a string is called an **index**.

The **Replace method** returns a string with all occurrences of a sequence of characters replaced with another sequence of characters.

The **Mid statement** replaces a portion of a string with another string.

The **PadLeft**, **PadRight**, and **Insert methods** return a string with the appropriate characters inserted.

The **StartsWith** and **EndsWith methods** return the Boolean value True when a specific sequence of characters occurs at the beginning and end, respectively, of a string; otherwise, they return the Boolean value False.

The **Contains method** returns the Boolean value True when a specific sequence of characters appears in a string; otherwise, it returns the Boolean value False.

The **IndexOf method** searches a *string* for a *subString*, and returns the number –1 when the *subString* is not found in the *string*; otherwise, it returns the index of the starting position of *subString* within *string*.

The **Substring method** returns characters from a string.

The **String.Compare method** compares two strings, *string1* and *string2*. It returns the number 0 when both strings are equal. It returns the number 1 when *string1* is greater than *string2*, and returns the number –1 when *string1* is less than *string2*.

The String.Compare method uses **word sort rules** when comparing strings. Following the rules, a number is considered less than a lowercase letter, which is considered less than an uppercase letter.

The **Like operator** allows you to use pattern-matching characters to determine whether one string is equal to another string.

You use the **RadioButton tool** to add a radio button to an interface.

A **radio button** allows you to limit the user to only one choice in a group of two or more related and mutually exclusive choices.

The **default radio button** is the radio button that is automatically selected when the interface first appears.

You use the **CheckBox tool** to add a check box to an interface.

**Check boxes** allow the user to select any number of choices from a group of one or more independent and nonexclusive choices.

## Self-Check Questions and Answers

1. You can use the _____ to determine the number of characters in a string.
   a. Length method
   b. Length property
   c. NumChars property
   d. Size property

2. Which of the following removes the leading and trailing spaces from the addressTextBox?
   a. `addressTextBox.Text = addressTextBox.Text.Trim()`
   b. `addressTextBox.Text = addressTextBox.Text.TrimAll()`
   c. `addressTextBox.Text = addressTextBox.Trim()`
   d. None of the above.

3. Which of the following changes the name "Mary Smyth" to "Mark Smyth"? The name is stored in the `fullName` variable.
   a. `fullName = fullName.Change("y", "k")`
   b. `fullName =fullName.Replace("y", "k")`
   c. `Mid(fullName, 4) = "k"`
   d. Both b and c.

4. You can use the _____ method to right-align a string within a control.
   a. Align
   b. PadLeft
   c. StartsWith
   d. None of the above.

5. Which of the following changes the name "Mary Smyth" to "Mary"? The name is stored in the `fullName` variable.
   a. `fullName = fullName.Replace(" Smyth", "")`
   b. `fullName = fullName.Remove("Smyth")`
   c. `fullName = fullName.TrimEnd(" Smyth")`
   d. All of the above.

6. The `String.Compare("dog", "Dog")` method will return _____.
   a. -1
   b. 0
   c. 1
   d. None of the above.

7. Which of the following methods will return the Boolean value True when the `petName` variable contains the string "Micki"?
   a. `petName.StartsWith("M")`
   b. `petName.Contains("k")`
   c. `petName Like "M*"`
   d. All of the above.

8. Which of the following statements changes the name "Mary Smyth" to "Mary E. Smyth"? The name is stored in the `fullName` variable.
   a. `fullName = fullName.Insert(4, " E.")`
   b. `fullName = fullName.Insert(5, "E. ")`
   c. `fullName = fullName.Replace(" ", " E. ")`
   d. All of the above.

9. Which of the following expressions evaluates to True when the `partNum` variable contains the string "123X45"?
   a. `partNum Like "999[A-Z]99"`
   b. `partNum Like "######"`
   c. `partNum Like "###[A-Z]##"`
   d. None of the above.

10. What will the `address.IndexOf("Main")` method return when the `address` variable contains "34 Main Street"?
    a. 3
    b. 4
    c. True
    d. None of the above.

Answers: 1) b, 2) a, 3) c, 4) b, 5) a, 6) a, 7) d, 8) d, 9) c, 10) a

## Review Questions

1. Assume that the `amount` variable contains the string "$56.55". Which of the following statements removes the dollar sign from the variable's contents?
   a. `amount = amount.Remove("$")`
   b. `amount = amount.Remove(0, 1)`
   c. `amount = amount.TrimStart("$"c)`
   d. Both b and c.

2. Assume that the `state` variable contains the string "MI   " (the letters M and I followed by three spaces). Which of the following statements removes the three spaces from the variable's contents?
   a. `state = state.Remove(2, 3)`
   b. `state = state.Remove(3, 3)`
   c. `state = state.TrimEnd(2, 3)`
   d. Both a and c.

3. Which of the following statements removes any dollar signs and percent signs from the beginning and end of the string stored in the `amount` variable?
   a. `amount = amount.Trim("$"c, "%"c)`
   b. `amount = amount.Trim("$, %"c)`
   c. `amount = amount.TrimAll("$"c, "%"c)`
   d. `amount = amount.TrimAll("$, %"c)`

4. Which of the following methods can be used to determine whether the string stored in the `partNum` variable begins with the letter A?
   a. `partNum.BeginsWith("A")`
   b. `partNum.Starts("A")`
   c. `partNum.StartsWith("A")`
   d. `partNum.StartsWith = "A"`

5. Which of the following methods can be used to determine whether the string stored in the `partNum` variable ends with either the letter B or the letter b?
   a. `partNum.Ends("B, b")`
   b. `partNum.Ends("B", "b")`
   c. `partNum.EndsWith("B", "b")`
   d. `partNum.ToUpper().EndsWith("B")`

6. Which of the following statements assigns the first three characters in the `partNum` variable to the code variable?
   a. `code = partNum.Assign(0, 3)`
   b. `code = partNum.Sub(0, 3)`
   c. `code = partNum.Substring(0, 3)`
   d. `code = partNum.Substring(1, 3)`

7. Assume that the `word` variable contains the string "Bells". Which of the following statements changes the contents of the `word` variable to "Bell"?
   a. `word = word.Remove(word.Length - 1, 1)`
   b. `word = word.Substring(0, word.Length - 1)`
   c. `word = word.Replace("s", "")`
   d. All of the above.

8. Which of the following statements changes the contents of the `zip` variable from "60121" to "60323"?
   a. `Replace(zip, "1", "3")`
   b. `zip.Replace("1", "3")`
   c. `zip = zip.Replace("1", "3")`
   d. `zip = zip.Replace("3", "1")`

9. Which of the following methods can be used to determine whether the `amount` variable contains the dollar sign?
   a. `amount.Contains("$")`
   b. `amount.IndexOf("$")`
   c. `amount.IndexOf("$", 0)`
   d. All of the above.

10. Which of the following statements changes the contents of the `zip` variable from "60537" to "60536"?
    a. `Mid(zip, "7", "6")`
    b. `Mid(zip, 4, "6")`
    c. `zip = Mid(zip, 4, "6")`
    d. None of the above.

11. Which of the following statements changes the contents of the `word` variable from "men" to "mean"?
    a. `word = word.AddTo(2, "a")`
    b. `word = word.Insert(2, "a")`
    c. `word = word.Insert(3, "a")`
    d. `word = word.Replace(2, "a")`

12. When the `message` variable contains the string "Happy holidays", the `message.IndexOf("day")` method returns _____.
    a. -1
    b. 0
    c. 10
    d. 11

13. When the `message` variable contains the string "Good morning", the statement `Mid(message, 6) = "night"` changes the contents of the variable to _____.
    a. Good mnight
    b. Good mnightg
    c. Good night
    d. Good nightng

14. Which of the following If clauses can be used to determine whether the `amount` variable contains a comma?
    a. `If amount.Contains(",") Then`
    b. `If amount.Substring(",") Then`
    c. `If amount.IndexOf(",") > -1 Then`
    d. Both a and c.

15. Which of the following can be used to assign the fifth character in the `word` variable to the `letter` variable?
    a. `letter = word.Substring(4)`
    b. `letter = word.Substring(5, 1)`
    c. `letter = word(5).Substring`
    d. None of the above.

16. If a check box or radio button is selected, its _____ property contains the Boolean value True.
    a. Checked
    b. On
    c. Selected
    d. Value

17. Which of the following can be used to determine whether the `partNum` variable contains two characters followed by a digit?
    a. `If partNum Like "??#" Then`
    b. `If partNum Like "**?" Then`
    c. `If partNum Like "##?" Then`
    d. None of the above.

18. Which of the following can be used to determine whether the `item` variable contains either the word "shirt" or the word "skirt"? You can assume that the `item` variable contains uppercase letters only.
    a. `If item = "SHIRT" AndAlso item = "SKIRT" Then`
    b. `If item = "S[HK]IRT" Then`
    c. `If item Like "S[HK]IRT" Then`
    d. `If item Like "S[H-K]IRT" Then`

19. The `String.Compare(city, "Paris", True)` method returns _____ when the `city` variable contains the string "PARIS".
    a. True
    b. False
    c. 0
    d. 1

20. Which of the following assigns the contents of the `message` variable followed by four exclamation points (!) to the `newMessage` variable? The `message` variable contains the string "Great job".
    a. `newMessage = message.PadLeft(4, "!"c)`
    b. `newMessage = message.PadLeft(13, "!")`
    c. `newMessage = message.PadRight(4, "!")`
    d. `newMessage = message.PadRight(13, "!"c)`

## Review Exercises – Short Answer

1.  Write the Visual Basic statement that displays in the sizeLabel the number of characters contained in the message variable.

2.  Write the Visual Basic statement that removes the leading spaces from the city variable.

3.  Write the Visual Basic statement that removes the leading and trailing spaces from a String variable named number.

4.  Write the Visual Basic statement that removes any trailing spaces, commas, and periods from a String variable named amount.

5.  Write the Visual Basic statement that uses the Remove method to remove the first two characters from the fullName variable.

6.  Write the Visual Basic code that uses the EndsWith method to determine whether the string stored in the inputRate variable ends with the percent sign. If it does, the code should use the TrimEnd method to remove the percent sign from the variable's contents.

7.  Assume that the partNum variable contains the string "ABCD34G". Write the Visual Basic statement that assigns the number 34 in the partNum variable to the code variable.

8.  Assume that the amount variable contains the string "3,123,560". Write the Visual Basic statement that assigns the contents of the variable, excluding the commas, to the amount variable.

9.  Write the Mid statement that changes the contents of the word variable from "mouse" to "mouth".

10. Write the Visual Basic statement that uses the Insert method to change the contents of the word variable from "mend" to "amend".

11. Write the Visual Basic statement that uses the IndexOf method to determine whether the address variable contains the street name "Elm Street" (entered in uppercase, lowercase, or a combination of uppercase and lowercase). Begin the search with the first character in the address variable, and assign the method's return value to the indexNum variable.

12. Write the Visual Basic statement that uses the Contains method to determine whether the address variable contains the street name "Elm Street" (entered in uppercase, lowercase, or a combination of uppercase and lowercase). Assign the method's return value to a Boolean variable named isContained.

13. Write the Visual Basic statement that uses the String.Compare method to determine whether the string stored in the item variable is equal to the string stored in the itemOrdered variable. Assign the method's return value to an Integer variable named result.

14. Write an If clause that uses the Like operator to determine whether the string stored in the state variable is equal to any of the following strings: "New York", "New Jersey", or "New Mexico".

15. Write the Visual Basic statement that changes the contents of the pay variable from "235.67" to "****235.67".

16. What will the newPhone = phone.Replace("800", "877") statement assign to the newPhone variable when the phone variable contains the string "1-800-999-9980"?  What will it assign when the phone variable contains the string "1-800-999-8006"?

17.  Sort the following strings using word sort rules: "Cat", "dog", "123", "MARY", "mary".

18. If the inventoryNum variable contains the string "ABX34", the inventoryNum = inventoryNum.Replace("X", "Z") statement changes the contents of the variable to "ABZ34". Rather than replace the letter X with the letter Z, you can remove the letter X and then insert the letter Z. Write the Visual Basic statements to accomplish the remove and insert operations.

19. Write the Visual Basic statement to compare the string stored in the departmentName variable with the string "Accounting". Ignore the case of the string when performing the comparison. Store the result of the comparison in an Integer variable named result.

20. Write the Visual Basic statement to search for the period in a string named price. Assign the location of the period to an Integer variable named location.

## Computer Exercises

1. In this exercise, you modify the Hangman Game application you created in the chapter's Programming Tutorial.
   a. Use Windows to make a copy of the Hangman Game Solution folder, which is contained in the VbReloaded\Chap06 folder. Rename the copy Hangman Game Solution-Ex1.
   b. Open the Hangman Game Solution (Hangman Game Solution.sln) file contained in the VbReloaded\Chap06\Hangman Game Solution-Ex1 folder.
   c. The application should verify that the word entered by the first player contains only letters of the alphabet. It also should verify that the character entered by the second player is a letter of the alphabet.
   d. Save the solution, then start and test the application. Click the Exit button to end the application, then close the solution.

2. In this exercise, you modify the Hangman Game application you created in the chapter's Programming Tutorial.
   a. Use Windows to make a copy of the Hangman Game Solution folder, which is contained in the VbReloaded\Chap06 folder. Rename the copy Hangman Game Solution-Ex2.
   b. Open the Hangman Game Solution (Hangman Game Solution.sln) file contained in the VbReloaded\Chap06\Hangman Game Solution-Ex2 folder.
   c. Modify the application so it allows the first player to enter a word that contains any number of characters.
   d. Save the solution, then start and test the application. Click the Exit button to end the application, then close the solution.

3.  In this exercise, you modify the Hangman Game application you created in the chapter's Programming Tutorial.
    a.  Use Windows to make a copy of the Hangman Game Solution folder, which is contained in the VbReloaded\Chap06 folder. Rename the copy Hangman Game Solution-Ex3.
    b.  Open the Hangman Game Solution (Hangman Game Solution.sln) file contained in the VbReloaded\Chap06\Hangman Game Solution-Ex3 folder.
    c.  Modify the application so it stops the game when the user clicks the Cancel button in the Letter dialog box.
    d.  Save the solution, then start and test the application. Click the Exit button to end the application, then close the solution.

4.  In this exercise, you complete an application that displays a shipping charge based on the ZIP code entered by the user.
    a.  Open the Zip Solution (Zip Solution.sln) file, which is contained in the VbReloaded\Chap06\Zip Solution folder.
    b.  The Display Shipping Charge button's Click event procedure should display the appropriate shipping charge based on the ZIP code entered by the user. To be valid, the ZIP code must contain exactly five digits, and the first three digits must be either "605" or "606". All ZIP codes beginning with "605" have a $25 shipping charge. All ZIP codes beginning with "606" have a $30 shipping charge. All other ZIP codes are invalid and the procedure should display an appropriate message. Code the procedure appropriately.
    c.  Save the solution, then start the application. Test the application using the following ZIP codes: 60677, 60511, 60344, and 7130.
    d.  Click the Exit button to end the application, then close the solution.

5.  In this exercise, you complete an application that displays the name of the month corresponding to three letters entered by the user.
    a.  Open the Month Solution (Month Solution.sln) file, which is contained in the VbReloaded\Chap06\Month Solution folder.
    b.  The user will enter the first three characters of the month's name in the monthTextBox. The Display Month button's Click event procedure should display the name of the month corresponding to the characters entered by the user. For example, if the user enters the three characters "Jan" (in any case), the procedure should display the string "January" in the monthLabel. If the user enters "Jun", the procedure should display "June". If the three characters entered by the user do not match any of the 12 months, or if the user does not enter exactly three characters, the procedure should display an appropriate message.
    c.  Save the solution, then start the application. Test the application using the following data: jun, dec, xyz, ju.
    d.  Click the Exit button to end the application, then close the solution.

6.  In this exercise, you code an application that displays the color of an item.
    a.  Open the Color Solution (Color Solution.sln) file, which is contained in the VbReloaded\Chap06\Color Solution folder.

b. The Display Color button's Click event procedure should display the color of the item whose item number is entered by the user. All item numbers contain exactly five characters. All items are available in four colors: blue, green, red, and white. The third character in the item number indicates the item's color, as follows:

| Character | Color |
|-----------|-------|
| B or b    | Blue  |
| G or g    | Green |
| R or r    | Red   |
| W or w    | White |

For example, if the user enters 12b45, the procedure should display the word "Blue" in the colorLabel. If the item number does not contain exactly five characters, or if the third character is not one of the characters listed above, the procedure should display an appropriate message in a message box.

c. Save the solution, then start the application. Test the application using the following item numbers: 12x, 12b45, 99G44, abr55, 78w99, and 23abc.

d. Click the Exit button to end the application, then close the solution.

7. In this exercise, you code an application that allows the user to enter a name (the first name followed by a space and the last name). The application then displays the name (the last name followed by a comma, a space, and the first name).

a. Build an appropriate interface. Name the solution Reverse Name Solution. Name the project Reverse Name Project. Save the application in the VbReloaded\Chap06 folder.

b. Code the application.

c. Save the solution, and then start the application. Test the application using the following names: Carol Smith, Jose Martinez, Sven Miller, and Susan.

d. Stop the application, then close the solution.

8. In this exercise, you modify the application that you created in Computer Exercise 7 so that it displays the names using proper case.

a. Use Windows to make a copy of the Reverse Name Solution folder, which is contained in the VbReloaded\Chap06 folder. Rename the folder Proper Case Solution.

b. Open the Reverse Name Solution (Reverse Name Solution.sln) file contained in the Proper Case Solution folder.

c. Modify the application so that it displays the first and last names in the proper case. In other words, the first and last names should begin with an uppercase letter, and the remaining letters should be lowercase.

d. Save the solution, then start the application. Test the application using jAke millEr as the name. The application should display Miller, Jake.

e. Stop the application, then close the solution.

9. In this exercise, you code an application that allows the user to enter a phone number. The application then removes any hyphens, spaces, and parentheses from the phone number before displaying the phone number.

a. Build an appropriate interface. Name the solution Phone Solution. Name the project Phone Project. Save the application in the VbReloaded\ Chap06 folder.

b. Code the application.

    c.  Save the solution, then start the application. Test the application using the following phone numbers: (555) 111-1111, 555-5555, and 123-456-1111.

    d.  Stop the application, then close the solution.

10.  In this exercise, you code an application that displays a message indicating whether a portion of a string begins with another string.

    a.  Open the String Solution (String Solution.sln) file, which is contained in the VbReloaded\Chap06\String Solution folder.

    b.  The application allows the user to enter a name (first name followed by a space and the last name) and the search text. If the last name (entered in any case) begins with the search text (entered in any case), the Display Message button's Click event procedure should display the message "The last name begins with" followed by a space and the search text. If the characters in the last name come before the search text (using word sort rules), display the message "The last name comes before" followed by a space and the search text. Finally, if the characters in the last name come after the search text (using word sort rules), display the message "The last name comes after" followed by a space and the search text.

    c.  Save the solution, then start the application. To test the application, enter Helga Swanson as the name, then use the following strings for the search text: g, ab, he, s, SY, sw, swan, and wan.

    d.  Click the Exit button to end the application, then close the solution.

11.  In this exercise, you modify the Glasgow Health Club application you created in the chapter's Programming Example. The modified application keeps track of the additional charges as the check boxes are selected and deselected.

    a.  Create the Glasgow Health Club application shown in the chapter's Programming Example.

    b.  Use Windows to make a copy of the Glasgow Health Solution folder, which is contained in the VbReloaded\Chap06 folder. Rename the copy Glasgow Health Solution-Modified.

    c.  Open the Glasgow Health Solution (Glasgow Health Solution.sln) file contained in the VbReloaded\Chap06\Glasgow Health Solution-Modified folder.

    d.  Declare a module-level variable named `additionalCharges`. The variable will accumulate the additional charges as the check boxes are selected and deselected.

    e.  Code each check box's Click event procedure so that it adds the appropriate additional charge to the `additionalCharges` variable when the check box is selected, and subtracts the appropriate additional amount from the `additionalCharges` variable when the check box is deselected. The additional charges are $30 per month for tennis, $25 per month for golf, and $20 per month for racquetball. (The additional charges are the same for Single and Family memberships.)

    f.  Make the appropriate changes to the Calculate button's Click event procedure.

    g.  Save the solution, then start and test the application. Click the Exit button to end the application, then close the solution.

12.  In this exercise, you create an application that allows the user to enter a word. The application should display the word in pig latin form. The rules for converting a word into pig latin form are as follows:

    1.  If the word begins with a vowel (A, E, I, O, or U), then add the string "-way" (a dash followed by the letters w, a, and y) to the end of the word. For example, the pig latin form of the word "ant" is "ant-way".

2. If the word does not begin with a vowel, first add a dash to the end of the word. Then continue moving the first character in the word to the end of the word until the first character is the letter A, E, I, O, U, or Y. Then add the string "ay" to the end of the word. For example, the pig latin form of the word "Chair" is "air-Chay".

3. If the word does not contain the letter A, E, I, O, U, or Y, then add the string "-way" to the end of the word. For example, the pig latin form of "56" is "56-way".

   a. Build an appropriate interface. Name the solution Pig Latin Solution. Name the project Pig latin Project. Save the application in the VbReloaded\Chap06 folder.

   b. Code the application.

   c. Save the solution, then start and test the application.

   d. Stop the application, then close the solution.

13. In this exercise, you code an application for Woodland School. The application allows a student to select the name of a state and the name of a capital city. After making his or her selections, the student can click the Verify Answer button to verify that the selected city is the capital of the selected state.

   a. Open the Capitals Solution (Capitals Solution.sln) file, which is contained in the VbReloaded\Chap06\Capitals Solution folder.

   b. Place the state radio buttons in a group box, and place the capital radio buttons in a different group box. Set the Tab order.

   c. Designate the first radio button in each group as the default radio button for the group.

   d. Declare two module-level String variables named `capital` and `choice`.

   e. Code the state radio buttons' Click event procedures so that each assigns the appropriate capital to the `capital` variable, and each removes the contents of the messageLabel.

   f. Code the capital radio buttons' Click event procedures so that each assigns the selected capital to the `choice` variable, and each removes the contents of the messageLabel.

   g. Code the Verify Answer button's Click event procedure so that it displays the word "Correct" in the messageLabel if the student selected the appropriate capital; otherwise, display the word "Incorrect".

   h. Save the solution, then start the application. Click Little Rock in the capital group, then click the Verify Answer button. Notice that the application is not working correctly. Click Illinois, then click Springfield, and then click the Verify Answer button. The application displays "Correct" in the messageLabel, which is correct. Click Salem, then click the Verify Answer button. The application displays "Incorrect" in the messageLabel, which is correct. Click the Exit button to stop the application.

   i. Why didn't the application work the first time?

   j. You can use the PerformClick method to fix the application. Research the method, then enter the appropriate code. Save the solution, then start and test the application.

   k. Click the Exit button to end the application, then close the solution.

14. In this exercise, you find and correct an error in an application. The process of finding and correcting errors is called debugging.

   a. Open the Debug Solution (Debug Solution.sln) file, which is contained in the VbReloaded\Chap06\Debug Solution folder.

   b. Open the Code Editor window. Review the existing code.

c. Start the application. Enter Tampa, Florida in the Address text box, then click the Display City button. The button displays the letter T in a message box, which is incorrect; it should display the word Tampa. Click the OK button to close the dialog box, then click the Exit button to end the application.

d. Correct the application's code, then save the solution and start the application.

e. Enter Tampa, Florida in the Address text box, then click the Display City button. The button should display the word Tampa in a message box. Close the dialog box.

f. Click the Exit button to end the application, then close the solution.

## Case Projects

### Georgetown Credit

Credit card companies typically assign a special digit, called a check digit, to the end of each customer's credit card number. Many methods for creating the check digit have been developed. One simple method is to multiply every other number in the credit card number by two, then add the products to the remaining numbers to get the total. You then take the last digit in the total and append it to the end of the number, as illustrated in Figure 6.66.

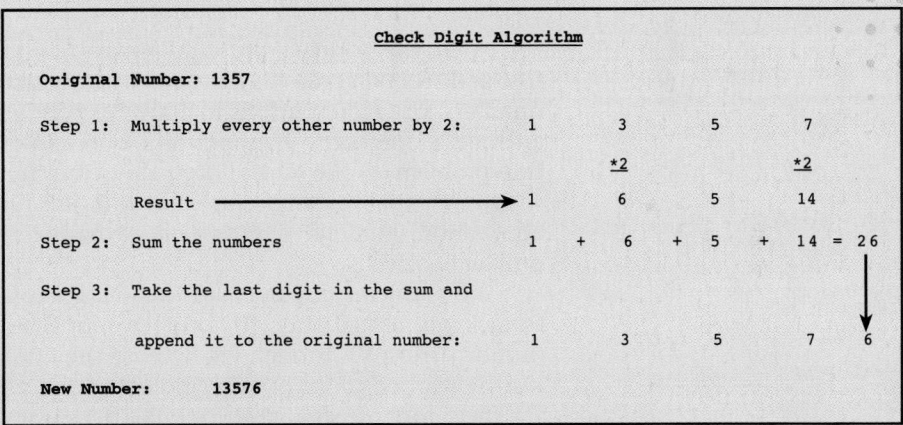

**FIGURE 6.66**

Create an application that allows the user to enter a five-digit credit card number; assume that the fifth digit is the check digit. The application should use the method illustrated in Figure 6.66 to verify that the credit card number is valid. Display appropriate messages indicating whether the credit card number is valid or invalid.

## Jacobson Finance

Create an application that allows the user to enter a password that contains five, six, or seven characters. The application then should create and display a new password as follows:

1.  Replace all vowels (A, E, I, O, and U) with the letter X.

2.  Replace all numbers with the letter Z.

3.  Reverse the characters in the password.

## BobCat Motors

Each salesperson at BobCat Motors is assigned an ID number, which consists of four characters. The first character is either the letter F or the letter P. The letter F indicates that the salesperson is a full-time employee; the letter P indicates that he or she is a part-time employee. The middle two characters are the salesperson's initials, and the last character is either a 1 or a 2. A 1 indicates that the salesperson sells new cars, and a 2 indicates that the salesperson sells used cars. Create an application that allows the sales manager to enter a salesperson's ID and the number of cars the salesperson sold during the month. The application should allow the sales manager to enter this information for as many salespeople as needed. The application should calculate and display the total number of cars sold by each of the following four categories of employees: full-time employees, part-time employees, employees selling new cars, and employees selling used cars.

## Delta Primary School

Ms. Chen, the principal of Delta Primary School, needs an application that the first and second grade students can use to practice both adding and subtracting numbers. Use radio buttons to allow Ms. Chen to select the grade level and arithmetic operation. The application should display the addition or subtraction problem on the screen, then allow the student to enter the answer, and then verify that the answer is correct. If the student's answer is not correct, the application should give him or her as many chances as necessary to answer the problem correctly.

The problems displayed for the first grade students should use numbers from 1 through 10 only. The problems for the second grade students should use numbers from 10 through 99. Because the first and second grade students have not yet learned about negative numbers, the subtraction problems should never ask them to subtract a larger number from a smaller one.

Ms. Chen also wants the application to keep track of how many correct and incorrect responses the student makes; this information will help her assess the student's math ability. Finally, she wants to be able to control the display of this information to keep students from being distracted or pressured by the number of right and wrong answers. Use a check box to allow Ms. Chen to show or hide the information.

CHAPTER

# 7

# Sub and Function Procedures

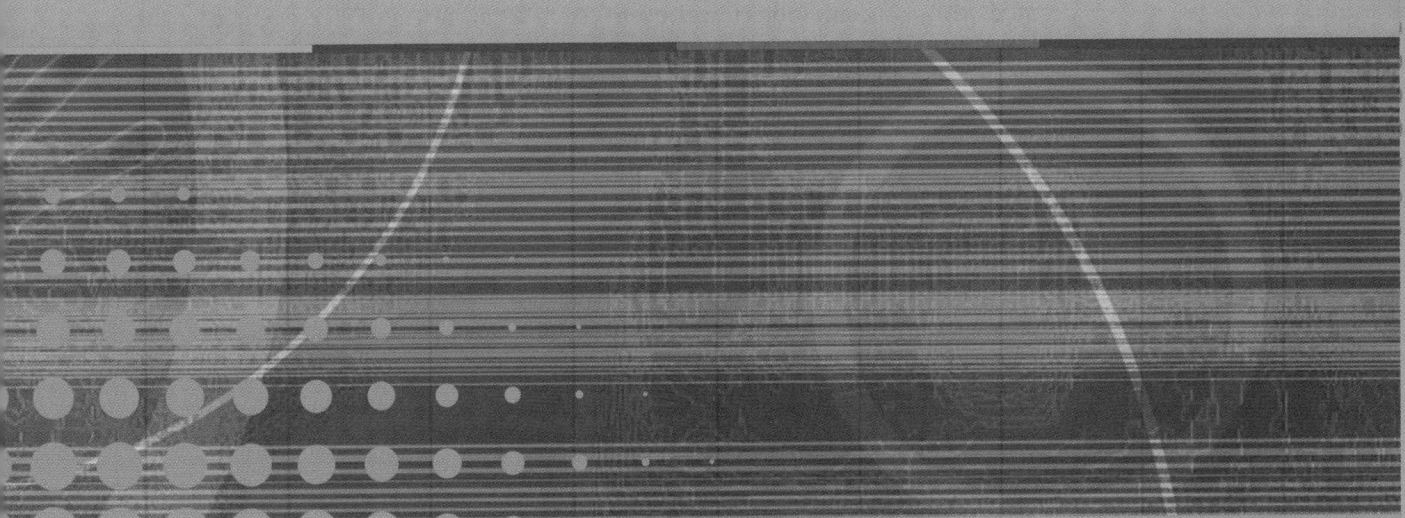

**After studying Chapter 7, you should be able to:**

- Explain the difference between a Sub procedure and a Function procedure
- Create a Sub procedure
- Create a procedure that receives information passed to it
- Explain the difference between passing data *by value* and passing data *by reference*
- Explain the purpose of the `sender` and e parameters
- Associate a procedure with more than one object and event
- Create a Function procedure
- Convert an object to a different type using the `TryCast` keyword

## PROCEDURES

A **procedure** is a block of program code that performs a specific task. Most procedures in Visual Basic are either Sub procedures or Function procedures. The difference between both types of procedures is that a **Function procedure** returns a value after performing its assigned task, whereas a **Sub procedure** does not return a value. Although you have been using Sub procedures since Chapter 1, this chapter provides a more in-depth look into their creation and use. After exploring the topic of Sub procedures, you then will learn how to create and use Function procedures.

## SUB PROCEDURES

There are two types of Sub procedures in Visual Basic: event procedures and independent Sub procedures. The procedures that you coded in previous chapters were event procedures. An event procedure is a Sub procedure that is associated with a specific object and event, such as a button's Click event or a text box's TextChanged event. Recall that the computer automatically processes an event procedure when the event occurs. An **independent Sub procedure**, on the other hand, is a collection of code that can be invoked from one or more places in an application. Unlike an event procedure, an independent Sub procedure is independent of any object and event, and is processed only when called, or invoked, from code.

Programmers use independent Sub procedures for two reasons. First, they allow the programmer to avoid duplicating code in different parts of a program. If a program needs to perform the same task several times, it is more efficient to enter the appropriate code once, in a procedure, and then call the procedure to perform its task when needed. Second, procedures allow large and complex applications, which typically are written by a team of programmers, to be broken into small and manageable tasks; each member of the team is assigned one or more tasks to code as a procedure. When each programmer completes his or her procedure, all of the procedures are gathered together into one application.

Figure 7.1 shows the syntax you use to create an independent Sub procedure. It also includes an example of an independent Sub procedure, as well as the steps you follow to enter an independent Sub procedure in the Code Editor window.

## HOW TO...

### Create an Independent Sub Procedure

*Procedure header*

*Procedure footer*

**Syntax**
**Private Sub** *procedurename*(*[parameterlist]*)
    *[statements]*
**End Sub**

**Example**
```
Private Sub ClearLabels()
    ' removes the contents of the labels that
    ' display the regular, overtime, and gross pay
```

*(Figure is continued on next page)*

```
        regularLabel.Text = String.Empty
        overtimeLabel.Text = String.Empty
        grossLabel.Text = String.Empty
End Sub
```

**Steps for entering an independent Sub procedure in the Code Editor window**

1. Open the Code Editor window.
2. Click a blank line in the Code Editor window. The blank line can be anywhere between the `Public Class` clause and the `End Class` clause. However, it must be outside of any other Sub or Function procedure.
3. Type the Sub procedure header and press the Enter key on your keyboard. When you press the Enter key, the Code Editor will automatically enter the Sub procedure footer (`End Sub`) for you.

**FIGURE 7.1** How to create an independent Sub procedure

As do all procedures, independent Sub procedures have both a procedure header and procedure footer. In most cases, the procedure header begins with the keyword `Private`, which indicates that the procedure can be used only by the other procedures in the current form. Following the `Private` keyword in the procedure header is the keyword `Sub`, which identifies the procedure as a Sub procedure. After the `Sub` keyword is the *procedurename*. The rules for naming an independent Sub procedure are the same as those for naming variables and constants. Recall that the rules state that the name must begin with a letter or an underscore and can contain only letters, numbers, and the underscore character. No punctuation characters or spaces are allowed in the name, and the name cannot be a reserved word. Additionally, the recommended maximum number of characters to include in a procedure name is 32.

Procedure names are entered using Pascal case, which means that you capitalize the first letter in the name and the first letter of each subsequent word in the name. You should select a descriptive name for the Sub procedure. The name should indicate the task the procedure performs. It is a common practice to begin the name with a verb. For example, a good name for a Sub procedure that clears the contents of the label controls in an interface is ClearLabels.

Following the *procedurename* in the procedure header is a set of parentheses that contains an optional *parameterlist*. The *parameterlist* lists the data type and name of one or more memory locations, called **parameters**. The parameters store the information passed to the procedure when it is invoked. The *parameterlist* also specifies how each parameter is passed—either *by value* or *by reference*. You learn more about the *parameterlist*, and about passing information *by value* and *by reference*, later in the chapter.

Unlike the procedure header, which varies with each procedure, the procedure footer for a Sub procedure is always `End Sub`. Between the procedure header and procedure footer, you enter the instructions you want the computer to process when the procedure is invoked. For example, when the ClearLabels procedure shown in Figure 7.1 is invoked, the computer will process the three assignment statements contained in the procedure.

You can invoke an independent Sub procedure using the **Call statement**. Figure 7.2 shows the syntax of the Call statement and includes an example of using the statement to invoke the ClearLabels procedure shown in Figure 7.1.

HOW TO...

**Call an Independent Sub Procedure**

**Syntax**
**Call** *procedurename*([*argumentlist*])

**Example**
```
Call ClearLabels()
```

**FIGURE 7.2**     How to call an independent Sub procedure

In the Call statement's syntax, *procedurename* is the name of the procedure you are invoking (calling), and *argumentlist* (which is optional) is a comma-separated list of arguments you want passed to the procedure. If you have no information to pass to the procedure that you are calling, as is the case in the ClearLabels procedure, you simply include an empty set of parentheses after the *procedurename*, as shown in Figure 7.2. The ClearLabels procedure is used in the Gadis Antiques application, which you view next.

## The Gadis Antiques Application

The manager at Gadis Antiques wants an application that he can use to calculate an employee's regular pay, overtime pay, and gross pay. Employees are paid on an hourly basis and are given time and one-half for the hours worked over 40. Figure 7.3 shows a sample run of the Gadis Antiques application, and Figure 7.4 shows the application's code.

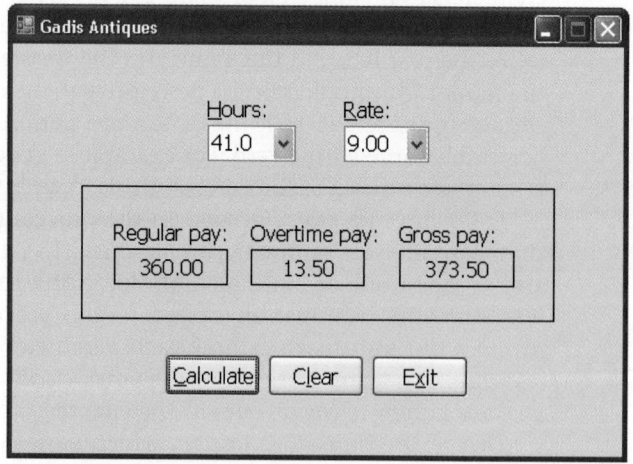

**FIGURE 7.3**     Sample run of the Gadis Antiques application

**Visual Basic code**

```vb
' Project name:        Gadis Antiques Project
' Project purpose:     The project calculates an employee's
'                      regular, overtime, and gross pay
' Created/revised by:  <your name> on <current date>

Option Strict On
Option Explicit On

Public Class MainForm

    Private Sub ClearLabels()
        ' clears the labels that display the
        ' regular, overtime, and gross pay

        regularLabel.Text = String.Empty
        overtimeLabel.Text = String.Empty
        grossLabel.Text = String.Empty
    End Sub

    Private Sub MainForm_Load(ByVal sender As Object, _
        ByVal e As System.EventArgs) Handles Me.Load
        ' fills the combo boxes with values

        For hours As Decimal = 30D To 50D Step 0.5D
            hoursComboBox.Items.Add(hours.ToString("N1"))
        Next hours

        For rates As Decimal = 7.75D To 12.5D Step 0.25D
            rateComboBox.Items.Add(rates.ToString("N2"))
        Next rates
    End Sub

    Private Sub exitButton_Click(ByVal sender As Object, _
        ByVal e As System.EventArgs) Handles exitButton.Click
        Me.Close()
    End Sub

    Private Sub calcButton_Click(ByVal sender As Object, _
        ByVal e As System.EventArgs) Handles calcButton.Click
        ' calculates the regular pay, overtime pay,
        ' and gross pay

        Const Message As String = _
            "The hours and rate entries must be numeric."
        Dim hoursWorked As Decimal
        Dim payRate As Decimal
        Dim regularPay As Decimal
```

*ClearLabels Sub procedure*

*(Figure is continued on next page)*

```
            Dim overtimePay As Decimal
            Dim grossPay As Decimal
            Dim isConvertedHours As Boolean
            Dim isConvertedRate As Boolean

            ' convert input to Decimal
            isConvertedHours = _
                Decimal.TryParse(hoursComboBox.Text, hoursWorked)
            isConvertedRate = _
                Decimal.TryParse(rateComboBox.Text, payRate)

            ' if input can be converted to a number,
            ' perform calculations and display results
            ' otherwise, clear labels and display message
            If isConvertedHours AndAlso isConvertedRate Then
                If hoursWorked <= 40D Then
                    ' calculate regular pay only
                    regularPay = hoursWorked * payRate
                Else
                    ' calculate regular and overtime pay
                    regularPay = 40 * payRate
                    overtimePay = (hoursWorked - 40) * payRate * 1.5D
                End If

                ' calculate gross pay
                grossPay = regularPay + overtimePay

                ' display calculated results
                regularLabel.Text = regularPay.ToString("N2")
                overtimeLabel.Text = overtimePay.ToString("N2")
                grossLabel.Text = grossPay.ToString("N2")
            Else
                MessageBox.Show(Message, "Gadis Antiques", _
                    MessageBoxButtons.OK, MessageBoxIcon.Information)
            End If

        End Sub

        Private Sub clearButton_Click(ByVal sender As Object, _
            ByVal e As System.EventArgs) Handles clearButton.Click
            Call ClearLabels()
        End Sub

        Private Sub hoursComboBox_TextChanged(ByVal sender As Object, _
            ByVal e As System.EventArgs) Handles hoursComboBox.TextChanged
            Call ClearLabels()
        End Sub
```

*Invokes the ClearLabels procedure*

*Invokes the ClearLabels procedure*

**(Figure is continued on next page)**

```
        Private Sub rateComboBox_TextChanged(ByVal sender As Object, _
          ByVal e As System.EventArgs) Handles rateComboBox.TextChanged
                              Call ClearLabels()
              End Sub
    End Class
```

*Invokes the
ClearLabels
procedure*

**FIGURE 7.4**    Code for the Gadis Antiques application

**TIP**

When you enter a procedure below the last event procedure in the Code Editor window, be sure to enter it above the **End Class** statement.

In Figure 7.4, the ClearLabels procedure is entered above the event procedures in the Code Editor window. Rather than entering it in this area, it also could have been entered below any of the event procedures in the code. However, it is a good programming practice to enter the procedures you create either above the first event procedure (as shown in Figure 7.4) or below the last event procedure. By organizing the code in this manner, you can more easily locate the independent Sub and Function procedures in the Code Editor window.

As Figure 7.4 indicates, three event procedures need to clear the contents of the regularLabel, overtimeLabel, and grossLabel controls: the clearButton's Click event procedure, the hoursComboBox's TextChanged event procedure, and the rateComboBox's TextChanged event procedure. You can accomplish the task by entering the appropriate assignment statements in each of the three event procedures. Or, you can enter the assignment statements in an independent Sub procedure, and then call the Sub procedure from each of the three event procedures, as shown in Figure 7.4. Entering the code in an independent Sub procedure saves you from having to enter the same statements more than once. Additionally, if the application is modified—for example, if the user prefers to assign the string "0.00" rather than the empty string to the labels—you need to make the change in only one place in the code.

First study the code that appears in the clearButton's Click event procedure, which is processed when the user clicks the Clear button in the interface. When the computer processes the `Call ClearLabels()` statement in the procedure, it temporarily leaves the clearButton's Click event procedure to process the code in the ClearLabels procedure. The assignment statements in the ClearLabels procedure remove the contents of three label controls in the interface. After processing the assignment statements, the computer processes the ClearLabels procedure's `End Sub` statement, which ends the procedure. The computer then returns to the clearButton's Click event procedure and processes the statement located immediately below the Call statement. The statement below the Call statement is `End Sub`, which ends the clearButton's Click event procedure.

Next, study the code in the TextChanged event procedures for the two combo boxes. As you learned in Chapter 5, a combo box's TextChanged event occurs when the user either selects an item from the list portion of the combo box or types a value in the text portion. In this case, the computer processes the `Call ClearLabels()` statement when the TextChanged event for either combo box occurs. As before, when processing the `Call ClearLabels()` statement, the computer temporarily leaves the current event procedure to process the code contained in the ClearLabels procedure. When the ClearLabels procedure ends, the computer returns to the current event procedure and processes the code immediately below the Call statement.

## INCLUDING PARAMETERS IN AN INDEPENDENT SUB PROCEDURE

As mentioned earlier, an independent Sub procedure can contain one or more parameters in its procedure header. Each parameter stores data that is passed to the procedure when the procedure is invoked by the Call statement. The Call statement passes the information in its optional *argumentlist*. The number of arguments listed in the Call statement's *argumentlist* should agree with the number of parameters listed in the *parameterlist* in the procedure header. If the *argumentlist* includes one argument, then the procedure header should have one parameter in its *parameterlist*. Similarly, a procedure that is passed three arguments when called requires three parameters in its *parameterlist*. (Refer to the Tip on this page for an exception to this general rule.)

In addition to having the same number of parameters as arguments, the data type and position of each parameter in the *parameterlist* should agree with the data type and position of its corresponding argument in the *argumentlist*. For instance, if the argument is an integer, then the parameter that will store the integer should have a data type of Integer, Short, or Long, depending on the size of the integer. Likewise, if two arguments are passed to a procedure—the first one being a String variable and the second one being a Decimal variable—the first parameter should have a data type of String and the second parameter should have a data type of Decimal.

You can pass a literal constant, named constant, keyword, or variable to an independent Sub procedure; in most cases, you will pass a variable.

## PASSING VARIABLES

Each variable you declare in an application has both a value and a unique address that represents the location of the variable in the computer's internal memory. Visual Basic allows you to pass either the variable's value or its address to the receiving procedure. Passing a variable's value is referred to as **passing by value**. Passing a variable's address is referred to as **passing by reference**. The method you choose—*by value* or *by reference*—depends on whether you want the receiving procedure to have access to the variable in memory. In other words, it depends on whether you want to allow the receiving procedure to change the contents of the variable.

Although the idea of passing information *by value* and *by reference* may sound confusing at first, it is a concept with which you already are familiar. To illustrate, assume that you have a savings account at a local bank. During a conversation with a friend, you mention the amount of money you have in the account. Telling someone the amount of money in your account is similar to passing a variable *by value*. Knowing the balance in your account does not give your friend access to your bank account. It merely gives your friend some information that he or she can use—perhaps to compare to the amount of money he or she has saved.

The savings account example also provides an illustration of passing information *by reference*. To deposit money to or withdraw money from your account, you must provide the bank teller with your account number. The account number represents the location of your account at the bank and allows the teller to change the account balance. Giving the teller your bank account number is similar to passing a variable *by reference*. The account number allows the teller to change the contents of your bank account, similar to the way the variable's address allows the receiving procedure to change the contents of the variable passed to the procedure.

## Passing Variables by Value

To pass a variable *by value* in Visual Basic, you include the keyword `ByVal` (which stands for "by value") before the variable's corresponding parameter in the *parameterlist*. When you pass a variable *by value*, the computer passes only the contents of the variable to the receiving procedure. When only the contents are passed, the receiving procedure is not given access to the variable in memory, so it cannot change the value stored inside the variable. You pass a variable *by value* when the receiving procedure needs to *know* the variable's contents, but the receiving procedure does not need to *change* the contents. Unless specified otherwise, variables are passed *by value* in Visual Basic.

Figure 7.5 shows a sample run of the Pet Information application, and Figure 7.6 shows the application's code, which passes two String variables *by value* to an independent Sub procedure.

**FIGURE 7.5**    Sample run of the Pet Information application

---

**Visual Basic code**

```
' Project name:        Pet Information Project
' Project purpose:     The project displays a message
'                      that contains a pet's name and age.
' Created/revised by:  <your name> on <current date>

Option Explicit On
Option Strict On

Public Class MainForm

    Private Sub DisplayMessage(ByVal pet As String, ByVal years As String)
        ' displays the pet information passed to it

        messageLabel.Text = "Your pet " & pet & " is " _
            & years & " years old."
    End Sub

    Private Sub getInfoButton_Click(ByVal sender As Object, _
        ByVal e As System.EventArgs) Handles getInfoButton.Click
        ' gets the pet information, then displays the
        ' information in a message
```

*Parameterlist*

*(Figure is continued on next page)*

```
        Dim petName As String
        Dim petAge As String

        petName = InputBox("Pet's name:", "Name Entry")
        petAge = InputBox("Pet's age (years):", "Age Entry")

        Call DisplayMessage(petName, petAge)
    End Sub

    Private Sub exitButton_Click(ByVal sender As Object, _
        ByVal e As System.EventArgs) Handles exitButton.Click
        Me.Close()
    End Sub
End Class
```

*Argumentlist*

**FIGURE 7.6**   Code for the Pet Information application

Notice that the number, data type, and sequence of the arguments in the Call statement match the number, data type, and sequence of the corresponding parameters in the procedure header. Also notice that the names of the parameters do not need to be identical to the names of the corresponding arguments. In fact, to avoid confusion, it usually is better to use different names for the arguments and parameters.

Study the code shown in Figure 7.6. The getInfoButton's Click event procedure first declares two String variables named `petName` and `petAge`. The next two statements in the procedure use the InputBox function to prompt the user to enter the name and age (in years) of his or her pet. If the user enters "Spot" as the name and "4" as the age, the computer stores the string "Spot" in the `petName` variable and stores the string "4" in the `petAge` variable.

Next, the `Call DisplayMessage(petName, petAge)` statement calls the DisplayMessage procedure, passing it the `petName` and `petAge` variables *by value*, which means that only the contents of the variables—in this case, "Spot" and "4"—are passed to the procedure. You know that the variables are passed *by value* because the keyword `ByVal` appears before each variable's corresponding parameter in the DisplayMessage procedure header. At this point, the computer temporarily leaves the getInfoButton's Click event procedure to process the code contained in the DisplayMessage procedure.

The first instruction processed in the DisplayMessage procedure is the procedure header. When processing the procedure header, the computer creates the variables listed in the *parameterlist*, and stores the information passed to the procedure in those variables. In this case, the computer creates the `pet` and `years` variables, storing the string "Spot" in the `pet` variable and the string "4" in the `years` variable. The variables that appear in a procedure header are procedure-level variables, which means they can be used only by the procedure in which they are declared. In this case, the `pet` and `years` variables can be used only by the DisplayMessage procedure.

After processing the DisplayMessage procedure header, the computer processes the assignment statement contained in the procedure. The assignment statement uses the values stored in the procedure's parameters (`pet` and `years`) to display the appropriate message in the messageLabel. In this case, the statement displays the message "Your pet Spot is 4 years old."

**TIP**

You cannot determine by looking at the Call statement whether a variable is being passed *by value* or *by reference*. You must look at the procedure header to make the determination.

Next, the computer processes the DisplayMessage procedure footer (`End Sub`), which ends the DisplayMessage procedure. At this point, the `pet` and `years` variables are removed from the computer's internal memory. (Recall that a procedure-level variable is removed from the computer's memory when the procedure in which it is declared ends.) The computer then returns to the getInfoButton's Click event procedure to process the statement immediately following the `Call DisplayMessage(petName, petAge)` statement. In this case, the statement following the Call statement is `End Sub`, which ends the getInfoButton's Click event procedure. The computer then removes the `petName` and `petAge` procedure-level variables from its internal memory.

Next, you view another example of passing information *by value*. Figure 7.7 shows a sample run of the Bonus Calculator application, and Figure 7.8 shows the application's code. In the code, the calcButton's Click event procedure passes three values to the CalcAndDisplayBonus procedure: the values contained in two variables and the value contained in a named constant.

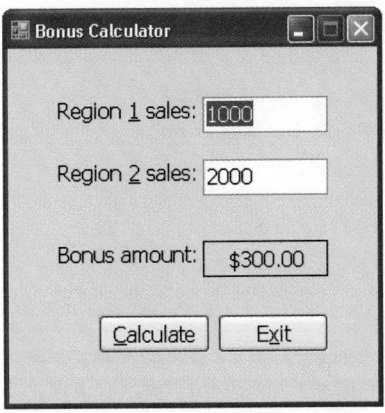

**FIGURE 7.7**    Sample run of the Bonus Calculator application

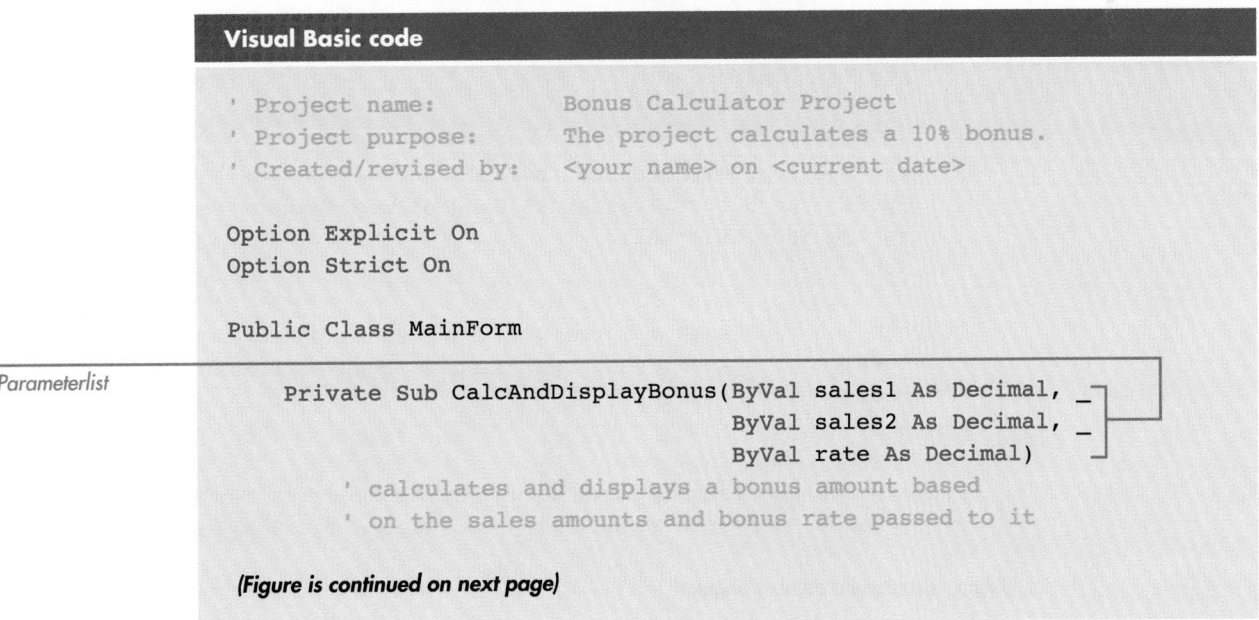

**Visual Basic code**

```
' Project name:        Bonus Calculator Project
' Project purpose:     The project calculates a 10% bonus.
' Created/revised by:  <your name> on <current date>

Option Explicit On
Option Strict On

Public Class MainForm

    Private Sub CalcAndDisplayBonus(ByVal sales1 As Decimal, _
                                    ByVal sales2 As Decimal, _
                                    ByVal rate As Decimal)
        ' calculates and displays a bonus amount based
        ' on the sales amounts and bonus rate passed to it
```

*Parameterlist*

**(Figure is continued on next page)**

```
        Dim bonus As Decimal

        bonus = (sales1 + sales2) * rate
        bonusLabel.Text = bonus.ToString("C2")
    End Sub

    Private Sub exitButton_Click(ByVal sender As Object, _
        ByVal e As System.EventArgs) Handles exitButton.Click
        Me.Close()
    End Sub

    Private Sub calcButton_Click(ByVal sender As Object, _
        ByVal e As System.EventArgs) Handles calcButton.Click
        ' calculates a 10% bonus amount

        Const BonusRate As Decimal = 0.1D
        Dim reg1Sales As Decimal
        Dim reg2Sales As Decimal
        Dim isConvertedReg1 As Boolean
        Dim isConvertedReg2 As Boolean

        isConvertedReg1 = _
            Decimal.TryParse(reg1TextBox.Text, reg1Sales)
        isConvertedReg2 = _
            Decimal.TryParse(reg2TextBox.Text, reg2Sales)

        If isConvertedReg1 AndAlso isConvertedReg2 Then
            Call CalcAndDisplayBonus(reg1Sales, reg2Sales, BonusRate)
        Else
            MessageBox.Show("The sales amounts must be numeric.", _
                "Bonus Calculator", MessageBoxButtons.OK, _
                MessageBoxIcon.Information)
        End If

        reg1TextBox.Focus()
    End Sub

    Private Sub reg1TextBox_Enter(ByVal sender As Object, _
        ByVal e As System.EventArgs) Handles reg1TextBox.Enter
        reg1TextBox.SelectAll()
    End Sub

    Private Sub reg2TextBox_Enter(ByVal sender As Object, _
        ByVal e As System.EventArgs) Handles reg2TextBox.Enter
        reg2TextBox.SelectAll()
    End Sub

    Private Sub reg1TextBox_TextChanged(ByVal sender As Object, _
        ByVal e As System.EventArgs) Handles reg1TextBox.TextChanged
```

*Argumentlist*

*(Figure is continued on next page)*

```
         bonusLabel.Text = String.Empty
     End Sub

     Private Sub reg2TextBox_TextChanged(ByVal sender As Object, _
         ByVal e As System.EventArgs) Handles reg2TextBox.TextChanged
         bonusLabel.Text = String.Empty
     End Sub

 End Class
```

**FIGURE 7.8**    Code for the Bonus Calculator application

Study the code shown in Figure 7.8. The calcButton's Click event procedure first declares a Decimal named constant, two Decimal variables, and two Boolean variables. The next two statements in the procedure use the TryParse method to convert the contents of the text boxes to Decimal numbers. The procedure then uses a selection structure to check whether the conversions were successful. If one or both conversions were not successful, the instruction in the selection structure's false path displays an appropriate message. However, if both conversions were successful, the Call CalcAndDisplayBonus(reg1Sales, reg2Sales, BonusRate) statement in the selection structure's true path calls the CalcAndDisplayBonus procedure, passing it two variables and a named constant *by value*, which means that only the contents of the variables and named constant are passed to the procedure. Here again, you know that the variables and named constant are passed *by value* because the keyword ByVal appears before each corresponding parameter in the CalcAndDisplayBonus procedure header. At this point, the computer temporarily leaves the calcButton's Click event procedure to process the code contained in the CalcAndDisplayBonus procedure.

The first instruction processed in the CalcAndDisplayBonus procedure is the procedure header. When processing the procedure header, the computer creates the three procedure-level variables listed in the *parameterlist* (sales1, sales2, and rate), and stores the information passed to the procedure in those variables. After processing the procedure header, the computer processes the statements contained in the procedure. The first statement declares an additional procedure-level variable named bonus. The next statement calculates the bonus by adding the value stored in the sales1 variable to the value stored in the sales2 variable, and then multiplying the sum by the value stored in the rate variable. The third statement in the procedure displays the bonus, formatted with a dollar sign and two decimal places, in the bonusLabel. As Figure 7.7 shows, the procedure displays a bonus amount of $300.00 when the user enters the numbers 1000 and 2000 as the sales amounts for Region 1 and Region 2.

Next, the computer processes the CalcAndDisplayBonus procedure footer, which ends the CalcAndDisplayBonus procedure. At this point, the procedure's variables (sales1, sales2, rate, and bonus) are removed from the computer's internal memory. The computer then returns to the calcButton's Click event procedure and processes the reg1TextBox.Focus() statement. After setting the focus, the computer processes the End Sub statement, which ends the calcButton's Click event procedure. The computer then removes the BonusRate named constant and the reg1Sales, reg2Sales, isConvertedReg1, and isConvertedReg2 variables from its internal memory.

## Passing Variables by Reference

In addition to passing a variable's value to a procedure, you also can pass a variable's address—in other words, its location in the computer's internal memory. As you learned earlier, passing a variable's address is referred to as passing *by reference*, and it gives the receiving procedure access to the variable being passed. You pass a variable *by reference* when you want the receiving procedure to change the contents of the variable.

To pass a variable *by reference* in Visual Basic, you include the keyword `ByRef` (which stands for "by reference") before the variable's corresponding parameter in the receiving procedure's header. The `ByRef` keyword tells the computer to pass the variable's address rather than its contents.

Figure 7.9 shows a sample run of the Gross Pay application, and Figure 7.10 shows the application's code. In the code, the calcButton's Click event procedure passes three variables to the CalcGrossPay procedure: two *by value* and one *by reference*.

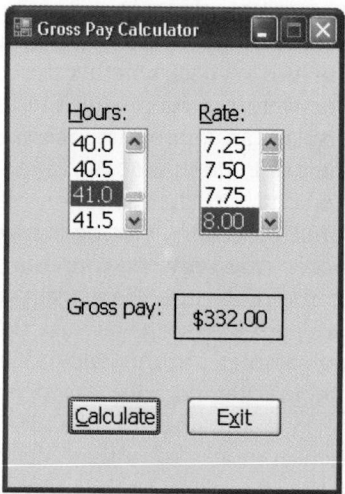

**FIGURE 7.9**    Sample run of the Gross Pay application

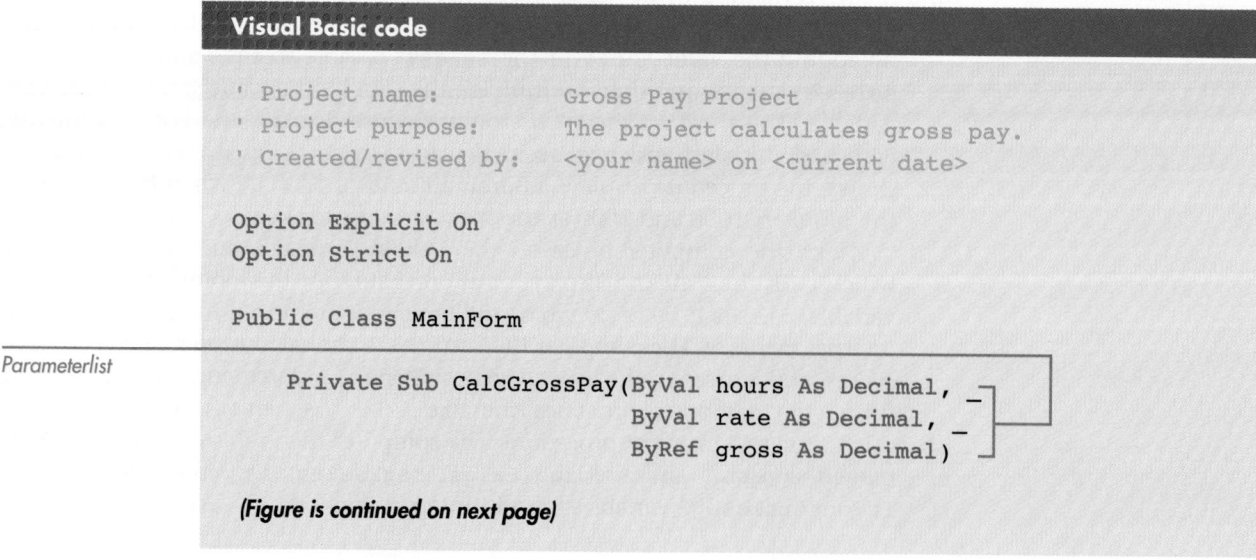

**Visual Basic code**

```
' Project name:          Gross Pay Project
' Project purpose:       The project calculates gross pay.
' Created/revised by:    <your name> on <current date>

Option Explicit On
Option Strict On


Public Class MainForm

    Private Sub CalcGrossPay(ByVal hours As Decimal, _
                             ByVal rate As Decimal, _
                             ByRef gross As Decimal)
```

*Parameterlist*

**(Figure is continued on next page)**

```
                ' calculates gross pay
            If hours <= 40D Then
                gross = hours * rate
            Else
                gross = hours * rate + (hours - 40D) * rate / 2D
            End If
        End Sub

        Private Sub MainForm_Load(ByVal sender As Object, _
            ByVal e As System.EventArgs) Handles Me.Load
            ' fills list boxes with values, then
            ' selects a default item

            For hours As Decimal = 0.5D To 50D Step 0.5D
                hoursListBox.Items.Add(hours.ToString)
            Next hours

            For rates As Decimal = 7.25D To 10.5D Step 0.25D
                rateListBox.Items.Add(rates.ToString)
            Next rates

            hoursListBox.SelectedItem = "40.0"
            rateListBox.SelectedIndex = 0
        End Sub

        Private Sub calcButton_Click(ByVal sender As Object, _
            ByVal e As System.EventArgs) Handles calcButton.Click
            ' calculates and displays a gross pay amount

            Dim hoursWkd As Decimal
            Dim rateOfPay As Decimal
            Dim grossPay As Decimal

            hoursWkd = Convert.ToDecimal(hoursListBox.SelectedItem)
            rateOfPay = Convert.ToDecimal(rateListBox.SelectedItem)

            Call CalcGrossPay(hoursWkd, rateOfPay, grossPay)

            grossLabel.Text = grossPay.ToString("C2")
        End Sub

        Private Sub exitButton_Click(ByVal sender As Object, _
            ByVal e As System.EventArgs) Handles exitButton.Click
            Me.Close()
        End Sub

        Private Sub hoursListBox_SelectedValueChanged _
            (ByVal sender As Object, ByVal e As System.EventArgs) _
```

*Argumentlist*

**(Figure is continued on next page)**

```
            Handles hoursListBox.SelectedValueChanged
            grossLabel.Text = String.Empty
        End Sub
        Private Sub rateListBox_SelectedValueChanged _
            (ByVal sender As Object, ByVal e As System.EventArgs) _
            Handles rateListBox.SelectedValueChanged
            grossLabel.Text = String.Empty
        End Sub
    End Class
```

**FIGURE 7.10**     Code for the Gross Pay application

Notice that the number, data type, and sequence of the arguments in the Call statement match the number, data type, and sequence of the corresponding parameters in the procedure header. Also notice that the names of the parameters do not need to be identical to the names of the arguments to which they correspond.

Study the code shown in Figure 7.10. The calcButton's Click event procedure first declares three Decimal variables. The next two statements in the procedure convert the items selected in the list boxes to Decimal numbers. The `Call CalcGrossPay(hoursWkd, rateOfPay, grossPay)` statement then calls the CalcGrossPay procedure, passing it three variables. Two of the variables (`hoursWkd` and `rateOfPay`) are passed *by value*, which means that only the contents of the variables are passed to the procedure. The `grossPay` variable, however, is passed *by reference*, which means that the variable's address in memory, rather than its contents, is passed to the procedure. Here again, you know that the `hoursWkd` and `rateOfPay` variables are passed *by value* because the keyword `ByVal` appears before the corresponding parameters in the CalcGrossPay procedure header. You know that the `grossPay` variable is passed *by reference* because the keyword `ByRef` appears before the corresponding parameter in the CalcGrossPay procedure header. When processing the Call statement, the computer temporarily leaves the calcButton's Click event procedure to process the code contained in the CalcGrossPay procedure.

The first instruction processed in the CalcGrossPay procedure is the procedure header. The `ByVal` keyword that appears before the names of the first two parameters in the procedure header indicates that the procedure will be receiving the contents of the `hoursWkd` and `rateOfPay` variables. The `ByRef` keyword that appears before the last parameter in the procedure header indicates that the procedure will be receiving the address of the `grossPay` variable.

When you pass a variable's address to a procedure, the computer uses the address to locate the variable in memory. It then assigns the name appearing in the procedure header to the memory location. In this case, for example, the computer first locates the `grossPay` variable in memory. It then assigns the name `gross` to the location. At this point, the memory location has two names: one assigned by the calcButton's Click event procedure, and the other assigned by the CalcGrossPay procedure.

After processing the CalcGrossPay procedure header, the computer processes the selection structure contained in the procedure. In this case, if the contents of the `hours` variable is less than or equal to the number 40, the selection structure's true path calculates the gross pay by multiplying the contents of the

**TIP**

Although the **grossPay** and **gross** variables refer to the same location in memory, the **grossPay** variable is recognized only within the calcButton's Click event procedure. Similarly, the **gross** variable is recognized only within the CalcGrossPay procedure.

hours variable by the contents of the rate variable, assigning the result to the gross variable. However, if the contents of the hours variable is greater than the number 40, the selection structure's false path calculates the gross pay by multiplying the contents of the hours variable by the contents of the rate variable, and then adding to that an additional half-time for the hours worked over 40. The result is assigned to the gross variable.

Figure 7.11 shows the contents of memory after the CalcGrossPay procedure header and selection structure are processed. The figure is based on the user selecting 41.0 in the hoursListBox and 8.00 in the rateListBox. Notice that changing the contents of the gross variable also changes the contents of the grossPay variable. This is because the names refer to the same location in memory.

**Memory locations belonging only to the calcButton's Click event procedure:**

| hoursWkd | rateOfPay |
|----------|-----------|
| 41.0 | 8.00 |

**Memory locations belonging only to the CalcGrossPay procedure:**

| hours | rate |
|-------|------|
| 41.0 | 8.00 |

**Memory location belonging to both procedures:**

grossPay **(calcButton's Click event procedure)**
gross      **(CalcGrossPay procedure)**

332.00

**FIGURE 7.11**   Contents of memory after the CalcGrossPay procedure header and selection structure are processed

As Figure 7.11 indicates, one memory location belongs to both the calcButton's Click event procedure and the CalcGrossPay procedure. Although both procedures can access the memory location, each procedure uses a different name to do so. The calcButton's Click event procedure uses the name grossPay to refer to the memory location, whereas the CalcGrossPay procedure uses the name gross.

The End Sub statement in the CalcGrossPay procedure is processed next and ends the procedure. At this point, the computer removes the memory locations that belong only to the CalcGrossPay procedure; those memory locations are the hours and rate variables. Additionally, it removes the name gross, which is assigned to the memory location that belongs to both procedures. Figure 7.12 shows the contents of memory after the hours and rate variables, as well as the gross variable name, are removed from memory. Notice that the grossPay memory location now has only one name, which is the name assigned to it by the calcButton's Click event procedure.

| Memory locations belonging only to the calcButton's Click event procedure: | | |
|---|---|---|
| hoursWkd | rateOfpay | grossPay |
| 41.0 | 8.00 | 332.00 |

**FIGURE 7.12**     Contents of memory after the appropriate variables and variable name are removed

The computer then returns to the calcButton's Click event procedure, to the statement located immediately below the Call statement. The statement displays the gross pay—in this case, $332.00—in the grossLabel, as shown earlier in Figure 7.9. Next, the computer processes the End  Sub statement in the calcButton's Click event procedure, which ends the procedure. The computer then removes the hoursWkd, rateOfPay, and grossPay variables from its internal memory.

## ASSOCIATING A PROCEDURE WITH DIFFERENT OBJECTS AND EVENTS

As you learned in Chapter 1, the Handles keyword appears in an event procedure's header and indicates the object and event associated with the procedure. For example, the Handles clearButton.Click clause that appears in the code shown in Figure 7.13 indicates that the clearButton_Click procedure is associated with the Click event of the clearButton. In other words, the clearButton_Click procedure will be processed when the clearButton's Click event occurs. (The MainForm's Load event procedure and the Click event procedures for the exitButton and calcButton are collapsed in Figure 7.13. The entire code for the Gadis Antiques application appears earlier in Figure 7.4, and its interface appears in Figure 7.3.)

**Visual Basic code**

```
' Project name:        Gadis Antiques Project
' Project purpose:     The project calculates an employee's
'                      regular, overtime, and gross pay
' Created/revised by:  <your name> on <current date>

Option Strict On
Option Explicit On

Public Class MainForm

    Private Sub ClearLabels()
        ' clears the labels that display the
        ' regular, overtime, and gross pay

        regularLabel.Text = String.Empty
        overtimeLabel.Text = String.Empty
```

*(Figure is continued on next page)*

```
                     grossLabel.Text = String.Empty
                 End Sub

                ┌Private Sub MainForm_Load ...

                 Private Sub exitButton_Click ...

                └Private Sub calcButton_Click ...

                 Private Sub clearButton_Click(ByVal sender As Object, _
                     ByVal e As System.EventArgs) Handles clearButton.Click
                     Call ClearLabels()
                 End Sub

                 Private Sub hoursComboBox_TextChanged(ByVal sender As Object, _
                     ByVal e As System.EventArgs) Handles hoursComboBox.TextChanged
                     Call ClearLabels()
                 End Sub

                 Private Sub rateComboBox_TextChanged(ByVal sender As Object, _
                     ByVal e As System.EventArgs) Handles rateComboBox.TextChanged
                     Call ClearLabels()
                 End Sub
             End Class
```

*These three procedures are collapsed*

*Procedure name*

*Handles keyword*

*Object and event names*

**FIGURE 7.13**  Partial code for the Gadis Antiques application

Although the name of an event procedure includes both the object name and the event name, both of which appear after the Handles keyword, that is not a requirement. You can change the name of an event procedure to anything you like, as long as the name follows the naming rules for procedures. For example, you can change the name clearButton_Click in Figure 7.13 to simply Clear and the procedure will still work correctly. This is because the Handles clause, rather than the event procedure's name, determines when the procedure is invoked.

You also can associate a procedure with more than one object and event, as long as each event contains the same parameters in its procedure header. For example, in the code shown in Figure 7.13, you can associate the ClearLabels procedure with the clearButton's Click event, the hoursComboBox's TextChanged event, and the rateComboBox's TextChanged event, because the three event procedures have the same parameters in their procedure header. In this case, the three event procedures contain the ByVal sender As Object, ByVal e As System.EventArgs parameters.

You may have noticed that all event procedures contain a sender parameter and an e parameter. The sender parameter contains the memory address of the object that raised the event. For example, when the clearButton's Click event occurs, the button's address in memory is stored in the sender parameter. Similarly, when either of the combo box's TextChanged event occurs, the corresponding combo box's memory address is stored in the sender parameter.

The e parameter in an event procedure contains any additional information provided by the object that raised the event. For example, the e parameter in a text box's KeyPress event contains information regarding the key that the user pressed on the keyboard. You can determine the items of information contained in an event procedure's **e** parameter by viewing its properties. To view the properties of an event procedure's **e** parameter, you first display the event procedure's code template in the Code Editor window, and then type the letter **e** followed by a period. Doing this displays a list that includes the properties of the **e** parameter.

To associate a procedure with more than one object and event, you list each parameter in the procedure's *parameterlist*, and list each object and event in the **Handles** clause, as shown in Figure 7.14. You use commas to separate each parameter, as well as to separate each object and event.

**Visual Basic code**

```
' Project name:        Gadis Antiques Project
' Project purpose:     The project calculates an employee's
'                      regular, overtime, and gross pay
' Created/revised by:  <your name> on <current date>

Option Strict On
Option Explicit On

Public Class MainForm

    Private Sub ClearLabels(ByVal sender As Object, _
        ByVal e As System.EventArgs) _
        Handles clearButton.Click, hoursComboBox.TextChanged, _
        rateComboBox.TextChanged
        ' clears the labels that display the
        ' regular, overtime, and gross pay

        regularLabel.Text = String.Empty
        overtimeLabel.Text = String.Empty
        grossLabel.Text = String.Empty
    End Sub

    Private Sub MainForm_Load ...

    Private Sub exitButton_Click ...

    Private Sub calcButton_Click ...

End Class
```

*Parameters*

*Procedure name*

*Handles clause now contains the names of three objects and events*

**FIGURE 7.14**   A different version of the code for the Gadis Antiques application

The Handles clause in the ClearLabels procedure tells the computer to invoke the procedure when any of the following occurs: the clearButton's Click event, the hoursComboBox's TextChanged event, or the rateComboBox's TextChanged event.

As you learned earlier, in addition to creating Sub procedures, you also can create Function procedures in Visual Basic.

## FUNCTION PROCEDURES

Like a Sub procedure, a Function procedure, which is typically referred to simply as a **function**, is a block of code that performs a specific task. However, unlike a Sub procedure, a function returns a value after completing its task. Some functions, such as the InputBox function, are built into Visual Basic. Recall from Chapter 5 that the InputBox function returns the user's response to a prompt that appears in a dialog box.

You also can create your own functions in Visual Basic. After creating a function, you then can invoke it from one or more places in an application. You invoke a function that you create in exactly the same way as you invoke a built-in function: you simply include the function's name in a statement. Usually the statement will display the function's return value, or use the return value in a calculation, or assign the return value to a variable.

As is true with Sub procedures, you also can pass (send) information to a function that you create, and the information can be passed either *by value* or *by reference*. Figure 7.15 shows the syntax you use to create a Function procedure. It also includes an example of a Function procedure, and the steps you follow to enter a Function procedure in the Code Editor window.

**HOW TO...**

*Procedure header*

*Procedure footer*

### Create a Function Procedure

**Syntax**
**Private Function** *procedurename*([*parameterlist*]) **As** *datatype*
       [*statements*]
       **Return** *expression*
**End Function**

**Example**
```
Private Function CalcNew(ByVal price As Decimal) As Decimal
     ' calculates and returns a new price using the current
     ' price passed to it and a 5% price increase rate

     Return price * 1.05D
End Function
```

**Steps for entering a Function procedure in the Code Editor window**

1. Open the Code Editor window.
2. Click a blank line in the Code Editor window. The blank line can be anywhere between the `Public Class` clause and the `End Class` clause. However, it must be outside of any other Sub or Function procedure.
3. Type the Function procedure header and press the Enter key on your keyboard. When you press the Enter key, the Code Editor will automatically enter the Function procedure footer (`End Function`) for you.

**FIGURE 7.15**  How to create a Function procedure

Like Sub procedures, Function procedures have both a procedure header and procedure footer. The procedure header for a Function procedure is almost identical to the procedure header for a Sub procedure, except it includes the Function keyword rather than the Sub keyword. The Function keyword identifies the procedure as a Function procedure, which returns a value after completing its task.

Also different from a Sub procedure header, a Function procedure header includes the **As** *datatype* clause. You use the clause to specify the data type of the value returned by the function. For example, if the function returns a string, you include As String at the end of the procedure header. Similarly, if the function returns a number having a decimal place, you can include As Decimal, or As Double, or As Single in the procedure header. The *datatype* you use depends on the size of the number, and whether you want the number stored with a fixed decimal point or a floating decimal point.

The procedure footer in a Function procedure is always End Function. Between the procedure header and procedure footer, you enter the instructions you want the computer to process when the function is invoked. In most cases, the last statement in a Function procedure is Return *expression*, where *expression* represents the one and only value that will be returned to the statement that called the function. The data type of the *expression* in the Return statement must agree with the data type specified in the **As** *datatype* clause in the procedure header. The **Return statement** alerts the computer that the function has completed its task and ends the function after returning the value of its *expression*.

In the example shown in Figure 7.15, the CalcNew function is passed the current price of an item. The current price is passed *by value* and stored in the price variable. The Return price * 1.05D statement in the function first calculates the new price, and then returns the new price to the statement that called the function. In the next section, you view an application that creates and uses a function.

## The Pine Lodge Application

The owner of the Pine Lodge wants an application that allows her to calculate an employee's new hourly pay, given the employee's current hourly pay and raise rate. Figure 7.16 shows a sample run of the Pine Lodge application, and Figure 7.17 shows the application's code.

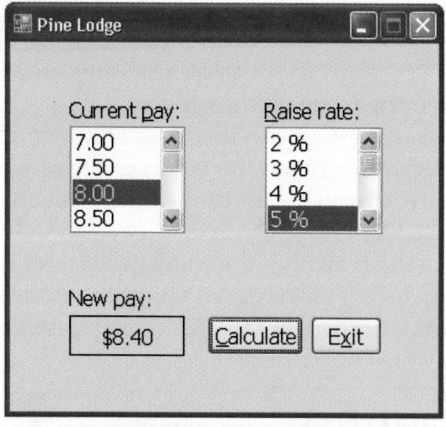

**FIGURE 7.16**   Sample run of the Pine Lodge application

**Visual Basic code**

```vb
' Project name:        Pine Lodge Project
' Project purpose:     The project calculates an employee's
'                      new pay amount.
' Created/revised by:  <your name> on <current date>

Option Explicit On
Option Strict On

Public Class MainForm

    Private Function GetNewPay(ByVal current As Decimal, _
        ByVal rate As Decimal) As Decimal
        ' calculates and returns the new hourly pay
        ' based on the current hourly pay and raise rate
        ' passed to it

        Dim raise As Decimal
        Dim newPay As Decimal

        raise = current * rate
        newPay = current + raise

        Return newPay
    End Function

    Private Sub ClearLabel(ByVal sender As Object, _
        ByVal e As System.EventArgs) Handles _
        currentListBox.SelectedValueChanged, _
        rateListBox.SelectedValueChanged
        newPayLabel.Text = String.Empty
    End Sub

    Private Sub calcButton_Click(ByVal sender As Object, _
        ByVal e As System.EventArgs) Handles calcButton.Click
        ' calls a function to calculate an employee's new
        ' hourly pay, then displays the new hourly pay

        Dim currentPay As Decimal
        Dim rateChoice As String
        Dim raiseRate As Decimal
        Dim newHourlyPay As Decimal

        currentPay = Convert.ToDecimal(currentListBox.SelectedItem)
        rateChoice = rateListBox.SelectedItem.ToString.TrimEnd("%"c)
        raiseRate = Convert.ToDecimal(rateChoice) / 100D

        newHourlyPay = GetNewPay(currentPay, raiseRate)
```

*GetNewPay function*

*Invokes the GetNewPay function and assigns the function's return value to the newHourlyPay variable*

**(Figure is continued on next page)**

```
            newPayLabel.Text = newHourlyPay.ToString("C2")
        End Sub

        Private Sub MainForm_Load(ByVal sender As Object, _
            ByVal e As System.EventArgs) Handles Me.Load
            ' fills the list boxes with values, then selects
            ' the first value

            For pay As Decimal = 7D To 12D Step 0.5D
                currentListBox.Items.Add(pay.ToString("N2"))
            Next pay

            For rate As Decimal = 0.02D To 0.11D Step 0.01D
                rateListBox.Items.Add(rate.ToString("P0"))
            Next rate

            currentListBox.SelectedIndex = 0
            rateListBox.SelectedIndex = 0
        End Sub

        Private Sub exitButton_Click(ByVal sender As Object, _
            ByVal e As System.EventArgs) Handles exitButton.Click
            Me.Close()
        End Sub
    End Class
```

**FIGURE 7.17**    Code for the Pine Lodge application

Study the code shown in Figure 7.17. The MainForm's Load event procedure fills the two list boxes with values, and then selects the first value in each list. Notice that the values added to the currentListBox are formatted using the "N2" *formatString*, which you learned about in Chapter 3. The "N2" *formatString* displays two decimal places in each value added to the currentListBox. The values added to the rateListBox are formatted using the "P0" *formatString*, which multiplies each value added to the rateListBox by 100 before displaying it with a percent sign and, in this case, zero decimal places.

The ClearLabel Sub procedure in the code removes the contents of the newPayLabel when the SelectedValueChanged event occurs for either list box. The exitButton's Click event procedure ends the application.

The calcButton's Click event procedure declares a String variable and three Decimal variables. It then converts the item selected in the currentListBox to Decimal and assigns the result to the currentPay variable. The next statement in the procedure removes the percent sign that appears at the end of the item selected in the rateListBox, and assigns the result to the rateChoice variable. Next, the procedure converts the contents of the rateChoice variable to Decimal and assigns the result, divided by the number 100, to the raiseRate variable. (Because the values listed in the rateListBox represent percentages, you need to divide the selected value by 100 to change the percentage to its decimal equivalent.)

The newHourlyPay = GetNewPay(currentPay, raiseRate) statement calls the GetNewPay function, passing it the values stored in the currentPay and `raiseRate` variables. The computer stores the values in the `current` and `rate` variables that appear in the GetNewPay procedure header.

After processing the GetNewPay procedure header, the computer processes the statements contained in the function. The first two statements declare procedure-level variables named `raise` and `newPay`. The next statement calculates the employee's raise by multiplying the value stored in the `current` variable by the value stored in the `rate` variable; the statement assigns the raise amount to the `raise` variable. The next statement calculates the new pay by adding the value stored in the `current` variable to the value stored in the `raise` variable, assigning the result to the `newPay` variable. The `Return newPay` statement in the function returns the contents of the `newPay` variable to the statement that called the function. That statement is the `newHourlyPay = GetNewPay(currentPay, raiseRate)` statement in the calcButton's Click event procedure. After processing the `Return` statement, the GetNewPay function ends, and the computer removes the `current`, `rate`, `raise`, and `newPay` variables from its internal memory.

When the `newHourlyPay = GetNewPay(currentPay, raiseRate)` statement receives the value returned by the GetNewPay function, it assigns the value to the `newHourlyPay` variable. The `newPayLabel.Text = newHourlyPay.ToString("C2")` statement then displays the new hourly pay in the newPayLabel, as shown earlier in Figure 7.16. Finally, the computer processes the `End Sub` statement in the calcButton's Click event procedure, which ends the procedure. The computer then removes the `rateChoice`, `currentPay`, `raiseRate`, and `newHourlyPay` variables from its internal memory.

You have completed the concepts section of Chapter 7. The next section is the Programming Tutorial section, which gives you step-by-step instructions on how to apply the chapter's concepts to an application. A Programming Example follows the Programming Tutorial. The Programming Example is a completed program that demonstrates the concepts taught in the chapter. Following the Programming Example are the Quick Review, Key Terms, Self-Check Questions and Answers, Review Questions, Review Exercises – Short Answer, Computer Exercises, and Case Projects sections.

# PROGRAMMING TUTORIAL

## Concentration Game Application

In this tutorial, you create an application that simulates a game called Concentration. The game board contains 16 label controls. Scattered among the labels are eight pairs of matching words, which are hidden from view. The user begins by clicking one of the labels to reveal a word. He or she then clicks another label to reveal another word. If the two words match, the words remain on the screen. However, if the words do not match, they are hidden once again. The game is over when all of the matching words are revealed. The user can start a new game by clicking the New Game button in the interface. In each game, the words will appear in different locations on the game board. This is accomplished using an independent Sub procedure that generates random numbers. The Concentration Game application's user interface is shown in Figure 7.18, and its TOE chart is shown in Figure 7.19.

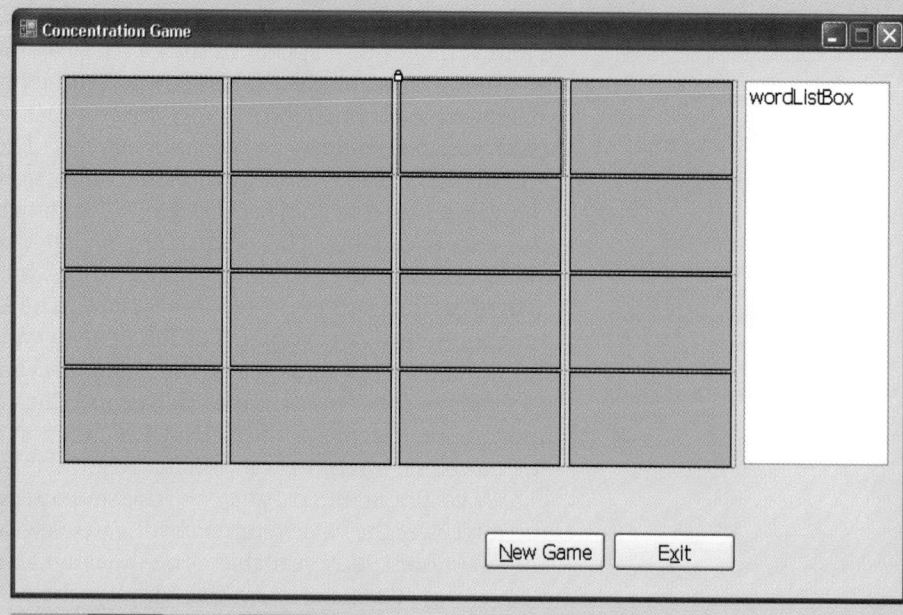

**FIGURE 7.18**    MainForm

**TOE Chart:**

| Task | Object | Event |
|------|--------|-------|
| 1. Fill the list box with 8 pairs of matching words<br>2. Call a procedure to shuffle the words in the list box | MainForm | Load |
| End the application | exitButton | Click |
| 1. Clear the label controls, then enable them<br>2. Reset the counter to 0<br>3. Call a procedure to shuffle the words in the list box | newButton | Click |
| 1. Enable the boardTableLayoutPanel<br>2. Disable the matchTimer | matchTimer | Tick |
| 1. Clear the words from the chosen labels<br>2. Enable the boardTableLayoutPanel<br>3. Disable the noMatchTimer | noMatchTimer | Tick |
| 1. Use a counter to keep track of whether this is the first or second label clicked<br>2. If this is the first label clicked, display a word from the list box in the label<br>3. If this is the second label clicked, disable the boardTableLayoutPanel, display a word from the list box in the label, and then compare both words<br>4. If both words match, disable both labels, then turn on the matchTimer<br><br>*(Figure is continued on next page)* | 16 Label controls | Click |

| | | |
|---|---|---|
| 5. If both words do not match, turn on the noMatchTimer<br>6. Reset the counter to 0 | | |
| Store the 16 words | wordListBox | None |
| Display the game board | boardTableLayoutPanel | None |

**FIGURE 7.19** TOE chart

## Coding the Concentration Game Application

According to the application's TOE chart, the MainForm's Load event procedure, and the Click event procedures for the exitButton, the newButton, and the 16 labels need to be coded. You also need to code the Tick event procedures for the two timer controls in the application.

**To begin coding the Concentration Game application:**

1. Start Visual Studio. If necessary, close the Start Page window.
2. Open the **Concentration Game Solution** (Concentration Game Solution.sln) file, which is contained in the VbReloaded\Chap07\Concentration Game Solution folder. The user interface shown in Figure 7.20 appears on the screen. The interface contains a table layout panel, 16 labels, two buttons, two timers, and a list box.

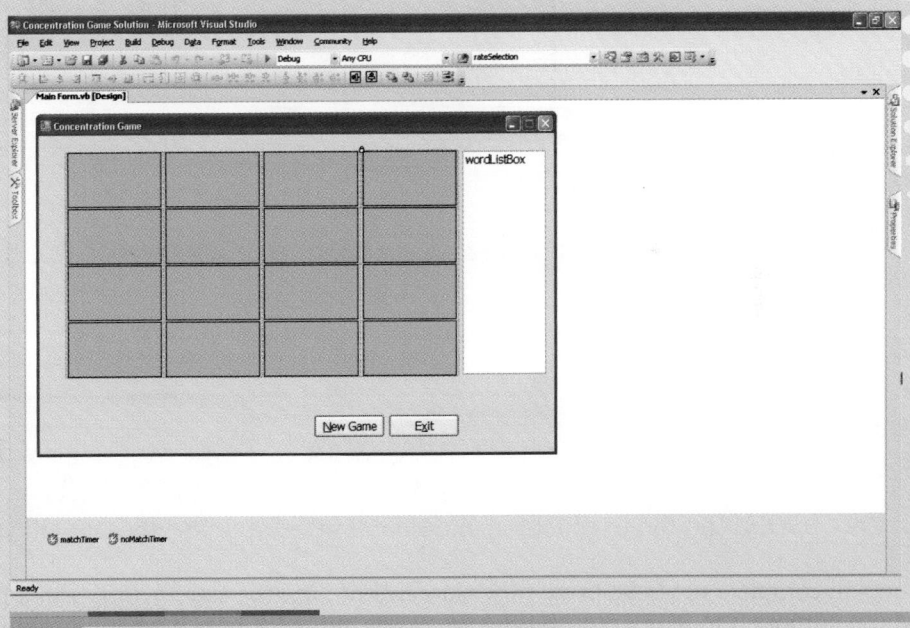

**FIGURE 7.20** The Concentration Game application's user interface

3. Open the Code Editor window, which already contains some of the application's code.
4. Replace the <your name> and <current date> text in the comments with your name and the current date.

First, you will complete the MainForm's Load event procedure, which is responsible for filling the wordListBox with eight pairs of matching words, and then reordering the words. The list box provides the words that the user will try to match on the game board. The procedure's pseudocode is shown in Figure 7.21.

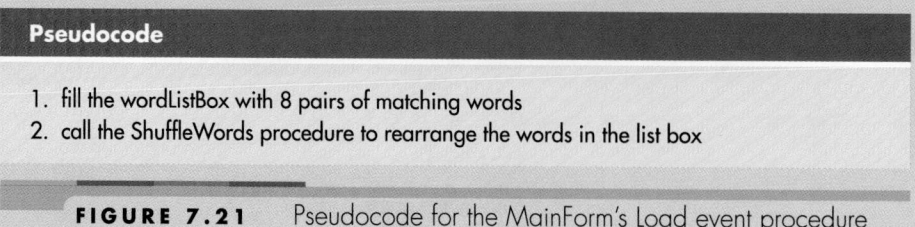

**Pseudocode**

1. fill the wordListBox with 8 pairs of matching words
2. call the ShuffleWords procedure to rearrange the words in the list box

**FIGURE 7.21**     Pseudocode for the MainForm's Load event procedure

**To complete the MainForm's Load event procedure:**

1. Scroll down the Code Editor window to view the code already entered in the MainForm's Load event procedure. Notice that the first eight statements in the procedure add eight unique words to the wordListBox control, and the last eight statements duplicate the words in the control.

2. Save the solution, then run the application. The Load event procedure adds the 16 words to the list box, as shown in Figure 7.22. Notice that the words appear in the order in which they are added in the Load event procedure.

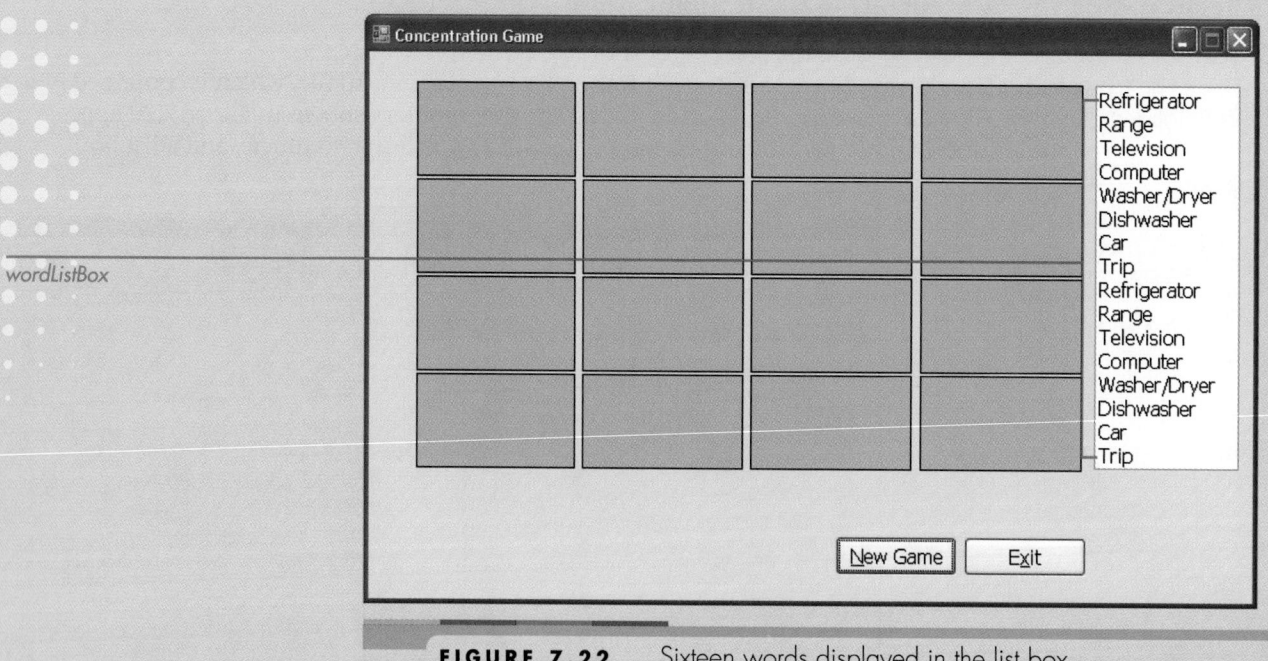

**FIGURE 7.22**     Sixteen words displayed in the list box

3. Click the **Exit** button to end the application. If necessary, close the Output window.

You will complete the Load event procedure by entering the statement to call a procedure named ShuffleWords, whose purpose is to reorder (or shuffle) the words in the list box. If you do not shuffle the words, they will appear in the exact same location on the game board each time the application is started. Shuffling the words makes the game more challenging, because the user will never be sure exactly where each word will appear on the game board. The ShuffleWords procedure will be a Sub procedure, because it will not need to return a value.

4. Type the Call statement shown in Figure 7.23, which contains the completed Load event procedure. Do not be concerned about the jagged line that appears below the ShuffleWords procedure name in the Code Editor window. The line will disappear when you create the procedure.

```
            Private Sub MainForm_Load(ByVal sender As Object, _
                ByVal e As System.EventArgs) Handles Me.Load
                ' fills the list box with 8 pairs of matching words,
                ' then calls a procedure to shuffle the words

                wordListBox.Items.Add("Refrigerator")
                wordListBox.Items.Add("Range")
                wordListBox.Items.Add("Television")
                wordListBox.Items.Add("Computer")
                wordListBox.Items.Add("Washer/Dryer")
                wordListBox.Items.Add("Dishwasher")
                wordListBox.Items.Add("Car")
                wordListBox.Items.Add("Trip")
                wordListBox.Items.Add("Refrigerator")
                wordListBox.Items.Add("Range")
                wordListBox.Items.Add("Television")
                wordListBox.Items.Add("Computer")
                wordListBox.Items.Add("Washer/Dryer")
                wordListBox.Items.Add("Dishwasher")
                wordListBox.Items.Add("Car")
                wordListBox.Items.Add("Trip")

                Call ShuffleWords()
            End Sub
```

*These statements fill the list box with 16 words*

*Enter the Call statement*

**FIGURE 7.23**    Completed MainForm's Load event procedure

Next, you will create the ShuffleWords procedure. As mentioned earlier, the procedure is responsible for reordering the words in the list box. Reordering the words will ensure that most of the words appear in different locations in each game. An easy way to reorder a list of words is to swap one word with another word. For example, you can swap the word that appears at the top of the list with the word that appears in the middle of the list.

In this application, you will use random numbers to select the positions of the two words to be swapped. Because there are 16 words in the list box, you will perform the swap 16 times to ensure that the words are sufficiently reordered. The pseudocode for the ShuffleWords procedure is shown in Figure 7.24.

**Pseudocode**

1. repeat 16 times
   generate two random numbers that are greater than or equal to 0, but less than 16
   use the random numbers to swap the words in the list box
   end repeat

**FIGURE 7.24**    Pseudocode for the ShuffleWords procedure

**To code the ShuffleWords procedure, then test the procedure:**

1. Position the insertion point in the line immediately above the MainForm's Load event procedure. Type **private sub ShuffleWords()** and press **Enter**. Notice that the Code Editor enters the procedure footer (End Sub) for you. Also notice that a jagged line no longer appears below the ShuffleWords name in the Load event procedure.
2. Type **' shuffles the words in the list box** and press **Enter** twice.

The ShuffleWords procedure will use four variables named randomGenerator, index1, index2, and temp. The randomGenerator variable will represent Visual Basic's pseudo-random number generator in the procedure. The index1 and index2 variables will store two random integers that are greater than or equal to zero, but less than 16. Each integer corresponds to the index of a word in the wordListBox. The temp variable will be used during the swapping process.

3. Enter the following Dim statements. Press **Enter** twice after typing the last Dim statement.
   **Dim randomGenerator As New Random**
   **Dim index1 As Integer**
   **Dim index2 As Integer**
   **Dim temp As String**
4. The first step in the pseudocode shown in Figure 7.24 is a repetition structure that repeats its instructions 16 times. Type **for counter as integer = 1 to 16** and press **Enter**.

The first task in the repetition structure is to generate two random numbers that are greater than or equal to zero, but less than 16. The random numbers will represent the locations, or indexes, of the words to be swapped in the list box. Recall that the first item in a list box has an index of zero; the second has an index of 1, and so on. Therefore, although the list box contains 16 words, you use indexes of 0 through 15 to access the words.

5. Type **'generate two random numbers** and press **Enter**. Type **index1 = randomgenerator.next(0, 16)** and press **Enter**, then type **index2 = randomgenerator.next(0, 16)** and press **Enter**.

The second task in the repetition structure is to use the random numbers to swap the words in the list box. You learned how to swap the contents of two variables in Chapter 4. You can use a similar process to swap two words in the wordListBox.

6. First you need to store the first word, temporarily, in a variable. The index1 variable contains the position of the first word you want to swap in the list box. Type **' swap the two words** and press **Enter**, then type **temp = wordlistbox.items(index1).tostring** and press **Enter**.
7. Next, you replace the word located in the index1 position in the list box with the word located in the index2 position in the list box. Type **wordlistbox.items(index1) = wordlistbox.items(index2)** and press **Enter**.
8. Finally, you replace the word located in the index2 position in the list box with the word stored in the temp variable. Type **wordlistbox.items(index2) = temp**.
9. Change the Next clause in the procedure to **Next counter**. Figure 7.25 shows the completed ShuffleWords procedure.

```
Private Sub ShuffleWords()
    ' shuffles the words in the list box

    Dim randomGenerator As New Random
    Dim index1 As Integer
    Dim index2 As Integer
    Dim temp As String

    For counter As Integer = 1 To 16
        ' generate two random numbers
        index1 = randomGenerator.Next(0, 16)
        index2 = randomGenerator.Next(0, 16)
        ' swap the two words
        temp = wordListBox.Items(index1).ToString
        wordListBox.Items(index1) = wordListBox.Items(index2)
        wordListBox.Items(index2) = temp
    Next counter
End Sub
```

**FIGURE 7.25**    Completed ShuffleWords procedure

10. Save the solution, then start the application. The 16 words appear in the wordListBox. This time, however, they do not appear in the order in which they are entered in the Load event procedure. Instead, they appear in a random order, as shown in Figure 7.26. (Because the ShuffleWords procedure uses random numbers to swap the words, your words may appear in different locations in the list box.)

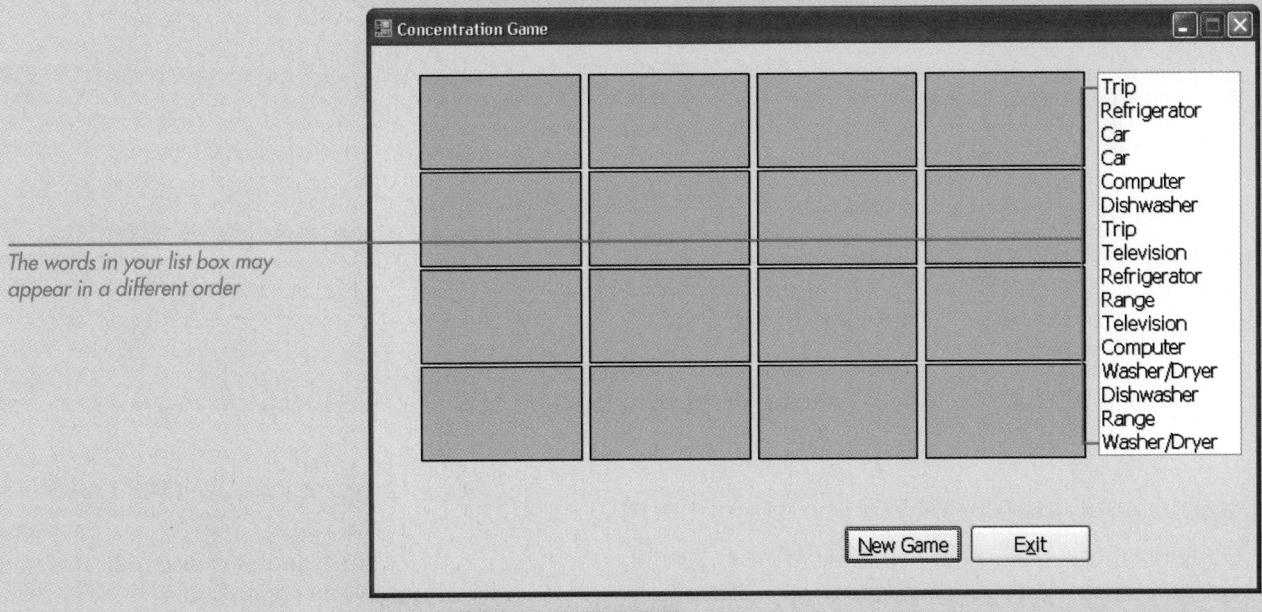

*The words in your list box may appear in a different order*

**FIGURE 7.26**    Words appear in a random order in the list box

11. Click the **Exit** button to end the application. If necessary, close the Output window.

Next, you will code the Click event procedures for the 16 labels in the interface. In this application, each label on the game board is associated with a word in the list box. The first label is associated with the first word; the second label is associated with the second word, and so on. When the user clicks a label, the label's Click event procedure will access the appropriate word in the list box, and then display the word in the label. For example, if the user clicks the first label on the game board, the Click event procedure will assign the first word in the list box to the label's Text property.

After the user selects two labels, the procedure will determine whether the labels contain matching words. If the words match, they will remain visible in their respective labels. However, if the words do not match, the user will be given a short amount of time to memorize the location of the words before the procedure removes the words from the labels. The pseudocode for the labels' Click event procedures is shown in Figure 7.27.

## Pseudocode

1. add 1 to the selection counter, which indicates whether this is the first or second label selected on the game board
2. if this is the first label selected
    extract the number from the label's name and assign it to the labelNum variable
    subtract 1 from the labelNum variable and assign the result to the index1 variable
    use the index1 variable to access the appropriate word in the list box, and display the word in the label

    else (which means it is the second label selected)
        disable the game board to prevent the user from making another selection
        extract the number from the label's name and assign it to the labelNum variable
        subtract 1 from the labelNum variable and assign the result to the index2 variable
        use the index2 variable to access the appropriate word in the list box, and display the word in the label

        if both labels contain the same word
            disable both labels on the game board
            turn the matchTimer on
        else
            turn the noMatchTimer on
        end if

        reset the selection counter to 0
    end if

**FIGURE 7.27**     Pseudocode for the Click event procedures of the 16 label controls

**To begin coding the Click event procedures for the 16 label controls:**

1. Scroll down the Code Editor window to view the TestForMatch procedure. The Handles clause indicates that the procedure will be processed when the Click event occurs for any of the 16 label controls.

The TestForMatch procedure will use a procedure-level String variable named `labelNum`, and two procedure-level Integer variables named `index1` and `index2`. When the user clicks a label on the game board, the procedure will assign the number portion of the label's name to the `labelNum` variable. For example, if the user clicks the Label1 control, the number 1 will be assigned to the variable. Similarly, if the user clicks the Label12 control, the number 12 will be assigned to the variable.

As you learned earlier, each label control on the game board is associated with a word in the list box. The Label1 control, for example, is associated with the word whose index is 0 in the list box. Likewise, the Label12 control is associated with the word whose index is 11. Notice that the label's number (1 and 12) is always one number more than the word's index (0 and 11). Therefore, you can determine the index of the word associated with a label by subtracting the number one from the label's number. The procedure will use the `index1` and `index2` variables to store the indexes.

2. Position the insertion point below the last line in the procedure header, then type **' displays the appropriate words, and determines whether** and press **Enter**. Type **' the user selected a matching pair of words** and press **Enter** twice.
3. Enter the following three Dim statements. Press **Enter** twice after typing the last Dim statement.
   **Dim labelNum as String**
   **Dim index1 as Integer**
   **Dim index2 as Integer**

The procedure also will use three module-level variables named `selectionCounter`, `firstLabel`, and `secondLabel`. The variables need to be module-level variables because they will be used by more than one procedure in the application. The `selectionCounter` variable will keep track of whether the user has clicked one or two labels. The `firstLabel` and `secondLabel` variables will keep track of the labels the user clicked.

4. Position the insertion point in the blank line below the `Public Class MainForm` statement, then press **Enter**. Enter the following three Private statements in the MainForm's Declarations section:
   **Private firstLabel As Label**
   **Private secondLabel As Label**
   **Private selectionCounter As Integer**

5. The first step in the pseudocode shown in Figure 7.27 is to add the number one to the selection counter. Position the insertion point two blank lines below the last Dim statement in the TestForMatch procedure. Type **' update the selection counter** and press **Enter**, then type **selectioncounter = selectioncounter + 1** and press **Enter** twice.
6. The next step is a selection structure that determines whether this is the first label control selected. Type **' determine whether this is the first or second selection** and press **Enter**. Type **if selectioncounter = 1 then** and press **Enter**.

According to the pseudocode, if this is the first of two labels selected on the game board, you should extract the numeric portion of the label's name and assign it to the `labelNum` variable. At this point, you may be wondering how you will know which label name to use, because the TestForMatch procedure will be processed when any of the 16 labels are clicked. You can use the `sender` parameter to determine the appropriate name. As you learned earlier, the `sender` parameter contains the address of the object that raised the event. In this case, it will contain the address of the label that was clicked. Therefore, you should be able to access the label's name using the syntax `sender.Name`.

7. Type **sender.** (be sure to type the period). See Figure 7.28.

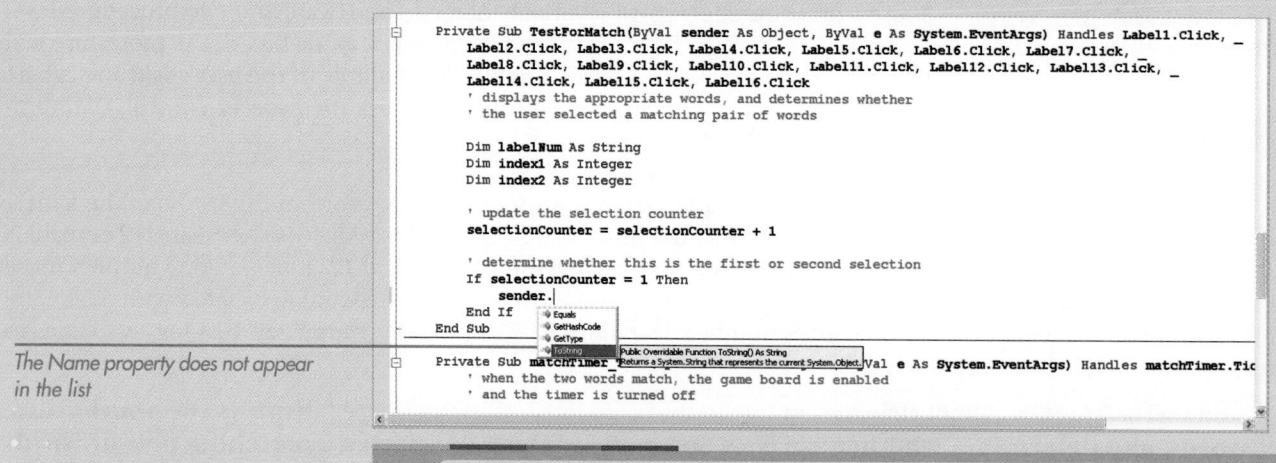

```
Private Sub TestForMatch(ByVal sender As Object, ByVal e As System.EventArgs) Handles Label1.Click, _
    Label2.Click, Label3.Click, Label4.Click, Label5.Click, Label6.Click, Label7.Click, _
    Label8.Click, Label9.Click, Label10.Click, Label11.Click, Label12.Click, Label13.Click, _
    Label14.Click, Label15.Click, Label16.Click
    ' displays the appropriate words, and determines whether
    ' the user selected a matching pair of words

    Dim labelNum As String
    Dim index1 As Integer
    Dim index2 As Integer

    ' update the selection counter
    selectionCounter = selectionCounter + 1

    ' determine whether this is the first or second selection
    If selectionCounter = 1 Then
        sender.
    End If
End Sub
```

*The Name property does not appear in the list*

```
Private Sub matchTimer ...(...Val e As System.EventArgs) Handles matchTimer.Tic...
    ' when the two words match, the game board is enabled
    ' and the timer is turned off
```

**FIGURE 7.28**　　List of choices for the **sender** parameter

Notice that the Name property does not appear in the list of choices shown in Figure 7.28. This is because the **sender** parameter in the procedure header is declared using the Object data type, and Object variables do not have a Name property. Before you can continue coding the procedure, you need to learn how to convert an Object variable to a different type.

8. Press the **Backspace** key seven times to delete the sender. text.
9. Save the solution.

### Converting Object Variables

The `ByVal sender As Object` text that appears in a procedure header creates a variable named `sender` and assigns the Object data type to it. As you learned in Chapter 3, an Object variable can store many different types of data, and it also can freely change the type of stored data while the application is running. For example, you can store the number 40 in an Object variable at the beginning of the application and then, later on in the application, store the text "John Smith" in that same variable. You also can store the address of an object in an Object variable. For example, you can store the address of a label, or a text box, or a button. Unlike variables declared using the String or Decimal data type, variables declared using the Object data type do not have a set of properties. This is because there are no common attributes for all of the different types of data that can be stored in an Object variable. Additionally, the computer cannot determine the type of data stored in an Object variable until the application is run.

To access the properties of the object whose address is stored in the `sender` parameter, you first declare a variable of the appropriate data type. You then convert the `sender` parameter to the data type, assigning the result to the variable. You can use the `TryCast` keyword to perform the conversion. Figure 7.29 shows the syntax of the `TryCast` keyword and contains two examples of using the keyword.

HOW TO...

**Use the TryCast Keyword**

**Syntax**
**TryCast**(*object, datatype*)

**Examples**
```
Dim myLabel As Label
myLabel = TryCast(sender, Label)
```
converts the sender parameter to the Label data type, then assigns the
label's address to the myLabel variable

```
Dim firstTextBox As TextBox
firstTextBox = TryCast(sender, TextBox)
```
converts the sender parameter to the TextBox data type, then assigns
the text box's address to the firstTextBox variable

**FIGURE 7.29**    How to use the TryCast keyword

In the syntax, *object* is the name of the object you want to convert to the data type specified in the *datatype* argument. To convert the sender parameter from the Object data type to the Label data type, you use TryCast(sender, Label). Similarly, to convert it to the TextBox data type, you use TryCast(sender, TextBox). If the TryCast keyword cannot convert the *object* to the *datatype*, it returns the keyword Nothing.

In the TestForMatch procedure, which is processed when any of the 16 labels are clicked, you will use the TryCast keyword to convert the sender parameter to the Label data type. This will allow you to extract the number from the name of the label that was clicked. Recall that you will use the number to access the label's corresponding word in the list box.

**To continue coding the Click event procedures for the 16 label controls:**

1. The insertion point should be positioned below the If selectionCounter = 1 Then clause in the TestForMatch procedure.
2. Type ' **if this is the first label, extract the number from** and press **Enter**, then type ' **the label's name, then use the number to display the** and press **Enter**, and then type ' **appropriate word from the list box** and press **Enter**.
3. First convert the sender parameter to the Label data type, and assign the result to the module-level firstLabel variable. Type **firstlabel = trycast(sender, label)** and press **Enter**.
4. Now extract the number from the label's name and assign it to the labelNum variable. The number in each label's name begins with the character whose index is 5. (The word "Label" in each name is in index positions 0 through 4.) Type **labelnum = firstlabel.name.substring(5)** and press **Enter**.
5. Next, convert the contents of the labelNum variable to Integer, and then subtract the number one from the integer and assign the result to the index1 variable. (Recall that the label's number is one number more than the word's index.) Type **index1 = convert.toint32(labelnum) – 1** and press **Enter**.
6. Now use the number stored in the index1 variable to access the appropriate word in the list box. Display the word in the label whose address is stored in the firstLabel variable. Type **firstlabel.text = wordlistbox. items(index1).tostring** and press **Enter**.
7. Type **else** and press **Enter**.

If this is the second label the user clicked, you first will disable the game board. This will allow the application to compare the contents of both labels before the user makes the next selection.

8. Type ' **this is the second label, so disable the game board,** and press **Enter**. Type ' **then extract the number from the label's name, then** and press **Enter**. Type ' **use the number to display the appropriate word from** and press **Enter**, then type ' **the list box** and press **Enter**.

9. Type **boardtablelayoutpanel.enabled = false** and press **Enter**.

10. Now convert the `sender` parameter to the Label data type, assigning the result to the module-level `secondLabel` variable. Then extract the number from the label's name. Type **secondlabel = trycast(sender, label)** and press **Enter**. Type **labelnum = secondlabel.name.substring(5)** and press **Enter**.

11. Now calculate the index, then use the index to display the appropriate word. Type **index2 = convert. toint32(labelnum) – 1** and press **Enter**. Type **secondlabel.text = wordlistbox.items(index2). tostring** and press **Enter** twice.

The next task in the pseudocode is to compare the contents of both labels. If both labels contain the same word, you will disable the labels to prevent the user from inadvertently clicking them again. You also will turn on the matchTimer. However, if the labels do not contain the same word, you will turn on the noMatchTimer.

12. Type the following comments and selection structure. Press **Enter** twice after typing the `End If` clause.

```
' if both words match, disable the corresponding
' label controls, then turn on the matchTimer;
' otherwise, turn on the noMatchTimer
If firstLabel.Text = secondLabel.Text Then
    firstLabel.Enabled = False
    secondLabel.Enabled = False
    matchTimer.Enabled = True
Else
    noMatchTimer.Enabled = True
End If
```

13. The last task in the pseudocode is to reset the selection counter to zero. Recall that the selection counter keeps track of whether the user has clicked one or two labels. Type ' **reset the selection counter** and press **Enter**, then type **selectioncounter = 0**.

14. Save the solution. Figure 7.30 shows the code for the TestForMatch procedure, which is processed when any of the 16 label controls are clicked.

```
Private Sub TestForMatch(ByVal sender As Object, _
    ByVal e As System.EventArgs) Handles Label1.Click, _
    Label2.Click, Label3.Click, Label4.Click, _
    Label5.Click, Label6.Click, Label7.Click, _
    Label8.Click, Label9.Click, Label10.Click, _
    Label11.Click, Label12.Click, Label13.Click, _
    Label14.Click, Label15.Click, Label16.Click
    ' displays the appropriate words, and determines whether
    ' the user selected a matching pair of words

    Dim labelNum As String
    Dim index1 As Integer
    Dim index2 As Integer
```

*(Figure is continued on next page)*

```
        ' update the selection counter
        selectionCounter = selectionCounter + 1

        ' determine whether this is the first or second selection
        If selectionCounter = 1 Then
            ' if this is the first label, extract the number from
            ' the label's name, then use the number to display the
            ' appropriate word from the list box
            firstLabel = TryCast(sender, Label)
            labelNum = firstLabel.Name.Substring(5)
            index1 = Convert.ToInt32(labelNum) - 1
            firstLabel.Text = wordListBox.Items(index1).ToString
        Else
            ' this is the second label, so disable the game board,
            ' then extract the number from the label's name, then
            ' use the number to display the appropriate word from
            ' the list box
            boardTableLayoutPanel.Enabled = False
            secondLabel = TryCast(sender, Label)
            labelNum = secondLabel.Name.Substring(5)
            index2 = Convert.ToInt32(labelNum) - 1
            secondLabel.Text = wordListBox.Items(index2).ToString

            ' if both words match, disable the corresponding
            ' label controls, then turn on the matchTimer;
            ' otherwise, turn on the noMatchTimer
            If firstLabel.Text = secondLabel.Text Then
                firstLabel.Enabled = False
                secondLabel.Enabled = False
                matchTimer.Enabled = True
            Else
                noMatchTimer.Enabled = True
            End If

            ' reset the selection counter
            selectionCounter = 0
        End If
    End Sub
```

**FIGURE 7.30**      TestForMatch procedure

Before testing the TestForMatch procedure, you will code the Tick event procedures for the two timers, and also complete the newButton's Click event procedure.

### Completing the Concentration Game Application

Figure 7.31 shows the pseudocode for the matchTimer's Tick event procedure, which perform two tasks. First, it enables the game board so the user can make another selection. Second, it turns off the matchTimer. Turning off the timer stops the timer's Tick event and prevents its code from being processed again. The matchTimer's Tick event procedure will not be processed again until the timer is turned back on, which happens when the user locates a matching pair of words on the game board.

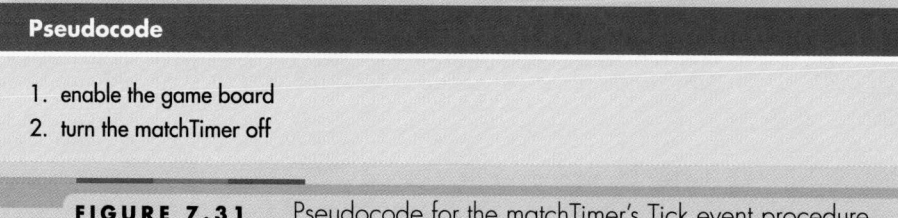

**Pseudocode**

1. enable the game board
2. turn the matchTimer off

**FIGURE 7.31**    Pseudocode for the matchTimer's Tick event procedure

**To code the matchTimer's Tick event procedure:**

1. Locate the matchTimer's Tick event procedure in the Code Editor window.
2. Enter the two assignment statements indicated in Figure 7.32, which shows the completed Tick event procedure.

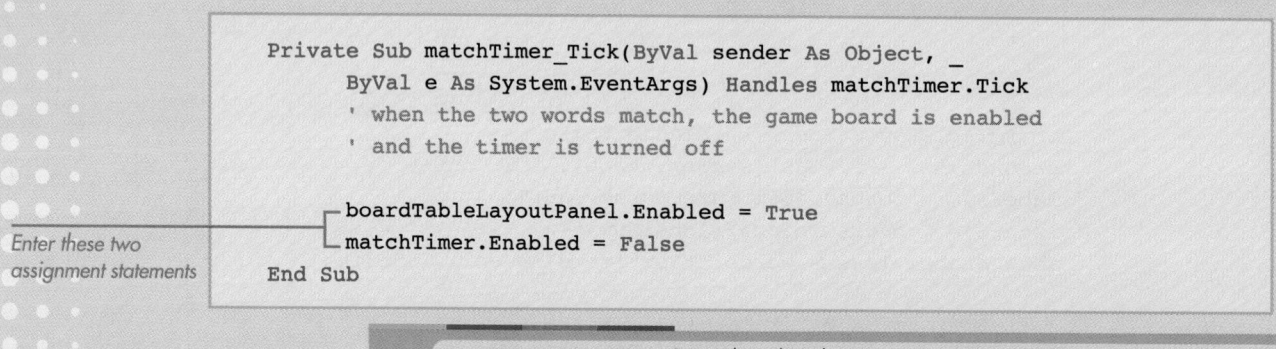

```
Private Sub matchTimer_Tick(ByVal sender As Object, _
       ByVal e As System.EventArgs) Handles matchTimer.Tick
       ' when the two words match, the game board is enabled
       ' and the timer is turned off

       boardTableLayoutPanel.Enabled = True
       matchTimer.Enabled = False
End Sub
```

*Enter these two assignment statements*

**FIGURE 7.32**    Completed Tick event procedure for the matchTimer

Figure 7.33 shows the pseudocode for the noMatchTimer's Tick event procedure, which performs four tasks. The first two tasks clear the contents of the labels whose addresses are stored in the firstLabel and secondLabel variables. The third task enables the game board so the user can make another selection. And the last task turns off the noMatchTimer to prevent the timer's Tick event from occurring and its code being processed. The noMatchTimer's Tick event procedure will not be processed again until the timer is turned back on, which happens when the two labels selected by the user contain different words.

**Pseudocode**

1. clear the contents of the firstLabel
2. clear the contents of the secondLabel
3. enable the game board
4. turn the noMatchTimer off

**FIGURE 7.33**    Pseudocode for the noMatchTimer's Tick event procedure

**To code the noMatchTimer's Tick event procedure, then test the code:**

1. Locate the noMatchTimer's Tick event procedure in the Code Editor window.
2. Enter the four assignment statements indicated in Figure 7.34, which shows the completed Tick event procedure.

```
        Private Sub noMatchTimer_Tick(ByVal sender As Object, _
            ByVal e As System.EventArgs) Handles noMatchTimer.Tick
            ' when the words do not match, the words are
            ' removed from the labels, the game board is enabled,
            ' and the timer is turned off

            firstLabel.Text = String.Empty
            secondLabel.Text = String.Empty
            boardTableLayoutPanel.Enabled = True
            noMatchTimer.Enabled = False
        End Sub
```

*Enter these four assignment statements*

**FIGURE 7.34**     Completed Tick event procedure for the noMatchTimer

Finally, you will complete the code for the newButton's Click event procedure. Figure 7.35 shows the procedure's pseudocode.

### Pseudocode

1. clear the contents of the 16 labels
2. enable the 16 labels
3. reset the selection counter to zero
4. call the ShuffleWords procedure to rearrange the words in the list box

**FIGURE 7.35**     Pseudocode for the newButton's Click event procedure

**To complete the newButton's Click event procedure, then test the code:**

1. Locate the newButton's Click event procedure in the Code Editor window. Position the insertion point in the blank line immediately above the procedure's End Sub statement, then press **Tab** twice.
2. Type **selectioncounter = 0** and press **Enter**, then type **call shufflewords( )**.
3. Save the solution. Figure 7.36 shows the Concentration Game application's code.

```
    ' Project name:          Concentration Game Project
    ' Project purpose:       The project simulates a game called
    '                        Concentration, where a player tries
    '                        to find matching pairs on the playing
    '                        board.
    ' Created/revised by:    <your name> on <current date>

    Option Explicit On
    Option Strict On

    (Figure is continued on next page)
```

```
Public Class MainForm

    Private firstLabel As Label
    Private secondLabel As Label
    Private selectionCounter As Integer

    Private Sub ShuffleWords()
        ' shuffles the words in the list box

        Dim randomGenerator As New Random
        Dim index1 As Integer
        Dim index2 As Integer
        Dim temp As String

        For counter As Integer = 1 To 16
            ' generate two random numbers
            index1 = randomGenerator.Next(0, 16)
            index2 = randomGenerator.Next(0, 16)
            ' swap the two words
            temp = wordListBox.Items(index1).ToString
            wordListBox.Items(index1) = wordListBox.Items(index2)
            wordListBox.Items(index2) = temp
        Next counter
    End Sub

    Private Sub MainForm_Load(ByVal sender As Object, _
        ByVal e As System.EventArgs) Handles Me.Load
        ' fills the list box with 8 pairs of matching words,
        ' then calls a procedure to shuffle the words

        wordListBox.Items.Add("Refrigerator")
        wordListBox.Items.Add("Range")
        wordListBox.Items.Add("Television")
        wordListBox.Items.Add("Computer")
        wordListBox.Items.Add("Washer/Dryer")
        wordListBox.Items.Add("Dishwasher")
        wordListBox.Items.Add("Car")
        wordListBox.Items.Add("Trip")
        wordListBox.Items.Add("Refrigerator")
        wordListBox.Items.Add("Range")
        wordListBox.Items.Add("Television")
        wordListBox.Items.Add("Computer")
        wordListBox.Items.Add("Washer/Dryer")
        wordListBox.Items.Add("Dishwasher")
        wordListBox.Items.Add("Car")
        wordListBox.Items.Add("Trip")

        Call ShuffleWords()
    End Sub
```

*(Figure is continued on next page)*

```
    Private Sub exitButton_Click(ByVal sender As Object, _
        ByVal e As System.EventArgs) Handles exitButton.Click
        Me.Close()
    End Sub

    Private Sub newButton_Click(ByVal sender As Object, _
        ByVal e As System.EventArgs) Handles newButton.Click
        ' removes any words from the label controls, then
        ' enables the label controls, then resets the
        ' selection counter, and then calls a procedure
        ' to shuffle the words

        Label1.Text = String.Empty
        Label2.Text = String.Empty
        Label3.Text = String.Empty
        Label4.Text = String.Empty
        Label5.Text = String.Empty
        Label6.Text = String.Empty
        Label7.Text = String.Empty
        Label8.Text = String.Empty
        Label9.Text = String.Empty
        Label10.Text = String.Empty
        Label11.Text = String.Empty
        Label12.Text = String.Empty
        Label13.Text = String.Empty
        Label14.Text = String.Empty
        Label15.Text = String.Empty
        Label16.Text = String.Empty

        Label1.Enabled = True
        Label2.Enabled = True
        Label3.Enabled = True
        Label4.Enabled = True
        Label5.Enabled = True
        Label6.Enabled = True
        Label7.Enabled = True
        Label8.Enabled = True
        Label9.Enabled = True
        Label10.Enabled = True
        Label11.Enabled = True
        Label12.Enabled = True
        Label13.Enabled = True
        Label14.Enabled = True
        Label15.Enabled = True
        Label16.Enabled = True

        selectionCounter = 0
        Call ShuffleWords()
    End Sub
```

*(Figure is continued on next page)*

```
Private Sub TestForMatch(ByVal sender As Object, _
    ByVal e As System.EventArgs) Handles Label1.Click, _
    Label2.Click, Label3.Click, Label4.Click, _
    Label5.Click, Label6.Click, Label7.Click, _
    Label8.Click, Label9.Click, Label10.Click, _
    Label11.Click, Label12.Click, Label13.Click, _
    Label14.Click, Label15.Click, Label16.Click
    ' displays the appropriate words, and determines whether
    ' the user selected a matching pair of words

    Dim labelNum As String
    Dim index1 As Integer
    Dim index2 As Integer

    ' update the selection counter
    selectionCounter = selectionCounter + 1

    ' determine whether this is the first or second selection
    If selectionCounter = 1 Then
        ' if this is the first label, extract the number from
        ' the label's name, then use the number to display the
        ' appropriate word from the list box
        firstLabel = TryCast(sender, Label)
        labelNum = firstLabel.Name.Substring(5)
        index1 = Convert.ToInt32(labelNum) - 1
        firstLabel.Text = wordListBox.Items(index1).ToString
    Else
        ' this is the second label, so disable the game board,
        ' then extract the number from the label's name, then
        ' use the number to display the appropriate word from
        ' the list box
        boardTableLayoutPanel.Enabled = False
        secondLabel = TryCast(sender, Label)
        labelNum = secondLabel.Name.Substring(5)
        index2 = Convert.ToInt32(labelNum) - 1
        secondLabel.Text = wordListBox.Items(index2).ToString

        ' if both words match, disable the corresponding
        ' label controls, then turn on the matchTimer;
        ' otherwise, turn on the noMatchTimer
        If firstLabel.Text = secondLabel.Text Then
            firstLabel.Enabled = False
            secondLabel.Enabled = False
            matchTimer.Enabled = True
        Else
            noMatchTimer.Enabled = True
        End If
```

*(Figure is continued on next page)*

```
                 ' reset the selection counter
                 selectionCounter = 0
          End If
     End Sub

     Private Sub matchTimer_Tick(ByVal sender As Object, _
          ByVal e As System.EventArgs) Handles matchTimer.Tick
          ' when the two words match, the game board is enabled
          ' and the timer is turned off

          boardTableLayoutPanel.Enabled = True
          matchTimer.Enabled = False
     End Sub

     Private Sub noMatchTimer_Tick(ByVal sender As Object, _
          ByVal e As System.EventArgs) Handles noMatchTimer.Tick
          ' when the words do not match, the words are
          ' removed from the labels, the game board is enabled,
          ' and the timer is turned off

          firstLabel.Text = String.Empty
          secondLabel.Text = String.Empty
          boardTableLayoutPanel.Enabled = True
          noMatchTimer.Enabled = False
     End Sub
End Class
```

**FIGURE 7.36**    Code for the Concentration Game application

Now test the application to verify that it is working correctly.

**To test the Concentration Game application:**

1. Start the application.
2. Click the **label in the upper-left corner of the game board**. The TestForMatch procedure assigns the first word in the wordListBox to the label's Text property. The word appears in the label, as shown in Figure 7.37. (Recall that the ShuffleWords procedure uses random numbers to reorder the list of words in the list box. Therefore, the first word in your list box, and therefore the word that appears in the Label1 control, might be different than the one shown in Figure 7.37.)

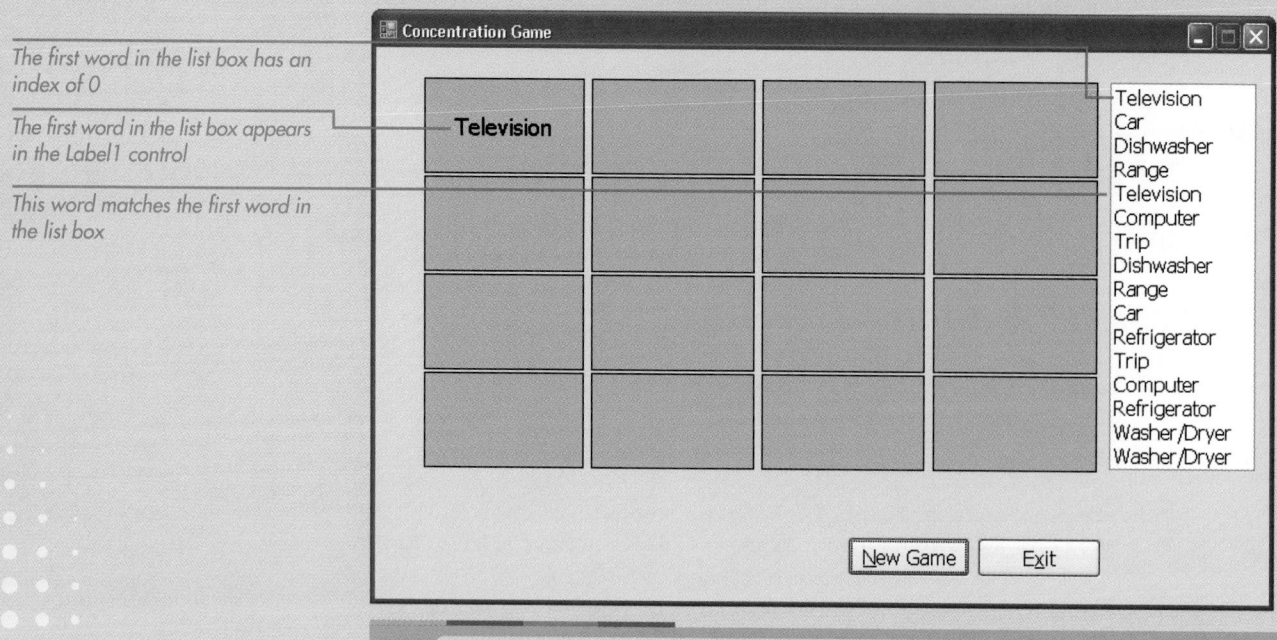

*The first word in the list box has an index of 0*

*The first word in the list box appears in the Label1 control*

*This word matches the first word in the list box*

**FIGURE 7.37**     First word appears in the label on the game board

First you will test the code that handles two matching words. To do this, you will need to find the word in the list box that matches the first word, and then click its associated label.

3. Count down the list of words in the list box, stopping when you reach the word that matches the first word in the list box. In Figure 7.37, the word that matches the first word (Television) is the fifth word in the list box.

4. Now count each label control, from left to right, beginning with the first row on the game board. Stop counting when you reach the label control whose number is the same as in the previous step. In Figure 7.37, for example, you would stop counting when you reached the fifth label control, which is located in the first column of the second row.

5. Click the **label control associated with the matching word**. The word appears in the label, as shown in Figure 7.38.

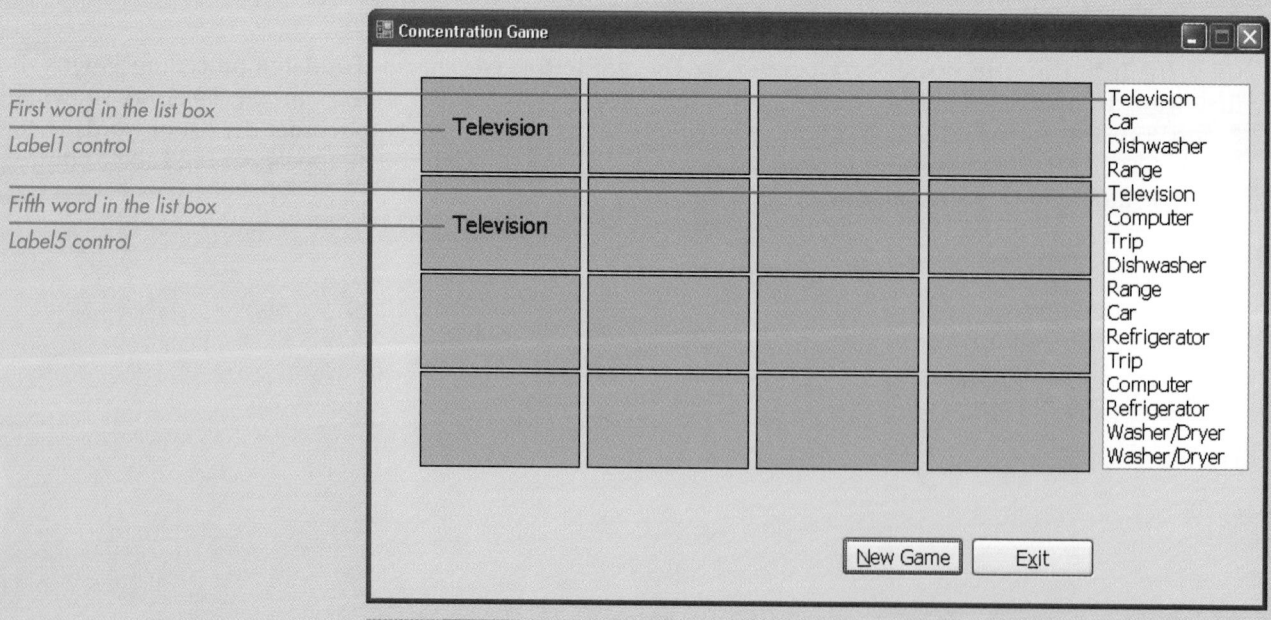

*First word in the list box*

*Label1 control*

*Fifth word in the list box*

*Label5 control*

**FIGURE 7.38**     Both labels contain the same word

6. Click the **Label1 control** again. Nothing happens because the TestForMatch procedure disables the label when the matching word is found.

Next, you will test the code that handles two words that do not match.

7. Click **a blank label control on the game board**, then click **another blank label control**, being sure that the second label's word is not the same as the first label's word. Because both words are not the same, they are removed from the game board after a short time.

Finally, you will verify that the code entered in the newButton's Click event procedure works correctly.

8. Click the **New Game** button. The button's Click event procedure clears the contents of the label controls and also enables them. Additionally, it resets the selection counter to zero, and calls the ShuffleWords procedure to reorder the words in the list box. See Figure 7.39.

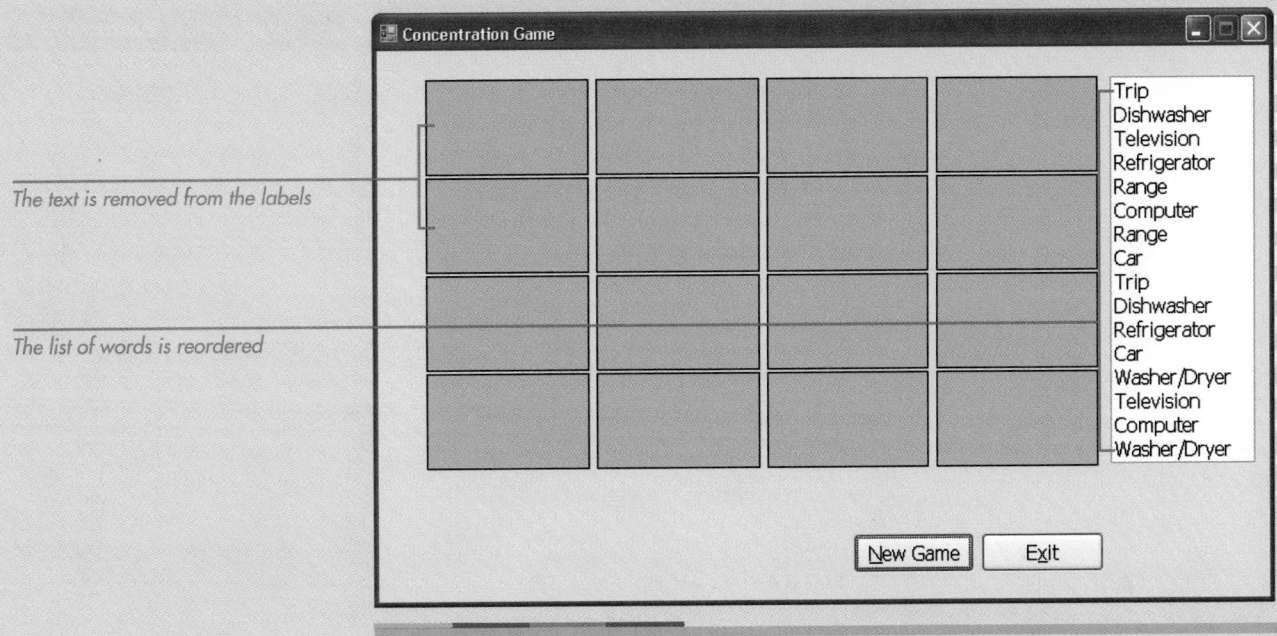

**FIGURE 7.39**   Result of clicking the New Game button

9. On your own, test the application several more times.
10. When you are finished testing, click the **Exit** button to end the application. If necessary, close the Output window.

Now that you know the application works correctly, you will hide the list box and resize the form.

**To hide the list box and resize the form:**

1. Close the Code Editor window.
2. Set the wordListBox's Visible property to **False**.
3. Change the form's Size property to **645, 473**.
4. Save the solution, then start the application to verify that the list box is no longer visible in the interface.
5. Click the **Exit** button to end the application. If necessary, close the Output window.
6. Close the solution.

# PROGRAMMING EXAMPLE

## Rainfall Application

Create an application that allows the user to enter any number of monthly rainfall amounts. The application should calculate and display the total rainfall amount and the average rainfall amount. Name the solution Rainfall Solution. Name the project Rainfall Project. Name the form file Main Form.vb. Save the application in the VbReloaded\Chap07 folder.

**TOE Chart:**

| Task | Object | Event |
|------|--------|-------|
| 1. Call the CalcTotalAndAverage procedure to calculate the total and average rainfall amounts<br>2. Display the total rainfall amount and average rainfall amount in totalLabel and averageLabel | calcButton | Click |
| End the application | exitButton | Click |
| Display the total rainfall amount and the average rainfall amount (from calcButton) | totalLabel, averageLabel | None |
| Get and display the monthly rainfall amounts<br>Select the existing text<br>Clear the totalLabel and averageLabel | monthlyTextBox | None<br>Enter<br>TextChanged |

**FIGURE 7.40**

**User Interface:**

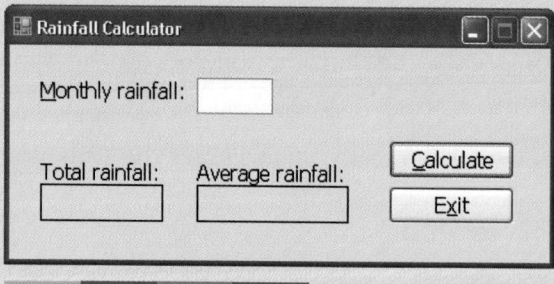

**FIGURE 7.41**

## Objects, Properties, and Settings:

| Object | Property | Setting |
|--------|----------|---------|
| Form1 | Name | MainForm |
|  | AcceptButton | calcButton |
|  | Font | Tahoma, 12 point |
|  | MaximizeBox | False |
|  | Size | 430, 195 |
|  | StartPosition | CenterScreen |
|  | Text | Rainfall Calculator |
| Label1 | Text | &Monthly rainfall: |
|  | Location | 22, 24 |
| Label2 | Text | Total rainfall: |
|  | Location | 22, 85 |
| Label3 | Text | Average rainfall: |
|  | Location | 145, 85 |
| Label4 | Name | totalLabel |
|  | AutoSize | False |
|  | BorderStyle | FixedSingle |
|  | Location | 24, 104 |
|  | Size | 97, 28 |
|  | Text | (empty) |
|  | TextAlign | MiddleCenter |
| Label5 | Name | averageLabel |
|  | AutoSize | False |
|  | BorderStyle | FixedSingle |
|  | Location | 147, 104 |
|  | Size | 119, 28 |
|  | Text | (empty) |
|  | TextAlign | MiddleCenter |
| TextBox1 | Name | monthlyTextBox |
|  | Location | 147, 24 |
|  | Size | 60, 27 |
| Button1 | Name | calcButton |
|  | Location | 297, 70 |
|  | Size | 97, 28 |
|  | Text | &Calculate |
| Button2 | Name | exitButton |
|  | Location | 297, 104 |
|  | Size | 97, 28 |
|  | Text | E&xit |

**FIGURE 7.42**

**Tab Order:**

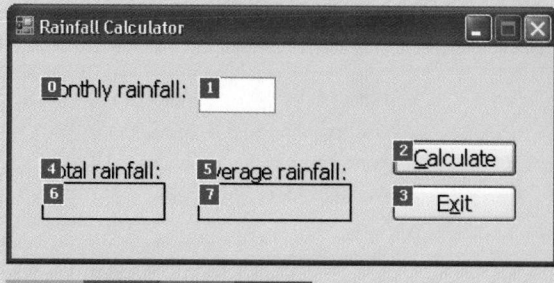

**FIGURE 7.43**

**Pseudocode:**

**exitButton Click event procedure**

1. close application

**monthlyTextBox Enter event procedure**

1. select the existing text

**monthlyTextBox TextChanged event procedure**

1. remove the contents of the totalLabel
2. remove the contents of the averageLabel

**calcButton Click event procedure**

1. call the CalcTotalAndAverage procedure to calculate the total and average rainfall amounts
2. display the total and average rainfall amounts in the totalLabel and averageLabel
3. send the focus to the monthlyTextBox
4. select the existing text in the monthlyTextBox

**CalcTotalAndAverage procedure**

1. convert the rainfall amount contained in the text box to a Decimal number
2. if the conversion is successful
    add 1 to the counter
    add the rainfall amount to the accumulator
    if the counter contains a number that is greater than 0
        calculate the average by dividing the accumulator by the counter
    end if
else
    display a message informing the user to enter a number
end if

**Code:**

```
' Project name:          Rainfall Project
' Project purpose:       The project allows the user to enter monthly
'                        rainfall amounts. It calculates the total
'                        amount and the average amount.
' Created/revised by:    <your name> on <current date>

Option Explicit On
Option Strict On

Public Class MainForm

    Private Sub CalcTotalAndAverage(ByRef counter As Integer, _
                                    ByRef accumulator As Decimal, _
                                    ByRef avg As Decimal)
        ' calculates the total and average rainfall amount

        Dim monthRain As Decimal
        Dim isConverted As Boolean

        isConverted = Decimal.TryParse(monthlyTextBox.Text, monthRain)

        ' if the rainfall amount can be converted to a number,
        ' then update the counter and accumulator, and calculate the
        ' average rainfall; otherwise, display an appropriate
        ' message
        If isConverted Then
            counter = counter + 1
            accumulator = accumulator + monthRain

            If counter > 0 Then
                avg = accumulator / (Convert.ToDecimal(counter))
            End If

        Else
            MessageBox.Show("The rainfall amount must be a number.", _
                "Rainfall Calculator", MessageBoxButtons.OK, _
                MessageBoxIcon.Information)
        End If

    End Sub

    Private Sub exitButton_Click(ByVal sender As Object, _
        ByVal e As System.EventArgs) Handles exitButton.Click
        Me.Close()
    End Sub
```

*(Figure is continued on next page)*

```
Private Sub calcButton_Click(ByVal sender As Object, _
    ByVal e As System.EventArgs) Handles calcButton.Click
    ' calls a procedure to calculate the total and average
    ' rainfall amounts, then displays both amounts

    Static rainCounter As Integer
    Static rainAccum As Decimal
    Dim avgRain As Decimal

    Call CalcTotalAndAverage(rainCounter, rainAccum, avgRain)

    totalLabel.Text = rainAccum.ToString("N2")
    averageLabel.Text = avgRain.ToString("N2")

    monthlyTextBox.Focus()
    monthlyTextBox.SelectAll()
End Sub

Private Sub monthlyTextBox_Enter(ByVal sender As Object, _
    ByVal e As System.EventArgs) Handles monthlyTextBox.Enter
    monthlyTextBox.SelectAll()
End Sub

Private Sub monthlyTextBox_TextChanged(ByVal sender As Object, _
    ByVal e As System.EventArgs) Handles monthlyTextBox.TextChanged
    totalLabel.Text = String.Empty
    averageLabel.Text = String.Empty
End Sub
End Class
```

**FIGURE 7.44**

## Quick Review

- The difference between a Sub procedure and a Function procedure is that a Function procedure returns a value, whereas a Sub procedure does not return a value.
- An event procedure is a Sub procedure that is associated with one or more objects and events.
- Independent Sub procedures and Function procedures are not associated with any specific object or event. The names of independent Sub procedures and Function procedures typically begin with a verb.
- Procedures allow programmers to avoid duplicating code in different parts of a program. Procedures also allow a team of programmers to work on large and complex programs.
- You enter Sub and Function procedures in the Code Editor window.

- You can use the Call statement to invoke an independent Sub procedure. The Call statement allows you to pass arguments to the Sub procedure.
- You invoke a Function procedure by including its name and any arguments in a statement.
- When calling a procedure, the number of arguments listed in the *argumentlist* should agree with the number of parameters listed in the *parameterlist* in the procedure header. Also, the data type and position of each parameter in the *parameterlist* should agree with the data type and position of its corresponding argument in the *argumentlist*.
- You can pass information to a Sub or Function procedure either *by value* or *by reference*.
- To pass a variable *by value*, you precede the variable's corresponding parameter with the keyword `ByVal`.
- To pass a variable *by reference*, you precede the variable's corresponding parameter with the keyword `ByRef`.
- The procedure header indicates whether a variable is being passed *by value* or *by reference*.
- When you pass a variable *by value*, only the contents of the variable are passed.
- When you pass a variable *by reference*, the variable's address is passed.
- Variables that appear in the *parameterlist* in a procedure header are procedure-level, which means they can be used only by the procedure.
- The `TryCast` keyword allows you to convert an object from one data type to another.

## Key Terms

A **procedure** is a block of program code that performs a specific task.

A **Sub procedure** is a procedure that does not return a value after performing its assigned task.

A **Function procedure** is a procedure that returns a value after performing its assigned task.

An **independent Sub procedure** is a procedure that is not associated with any specific object or event, and is processed only when invoked (called) from code.

The memory locations listed in a procedure header are called **parameters**.

The **Call statement** is used to invoke an independent Sub procedure in a program.

When you pass a variable's contents to a procedure, you are **passing by value**.

When you pass a variable's address to a procedure, you are **passing by reference**.

A Function procedure is more simply referred to as a **function**.

You use the **Return statement** to return a function's value to the statement that invoked the function.

You use the **TryCast keyword** to convert an object from one type to another.

## Self-Check Questions and Answers

1. The items listed in the Call statement are referred to as _____.
   a. arguments
   b. parameters
   c. passers
   d. None of the above.

2. Which of the following is a valid procedure header for a procedure that receives the contents of two String variables?
   a. `Private Sub Display(ByRef x As String, ByRef y As String)`
   b. `Private Sub Display(ByVal x As String, ByVal y As String)`
   c. `Private Sub Display(ByValue x As String, ByValue y As String)`
   d. None of the above.

3. Which of the following is a valid procedure header for a procedure that receives the address of a Decimal variable?
   a. `Private Sub Calculate(ByAddress num As Decimal)`
   b. `Private Sub Calculate(ByVal num As Decimal)`
   c. `Private Sub Calculate(ByValue num As Decimal)`
   d. None of the above.

4. Which of the following is a valid procedure header for a procedure that returns a Decimal number?
   a. `Private Function Calculate() As Decimal`
   b. `Private Sub Calculate() As Decimal`
   c. `Private Sub Calculate(Decimal)`
   d. Both a and b.

5. Which of the following statements invokes a Sub procedure named Display, passing it the contents of a String variable named `empName`?
   a. `Call Display(empName As String)`
   b. `Call Display(String empName)`
   c. `Call Display(empName)`
   d. None of the above.

6. Which of the following statements invokes a Function procedure named Calculate, passing it the contents of two Decimal variables named `hours` and `rate`? The statement should assign the function's return value to a variable named `grossPay`.
   a. `grossPay = Call Calculate(hours, rate)`
   b. `Call Calculate(hours, rate, grossPay)`
   c. `grossPay = Calculate(hours, rate)`
   d. None of the above.

7. Which of the following procedure headers tells the computer to process the procedure when the Click event occurs for either the singleRadioButton or the marriedRadioButton?
   a. `Private Sub ClearTaxLabel() Handles singleRadioButton.Click, marriedRadioButton.Click`
   b. `Private Sub ClearTaxLabel(ByVal sender As Object, ByVal e As system.EventArgs) Handles singleRadioButton.Click, marriedRadioButton.Click`

c. `Private Sub ClearTaxLabel(ByRef sender As Object, ByRef e As system.EventArgs) Handles singleRadioButton.Click, marriedRadioButton.Click`
d. All of the above.

8. When the CalculateGross function completes its processing, it should send the value stored in the `grossPay` variable to the statement that invoked the function. Which of the following statements tells the computer to perform that task?
   a. `Return(grossPay)`
   b. `Send(grossPay)`
   c. `SendBack grossPay`
   d. None of the above.

9. Which of the following converts the `sender` parameter to a TextBox object named myTextBox?
   a. `myTextBox = TryCast(sender, TextBox)`
   b. `myTextBox = TryConvert(sender, TextBox)`
   c. `myTextBox = TryParse(sender, TextBox)`
   d. Both a and c.

10. A function procedure can return _____.
    a. one value only
    b. one or more values
    c. zero or more values

Answers: 1) a, 2) b, 3) d, 4) a, 5) c, 6) c, 7) b, 8) d, 9) a, 10) a

## Review Questions

1. Which of the following is false?
   a. A Function procedure can return one or more values to the statement that called it.
   b. A procedure can accept one or more items of data passed to it.
   c. The *parameterlist* in a procedure header is optional.
   d. At times, a memory location inside the computer's internal memory may have more than one name.

2. Each memory location listed in the *parameterlist* in the procedure header is referred to as _____.
   a. an address
   b. a constraint
   c. a parameter
   d. a value

3. To determine whether a variable is being passed to a procedure either *by value* or *by reference*, you will need to examine _____.
   a. the Call statement
   b. the procedure header
   c. the statements entered in the procedure
   d. Either a or b.

4. Which of the following statements can be used to call the CalcArea Sub procedure, passing it two variables *by value*?
   a. `Call CalcArea(length, width)`
   b. `Call CalcArea(ByVal length, ByVal width)`
   c. `Call CalcArea ByVal(length, width)`
   d. `Call ByVal CalcArea(length, width)`

5. Which of the following procedure headers receives the value stored in a String variable?
   a. `Private Sub DisplayName(ByValue empName As String)`
   b. `Private Sub DisplayName(ByRef empName As String)`
   c. `Private Sub DisplayName ByVal(empName As String)`
   d. None of the above.

6. Which of the following is a valid procedure header for a procedure that receives an integer first and a number with a decimal place second?
   a. `Private Sub CalcFee(base As Integer, rate As Decimal)`
   b. `Private Sub CalcFee(ByRef base As Integer, ByRef rate As Decimal)`
   c. `Private Sub CalcFee(ByVal base As Integer, ByVal rate As Decimal)`
   d. None of the above.

7. Which of the following procedure headers indicates that the procedure should be processed when the user clicks either the firstCheckBox or the secondCheckBox?
   a. `Private Sub Clear(ByVal sender As Object, ByVal e As System.EventArgs) Handles firstCheckBox.Click, secondCheckBox.Click`
   b. `Private Sub Clear(ByVal sender As Object, ByVal e As System.EventArgs) Handles firstCheckBox_Click, secondCheckBox_Click`
   c. `Private Sub Clear_Click(ByVal sender As Object, ByVal e As System.EventArgs) Handles firstCheckBox, secondCheckBox`
   d. `Private Sub Clear(ByVal sender As Object, ByVal e As System.EventArgs) Handles firstCheckBox.Click and secondCheckBox.Click`

8. The procedure header specifies the procedure's _____.
   a. name
   b. parameters
   c. type (either Sub or Function)
   d. All of the above.

9. Which of the following is false?
   a. In most cases, the number of arguments should agree with the number of parameters.
   b. The data type of each argument should match the data type of its corresponding parameter.
   c. The name of each argument should be identical to the name of its corresponding parameter.
   d. When you pass information to a procedure *by value*, the procedure stores the value of each item it receives in a separate memory location.

10. Which of the following instructs a function to return the contents of the `stateTax` variable to the statement that called the function?
    a. `Return stateTax`
    b. `Return stateTax ByVal`
    c. `Return ByVal stateTax`
    d. `Return ByRef stateTax`

11. Which of the following is a valid procedure header for a procedure that receives the value stored in an Integer variable first, and the address of a Decimal variable second?
    a. `Private Sub CalcFee(ByVal base As Integer, ByAdd rate As Decimal)`
    b. `Private Sub CalcFee(base As Integer, rate As Decimal)`
    c. `Private Sub CalcFee(ByVal base As Integer, ByRef rate As Decimal)`
    d None of the above.

12. Which of the following is a valid procedure header for a procedure that receives the number 15?
    a. `Private Function CalcTax(ByVal rate As Integer) As Decimal`
    b. `Private Function CalcTax(ByAdd rate As Integer) As Decimal`
    c. `Private Sub CalcTax(ByVal rate As Integer)`
    d. Both a and c.

13. If the statement `Call CalcNet(netPay)` passes the address of the `netPay` variable to the CalcNet procedure, the variable is said to be passed _____.
    a. *by address*
    b. *by content*
    c. *by reference*
    d. *by value*

14. If the statement `Call CalcNet(netPay)` passes the contents of the `netPay` variable to the CalcNet procedure, the variable is said to be passed _____.
    a. *by address*
    b. *by content*
    c. *by reference*
    d. *by value*

15. Which of the following is false?
    a. When you pass a variable *by reference*, the receiving procedure can change its contents.
    b. When you pass a variable *by value*, the receiving procedure creates a procedure-level variable that it uses to store the passed value.
    c. Unless specified otherwise, all variables in Visual Basic are passed *by value*.
    d. To pass a variable *by reference* in Visual Basic, you include the keyword `ByRef` before the variable's name in the Call statement.

16. Assume that a Sub procedure named CalcEndingInventory is passed four Integer variables named `begin`, `sales`, `purchases`, and `ending`. The procedure's task is to calculate the ending inventory, based on the beginning inventory, sales, and purchase amounts passed to the procedure. The

procedure should store the result in the ending memory location. Which of the following procedure headers is correct?

a. `Private Sub CalcEndingInventory(ByVal b As Integer, ByVal s As Integer, ByVal p As Integer, ByRef final As Integer)`

b. `Private Sub CalcEndingInventory(ByVal b As Integer, ByVal s As Integer, ByVal p As Integer, ByVal final As Integer)`

c. `Private Sub CalcEndingInventory(ByRef b As Integer, ByRef s As Integer, ByRef p As Integer, ByVal final As Integer)`

d. `Private Sub CalcEndingInventory(ByRef b As Integer, ByRef s As Integer, ByRef p As Integer, ByRef final As Integer)`

17. Which of the following statements should you use to call the CalcEndingInventory procedure described in Question 16?

a. `Call CalcEndingInventory(begin, sales, purchases, ending)`

b. `Call CalcEndingInventory(ByVal begin, ByVal sales, ByVal purchases, ByRef ending)`

c. `Call CalcEndingInventory(ByRef begin, ByRef sales, ByRef purchases, ByRef ending)`

d. `Call CalcEndingInventory(ByVal begin, ByVal sales, ByVal purchases, ByVal ending)`

18. The memory locations listed in the *parameterlist* in a procedure header are procedure-level and are removed from the computer's internal memory when the procedure ends.

a. True

b. False

19. The CalcTax function's procedure header is `Private Function CalcTax(ByVal sales As Decimal) As Decimal`. Which of the following is a valid Return statement for the function? (The `tax` and `rate` variables are Decimal variables declared in the function.)

a. `Return sales * .06D`

b. `Return tax`

c. `Return sales * rate`

d. All of the above.

20. Which of the following statements converts the `sender` parameter to a Label object named `netLabel`?

a. `Cast(sender, netLabel)`

b. `netLabel = Cast(sender, Label)`

c. `netLabel = TryCast(Label, sender)`

d. None of the above.

## Review Exercises – Short Answer

1. Explain the difference between a Sub procedure and a Function procedure.

2. Explain the difference between passing a variable *by value* and passing it *by reference*.

3. Write the Visual Basic code for a Sub procedure that receives an integer passed to it. The procedure, named HalveNumber, should divide the integer by 2 and then display the result in the numLabel.

4. Write an appropriate statement to invoke the HalveNumber procedure created in Exercise 3. Pass the integer 87 to the procedure.

5. Write the Visual Basic code for a Sub procedure that prompts the user to enter the name of a city, and then stores the user's response in the String variable whose address is passed to the procedure. Name the procedure GetCity.

6. Write an appropriate statement to invoke the GetCity procedure created in Exercise 5. Pass a String variable named `city`.

7. Write the Visual Basic code for a Sub procedure that receives four Integer variables: the first two *by value* and the last two *by reference*. The procedure should calculate the sum and the difference of the two variables passed *by value*, and then store the results in the variables passed *by reference*. (When calculating the difference, subtract the contents of the second variable from the contents of the first variable.) Name the procedure CalcSumAndDiff.

8. Write an appropriate statement to invoke the CalcSumAndDiff procedure created in Exercise 7. Pass the Integer variables named `firstNum`, `secondNum`, `sum`, and `difference`.

9. Write the Visual Basic code for a Sub procedure that receives three Decimal variables: the first two *by value* and the last one *by reference*. The procedure should divide the first variable by the second variable, and then store the result in the third variable. Name the procedure CalcQuotient.

10. Write the Visual Basic code for a Function procedure that receives the value stored in an Integer variable. Name the procedure DivideNumber. The procedure should divide the integer by 2 and then return the result (which may contain a decimal place).

11. Write an appropriate statement to call the DivideNumber function created in Exercise 10. The name of the Integer variable passed to the function is `number`. Assign the value returned by the function to the `answer` variable.

12. Write the Visual Basic code for a Function procedure that prompts the user to enter the name of a state, and then returns the user's response to the calling procedure. Name the procedure GetState.

13. Write an appropriate statement to invoke the GetState function created in Exercise 12. Display the function's return value in a message box.

14. Write the Visual Basic code for a Function procedure that receives the contents of four Integer variables. The procedure should calculate the average of the four integers and then return the result (which may contain a decimal place). Name the procedure CalcAverage.

15. Write an appropriate statement to invoke the CalcAverage function created in Exercise 14. The Integer variables passed to the function are named num1, num2, num3, and num4. Assign the function's return value to a Decimal variable named `average`.

16. Write the Visual Basic code for a Function procedure that receives two numbers that both have a decimal place. The procedure should divide the first number by the second number and then return the result. Name the procedure CalcQuotient.

17. Write the procedure header for a Sub procedure named CalculateTax. The procedure should be invoked when any of the following occurs: the rate1Button's Click event, the rate2Button's Click event, and the salesListBox's SelectedValueChanged event.

18. Write the statement to convert the `sender` parameter to a radio button object named `currentRadioButton`.

19. In the Bonus Calculator application's code, which is shown in Figure 7.8 in the chapter, both the reg1TextBox_TextChanged procedure and the reg2TextBox_TextChanged procedure contain an instruction to remove the contents of the bonusLabel. Rewrite that portion of the code so that it uses one procedure to clear the contents of the bonusLabel. The procedure should be invoked automatically when the TextChanged event occurs for either text box.

20. In the Gross Pay application's code, which is shown in Figure 7.10 in the chapter, both the hoursListBox_SelectedValueChanged procedure and the rateListBox_SelectedValueChanged procedure contain an instruction to remove the contents of the grossLabel. Rewrite that portion of the code so that it uses one procedure to clear the contents of the grossLabel. The procedure should be invoked automatically when the SelectedValueChanged event occurs for either list box.

## Computer Exercises

1. In this exercise, you complete an application that calculates an employee's regular, overtime, and gross pay.
   a. Open the Gadis Antiques Solution (Gadis Antiques Solution.sln) file, which is contained in the VbReloaded\Chap07\Gadis Antiques Solution folder.
   b. Enter the code shown in Figure 7.4.
   c. Save the solution, then start and test the application.
   d. Use the code shown in Figure 7.14 to modify the application.
   e. Save the solution, then start and test the application.
   f. Click the Exit button to end the application, then close the solution.

2. In this exercise, you complete an application that displays a message containing a pet's name and age.
   a. Open the Pet Information Solution (Pet Information Solution.sln) file, which is contained in the VbReloaded\Chap07\Pet Information Solution folder.
   b. Enter the code shown in Figure 7.6.
   c. Save the solution, then start and test the application.
   d. Click the Exit button to end the application, then close the solution.

3. In this exercise, you complete an application that calculates a 10% bonus amount.
   a. Open the Bonus Calculator Solution (Bonus Calculator Solution.sln) file, which is contained in the VbReloaded\Chap07\Bonus Calculator Solution folder.
   b. Enter the code shown in Figure 7.8.
   c. Save the solution, then start and test the application.

d. Modify the application so that it uses one procedure to clear the contents of the bonusLabel. The procedure should be invoked when the TextChanged event occurs for either text box.
e. Save the solution, then start and test the application.
f. Click the Exit button to end the application, then close the solution.

4. In this exercise, you complete an application that calculates gross pay.
a. Open the Gross Pay Solution (Gross Pay Solution.sln) file, which is contained in the VbReloaded\Chap07\Gross Pay Solution folder.
b. Enter the code shown in Figure 7.10.
c. Save the solution, then start and test the application.
d. Modify the application so that it uses one procedure to clear the contents of the grossLabel. The procedure should be invoked when the SelectedValueChanged event occurs for either list box.
e. Save the solution, then start and test the application.
f. Click the Exit button to end the application, then close the solution.

5. In this exercise, you complete an application that calculates an employee's new pay.
a. Open the Pine Lodge Solution (Pine Lodge Solution.sln) file, which is contained in the VbReloaded\Chap07\Pine Lodge Solution folder.
b. Enter the code shown in Figure 7.17.
c. Save the solution, then start and test the application.
d. Click the Exit button to end the application, then close the solution.

6. In this exercise, you modify the application completed in Computer Exercise 4.
a. Use Windows to make a copy of the Gross Pay Solution folder, which is contained in the VbReloaded\Chap07 folder. Rename the copy Modified Gross Pay Solution.
b. Open the Gross Pay Solution (Gross Pay Solution.sln) file contained in the VbReloaded\Chap07\Modified Gross Pay Solution folder.
c. Modify the code so that it uses a Function procedure rather than a Sub procedure to calculate and return the gross pay amount.
d. Save the solution, then start and test the application.
e. Click the Exit button to end the application, then close the solution.

7. In this exercise, you modify the application completed in Computer Exercise 5.
a. Use Windows to make a copy of the Pine Lodge Solution folder, which is contained in the VbReloaded\Chap07 folder. Rename the copy Modified Pine Lodge Solution.
b. Open the Pine Lodge Solution (Pine Lodge Solution.sln) file contained in the VbReloaded\Chap07\Modified Pine Lodge Solution folder.
c. Modify the code so that it uses a Sub procedure rather than a Function procedure to calculate the new pay amount.
d. Save the solution, then start and test the application.
e. Click the Exit button to end the application, then close the solution.

8. In this exercise, you modify the Concentration Game application you created in the chapter's Programming Tutorial.
a. Use Windows to make a copy of the Concentration Game Solution folder, which is contained in the VbReloaded\Chap07 folder. Rename the copy Concentration Game Solution-Color.
b. Open the Concentration Game Solution (Concentration Game Solution.sln) file contained in the VbReloaded\Chap07\Concentration Game Solution-Color folder.

   c. When the user finds a matching pair of items, change the BackColor property of the corresponding labels to a different color. Be sure to return the labels to their original color when the user clicks the New Game button.

   d. Also modify the application so that it displays the message "Game Over" when the user has located all of the matching pairs.

   e. Save the solution, then start and test the application. Click the Exit button to end the application, then close the solution.

9. In this exercise, you modify the Concentration Game application you created in the chapter's Programming Tutorial.

   a. Use Windows to make a copy of the Concentration Game Solution folder, which is contained in the VbReloaded\Chap07 folder. Rename the copy Concentration Game Solution-Wild.

   b. Open the Concentration Game Solution (Concentration Game Solution.sln) file contained in the VbReloaded\Chap07\Concentration Game Solution-Wild folder.

   c. Replace the Washer/Dryer values in the list box with two Wild Card values. A Wild Card value matches any other value on the board. Modify the code appropriately.

   d. Save the solution, then start and test the application. Click the Exit button to end the application, then close the solution.

10. In this exercise, you modify the Rainfall application you created in the chapter's Programming Example.

   a. Create the Rainfall application shown in the chapter's Programming Example. Save the application in the VbReloaded\Chap07 folder.

   b. Modify the application so that it uses two function procedures rather than a Sub procedure to calculate the total and average rainfall amounts.

   c. Save the solution, then start and test the application. Click the Exit button to end the application, then close the solution.

11. In this exercise, you code an application that uses two independent Sub procedures: one to convert a temperature from Fahrenheit to Celsius, and the other to convert a temperature from Celsius to Fahrenheit.

   a. Build an appropriate interface. Name the solution Temperature Solution. Name the project Temperature Project. Save the application in the VbReloaded\Chap07 folder.

   b. Code the application.

   c. Save the solution, and then start the application. Test the application.

   d. Stop the application, then close the solution.

12. In this exercise, you modify the application that you created in Computer Exercise 11 so that it uses two functions rather than two Sub procedures.

   a. Use Windows to make a copy of the Temperature Solution folder, which is contained in the VbReloaded\Chap07 folder. Rename the copy Modified Temperature Solution.

   b. Open the Temperature Solution (Temperature Solution.sln) file contained in the VbReloaded\Chap07\Modified Temperature Solution folder.

   c. Modify the code so that it uses two functions rather than two Sub procedures to convert the temperatures.

   d. Save the solution, and then start the application. Test the application.

   e. Stop the application, then close the solution.

13. In this exercise, you modify the Concentration Game application you created in the chapter's Programming Tutorial.
    a. Use Windows to make a copy of the Concentration Game Solution folder, which is contained in the VbReloaded\Chap07 folder. Rename the copy Concentration Game Solution-Counters.
    b. Open the Concentration Game Solution (Concentration Game Solution.sln) file contained in the VbReloaded\Chap07\Concentration Game Solution-Counters folder.
    c. Modify the application so that it displays (in two labels) the number of times the user selects a matching pair of words, and the number of times the user does not select a matching pair of words.
    d. Save the solution, then start and test the application. Click the Exit button to end the application, then close the solution.

14. In this exercise, you learn how to specify that one or more arguments are optional in a Call statement.
    a. Open the Optional Solution (Optional Solution.sln) file, which is contained in the VbReloaded\Chap07\Optional Solution folder.
    b. Study the application's existing code. Notice that the calcButton's Click event procedure contains two Call statements. The first Call statement passes three variables (`sales`, `bonus`, and `rate`) to the GetBonus procedure. The second Call statement, however, passes only two variables (`sales` and `bonus`) to the procedure. (Do not be concerned about the jagged line that appears below the second Call statement.) Notice that the `rate` variable is omitted from the second Call statement. You indicate that the `rate` variable is optional in the Call statement by including the keyword `Optional` before the variable's corresponding parameter in the procedure header; you enter the `Optional` keyword before the `ByVal` keyword. You also assign a default value that the procedure will use for the missing parameter when the procedure is called. You assign the default value by entering the assignment operator followed by the default value after the parameter in the function header. In this case, you will assign the number .1 as the default value for the `rate` variable. (Optional parameters must be listed at the end of the procedure header.)
    c. Change the `ByVal bonusRate As Decimal` in the procedure header appropriately.
    d. Save the solution, then start the application. Calculate the bonus for a salesperson with an "A" code, $1000 in sales, and a rate of .05. The `Call GetBonus(sales, bonus, rate)` statement calls the GetBonus procedure, passing it the number 1000, the address of the `bonus` variable, and the number .05. The GetBonus procedure stores the number 1000 in the `totalSales` variable. It also assigns the name `bonusAmount` to the `bonus` variable, and stores the number .05 in the `bonusRate` variable. The procedure then multiplies the contents of the `totalSales` variable (1000) by the contents of the `bonusRate` variable (.05), and assigns the result (50) to the `bonusAmount` variable. The `bonusLabel.Text = bonus.ToString("C2")` statement then displays the number $50.00 in the bonusLabel.
    e. Now calculate the bonus for a salesperson with a code of "B" and a sales amount of $2000. The `Call GetBonus(sales, bonus)` statement calls the GetBonus procedure, passing it the number 2000 and the address of the `bonus` variable. The GetBonus procedure stores the number 2000 in the `totalSales` variable, and assigns the name `bonusAmount` to the `bonus` variable. Because the Call statement did not

supply a value for the `bonusRate` variable, the default value (.1) is assigned to the variable. The procedure then multiplies the contents of the `totalSales` variable (2000) by the contents of the `bonusRate` variable (.1), and assigns the result (200) to the `bonusAmount` variable. The `bonusLabel.Text = bonus.ToString("C2")` statement then displays the number $200.00 in the bonusLabel.

   f.  Click the Exit button to end the application, then close the solution.

15.  In this exercise, you modify the Bonus Calculator application that you coded in Computer Exercise 3.

   a.  Open the Bonus Calculator Solution (Bonus Calculator Solution.sln) file, which is contained in the VbReloaded\Chap07\Bonus Calculator Solution folder.

   b.  Modify the code so that it uses one procedure (rather than two, as it currently does) to select the existing text in the text box. The procedure should be processed when the Enter event of either text box occurs.

   c.  Save the solution, then start and test the application.

   d.  Click the Exit button to end the application, then close the solution.

16.  In this exercise, you find and correct an error in an application. The process of finding and correcting errors is called debugging.

   a.  Open the Debug Solution (Debug Solution.sln) file, which is contained in the VbReloaded\Chap07\Debug Solution folder.

   b.  Open the Code Editor window. Review the existing code.

   c.  Start the application. Click the Display Name button. When prompted to enter a name, type your name and press Enter. Notice that your name did not appear in the nameLabel, which is incorrect. Click the Exit button to end the application.

   d.  Modify the application's code appropriately.

   e.  Save the solution, then start the application. Click the Display Name button. When prompted to enter a name, type your name and press Enter. This time, your name should appear in the nameLabel.

   f.  Click the Exit button to end the application, then close the solution.

## Case Projects

### Car Shoppers Inc.

Recently, in an effort to boost sales, Car Shoppers Inc. is offering buyers a choice of either a large cash rebate or an extremely low financing rate, much lower than the rate most buyers would pay by financing the car through their local bank. Jake Miller, the manager of Car Shoppers Inc., wants you to create an application that he can use to help buyers decide whether to take the lower financing rate from his dealership, or take the rebate and then finance the car through their local bank. Be sure to use one or more independent Sub or Function procedures in the application. (Payments are due at the beginning of the month.)

### Wallpaper Warehouse

Last year, Johanna Liu opened a new wallpaper store named Wallpaper Warehouse. Business is booming at the store, and Johanna and her salesclerks are always busy. Recently, however, Johanna has received several complaints from customers about the store's slow service, and she has decided to ask her salesclerks for suggestions on how the service can be improved. The overwhelming response from the salesclerks is that they need a more convenient way to calculate the number of single rolls of wallpaper required to cover a room. Currently, the salesclerks perform this calculation manually, using pencil and paper. Doing this for so many customers, however, takes a great deal of time, and service has begun to suffer. Johanna has asked for your assistance in this matter. She would like you to create an application that the salesclerks can use to quickly calculate and display the required number of rolls. Be sure to use one or more independent Sub or Function procedures in the application.

## Cable Direct

Sharon Barrow, the billing supervisor at Cable Direct (a local cable company) has asked you to create an application that she can use to calculate and display a customer's bill. The cable rates are as follows:

Residential customers:

| | |
|---|---|
| Processing fee: | $4.50 |
| Basic service fee: | $30 |
| Premium channels: | $5 per channel |

Business customers:

| | |
|---|---|
| Processing fee: | $16.50 |
| Basic service fee: | $80 for first 10 connections; $4 for each additional connection |
| Premium channels: | $50 per channel for any number of connections |

Business customers must have at least one connection. Be sure to use one or more independent Sub or Function procedures in the application.

## Harvey Industries

Currently, Khalid Patel, the payroll manager at Harvey Industries, manually calculates each employee's weekly gross pay, Social Security and Medicare (FICA) tax, federal withholding tax (FWT), and net pay—a very time-consuming process and one that is prone to mathematical errors. Mr. Patel has asked you to create an application that he can use to perform the payroll calculations both efficiently and accurately.

Employees at Harvey Industries are paid every Friday. All employees are paid on an hourly basis, with time and one-half paid for the hours worked over 40.

The amount of FICA tax to deduct from an employee's weekly gross pay is calculated by multiplying the gross pay amount by 7.65%.

The amount of FWT to deduct from an employee's weekly gross pay is based on the employee's filing status—either single (including head of household) or married—and his or her weekly taxable wages. You calculate the weekly taxable wages by first multiplying the number of withholding allowances by $55.77 (the value of a withholding allowance), and then subtracting the result from the weekly gross pay. For example, if your weekly gross pay is $400 and you have two withholding allowances, your weekly taxable wages are $288.46. You use the weekly taxable wages, along with the filing status and the weekly Federal Withholding Tax table, to determine the amount of FWT tax to withhold. The weekly tax tables are shown in Figure 7.45.

## FWT Tables – Weekly Payroll Period

### Single person (including head of household)

| If the taxable wages are: | | The amount of income tax to withhold is | | |
|---|---|---|---|---|
| Over | But not over | Base amount | Percentage | Of excess over |
|  | $ 51 | 0 |  |  |
| $ 51 | $ 552 | 0 | 15% | $ 51 |
| $ 552 | $1,196 | $ 75.15 plus | 28% | $ 552 |
| $1,196 | $2,662 | $ 255.47 plus | 31% | $1,196 |
| $2,662 | $5,750 | $ 709.93 plus | 36% | $2,662 |
| $5,750 |  | $1,821.61 plus | 39.6% | $5,750 |

### Married person

| If the taxable wages are: | | The amount of income tax to withhold is | | |
|---|---|---|---|---|
| Over | But not over | Base amount | Percentage | Of excess over |
|  | $ 124 | 0 |  |  |
| $ 124 | $ 960 | 0 | 15% | $ 124 |
| $ 960 | $2,023 | $ 125.40 plus | 28% | $ 960 |
| $2,023 | $3,292 | $ 423.04 plus | 31% | $2,023 |
| $3,292 | $5,809 | $ 816.43 plus | 36% | $3,292 |
| $5,809 |  | $1,722.55 plus | 39.6% | $5,809 |

**FIGURE 7.45**

Be sure to use one or more independent Sub or Function procedures in the application.

# 8

# Arrays

## After studying Chapter 8, you should be able to:

- Declare and initialize a one-dimensional array
- Store data in a one-dimensional array
- Display the contents of a one-dimensional array
- Code a loop using the For Each...Next statement
- Access an element in a one-dimensional array
- Search a one-dimensional array
- Compute the average of a one-dimensional array's contents
- Find the highest entry in a one-dimensional array
- Update the contents of a one-dimensional array
- Sort a one-dimensional array
- Create and manipulate parallel one-dimensional arrays
- Create and initialize a two-dimensional array
- Store data in a two-dimensional array
- Search a two-dimensional array

## USING ARRAYS

All of the variables you have used so far have been simple variables. A **simple variable**, also called a **scalar variable**, is one that is unrelated to any other variable in memory. In many applications, however, you may need to reserve a block of related variables, referred to as an array.

An **array** is a group of variables that have the same name and data type and are related in some way. For example, each variable in the array might contain an inventory quantity, or each might contain a state name, or each might contain an employee record (name, Social Security number, pay rate, and so on). It may be helpful to picture an array as a group of small, adjacent boxes inside the computer's memory. You can write information to the boxes and you can read information from the boxes; you just cannot *see* the boxes.

Programmers use arrays to temporarily store related data in the internal memory of the computer. Examples of data stored in an array would include the federal withholding tax tables in a payroll program, and a price list in an order entry program. Storing data in an array increases the efficiency of a program, because data can be both written to and read from internal memory much faster than it can be written to and read from a file on a disk. Additionally, after the data is entered into an array, which typically is done at the beginning of the program, the program can use the data as many times as desired. A payroll program, for example, can use the federal withholding tax tables stored in an array to calculate the amount of each employee's federal withholding tax.

The most commonly used arrays are one-dimensional and two-dimensional.

## ONE-DIMENSIONAL ARRAYS

You can visualize a **one-dimensional** array as a column of variables. A unique number called a **subscript** identifies each variable in a one-dimensional array. The computer assigns the subscripts to the array variables when the array is created. The subscript indicates the variable's position in the array. The first variable in a one-dimensional array has a subscript of 0 (zero), the second a subscript of 1 (one), and so on. You refer to each variable in an array by the array's name and the variable's subscript, which is specified in a set of parentheses immediately following the array name. For example, to refer to the first variable in a one-dimensional array named `states`, you use `states(0)`—read "states sub zero." Similarly, to refer to the third variable in the `states` array, you use `states(2)`. Figure 8.1 illustrates this naming convention.

| | |
|---|---|
| *states(0)* | Alaska |
| *states(1)* | Montana |
| *states(2)* | South Carolina |
| *states(3)* | Tennessee |

**FIGURE 8.1**   Names of the variables in a one-dimensional array named `states`

**TIP**

The variables in an array are stored in consecutive memory locations in the computer's internal memory.

**TIP**

It takes longer for the computer to access the information stored in a disk file, because the computer must wait for the disk drive to locate the needed information and then read the information into internal memory.

**TIP**

You also can visualize a one-dimensional array as a row of variables, rather than as a column of variables.

Before you can use an array, you first must declare (create) it. Figure 8.2 shows two versions of the syntax you use to declare a one-dimensional array in Visual Basic. The figure also includes examples of using each syntax.

**HOW TO...**

TIP

A subscript is also called an index.

> ### Declare a One-Dimensional Array
>
> **Syntax – Version 1**
> {Dim | Private} *arrayname*(*highestSubscript*) As *datatype*
>
> **Syntax – Version 2**
> {Dim | Private} *arrayname*() As *datatype* = {*initialValues*}
>
> **Examples**
> ```
> Dim cities(3) As String
> ```
> declares a four-element procedure-level array named `cities`; each element is automatically initialized using the keyword `Nothing`
>
> ```
> Private numbers(5) As Integer
> ```
> declares a six-element module-level array named `numbers`; each element is automatically initialized to the number zero
>
> ```
> Private states() As String = {"Hawaii", "Alaska", "Maine"}
> ```
> declares and initializes a three-element module-level array named `states`
>
> ```
> Dim sales() As Decimal = {75.33D, 9.65D, 23.55D, 6.89D}
> ```
> declares and initializes a four-element procedure-level array named `sales`

**FIGURE 8.2**   How to declare a one-dimensional array

The {**Dim** | **Private**} portion in each syntax version indicates that you can select only one of the keywords appearing within the braces. In this case, you can select either the `Dim` keyword or the `Private` keyword. The appropriate keyword to use depends on whether you are creating a procedure-level array or a module-level array. *Arrayname* is the name of the array, and *datatype* is the type of data the array variables, referred to as **elements**, will store. Recall that each of the elements (variables) in an array has the same data type.

In Version 1 of the syntax, *highestSubscript* is an integer that specifies the highest subscript in the array. When the array is created, it will contain one element more than the number specified in the *highestSubscript* argument; this is because the first element in a one-dimensional array has a subscript of zero. For instance, the `Dim cities(3) As String` statement, which is shown in the first example in Figure 8.2, creates a procedure-level one-dimensional array named `cities`. The `cities` array contains four elements with subscripts of 0, 1, 2, and 3; each element can store a string. Similarly, the statement shown in the second example, `Private numbers(5) As Integer`, creates a module-level one-dimensional array named `numbers`. The `numbers` array contains six elements with subscripts of 0, 1, 2, 3, 4, and 5; in this case, each element can store an integer.

When you use the syntax shown in Version 1 to declare a one-dimensional array, the computer automatically initializes each element in the array when the array is created. If the array's data type is String, each element in the array is initialized using the keyword `Nothing`. As you learned in Chapter 3, variables initialized to `Nothing` do not actually contain the word "Nothing"; rather, they contain no data at all. Elements in a numeric array are initialized to the number zero, and elements in a Boolean array are initialized to the Boolean value False. Date array elements are initialized to 12:00 AM January 1, 0001.

You use the syntax shown in Version 2 in Figure 8.2 to declare an array and, at the same time, specify each element's initial value. You list the initial values in the *initialValues* section of the syntax, using commas to separate the values, and you enclose the list of values in braces ({}). Notice that the syntax shown in Version 2 does not include the *highestSubscript* argument; instead, an empty set of parentheses follows the array name. The computer automatically calculates the highest subscript based on the number of values listed in the *initialValues* section. If the *initialValues* section contains five values, the highest subscript in the array is 4. Likewise, if the *initialValues* section contains 100 values, the highest subscript in the array is 99. Notice that the highest subscript is always one number less than the number of values listed in the *initialValues* section; this is because the first subscript in a one-dimensional array is the number zero.

In the third example shown in Figure 8.2, the `Private states() As String = {"Hawaii", "Alaska", "Maine"}` statement declares a module-level one-dimensional String array named `states`. The `states` array contains three elements with subscripts of 0, 1, and 2. When the array is created, the computer assigns the string "Hawaii" to the `states(0)` element, "Alaska" to the `states(1)` element, and "Maine" to the `states(2)` element. Similarly, the `Dim sales() As Decimal = {75.33D, 9.65D, 23.55D, 6.89D}` statement shown in the last example declares a procedure-level one-dimensional Decimal array named `sales`. The `sales` array contains four elements with subscripts of 0, 1, 2, and 3. The computer assigns the number 75.33 to the `sales(0)` element, 9.65 to the `sales(1)` element, 23.55 to the `sales(2)` element, and 6.89 to the `sales(3)` element.

## STORING DATA IN A ONE-DIMENSIONAL ARRAY

In most cases, you use an assignment statement to enter data into an existing array. Figure 8.3 shows the syntax of such an assignment statement and includes several examples of using the syntax to enter data into the arrays declared in Figure 8.2. In the syntax, *arrayname*(*subscript*) is the name and subscript of the array variable to which you want the *value* (data) assigned.

HOW TO...

**Store Data in a One-Dimensional Array**

**Syntax**
*arrayname*(*subscript*) = *value*

**Examples**
```
cities(0) = "Madrid"
cities(1) = "Paris"
cities(2) = "Rome"
```
assigns the strings "Madrid", "Paris", and "Rome" to the `cities` array

```
For x As Integer = 1 To 6
    numbers(x - 1) = x * x
Next x
```
assigns the squares of the numbers from one through six to the `numbers` array

```
states(1) = "Virginia"
```
assigns the string "Virginia" to the second element in the `states` array

```
isConverted = Decimal.TryParse(salesTextBox.Text, sales(0))
```
assigns either the value entered in the salesTextBox (converted to Decimal) or the number zero to the first element in the `sales` array

**FIGURE 8.3**    How to store data in a one-dimensional array

The three assignment statements shown in the first example in Figure 8.3 assign the strings "Madrid", "Paris", and "Rome" to the first three elements in the `cities` array, replacing the values stored in the array elements when the array was created. The code shown in the second example assigns the squares of the numbers from one through six to the `numbers` array, writing over the array's initial values. Notice that the number one must be subtracted from the value stored in the x variable when assigning the squares to the array; this is because the first array element has a subscript of zero rather than one.

The `states(1) = "Virginia"` statement shown in the third example in Figure 8.3 assigns the string "Virginia" to the second element in the `states` array, replacing the string "Alaska" that was stored in the element when the array was created. In the last example, the `isConverted = Decimal.TryParse(salesTextBox.Text, sales(0))` statement converts the value entered in the salesTextBox to Decimal. If the conversion is successful, the statement assigns the Decimal result to the first element in the `sales` array; otherwise, it assigns the number zero to the first element in the array.

## MANIPULATING ONE-DIMENSIONAL ARRAYS

The variables (elements) in an array can be used just like any other variables. For example, you can assign values to them, use them in calculations, display their contents, and so on. In the next several sections, you view sample procedures that demonstrate how one-dimensional arrays are used in an application. More specifically, the procedures will show you how to perform the following tasks using a one-dimensional array:

1. Display the contents of an array.
2. Access an array element using its subscript.
3. Search the array.
4. Calculate the average of the data stored in a numeric array.
5. Find the highest value stored in an array.
6. Update the array elements.
7. Sort the array elements.

In most applications, the values stored in an array come from a file on the computer's disk and are assigned to the array after it is declared. However, so that you can follow the code and its results more easily, most of the procedures you view in this chapter use the Dim statement to assign the appropriate values to the array. The first procedure you view displays the contents of a one-dimensional array.

### Displaying the Contents of a One-Dimensional Array

Figure 8.4 shows a sample run of the Months application, which assigns to a label control the item selected in a list box. Figure 8.5 shows the pseudocode for the MainForm's Load event procedure contained in the application, and Figure 8.6 shows the corresponding Visual Basic code. The Load event procedure demonstrates how you can display the contents of an array in a list box.

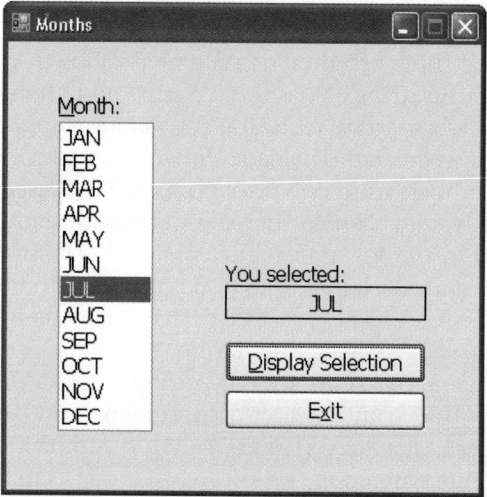

**FIGURE 8.4**    Sample run of the Months application

---

**Pseudocode**

1. declare and initialize a String array named months
2. repeat for each element in the months array
       display the contents of the current array element in the monthListBox
   end repeat

---

**FIGURE 8.5**    Pseudocode for the MainForm's Load event procedure

**Visual Basic code**

```
' Project name:            Months Project
' Project purpose:         The project displays the contents of an
'                          array in a list box. It also displays
'                          the item selected in the list box.
' Created/revised by:      <your name> on <current date>

Option Explicit On
Option Strict On

Public Class MainForm

    Private Sub MainForm_Load(ByVal sender As Object, _
        ByVal e As System.EventArgs) Handles Me.Load
        ' fills the list box with array values, then selects
        ' the first item

        Dim months() As String = {"JAN", "FEB", "MAR", _
            "APR", "MAY", "JUN", "JUL", "AUG", "SEP", _
            "OCT", "NOV", "DEC"}

        For subscript As Integer = 0 To 11
            monthListBox.Items.Add(months(subscript))
        Next subscript

        monthListBox.SelectedIndex = 0
    End Sub

    Private Sub exitButton_Click(ByVal sender As Object, _
        ByVal e As System.EventArgs) Handles exitButton.Click
        Me.Close()
    End Sub


    Private Sub displayButton_Click(ByVal sender As Object, _
        ByVal e As System.EventArgs) Handles displayButton.Click
        selectedItemLabel.Text = monthListBox.SelectedItem.ToString
    End Sub

    Private Sub monthListBox_SelectedValueChanged(ByVal sender As _
        Object, ByVal e As System.EventArgs) _
        Handles monthListBox.SelectedValueChanged
        selectedItemLabel.Text = String.Empty
    End Sub
End Class
```

*Array declaration* → `Dim months() As String = {"JAN", "FEB", "MAR", ...`

*Displays the array values in a list box* → `For subscript As Integer = 0 To 11 ... Next subscript`

**FIGURE 8.6**    Code for the Months application

The MainForm's Load event procedure declares a 12-element String array named months, using the names of the 12 months to initialize the array. The procedure then uses a For...Next loop to display the contents of each array element in the monthListBox. The first time the loop is processed, the subscript variable contains the number zero, and the monthListBox.Items.Add(months (subscript)) statement displays the contents of the months(0) element—JAN—in the monthListBox. The Next subscript statement then adds the number one to the value stored in the subscript variable, giving one. When the loop is processed the second time, the monthListBox.Items.Add(months (subscript)) statement adds the contents of the months(1) element—FEB—to the monthListBox, and so on. The computer repeats the loop instructions for each element in the months array, beginning with the element whose subscript is zero (JAN) and ending with the element whose subscript is 11 (DEC). The computer stops processing the loop when the value contained in the subscript variable is 12, which is one number more than the highest subscript in the array.

In Figure 8.6, the MainForm's Load event procedure uses the For...Next statement to display each array element. You also could use the Do...Loop statement (which you learned about in Chapter 5) or the For Each...Next statement (which you learn about next).

## The For Each...Next Statement

You can use the **For Each...Next statement** to code a loop whose instructions you want processed for each element in a group—for example, for each array variable in an array. Figure 8.7 shows the syntax of the For Each...Next statement. It also shows two ways of writing the loop from Figure 8.6 using the For Each...Next statement.

**HOW TO...**

### Use the For Each...Next Statement

**Syntax**
For Each *element* [As *datatype*] In *group*
    [*statements*]
Next *element*

**Examples**
```
For Each monthName As String In months
    monthListBox.Items.Add(monthName)
Next monthName
```
displays the contents of the months array in the monthListBox

```
Dim monthName As String
For Each monthName In months
    monthListBox.Items.Add(monthName)
Next monthName
```
same as the previous example

**FIGURE 8.7**        How to use the For Each...Next statement

The For Each...Next statement begins with the For Each clause and ends with the Next clause. Between the two clauses, you enter the instructions you want the loop to repeat for each *element* in the *group*.

When using the For Each...Next statement to process an array, *element* is the name of a variable that the computer can use to keep track of each array variable, and *group* is the name of the array. You can use the **As** *datatype* portion of the For Each clause to declare the *element* variable, as shown in the first example in Figure 8.7. When you declare a variable in the For Each clause, the variable has block scope and can be used only by the For Each...Next loop. Alternatively, you can declare the *element* variable in a Dim statement, as shown in the last example in Figure 8.7. As you know, when a variable is declared in a Dim statement at the beginning of a procedure, it has procedure scope and can be used by the entire procedure.

The data type of the *element* must match the data type of the *group*. For example, if the *group* is an Integer array, then the *element*'s data type must be Integer. Likewise, if the *group* is a String array, then the *element*'s data type must be String.

TIP

You can nest For Each...Next statements, which means that you can place one For Each...Next statement within another For Each...Next statement.

In the examples shown in Figure 8.7, *group* is a String array named `months`, and *element* is a String variable named `monthName`.

The `monthListBox.Items.Add(monthName)` statement in both examples in Figure 8.7 displays the current array element in the `monthListBox` and will be processed for each element in the `months` array. The code shown in both examples will display the same result as shown earlier in Figure 8.4.

Next, you view a procedure that uses the array subscript to access the appropriate element in an array.

## Using the Subscript to Access an Element in a One-Dimensional Array

XYZ Corporation pays its managers based on six different salary codes, 1 through 6. Each code corresponds to a different salary amount. Your task is to create an application that displays the salary amount associated with the salary code entered by the user. Figure 8.8 shows a sample run of the Salary Code application. Figure 8.9 shows the pseudocode for the displayButton's Click event procedure contained in the application, and Figure 8.10 shows the corresponding Visual Basic code. The Click event procedure uses an array element's subscript to access the element in the array.

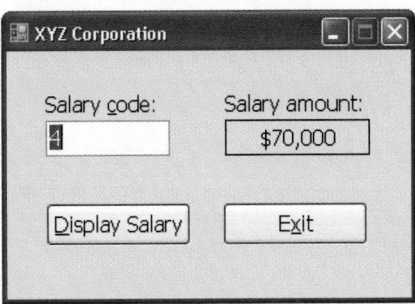

**FIGURE 8.8**   Sample run of the Salary Code application

---

**Pseudocode**

1. declare and initialize an Integer array named salaries
2. convert the salary code entered by the user to Integer
3. if the salary code can be converted to a number
   if the salary code is between 1 and 6, inclusive
      display the salary amount stored in the element located in position (salary code − 1) in the array
   else
      display the message "Enter a code from 1 through 6." in a message box
   end if
else
   display the message "The salary code must be numeric." in a message box
end if

**FIGURE 8.9**   Pseudocode for the displayButton's Click event procedure

**Visual Basic code**

```vb
' Project name:         Salary Code Project
' Project purpose:      The project displays the salary amount
'                       corresponding to the salary code entered
'                       by the user.
' Created/revised by:   <your name> on <current date>

Option Explicit On
Option Strict On

Public Class MainForm

    Private Sub exitButton_Click(ByVal sender As Object, _
        ByVal e As System.EventArgs) Handles exitButton.Click
        Me.Close()
    End Sub

    Private Sub codeTextBox_Enter(ByVal sender As Object, _
        ByVal e As System.EventArgs) Handles codeTextBox.Enter
        codeTextBox.SelectAll()
    End Sub

    Private Sub codeTextBox_TextChanged(ByVal sender As Object, _
        ByVal e As System.EventArgs) Handles codeTextBox.TextChanged
        salaryLabel.Text = String.Empty
    End Sub

    Private Sub displayButton_Click(ByVal sender As Object, _
        ByVal e As System.EventArgs) Handles displayButton.Click
        ' displays the salary amount associated with the
        ' salary code entered by the user

        Dim salaries() As Integer = {25000, 35000, 55000, _
                                     70000, 80200, 90500}
        Dim code As Integer
        Dim isConverted As Boolean

        ' use the salary code to display the appropriate
        ' salary amount from the array
        isConverted = Integer.TryParse(codeTextBox.Text, code)
        If isConverted Then

            ' verify that the salary code is valid
            If code >= 1 AndAlso code <= 6 Then
                salaryLabel.Text = salaries(code - 1).ToString("C0")
            Else
                MessageBox.Show("Enter a code from 1 through 6.", _
                    "XYZ Corporation", MessageBoxButtons.OK, _
                    MessageBoxIcon.Information)
            End If

        Else
            MessageBox.Show("The salary code must be numeric.", _
                "XYZ Corporation", MessageBoxButtons.OK, _
                MessageBoxIcon.Information)
        End If

        codeTextBox.Focus()
    End Sub
End Class
```

*Array declaration*

*Displays the salary amount associated with the salary code*

**FIGURE 8.10**    Code for the Salary Code application

The displayButton's Click event procedure shown in Figure 8.10 declares an Integer array named `salaries`, using six salary amounts to initialize the array. The salary amount for salary code 1 is stored in `salaries(0)`. Salary code 2's salary amount is stored in `salaries(1)`, and so on. Notice that the salary code is one number more than the subscript of its corresponding salary amount in the array.

After creating and initializing the array, the procedure declares an Integer variable named `code` and a Boolean variable named `isConverted`. It then uses the TryParse method to convert the salary code entered in the codeTextBox to Integer. If the conversion is not successful, an appropriate message is displayed in a message box. However, if the conversion is successful, the procedure verifies that the salary code is valid. To be valid, the salary code must be greater than or equal to the number one and, at the same time, less than or equal to the number six.

If the salary code is not valid, the procedure displays an appropriate message in a message box. Otherwise, it uses the salary code, which is stored in the `code` variable, to access the appropriate salary amount from the array. Notice that, to access the correct element in the `salaries` array, the number one must be subtracted from the contents of the `code` variable; this is because the salary code is one number more than the subscript of its associated salary amount in the array. As Figure 8.8 indicates, the procedure displays $70,000 when the user enters the number four as the salary code.

## Searching a One-Dimensional Array

The sales manager at Jacobsen Motors wants an application that allows him to determine the number of salespeople selling above a certain amount, which he will enter. To accomplish this task, the application will search an array that contains the amount sold by each salesperson. The application will look for array values that are greater than the amount entered by the sales manager. Figure 8.11 shows a sample run of the Sales application. Figure 8.12 shows the pseudocode for the searchButton's Click event procedure contained in the application, and Figure 8.13 shows the corresponding Visual Basic code.

**TIP**

Before accessing an array element, a procedure always should verify that the subscript is valid—in other words, that it is in range. If the procedure uses a subscript that is not in range, Visual Basic displays an error message and the procedure ends abruptly.

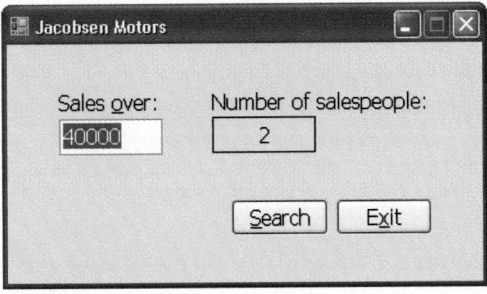

**FIGURE 8.11**   Sample run of the Sales application

## Pseudocode

1. declare and initialize an Integer array named sales
2. convert the sales amount entered in the salesTextBox to Integer
3. if the sales amount can be converted to a number
    repeat for each element in the sales array
        if the value in the current array element is greater than the value entered by the user
            add 1 to the counter variable
        end if
    end repeat
     display the contents of the counter variable in the countLabel
  else
     display the message "The sales amount must be numeric." in a message box
  end if

**FIGURE 8.12**      Pseudocode for the searchButton's Click event procedure

## Visual Basic code

```
' Project name:        Jacobsen Motors Project
' Project purpose:     The project determines the number of
'                      salespeople selling over an amount
'                      entered by the user.
' Created/revised by:  <your name> on <current date>

Option Explicit On
Option Strict On

Public Class MainForm

    Private Sub exitButton_Click(ByVal sender As Object, _
     ByVal e As System.EventArgs) Handles exitButton.Click
        Me.Close()
    End Sub

    Private Sub salesTextBox_Enter(ByVal sender As Object, _
     ByVal e As System.EventArgs) Handles salesTextBox.Enter
        salesTextBox.SelectAll()
    End Sub

    Private Sub salesTextBox_TextChanged(ByVal sender As Object, _
     ByVal e As System.EventArgs) Handles salesTextBox.TextChanged
        countLabel.Text = String.Empty
    End Sub

    Private Sub searchButton_Click(ByVal sender As Object, _
     ByVal e As System.EventArgs) Handles searchButton.Click
        ' searches the array, looking for values that are
        ' greater than the value entered by the user

        Dim sales() As Integer = {45000, 35000, 25000, 60000, 23000}
        Dim counter As Integer
        Dim searchFor As Integer
        Dim isConverted As Boolean

        isConverted = Integer.TryParse(salesTextBox.Text, searchFor)
```

*Array declaration*

**(Figure is continued on next page)**

```
            If isConverted Then
                ' search the array, updating the counter
                ' when the array value is greater than
                ' the searchFor value
                For Each salesAmount As Integer In sales
                    If salesAmount > searchFor Then
                        counter = counter + 1
                    End If
                Next salesAmount

                ' display the counter value
                countLabel.Text = Convert.ToString(counter)

            Else
                MessageBox.Show("The sales amount must be numeric.", _
                    "Jacobsen Motors", MessageBoxButtons.OK, _
                    MessageBoxIcon.Information)
            End If

            salesTextBox.Focus()
        End Sub
End Class
```

*Searches the array for values greater than a specific amount*

**FIGURE 8.13**    Code for the Sales application

The searchButton's Click event procedure declares an Integer array named sales, using five sales amounts to initialize the array. The procedure also declares two Integer variables named `counter` and `searchFor`, and a Boolean variable named `isConverted`.

After declaring the array and variables, the procedure uses the TryParse method to convert the sales amount entered in the salesTextBox to Integer. If the conversion is not successful, an appropriate message is displayed in a message box. If the conversion is successful, however, the procedure uses a loop that repeats its instructions for each element in the `sales` array. Notice that the loop uses the `salesAmount` variable to represent each element in the array.

The selection structure in the loop compares the contents of the current array element with the contents of the `searchFor` variable. If the array element contains a number that is greater than the number stored in the `searchFor` variable, the selection structure's true path adds the number one to the value stored in the `counter` variable. In the searchButton's Click event procedure, the `counter` variable is used as a counter to keep track of the number of salespeople selling over the amount entered by the sales manager.

When the loop ends, which is when there are no more array elements to search, the procedure displays the contents of the `counter` variable in the countLabel. As Figure 8.11 indicates, the procedure displays the number two when the sales manager enters 40000 as the sales amount.

## Calculating the Average Amount Stored in a One-Dimensional Numeric Array

Professor Jeremiah wants an application that calculates and displays the average test score earned by his students on the final exam. To accomplish this task, the application will add together the test scores stored in an array, and then divide the sum by the number of array elements. Figure 8.14 shows a sample run of the Average application. Figure 8.15 shows the pseudocode for the calcButton's Click event procedure contained in the application, and Figure 8.16 shows the corresponding Visual Basic code.

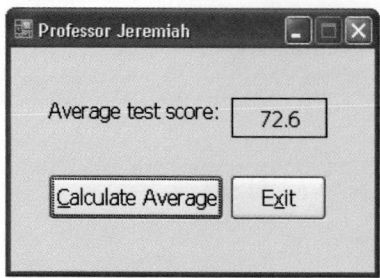

## Pseudocode

1. declare and initialize an Integer array named scores
2. repeat for each element in the scores array
       add the contents of the current array element to an accumulator variable
   end repeat
3. calculate the average score by dividing the contents of the accumulator variable by the number of array elements
4. display the average score in the averageLabel

## Visual Basic code

```vb
' Project name:        Average Project
' Project purpose:     The project calculates and displays
                       the average of the test scores stored
                       in an array.
' Created/revised by:  <your name> on <current date>

Option Explicit On
Option Strict On

Public Class MainForm

    Private Sub exitButton_Click(ByVal sender As Object, _
        ByVal e As System.EventArgs) Handles exitButton.Click
        Me.Close()
    End Sub

    Private Sub calcButton_Click(ByVal sender As Object, _
        ByVal e As System.EventArgs) Handles calcButton.Click
        ' calculates and displays the average test score

        Dim scores() As Integer = {98, 100, 56, 74, 35}
        Dim scoresAccumulator As Integer
        Dim averageScore As Double
```

*Array declaration*

**(Figure is continued on next page)**

*Accumulates the values stored in the array*

```
' accumulate scores
For Each score As Integer In scores
    scoresAccumulator = scoresAccumulator + score
Next score

' calculate and display the average score
averageScore = scoresAccumulator / scores.Length
averageLabel.Text = Convert.ToString(averageScore)
        End Sub
End Class
```

**FIGURE 8.16**  Code for the Average application

The calcButton's Click event procedure declares an Integer array named scores, using five test scores to initialize the array. It also declares an Integer variable named scoresAccumulator and a Double variable named averageScore. The loop in the procedure repeats its instruction for each element in the scores array. The instruction in the loop adds the score contained in the current array element to the scoresAccumulator variable. When the loop ends, the averageScore = scoresAccumulator / scores.Length statement uses the salesAccumulator variable and the array's Length property to calculate the average test score. An array's **Length property**, whose syntax is *arrayname*.**Length**, stores an integer that represents the number of elements in the array. In this case, the Length property stores the number five, because the scores array contains five elements. The calcButton's Click event procedure then displays the average test score in the averageLabel. As Figure 8.14 indicates, the procedure displays the number 72.6.

## Determining the Highest Value Stored in a One-Dimensional Array

Sharon Johnson keeps track of the amount of money she earns each week. She would like an application that displays the highest amount earned in a week. The application will store the pay amounts in a one-dimensional array. Similar to the Sales application's code shown earlier in Figure 8.13, the Pay application's code will need to search the array. However, rather than looking in the array for values that are greater than a specific amount, the Pay application will look for the highest amount in the array. Figure 8.17 shows a sample run of the Pay application. Figure 8.18 shows the pseudocode for the displayHighButton's Click event procedure contained in the application, and Figure 8.19 shows the corresponding Visual Basic code.

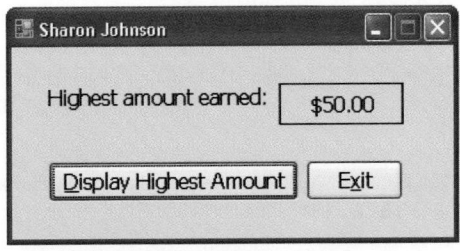

**FIGURE 8.17**  Sample run of the Pay application

**Pseudocode**

1. declare and initialize a Decimal array named pays
2. declare a Decimal variable named highestPay, and initialize the variable using the contents of the first element in the pays array
3. repeat for the second through the last array element
   if the value in the current array element is greater than the value in the highestPay variable
      assign the value in the current array element to the highestPay variable
   end if
   end repeat
4. display the contents of the highestPay variable in the highestLabel

**FIGURE 8.18**   Pseudocode for the displayHighButton's Click event procedure

**Visual Basic code**

```
' Project name:       Pay Project
' Project purpose:    The project displays the highest pay
'                     amount stored in an array.
' Created/revised by: <your name> on <current date>

Option Explicit On
Option Strict On

Public Class MainForm

    Private Sub exitButton_Click(ByVal sender As Object, _
        ByVal e As System.EventArgs) Handles exitButton.Click
        Me.Close()
    End Sub

    Private Sub displayHighButton_Click(ByVal sender As Object, _
        ByVal e As System.EventArgs) Handles displayHighButton.Click
        ' displays the highest amount stored in an array

        Dim pays() As Decimal = {25.6D, 30.25D, 50D, 20D, 25.45D}
        Dim highestPay As Decimal = pays(0)

        ' search the array, beginning with the second element
        For subscript As Integer = 1 To pays.Length - 1
            If pays(subscript) > highestPay Then
                ' store the higher value in the highestPay variable
                highestPay = pays(subscript)
            End If
        Next subscript

        ' displays the highest value
        highestLabel.Text = highestPay.ToString("C2")
    End Sub
End Class
```

*Array declaration*

*Searches the array for the highest amount*

**FIGURE 8.19**   Code for the Pay application

TIP

Notice that the loop shown in Figure 8.19 searches the second through the last element in the **pays** array. The first element is not included in the search because it is already stored in the **highestPay** variable.

The displayHighButton's Click event procedure declares a Decimal array named **pays**, and it initializes the array to the amounts that Sharon earned during the last five weeks. The procedure also declares a Decimal variable named **highestPay**, which will keep track of the highest value stored in the **pays** array. Notice that the **highestPay** variable is initialized using the value stored in the first array element.

The first time the loop in the displayHighButton's Click event procedure is processed, the selection structure within the loop compares the value stored in the second array element—**pays(1)**—with the value stored in the **highestPay** variable. At this point, the **highestPay** variable contains the same value as the first array element. If the value stored in the second array element is greater than the value stored in the **highestPay** variable, then the **highestPay = pays (subscript)** statement assigns the array element value to the **highestPay** variable. The **Next subscript** clause then adds the number one to the **subscript** variable, giving 2. The next time the loop is processed, the selection structure compares the value stored in the third array element—**pays(2)**—with the value stored in the **highestPay** variable, and so on. When the loop ends, which is when the **subscript** variable contains the number five, the procedure displays the contents of the **highestPay** variable in the highestLabel. As Figure 8.17 indicates, the procedure displays $50.00.

## Updating the Values Stored in a One-Dimensional Array

The sales manager at Jillian Company wants an application that allows her to increase the price of each item the company sells. The application will store the prices in a one-dimensional array. It then will increase the value stored in each array element. Additionally, the sales manager wants the procedure to display each item's new price in the newPricesLabel. Figure 8.20 shows a sample run of the Prices application. Figure 8.21 shows the pseudocode for the updateButton's Click event procedure contained in the application, and Figure 8.22 shows the corresponding Visual Basic code.

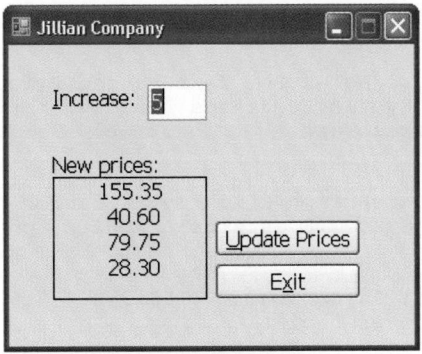

**FIGURE 8.20**    Sample run of the Prices application

**Pseudocode**

1. declare a Decimal array named prices
2. convert the increase amount entered in the increaseTextBox to Decimal
3. if the increase amount can be converted to a number
      repeat for each element in the prices array
            add the increase amount to the value stored in the current array element
            display the contents of the current array element in the newPricesLabel
      end repeat
   else
      display the message "The increase amount must be numeric." in a message box
   end if

**FIGURE 8.21**     Pseudocode for the updateButton's Click event procedure

**Visual Basic code**

```vb
' Project name:         Price Project
' Project purpose:      The project updates the prices
'                       stored in an array.
' Created/revised by:   <your name> on <current date>

Option Explicit On
Option Strict On

Public Class MainForm

    Private Sub exitButton_Click(ByVal sender As Object, _
        ByVal e As System.EventArgs) Handles exitButton.Click
        Me.Close()
    End Sub

    Private Sub increaseTextBox_Enter(ByVal sender As Object, _
        ByVal e As System.EventArgs) Handles increaseTextBox.Enter
        increaseTextBox.SelectAll()
    End Sub

    Private Sub increaseTextBox_TextChanged(ByVal sender As Object, _
        ByVal e As System.EventArgs) Handles increaseTextBox.TextChanged
        newPricesLabel.Text = String.Empty
    End Sub

    Private Sub updateButton_Click(ByVal sender As Object, _
        ByVal e As System.EventArgs) Handles updateButton.Click
        ' updates the prices stored in the array

        Dim prices() As Decimal = {150.35D, 35.6D, 74.75D, 23.3D}
        Dim increase As Decimal
        Dim isConverted As Boolean

        isConverted = Decimal.TryParse(increaseTextBox.Text, increase)
```

*Array declaration*

*(Figure is continued on next page)*

Updates and
displays the value
stored in each
array element

```
        If isConverted Then
            For Each price As Decimal In prices
                price = price + increase
                newPricesLabel.Text = newPricesLabel.Text _
                    & price.ToString("N2").PadLeft(6) _
                    & ControlChars.NewLine
            Next price
        Else
            MessageBox.Show("The increase amount must be numeric.", _
                "Jullian Company", MessageBoxButtons.OK, _
                MessageBoxIcon.Information)
        End If

        increaseTextBox.Focus()
    End Sub
End Class
```

**FIGURE 8.22**    Code for the Prices application

The updateButton's Click event procedure declares a Decimal array named prices, using four values to initialize the array. The procedure also declares a Decimal variable named increase and a Boolean variable named isConverted. The procedure uses the TryParse method to convert the increase amount entered in the increaseTextBox to Decimal. If the conversion is not successful, the procedure displays an appropriate message. If the conversion is successful, however, the procedure uses a loop to access each element in the prices array. Notice that the procedure uses a Decimal variable named price to represent each array element.

The first instruction in the loop, price = price + increase, updates the contents of the current array element by adding the increase amount to it. The second instruction in the loop then displays the updated contents in the newPricesLabel. The loop ends when all of the array elements have been updated. Figure 8.20 shows the results of the application when the user enters the number five as the increase amount. Notice that each new price is five dollars more than its corresponding original price.

## Sorting the Data Stored in a One-Dimensional Array

In some applications, you might need to arrange the contents of an array in either ascending or descending order. Arranging data in a specific order is called **sorting**. When an array is sorted in ascending order, the first element in the array contains the smallest value, and the last element contains the largest value. When an array is sorted in descending order, on the other hand, the first element contains the largest value, and the last element contains the smallest value.

You use the **Array.Sort method** to sort the elements in a one-dimensional array in ascending order. The method's syntax is **Array.Sort(*arrayname*)**, where *arrayname* is the name of the one-dimensional array to be sorted. To sort a one-dimensional array in descending order, you first use the Array.Sort method to sort the array in ascending order, and then use the **Array.Reverse method** to reverse the array elements. The syntax of the Array.Reverse method is **Array.Reverse(*arrayname*)**, where *arrayname* is the name of the one-dimensional array whose elements you want reversed.

The State application that you view in this section uses both the Array.Sort and Array.Reverse methods. The application allows the user to enter the names of five states. It stores the state names in a module-level, one-dimensional String array named states. The user then can choose to display the state names in either ascending or descending order. Figures 8.23 and 8.24 show sample runs of the State application when the user enters the following state names: Illinois, Texas, Alaska, New York, and Idaho. In Figure 8.23, the state names appear in ascending order, while in Figure 8.24 they appear in descending order. Figure 8.25 shows the Visual Basic code for the State application.

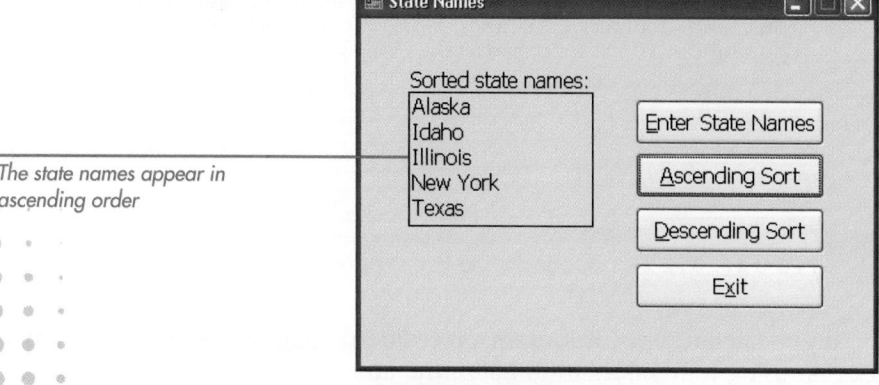

The state names appear in ascending order

**FIGURE 8.23**    Sample run of the State application showing the state names in ascending order

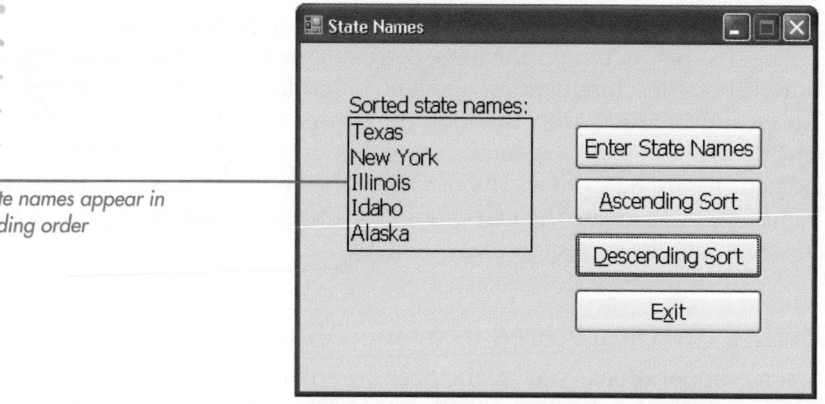

The state names appear in descending order

**FIGURE 8.24**    Sample run of the State application showing the state names in descending order

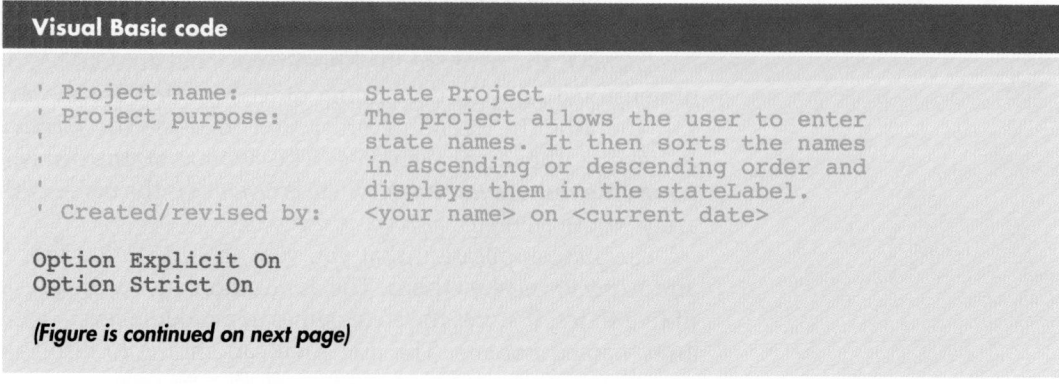

## Visual Basic code

```
' Project name:         State Project
' Project purpose:      The project allows the user to enter
'                       state names. It then sorts the names
'                       in ascending or descending order and
'                       displays them in the stateLabel.
' Created/revised by:   <your name> on <current date>

Option Explicit On
Option Strict On
```

**(Figure is continued on next page)**

```
Public Class MainForm

        ' module-level array
        Private stateNames(4) As String

        Private Sub exitButton_Click(ByVal sender As Object, _
            ByVal e As System.EventArgs) Handles exitButton.Click
            Me.Close()
        End Sub

        Private Sub enterButton_Click(ByVal sender As Object, _
            ByVal e As System.EventArgs) Handles enterButton.Click
            ' allows the user to enter five state names
            ' stores the state names in the module-level
            ' stateNames array

            For subscript As Integer = 0 To stateNames.Length - 1
                stateNames(subscript) = _
                    InputBox("State name", "State Names")
            Next subscript
        End Sub

        Private Sub sortAscendButton_Click(ByVal sender As Object, _
            ByVal e As System.EventArgs) Handles sortAscendButton.Click
            ' sorts the array values in ascending order, then
            ' displays them in the stateLabel

            Array.Sort(stateNames)

            stateLabel.Text = String.Empty
            For Each name As String In stateNames
                stateLabel.Text = _
                    stateLabel.Text & name & ControlChars.NewLine
            Next name
        End Sub

        Private Sub sortDescendButton_Click(ByVal sender As Object, _
            ByVal e As System.EventArgs) Handles sortDescendButton.Click
            ' sorts the array values in descending order, then
            ' displays them in the stateLabel

            Array.Sort(stateNames)
            Array.Reverse(stateNames)

            stateLabel.Text = String.Empty
            For Each name As String In stateNames
                stateLabel.Text = _
                    stateLabel.Text & name & ControlChars.NewLine
            Next name
        End Sub
End Class
```

*Module-level array declaration*

*Sorts the array values in ascending order*

*Sorts the array values in descending order*

**FIGURE 8.25**     Code for the State application

**TIP**

Recall that an array's Length property stores the number of elements in the array and is always one number more than the highest subscript in the array.

The `Private stateNames(4) As String` statement in Figure 8.25 declares a module-level, one-dimensional String array named `stateNames`. The array contains five elements having subscripts of 0, 1, 2, 3, and 4. You typically use a module-level array when you need more than one procedure in the *same* form to use the *same* array, because a module-level array can be used by all of the procedures in the form, including the procedures associated with the controls contained on the form. In this application, the stateNames array will be used by the Click event procedures for the enterButton, sortAscendButton, and sortDescendButton.

The enterButton's Click event procedure uses a For...Next statement and the InputBox function to prompt the user for five state names. The procedure stores the names in the `stateNames` array.

The sortAscendButton's Click event procedure uses the Array.Sort method to sort in ascending order the values stored in the `stateNames` array. It then uses a For Each...Next statement to display the sorted values in the stateLabel.

The sortDescendButton's Click event procedure uses both the Array.Sort and Array.Reverse methods to sort in descending order the values stored in the `stateNames` array. It then uses a For Each...Next statement to display the sorted values in the stateLabel.

## PARALLEL ONE-DIMENSIONAL ARRAYS

Takoda Tapahe owns a small gift shop named Treasures. She wants an application that allows her to display the price of the item whose product ID she enters. Figure 8.26 shows a portion of the gift shop's price list.

| Product ID | Price |
|------------|-------|
| BX35 | 13 |
| CR20 | 10 |
| FE15 | 12 |
| KW10 | 24 |
| MM67 | 4 |

**FIGURE 8.26**     A portion of the gift shop's price list

Recall that all of the variables in an array have the same data type. So how can you store a price list, which includes a string (the product ID) and a number (the price), in an array? One solution is to use two one-dimensional arrays: a String array to store the product IDs and an Integer array to store the prices. Both arrays are illustrated in Figure 8.27.

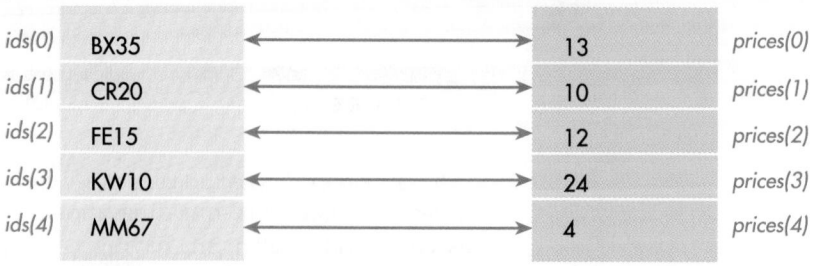

**FIGURE 8.27**     Illustration of a price list stored in two one-dimensional arrays

The arrays shown in Figure 8.27 are referred to as parallel arrays. **Parallel arrays** are two or more arrays whose elements are related by their position in the arrays. In other words, they are related by their subscript. The `ids` and `prices` arrays shown in Figure 8.27 are parallel because each element in the `ids` array corresponds to the element located in the same position in the `prices` array. For example, the first element in the `ids` array corresponds to the first element in the `prices` array. In other words, the item whose product ID is BX35 [`ids(0)`] has a price of $13 [`prices(0)`]. Likewise, the second elements in both arrays—the elements with a subscript of 1—also are related; the item whose product ID is CR20 has a price of $10. The same relationship is true for the remaining elements in both arrays. To determine an item's price, you simply locate the item's ID in the `ids` array and then view its corresponding element in the `prices` array.

Figure 8.28 shows a sample run of the Price List application. Figure 8.29 shows the pseudocode for the displayButton's Click event procedure contained in the application, and Figure 8.30 shows the corresponding Visual Basic code.

*The idTextBox's CharacterCasing and MaxLength properties are set to Upper and 4, respectively*

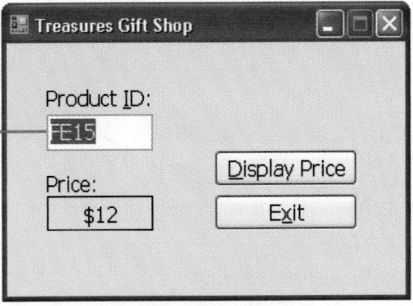

**FIGURE 8.28**  Sample run of the Price List application

**Pseudocode**

1. declare and initialize a String array named ids
2. declare and initialize an Integer array named prices
3. search the ids array for the product ID entered in the idTextBox; stop the search when there are no more array elements to search, or when the product ID is located in the array
4. if the product ID is in the ids array
    use its location in the array to display the corresponding price from the prices array
  else
    display the message "Invalid product ID." in a message box
  end if

**FIGURE 8.29**  Pseudocode for the displayButton's Click event procedure

**Visual Basic code**

```
' Project name:        Price List Project
' Project purpose:     The project displays the price
'                      associated with a product ID.
' Created/revised by:  <your name> on <current date>

Option Explicit On
Option Strict On
```

*(Figure is continued on next page)*

```
Public Class MainForm

    Private Sub exitButton_Click(ByVal sender As Object, _
        ByVal e As System.EventArgs) Handles exitButton.Click
        Me.Close()
    End Sub

    Private Sub idTextBox_Enter(ByVal sender As Object, _
        ByVal e As System.EventArgs) Handles idTextBox.Enter
        idTextBox.SelectAll()
    End Sub

    Private Sub idTextBox_TextChanged(ByVal sender As Object, _
        ByVal e As System.EventArgs) Handles idTextBox.TextChanged
        priceLabel.Text = String.Empty
    End Sub

    Private Sub displayButton_Click(ByVal sender As Object, _
        ByVal e As System.EventArgs) Handles displayButton.Click
        ' displays the price associated with the product
        ' ID entered by the user

        Dim ids() As String = {"BX35", "CR20", "FE15", "KW10", "MM67"}
        Dim prices() As Integer = {13, 10, 12, 24, 4}
        Dim searchFor As String
        Dim subscript As Integer

        ' assign the product ID to a variable
        searchFor = idTextBox.Text

        ' search the ids array for the product ID
        ' continue searching until there are
        ' no more array elements to search or
        ' the product ID is found
        Do Until subscript = ids.Length _
            OrElse searchFor = ids(subscript)
            subscript = subscript + 1
        Loop

        ' determine whether the product ID
        ' was found in the ids array
        If subscript < ids.Length Then
            priceLabel.Text = prices(subscript).ToString("C0")
        Else
            MessageBox.Show("Invalid product ID.", _
                "Treasures Gift Shop", MessageBoxButtons.OK, _
                MessageBoxIcon.Information)
        End If

        idTextBox.Focus()
    End Sub
End Class
```

*Parallel one-dimensional array declarations*

*Searches for the product ID in the ids array*

*Displays the corresponding price from the prices array*

**FIGURE 8.30**     Code for the Price List application using parallel one-dimensional arrays

    The displayButton's Click event procedure declares and initializes two parallel one-dimensional arrays: a five-element String array named ids and a five-element Integer array named prices. Notice that each product ID is stored in the ids array, and its price is stored in the corresponding location in the prices array. The procedure also declares a String variable named searchFor and an Integer variable named subscript. After declaring the arrays and variables, the procedure assigns the contents of the idTextBox to the searchFor variable. (As Figure 8.28 indicates, the idTextBox's CharacterCasing and MaxLength properties are set to Upper and 4, respectively.)

The loop in the displayButton's Click event procedure searches for the product ID in each element in the `ids` array, stopping when there are no more array elements to search or when the product ID is located in the array. After the loop completes its processing, the selection structure in the procedure compares the number stored in the `subscript` variable with the value stored in the `ids` array's Length property. In this case, the Length property contains the number 5, because there are five elements in the `ids` array. If the `subscript` variable contains a number that is less than the number of elements in the `ids` array, it indicates that the loop stopped processing because the product ID was located in the array. In that case, the procedure displays the price located in the same position in the `prices` array. However, if the `subscript` variable's value is not less than the number of elements in the `ids` array, it indicates that the loop stopped processing because it reached the end of the array without finding the product ID. In that case, the message "Invalid product ID." is displayed in a message box. As Figure 8.28 indicates, the procedure displays a price of $12 when the user enters FE15 as the product ID.

Using two parallel one-dimensional arrays is only one way of coding the Price List application. You also can use a two-dimensional array.

## TWO-DIMENSIONAL ARRAYS

Recall that you can visualize a one-dimensional array as a column of variables. A **two-dimensional array**, however, resembles a table in that the variables are in rows and columns. Figure 8.31 illustrates a two-dimensional array.

| | | |
|---|---|---|
| AC34 | Shirt | Red |
| BD12 | Coat | Blue |
| CP14 | Blouse | White |

**FIGURE 8.31**  Illustration of a two-dimensional array

Each variable (element) in a two-dimensional array is identified by a unique combination of two subscripts, which the computer assigns to the variable when the array is created. The subscripts specify the variable's row and column position in the array. Variables located in the first row in a two-dimensional array are assigned a row subscript of 0 (zero). Variables located in the second row are assigned a row subscript of 1 (one), and so on. Similarly, variables located in the first column in a two-dimensional array are assigned a column subscript of 0 (zero). Variables located in the second column are assigned a column subscript of 1 (one), and so on. You refer to each variable in a two-dimensional array by the array's name and the variable's row and column subscripts, which are separated by a comma and specified in a set of parentheses immediately following the array name. For example, to refer to the variable located in the first row, first column in a two-dimensional array named `products`, you use `products(0, 0)`—read "products sub zero comma zero." Similarly, you use `products(1, 2)` to refer to the variable located in the second row, third column in the `products` array. Figure 8.32 illustrates this naming convention. Notice that the row subscript is listed first within the parentheses.

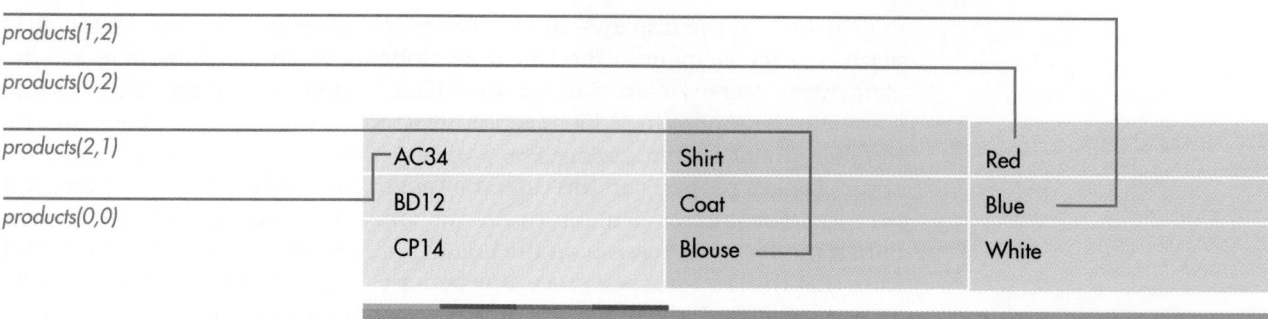

products(1,2)
products(0,2)
products(2,1)
products(0,0)

| AC34 | Shirt  | Red   |
| BD12 | Coat   | Blue  |
| CP14 | Blouse | White |

**FIGURE 8.32**    Names of some of the variables contained in the **products** array

Recall that you first must declare (create) an array before you can use it. Figure 8.33 shows two versions of the syntax you use to declare a two-dimensional array in Visual Basic. The figure also includes an example of using each syntax.

HOW TO...

### Declare a Two-Dimensional Array

**Syntax - Version 1**
{**Dim** | **Private**} *arrayname*(*highestRowSubscript*, *highestColumnSubscript*) **As** *datatype*

**Syntax - Version 2**
{**Dim** | **Private**} *arrayname*(,) **As** *datatype* = {{*initialValues*},…{*initialValues*}}

**Examples**
```
Dim cities(5, 3) As String
```
declares a six-row, four-column array named `cities`; each element is automatically initialized using the keyword `Nothing`

```
Dim scores(,) As Integer = {{75, 90}, _
                            {9, 25}, _
                            {23, 56}, _
                            {6, 12}}
```
declares and initializes a four-row, two-column array named `scores`

**FIGURE 8.33**    How to declare a two-dimensional array

You use the `Dim` keyword to declare a procedure-level array, and use the `Private` keyword to declare a module-level array. In each syntax version, *arrayname* is the name of the array, and *datatype* is the type of data the array variables will store. Recall that each of the variables in an array has the same data type.

In Version 1 of the syntax, *highestRowSubscript* and *highestColumnSubscript* are integers that specify the highest row and column subscripts, respectively, in the array. When the array is created, it will contain one row more than the number specified in the *highestRowSubscript* argument, and one column more than the number specified in the *highestColumnSubscript* argument. This is because the first row subscript in a two-dimensional array is zero, and the first column subscript also is zero. When you declare a two-dimensional array using the syntax shown in Version 1 in Figure 8.33, the computer automatically initializes each element in the array when the array is created.

You use the syntax shown in Version 2 in Figure 8.33 to declare a two-dimensional array and, at the same time, specify each variable's initial value. Using Version 2's syntax, you include a separate *initialValues* section, enclosed in braces, for each row in the array. If the array has two rows, then the statement that declares and initializes the array should have two *initialValues* sections. If the array has five rows, then the declaration statement should have five *initialValues* sections.

Within the individual *initialValues* sections, you enter one or more values separated by commas. The number of values to enter corresponds to the number of columns in the array. If the array contains 10 columns, then each individual *initialValues* section should contain 10 values.

In addition to the set of braces that surrounds each individual *initialValues* section, notice in the syntax that a set of braces also surrounds all of the *initialValues* sections. Also notice that a comma appears within the parentheses that follow the array name. The comma indicates that the array is a two-dimensional array. (Recall that a comma is used to separate the row subscript from the column subscript in a two-dimensional array.)

Study the two examples shown in Figure 8.33. The statement shown in the first example creates a two-dimensional String array named `cities`; the array has six rows and four columns. The computer automatically initializes each variable in the `cities` array using the keyword `Nothing`. The statement shown in the second example creates a two-dimensional Integer array named `scores`; the array has four rows and two columns. The statement initializes the `scores(0, 0)` variable to the number 75, and initializes the `scores(0, 1)` variable to the number 90. The `scores(1, 0)` and `scores(1, 1)` variables are initialized to the numbers 9 and 25, respectively. The `scores(2, 0)` and `scores(2, 1)` variables are initialized to the numbers 23 and 56, respectively, and the `scores(3, 0)` and `scores(3, 1)` variables are initialized to the numbers 6 and 12, respectively.

## Storing Data in a Two-Dimensional Array

As with one-dimensional arrays, you generally use an assignment statement to enter data into a two-dimensional array. Figure 8.34 shows the syntax of such an assignment statement and includes several examples of using the syntax to enter data into the arrays declared in Figure 8.33. In the syntax, *arrayname*(*rowSubscript*, *columnSubscript*) is the name and subscripts of the array variable to which you want the *value* (data) assigned.

## HOW TO...

### Store Data in a Two-Dimensional Array

**Syntax**
*arrayname*(*rowSubscript*, *columnSubscript*) = *value*

**Examples**
```
cities(0, 0) = "Madrid"
cities(0, 1) = "Paris"
cities(0, 2) = "Rome"
cities(0, 3) = "London"
```
assigns the strings "Madrid", "Paris", "Rome", and "London" to the variables contained in the first row in the `cities` array

*(Figure is continued on next page)*

```
For row As Integer = 0 To 3
     For column As Integer = 0 To 1
          scores(row, column) = 0
     Next column
Next row
```
assigns the number zero to each variable in the **scores** array

```
For Each number As Integer In scores
     number = 0
Next number
```
assigns the number zero to each variable in the **scores** array

**FIGURE 8.34**    How to store data in a two-dimensional array

The code shown in the first example in Figure 8.34 uses four assignment statements to assign values to the elements contained in the first row in the **cities** array. The code shown in the second and third examples assigns the number zero to each element in the **scores** array. The second example uses a nested For...Next loop to make the assignments, while the third example uses a For Each...Next statement.

## Searching a Two-Dimensional Array

Earlier, in the *Parallel One-Dimensional Arrays* section, you viewed an application created for Takoda Tapahe, the owner of a small gift shop named Treasures. As you may remember, the application allows Takoda to display the price of the item whose product ID she enters. In the application's code, shown earlier in Figure 8.30, you used two parallel one-dimensional arrays to store the gift shop's price list. In this section of the chapter, you modify the application's code so that it stores the price list in a two-dimensional array.

Figure 8.35 shows a sample run of the modified Price List application. Figure 8.36 shows the modified pseudocode for the displayButton's Click event procedure, and Figure 8.37 shows the application's code using a two-dimensional array. Notice that, to store the price list in a two-dimensional array, you will need to treat both the product IDs and the prices as Strings. This is because all of the variables in an array must have the same data type.

*The idTextBox's CharacterCasing and MaxLength properties are set to Upper and 4, respectively*

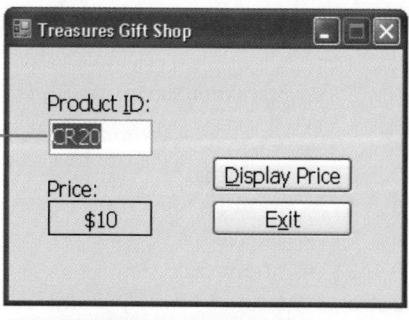

**FIGURE 8.35**    Sample run of the modified Price List application

**Pseudocode**

1. declare and initialize a String array named products
2. search the first column in the products array, looking for the product ID entered in the idTextBox; stop the search when there are no more array elements to search, or when the product ID is located
3. if the product ID is in the first column of the products array
      use its location in the array to display the corresponding price from the second
      column in the array
   else
      display the message "Invalid product ID." in a message box
   end if

**FIGURE 8.36**    Modified pseudocode for the displayButton's Click event procedure

**Visual Basic code**

```
' Project name:        Price List Project
' Project purpose:     The project displays the price
'                      associated with a product ID.
' Created/revised by:  <your name> on <current date>

Option Explicit On
Option Strict On

Public Class MainForm

    Private Sub exitButton_Click(ByVal sender As Object, _
        ByVal e As System.EventArgs) Handles exitButton.Click
        Me.Close()
    End Sub

    Private Sub idTextBox_Enter(ByVal sender As Object, _
        ByVal e As System.EventArgs) Handles idTextBox.Enter
        idTextBox.SelectAll()
    End Sub

    Private Sub idTextBox_TextChanged(ByVal sender As Object, _
        ByVal e As System.EventArgs) Handles idTextBox.TextChanged
        priceLabel.Text = String.Empty
    End Sub

    Private Sub displayButton_Click(ByVal sender As Object, _
        ByVal e As System.EventArgs) Handles displayButton.Click
        ' displays the price associated with the product
        ' ID entered by the user

        Dim products(,) As String = {{"BX35", "13"}, _
                                      {"CR20", "10"}, _
                                      {"FE15", "12"}, _
                                      {"KW10", "24"}, _
                                      {"MM67", "4"}}
        Dim searchFor As String
        Dim row As Integer

        ' assign the product ID to a variable
        searchFor = idTextBox.Text
```

*Two-dimensional array declaration*

**(Figure is continued on next page)**

```
        ' search for the product ID in the first column
        ' of the products array
        ' continue searching until there are
        ' no more array elements to search or
        ' the product ID is found
        Do Until row = 5 OrElse searchFor = products(row, 0)
            row = row + 1
        Loop

        ' determine whether the product ID
        ' was found in the ids array
        If row < 5 Then
            priceLabel.Text = "$" & products(row, 1)
        Else
            MessageBox.Show("Invalid product ID.", _
                "Treasures Gift Shop", MessageBoxButtons.OK, _
                MessageBoxIcon.Information)
        End If

        idTextBox.Focus()
    End Sub
End Class
```

*Searches for the product ID in the first column of the products array*

*Displays the corresponding price from the second column of the products array*

**FIGURE 8.37**    Code for the Price List application using a two-dimensional array

In the modified code shown in Figure 8.37, the displayButton's Click event procedure declares and initializes a two-dimensional array named products; the array has five rows and two columns. Notice that each product ID is stored in the first column of the products array, and its price is stored in the corresponding row in the second column. The procedure also declares a String variable named searchFor and an Integer variable named row. After declaring the arrays and variables, the procedure assigns the contents of the idTextBox to the searchFor variable. (As Figure 8.35 indicates, the idTextBox's CharacterCasing and MaxLength properties are set to Upper and 4, respectively.)

The loop in the displayButton's Click event procedure searches for the product ID in the first column in the products array, stopping when there are no more array elements to search or when the product ID is located in the array. After the loop completes its processing, the selection structure in the procedure compares the number stored in the row variable with the number 5, which is the number of rows contained in the array. If the row variable contains a number that is less than 5, it indicates that the loop stopped processing because the product ID was located in the array. In that case, the procedure displays the price located in the same row as the product ID in the products array, but in the second column. However, if the row variable's value is not less than 5, it indicates that the loop stopped processing because it reached the end of the array's first column without finding the product ID. In that case, the message "Invalid product ID." is displayed in a message box. As Figure 8.35 indicates, the procedure displays a price of $10 when the user enters CR20 as the product ID.

You have completed the concepts section of Chapter 8. The next section is the Programming Tutorial section, which gives you step-by-step instructions on how to apply the chapter's concepts to an application. A Programming Example follows the Programming Tutorial. The Programming Example is a completed program that demonstrates the concepts taught in the chapter. Following the Programming Example are the Quick Review, Key Terms, Self-Check Questions and Answers, Review Questions, Review Exercises – Short Answer, Computer Exercises, and Case Projects sections.

# PROGRAMMING TUTORIAL

## Lottery Game Application

In this tutorial, you create an application that generates and displays six unique random numbers for a Lottery Game. Each lottery number can range from 1 through 54 only. The Lottery Game application's user interface is shown in Figure 8.38, and its TOE chart is shown in Figure 8.39.

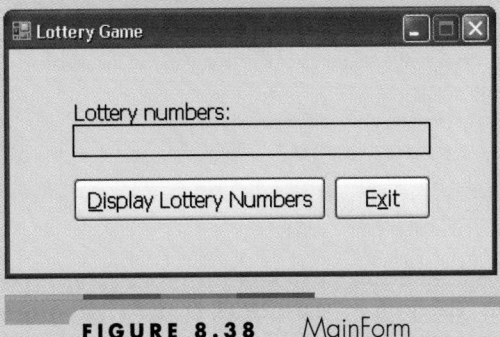

**FIGURE 8.38**   MainForm

**TOE Chart:**

| Task | Object | Event |
|------|--------|-------|
| End the application | exitButton | Click |
| 1.  Generate random numbers<br>2.  Store six unique random numbers in a one-dimensional array<br>3.  Display the contents of the array in the lotteryLabel | displayButton | Click |
| Show the six lottery numbers | lotteryLabel | None |

**FIGURE 8.39**   TOE chart

### Coding the Lottery Game Application

According to the application's TOE chart, only two procedures need to be coded: the exitButton's Click event procedure and the displayButton's Click event procedure.

**To begin coding the Lottery Game application:**

1. Start Visual Studio. If necessary, close the Start Page window.
2. Open the **Lottery Game Solution** (Lottery Game Solution.sln) file, which is contained in the VbReloaded\Chap08\Lottery Game Solution folder. If necessary, open the Form Designer window. The user interface shown earlier in Figure 8.38 appears on the screen. The interface contains two labels and two buttons.
3. Open the Code Editor window, which already contains the appropriate comments and Option statements. It also contains the code for the exitButton's Click event procedure.
4. Replace the <your name> and <current date> text in the comments with your name and the current date.

Figure 8.40 shows the pseudocode for the displayButton's Click event procedure.

> **Pseudocode**
>
> 1. generate a random number from 1 through 54, and store it in the first array element
> 2. repeat the following until all of the remaining array elements contain a unique random number:
>      generate a random number from 1 through 54
>      search the array elements that contain numbers
>      if the random number is not already in the array
>          store the random number in the current array element, then continue with the next array element
>      end if
>    end repeat
> 3. display the contents of the array in the lotteryLabel

**FIGURE 8.40**    Pseudocode for the displayButton's Click event procedure

### To code the displayButton's Click event procedure:

1. Open the code template for the displayButton's Click event procedure. Type ' **generates and displays six unique random** and press **Enter**, then type ' **numbers from 1 through 54** and press **Enter** twice.
2. The procedure will store the six unique random numbers in a six-element one-dimensional array named `numbers`. Type **dim numbers(5) as integer** and press **Enter**.
3. While filling the array with numbers, the procedure will use an Integer variable to keep track of the array subscripts. Type **dim subscript as integer** and press **Enter**.
4. While searching the array to verify that it does not already contain the random number, the procedure will use an Integer variable to keep track of the array subscripts. Type **dim searchSubscript as integer** and press **Enter**.
5. The procedure will use an Integer variable to store the random number before it is added to the array. Type **dim randomNum as integer** and press **Enter**.
6. The procedure will use a Random object to represent Visual Basic's pseudo-random number generator. Type **dim randomGenerator as new random** and press **Enter**.
7. The procedure will use a Boolean variable to indicate whether the random number is already contained in the array. Type **dim isFound as boolean** and press **Enter** twice.
8. The first step in the procedure's pseudocode (shown in Figure 8.40) is to generate a random number from 1 through 54, and store it in the first element in the array. Type ' **generate the first random number, and** and press **Enter**. Type ' **store it in the first array element** and press **Enter**. Type **numbers(0) = randomgenerator.next(1, 55)** and press **Enter** twice.
9. Next, the procedure should fill the remaining array elements—the elements with subscripts of 1 through 5—with unique random numbers. Type ' **fill remaining array elements with unique** and press **Enter**. Type ' **random numbers** and press **Enter**. Type **subscript = 1** and press **Enter**.
10. Type **do while subscript < numbers.length** and press **Enter**.
11. Type ' **generate another random number** and press **Enter**. Type **randomnum = randomgenerator.next(1, 55)** and press **Enter** twice.

Now you need to search the array to verify that it does not contain the random number stored in the `randomNum` variable. You need to search only the array elements that already contain numbers. The elements that already contain numbers have subscripts starting with zero and ending with the subscript that is one less than the current subscript. In other words, if the current subscript is 1, you need to search for the random number only in the `numbers(0)` element, because that is the only element that contains a number. Similarly, if the current subscript is 5, you need to search for the random number in the `numbers(0)`, `numbers(1)`, `numbers(2)`, `numbers(3)`, and `numbers(4)` elements.

12. Type **' search the array to determine whether it** and press **Enter**, then type **' already contains the random number** and press **Enter**. Type **' stop the search when there are no more array** and press **Enter**, then type **' elements or when the random number is found** and press **Enter**.

13. Type **searchsubscript = 0** and press **Enter**, then type **isfound = false** and press **Enter**.

14. Type **do while searchsubscript < subscript andalso isfound = false** and press **Enter**.

15. Type **' if the random number is in the current array** and press **Enter**, then type **' element, assign True to isFound** and press **Enter**. Type **' otherwise, search the next element** and press **Enter**.

16. Type **if numbers(searchsubscript) = randomnum then** and press **Enter**, then type **isfound = true** and press **Enter**. Type **else** and press **Enter**, then type **searchsubscript = searchsubscript + 1**.

17. If the random number is not in the array, the procedure should assign the random number to the current array element, and then prepare to fill the next array element. Type the comments and selection structure shown in Figure 8.41, then position the insertion point as shown in the figure.

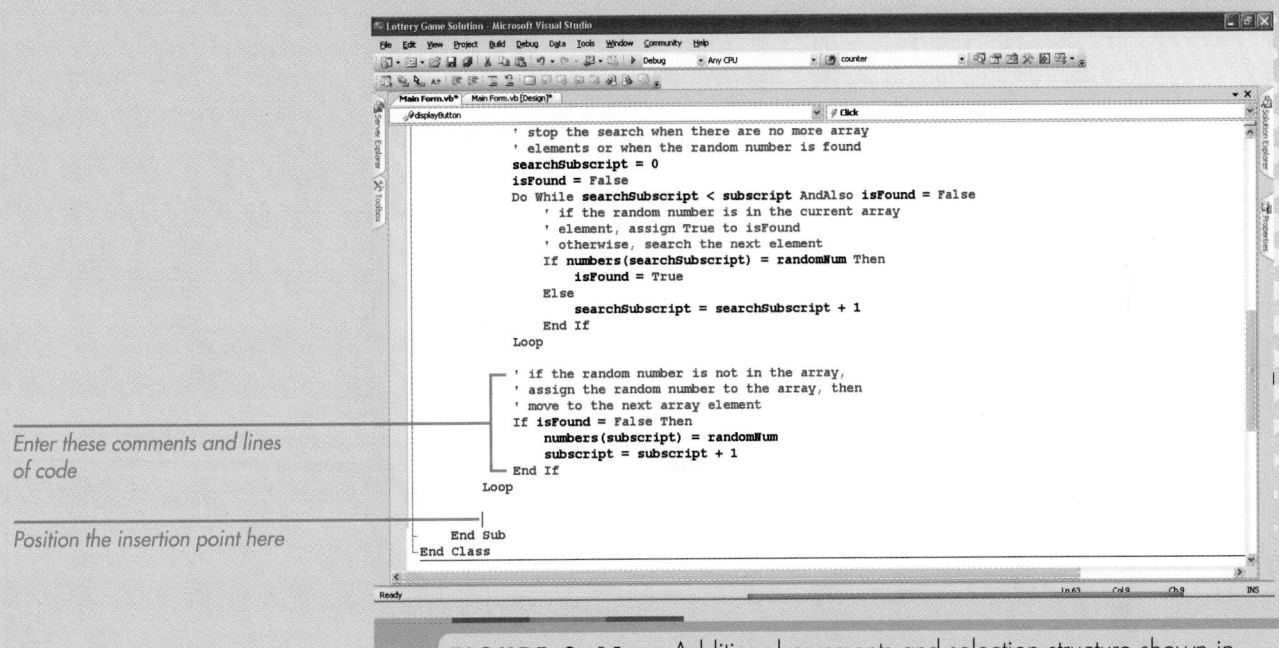

Enter these comments and lines
of code

Position the insertion point here

**FIGURE 8.41**   Additional comments and selection structure shown in the procedure

18. The last step in the procedure's pseudocode (shown in Figure 8.40) is to display the contents of the numbers array, which now contains the six lottery numbers, in the lotteryLabel. Type **' display the contents of the array** and press **Enter**. Type **lotterylabel.text = string.empty** and press **Enter**.

19. Type **for each num as integer in numbers** and press **Enter**. Type **lotterylabel.text = lotterylabel.text & " " _** (be sure to include two spaces between the quotation marks, as well as a space before the line continuation character) and press **Enter**. Press **Tab**, then type **& num.tostring**.

20. Change the Next clause to **Next num**. Figure 8.42 shows the Lottery Game application's code.

```
' Project name:        Lottery Game Project
' Project purpose:     The project displays six unique
'                      random numbers from 1 through 54.
' Created/revised by:  <your name> on <current date>


Option Explicit On
Option Strict On


(Figure is continued on next page)
```

```
Public Class MainForm

    Private Sub exitButton_Click(ByVal sender As Object, _
        ByVal e As System.EventArgs) Handles exitButton.Click
        Me.Close()
    End Sub

    Private Sub displayButton_Click(ByVal sender As Object, _
        ByVal e As System.EventArgs) Handles displayButton.Click
        ' generates and displays six unique random
        ' numbers from 1 through 54

        Dim numbers(5) As Integer
        Dim subscript As Integer
        Dim searchSubscript As Integer
        Dim randomNum As Integer
        Dim randomGenerator As New Random
        Dim isFound As Boolean

        ' generate the first random number, and
        ' store it in the first array element
        numbers(0) = randomGenerator.Next(1, 55)

        ' fill remaining array elements with unique
        ' random numbers
        subscript = 1
        Do While subscript < numbers.Length
            ' generate another random number
            randomNum = randomGenerator.Next(1, 55)

            ' search the array to determine whether it
            ' already contains the random number
            ' stop the search when there are no more array
            ' elements or when the random number is found
            searchSubscript = 0
            isFound = False
            Do While searchSubscript < subscript AndAlso isFound = False
                ' if the random number is in the current array
                ' element, assign True to isFound
                ' otherwise, search the next element
                If numbers(searchSubscript) = randomNum Then
                    isFound = True
                Else
                    searchSubscript = searchSubscript + 1
                End If
            Loop
```

*(Figure is continued on next page)*

```
                        ' if the random number is not in the array,
                        ' assign the random number to the array, then
                        ' move to the next array element
                        If isFound = False Then
                            numbers(subscript) = randomNum
                            subscript = subscript + 1
                        End If
                    Loop

                    ' display the contents of the array
                    lotteryLabel.Text = String.Empty
                    For Each num As Integer In numbers
                        lotteryLabel.Text = lotteryLabel.Text & "   " _
                            & num.ToString
                    Next num
                End Sub
            End Class
```

**FIGURE 8.42**     Code for the Lottery Game application

Now test the application to verify that it is working correctly.

**To test the Lottery Game application:**

1. Save the solution, then start the application. Click the **Display Lottery Numbers** button. Six unique numbers appear in the interface, as shown in Figure 8.43. (Because the numbers are random, your numbers might be different from those shown in the figure.)

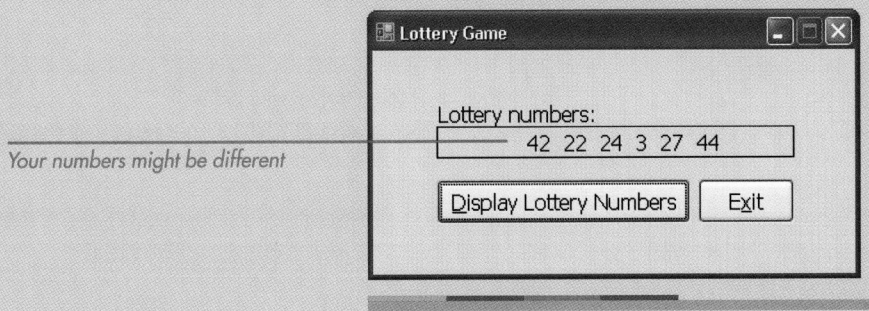

Your numbers might be different

**FIGURE 8.43**     Lottery numbers in the interface

2. Click the **Display Lottery Numbers** button several more times. When you are finished testing the application, click the **Exit** button to end the application. If necessary, close the Output window.
3. Close the Code Editor window, then close the solution.

# PROGRAMMING EXAMPLE

## Perrytown Gift Shop Application

Stanley Habeggar is the owner and manager of Perrytown Gift Shop. Every Friday afternoon, Mr. Habeggar calculates the weekly pay for his six employees. The most time-consuming part of this task, and the one prone to the most errors, is the calculation of the federal withholding tax (FWT). Create an application that Mr. Habeggar can use to quickly and accurately calculate the FWT. Name the solution Perrytown Solution. Name the project Perrytown Project. Name the form file Main Form.vb. The federal withholding tax tables are shown in Figure 8.44.

### FWT Tables – Weekly Payroll Period

**Single person (including head of household)**

| If the taxable wages are: | | The amount of income tax to withhold is | | |
|---|---|---|---|---|
| Over | But not over | Base amount | Percentage | Of excess over |
|  | $ 51 | 0 |  |  |
| $ 51 | $ 552 | 0 | 15% | $ 51 |
| $ 552 | $1,196 | $ 75.15 plus | 28% | $ 552 |
| $1,196 | $2,662 | $ 255.47 plus | 31% | $1,196 |
| $2,662 | $5,750 | $ 709.93 plus | 36% | $2,662 |
| $5,750 |  | $1,821.61 plus | 39.6% | $5,750 |

**Married person**

| If the taxable wages are: | | The amount of income tax to withhold is | | |
|---|---|---|---|---|
| Over | But not over | Base amount | Percentage | Of excess over |
|  | $ 124 | 0 |  |  |
| $ 124 | $ 960 | 0 | 15% | $ 124 |
| $ 960 | $2,023 | $ 125.40 plus | 28% | $ 960 |
| $2,023 | $3,292 | $ 423.04 plus | 31% | $2,023 |
| $3,292 | $5,809 | $ 816.43 plus | 36% | $3,292 |
| $5,809 |  | $1,722.55 plus | 39.6% | $5,809 |

**FIGURE 8.44**    Federal Withholding Tax tables

Notice that both tables shown in Figure 8.44 contain five columns of information. The first two columns list the various ranges, also called brackets, of taxable wage amounts. The first column (the Over column) lists the amount that a taxable wage in that range must be over, and the second column (the But not over column) lists the maximum amount included in the range. The remaining three columns (Base amount, percentage, and Of excess over) tell you how to calculate the tax for each range. For example, assume that you are married and your weekly taxable wages are $280. Before you can calculate the amount of your tax, you need to locate your taxable wages in the first two columns of the Married table. In this case, your taxable wages fall within the $124 through $960 range. After locating the range that contains your taxable wages, you then use the remaining three columns in the table to calculate your tax. According to the Married table, taxable wages in the $124 through $960 bracket have a tax of 15% of the amount over $124; therefore, your tax is $23.40.

**TOE Chart:**

| Task | Object | Event |
|---|---|---|
| 1. Calculate the federal withholding tax<br>2. Display the federal withholding tax in the fwtLabel | calcButton | Click |
| End the application | exitButton | Click |
| Display the federal withholding tax (from calcButton) | fwtLabel | None |
| Get and display the taxable wages | taxableTextBox | None |
| Get the marital status | singleRadioButton, marriedRadioButton | None |

**FIGURE 8.45**

**User Interface:**

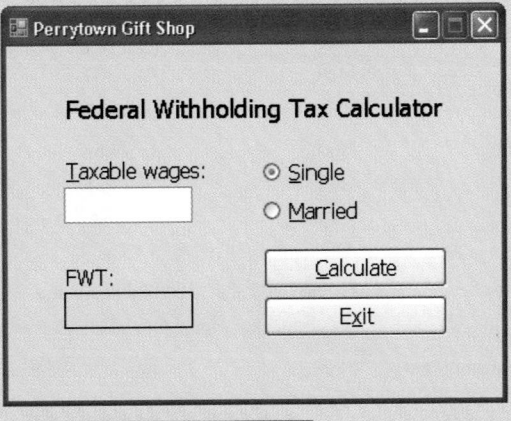

**FIGURE 8.46**

**Objects, Properties, and Settings:**

| Object | Property | Setting |
|---|---|---|
| Form1 | Name | MainForm |
| | Font | Tahoma, 12 point |
| | Size | 392, 300 |
| | StartPosition | CenterScreen |
| | Text | Perrytown Gift Shop |
| Label1 | Font | Tahoma, 14 point |
| | Location | 44, 36 |
| | Text | Federal Withholding Tax Calculator |
| Label2 | Text | &Taxable wages: |
| | Location | 44, 84 |
| Label3 | Text | FWT: |
| | Location | 44, 164 |
| Label4 | Name | fwtLabel |
| | AutoSize | False |
| | BorderStyle | FixedSingle |
| | Location | 44, 185 |
| | Size | 100, 27 |
| | Text | (empty) |
| | TextAlign | MiddleCenter |
| Button1 | Name | calcButton |
| | Location | 199, 153 |
| | Size | 142, 30 |
| | Text | &Calculate |
| Button2 | Name | exitButton |
| | Location | 199, 189 |
| | Size | 142, 30 |
| | Text | E&xit |
| TextBox1 | Name | taxableTextBox |
| | Location | 44, 106 |
| RadioButton1 | Name | singleRadioButton |
| | Checked | True |
| | Location | 199, 84 |
| | Text | &Single |
| RadioButton2 | Name | marriedRadioButton |
| | Location | 199, 113 |
| | Text | &Married |

**FIGURE 8.47**

**Tab Order:**

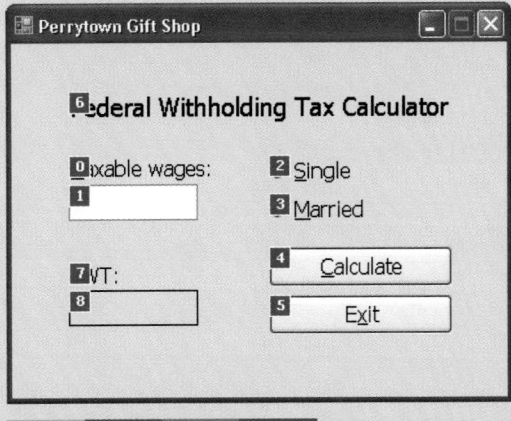

**FIGURE 8.48**

**Pseudocode:**

**exitButton Click event procedure**

1. close application

**taxableTextBox Enter event procedure**

1. select the existing text in the text box

**taxableTextBox TextChanged, singleRadioButton Click, marriedRadioButton Click event procedures**

1. clear the contents of the fwtLabel

**calcButton Click event procedure**

1. convert the taxable wages stored in the taxableTextBox to Decimal
2. if the taxable wages cannot be converted to a number
      display the message "The taxable wages must be numeric."
  else
      if the singleRadioButton is selected
         use the Single tax table, which is stored in the singleTable array
      else
         use the Married tax table, which is stored in the marriedTable array
      end if

      repeat while there are still rows in the tax table to search and the taxable wages have not been found
         if the taxable wages are less than or equal to the value stored in the first column of the current row in
         the tax table
            use the information stored in the second, third, and fourth columns in the tax table to calculate
            the federal withholding tax
            indicate that the taxable wages were found by assigning the value True to the isFound variable
        else
            add 1 to the contents of the row variable to continue the search in the next row in the tax table
        end if
      end repeat
      display the federal withholding tax in the fwtLabel
  end if

**Code:**

```
' Project name:          Perrytown Project
' Project purpose:       The project calculates the Federal
'                        Withholding Tax (FWT) based on the
'                        taxable wages and marital status
'                        entered by the user.
' Created/revised by:    <your name> on <current date>

Option Explicit On
Option Strict On

Public Class MainForm

    Private singleTable(,) As Decimal = {{51D, 0D, 0D, 0D}, _
                                         {552D, 0D, 0.15D, 51D}, _
                                         {1196D, 75.15D, 0.28D, 552D}, _
                                         {2662D, 255.47D, 0.31D, 1196D}, _
                                         {5750D, 709.93D, 0.36D, 2662D}, _
                                         {99999D, 1821.61D, 0.396D, 5750D}}

    Private marriedTable(,) As Decimal = {{124D, 0D, 0D, 0D}, _
                                          {960D, 0D, 0.15D, 124D}, _
                                          {2023D, 125.4D, 0.28D, 960D}, _
                                          {3292D, 423.04D, 0.31D, 2023D}, _
                                          {5809D, 816.43D, 0.36D, 3292D}, _
                                          {99999D, 1722.55D, 0.396D, 5809D}}


    Private Sub exitButton_Click(ByVal sender As Object, _
        ByVal e As System.EventArgs) Handles exitButton.Click
        Me.Close()
    End Sub

    Private Sub taxableTextBox_Enter(ByVal sender As Object, _
        ByVal e As System.EventArgs) Handles taxableTextBox.Enter
        taxableTextBox.SelectAll()
    End Sub

    Private Sub ClearLabel(ByVal sender As Object, _
        ByVal e As System.EventArgs) Handles taxableTextBox.TextChanged, _
        singleRadioButton.Click, marriedRadioButton.Click
        fwtLabel.Text = String.Empty
    End Sub

    Private Sub calcButton_Click(ByVal sender As Object, _
        ByVal e As System.EventArgs) Handles calcButton.Click
        ' calculates and displays the FWT
```

*(Figure is continued on next page)*

```
            Dim taxTable(5, 3) As Decimal
            Dim taxableWages As Decimal
            Dim fwt As Decimal
            Dim row As Integer
            Dim isFound As Boolean
            Dim isConverted As Boolean

            isConverted = Decimal.TryParse(taxableTextBox.Text, taxableWages)

            If isConverted = False Then
                MessageBox.Show("The taxable wages must be numeric.", _
                    "Perrytown Gift Shop", MessageBoxButtons.OK, _
                    MessageBoxIcon.Information)
            Else
                ' determine the appropriate tax table
                If singleRadioButton.Checked Then
                    taxTable = singleTable
                Else
                    taxTable = marriedTable
                End If

                ' search for the taxable wages in the first column
                ' in the array
                Do Until row = 6 OrElse isFound
                    If taxableWages <= taxTable(row, 0) Then
                        ' calculate the FWT
                        fwt = taxTable(row, 1) + taxTable(row, 2) _
                            * (taxableWages - taxTable(row, 3))
                        isFound = True
                    Else
                        ' continue searching for the taxable wages
                        row = row + 1
                    End If
                Loop

                ' display the FWT
                fwtLabel.Text = fwt.ToString("C2")
            End If

            taxableTextBox.Focus()
        End Sub
End Class
```

**FIGURE 8.49**

## Quick Review

- Programmers use arrays to temporarily store related data in the internal memory of the computer.
- All of the variables in an array have the same name and data type.
- Each element in a one-dimensional array is identified by a unique subscript, which appears in parentheses after the array's name.
- Each element in a two-dimensional array is identified by a unique combination of two subscripts: a row subscript and a column subscript. The subscripts appear in parentheses after the array's name. You list the row subscript first, followed by a comma and the column subscript.
- The first subscript in a one-dimensional array is 0 (zero).
- The first row subscript in a two-dimensional array is 0 (zero). Likewise, the first column subscript also is 0 (zero).
- When declaring a one-dimensional array, you provide either the highest subscript or the initial values.
- When declaring a two-dimensional array, you provide either the highest row and column subscripts or the initial values.
- The number of elements in a one-dimensional array is one number more than its highest subscript.
- The number of rows in a two-dimensional array is one number more than its highest row subscript. Likewise, the number of columns is one number more than its highest column subscript.
- You usually use an assignment statement to store data in an array.
- You refer to an element in a one-dimensional array using the array's name followed by the element's subscript.
- You refer to an element in a two-dimensional array using the array's name followed by the element's row and column subscripts, which are separated by a comma.
- You can use the For Each...Next statement to code a loop whose instructions you want processed for each element in an array. You also can use the For...Next statement or the Do...Loop statement.
- You can use the Length property to determine the number of elements in an array.
- You use the Array.Sort method to sort the elements in a one-dimensional array in ascending order.
- You use the Array.Reverse method to reverse the order of the elements in a one-dimensional array.
- The elements in parallel arrays are related by their subscript (or position) in the arrays.

## Key Terms

A **simple variable** is a variable that is unrelated to any other variable in the computer's internal memory.

A simple variable is also called a **scalar variable**.

An **array** is a group of variables that have the same name and data type and are related in some way.

A **one-dimensional** array is a group of related variables. A unique number, called a **subscript**, identifies each variable in a one-dimensional array.

The variables in an array are also called **elements**.

The **For Each...Next statement** can be used to code a loop whose instructions you want processed for each element in an array.

An array's **Length property** stores an integer that represents the number of elements in the array.

The **Array.Sort method** sorts the elements in a one-dimensional array in ascending order.

The **Array.Reverse method** reverses the order of the elements in a one-dimensional array.

Arrays whose elements are related by their subscript (position) in the arrays are called **parallel arrays**.

A **two-dimensional array** is a group of related variables. Each variable in a two-dimensional array is identified by a unique combination of two numbers: a row subscript and a column subscript.

## Self-Check Questions and Answers

1. Which of the following statements declares a one-dimensional, four-element String array named letters?
   a. Dim letters(3) As String
   b. Dim letters() As String = "A", "B", "C", "D"
   c. Dim letters(4) As String = {"A", "B", "C", "D"}
   d. All of the above.

2. Which of the following declares a two-dimensional String array named letters that contains four rows and two columns?
   a. Dim letters(3, 1) As String
   b. Private letters(3, 1) As String
   c. Dim letters() = {{"A", "B"}, {"C", "D"}, _
                      {"E", "F"}, {"G", "H"}}
   d. All of the above.

3. Which of the following statements determines the number of elements contained in a one-dimensional array named items, and then assigns the result to the countLabel?
   a. countLabel.Text = items.Len.ToString
   b. countLabel.Text = items.Length.ToString()
   c. countLabel.Text = Length(items).ToString()
   d. None of the above.

4. Which of the following statements sorts (in ascending order) the numbers stored in the population array?
   a. population.Sort
   b. SortArray(population)
   c. Array.Sort(population)
   d. Sort.Array(population)

5. The `numberOrdered` array is declared using the `Dim numberOrdered()`
   `As Integer = {5, 2, 9, 1, 7}` statement. Which of the following
   statements changes the values stored in the array to 7, 1, 9, 2, and 5?
   a. `Array.Reorder(numberOrdered)`
   b. `Array.Reverse(numberOrdered)`
   c. `Reorder.Array(numberOrdered)`
   d. `Reverse.Array(numberOrdered)`

6. Which of the following statements changes the values stored in the
   `numberOrdered` array from Question 5 to 1, 2, 5, 7, and 9?
   a. `Array.ReorderAscending(numberOrdered)`
   b. `Array.AscendingSort(numberOrdered)`
   c. `Array.Sort(numberOrdered)`
   d. `Resort.Array(numberOrdered)`

7. Which of the following statements changes the values stored in the
   `numberOrdered` array from Question 5 to 9, 7, 5, 2, and 1?
   a. `Array.ReorderDescending(numberOrdered)`
   b. `Array.SortAscending(numberOrdered)`
      `Array.Reverse(numberOrdered)`
   c. `Array.SortDescending(numberOrdered)`
   d. `Array.Sort(numberOrdered)`
      `Array.Reverse(numberOrdered)`

8. Which of the following statements assigns the string "Paris" to the fifth element in a one-dimensional array named `cities`?
   a. `cities(4) = "Paris"`
   b. `cities[4] = "Paris"`
   c. `cities(5) = "Paris"`
   d. None of the above.

9. Which of the following statements assigns the Boolean value True to the
   element located in the third row, first column of a two-dimensional Boolean
   array named `testAnswers`?
   a. `testAnswers(0, 2) = True`
   b. `testAnswers(1, 3) = True`
   c. `testAnswers(3, 1) = True`
   d. None of the above.

10. If the `states` and `capitals` arrays are parallel arrays, the capital of the
    state stored in the `states(21)` element is contained in the `capitals(21)`
    element.
    a. True
    b. False

Answers: 1) a, 2) d, 3) b, 4) c, 5) b, 6) c, 7) d, 8) a, 9) d, 10) a

## Review Questions

1. Which of the following statements declares a one-dimensional array named
   prices that contains five elements?
   a. `Dim prices(4) As Decimal`
   b. `Dim prices(5) As Decimal`
   c. `Dim prices(4) As Decimal = {3.55D, 6.7D, 8D, 4D, 2.34D}`
   d. Both a and c.

2. The `items` array is declared using the `Dim items(20) As String` statement. The `x` variable keeps track of the array subscripts and is initialized to the number zero. Which of the following Do clauses will process the loop instructions for each element in the array?
   a. `Do While x > 20`
   b. `Do While x < 20`
   c. `Do While x >= 20`
   d. `Do While x <= 20`

Use the `sales` array to answer Questions 3 through 6. The array was declared using the following statement: `Dim sales() As Integer = {10000, 12000, 900, 500, 20000}`.

3. The statement `sales(3) = sales(3) + 10` will _____.
   a. replace the 500 amount with 10
   b. replace the 500 amount with 510
   c. replace the 900 amount with 10
   d. replace the 900 amount with 910

4. Which of the following If clauses can be used to verify that the array subscript, named x, is valid for the `sales` array?
   a. `If sales(x) >= 0 AndAlso sales(x) < 4 Then`
   b. `If sales(x) >= 0 AndAlso sales(x) <= 4 Then`
   c. `If x >= 0 AndAlso x < 4 Then`
   d. `If x >= 0 AndAlso x <= 4 Then`

5. Which of the following loops will correctly add 100 to each element in the `sales` array? The x variable was declared as an Integer variable and was initialized to the number zero.
   a. 
```
Do While x <= 4
    x = x + 100
Loop
```
   b. 
```
Do While x <= 4
    sales = sales + 100
Loop
```
   c. 
```
Do While sales < 5
    sales(x) = sales(x) + 100
Loop
```
   d. 
```
Do While x < 5
    sales(x) = sales(x) + 100
    x = x + 1
Loop
```

6. Which of the following statements sorts the `sales` array in ascending order?
   a. `Array.Sort(sales)`
   b. `sales.Sort()`
   c. `Sort(sales)`
   d. `SortArray(sales)`

Use the `numbers` array to answer Questions 7 through 12. The array was declared using the following statement: `Dim numbers() As Integer = {10, 5, 7, 2}`. The `total` and `x` variables were declared as Integer variables and were initialized to the number zero. The `avg` variable was declared as a Decimal variable and was initialized to the number zero.

7. Which of the following will correctly calculate the average of the elements included in the numbers array?

a.
```
Do While x < 4
    numbers(x) = total + total
    x = x + 1
Loop
avg = Convert.ToDecimal(total / x)
```
b.
```
Do While x < 4
    total = total + numbers(x)
    x = x + 1
Loop
avg = Convert.ToDecimal(total / x)
```
c.
```
Do While x < 4
    total = total + numbers(x)
    x = x + 1
Loop
avg = Convert.ToDecimal(total / x - 1)
```
d.
```
Do While x < 4
    total = total + numbers(x)
    x = x + 1
Loop
avg = Convert.ToDecimal(total / (x - 1))
```

8. The code in Question 7's answer a will assign _____ to the avg variable.
   a. 0
   b. 5
   c. 6
   d. 8

9. The code in Question 7's answer b will assign _____ to the avg variable.
   a. 0
   b. 5
   c. 6
   d. 8

10. The code in Question 7's answer c will assign _____ to the avg variable.
    a. 0
    b. 5
    c. 6
    d. 8

11. The code in Question 7's answer d will assign _____ to the avg variable.
    a. 0
    b. 5
    c. 6
    d. 8

12. Which of the following statements determines the number of elements included in the numbers array, and then assigns the result to an Integer variable named elements?
    a. elements = Len(numbers)
    b. elements = Length(numbers)
    c. elements = numbers.Len
    d. elements = numbers.Length

13. Which of the following statements creates a two-dimensional array that contains three rows and four columns?
    a. `Dim temps(2, 3) As Decimal`
    b. `Dim temps(3, 4) As Decimal`
    c. `Dim temps(3, 2) As Decimal`
    d. `Dim temps(4, 3) As Decimal`

Use the `sales` array to answer Questions 14 through 16. The array was declared using the following statement:

```
Dim sales(,) As Decimal = {{1000, 1200, 900, 500, 2000}, _
                           {350, 600, 700, 800, 100}}
```

14. The `sales(1, 3) = sales(1, 3) + 10` statement will _____.
    a. replace the 900 amount with 910
    b. replace the 500 amount with 510
    c. replace the 700 amount with 710
    d. replace the 800 amount with 810

15. The `sales(0, 4) = sales(0, 4 - 2)` statement will _____.
    a. replace the 500 amount with 1200
    b. replace the 2000 amount with 900
    c. replace the 2000 amount with 1998
    d. result in an error

16. Which of the following If clauses can be used to verify that the array subscripts named `row` and `col` are valid for the `sales` array?
    a. `If sales(row, col) >= 0 AndAlso sales(row, col) < 5 Then`
    b. `If sales(row, col) >= 0 AndAlso sales(row, col) <= 5 Then`
    c. `If row >= 0 AndAlso row < 3 AndAlso col >= 0 AndAlso`
       `col < 6 Then`
    d. `If row >= 0 AndAlso row < 2 AndAlso col >= 0 AndAlso`
       `col < 5 Then`

17. Which of the following statements assigns the string "California" to the variable located in the third column, fifth row of a two-dimensional array named `states`?
    a. `states(3, 5) = "California"`
    b. `states(5, 3) = "California"`
    c. `states(2, 4) = "California"`
    d. `states(4, 2) = "California"`

18. Which of the following assigns the number one to each element in a one-dimensional Integer array named `counters`? The `counters` array contains five elements.
    a. ```
       For row As Integer = 0 To 4
           counters(row) = 1
       Next row
       ```
    b. ```
       Dim row As Integer
           Do While row < 5
           counters(row) = 1
           row = row + 1
       Loop
       ```
    c. ```
       For Each row As Integer In counters
           row = 1
       Next row
       ```
    d. All of the above.
       ```

19. Which of the following assigns the number zero to each element in a two-dimensional Integer array named sums? The sums array contains two rows and four columns.

    a. 
    ```
    For row As Integer = 0 To 1
        For column As Integer = 0 To 3
            sums(row, column) = 0
        Next column
    Next row
    ```

    b. 
    ```
    Dim row As Integer
    Dim column As Integer
    Do While row < 2
        column = 0
        Do While column < 4
            sums(row, column) = 0
            column = column + 1
        Loop
        row = row + 1
    Loop
    ```

    c. 
    ```
    For Each element As Integer In sums
        element = 0
    Next element
    ```

    d. All of the above.

20. If the elements in two arrays are related by their subscripts, the arrays are called _____ arrays.

    a. associated
    b. coupled
    c. matching
    d. parallel

## Review Exercises – Short Answer

1. Write the statement to declare a procedure-level one-dimensional array named numbers. The array should be able to store 20 integers.

2. Write the statement to store the number seven in the second element contained in the numbers array.

3. Write the statement to declare a module-level one-dimensional array named products. The array should be able to store 10 strings.

4. Write the statement to store the string "Paper" in the third element contained in the products array.

5. Write the statement to declare and initialize a procedure-level one-dimensional array named rates that has five elements. Use the following numbers to initialize the array: 6.5, 8.3, 4, 2, 10.5.

6. Write the code to display the contents of the rates array from Review Exercise 5 in the ratesLabel. Use the For...Next statement.

7. Rewrite the code from Review Exercise 6 using the Do...Loop statement.

8. Rewrite the code from Review Exercise 6 using the For Each...Next statement.

9. Write the statement to sort the rates array in ascending order.

10. Write the statement to reverse the contents of the `rates` array.

11. Write the code to calculate the average of the elements stored in the `rates` array from Review Exercise 5. Display the average in the averageLabel. Use the For...Next statement.

12. Rewrite the code from Review Exercise 11 using the Do...Loop statement.

13. Rewrite the code from Review Exercise 11 using the For Each...Next statement.

14. Write the code to display, in the smallestLabel, the smallest number stored in the `rates` array from Review Exercise 5. Use the Do...Loop statement.

15. Rewrite the code from Review Exercise 14 using the For...Next statement.

16. Rewrite the code from Review Exercise 14 using the For Each...Next statement.

17. Write the code to subtract the number one from each element in the `rates` array from Review Exercise 5. Use the Do...Loop statement.

18. Rewrite the code from Review Exercise 17 using the For...Next statement.

19. Rewrite the code from Review Exercise 17 using the For Each...Next statement.

20. Write the code to multiply by two the number stored in the first element of a one-dimensional array named `numbers`. Store the result in the `doubleNum` variable.

21. Write the code to add together the numbers stored in the first and second elements of a one-dimensional array named `numbers`. Display the sum in the `sumLabel`.

22. Write the statement to declare a two-dimensional Decimal array named `balances`. The array should have four rows and six columns.

23. Write a loop that stores the number 10 in each element in the `balances` array from Review Exercise 22. Use the For...Next statement.

24. Rewrite the code from Review Exercise 23 using a Do...Loop statement.

25. Rewrite the code from Review Exercise 23 using a For Each...Next statement.

## Computer Exercises

1. In this exercise, you modify the Lottery Game application you created in the chapter's Programming Tutorial.
   a. Use Windows to make a copy of the Lottery Game Solution folder, which is contained in the VbReloaded\Chap08 folder. Rename the folder Modified Lottery Game Solution.
   b. Open the Lottery Game Solution (Lottery Game Solution.sln) file contained in the VbReloaded\Chap08\Modified Lottery Game Solution folder.
   c. Open the Code Editor window. Change both Do While clauses to Do Until clauses.
   d. Save the solution, then start and test the application.
   e. Click the Exit button to end the application, then close the solution.

2. In this exercise, you modify the chapter's Programming Example.
   a. Create the Perrytown Gift Shop application shown in the chapter's Programming Example. Save the application in the VbReloaded\Chap08 folder.

b. Open the Code Editor window. Remove the `Dim taxTable(5,3) As Decimal` statement from the calcButton's Click event procedure. Modify the selection structure so that it passes the taxable wages and the appropriate array (either the singleTable or marriedTable array) to a function named CalculateFwt.

c. Create a function named CalculateFwt. The function will need to accept the taxable wages and the array passed to it. Move the code that calculates the federal withholding tax from the calcButton's Click event procedure to the CalculateFwt function.

d. Save the solution, then start the application. Use the application to display the tax for a married employee with taxable wages of $288.46. The application should display $24.67 as the tax. Now use the application to display the tax for a single employee with taxable wages of $600. The application should display $88.59 as the tax.

e. Click the Exit button to end the application, then close the solution.

3. In this exercise, you code the Salary Code application that you viewed in the chapter.

a. Open the Salary Code Solution (Salary Code Solution.sln) file, which is contained in the VbReloaded\Chap08\Salary Code Solution folder.

b. Open the Code Editor window, then enter the code shown in Figure 8.10.

c. Save the solution, then start and test the application.

d. Click the Exit button to end the application, then close the solution.

4. In this exercise, you modify the Salary Code application you coded in Computer Exercise 3. The modified application will allow the user to enter the salary code by selecting it from a list box.

a. Use Windows to make a copy of the Salary Code Solution folder. Rename the folder Salary Code Solution-ListBox.

b. Open the Salary Code Solution (Salary Code Solution.sln) file contained in the VbReloaded\Chap08\Salary Code Solution-ListBox folder.

c. Modify the application's interface so that it uses a list box to display the salary codes. Also make the appropriate modifications to the application's code.

d. Save the solution, then start and test the application.

e. Click the Exit button to end the application, then close the solution.

5. In this exercise, you code an application that displays the number of days in a month.

a. Open the Month Solution (Month Solution.sln) file, which is contained in the VbReloaded\Chap08\Month Solution folder.

b. Open the Display Days button's Click event procedure. Declare a 12-element, one-dimensional array named **days**. Use the number of days in each month to initialize the array. (Use 28 for February.)

c. Code the displayButton's Click event procedure so that it displays (in the daysLabel) the number of days in the month whose month number is entered in the monthTextBox. For example, if the monthTextBox contains the number one, the procedure should display 31 in the daysLabel, because there are 31 days in January. The procedure should display an appropriate message in a message box when the user enters an invalid number in the monthTextBox.

d. Save the solution, then start the application. Enter the number 20 in the monthTextBox, then click the Display Days button. An appropriate message should appear in a message box. Close the message box.

e. Now test the application by entering numbers from 1 through 12 in the monthTextBox. Click the Display Days button after entering each number.

f. Click the Exit button to end the application, then close the solution.

6. In this exercise, you code an application that displays the lowest value stored in an array.

a. Open the Lowest Solution (Lowest Solution.sln) file, which is contained in the VbReloaded\Chap08\Lowest Solution folder.

b. Locate the Display Lowest button's Click event procedure. The procedure declares and initializes a 20-element, one-dimensional Integer array named scores.

c. Code the displayButton's Click event procedure so that it displays (in the lowestLabel) the lowest score stored in the array.

d. Save the solution, then start the application. Click the Display Lowest button. The number 13, which is the lowest score in the scores array, should appear in the lowestLabel.

e. Click the Exit button to end the application, then close the solution.

7. In this exercise, you code an application that updates each value stored in an array.

a. Open the Update Prices Solution (Update Prices Solution.sln) file, which is contained in the VbReloaded\Chap08\Update Prices Solution folder.

b. Open the Increase button's Click event procedure. Declare a one-dimensional Decimal array named prices. The array should contain 10 elements and be initialized using the following prices: 6.75, 12.50, 33.50, 10, 9.50, 25.50, 7.65, 8.35, 9.75, 3.50.

c. The procedure should ask the user for a percentage amount by which each price should be increased. It then should increase each price by that amount, and then display the increased prices in the interface.

d. Save the solution, then start the application. Click the Increase button. Increase each price by 5%.

e. Click the Exit button to end the application, then close the solution.

8. In this exercise, you modify the application from Computer Exercise 7. The modified application allows the user to update a specific price.

a. Use Windows to make a copy of the Update Prices Solution folder, which is contained in the VbReloaded\Chap08 folder. Rename the copy Modified Update Prices Solution.

b. Open the Update Prices Solution (Update Prices Solution.sln) file contained in the VbReloaded\Chap08\Modified Update Prices Solution folder.

c. Open the Increase button's Click event procedure. Modify the procedure so that it also asks the user to enter a number from one through 10. If the user enters the number one, the procedure should update the first price in the array. If the user enters the number two, the procedure should update the second price in the array, and so on.

d. Save the solution, then start the application. Click the Increase button. Increase the second price by 10%. Click the Increase button again. This time, increase the tenth price by 2%.

e. Click the Exit button to end the application, then close the solution.

9. In this exercise, you code an application that displays the number of students earning a specific score.

a. Open the Scores Solution (Scores Solution.sln) file, which is contained in the VbReloaded\Chap08\Scores Solution folder.

b. Open the Display button's Click event procedure. Declare a 20-element, one-dimensional Integer array named scores. Assign the following numbers to the array: 88, 72, 99, 20, 66, 95, 99, 100, 72, 88, 78, 45, 57, 89, 85, 78, 75, 88, 72, 88.

c. Code the procedure so that it prompts the user to enter a score from zero through 100. The procedure then should display (in a message box) the number of students who earned that score.

d. Save the solution, then start the application. Use the application to answer the following questions:
How many students earned a score of 72?
How many students earned a score of 88?
How many students earned a score of 20?
How many students earned a score of 99?

e. Click the Exit button to end the application, then close the solution.

10. In this exercise, you modify the application that you coded in Computer Exercise 9. The modified application allows the user to display the number of students earning a score in a specific range.

a. Use Windows to make a copy of the Scores Solution folder, which is contained in the VbReloaded\Chap08 folder. Rename the copy Modified Scores Solution.

b. Open the Scores Solution (Scores Solution.sln) file contained in the VbReloaded\Chap08\Modified Scores Solution folder.

c. Open the Display button's Click event procedure. Modify the procedure so that it prompts the user to enter a minimum score and a maximum score. The procedure then should display (in a message box) the number of students who earned a score within that range.

d. Save the solution, then start the application. Use the application to answer the following questions:
How many students earned a score between 70 and 79, including 70 and 79?
How many students earned a score between 65 and 85, including 65 and 85?
How many students earned a score between 0 and 50, including 0 and 50?

e. Click the Exit button to end the application, then close the solution.

11. In this exercise, you code an application that allows Professor Carver to display a grade based on the number of points he enters. The grading scale is shown in Figure 8.50.

| Minimum points | Maximum points | Grade |
| --- | --- | --- |
| 0 | 299 | F |
| 300 | 349 | D |
| 350 | 399 | C |
| 400 | 449 | B |
| 450 | 500 | A |

**FIGURE 8.50**

a. Open the Carver Solution (Carver Solution.sln) file, which is contained in the VbReloaded\Chap08\Carver Solution folder.

    b. Store the minimum points in a five-element, one-dimensional Integer array named `points`. Store the grades in a five-element, one-dimensional String array named `grades`. The arrays should be parallel arrays.

    c. Code the Display Grade button's Click event procedure so that it searches the `points` array for the number of points entered by the user, and then displays the corresponding grade from the `grade` array.

    d. Save the solution, and then start the application. Enter 455 in the Points text box, then click the Display Grade button. A grade of A appears in the interface.

    e. Enter 210 in the Points text box, then click the Display Grade button. A grade of F appears in the interface.

    f. Click the Exit button to end the application, then close the solution.

12. In this exercise, you modify the application that you coded in Computer Exercise 11. The modified application allows the user to change the grading scale when the application is started.

    a. Use Windows to make a copy of the Carver Solution folder, which is contained in the VbReloaded\Chap08 folder. Rename the copy Modified Carver Solution.

    b. Open the Carver Solution (Carver Solution.sln) file contained in the VbReloaded\Chap08\Modified Carver Solution folder.

    c. When the form is loaded into the computer's memory, the application should use the InputBox function to prompt the user to enter the total number of possible points—in other words, the total number of points a student can earn in the course. Modify the application's code to perform this task.

    d. Modify the application's code so that it uses the grading scale shown in Figure 8.51. For example, if the user enters the number 500 in response to the InputBox function, the code should enter 450, which is 90% of 500, as the minimum number of points for an A. If the user enters the number 300, the code should enter 270, which is 90% of 300, as the minimum number of points for an A.

| Minimum points | Grade |
| --- | --- |
| Less than 60% of the possible points | F |
| 60% of the possible points | D |
| 70% of the possible points | C |
| 80% of the possible points | B |
| 90% of the possible points | A |

**FIGURE 8.51**

    e. Save the solution, and then start the application. Enter 300 as the number of possible points, then enter 185 in the Points text box. Click the Display Grade button. A grade of D appears in the interface.

    f. Click the Exit button to end the application.

    g. Start the application again. Enter 500 as the number of possible points, then enter 363 in the Points text box. Click the Display Grade button. A grade of C appears in the interface.

    h. Click the Exit button to end the application, then close the solution.

13. In this exercise, you code an application that sums the values contained in a two-dimensional array.
    a. Open the Inventory Solution (Inventory Solution.sln) file, which is contained in the VbReloaded\Chap08\Inventory Solution folder.
    b. Code the Display Total button's Click event procedure so that it adds together the values stored in the `inventory` array. Display the sum in the totalLabel.
    c. Save the solution, and then start the application. Click the Display Total button to display the sum of the array values.
    d. Click the Exit button to end the application, then close the solution.

14. In this exercise, you code an application that displays the highest score earned on the midterm exam and the highest score earned on the final exam.
    a. Open the Highest Solution (Highest Solution.sln) file, which is contained in the VbReloaded\Chap08\Highest Solution folder.
    b. Code the Display Highest button's Click event procedure so that it displays (in the appropriate label controls) the highest score earned on the midterm exam and the highest score earned on the final exam.
    c. Save the solution, and then start the application. Click the Display Highest button to display the highest scores.
    d. Click the Exit button to end the application, then close the solution.

15. In this exercise, you learn about the ReDim statement.
    a. Display the Help screen for the ReDim statement. What is the purpose of the statement?
    b. What is the purpose of the `Preserve` keyword?
    c. Open the ReDim Solution (ReDim Solution.sln) file, which is contained in the VbReloaded\Chap08\ReDim Solution folder.
    d. Open the Code Editor window and view the displayButton's Click event procedure. Study the existing code, then modify the procedure so that it stores any number of sales amounts in the `sales` array.
    e. Save the solution, then start the application. Click the Display Sales button, then enter the following sales amounts: 700, 550, and 800. The button's Click event procedure should display each sales amount in a separate message box.
    f. Click the Display Sales button again, then enter the following sales amounts: 5, 9, 45, 67, 8, and 0. The button's Click event procedure should display each sales amount in a separate message box.
    g. Click the Exit button to end the application, then close the solution.

16. In this exercise, you learn about the Array.GetUpperBound method.
    a. Display the Help screen for the Array.GetUpperBound method. What is the purpose of the method?
    b. Open the Price List Solution (Price List Solution.sln) file, which is contained in the VbReloaded\Chap08\Price List Solution folder.
    c. Open the Code Editor window, then enter the code shown earlier in Figure 8.37.
    d. Save the solution, then start and test the application. Click the Exit button to end the application.
    e. Modify the code so that it uses the Array.GetUpperBound method rather than the number 5.
    f. Save the solution, then start and test the application. Click the Exit button to end the application, then close the solution.

17. In this exercise, you find and correct an error in an application. The process of finding and correcting errors is called debugging.
    a. Open the Debug Solution (Debug Solution.sln) file, which is contained in the VbReloaded\Chap08\Debug Solution folder.
    b. Open the Code Editor window. Review the existing code. Notice that the names array contains five rows and two columns. Column one contains five first names, and column two contains five last names. The displayButton's Click event procedure should display the first and last names in the firstLabel and lastLabel, respectively.
    c. Notice that a jagged line appears below some of the lines of code in the Code Editor window. Correct the code to remove the jagged lines.
    d. Save the solution, then start the application. Click the Display button. If an error message appears in a dialog box, click the No button.
    e. Correct the errors in the application's code, then save the solution and start the application. Click the Display button to display the first and last names in the appropriate labels.
    f. Click the Exit button to end the application, then close the solution.

## Case Projects

### JM Sales

JM Sales employs 10 salespeople. The sales made by the salespeople during the months of January, February, and March are shown in Figure 8.52. The sales manager wants an application that allows him to enter the current bonus rate. The application should display each salesperson's number (1 through 10), total sales amount, and total bonus amount. It also should display the total bonus paid to all salespeople. Be sure to use one or more arrays in the application.

| Salesperson | January | February | March |
|---|---|---|---|
| 1 | 2400 | 3500 | 2000 |
| 2 | 1500 | 7000 | 1000 |
| 3 | 600 | 450 | 2100 |
| 4 | 790 | 240 | 500 |
| 5 | 1000 | 1000 | 1000 |
| 6 | 6300 | 7000 | 8000 |
| 7 | 1300 | 450 | 700 |
| 8 | 2700 | 5500 | 6000 |
| 9 | 4700 | 4800 | 4900 |
| 10 | 1200 | 1300 | 1400 |

**FIGURE 8.52**

### Waterglen Horse Farms

Each year, Sabrina Cantrell, the owner of Waterglen Horse Farms, enters four of her horses in five local horse races. She uses the table shown in Figure 8.53 to keep track of how her horses performed in each race. In the table, a 1 means that the horse won the race, a 2 means that the horse finished in second place, and a 3 means that the horse finished in third place. A 0 means that the horse did not finish in the top three. Sabrina wants an application that she can use to display a summary of how each horse performed individually, as well as how all of the horses performed. For example, using the table shown in Figure 8.53, horse 1 won one race, finished second in one race, finished third in one race, and didn't finish in the top three in two races. Overall, Sabrina's horses won four races, finished second in three races, finished third in three races, and didn't finish in the top three in ten races. Be sure to use one or more arrays in the application.

Each column represents a race

Each row represents a horse

|   | 1 | 2 | 3 | 4 | 5 |
|---|---|---|---|---|---|
| 1 | 0 | 1 | 0 | 3 | 2 |
| 2 | 1 | 0 | 2 | 0 | 0 |
| 3 | 0 | 3 | 3 | 0 | 1 | 0 |
| 4 | 3 | 2 | 1 | 0 | 0 |

**FIGURE 8.53**

## Conway Enterprises

Conway Enterprises has both domestic and international sales operations. The company's sales manager wants an application that she can use to display the total domestic, total international, and total company sales made during a six-month period. The sales amounts are shown in Figure 8.54. Be sure to use one or more arrays in the application.

| Month | Domestic | International |
|-------|----------|--------------|
| 1 | 100,000 | 150,000 |
| 2 | 90,000 | 120,000 |
| 3 | 75,000 | 210,000 |
| 4 | 88,000 | 50,000 |
| 5 | 125,000 | 220,000 |
| 6 | 63,000 | 80,000 |

**FIGURE 8.54**

## Tic-Tac-Toe

Create an application that simulates the Tic-Tac-Toe game, which requires two players. Be sure to use one or more arrays in the application.

# Structures and Sequential Access Files

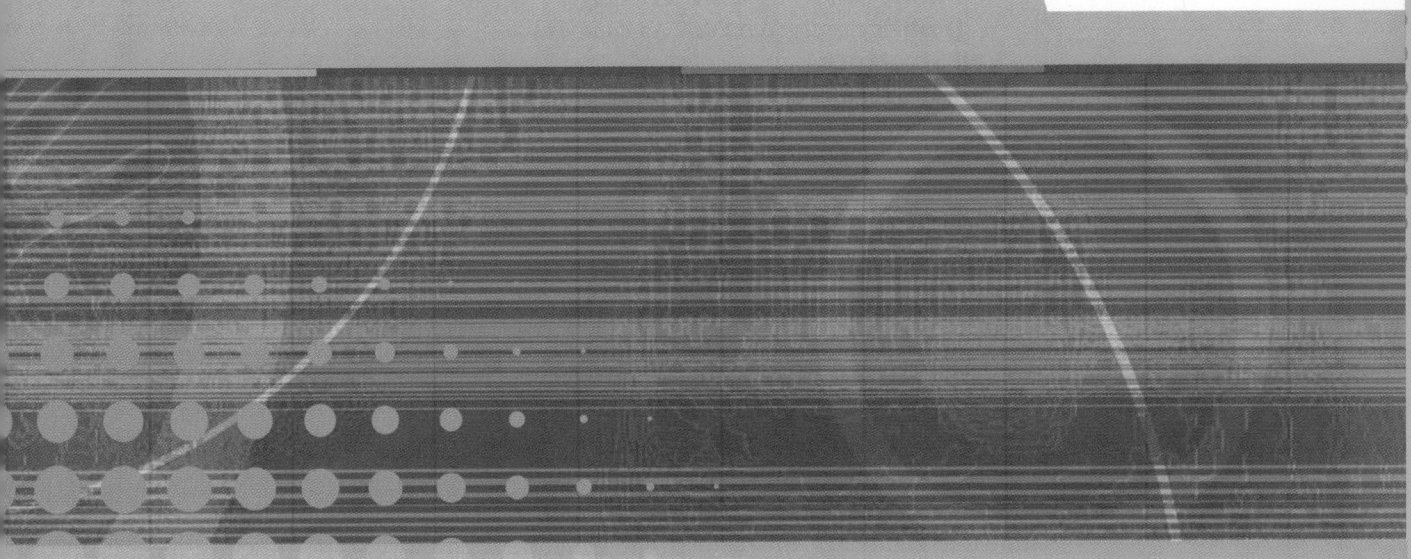

## After studying Chapter 9, you should be able to:

- Create a structure
- Declare and manipulate a structure variable
- Create an array of structure variables
- Write information to a sequential access file
- Align the text written to a sequential access file
- Read information from a sequential access file
- Determine whether a file exists
- Code the FormClosing event
- Prevent a form from closing

## STRUCTURES

In previous chapters, you used only the data types built into Visual Basic, such as the Integer, Decimal, and String data types. You also can create your own data types in Visual Basic using the **Structure statement**. Data types created using the Structure statement are referred to as **user-defined data types** or **structures**. Figure 9.1 shows the syntax of the Structure statement and includes an example of using the statement to create a structure (user-defined data type) named Employee.

**HOW TO...**

**Create a Structure (User-Defined Data Type)**

**Syntax**
**Structure** *structureName*
    **Public** *memberVariable1* **As** *datatype*
    [**Public** *memberVariableN* **As** *datatype*]
**End Structure**

**Example**
```
Structure Employee
    Public number As String
    Public firstName As String
    Public lastName As String
    Public salary As Decimal
End Structure
```

**FIGURE 9.1**    How to create a structure (user-defined data type)

The Structure statement begins with the Structure clause, which contains the keyword `Structure` followed by the name of the structure. In the example shown in Figure 9.1, the name of the structure is Employee. The Structure statement ends with the End Structure clause, which contains the keywords `End Structure`. Between the Structure and End Structure clauses, you define the members included in the structure. The members can be variables, constants, or procedures. However, in most cases, the members will be variables; such variables are referred to as **member variables**. In this book, you learn how to include only member variables in a structure.

As the syntax shown in Figure 9.1 indicates, each member variable's definition contains the keyword `Public` followed by the name of the variable, the keyword `As`, and the variable's *datatype*. The *datatype* identifies the type of data the member variable will store and can be any of the standard data types available in Visual Basic; it also can be another structure (user-defined data type). The Employee structure shown in Figure 9.1 contains four member variables: three are String variables and one is a Decimal variable.

In most applications, you enter the Structure statement in the form's Declarations section in the Code Editor window. Recall that the form's Declarations section begins with the Public Class clause and ends with the End Class clause. After entering the Structure statement, you then can use the structure to declare a variable.

**TIP**

Most programmers use the Class statement, rather than the Structure statement, to create data types that contain procedures. You learn about the Class statement in Chapter 10.

**TIP**

The Structure statement merely defines the structure. It does not actually create a structure variable.

## Using a Structure to Declare a Variable

As you can with the standard data types built into Visual Basic, you also can use a structure (user-defined data type) to declare a variable. Variables declared using a structure are often referred to as **structure variables**. Figure 9.2 shows the syntax for creating a structure variable. The figure also includes examples of declaring structure variables using the Employee structure from Figure 9.1.

**HOW TO...**

**Declare a Structure Variable**

**Syntax**
{Dim | **Private**} *structureVariableName* **As** *structureName*

**Examples**
```
Dim manager As Employee
```
declares a procedure-level Employee variable named `manager`

```
Private salaried As Employee
```
declares a module-level Employee variable named `salaried`

**FIGURE 9.2**    How to declare a structure variable

You use the `Dim` keyword to create a procedure-level structure variable, and use the `Private` keyword to declare a module-level structure variable. In the syntax, *structureVariableName* is the name of the structure variable you are declaring and *structureName* is the name of the structure (user-defined data type).

Similar to the way the `Dim age As Integer` instruction declares an Integer variable named `age`, the `Dim manager As Employee` instruction, which is shown in the first example in Figure 9.2, declares an Employee structure variable named `manager`. However, unlike the `age` variable, the `manager` variable itself contains four member variables. In code, you refer to the entire structure variable by its name; in this case, you refer to it using the name `manager`. To refer to an individual member variable within a structure variable, you precede the member variable's name with the name of the structure variable in which it is defined. You use the dot member access operator (a period) to separate the structure variable's name from the member variable's name. For instance, the names of the member variables within the `manager` structure variable are `manager.number`, `manager.firstName`, `manager.lastName`, and `manager.salary`.

The `Private salaried As Employee` instruction shown in the second example in Figure 9.2 declares a module-level Employee structure variable named `salaried`. The names of the member variables within the `salaried` variable are `salaried.number`, `salaried.firstName`, `salaried.lastName`, and `salaried.salary`.

The member variables contained in a structure variable can be used just like any other variables. For example, you can assign values to them, use them in calculations, display their contents, and so on. Figure 9.3 shows various ways of manipulating the member variables created by the statements shown in Figure 9.2.

**TIP**

The dot member access operator indicates that **number**, **firstName**, **lastName**, and **salary** are members of the **manager** and **salaried** variables.

HOW TO...

### Manipulate Member Variables

```
manager.number = "0477"
manager.firstName = "Janice"
manager.lastName = "Lopenski"
manager.salary = 34500D
```
assigns data to the member variables contained in the `manager` variable

```
manager.salary = manager.salary * 1.05D
```
multiplies the contents of the `manager.salary` member variable by 1.05, and then assigns the result to the member variable

```
salaried.firstName = firstTextBox.Text
```
assigns the value entered in the firstTextBox to the `salaried.firstName` member variable

```
salaryTextBox.Text = salaried.salary.ToString("C2")
```
formats the value contained in the `salaried.salary` member variable to Currency with two decimal places, and then displays the result in the salaryTextBox

**FIGURE 9.3** How to manipulate member variables

In the first example shown in Figure 9.3, the first three assignment statements assign the strings "0477", "Janice", and "Lopenski" to the String members of the `manager` variable. The fourth assignment statement in the example assigns a Decimal number to the Decimal member of the `manager` variable.

The second example in Figure 9.3 multiplies the contents of the `manager.salary` member variable by 1.05, and then assigns the result to the member variable. The third example assigns the value entered in the firstTextBox to the `salaried.firstName` member variable. The last example displays the value stored in the `salaried.salary` member variable, formatted with a dollar sign and two decimal places, in the salaryTextBox.

Programmers use structures (user-defined data types) to group related items into one unit. The advantages of doing this will become more apparent as you read through the next two sections.

### Passing a Structure Variable to a Procedure

The sales manager at Willow Pools wants an application that allows the salespeople to enter the length, width, and depth of a rectangular pool. The application should determine the amount of water required to fill the pool. You can make this determination by calculating the volume of the pool. To calculate the volume, you multiply the pool's length by its width, and then multiply the result by the pool's depth. Figure 9.4 shows a sample run of the Willow Pools application, and Figure 9.5 shows how you can code the application without using a structure.

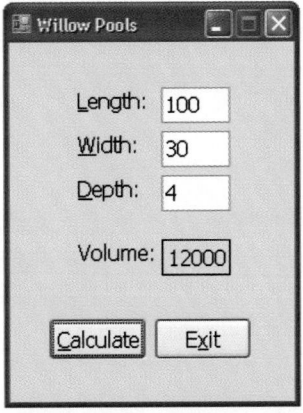

**FIGURE 9.4**    Sample run of the Willow Pools application

**Visual Basic code**

```vb
' Project name:        Pool Project
' Project purpose:     The project calculates the volume
'                      of a rectangular pool.
' Created/revised by:  <your name> on <current date>


Option Explicit On
Option Strict On


Public Class MainForm

    Private Function ValidateInput(ByRef len As Decimal, _
                                   ByRef wid As Decimal, _
                                   ByRef dep As Decimal) As Boolean

        Dim isLenValid As Boolean
        Dim isWidValid As Boolean
        Dim isDepValid As Boolean

        isLenValid = Decimal.TryParse(lengthTextBox.Text, len)
        isWidValid = Decimal.TryParse(widthTextBox.Text, wid)
        isDepValid = Decimal.TryParse(depthTextBox.Text, dep)

        If isLenValid AndAlso isWidValid AndAlso isDepValid Then
            Return True
        Else
            Return False
        End If
    End Function

    Private Function CalcVolume(ByVal len As Decimal, _
                                ByVal wid As Decimal, _
                                ByVal dep As Decimal) As Decimal
        Return len * wid * dep
    End Function
```

*Receives three variables by reference and assigns data to the variables*

*Receives three variables by value and uses the values to calculate the volume*

*(Figure is continued on next page)*

*These three procedures are collapsed*

*Declares three variables to store the input data*

*Passes three variables to the ValidateInput function*

*Passes three variables to the CalcVolume function*

```
Private Sub exitButton_Click ...

Private Sub SelectText ...

Private Sub ClearVolume ...

Private Sub calcButton_Click(ByVal sender As Object, _
    ByVal e As System.EventArgs) Handles calcButton.Click
    ' validates the user's input, then displays either
    ' the volume or an error message

    Dim poolLength As Decimal
    Dim poolWidth As Decimal
    Dim poolDepth As Decimal
    Dim isValid As Boolean
    Dim poolVolume As Decimal

    isValid = ValidateInput(poolLength, poolWidth, poolDepth)

    If isValid = True Then
        poolVolume = CalcVolume(poolLength, poolWidth, poolDepth)
        volumeLabel.Text = Convert.ToString(poolVolume)
    Else
        MessageBox.Show("The pool measurements must be numeric.", _
            "Willow Pools", MessageBoxButtons.OK, _
            MessageBoxIcon.Information)
    End If
End Sub
End Class
```

**FIGURE 9.5**   Code for the Willow Pools application (without a structure)

When the user clicks the Calculate button in the interface, the calcButton's Click event procedure shown in Figure 9.5 declares the necessary variables. It then calls the ValidateInput function, passing it three variables *by reference*. The ValidateInput function uses the TryParse method to convert the user's input (length, width, and depth) to Decimal, assigning the result of each conversion to the appropriate variable passed to it. The function returns the Boolean value True when the three conversions are successful; otherwise, it returns the Boolean value False. The calcButton's Click event procedure assigns the function's return value to the isValid variable.

If the isValid variable contains the Boolean value False, the calcButton's Click event procedure displays an appropriate message. If, on the other hand, the isValid variable contains the Boolean value True, the calcButton's Click event procedure calls the CalcVolume function, passing it three variables *by value*. The CalcVolume function uses the values stored in the variables to calculate the volume of the pool, which it returns as a Decimal number. The calcButton's Click event procedure assigns the function's return value to the poolVolume variable. It then converts the contents of the poolVolume variable to String and displays the result in the volumeLabel.

Figure 9.6 shows a more convenient way of writing the code for the Willow Pools application. In this version of the code, a structure named Dimensions is used to group together the input data.

**Visual Basic code**

```vb
' Project name:          Pool Project
' Project purpose:       The project calculates the volume
'                        of a rectangular pool.
' Created/revised by:    <your name> on <current date>

Option Explicit On
Option Strict On

Public Class MainForm

    Structure Dimensions
        Public length As Decimal
        Public width As Decimal
        Public depth As Decimal
    End Structure

    Private Function ValidateInput(ByRef pool As Dimensions) As Boolean

        Dim isLenValid As Boolean
        Dim isWidValid As Boolean
        Dim isDepValid As Boolean

        isLenValid = Decimal.TryParse(lengthTextBox.Text, pool.length)
        isWidValid = Decimal.TryParse(widthTextBox.Text, pool.width)
        isDepValid = Decimal.TryParse(depthTextBox.Text, pool.depth)

        If isLenValid AndAlso isWidValid AndAlso isDepValid Then
            Return True
        Else
            Return False
        End If
    End Function

    Private Function CalcVolume(ByVal pool As Dimensions) As Decimal
        Return pool.length * pool.width * pool.depth
    End Function

    Private Sub exitButton_Click ...

    Private Sub SelectText ...

    Private Sub ClearVolume ...

    Private Sub calcButton_Click(ByVal sender As Object, _
        ByVal e As System.EventArgs) Handles calcButton.Click
        ' validates the user's input, then displays either
        ' the volume or an error message
```

*Defines the Dimensions structure*

*Receives a Dimensions structure variable by reference and assigns data to the member variables*

*Receives a Dimensions structure variable by value and uses the values to calculate the volume*

*These three procedures are collapsed*

**(Figure is continued on next page)**

*Declares a Dimensions structure variable to store the input data*

*Passes the Dimensions structure variable to the ValidateInput function*

*Passes the Dimensions structure variable to the CalcVolume function*

```
Dim poolDims As Dimensions
Dim isValid As Boolean
Dim poolVolume As Decimal

isValid = ValidateInput(poolDims)

If isValid = True Then
    poolVolume = CalcVolume(poolDims)
    volumeLabel.Text = Convert.ToString(poolVolume)
Else
    MessageBox.Show("The pool measurements must be numeric.", _
        "Willow Pools", MessageBoxButtons.OK, _
        MessageBoxIcon.Information)
End If
    End Sub
End Class
```

**FIGURE 9.6**    Code for the Willow Pools application (with a structure)

In the code shown in Figure 9.6, the Structure statement that defines the Dimensions structure is entered in the MainForm's Declarations section. Notice that the structure contains three member variables named `length`, `width`, and `depth`.

The `Dim poolDims As Dimensions` statement in the calcButton's Click event procedure uses the Dimensions structure to declare a structure variable named `poolDims`. The `isValid = ValidateInput(poolDims)` statement in the procedure calls the ValidateInput function, passing it the `poolDims` structure variable *by reference*. When you pass a structure variable, all of the member variables are automatically passed.

The ValidateInput function uses the TryParse method to convert the user's input (length, width, and depth) to Decimal, assigning the result of each conversion to the appropriate member variable passed to it. The function returns the Boolean value True when the three conversions are successful; otherwise, it returns the Boolean value False. The calcButton's Click event procedure assigns the function's return value to the `isValid` variable.

If the `isValid` variable contains the Boolean value False, the calcButton's Click event procedure displays an appropriate message. If, on the other hand, the `isValid` variable contains the Boolean value True, the calcButton's Click event procedure calls the CalcVolume function, passing it the `poolDims` structure variable *by value*. The CalcVolume function uses the values stored in the member variables to calculate the volume of the pool, which it returns as a Decimal number. The calcButton's Click event procedure assigns the function's return value to the `poolVolume` variable. It then converts the contents of the `poolVolume` variable to String and displays the result in the volumeLabel.

Notice that the calcButton's Click event procedure shown earlier in Figure 9.5 uses three scalar variables to store the input data. However, in Figure 9.6's code, the procedure uses only one structure variable for this purpose. The calcButton's Click event procedure in Figure 9.5 also must pass three scalar variables (rather than one structure variable) to both the ValidateInput and CalcVolume functions, which must use three scalar variables (rather than one structure variable) to accept the data. Imagine if the input data consisted of 20 items rather than

**TIP**

As you learned in Chapter 8, a scalar variable, also called a simple variable, is one that is unrelated to any other variable in memory.

just three items! Passing a structure variable would be much less work than passing 20 individual scalar variables.

As you will learn in the next section, another advantage of grouping related data into one unit is that the unit then can be stored in an array.

### Creating an Array of Structure Variables

In Chapter 8, you learned how to use two parallel one-dimensional arrays to store a price list for Takoda Tapahe, the owner of a small gift shop named Treasures. (The code is shown in Figure 8.30 in Chapter 8.) As you may remember, you stored each product's ID in a one-dimensional String array, and stored each product's price in the corresponding location in a one-dimensional Integer array. Also in Chapter 8, you learned how to store the Treasures price list in a two-dimensional String array. (The code is shown in Figure 8.37 in Chapter 8.) In addition to using parallel one-dimensional arrays or a two-dimensional array, you also can use a one-dimensional array of structure variables.

Figure 9.7 shows a sample run of the Treasures application, and Figure 9.8 shows the application's code using an array of structure variables.

**TIP**

Notice that there are many different ways to solve the same problem.

The idTextBox's CharacterCasing and MaxLength properties are set to Upper and 4, respectively

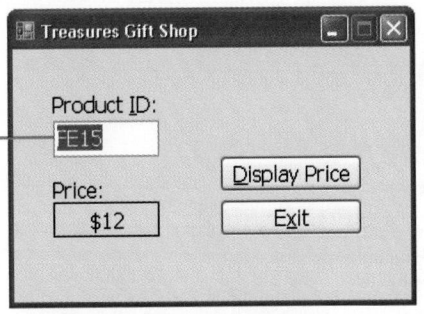

**FIGURE 9.7**   Sample run of the Treasures application

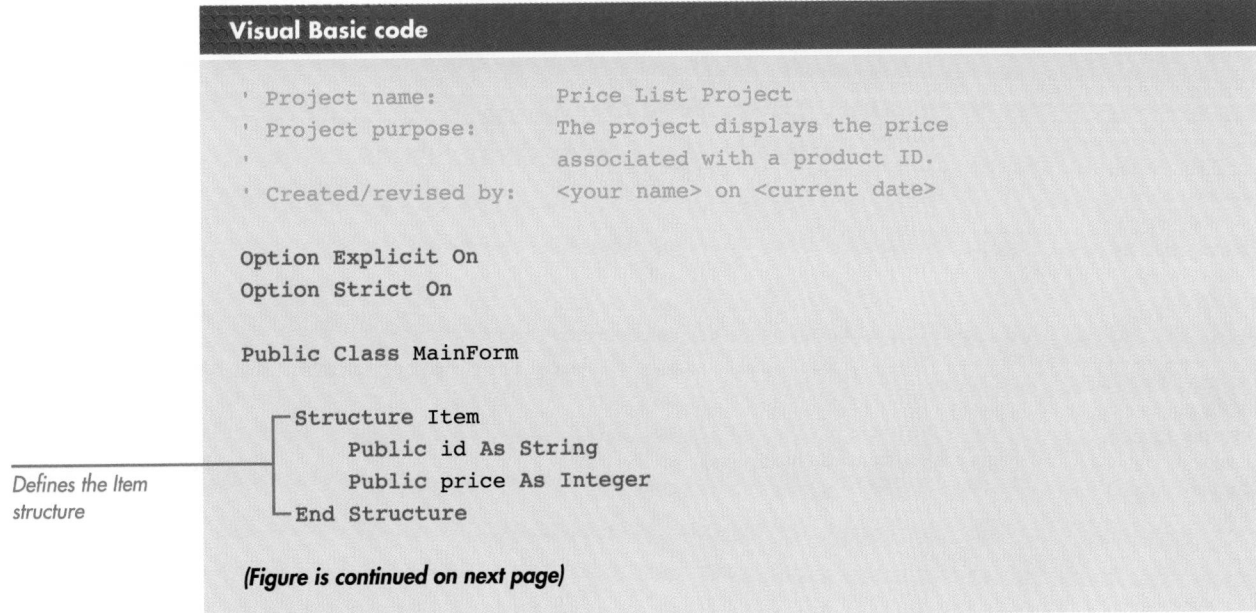

Defines the Item structure

```
Visual Basic code

' Project name:          Price List Project
' Project purpose:       The project displays the price
'                        associated with a product ID.
' Created/revised by:    <your name> on <current date>

Option Explicit On
Option Strict On


Public Class MainForm


    Structure Item
        Public id As String
        Public price As Integer
    End Structure
```

*(Figure is continued on next page)*

*These three procedures are collapsed*

```vbnet
Private Sub exitButton_Click ...

Private Sub idTextBox_Enter ...

Private Sub idTextBox_TextChanged ...

Private Sub displayButton_Click(ByVal sender As Object, _
    ByVal e As System.EventArgs) Handles displayButton.Click
    ' displays the price associated with the product
    ' ID entered by the user

    Dim searchFor As String
    Dim subscript As Integer

    ' declare an array of structure variables
    Dim gifts(4) As Item

    ' assign product IDs and prices to the array
    gifts(0).id = "BX35"
    gifts(0).price = 13
    gifts(1).id = "CR20"
    gifts(1).price = 10
    gifts(2).id = "FE15"
    gifts(2).price = 12
    gifts(3).id = "KW10"
    gifts(3).price = 24
    gifts(4).id = "MM67"
    gifts(4).price = 4

    ' assign the product ID to a variable
    searchFor = idTextBox.Text

    ' search the gifts array for the product ID
    ' continue searching until there are
    ' no more array elements to search or
    ' the product ID is found
    Do Until subscript = gifts.Length _
        OrElse searchFor = gifts(subscript).id
        subscript = subscript + 1
    Loop

    ' determine whether the product ID
    ' was found in the gifts array
    If subscript < gifts.Length Then
        priceLabel.Text = gifts(subscript).price.ToString("C0")
    Else
```

*Declares an array of Item structure variables*

*Fills the member variables with data*

*Accesses the length of the array and the contents of the id member variable contained in the current array element*

*Accesses the contents of the price member variable contained in the current array element*

**(Figure is continued on next page)**

```
            MessageBox.Show("Invalid product ID.", _
                "Treasures Gift Shop", MessageBoxButtons.OK, _
                MessageBoxIcon.Information)
        End If

        idTextBox.Focus()
    End Sub
End Class
```

**FIGURE 9.8**    Code for the Treasures application using an array of structure variables

The displayButton's Click event procedure declares a String variable named searchFor and an Integer variable named subscript. The searchFor variable will store the product ID entered by the user, and the subscript variable will keep track of the array subscripts. The procedure also declares a five-element, one-dimensional array named gifts, using the Item structure defined in the MainForm's Declarations section as the array's data type. Each element in the gifts array is a structure variable that contains two member variables: a String variable named id and an Integer variable named price.

After declaring the array, the procedure populates the array by assigning the appropriate IDs and prices to it. Notice that you refer to a member variable in an array element using the syntax *arrayname*(*subscript*).*memberVariableName*. For example, you use gifts(0).id to refer to the id member contained in the first element in the gifts array. Likewise, you use gifts(4).price to refer to the price member contained in the last element in the gifts array. Figure 9.9 illustrates this naming convention.

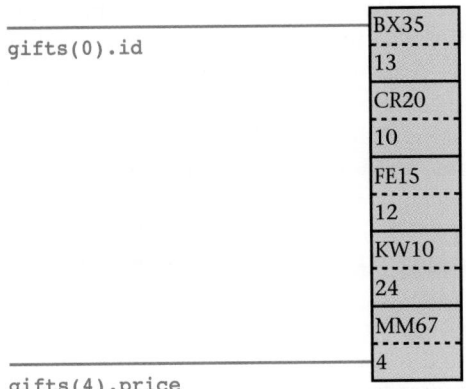

gifts(0).id

gifts(4).price

**FIGURE 9.9**    Names of some of the member variables in the gifts array

After populating the gifts array, the displayButton's Click event procedure assigns the contents of the idTextBox to the searchFor variable. The loop in the procedure then searches for the product ID in each id member in the gifts array, stopping when there are no more id member elements to search or when

**TIP**

Recall that the value stored in an array's Length property is always one number more than the highest subscript in the array.

the product ID is located. After the loop completes its processing, the selection structure in the procedure compares the number stored in the `subscript` variable with the value stored in the `gifts` array's Length property. In this case, the Length property contains the number five, because there are five elements in the `gifts` array. If the `subscript` variable contains a number that is less than five, it indicates that the loop stopped processing because the product ID was located in an `id` member in the array. In that case, the procedure displays the price from the corresponding `price` member in the array. However, if the `subscript` variable's value is not less than five, it indicates that the loop stopped processing because it reached the end of the array without finding the product ID. In that case, the message "Invalid product ID." is displayed in a message box. As Figure 9.7 indicates, the procedure displays a price of $12 when the user enters FE15 as the product ID.

As mentioned in Chapter 8, in most applications, the values stored in an array come from a file on the computer's disk and are assigned to the array after it is declared. You learn about files in the next several sections.

## FILE TYPES

In addition to getting information from the keyboard and sending information to the computer screen, an application also can get information from and send information to a file on a disk. Getting information from a file is referred to as "reading the file," and sending information to a file is referred to as "writing to the file." Files to which information is written are called **output files**, because the files store the output produced by an application. Files that are read by the computer are called **input files**, because an application uses the information in these files as input.

You can create three different types of files in Visual Basic: sequential, random, and binary. The file type refers to how the information in the file is accessed. The information in a sequential access file is always accessed sequentially. In other words, it is always accessed in consecutive order from the beginning of the file through the end of the file. The information stored in a random access file can be accessed either in consecutive order or in random order. The information in a binary access file can be accessed by its byte location in the file. You learn about sequential access files in this chapter. Random access and binary access files are used less often in programs, so these file types are not covered in this book.

## SEQUENTIAL ACCESS FILES

A **sequential access file** is often referred to as a **text file**, because it is composed of lines of text. The text might represent an employee list, as shown in Example 1 in Figure 9.10. Or, it might be a memo or a report, as shown in Examples 2 and 3 in the figure.

**Examples**

**Example 1 — employee list**
```
Bonnel, Jacob
Carlisle, Donald
Eberg, Jack
Hou, Chang
```

**Example 2 — memo**
```
To all employees:

Effective January 1, 2008, the cost of dependent coverage will
increase from $35 to $38.50 per month.

Jefferson Williams
Insurance Manager
```

**Example 3 — report**
```
ABC Industries Sales Report

State          Sales
California      15000
Montana         10000
Wyoming          7000
               -----
Total sales:   $32000
```

**FIGURE 9.10** Examples of text stored in a sequential access file

Sequential access files are similar to cassette tapes in that each line in the file, like each song on a cassette tape, is both stored and retrieved in consecutive order (sequentially). In other words, before you can record (store) the fourth song on a cassette tape, you first must record songs one through three. Likewise, before you can write (store) the fourth line in a sequential access file, you first must write lines one through three. The same holds true for retrieving a song from a cassette tape and a line of text from a sequential access file. To listen to the fourth song on a cassette tape, you must play (or fast-forward through) the first three songs. Likewise, to read the fourth line in a sequential access file, you first must read the three lines that precede it.

## WRITING INFORMATION TO A SEQUENTIAL ACCESS FILE

You can use the **WriteAllText method** to write information to a sequential access file. Figure 9.11 shows the syntax of the WriteAllText method and includes examples of using the method to write text to a sequential access file.

# HOW TO...

## Write Information to a Sequential Access File

### Syntax
**My.Computer.FileSystem.WriteAllText**(*file*, *text*, *append*)

### Example 1
```
My.Computer.FileSystem.WriteAllText("msg.txt", "Hi", False)
```

### Result
Hi

*File pointer*

### Example 2
```
My.Computer.FileSystem.WriteAllText("msg.txt", _
    "Hi" & ControlChars.NewLine, False)
```

### Result
Hi

*File pointer*

### Example 3
```
Dim file As String = "C:\VbReloaded\Chap09\report.txt"
Dim line As String = "The top salesperson is "
Dim name As String = "Carolyn"
My.Computer.FileSystem.WriteAllText(file, line, False)
My.Computer.FileSystem.WriteAllText(file, name & ".", True)
My.Computer.FileSystem.WriteAllText(file, _
    ControlChars.NewLine & ControlChars.NewLine, True)
My.Computer.FileSystem.WriteAllText(file, "ABC Sales", True)
```

### Result
The top salesperson is Carolyn.

ABC Sales

*File pointer*

### Example 4
```
Dim file As String = "C:\VbReloaded\Chap09\report.txt"
Dim price As Decimal = 5.6D
My.Computer.FileSystem.WriteAllText(file, _
    "Total price: ", False)
My.Computer.FileSystem.WriteAllText(file, _
    Price.ToString("C2") & ControlChars.NewLine, True)
```

### Result
Total price: $5.60

*File pointer*

### Example 5
```
Dim file As String = "C:\VbReloaded\Chap09\letters.txt"
My.Computer.FileSystem.WriteAllText(file, _
    Strings.Space(10) & "A" & Strings.Space(5) & "B", False)
```

### Result
          A     B

*File pointer*

**FIGURE 9.11**    How to write information to a sequential access file

The "My" in the syntax shown in Figure 9.11 is a new feature in Visual Basic 2005. The **My feature** exposes a set of commonly used objects to the programmer. One of the objects exposed by the My feature is the My.Computer object.

Using the **My.Computer object**, you can easily access other objects and methods used to manipulate files. For example, to write information to a file on your computer's disk, you use the WriteAllText method, which is available through the FileSystem object exposed by the My.Computer object.

In the WriteAllText method's syntax (shown in Figure 9.11), the *file* argument is a string that contains the name of the sequential access file to which you want to write information. The *file* argument can contain an optional folder path. If the folder path is not specified, the computer looks for the file in the current project's bin\Debug folder. For example, if the current project is stored in the VbReloaded\Chap09\Payroll Solution\Payroll Project folder, the computer will look for the file in the VbReloaded\Chap09\Payroll Solution\Payroll Project\bin\Debug folder. If the file whose name is specified in the *file* argument does not exist, the computer creates the file before writing the information to the file.

The information to write to the sequential access file is specified in the *text* argument in the WriteAllText method's syntax. Like the *file* argument, the *text* argument must be a string.

The *append* argument in the syntax is a Boolean value, either True or False. If *append* is True, the information contained in the *text* argument is added to the end of any existing information in the file. If *append* is False, the existing information in the file is erased before the information in the *text* argument is written to the file.

The `My.Computer.FileSystem.WriteAllText("msg.txt", "Hi", False)` statement shown in Example 1 in Figure 9.11 tells the computer to write the string "Hi" to a file named msg.txt. If the msg.txt file does not exist, the computer creates it before writing the string "Hi" to it. However, if the msg.txt file exists, the False value that appears in the *append* argument tells the computer to erase the file's contents before writing the string to the file.

The computer uses a file pointer to keep track of the next character to either write to a file or read from a file. After processing the `My.Computer.FileSystem.WriteAllText("msg.txt", "Hi", False)` statement in Example 1, the computer positions the file pointer immediately after the last letter in the string "Hi", as indicated in the figure. To position the file pointer on the next line in the file, you concatenate the `ControlChars.NewLine` constant with the *text* argument, as shown in the second example in Figure 9.11.

The `My.Computer.FileSystem.WriteAllText(file, line, False)` statement shown in Example 3 tells the computer to write the string "The top salesperson is " to the report.txt file located in the C:\VbReloaded\Chap09 folder. If the file does not exist, the computer creates it before writing the string to it. If the file exists, the False value that appears in the *append* argument tells the computer to erase the file's contents before writing the string to the file. After processing the statement, the computer positions the file pointer after the last character in the string (in this case, after the space character).

The next statement in Example 3, `My.Computer.FileSystem.WriteAllText(file, name & ".", True)`, tells the computer to concatenate the contents of the `name` variable with a period, and then write the result to the report.txt file. The True value that appears in the *append* argument tells the computer to append, or add, the concatenated string to the file. In this case, the concatenated string will be written on the same line as the previous string, immediately after the last space character in the string. The next statement, `My.Computer.FileSystem.WriteAllText(file, ControlChars.NewLine & ControlChars.NewLine, True)` writes two new line characters to the file, which positions the file pointer two lines below the previously written text in the file. The last statement in Example 3, `My.Computer.FileSystem.`

**TIP**

Although it is not a requirement, the "txt" (short for "text") file-name extension is typically used when naming sequential access files. This is because sequential access files are text files.

`WriteAllText(file, "ABC Sales", True)`, writes the string "ABC Sales" to the file, adding the string immediately below the two new line characters. After the statement is processed, the file pointer is located after the last character in the string, as indicated in the example.

The WriteAllText methods shown in Example 4 write the string "Total price: " and the contents of the `price` variable (formatted with a dollar sign and two decimal places) on the same line in the file. The file pointer is then positioned at the beginning of the next line in the file.

Example 5 in Figure 9.11 shows how you can use the **Strings.Space method** to write a specific number of spaces to a file. The syntax of the Strings.Space method is **Strings.Space(*number*)**, where *number* represents the number of spaces you want to write. The `My.Computer.FileSystem.WriteAllText(file, Strings.Space(10) & "A" & Strings.Space(5) & "B", False)` statement writes 10 spaces, the letter "A", five spaces, and the letter "B" to the file. After the statement is processed, the file pointer is positioned immediately after the letter B in the file.

## Aligning Columns of Information in a Sequential Access File

In Chapter 6, you learned how to use the PadLeft and PadRight methods to pad a string with a character until the string is a specified length. Recall that the syntax of the PadLeft method is *string*.**PadLeft(***length*[, *character*]**)**, and the syntax of the PadRight method is *string*.**PadRight(***length*[, *character*]**)**. In each syntax, *length* is an integer that represents the desired length of the *string*, and *character* (which is optional) is the character that each method uses to pad the *string* until it reaches the desired *length*. If the *character* argument is omitted, the default *character* is the space character. Figure 9.12 shows examples of using the PadLeft and PadRight methods to align columns of information written to a sequential access file.

---

## HOW TO...    Align Columns of Information in a Sequential Access File

### Example 1

```
Dim formatPrice As String
For price As Decimal = 1D To 3D Step .5D
    formatPrice = price.ToString("N2")
    My.Computer.FileSystem.WriteAllText("prices.txt", _
        formatPrice.PadLeft(4), True)
    My.Computer.FileSystem.WriteAllText("prices.txt", _
        ControlChars.NewLine, True)
Next price
```

### Result
```
1.00
1.50
2.00
2.50
3.00
```

*(Figure is continued on next page)*

**Example 2**
```
Dim name As String
Dim age As String
Dim path As String = "C:\VbReloaded\Chap09\"
Dim heading As String = "Name" & Strings.Space(11) & "Age"
My.Computer.FileSystem.WriteAllText(path & "info.txt", _
        heading & ControlChars.NewLine, True)
name = InputBox("Enter name:", "Name")
Do While name <> String.Empty
        age = InputBox("Enter age:", "Age")
        My.Computer.FileSystem.WriteAllText(path & "info.txt", _
            name.PadRight(15) & age _
            & ControlChars.NewLine, True)
        name = InputBox("Enter name:", "Name")
Loop
```

**Result (when the user enters the following names and ages: Janice, 23, Sue, 67)**
```
Name           Age
Janice         23
Sue            67
```

**FIGURE 9.12**    How to align columns of information in a sequential access file

The code in Example 1 shows how you can align a column of numbers by the decimal point. First, you format each number in the column to ensure that each has the same number of digits to the right of the decimal point. You then use the PadLeft method to insert spaces at the beginning of the number; this right-aligns the number within the column. Because each number has the same number of digits to the right of the decimal point, aligning each number on the right will, in effect, align each by its decimal point.

The code in Example 2 in Figure 9.12 shows how you can align the second column of information when the first column contains strings whose lengths vary. To align the second column, you first use either the PadRight or PadLeft method to ensure that each string in the first column contains the same number of characters. You then concatenate the padded string to the information in the second column before writing the concatenated string to the file. The code shown in Example 2, for instance, uses the PadRight method to ensure that each name in the first column contains exactly 15 characters. It then concatenates the 15 characters with the age stored in the age variable, and then writes the concatenated string to the file. Because each name has 15 characters, each age will automatically appear beginning in character position 16 in the file.

## READING INFORMATION FROM A SEQUENTIAL ACCESS FILE

You can use the **ReadAllText method** to read the information stored in a sequential access file. Figure 9.13 shows the syntax of the ReadAllText method and includes examples of using the method to read information from a sequential access file.

## HOW TO...

**Read Information From a Sequential Access File**

**Syntax**
**My.Computer.FileSystem.ReadAllText**(*file*)

**Examples**
```
Dim contents As String
contents = My.Computer.FileSystem.ReadAllText("prices.txt")
```
reads the text contained in the prices.txt file, and then assigns the text to
the contents variable

```
Dim path As String = "C:\VbReloaded\Chap09\"
reportTextBox.Text = _
      My.Computer.FileSystem.ReadAllText(path & "info.txt")
```
reads the text contained in the info.txt file, and then displays the text in
the reportTextBox

**FIGURE 9.13**    How to read information from a sequential access file

In the syntax shown in Figure 9.13, the *file* argument is a string that contains
the name of the sequential access file from which you want to read information.
Here again, the *file* argument can contain an optional folder path. If the folder
path is not specified, the computer looks for the file in the current project's
bin\Debug folder. If the file whose name is specified in the *file* argument does
not exist, an error occurs and your application will end abruptly. You will learn
how to handle this situation in the next section.

In the first example shown in Figure 9.13, the contents = My.Computer.
FileSystem.ReadAllText("prices.txt") statement reads the text contained in a sequential access file named prices.txt, and it assigns the text to a
String variable named contents. Because no folder path is specified in the file
argument, the computer will look for the prices.txt file in the current project's
bin\Debug folder.

In the second example shown in Figure 9.13, the reportTextBox.Text =
My.Computer.FileSystem.ReadAllText(path & "info.txt") statement
reads the text contained in the info.txt file and assigns the text to the
reportTextBox's Text property. In this case, the computer will look for the
info.txt file in the VbReloaded\Chap09 folder on the computer's hard disk.

### Determining Whether a File Exists

As you learned earlier, an error occurs when the computer attempts to read a
sequential access file that does not exist. You can prevent the error from occurring by first determining whether the file exists. You can make the determination using the **FileExists method**. Figure 9.14 shows the syntax of the
FileExists method and includes two examples of using the method.

# HOW TO...

## Determine Whether a File Exists

**Syntax**
**My.Computer.FileSystem.FileExists(***file***)**

**Examples**
```
Dim text As String
If My.Computer.FileSystem.FileExists("prices.txt") Then
     text = My.Computer.FileSystem.ReadAllText("prices.txt")
Else
     MessageBox.Show("File does not exist", "Prices", _
          MessageBoxButtons.OK, MessageBoxIcon.Information)
End If
```
reads the prices.txt file if the file exists; otherwise, displays the "File does not exist" message in a message box

```
Dim path As String = "C:\VbReloaded\Chap09\"
Dim button As DialogResult
If My.Computer.FileSystem.FileExists(path & "info.txt") Then
     button = MessageBox.Show("Erase the file?", _
          "Information", MessageBoxButtons.YesNo, _
          MessageBoxIcon.Exclamation, _
          MessageBoxDefaultButton.Button2)
     If button = DialogResult.Yes Then
          My.Computer.FileSystem.WriteAllText("info.txt", _
               String.Empty, False)
     End If
End If
```
if the info.txt file exists, displays the "Erase the file?" message in a message box; the file is erased if the user clicks the Yes button in the message box

**FIGURE 9.14**    How to determine whether a file exists

In the syntax shown in Figure 9.14, *file* is the name of the file whose existence you want to verify. If you do not include a folder path in the *file* argument, the computer searches for the file in the current project's bin\Debug folder. The FileExists method returns the Boolean value True if the file exists; otherwise, it returns the Boolean value False.

In the first example shown in Figure 9.14, the `If  My.Computer.FileSystem.FileExists("prices.txt")`  Then clause determines whether the prices.txt file exists in the current project's bin\Debug folder. If the file exists, the `text = My.Computer.FileSystem.ReadAllText("prices.txt")` statement assigns the contents of the file to the `text` variable. If the file does not exist, an appropriate message is displayed in a message box.

In the last example shown in Figure 9.14, the `If My.Computer.FileSystem.FileExists(path & "info.txt")` Then clause determines whether the info.txt file exists in the VbReloaded\Chap09 folder on the computer's hard disk. If the file exists, the "Erase the file?" message is displayed in a message box, along with Yes and No buttons. If the user clicks the Yes button in the message box, the `My.Computer.FileSystem.WriteAllText("info.txt", String.Empty, False)` statement erases the contents of the file by writing the empty string to it.

Before viewing a complete application that uses a sequential access file, you will learn about a form's FormClosing event. You often will enter code related to files in the FormClosing event procedure.

## THE FORMCLOSING EVENT

A form's **FormClosing event** occurs when a form is about to be closed. In most cases, this happens when the computer processes the `Me.Close()` statement in the form's code. However, it also occurs when the user clicks the Close button on the form's title bar. Figure 9.15 shows examples of code you might enter in the FormClosing event procedure.

HOW TO...

### Use the FormClosing Event Procedure

**Example 1 — writes information to a sequential access file**

```
Private Sub MainForm_FormClosing(ByVal sender As Object, _
    ByVal e As System.Windows.Forms.FormClosingEventArgs) _
    Handles Me.FormClosing

    My.Computer.FileSystem.WriteAllText("date.txt", _
        dateLabel.Text, True)
End Sub
```

**Example 2 — verifies that the user wants to exit the application**

```
Private Sub MainForm_FormClosing(ByVal sender As Object, _
    ByVal e As System.Windows.Forms.FormClosingEventArgs) _
    Handles Me.FormClosing

    Dim button As DialogResult
    button = MessageBox.Show("Do you want to exit?", "Payroll", _
        MessageBoxButtons.YesNo, MessageBoxIcon.Exclamation, _
        MessageBoxDefaultButton.Button2)
    If button = DialogResult.No Then
        ' stop the form from closing
        e.Cancel = True
    End If
End Sub
```

**FIGURE 9.15**   How to use the FormClosing event procedure

The FormClosing event procedure shown in Example 1 in Figure 9.15 writes the contents of the dateLabel to the date.txt file. The FormClosing event procedure shown in Example 2 displays the "Do you want to exit?" message in a message box, along with Yes and No buttons. If the user clicks the No button in the message box, it indicates that he or she does not want to exit the application. In that case, the FormClosing event procedure should stop the computer from closing the MainForm. You prevent the computer from closing a form by setting the Cancel property of the FormClosing procedure's e parameter to True. This is accomplished using the statement `e.Cancel = True`, as shown in Example 2's code.

Next, you view an application that demonstrates what you have learned about sequential access files and the FormClosing event procedure.

## THE FRIENDS APPLICATION

Figure 9.16 shows a sample run of the Friends application, which you can use to record the names of your friends in a sequential access file. Figure 9.17 shows the application's code. (The code for both the exitButton's Click event procedure and the nameTextBox's Enter event procedure are collapsed in the figure.)

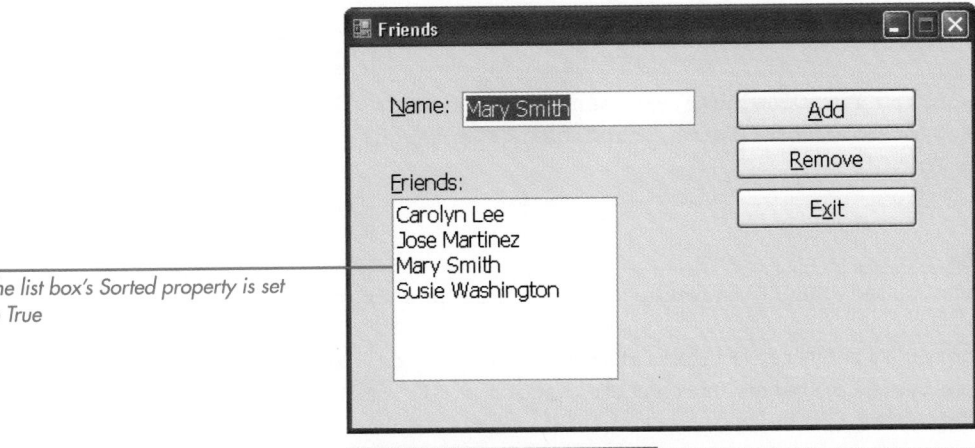

The list box's Sorted property is set to True

**FIGURE 9.16**  Sample run of the Friends application

### Visual Basic code

```
' Project name:        Friends Project
' Project purpose:     The project writes information to
'                      and reads information from a
'                      sequential access file.
' Created/revised by:  <your name> on <current date>

Option Explicit On
Option Strict On

Public Class MainForm

    Private Sub exitButton_Click ...

    Private Sub nameTextBox_Enter ...

    Private Sub addButton_Click(ByVal sender As Object, _
        ByVal e As System.EventArgs) Handles addButton.Click
        ' adds a name to the list box
```

**(Figure is continued on next page)**

```
            friendListBox.Items.Add(nameTextBox.Text)
            nameTextBox.Focus()
    End Sub

    Private Sub removeButton_Click(ByVal sender As Object, _
        ByVal e As System.EventArgs) Handles removeButton.Click
        ' removes a name from the list box

        If friendListBox.SelectedIndex > -1 Then
            friendListBox.Items.RemoveAt(friendListBox.SelectedIndex)
        End If
    End Sub

    Private Sub MainForm_FormClosing(ByVal sender As Object, _
        ByVal e As System.Windows.Forms.FormClosingEventArgs) _
        Handles Me.FormClosing
        ' writes the contents of the list box to the sequential access file

        Dim path As String = _
            "C:\VbReloaded\Chap09\Friends Solution\Friends Project\"

        If My.Computer.FileSystem.FileExists(path & "friends.txt") Then
            My.Computer.FileSystem.WriteAllText(path & "friends.txt", _
                String.Empty, False)
        End If

        For Each item As String In friendListBox.Items
            My.Computer.FileSystem.WriteAllText(path & "friends.txt", _
                item & ControlChars.NewLine, True)
        Next item
    End Sub

    Private Sub MainForm_Load(ByVal sender As Object, _
        ByVal e As System.EventArgs) Handles Me.Load
        ' reads names from a sequential access file and displays
        ' the names in a list box

        Dim path As String = _
            "C:\VbReloaded\Chap09\Friends Solution\Friends Project\"
        Dim text As String
        Dim name As String
        Dim newLineIndex As Integer
        Dim nameIndex As Integer

        ' clear the contents of the list box
        friendListBox.Items.Clear()

        If My.Computer.FileSystem.FileExists(path & "friends.txt") Then
            ' if the file exists, assign its contents to a variable
            text = My.Computer.FileSystem.ReadAllText(path & "friends.txt")
```

*(Figure is continued on next page)*

```
            ' search for the newline character that separates
            ' each name; continue the search until there are
            ' no more newline characters
            newLineIndex = text.IndexOf(ControlChars.NewLine, nameIndex)
            Do Until newLineIndex = -1
                ' the name begins with the character located in the
                ' nameIndex position; its length is the difference
                ' between the location of the newline
                ' character (newLineIndex) and the location of the
                ' first character in the name (nameIndex)
                name = text.Substring(nameIndex, newLineIndex - nameIndex)

                ' add the name to the list box
                friendListBox.Items.Add(name)

                ' start the next search after the newline
                ' character, which has a length of 2
                nameIndex = newLineIndex + 2
                newLineIndex = text.IndexOf(ControlChars.NewLine, nameIndex)
            Loop
        End If
    End Sub
End Class
```

**FIGURE 9.17**    Code for the Friends application

**TIP**

As you learned in Chapter 5, if no item is selected in a list box, the list box's SelectedIndex property contains the number −1.

Study the code shown in Figure 9.17. When the user clicks the Add button in the interface, the button's Click event procedure adds to the list box the name entered in the text box. When the user clicks the Remove button, the button's Click event procedure first verifies that a name is selected in the list box. If a name is selected, the procedure removes the selected name from the list box.

When the user clicks the Exit button in the interface, the computer processes the `Me.Close()` statement, which triggers the MainForm's FormClosing event. (Keep in mind that the FormClosing event is also triggered when the user clicks the Close button on the MainForm's title bar.) After assigning a folder path to a variable, the FormClosing event procedure determines whether the friends.txt file exists in the folder. If it does, the contents of the file are erased; this is accomplished by writing the empty string to the file. The For Each...Next statement in the procedure then writes the contents of the list box, one name at a time, to the friends.txt file. Notice that the newline character, which is represented by the `ControlChars.NewLine` constant, is appended to the end of each name before the name is written to the file. Appending the newline character to the end of the name ensures that each name will appear on a separate line in the file, as shown in Figure 9.18.

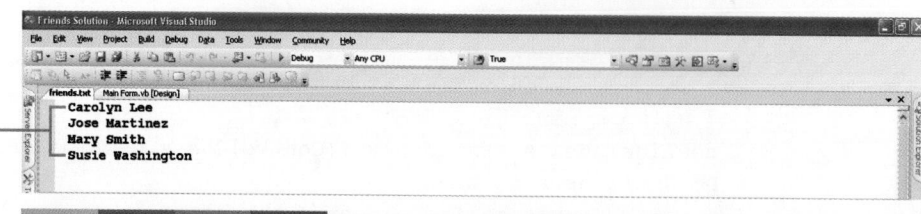

*Each name appears on a separate line in the file*

**FIGURE 9.18**    Contents of the friends.txt file

**TIP**

To view the contents of a file in a separate window in the IDE, click File on the menu bar, point to Open, and then click File. Open the folder containing the file, then click the filename, then click the Open button. To close the window, click its Close button.

Each time the application is started, the computer processes the code in the MainForm's Load event procedure (shown earlier in Figure 9.17). After declaring the necessary variables, the procedure clears the contents of the list box in the interface. It then uses the FileExists method to determine whether the friends.txt file exists. If the file exists, the procedure reads the contents of the file and assigns the contents to a String variable named `text`.

The `newLineIndex = text.IndexOf(ControlChars.NewLine, nameIndex)` statement that appears above the loop uses the IndexOf method to search for the newline character in the `text` variable. As you learned in Chapter 6, the IndexOf method's syntax is *string*.**IndexOf(***subString*[, *startIndex*]**)**, where *subString* is the string you are looking for, and *startIndex* specifies the starting position for the search. When the `newLineIndex = text.IndexOf(ControlChars.NewLine, nameIndex)` statement is processed, the `nameIndex` variable (which is used as the *startIndex* argument) contains the number zero. Therefore, the statement tells the computer to begin the search with the first character in the `text` variable. The computer stops searching when it locates the first newline character; it then assigns the character's index to the `newLineIndex` variable. If the first name in the file is Carolyn Lee, as shown in Figure 9.18, the statement assigns the number 11 to the `newLineIndex` variable because that is the index of the first newline character.

The `Do Until newLineIndex = -1` clause in the Load event procedure tells the computer to repeat the loop instructions until the IndexOf method returns the number –1, which indicates that the method did not find a newline character. The first instruction in the loop, `name = text.Substring(nameIndex, newLineIndex - nameIndex)`, uses the Substring method to access a name from the `text` variable. As you learned in Chapter 6, the syntax of the Substring method is *string*.**Substring(***startIndex*[, *count*]**)**, where *startIndex* is the index of the first character you want to access in the *string*, and *count* specifies the number of characters you want to access. Each time the loop instructions are processed, the statement assigns a name from the `text` variable to the `name` variable. The first time the `name = text.Substring(nameIndex, newLineIndex - nameIndex)` statement is processed, the `nameIndex` variable contains the number zero, and the `newLineIndex` variable contains the number 11. Therefore, the statement assigns the first 11 characters from the `text` variable (Carolyn Lee) to the `name` variable.

The second instruction in the loop, `friendListBox.Items.Add(name)`, adds the name "Carolyn Lee" to the friendListBox. The third instruction, `nameIndex = newLineIndex + 2`, updates the `nameIndex` variable, which keeps track of where the search for the next newline character should begin. In this case, it should begin with the character located immediately after the first newline character. Because the first newline character is located in index position 11, it would seem that the next search should begin with the character located in index position 12. So why is the `nameIndex` variable assigned a number that is two more than, rather than one more than, the value stored in the `newLineIndex` variable? Although the `ControlChars.NewLine` constant is referred to as the newline character, it actually consists of two characters: a carriage return and a line feed. In other words, the first newline character in the `text` variable actually takes up two index positions; in this case, it begins in position 11 and ends in position 12. To begin the next search with the character located immediately after the newline character, you need to add the number two (rather than the number one) to the newline character's index. In this case, for example, the next search will begin with the character whose index is 13. Using the information shown in Figure 9.18, the next search will begin with the letter J in the name Jose.

The last instruction in the loop, `newLineIndex = text.IndexOf (ControlChars.NewLine, nameIndex)`, tells the computer to search for the next newline character in the `text` variable. As already mentioned, the search will begin with the character whose index is 13.

You have completed the concepts section of Chapter 9. The next section is the Programming Tutorial section, which gives you step-by-step instructions on how to apply the chapter's concepts to an application. A Programming Example follows the Programming Tutorial. The Programming Example is a completed program that demonstrates the concepts taught in the chapter. Following the Programming Example are the Quick Review, Key Terms, Self-Check Questions and Answers, Review Questions, Review Exercises – Short Answer, Computer Exercises, and Case Projects sections.

# PROGRAMMING TUTORIAL

## Modified Car Race Game Application

In the Programming Tutorial section of Chapter 5, you created the Car Race Game application, which simulates a race between two cars. As you may remember, the application allows the user to guess the race results by selecting an item from a list box. The list box items are "Tie", "Red car wins", "White car wins", and "No guess". Recall that the "No guess" item is provided in case the user does not want to make a guess. The application keeps track of the number of times the user guesses the correct race results, as well as the number of times the user selects an incorrect race result. However, that information is lost when the user exits the application. In this tutorial, you modify the application so that it saves, in a sequential access file, the number of correct and incorrect guesses made by the user. The task of saving the information will be performed by the MainForm's FormClosing event procedure. Each time the application is started, the MainForm's Load event procedure will read the information from the file and display the information in the appropriate label controls in the interface. The Car Race Game application's user interface is shown in Figure 9.19.

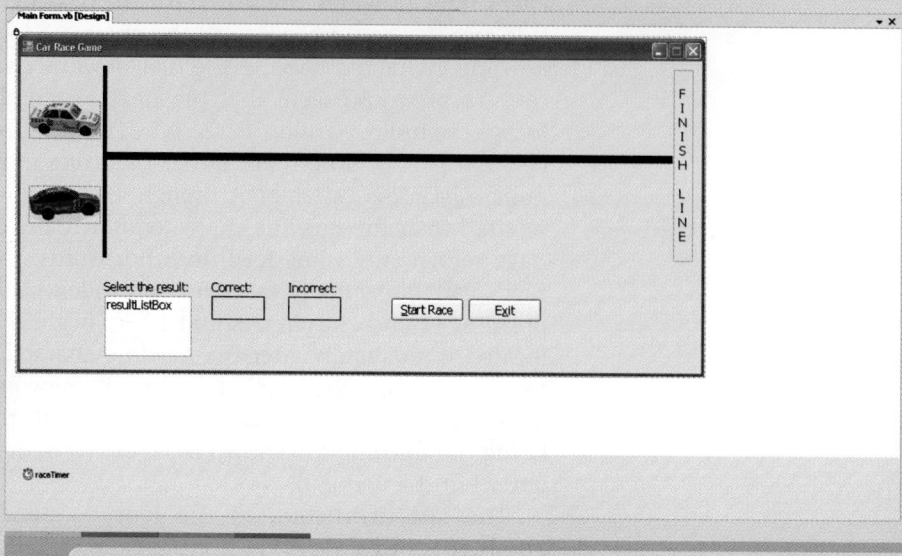

**FIGURE 9.19**  MainForm

## Modifying the Car Race Game Application

The first procedure you will code is the MainForm's FormClosing event procedure, which is responsible for saving the number of correct and incorrect guesses in a sequential access file.

**To code the MainForm's FormClosing event procedure:**

1. Start Visual Studio. If necessary, close the Start Page window.
2. Open the **Car Race Game Solution** (Car Race Game Solution.sln) file, which is contained in the VbReloaded\Chap09\Car Race Game Solution folder. The user interface shown earlier in Figure 9.19 appears on the screen.
3. Open the Code Editor window. Replace the <your name> and <current date> text in the comments with your name and the current date.
4. Click the **Class Name** list arrow, then click **(MainForm Events)** in the list. Click the **Method Name** list arrow, then click **FormClosing** in the list.

While the application is running, the number of correct responses is stored in the correctLabel, and the number of incorrect responses is stored in the incorrectLabel. Before the form is closed, the FormClosing event procedure should save the contents of the labels to the responses.txt file. You will use the ControlChars.Tab constant to separate the contents of the correctLabel from the contents of the incorrectLabel in the file. The **ControlChars.Tab constant** represents the Tab key on the computer keyboard.

5. Type **' saves the number of correct and incorrect responses** and press **Enter**, then type **' to the responses.txt sequential access file** and press **Enter** twice.
6. Type **my.computer.filesystem.writealltext("responses.txt", _** and press **Enter**. Press **Tab**, then type **correctlabel.text & controlchars.tab, false)** and press **Enter**.
7. Type **my.computer.filesystem.writealltext("responses.txt", _** and press **Enter**. Press **Tab**, then type **incorrectlabel.text, true)**.

Next, you will modify the code contained in the MainForm's Load event procedure. The procedure will now need to read the two numbers from the responses.txt file, displaying the first number in the correctLabel and displaying the second number in the incorrectLabel.

**To modify the MainForm's Load event procedure:**

1. Locate the MainForm's Load event procedure in the Code Editor window.
2. Position the cursor below the comment in the procedure. Type **' displays the number of correct and incorrect responses** and press **Enter**. Type **' stored in the responses.txt sequential access file** and press **Enter** twice.
3. Type **dim text as string** and press **Enter**. The text variable will store the contents of the responses.txt file.
4. Type **dim tabIndex as integer** and press **Enter**. The tabIndex variable will store the index of the ControlChars.Tab constant.
5. Insert two blank lines above the End Sub clause in the Load event procedure, then position the cursor in the blank line immediately above the End Sub clause.
6. Before telling the computer to read a file, it is a good programming practice to first verify that the file exists. Type **if my.computer.filesystem.fileexists("responses.txt") then** and press **Enter**.
7. If the responses.txt file exists, the procedure should read the file, assigning its contents to the text variable. Type **text = my.computer.filesystem.readalltext("responses.txt")** and press **Enter**.
8. Now locate the ControlChars.Tab character in the text variable, and assign its index to the tabIndex variable. Recall that the ControlChars.Tab constant separates the number of correct responses from the number of incorrect responses in the file. Type **tabIndex = text.indexof(controlchars.tab, 0)** and press **Enter**.
9. The value that precedes the ControlChars.Tab constant in the text variable represents the number of correct responses. Type **correctlabel.text = text.substring(0, tabindex)** and press **Enter**.
10. The value that follows the ControlChars.Tab constant in the text variable represents the number of incorrect responses. Type **incorrectlabel.text = text.substring(tabindex + 1)** and press **Enter**.
11. If the responses.txt file does not exist, the Load event procedure will display the number zero in the correctLabel and incorrectLabel. Type **else** and press **Enter**. Type **correctlabel.text = "0"** and press **Enter**, then type **incorrectlabel.text = "0"**.

Finally, you will modify the raceTimer's Tick event procedure. The procedure will now assign the contents of the correctLabel to the numberCorrect variable, and assign the contents of the incorrectLabel to the numberIncorrect variable.

**To modify the raceTimer's Tick event procedure:**

1. Locate the raceTimer's Tick event procedure in the Code Editor window.
2. Change the Static numberCorrect As Integer statement to **Static numberCorrect As Integer = Convert.ToInt32(correctLabel.Text)**.
3. Change the Static numberIncorrect As Integer statement to **Static numberIncorrect As Integer = Convert.ToInt32(incorrectLabel.Text)**.

Figure 9.20 shows the application's code. Changes made to the original code are shaded in the figure.

```vb
' Project name:        Car Race Game Project
' Project purpose:     The project simulates a car race. It allows thee
'                      user to select the race results from a list box. The
'                      project keeps track of the number of correct selections
'                      and the number of incorrect selections.
' Created/revised by:  <your name> on <current date>

Option Explicit On
Option Strict On

Public Class MainForm

    Private Sub exitButton_Click(ByVal sender As Object, _
        ByVal e As System.EventArgs) Handles exitButton.Click
        Me.Close()
    End Sub

    Private Sub MainForm_FormClosing(ByVal sender As Object, _
        ByVal e As System.Windows.Forms.FormClosingEventArgs) _
        Handles Me.FormClosing
        ' saves the number of correct and incorrect responses
        ' to the responses.txt sequential access file

        My.Computer.FileSystem.WriteAllText("responses.txt", _
            correctLabel.Text & ControlChars.Tab, False)
        My.Computer.FileSystem.WriteAllText("responses.txt", _
            incorrectLabel.Text, True)
    End Sub

    Private Sub MainForm_Load(ByVal sender As Object, _
        ByVal e As System.EventArgs) Handles Me.Load
        ' fills the list box with items, then selects the first item
        ' displays the number of correct and incorrect responses
        ' stored in the responses.txt sequential access file

        Dim text As String
        Dim tabIndex As Integer

        resultListBox.Items.Add("No guess")
        resultListBox.Items.Add("Tie")
        resultListBox.Items.Add("Red car wins")
        resultListBox.Items.Add("White car wins")
        resultListBox.SelectedIndex = 0

        If My.Computer.FileSystem.FileExists("responses.txt") Then
            text = My.Computer.FileSystem.ReadAllText("responses.txt")
            tabIndex = text.IndexOf(ControlChars.Tab, 0)
            correctLabel.Text = text.Substring(0, tabIndex)
            incorrectLabel.Text = text.Substring(tabIndex + 1)
```

*(Figure is continued on next page)*

```vbnet
        Else
            correctLabel.Text = "0"
            incorrectLabel.Text = "0"
        End If
    End Sub

    Private Sub startButton_Click(ByVal sender As Object, _
        ByVal e As System.EventArgs) Handles startButton.Click
        raceTimer.Enabled = True
    End Sub

    Private Sub raceTimer_Tick(ByVal sender As Object, _
        ByVal e As System.EventArgs) Handles raceTimer.Tick
        ' moves two cars from a starting line to a finish line on the form
        ' displays a message indicating the race results
        ' calculates and displays the number of times the user selects the
        ' correct race result from the resultListBox, and the number of
        ' times the user selects an incorrect race result

        Dim randomGenerator As New Random
        Dim whiteNewLocation As Integer
        Dim redNewLocation As Integer
        Dim raceResult As String
        Dim userChoice As String
        Dim finishLine As Integer = finishTextBox.Left + 1
        Static numberCorrect As Integer = Convert.ToInt32(correctLabel.Text)
        Static numberIncorrect As Integer = Convert.ToInt32(incorrectLabel.Text)

        ' save the user's list box selection, then disable the list box
        userChoice = resultListBox.SelectedItem.ToString
        resultListBox.Enabled = False

        ' calculate the new location of each picture box's right border
        ' don't allow the right border to go beyond the finish line
        whiteNewLocation = whitePictureBox.Right + randomGenerator.Next(0, 11)
        If whiteNewLocation > finishLine Then
            whiteNewLocation = finishLine
        End If
        redNewLocation = redPictureBox.Right + randomGenerator.Next(0, 11)
        If redNewLocation > finishLine Then
            redNewLocation = finishLine
        End If

        ' move each picture box toward the finish line
        whitePictureBox.SetBounds(whiteNewLocation - whitePictureBox.Width, _
            0, 0, 0, BoundsSpecified.X)
        redPictureBox.SetBounds(redNewLocation - redPictureBox.Width, _
            0, 0, 0, BoundsSpecified.X)
```

*(Figure is continued on next page)*

```
        ' the following selection structure is processed only when at least
        ' one of the picture boxes is at the finish line
        If whitePictureBox.Right = finishLine _
            OrElse redPictureBox.Right = finishLine Then
            ' disable the timer
            raceTimer.Enabled = False

            ' sound a beep to indicate the end of the race
            For x As Integer = 1 To 5
                Console.Beep(100, 100)
            Next x

            ' store the result of the race in a variable
            If whiteNewLocation = redNewLocation Then
                raceResult = "Tie"
            ElseIf whiteNewLocation > redNewLocation Then
                raceResult = "White car wins"
            Else
                raceResult = "Red car wins"
            End If

            ' display the race results
            MessageBox.Show("Race Over!" & ControlChars.NewLine & raceResult, _
                "Car Race", MessageBoxButtons.OK, MessageBoxIcon.Information)

            ' move the picture boxes back to the starting line
            whitePictureBox.SetBounds(12, 0, 0, 0, BoundsSpecified.X)
            redPictureBox.SetBounds(12, 0, 0, 0, BoundsSpecified.X)

            ' if the user did not want to guess the race results, then
            ' don't update or display the counter values; otherwise,
            ' compare the race results to the user's selection and update
            ' the appropriate counter, then display both counter values
            If userChoice <> "No guess" Then
                If raceResult = userChoice Then
                    numberCorrect = numberCorrect + 1
                Else
                    numberIncorrect = numberIncorrect + 1
                End If
                correctLabel.Text = Convert.ToString(numberCorrect)
                incorrectLabel.Text = Convert.ToString(numberIncorrect)
            End If

            ' enable the list box
            resultListBox.Enabled = True
        End If

    End Sub
End Class
```

**FIGURE 9.20**     Modified code for the Car Race Game application

Now that you have finished modifying the application's code, you will test the application to verify that it works correctly.

**To test the Car Race Game application:**

1. Close the Code Editor window. Save the solution, then start the application. Because the responses.txt file does not yet exist, the MainForm's Load event procedure displays the number zero in the correctLabel and incorrectLabel controls.
2. Click **Tie** in the list box, then click the **Start Race** button. Depending on the result of your car race, the number one appears in either the correctLabel or incorrectLabel.
3. When the race is over, click the **OK** button to close the Car Race message box.
4. Click **Red car wins** in the list box, then click the **Start Race** button.
5. Click the **OK** button to close the Car Race message box. Make a mental note of the numbers that appear in the correctLabel and incorrectLabel controls.
6. Click the **Exit** button to end the application. The `Me.Close()` statement in the exitButton's Click event procedure triggers the MainForm's FormClosing event. The code in the FormClosing event procedure writes the contents of the correctLabel and incorrectLabel to the responses.txt file.
7. If necessary, close the Output window.
8. Before starting the application again, view the contents of the responses.txt file. Click **File** on the menu bar, point to **Open**, and then click **File**. Open the VbReloaded\Chap09\Car Race Game Solution\Car Race Game Project\bin\Debug folder. Click **responses.txt** in the list of filenames, then click the **Open** button. The contents of the responses.txt file appear in a separate window in the IDE, as shown in Figure 9.21. (The two numbers in your file may be different from the ones shown in Figure 9.21.)

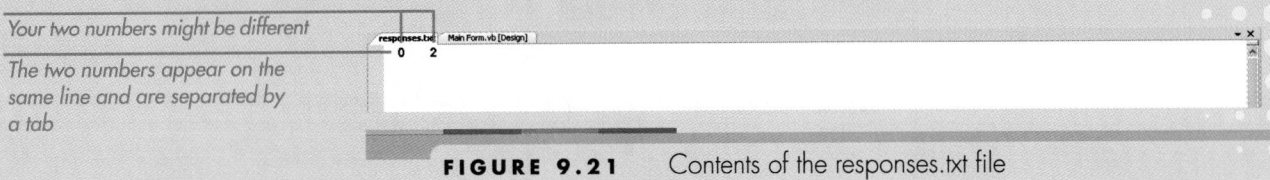

**FIGURE 9.21**   Contents of the responses.txt file

Notice that the two numbers appear on the same line in the responses.txt file. The first number represents the number of correct responses, and the second number represents the number of incorrect responses. A tab separates both numbers.

9. Click the **Close** button on the responses.txt window to close the window.
10. Start the application. Now that the responses.txt file exists, the MainForm's Load event procedure uses the information in the file to display the number of correct and incorrect responses in the appropriate label controls.
11. On your own, test the application several more times. When you are finished testing the application, close the Output window (if necessary), then close the solution.

# PROGRAMMING EXAMPLE

## Glovers Application

Glovers Industries stores the item numbers and prices of the items it sells in a sequential access file named itemInfo.txt. Opal Jacoby, the company's sales manager, wants an application that allows her to display the price of an item. Open the Glovers Solution (Glovers Solution.sln) file, which is contained in the

VbReloaded\Chap09\Glovers Solution folder. Open the itemInfo.txt file, which is contained in the VbReloaded\Chap09\Glovers Solution\Glovers Project folder. Notice that each item's number and price appear on a separate line in the file. Close the itemInfo.txt window, then complete the Glovers Industries application.

**TOE Chart:**

| Task | Object | Event |
|---|---|---|
| 1. Fill the items array with the item numbers and prices stored in the itemInfo.txt file<br>2. Fill the numbersListBox with the item numbers<br>3. Select the first item in the numbersListBox | MainForm | Load |
| Display the price of the item whose number is selected in the numbersListBox | numbersListBox | SelectedIndexChanged |
| End the application | exitButton | Click |

**FIGURE 9.22**

**User Interface:**

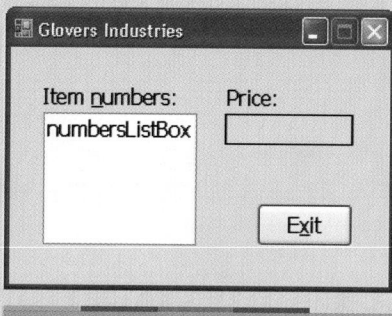

**FIGURE 9.23**

**Objects, Properties, and Settings:**

| Object | Property | Setting |
|---|---|---|
| MainForm | Size | 305, 212 |
| Label1 | Location<br>Text | 24, 27<br>Item &numbers: |
| Label2 | Location<br>Text | 169, 27<br>Price: |
| *(Figure is continued on next page)* | | |

| Label3 | Name | priceLabel |
|---|---|---|
| | AutoSize | False |
| | BorderStyle | FixedSingle |
| | Location | 169, 49 |
| | Size | 100, 23 |
| | Text | (empty) |
| | TextAlign | MiddleCenter |
| ListBox1 | Name | numbersListBox |
| | Location | 26, 49 |
| | Size | 120, 99 |
| | Sorted | False |
| Button1 | Name | exitButton |
| | Location | 194, 116 |
| | Size | 75, 32 |
| | Text | E&xit |

**FIGURE 9.24**

**Tab Order:**

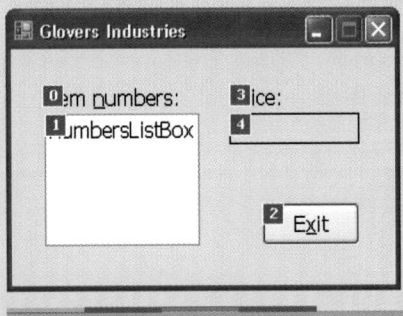

**FIGURE 9.25**

**Pseudocode:**

**exitButton Click event procedure**

1. close the application

**MainForm Load event procedure**

1. if the itemInfo.txt file exists

    assign the file's contents to the text variable

    repeat for subscripts of 0 through 4

        search for the newline character in the text variable and assign its index to the newLineIndex variable

        assign a line from the text variable to the record variable; the line begins with the first character in the item number and ends with the character immediately before the newline character

locate the comma in the record variable and assign its index to the commaIndex variable

assign all of the characters that appear to the left of the comma in the record variable to the number member of the items array

assign all of the characters that appear to the right of the comma in the record variable to the price member of the items array

add the item number to the numbersListBox

add 2 (which is the length of the newline character) to the recordIndex, which keeps track of where the next search for the newline character should begin

    end repeat

end if

### numbersListBox SelectedIndexChanged event procedure

1. display the price associated with the item number selected in the list box

### Code:

```
' Project name:        Glovers Project
' Project purpose:     The project displays the price of an item.
' Created/revised by:  <your name> on <current date>

Option Explicit On
Option Strict On

Public Class MainForm

    ' define the Product structure
    Structure Product
        Public number As String
        Public price As Decimal
    End Structure

    ' declare module-level array
    Private items(4) As Product

    Private Sub MainForm_Load(ByVal sender As Object, _
        ByVal e As System.EventArgs) Handles Me.Load
        ' fills the items array and numbersListBox
        ' with the data stored in a sequential access file

        Dim path As String = _
            "C:\VbReloaded\Chap09\Glovers Solution\Glovers Project\"
        Dim text As String
        Dim newLineIndex As Integer
        Dim recordIndex As Integer
```

*(Figure is continued on next page)*

```
        Dim record As String
        Dim commaIndex As Integer

        If My.Computer.FileSystem.FileExists(path & "itemInfo.txt") Then
            ' if the file exists, assign its contents to a variable
            text = My.Computer.FileSystem.ReadAllText(path & "itemInfo.txt")

            For subscript As Integer = 0 To 4
                ' locate the newline character in the text variable
                newLineIndex = _
                    text.IndexOf(ControlChars.NewLine, recordIndex)

                ' assign a line from the text variable to the record variable
                record = _
                    text.Substring(recordIndex, newLineIndex - recordIndex)

                ' locate the comma in the record variable
                commaIndex = record.IndexOf(",", 0)

                ' assign the item number and price to the array
                items(subscript).number = record.Substring(0, commaIndex)
                items(subscript).price = _
                    Convert.ToDecimal(record.Substring(commaIndex + 1))

                ' add the item number to the list box
                numbersListBox.Items.Add(items(subscript).number)

                ' update the record index by 2, which is the
                ' length of the ControlChars.NewLine constant
                recordIndex = newLineIndex + 2
            Next subscript
        End If

        ' select the first item in the list box
        numbersListBox.SelectedIndex = 0
    End Sub

    Private Sub numbersListBox_SelectedIndexChanged(ByVal sender As Object, _
        ByVal e As System.EventArgs) Handles numbersListBox.SelectedIndexChanged
        ' displays the price corresponding to the item selected
        ' in the list box

        priceLabel.Text = _
            items(numbersListBox.SelectedIndex).price.ToString("N2")
    End Sub

    Private Sub exitButton_Click(ByVal sender As Object, _
        ByVal e As System.EventArgs) Handles exitButton.Click
        Me.Close()
    End Sub
End Class
```

**FIGURE 9.26**

## Quick Review

- You can use the Structure statement to define a user-defined data type (or structure) in Visual Basic. You typically enter the Structure statement in the form's Declarations section in the Code Editor window.
- After defining a structure, you can use the structure to declare a structure variable.
- A structure variable contains one or more member variables. You access a member variable using the structure variable's name, followed by the dot member access operator and the member variable's name.
- The member variables contained in a structure variable can be used just like any other variables.
- A structure variable can be passed to procedures.
- You can create a one-dimensional array of structure variables. You access a member variable in an array element using the array's name, followed by the element's subscript enclosed in parentheses, the dot member access operator, and the member variable's name.
- An application can write information to a file and also read information from a file.
- The information in a sequential access file is always accessed in consecutive order (sequentially) from the beginning of the file through the end of the file.
- In Visual Basic, you can use the WriteAllText method to write text to a sequential access file. You can use the ReadAllText method to read the text contained in a sequential access file.
- You can use the Strings.Space method to write a specific number of spaces to a file.
- You can use the PadLeft and PadRight methods to align the text stored in a sequential access file.
- An error occurs when the computer attempts to read a non-existent file.
- You can use the FileExists method to determine whether a file exists. The method returns the Boolean value True if the file exists; otherwise, it returns the Boolean value False.
- The FormClosing event occurs when a form is about to be closed.
- You can use the FormClosing event procedure to prevent a form from being closed. To do so, you set the Cancel property of the procedure's e parameter to True.

## Key Terms

You use the **Structure statement** to create **user-defined data types** or **structures** in Visual Basic.

The variables contained in a **structure variable**, which is a variable declared using a structure (user-defined data type), are called **member variables**.

An application writes information to an **output file**, and reads information from an **input file**.

A **sequential access file** is composed of lines of text that are both stored and retrieved sequentially. A sequential access file is often referred to as a **text file**.

The **WriteAllText method** writes information to a sequential access file.

The **My feature** exposes a set of commonly used objects to the programmer.

The **My.Computer object** allows you to easily access other objects and methods used to manipulate files.

You can use the **Strings.Space method** to write a specific number of spaces to a file.

The **ReadAllText method** reads the text contained in a sequential access file.

You can use the **FileExists method** to determine whether a file exists.

A form's **FormClosing event** occurs when the computer processes the `Me.Close()` statement, and when the user clicks the Close button on the form's title bar.

## Self-Check Questions and Answers

1. You use the _____ statement to declare a user-defined data type.
   a. Declare
   b. Define
   c. Structure
   d. UserType

2. In most applications, the code to define a user-defined data type is entered in the form's _____.
   a. Declarations section
   b. Definition section
   c. Load event procedure
   d. User-defined section

3. Which of the following statements assigns the string "Maple" to the `street` member variable within a structure variable named `address`?
   a. `address&street = "Maple"`
   b. `address.street = "Maple"`
   c. `street.address = "Maple"`
   d. None of the above.

4. An array is declared using the following statement: `Dim inventory(4) As Product`. Which of the following statements assigns the number 100 to the `quantity` member variable contained in the last array element?
   a. `inventory.quantity(4) = 100`
   b. `inventory(4).Product.quantity = 100`
   c. `inventory(3).quantity = 100`
   d. None of the above.

5. Which of the following statements writes the contents of the addressTextBox to a sequential access files named address.txt, replacing the file's existing text?
   a. `My.Computer.FileSystem.WriteAll("address.txt", addressTextBox.Text, False)`
   b. `My.Computer.FileSystem.WriteAllText("address.txt", addressTextBox.Text, False)`
   c. `My.Computer.FileSystem.WriteAllText("address.txt", addressTextBox.Text, True)`
   d. `My.Computer.FileSystem.WriteText("address.txt", addressTextBox.Text, Replace)`

6. Which of the following statements reads the contents of a sequential access file named address.txt, and assigns the contents to a String variable named `fileContents`?
   a. `fileContents = My.Computer.File.Read("address.txt")`
   b. `fileContents = My.Computer.File.ReadAll("address.txt")`
   c. `fileContents =`
      `My.Computer.FileSystem.ReadAll("address.txt")`
   d. `fileContents =`
      `My.Computer.FileSystem.ReadAllText("address.txt")`

7. Which of the following clauses verifies the existence of a sequential access file named address.txt?
   a. `If My.FileExists("address.txt") Then`
   b. `If My.Computer.FileExists("address.txt") Then`
   c. `If My.Computer.FileSystem.FileExists("address.txt") Then`
   d. None of the above.

8. The _____ event occurs when the computer processes the `Me.Close()` statement, and when the user clicks the Close button on the form's title bar.
   a. FormClosing
   b. FormFinish
   c. Finish
   d. None of the above.

9. You can prevent a form from being closed by setting the _____ property of the e parameter to True.
   a. Cancel
   b. CancelClose
   c. Open
   d. None of the above.

10. An error occurs when the computer attempts to write to a file that does not exist.
    a. True
    b. False

Answers: 1) c, 2) a, 3) b, 4) d, 5) b, 6) d, 7) c, 8) a, 9) a, 10) b

## Review Questions

1. Which of the following statements declares a Country variable named spain?
   a. `Private spain As Country`
   b. `Dim spain As Country`
   c. `Dim Country As spain`
   d. Both a and b.

2. Which of the following statements assigns the string "Madrid" to the city member of a Country variable named spain?
   a. `city.spain = "Madrid"`
   b. `Country.city = "Madrid"`
   c. `Country.spain.city = "Madrid"`
   d. `spain.city = "Madrid"`

3. An application uses a structure named Employee. Which of the following statements creates a five-element, one-dimensional array of Employee structure variables?
   a. `Dim workers(4) As Employee`
   b. `Dim workers(5) As Employee`
   c. `Dim workers As Employee(4)`
   d. `Dim workers As Employee(5)`

4. Each structure variable in the `items` array contains two members: a String variable named `number` and an Integer variable named `quantity`. Which of the following statements assigns the inventory number "123XY" to the first element in the array?
   a. `items(0).number = "123XY"`
   b. `items(1).number = "123XY"`
   c. `items.number(0) = "123XY"`
   d. `items.number(1) = "123XY"`

5. If the specified file does not exist, the _____ method results in an error when the computer processes it.
   a. AddText
   b. AppendText
   c. ReadText
   d. None of the above.

6. Which of the following can be used to write the string "Your pay is $56" to a sequential access file? The file's name is stored in the `file` variable. The pay variable contains the number 56.
   a. `My.Computer.FileSystem.WriteAllText(file, "Your pay is $", False)`
      `My.Computer.FileSystem.WriteAllText(file, pay.ToString(), True)`
   b. `My.Computer.FileSystem.WriteAllText(file, "Your pay is $" & pay.ToString(), False)`
   c. `My.Computer.FileSystem.WriteAllText(file, "Your ", False)`
      `My.Computer.FileSystem.WriteAllText(file, "pay is ", True)`
      `My.Computer.FileSystem.WriteAllText(Convert.ToString(pay), True)`
   d. All of the above.

7. Which of the following statements can be used to write 15 space characters to a sequential access file named msg.txt?
   a. `My.Computer.FileSystem.WriteAllText("msg.txt", Blank(15, " "), True)`
   b. `My.Computer.FileSystem.WriteAllText("msg.txt", Chars(15, " "), True)`
   c. `My.Computer.FileSystem.WriteAllText("msg.txt", Strings.Space(15, " "), True)`
   d. `My.Computer.FileSystem.WriteAllText("msg.txt", Strings.Space(15), True)`

8.  Which of the following reads the text from a sequential access file, and assigns the text to the `text` variable? The file's name is stored in the `file` variable.
    a.  `My.Computer.FileSystem.ReadText(file, text)`
    b.  `My.Computer.FileSystem.ReadAllText(file, text)`
    c.  `text = My.Computer.FileSystem.ReadText(file)`
    d.  `text = My.Computer.FileSystem.ReadAllText(file)`

9.  Which of the following clauses can be used to determine whether the employ.txt file exists?
    a.  `If FileExists("employ.txt") Then`
    b.  `If My.FileExists("employ.txt") Then`
    c.  `If My.Computer.FileSystem.FileExists("employ.txt") Then`
    d.  None of the above.

10. When entered in the FormClosing event, which of the following statements keeps the form open?
    a.  `e.Cancel = True`
    b.  `e.Cancel = False`
    c.  `e.Open = True`
    d.  `e.Open = False`

## Review Exercises – Short Answer

1.  Write a Structure statement that defines a structure named Book. The structure contains two String member variables named `title` and `author`, and a Decimal member variable named `cost`.

2.  Write a Structure statement that defines a structure named Tape. The structure contains three String member variables named `name`, `artist`, and `songLength`, and an Integer member variable named `songNum`.

3.  Write a Private statement that declares a Book variable named `fiction`.

4.  Write a Dim statement that declares a Tape variable named `blues`.

5.  An application contains the following Structure statement:

```
Structure Computer

        Public model As String

        Public cost As Decimal

End Structure
```

    a.  Write a Dim statement that declares a Computer variable named homeUse.
    b.  Write an assignment statement that assigns the string "IB-50" to the model member variable.
    c.  Write an assignment statement that assigns the number 2400 to the cost member variable.

6. An application contains the following Structure statement:

```
Structure Friend

        Public last As String

        Public first As String

End Structure
```

   a. Write a Dim statement that declares a Friend variable named `school`.
   b. Write an assignment statement that assigns the value in the firstTextBox to the `first` member variable.
   c. Write an assignment statement that assigns the value in the lastTextBox to the `last` member variable.
   d. Write an assignment statement that assigns the value in the `last` member variable to the lastLabel.
   e. Write an assignment statement that assigns the value in the `first` member variable to the firstLabel.

7. An application contains the following Structure statement:

```
Structure Computer

        Public model As String

        Public cost As Decimal

End Structure
```

   a. Write a Private statement that declares a 10-element, one-dimensional array of Computer variables. Name the array `business`.
   b. Write an assignment statement that assigns the string "HPP405" to the `model` member variable contained in the first array element.
   c. Write an assignment statement that assigns the number 3600 to the `cost` member variable contained in the first array element.

8. An application contains the following Structure statement:

```
Structure Friend

        Public last As String

        Public first As String

End Structure
```

   a. Write a Private statement that declares a 5-element, one-dimensional array of Friend variables. Name the array `home`.
   b. Write an assignment statement that assigns the value in the firstTextBox to the `first` member variable contained in the last array element.
   c. Write an assignment statement that assigns the value in the lastTextBox to the `last` member variable contained in the last array element.

9. Write the string "Employee" and the string "Name" to a sequential access file named report.txt. Each string should appear on a separate line in the file.

10. Write the contents of a String variable named `capital`, followed by 20 spaces, the contents of a string variable named `state`, and the ControlChars.NewLine constant to a sequential access file named geography.txt.

11. Write the statement to assign the contents of the report.txt file to a String variable named `text`.

12. Write the statement to assign the contents of the report.txt file to the reportTextBox.

13. Write the code to determine whether the jansales.txt file exists. If it does, the code should display the string "File exists" in the messageLabel; otherwise, it should display the string "File does not exist" in the messageLabel.

14. What are the three central objects exposed by the My feature, and what is the purpose of each?

15. In Figure 9.17 in the chapter, the code in the FormClosing event erases the contents of the friends.txt file when the file exists. Rather than erase the contents of the file, you also can delete the file. Write the statement to delete the friends.txt file.

## Computer Exercises

1. In this exercise, you code an application that uses a structure.
   a. Open the Pool Solution (Pool Solution.sln) file, which is contained in the VbReloaded\Chap09\Pool Solution folder.
   b. Open the Code Editor window, which contains the code shown in Figure 9.5 in the chapter. Currently, the code does not use a structure.
   c. Use Figure 9.6 in the chapter to modify the application's code so that it uses a structure.
   d. Save the solution, and then start and test the application.
   e. Click the Exit button to end the application, then close the solution.

2. In this exercise, you code an application that uses an array of structure variables.
   a. Open the Price List Solution (Price List Solution.sln) file, which is contained in the VbReloaded\Chap09\Price List Solution folder.
   b. Code the application using the code shown in Figure 9.8 in the chapter.
   c. Save the solution, and then start and test the application.
   d. Click the Exit button to end the application, then close the solution.

3. In this exercise, you code an application that writes information to a sequential access file.
   a. Open the Employee List Solution (Employee List Solution.sln) file, which is contained in the VbReloaded\Chap09\Employee List Solution folder.
   b. The Write button should write the contents of the nameTextBox to a sequential access file named names.txt. Each name should appear on a separate line in the file. Save the names.txt file in the VbReloaded\Chap09\Employee List Solution\Employee List Project folder.
   c. Save the solution, and then start the application. Test the application by writing five names to the file, then click the Exit button to end the application.
   d. Open the names.txt file to verify that it contains five names. Close the names.txt window, then close the solution.

4. In this exercise, you code an application that writes information to a sequential access file.
   a. Open the Memo Solution (Memo Solution.sln) file, which is contained in the VbReloaded\Chap09\Memo Solution folder.
   b. The Write button should write the contents of the memoTextBox to a sequential access file named memo.txt. Save the memo.txt file in the VbReloaded\Chap09\Memo Solution\Memo Project folder.
   c. Save the solution, and then start the application. Test the application by writing the following memo to the file:

   To all employees:

   The annual picnic will be held at Rogers Park on Saturday, July 13. Bring your family for a day full of fun!

   Carolyn Meyer
   Personnel Manager

   d. Click the Exit button to end the application.
   e. Open the memo.txt file to verify that it contains the memo. Close the memo.txt window, then close the solution.

5. In this exercise, you code an application that writes information to a sequential access file.
   a. Open the Report Solution (Report Solution.sln) file, which is contained in the VbReloaded\Chap09\Report Solution folder.
   b. Open the Code Editor window. The application uses an array to store three state names and their corresponding sales. Code the application so that it creates the report shown in Example 3 in Figure 9.10. Save the report in a sequential access file named report.txt. Save the report.txt file in the VbReloaded\Chap09\Report Solution\Report Project folder.
   c. Save the solution, and then start and test the application.
   d. Click the Exit button to end the application.
   e. Open the report.txt file to verify that it contains the report. Close the report.txt window, then close the solution.

6. In this exercise, you code an application that writes information to and reads information from a sequential access file.
   a. Create the Friends interface shown in Figure 9.16. Name the solution Friends Solution. Name the project Friends Project. Save the application in the VbReloaded\Chap09 folder.
   b. Use the code shown in Figure 9.17 to code the application. If necessary, change the path to the file.
   c. Save the solution, and then start the application. Test the application by entering six names, then removing the second name.
   d. Click the Exit button to end the application.
   e. Open the friends.txt file to verify that it contains five names.
   f. Close the friends.txt window, then close the solution.

7. In this exercise, you modify the application that you created in Computer Exercise 3. The modified application allows the user to either create a new file or append information to the end of an existing file.
   a. Use Windows to make a copy of the Employee List Solution folder, which is contained in the VbReloaded\Chap09 folder. Rename the copy Modified Employee List Solution.
   b. Use Windows to delete the names.txt file contained in the VbReloaded\Chap09\Modified Employee List Solution\Employee List Project folder.

c. Open the Employee List Solution (Employee List Solution.sln) file contained in the VbReloaded\Chap09\Modified Employee List Solution folder.

d. When the writeButton's Click event procedure is processed the first time, the procedure should determine whether the names.txt file exists in the VbReloaded\Chap09\Modified Employee List Solution\Employee List Project folder. If the file exists, the procedure should use the MessageBox.Show method to ask the user whether he or she wants to replace the existing file. Include Yes and No buttons in the message box. If the user clicks the Yes button, then replace the existing file; otherwise, append to the existing file.

e. Save the solution, then start the application. Type Helen in the Name text box, and then click the Write button.

f. Click the Exit button to end the application, then start the application again. Type Ginger in the Name text box, and then click the Write button. The application should ask if you want to replace the existing file. Click the No button.

g. Click the Exit button to end the application, then use the File menu to open the names.txt file in a window. The file should contain two names: Helen and Ginger. Close the names.txt window.

h. Start the application again. Type George in the Name text box, and then click the Write button. The application should ask if you want to replace the existing file. Click the Yes button.

i. Click the Exit button to end the application, then use the File menu to open the names.txt file in a window. The file should contain one name: George. Close the names.txt window, then close the solution.

8. In this exercise, you make another modification to the Car Race Game application, which you modified in the chapter's Programming Tutorial.

a. Use Windows to make a copy of the Car Race Game Solution folder, which is contained in the VbReloaded\Chap09 folder. Rename the copy Modified Car Race Game Solution.

b. Open the Car Race Game Solution (Car Race Game Solution.sln) file contained in the VbReloaded\Chap09\Modified Car Race Game Solution folder. Modify the FormClosing event procedure so that it asks the user whether he or she wants to exit the application. If the user chooses to exit, the procedure should ask the user if he or she wants to save the number of correct and incorrect responses.

c. Save the solution, then start and test the application.

d. Click the Exit button to end the application, then close the solution.

9. In this exercise, you update the contents of a sequential access file.

a. Open the Pay Solution (Pay Solution.sln) file, which is contained in the VbReloaded\Chap09\Pay Solution folder.

b. Open the payrates.txt file, which is contained in the VbReloaded\Chap09\Pay Solution\Pay Project folder. View the file's contents, then close the payrates.txt window.

c. Code the Increase button's Click event procedure so that it increases each pay rate by 10%. Save the increased prices in a sequential access file named updated.txt. Save the file in the VbReloaded\Chap09\Pay Solution\Pay Project folder.

d. Save the solution, then start the application. Click the Increase button to update the pay rates.

e. Click the Exit button to end the application.

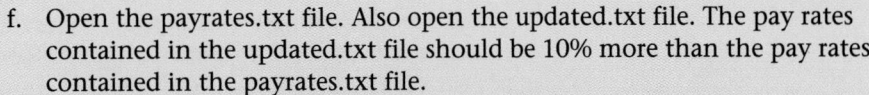

    f.  Open the payrates.txt file. Also open the updated.txt file. The pay rates contained in the updated.txt file should be 10% more than the pay rates contained in the payrates.txt file.

    g.  Close the updated.txt and payrates.txt windows, then close the solution.

10.  In this exercise, you find and correct an error in an application. The process of finding and correcting errors is called debugging.

    a.  Open the Debug Solution (Debug Solution.sln) file, which is contained in the VbReloaded\Chap09\Debug Solution folder.

    b.  Open the Code Editor window. Review the existing code.

    c.  Start and test the application. Notice that the application is not working correctly.

    d.  Correct the application's code, then save the solution.

    e.  Start and test the application. When the application is working correctly, close the solution.

## Case Projects

### Warren High School

This year, three students are running for senior class president: Mark Stone, Sheima Patel, and Sam Perez. Create an application that allows the current class president to keep track of the voting. Save the voting information in a sequential access file. The application also should display the number of votes per candidate.

### WKRK-Radio

Each year, WKRK-Radio polls its audience to determine which Super Bowl commercial was the best. The choices are as follows: Budweiser, FedEx, MasterCard, and Pepsi. The station manager has asked you to create an application that allows him to enter a caller's choice. The choice should be saved in a sequential access file. The application also should display the number of votes for each commercial.

### Shoe Circus

Shoe Circus sells 10 styles of children's shoes. The style numbers and prices are stored in a sequential access file named shoeinfo.txt. The file is contained in the VbReloaded\Chap09\Shoe Circus Solution\Shoe Circus Project folder. The store manager has asked you to create an application that she can use to enter a style number and then display the style's price. Use an array of structure variables to store the style number and price information for the 10 shoe styles.

### Revellos

Revellos has stores located in several states. The sales manager has asked you to create an application that he can use to enter the following information for each store: the store number, the state in which the store is located, and the name of the store manager. The application should save the information in a sequential access file. Each store's information should appear on a separate line in the file. In other words, the first store's number, state name, and manager name should appear on the first line in the file. The application also should allow the sales manager to enter a store number, and then display the state in which the store is located and the store manager's name. Use the following data:

| Number | State | Manager |
|--------|-------|---------|
| 1004 | Texas | Jeffrey Jefferson |
| 1005 | Texas | Paula Hendricks |
| 1007 | Arizona | Jake Johansen |
| 1010 | Arizona | Henry Abernathy |
| 1011 | California | Barbara Millerton |
| 1013 | California | Inez Baily |
| 1015 | California | Sung Lee |
| 1016 | California | Lou Chan |
| 1017 | California | Homer Gomez |
| 1019 | New Mexico | Ingrid Nadkarni |

# CHAPTER

# 10 Creating Classes and Objects

After studying Chapter 10, you should be able to:

- Define a class
- Instantiate an object from a class that you define
- Add Property procedures to a class
- Include data validation in a class
- Create default and parameterized constructors
- Include methods in a class
- Overload the methods in a class
- Create a derived class using inheritance

## CLASSES AND OBJECTS

As you learned in Chapter 1, object-oriented programs are based on objects that are instantiated (created) from classes. Each object is an instance of the class from which it is created. A text box, for example, is an instance of the TextBox class. Similarly, buttons and labels are instances of the Button class and Label class, respectively.

Recall that a class encapsulates (contains) the attributes (properties) that describe the object it creates, and the behaviors (methods) that allow the object to perform tasks. The TextBox class, for instance, contains the Name, CharacterCasing, and Text properties. Examples of methods contained in the TextBox class include Focus and SelectAll.

In previous chapters, you instantiated objects using classes that are built into Visual Basic, such as the TextBox and Label classes. You used the instantiated objects in a variety of ways in many different applications. For example, in some applications you used a text box to enter a name, while in other applications you used it to enter a sales tax rate. Similarly, you used label controls to identify text boxes and also to display the result of calculations. The ability to use an object for more than one purpose saves programming time and money—an advantage that contributes to the popularity of object-oriented programming.

In addition to using the classes built into Visual Basic, you also can define your own classes and then create instances (objects) from those classes. The classes that you define can represent something encountered in real life, such as a credit card receipt, a check, and an employee.

**TIP**

Recall from Chapter 1 that each tool in the toolbox represents a class. When you drag a tool from the toolbox to the form, the computer uses the class to instantiate the appropriate object.

## DEFINING A CLASS

Like the Visual Basic classes, your classes must specify the attributes and behaviors of the objects they create. The attributes describe the characteristics of the objects, and the behaviors specify the tasks that the objects can perform.

You use the **Class statement** to define a class in Visual Basic. Figure 10.1 shows the syntax of the Class statement and includes an example of using the statement to create a class named TimeCard.

---

**HOW TO...**     **Define a Class**

**Syntax**
**Public Class** *classname*
    *attributes section*
    *behaviors section*
**End Class**

**Example**
```
Public Class TimeCard
    variables and Property procedures appear in the attributes section
    Sub and Function procedures, referred to as methods, appear in the
    behaviors section
End Class
```

**FIGURE 10.1**    How to define a class

The Class statement begins with the keywords `Public Class`, followed by the name of the class; it ends with the keywords `End Class`. Although it is not required by the syntax, the convention is to enter the class name using Pascal case, which means that you capitalize the first letter in the name and the first letter in any subsequent words in the name. The names of Visual Basic classes (for example, String and TextBox) also follow this naming convention.

Within the Class statement, you define the attributes and behaviors of the class. The attributes are represented by variables and Property procedures, and the behaviors are represented by Sub and Function procedures, more commonly referred to as methods. You learn various ways of defining the attributes and behaviors later in this chapter.

You enter the Class statement in a class file. Figure 10.2 shows how to add a class file to the current project, and Figure 10.3 shows an example of a completed Add New Item – *projectname* dialog box.

## HOW TO...

### Add a Class File to the Current Project

1. Click Project on the menu bar.
2. Click Add Class. The Add New Item – *projectname* dialog box opens with Class selected in the Visual Studio installed templates box.
3. Type the name of the class followed by a period and the letters vb in the Name box.
4. Click the Add button.

**FIGURE 10.2**    How to add a class file to the current project

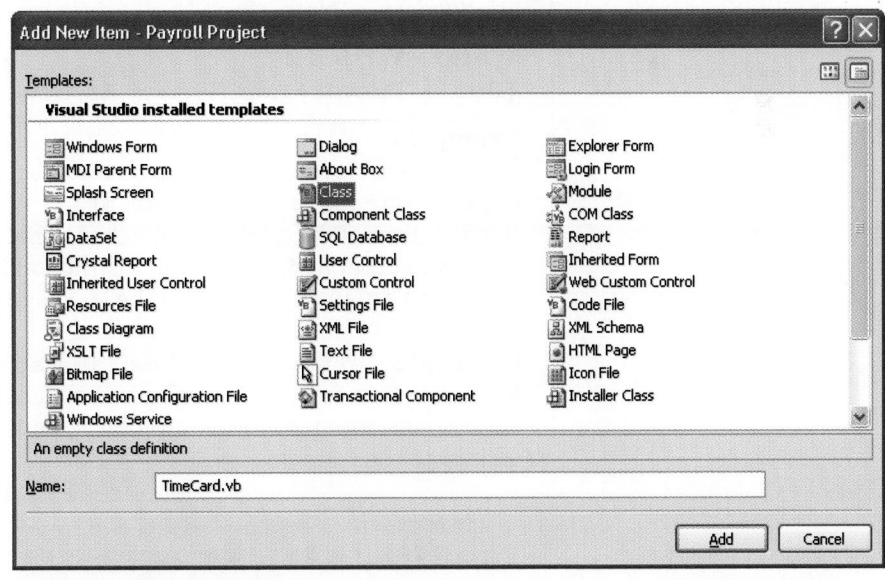

**FIGURE 10.3**    Completed Add New Item – *projectname* dialog box

When you click the Add button in the Add New Item – Payroll Project dialog box shown in Figure 10.3, the computer adds a file named TimeCard.vb to the current project. It also opens the file in the Code Editor window, as shown in Figure 10.4.

Form filename

Class filename

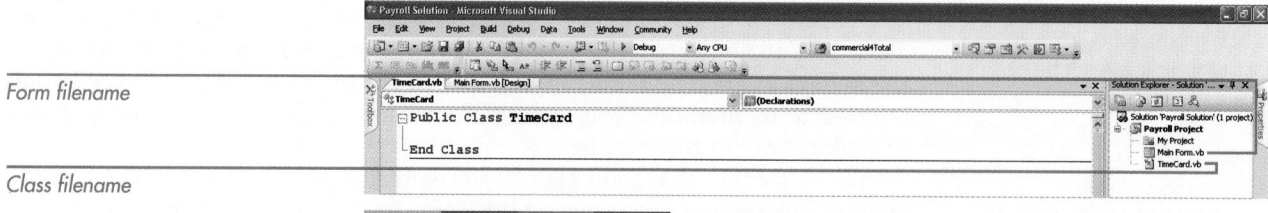

**FIGURE 10.4**   TimeCard.vb file opened in the Code Editor window

The Code Editor automatically enters the Class statement in the class file. You complete the Class statement by entering the attributes and behaviors of the class. (Recall that you learn how to enter the attributes and behaviors later in this chapter.)

After you define a class, you then can use the class to instantiate one or more objects. Figure 10.5 shows two versions of the syntax you use to instantiate an object from a class. It also includes an example of using each version.

## HOW TO...

### Instantiate an Object From a Class

**Syntax - Version 1**
**{Dim | Private}** *objectVariable* **As** *class*
*objectVariable* **= New** *class*

**Syntax - Version 2**
**{Dim | Private}** *objectVariable* **As New** *class*

**Examples**
```
Private employeeTimeCard As TimeCard
employeeTimeCard = New TimeCard
```
the first instruction creates a TimeCard variable named `employeeTimeCard`; the second instruction instantiates a TimeCard object and assigns its address to the `employeeTimeCard` variable

```
Dim employeeTimeCard As New TimeCard
```
the instruction creates a TimeCard variable named `employeeTimeCard` and also instantiates a TimeCard object, and it assigns the object's address to the variable

**FIGURE 10.5**   How to instantiate an object from a class

In both versions of the syntax for instantiating an object, *class* is the name of the class the computer will use to instantiate the object, and *objectVariable* is the name of a variable that will store the object's address. You use the `Dim` keyword to create a procedure-level *objectVariable*. To create a module-level *objectVariable*, you use the `Private` keyword.

Example 1—Using a Class that Contains Public Variables Only **601**

The first example in Figure 10.5 uses Version 1 of the syntax. The `Private employeeTimeCard As TimeCard` statement creates a module-level variable named `employeeTimeCard` that can store the address of a TimeCard object. The `employeeTimeCard = New TimeCard` statement in the example uses the TimeCard class to instantiate a TimeCard object, and it assigns the object's address to the `employeeTimeCard` variable.

The second example in Figure 10.5 uses Version 2 of the syntax. In the example, the `Dim employeeTimeCard As New TimeCard` statement creates a variable named `employeeTimeCard`. It also uses the TimeCard class to instantiate a TimeCard object, assigning the object's address to the variable. Notice that the difference between both versions of the syntax used to instantiate an object relates to when the object is actually created. In Visual Basic, the statement containing the `New` keyword creates the object.

The easiest way to learn how to define classes and instantiate objects is to view examples of doing so. You begin with a simple example of a class that contains attributes only. In the example, each of the class's attributes is represented by a Public variable.

## EXAMPLE 1—USING A CLASS THAT CONTAINS PUBLIC VARIABLES ONLY

The sales manager at Sweets Unlimited wants an application that allows him to save each salesperson's name, sales amount, and bonus amount in a sequential access file. Notice that each salesperson is associated with three items of information: a name, a sales amount, and a bonus amount. In the context of object-oriented programming (OOP), each salesperson can be treated as an object having three attributes. By including the attributes in the Class statement, you can create a pattern that any application can use to instantiate a salesperson object. In this case, the Sweets Unlimited application will use a salesperson object to store each salesperson's information before writing the information to the sequential access file. Figure 10.6 shows the Salesperson class defined in a class file named Salesperson.vb file.

*Defines the Salesperson class*

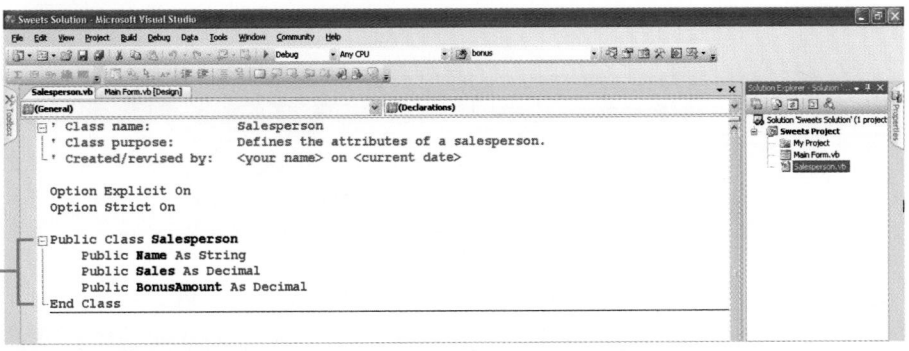

**FIGURE 10.6**  Salesperson class defined in the Salesperson.vb file

Notice that the Salesperson.vb file contains the `Option Explicit On` and `Option Strict On` statements. As is true when coding a form, it's a good programming practice to enter both Option statements when coding a class. The `Option Explicit On` and `Option Strict On` statements have the same meaning in a class file as they do in a form file.

The Salesperson class shown in Figure 10.6 contains three attributes; each attribute is represented by a Public variable. When a variable in a class is declared using the `Public` keyword, it can be accessed by any application that contains an instance of the class. In this case, the variables included in the Salesperson class can be used by any application that instantiates a Salesperson object.

Notice that, unlike most variable names, the variable names in the Salesperson class are not entered using camel case. This is because the convention is to use Pascal case for the names of the Public variables in a class.

Figure 10.7 shows the interface for the Sweets Unlimited application, and Figure 10.8 shows a sample of the sequential access file created by the application. Figure 10.9 shows the code for the Sweets Unlimited application.

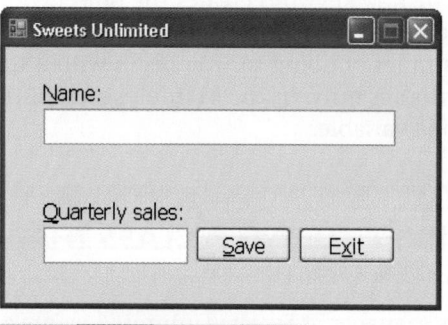

**FIGURE 10.7**    Interface for the Sweets Unlimited application

*Sales amounts*

*Names*

*5% bonus amounts*

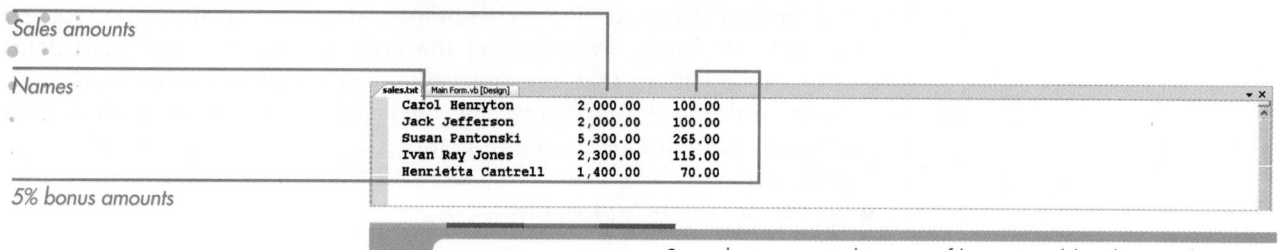

| sales.txt | Main Form.vb [Design] |
| --- | --- |

```
Carol Henryton      2,000.00    100.00
Jack Jefferson      2,000.00    100.00
Susan Pantonski     5,300.00    265.00
Ivan Ray Jones      2,300.00    115.00
Henrietta Cantrell  1,400.00     70.00
```

**FIGURE 10.8**    Sample sequential access file created by the application

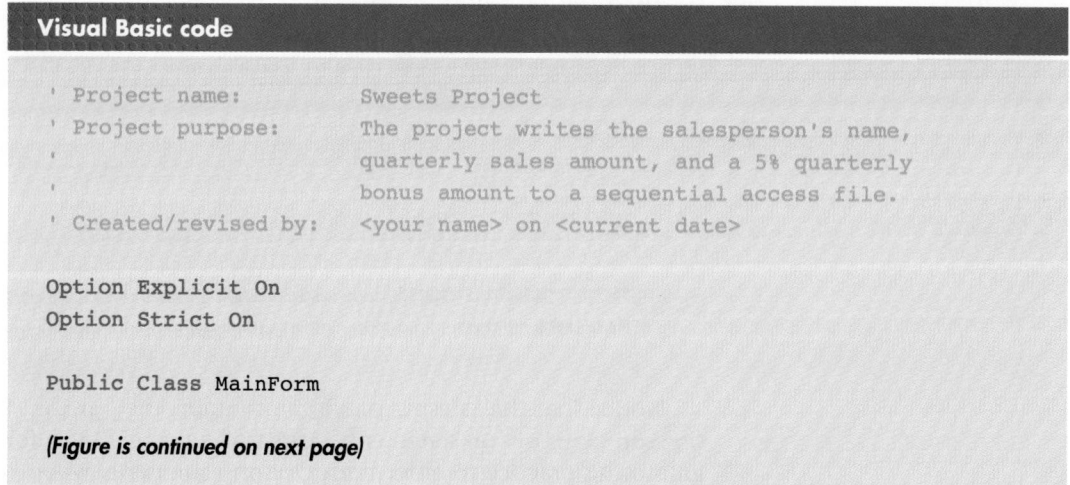

**Visual Basic code**

```
' Project name:        Sweets Project
' Project purpose:     The project writes the salesperson's name,
'                      quarterly sales amount, and a 5% quarterly
'                      bonus amount to a sequential access file.
' Created/revised by:  <your name> on <current date>

Option Explicit On
Option Strict On

Public Class MainForm
```

**(Figure is continued on next page)**

Example 1—Using a Class that Contains Public Variables Only                                        **603**

*These three procedures are collapsed*

```
      ┌─ Private Sub exitButton_Click...

      ├─ Private Sub nameTextBox_Enter...

      └─ Private Sub salesTextBox_Enter...

         Private Sub saveButton_Click(ByVal sender As Object, _
             ByVal e As System.EventArgs) Handles saveButton.Click
             ' saves the sales information to a sequential access file

             Dim path As String = _
                 "C:\VbReloaded\Chap10\Sweets Solution\Sweets Project\"
         ──  Dim ourEmployee As New Salesperson
             Dim isConverted As Boolean

             If nameTextBox.Text <> String.Empty _
                AndAlso salesTextBox.Text <> String.Empty Then
                ' if both text boxes contain data, assign the
                ' name and sales amount (converted to Decimal)
                ' to the ourEmployee object
           ┌─  ourEmployee.Name = nameTextBox.Text
           │   isConverted = _
           │      Decimal.TryParse(salesTextBox.Text, ourEmployee.Sales)
           │   If isConverted Then
           │      ' if the conversion is successful, calculate the bonus,
           │      ' then save the information to the file
           └─     ourEmployee.BonusAmount = ourEmployee.Sales * 0.05D
             ┌─  My.Computer.FileSystem.WriteAllText(path & "sales.txt", _
             │       ourEmployee.Name.PadRight(20) _
             │       & ourEmployee.Sales.ToString("N2").PadLeft(10) _
             │       & ourEmployee.BonusAmount.ToString("N2").PadLeft(10) _
             └─      & ControlChars.NewLine, True)

                    ' clear the text boxes
                    nameTextBox.Text = String.Empty
                    salesTextBox.Text = String.Empty
                Else
                    MessageBox.Show("The sales amount must be numeric.", _
                    "Sweets Unlimited", MessageBoxButtons.OK, _
                    MessageBoxIcon.Information)
                End If
             Else
                MessageBox.Show("Please enter a name and a sales amount.", _
                    "Sweets Unlimited", MessageBoxButtons.OK, _
                    MessageBoxIcon.Information)
             End If

             nameTextBox.Focus()
         End Sub
     End Class
```

*Instantiates a Salesperson object and assigns its address to the ourEmployee variable*

*Assigns values to the object's Public variables*

*Writes the contents of the object's Public variables to a sequential access file*

**FIGURE 10.9**    Code for the Sweets Unlimited application

**TIP**

When you type
**ouremployee.** in the Code
Editor window, the attributes of a
Salesperson object appear in a
list. You then can select the
appropriate attribute from the list.

In the saveButton's Click event procedure shown in Figure 10.9, the `Dim ourEmployee As New Salesperson` statement first instantiates a Salesperson object, and then assigns the object's address to the `ourEmployee` variable. After the statement is processed, you can access the object's attributes using the syntax *objectVariable.attribute*, where *objectVariable* is the name of the variable that stores the object's address, and *attribute* is the name of the attribute you want to access. For example, you use `ourEmployee.Name` to access the Name attribute of the Salesperson object created in Figure 10.9. Likewise, you use `ourEmployee.Sales` and `ourEmployee.BonusAmount` to access the Sales and BonusAmount attributes, respectively.

Notice that the saveButton's Click event procedure uses two assignment statements to assign values to the Name and BonusAmount attributes of the Salesperson object. The `ourEmployee.Name = nameTextBox.Text` statement assigns the contents of the nameTextBox to the object's Name attribute. Similarly, the `ourEmployee.BonusAmount = ourEmployee.Sales * 0.05D` statement multiplies the contents of the object's Sales attribute by 5%, and then stores the result in the object's BonusAmount attribute. The object's Sales attribute receives its value from the TryParse method contained in the `isConverted = Decimal.TryParse(salesTextBox.Text, ourEmployee.Sales)` statement in the procedure. The saveButton's Click event procedure uses the WriteAllText method to write the contents of the object's three attributes to the sales.txt file.

Although you can define a class that contains only attributes represented by Public variables—like the Salesperson class shown in Figure 10.6—that is rarely done. The disadvantage of using Public variables in a class is that a class cannot control the values assigned to its Public variables. For example, the class cannot validate the values to ensure that they are appropriate for the variables. Additionally, most classes contain both attributes and behaviors. This is because the purpose of a class in OOP is to encapsulate both the properties that describe an object and the methods that allow the object to perform tasks.

## EXAMPLE 2—USING A CLASS THAT CONTAINS A PRIVATE VARIABLE, A PROPERTY PROCEDURE, AND TWO METHODS

In this example, you view the code for a class named Square, which can be used to instantiate a Square object. Square objects have one attribute, which is the length of a side. Square objects also have two behaviors: they can initialize their side measurement when they are created, and they can calculate their area. Figure 10.10 shows the Square class defined in the Square.vb file.

**Visual Basic code**

```
' Class name:          Square
' Class purpose:       Calculates the area of a square.
' Created/revised by:  <your name> on <current date>


Option Explicit On
Option Strict On
```

*(Figure is continued on next page)*

```
Public Class Square
    Private _side As Integer

    Public Property Side() As Integer
        Get
            Return _side
        End Get
        Set(ByVal value As Integer)
            If value >= 0 Then
                _side = value
            Else
                _side = 0
            End If
        End Set
    End Property

    Public Sub New()        ' default constructor
        _side = 0
    End Sub

    Public Function CalculateArea() As Integer
        Return _side * _side
    End Function
End Class
```

*Private variable declaration*

*Property procedure*

*Methods*

**FIGURE 10.10**    Square class defined in the Square.vb file

**TIP**

When you type the **Public Property Side() As Integer** statement in the Code Editor window and then press the Enter key, the Code Editor automatically enters the **Get**, **End Get**, **Set(ByVal value As Integer)**, **End Set**, and **End Property** statements for you.

The Square class contains the `Private _side As Integer` statement, which declares a Private variable named `_side`. When naming the Private variables in a class, the convention is to use the underscore as the first character, and then use camel case for the remainder of the name.

The `Private` keyword in the `Private _side As Integer` statement indicates that only the class in which it is defined can use the `_side` variable. In this case, the `_side` variable can be used only by the code entered in the Square class. The code uses the variable to store the side measurement of the square whose area is to be calculated.

When you use a class to instantiate an object in an application, only the Public members of the class are exposed (made available) to the application; the Private members of the class are hidden from the application. When an application needs to assign data to or retrieve data from a Private variable in a class, it must use a Public property to do so. In other words, an application cannot refer, directly, to a Private variable in a class. Rather, it must refer to the variable indirectly, through the use of a Public property. You create a Public property using a **Property procedure**. Figure 10.11 shows the syntax of a Property procedure. The figure also includes examples of Property procedures.

# HOW TO...

*Property procedure header*

*Property procedure footer*

## Create a Property Procedure

**Syntax**
**Public [ReadOnly | WriteOnly] Property** *propertyName*() **As** *datatype*
   **Get**
      [*instructions*]
      **Return** *privateVariable*
   **End Get**
   **Set(ByVal value As** *datatype*)
      [*instructions*]
      *privateVariable* = {**value** | *defaultValue*}
   **End Set**
**End Property**

**Example 1–An application can both retrieve and set the Side property's value**

```
Public Property Side() As Integer
    Get
        Return _side
    End Get
    Set(ByVal value As Integer)
        If value > 0 Then
            _side = value
        Else
            _side = 0
        End If
    End Set
End Property
```

**Example 2–An application can retrieve the Bonus property's value, but not set it**

```
Public ReadOnly Property Bonus() As Decimal
    Get
        Return _bonus
    End Get
End Property
```

**Example 3–An application can set the AnnualSale property's value, but not retrieve it**

```
Public WriteOnly Property AnnualSale() As Integer
    Set(ByVal value As Integer)
        _annualSale = value
    End Set
End Property
```

**FIGURE 10.11** How to create a property procedure

In most cases, a Property procedure header begins with the keywords `Public Property`. However, as the syntax indicates, the header also can include either the keyword `ReadOnly` or the keyword `WriteOnly`. The `ReadOnly` keyword in a Property procedure header indicates that you are creating a property whose value can be retrieved (read) by an application, but the application cannot set (write to) the property. The WriteOnly keyword in a Property procedure header indicates that an application can set the property's value, but it cannot retrieve the value.

Following the Property keyword in the Property procedure header is the name of the property. You should use nouns and adjectives to name a property, as in Side, Bonus, and AnnualSale. Property names should be entered using Pascal case.

Following the property name in the Property procedure header is a set of parentheses, the keyword As, and the property's *datatype*. The data type of the property must match the data type of the Private variable associated with the Property procedure. A Public Property procedure creates a property that is visible to any application that contains an instance of the class.

A Property procedure ends with the procedure footer, which contains the keywords End Property. Between the procedure header and procedure footer, you include a Get block of code, or a Set block of code, or both Get and Set blocks of code. The appropriate block or blocks of code to include depends on the keywords contained in the Property procedure header. If the procedure header contains the ReadOnly keyword, you include only a Get block of code in the Property procedure. The code contained in the **Get block** allows an application to retrieve the contents of the Private variable associated with the property. In the Property procedure shown in Example 2 in Figure 10.11, the ReadOnly keyword indicates that an application can retrieve the contents of the Bonus property, but it cannot set the property's value.

If the Property procedure header contains the WriteOnly keyword, you include only a Set block of code in the procedure. The code in the **Set block** allows an application to assign a value to the Private variable associated with the property. In the Property procedure shown in Example 3 in Figure 10.11, the WriteOnly keyword indicates that an application can assign a value to the AnnualSale property, but it cannot retrieve the property's contents.

If the Property procedure header does not contain the ReadOnly or WriteOnly keywords, you include both a Get block of code and a Set block of code in the procedure, as shown in Example 1 in Figure 10.11. In this case, an application can both retrieve and set the Side property's value.

The Get block uses the **Get statement**, which begins with the keyword Get and ends with the keywords End Get. Most times, you will enter only the **Return** *privateVariable* instruction within the Get statement. The instruction directs the computer to return the contents of the Private variable associated with the property. For instance, in the first example shown in Figure 10.11, the Return _side statement tells the computer to return the contents of the _side variable, which is the Private variable associated with the Side property. Similarly, the Return _bonus statement in the second example tells the computer to return the contents of the _bonus variable, which is the Private variable associated with the Bonus property. Notice that Example 3 in Figure 10.11 does not contain a Get statement. This is because the AnnualSale property is designated as a WriteOnly property.

The Set block uses the **Set statement**, which begins with the keyword Set and ends with the keywords End Set. As shown in Figure 10.11, the Set keyword is followed by a parameter enclosed in parentheses. The parameter begins with the keywords ByVal value As, followed by a *datatype*, which must match the data type of the Private variable associated with the Property procedure. The value parameter temporarily stores the value that is passed to the property by the application.

You can enter one or more instructions within the Set statement. One of the instructions should assign the contents of the `value` parameter to the Private variable associated with the property. For instance, in the AnnualSale Property procedure shown in Example 3 in Figure 10.11, the `_annualSale = value` statement assigns the contents of the procedure's `value` parameter to the Private `_annualSale` variable.

In the Set statement, you often will include instructions to validate the value received from the application before assigning it to the Private variable. For instance, the Set statement shown in Example 1 in Figure 10.11 includes a selection structure that determines whether the side measurement received from the application is valid. In this case, a valid side measurement is an integer that is greater than zero. If the side measurement is valid, the `_side = value` instruction in the selection structure's true path assigns the integer stored in the `value` parameter to the Private `_side` variable. However, if the side measurement is not valid, the `_side = 0` instruction in the selection structure's false path assigns a default value—in this case, the number zero—to the Private `_side` variable.

Notice that the Property procedure shown in Example 2 in Figure 10.11 does not contain a Set statement. This is because the Bonus property is designated as a `ReadOnly` property.

As shown earlier in Figure 10.10, the Square class also contains two methods, which are named New and CalculateArea. The New method is the default constructor for the class.

## Constructors

A **constructor** is a method whose instructions the computer automatically processes each time an object is instantiated from the class. The sole purpose of a constructor is to initialize the class's Private variables. Figure 10.12 shows the syntax of a constructor. It also includes the constructor entered in the Square class.

**HOW TO...**

**How to Create a Constructor**

**Syntax**
**Public Sub New(**[*parameterlist*]**)**
    *instructions to initialize the class's Private variables*
**End Sub**

**Example**
```
Public Sub New()
    _side = 0
End Sub
```

**FIGURE 10.12**    How to create a constructor

A constructor begins with the keywords `Public Sub New`, followed by a set of parentheses that contains an optional *parameterlist*. A constructor that has no parameters is called the **default constructor**.

A constructor ends with the keywords `End Sub`. Within the constructor you enter the code to initialize the class's Private variables. The variables will be initialized when the class is used to instantiate an object.

**TIP**

Constructors never return a value, so they are always Sub procedures rather than Function procedures.

A class can have more than one constructor. Each constructor included in a class has the same name, New, but its parameters (if any) must be different from any other constructor in the class. Only one of the class's constructors is the default constructor, and that constructor is always the one without any parameters. You will learn how to create a class containing multiple constructors in the next example.

The Square class contains one constructor, which is shown in the example in Figure 10.12. (It also is shown in Figure 10.10.) Notice that the constructor simply initializes the class's Private variable, named _side, to the number zero. The constructor is the Square class's default constructor, because it has no parameters. The computer automatically processes the default constructor when you use the Square class to instantiate an object. Examples of statements that you can use to instantiate a Square object include Dim mySquare As New Square and mySquare = New Square.

A class also can contain methods other than constructors. The Square class, for example, contains a method named CalculateArea.

## Methods Other Than Constructors

Except for constructors, which must be Sub procedures, the methods included in a class can be either Sub procedures or Function procedures. As you learned in Chapter 7, the difference between both types of procedures is that a Function procedure returns a value after performing its assigned task, whereas a Sub procedure does not return a value.

Figure 10.13 shows the syntax of a method that is not a constructor. The figure also includes the CalculateArea method entered in the Square class.

**HOW TO...**

**How to Create a Method That Is Not a Constructor**

**Syntax**
**Public {Sub | Function}** *methodname*(*[parameterlist]*) **As** *datatype*
   *instructions*
**End {Sub | Function}**

**Example**
```
Public Function CalculateArea() As Integer
     Return _side * _side
End Function
```

**FIGURE 10.13** How to create a method that is not a constructor

The **{Sub | Function}** in the syntax shown in Figure 10.13 indicates that you can select only one of the keywords appearing within the braces. In this case, you can choose either the Sub keyword or the Function keyword.

The rules for naming methods are similar to the rules for naming properties. Like property names, method names should be entered using Pascal case. However, unlike property names, the first word in a method name should be a verb; any subsequent words should be nouns and adjectives. The name CalculateArea follows this naming convention.

The CalculateArea method in the Square class is represented by a Function procedure. The `Return _side * _side` statement within the procedure uses the contents of the class's Private variable, `_side`, to calculate the area of a square. The statement then returns the area to the application that called the procedure.

The Area application, which you view next, uses the Square class to instantiate and manipulate a Square object. Figure 10.14 shows a sample run of the application, and Figure 10.15 shows the application's code.

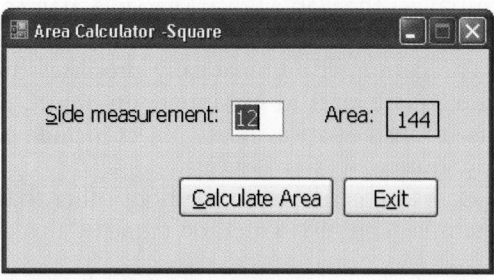

**FIGURE 10.14**     Sample run of the Area application

### Visual Basic code

```
' Project name:         Area Project
' Project purpose:      The project displays the area of a square.
' Created/revised by:   <your name> on <current date>

Option Explicit On
Option Strict On

Public Class MainForm

    Private Sub exitButton_Click...

    Private Sub sideTextBox_Enter...

    Private Sub sideTextBox_TextChanged...

    Private Sub calcButton_Click(ByVal sender As Object, _
        ByVal e As System.EventArgs) Handles calcButton.Click
        ' calculates and displays the area of a square

        Dim mySquare As New Square
        Dim isConverted As Boolean
        Dim area As Integer
```

*These three procedures are collapsed*

*Creates a Square object and assigns its address to the mySquare variable*

**(Figure is continued on next page)**

```
                     ' assign side measurement to the
                     ' Square object's property
                     isConverted = _
                         Integer.TryParse(sideTextBox.Text, mySquare.Side)


                     If isConverted Then
                         ' calculate and display the area
                         area = mySquare.CalculateArea()
                         areaLabel.Text = Convert.ToString(area)
                     Else
                         MessageBox.Show("The side measurement must be numeric.", _
                             "Area Calculator", MessageBoxButtons.OK, _
                             MessageBoxIcon.Information)
                     End If

                     sideTextBox.Focus()
                 End Sub
             End Class
```

*Assigns a value to the object's Side property*

*Uses the object's CalculateArea method to calculate the area*

**FIGURE 10.15**    Code for the Area application

The `Dim mySquare As New Square` statement contained in the calcButton's Click event procedure tells the computer to instantiate a Square object, and then assign the object's address to the `mySquare` variable. When creating the Square object, the computer uses the class's default constructor to initialize the class's Private variable (named `_side`).

The `isConverted = Integer.TryParse(sideTextBox.Text, mySquare.Side)` statement in the procedure uses the TryParse method to convert the contents of the sideTextBox to Integer. If the conversion is successful, the integer is stored in the Square object's Side property, and the Boolean value True is assigned to the `isConverted` variable. However, if the conversion is not successful, the number zero is stored in the Square object's Side property, and the Boolean value False is assigned to the `isConverted` variable.

Next, the calcButton's Click event procedure uses a selection structure to determine whether the text box's contents were converted to Integer. If the `isConverted` variable does not contain the Boolean value True, it means that the conversion was not successful. In that case, the statement in the selection structure's false path displays an appropriate message in a message box. However, if the `isConverted` variable contains the Boolean value True, it means that the conversion was successful. In that case, the two statements in the selection structure's true path are processed. The first statement, `area = mySquare.CalculateArea()`, uses the Square object's CalculateArea method to calculate and return the area, assigning the result to the `area` variable. The second statement, `areaLabel.Text = Convert.ToString(area)`, displays the contents of the `area` variable in the areaLabel.

Next, you view an example of a class that contains more than one constructor.

## EXAMPLE 3—USING A CLASS THAT CONTAINS TWO CONSTRUCTORS

In this example, you view the code for a class named FormattedDate, which can be used to instantiate a FormattedDate object. FormatttedDate objects have two attributes: a month number and a day number. FormattedDate objects also have three behaviors. First, they can initialize their attributes using values provided by the class. Second, they can initialize their attributes using values passed by the application in which they are instantiated. Third, they can return their month number attribute, followed by a slash and their day number attribute. Figure 10.16 shows the FormattedDate class defined in the FormattedDate.vb file.

**Visual Basic code**

```vb
' Class name:          FormattedDate
' Class purpose:       Inserts a slash between the month number
'                      and day number.
' Created/revised by:  <your name> on <current date>

Option Explicit On
Option Strict On

Public Class FormattedDate
    Private _month As String
    Private _day As String

    Public Property Month() As String
        Get
            Return _month
        End Get
        Set(ByVal value As String)
            _month = value
        End Set
    End Property

    Public Property Day() As String
        Get
            Return _day
        End Get
        Set(ByVal value As String)
            _day = value
        End Set
    End Property

    Public Sub New()      ' default constructor
        _month = String.Empty
        _day = String.Empty
    End Sub
```

*Accesses the Private _month variable directly*

**(Figure is continued on next page)**

Example 3—Using a Class that Contains Two Constructors          **613**

*Uses the Month property to access the Private _month variable indirectly*

*Accesses the Private variables directly*

```
        Public Sub New(ByVal monthNum As String, ByVal dayNum As String)
            Month = monthNum
            Day = dayNum
        End Sub

        Public Function GetNewDate() As String
            Dim newDate As String
            newDate = _month & "/" & _day
            Return newDate
        End Function
    End Class
```

**FIGURE 10.16**    FormattedDate class defined in the FormattedDate.vb file

The FormattedDate class contains two Private variables named _month and _day. It also contains two Property procedures named Month and Day. The Month Property procedure is associated with the _month variable, and the Day Property procedure is associated with the _day variable.

In addition to the Private variables and Property procedures, the FormattedDate class also contains three methods: two are named New and one is named GetNewDate. The two New methods are the class's constructors. The first constructor is the default constructor, because it does not have any parameters. The computer processes the default constructor when you use a statement such as `Dim payDate As New FormatttedDate` to instantiate a FormattedDate object. It also processes the default constructor when you use the `payDate = New FormattedDate` statement to create an instance of the FormattedDate class.

The second constructor in the FormattedDate class allows you to specify the initial values for a FormattedDate object when the object is created. In this case, the initial values must be strings, because the constructor's *parameterlist* contains two String variables. You include the initial values, enclosed in a set of parentheses, in the statement that instantiates the object. For example, the `Dim payDate As New FormattedDate(monNum, dayNum)` statement creates a FormattedDate object and passes two String variables (arguments) to the FormattedDate class. The computer determines which class constructor to use by matching the number, data type, and position of the arguments with the number, data type, and position of the parameters listed in each constructor's *parameterlist*. In this case, the computer will use the second constructor in the FormattedDate class, because that is the constructor that contains two String variables in its *parameterlist*. Constructors that contain parameters are called **parameterized constructors**. The method name combined with its optional *parameterlist* is called the method's **signature**.

The third method in the FormattedDate class is a Function procedure named GetNewDate. The function's purpose is to return the month and day numbers, separated by a slash. The month and day numbers are stored in the class's Private variables.

The methods in a class can access the class's Private variables either directly (by name) or indirectly (through the Public properties). In the FormattedDate class shown in Figure 10.16, both the default constructor and the GetNewDate method use the names of the Private variables to access the variables directly. The default constructor assigns values to the Private variables, and the GetNewDate method retrieves the values stored in the Private variables.

The parameterized New constructor, on the other hand, uses the Public properties to access the Private variables indirectly. This is because the values passed to the parameterized constructor come from the application rather than from the class itself. Values that originate outside the class should always be assigned to the Private variables indirectly, through the Public properties. Doing this ensures that the Property procedure's Set block, which typically contains validation code, is processed. Currently, the Month and Day Property procedures in the FormattedDate class do not contain any data validation code. However, if validation code is added at a later date, the code in the parameterized constructor will not need to be modified.

Next, you view the Personnel application, which uses the FormattedDate class to instantiate and manipulate a FormatttedDate object. Figure 10.17 shows a sample run of the application, and Figure 10.18 shows the application's code.

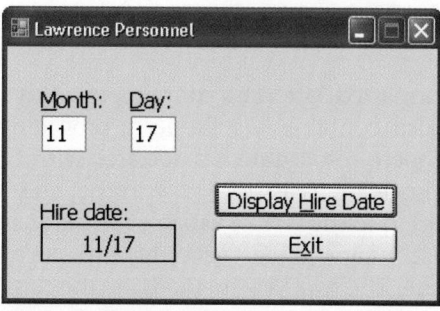

**FIGURE 10.17**    Sample run of the Personnel application

**Visual Basic code**

```
' Project name:          Personnel Project
' Project purpose:       The project displays the month number
'                        and day number, separated by a slash
' Created/revised by:    <your name> on <current date>

Option Explicit On
Option Strict On

Public Class MainForm

      Private Sub ClearLabel...

      Private Sub exitButton_Click...

      Private Sub monTextBox_Enter...

      Private Sub dayTextBox_Enter...
```

*These four procedures are collapsed*

*(Figure is continued on next page)*

Example 3—Using a Class that Contains Two Constructors **615**

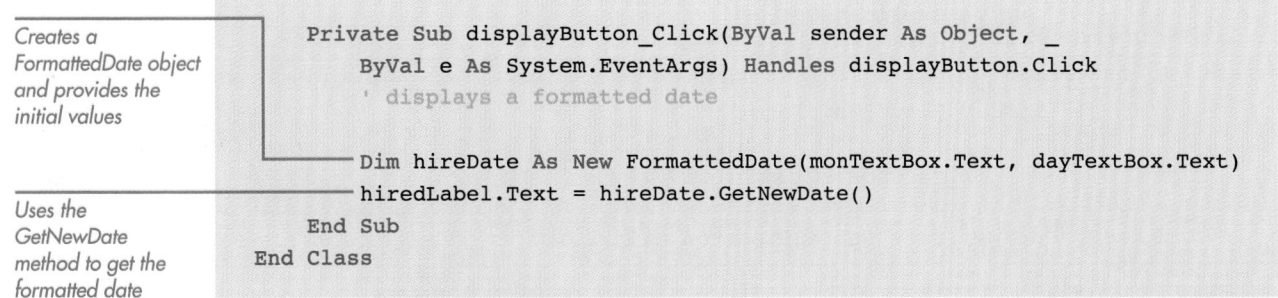

Creates a FormattedDate object and provides the initial values

Uses the GetNewDate method to get the formatted date

```
Private Sub displayButton_Click(ByVal sender As Object, _
    ByVal e As System.EventArgs) Handles displayButton.Click
    ' displays a formatted date

    Dim hireDate As New FormattedDate(monTextBox.Text, dayTextBox.Text)
    hiredLabel.Text = hireDate.GetNewDate()
End Sub
End Class
```

**FIGURE 10.18**   Code for the Personnel application using the parameterized constructor

The `Dim hireDate As New FormattedDate(monTextBox.Text, dayTextBox.Text)` statement tells the computer to create a FormattedDate object and assign its address to the `hireDate` variable. The computer will use the parameterized constructor to initialize the object. This is because the Dim statement contains two String arguments, which agrees with the *parameterlist* in the second constructor. The computer passes the two String arguments, *by value*, to the parameterized constructor. The constructor receives the values and stores them in the `monthNum` and `dayNum` variables listed in its procedure header.

The `Month = monthNum` instruction in the parameterized constructor assigns the value stored in the `monthNum` variable to the Month property. When you assign a value to a property, the computer passes the value to the property's Set statement, where it is stored in the Set statement's `value` parameter. The `_month = value` instruction in the Set statement assigns the contents of the `value` parameter to the Private `_month` variable.

Next, the `Day = dayNum` instruction in the parameterized constructor assigns the value stored in the `dayNum` variable to the Day property. In this case, the computer passes the value to the Day property's Set statement, where it is stored in the statement's `value` parameter. The `_day = value` instruction in the Set statement then assigns the contents of the `value` parameter to the Private `_day` variable.

The `hiredLabel.Text = hireDate.GetNewDate()` statement uses the FormattedDate object's GetNewDate method to return the month and day numbers, separated by a slash. The statement displays the formatted date in the hiredLabel.

Figure 10.19 shows a different version of the Personnel application's code. When processing this version of the code, the computer will use the default constructor to initialize the FormattedDate object.

**Visual Basic code**

```
' Project name:        Personnel Project
' Project purpose:     The project displays the month number
'                      and day number, separated by a slash
' Created/revised by:  <your name> on <current date>
```

*(Figure is continued on next page)*

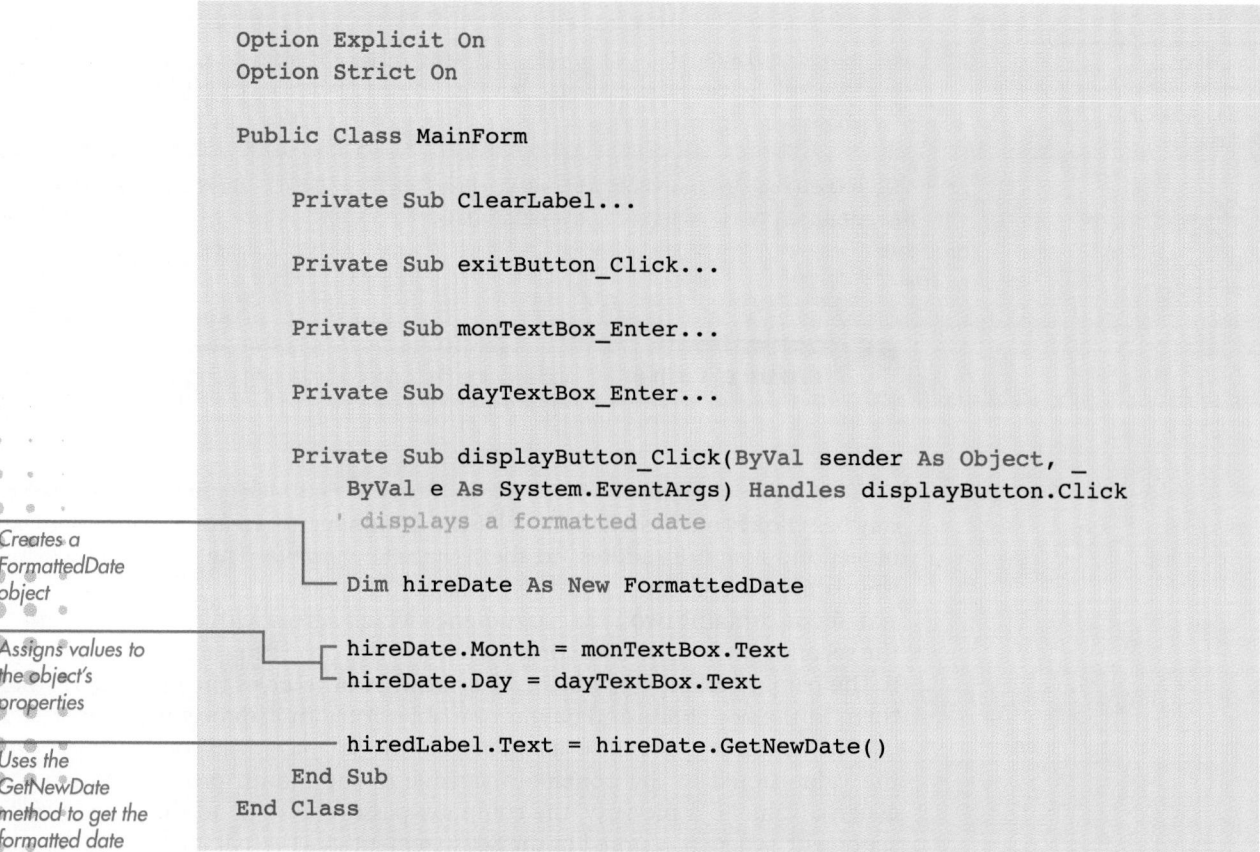

```
Option Explicit On
Option Strict On

Public Class MainForm

    Private Sub ClearLabel...

    Private Sub exitButton_Click...

    Private Sub monTextBox_Enter...

    Private Sub dayTextBox_Enter...

    Private Sub displayButton_Click(ByVal sender As Object, _
        ByVal e As System.EventArgs) Handles displayButton.Click
        ' displays a formatted date

        Dim hireDate As New FormattedDate

        hireDate.Month = monTextBox.Text
        hireDate.Day = dayTextBox.Text

        hiredLabel.Text = hireDate.GetNewDate()
    End Sub
End Class
```

Creates a
FormattedDate
object

Assigns values to
the object's
properties

Uses the
GetNewDate
method to get the
formatted date

**FIGURE 10.19**     Code for the Personnel application using the default
constructor

Comparing the code shown in Figure 10.18 with the code shown in Figure 10.19, you will notice that the `Dim hireDate As New FormattedDate (monTextBox.Text, dayTextBox.Text)` statement in Figure 10.18 was replaced with the following three lines of code in Figure 10.19:

```
Dim hireDate As New FormattedDate
hireDate.Month = monTextBox.Text
hireDate.Day = dayTextBox.Text
```

When processing the `Dim hireDate As New FormattedDate` statement, the computer instantiates a FormattedDate object, and it assigns the object's address to the `hireDate` variable. In this case, the computer uses the default constructor to initialize the class's Private variables. This is because the Dim statement does not contain any arguments, which agrees with the empty *parameterlist* in the default constructor. The `hireDate.Month = monTextBox.Text` statement then assigns the contents of the monTextBox to the object's Month property. Recall that the Month property is a Public member of the class, and all Public members are exposed to any application that uses an instance of the class. Similarly, the `hireDate.Day = dayTextBox.Text` statement assigns the contents of the dayTextBox to the object's Day property.

Example 4—Using a Class that Contains Overloaded Methods                617

## EXAMPLE 4—USING A CLASS THAT CONTAINS OVERLOADED METHODS

In this example, you view the code for a class named Employee, which can be used to instantiate an Employee object. Employee objects have two attributes: an employee number and an employee name. Employee objects also have the following four behaviors:

1. They can initialize their attributes using values provided by the class.
2. They can initialize their attributes using values passed by the application in which they are instantiated.
3. They can calculate and return the gross pay for salaried employees. The gross pay is calculated by dividing the salaried employee's annual salary by 24, because salaried employees are paid twice per month.
4. They can calculate and return the gross pay for hourly employees. The gross pay is calculated by multiplying the number of hours the employee worked during the week by his or her pay rate.

Figure 10.20 shows the Employee class defined in the Employee.vb file.

**Visual Basic code**

```vb
' Class name:          Employee
' Class purpose:       Calculates the gross pay for salaried
'                      and hourly employees.
' Created/revised by:  <your name> on <current date>

Option Explicit On
Option Strict On

Public Class Employee
    Private _number As String
    Private _empName As String

    Public Property Number() As String
        Get
            Return _number
        End Get
        Set(ByVal value As String)
            _number = value
        End Set
    End Property

    Public Property EmpName() As String
        Get
            Return _empName
        End Get
```

*(Figure is continued on next page)*

```
            Set(ByVal value As String)
                _empName = value
            End Set
        End Property

        Public Sub New()
            _number = String.Empty
            _empName = String.Empty
        End Sub

        Public Sub New(ByVal num As String, ByVal name As String)
            Number = num
            EmpName = name
        End Sub

        Public Overloads Function CalculateGross(ByVal salary As Decimal) _
            As Decimal
            ' calculates the gross pay for salaried
            ' employees, who are paid twice per month

            Return salary / 24D
        End Function

        Public Overloads Function CalculateGross(ByVal hours As Decimal, _
            ByVal rate As Decimal) As Decimal
            ' calculates the weekly pay for
            ' hourly employees

            Return hours * rate
        End Function
End Class
```

*Overloaded constructors*

*Overloaded CalculateGross method*

*Overloaded CalculateGross method*

**FIGURE 10.20**     Employee class defined in the Employee.vb file

The Employee class contains two Private variables named _number and _empName. It also contains two Property procedures named Number and EmpName. The Number Property procedure is associated with the _number variable, and the EmpName Property procedure is associated with the _empName variable.

In addition to the Private variables and Property procedures, the Employee class also contains four methods. The two methods named New are the class's constructors. The first New method is the default constructor, and the second New method is a parameterized constructor. When two or more methods have the same name but different parameters, the methods are referred to as **overloaded methods**. The two constructors contained in the Employee class are overloaded methods, because each is named New and each has a different *parameterlist*.

**TIP**

The New methods in the FormattedDate class shown earlier in Figure 10.16 are overloaded methods.

Example 4—Using a Class that Contains Overloaded Methods　　　　　　　　**619**

You already are familiar with overloaded methods, as you have used several of the overloaded methods built into Visual Basic. Examples of such methods include ToString, TryParse, Convert.ToDecimal, and MessageBox.Show. The IntelliSense feature in the Code Editor window displays a box that allows you to view a method's signatures, one signature at a time. The box shown in Figure 10.21, for example, displays the second of the ToString method's four signatures. You use the up and down arrows in the box to display the other signatures. The IntelliSense feature will also display the signatures of the overloaded methods contained in the classes you create.

*Signature*

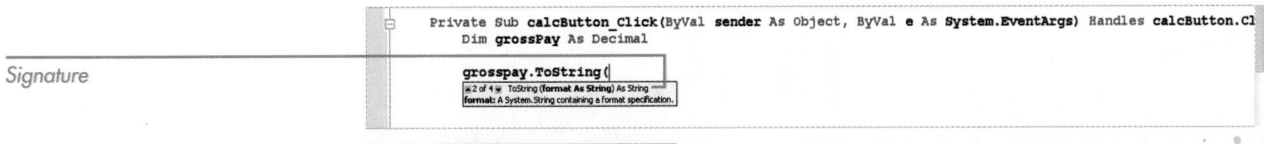

```
Private Sub calcButton_Click(ByVal sender As Object, ByVal e As System.EventArgs) Handles calcButton.Cl
    Dim grossPay As Decimal

    grosspay.ToString (
    ▲ 2 of 4 ▼  ToString (format As String) As String
    format: A System.String containing a format specification.
```

**FIGURE 10.21**　　Box displaying one signature of the ToString method

You can overload any methods contained in the classes you create, not just constructors. The two CalculateGross methods contained in the Employee class, for example, are overloaded methods: each has the same name but a different *parameterlist*. However, if the methods being overloaded are not constructors, you must use the keyword Overloads in the procedure header, as shown earlier in Figure 10.20. The Overloads keyword is not used when overloading constructors.

Overloading is useful when two or more methods require different parameters to perform the same task. For example, both overloaded constructors in the Employee class initialize the class's Private variables. However, the default constructor does not need to be passed any information to perform the task, while the parameterized constructor requires two items of information (the employee number and name). Similarly, both CalculateGross methods in the Employee class calculate and return a gross pay amount. However, the first CalculateGross method, which calculates and returns the gross pay amount for salaried employees, requires an application to pass it one item of information: the employee's annual salary. The second CalculateGross method, on the other hand, calculates and returns the gross pay amount for hourly employees and requires two items of information: the number of hours the employee worked and his or her rate of pay.

Rather than using two overloaded CalculateGross methods in the Employee class, you could have used two methods having different names. For example, you could have used a method named CalcSalariedGross to calculate and return the gross pay amount for salaried employees, and a method named CalcHourlyGross to calculate and return the gross pay amount for hourly employees. However, by overloading the CalculateGross method, you need to remember the name of only one method.

Next, you view the ABC Company application, which uses the Employee class to instantiate and manipulate an Employee object. Figures 10.22 and 10.23 show sample runs of the application, and Figure 10.24 shows the application's code.

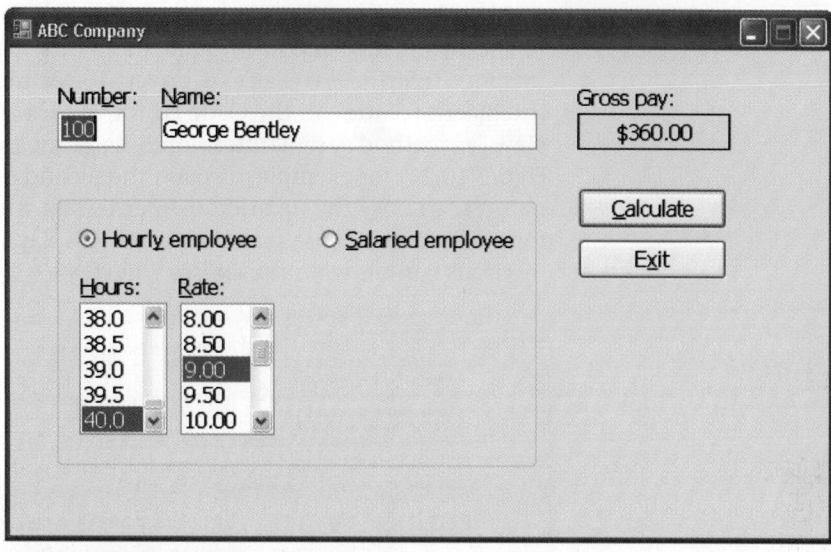

**FIGURE 10.22**  Sample run showing the gross pay for an hourly worker

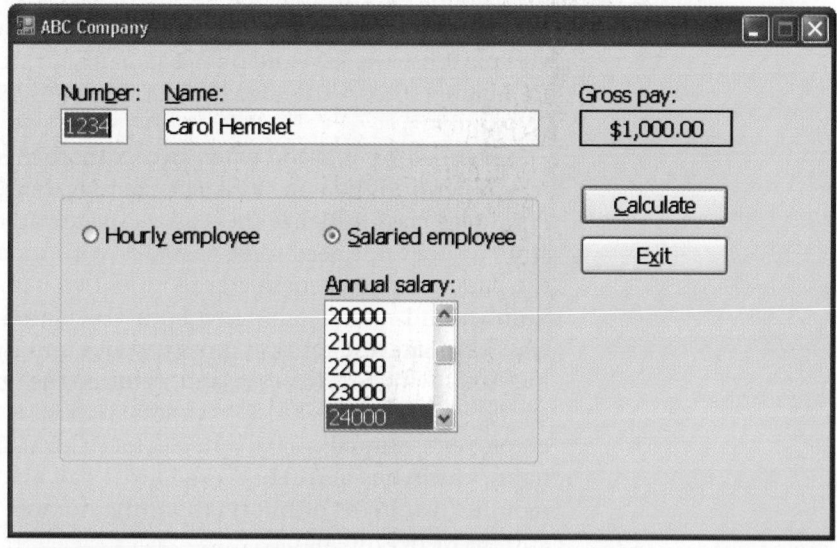

**FIGURE 10.23**  Sample run showing the gross pay for a salaried worker

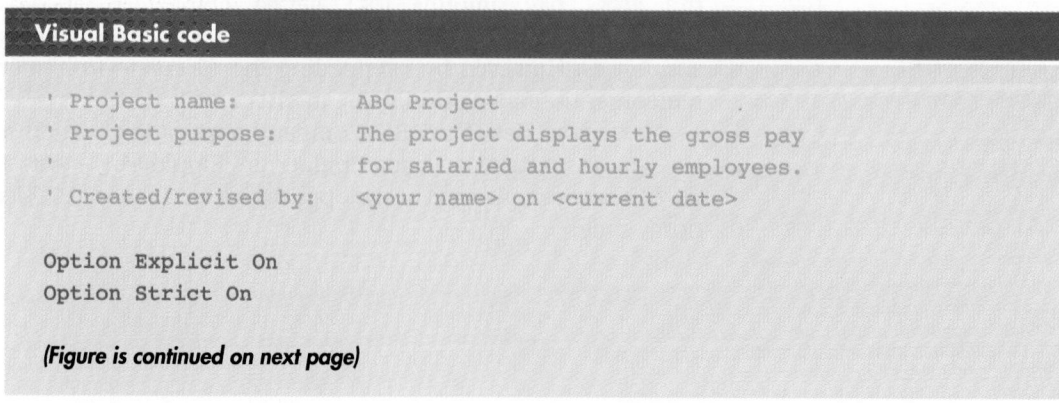

**Visual Basic code**

```
' Project name:        ABC Project
' Project purpose:     The project displays the gross pay
'                      for salaried and hourly employees.
' Created/revised by:  <your name> on <current date>

Option Explicit On
Option Strict On
```

*(Figure is continued on next page)*

Example 4—Using a Class that Contains Overloaded Methods

**621**

```
Public Class MainForm

    Private Sub Clearlabel...

    Private Sub exitButton_Click...

    Private Sub numTextBox_Enter...

    Private Sub nameTextBox_Enter...

    Private Sub hourlyRadioButton_Click...

    Private Sub salariedRadioButton_Click...

    Private Sub MainForm_Load...

    Private Sub calcButton_Click(ByVal sender As Object, _
        ByVal e As System.EventArgs) Handles calcButton.Click
        ' calculates and displays the gross pay

        Dim abcEmployee As Employee
        Dim annualSalary As Decimal
        Dim hoursWorked As Decimal
        Dim hourlyRate As Decimal
        Dim grossPay As Decimal

        ' create an Employee object and assign the
        ' employee number and name to the object
        abcEmployee = New Employee(numTextBox.Text, nameTextBox.Text)

        ' determine which radio button is checked
        If hourlyRadioButton.Checked Then
            ' calculate the gross pay for an hourly worker
            hoursWorked = Convert.ToDecimal(hoursListBox.SelectedItem)
            hourlyRate = Convert.ToDecimal(rateListBox.SelectedItem)
            grossPay = _
                abcEmployee.CalculateGross(hoursWorked, hourlyRate)
        Else
            ' calculate the gross pay for a salaried worker
            annualSalary = Convert.ToDecimal(salaryListBox.SelectedItem)
            grossPay = abcEmployee.CalculateGross(annualSalary)
        End If

        ' display the gross pay
        grossLabel.Text = grossPay.ToString("C2")

        numTextBox.Focus()
    End Sub
End Class
```

*Declares a variable that will store the address of an Employee object*

*Instantiates an Employee object using the parameterized constructor*

*Calculates the gross pay for an hourly worker*

*Calculates the gross pay for a salaried worker*

**FIGURE 10.24** Code for the ABC Company application

The `Dim abcEmployee As Employee` statement in the calcButton's Click event procedure declares a variable that will store the address of an Employee object. The Employee object is instantiated using the `abcEmployee = New Employee(numTextBox.Text, nameTextBox.Text)` statement. When instantiating the object, the computer will use the class's parameterized constructor to initialize the object's Private variables.

Notice that the CalculateGross method appears in two statements in the calcButton's Click event procedure. The computer uses the signature of the CalculateGross method in each statement to determine which of the class's CalculateGross methods to process. In this case, the `grossPay = abcEmployee.CalculateGross(hoursWorked, hourlyRate)` statement tells the computer to process the CalculateGross method that contains two parameters, and then assign the return value to the `grossPay` variable. In the Employee class, the CalculateGross method that contains two parameters calculates and returns the gross pay amount for an hourly worker. The `grossPay = abcEmployee.CalculateGross(annualSalary)` statement, on the other hand, tells the computer to process the CalculateGross method that contains one parameter, and then assign the return value to the `grossPay` variable. In the Employee class, the CalculateGross method that contains one parameter calculates and returns the gross pay amount for a salaried worker. The calcButton's Click event procedure displays the contents of the `grossPay` variable, formatted with a dollar sign and two decimal places, in the grossLabel.

## EXAMPLE 5—USING A BASE CLASS AND A DERIVED CLASS

As you learned in Chapter 1, you can create one class from another class. In OOP, this is referred to as inheritance. The new class is called the derived class, and it inherits the attributes and behaviors of the original class, called the base class. You indicate that a class is a derived class by including the Inherits clause in the derived class's Class statement. The syntax of the Inherits clause is **Inherits** *base*, where *base* is the name of the base class whose attributes and behaviors the derived class will inherit (be provided). You enter the Inherits clause below the Public Class header in the derived class.

Figure 10.25 shows the code for a base class named Employee and a derived class named Salaried. Both class definitions are contained in the CompanyClass.vb file. (In Computer Exercise 11, you will add another class to the file. The new class will be named Hourly.)

**Visual Basic code**

```
' Class name:          Employee
' Class purpose:       Base class.
' Created/revised by:  <your name> on <current date>

Option Explicit On
Option Strict On

Public Class Employee
    Private _number As String
    Private _empName As String
```

*Beginning of base Employee class*

*(Figure is continued on next page)*

Example 5—Using a Base Class and a Derived Class                                             **623**

```
        Public Property Number() As String
            Get
                Return _number
            End Get
            Set(ByVal value As String)
                _number = value
            End Set
        End Property

        Public Property EmpName() As String
            Get
                Return _empName
            End Get
            Set(ByVal value As String)
                _empName = value
            End Set
        End Property

        Public Sub New()
            _number = String.Empty
            _empName = String.Empty
        End Sub

        Public Sub New(ByVal num As String, ByVal name As String)
            Number = num
            EmpName = name
        End Sub

        Public Overridable Function CalculateGross() As Decimal
            ' this function will be overriden
            ' in the derived classes
        End Function
    End Class

' Class name:          Salaried
' Class purpose:       Calculates the gross pay for salaried workers.
' Created/revised by:  <your name> on <current date>

Public Class Salaried
    Inherits Employee

    Private _salary As Decimal

    Public Property Salary() As Decimal
        Get
            Return _salary
        End Get
        Set(ByVal value As Decimal)
            _salary = value
        End Set
    End Property
```

The method can be overridden in the derived class

Beginning of the derived Salaried class

The derived class inherits from the base class

**(Figure is continued on next page)**

```
                    Public Sub New()
                        MyBase.New()
                        _salary = 0
                    End Sub

                    Public Sub New(ByVal num As String, ByVal name As String, _
                        ByVal annualSalary As Decimal)
                        MyBase.New(num, name)
                        Salary = annualSalary
                    End Sub

                    Public Overrides Function CalculateGross() As Decimal
                        Dim gross As Decimal
                        gross = _salary / 24D
                        Return gross
                    End Function

                End Class
```

*Calls the base class's default constructor*

*Calls the base class's parameterized constructor*

*This method overrides the one in the base class*

**FIGURE 10.25** Base Employee class and derived Salaried class

The Employee class definition shown in Figure 10.25 is almost identical to the Employee class definition shown in Figure 10.20; only the CalculateGross method in both class definitions differs. For instance, the CalculateGross method in Figure 10.20 is an overloaded method that can calculate the gross pay for either a salaried employee or an hourly employee. The CalculateGross method in the Employee class shown in Figure 10.25, on the other hand, does not perform any calculations; it doesn't even contain any code. Additionally, its procedure header contains the `Overridable` keyword, which indicates that the method can be overridden by any class that is derived from the Employee class. In other words, classes derived from the Employee class will provide their own CalculateGross method.

Study the code contained in the Salaried class shown in Figure 10.25. The `Inherits Employee` clause that appears below the `Public Class Salaried` clause indicates that the Salaried class is derived from the Employee class. This means that the Salaried class includes all of the attributes and behaviors of the Employee class. The Salaried class also contains an attribute of its own: salary. The salary attribute is represented by the Private `_salary` variable and the Public Salary Property procedure in the class. The salary attribute belongs to the Salaried class only.

Both constructors in the Salaried class contain the **MyBase.New** (*parameterlist*) statement. This statement tells the computer to process the code contained in the appropriate constructor in the base class. You refer to the base class using the `MyBase` keyword. For example, the `MyBase.New()` statement in the default constructor tells the computer to process the code contained in the base class's default constructor. The `MyBase.New(num, name)` statement in the Salaried class's parameterized constructor indicates that the code in the base class's parameterized constructor should be processed.

Notice that the Salaried class contains a CalculateGross method, which calculates the gross pay for a salaried employee. The method's header contains the

TIP

Recall that all constructors are named New.

Example 5—Using a Base Class and a Derived Class **625**

keyword Overrides to indicate that the method overrides (replaces) the CalculateGross method contained in the base Employee class.

In Figure 10.24, you viewed the code for the ABC Company application, which used the overloaded methods defined in the Employee class shown in Figure 10.20. Figure 10.26 shows a different version of the calcButton's Click event procedure from the application. In this version, the procedure uses the derived Salaried class shown in Figure 10.25. The code pertaining to the Salaried class is shaded in the figure. (You will complete the calcButton's Click event procedure in Computer Exercise 11.)

**TIP**

The three statements in the Salaried class's CalculateGross method are equivalent to the statement Return _salary / 24D.

You will complete this section of the code in Computer Exercise 11

**Visual Basic code**

```vb
Private Sub calcButton_Click(ByVal sender As Object, _
        ByVal e As System.EventArgs) Handles calcButton.Click
    ' calculates and displays the gross pay

    Dim salEmployee As Salaried
    Dim annualSalary As Decimal
    Dim hoursWorked As Decimal
    Dim hourlyRate As Decimal
    Dim grossPay As Decimal

    ' determine which radio button is checked
    If hourlyRadioButton.Checked Then
        ' calculate the gross pay for an hourly worker

    Else
        ' calculate the gross pay for a salaried worker
        annualSalary = Convert.ToDecimal(salaryListBox.SelectedItem)
        salEmployee = _
            New Salaried(numTextBox.Text, nameTextBox.Text, _
            annualSalary)
        grossPay = salEmployee.CalculateGross()
    End If

    ' display the gross pay
    grossLabel.Text = grossPay.ToString("C2")

    numTextBox.Focus()
End Sub
```

**FIGURE 10.26**    Salaried class used in the calcButton's Click event procedure

The Dim salEmployee As Salaried statement declares a variable that can store the address of a Salaried object. The salEmployee = New Salaried (numTextBox.Text, nameTextBox.Text, annualSalary) statement instantiates a Salaried object, and it assigns the object's address to the salEmployee variable. The statement passes three items of information to the Salaried class's parameterized constructor, which uses the items to initialize the object when it is

**TIP**

Sample runs of the ABC Company application appear in Figures 10.22 and 10.23.

created. The `grossPay = salEmployee.CalculateGross()` statement uses the Salaried class's CalculateGross method to calculate and return the gross pay, which the statement assigns to the `grossPay` variable.

You have completed the concepts section of Chapter 10. The next section is the Programming Tutorial section, which gives you step-by-step instructions on how to apply the chapter's concepts to an application. A Programming Example follows the Programming Tutorial. The Programming Example is a completed program that demonstrates the concepts taught in the chapter. Following the Programming Example are the Quick Review, Key Terms, Self-Check Questions and Answers, Review Questions, Review Exercises – Short Answer, Computer Exercises, and Case Projects sections.

# PROGRAMMING TUTORIAL

## Card Game

In this tutorial, you create an application that uses 13 cards from a deck of playing cards; the 13 cards belong to the suit of Hearts. When the player clicks the Deal button in the interface, the application will display two of the 13 cards, face down. The object of the game is for the player to click the card having the highest value. The cards associated with the two of Hearts through the 10 of Hearts are worth their face value. The Jack of Hearts has a value of 11, the Queen a value of 12, the King a value of 13, and the Ace a value of 14. After the player makes his or her selection, the application displays the two cards face-up. It then displays a message indicating whether the player's selection was correct or incorrect. The application also displays the number of correct and incorrect selections made by the player. The Card Game application's user interface is shown in Figure 10.27, and its TOE chart is shown in Figure 10.28.

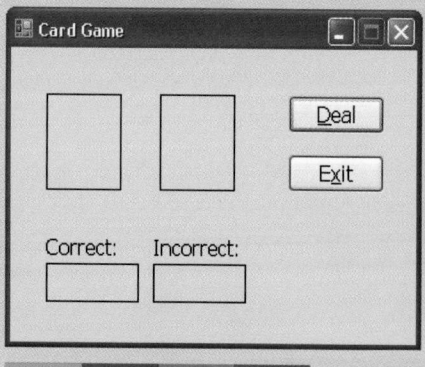

**FIGURE 10.27**    MainForm

**TOE Chart:**

| Task | Object | Event |
|---|---|---|
| End the application | exitButton | Click |
| 1. Shuffle the cards<br>2. Display the first two cards, face down, in the card1PictureBox and card2PictureBox | dealButton | Click |
| Store the 13 cards in an array | MainForm | Load |
| 1. Display the first two cards face-up<br>2. Convert the face values of the two cards to numbers<br>3. Determine the highest card<br>4. Determine whether the player selected the highest card; display appropriate messages<br>5. Update the appropriate counter<br>6. Display the counters in the correctLabel and incorrectLabel | card1PictureBox, card2PictureBox | Click |
| Display the number of correct selections | correctLabel | None |
| Display the number of incorrect selections | incorrectLabel | None |

**FIGURE 10.28**   TOE chart

## Coding the Card Game Application

Before you can begin coding the Card Game application, you need to open the Card Game Solution file.

**To open the Card Game Solution file:**

1. Start Visual Studio. If necessary, close the Start Page window.
2. Open the **Card Game Solution** (Card Game Solution.sln) file, which is contained in the VbReloaded\Chap10\Card Game Solution folder. The user interface shown earlier in Figure 10.27 appears on the screen.
3. Open the Code Editor window. Replace the <your name> and <current date> text in the comments with your name and the current date.

First, you will define a class named Card, which the Card Game application can use to instantiate 13 Card objects. Each Card object will represent a card from the suit of Hearts in a deck of playing cards.

Card objects have four attributes: the picture that appears on the front of the card, the picture that appears on the back of the card, the card's value, and the card's suit. The front and back pictures of each card are stored in image files contained in the VbReloaded\Chap10 folder. For example, an image of the front of the Ace of Hearts card is stored in a file named AH.tif. (The "A" stands for "Ace", and the "H" stands for "Hearts.") An image of the back of each card is stored in the CardBack.tif file.

Card objects also have three behaviors. First, they can initialize their attributes using values provided by the class. Second, they can initialize their attributes using values passed by the Card Game application. And third, they can shuffle themselves.

**To code the Card class:**

1. First, you will add a class file to the project. Click **Project** on the menu bar, and then click **Add Class**. The Add New Item – Card Game Project dialog box opens with Class selected in the Visual Studio installed templates list. Change the filename in the Name box to **Card.vb**, then click the **Add** button.

2. Enter the comments and Option statements shown in Figure 10.29, then position the insertion point as shown in the figure. If necessary, temporarily display the Solution Explorer window, which contains the name of the class file.

*Class filename*

*Enter these comments and Option statements*

*Position the insertion point here*

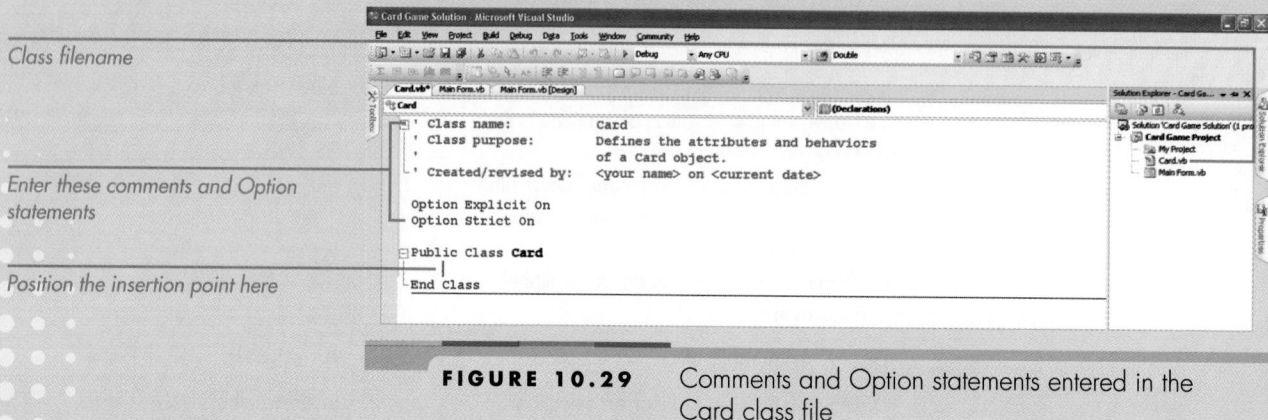

**FIGURE 10.29**    Comments and Option statements entered in the Card class file

3. Now you will create Private variables for the four attributes. Enter the following Private statements, pressing **Enter** twice after typing the last statement:
   **private _front as string**
   **private _back as string**
   **private _faceValue as string**
   **private _suit as string**

Next, you will create a Public property for each Private variable in the class. A Public property allows an application indirect access to the Private variable with which it is associated. (Recall that an application cannot directly access a Private variable in a class.)

4. Type **public property Front as string** and press **Enter**. Notice that the Code Editor inserts a set of parentheses after the Front property name. Also notice that it enters the Get and Set statements for you, and positions the insertion point within the Get statement.

5. Recall that the Get block in a Property procedure simply returns the contents of the Private variable. Type **return _front**.

6. The Set block in the Property procedure should assign the contents of the value parameter to the Private variable. Position the insertion point within the Set statement, and then type **_front = value**. Figure 10.30 shows the completed Front Property procedure.

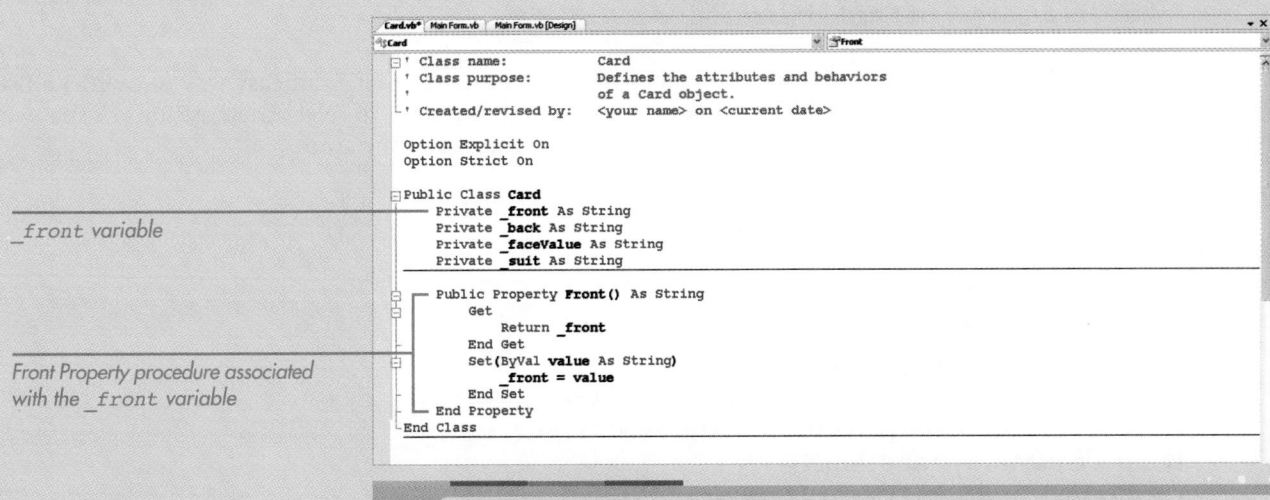

_front variable

Front Property procedure associated
with the _front variable

```
' Class name:          Card
' Class purpose:       Defines the attributes and behaviors
'                      of a Card object.
' Created/revised by:  <your name> on <current date>

Option Explicit On
Option Strict On

Public Class Card
    Private _front As String
    Private _back As String
    Private _faceValue As String
    Private _suit As String

    Public Property Front() As String
        Get
            Return _front
        End Get
        Set(ByVal value As String)
            _front = value
        End Set
    End Property
End Class
```

**FIGURE 10.30**   Completed Front Property procedure

7. Position the insertion point two lines below the `End Property` statement. Now you will enter the Property procedure for the `_back` Private variable. Type **public property Back as string** and press **Enter**. Within the Get statement, type **return _back**. Within the Set statement, type **_back = value**.

8. Position the insertion point two lines below the Back property's `End Property` statement. Now enter the Property procedure for the `_faceValue` Private variable. Type **public property FaceValue as string** and press **Enter**. Within the Get statement, type **return _facevalue**. Within the Set statement, type **_facevalue = value**.

9. Position the insertion point two lines below the FaceValue property's `End Property` statement. Now enter the Property procedure for the `_suit` Private variable. Type **public property Suit as string** and press **Enter**. Within the Get statement, type **return _suit**. Within the Set statement, type **_suit = value**.

Now you can enter the class's behaviors.

10. First you will enter the default constructor. Position the insertion point two lines below the Suit property's `End Property` statement, then enter the following code:
    **public sub new()**
        **_front = string.empty**
        **_back = string.empty**
        **_faceValue = string.empty**
        **_suit = string.empty**
    **end sub**

11. Now you will enter a parameterized constructor that allows an application to pass the initial values for the class's Private variables. Position the insertion point two lines below the default constructor's `End Sub` statement. Type **public sub new(byval frontFile as string, byval backFile as string, _** and press **Enter**. Press **Tab**, then type **byval faceCharacter as string, byval faceSuit as string)** and press **Enter**.

12. Complete the parameterized constructor by entering the following code:
    **front = frontfile**
    **back = backfile**
    **facevalue = facecharacter**
    **suit = facesuit**

Finally, you will enter a method that can shuffle any number of cards stored in an array. The method will require the application to pass it the array and the number of times the cards should be shuffled. You will pass the array *by reference* because the method will need to change the array's contents.

13. Position the insertion point two lines below the parameterized constructor's `End Sub` statement. Type **public sub shufflecards(byref cardArray() as card, byval numShuffles as integer)** and press **Enter**.

**14.** Type **' shuffles an array of Card objects** and press **Enter** twice.

As you learned when you coded the Concentration Game application in Chapter 7, an easy way to reorder a list of items is to swap one item with another item. You can use random numbers to select the positions of the two items to be swapped. In this case, the items will be the Card objects stored in the array.

**15.** Type the following lines of code:

```
Dim randomGenerator As New Random
Dim randNum1 As Integer
Dim randNum2 As Integer
Dim temp As New Card

For x As Integer = 0 To numShuffles
    randNum1 = randomGenerator.Next(0, cardArray.Length)
    randNum2 = randomGenerator.Next(0, cardArray.Length)
    temp = cardArray(randNum1)
    cardArray(randNum1) = cardArray(randNum2)
    cardArray(randNum2) = temp
Next x
```

**16.** Save the solution. Figure 10.31 shows the code entered in the Card class.

```
Visual Basic code

' Class name:          Card
' Class purpose:       Defines the attributes and behaviors
'                      of a Card object.
' Created/revised by:  <your name> on <current date>

Option Explicit On
Option Strict On

Public Class Card
    Private _front As String
    Private _back As String
    Private _faceValue As String
    Private _suit As String

    Public Property Front() As String
        Get
            Return _front
        End Get
        Set(ByVal value As String)
            _front = value
        End Set
    End Property

    Public Property Back() As String
        Get
            Return _back
        End Get
        Set(ByVal value As String)
            _back = value
        End Set
```

*(Figure is continued on next page)*

```
        End Property
        Public Property FaceValue() As String
            Get
                Return _faceValue
            End Get
            Set(ByVal value As String)
                _faceValue = value
            End Set
        End Property

        Public Property Suit() As String
            Get
                Return _suit
            End Get
            Set(ByVal value As String)
                _suit = value
            End Set
        End Property

        Public Sub New()
            _front = String.Empty
            _back = String.Empty
            _faceValue = String.Empty
            _suit = String.Empty
        End Sub

        Public Sub New(ByVal frontFile As String, ByVal backFile As String, _
            ByVal faceCharacter As String, ByVal faceSuit As String)
            Front = frontFile
            Back = backFile
            FaceValue = faceCharacter
            Suit = faceSuit
        End Sub

        Public Sub shufflecards(ByRef cardArray() As Card, _
            ByVal numShuffles As Integer)
            ' shuffles an array of Card objects

            Dim randomGenerator As New Random
            Dim randNum1 As Integer
            Dim randNum2 As Integer
            Dim temp As New Card

            For x As Integer = 0 To numShuffles
                randNum1 = randomGenerator.Next(0, cardArray.Length)
                randNum2 = randomGenerator.Next(0, cardArray.Length)
                temp = cardArray(randNum1)
                cardArray(randNum1) = cardArray(randNum2)
                cardArray(randNum2) = temp
            Next x
        End Sub
    End Class
```

**FIGURE 10.31**   Code entered in the Card class

Now that the Card class is defined, you can begin coding the Card Game application. According to the TOE chart shown earlier in Figure 10.28, five event procedures need to be coded.

**To begin coding the Card Game application:**

1. Click the **Main Form.vb tab** to display the Code Editor window for the MainForm.

Notice that the window contains a function named GetNumber. The GetNumber function receives a String value that represents the character appearing on the face of the card. Examples of String values passed to the function include "5", "Q" (for Queen), and "A" (for Ace). The function returns the Integer value associated with the String value. For example, when the String value is "5", the function returns the number 5. Similarly, the function returns the number 12 when the String value is "Q", and returns the number 14 when the String value is "A".

The Code Editor window also contains the code for the exitButton's Click event procedure. Additionally, it contains most of the code for the MainForm's Load event procedure. Before completing the Load event procedure, you will declare a module-level array. The array will contain 13 elements, with each element capable of storing a Card object.

2. Position the insertion point in the blank line below the `Public Class MainForm` statement, then press **Enter**. Type **private cards(12) as card** and press **Enter**.
3. Locate the MainForm's Load event procedure. The first statement in the procedure creates a variable named `path`. The `path` variable stores the folder path to the card image files on your computer's disk. If necessary, change the path to reflect the location of the files on your system.

The 12 assignment statements in the procedure instantiate 12 Card objects, assigning each to an element in the `cards` array. Notice that the statements use the Card class's parameterized constructor to provide initial values for each object.

4. Missing from the procedure is the statement to instantiate and initialize the thirteenth Card object. Position the insertion point in the blank line below the last assignment statement. If necessary, press **Tab** to align the insertion point with the preceding assignment statement. Type **cards(12) = new card(**. The IntelliSense feature displays the first signature of the New method in a box. Click the **up arrow** in the box to display the method's second signature. As Figure 10.32 shows, the signature indicates the data type, number, and position of the method's parameters.

*If necessary, modify the path*

*Box displayed by the IntelliSense feature*

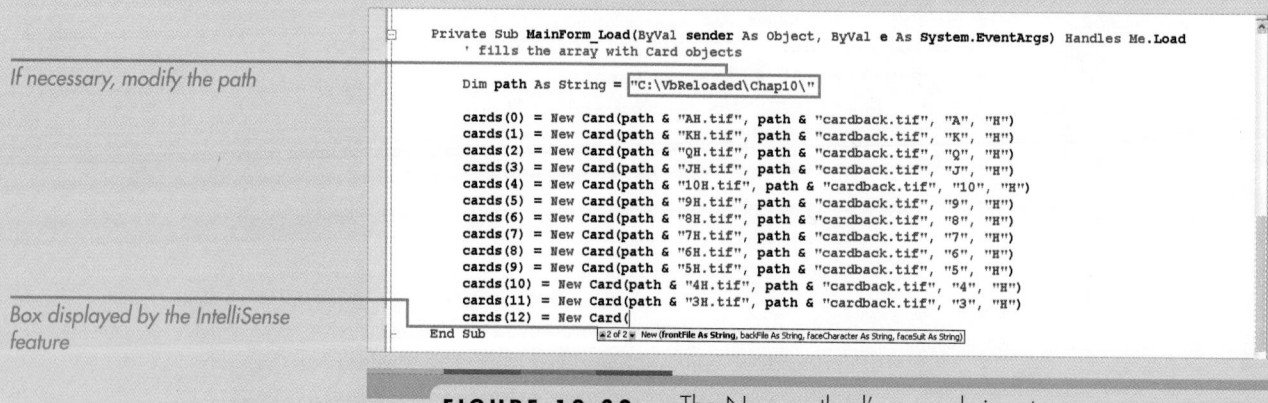

```
Private Sub MainForm_Load(ByVal sender As Object, ByVal e As System.EventArgs) Handles Me.Load
    ' fills the array with Card objects

    Dim path As String = "C:\VbReloaded\Chap10\"

    cards(0) = New Card(path & "AH.tif", path & "cardback.tif", "A", "H")
    cards(1) = New Card(path & "KH.tif", path & "cardback.tif", "K", "H")
    cards(2) = New Card(path & "QH.tif", path & "cardback.tif", "Q", "H")
    cards(3) = New Card(path & "JH.tif", path & "cardback.tif", "J", "H")
    cards(4) = New Card(path & "10H.tif", path & "cardback.tif", "10", "H")
    cards(5) = New Card(path & "9H.tif", path & "cardback.tif", "9", "H")
    cards(6) = New Card(path & "8H.tif", path & "cardback.tif", "8", "H")
    cards(7) = New Card(path & "7H.tif", path & "cardback.tif", "7", "H")
    cards(8) = New Card(path & "6H.tif", path & "cardback.tif", "6", "H")
    cards(9) = New Card(path & "5H.tif", path & "cardback.tif", "5", "H")
    cards(10) = New Card(path & "4H.tif", path & "cardback.tif", "4", "H")
    cards(11) = New Card(path & "3H.tif", path & "cardback.tif", "3", "H")
    cards(12) = New Card(
End Sub            ▲ 2 of 2 ▼  New (frontFile As String, backFile As String, faceCharacter As String, faceSuit As String)
```

**FIGURE 10.32**    The New method's second signature

5. Type **path & "2H.tif", path & "cardback.tif", "2", "H")**.
6. Save the solution.

Next, you will code the dealButton's Click event procedure. According to the TOE chart, the procedure should shuffle the cards, and then display the first two cards face down in the card1PictureBox and card2PictureBox.

**To code the dealButton's Click event procedure:**

1. Open the code template for the dealButton's Click event procedure. Type ' **shuffles the cards, then deals the first two cards** and press **Enter** twice.
2. You can shuffle the cards using the ShuffleCards method defined in the Card class. You can access the method using any of the Card objects stored in the array; in this case, you will use the first Card object. Type **cards(0).shufflecards(**. The IntelliSense feature displays the method's one signature, as shown in Figure 10.33.

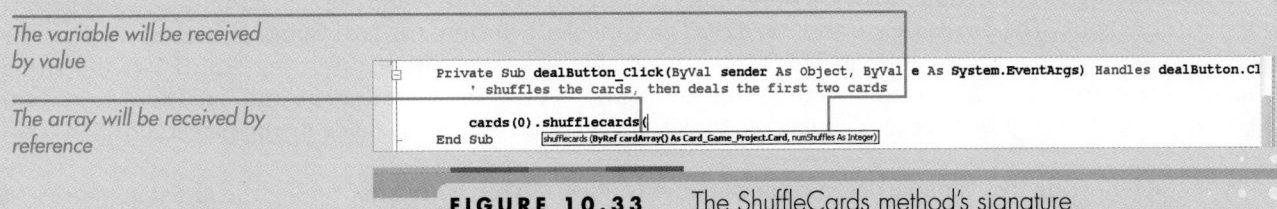

*The variable will be received by value*

*The array will be received by reference*

```
Private Sub dealButton_Click(ByVal sender As Object, ByVal e As System.EventArgs) Handles dealButton.Cl
        ' shuffles the cards, then deals the first two cards

        cards(0).shufflecards(
End Sub     shufflecards (ByRef cardArray() As Card_Game_Project.Card, numShuffles As Integer)
```

**FIGURE 10.33**   The ShuffleCards method's signature

The signature shown in Figure 10.33 specifies that the method's first parameter must be an array of Card objects. The ByRef keyword indicates that the array will be received *by reference*. The method's second parameter, which represents the number of times the Card objects should be shuffled, must be an integer. Notice that the signature does not specify how the second parameter will be received. If the ByRef keyword does not appear before the parameter's name, it means that the parameter will be received *by value*.

3. You will pass the cards array to the ShuffleCards method, and you will have the cards shuffled 13 times. Type **cards, 13)** and press **Enter** twice.

Now you need to display the first two cards from the array, face down, in the card1PictureBox and card2PictureBox. You can display a card face down in a picture box control by assigning the Card object's Back property to the control's Image property. Because the Back property of each Card object contains the name of a file (in this case, it contains cardback.tif) on your computer's disk, you need to use the **Image.FromFile method** to retrieve the file. The Image.FromFile method's syntax is **Image.FromFile(***string***)**, where *string* is the name of the file you want to retrieve.

4. Type ' **display the back of the first two cards** and press **Enter**. Type **card1picturebox.image = image.fromfile(cards(0).back)** and press **Enter**. Then type **card2picturebox.image = image. fromfile(cards(1).back)**.
5. Save the solution.

Next, you need to code the Click event procedures for the two picture boxes. As the TOE chart shown earlier in Figure 10.28 indicates, both Click event procedures will perform the same set of tasks. Therefore, you will enter most of their code in an independent Sub procedure, which then can be called from within both Click event procedures. First code the Click event procedures for the two picture boxes.

**To code the Click event procedures for the two picture boxes:**

1. Open the code template for the card1PictureBox's Click event procedure. Type ' **call the DetermineHighest procedure** and press **Enter**. The Click event procedure will pass one argument to the DetermineHighest procedure. In this case, it will pass the string "card1" to indicate that the player selected the card1PictureBox. Type **call DetermineHighest("card1")**.
2. Open the code template for the card2PictureBox's Click event procedure. Type ' **call the DetermineHighest procedure** and press **Enter**. In this case, the Click event procedure will pass the string "card2" to the DetermineHighest procedure. The "card2" string indicates that the player selected the card2PictureBox. Type **call DetermineHighest("card2")**.
3. Save the solution.

The last procedure you will code is the DetermineHighest procedure.

**To code the DetermineHighest procedure:**

1. Position the insertion point in the blank line above the Private Function GetNumber procedure header, then press **Enter**.
2. Type **private sub DetermineHighest(byval selection as string)** and press **Enter**.
3. Type ' **turns the cards face-up, then displays a message** and press **Enter**. Type ' **indicating whether the player selected the highest** and press **Enter**. Type ' **card; also displays the number of correct** and press **Enter**, then type ' **and incorrect selections** and press **Enter** twice.

The DetermineHighest procedure will use five variables named card1Value, card2Value, highest, numCorrect, and numIncorrect. The card1Value and card2Value variables will store the face values of both cards after the values have been converted to Integer. The highest variable will store either the string "card1" or the string "card2", depending on which of the two cards has the highest value. The numCorrect and numIncorrect variables will be used to keep track of the number of correct and incorrect selections made by the player.

4. Type the following five variable declaration statements. Press **Enter** twice after typing the last statement.
   **dim card1Value as integer**
   **dim card2Value as integer**
   **dim highest as String**
   **static numCorrect as integer**
   **static numIncorrect as integer**
5. The first task is to display the two cards face-up in the picture boxes. You can accomplish this task by assigning the Card object's Front property to the Image property of the picture boxes. Recall that the Front property contains the name of an image file. Type ' **display cards face-up** and press **Enter**. Type **card1picturebox.image = image.fromfile(cards(0).front)** and press **Enter**, then type **card2picturebox.image = image.fromfile (cards(1).front)** and press **Enter** twice.

Next, the procedure must determine the card that has the highest face value. To do so, it first will convert both cards' face values from a String to a number. (Recall that the face value is stored as a String in the Card class.) The procedure will use the GetNumber function to make the conversion and return the result. It will store the result in the card1Value and card2Value variables.

6. Type ' **convert the face values to numbers** and press **Enter**. The GetNumber function requires one argument: a String that represents the card's face value. You access a Card object's face value using the object's FaceValue property. Type **card1value = getnumber(cards(0).facevalue)** and press **Enter**, then type **card2value = getnumber(cards(1).facevalue)** and press **Enter** twice.
7. If the number stored in the card1Value variable is greater than the number stored in the card2Value variable, it means that the first card has the highest face value; otherwise, the second card has the highest face value. Type ' **determine the highest card** and press **Enter**. Then type the following selection structure:
   **if card1value > card2value then**
       **highest = "card1"**
   **else**
       **highest = "card2"**
   **end if**
8. Now compare the string stored in the selection variable, which indicates the card selected by the player, with the string stored in the highest variable. Position the insertion point two lines below the End If clause. Type ' **determine whether the player's choice is correct** and press **Enter**. Type **if selection = highest then** and press **Enter**.
9. If both strings are equal, display the "You chose correctly." message in a message box, and also add the number one to the numCorrect variable. Type **messagebox.show("You chose correctly.", "Card Game", _** and press **Enter**. Press **Tab**, then type **messageboxbuttons.ok, messageboxicon.information)** and press **Enter**. Type **numcorrect = numcorrect + 1** and press **Enter**.
10. Otherwise, display the "Sorry." message in a message box, and also add the number one to the numIncorrect variable. Type **else** and press **Enter**, then type **messagebox.show("Sorry!", "Card Game", _** and press **Enter**. Press **Tab**, then type **messageboxbuttons.ok, messageboxicon.information)** and press **Enter**. Type **numincorrect = numincorrect + 1**.

11. Finally, display the contents of the counter variables in the correctLabel and incorrectLabel. Position the insertion point two lines below the last End If clause, then type the following three lines of code:

**' display the counters**
**correctlabel.text = convert.tostring(numcorrect)**
**incorrectlabel.text = convert.tostring(numincorrect)**

12. Save the solution. Figure 10.34 shows the code entered in the Main Form.vb file.

```vb
Visual Basic code

' Project name:        Card Game Project
' Project purpose:     The project displays two cards
'                      and allows the player to guess
'                      which card has the highest value.
' Created/revised by:  <your name> on <current date>

Option Explicit On
Option Strict On

Public Class MainForm

    Private cards(12) As Card

    Private Sub DetermineHighest(ByVal selection As String)
        ' turns the cards face-up, then displays a message
        ' indicating whether the player selected the highest
        ' card; also displays the number of correct
        ' and incorrect selections

        Dim card1Value As Integer
        Dim card2Value As Integer
        Dim highest As String
        Static numCorrect As Integer
        Static numIncorrect As Integer

        ' display cards face-up
        card1PictureBox.Image = Image.FromFile(cards(0).Front)
        card2PictureBox.Image = Image.FromFile(cards(1).Front)

        ' convert the face values to numbers
        card1Value = GetNumber(cards(0).FaceValue)
        card2Value = GetNumber(cards(1).FaceValue)

        ' determine the highest card
        If card1Value > card2Value Then
            highest = "card1"
        Else
            highest = "card2"
        End If
```

*(Figure is continued on next page)*

```vb
        ' determine whether the player's choice is correct
        If selection = highest Then
            MessageBox.Show("You chose correctly.", "Card Game", _
                MessageBoxButtons.OK, MessageBoxIcon.Information)
            numCorrect = numCorrect + 1
        Else
            MessageBox.Show("Sorry!", "Card Game", _
                MessageBoxButtons.OK, MessageBoxIcon.Information)
            numIncorrect = numIncorrect + 1
        End If

        ' display the counters
        correctLabel.Text = Convert.ToString(numCorrect)
        incorrectLabel.Text = Convert.ToString(numIncorrect)
    End Sub

    Private Function GetNumber(ByVal faceChar As String) As Integer
        ' returns the numeric value of the Card object

        Dim number As Integer

        Select Case faceChar
            Case "2", "3", "4", "5", "6", "7", "8", "9", "10"
                number = Convert.ToInt32(faceChar)
            Case "J"
                number = 11
            Case "Q"
                number = 12
            Case "K"
                number = 13
            Case "A"
                number = 14
        End Select

        Return number
    End Function

    Private Sub exitButton_Click(ByVal sender As Object, _
        ByVal e As System.EventArgs) Handles exitButton.Click
        Me.Close()
    End Sub

    Private Sub MainForm_Load(ByVal sender As Object, _
        ByVal e As System.EventArgs) Handles Me.Load
        ' fills the array with Card objects

        Dim path As String = "C:\VbReloaded\Chap10\"

        cards(0) = New Card(path & "AH.tif", path & "cardback.tif", "A", "H")
        cards(1) = New Card(path & "KH.tif", path & "cardback.tif", "K", "H")
```

*(Figure is continued on next page)*

```
                    cards(2) = New Card(path & "QH.tif", path & "cardback.tif", "Q", "H")
                    cards(3) = New Card(path & "JH.tif", path & "cardback.tif", "J", "H")
                    cards(4) = New Card(path & "10H.tif", path & "cardback.tif", "10", "H")
                    cards(5) = New Card(path & "9H.tif", path & "cardback.tif", "9", "H")
                    cards(6) = New Card(path & "8H.tif", path & "cardback.tif", "8", "H")
                    cards(7) = New Card(path & "7H.tif", path & "cardback.tif", "7", "H")
                    cards(8) = New Card(path & "6H.tif", path & "cardback.tif", "6", "H")
                    cards(9) = New Card(path & "5H.tif", path & "cardback.tif", "5", "H")
                    cards(10) = New Card(path & "4H.tif", path & "cardback.tif", "4", "H")
                    cards(11) = New Card(path & "3H.tif", path & "cardback.tif", "3", "H")
                    cards(12) = New Card(path & "2H.tif", path & "cardback.tif", "2", "H")
        End Sub

        Private Sub dealButton_Click(ByVal sender As Object, _
            ByVal e As System.EventArgs) Handles dealButton.Click
            ' shuffles the cards, then deals the first two cards

            cards(0).shufflecards(cards, 13)

            ' display the back of the first two cards
            card1PictureBox.Image = Image.FromFile(cards(0).Back)
            card2PictureBox.Image = Image.FromFile(cards(1).Back)
        End Sub

        Private Sub card1PictureBox_Click(ByVal sender As Object, _
            ByVal e As System.EventArgs) Handles card1PictureBox.Click
            ' call the DetermineHighest procedure
            Call DetermineHighest("card1")
        End Sub

        Private Sub card2PictureBox_Click(ByVal sender As Object, _
            ByVal e As System.EventArgs) Handles card2PictureBox.Click
            ' call the DetermineHighest procedure
            Call DetermineHighest("card2")
        End Sub
End Class
```

**FIGURE 10.34**    Code entered in the Main Form.vb file

Now test the application to verify that it is working correctly.

**To test the application:**
1. Start the application. Press **Enter** to select the Deal button, which is the form's default button. Two cards appear face down in the interface, as shown in Figure 10.35.

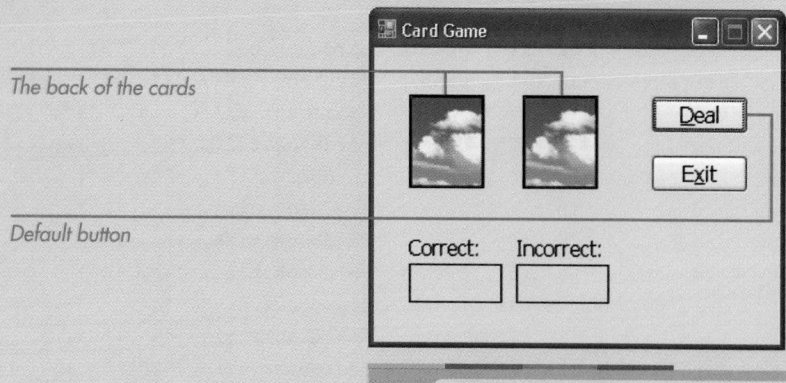

**FIGURE 10.35**    Cards are dealt face down

2. Click **one of the cards** in the interface. The application displays the cards face-up, and the appropriate message (either "You chose correctly." or "Sorry!") appears in a message box, as shown in Figure 10.36. (Your cards and message might be different.)

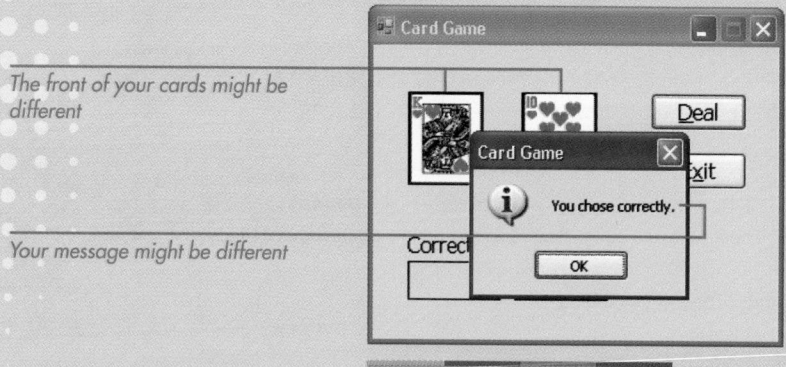

**FIGURE 10.36**    The application displays the front of the cards and a message box

3. Click the **OK** button to close the message box. Depending on the result of your game, the application displays the number one in either the correctLabel or the incorrectLabel.
4. On your own, test the application several more times. When you are finished testing the application, click the **Exit** button. If necessary, close the Output window.
5. Close the Code Editor window, then close the solution.

# PROGRAMMING EXAMPLE

## Kessler Landscaping Application

Monica Kessler, the owner of Kessler Landscaping, wants an application that she can use to estimate the cost of laying sod. In this application, you will use a MyRectangle class. Open the Kessler Solution (Kessler Solution.sln) file, which is contained in the VbReloaded\Chap10\Kessler Solution folder.

**TOE Chart:**

| Task | Object | Event |
|------|--------|-------|
| 1. Calculate the area of the rectangle<br>2. Calculate the total price<br>3. Display the total price in the totalPriceLabel | calcButton | Click |
| End the application | exitButton | Click |
| Display the total price (from calcButton) | totalPriceLabel | None |
| Get the length in feet | lengthTextBox | None |
| Get the width in feet | widthTextBox | None |
| Get the price of the sod per square yard | priceTextBox | None |
| Clear the contents of the totalPriceLabel | lengthTextBox,<br>widthTextBox,<br>priceTextBox | TextChanged |

**FIGURE 10.37**

**User Interface:**

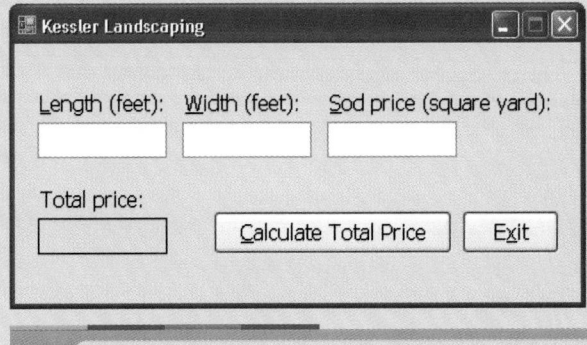

**FIGURE 10.38**

**Pseudocode:**

**exitButton Click event procedure**

1. close the application

**calcButton Click event procedure**

1. declare a MyRectangle object
2. assign the length and width to the MyRectangle object's properties
3. assign the sod price to a variable
4. calculate the area of the rectangle
5. calculate the total price of the sod
6. display the total price of the sod in totalPriceLabel

**lengthTextBox, widthTextBox, and priceTextBox TextChanged event procedures**

1. clear the contents of the totalPriceLabel

**Code (MyRectangle.vb file):**

```vb
' Class name:           MyRectangle
' Class purpose:        Calculates the area of a rectangle.
' Created/revised by:   <your name> on <current date>

Option Explicit On
Option Strict On

Public Class MyRectangle
    Private _length As Decimal
    Private _width As Decimal

    Public Property Length() As Decimal
        Get
            return _length
        End Get
        Set(ByVal value As Decimal)
            _length = Value
        End Set
    End Property

    Public Property Width() As Decimal
        Get
            return _width
        End Get
        Set(ByVal value As Decimal)
            _width = value
        End Set
    End Property

    Public Sub New()      'default constructor
        _length = 0D
        _width = 0D
    End Sub

    Public Sub New(ByVal len As Decimal, ByVal wid As Decimal)
        Length = len
        Width = wid
    End Sub

    Public Function CalculateArea() As Decimal
        Return _length * _width
    End Function
End Class
```

**FIGURE 10.39**

**Code (Main Form.vb file):**

```vb
'Project name:            Kessler Project
'Project purpose:         The project calculates the cost of laying sod.
'Created/revised by:      <your name> on <current date>

Option Explicit On
Option Strict On

Public Class MainForm

    Private Sub SelectText(ByVal sender As Object, ByVal e As System.EventArgs) _
        Handles lengthTextBox.Enter, widthTextBox.Enter, priceTextBox.Enter
        ' selects the existing text
        Dim current As TextBox
        current = TryCast(sender, TextBox)
        current.SelectAll()
    End Sub

    Private Sub ClearLabel(ByVal sender As Object, ByVal e As System.EventArgs) _
        Handles lengthTextBox.TextChanged, widthTextBox.TextChanged, _
        priceTextBox.TextChanged
        ' clears the total price label
    End Sub

    Private Sub exitButton_Click(ByVal sender As Object, _
        ByVal e As System.EventArgs) Handles exitButton.Click
        Me.Close()
    End Sub

    Private Sub calcButton_Click(ByVal sender As Object, _
        ByVal e As System.EventArgs) Handles calcButton.Click
        ' calculates the cost of laying sod

        Dim lawn As New MyRectangle
        Dim sodPrice As Decimal
        Dim area As Decimal
        Dim totalPrice As Decimal
        Dim isConvertedLen As Boolean
        Dim isConvertedWid As Boolean
        Dim isConvertedPrice As Boolean

        isConvertedLen = _
            Decimal.TryParse(lengthTextBox.Text, lawn.length)
        isConvertedWid = _
            Decimal.TryParse(widthTextBox.Text, lawn.width)
        isConvertedPrice = _
            Decimal.TryParse(priceTextBox.Text, sodPrice)
```

*(Figure is continued on next page)*

```
        If isConvertedLen AndAlso isConvertedWid _
            AndAlso isConvertedPrice Then
            ' calculate the area (in square yards)
            area = lawn.CalculateArea / 9D
        End If

        ' calculate and display the total price
        totalPrice = area * sodPrice
        totalPriceLabel.Text = totalPrice.ToString("C2")
    End Sub
End Class
```

**FIGURE 10.40**

## Quick Review

• The objects used in an object-oriented program are created, or instantiated, from classes.

• A class encapsulates the attributes that describe the object it creates, and the behaviors that allow the object to perform tasks.

• In Visual Basic, you can create (instantiate) objects from classes that you define with the Class statement.

• Class names are entered using Pascal case.

• You enter the class definition in a class file, which you can add to the current project using the Project menu.

• It is a good programming practice to enter the Option Explicit On and Option Strict On statements in both the form file and the class file.

• The names of the Public variables in a class are entered using Pascal case.

• Variables declared using the Public keyword in a class definition can be accessed by any application that uses an object created from the class.

• A class cannot control the values assigned to its Public variables.

• Most classes contain properties and methods.

• The names of the Private variables in a class should begin with the underscore character. The subsequent characters in the name should be entered using camel case.

• When an object is instantiated in an application, the Public members of the class are exposed to the application; the Private members are hidden from the application.

• When an application needs to assign data to or retrieve data from a Private variable in a class, it must use a Public property to do so. You create a Public property using a Property procedure.

• You use the ReadOnly keyword in a Property procedure header to create a property whose value can be retrieved (read), but not set. You use the WriteOnly keyword in a Property procedure header to create a property whose value can be set, but not retrieved.

• The names of the properties in a class should be entered using Pascal case. You should use nouns and adjectives to name a property.

• The Get block in a Property procedure allows an application to access the contents of the Private variable associated with the property.

- The Set block in a Property procedure allows an application to assign a value to the Private variable associated with the property.
- A class can have one or more constructors. All constructors are Sub procedures that are named New. Each constructor must have a different *parameterlist* (if any).
- A constructor that has no parameters is the default constructor. Constructors that contain parameters are called parameterized constructors.
- The computer processes the constructor whose parameters match (in number, data type, and position) the arguments contained in the statement that instantiates the object.
- The names of the methods in a class should be entered using Pascal case. You should use a verb for the first word in the name, and nouns and adjectives for any subsequent words in the name.
- Values that originate outside the class should always be assigned to the Private variables indirectly, through the Public properties.
- You use the `Overridable` keyword to indicate that a method in the base class can be overridden (replaced) in the derived class.
- You use the `Overrides` keyword to indicate that a method in the derived class overrides (replaces) a method in the base class.
- You use the Inherits clause to create a derived class.
- The `MyBase` keyword refers to the base class.
- While an application is running, you can use the Image.FromFile method to retrieve an image file from the computer's disk.

## Key Terms

The **Class statement** allows you to define a class in Visual Basic.

You use a **Property procedure** to create a Public property that allows the user to access the Private variables in a class.

The **Get block** in a Property procedure contains the **Get statement**. Within the Get statement, you enter the code that allows an application to retrieve the contents of the Private variable associated with the property.

The **Set block** in a Property procedure contains the **Set statement**. Within the Set statement, you enter the code that allows an application to assign a value to the Private variable associated with the property.

A **constructor** is a method whose instructions are automatically processed each time you use the class to create (instantiate) an object. The purpose of a constructor is to initialize the class's variables.

A constructor that has no parameters is called the **default constructor**.

Constructors that contain parameters are called **parameterized constructors**.

The method name combined with its *parameterlist* is called the method's **signature**.

You can use the **Image.FromFile method** to retrieve an image file from the computer's disk while an application is running.

## Self-Check Questions and Answers

1. In Visual Basic, you enter the Class statement in _____.
   a. a class file whose filename ends with .vb
   b. a class file whose filename ends with .cls
   c. a form file whose filename ends with .cla
   d. a form file whose filename ends with .cls

2. The attributes of an object are represented by _____ in a class.
   a. constants
   b. methods
   c. functions
   d. variables

3. If a variable in a class is declared using the Public keyword, the variable can be accessed by any application that uses an instance of the class.
   a. True
   b. False

4. When two methods have the same name but different *parameterlists*, the methods are referred to as _____ methods.
   a. loaded
   b. overloaded
   c. parallel
   d. None of the above.

5. Some constructors return a value.
   a. True
   b. False

6. Following the naming convention discussed in the chapter, which of the following would be considered a good name for a method contained in a class?
   a. Bonus
   b. SalesIncome
   c. SetDate
   d. Expenses

7. Following the naming convention discussed in the chapter, which of the following would be considered a good name for a property contained in a class?
   a. CalcBonus
   b. decSales
   c. FirstName
   d. Both b and c.

8. A constructor that has no parameters is called the _____ constructor.
   a. default
   b. empty
   c. parameterless
   d. parameter-free

9. The Product class contains a Private variable named _price and a Public method named CalculateNewPrice. The _price variable is associated with a Public property named Price. An application instantiates a Product object and assigns its address to a variable named item. Which of the following statements can the application use to assign the number 45 to the _price variable?
   a. `_price = 45`
   b. `Price = 45`
   c. `_price.item = 45`
   d. None of the above.

10. Which of the following can be used by the application in Question 9 to call the CalculateNewPrice method?
    a. `newPrice = Call CalculateNewPrice()`
    b. `newPrice = Price.CalculateNewPrice()`
    c. `newPrice = item.CalculateNewPrice()`
    d. `newPrice = item.CalculateNewPrice(_price)`

Answers: 1) a, 2) d, 3) a, 4) b, 5) b, 6) c, 7) c, 8) a, 9) d, 10) c

## Review Questions

1. Which of the following statements is false?
   a. An example of an attribute is the _minutes variable in a Time class.
   b. An example of a behavior is the SetTime method in a Time class.
   c. An object created from a class is referred to as an instance of the class.
   d. A class is considered an object.

2. A Private variable in a class can be accessed directly by a Public method in the same class.
   a. True
   b. False

3. An application can access the Private variables in a class _____.
   a. directly
   b. using properties created by Property procedures
   c. through Private procedures contained in the class
   d. None of the above.

4. To expose a variable or method contained in a class, you declare the variable or method using the _____ keyword.
   a. `Exposed`
   b. `Private`
   c. `Public`
   d. `Viewed`

5. The name of the default constructor for a class named Animal is _____.
   a. Animal
   b. AnimalConstructor
   c. Constructor
   d. None of the above.

6. An overloaded method must contain the keyword _____ in its procedure header.
   a. Loaded
   b. Overload
   c. Overloaded
   d. None of the above.

7. The method name combined with the method's optional *parameterlist* is called the method's _____.
   a. autograph
   b. inscription
   c. signature
   d. None of the above.

8. A constructor is _____.
   a. a Function procedure
   b. a Property procedure
   c. a Sub procedure
   d. either a Function procedure or a Sub procedure

9. Which of the following creates an Animal object and assigns the object's address to the dog variable?
   a. Dim dog As Animal
   b. Dim dog As New Animal
   c. Dim dog As Animal
      dog = New Animal
   d. Both b and c.

10. An application creates an Animal object and assigns its address to the dog variable. Which of the following calls the DisplayBreed method contained in the Animal class?
    a. Animal.DisplayBreed()
    b. DisplayBreed.Animal()
    c. DisplayBreed().objDog
    d. dog.DisplayBreed()

11. If you need to validate a value before assigning it to a Private variable, you enter the validation code in the _____ block in a Property procedure.
    a. Assign
    b. Get
    c. Set
    d. Validate

12. The Option Explicit On and Option Strict On statements can be entered in a form file only; they cannot be entered in a class file.
    a. True
    b. False

13. An application creates a Date object and assigns its address to the payDate variable. The Date class contains a Month property, which is associated with a String variable named _month. Which of the following assigns the number 12 to the Month property?
    a. payDate.Month = "12"
    b. payDate.Month._Month = "12"
    c. payDate._Month = "12"
    d. Date.Month = "12"

14. The Return statement is entered in the _____ block in a Property procedure.
    a. Get
    b. Set

15. Which of the following statements retrieves the image stored in the "Dog.gif" file, and displays the image in the animalPictureBox.
    a. `animalPictureBox.Image = Image.FromFile("Dog.gif")`
    b. `animalPictureBox.Image.FromFile("Dog.gif")`
    c. `animalPictureBox.FileImage("Dog.gif")`
    d. `animalPictureBox.Image = ImageFile("Dog.gif")`

## Review Exercises – Short Answer

1. Write a Class statement that defines a class named Book. The class contains three Public variables named `Title`, `Author`, and `Cost`. The `Title` and `Author` variables are String variables. The `Cost` variable is a Decimal variable.

2. Write a Class statement that defines a class named Tape. The class contains four Public String variables named `Name`, `Artist`, `SongNumber`, and `Length`.

3. Use the syntax shown in Version 1 in Figure 10.5 to declare a variable named `fiction` that can store the address of a Book object. Create the Book object and assign its address to the `fiction` variable.

4. Use the syntax shown in Version 2 in Figure 10.5 to create a Tape object and assign its address to a variable named `blues`.

5. An application contains the class definition shown in Figure 10.41.

```
Public Class Computer
    Private _model As String
    Private _cost As Decimal


    Public Property Model() As String
        Get
            Return _model
        End Get
        Set(ByVal value As String)
            _model = value
        End Set
    End Property
```

*(Figure is continued on next page)*

```
    Public Property Cost() As Decimal
        Get
             Return _cost
        End Get
      Set(ByVal value As String)
             _cost = value
        End Set
    End Property

    Public Sub New()
        _model = String.Empty
        _cost = 0D
    End Sub

    Public Sub New(ByVal comType As String, ByVal price As Decimal)
        Model = comType
        Cost = price
    End Sub

    Public Function IncreasePrice() As Decimal
        Return _cost * 1.2D
    End Function
End Class
```

**FIGURE 10.41**

a. Write a Dim statement that creates a Computer object and initializes it using the default constructor. Assign the object's address to a variable named homeUse.

b. Write an assignment statement that uses the Computer object created in Step a to assign the string "IB-50" to the Model property.

c. Write an assignment statement that uses the Computer object created in Step a to assign the number 2400 to the Cost property.

d. Write an assignment statement that uses the Computer object created in Step a to call the IncreasePrice function. Assign the function's return value to a variable named newPrice.

e. Write a Dim statement that creates a Computer object and initializes it using the parameterized constructor. Assign the object's address to a variable named companyUse. Use the following values to initialize the object: "IBM" and 1236.99.

6. Write the class definition for a class named Employee. The class should include Private variables and Property procedures for an Employee object's name and salary. The salary may contain a decimal place. The class also should contain two constructors: the default constructor and a constructor that allows an application to assign values to the Private variables.

7. Add another method to the Employee class you defined in Review Exercise 6. The method should calculate an Employee object's new salary, based on a raise percentage provided by the application using the object. Before calculating the new salary, the method should verify that the raise percentage is greater than or equal to zero. If the raise percentage is less than zero, the method should assign the number 0 as the new salary.

8. Write the Property procedure for a ReadOnly property named BonusRate. The property's data type is Decimal.

9. Write the Property procedure for a WriteOnly property named SetBonusRate. The property's data type is Decimal.

10. What are overloaded methods and why are they used?

## Computer Exercises

1. In this exercise, you create an application that uses a class.
   a. Create the Sweets Unlimited interface shown in Figure 10.7. Name the solution Sweets Solution. Name the project Sweets Project. Save the application in the VbReloaded\Chap10 folder.
   b. Add a class file to the project. Name the class file Salesperson.vb. Use the code shown in Figure 10.6 to define the class.
   c. Use the code shown in Figure 10.9 to code the Sweets Unlimited application.
   d. Save the solution, and then start the application. Use the information shown in Figure 10.8 to test the application.
   e. Click the Exit button to end the application, then close the solution.

2. In this exercise, you code an application that uses a class.
   a. Open the Area Solution (Area Solution.sln) file, which is contained in the VbReloaded\Chap10\Area Solution folder.
   b. Add a class file to the project. Name the class file Square.vb. Use the code shown in Figure 10.10 to define the class.
   c. Use the code shown in Figure 10.15 to code the Area application.
   d. Save the solution, and then start and test the application.
   e. Click the Exit button to end the application, then close the solution.

3. In this exercise, you modify the application created in Computer Exercise 2.
   a. Use Windows to make a copy of the Area Solution folder, which is contained in the VbReloaded\Chap10 folder. Rename the folder Modified Area Solution.
   b. Open the Area Solution (Area Solution.sln) file contained in the VbReloaded\Chap10\Modified Area Solution folder.
   c. Make the following modifications to the Square class:
      1) Add a Private variable named _area.
      2) Associate the _area variable with a Property procedure named Area.
      3) Change the CalculateArea method to a Sub procedure. The method should calculate the area and then assign the result to the Area property.
      4) Include a parameterized constructor in the class. The constructor should accept one argument: the side measurement. After initializing the Private variable, the constructor should automatically call the CalculateArea method.
   d. Modify the calcButton's Click event procedure so that it uses the parameterized constructor to instantiate the Square object. The parameterized constructor will automatically calculate the area of the square; therefore, you can delete the line of code that calls the CalculateArea method in the event procedure.
   e. Save the solution, and then start and test the application.
   f. Click the Exit button to end the application, then close the solution.

4. In this exercise, you code an application that uses a class.
   a. Open the Personnel Solution (Personnel Solution.sln) file, which is contained in the VbReloaded\Chap10\Personnel Solution folder.
   b. Add a class file to the project. Name the class file FormattedDate.vb. Use the code shown in Figure 10.16 to define the class.
   c. Use the code shown in Figure 10.18 to code the Personnel application.
   d. Save the solution, and then start and test the application.
   e. Click the Exit button to end the application, then close the solution.

5. In this exercise, you modify the application that you created in Computer Exercise 4.
   a. Use Windows to make a copy of the Personnel Solution folder, which is contained in the VbReloaded\Chap10 folder. Rename the folder Modified Personnel Solution.
   b. Open the Personnel Solution (Personnel Solution.sln) file contained in the VbReloaded\Chap10\Modified Personnel Solution folder.
   c. Modify the interface to allow the user to enter the year number.
   d. The FormattedDate class should create an object that returns a month number, followed by a slash, a day number, a slash, and a year number. Modify the class appropriately.
   e. Modify the FormattedDate class to validate the day number, which should be from 1 through 31.
   f. Make the necessary modifications to the Personnel application's code.
   g. Save the solution, and then start and test the application.
   h. Click the Exit button to end the application, then close the solution.

6. In this exercise, you code an application that uses a class.
   a. Open the ABC Solution (ABC Solution.sln) file, which is contained in the VbReloaded\Chap10\ABC Solution folder.
   b. Open the Employee.vb class file in the Code Editor window. Use the code shown in Figure 10.20 to code the class.
   c. Use the code shown in Figure 10.24 to code the application.
   d. Save the solution, and then start and test the application, using Figure 10.22 and 10.23 as a guide.
   e. Click the Exit button to end the application, then close the solution.

7. In this exercise, you use the Employee class from Review Exercise 7 to create an object in an application.
   a. Open the Salary Solution (Salary Solution.sln) file, which is contained in the VbReloaded\Chap10\Salary Solution folder.
   b. Open the Employee.vb class file in the Code Editor window, then enter the class definition from Review Exercise 7.
   c. View the Salary Form.vb file in the Code Editor window. Use the comments that appear in the code to enter the missing instructions.
   d. Save the solution, and then start the application.
   e. Test the application by entering your name, a current salary amount of 54000, and a raise percentage of 10 (for 10%). The application should display the number $59,400.
   f. Click the Exit button to end the application, then close the solution.

8. In this exercise, you modify the MyRectangle class, which you created in the chapter's Programming Example, and then use the class in a different application.

   a. Jack Sysmanski, the owner of All-Around Fence Company, wants an application that he can use to calculate the cost of installing a fence. Create an interface that allows the user to enter the length and width (both in feet) of a rectangle, as well as the fence cost per linear foot. Name the solution Fence Solution. Name the project Fence Project. Save the application in the VbReloaded\Chap10 folder.

   b. Use Windows to copy the MyRectangle.vb file from the VbReloaded\Chap10\Kessler Solution\Kessler Project folder to the VbReloaded\Chap10\Fence Solution\Fence Project folder.

   c. Use the Project menu to add the existing MyRectangle.vb class file to the Fence project.

   d. Modify the MyRectangle class so that it calculates the perimeter of a rectangle. To calculate the perimeter, the class will need to add together the length and width measurements, and then multiply the sum by two.

   e. Code the Fence application so that it displays the cost of installing the fence.

   f. Save the solution, and then start the application. Test the application using 120 as the length, 75 as the width, and 10 as the cost per linear foot. The application should display $3,900.00 as the installation cost.

   g. End the application, then close the solution.

9. In this exercise, you modify the MyRectangle class, which you created in this chapter's Programming Example, and then use the class in a different application.

   a. The manager of Pool-Time, which sells in-ground pools, wants an application that the salespeople can use to determine the number of gallons of water required to fill an in-ground pool—a question commonly asked by customers. (*Hint:* To calculate the number of gallons, you need to find the volume of the pool. You can do so using the formula length * width * depth.) Create an appropriate interface. Name the solution Pool Solution. Name the project Pool Project. Save the application in the VbReloaded\Chap10 folder.

   b. Use Windows to copy the MyRectangle.vb file from the VbReloaded\Chap10\Kessler Solution\Kessler Project folder to the VbReloaded\Chap10\Pool Solution\Pool Project folder.

   c. Use the Project menu to add the existing MyRectangle.vb class file to the Pool project.

   d. Modify the MyRectangle class appropriately.

   e. Code the Pool application so that it displays the number of gallons. To calculate the number of gallons, you divide the volume by .13368.

   f. Save the solution, and then start the application. Test the application using 25 feet as the length, 15 as the width, and 6.5 feet as the depth. The application should display 18,233.84 as the number of gallons.

   g. Click the Exit button to end the application, then close the solution.

10. In this exercise, you define a Triangle class. You also create an application that uses the Triangle class to create a Triangle object.
    a. Create an interface that allows the user to display either the area of a triangle or the perimeter of a triangle. (*Hint:* The formula for calculating the area of a triangle is ½ * base * height. The formula for calculating the perimeter of a triangle is a + b + c, where a, b, and c are the lengths of the sides.) Name the solution Math Solution. Name the project Math Project. Save the application in the VbReloaded\Chap10 folder.
    b. Add a class file to the project. Name the class file Triangle.vb. The Triangle class should verify that the dimensions are greater than zero before assigning the values to the Private variables. The class also should include a method to calculate the area of a triangle and a method to calculate the perimeter of a triangle.
    c. Save the solution, and then start and test the application.
    d. Stop the application, then close the solution.

11. In this exercise, you modify the application you coded in Computer Exercise 6. The modified application uses a base class and a derived class.
    a. Use Windows to make a copy of the ABC Solution folder, which is contained in the VbReloaded\Chap10 folder. Rename the copy Modified ABC Solution. Open the ABC Solution (ABC Solution.sln) file contained in the VbReloaded\Chap10\Modified ABC Solution folder.
    b. Open the Employee.vb class file in the Code Editor window. Use the code shown in Figure 10.25 to modify the class.
    c. Include another class definition in the Employee.vb file. Name the class Hourly. The Hourly class should contain a CalculateGross method that calculates the gross pay for an hourly employee. Calculate the gross by multiplying the hours worked by the pay rate.
    d. Use the code shown in Figure 10.26 to modify the application's code. Also complete the true path of the selection structure.
    e. Save the solution, and then start and test the application, using Figure 10.22 and 10.23 as a guide.
    f. Click the Exit button to end the application, then close the solution.

12. In this exercise, you modify the Card Game application that you created in the chapter's Programming Tutorial.
    a. Use Windows to make a copy of the Card Game Solution folder, which is contained in the VbReloaded\Chap10 folder. Rename the copy Card Game Solution-Mod1.
    b. Open the Card Game Solution (Card Game Solution.sln) file contained in the VbReloaded\Chap10\Card Game Solution-Mod1 folder.
    c. In the Card Game application, the suit of the cards is not important. Add another parameterized constructor to the Card class. The constructor should accept three arguments: the image file for the front of the card, the image file for the back of the card, and the face value of the card.
    d. Modify the MainForm's Load event procedure so that it uses the constructor containing three parameters.
    e. Also modify the application so that it allows the user to click a card only after the Deal button is clicked. Once the user clicks a card, both cards should be disabled.
    f. Save the solution, and then start and test the application.
    g. Click the Exit button to end the application, then close the solution.

13. In this exercise, you modify the Card Game application that you created in the chapter's Programming Tutorial.
    a. Use Windows to make a copy of the Card Game Solution folder, which is contained in the VbReloaded\Chap10 folder. Rename the copy Card Game Solution-Mod2.
    b. Open the Card Game Solution (Card Game Solution.sln) file contained in the VbReloaded\Chap10\Card Game Solution-Mod2 folder.
    c. Currently, the application shuffles the cards each time the user clicks the Deal button. It also displays only the first two cards from the array. Modify the application so that it displays the first two cards when the Deal button is clicked the first time, the next two cards when the Deal button is clicked the second time, and so on. Shuffle the cards only after each of the 13 cards has been displayed.
    d. Save the solution, and then start and test the application.
    e. Click the Exit button to end the application, then close the solution.

14. In this exercise, you modify the Card Game application from Computer Exercise 13.
    a. Use Windows to make a copy of the Card Game Solution-Mod2 folder, which is contained in the VbReloaded\Chap10 folder. Rename the copy Card Game Solution-Mod3.
    b. Open the Card Game Solution (Card Game Solution.sln) file contained in the VbReloaded\Chap10\Card Game Solution-Mod3 folder.
    c. Modify the application so that it uses the 52 cards found in a typical deck of playing cards. The application should shuffle the cards only after each of the 52 cards has been displayed.
    d. If the two cards in the interface have the same face value, use the following rules to determine the higher card: Hearts are the highest, followed by Diamonds, then Clubs, and then Spades. For example, if the two cards are the 10 of Diamonds and the 10 of Clubs, the 10 of Diamonds is the higher card.
    e. Save the solution, and then start and test the application.
    f. Click the Exit button to end the application, then close the solution.

15. In this exercise, you modify the Card Game application that you created in the chapter's Programming Tutorial.
    a. Use Windows to make a copy of the Card Game Solution folder, which is contained in the VbReloaded\Chap10 folder. Rename the copy Card Game Solution-Mod4.
    b. Open the Card Game Solution (Card Game Solution.sln) file contained in the VbReloaded\Chap10\Card Game Solution-Mod4 folder.
    c. Modify the application so that it displays three cards rather than two cards.
    d. Save the solution, and then start and test the application.
    e. Click the Exit button to end the application, then close the solution.

16. In this exercise, you modify the Card Game application that you created in the chapter's Programming Tutorial.
    a. Use Windows to make a copy of the Card Game Solution folder, which is contained in the VbReloaded\Chap10 folder. Rename the copy Card Game Solution-Disc1.
    b. Open the Card Game Solution (Card Game Solution.sln) file contained in the VbReloaded\Chap10\Card Game Solution-Disc1 folder.
    c. Currently, the only way to access the Card class's ShuffleCards method is through a Card object. This is the reason you used the `cards(0).ShuffleCards(cards, 13)` statement in the dealButton's

Click event procedure. You also can create a method that can be accessed through the class itself, rather than through an instance of the class. Such a method is created using the `Shared` keyword. Include the `Shared` keyword in the ShuffleCards procedure header, then change the `cards(0).ShuffleCards(cards, 13)` statement in the dealButton's Click event procedure to `Card.ShuffleCards(cards, 13)`.

  d. Save the solution, and then start and test the application.

  e. Click the Exit button to end the application, then close the solution.

17. In this exercise, you modify the Card Game application that you created in the chapter's Programming Tutorial.

  a. Use Windows to make a copy of the Card Game Solution folder, which is contained in the VbReloaded\Chap10 folder. Rename the copy Card Game Solution-Disc2.

  b. Open the Card Game Solution (Card Game Solution.sln) file contained in the VbReloaded\Chap10\Card Game Solution-Disc2 folder.

  c. Create a class named DeckOfCards that represents the 52 cards typically found in a deck of playing cards. The class should inherit the attributes and methods of the Card class.

  d. Modify the application's code so that it uses the 52 cards contained in the DeckOfCards class.

  e. Save the solution, and then start and test the application.

  f. Click the Exit button to end the application, then close the solution.

18. In this exercise, you find and correct an error in an application. The process of finding and correcting errors is called debugging.

  a. Open the Debug Solution (Debug Solution.sln) file, which is contained in the VbReloaded\Chap10\Debug Solution folder.

  b. Open the Code Editor window. Review the existing code.

  c. Notice that a jagged line appears below some of the lines of code in the Code Editor window. Correct the code to remove the jagged lines.

  d. Save the solution, then start the application.

  e. Correct the errors in the application's code, then save the solution and start the application. Test the application.

  f. Click the Exit button to end the application, then close the solution.

## Case Projects

### Glasgow Health Club

In Chapter 6's Programming Example, you created an application for the Glasgow Health Club. As you may remember, each member of the Glasgow Health Club must pay monthly dues that consist of a basic fee and, optionally, one or more additional charges. The basic fee for a single membership is $50 per month. The basic fee for a family membership is $90 per month. If the member has a single membership, the additional charges are $30 per month for tennis, $25 per month for golf, and $20 per month for racquetball. If the member has a family membership, the additional charges are $50 per month for tennis, $35 per month for golf, and $30 per month for racquetball. The application should calculate and display a member's monthly dues. Copy the solution's folder from the VbReloaded\Chap06 folder to the VbReloaded\Chap10 folder, then modify the application so that it uses a class.

### Franklin Calendars

Jeremiah Carter, the manager of the Accounts Payable department at Franklin Calendars, wants an application that he can use to keep track of the checks written by his department. More specifically, he wants to record (in a sequential access file) the check number, date, payee, and amount of each check. Create an appropriate interface and class, then code the application.

### Bingo Game

Create an application that simulates the game of Bingo. Be sure to use a class in the application.

### Pennington Book Store

Shelly Jones, the manager of Pennington Book Store, wants an application that she can use to calculate and display the total amount a customer owes. Create the interface shown in Figure 10.42. Assume that a customer can purchase one or more books at either the same price or different prices. The application should keep a running total of the amount the customer owes, and display the total in the Total due control. For example, a customer might purchase two books at $6 and three books at $10. To calculate the total due, Shelly will need to enter 2 in the Quantity box and 6 in the Price box, and then click the Add to Sale button. The Total due control should display $12.00. To complete the order, Shelly will need to enter 3 in the Quantity box and 10 in the Price box, and then click the Add to Sale button. The Total due control should display $42.00. Before calculating the next customer's order, Shelly will need to click the New Order button.

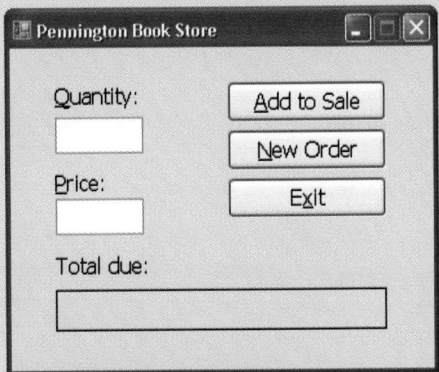

**FIGURE 10.42**

# Using ADO.NET 2.0

- Define the terms used when talking about databases
- Connect a database to an application
- Bind table and field objects to controls
- Explain the purpose of the DataSet, BindingSource, TableAdapter, and BindingNavigator objects
- Access the records in a dataset
- Write SQL SELECT statements
- Create a query using the Query Configuration Wizard
- Associate a ToolStrip control with a query

## DATABASE TERMINOLOGY

In order to maintain accurate records, most businesses store information about their employees, customers, and inventory in files called databases. In general, a **database** is simply an organized collection of related information stored in a file on a disk.

Many computer products exist for creating databases; some of the most popular are Microsoft Access, Oracle, and Microsoft SQL Server. You can use Visual Basic to access the data stored in databases created by these products. This allows a company to create a standard interface in Visual Basic that employees can use to access database information stored in a variety of formats. Instead of learning each product's user interface, the employee needs to know only one interface. The actual format of the database is unimportant and will be transparent to the user.

In this chapter, you learn how to access the data stored in a Microsoft SQL Server database. Databases created by Microsoft SQL Server are relational databases. A **relational database** is one that stores information in tables, which are composed of columns and rows, similar to the format used in a spreadsheet. Each column in a table represents a field, and each row represents a record.

A **field** is a single item of information about a person, place, or thing—for example, a name, a salary amount, a Social Security number, or a price. A **record** is a group of related fields that contain all of the necessary data about a specific person, place, or thing. The college you are attending keeps a student record on you. Examples of fields contained in your student record include your Social Security number, name, address, phone number, credits earned, grades earned, and grade point average. The place where you are employed also keeps a record on you. Your employee record contains your Social Security number, name, address, phone number, starting date, salary or hourly wage, and so on. A group of related records is called a **table**. Each record in a table pertains to the same topic, and each contains the same type of information. In other words, each record in a table contains the same fields.

A relational database can contain one or more tables. A one-table database would be a good choice for storing the information regarding the college courses you have taken. An example of such a table is shown in Figure 11.1.

| ID | Title | Hours | Grade |
|---|---|---|---|
| CIS100 | Intro to Computers | 3 | A |
| Eng100 | English Composition | 3 | B |
| Phil105 | Philosophy Seminar | 2 | C |
| CIS201 | Visual Basic 2005 | 3 | A |

**FIGURE 11.1**   Example of a one-table relational database

Notice that each record in the table contains four fields: an ID field that indicates the department name and course number, a course title field, a number of credit hours field, and a grade field. In most tables, one of the fields uniquely identifies each record and is called the **primary key**. In the table shown in Figure 11.1, you could use either the ID field or the Title field as the primary key, because the data in those fields will be unique for each record.

To store information about your CD (compact disc) collection, you typically use a two-table database: one table to store the general information about each CD (such as the CD's name and the artist's name) and the other table to store the information about the songs on each CD (such as their title and track number). You then use a common field—for example, a CD number—to relate the records contained in both tables. Figure 11.2 shows an example of a two-table database that stores CD information.

*The two tables are related by the Number field*

| Number | Name | Artist |
|--------|------|--------|
| 01 | Western Way | Dolly Draton |
| 02 | Midnight Blue | Paul Elliot |

| Number | Song title | Track |
|--------|-----------|-------|
| 01 | Country | 1 |
| 01 | Night on the Road | 2 |
| 01 | Old Times | 3 |
| 02 | Lovely Nights | 1 |
| 02 | Colors | 2 |
| 02 | Heavens | 3 |

**FIGURE 11.2**  Example of a two-table relational database

The first table shown in Figure 11.2 is often referred to as the **parent table**, and the second table is referred to as the **child table**. In the parent table, the Number field is the primary key, because it uniquely identifies each record in that table. In the child table, the Number field is used solely to link the song title and track information to the appropriate CD in the parent table. In the child table, the Number field is called the **foreign key**.

Storing data in a relational database offers many advantages. The computer can retrieve data stored in a relational format both quickly and easily, and the data can be displayed in any order. For example, the information in the CD database shown in Figure 11.2 can be arranged by artist name, song title, and so on. A relational database also allows you to control the amount of information you want to view at a time. You can view all of the information in the CD database, or you can view only the information pertaining to a certain artist, or only the names of the songs contained on a specific CD.

## ADO.NET 2.0

When a Visual Basic 2005 application needs to access the information stored in a database, the computer uses a technology called **ADO.NET 2.0** to connect the application to the database. (ADO stands for ActiveX Data Objects.) The connection allows the application to read information from and write information to the database.

After creating the connection between the database and the application, the computer opens the database and then makes a copy of the fields and records the application wants to access. The computer stores the copy, called a **dataset**, in its internal memory. The computer then closes both the database and the connection to the database. Notice that the connection is only a temporary one. The computer reconnects the application to the database only when the application requests further information from the database, or when changes made to the dataset (which is in internal memory) need to be saved. After retrieving the additional information or saving any changes, the computer again closes the database and the connection to the database.

In the concepts section of this chapter, you learn how to access the data contained in a Microsoft SQL Server database named Employees. The database is stored in a file named Employees.mdf, which is located in the VbReloaded\Chap11\SQL Databases folder. The Employees database contains one table, which is named tblEmploy. (It is not necessary to begin a table name with "tbl".) Figure 11.3 shows the table data displayed in a window in the IDE. (To learn how to access the data contained in a Microsoft Access database, refer to Appendix H. You can obtain Appendix H and the Access database files electronically from the Course Technology Web site by connecting to **www.course.com** and then navigating to the page for this book.)

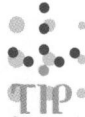

Table name

Field names

Records

| Number | Last | First | Hired | Rate | Status | Code |
|--------|------|-------|-------|------|--------|------|
| 100 | Benton | Jack | 3/5/1999 | 15.00 | F | 2 |
| 101 | Jones | Carol | 4/2/1999 | 15.60 | F | 2 |
| 102 | Ismal | Asaad | 1/15/2000 | 10.00 | P | 1 |
| 103 | Rodriguez | Carl | 5/6/2000 | 12.00 | P | 3 |
| 104 | Iovanelli | Sam | 8/15/2000 | 20.00 | F | 1 |
| 105 | Nyugen | Thomas | 10/20/2000 | 11.00 | P | 3 |
| 106 | Vine | Martha | 2/5/2001 | 9.50 | P | 2 |
| 107 | Smith | Paul | 5/14/2001 | 17.50 | F | 2 |
| 108 | Gerber | Wanda | 9/24/2001 | 21.00 | F | 3 |
| 109 | Zonten | Mary | 12/4/2001 | 13.50 | F | 4 |
| 110 | Sparrow | John | 1/5/2002 | 9.00 | P | 4 |
| 111 | Krutchen | Jerry | 5/7/2002 | 9.00 | P | 4 |

**FIGURE 11.3**     Data contained in the tblEmploy table

The tblEmploy table contains seven fields and 12 records. The Number, Last, First, Hired, and Rate fields store employee numbers, last names, first names, hire dates, and rates of pay, respectively. The Status field contains the employment status, which is either the letter F (for fulltime) or the letter P (for part-time). The Code field identifies the employee's department: 1 for Accounting, 2 for Advertising, 3 for Personnel, and 4 for Inventory. In the tblEmploy table, the Number field is the primary key, because it uniquely identifies each record.

## CONNECTING A DATABASE TO AN APPLICATION

Before an application can access the data stored in a database, you need to connect the database to the application. You can use the Data Source Configuration Wizard to make the connection. Figure 11.4 shows the procedure you follow when using the Data Source Configuration Wizard to connect a database to an application.

HOW TO...

### Connect a Database to an Application

1. Open the application's solution file. Click Data on the menu bar, and then click Show Data Sources to open the Data Sources window.

2. Click the Add New Data Source Link in the Data Sources window. This opens the Data Source Configuration Wizard dialog box and displays the Choose a Data Source type screen. If necessary, click Database. See Figure 11.5. As the figure indicates, the Database option in the dialog box allows you to connect to a database and choose the database objects (such as tables and fields) for your application. The option also creates a dataset that contains the chosen objects.

3. Click the Next button, and then continue using the Data Source Configuration Wizard to specify the data source. The Wizard will add several files to the project. The names of the files will appear in the Solution Explorer window. (Detailed steps for using the wizard can be found in the Programming Tutorial section of this chapter.)

4. When the Wizard is finished, it adds a dataset to the Data Sources window. Figure 11.6 shows an example of a dataset added to the Data Sources window in the Morgan Industries application. In this case, the dataset's name is EmployeesDataSet, and it contains one table object and seven field objects. The table object is the tblEmploy table contained in the Employees database, and the seven field objects correspond to the seven fields in the table.

**FIGURE 11.4**   How to connect a database to an application

*Data Sources window*

*Data Source Configuration Wizard*

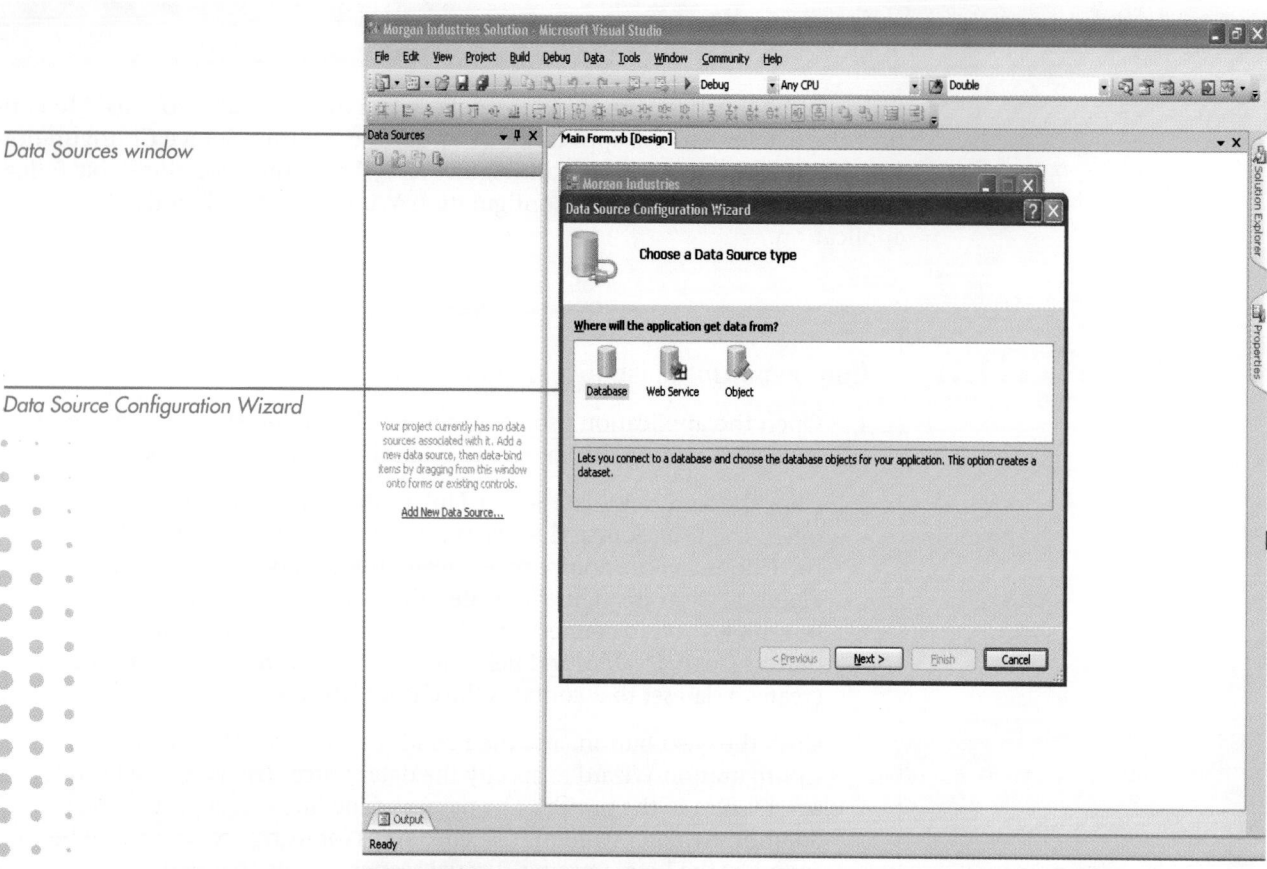

**FIGURE 11.5** Data Source Configuration Wizard dialog box

*Dataset*

*Table and field objects included in the dataset*

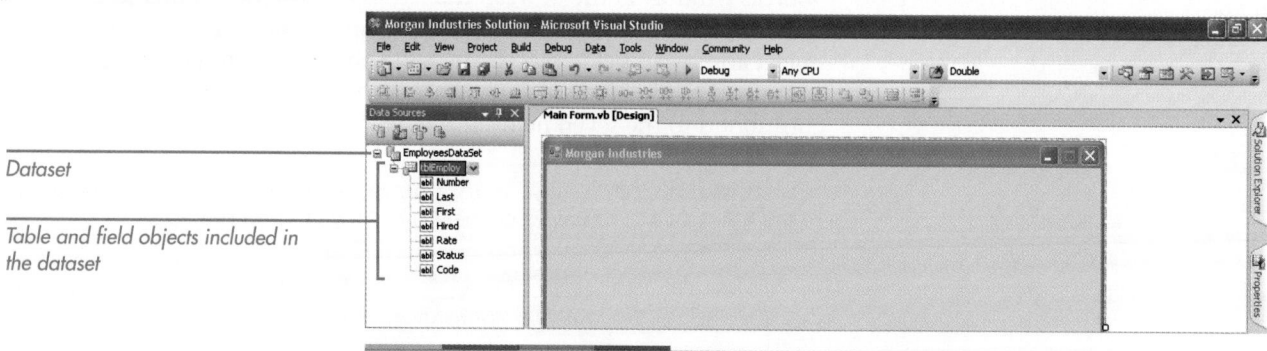

**FIGURE 11.6** Dataset added to the Data Sources window in the Morgan Industries application

## Previewing the Data Contained in a Dataset

As you learned in the previous section, the Data Source Configuration Wizard creates a dataset and adds it to the Data Sources window. You can use the procedure shown in Figure 11.7 to preview the contents of the dataset.

# HOW TO...

## Preview the Contents of a Dataset

1.  Right-click the Data Sources window, and then click Preview Data. This opens the Preview Data dialog box. (Alternatively, you can click the form, then click Data on the menu bar, and then click Preview Data on the menu.)

2.  Select the object to preview, and then click the Preview button. The Preview Data dialog box in Figure 11.8 shows the contents of the EmployeesDataSet.

3.  When you are finished previewing the data, click the Close button in the dialog box.

**FIGURE 11.7**    How to preview the contents of a dataset

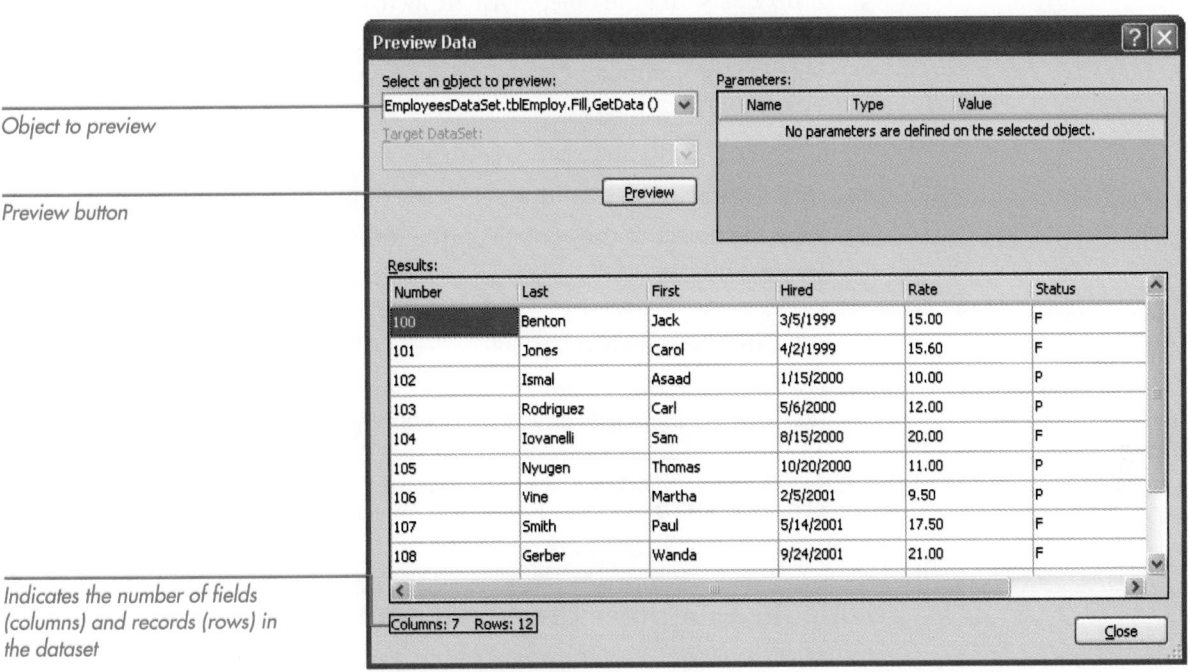

Object to preview

Preview button

Indicates the number of fields (columns) and records (rows) in the dataset

**FIGURE 11.8**    Contents of the EmployeesDataSet displayed in the Preview Data dialog box

Notice that `EmployeesDataSet.tblEmploy.Fill, GetData()` appears in the Select an object to preview box in Figure 11.8. EmployeesDataSet is the name of the dataset in the application, and tblEmploy is the name of the table included in the dataset. Fill and GetData are methods. The Fill method populates an existing table with data, while the GetData method creates a new table and populates it with data.

## BINDING THE OBJECTS IN A DATASET

For the user to view the contents of a dataset while an application is running, you need to connect one or more objects in the dataset to one or more controls in the interface. Connecting an object to a control is called **binding**, and the connected controls are called **bound controls**. Figure 11.9 shows various ways of binding the objects in a dataset. Notice that you can bind an object either to a control that the computer creates for you, or to an existing control in the interface.

## HOW TO...

### Bind the Objects in a Dataset

To have the computer create a control and then bind an object to it:

1. In the Data Sources window, click the object you want to bind.
2. If necessary, use the object's list arrow to change the control type.
3. Drag the object to an empty area on the form, then release the mouse button. The computer creates the appropriate control and binds the object to it.

To bind an object to an existing control:

1. In the Data Sources window, click the object you want to bind.
2. Drag the object to the control on the form, then release the mouse button.

   *OR*

1. Click the control on the form.
2. Use the Properties window to set the appropriate property or properties. (Refer to the *Binding to an Existing Control* section.)

**FIGURE 11.9**     How to bind the objects in a dataset

### Having the Computer Create a Bound Control

As indicated in Figure 11.9, one way to bind an object from a dataset is to drag the object to an empty area on the form. When you do this, the computer creates the necessary control and automatically binds the object to it. The icon that appears before the object's name in the Data Sources window indicates the type of control the computer will create. For example, the ▦ icon, which is shown in Figure 11.10, indicates that the computer will create a DataGridView control when you drag the tblEmploy table object to the form. A **DataGridView control** displays the table data in a row and columnar format, similar to a spreadsheet. Each row in the control represents a record, and each column represents a field. The abl icon, on the other hand, indicates that the computer will create a text box when you drag the Last field object to the form.

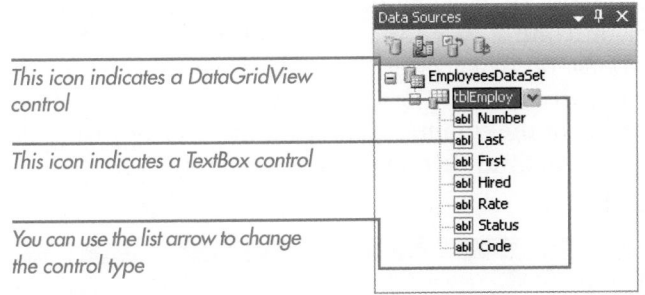

This icon indicates a DataGridView control

This icon indicates a TextBox control

You can use the list arrow to change the control type

**FIGURE 11.10**    Icons displayed in the Data Sources window

You can use the list arrow that appears next to an object's name to change the type of control the computer will create. For example, to display the tblEmploy data in separate text box controls, rather than in a DataGridView control, you first click tblEmploy in the Data Sources window. You then click its list arrow, as shown in Figure 11.11, and then click Details in the list. The Details option tells the computer to create a separate control for each field in the table.

**FIGURE 11.11**    Result of clicking the tblEmploy table object's list arrow

Similarly, to display the Last field data in a label control rather than in a text box, you first click Last in the Data Sources window. You then click its list arrow, as shown in Figure 11.12, and then click Label in the list.

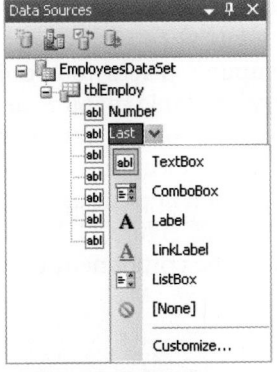

**FIGURE 11.12**    Result of clicking the Last field object's list arrow

Figure 11.13 shows the result of dragging the tblEmploy table object to the MainForm, using the default control type for a table, and then sizing the control. In this case, the DataGridView control was sized by first setting its AutoSizeColumnsMode property to Fill. The Fill setting automatically adjusts the column widths so that all of the columns exactly fill the display area of the control. The control's right border was then dragged to the desired width.

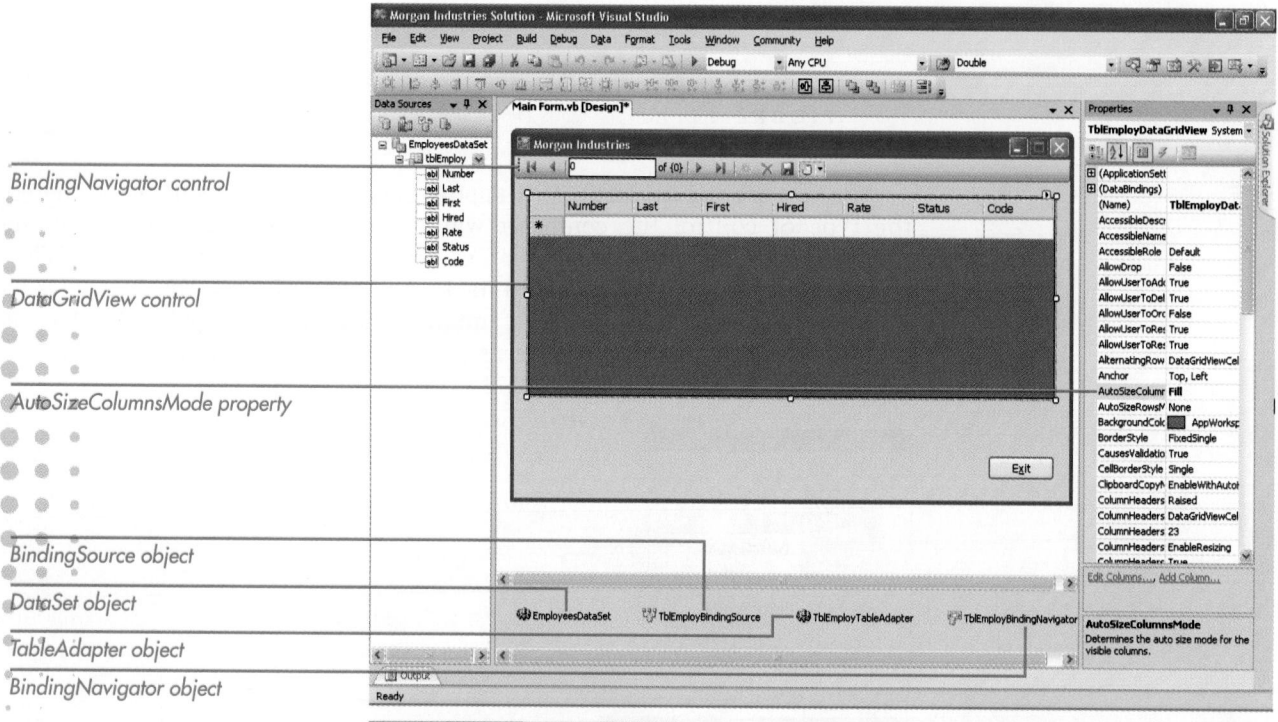

**FIGURE 11.13**      Result of dragging the tblEmploy table object to the form in the Morgan Industries application

Besides adding a DataGridView control to the form, the computer also adds a BindingNavigator control. When an application is running, the **BindingNavigator control** allows you to move from one record to the next in the dataset. It also allows you to add and delete a record, as well as save any changes made to the dataset.

Additionally, the computer places four objects in the component tray: a DataSet, a BindingSource, a TableAdapter, and a BindingNavigator. As you learned in Chapter 2, the component tray stores objects that do not appear in the user interface when an application is running. An exception to this is the BindingNavigator object, which appears as the BindingNavigator control during both design time and run time. Figure 11.14 illustrates the relationships among the database, the objects in the component tray, and the controls on the form.

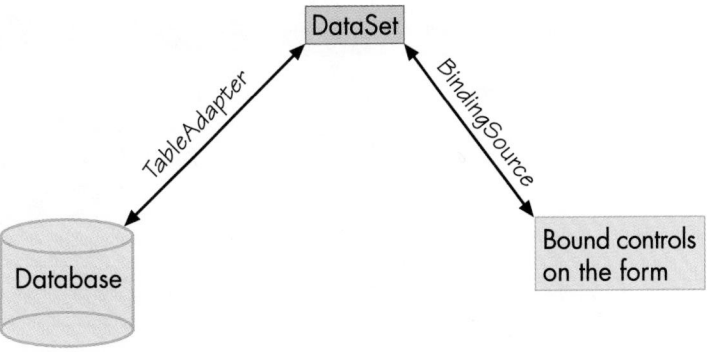

**TIP**

The DataSet, BindingSource, and TableAdapter objects, as well as the Timer control you learned about in Chapter 2, are examples of objects that appear in the component tray during design time, but are not visible during run time.

The **TableAdapter object** connects the database to the **DataSet object**, which stores the information you want to access from the database. The TableAdapter is responsible for retrieving the appropriate information from the database and storing it in the DataSet. It also is responsible for saving to the database any changes made to the data contained in the DataSet.

The **BindingSource object** provides the connection between the DataSet object and the bound controls on the form. For example, the TblEmployBindingSource object (shown earlier in Figure 11.13) connects the EmployeesDataSet object to two bound controls: the DataGridView control and the BindingNavigator control. The BindingSource object allows the DataGridView control to display the data contained in the dataset. It also allows the BindingNavigator control to access the records stored in the dataset.

If a table object's control type is changed from DataGridView to Details, the computer automatically provides the appropriate controls (such as text boxes, labels, and so on) when you drag the table object to the form. It also adds the BindingNavigator control to the form, and adds the DataSet, BindingSource, TableAdapter, and BindingNavigator objects to the component tray. The appropriate controls and objects are also automatically included when you drag a field object to an empty area on the form.

When a table or field object is dragged to the form, the computer not only adds the appropriate controls and objects to the application, but it also enters some code in the Code Editor window. Figure 11.15 shows the code that is automatically entered in the Code Editor window when the tblEmploy object is dragged to the form.

**Visual Basic code**

```
' Project name:          Morgan Industries Project
' Project purpose:       The project displays the employee
'                        records stored in a database.
' Created/revised by:    <your name> on <current date>

Option Explicit On
Option Strict On

Public Class MainForm

    Private Sub exitButton_Click ...

    Private Sub bindingNavigatorSaveItem_Click(ByVal sender _
        As System.Object, ByVal e As System.EventArgs) _
        Handles bindingNavigatorSaveItem.Click
        If Me.Validate Then
            Me.TblEmployBindingSource.EndEdit()
            Me.TblEmployTableAdapter.Update(Me.EmployeesDataSet.tblEmploy)
        Else
            System.Windows.Forms.MessageBox.Show(Me, _
                "Validation errors occurred.", "Save", _
                System.Windows.Forms.MessageBoxButtons.OK, _
                System.Windows.Forms.MessageBoxIcon.Warning)
        End If
    End Sub

    Private Sub MainForm_Load(ByVal sender As System.Object, _
        ByVal e As System.EventArgs) Handles MyBase.Load
        'TODO: This line of code loads data into the
        'EmployeesDataSet.tblEmploy' table. You can move,
        'or remove, it as needed.
        Me.TblEmployTableAdapter.Fill(Me.EmployeesDataSet.tblEmploy)
    End Sub

End Class
```

*This code is automatically entered when the table object is dragged to the form*

**FIGURE 11.15**    Code entered in the Code Editor window

As Figure 11.15 indicates, two event procedures are automatically entered in the Code Editor window: bindingNavigatorSaveItem_Click and MainForm_Load. The bindingNavigatorSaveItem_Click procedure is processed when you click the Save button on the BindingNavigator control. The code in the procedure saves, to the database, any changes made to the dataset. It does this using two methods: the EndEdit method of the BindingSource object and the Update method of the TableAdapter object. The **EndEdit method** applies any pending changes (such as new records, deleted records, or changed records) to the dataset. The **Update method** commits, to the database, the changes made to the dataset.

The syntax of the EndEdit method is [**Me.**]*bindingSourceName*.**EndEdit()**, where *bindingSourceName* is the name of the BindingSource object in the application. The syntax of the Update method is [**Me.**]*tableAdapterName*. **Update([Me.]***dataSetName*.*tableName***)**. In the syntax, *tableAdapterName* is the name of the TableAdapter object in the application. *DataSetName* is the name of the DataSet object, and *tableName* is the name of the table object contained in the dataset. The Me. in the syntax for both methods is optional, as indicated by the square brackets; when used, it refers to the current form.

The MainForm's Load procedure, on the other hand, is processed when an application is started and the form is loaded into the computer's internal memory. Notice that the Load procedure contains one statement: Me.TblEmployTableAdapter.Fill(Me.EmployeesDataSet.tblEmploy). The statement uses the TableAdapter object's **Fill method** to retrieve data from the database and store it in the dataset. The Fill method's syntax is [**Me.**]*tableAdapterName*.**Fill([Me.]***dataSetName*.*tableName***)**. In the syntax, *tableAdapterName* is the name of the TableAdapter object in the application. *DataSetName* is the name of the DataSet object, and *tableName* is the name of the table object contained in the dataset.

In most applications, the statement to fill a dataset with data belongs in the form's Load event procedure, as shown in Figure 11.15. However, as the comments in the Load procedure indicate, you can move the statement to another procedure; or, you can remove the statement from the Code Editor window.

Figure 11.16 shows a sample run of the Morgan Industries application. When the application is started, the statement in the MainForm's Load event procedure retrieves the appropriate data from the Employees database and loads the data into the EmployeesDataSet object. As the figure shows, the data is displayed in the DataGridView control, which is bound to the tblEmploy table contained in the EmployeesDataSet.

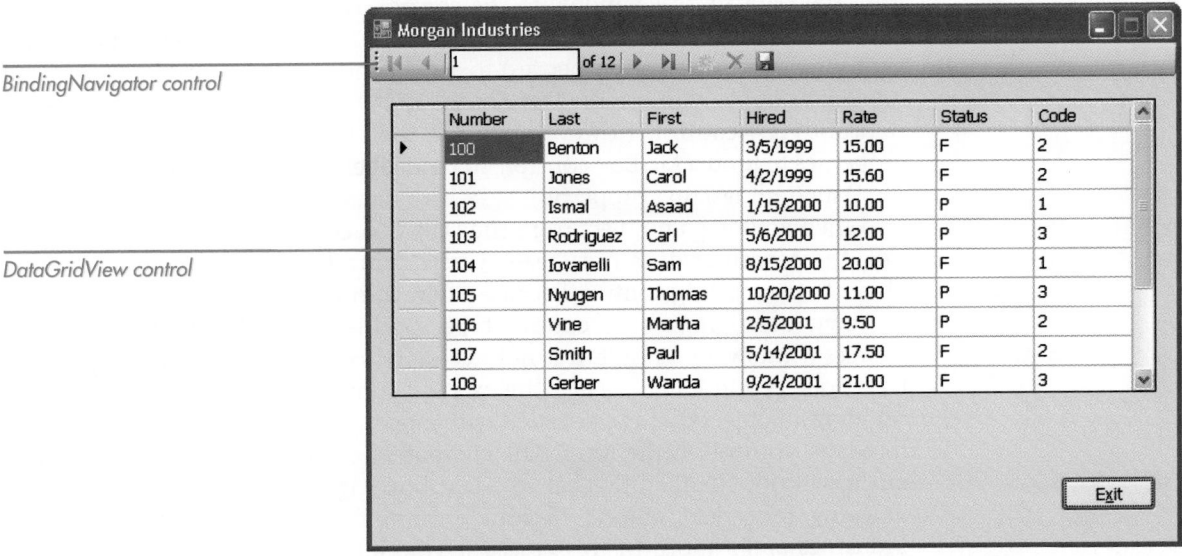

*BindingNavigator control*

*DataGridView control*

**FIGURE 11.16**   Sample run of the Morgan Industries application

You can make a change to an existing record by modifying the data in the appropriate cell in the DataGridView control. A cell is an intersection of a row and column in the control. For example, to change Martha Vine's status from part-time to full-time, you position the cursor in the cell located in the seventh row, sixth column. You then replace the letter P with the letter F.

Recall that the EmployeesDataSet object is also bound to the TblEmployBindingNavigator control, which is shown in Figure 11.17.

Save button
Add and Delete buttons
Use to access specific records
Current record number

**FIGURE 11.17**     TblEmployBindingNavigator control

You can use the buttons on the TblEmployBindingNavigator control to access the first and last records in the EmployeesDataSet, as well as to access the previous and next records. You also can use the TblEmployBindingNavigator control to access a record by its record number. The first record in a dataset has a record number of one, the second has a record number of two, and so on. To access record number five, you type the number 5 in the box that contains the current record number, and you then press the Enter key on your keyboard. As shown in Figure 11.17, the TblEmployBindingNavigator control also contains buttons that allow you to add a record to the dataset, delete a record from the dataset, and save the changes made to the dataset.

## Binding to an Existing Control

As indicated earlier in Figure 11.9, you also can bind an object in a dataset to an existing control on the form. The easiest way to do this is by dragging the object from the Data Sources window to the control. However, you also can click the control and then set one or more properties in the Properties window. The appropriate property (or properties) to set depends on the control you are binding. For example, you use the DataSource and DataMember properties to bind a DataGridView control. However, you use the DataSource and DisplayMember properties to bind a ListBox control. To bind label and text box controls, you use the DataBindings/Text property.

When you drag an object from the Data Sources window to an existing control, the computer does not create a new control; rather, it merely binds the object to the existing control. Because a new control does not need to be created, the computer ignores the control type specified for the object in the Data Sources window. As a result, it is not necessary to change the control type in the Data Sources window to match the existing control's type. In other words, you can drag an object that is associated with a text box in the Data Sources window to a label control on the form. The computer will bind the object to the label, but it will not change the label to a text box. Figure 11.18 shows the result of dragging four field objects to four existing label controls in the Morgan Industries application. In this case, the computer will bind the Number, Last, Status, and Code field objects to the numberLabel, lastNameLabel, statusLabel, and codeLabel controls, respectively.

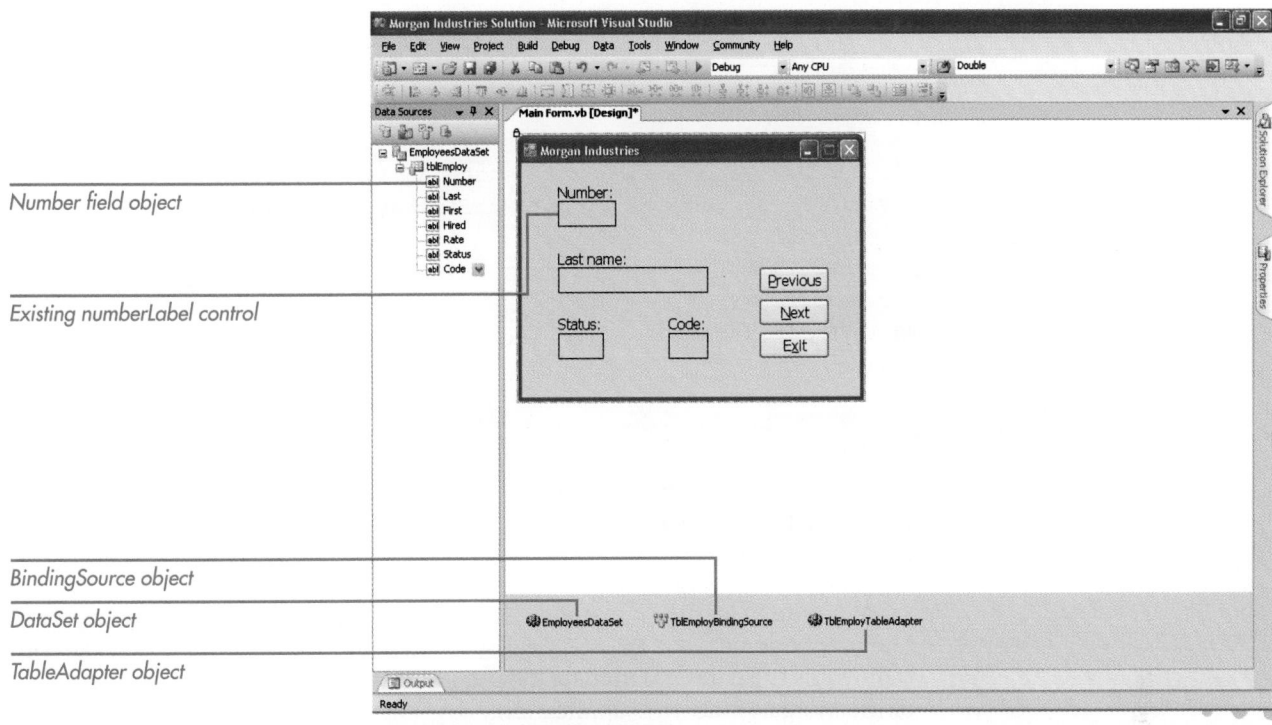

*Number field object*

*Existing numberLabel control*

*BindingSource object*

*DataSet object*

*TableAdapter object*

**FIGURE 11.18**   Result of dragging field objects to existing label controls in the Morgan Industries application

In addition to binding the field objects to the appropriate controls, the computer also adds the DataSet, BindingSource, and TableAdapter objects to the component tray. However, notice that it does not include the BindingNavigator object and BindingNavigator control in the application. You can use the BindingNavigator tool in the Toolbox to add a BindingNavigator control to the form; doing this also adds a BindingNavigator object to the component tray. You then must set the BindingNavigator control's DataSource property to the name of the BindingSource object in the application. In this case, for example, you would set the control's DataSource property to TblEmployBindingSource.

Figure 11.19 shows the code that is automatically entered in the Code Editor window when you drag an object from the Data Sources window to an existing control on the form.

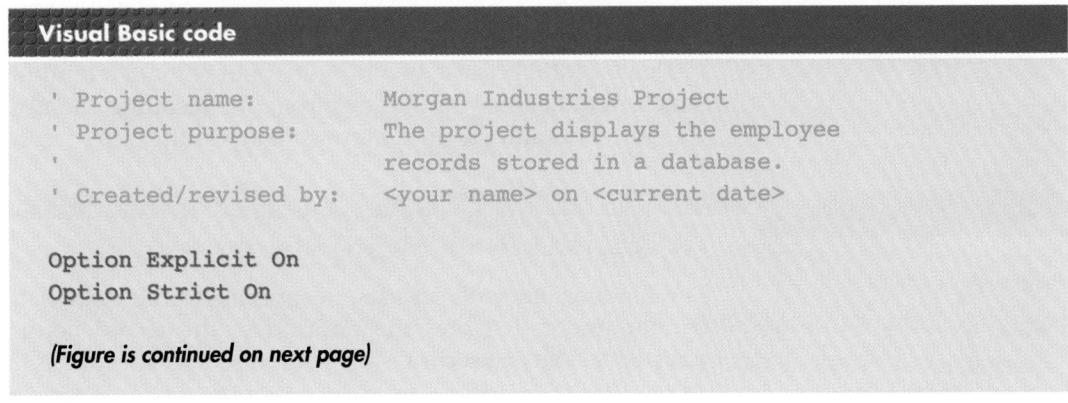

**Visual Basic code**

```
' Project name:        Morgan Industries Project
' Project purpose:     The project displays the employee
'                      records stored in a database.
' Created/revised by:  <your name> on <current date>


Option Explicit On
Option Strict On
```

**(Figure is continued on next page)**

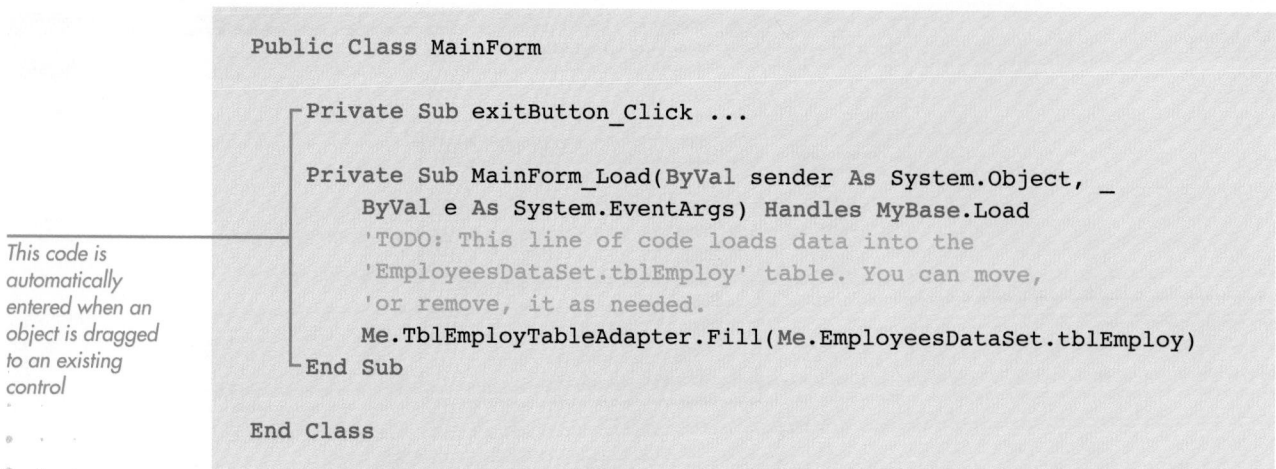

*This code is automatically entered when an object is dragged to an existing control*

```
Public Class MainForm

    Private Sub exitButton_Click ...

    Private Sub MainForm_Load(ByVal sender As System.Object, _
        ByVal e As System.EventArgs) Handles MyBase.Load
        'TODO: This line of code loads data into the
        'EmployeesDataSet.tblEmploy' table. You can move,
        'or remove, it as needed.
        Me.TblEmployTableAdapter.Fill(Me.EmployeesDataSet.tblEmploy)
    End Sub

End Class
```

**FIGURE 11.19**      Code entered in the Code Editor window

As you learned earlier, the `Me.TblEmployTableAdapter.Fill` `(Me.EmployeesDataSet.tblEmploy)` statement in the form's Load event procedure fills the dataset with data. Figure 11.20 shows a sample run of this version of the Morgan Industries application.

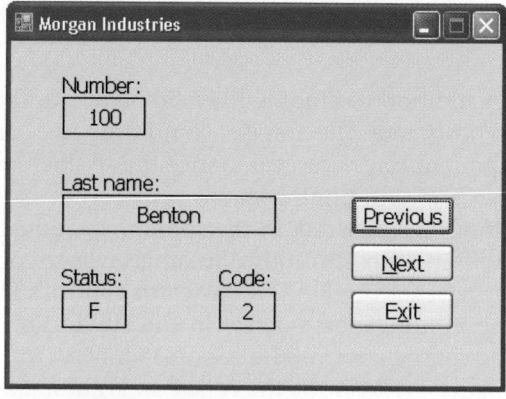

**FIGURE 11.20**      Sample run of a different version of the Morgan Industries application

Notice that only the first record in the dataset appears in the interface shown in Figure 11.20. Because the form does not contain a BindingNavigator control, which would allow you to move from one record to the next, you will need to code the Next and Previous buttons to access the other records in the dataset.

## ACCESSING THE RECORDS IN A DATASET

The BindingSource object uses an invisible record pointer to keep track of the current record. It stores the position of the record pointer in its **Position property**. The first record is in position zero, the second is in position one, and so on. For example, if the record pointer is pointing to the third record, the Position property contains the integer 2. Figure 11.21 shows the Position property's syntax and includes examples of using the property.

**HOW TO...**

**Use the BindingSource Object's Position Property**

**Syntax**
*bindingSourceName*.**Position**

**Examples**
`recordNum = TblEmployBindingSource.Position`
assigns the position of the current record to the `recordNum` variable

`TblEmployBindingSource.Position = 4`
moves the record pointer to the fifth record in the dataset

`TblEmployBindingSource.Position = _`
    `TblEmployBindingSource.Position + 1`
moves the record pointer to the next record in the dataset

**FIGURE 11.21**   How to use the BindingSource object's Position property

In the first example shown in Figure 11.21, the `recordNum = TblEmployBindingSource.Position` statement assigns the record pointer's position to the `recordNum` variable. The `TblEmployBindingSource.Position = 4` statement in the second example moves the record pointer to the fifth record in the dataset. (Recall that the first record is in position zero.) In the last example, the `TblEmployBindingSource.Position = TblEmployBindingSource.Position + 1` moves the record pointer to the next record in the dataset.

In addition to using the Position property to move the record pointer in a dataset, you also can use the Move methods of the BindingSource object. Figure 11.22 shows each Move method's syntax and includes an example of using each method. Notice that you can use the Move methods to move the record pointer to the first, last, next, and previous record in the dataset associated with the BindingSource object.

**HOW TO...**

**Use the BindingSource Object's Move Methods**

**Syntax**
*bindingSourceName*.**MoveFirst()**
*bindingSourceName*.**MoveLast()**
*bindingSourceName*.**MoveNext()**
*bindingSourceName*.**MovePrevious()**

*(Figure is continued on next page)*

**Examples**
```
TblEmployBindingSource.MoveFirst()
```
moves the record pointer to the first record in the dataset

```
TblEmployBindingSource.MoveLast()
```
moves the record pointer to the last record in the dataset

```
TblEmployBindingSource.MoveNext()
```
moves the record pointer to the next record in the dataset

```
TblEmployBindingSource.MovePrevious()
```
moves the record pointer to the previous record in the dataset

**FIGURE 11.22**     How to use the BindingSource object's Move methods

When the Next button in the Morgan Industries application is clicked, its Click event procedure should move the record pointer to the next record in the dataset. Similarly, when the Previous button is clicked, its Click event procedure should move the record pointer to the previous record in the dataset. You can use the TblEmployBindingSource object's MoveNext and MovePrevious methods to code the procedures, as shown in Figure 11.23.

**Visual Basic code**

```
Private Sub nextButton_Click(ByVal sender As Object, _
    ByVal e As System.EventArgs) Handles nextButton.Click
    TblEmployBindingSource.MoveNext()
End Sub


Private Sub previousButton_Click(ByVal sender As Object, _
    ByVal e As System.EventArgs) Handles previousButton.Click
    TblEmployBindingSource.MovePrevious()
End Sub
```

*Moves the record pointer to the next record in the dataset*

*Moves the record pointer to the previous record in the dataset*

**FIGURE 11.23**     Code entered in the Next and Previous buttons' Click event procedures

## DATASET DESIGNER

As you learned earlier, data stored in a relational database can be displayed in any order. For example, you can arrange the data contained in the Employees database by employee number, pay rate, status, and so on. A relational database also allows you to control the amount of information you want to view at a time. You can view all of the information in the Employees database, or you can view only the employee numbers and corresponding pay rates. You also can choose to view only the records for the part-time employees.

You can use the DataSet Designer to indicate the order in which you want data displayed, and also to specify the fields and records you want to view from the database. Figure 11.24 shows various ways of opening the DataSet Designer, and Figure 11.25 shows the DataSet Designer open in the IDE.

## HOW TO...

**Open the DataSet Designer**

- Right-click the Data Sources window, then click Edit DataSet with Designer.
- In the Solution Explorer window, right-click the name of the schema file, which has an .xsd extension, then click View Designer.
- Right-click the TableAdapter object in the component tray, then click Edit Queries in DataSet Designer.

**FIGURE 11.24**   How to open the DataSet Designer

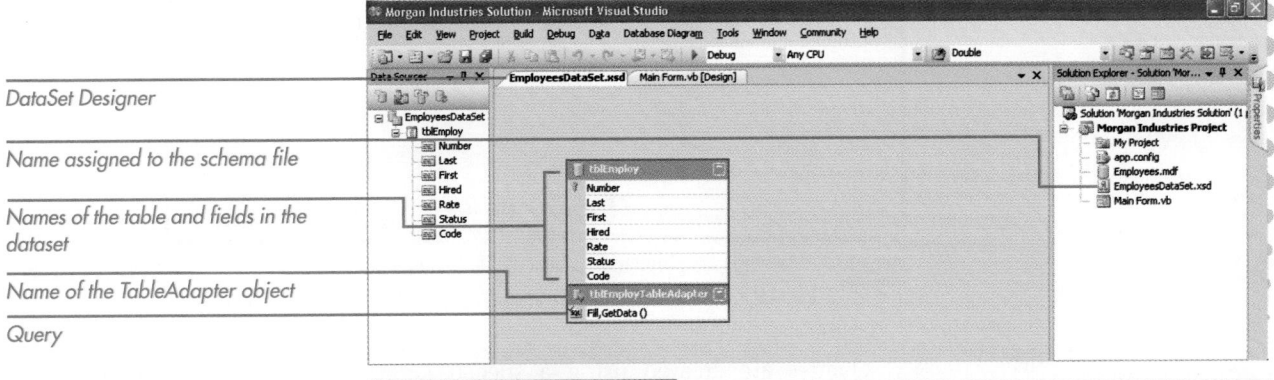

DataSet Designer

Name assigned to the schema file

Names of the table and fields in the dataset

Name of the TableAdapter object

Query

**FIGURE 11.25**   DataSet Designer

Notice that the Solution Explorer window shown in Figure 11.25 contains a file named EmployeesDataSet.xsd. The filename also appears on the tab in the DataSet Designer. The .xsd extension on the filename indicates that the file is an XML schema definition file. **XML**, which stands for **Extensible Markup Language**, is a text-based language used to store and share data between applications and across networks and the Internet. An **XML schema definition file** defines the tables and fields that make up the dataset. The .xsd file is added to the Solution Explorer window when you connect a database to an application.

The DataSet Designer in Figure 11.25 shows the name of the table object included in the EmployeesDataSet. It also lists the names of the seven field objects included in the dataset. Additionally, it shows the name of the application's TableAdapter object, which connects the dataset to its underlying database.

Every TableAdapter object contains one or more queries, which are listed below the TableAdapter object's name in the DataSet Designer. A **query** specifies the fields and records to retrieve from the database, as well as the order in which to arrange the fields and records. As Figure 11.25 indicates, the tblEmployTableAdapter in the

**TIP**

The key icon in Figure 11.25 indicates that the Number field is the primary field in the tblEmploy table.

Morgan Industries application contains one query. The query is associated with two methods named Fill and GetData. As you learned earlier, you use the Fill method to populate an existing table with data, and use the GetData method to create a new table and populate it with data.

You can view the information contained in a query by right-clicking the query in the DataSet Designer window, and then clicking Configure. Doing this opens the TableAdapter Configuration Wizard, as shown in Figure 11.26.

*SQL SELECT statement*

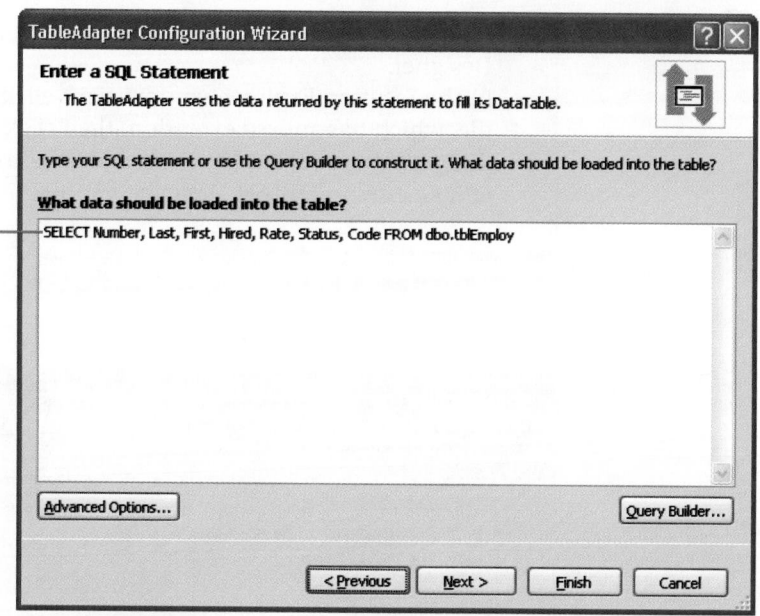

**FIGURE 11.26**     TableAdapter Configuration Wizard

Queries are created using a special language called **Structured Query Language** or, more simply, SQL. **SQL**, which is pronounced *ess-cue-el*, is a set of commands that allows you to access and manipulate the data stored in many database management systems on computers of all sizes, from large mainframes to small microcomputers. You can use SQL commands to perform database tasks such as storing, retrieving, updating, deleting, and sorting data.

The SELECT statement, which appears in Figure 11.26, is the most commonly used command in SQL. The **SELECT statement** allows you to specify the fields and records you want to view, as well as control the order in which the fields and records appear when displayed. Figure 11.27 shows the basic syntax of the SELECT statement and includes several examples of using the statement to access the data stored in the Employees database (shown earlier in Figure 11.3). As you may remember, the database contains one table (named tblEmploy) and seven fields. The Number, Rate, and Code fields contain numeric data. The Last, First, and Hired fields contain text data, and the Status field contains one character.

HOW TO...

## Use the SELECT Statement

**Syntax**
**SELECT** *fields* **FROM** *table* [**WHERE** *condition*] [**ORDER BY** *field*]

**Examples**

**Example 1**
```
SELECT Number, Last, First, Hired, Rate, Status, Code
FROM dbo.tblEmploy
```
selects all of the fields and records in the table

**Example 2**
```
SELECT Number, First, Last FROM dbo.tblEmploy
```
selects the Number, First, and Last fields from each record in the table

**Example 3**
```
SELECT Number, Last, First, Hired, Rate, Status, Code FROM
dbo.tblEmploy WHERE Status = 'F'
```
selects the records for full-time employees

**Example 4**
```
SELECT Number, Rate FROM dbo.tblEmploy WHERE Code = 3
```
selects the Number and Rate fields for employees in the Personnel
department

**Example 5**
```
SELECT Number FROM dbo.tblEmploy WHERE Last LIKE 'Smith'
```
selects the Number field for records that have a last name of Smith

**Example 6**
```
SELECT Number FROM dbo.tblEmploy WHERE Last LIKE 'S%'
```
selects the Number field for records whose last name begins with the letter S

**Example 7**
```
SELECT Number, Last, First, Hired, Rate, Status, Code
FROM dbo.tblEmploy ORDER BY Code
```
selects all of the fields and records in the table, and sorts the records in
ascending order by the Code field

**Example 8**
```
SELECT Number, Last, First, Hired, Rate, Status, Code
FROM dbo.tblEmploy WHERE Status = 'p' ORDER BY Code
```
selects the records for part-time employees, and sorts the records in
ascending order by the Code field

**FIGURE 11.27**   How to use the SELECT statement

TIP

The full syntax of the Select
statement contains other clauses
and options that are beyond the
scope of this book.

In the SELECT statement's syntax, *fields* is one or more field names (separated
by commas), and *table* is the name of the table containing the fields. Notice that
the SELECT statement's syntax contains two clauses that are optional: the
WHERE clause and the ORDER BY clause. The **WHERE clause** allows you to
limit the records that will be selected, and the **ORDER BY clause** allows you
to control the order in which the records appear when displayed. Although

you do not have to capitalize the keywords SELECT, FROM, WHERE, and ORDER BY in a SELECT statement, many programmers do so for clarity.

Study the examples shown in Figure 11.27. The SELECT statement in Example 1 selects all of the fields and records from the tblEmploy table. Notice that three letters ("dbo") and a period precede the table name in the example. The letters "dbo" stand for "database object."

The SELECT statement in Example 2 selects only three of the fields from each record in the table. The SELECT statement in Example 3 uses the WHERE clause to limit the records that will be selected. In this case, the statement indicates that only records for full-time employees should be selected. Notice that, when comparing the contents of the Status field (which contains one character only) with a character, you enclose the character in single quotation marks.

The SELECT statement in Example 4 selects only the Number and Rate fields for employees working in the Personnel department. The SELECT statement in Example 5 shows how you can compare the contents of a text field with a string. You do so using the Like operator in the WHERE clause, and you enclose the string in single quotation marks. The SELECT statement in Example 5 will select the Number field for all records that have Smith as the last name.

The SELECT statement in Example 6 shows how you can use the Like operator along with the % (percent sign) wildcard in the WHERE clause. As the example indicates, the `SELECT Number FROM dbo.tblEmploy WHERE Last LIKE 'S%'` statement will select the Number field for all records with a last name that begins with the letter S.

Example 7's SELECT statement selects all of the fields and records from the tblEmploy table, and then uses the ORDER BY clause to sort the records in ascending order by the Code field. To sort the records in descending order, you use `SELECT Number, Last, First, Hired, Rate, Status, Code FROM dbo.tblEmploy ORDER BY Code DESC`. The "DESC" stands for "descending".

The last SELECT statement shown in Figure 11.27 selects the records for part-time employees, and it sorts the records in ascending order by the Code field. Notice that the statement compares the contents of the Status field (which contains uppercase letters) with a lowercase 'p'. The statement works correctly because SQL commands are not case sensitive.

## Creating a New Query

As mentioned earlier, a TableAdapter object can contain more than one query. Figure 11.28 shows how to use the Query Configuration Wizard to create a new query.

## HOW TO...

### Create a Query Using the Query Configuration Wizard

1.  Right-click the name of the TableAdapter in the DataSet Designer, then click Add Query to open the Query Configuration Wizard. (Alternatively, you can right-click the DataSet Designer, point to Add, and then click Query. Or, you can click the DataSet Designer, then click Data on the menu bar, then point to Add, and then click Query.)

2.  Depending on the way you opened the Query Configuration Wizard, you may need to specify the data connection. If necessary, select the appropriate data connection, then click the Next button.

*(Figure is continued on next page)*

3. In the Choose a Command Type screen, select the Use SQL statements radio button, if necessary, then click the Next button.

4. In the Choose a Query Type screen, select the SELECT which returns rows radio button, if necessary, then click the Next button.

5. When the Specify a SQL SELECT statement screen appears, you can either type the SELECT statement yourself, or you can use the Query Builder dialog box to construct the statement for you. Figure 11.29 shows a SELECT statement entered on the Specify a SQL SELECT statement screen. (You learn how to use the Query Builder dialog box in the next section.)

6. When you have completed the SELECT statement, click the Next button in the Specify a SQL SELECT statement screen.

7. In the Choose Methods to Generate screen, select the Fill a DataTable and Return a DataTable check boxes, if necessary. Enter appropriate names for the query's FillBy and GetDataBy methods. For example, if the query retrieves the records of full-time employees only, you might assign the names FillByFulltime and GetDataByFulltime to their associated methods, as shown in Figure 11.30. Click the Next button.

8. In the Wizard Results screen, click the Finish button. The query is added to the DataSet Designer, as shown in Figure 11.31.

**FIGURE 11.28**   How to create a query using the Query Configuration Wizard

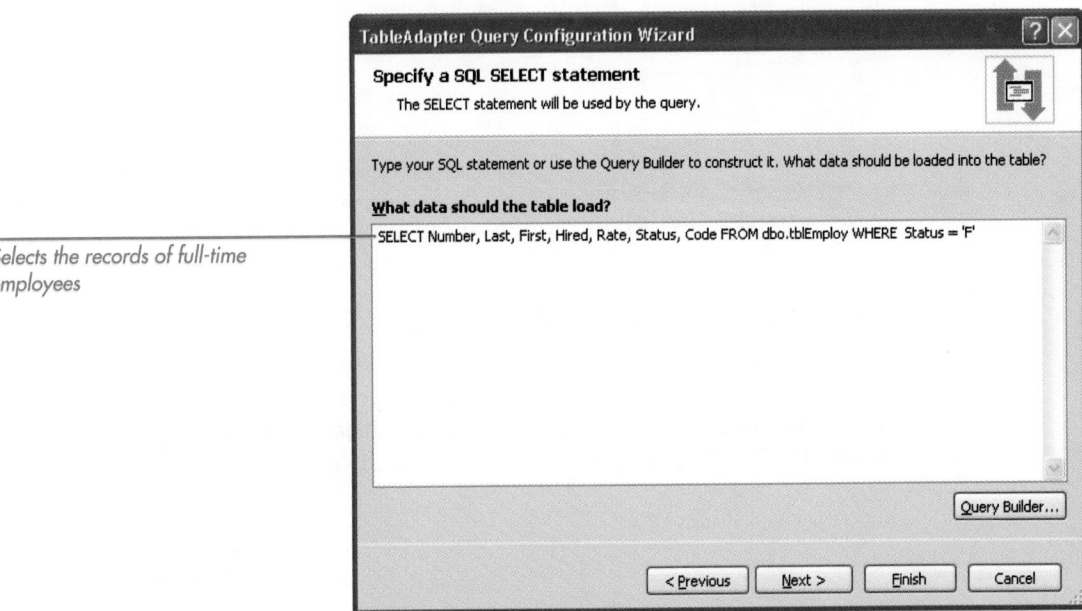

*Selects the records of full-time employees*

**FIGURE 11.29**   SELECT statement entered on the Specify a SQL SELECT statement screen

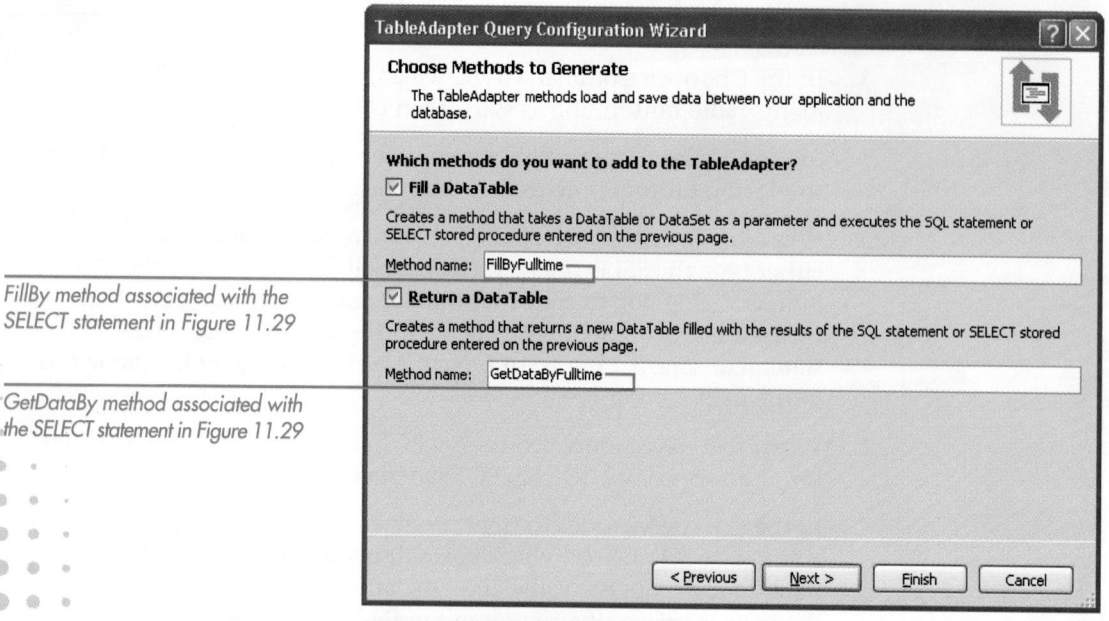

*FillBy method associated with the SELECT statement in Figure 11.29*

*GetDataBy method associated with the SELECT statement in Figure 11.29*

**FIGURE 11.30**        Names assigned to the FillBy and GetDataBy methods

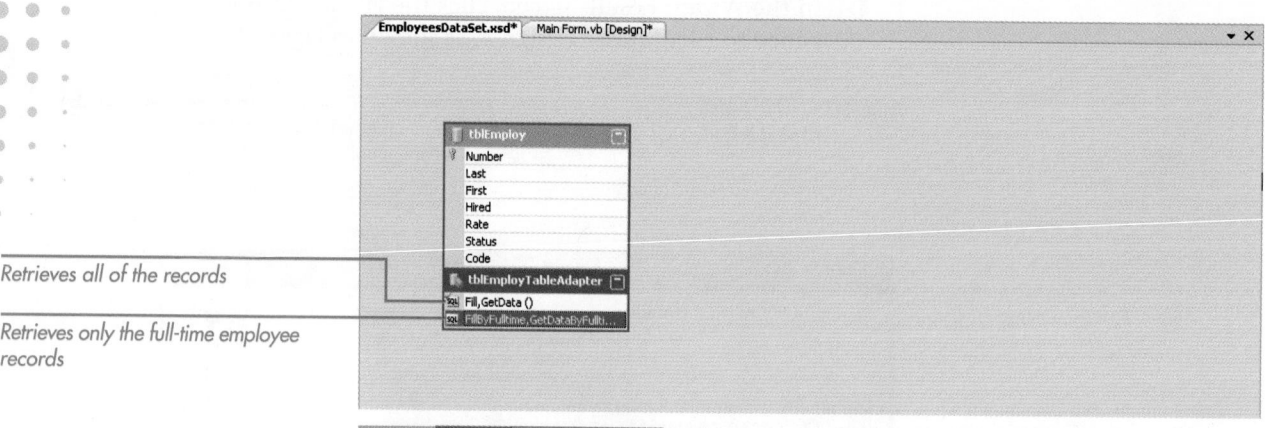

*Retrieves all of the records*

*Retrieves only the full-time employee records*

**FIGURE 11.31**        Queries shown in the DataSet Designer

## Using the Query Builder Dialog Box

Earlier, in Figure 11.29, you viewed a SELECT statement entered on the Specify a SQL SELECT statement screen. Rather than typing the SELECT statement on your own, you can use the Query Builder dialog box to construct it for you. Figure 11.32 shows an example of a completed Query Builder dialog box.

Used by the WHERE clause

Used by the ORDER BY clause

Selects only the Personnel records
and arranges them in descending
order by the pay rate

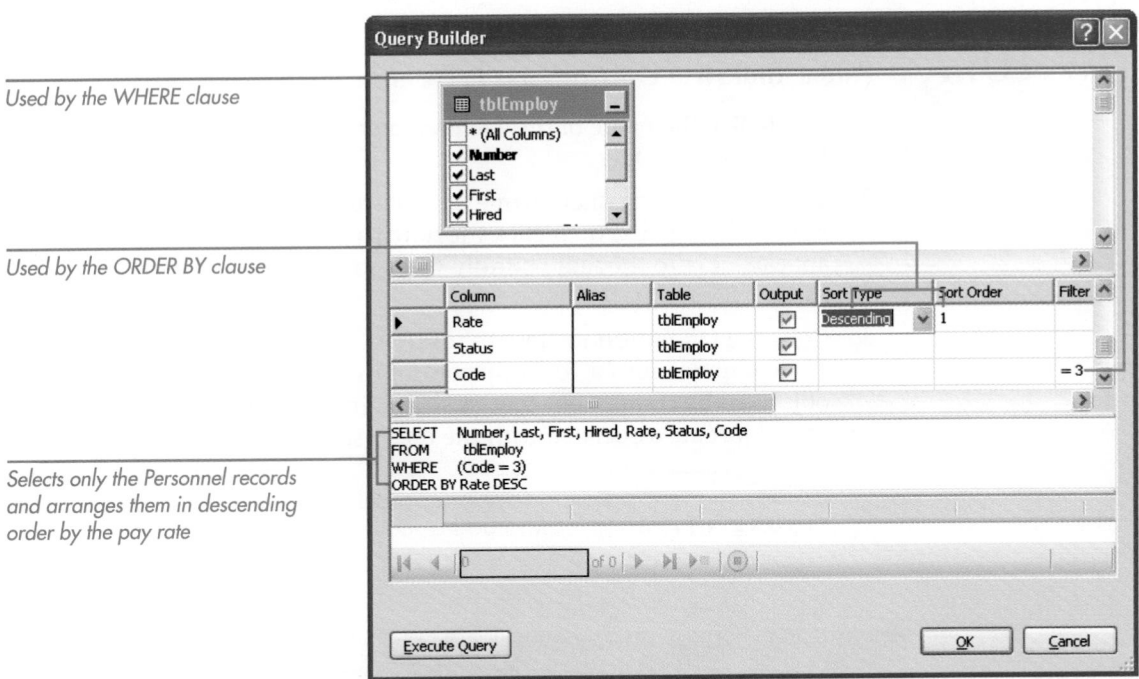

**FIGURE 11.32**    Example of a completed Query Builder dialog box

In the Query Builder dialog box shown in Figure 11.32, the word Descending and the number 1 appear in the Sort Type and Sort Order columns, respectively, for the Rate field. As a result, the Query Builder adds the `ORDER BY Rate DESC` clause to the SELECT statement. The =3 that appears in the Filter column for the Code field in the dialog box tells the Query Builder to include the `WHERE (Code = 3)` clause in the statement. When it is processed, the SELECT statement in the dialog box will select all of the fields from the tblEmploy table, but only for records having the number 3 in their Code field. In other words, it will select only the records of employees in the Personnel department. The records will be arranged in descending order by their pay rate.

## Allowing the User to Run a Query

You can provide a ToolStrip control that allows the user to run a query after an application has been started. Figure 11.33 shows the steps you follow to include on a form a ToolStrip control that is associated with a query.

# HOW TO...

## Add a ToolStrip Control That Is Associated with a Query

1. Right-click the name of the TableAdapter in the component tray, then click Add Query.

2. Select the Existing query name radio button in the Search Criteria Builder dialog box, then click the down arrow in the list box that appears next to the radio button. Click the name of the query in the list. See Figure 11.34.

3. Click the OK button to close the Search Criteria Builder dialog box. The computer adds a ToolStrip control to the form and a ToolStrip object to the component tray, as shown in Figure 11.35. The control and object are associated with the query selected in Step 2.

**FIGURE 11.33**     How to add a ToolStrip control that is associated with a query

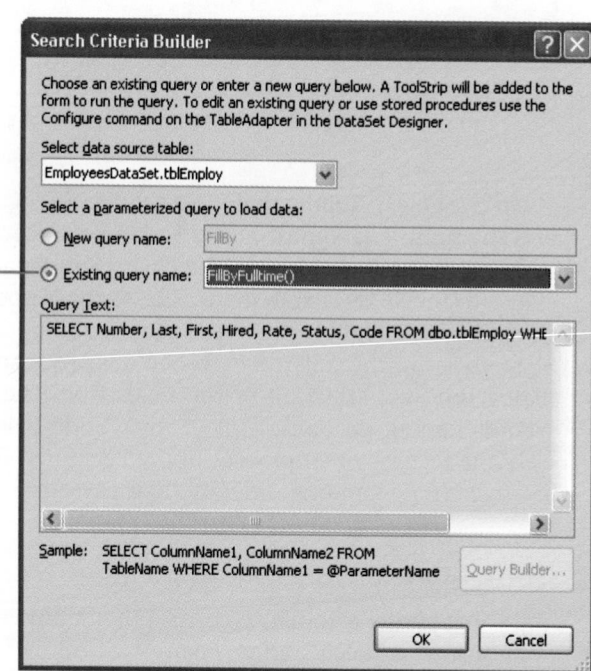

*The ToolStrip control will allow the user to run the FillByFulltime query*

**FIGURE 11.34**     Search Criteria Builder dialog box

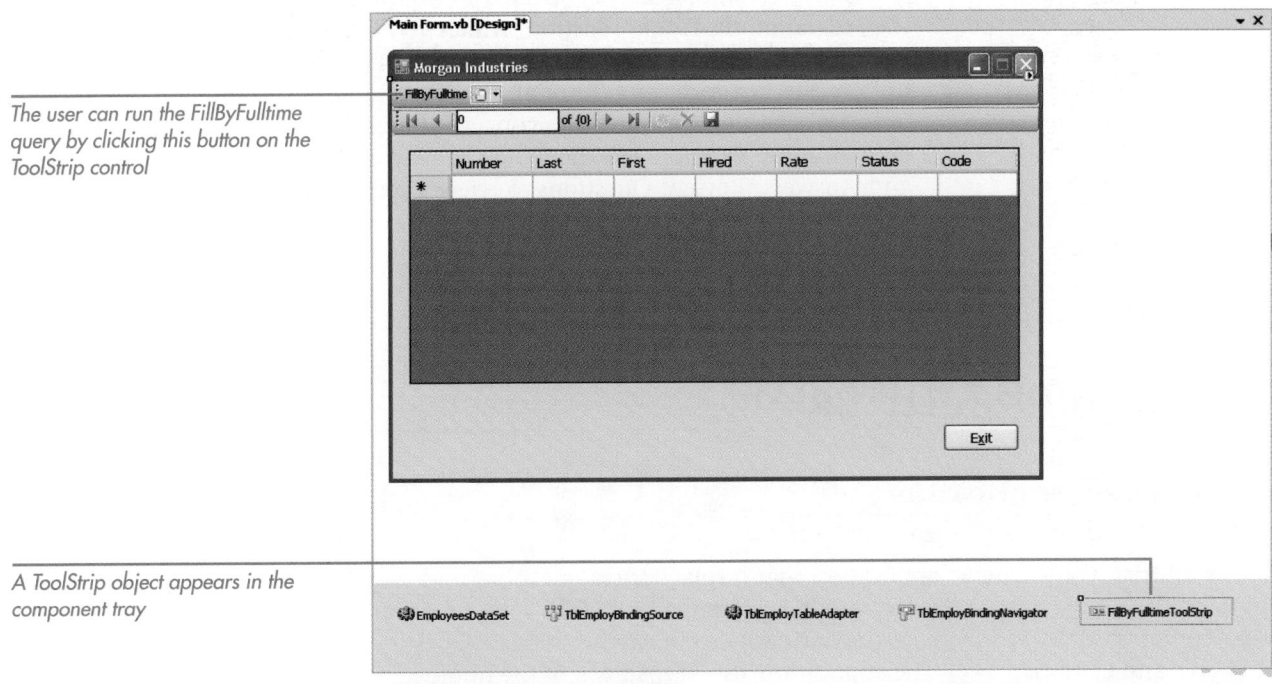

The user can run the FillByFulltime query by clicking this button on the ToolStrip control

A ToolStrip object appears in the component tray

**FIGURE 11.35** ToolStrip control and object added to the application

To run the FillByFulltime query in the Morgan Industries application shown in Figure 11.35, the user needs to start the application and then click the FillByFulltime button on the ToolStrip control. Figure 11.36 shows the result of clicking the button.

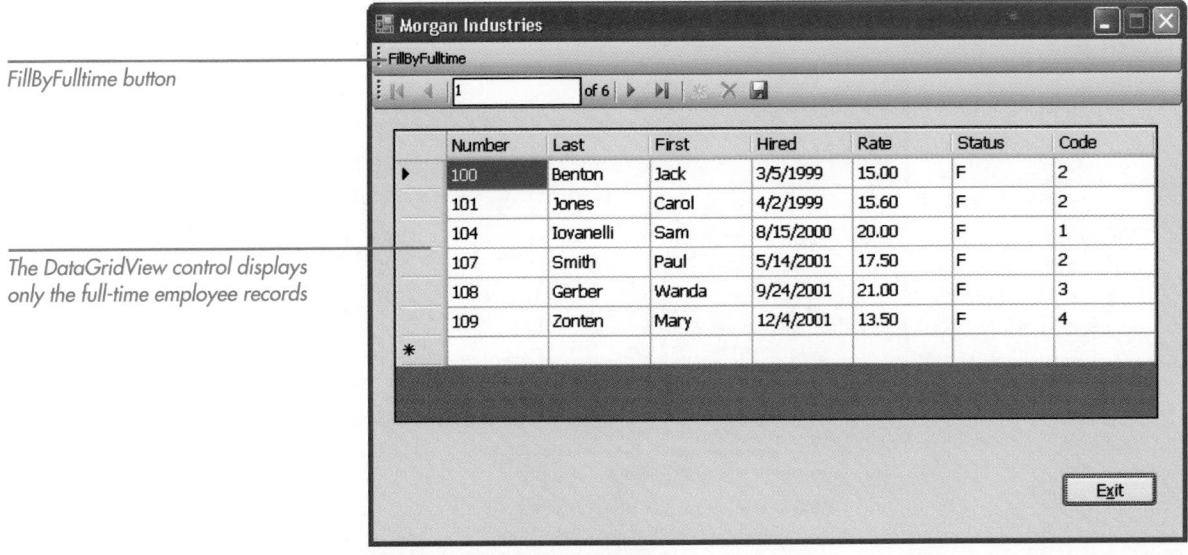

FillByFulltime button

The DataGridView control displays only the full-time employee records

**FIGURE 11.36** Result of clicking the FillByFulltime button on the ToolStrip control

You have completed the concepts section of Chapter 11. The next section is the Programming Tutorial section, which gives you step-by-step instructions on how to apply the chapter's concepts to an application. A Programming Example follows the Programming Tutorial. The Programming Example is a completed program that demonstrates the concepts taught in the chapter. Following the Programming Example are the Quick Review, Key Terms, Self-Check Questions and Answers, Review Questions, Review Exercises – Short Answer, Computer Exercises, and Case Projects sections.

# PROGRAMMING TUTORIAL

## Trivia Game Application

In this tutorial, you create an application that displays trivia questions and answers. The questions and answers are stored in a table named Game1, which is contained in a SQL Server database named Trivia.mdf. The Game1 table contains nine records. Each record contains six fields named Question, AnswerA, AnswerB, AnswerC, AnswerD, and CorrectAnswer. The application also keeps track of the number of incorrect responses made by the user, and it displays that information after all nine questions have been answered. The Trivia Game application's user interface is shown in Figure 11.37, and its TOE chart is shown in Figure 11.38.

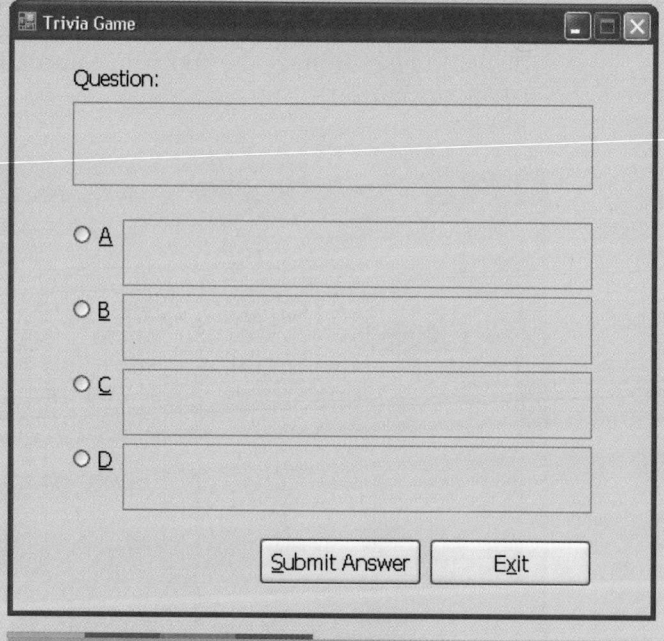

**FIGURE 11.37**    MainForm

**TOE Chart:**

| Task | Object | Event |
|---|---|---|
| End the application | exitButton | Click |
| Fill the dataset with data | MainForm | Load |
| 1. Compare the user's answer to the correct answer<br>2. Keep track of the number of incorrect answers<br>3. Display the next question and answers from the dataset<br>4. Display the number of incorrect answers | submitButton | Click |
| Display questions from the dataset | questionTextBox | None |
| Display answers from the dataset | aTextBox,<br>bTextBox,<br>cTextBox,<br>dTextBox | None |
| Display the user choices | aRadioButton,<br>bRadioButton,<br>cRadioButton,<br>dRadioButton | None |

**FIGURE 11.38**  TOE chart

## Coding the Trivia Game Application

Before you can begin coding the Trivia Game application, you need to open the Trivia Game Solution file.

**To open the Trivia Game solution file:**

1. Start Visual Studio. If necessary, close the Start Page window.
2. Open the **Trivia Game Solution** (Trivia Game Solution.sln) file, which is contained in the VbReloaded\ Chap11\Trivia Game Solution folder. The user interface shown earlier in Figure 11.37 appears on the screen.

First, you will connect the Trivia database to the application, and then you will preview the data.

**To connect the Trivia database to the application, then preview the data:**

1. Click **Data** on the menu bar, and then click **Show Data Sources** to display the Data Sources window.
2. Click **Add New Data Source** in the Data Sources window to start the Data Source Configuration Wizard. See Figure 11.39.

*Data Sources window*

*The data source for the application will be a database*

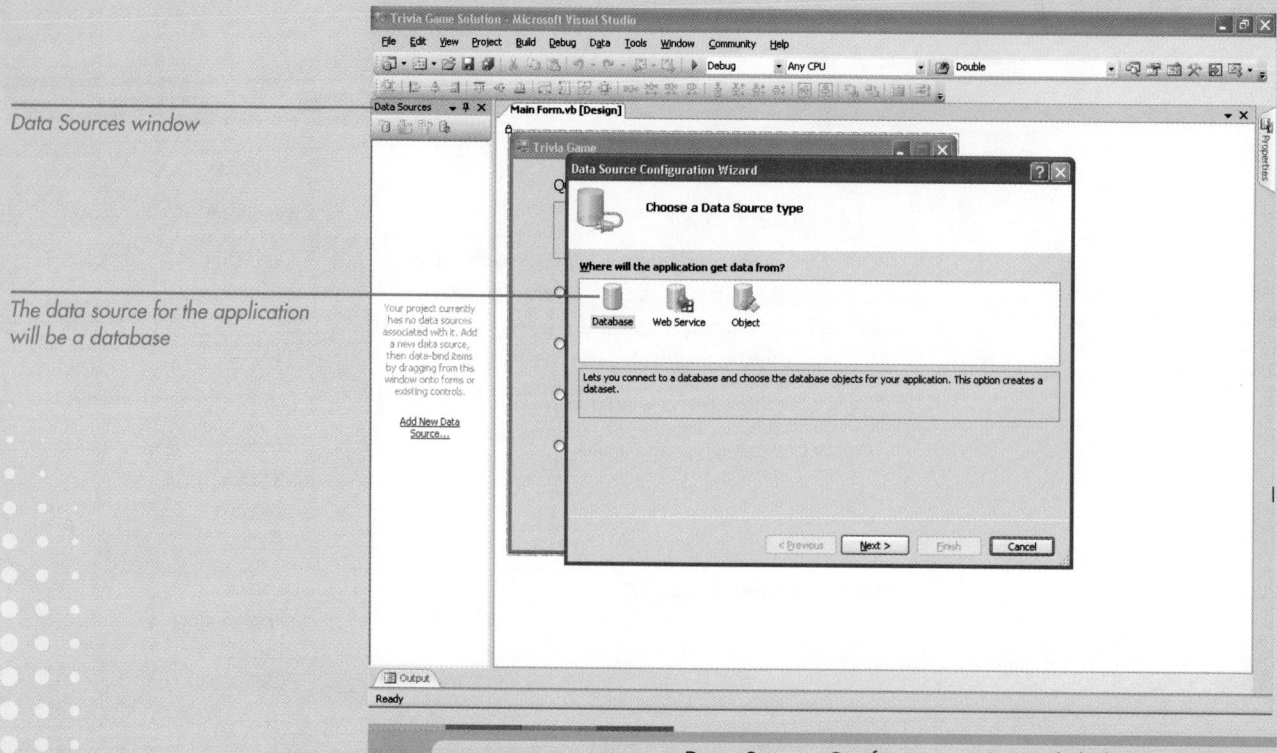

**FIGURE 11.39** Data Source Configuration Wizard dialog box

3. Click the **Next** button to display the Choose your data connection screen.
4. Click the **New Connection** button to display the Add Connection dialog box. If Microsoft SQL Server Database File (SqlClient) does not appear in the Data source box, click the **Change** button to open the Change Data Source dialog box, then click **Microsoft SQL Server Database File**, and then click the **OK** button to return to the Add Connection dialog box.
5. Click the **Browse** button in the Add Connection dialog box. Open the VbReloaded\Chap11\SQL Databases folder, then click **Trivia.mdf** in the list of filenames. Click the **Open** button. Figure 11.40 shows the completed Add Connection dialog box.

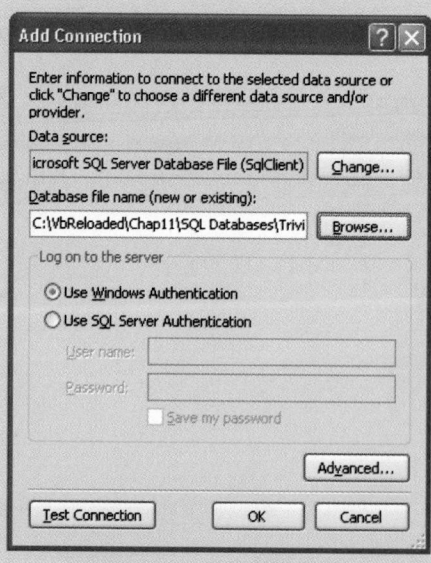

**FIGURE 11.40** Completed Add Connection dialog box

6. Click the **Test Connection** button in the Add Connection dialog box. The "Test connection succeeded." message appears in a dialog box. Click the **OK** button to close the dialog box.
7. Click the **OK** button to close the Add Connection dialog box. Trivia.mdf now appears in the Choose your data connection screen. Click the **Next** button. The computer displays the Local database file dialog box shown in Figure 11.41.

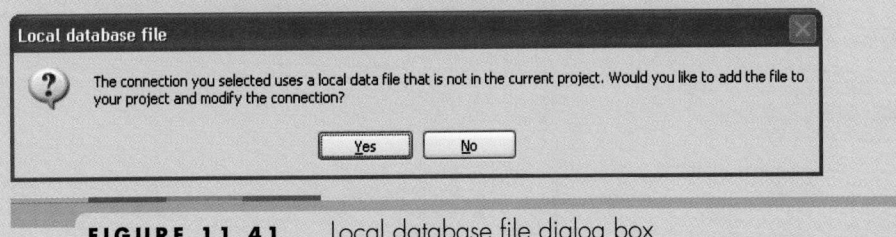

**FIGURE 11.41**    Local database file dialog box

8. Click the **Yes** button to add the Trivia.mdf file to the current project. The Save the connection string to the application configuration file screen shown in Figure 11.42 appears next. If necessary, select the check box.

*Verify that this check box is selected*

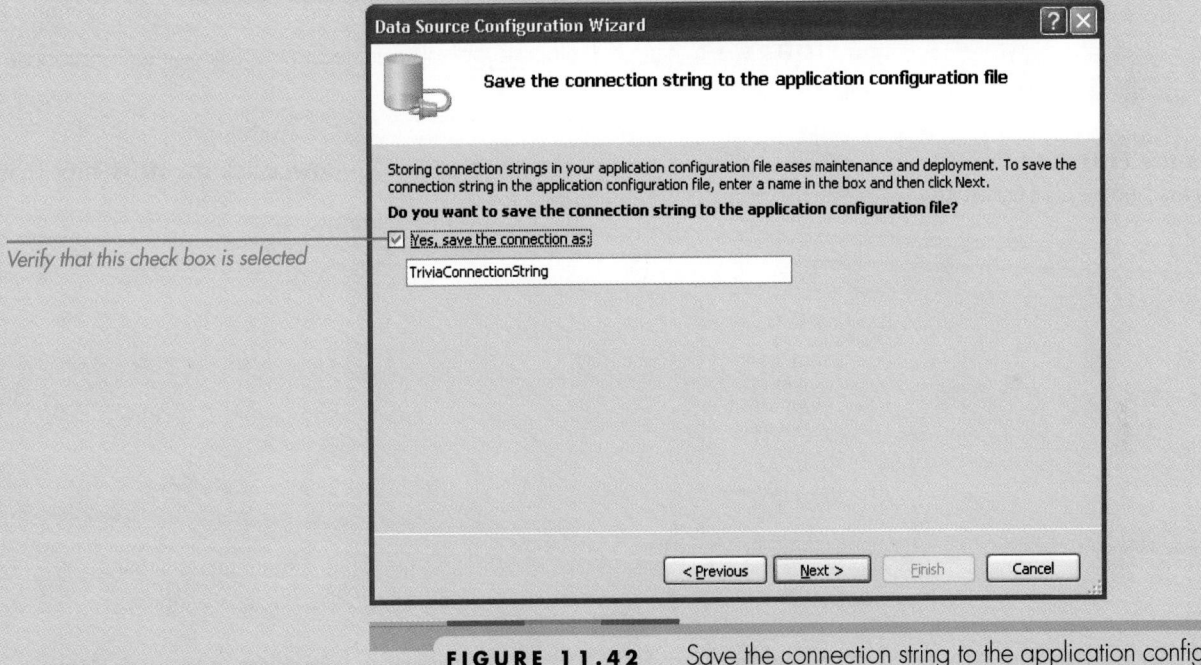

**FIGURE 11.42**    Save the connection string to the application configuration file screen

9. Click the **Next** button to display the Choose your database objects screen. Click the **plus box** that appears before Tables, then click the **plus box** that appears before Game1. Notice that the database contains one table (named Game1) and six fields. You can use this screen to select the table and/or field objects to include in the dataset.
10. In this application, you need to include all of the fields in the dataset. Click the **empty box** that appears before Game1. Doing this selects the table and field check boxes, as shown in Figure 11.43.

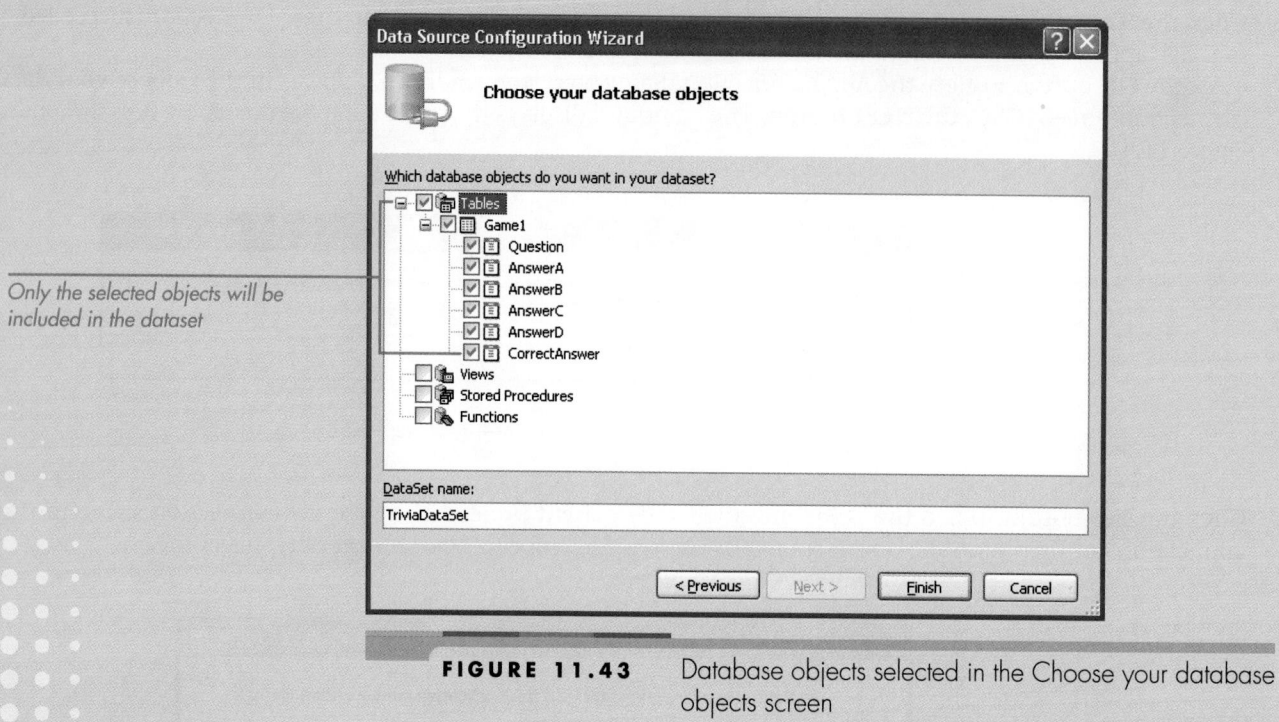

Only the selected objects will be
included in the dataset

**FIGURE 11.43**     Database objects selected in the Choose your database
objects screen

11. Click the **Finish** button. The computer adds a dataset to the Data Sources window. Click the **plus box** that appears before Game1 in the Data Sources window. See Figure 11.44.

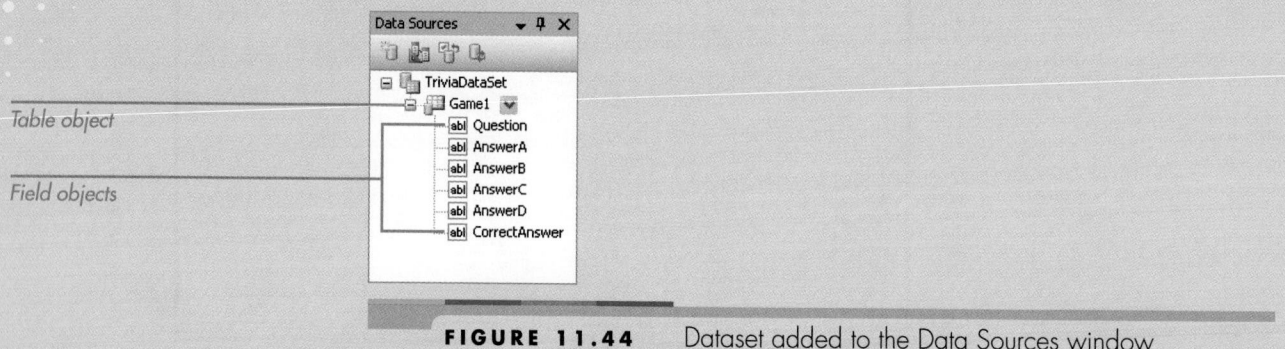

Table object

Field objects

**FIGURE 11.44**     Dataset added to the Data Sources window

12. Now preview the data contained in the dataset. Right-click the **Data Sources window**, then click **Preview Data**, and then click the **Preview** button in the Preview Data dialog box. See Figure 11.45.

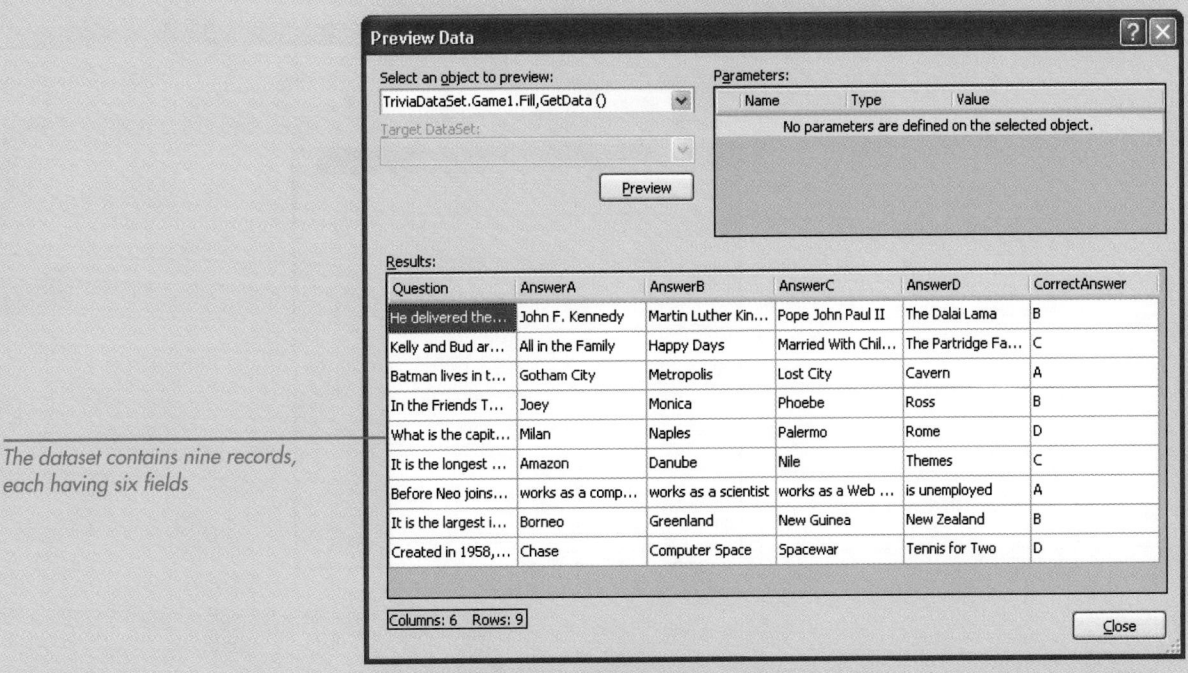

**FIGURE 11.45**      Data displayed in the Preview Data dialog box

*The dataset contains nine records, each having six fields*

13. Click the **Close** button in the Preview Data dialog box, then save the solution.

Next, you will bind the field objects in the dataset to the appropriate text boxes on the form.

**To bind the field objects to the text boxes, then test the application:**

1. Click the **Question** field object in the Data Sources window, then drag the Question field object to the questionTextBox, as shown in Figure 11.46.

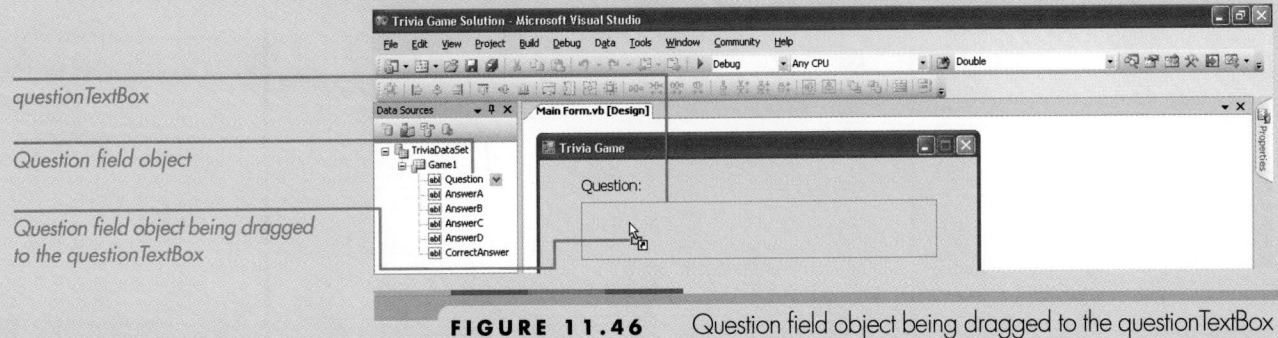

*questionTextBox*

*Question field object*

*Question field object being dragged to the questionTextBox*

**FIGURE 11.46**      Question field object being dragged to the questionTextBox

2. Release the mouse button. The computer binds the Question field object to the questionTextBox. It also adds the TriviaDataSet, Game1BindingSource, and Game1TableAdapter objects to the component tray, as shown in Figure 11.47.

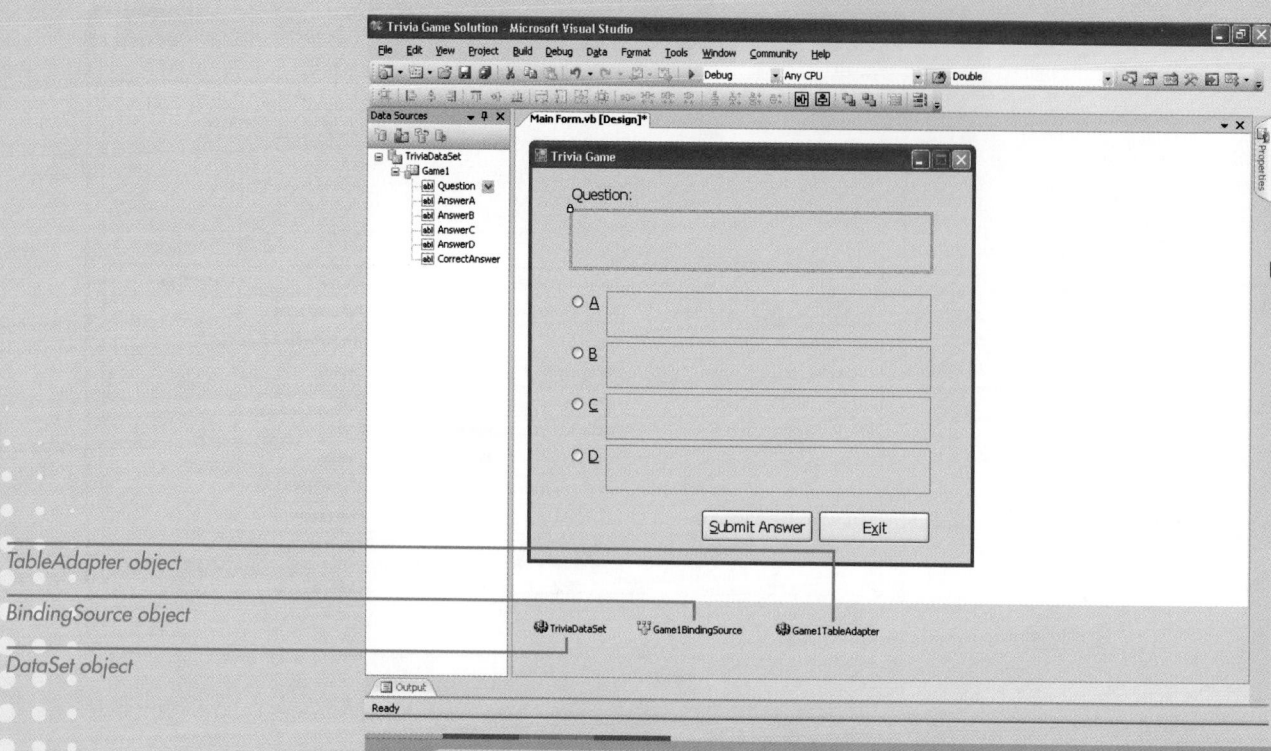

TableAdapter object

BindingSource object

DataSet object

**FIGURE 11.47**   Objects added to the component tray

3. Drag the AnswerA field object to the aTextBox, then drag the AnswerB field object to the bTextBox. Drag the AnswerC object to the cTextBox, then drag the AnswerD object to the dTextBox.
4. Save the solution, then start the application. The first record in the dataset appears in the interface, as shown in Figure 11.48.

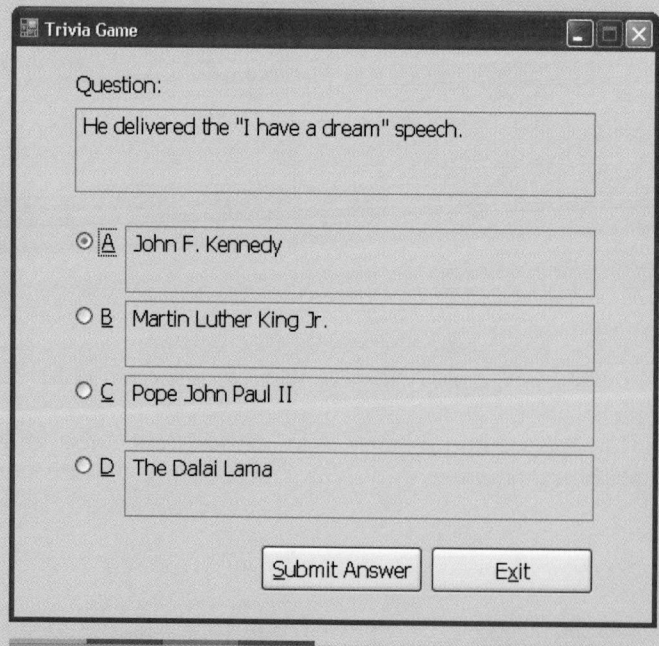

**FIGURE 11.48**   First record appears in the interface

5.  Click the **Exit** button to end the application. If necessary, close the Output window.
6.  Close the Data Sources window.

Now you can begin coding the application. According to the TOE chart, shown earlier in Figure 11.38, only three event procedures need to be coded: the Exit button's Click event procedure, the MainForm's Load event procedure, and the submitButton's Click event procedure.

**To begin coding the application:**

1.  Open the Code Editor window. Notice that the exitButton's Click event procedure and the MainForm's Load event procedure are already coded for you. The only procedure you need to code is the submitButton's Click event procedure. [Recall that the computer automatically enters the `Me.Game1TableAdapter.Fill (Me.TriviaDataSet.Game1)` statement when you drag an object from the Data Sources window to the form.]
2.  Replace the <your name> and <current date> text in the comments with your name and the current date.

Figure 11.49 shows the pseudocode for the submitButton's Click event procedure.

---

### Pseudocode

1.  store the position of the record pointer in a variable
2.  determine which radio button is selected, and assign its Text property (without the ampersand that designates the access key) to a variable named userAnswer
3.  if the userAnswer variable's contents does not match the correct answer from the dataset
    add 1 to a counter variable named numIncorrect
    end if
4.  if the record pointer is not pointing to the last record
    move the record pointer to the next record in the dataset
    else
    display the number of incorrect answers in a message box
    end if

---

**FIGURE 11.49**    Pseudocode for the submitButton's Click event procedure

---

**To finish coding the application:**

1.  Open the code template for the submitButton's Click event procedure.
2.  Type '  **determines whether the user's answer is correct** and press **Enter**, then type '  **keeps track of the number of incorrect answers** and press **Enter**. Type '  **displays the next record or the number of** and press **Enter**, then type '  **incorrect answers** and press **Enter** twice.
3.  Type **dim recPtrPos as integer** and press **Enter**, then type **dim userAnswer as string = ""** and press **Enter**. The `recPtrPos` variable will keep track of the position of the record pointer, and the `userAnswer` variable will store the user's answer to the question displayed in the questionTextBox (either A, B, C, or D).
4.  Type **static numIncorrect as integer** and press **Enter** twice. The `numIncorrect` variable will be used as a counter to keep track of the number of incorrect answers made by the user.
5.  The first step in the pseudocode is to store the position of the record pointer in a variable. Recall that you can use the BindingSource object's Position property to determine the current position of the record pointer in a dataset. Type '  **store position of record pointer** and press **Enter**, then type **recptrpos = game1bindingsource.position** and press **Enter** twice.
6.  Now you will determine which radio button is selected, and assign its Text property (without the ampersand that designates the access key) to the `userAnswer` variable. Type the comments and Select Case statement shown in Figure 11.50.

```
' determine selected radio button, which
' represents the user's answer
select case true
    case aradiobutton.checked
        useranswer = aradiobutton.text.replace("&", "")
    case bradiobutton.checked
        useranswer = bradiobutton.text.replace("&", "")
    case cradiobutton.checked
        useranswer = cradiobutton.text.replace("&", "")
    case dradiobutton.checked
        useranswer = dradiobutton.text.replace("&", "")
end select
```

*Enter these comments and lines of code*

**FIGURE 11.50**   Comments and Select Case statement

The next step is to compare the contents of the userAnswer variable to the contents of the CorrectAnswer field in the current record. If they are not the same, then you need to increase (by one) the contents of the numIncorrect counter variable. You can access the value stored in a field in the current record using the syntax *dataSetName*.*tableName*(*recordNumber*).*fieldname*.

7. Position the insertion point two lines below the End Select clause, then type ' **if necessary, update number of incorrect answers** and press **Enter**. Then type **if useranswer <> _** and press **Enter**. Press **Tab**, then type **triviadataset.game1(recptrpos).correctanswer then** and press **Enter**. Type **numincorrect = numincorrect + 1**.

The last step in the pseudocode is to determine whether to move to the next record or display a message box indicating the number of incorrect answers. If the record pointer is not pointing to the last record in the dataset, then the procedure should move the record pointer to the next record; doing this will display that record's question and answers. However, if the record pointer is pointing to the last record, it means that there are no more questions and answers to display. In that case, the procedure should display the number of incorrect answers made by the user.

8. Position the insertion point two lines below the End If clause, then type ' **determine position of record pointer** and press **Enter**. Type **if recptrpos <= 7 then** and press **Enter**.
9. Recall that you can use the BindingSource object's MoveNext method to move the record pointer to the next record. Type **game1bindingsource.movenext()** and press **Enter**.
10. Type **else** and press **Enter**. Type **messagebox.show("Number incorrect: " _** and press **Enter**. Press **Tab**, then type **& numincorrect.tostring, "Trivia Game", _** and press **Enter**. Type **messageboxbuttons.ok, messageboxicon.information)**.
11. Save the solution. Figure 11.51 shows the code for the Trivia Game application.

**Visual Basic code**

```
' Project name:        Trivia Game Project
' Project purpose:     The project displays trivia
'                      questions and answers from
'                      a database.
' Created/revised by:  <your name> on <current date>
```

**(Figure is continued on next page)**

```vb
Option Explicit On
Option Strict On

Public Class MainForm

    Private Sub exitButton_Click(ByVal sender As Object, _
        ByVal e As System.EventArgs) Handles exitButton.Click
        Me.Close()
    End Sub

    Private Sub MainForm_Load(ByVal sender As System.Object, _
        ByVal e As System.EventArgs) Handles MyBase.Load
        'TODO: This line of code loads data into the
        'TriviaDataSet.Game1' table. You can move,
        'or remove, it as needed.
        Me.Game1TableAdapter.Fill(Me.TriviaDataSet.Game1)

    End Sub

    Private Sub submitButton_Click(ByVal sender As Object, _
        ByVal e As System.EventArgs) Handles submitButton.Click
        ' determines whether the user's answer is correct
        ' keeps track of the number of incorrect answers
        ' displays the next record or the number of
        ' incorrect answers

        Dim recPtrPos As Integer
        Dim userAnswer As String = ""
        Static numIncorrect As Integer

        ' store position of record pointer
        recPtrPos = Game1BindingSource.Position

        ' determine selected radio button, which
        ' represents the user's answer
        Select Case True
            Case aRadioButton.Checked
                userAnswer = aRadioButton.Text.Replace("&", "")
            Case bRadioButton.Checked
                userAnswer = bRadioButton.Text.Replace("&", "")
            Case cRadioButton.Checked
                userAnswer = cRadioButton.Text.Replace("&", "")
            Case dRadioButton.Checked
                userAnswer = dRadioButton.Text.Replace("&", "")
        End Select

        ' if necessary, update number of incorrect answers
        If userAnswer <> _
            TriviaDataSet.Game1(recPtrPos).CorrectAnswer Then
            numIncorrect = numIncorrect + 1
        End If
```

*(Figure is continued on next page)*

```
' determine position of record pointer
If recPtrPos <= 7 Then
    Game1BindingSource.MoveNext()
Else
    MessageBox.Show("Number incorrect: " _
        & numIncorrect.ToString, "Trivia Game", _
        MessageBoxButtons.OK, MessageBoxIcon.Information)
End If
End Sub
```

**FIGURE 11.51**    Trivia Game application's code

**To test the application:**

1. Start the application. When the first question appears on the screen, answer the question correctly by clicking the **B** radio button, and then clicking the **Submit Answer** button.
2. When the second question appears on the screen, answer the question incorrectly by clicking the **D** radio button, and then clicking the **Submit Answer** button.
3. Answer the remaining seven questions on your own. When you have submitted the answer for the last question, the submitButton's Click event procedure displays the number of incorrect responses in a message box.
4. Click the **OK** button to close the message box.
5. Click the **Exit** button to end the application. If necessary, close the Output window.
6. Close the Code Editor window, then close the solution.

# PROGRAMMING EXAMPLE

## Cartwright Industries Application

Carl Simons, the sales manager at Cartwright Industries, records the item number, name, and price of each product the company sells in a database named Items. The Items database is stored in the Items.mdf file contained in the VbReloaded\Chap11\SQL Databases folder. Mr. Simons wants an application that allows the sales clerks to view the numbers, names, and prices of the items in the database. The application also should allow the sales clerk to add, delete, and save changes to the database. Name the solution Cartwright Solution. Name the project Cartwright Project. Name the form file Main Form.vb. Save the application in the VbReloaded\Chap11 folder.

Figure 11.52 shows the Items database opened in a window in the IDE. The database contains one table named tblItems. The Number and Name fields contain text, and the Price field contains numbers.

| Number | Name | Price |
|---|---|---|
| ABX12 | Chair | 45.00 |
| CSR14 | Desk | 175.00 |
| JTR23 | Table | 65.00 |
| NRE09 | End Table | 46.00 |
| OOE68 | Bookcase | 300.00 |
| PPR00 | Coffee Table | 190.00 |
| PRT45 | Lamp | 30.00 |
| REZ04 | Love Seat | 700.00 |
| THR98 | Side Chair | 33.00 |
| WKP10 | Sofa | 873.00 |

**FIGURE 11.52**    Data contained in the tblItems table

**TOE Chart:**

| Task | Object | Event |
|------|--------|-------|
| End the application | exitButton | Click |
| Display the dataset | TblItemsDataGridView | None |
| 1. Move from record to record<br>2. Add a record<br>3. Delete a record<br>4. Save changes to the dataset | TblItemsBindingNavigator | None |
| Fill the dataset with data | MainForm | Load |

**FIGURE 11.53**

**User Interface (drag the table to the form):**

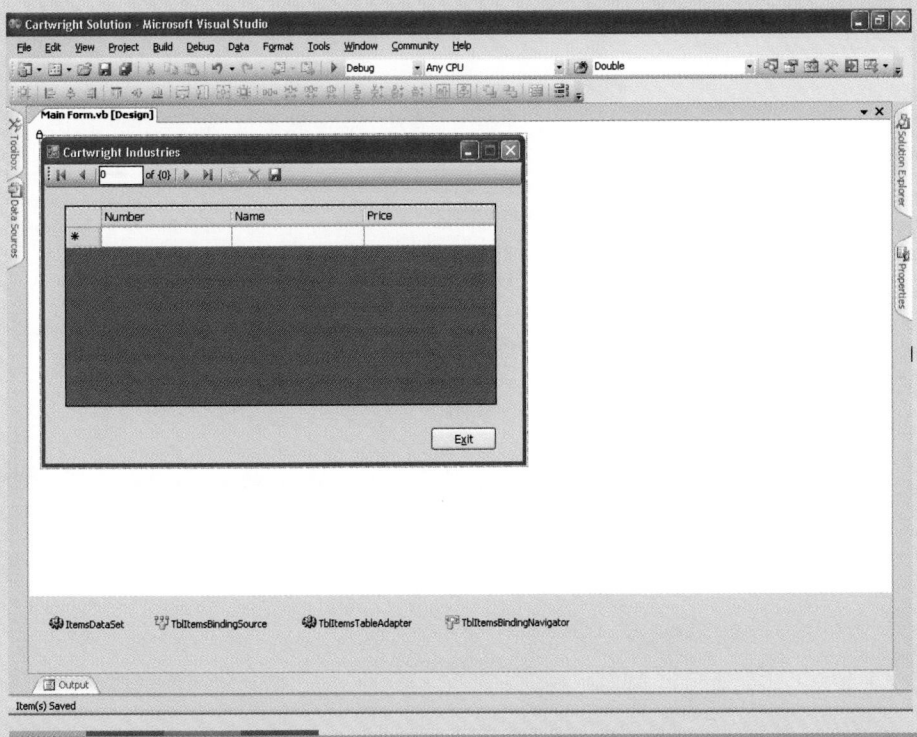

**FIGURE 11.54**

## Objects, Properties, and Settings:

| Object | Property | Setting |
|---|---|---|
| Form1 | Name | MainForm |
| | Font | Tahoma, 10 point |
| | MaximizeBox | False |
| | Size | 547, 361 |
| | StartPosition | CenterScreen |
| | Text | Cartwright Industries |
| Button1 | Name | exitButton |
| | Location | 435, 289 |
| | Size | 75, 26 |
| | Text | E&xit |
| TblItemsDataGridView | AutoSizeColumnsMode | Fill |
| | Location | 23, 45 |
| | Size | 487, 220 |

**FIGURE 11.55**

## Code:

```
' Project name:        Cartwright Project
' Project purpose:     The project displays the data
'                      contained in a database. It also
'                      allows the user to add records,
'                      delete records, and save the
'                      changes made to records.
' Created/revised by:  <your name> on <current date>

Option Explicit On
Option Strict On

Public Class MainForm

    Private Sub bindingNavigatorSaveItem_Click_
    (ByVal sender As System.Object, ByVal e As System.EventArgs) _
    Handles bindingNavigatorSaveItem.Click
        If Me.Validate Then
            Me.TblItemsBindingSource.EndEdit()
            Me.TblItemsTableAdapter.Update(Me.ItemsDataSet.tblItems)
        Else
            System.Windows.Forms.MessageBox.Show _
            (Me, "Validation errors occurred.", "Save", _
            System.Windows.Forms.MessageBoxButtons.OK, _
            System.Windows.Forms.MessageBoxIcon.Warning)
        End If
    End Sub
```

*(Figure is continued on next page)*

```
    Private Sub MainForm_Load(ByVal sender As System.Object, _
        ByVal e As System.EventArgs) Handles MyBase.Load
        'TODO: This line of code loads data into the
        'ItemsDataSet.tblItems' table. You can move,
        'or remove, it as needed.
        Me.TblItemsTableAdapter.Fill(Me.ItemsDataSet.tblItems)
    End Sub

    Private Sub exitButton_Click(ByVal sender As Object, _
        ByVal e As System.EventArgs) Handles exitButton.Click
        Me.Close()
    End Sub
End Class
```

**FIGURE 11.56**

## Quick Review

- Companies and individuals use databases to organize information.
- You can use Visual Basic to access the data stored in many different types of databases.
- Databases created by Microsoft SQL Server are relational databases. A relational database can contain one or more tables. Each table contains fields and records.
- Most tables contain a primary key that uniquely identifies each record.
- The data in a relational database can be displayed in any order, and you can control the amount of information you want to view.
- Visual Basic 2005 uses a technology called ADO.NET 2.0 to access the data stored in a database.
- The connection between a database and an application that uses ADO.NET 2.0 is only temporary.
- To access the data stored in a database, you first connect the database to an application. Doing this creates a dataset that contains objects, such as table objects and field objects.
- You can display the information contained in a dataset by binding one or more of the dataset objects to one or more controls in the application's interface.
- A TableAdapter object connects a database to a DataSet object.
- A BindingSource object connects a DataSet object to the bound controls on a form.
- In most applications, the statement to fill a dataset with data is entered in the form's Load event procedure.
- The BindingSource object uses an invisible record pointer to keep track of the current record.
- The location of the record pointer in a dataset is stored in the BindingSource object's Position property.
- You can use the BindingSource object's Move methods to move the record pointer in a dataset.
- You use a SQL SELECT statement to specify the fields and records to include in a dataset.

- You can use the Query Configuration Wizard to create queries.
- The Query Builder dialog box provides a convenient way to create a SELECT statement.
- You can associate a query with a ToolStrip control on a form.

## Key Terms

A **database** is an organized collection of related information stored in a file on a disk.

A **relational database** is a database that stores information in tables, which are composed of columns (fields) and rows (records).

A **field** is a single item of information about a person, place, or thing.

A **record** is a group of related fields that contain all of the necessary data about a specific person, place, or thing.

A **table** is a group of related records.

A **primary key** is the field that uniquely identifies each record in a table.

A **parent table** is a table to which another table, called a **child table**, links. The tables are linked using a common field. The common field is called the primary key in the parent table. It is called the **foreign key** in the child table.

**ADO.NET 2.0** refers to the technology used in Visual Basic 2005 to connect an application to a database.

A **dataset** is a copy of some or all of the records and fields contained in a database. A dataset is stored in the computer's internal memory.

**Binding** refers to the process of connecting a dataset object to a control on a form.

Controls connected to a dataset object are called **bound controls**.

You can use a **DataGridView control** to display the data contained in a dataset. The control displays the data in a row and columnar format.

You can use the **BindingNavigator control** to move from one record to another in the dataset, as well as to add, delete, and save records.

A **DataSet object** stores the information contained in a dataset.

A **TableAdapter object** connects a database to a DataSet object.

A **BindingSource object** connects a DataSet object to the bound controls on the form.

The BindingSource object's **EndEdit method** applies any pending changes (such as new records, deleted records, or changed records) to the dataset.

The TableAdapter object's **Update method** commits, to the database, the changes made to the dataset.

You can use a TableAdapter object's **Fill method** to load data into a table contained in a dataset.

The BindingSource object stores the position of the record pointer in its **Position property**.

**XML**, which stands for **Extensible Markup Language**, is a text-based language used to store and share data between applications and across networks and the Internet.

An **XML schema definition file** defines the tables and fields that make up the dataset.

A **query** specifies the fields and records to retrieve from a database, as well as the order in which to arrange the fields and records.

**SQL** stands for **Structured Query Language**, and is a set of commands that allows you to access and manipulate the data stored in databases.

The **SELECT statement** is the most commonly used SQL command. It allows you to specify the fields and records you want to access from a database, as well as control the order in which the fields and records appear when displayed.

You use the **WHERE clause** in a SELECT statement to limit the records that will be selected.

You use the **ORDER BY clause** in a SELECT statement to control the order in which the records are arranged.

## Self-Check Questions and Answers

1. The field that links a child table to a parent table is called the _____.
   a. foreign key in the child table
   b. foreign key in the parent table
   c. link key in the parent table
   d. primary key in the child table

2. When using ADO.NET 2.0 to access the information contained in a database, the computer stores a copy of the information in a _____.
   a. databaseSet in internal memory
   b. dataset in internal memory
   c. dataset on the computer's hard drive
   d. recordset on the computer's hard drive

3. The process of connecting a control to a dataset is called _____.
   a. assigning
   b. attaching
   c. joining
   d. None of the above.

4. The _____ object connects a database to a DataSet object.
   a. BindingSource
   b. DataBase
   c. DataGridView
   d. TableAdapter

5. The _____ property stores an integer that represents the location of the record pointer in a dataset.
   a. BindingNavigator object's Position
   b. BindingSource object's Position
   c. TableAdapter object's Position
   d. None of the above.

6. If the record pointer is positioned on record number five in a dataset, which of the following methods can be used to move the record pointer to record number four?
   a. GoPrevious()
   b. Move(4)
   c. MovePrevious()
   d. PositionPrevious

7. SQL stands for _____.
   a. Select Query Language
   b. Semi-Quick Language
   c. Structured Quick Language
   d. Structured Query Language

8. Which of the following will select the First, Middle, and Last fields from a table named tblNames?
   a. `SELECT First, Middle, AND Last FROM dbo.tblNames`
   b. `SELECT First, Middle, OR Last FROM dbo.tblNames`
   c. `SELECT First, Middle, Last FROM dbo.tblNames`
   d. None of the above.

9. Which of the following will arrange the SocialNum field data in descending order? The field is contained in a table named PensionInfo.
   a. `SELECT SocialNum FROM dbo.PensionInfo DESC`
   b. `SELECT SocialNum FROM dbo.PensionInfo ORDER BY SocialNum DESC`
   c. `SELECT SocialNum FROM dbo.PensionInfo WHERE SocialNum DESC`
   d. None of the above.

10. Which of the following will select only records that have the letter A in their Status field? The field is contained in the Worker table.
    a. `SELECT Id, Name, Status FROM dbo.Worker WHERE Status = 'A'`
    b. `SELECT Id, Name, Status FROM dbo.Worker ORDER BY Status = 'A'`
    c. `SELECT Id, Name, Status FROM dbo.Worker FOR Status = "A"`
    d. None of the above.

Answers: 1) a, 2) b, 3) d, 4) d, 5) b, 6) c, 7) d, 8) c, 9) b, 10) a

## Review Questions

1. A(n) _____ is an organized collection of related information stored in a file on a disk.
   a. database
   b. field
   c. object
   d. record

2. A _____ database is one that stores information in tables.
   a. columnar
   b. relational
   c. sorted
   d. tabular

3. A group of related records in a database is called a _____.
   a. column
   b. field
   c. row
   d. table

4. Which of the following statements is true about a relational database?
   a. Data stored in a relational database can be retrieved both quickly and easily by the computer.
   b. Data stored in a relational database can be displayed in any order.
   c. A relational database stores data in a column and row format.
   d. All of the above are true.

5. The _____ object provides the connection between a DataSet object and a control.
   a. Binding
   b. BindingSource
   c. Connecting
   d. None of the above.

6. An application contains DataSet, BindingSource, TableAdapter, and BindingNavigator objects named FriendsDataSet, TblNamesBindingSource, TblNamesTableAdapter, and TblNamesBindingNavigator, respectively. Which of the following statements retrieves data from the Friends database and stores it in the FriendsDataSet?
   a. `Me.FriendsDataSet.Fill(Friends.mdf)`
   b. `Me.TblNamesBindingSource.Fill(Me.FriendsDataSet)`
   c. `Me.TblNamesBindingNavigator.Fill(Me.FriendsDataSet.tblNames)`
   d. `Me.TblNamesTableAdapter.Fill(Me.FriendsDataSet.tblNames)`

Use the following database table, named tblState, to answer Questions 7 and 8.

| Field name | Data type |
| --- | --- |
| State | Text |
| Capital | Text |
| Population | Numeric |

7. Which of the following statements allows you to view all of the records in the table?
   a. `SELECT ALL records FROM tblState`
   b. `SELECT State, Capital, Population FROM tblState`
   c. `VIEW ALL records FROM tblState`
   d. `VIEW State, Capital, Population FROM tblState`

8. Which of the following statements will retrieve all records having a population that exceeds 5,000,000?
   a. `SELECT ALL FROM tblState FOR Population > 5000000`
   b. `SELECT State, Capital, Population FROM tblState WHERE Population > "5000000"`
   c. `SELECT State, Capital, Population FROM tblState WHERE Population > '5000000'`
   d. None of the above.

9. A field that uniquely identifies each record in a table is called a _____.
   a. foreign field
   b. foreign key
   c. primary field
   d. primary key

10. In a SELECT statement, the _____ clause is used to limit the records that will be selected.
    a. LIMIT
    b. ORDER BY
    c. SET
    d. None of the above.

11. Controls connected to a DataSet object are called _____ controls.
    a. bound
    b. connected
    c. data
    d. None of the above.

12. You can use the _____ dialog box to build a SELECT statement.
    a. Query Builder
    b. Select Builder
    c. SQL Builder
    d. SQL Helper

13. If the current record is the second record in the dataset, which of the following statements will position the record pointer on the first record?
    a. `TblEmployBindingSource.Position = 0`
    b. `TblEmployBindingSource.Position = TblEmployBindingSource.Position - 1`
    c. `TblEmployBindingSource.MoveFirst()`
    d. All of the above.

14. Which of the following tells the TblWorkerTableAdapter object to load the WorkersDataSet object with data?
    a. `TblWorkerTableAdapter.Fill(WorkersDataSet.tblWorker)`
    b. `TblWorkerTableAdapter.Load(tblWorker.WorkersDataSet)`
    c. `TblWorkerTableAdapter.FillInto(tblWorker)`
    d. None of the above.

15. The SQL SELECT statement is case sensitive.
    a. True
    b. False

## Review Exercises – Short Answer

Use the following database table to complete Review Exercises 1 through 6. The table is named tblMagInfo.

| Field name | Data type |
| --- | --- |
| Code | Character |
| Magazine | Text |
| Cost | Numeric |

1. Write a SELECT statement that will select the Code and Magazine fields.

2. Write a SELECT statement that will select the Code and Cost fields. Arrange the records in descending order by the Cost field.

3. Write a SELECT statement that will select all of the fields, but only for records having a code of 9.

4. Write a SELECT statement that will select all of the fields, but only for magazines having a cost of $3 or more.

5. Write a SELECT statement that will select the Magazine and Cost fields, but only for the Daily Food Guide magazine.

6. Write a SELECT statement that will select the Magazine and Cost fields, but only for magazines whose names begin with the letter G.

7. Write the statement to assign the location of the record pointer to an Integer variable named recNum.

8. Write the statement to move the record pointer to the last record in the dataset.

9. Explain the purpose of each of the following objects: DataSet, TableAdapter, BindingSource.

10. How do you remove the Delete button from a BindingNavigator control?

## Computer Exercises

1. In this exercise, you create an application that accesses the data stored in a database. The application displays the data in a DataGridView control.
   a. Open the Morgan Industries Solution (Morgan Industries Solution.sln) file, which is contained in the VbReloaded\Chap11\Morgan Industries Solution-Ex1 folder.
   b. Complete the interface, using Figure 11.13 as a guide.
   c. Save the solution, then start the application. The interface should appear as shown in Figure 11.16. Verify that the BindingNavigator control works appropriately. (Do not try to save an empty record.)
   d. Click the Exit button to end the application, then close the solution.

2. In this exercise, you create an application that accesses the data stored in a database. The application displays the data in label controls.
   a. Open the Morgan Industries Solution (Morgan Industries Solution.sln) file, which is contained in the VbReloaded\Chap11\Morgan Industries Solution-Ex2 folder.
   b. Complete the interface, using Figure 11.18 as a guide. Also be sure to code the Next and Previous buttons. (The code is shown in Figure 11.23.)
   c. Save the solution, then start the application. The interface should appear as shown in Figure 11.20. Test the Next and Previous buttons to verify that they are working correctly.
   d. Click the Exit button to end the application, then close the solution.

3. In this exercise, you modify the application from Computer Exercise 1. The modified application will allow the user to display the full-time records, part-time records, and all of the records.
   a. Use Windows to make a copy of the Morgan Industries Solution-Ex1 folder, which is contained in the VbReloaded\Chap11 folder. Rename the copy Morgan Industries Solution-Ex3.
   b. Open the Morgan Industries Solution (Morgan Industries Solution.sln) file contained in the VbReloaded\Chap11\Morgan Industries Solution-Ex3 folder.

   c. Add the FillByFulltime query to the TblEmployTableAdapter object. (You can use Figures 11.28 through Figure 11.31 as a guide.)

   d. Associate the FillByFulltime query with a ToolStrip control. (You can use Figures 11.33 through 11.35 as a guide.)

   e. Save the solution, then start the application. Test the FillByFulltime button on the ToolStrip control. The interface should appear as shown in Figure 11.36.

   f. Click the Exit button to end the application.

   g. Create another query. The query should select only the records for part-time employees. Arrange the records in order by the Rate field. Use FillByParttime as the name for the query's Fill method, and use GetDataByParttime as the name for its GetData method.

   h. Associate the FillByParttime query with a ToolStrip control. Also associate the Fill query with a ToolStrip control.

   i. Save the solution, then start the application. Test the FillByFulltime, FillByParttime, and Fill buttons on the ToolStrip controls.

   j. Click the Exit button to end the application, then close the solution.

4. In this exercise, you modify the application from the chapter's Programming Example.

   a. Create the Cartwright Industries application shown in the chapter's Programming Example. Save the application in the VbReloaded\Chap11 folder.

   b. Create a query that allows you to display the data in ascending order by the item number. Also create a query that allows you to display the data in descending order by the price.

   c. Associate the two queries with two ToolStrip controls.

   d. Save the solution, then start and test the application.

   e. Click the Exit button to end the application, then close the solution.

5. In this exercise, you modify the application you created in the chapter's Programming Tutorial.

   a. Use Windows to make a copy of the Trivia Game Solution folder, which is contained in the VbReloaded\Chap11 folder. Rename the copy Modified Trivia Game Solution.

   b. Open the Trivia Game Solution (Trivia Game Solution.sln) file contained in the VbReloaded\Chap11\Modified Trivia Game Solution folder.

   c. Display the question number (from 1 through 9) along with the word "Question" in the interface.

   d. Add another button to the interface. The button should allow the user to start a new game. Allow the user to click the New Game button only after he or she has answered all nine questions.

   e. Save the solution, and then start and test the application.

   f. End the application, then close the solution.

6. In this exercise, you modify the application you created in the chapter's Programming Tutorial.

   a. Use Windows to make a copy of the Trivia Game Solution folder, which is contained in the VbReloaded\Chap11 folder. Rename the copy Disc Trivia Game Solution.

   b. Open the Trivia Game Solution (Trivia Game Solution.sln) file contained in the VbReloaded\Chap11\Disc Trivia Game Solution folder.

   c. Allow the user to answer the questions in any order, and also to change his or her answers. (You will probably need to modify the interface by including additional buttons.) Only display the number of incorrect answers when the user requests that information.

d. Save the solution, and then start and test the application.

e. End the application, and then close the solution.

7. In this exercise, you find and correct an error in an application. The process of finding and correcting errors is called debugging.

a. Open the Debug Solution (Debug Solution.sln) file, which is contained in the VbReloaded\Chap11\Debug Solution folder.

b. Open the Code Editor window. Review the existing code.

c. Notice that a jagged line appears below one of the lines of code in the Code Editor window. Correct the code to remove the jagged line.

d. Save the solution, and then start and test the application. Notice that the application is not working correctly. Click the Exit button to end the application.

e. Correct the errors in the application's code, and then save the solution and start the application. Test the application.

f. Click the Exit button to end the application, and then close the solution.

## Case Projects

### Addison Playhouse

In this Case Project, you use a SQL Server database named Play. The Play.mdf database file is located in the VbReloaded\Chap11\SQL Databases folder. The Play database contains one table named tblReservations. The table contains 20 records, each having three fields: a numeric field named Seat and two text fields named Name and Phone. Create an application that allows the user to display the contents of the dataset, and also to add, delete, and save records.

### College Courses

In this Case Project, you use a SQL Server database named Courses. The Courses.mdf database file is located in the VbReloaded\Chap11\SQL Databases folder. The Courses database contains one table named tblCourses. The table contains 10 records, each having four fields: course ID, course title, credit hours, and grade. The credit hours field is numeric; the other fields contain text. Create an application that uses six queries. Five of the queries should allow you to display the data for a specific grade (A, B, C, D, F). The sixth query should display all of the records in their original order.

### Sports Action

In this Case Project, you use a SQL Server database named Sports. The Sports.mdf database file is located in the VbReloaded\Chap11\SQL Databases folder. The Sports database contains one table named tblScores. The table contains 10 records, each having four fields that store the following information: name of the opposing team, the date of the game, your favorite team's score, and the opposing team's score. Create an application that allows you to view each record, and also to add, delete, and save records.

## The Fiction Bookstore

Jerry Schmidt, the manager of the Fiction Bookstore, uses a Microsoft SQL Server database named Books to keep track of the books in his store. The Books.mdf database file is contained in the VbReloaded\Chap11\SQL Databases folder. The database has one table named tblBooks. The table has three fields: a numeric field named BookNumber and two text fields named Title and Author. Mr. Schmidt wants an application that he can use to enter an author's name, and then display only the titles of books written by the author. Display the information in a DataGridView control. (*Hint*: In this application, you need to allow the user to specify the records he or she wants to select while the application is running. You can use a parameterized query to accomplish this task. A parameterized query is simply a SELECT statement that contains an @ sign followed by a *parameter* name in the WHERE clause. The *@parameterName* is a placeholder for the missing data. For example, you can create a parameterized query using @author in the WHERE clause. Associate the query with a ToolStrip control in the interface.)

# How To Boxes

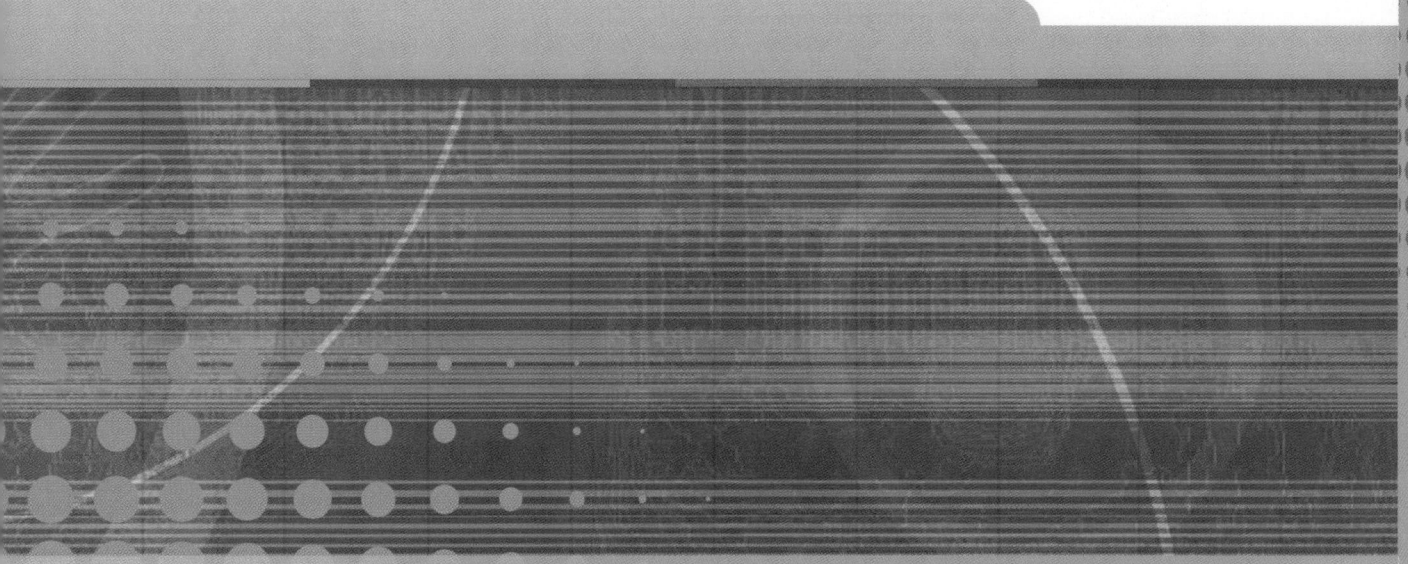

| How to | Chapter | Figure |
|---|---|---|
| Add a class file to the current project | 10 | 10.2 |
| Add a control to a form | 1 | 1.20 |
| Add a splash screen and a dialog box to an application | 2 | 2.22 |
| Add a ToolStrip control that is associated with a query | 11 | 11.33 |
| Add items to a list box | 5 | 5.16 |
| Align columns of information in a sequential access file | 9 | 9.12 |
| Assign a value to a variable | 3 | 3.4 |
| Bind the objects in a dataset | 11 | 11.9 |
| Call an independent Sub procedure | 7 | 7.2 |
| Clear a control's Text property while an application is running | 3 | 3.28 |
| Close a solution | 1 | 1.40 |
| *(Table is continued on next page)* | | |

| How to | Chapter | Figure |
|---|---|---|
| Concatenate strings | 4 | 4.12 |
| Connect a database to an application | 11 | 11.4 |
| Create a constructor | 10 | 10.12 |
| Create a Function procedure | 7 | 7.15 |
| Create a method that is not a constructor | 10 | 10.13 |
| Create a property procedure | 10 | 10.11 |
| Create a query using the Query Configuration Wizard | 11 | 11.28 |
| Create a structure (user-defined data type) | 9 | 9.1 |
| Create a Visual Basic 2005 Windows-based application | 1 | 1.7 |
| Create an independent Sub procedure | 7 | 7.1 |
| Declare a named constant | 3 | 3.18 |
| Declare a one-dimensional array | 8 | 8.2 |
| Declare a structure variable | 9 | 9.2 |
| Declare a two-dimensional array | 8 | 8.33 |
| Declare a variable | 3 | 3.3 |
| Define a class | 10 | 10.1 |
| Determine whether a file exists | 9 | 9.14 |
| End an application | 1 | 1.36 |
| Format a number | 3 | 3.36 |
| Generate random numbers | 4 | 4.48 |
| Include arithmetic expressions in assignment statements | 3 | 3.12 |
| Instantiate an object from a class | 10 | 10.5 |
| Manage the windows in the IDE | 1 | 1.10 |
| Manipulate member variables | 9 | 9.3 |
| Name a variable | 3 | 3.2 |
| Open an existing solution | 1 | 1.41 |
| Open the Code Editor window | 1 | 1.26 |
| Open the DataSet Designer | 11 | 11.24 |
| Plan an application | 2 | 2.1 |
| Preview the contents of a dataset | 11 | 11.7 |
| Print an application's code | 1 | 1.39 |
| Read information from a sequential access file | 9 | 9.13 |
| Save a solution | 1 | 1.31 |
| Select the existing text in a text box | 5 | 5.9 |
| *(Table is continued on next page)* | | |

| How to | Chapter | Figure |
|---|---|---|
| Specify the startup form | 1 | 1.32 |
| Start an application | 1 | 1.34 |
| Start Microsoft Visual Studio 2005 | 1 | 1.4 |
| Store data in a one-dimensional array | 8 | 8.3 |
| Store data in a two-dimensional array | 8 | 8.34 |
| Turn on Option Explicit and Option Strict | 3 | 3.21 |
| Use a button control | 1 | 1.25 |
| Use a check box | 6 | 6.46 |
| Use a combo box | 5 | 5.26 |
| Use a group box | 2 | 2.14 |
| Use a label control | 1 | 1.23 |
| Use a list box | 5 | 5.15 |
| Use a panel | 2 | 2.15 |
| Use a radio button | 6 | 6.41 |
| Use a table layout panel | 2 | 2.16 |
| Use a text box | 2 | 2.4 |
| Use a timer | 2 | 2.25 |
| Use a Windows Form object | 1 | 1.17 |
| Use the BindingSource object's Move methods | 11 | 11.22 |
| Use the BindingSource object's Position property | 11 | 11.21 |
| Use the Console.Beep method | 5 | 5.53 |
| Use the Contains method | 6 | 6.25 |
| Use the Do...Loop statement | 5 | 5.29 |
| Use the Financial.Pmt method | 5 | 5.6 |
| Use the Focus method | 3 | 3.29 |
| Use the For Each...Next statement | 8 | 8.7 |
| Use the For...Next statement | 5 | 5.1 |
| Use the FormClosing event procedure | 9 | 9.15 |
| Use the If...Then...Else statement to code the If and If/Else selection structures | 4 | 4.4 |
| Use the IndexOf method | 6 | 6.28 |
| Use the InputBox function | 5 | 5.36 |
| Use the Insert method | 6 | 6.19 |
| Use the Length property of a string | 6 | 6.1 |
| *(Table is continued on next page)* | | |

| How to | Chapter | Figure |
|---|---|---|
| Use the Like operator | 6 | 6.37 |
| Use the literal type characters | 3 | 3.5 |
| Use the logical operators | 4 | 4.20 |
| Use the MessageBox.Show method | 4 | 4.30 |
| Use the methods contained in the Convert class | 3 | 3.10 |
| Use the Mid statement | 6 | 6.13 |
| Use the most commonly used comparison operators | 4 | 4.5 |
| Use the PadLeft and PadRight methods | 6 | 6.16 |
| Use the Remove method | 6 | 6.7 |
| Use the Replace method | 6 | 6.10 |
| Use the Select Case statement | 4 | 4.45 |
| Use the SELECT statement | 11 | 11.27 |
| Use the SelectedItem and SelectedIndex properties | 5 | 5.20 |
| Use the SetBounds method | 5 | 5.48 |
| Use the Show and ShowDialog methods | 2 | 2.24 |
| Use the StartsWith and EndsWith methods | 6 | 6.22 |
| Use the String.Compare method | 6 | 6.34 |
| Use the String.IsNullOrEmpty method | 4 | 4.26 |
| Use the Substring method | 6 | 6.31 |
| Use the ToUpper and ToLower methods | 4 | 4.17 |
| Use the TrimStart, TrimEnd, and Trim methods | 6 | 6.4 |
| Use the TryCast keyword | 7 | 7.29 |
| Use the TryParse method | 3 | 3.6 |
| Use the value returned by the MessageBox.Show method | 4 | 4.33 |
| Write information to a sequential access file | 9 | 9.11 |

# B GUI Design Rules

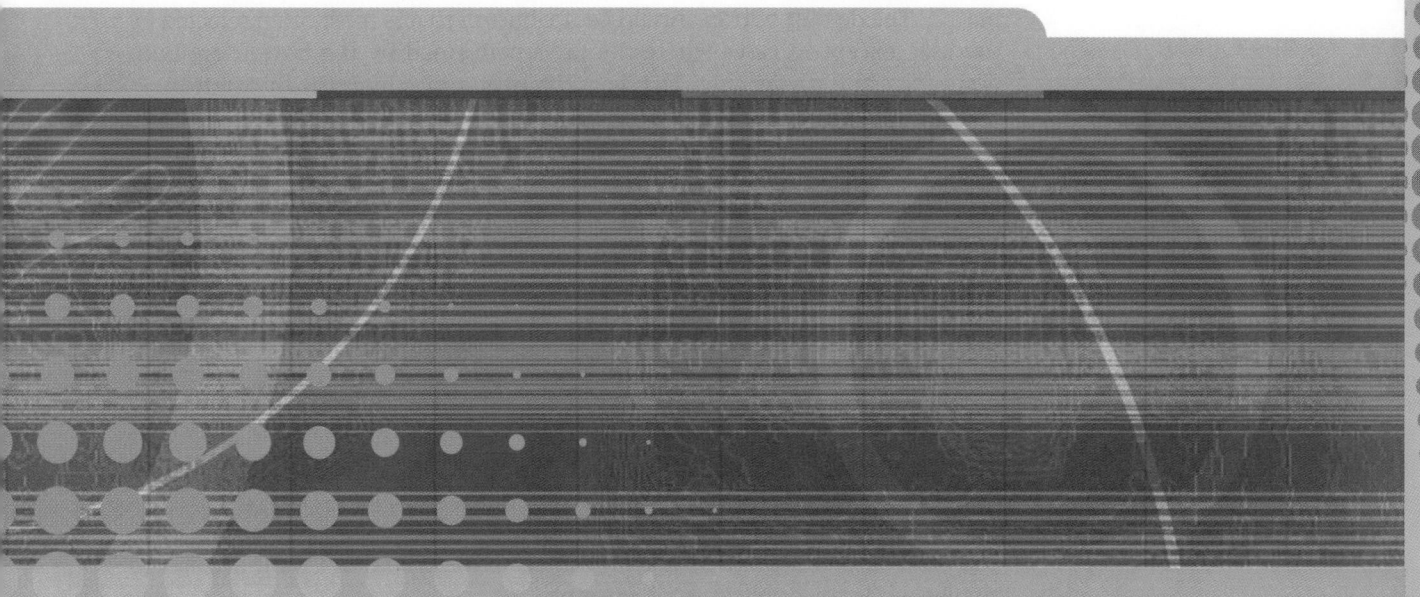

The following list summarizes the GUI design guidelines you have learned. You can use this list to verify that the interfaces you create in the Computer Exercises and Case Projects adhere to the GUI standards outlined in the book.

- A splash screen should not have a Minimize, Maximize, or Close button, and its borders should not be sizable.
- A form that is not a splash screen should always have a Minimize button and a Close button. Usually, it also contains a Maximize button. In most cases, the FormBorderStyle property is set to Sizable.
- If the form is a dialog box, it should have a Close button, but no Minimize or Maximize buttons, and its FormBorderStyle property should be set to FixedDialog.
- Set the form's StartPosition property; in most cases, you will set it to CenterScreen.
- Graphics and color should be used sparingly in an interface.
- If you use a graphic in the interface, use a small one and place it in a location that will not distract the user.

- Build the interface using black, white, and gray first, then add color only if you have a good reason to do so.
- Use white, off-white, or light gray for an application's background, and black for the text.
- Limit the number of colors in an interface to three, not including white, black, and gray. The colors you choose should complement each other.
- Never use color as the only means of identification for an element in the user interface.
- It is recommended that you use the Tahoma font for applications that will run on systems running Windows 2000 or Windows XP.
- Use 8-, 9-, 10-, 11-, or 12-point fonts for the text in an interface. Use no more than two different font sizes.
- Avoid using italics and underlining in an interface, and limit the use of bold text to titles, headings, and key items that you want to emphasize.
- Use only one font type, which should be a sans serif font, in the interface.
- You can use the form's AcceptButton property to designate an optional default button, and its CancelButton property to designate an optional cancel button. The default button should be the button that is most often selected by the user, except in cases where the tasks performed by the button are both destructive and irreversible. The default button typically is the first button.
- The information in an interface should flow either vertically or horizontally, with the most important information always located in the upper-left corner of the screen.
- When positioning the controls on a form, you should maintain a consistent margin from the edge of the form.
- Align the borders of the controls wherever possible to minimize the number of different margins used in the interface.
- Try to create a user interface that no one notices.
- Related controls should be grouped together using either white space or one of the tools listed in the Containers section of the toolbox.
- Related controls typically are placed close together on the form. Controls that are not part of any logical grouping may be positioned farther away from other controls.
- You can use a text box control to give the user an area in which to enter data.
- You use a label control to display information that you don't want the user to change while the application is running.
- In Windows applications, a button control is used to perform an immediate action when clicked.
- Labels that identify text boxes should be left aligned and positioned either above or to the left of the text box. They also should end with a colon and be entered using sentence capitalization.
- Identifying labels and button captions should be from one to three words only, and each should appear on one line.
- Identifying labels and button captions should be meaningful.
- Labels that identify controls should have their BorderStyle property set to None.
- Labels that display program output, such as the result of a calculation, usually have their BorderStyle property set to FixedSingle.
- Button captions should be entered using book title capitalization.
- When buttons are positioned horizontally on the screen, all the buttons should be the same height; their widths, however, may vary if necessary. When buttons are stacked vertically on the screen, all the buttons should be the same height and the same width. The most commonly used button should be placed first.

- Use radio buttons when you want to limit the user to one of two or more related and mutually exclusive choices.
- The minimum number of radio buttons in a group is two, and the recommended maximum is seven.
- The label in the radio button's Text property should be entered using sentence capitalization.
- Use a group box, panel, or table layout panel control to create separate groups of radio buttons. Only one button in each group can be selected at any one time. Use sentence capitalization for the optional identifying label in a group box control.
- Designate a default radio button in each group of radio buttons.
- Use check boxes when you want to allow the user to select any number of choices from a group of one or more independent and nonexclusive choices.
- The label in the check box's Text property should be entered using sentence capitalization.
- A list box should display a minimum of three selections and a maximum of eight selections at a time.
- Use a label control to provide keyboard access to a list box or combo box. Set the label control's TabIndex property to a value that is one less than the TabIndex value of the list box or combo box.
- List box items are either arranged by use, with the most used entries appearing first in the list, or sorted in ascending order.
- If a list box allows the user to make only one selection at a time, then a default item should be selected in the list box when the interface first appears. The default item should be either the most used selection or the first selection in the list. However, if a list box allows more than one selection at a time, you do not select a default item.
- Assign a unique access key to each control (in the interface) that can receive user input (text boxes, buttons, and so on).
- When assigning an access key to a control, use the first letter of the caption or identifying label, unless another letter provides a more meaningful association. If you can't use the first letter and no other letter provides a more meaningful association, then use a distinctive consonant. Lastly, use a vowel or a number.
- Set each control's TabIndex property to a number that represents the order in which you want the control to receive the focus (begin with 0).
- Lock the controls in place on the form.
- In the InputBox function, use sentence capitalization for the *prompt*, and book title capitalization for the *title*.
- Use sentence capitalization for the *text* argument in the MessageBox.Show method, but book title capitalization for the *caption* argument. The name of the application typically appears in the *caption* argument.
- Avoid using the words "error," "warning," or "mistake" in the MessageBox.Show method's message, as these words imply that the user has done something wrong.
- Display the Warning Message icon in a message box that alerts the user that he or she must make a decision before the application can continue. You can phrase the message as a question.
- Display the Information Message icon in a message box that displays an informational message along with an OK button only.
- Display the Stop Message icon when you want to alert the user of a serious problem that must be corrected before the application can continue.

- The default button in a message box should be the one that represents the user's most likely action, as long as that action is not destructive.
- If appropriate, format an application's numeric output so that it displays special characters (such as dollar signs and percent signs) and the desired number of decimal places.
- You can use the Focus method to move the focus to a control while the application is running.
- Highlight, or select, the existing text in a text box when the text box receives the focus.

# C

# Visual Basic Type Conversion Functions

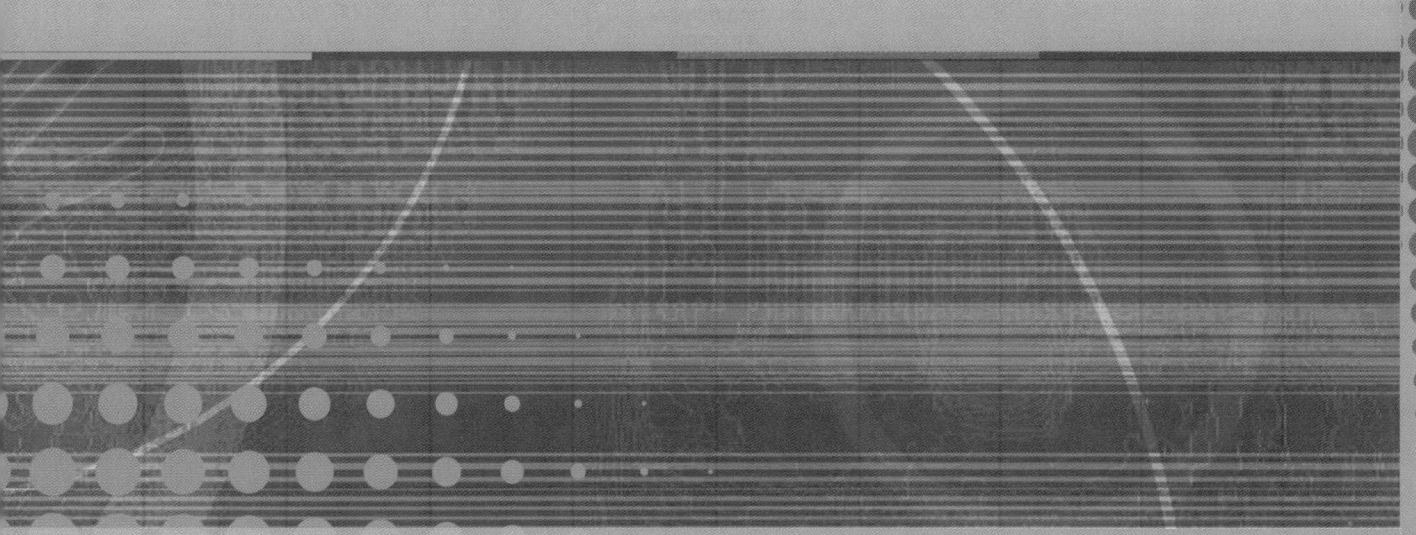

This appendix lists the Visual Basic type conversion functions. As you learned in Chapter 3, you can use the conversion functions (rather than the Convert methods) to convert an expression from one data type to another.

| Syntax | Return data type | Range for *expression* |
|--------|------------------|------------------------|
| CBool(*expression*) | Boolean | Any valid String or numeric expression |
| CByte(*expression*) | Byte | 0 through 255 (unsigned) |
| CChar(*expression*) | Char | Any valid String expression; value can be 0 through 65535 (unsigned); only first character is converted |
| CDate(*expression*) | Date | Any valid representation of a date and time |
| CDbl(*expression*) | Double | −1.79769313486231570E+308 through −4.94065645841246544E−324 for negative values; 4.94065645841246544E−324 through 1.79769313486231570E+308 for positive values |
| CDec(*expression*) | Decimal | +/−79,228,162,514,264,337,593,543,950,335 for zero-scaled numbers, that is, numbers with no decimal places. For numbers with 28 decimal places, the range is +/−7.9228162514264337593543950335. The smallest possible non-zero number is 0.0000000000000000000000000001 (+/−1E−28) |
| CInt(*expression*) | Integer | −2,147,483,648 through 2,147,483,647; fractional parts are rounded |
| CLng(*expression*) | Long | −9,223,372,036,854,775,808 through 9,223,372,036,854,775,807; fractional parts are rounded |
| CObj(*expression*) | Object | Any valid expression |
| CSByte(*expression*) | SByte (signed Byte) | −128 through 127; fractional parts are rounded |
| CShort(*expression*) | Short | −32,768 through 32,767; fractional parts are rounded |
| CSng(*expression*) | Single | −3.402823E+38 through −1.401298E−45 for negative values; 1.401298E−45 through 3.402823E+38 for positive values |
| CStr(*expression*) | String | Depends on the *expression* |
| CUInt(*expression*) | UInt | 0 through 4,294,967,295 (unsigned) |
| CULng(*expression*) | ULng | 0 through 18,446,744,073,709,551,615 (unsigned) |
| CUShort(*expression*) | UShort | 0 through 65,535 (unsigned) |

# Creating a SQL Server Database

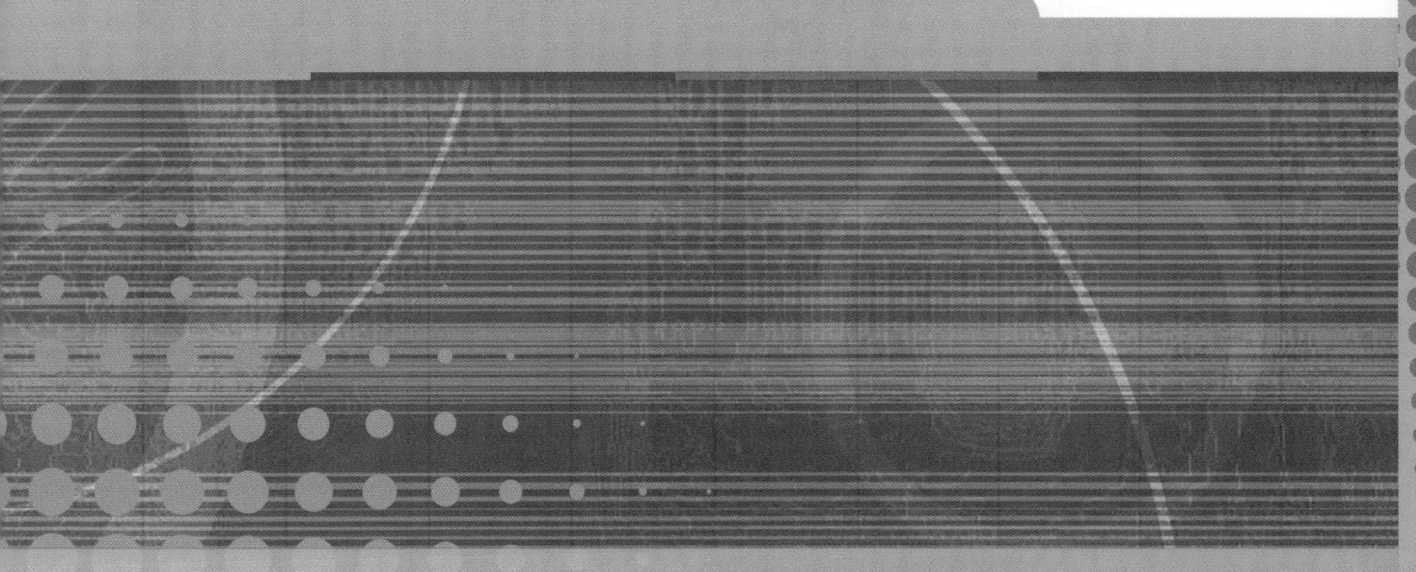

In this appendix, you learn how to use Visual Studio 2005 to create a SQL Server database.

**To create a SQL Server database:**

1. Start Visual Studio, then use the View menu to open the Server Explorer window.
2. Right-click the **Server Explorer** window, then click **Create New SQL Server Database** to open the Create New SQL Server Database dialog box.
3. In the Create New SQL Server Database dialog box, you enter the server name (which typically is .\SQLEXPRESS), your security preference, and the database name. Type **.\SQLEXPRESS** in the Server name box, then type **MyDatabase** in the New database name box. Also verify that the Use Windows Authentication radio button is selected. See Figure D.1.

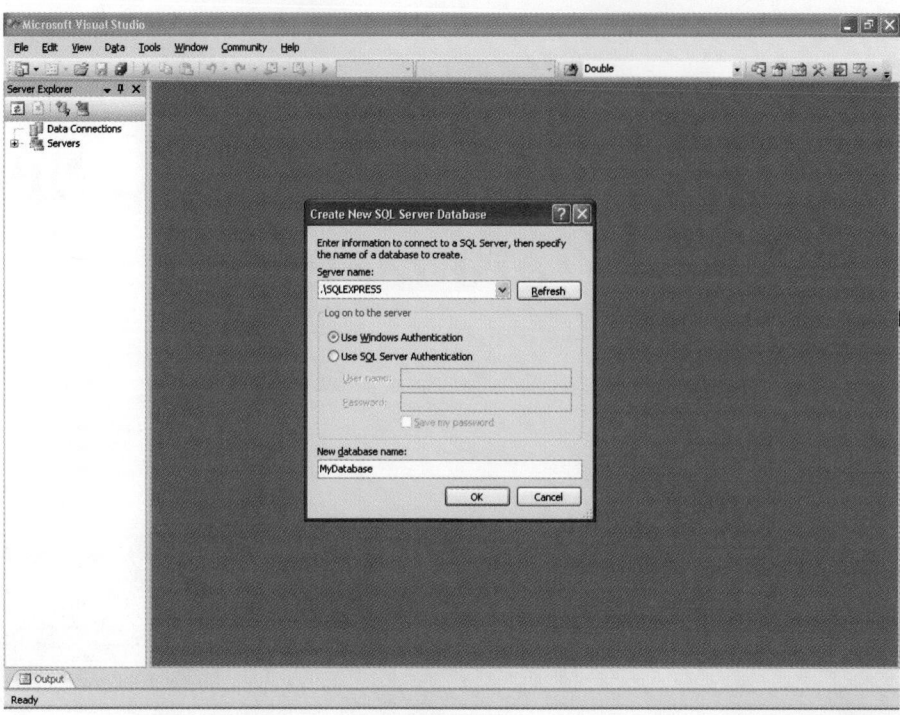

**FIGURE D.1**    Completed Create New SQL Server Database dialog box

4. Click the **OK** button to close the Create New SQL Server Database dialog box. Visual Studio creates two files named MyDatabase.mdf and MyDatabase_log.LDF. The files are located in the Program Files\Microsoft SQL Server\MSSQL.1\ MSSQL\Data folder.

5. Click the **plus box** that appears next to the MyDatabase.dbo entry in the Server Explorer window. Doing this displays the objects that can be included in a database. See Figure D.2.

**FIGURE D.2**    Server Explorer window showing database name and objects

6. You include a table in the database by right-clicking **Tables** in the Server Explorer window, and then clicking **Add New Table**. Doing this displays a window in which you define the table. See Figure D.3.

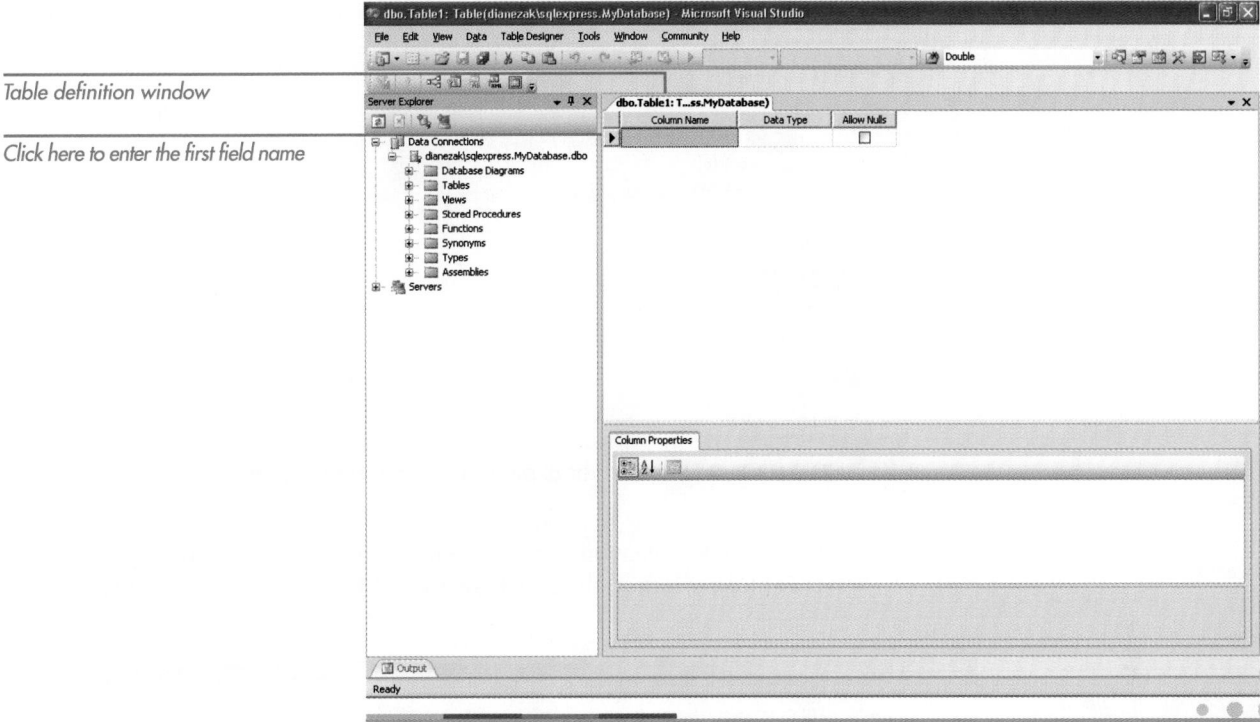

*Table definition window*

*Click here to enter the first field name*

**FIGURE D.3** Table definition window

7. The MyDatabase database will contain one table named tblEmpInfo. The tblEmpInfo table will contain three fields named EmpNum, First, and Last. Click the **box below the Column Name heading**. Type **EmpNum**, then press **Tab**. The EmpNum field will contain integers that represent employee numbers. Click the **down arrow in the Data Type column**. Scroll up the list, and then click **int**. Click the **check box in the Allow Nulls column** to deselect it.

8. The EmpNum field will be the primary key for the table. Right-click **EmpNum**, then click **Set Primary Key**.

9. Use Figure D.4 to define the First and Last fields, which will contain the first and last names of the employees.

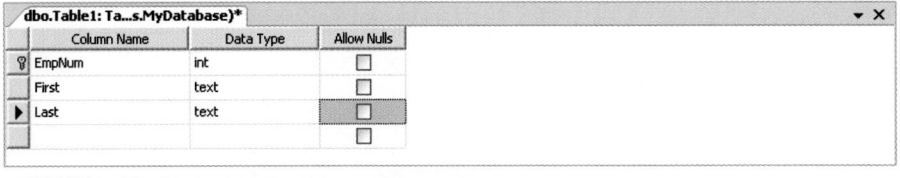

**FIGURE D.4** Completed table definition

10. Click **File** on the menu bar, and then click **Save Table1** to open the Choose Name dialog box. Type **tblEmpInfo** in the Enter a name for the table box, then click the **OK** button.

11. Click the **plus box that appears next to Tables** in the Server Explorer window, if necessary, then click the **plus box that appears next to tblEmpInfo**. See Figure D.5.

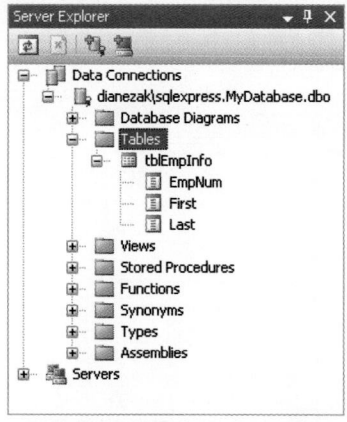

**FIGURE D.5**   Server Explorer window showing table and field names

12. After defining a table, you can fill it with data. Right-click **tblEmpInfo** in the Server Explorer window, then click **Show Table Data**. See Figure D.6.

*Table definition window*

*Data entry window*

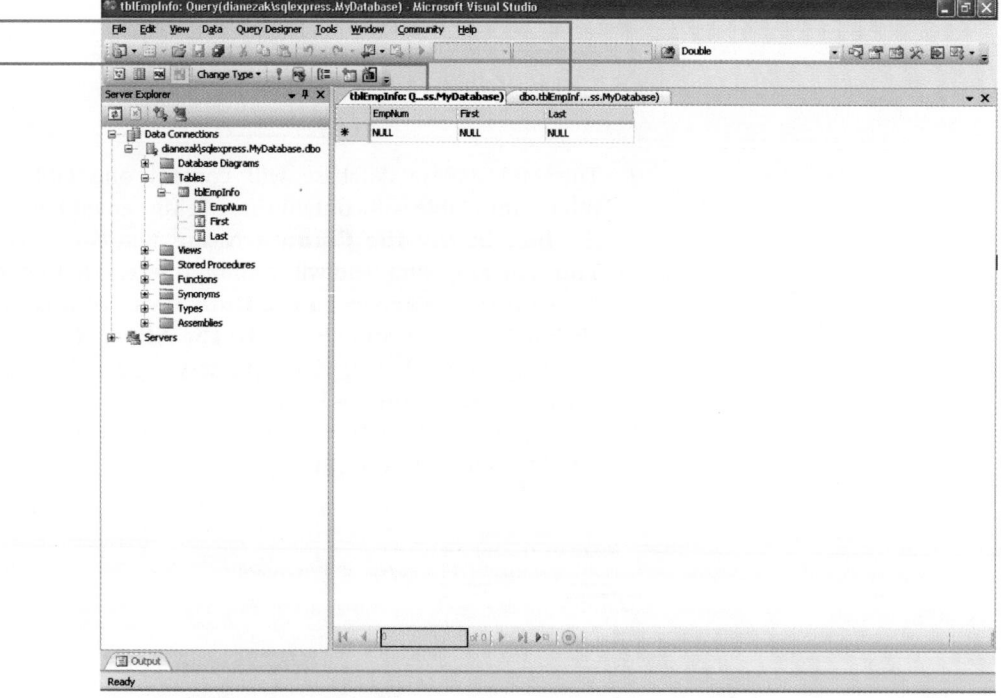

**FIGURE D.6**   Data entry window

13. Click the **box below the EmpNum column heading**, then type **12** as the employee number and press **Tab**. Type **Harold** as the first name and press **Tab**, then type **Jones** as the last name and press **Tab**.
14. Use Figure D.7 to enter the remaining records.

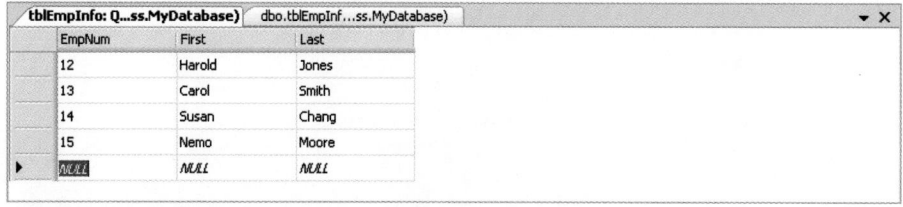

| tblEmpInfo: Q...ss.MyDatabase) | dbo.tblEmpInf...ss.MyDatabase) | |
|---|---|---|
| EmpNum | First | Last |
| 12 | Harold | Jones |
| 13 | Carol | Smith |
| 14 | Susan | Chang |
| 15 | Nemo | Moore |
| NULL | NULL | NULL |

**FIGURE D.7**    Records contained in the tblEmpInfo table

15. Close the data entry window, then close the table definition window.
16. Close Visual Studio.

# Glossary

## A

**abstraction** Refers to the hiding of the internal details of an object from the user. (1)

**AcceptButton property** The form property that specifies the default button. (2)

**access key** The underlined character in an object's identifying label or caption. An access key allows the user to select the object using the Alt key in combination with the character. (2)

**accumulator** A numeric variable used for accumulating (adding together) something. It allows you to answer the question "How much?". (5)

**Add method** A method of the Items collection; used to specify the items you want displayed in a list box. (5)

**ADO.NET 2.0** Refers to the technology used in Visual Basic 2005 to connect an application to a database. (11)

**application** Another name for a program. (1)

**applications programmers** Programmers who write and maintain programs that handle a specific task. (1)

**array** A group of variables that have the same name and data type and are related in some way. (8)

**Array.Reverse method** Reverses the order of the elements in a one-dimensional array. (8)

**Array.Sort method** Sorts the elements in a one-dimensional array in ascending order. (8)

**assembler** A program that converts assembly instructions into machine code. (1)

**assembly languages** These languages were developed after machine languages. They allow the programmer to use mnemonics in place of the 0s and 1s in a program. (1)

**assignment operator** The equal sign (=) in an assignment statement. (1)

**assignment statement** An instruction that assigns a value to something, such as a property of a control. (1)

**attributes** The characteristics that describe an object. Attributes are also called properties. (1)

## B

**BackColor property** Specifies the background color of a control. (2)

**base class** The original class from which another class is created. (1)

**behaviors** The operations or actions that an object is capable of performing (methods), as well as the actions to which an object can respond (events). (1)

**binding** Refers to the process of connecting a dataset object to a control on the form. (11)

**BindingNavigator control** Allows you to move from one record to the next in a dataset, as well as to add, delete, and save records. (11)

**BindingSource object** Connects a DataSet object to the bound controls on a form. (11)

**block scope** The scope of block-level variables, which can be used only within the statement block in which they are declared. (3, 4)

**block-level variables** Variables declared within a specific block of code; have block scope. (3)

**book title capitalization** When using this form of capitalization, you capitalize the first letter in each word, except for articles, conjunctions, and prepositions that do not occur at either the beginning or the end of the caption. (2)

**Boolean operators** The operators that allow you to combine two or more *conditions* into one compound *condition*; also called logical operators. (4)

**bound controls** Controls that are connected to a dataset object. (11)

**bug** An error in a program. (3)

**button control** The control used in a Windows application to perform an immediate action when clicked. (1)

**Button tool** The tool used to instantiate a button control. (1)

## C

**Call statement** The statement used to invoke an independent Sub procedure in a program. (7)

**camel case** A naming convention that uses lowercase letters for the first word in the name (or, in the case of Hungarian notation, the characters that represent the object's type), and then uses uppercase letters for the first letter of each subsequent word in the name. (1)

**cancel button** The button that can be selected on a form by pressing the Esc key. (2)

**CancelButton property** The form property that specifies the cancel button. (2)

**check box** Allows the user to select any number of choices from a group of one or more independent and nonexclusive choices. (6)

**CheckBox tool** The tool used to instantiate a check box. (6)

**child table** The table linked by a common field to a parent table. (11)

**class** A pattern or blueprint used to create an object. (1)

**class definition** A block of code that specifies (or defines) the attributes and behaviors of an object. (1)

**Class statement** Used to define a class. (10)

**Class Name list box** Located in the Code Editor window, it lists the names of the objects included in the user interface. (1)

**Clear method** Used to remove the contents of a text box. (3)

**CLR** Stands for "Common Language Runtime"; it is responsible for managing the execution of the IL (MSIL) instructions. (1)

**code** Another name for program instructions. (1)

**collection** A group of one or more individual objects treated as one unit. (5)

**combo box** Allows the user to select from a list of choices. It also can have a text field that allows the user to enter an item. (5)

**ComboBox tool** The tool used to instantiate a combo box. (5)

**Comments** Used to document a program internally; created using the apostrophe. (3)

**Common Language Runtime** CLR; responsible for managing the execution of the IL (MSIL) instructions. (1)

**comparison operators** The operators that allow you to compare values in a condition; also called relational operators. (4)

**compiler** In most cases, a program that translates all of a program's high-level instructions into machine code before running the program. The .NET language-specific compilers, however, translate the program instructions into IL (or MSIL). The JIT compiler then translates the IL into machine code. (1)

**component tray** A special area in the IDE; it stores controls that do not appear in the interface when an application is running. (2)

**concatenation operator** The operator used to concatenate strings; the ampersand (&), which must be preceded by and followed by a space. (4)

**condition** Specifies the decision you are making and must be phrased so that it results in either a true or false answer only. (4)

**Console.Beep method** Allows you to play the sound of a beep through the computer console speaker. (5)

**constructor** A method whose instructions are automatically processed each time you use the class to create (instantiate) an object. The purpose of a constructor is to initialize the class's variables. (10)

**Const statement** Used to create a named constant. (3)

**Contains method** Returns the Boolean value True when a specific sequence of characters appears in a string; otherwise, it returns the Boolean value False. (6)

**control** Another name for an object displayed on a form. (1)

**ControlBox property** Allows you to remove the Control menu box, as well as the Minimize, Maximize, and Close buttons, from a form's title bar. (2)

**ControlChars.NewLine constant** The constant used to advance the insertion point to the next line in a control. (4)

**Convert class** This class contains methods that return the result of converting a value to a specified data type. (3)

**counter** A numeric variable used for counting something. It allows you to answer the question "How many?". (5)

## D

**database** An organized collection of related information stored in a file on a disk. (11)

**DataGridView control** Used to display the data from a dataset; displays the data in a row and column format, similar to a spreadsheet. (11)

**dataset** A copy of some or all of the records and fields contained in a database; it is stored in the computer's internal memory. (11)

**DataSet object** Stores the information contained in a dataset. (11)

**data type** Determines the type of data a variable can store. (3)

**data validation** The process of verifying that a program's input data is within the expected range. (4)

**debugging** The process of locating errors in a program. (3)

**decision structure** Allows a program to make a decision or comparison and then select the appropriate path, depending on the result of that decision or comparison; also called the selection structure. (4)

**default button** The button that can be selected on a form by pressing the Enter key when the button does not have the focus. (2)

**default constructor** A constructor that has no parameters. (10)

**default list box item** The item that is automatically selected when the interface first appears. (5)

**default radio button** The radio button that is automatically selected when the interface first appears. (6)

**demoted** Occurs when a value is converted from one data type to another that can store only smaller numbers. (3)

**derived class** The class that inherits from a base class. (1)

**dialog box** A window that supports and supplements a user's activities in a primary window. (2)

**Do...Loop statement** Can be used to code both a pretest loop and a posttest loop. (5)

**dot member access operator** The period used to indicate a hierarchy of namespaces. (1)

**E**

**elements** The variables in an array. (8)

**Else clause** Contains the instructions that are processed when the condition in an If...Then...Else statement evaluates to False. (4)

**empty string** A set of quotation marks with nothing between them; also called a zero-length string. (3)

**Enabled property** Indicates a timer's state, which is either running or stopped. (2)

**encapsulates** An OOP term that means "contains." For example, a class encapsulates (contains) all of the attributes and behaviors that describe the object created by the class. (1)

**EndEdit method** A method of the BindingSource object; applies any pending changes (such as new records, deleted records, or changed records) to a dataset. (11)

**EndsWith method** Returns the Boolean value True when a specific sequence of characters occurs at the end of a string; otherwise, it returns the Boolean value False. (6)

**Enter event** Occurs when the user tabs to a control or uses the control's access key. Also occurs when the Focus method is used in code to send the focus to the control. (5)

**event procedure** A set of Visual Basic instructions that tells an object how to respond to an event. (1)

**events** Actions (such as clicking) to which an object can respond. (1)

**executable file** A file that can be run outside of the Visual Studio 2005 IDE. (1)

**exposed** An OOP term that refers to the accessible attributes and behaviors of an object. (1)

**extended selection structures** The If/ElseIf/Else and Case forms of the selection structure; also called multiple-path selection structures, because they have several alternatives from which to choose. (4)

**Extensible Markup Language** XML; a text-based language used to store and share data between applications and across networks and the Internet. (11)

**F**

**false path** Contains the instructions that are processed when the condition in a selection structure evaluates to False. (4)

**field** A single item of information about a person, place, or thing. (11)

**FileExists method** Used to determine whether a file exists. (9)

**Fill method** Used to load data into a table contained in a dataset while an application is running. (11)

**Financial.Pmt method** Calculates a periodic payment on either a loan or an investment. (5)

**floating-point number** A number that is expressed as a multiple of some power of 10. (3)

**flowchart** Uses standardized symbols to show the steps a procedure needs to take to accomplish its goal. (3)

**flowlines** The lines connecting the symbols in a flowchart. (3)

**focus** When a control has the focus, it can accept user input. (2)

**Focus method** Used to move the focus to a control while an application is running. (3)

**font** The general shape of the characters in the text. (2)

**Font property** Allows you to change the type, style, and size of the font used to display the text in an object. (2)

**For Each...Next statement** Can be used to code a loop whose instructions you want processed for each element in a group (such as an array). (8)

**ForeColor property** Specifies the color of a control's text. (2)

**foreign key** The field in the child table that links the child table to a parent table. (11)

**form** The foundation for the user interface in a Windows-based application; also called a Windows Form object. (1)

**format specifier** Determines the special characters that will appear in a formatted number. (3)

**formatting** Refers to the process of specifying the number of decimal places and the special characters to display in a number. (3)

**FormBorderStyle property** Allows you to specify the border style of the form. (2)

**FormClosing event** Occurs when the computer processes the `Me.Close()` statement, and when the user clicks the Close button on the form's title bar. (9)

**form file** Contains the code associated with a Windows Form object. (1)

**For...Next statement** Can be used to code a pretest loop whose instructions you want processed a precise number of times. (5)

**function** A predefined procedure that performs a specific task and then returns a value after completing the task. (5, 7)

**Function procedure** A procedure that returns a value after performing its assigned task; also called a function. (7)

## G

**Get block** Located in a Property procedure, the Get block contains the Get statement. (10)

**Get statement** Within the Get statement, you enter the code that allows an application to retrieve the contents of a Private variable in the class. (10)

**group box control** Used to group related controls together. (2)

**GUI** Stands for "graphical user interface." (1)

## H

**hidden** Refers to the inaccessible attributes and behaviors of an object. (1)

**high-level languages** These languages were developed after assembly languages. They allow the programmer to use computer instructions that more closely resemble the English language. (1)

**Hungarian notation** A naming convention that uses the first three (or more) characters in the name to represent the object's type, and the remaining characters to represent the object's purpose. (1)

## I

**IDE** Stands for "integrated development environment," which is an environment that contains all of the tools and features you need to create, run, and test your programs. (1)

**identifier** The name of an object. (3)

**If selection structure** Contains only one set of instructions, which are processed when the condition is true. (4)

**If/ElseIf/Else selection structure** Commonly referred to as an extended selection structure or multiple-path selection structure, because it has several alternatives from which to choose. (4)

**If/Else selection structure** Contains two sets of instructions: one set is processed when the condition is true and the other set is processed when the condition is false. (4)

**If...Then...Else statement** Used to code the If, If/Else, and If/ElseIf/Else forms of the selection structure. (4)

**IL** Stands for "Intermediate Language"; each language-specific compiler in .NET translates program instructions into this language; also called MSIL (Microsoft Intermediate Language). (1)

**Image.FromFile method** Used to retrieve an image file from the computer's disk while an application is running. (10)

**implicit type conversion** The process by which a value is automatically converted to fit the memory location to which it is assigned. (3)

**incrementing** Adding a number to the value stored in a counter or accumulator variable; also called updating. (5)

**independent Sub procedure** A procedure that is not associated with any specific object or event, and is processed only when invoked (called) from code. (7)

**index** The unique number assigned to each item in a collection, and to each character in a string. (5, 6)

**IndexOf method** Searches a *string* for a *subString*, and returns the number –1 when the *subString* is not found in the *string*; otherwise, it returns the index of the starting position of *subString* within *string*. (6)

**inheritance** Refers to the fact that you can create one class from another class. (1)

**initializing** Assign a beginning value to a variable. (5)

**InputBox function** Displays a dialog box that contains a message, OK and Cancel buttons, and an input area. (5)

**input file** The type of file from which an application reads information. (9)

**input/output symbol** The parallelogram in a flowchart. (3)

**Insert method** Returns a string with the appropriate characters inserted. (6)

**instances** The objects created from a class. (1)

**integer** A whole number; a number without any decimal places. (3)

**integer division operator** The backslash (\); divides two integers, and then returns the result as an integer. (3)

**integrated development environment** IDE; an environment that contains all of the tools and features you need to create, run, and test your programs. (1)

**Intermediate Language** IL; each language-specific compiler in .NET translates program instructions into this language; also called Microsoft Intermediate Language (MSIL). (1)

**interpreter** A program that translates high-level instructions into machine code, line by line, as the program is running. (1)

**Interval property** A property of a timer control; specifies the intervals for executing the code contained in the control's Tick event procedure. (2)

**Invalid data** Data that an application is not expecting. (3)

**Items collection** Contains the items in a list box. (5)

## J

**JIT** Stands for "just-in-time"; the compiler that converts IL (MSIL) into native machine code. (1)

**just-in-time** JIT; refers to the compiler that converts IL (MSIL) into native machine code. (1)

## K

**keyword** A word that has a special meaning in a programming language. (1)

## L

**label control** Displays text that the user is not allowed to edit while the application is running. (1)

**Label tool** The tool used to instantiate a label control. (1)

**Length property** Stores an integer that represents the number of characters contained in a string, or the number of elements contained in an array. (6, 8)

**lifetime** Indicates how long a variable remains in the computer's internal memory. (3)

**Like operator** Allows you to use pattern-matching characters to determine whether one string is equal to another string. (6)

**line continuation character** An underscore, which must be preceded by a space; used to break up a long instruction into two or more physical lines in the Code Editor window. (3)

**list box** Allows you to display a list of choices from which the user can select zero choices, one choice, or more than one choice. (5)

**ListBox tool** The tool used to instantiate a list box. (5)

**literal constant** An item of data whose value does not change while an application is running. (3)

**literal type character** A character used to convert a literal constant to a different data type. (3)

**Load event** Occurs when an application is started and the form is displayed the first time. (2)

**logical operators** Allow you to combine two or more *conditions* into one compound *condition*; also referred to as Boolean operators. (4)

**logic error** Occurs when you enter an instruction that is syntactically correct, but it does not give you the expected results. (3)

**loop** Another name for a repetition structure; used to repeatedly process one or more program instructions until some condition is met, at which time the loop ends. (5)

## M

**machine code** Computer instructions written in 0s and 1s; also called machine language. (1)

**machine language** Computer instructions written in 0s and 1s; also called machine code. (1)

**MaximizeBox property** Controls the display of the Maximize button on a form's title bar. (2)

**Me.Close method** Instructs the computer to terminate the current application. (1)

**member variables** The variables contained in a structure variable. (9)

**MessageBox.Show method** Displays a message box that contains text, one or more buttons, and an icon. (4)

**method** A predefined Visual Basic procedure that you can call (or invoke) when needed. A method performs a task for the class in which it is defined. (1, 3)

**Method Name list box** Located in the Code Editor window, it lists the events to which the selected object is capable of responding. (1)

**methods** The operations (actions) that an object is capable of performing. (1)

**Microsoft Intermediate Language** MSIL; each language-specific compiler in .NET translates program instructions into this language; also called Intermediate Language (IL). (1)

**Microsoft .NET Framework 2.0** The platform on which you create .NET applications. (1)

**Mid statement** Replaces a portion of a string with another string. (6)

**MinimizeBox property** Controls the display of the Minimize button on a form's title bar. (2)

**mnemonics** The alphabetic abbreviations used to represent instructions in assembly languages. (1)

**modal form** A form that requires the user to take some action in the form before he or she can continue working in the application. (2)

**modeless form** A form that can remain on the screen while the user completes other actions in the application. (2)

**module-level variable** A variable declared in the form's Declarations section. (3)

**module scope** Refers to the scope of a module-level variable, which can be used by all of the procedures in the current form. (3)

**modulus arithmetic operator** Mod; returns the remainder of a division. (3)

**MSIL** Stands for "Microsoft Intermediate Language"; each language-specific compiler in .NET translates program instructions into this language; also called IL (Intermediate Language). (1)

**multiple-path selection structures** The If/ElseIf/Else and Case forms of the selection structure; also referred to as extended selection structures, because they have several alternatives from which to choose. (4)

**My feature** Exposes a set of commonly used objects to the programmer. (9)

**My.Computer object** Allows you to easily access other objects and methods used to manipulate files. (9)

## N

**Name property** Used to refer to an object in code. (1)

**named constant** A computer memory location whose contents cannot be changed while the application is running; created with the Const statement. (3)

**namespace** An area in the computer's internal memory that contains the code definitions for a group of related classes. (1)

**.NET application** An application created using a .NET language. (1)

**.NET language** A language that runs in the .NET Framework. (1)

**.NET Framework class library** Contains an extensive set of classes that can be used in any .NET application. (1)

## O

**object** Anything that can be seen, touched, or used. (1)

**Object box** Located in the Properties window, it contains the name of the selected object. (1)

**object-oriented program** When writing this type of program, the programmer concentrates on the objects that the program can use to accomplish its goal. However, the programmer uses procedure-oriented programming when coding an object's tasks. (1)

**one-dimensional array** A group of related variables, with each variable identified by a unique number called a subscript. (8)

**OOD** An acronym for object-oriented design, which is the design methodology used to plan object-oriented programs. (1)

**OOP** An acronym for object-oriented programming, which means that you are using an object-oriented language to create a program that contains one or more objects. (1)

**ORDER BY clause** Used in a SELECT statement to control the order in which the records appear when displayed. (11)

**output file** The type of file to which an application writes information. (9)

## P

**PadLeft method** Returns a string with the appropriate characters inserted at the beginning of the string. (6)

**PadRight method** Returns a string with the appropriate characters inserted at the end of the string. (6)

**panel control** Used to group related controls together. (2)

**parallel arrays** Arrays whose elements are related by their subscript (position) in the arrays. (8)

**parameterized constructors** Constructors that have parameters. (10)

**parameters** The memory locations listed in a procedure header. (7)

**parent table** A table to which another table, called a child table, links. (11)

**Pascal case** A naming convention in which you capitalize the first letter in each word in the name. (1)

**passing by reference** The process of passing a variable's address to a procedure. (7)

**passing by value** The process of passing a variable's contents to a procedure. (7)

**pixel** Short for "picture element"; one spot in a grid of thousands of such spots that form an image produced on the screen by a computer or printed on a page by a printer. (5)

**point** A font measurement that is equal to $1/72$ of an inch. (2)

**Polymorphism** The object-oriented feature that allows the same instruction to be carried out differently depending on the object. (1)

**Position property** This property of the BindingSource object stores the position of the record pointer. (11)

**posttest loop** The type of repetition structure where the condition is evaluated after the instructions within the loop are processed. (5)

**precedence numbers** Indicate the order in which the computer performs an operation (such as an arithmetic operation) in an expression. (3)

**precision specifier** Controls the number of significant digits or zeros to the right of the decimal point in a formatted number. (3)

**pretest loop** The type of repetition structure where the condition is evaluated before the instructions within the loop are processed. (5)

**primary decision** In a nested selection structure, this decision is always made by the outer selection structure. (4)

**primary key** The field that uniquely identifies each record in a table. (11)

**primary window** A window in which the primary viewing and editing of your application's data takes place. (2)

**priming read** The read operation that prepares a loop for processing. (5)

**procedure** A block of program code that performs a specific task. (7)

**procedure footer** The last line in a procedure. (1)

**procedure header** The first line in a procedure. (1)

**procedure-level variable** A variable that is declared in a procedure. (3)

**procedure-oriented program** In this type of program, the programmer concentrates on the major tasks that the program needs to perform. (1)

**procedure scope** The scope of a procedure-level variable. (3)

**process symbol** The rectangle symbol in a flowchart. (3)

**programmers** The people who write programs. (1)

**programming languages** The languages that programmers use to communicate with the computer. (1)

**programs** The directions given to computers. (1)

**project** A container that stores files associated with only a specific piece of a solution. (1)

**Project Designer window** Allows you to access various settings for the project. (1)

**promoted** Occurs when a value is converted from one data type to another that can store larger numbers. (3)

**properties** The characteristics that describe an object; also called attributes. (1)

**Properties list** The left column in the Properties window; displays the names of the properties associated with the selected object. (1)

**Properties window** The window that lists an object's attributes (properties). (1)

**Property procedure** Used to create a Public property that allows the user to access the Private variables in a class. (10)

**pseudocode** Uses phrases to describe the steps a procedure needs to take to accomplish its goal. (3)

**pseudo-random number generator** Used to generate random numbers. (4)

**Q**

**query** Specifies the fields and records to retrieve from a database, as well as the order in which to arrange the fields and records. (11)

**R**

**radio button** Allows you to limit the user to only one choice in a group of two or more related and mutually exclusive choices. (6)

**RadioButton tool** The tool used to instantiate a radio button. (6)

**Random.Next method** Generates a random integer that is greater than or equal to a minimum value, but less than a maximum value. (4)

**ReadAllText method** Reads the text contained in a sequential access file. (9)

**record** A group of related fields that contain all of the necessary data about a specific person, place, or thing. (11)

**relational database** A database that stores information in tables, which are composed of columns (fields) and rows (records). (11)

**relational operators** The operators that allow you to compare values in a condition; also called comparison operators. (4)

**Remove method** Removes one or more characters from a string, and then returns a string with the appropriate characters removed. (6)

**repetition structure** Another name for a loop; allows you to repeatedly process one or more program instructions until some condition is met, at which time the loop ends. (5)

**Replace method** Returns a string with all occurrences of a sequence of characters replaced with another sequence of characters. (6)

**Return statement** Used to return a function's value to the statement that invoked the function. (7)

## S

**scalar variable** A variable that is unrelated to any other variable in the computer's internal memory; also called a simple variable. (8)

**scope** Indicates where a variable can be used in the application's code. (3)

**secondary decision** In a nested selection structure, this decision depends on the result of the primary decision and is always made by the inner (nested) selection structure. (4)

**SelectAll method** Used to select all of the text contained in a control. (5)

**Select Case statement** Used to code the Case selection structure. (4)

**SelectedIndexChanged event** Occurs when a different value is selected in a list box. (5)

**SelectedValueChanged event** Occurs when a different value is selected in a list box. (5)

**selection/repetition symbol** The diamond symbol in a flowchart. (4)

**selection structure** Allows a program to make a decision or comparison and then select the appropriate path, depending on the result of that decision or comparison; also called the decision structure. (4)

**SELECT statement** The most commonly used SQL command. It allows you to specify the fields and records you want to access from a database, as well as control the order in which the fields and records appear when displayed. (11)

**sentence capitalization** When using this form of capitalization, you capitalize only the first letter in the first word and in any words that are customarily capitalized. (2)

**sequence structure** Refers to the fact that the computer processes a procedure's instructions, one after another, in the order in which they appear in the procedure; also called sequential processing. (1)

**sequential access file** A file composed of lines of text that are both stored and retrieved sequentially; often referred to as a text file. (9)

**sequential processing** Refers to the fact that the computer processes a procedure's instructions, one after another, in the order in which they appear in the procedure; also called the sequence structure. (1)

**serif** A light cross stroke that appears at the top or bottom of a character. (2)

**Set block** Located in a Property procedure, the Set block contains the Set statement. (10)

**SetBounds method** Allows you to change the location and/or size of a control while an application is running. (5)

**Set statement** Within the Set statement, you enter the code that allows an application to assign a value to a Private variable in the class. (10)

**Settings box** The right column in the Properties window; displays the current value (setting) of each of the properties. (1)

**short-circuit evaluation** Refers to the fact that when using the AndAlso and OrElse logical operators in a condition, the computer does not always evaluate the second condition in a compound condition. (4)

**Show method** Displays a modeless form. (2)

**ShowDialog method** Displays a modal form. (2)

**signature** A method name combined with its *parameterlist*. (10)

**simple variable** A variable that is unrelated to any other variable in the computer's internal memory; also called a scalar variable. (8)

**solution** A container that stores the projects and files for an entire application. (1)

**Solution Explorer window** Displays a list of the projects contained in the current solution, and the items contained in each project. (1)

**source file** A file that contains code. (1)

**splash screen** The first image that appears when an application is started. It is used to introduce the application and hold the user's attention while the application is being read into the computer's internal memory. (1)

**SQL** Acronym for Structured Query Language, which is a set of commands that allows you to access and manipulate the data stored in databases. (11)

**StartPosition property** Determines where the form is positioned when the application is started and the form first appears on the screen. (1)

**start/stop symbol** The oval symbol in a flowchart. (3)

**StartsWith method** Returns the Boolean value True when a specific sequence of characters occurs at the beginning of a string; otherwise, it returns the Boolean value False. (6)

**startup form** The form that is automatically displayed when an application is started. (1)

**statement block** A set of statements terminated by an Else, End If, Loop, or Next statement. (4)

**static variable** A procedure-level variable that retains its value when the procedure ends. (3)

**string** A group of characters enclosed in quotation marks. (3)

**String.Compare method** Compares two strings and returns an integer that indicates the result of the comparison. (6)

**String.Empty** Represents the empty string; used to remove the contents of a control. (3)

**String.IsNullOrEmpty method** Used to determine whether a string contains data. (4)

**Strings.Space method** Used to write a specific number of spaces to a file. (9)

**Structured Query Language** SQL; a set of commands that allows you to access and manipulate the data stored in databases. (11)

**structures** User-defined data types created using the Structure statement. (9)

**Structure statement** Used to create structures (user-defined data types). (9)

**structure variable** A variable declared using a structure as the data type. (9)

**sub procedure** A block of code that performs a specific task. (1)

**Sub procedure** A procedure that does not return a value after performing its assigned task. (7)

**subscript** A unique number that identifies each element in an array. (8)

**Substring method** Returns characters from a string. (6)

**syntax** The rules of a programming language. (1)

**syntax errors** Typing errors that occur when entering instructions. (3)

**systems programmers** Programmers who write and maintain programs that help the computer carry out its basic operating functions. (1)

## T

**TabIndex property** Determines the order in which a control receives the focus when the user presses either the Tab key or an access key while the application is running. (2)

**table** A group of related records. (11)

**TableAdapter object** Connects a database to a DataSet object. (11)

**table layout panel control** Used to group related controls together. (2)

**text box** A control that gives the user an area in which to enter data. (2)

**TextBox tool** The tool used to instantiate a text box. (2)

**TextChanged event** Occurs when a change is made to the text contained in a control's Text property. (5)

**text file** A file composed of lines of text that are both stored and retrieved sequentially; often referred to as a sequential access file. (9)

**Text property** The Text property of a form appears in the form's title bar and on the taskbar while the application is running. The Text property of a control appears inside the control. (1)

**timer control** Used to process code at one or more regular intervals. (2)

**Timer tool** The tool used to instantiate a timer control. (2)

**ToLower method** Temporarily converts a string to lowercase. (4)

**toolbox** Refers to the Toolbox window. (1)

**ToUpper method** Temporarily converts a string to uppercase. (4)

**Toolbox window** Contains the tools you use when creating your application; each tool represents a class; also called the toolbox. (1)

**Trim method** Removes one or more characters from the beginning and end of a string, and then returns a string with the appropriate characters removed. (6)

**TrimEnd method** Removes one or more characters from the end of a string, and then returns a string with the appropriate characters removed. (6)

**TrimStart method** Removes one or more characters from the beginning of a string, and then returns a string with the appropriate characters removed. (6)

**true path** Contains the instructions that are processed when the condition in a selection structure evaluates to True. (4)

**truth tables** Summarize how Visual Basic evaluates the logical operators in an expression. (4)

**TryCast keyword** Converts an object from one type to another type. (7)

**TryParse method** Used to convert a string to a number. (3)

**two-dimensional array** A group of related variables, with each variable identified by a unique combination of two numbers: a row subscript and a column subscript. (8)

## U

**Unicode** The universal coding scheme that assigns a unique number to each character in the written languages of the world. (3)

**Update method** A method of the TableAdapter object; commits to the database any changes made to the dataset. (11)

**Updating** Adding a number to the value stored in a counter or accumulator variable; also called incrementing. (5)

**user-defined data types** Data types created using the Structure statement; also called structures. (9)

**user interface** What you see and interact with when using an application. (1)

## V

**valid data** Data that an application is expecting. (3)

**variables** Computer memory locations where programmers can temporarily store data while an application is running. (3)

## W

**Web-based application** An application that has a Web user interface and runs on a server. (1)

**WHERE clause** Used in a SELECT statement to limit the records that will be selected. (11)

**Windows-based application** An application that has a Windows user interface and runs on a desktop computer. (1)

**Windows Form Designer window** The window in which you create your Windows application's GUI. (1)

**Windows Form object** The foundation for the user interface in a Windows-based application; also called a form. (1)

**word sort rules** Using these rules, a number is considered less than a lowercase letter, which is considered less than an uppercase letter. (6)

**WriteAllText method** Writes information to a sequential access file. (9)

## X

**XML** Stands for "Extensible Markup Language," which is a text-based language used to store and share data between applications and across networks and the Internet. (11)

**XML schema definition file** Defines the tables and fields that make up a dataset. (11)

## Z

**zero-length string** A set of quotation marks with nothing between them; also called an empty string. (3)

# Index

## A

ABC Company application, 620–621
abstraction, 5
AcceptButton property, 18, 90
access keys, 86–87, 291
accumulators, 300–302, 305
Add button's Click event procedure, 573
Add method, 282–284, 290
Add New Item - <projectname> dialog box, 91–92, 102, 599–600
Add Query command, 678, 682
addition (+) operator, 142, 215
ADO.NET 2.0, 660
All Programs, Microsoft Visual Studio 2005 command, 8
Alphabet application code, 386–387, 390–391
And logical operator, 211–215
AndAlso logical operator, 211–216
annual payments, 274–276
ANSI (American National Standards Institute), 676
Application pane, 14, 27
applications, 6
  breaking into smaller tasks, 432
  Close button, 29, 30
  connecting to database, 660–663
  consistent with Windows standards, 78
  debugging, 164–166
  designing user interface, 78–86
  dialog boxes, 78–79, 91–93
  ending, 29–30
  planning, 72–78, 154
  primary windows, 78–79
  splash screen, 91–93
  starting and stopping, 27–29, 47–49
  tasks, 72–74
  terminating, 26–27
  testing, 164–166

applications programmers, 2
Area application code, 610–611
arithmetic expressions, 141–144
arithmetic operators, 215, 141–142
Array.Reverse method, 513–516
arrays, 496–498
  Length property, 509, 515
  module-level, 497, 520
  one-dimensional, 496–516
  parallel, 516–519
  populating, 498
  procedure-level, 497, 520
  structure variables, 559–562
  subscript, 497–498
  two-dimensional, 519–524
Array.Sort method, 513–516
As keyword, 607
assembler, 3
assembly languages, 3
assignment operator (=), 30, 132–133
assignment statements, 30, 132–133, 604
  arithmetic expressions, 143–144
  structures, 554
  two-dimensional arrays, 521
asterisk (*) pattern-matching character, 389
attributes, 5, 601–602, 604
auto-hiding windows, 11
AutoSize property, 22
Average application code, 509

## B

BackColor properties, 75
BackgroundImage property, 23
BackgroundImageLayout property, 23
base classes, 5, 622–626
Base Employee class code, 623–624
BASIC (Beginner's All-Purpose Symbolic Instruction Code), 3
behaviors, 5
binary file, 562

binary operators, 142
binding, 664–672
BindingNavigator control, 666–668, 671
bindingNavigatorSaveItem_Click procedure, 668
BindingSource object, 667, 672–674
block scope, 144, 148, 204
block-level variables, 148
Bonus Calculator application code, 441–443
book title capitalization, 84
Boolean data type, 128–129
Boolean operators, 211
Boolean variable, 136
BorderStyle property, 22, 83
bound controls, computer-created, 664–670
bugs, 164
button controls, 22–23, 74
Button tool, 22–23
buttons, 43, 84
ByRef keyword, 444
Byte data type, 128
ByVal keyword, 438, 440
ByVal value As keywords, 607

## C

C, 3
C++, 4
CalcAndDisplayBonus procedure, 443
calcButton's Click event procedure, 161–164, 173, 206–207, 218–220, 289, 305, 443, 446–447, 454–455, 507–509, 555, 558, 611, 622, 625
CalcGrossPay procedure, 446–448
calculations, 141, 144
CalcVolume function, 558
Call statement, 434, 438, 440, 446
camel case, 17, 22, 130
cancel button, 91

CancelButton property, 18, 91
captions, 63–64, 84
Car Race Game application
    code, 312–313, 321–323
    interface, 308–311
    modified code, 578–580
    modifying, 576–580
    picture boxes, 325
    testing, 324–325
Card class code, 628–630
Card Game application, 627–638
Card Game Solution file, 627
Case clauses, 235–237
Case Else clause, 237
Case selection structure, 233–237
case-insensitive searches, 380
CellBorderStyle property, 83
cells, 669
Change Game application, 171–177
Char data type, 128–129
CharacterCasing properties, 75
characters
    accessing in string, 382–384
    formatting numbers, dates, and
        times, 137
    inserting in string, 364–370
    number in string, 350–352
    removing from string, 352–358
    replacing in string, 358–363
    searching string for, 370–382
check boxes, 396–398
CheckBox tool, 396
Checked property, 393, 396
child table and foreign key, 659
City Names application code, 355
class definition, 17
class file, 599–501
Class statement, 24, 552,
    598–601, 622
Class View window, 9
classes, 5, 598
    base, 622–626
    constructors, 608–609
    defining, 598–601
    derived, 622–626
    encapsulation, 598
    inheritance, 5, 622
    instances, 5
    instantiating object from, 17,
        600–601
    methods, 609–611
    multiple constructors, 612–616
    overloaded methods, 617–622

Private members, 605
Private variables, 604–611
    property procedure, 604–611
Public members, 605
Public variables, 601–604
two methods in, 604–611
usable, 599
Clear method, 160
clearButton_Click procedure, 448
clearButton's Click event
    procedure, 158–160, 172, 448
ClearLabel Sub procedure, 454
ClearLabels procedure, 433, 437,
    449, 450
Click event, 25–25, 305, 448
Click event procedure, 50–51,
    101–102, 104–105, 437, 503, 674
    Add button, 573
    calcButton, 161–164, 173,
        206–207, 289, 443, 446–447,
        454–455, 507–509, 555, 558,
        611, 622, 625
    clearButton, 158–160, 172
    coding, 51–52
    dealButton, 633
    displayButton, 202–203,
        226–230, 505, 518–519,
        522–524, 526–527, 561
    displayHighButton, 509–511
    displayMsgButton, 231, 233
    displayPriceButton, 236
    enterButton, 516
    exitButton, 243
    generateButton, 238
    getInfoButton, 440–441
    label controls, 462–464,
        465–467
    modified for calcButton,
        218–220
    newButton, 469
    paperPictureBox, 245–246
    picture boxes, 633
    playButton, 402–405
    rockPictureBox, 244–245
    saveButton, 604
    scissorsPictureBox, 246
    searchButton, 505, 507
    sortAscendButton, 516
    sortDescendButton, 516
    updateButton, 511–513
CLR (Common Language
    Runtime), 7
COBOL, 3

code, 15
    bugs, 164
    hiding or collapsing, 25
    If selection structure, 199–200
    If/Else selection structure,
        199–200
    modifying, 29
    printing, 31, 53
    processing at intervals, 93
    self-documenting, 151
    syntax errors, 54–56
Code Editor window, 15, 24–27
    closing, 52–53
    comments, 158
    IntelliSense feature, 619
    opening, 49–50
    syntax errors, 164
code template procedure header
    and footer, 25–26
collections, 282
color and user interface, 85–86
ColumnCount property, 83
Columns property, 83
combo boxes, 290–294
ComboBox tool, 290
comments, 145–146, 242
comparing strings, 209–211,
    385–391
comparison operators, 200–206, 215
Compile pane, 14
compilers, 3, 7
component tray, 94, 667
compound condition, 211, 213–214
computer-created bound controls,
    664–670
concatenating strings, 205–206, 565
concatenation operator (&),
    205–206, 215
Concentration Game application
    code, 457–473, 470–473
conditions, 196–198, 211, 295
Console.Beep method, 319–320
Const statement, 150–151
constructors, 608–619
Contains method, 375–378
ControlBox property, 81
ControlChars.NewLine
    constant, 206
controls, 20–21
    adding, 37–40
    aligning borders, 84
    arranging on interface, 81–84
    assigning access keys, 86–87

binding object to, 664–672
binding to existing, 670–672
clearing Text property contents, 159–160
identifying, 21–22
locking and unlocking, 21, 46
manipulating, 37–40, 43
modifying, 21
moving, 21
   focus to, 160
      while application is running, 313–315, 318
order receiving focus, 87–90
selecting, 21
separate for each field, 665
sizing handles, 21
TabIndex property, 87–90
TextChanged event procedure, 280–281
Convert class, 140–141
Convert.ToDecimal method, 368
Convert.ToString method, 270
Count application code, 380–382
counter variable, 271
counters, 300–302, 305
custom
   data types, 552
   formatString method, 168

**D**

data
   aligning columns in sequential access files, 566–567
   previewing from dataset, 662–663
   reading from sequential access file, 567–569
   sorting in one-dimensional arrays, 513–516
   storing in one-dimensional arrays, 498–499
   storing in two-dimensional arrays, 521–522
   writing to sequential access file, 563–566
Data, Query command, 678
Data, Show Data Sources command, 661
Data Source Configuration Wizard dialog box, 661
Data Sources window, 661, 663, 665, 670

data types, 552
   Case clauses, 235
   named constants, 150
   numbers, 139–141
   properties, 607
   values, 133–134
   variables, 128–129, 133–134
   widest, 144
data validation, 216–217
Database Explorer window, 9
databases, 658
   connecting applications to, 660–663
   order data displayed, 675
   queries, 675
   retrieving data from, 669
DataGridView control, 664, 666, 669
dataset, 660–661
   accessing records, 672–674
   applying pending changes, 668–669
   binding objects, 664–672
   binding to existing control, 670–672
   filling with data, 672
   moving between records, 666
   order data displayed, 675
   previewing data, 662–663
   retrieving database data, 669
   saving changes to database, 668–669
DataSet Designer, 674–684
DataSet object, 667
Date application code, 369–370
Date data type, 128
Date, Time, Language, and Regional Options dialog box, 137
dealButton's Click event procedure, 633
Debug pane, 14
Debug, Start Debugging command, 28
Debug, Stop Debugging command, 306
debugging applications, 164–166
Decimal data type, 128–129, 135
decision structures, 196
declaration statement, 131–132
Declarations section, 145–146, 552
default
   button, 90
   constructor, 608, 613, 616, 618
   list box item, 285
   radio button, 394

demoted, 153
derived classes, 5, 622–626
derived Salaried class code, 623–624
DetermineHighest procedure code, 634–635
dialog boxes, 78, 300–301
   adding, 91–93, 102–104
   border, 79–80
Dialog template, 92
DialogForm code, 104–105
Dim keyword, 131, 144, 497, 520, 553, 600
dimensional arrays, declaring, 520–521
displayButton's Click event procedure, 202–203, 226–230, 505, 518–519, 522–524, 526–527, 561
displayHighButton's Click event procedure, 509–511
DisplayMessage procedure, 440–441
displayMsgButton's Click event procedure, 233
displayPriceButton's Click event procedure, 236
division
   by zero, 303
   remainder of, 142
division (/) operator, 142, 215
Do clause, 295, 306, 372
Do...Loop statement, 294–299, 306
dot member access operator (.), 17, 553
Double data type, 128–129, 135
DropDownStyle property, 290=291

**E**

Edit DataSet with Designer command, 675
Edit, Find and Replace command, 92
Edit Queries command, 675
elements, 497–498
Else clause, 200
EmployeesDataSet object, 670
Employee.vb file code, 617–618
empty string, 159
Enabled property, 23, 93–94
encapsulation, 5, 598
End Class keyword, 599
End Class statement, 498
End Get keywords, 607
End Property keywords, 607

End Select clause, 235
End Structure clause, 552
End Structure keywords, 552
End Sub keywords, 26, 608
EndEdit method, 668–669
endless loops, 306
EndsWith method, 371–375, 383
Enter event, 279
enterButton's Click event
    procedure, 516
equal to (=) comparison operator,
    201, 215
"Error" message, 217
event procedures, 24, 432, 437,
    449–450, 599
events, 24–25
    associating with procedures,
        448–450
    identifying, 77
executable file, 29
Exit button, 43, 50–51
Exit For statement, 271, 502
exitButton object, 25–26
exitButton_Click procedure, 26
exitButton's Click event
    procedure, 243
exponentiation (^) operator,
    142, 215
expressions, evaluating logical
    operators, 212
extended selection structures,
    231–237

**F**

false condition, 196
false path, 198
fields, 658–659, 665
File, Close Solution command, 32
File, Exit command, 29, 30
File Name property, 16
File, New, Project command, 10
File, Open, File command, 574
File, Open, Project/Solution
    command, 32
file pointers, 565
File, Print command, 31
File, Save All command, 27
FileExists method, 568–569, 574
files, 7–8
    newline, 573–575
    reading, 562
    reading from, 565
    renaming, 16

types, 562
verifying existence, 568–569
viewing in separate window, 574
writing spaces to, 566
writing to, 565
Fill method, 669, 676
Financial.Pmt method, 274–276,
    278, 289
Find and Replace dialog box, 92
fixed-point numbers, 129
floating-point numbers, 129
flowcharts, 156–158, 198–199, 298
flowlines, 157
focus, 87–90, 160
Focus method, 160
Font property, 18, 22–23, 75, 85,
    282, 291, 393, 396
fonts, 41, 85
For clause, 271–272, 278
For Each clause, 502
For Each...Next statements,
    502–503, 522
ForeColor properties, 75
foreign key, 659
Form class, 17
form files, 15
Form object, 18
Form1 object, 17
Form1.vb file, 15
Format, Lock Controls
    command, 21
format specifier, 167
formatString argument, 167
formatString method, 168
FormattedDate.vb file code,
    612–613
formatting numeric output,
    166–169
FormBorderStyle property, 18,
    79–80
FormClosing event, 573
FormClosing event procedure,
    570, 576
forms, 13, 79
    adding
        controls, 37–40
        objects, 19–23, 36–40
    button controls, 22–23
    caption, 18
    closing, 570
    controls, 20–21
    Declarations section, 146, 552
    General Declarations
        section, 146

label controls, 21–22
location on screen, 18
manipulating controls, 37–40
maximizing and
    minimizing, 80
names, 17–18
naming conventions, 17
opening, 92
splash screens, 80–81
ToolStrip control, 681–683
For...Next statement, 148, 270–274,
    278, 501
Friends application code, 571–573
Function keyword, 452, 609
Function procedures, 432, 437,
    451–455, 609–610
functions, 302, 451–455

**G**

Gadis Antiques application code,
    435–437, 448–450
generateButton's Click event
    procedure, 238
Gentry Supplies application code,
    394–395, 397–398
Get block of code, 607
Get keyword, 607
Get statement, 607
GetData method, 676
getInfoButton's Click event
    procedure, 440–441
GetNewPay function, 454–455
global variables, 144
graphics and user interface, 84
greater than (>) comparison
    operator, 201, 215
greater than or equal to (>=)
    comparison operator, 201, 215
Gross Pay application code,
    444–446
group box control, 81–84
GroupBox tool, 81
GUI (graphical user interface),
    12–13
    design rules, 711–714
    guidelines, 78

**H**

Handles clause, 450
Handles keyword, 448–448, 449
Hangman Game application,
    400–410

Help, Index command, 168
high-level languages, 3–4
How to boxes, 707–710
Hungarian notation, 17–18, 22, 130

## I

IDE (integrated development
   environment), 6
   managing windows, 11–12,
     35–36
   opening database table, 660
identifier, 130
If selection structure, 197–200
If/Else selection structure, 197–200
If/ElseIf/Else selection structure,
   231–232
If...Then...Else statement, 148, 199
   comparison operators, 204
   essential components, 200
   If/ElseIf/Else selection structure,
     231–232
   logical operators, 216–217
   true path, 204
IL (Intermediate Language), 7
Image property, 23
ImageAlign property, 23
implicit type conversion, 152–153
incrementing, 300
independent Sub procedure,
   432–433, 437–438
index, 282, 356
IndexOf method, 378–382, 574
inheritance, 5, 622
Inherits clause, 622
initializing, 300
input files, 562
InputBox function, 300–302,
   305–306, 440
input/output symbol, 157, 199
Insert method, 368–370
instances, 5, 13
instructions and line continuation
   character, 138
Integer data type, 128–129, 135
integer division ( operator, 142, 215
integers, 129, 142
interfaces
   Add button, 573
   cancel button, 91
   combo box, 290–294
   default button, 90
   Exit button, 29–30, 573
   list box, 281–287

   order controls receive focus,
     87–88
interpreters, 3
Interval property, 93–94
invalid data, 164–166
Irritated Vowel Web site, 18
Is keyword, 235–237
Item Prices application code,
   366–367
Items collection, 282
Items.Count property, 282, 291

## J

Java, 4
JIT (just-in-time) compilers, 7

## K

keywords, 25

## L

label controls, 21–22, 74, 462–467
Label tool, 21–22
labels, 63–64, 84
Length property, 350–352, 509, 515
less than (<) comparison operator,
   201, 215
less than or equal to (<=)
   comparison operator, 201, 215
lifetime, 144–148
Like operator, 388–391
line continuation character, 138
list box, 281–287, 317
ListBox tool, 281
literal constants, 133, 354
literal type characters, 133, 354
Load event procedure, 108, 289,
   458–459, 500–502, 574, 577, 669
loans, periodic payment, 274–276
logic errors, 164
logical operators, 211–212, 215–217
Long data type, 128–129
Loop clause, 295, 306–307
loop instruction, 351
loops, 270, 303, 506
   counters or accumulators,
     300–302
   Do...Loop statement, 294–299
   endless, 306
   For Each...Next statement,
     502–503
   For...Next statements, 270–274

   instructions, 306
   number of times processed, 272
   priming, 303
Lottery game application code,
   525–529

## M

machine code, 3
machine languages, 3
MainForm
   code, 100–102, 108–110
   FormClosing event procedure,
     573, 576
   Load event procedure, 289,
     458–459, 500–502, 574,
     577, 669
   user interface, 96–100
Margin property, 22–23, 75
matchTimer's Tick event
   procedure, 468
MaximizeBox property, 80
MaxLength properties, 75
.mdf filename extension, 660
Me.Close method, 26–27, 570, 573
member variables, 552–554
members, 552
memory location, converting value
   to fit, 152
message box, 221–225, 303
MessageBox.Show method,
   221–225, 306
methods, 5, 25–26, 134, 604–611
   accessing commonly used, 565
   overloaded, 617–622
   signature, 613
   signatures, 619
Microsoft Access, 658
Microsoft .NET Framework 2.0, 6–7
Microsoft SQL Server, 658
Mid statement, 361–363
MinimizeBox property, 80
mnemonics, 3
modal form, 92–93
modeless form, 92–93
module scope, 144, 146–148
module-level
   arrays, 497–498, 520
   named constant, 151
   one-dimensional arrays, 497
   structure variables, 553
   variables, 146–148, 498, 600
modulus arithmetic (Mod)
   operator, 142, 215

Monthly Payment Calculator application, 277–279
Months application code, 501
Move method, 673–674
MoveNext method, 674
MovePrevious method, 674
MSIL (Microsoft Intermediate Language), 7
Multiline properties, 75
multiple-path selection structures, 231–237
multiplication (*) operator, 142, 215
My feature, 564–565
My Project folder, 13
MyBase keyword, 623
MyBase.New (parameterlist) statement, 623
My.Computer object, 564–565

**N**

Name application code, 384
Name property, 17–18, 22–23, 75, 83, 94, 282, 291, 393, 396
named constants, 150–152, 162
namespace scope, 144
namespace variables, 144
namespaces, 17
negation (-) operator, 142, 215
nested
    Do...Loop statement, 295
    For Each...Next statements, 503
    For...Next statement, 271, 522
    selection structures, 225–231, 320
.NET applications, 7
.NET Framework 2.0, 6–7
.NET Framework class library, 7
.NET languages, 7
New keyword, 601
New Project dialog box, 10
newButton's Click event procedures, 469
newline character, 573–575
Next clause, 271, 502
noMatchTimer's Tick event procedure, 468–469
not equal to (<>) comparison operator, 201, 215
Not logical operator, 211–213, 215
Nothing keyword, 498
number sign (#) pattern-matching character, 389

numbers
    aligning by decimal point, 567
    converting data type, 139–141
    monetary or percentage amounts, 166
numeric arrays, 498
numeric data type, 134–140
numeric output, formatting, 166–169
numeric values, swapping, 202–206
numeric variable, 167

**O**

Object data type, 128, 152, 464
object variables, converting, 464–465
object-oriented programs, 4
objects, 4, 17, 25, 598
    adding, 19–23, 36–40
    assigning tasks, 75–76
    associating with procedures, 448–450
    attributes, 5, 601–602, 604
    behaviors, 5
    binding, 664–672
    exposing commonly used, 564–565
    identifying, 74–76
    instances, 13
    instantiating, 17, 20, 598, 600–601
    methods, 5
    naming, 15, 17–18
    properties, 15–16
*Occupational Outlook Handbook* (OOH), 2
one-dimensional arrays
    declaring, 497
    displaying contents, 500–502
    elements, 497–498
    highest value stored in, 509–511
    manipulating, 499–516
    module-level, 497
    parallel, 516–519
    procedure-level, 497
    referring to variables in, 496
    searching, 505–507
    sorting data, 513–516
    storing data in, 498–499
    subscripts, 496, 503–505
    updating values, 511–513
one-dimensional numeric array, 507–509

OOD (object-oriented design), 4
OOP (object oriented programming), 4–5
Open command, 27
Open Project dialog box, 32
option explicit, 152–154
Option Explicit On statement, 158, 601
Option statements, 242
option strict, 152–154
Option Strict On statement, 158, 601
Options button, 104–105
Options dialog box, 153
Or logical operator, 211–215
Oracle, 658
ORDER BY clause, 677–678
OrElse logical operator, 211–217
output files, 562
overloaded methods, 617–622
Overloads keyword, 619
Overridable keyword, 623

**P**

Padding property, 83
padding strings, 566–567
PadLeft method, 364–368, 566–567
PadRight method, 364–368, 566–567
panel control, 81–84
Panel tool, 81
panels, 82–83
paperPictureBox's Click event procedure, 245–246
parallel arrays, 516–519
parallel one-dimensional arrays, 516–519
parameterized constructors, 613–615, 618
parameters, 25, 433, 438
parent table, 659
parsing strings, 136
Part Number application code, 377–378
Pascal case, 17–18, 150, 433
passing by reference, 438, 444–448, 555, 558
passing by value, 438, 439–443
passing variables, 438–448
PasswordChar properties, 75
pattern-matching characters, 388–391

Pay application code, 510
periodic payment, 274–276
Personnel application, 614–616
Pet Information application code, 438–440
Phone application code, 363
picture box control, 44–46
picture boxes, 633
Pine Lodge application code, 453–454
pixels, 314
planning applications, 72–78, 154
playButton's Click event procedure, 402–405
points, 85
polymorphism, 5
Position property, 672–673
posttest loop, 270, 294–299
precedence numbers, 141–142
precision specifier, 167–168
predefined dialog boxes, 300
pretest loop, 270, 294–299, 302, 351
Preview Data command, 663
Preview Data dialog box, 663
Previous button, 674
Price List application code, 517–518, 523–524
Prices application code, 512–513
primary decision, 226
primary field, 675
primary key, 659
primary windows, 78–80
priming read, 303
principalTextBox's TextChanged event procedure, 281
printing code, 31, 53
Private keyword, 25, 131, 146, 151, 433, 497, 520, 553, 600, 605
Private variables, 604–611, 613, 618
procedure footer, 25–26, 433
procedure header, 25–26, 433
procedure scope, 144–145
procedure-level
    arrays, 497, 520
    named constants, 151
    one-dimensional arrays, 497
    structure variables, 553
    variables, 144–145, 600
procedure-oriented programs, 3
procedures, 432–433
    associating with objects and events, 448–450

comments, 145–146
declaring variable in, 144–145
documenting, 145–146
indenting lines within, 26
passing structure variable to, 554–559
performing task several times, 432
planning with, 156–158
planning with pseudo code, 155–156
Static keyword, 148
process symbols, 157, 199
programmers, 2
programming languages, 2–4
programs, 2
Project, Add Class command, 599
Project, Add Windows Form command, 91
Project, <project name> Properties command, 27
Project Designer window, 13–14, 27, 153
projects, 7–8, 10
    adding class file to, 599
    listing, 13
promoted, 152
properties, 15–18, 42–43, 210, 607
Properties window, 11, 15–18, 24, 670
Property procedure, 604–611, 613, 618
pseudocode, 155–158, 197–198
pseudo-random number generator, 237–239, 317
Public Class keyword, 599
Public Class statement, 498
Public keyword, 24, 552
Public property, 605
Public Property keywords, 606
Public Sub New keywords, 608
public variables, 144, 601–604
Publish pane, 14

## Q

queries, 675
    allowing user to run, 681–683
    creation of, 678–680
    SQL (Structured Query Language), 676
    viewing information in, 676–678

Query Builder dialog box, 679–681
Query Configuration Wizard, 678–679
question mark (?) pattern-matching character, 389

## R

raceTimer's Tick event procedure, 315–324, 577
radio buttons, 282, 393–395
RadioButton tool, 393
random file, 562
random numbers, 237–239, 318, 460–461, 526–527
Random object, 238
Random.Next method, 238
ReadAllText method, 567–568
reading
    files, 562
    from files, 565
    information from sequential access files, 567–569
ReadOnly keyword, 606–607
Recent Projects list, 9
records, 658–659, 666, 672–673
References pane, 14
relational databases, 658–659
relational operations and Is keyword, 236–237
relational operators, 200
Remove method, 356–358
Rename command, 16
repetition structures, 270, 319–320, 320
    accumulators, 300–302
    counters, 300–302
    Do...Loop statement, 294–299
    For...Next statements, 270–274
Replace method, 358–361
Resources pane, 14
Return privateVariable instruction, 607
Return statement, 452
rockPictureBox's Click event procedure, 244–245
RowCount property, 83
Rows property, 83

## S

Salary Code application code, 504
Sales application code, 506–507

Sales Express application, 302–307
Sales Tax application code, 373–374
sans serif fonts, 85
saveButton, 604
SByte data type, 128
scalar variables, 496
scissorsPictureBox's Click event
    procedure, 246
scope, 144–148
ScrollBars properties, 75
Search Criteria Builder dialog
    box, 682
searchButton's Click event
    procedure, 505, 507
searching
    case-insensitive, 380
    case-sensitive, 370–380
    for character strings, 370–382
    one-dimensional arrays, 505–507
    two-dimensional arrays, 522–524
secondary decision, 226
Security pane, 14
Select Case clause, 235
Select Case statement, 234–235
SELECT statement, 676–679,
    679–681
SelectAll method, 278–280
SelectedIndex property, 282, 291
SelectedIndexChanged event,
    286–287
SelectedItem property, 282,
    284–286, 291
SelectedValueChanged event,
    286–287, 454
SelectedValueChanged event
    procedure, 289
selection structures, 270, 302, 306,
    319, 351
    choosing from several
        alternatives, 231–237
    conditions, 196
    nested, 225–231, 320
SelectionMode property, 281–282
sequence programming
    structure, 196
sequence structure, 26, 270
sequential access files, 562
    aligning columns of data,
        566–567
    reading information from,
        567–569
    writing information to, 563–566
sequential file, 562

sequential processing, 26
serif fonts, 85
Server Explorer window, 9
Server (Database) Explorer
    window, 9
Set block of code, 607–608
Set statement, 607–608
SetBounds method, 313–315,
    318–320
Settings pane, 14
Short data type, 128–129
short-circuit evaluation, 213
Show method, 92–93
Show Table Data command, 660
ShowDialog method, 92–93
ShuffleWords procedure code,
    460–462
signature, 613
Signing pane, 14
simple variables, 496
Single data type, 128–129
Social Security application code,
    357–360
Solution Explorer window, 9, 13, 27
solutions, 7–8, 10, 27
    listing projects, 13
    opening and closing, 32, 53
sortAscendButton's Click event
    procedure, 516
sortDescendButton's Click event
    procedure, 516
Sorted property, 282, 284, 291
sorting, 284, 513–516
source files, 15
space character (" "), 353
Specify a SQL SELECT statement
    screen, 679
Splash Screen template, 92
splash screens, 18, 80–81, 91–93
SplashScreenForm, 106
SQL (Structured Query
    Language), 676
SQL Server database creation,
    717–721
Square class, 604–605
Square.vb file, 604–605
Standard toolbar, 27
Start Page window, 9–10
StartPosition property, 18
start/stop symbol, 157, 199
StartsWith method, 371–375, 383
startup form, 27
State application code, 514–515

statement block, 200
Static keyword, 131, 148
static variables, 148–149
Stop Message icon, 223
String Collection Editor dialog
    box, 283
String data type, 128–129, 129
String variables, 210, 217–218
String.Compare method, 385–387
String.Empty value, 159
String.IsNullOrEmpty method,
    217–218
strings, 133
    accessing characters, 382–384
    comparing, 209–211, 385–391
    concatenating, 205–206, 565
    converting, 134–140, 209–211
    first character, 379
    formatting, 137–138, 166
    index, 356
    inserting characters, 364–370
    length, 350–352, 365
    manipulating, 350
    number of characters, 350–352
    padding, 364–370, 566–567
    parsing, 136
    pattern-matching characters,
        388–391
    removing characters, 352–358
    replacing characters, 358–363
    searching for characters,
        370–382
    substrings, 378–382
    writing, 565
Strings.Space method, 566
Structure clause, 552
Structure keyword, 552
Structure statement, 552, 558
structure variables
    arrays, 559–562
    member variables, 553
    module-level, 553
    passing to procedure, 554–559
    procedure-level, 553
structures, 552–554
Sub keyword, 25, 433, 609
Sub procedures, 25, 432–437, 609
subscripts, 496–497, 503–505
Substring method, 382–384, 574
substrings, 378–382
subtraction (–) operator, 142, 215
swapping numeric values, 202–206

Sweets Unlimited application code, 602–603
syntax errors, 54–56, 164
System.Globalization namespace, 139, 158
systems programmers, 2
System.Windows.Forms namespace, 17

**T**

TabIndex property, 22–23, 75, 87–90
table layout panel control, 81–84, 96–98
TableAdapter Configuration Wizard, 676
TableAdapter object, 667, 675–676
TableLayoutPanel tool, 81, 83
tables, 658, 676
    primary key, 659
    row and columnar format, 664
    structure, 82
TabStop properties, 75
taskbar, 8
tasks, 72–76, 432
TblEmployBindingNavigator control, 670
templates, 10
text
    modifying fonts, 41
    selecting in text box, 278–280
text box controls, 74
text boxes, 75, 160, 278–280, 284–286
text files, 562–563
Text property, 18, 22–23, 75, 83, 291, 393, 396
    changing contents, 280–281
    clearing contents, 159–160
    containing data, 217–218
    removing leading spaces from, 354
    String.Empty value, 159
    value stored in, 133
    zipTextBox, 351
TextAlign property, 22–23, 75
TextBox tool, 75
TextChanged event, 280
TextChanged event procedure, 280–281, 437

Tick event procedure, 107–108
    matchTimer, 468
    noMatchTimer, 468–469
    raceTimer, 315–324, 577
timer control, 93, 106
Timer tool, 93–94
timers, 93–94
To keyword, 235–237
ToDecimal method, 140
ToDouble method, 140
TOE (Task, Object, Event) chart, 72, 74–76, 77
ToInt32 method, 140
ToLower method, 209–211
Toolbox, 9, 11, 19–23, 36–40
tools, 19–20
ToolStrip control, 681–683
ToString method, 140, 167, 270, 283
ToUpper method, 209–211
Treasures application code, 559–561
Trim method, 352–355
TrimEnd method, 352–355
TrimStart method, 352–355
Trivia Game application
    binding field objects to text boxes, 689–691
    coding, 685–693
    connecting Trivia database, 685–689
    previewing data, 685–689
    testing, 689–691, 694
true condition, 196
true path, 197–198
truth tables, 212–215
TryCast keyword, 464
TryParse method, 134–140, 278, 305–306
two-dimensional arrays, 519–524
txt file extension, 565
type conversion functions, 715–716
type conversion rules, 153

**U**

UInteger data type, 128
ULong data type, 128
unary operators, 142
undeclared variables, 152

Unicode, 129
Until keyword, 295
Update method, 668–669
updateButton's Click event procedure, 511–513
updating, 300
user interface, 6, 12–13
    arranging controls, 81–84
    color, 85–86
    creation of, 241–252
    designing, 78–86
    fonts, 85
    graphics, 84
    MainForm, 96–100
user-defined data types, 552
users, allowing to run query, 681–683
UShort data type, 128

**V**

valid data, 164
values
    converting to fit memory location, 152
    data types, 133–134
    demoted, 153
    promoted, 152
variables, 128, 162
    assigning value, 132–140
    block scope, 204
    converting, 464–465
    data types, 128–129, 133–134
    declaring, 131–132
    declaring using structure, 553–554
    identifier, 130
    lifetime, 144–148
    literal constants, 133
    minimum scope needed, 148
    module-level, 600
    namespace scope, 144
    naming, 130, 136
    "on the fly," 152
    passing by reference, 438, 444–448, 555, 558
    passing by value, 438, 439–443
    procedure-level, 600
    scope, 144–148
    strings, 133
    undeclared, 152

.vb extension, 15
.vb file, 600
View Code command, 24
View Code (F7) keyboard
    shortcut, 24
View, Code command, 24
View, Designer command, 32
View, Start Page command, 11
View, Tab Order command, 89
View, Toolbox command, 11
View menu, 11
Visual Basic, 4
Visual Basic 2005, 6
Visual C#, 4
Visual C# 2005, 6
Visual C++, 4
Visual C++ 2005, 6
Visual J#, 4
Visual J# 2005, 6
Visual Studio 2005, 6, 8–13, 33

**W**

Web-based applications, 6
WHERE clause, 678
While keyword, 295
Willow Pools application code,
    555–558
windows, 11–12, 35–36
Windows Form class, 13
Windows Form Designer window,
    11–13, 32
Windows Form object, 13, 15–18, 79
Windows XP, 87
Windows-based applications, 6,
    10–13, 34–35
Wizard Results screen, 679
WriteAllText method, 563–566
WriteOnly keyword, 606–607
writing to files, 565

**X**

XML (Extensible Markup
    Language), 675
XML schema definition file, 675
Xor logical operator, 211–215
.xsd extension, 675

**Z**

zero-length string (" "), 159,
    306, 359
ZIP Codes application code,
    351–352
zipTextBox's Text property, 351